PENGUIN BOOKS

ONE WORLD DIVISIBLE

David Reynolds teaches twentieth-century international history at Cambridge University, where he is a Fellow of Christ's College. He has also held visiting appointments at Harvard University and Nihon University in Tokyo. He is the author of two prize-winning books on the Second World War: *The Creation of the Anglo-American Alliance 1937–1941* and *Rich Relations: The American Occupation of Britain 1942–1945*. He co-authored *An Ocean Apart*, which accompanied the BBC/PBS television series on twentieth-century Anglo-American relations for which he was principal historical adviser. Other publications include *Britannia Overruled: British Policy and World Power in the 20th Century*, as editor, *The Origins of the Cold War in Europe: International Perspectives*, and, as co-editor, *Allies at War: The Soviet, American and British Experience 1939–1945*.

Paul Kennedy is J. Richardson Dilworth Professor of History at Yale University, author of *The Rise and Fall of British Naval Mastery*, *The Rise and Fall of the Great Powers*, *Preparing for the Twenty-First Century* and other books, and general editor of this series.

D1121012

ONE WORLD DIVISIBLE

A Global History Since 1945

DAVID REYNOLDS

PENGUIN BOOKS

PENGUIN BOOKS

Published by the Penguin Group
Penguin Books Ltd, 27 Wrights Lane, London W8 5TZ, England
Penguin Putnam Inc., 375 Hudson Street, New York, New York 10014, USA
Penguin Books Australia Ltd, Ringwood, Victoria, Australia
Penguin Books Canada Ltd, 10 Alcorn Avenue, Toronto, Ontario, Canada M4V 3B2
Penguin Books India (P) Ltd, 11, Community Centre, Panchsheel Park, New Delhi – 110 017, India
Penguin Books (NZ) Ltd, Private Bag 102902, NSMC, Auckland, New Zealand
Penguin Books (South Africa) (Pty) Ltd, 5 Watkins Street, Denver Ext 4, Johannesburg 2094, South Africa

Penguin Books Ltd, Registered Offices: Harmondsworth, Middlesex, England

First published in the USA by W. W. Norton & Company Inc. 2000
First published in Great Britain by Allen Lane The Penguin Press 2000
Published in Penguin Books 2001
1

Copyright © David Reynolds, 2000
All rights reserved

The moral right of the author has been asserted

Printed in England by Clays Ltd, St Ives plc

For my students

TO TEACH IS TO LEARN

Contents

List of Maps

List of Illustrations

Between pages 64 and 65

Foreword

by Paul Kennedy

This brilliant history of our world since 1945 not only stands as a land-mark synthesis in its own right but also marks the first of a multivolume series, The Global Century, that seeks to recapture the major aspects of human experiences over the past, tumultuous, hundred years. In the near future, David Reynolds's work will be joined by a companion volume covering the years 1900–1945 and by a dozen others dealing with such themes as the environment, economic change, arts and ideas, science and technology, social patterns, war and peace, gender and the family, religion, and the relations of states.

Though varied in their themes, these volumes will share common features. They are all truly *global* in nature, seeking to recreate historical reality as it affected the greater part of the Earth's inhabitants: a merely Western viewpoint is not desired here. Each will cover the entire century and, by introducing strong themes and trying to make sense of the whole rather than merely detailing the parts, each will stand as an individual work of scholarship in its own right as well as being a key member of the overall series. All will be written in the clearest possible manner, with the intelligent general reader in mind.

Given these high ambitions of The Global Century series, nothing could be more welcome than to have it inaugurated by Reynolds's magisterial account of the history of the world since the end of the Second World War. As the reader will discover, it is global in its reach: transformations in places as distant from one another as Chile and Indonesia are treated as seriously as the unfolding of events in Hungary and California. Here, Reynolds's conscious decision to visit and study in Japan and Southeast Asia as part of the preparation for writing this book has paid off amply; the range of his discourse is remarkable, balanced, and thorough.

No less remarkable is the range of the *themes* covered in this volume. As Reynolds admits, the role and activities of the state loom large in this story; thus *One World Divisible* is underpinned by a strong political narrative: nuclear weapons, diplomatic crises, and the rise and fall of communism did and do count. But there was much more going on in this fast-changing half-century. The author is superb in his treatment of cultural and social transformations (especially the changing role of women), of youth movements and popular culture, and of the varied and sometimes contradictory impacts of technology. Indeed, it is this last perhaps that emerges as the strongest theme in this rich tapestry, since technology was and is simultaneously bringing peoples of our planet together and revealing their differences. *One World Divisible* is a volume that enriches and at the same time provokes deep thought about where humankind is coming from and where it may be headed. Appearing as it does at the onset of a new century, there could be no better reading for all concerned citizens of the Earth.

Acknowledgments

Writing a global history of the second half of this century is, of course, an impossible task. The vastness of the project, the bulk of material, one's own intellectual, linguistic, and cultural limitations—all are daunting in the extreme. I recognized this from the start. But that recognition was, in fact, liberating. It freed me from spurious notions of definitiveness and made clear that this would have to be a limited and personal view.

This book is necessarily a work of synthesis, rather than original scholarship. It cannot do more than scratch the surface of a vast and disparate literature. My hope is that the patterns I have detected in the past half-century may stimulate the reflection and research of other scholars.

Self-evidently this is also a *large* work of synthesis. The size of the book makes it possible to go beyond the schematized overview often provided by volumes of this sort. I have tried to put thematic flesh on the bones of narrative, to add color to a succession of silhouettes, to highlight people as much as process—in short to savor the contingency and particularity of general history.

In my research and writing, I was helped by the fact that, since 1985, I had taught a course for final-year history undergraduates at Cambridge University on twentieth-century international relations. This gave me a basic politico-military-economic foundation. On that, I built a fuller knowledge of social, technological, and cultural trends, and also used it as a base from which to spread my wings beyond the transatlantic world around which I had

migrated hitherto. The following institutions have assisted by providing research facilities and/or opportunities to debate my ideas: the Charles Warren
Center for Studies in American History and the Minda de Gunzburg Center for European Studies at Harvard University; the World Bank, Washington, D.C.; the Institutes for Contemporary History in Vienna and in Munich;
the Institute for Universal History, Academy of Sciences, Moscow; and the
Indonesian Center for Strategic and International Studies in Jakarta. I am
particularly grateful to the Department of Economics, Nihon University,
Tokyo, where, as a visiting professor in 1995, I was able to give a course of
lectures on Japan and the world since the Pacific War. Professor Takehiko
Noguchi was a most considerate host.

This book, like my others, would have been impossible without the University Library at Cambridge—uniquely in Britain, a copyright library with
facilities for borrowing and browsing. I am also grateful that Cambridge has
one of the world's leading history departments, with a global range of expertise, and that it is a collegiate university, enabling me to talk at lunch with
scholars from various disciplines.

My thanks to friends and family for reading parts of this work, particularly
Susan Bayly, Meg Graham, Warren Kimball, Alan Munro, and Jean Ray, and
also to several doctoral students for their comments and input, especially Ver-
ena Salzmann, Peter Speicher, and Kristina Spohr. On the business side
Peter Robinson has smoothed my path. I am especially grateful to Tony and
Jane Whitten for hospitality in both Indonesia and the United States. My ed-
itor at Norton, Steven Forman, has been a valuable and constructive critic.
I also appreciate the work of the production staff at Norton, particularly
Kate Nash. My principal debts are to Margaret and Jim—my small world—
for putting up with me.

—David Reynolds
Cambridge
June 1999

ONE WORLD
DIVISIBLE

1. The Americas in the 1990s

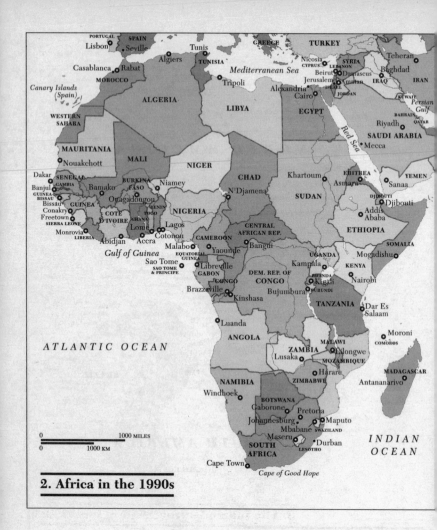

2. Africa in the 1990s

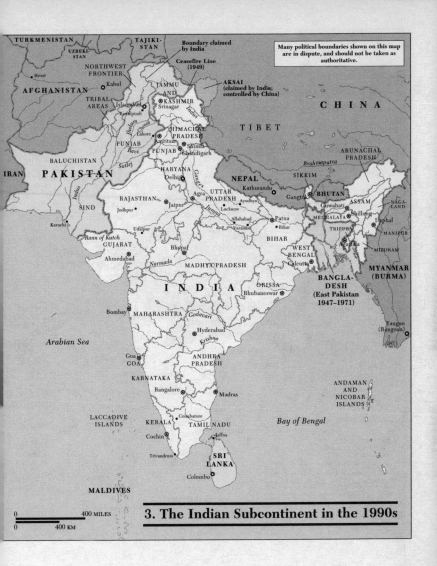

3. The Indian Subcontinent in the 1990s

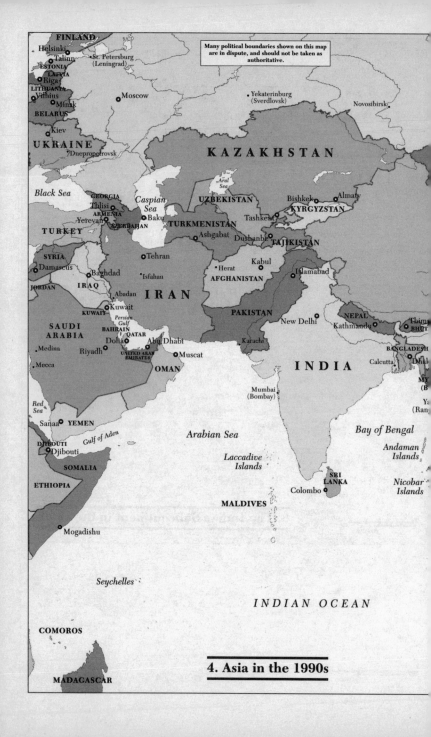

Many political boundaries shown on this map are in dispute, and should not be taken as authoritative.

FINLAND
Helsinki
Talinn
ESTONIA
St. Petersburg (Leningrad)
LATVIA
Riga
LITHUANIA
Vilnius
Minsk
BELARUS
Kiev
UKRAINE
Dnepropetrovsk
Moscow
Yekaterinburg (Sverdlovsk)
Novosibirsk

KAZAKHSTAN

Black Sea
Aral Sea
Caspian Sea
UZBEKISTAN
Bishkek
Almaty
KYRGYZSTAN
GEORGIA
Tbilisi
ARMENIA
Yerevan
AZERBAIJAN
Baku
TURKMENISTAN
Tashkent
TURKEY
Ashgabat
Dushanbe
TAJIKISTAN
SYRIA
Damascus
Tehran
Herat
Kabul
AFGHANISTAN
Islamabad
Baghdad
Isfahan
JORDAN
IRAQ
Abadan
IRAN
KUWAIT
Kuwait
PAKISTAN
New Delhi
NEPAL
Kathmandu
Thimp
BHUT
SAUDI ARABIA
Persian Gulf
BAHRAIN
QATAR
Doha
Abu Dhabi
Karachi
BANGLADESH
Medina
Riyadh
UNITED ARAB EMIRATES
Muscat
Calcutta
Dhak
Mecca
OMAN
INDIA
MY
(B

Red Sea
Sanaa
YEMEN
Mumbai (Bombay)
Ya
(Ran

DJIBOUTI
Djibouti
Gulf of Aden
Arabian Sea
Bay of Bengal
Andaman Islands

SOMALIA
Laccadive Islands

ETHIOPIA
SRI LANKA
Nicobar Islands
Colombo

MALDIVES

Mogadishu

Seychelles

INDIAN OCEAN

COMOROS

4. Asia in the 1990s

MADAGASCAR

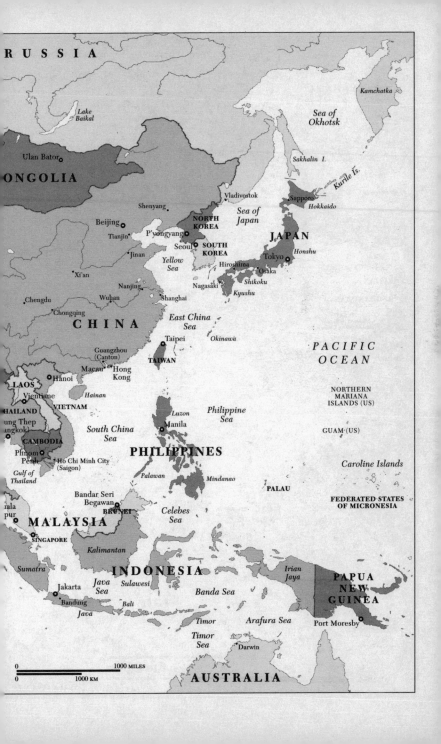

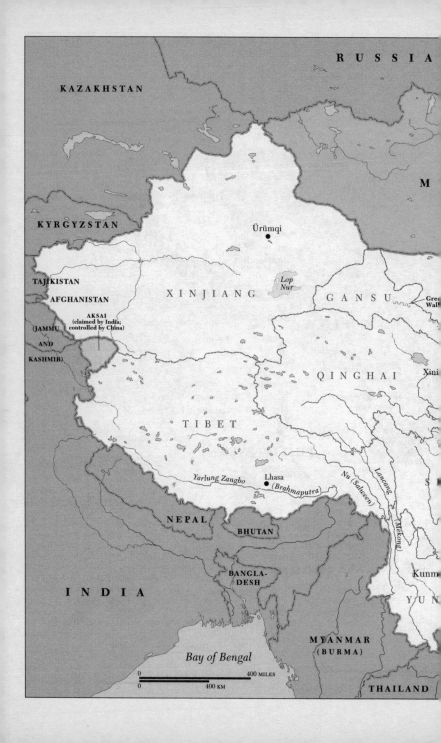

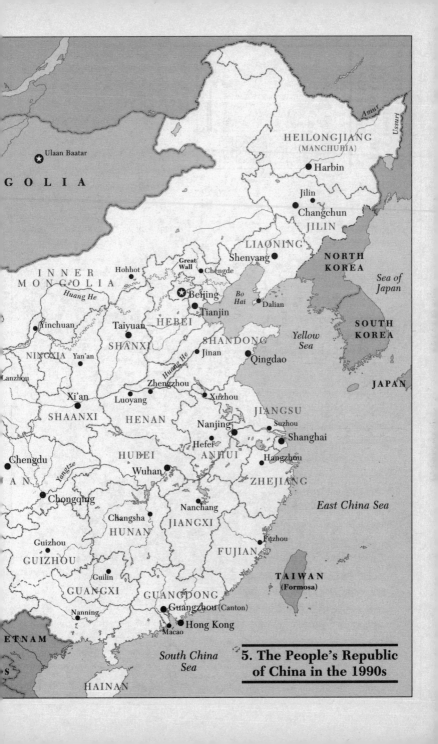

5. The People's Republic of China in the 1990s

6. The European Community/European Union since 1958

YEAR OF ENTRY

- Original members
- 1973
- 1981
- 1986
- 1990
- 1995
- 1997 negotiations

0 — 200 MILES
0 — 200 KM

What's past is prologue.

—WILLIAM SHAKESPEARE

History is bunk.

—HENRY FORD

Yesterday will be what tomorrow was.

—GÜNTER GRASS

History is the gradual instant.

—ANNE MICHAELS

Introduction

One World, published in New York in April 1943, was one of the biggest nonfiction bestsellers to date. It sold its first million copies in only seven weeks—quicker than either *The Outline of History* (1920) by H. G. Wells or Dale Carnegie's *How to Win Friends and Influence People* (1936). By October 1944, when its author, Wendell Willkie, died of a heart attack, *One World* had been translated into dozens of foreign languages and had notched up 4.5 million sales.

Willkie had been the Republican party's presidential candidate in 1940. On August 26, 1942, with the blessing of President Franklin D. Roosevelt, he set off in a converted U.S. bomber to view the war fronts. Around the world he went in forty-nine days (thirty of them spent on the ground)—a total of 31,000 miles—across the Atlantic to Cairo and Teheran, on to Moscow and Chongqing, then back via Siberia and Alaska. *One World* was Willkie's hastily composed travelogue. "The world has become small and completely interdependent," he wrote. The "myriad millions of human beings of the Far East are as close to us as Los Angeles is to New York by the fastest trains. . . . Our thinking in the future must be world-wide."[1]

In the 1940s, air travel was abolishing distance—at least for a few. Over the next half-century it became available to millions. The whole period is, on one trajectory, the story of a growing web of interconnectedness in travel and trade, ideas and information, that takes us on to the Internet of the late 1990s. It has also seen unprecedented migration of peoples, from country to country and even more important, from countryside to city. What mattered was not merely the fact of interconnection, but the growing awareness of it. This was fostered by mass education and by the spread of radio and television. A quarter-century after Willkie, space flight transformed one world into one planet, and TV allowed millions of human beings to share the astronauts' vision of earth (Plates 17 and 18). That image became an icon of our age—the fragile biosphere floating in the darkness of infinite space.

Unities—real and perceived, yet also divisions. Willkie's own book was full of them—the rifts caused by totalitarianism and imperialism, by religion and nationalism, by hierarchy, class, and landed wealth. Less than a year after his death, the atomic bomb gave humanity a truly novel weapon of destruction, around which the postwar era polarized in a struggle between the United States and the Soviet Union. Crisscrossing the "East-West" divide has been a "North-South" gulf between colonies and empires, between dominant industrial powers and dependent new nations. The South, in turn, fractured into Jew, Muslim, and Hindu, into the well oiled and oil-less, into Asian tigers, Indian elephants, and, at times, African jackals. Nor was the North a unity—Serbs battled with Croats, Ulstermen fought Irish Nationalists, and the politics of the European Community often seemed to be a continuation of war by other means. This was not just a divided world, therefore, but one that could apparently be almost endlessly divided. The tools of unification (from statehood to software) also served as weapons of disintegration—creating new states and sects, reinforcing old cultures and nations.

Greater unity and keener consciousness of interconnection; but also multiple divisions and the creation of many more: to adapt the U.S. pledge of allegiance, this is a story of one world, divisible.

But can one tell it as a story? After all, stories have beginnings and endings. By definition, a history of our own time has no ending. Contemporary historians are like interpreters, trying to comprehend a very long sentence in German, whose verb has yet to be uttered.[2] Back in the seventeenth century, Sir Walter Raleigh wisely prefaced his history of the world with the warning that "who-so-euer in writing a modern Historie, shall follow truth too neare the heeles, it may happily strike out his teeth."[3] Any contemporary historian must accept the risk that he will soon be reading his book with a wry, toothless grin.

The idea of narrative history is itself problematic. To postmodernists, stories are "explanatory fictions" created by the author to make sense of the world: they have no basis in reality, which is experienced as a mere sequence of events. I incline, however, to the view that storytelling is rooted in human consciousness. Remembrance and anticipation structure every conscious experience—the intermingling of time past, time present, and time future that informs the first of T. S. Eliot's *Four Quartets*.[4] This is why I have written a book not just about how people have acted, but about how they have understood their actions in the context of time. Sometimes the past has seemed a dead weight—"bunk," to quote Henry Ford—but often, in the line from Shakespeare that graces the portico of the U.S. National Archives, "What's past is prologue."[5]

Yet postmodernists are right to remind us that there is an element of construction in every narrative, be it avowed fiction or putative fact. They reserve particular contempt for "grand narratives" with an overarching theme, many of which are fabricated from present-day political agenda. Contemporary history is often victor's history. Whoever shapes the future determines interpretations of the past: "Yesterday will be what tomorrow was,"[6] to quote the German novelist Günter Grass.

It would, for instance, be tempting in a book of this sort to take a victor's history of the cold war as the grand narrative for the last half-century. President George Bush told the U.S. Congress in January 1992: "The biggest thing that has happened in the world in my life, in our lives, is this: By the grace of God, America won the cold war."[7] But, although this book takes seriously the impact of American power, wealth, and values on the postwar world, that does not constitute the totality, let alone the "end," of history. Even as a metaphor, it is deeply misleading to claim, in the words of a popular overview of the cold war, that "for 45 years the world held its breath."[8] As we shall see, much of moment happened in the postwar era, especially in the developing world, that cannot be squeezed into a cold war box. In particular, this interpretative scheme does not easily accommodate the rich and diverse past that has been uncovered by the "new social history"—about women and children, about families and social groups.

Nor can that social history be constructed around a Marxist framework—in the first half of our period the most fashionable "grand narrative" for interpreting current events. By the 1990s, it was hard to sustain the idea, however flexibly framed, that the dynamic of history is class struggle, from which the eventual outcome will be the triumph of the working class. As even Marxists had to admit, the collapse of the Soviet bloc contradicted their theory of history, "in which the idea of reverse movement from socialism to capitalism has no place."[9] While the teleology of class struggle became a victim of history, the concept of class as social description fell afoul of the new social historians, who found it too crude and myopic to serve as an overriding concept, even in industrial Europe, let alone the developing world.[10] For them, and for this book, class is only one of several (loose) concepts that matter in understanding economic and social relationships.

Marxist historiography is in retreat. Socialists, it seems, are turning into capitalists, workers are becoming consumers. Does that make "globalization" the interpretive key to the last half-century? I think not. If stated without qualification, globalization is just cold war victor's history conceptualized in a wider frame. As I have already suggested, the striking feature of recent decades has been the dialectical process of greater integration *and* greater fragmentation—the two being interrelated. If this book has a grand narrative, therefore, it is deliberately contrapuntal—*One World Divisible*. And that narrative is constructed mainly, but by no means exclusively, around what I take to be the central, political mechanism of the dialectic. This is the process of state building.

Since 1945, the membership of the United Nations has more than tripled to 185 states. Most of them were born out of the death of empires, from Japan's in 1945 to Russia's in 1991, and particularly from the demise of European colonialism in Asia, Africa, and the Middle East. The emergence and attempted consolidation of new states has generated much of the friction of this last half-century—both destructive and creative. From this has arisen endemic conflicts, such as those surrounding the state of Israel, and also innovative cooperation, notably the European Union. States have imploded in civil war in Africa and the Balkans; they have also forged alliances, voluntary and involuntary, such as NATO and the Warsaw Pact. All have struggled to regulate their relations within the arena of the UN. States are objects as well as actors. The revenue, resources, and weaponry at their disposal have been contested by rival social groups, from Peronist Argentina to Christian Democratic Italy. Although not every member of the UN figures in these pages, an emphasis on the proliferation and interplay of states may act as an antidote to the tendency in books of broad history to subsume local variety in global teleology.

A major source of conflict has been the attempt to relate territorial boundaries to ethnic and religious groupings—in other words, to make states congruent with nations. Yet this is an era in which *both* have been endlessly invented, from South Asia in the late 1940s to the Balkans in the early 1990s. The framework of the state is therefore a way to examine cultural and religious forces that are sometimes neglected by twentieth-century political historians—again treating them not as eternal essences but as part of the underlying dialectic of unifications and divisions. Religion plays a particularly important part in what follows, because it still provides a legitimizing authority for much of humankind and also because its politicization has been a feature of the period, from liberation theology in Latin America to the Christian right in the United States, from Islamic fundamentalism in the Middle East to militant Hindus and Buddhists in South Asia. Also central to the book is the concept of "race"—perhaps the classic modern example of an ethnic distinction reified by politics. This takes us from the Aryan megalomania of Nazism, which led to the systematic murder of millions of Jews, to the white supremacists of the American South and apartheid South Africa. But often, race was also an invented, unifying category for Third World militancy. The idea that racism was a whites-only virus is belied by the wartime record of Japanese imperialism, the conflicts over Chinese commercial minorities across Asia, and the "tribal" genocides of Nigeria in the 1960s or Rwanda in the 1990s.

Within this framework of the state, I pay particular attention to two themes, both stemming from the challenges to liberalism and capitalism that precipitated the Second World War. One was whether liberal traditions of representative government could cope with democracy—with universal adult suffrage. The "vanguard democracy" of the Soviet Union was one challenge to liberalism; the militarized mass democracy of Nazi Germany was another. Both were exported across the developing world after World War II, as new states experimented with a single mass-party and/or military government. The other question, posed sharply by the depression of the 1930s, was whether the management of modern industrial economies could be left to market forces, at home and abroad. The Soviet model of a planned, autarkic economy seemed to have been vindicated by victory in World War II, and it was taken up, to varying degrees, by developing states from Latin America to India. On the other hand, the American philosophy of private ownership and open trade was gradually (and patchily) adopted in Western Europe and East Asia.

On the face of it, these political and economic contests redounded to America's benefit. Certainly, on both counts, the Soviets "lost" the cold war. But although pluralist politics and civilian rule are now more common, most of the world does not operate on American principles of liberal democracy. And capitalism in East Asia has taken very different forms from those of the United States or Western Europe. The People's Republic of China (home to about a quarter of the world's population) is a reminder that one-party rule is not dead and that state capitalism is not a contradiction in terms.

In the more global market, however, the capacity of states has been eroded. Another theme of the period is the growing prominence of what political scientists call "transnational" forces, those transcending the polities of national states. Multinational corporations existed in the first half of the century, but they came into their own when barriers to commerce and capital began to fall in the 1950s and 1960s. Initially, most of these companies were based in North America and Western Europe, but multinationals from Japan and the Asian tigers soon became major players as well. Even more significant was the growth of transnational capital. By the 1970s, economic growth and financial deregulation had produced a large and turbulent pool of private capital, exceeding all government reserves and sloshing around in search of speculative opportunities. It became harder for governments to sustain fixed exchange rates, first in the West and then in the developing world, especially with the spread of currency markets and computerized trading.

Multinational business and private capital posed grave challenges to the capacity of even developed states to manage their own economies. Many developing countries simply could not cope. Economies still reliant on a few primary products were often dominated by the companies that extracted and marketed those minerals or cash crops. And as states opened up to foreign investment, many incurred debts that could not be sustained when commodity prices fell in the 1980s, with devastating consequences in Africa and Latin America. While the industrial economies established relationships of competitive interdependence, debt and dependence was the name of the game for much of the world. Western bailouts were conditional on greater openness to the world economy, but the restructuring also brought misery to millions. Economic integration went hand in hand with social fragmentation.

These are some of the broad themes of this book. They are traced in a broadly chronological progression, moving from one area of the world to another. The first three chapters look at facets of the postwar decade. Chapter 1 considers the impact of World War II, particularly on the two new superpowers and on Europe, while Chapter 2 examines the effect of the communist and nationalist revolutions on Asia, with special attention to China and Japan. Chapter 3 looks at the legacies of empire—both recent imperialisms as in South Asia, the Middle East, and Africa, and older ones in Latin America and the British "White Dominions."

The cold war is central to Chapters 4 and 6. The first of these deals with the character of divided Europe in the 1950s, including the economic growth of the German-led West. The second focuses on the apogee of superpower confrontation in the early 1960s, over the space race and Cuba, and on European attempts to break free of bipolarity—notably by de Gaulle's France and Dubček's Czechoslovakia.

Chapter 7 examines the sixties battle lines of race (especially in the United States and Africa) and of religion (the conflicts in the Middle East and South Asia), emphasizing the reliance of many developing states, particularly in Latin America and Africa, on the military as political backbone. In Chapter 8, attention turns to East and Southeast Asia in the 1960s—the turmoil in China, the upheavals in Indonesia, the war in Vietnam. By the 1970s, however (Chapter 10), the United States had eased its relations with Russia and China (likewise Western Europe with Eastern Europe), and the new round of Indochina wars pitted communist against communist. Chapter 11 shifts to the momentous events in the Middle East in the 1970s—the 1973 Arab-Israeli war, the oiling of the gulf states, and the Islamic revolution in Iran. Revolutions of a different and more durable sort are the theme of Chapter 12, which looks at the rise of Japan and the Asian tigers, at a time when the Western economies recorded slow growth and rapid inflation. It also compares the contrasting economic fortunes of China and India in the 1970s.

Our view of the 1980s is inevitably colored by the collapse of the Soviet bloc in 1989–1991. Yet, in the early 1980s, the West seemed to be facing graver challenges (Chapter 13), with capitalist ideology in flux, debt crises in Latin America, the collapse of Western client states in Africa, and a "new cold war" that threatened to rupture the Atlantic Alliance. Only in the late 1980s (Chapter 15), was the far more serious crisis of communism exposed, as Gorbachev's efforts at reform expedited revolutions in Eastern Europe and the breakup of the Soviet Union itself. Only in China, fatefully, did communist rule survive. The global aftermath of the cold war, for states and regions, is explored in Chapter 16. This highlights both the triumphs of "democracy" and "capitalism" and also the very real inadequacies of both of those concepts for understanding our contemporary world.

Not everything, however, can be fitted into a politically framed narrative. The explosion of social history, much of it written from the bottom up, not from the top down, has transformed the historical profession in the last few decades, opening the lives of peasants and workers, ethnic minorities and female majorities, to novel inspection and analysis. In particular, the idea that we are writing not merely history but *her-story* is now accepted in principle, if not in practice. How can these new insights be accommodated in a work of this sort?

I share the feeling that some recent social history has neglected the ubiquity of power in human affairs, and that we need to "bring the state back in."[11] Hence my overriding framework. Social attitudes and conduct also vary widely with political context—as we shall see, for example, when looking at women in Western and Eastern Europe during the cold war. Moreover, much social (and political) historiography is technologically illiterate. My own erudition in this area is strictly limited, but I have tried to take the issue seriously, particularly in a long chapter about the advanced technologies that have shaped the late twentieth century. Yet we should also bear in mind that, in the world as a whole, the decisive technologies have often been very basic. When we talk of the "wired world," for instance, what really matters to most people is electricity in the home, not access to the Internet.

Another complication is that social change operates on a different tempo and rhythm from the dramas of high politics. To quote the French historian Fernand Braudel, we must have an eye for both "conspicuous history which holds our attention by its continual and dramatic changes" and "submerged" history, whose motions are "almost silent and always discreet."[12] Each pattern is important. Moreover, what is submerged sometimes breaks the surface with seismic force—as in Paris in May 1968 or Berlin in November 1989. History is "the gradual instant."[13]

I have therefore interrupted my politically framed narrative at four points to explore underlying forces of social and cultural change. In Chapter 5, the focus is on demography, urbanization, and American consumer culture. Death rates and birth rates, cities and suburbs, cars and fridges, phones and TVs—these have been the dynamos of modernity. Chapter 9 looks at the consumption of culture (both "high" and "low") in art and music, which was made possible by the culture of consumption. It also examines the revolutions in child education and female labor (both reproductive and productive) that have loosened up patriarchal family life. The subject of Chapter 14 is science and technology—shifting emphasis from the familiar, cold war story of nuclear energy to the neglected histories of electronics (transistors and computers) and genetics (DNA and biotechnology), which, I stress, had greater impact on the postwar era.

These three chapters—on Cities and Consumers, on Cultures and Families, and on Chips and Genes—provide an essential counterpoint to the political theme. After each of these topics is examined, usually at a point when it is of particular political relevance, it is drawn into subsequent narrative chapters. But I return to these social-cultural-technological themes in Chapter 17 on Goods and Values, as part of a reflection on the material and the intellectual, the global and the local, in our contemporary world.

In a work of this sort, there can be no "conclusion" (like you, I am waiting for the verbs), but it would be impossible and improper to avoid ruminating on the changes and continuities, the evolutions and revolutions, examined in this book. So the epilogue pulls together some threads from the last half-century and offers a personal view of their significance.

1

The Mushroom Cloud and the Iron Curtain

The Cover Story That Never Was

At the end of July 1945, with Germany defeated and Japan encircled, the staff of *Time* magazine in New York began preparing a cover story about the weapon that had won the war. Tracing the development of radar took them back to decisive moments in the conflict—gaining early warning of German air raids in the Battle of Britain in 1940–1941, locating U-boats in the Atlantic in 1942–1943, identifying bombing targets in cloud-covered France and Germany in 1944–1945. In the 1930s, many governments had experimented with RAdio Detection And Ranging—the term was adopted by the U.S. Navy in late 1940—transmitting a pulsating radio wave and using the echo to calculate location and distance. But the decisive combination was Anglo-American. The Battle of Britain had been won with waves of more than one meter, using cumbersome "bedspring" antennae. In the autumn of 1940, the British shared their pioneering research on microwave radar (nearer the infrared part of the electromagnetic spectrum), which permitted reception by small and mobile "bowls." In a massive program centered on a new radiation laboratory (or RadLab) at the Massachusetts Institute of Technology (MIT), the Pentagon developed systems for use in ships and planes, as well as in early-warning defenses. After the war, radar had multitudinous civilian applications, ranging from microwave ovens and radio astronomy to systems for air traffic control. Equally important, hundreds of scientists had been diverted from nuclear and particle physics—the sexy subjects of the 1930s—and "exposed" to microwaves. Out of this came, directly, the transistor—one of the most important innovations of the last half-century. And without radar, the development of the computer would have been very different.[1]

The war saw other notable innovations. Hitler expended vast resources on what *he* judged the potential winning weapon—long-range rockets. The V-2s did not save the Third Reich, but these weapons (and their designers) were some of the most valuable booty that the superpowers looted in 1945. In them we find the origins of the space race of the cold war. Another development was the jet engine. Both the British and the Germans had jet fighters operational by the spring of 1944. When we remember that piston-engine monoplane fighters were novel at the beginning of the war in 1939, we can see again how the conflict accelerated technological change—destruction as the mother of invention.

Yet war was about saving life as well as destroying it. Many techniques of military medicine would also have vast civilian applications. Penicillin had been isolated and tested in Britain in the late 1930s. In the last two years of the war the Americans and British had manufactured enough of it for systematic use at the battlefronts, cutting fatalities by up to 15 percent.[2] By setting one microbe against another in this way, they began the antibiotic revolution. And so we could go on. Deaths caused by the explosion of a ship carrying mustard gas at the Italian port of Bari in December 1943 stimulated research into chemotherapy for cancers; a few months later, the use of the insecticide DDT in the Naples typhus epidemic launched the "miracle dust" that would help eliminate malaria.

In these and many other ways, the appliance of science helped turn the war and would shape the peace. I shall return to some of these technologies, especially electronics, in Chapter 14. But in the end, none of them figured in *Time* magazine's cover story on the war's winning weapon. In its issue of August 20, 1945, a highly condensed account of radar, plus the graphics originally commissioned for the cover, began on page 78. Instead, *Time* featured "an event so much more enormous that, relative to it, the war itself shrank to minor significance." *Time* called it simply "The Bomb."[3]

In vain, RadLab veterans insisted the bomb had only ended the war, radar had won it. In vain, they argued that their program had cost up to 50 percent more, with a price tag of some $3 billion. To no avail. The world war had ended with an atomic bang, not an electronic whimper. By the end of 1945, 140,000 inhabitants of Hiroshima had died from incineration or radiation;

likewise another 70,000 in the city of Nagasaki. And it had ended suddenly. Instead of months of fighting to capture the Japanese home islands, the bombs dropped on August 6 and 9 were followed on August 15 by the emperor's announcement of surrender. (Few Americans tried to factor in the impact of the Soviet declaration of war on the 8th.) Unlike that of radar, the power of the bomb was spectacularly visible. A brilliant fireball surged upward—white, orange, red, purple. Then it became streaked with black from the debris of what it had incinerated, before cooling into clouds as it hit the upper atmosphere to form its ethereal dome (Plate 1). The very term "mushroom cloud," quickly a commonplace, suggested a natural event rather than man-made destruction. With pictures of the dead and maimed suppressed by U.S. military censors, and the enormity of radiation sickness not yet grasped, the enduring image of 1945 was one of awesome, revolutionary power—monopolized by the United States. On hearing of Hiroshima, President Harry Truman exclaimed, "This is the greatest thing in history."[4]

So the creative potential of much wartime science was eclipsed by the destructive power of the bomb. In many ways, what followed was indeed the atomic age, whose unfolding will preoccupy us in subsequent chapters. But although other science seemed almost a footnote to history (and will be noted as such at places in this chapter), it is a fundamental contention of this book that we shall misunderstand much of the last half-century if we focus on the nuclear theme. Not only the world that emerged from the cold war, but the cold war itself, were legacies of radar as much as the bomb.

That is to anticipate, however. The world was fixated on the bomb in 1945, partly because it seemed to sum up the ferocious power of modern warfare. The European analogue of Hiroshima was Berlin—Germany's capital and industrial heart, arguably the cultural center of Europe in the 1920s—now battered into rubble by British and American bombers and by Russian tanks and artillery (Plate 2). In the city center, 60 percent of the housing had been destroyed. Only seven thousand trees out of two hundred thousand remained standing in the vast Tiergarten park. Hunger and misery were the lot of citizens who, five years before, had cheered their soldiers home through the Brandenburg Gate after a six-week campaign to crush France.

As at Hiroshima, foreign visitors were overwhelmed by an almost abstract sense of history. Hitler had boasted his empire would last for a thousand years. Now Berlin was "utter wasteland," wrote the American journalist William Shirer, adding "I don't think there has ever been such destruction on such a scale." The British author Stephen Spender predicted that the ruined Reichstag and Chancellery would be attracting sightseers for the next five hundred years—modern equivalents of the Colosseum at Rome. Alfred Döblin, author of a famous 1929 novel entitled *Berlin Alexanderplatz,* was also sobered by what he now saw: "You need to sit among the ruins for a long time, to let them get to you, and experience the pain and the judgment fully."[5]

Hiroshima and Berlin. The end of two empires—with a vengeance. Graphic evidence that war had given way to peace. Grim testimony to humanity's new technological powers. In time, the ruins would be rebuilt. But Japan had lost its independence. And Europe, especially Germany, was becoming partitioned by what Winston Churchill called the Iron Curtain. The division of Europe by two new "superpowers" is the theme of this chapter; the reactions of the Europeans will be considered more fully in Chapter 4.

The War and the Superpowers

Measured on the scale of human history, the greatest novelty of the war was indeed the scale of destruction. From the Seine to the Danube, the heartland of continental Europe had been ravaged. A few cities escaped—notably Paris, Rome, and Prague—but urban Germany was in ruins, ports from Rotterdam to Piraeus were choked with rubble, and everywhere bridges, roads and railways were wrecked. The Soviet Union had suffered even more severely, losing 30 percent of its prewar capital stock. Six million buildings were destroyed, and twenty-five million Soviet people rendered homeless.[6] Even Britain, which was never occupied by the enemy, lost about one-quarter of its national wealth. Across Asia the pattern was similar. Even before dropping the atomic bombs, the Americans had turned many of Japan's wooden cities into firebombed wasteland, particularly the area around Tokyo and Yokohama. In China, the war had destroyed most of the industrial plant of Manchuria; Japan's decision to blow up the dikes along the Yellow River had flooded three million acres of farmland. For all these countries, the immediate postwar years would be preoccupied with rebuilding and economic recovery.

On the other hand, some parts of the world were largely unscarred, including the Near East, most of Africa south of the Sahara, and the Western Hemisphere. It was particularly significant that the continental United States, unique among the major belligerents, was untouched by occupation or even bombing, apart from a handful of Japanese incendiaries. In fact, the war pulled the country out of its long depression, almost doubling the gross national product. Remarkably, the United States enjoyed guns *and* butter—producing more aircraft than Germany and Japan combined but also increasing its output of textiles and alcoholic drinks by 50 percent. To quote the historian Mark Leff, "War is hell. But for millions of Americans on the booming home front, World War II was also a hell of a war."[7] The contrast between America's new wealth and the enforced poverty of its former enemies and allies was of profound importance in the first postwar decade.

The human cost was even more appalling. Perhaps sixty million soldiers and civilians had lost their lives (compared with ten million in the fighting of 1914–1918). Again the Americans suffered least—three hundred thousand dead (fewer even than Britain's four hundred thousand) constituted less than 0.25 percent of the prewar population. By comparison, war-induced famines took the lives of more than a million in Bengal in 1943 and another million in Vietnam two years later. Of the dead, at least twenty-five million came from the Soviet Union, and perhaps another fifteen million were Chinese— although neither estimate can be precise.[8] The magnitude of Russian and Chinese losses was little known at the time, though, as we shall see, they must be taken seriously if we wish to understand the meaning and consequences of the war. What made more impact in 1945 was the extermination of nearly all the Jews of Europe, between five and six million people, half of them from Poland. Of these, about 60 percent had died in the Nazi camps, one million in Auschwitz alone.[9] The liberation of these camps in 1945, filmed extensively by Allied correspondents, gave a new moral meaning to the war. At Dachau, a nauseated American lieutenant machine-gunned 346 SS guards around the rotting corpses of the inmates. Incensed Allied commanders forced Germans from nearby towns to inspect the results. Under the Third Reich, evil had become domesticated, made "banal" in the term popularized by the scholar Hannah Arendt. The postwar world would never transcend that memory. And the provision of a safe homeland for the Jews became a major issue in international relations.

Globally, the conflict revolved around three epic struggles. One was between Germany and Russia over living space in Eastern Europe in 1941–1945. This was given added horror by Nazi policies of racial extermination against the Slavic *Untermenschen*. In the three-year siege of Leningrad alone, Russian deaths exceeded those of America and Britain combined for the whole war. The turning point of this struggle was the battle for Stalingrad, for which 800,000 Germans and 1.2 million Russians died. Although English-language histories of the war still concentrate on themes such as the Second Front debate and the Mediterranean campaign, their relative insignificance is suggested by the fact that between June 1941 and June 1944 (from the German invasion of Russia to the Allied landings in Normandy), 93 percent of the German Army's battle casualties were inflicted by the Soviets.[10] The fact that the Anglo-American invasion of France was delayed until 1944 helped ensure that the war would end with the USSR occupying much of Eastern Europe. That was a given of the postwar world.

The second main axis of World War II was a three-cornered struggle for mastery of China, involving Japan, the Chinese Nationalists, and the Chinese communists. This dated back to the breakup of the Qing dynasty in 1911 and the establishment of Japan's empire on the Asian mainland around the beginning of the twentieth century. But in its most recent phase, it began with the Japanese conquest of Manchuria in 1931 and of much of northeast China in 1937–1938. The Russians were actively involved in 1938–1939 and again in August 1945. After 1940, Japan's attention turned to Southeast Asia and then the Pacific, but at least one-third of its troops remained stuck in the China "quagmire." This was a conflict that none of the belligerents could win, even though the Japanese summer offensive of 1944 decimated Nationalist forces in the south. During this time, Nationalists and communists toned down their civil war, but from base areas in, respectively, southern and north-central China, they rebuilt their strength. After Japan's surrender in August 1945, they resumed their struggle for mastery of China. The outcome will be examined in Chapter 2.

In both of these conflicts, the British played a supporting role. Their main contribution to the outcome of the European war (a critical one) had been the refusal to surrender in 1940. This preserved Britain as a vital base for the bombing and eventual invasion of northwest Europe. In Asia they would have found it hard to recover the colonies they had lost in Japan's Pacific blitzkrieg of 1941–1942 but for the sudden Japanese capitulation in 1945. This enabled them to make a quick return to Malaya and Hong Kong and to piggy-back the French and Dutch into their lost territories in Southeast Asia. The Europeans therefore remained imperial powers after the war, as we shall see in Chapters 2 and 3.

The American contribution to the war came later than Britain's and cost less, but it was ultimately more important. In Asia, it constituted the third of the major global conflicts—the Pacific War (or *taiheiyō sensō*) in Japanese terminology, to distinguish it from the Greater East Asian War (*tōa sensō*) centered on China.[11] The United States was drawn into the conflict in December 1941 because its fleet and its territories of Hawaii and the Philippines (both relics of America's brief flurry of formal imperialism in 1898) blocked Japan's expansion. The humiliations America suffered in 1941–1942, particularly the attack on Pearl Harbor, inspired a war effort that eventually drove the Japanese back across the Pacific and ended with the United States dominating the occupation of Japan itself in 1945.

America's serious role in the European conflict began even later, with the invasion of France in June 1944. Until then, the British were the senior partner in their alliance against Germany and Italy. But in the last months of the war, American manpower became predominant in Western Europe, amounting to 60 percent of Allied troops there by the end of the war. And in both theaters, America's vast economic power was of critical importance, whether in the bombing of Germany and Japan or in material aid to Russia, China, and particularly Britain under Lend-Lease. By 1943–1944, for instance, virtually all Britain's raw material imports and a quarter of its military equipment came from the United States, while, ironically, U.S. trucks, jeeps and aircraft helped accelerate the Red Army's drive across Eastern Europe in 1944–1945.[12] By this time, however, American troops were deep into Western Europe as well. When the European war ended in May 1945, Americans and Russians eyed each other over the ruins of Hitler's Reich.

The dynamics of war shaped the patterns of peace. The events of 1941–1945 had created or at least mobilized two new "superpowers"—the word was coined in 1944 by the American political scientist William T. R. Fox to denote states with "great power plus great mobility of power."[13] At the end of the war, the Soviet Union and the United States had armed forces about 12 million strong. Yet the nature of their power was very different. The Soviet Union was a continuation of the old tsarist empire. Although its economy had made great strides since Stalin's forced industrialization of the late 1920s, its strength rested on vast resources of territory, raw materials, and manpower. It was not, for instance, a significant naval power, and its air force was mainly employed in support of land operations. In contrast, America boasted the world's greatest navy and air force, backed by an economy that produced half the world's manufactured goods using technology that was far in advance of Russia's. What enabled the Soviet Union to compete, at least in the short-term, was its "command economy," whereby the government was able to divert a large proportion of the country's resources into military activity. Stalin's prime postwar objective in this area was to break America's monopoly on the atomic bomb. "Hiroshima has shaken the world. The balance has been destroyed," he reportedly exclaimed on hearing the news. The Soviets' hitherto low-key atomic project was given top priority and placed under the personal direction of Lavrenti Beria, the chief of the secret police. Even if America had been willing to share the atomic secret (which it wasn't), Stalin would have wanted his own bomb—the ultimate, both as weapon and status symbol.[14]

The Soviet Union forged by Lenin and, after his death in 1924, by Stalin was, according to its constitution, a voluntary union of fifteen equal republics. Yet in practice, Soviet federalism was very different from that of the United States. It was a concession by Lenin and Stalin to the fact that they ruled a multinational empire of some two hundred million people (in 1940) from one hundred national groups and covering nearly nine million square miles, one-sixth of the earth's surface. This made it three times as large as the United States. What held it together was central domination. That domination was partly national. In 1950, 57 percent of the population was Russian; the Russian republic, which included the whole of Siberia across to the Pacific, accounted for most of the country's industry and key raw materials. Even the Ukraine, a major grain-producing area with 20 percent of the population, could not compare.

Even more important than Russian predominance was the one-party state. The Bolshevik coup in 1917 had not been followed by world revolution, but its leaders had survived a brutal civil war and they consolidated socialism in one country. Territorially, the Communist party spread down to three thousand urban and rural districts; there were also some two hundred thousand functional organizations in farms and factories, places of education and social institutions. The party was the government; society was subsumed in the state. The supreme organ of the party was its political bureau (Politburo), presided over by the general secretary. Since 1922, that post had been held by Josef Stalin.

Josef Vissarionovich Dzhugashvili (as he was born in 1879) seemed an unprepossessing autocrat. He was only five feet, four inches tall, and lacked charisma or oratorical skill. A childhood injury had left him with a withered left arm; his face was pockmarked and blotchy from smallpox contracted at the age of six. He came from a squalid town in rural Georgia, the only surviving son of a tyrannical father and a devoted mother, and left home in 1901 to join the revolutionary underground. He spent the next sixteen years on the run, in and out of tsarist prisons. This early life crystallized his isolated, suspicious, and brutal nature—the "man of steel" in his revolutionary pseudonym. But Stalin also had a methodical mind and an encyclopedic memory. Equally important, he was an accomplished actor. In the 1920s, he turned the paper-pushing post of party general secretary into the hub of a vast patronage network that enabled him to supplant and destroy the cosmopolitan sophisticates who thought of him as a coarse backroom boy. Many have judged that Stalin was clinically paranoid—the first to do so, a distinguished Russian neuropathologist in 1927, died a few days later![15] On one level, Stalin's purges were desperate efforts to hang on to power against real and imagined enemies. But the personal blurred into the political. "Stalin sought not simply power, but revolutionary power."[16] He saw himself as Lenin's successor, continuing and securing the tenuous revolution. In his view, Russia remained in a state of civil war during the 1920s and 1930s, necessitating the extermination of class enemies in the peasantry, the party, or the army. Throughout that period, he believed Russia was also in external danger: hence the need to impose breakneck industrial revolution regardless of the human cost.

Even so, Hitler's invasion in June 1941 was nearly disastrous. The country was ill prepared—indeed, Stalin's purges had decimated the military leadership—and in the early days of the invasion Stalin was psychologically and politically near to collapse. The German surrender at Stalingrad in February

1943 was therefore a personal as well as a national turning point, and victory in 1945 secured his regime completely. The great parades in Red Square, with captured German standards being piled beneath his feet at the base of the Lenin mausoleum, were a deliberate echo of Tsar Alexander's victory over Napoleon.

Although Stalin lived a fairly simple existence by the standard of dictators, the cult of personality now flourished, with statues, poems, and songs dedicated to him. Possible rivals in public esteem were quickly removed. For instance, Marshal Georgii Zhukov, the defender of Moscow and the conqueror of Berlin, was packed off to commands in Odessa and then the Urals.[17] Moreover, 1945 vindicated and entrenched the Stalinist elite as a whole. Although there were more purges, especially in Leningrad in 1948–1949, none matched the prewar horrors. The war years had taken their toll on Stalin's health, and autumn vacations on the Black Sea lengthened to three months in his final years. He was less involved in domestic matters—giving party, security forces, and local elites more leeway. Yet the result of this was not reform but atrophy—"mummified dogmas" enshrining "absolute bureaucracy," to quote one of his biographers.[18] As we shall see, Stalin's successors, notably Khrushchev and Gorbachev, would struggle with reform. But they were all beneficiaries of Stalinism. The system had a life of its own.

What did victory mean for the "average" Soviet citizen? There was undoubtedly pride in the achievement, which official propaganda cultivated assiduously, but the overwhelming emotions, however, must have been relief and sadness. The eternal flames burning not only beneath the Kremlin wall but in towns and villages across the western USSR bore silent witness to the grief that few families had escaped. European Russia, the Ukraine and Belorussia had been the main battlegrounds, and here the task of recovery was enormous. Some cities were rebuilt rapidly, but these were usually historic centers. By 1956, for instance, Kiev, capital of the Ukraine, had been wholly restored, but the city of Kremenchug, two hundred miles southeast, was still in ruins. The blueprint for recovery was the five-year plan promulgated in March 1946. Like previous plans, this concentrated on transport and heavy industry (particularly related to defense). In coal, steel, and electricity, the plan more than achieved its aim of exceeding prewar outputs by 1950. As before, the main casualty was agriculture. In 1946, the grain harvest was 20 percent down from the previous year, causing serious food shortages. Although this crisis was partly due to severe drought, it also reflected official priorities. In the race to rebuild industry, villages were starved of manpower, equipment, and building materials. True to form, Stalin also struck back at peasant independence by reasserting the prewar dominance of the inefficient collective farms and, from 1950, encouraging their amalgamation into larger units. In 1952, agricultural production had still not returned to the levels of 1940. The peasants were also the main victims of Stalin's currency reform of December 1947, when coins were exchanged at one-tenth of their face value, wiping out many people's hoarded savings. This was, admittedly, part of a general realignment of prices and wages to accompany the end of rationing— a welcome change—but, for most Soviet citizens, the last years of Stalin were a time of continued hardship.[19]

Life in the United States could hardly have been more different. Whereas Soviet federalism was a token concession from the top down, American federalism was a living reality emanating from the bottom up. The individual states had created the Union after their break with Britain in 1776, but this was mainly to satisfy basic common interests in defense and foreign policy. The federal government grew in authority over the next century and a half, particularly during the Civil War of 1861–1865, which held the Union together at the cost of 620,000 dead, but central authority remained weak. American democracy was an expression of this local self-government. By the 1830s, the elective principle had become the norm for most governmental offices, including the U.S. presidency. Abhorrence of centralized power was evident in Washington itself, where the Founding Fathers had deliberately given Congress substantial authority to check the president, through consent to appropriations and appointments. Although a nationwide party system provided some political coordination, the fact that the president and Congress were elected separately meant that the two branches of government might be in opposite political hands. This was the case in 1947–1948, when the Republicans controlled the Congress while a Democrat, Harry S. Truman, resided in the White House. Even when this bifurcation did not occur, as during the Democratic hegemony of President Franklin D. Roosevelt (1933–1945), Congressmen kept their eyes on the local interest groups that ensured their election, rather than following presidential preferences.

The aim of democratic localism was to keep government off people's backs and let them make their own decisions, particularly economic. With cheap land generally available, a quarter of the population still lived on farms in the 1930s, and most whites owned their freeholds. Others ran small businesses in small towns. Even the growing urban labor force was relatively prosperous: unlike in Europe, socialism enjoyed very little appeal in the United States. This was partly a reflection of American living standards, and partly because class consciousness was less potent than ethnic consciousness in the big cities of the early twentieth century. The federal structure and the democratic franchise also helped, for local concentrations of immigrants were able to wrest political power from the old "Anglo-Saxon" elites, as in Chicago or Boston. The United States proved much more successful than the Soviet

Union in assimilating its multinational population and turning them into "Americans."

If they were white, that is. The country had been created through extermination of its original native peoples and, particularly in the Southeast, through exploitation of the black population. Although freed from slavery in 1863 (two years after the tsarist government emancipated Russia's serfs), blacks remained second-class citizens, often working in serflike conditions on southern farms and denied civil and political rights by a network of "Jim Crow" laws and customs. Here the principle of democratic localism meant that the federal government turned a blind eye to breaches of the Constitution. In the cities of the North, blacks usually lived in segregated areas with inferior jobs, housing, and schools. By global standards their poverty was relative: in the 1940s the per capita income of Harlem, New York's black ghetto, ranked with that of the top five nations of the world.[20] But what mattered to most blacks were comparisons with their white American neighbors. By the 1940s these second-class black citizens constituted 10 per cent of the population. Although American liberal democracy had dealt relatively successfully with ethnicity, it had not even addressed "the persistent legacy of the original crime of slavery."[21]

"Race" was one area in which American reality diverged markedly from national ideology. Another was the country's political economy, which was not exactly the "free enterprise" lauded by classical liberalism. The industrial revolution of the late nineteenth century had been preeminently a revolution of scale. The United States was a vast, tariff-free common market, with a well-developed railroad network. Around 1900, a succession of mergers in transport, distribution, and eventually production brought the levers of economic power into a few hands. When titans such as J. P. Morgan or Andrew Carnegie then passed from the scene, capitalism lost its personal character, and these large firms were run by professional managers. But business remained big. In 1947 the two hundred largest industrial companies in the United States accounted for almost half of corporate assets and 30 percent of the value added in manufacturing.[22]

By this time, big business had been reinforced by big government as a consequence of the depression and the war. Between 1929 and 1933 unemployment soared from 3 percent of the work force to 25 percent, while manufacturing output collapsed by one-third. Franklin D. Roosevelt's New Deal programs tried to stimulate demand and provide work and relief for the distressed through increased government spending. The philosophy behind this was belatedly provided by the British economist John Maynard Keynes. Between 1933 and 1939, federal expenditure tripled, and Roosevelt's critics charged that he was turning America into a communist state. But the New

Deal was as nothing compared with World War II. In 1939, federal expenditure was $9 million; it had increased tenfold by 1945. And war spending finally cured the depression, pulling unemployment down from 14 percent in 1940 to less than 2 percent in 1943 as the labor force grew by ten million. Many Americans saw all this as vindicating American liberal capitalism. According to the *Saturday Evening Post:* "If Free Enterprise had not flourished here, the cause of world freedom might now be lost for centuries."[23] In fact, most of the war contracts were funneled through big business, with one hundred corporations receiving two-thirds of the money. And most of the decline in unemployment was due to the draft, as the government pulled the equivalent of 22 percent of the prewar work force into the armed forces.[24] The war economy was not so much a triumph of free enterprise as the result of big business being bankrolled by big government.

Americans ended the war with a prodigious sense of achievement, in marked contrast to the gloom and self-doubt of the depression. "The Great Republic has come into its own," declared the *New York Herald Tribune.* "It stands first among the peoples of the earth."[25] In the first full peacetime year of 1946, federal spending still amounted to $62 billion, or 30 percent of GNP. (In 1929, the proportion was only 3 percent.) But the pressures to "get back to normal" were intense. Congress wanted a return to low, balanced budgets, and families clamored to see the soldiers back home. Between June 1945 and June 1947 the armed forces fell from 12 million to 1.5 million, even though Congress reluctantly maintained the draft. The Truman Administration worried first about a postwar slump, then about the inflationary consequences of pent-up consumer demand. Either way, conversion to a postwar economy would be difficult.

The "GI Bill of Rights," adopted in 1944, was one answer—subsidizing veterans to complete their education rather than flood the job market and probably boost the unemployment figures. But the whole role of government was in question once again. Although America's military-industrial complex was born in World War II, it could easily have been stifled at birth. The federal government might have reverted mainly to domestic management, supplemented perhaps by a greater role in promoting international trade and monetary relations. There was nothing inevitable about "a postwar government looking like the wartime government, with the military establishment transcendent and military-security concerns dominant."[26] When in 1941 Roosevelt reluctantly approved plans for the army's new headquarters in Arlington, Virginia—a mile in circumference and the largest building in the world—he hoped that after the war the Pentagon could be used for storage.[27] That it was not, that the military-industrial complex dominated postwar American life, was largely the result of the cold war.

autarky - economic self-sufficiency, not reliant on imported goods

adjudicate - to settle a dispute or conflict

From Cold Peace to Cold War

There were, then, fundamental contrasts between the United States and the Soviet Union, between democratic localism and bureaucratic centralism, between capitalism and communism. And those contrasts had been simplified and refined in national ideologies to represent two ways of life— each vindicated in 1945 after previous disasters. Conflicting models of autarky versus exports, of state planning against free enterprise, were to vie for the allegiance of the developed and the developing world in the postwar years. Even so, however, the cold war was not inevitable in 1945.

Although the United States was now much more involved in world affairs, its postwar concerns were primarily domestic. Undersecretary of State Dean Acheson summed up the "popular attitude" to foreign policy in late 1945 in three sentences: "1. Bring the boys home; 2. Don't be a Santa Claus; 3. Don't be pushed around."[28] Even though air power had made America theoretically more vulnerable, it remained the most secure great power. Its neighbors in the Western Hemisphere posed no threat, no other country possessed nuclear weapons, and any assault on it would have to be mounted across thousands of miles of ocean guarded by the largest navy in the world. But, in at least two ways, attitudes had been fundamentally changed by the war. First, victory had created a new sense of America's power and, even more, of its moral right to adjudicate world affairs. Roosevelt's aide Harry Hopkins said in 1945 that it was America's business "to do everything within our diplomatic power to foster and encourage democratic governments throughout the world" because "we believe our dynamic democracy is the best in the world."[29] In addition, U.S. policy makers were now defining security in more expansive terms. After Pearl Harbor, the military wanted forward bases to keep an airborne enemy at bay. And the lesson of 1940 was that America dare not allow a hostile power to control the industrial resources of Europe, the other great center of world production. In June 1945 the Joint Chiefs of Staff warned that the Soviet Union was "the sole great power on the Continent—a position unique in modern history."[30] Much, therefore, depended on whether the wartime alliance could be maintained.

The Soviet Union was much less secure than the United States. This was the result of both geography and history. Despite its vast size, the country had only ten thousand miles of seacoast, most of which was either frozen over for most of the year or else controlled by other powers, particularly in the Baltic and Black seas. Improved maritime access had been a perennial aim of Russian foreign policy, before and after the Revolution. Moreover, the extremities of the Soviet Union were vital, yet hard to defend. Siberia provided much of the country's mineral resources, but it lay six thousand miles east of Moscow (twice the distance from New York to San Francisco) and was threatened by the powerful states of China and Japan. To the west, the Soviet Union's borders with Poland had been the cause of bloody dispute ever since World War I, and in 1941 Eastern Europe had been the base for Hitler's invasion. The memory of that surprise attack was even more potent for postwar Soviet leaders than was Pearl Harbor for the Americans. A secure Eastern Europe was deemed vital to prevent a third German war.

Exactly how Stalin intended to achieve that security is hard to ascertain, but he clearly had no wish for an immediate war. Soviet losses were too great and it was also hoped that continued Western aid would help reconstruction. Nor did Stalin share Hitler's grandiose plans for world hegemony. In general, he sought to push the boundaries of the USSR back to their full tsarist extent. These included the Baltic states of Lithuania, Latvia, and Estonia and the eastern part of prewar Poland. More specifically, he wanted no dangers along his western borders. His methods for attaining this varied. In Poland, Romania, and Bulgaria—springboards of Nazi assault—the Red Army quickly imposed governments dominated by Moscow-controlled communists. Stalin was slow to withdraw from northern Iran, and he also pressed the Turks for naval bases and free access out of the Black Sea. But in Finland, against which he had fought a bloody war, he accepted a friendly, noncommunist government, and in Czechoslovakia, whose leader Eduard Beneš had tried to keep a balance between East and West, Russian troops were withdrawn by the end of 1945. Stalin also observed his 1944 agreement with Churchill and did not aid the communists in the bloody civil war in Greece.

It is likely, of course, that his appetite would have grown in time. Stalin was hardly renowned for tolerance of political pluralism, and he also assumed that by the 1960s Germany and Japan would menace the USSR again. Nor did he doubt the underlying antipathy of the other capitalist powers, though in 1945–1946 he seems to have considered Britain, intent on retaining its empire in the Middle East, as a more serious challenge than America, which he did not expect to take much interest in Europe. His inveterate xenophobia reinforced the revolutionary paradigm to create a mental map of "them" and "us," made all the more lurid by his paranoia. And as in the 1920s, the ideology of revolution helped justify the tightening of party rule at home, which had been relaxed during wartime.[31]

All this being acknowledged, however, it seems that at this juncture, Stalin expected that his aspirations could be met within the framework of continued cooperation with America and Britain. When he spoke in November 1944 on the twenty-seventh anniversary of the Revolution, about the alliance resting not on "chance and passing considerations but vitally important and long-term interests," this was not mere rhetoric. Nevertheless, his words must be understood from the perspective of Marxist-Leninist ideology. Stalin assumed that the capitalist camp would soon resume its internal rivalry over colonies and trade. Economic advisers such as Eugen Varga predicted a post-war "crisis of overproduction" in capitalist countries which would culminate by 1947–1948 in another great depression. (This is why Stalin assumed the Americans would *need* to offer him economic aid.) Thus, the prospects of a united Anglo-American front against him seemed slim.[32] In any case, Winston Churchill, the British prime minister, and President Roosevelt particularly had gone out of their way at wartime conferences to accord him a sphere of influence in Eastern Europe. In return, Stalin had reined in communist parties in France and Italy, ordering them to eschew revolution and seek political power through coalition governments. In short, as the war drew to an end, the Soviet leader was hopeful that selective territorial expansion would not prejudice continued alliance cooperation.

The Western leaders also wanted continued entente—on *their* terms. From 1941, the main aim of Roosevelt and Churchill was to keep the Russians going against Hitler. Both, particularly Roosevelt, were also anxious to secure Russia's entry into the war against Japan once victory in Europe was won. These were the big issues, against which the configuration of Eastern Europe was secondary. In any case, both acknowledged that the Soviet Union had genuine security interests in the region and would, thanks to the Red Army's victories, be the dominant influence there at the end of the war. Roosevelt told some senators before leaving for the last wartime conference, at Yalta in the Crimea in February 1945, that "the only practicable course was to use what influence we had to ameliorate the situation."[33] Although Churchill, a visceral anticommunist, had always been more skeptical about Russian policy, this was also his objective at Yalta. What both leaders sought was a Russian commitment to at least a modicum of democracy and civil rights in Eastern Europe, especially Poland. They returned home from Yalta hopeful that this had been achieved. But Stalin understood Yalta (and the preceding conference at Teheran in 1943) very differently. He believed he had been granted a free hand in most of east-central Europe, much like that he had conceded to the Anglo-Americans in Italy and to the British in Greece. When communist-dominated governments were imposed in Poland, Romania, and Bulgaria, Churchill felt betrayed; when the British protested, Stalin, in turn, felt that they were reneging on the Yalta agreement.

Roosevelt had always played down difficulties with the Soviets in the interest of the war effort. But his sudden death in April 1945 brought a very different personality to the White House. Harry S. Truman—a short, dapper, bespectacled sixty-year-old—was a product of the American Midwest. He had graduated from farm work and small business to politics with the help of the local political machine. After a decade in the U.S. Senate, he was chosen as FDR's running mate in 1944 simply to balance the ticket. The new president had never been to college and had only left his country once before—for service in France in 1918. He was, however, a voracious reader, particularly of history, which he understood as "a story of men, battles and leadership, a uniquely personal process with little room for intangible forces."[34] Sure of his values, Truman compensated for his lack of experience with forthright decisiveness. His blunt lecture about Poland, days after becoming president, shook Vyacheslav Molotov, the Soviet foreign minister, and his decision to terminate Lend-Lease (mainly for domestic political reasons) was regarded in Moscow as economically damaging and diplomatically sinister.[35]

At this stage, however, Truman was still finding his feet. During the rest of 1945, the Americans accepted the governments in Poland, Romania, and Bulgaria with only cosmetic changes. But the months of haggling exacerbated suspicion on both sides. The Russians often took a stubborn line to show that they were not susceptible to American hints of nuclear blackmail. This in turn strengthened Western fears of Russian bellicosity.[36] There was a further row in early 1946 about Soviet slowness in withdrawing troops from northern Iran. In August 1946, Truman ordered warships into the eastern Mediterranean to counter Soviet pressure on Turkey. He readily accepted the Pentagon's warning: "The time has come when we must decide that we should resist with all means at our disposal any Soviet aggression."[37]

Stalin was no keener for war in 1946 than he had been in 1945. But U.S. policy makers did not forget that they had given Hitler the benefit of the doubt in the 1930s, with disastrous consequences. The lessons of appeasement were powerfully articulated by George Kennan, the acting head of the U.S. embassy in Moscow, in a widely read telegram in February 1946. He argued that the Soviets would back down "when strong resistance is encountered at any point" and that avoidance of war would therefore "depend on [the] degree of cohesion, firmness and vigor which [the] Western World can muster."[38] Here was the essence of what became known as the strategy of containment.

What particularly worried U.S. policy makers was Europe's swing to the left after the war. This reflected the prominent role of the communists in anti-Nazi resistance movements and also the general conviction that such appalling suffering *must* result in a better world. In Eastern Europe, of course, communists were often backed by the Red Army, but that was not true of Czechoslovakia, where party membership soared from twenty-eight thousand in May 1945 to 1.2 million a year later. And in Western Europe the appeal of the communists was entirely unconstrained. In 1945–1947, communists served for the first time in coalition governments in France and

Italy, where they were winning around 20 percent of the vote. Stalin found the European communists unruly clients, preoccupied with national interests, but Washington had no doubt that they were ultimately pawns of the Kremlin. The fear, therefore, was that Europe's resources might fall into Soviet hands by indirect, political means.

The stakes were highest in Germany. The country was divided into four occupation zones (Map 7)—the Soviets in the east; Britain in the north, including the devastated Ruhr; the Americans across the south from Frankfurt to Munich; and the French in the long-contested borderlands of the west.° Occupation was intended as a temporary measure until Germany had been denazified and the peace treaty agreed and signed. In the meantime, all policy decisions were supposed to be made by the Allies in concert: zonal divisions were purely administrative.

A fundamental dilemma soon emerged, however. Germany was, potentially, the economic powerhouse of continental Europe. Its coal and steel were crucial for the industrial recovery of France and the Low Countries. Yet, twice in the previous three decades, Germany had turned its economic power into military might. Understandably, the Russians fixated on Germany as a threat. Stalin demanded substantial reparations from Germany, in cash and equipment, to help rebuild his shattered economy, and the American and British governments conceded some of his demands. But in 1946 they became increasingly keen to accelerate German recovery. This would relieve their own taxpayers, who were providing food and supplies for western Germany's shattered cities—in effect, paying reparations *to* Germany. Yet the Russians would not accept recovery until reparations had been paid, and soon grain supplies from their zone to the urban west were stopped. Poverty and disease would only increase German discontent. As General Lucius D. Clay, the U.S. military governor in Germany, put it, "there is no choice between becoming a Communist on 1,500 calories [a day] and a believer in democracy on 1,000 calories."[39] In the summer of 1946, Clay suspended reparations deliveries to the Russians. The Americans and British agreed to fuse their two zones from January 1947, so they could push ahead with German recovery. The Russian zone in Germany was becoming a separate bloc.

American attitudes toward the Soviet Union had changed perceptibly. In March 1946 opinion polls indicated that only 35 percent of Americans believed Russia could be trusted, compared with 55 percent a year before. Yet barely 20 percent of Americans said they considered foreign affairs to be of "vital importance."[40] What led to a change of *policy* rather than merely a shift

---

°Or, as a contemporary joke put it, the Russians got the corn, the Americans got the scenery, the French got the wine, and the British got the ruins.

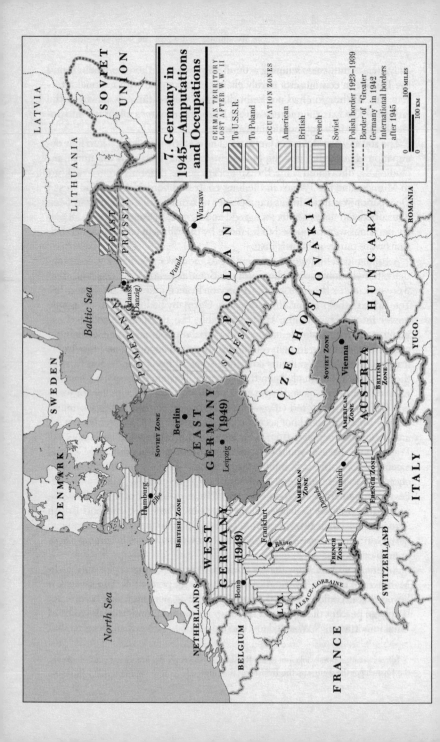

7. Germany in 1945—Amputations and Occupations

GERMAN TERRITORY
LOST AFTER W.W. II

To U.S.S.R.

To Poland

OCCUPATION ZONES

American

British

French

Soviet

········ Polish border 1923–1939

———— Border of "Greater
Germany" in 1942

———— International borders
after 1945

0 ——— 100 MILES
0 ——— 100 KM

SOVIET UNION

LATVIA

LITHUANIA

Warsaw

EAST PRUSSIA

Vistula

Baltic Sea

Gdańsk (Danzig)

POMERANIA

POLAND

SILESIA

SWEDEN

DENMARK

North Sea

Hamburg

BRITISH ZONE

Elbe

SOVIET ZONE

Berlin

EAST GERMANY (1949)

Leipzig

CZECHOSLOVAKIA

HUNGARY

ROMANIA

YUGO.

NETHERLANDS

WEST GERMANY (1949)

Frankfurt

Rhine

Bonn

BELGIUM

LUX.

FRENCH ZONE

ALSACE-LORRAINE

FRANCE

AMERICAN ZONE

Munich

Danube

FRENCH ZONE

SWITZERLAND

AMERICAN ZONE

FRENCH ZONE

AUSTRIA

SOVIET ZONE

Vienna

BRITISH ZONE

ITALY

of *attitude* was the awareness that the Europeans could not cope with this crisis alone. The crucial actor here was Britain.

In the late 1940s, Britain remained a great power. Despite conceding independence to India and Pakistan in 1947, it retained most of its empire. Even in the early 1950s its manufacturing output was greater than those of Germany and France combined.[41] Britain had the second-largest navy in the world, and in 1948 it still kept over one million men in the armed forces. Moreover, the country's postwar leaders were determined to maintain Britain's world role. When the Labour party won the election of July 1945, one senior Foreign Office official feared "a private revolution at home and the reduction of England to a 2nd-class power."[42] But although Labour began a vigorous program of socialism, its new foreign secretary, the burly ex-union boss Ernest Bevin, was almost Churchillian in his attitude to world affairs. In May 1947 he vehemently rejected the claim that Britain had "ceased to be a great Power, insisting that "we regard ourselves as one of the Powers most vital to the peace of the world."[43] Of particular moment was the government's decision, in January 1947, to develop its own atomic bomb. Britain had been a junior partner in the wartime project, but had been cut out of postwar collaboration when the Truman administration, partly for security reasons, reneged on previous agreements. Unsure of America's support and acutely vulnerable to bombing from the air, British leaders felt it essential to have their own bomb. Diplomatic status was also important. Bevin told colleagues: "We have got to have this thing over here whatever it costs. . . . We've got to have the bloody Union Jack flying on top of it."[44]

Britain's power base was fragile, however. Unlike the United States and the Soviet Union, it was not a continentwide state, commanding vast resources and manpower. It was a small island, about the size of Wyoming, with the equivalent of only one-third of America's population. Its wealth and power had depended on assets across the seas, such as Malayan rubber and Iranian oil. But the war had cost Britain a quarter of its imperial wealth. The country became the world's largest debtor nation, and a massive postwar loan from the United States proved essential to avoid a balance of payments crisis. Moreover, Indian independence eliminated a major source of military power. Retaining conscription and keeping thousands of men under arms meant fewer workers to boost Britain's recovery. Yet international tension meant that Britain could not easily cut back on commitments overseas. To keep feeding the Germans, for instance, using grain bought on credit from the United States, Britain had imposed bread rationing on its own people in mid-1946—an expedient avoided even in the darkest days of the war.

The crisis came to a head in early 1947, when the worst winter in more than eighty years paralyzed industry across Britain and most of northwest Europe. The chancellor of the exchequer warned his cabinet colleagues that "we were racing through our United States dollar credit at a reckless, and ever-accelerating, speed" and foresaw "a looming shadow of catastrophe."[45] In mid-February a rattled government decided to pull out of Palestine and India—with consequences that will be examined in Chapter 3. It also confirmed an earlier decision to end financial aid to Greece and Turkey—crunch points in the deepening cold war—and to do so by March 31.

The Americans acted to fill the vacuum created by this contraction of British power. The Truman administration had been preparing for some months to assume Britain's role in the eastern Mediterranean—financing anticommunists in the Greek civil war and bolstering Turkish resistance to Soviet pressure. It was concerned about the effect of any collapse in the eastern Mediterranean on communist strength in Italy and France. But the British decision to end aid to Greece and Turkey forced the administration to act publicly and quickly, which meant gaining approval for a replacement $400 million package from the Republican-dominated, cost-cutting Congress. To mobilize support, Truman depicted the world scene in stark black and white. Although not referring explicitly to the Soviet Union or communism, he told Congress on March 12, 1947, that the world was dividing into two ways of life, democracy and totalitarianism. "I believe," he said, "that it must be the policy of the United States to support free people who are resisting attempted subjugation by armed minorities or by outside pressures."[46] At this stage, America had no global strategy of containment: Truman was indulging in hyperbole to galvanize Congress. But the Truman Doctrine was an ideological marker for things to come.

The second great American initiative that spring came in response to the crisis in Germany. For seven weeks in March and April the foreign ministers of America, Russia, Britain and France conferred in Moscow. Despite forty-three meetings, they could not resolve their deadlock on Germany. George C. Marshall, the U.S. secretary of state, judged that Stalin, "looking over Europe, saw the best way to advance Soviet interests was to let matters drift," on the assumption that poverty and disease created "the kind of crisis that Communism thrived on." Marshall concluded that action must be taken to promote European recovery and that only America could provide the necessary leadership and funds. On June 5, 1947, Marshall announced that if the Europeans drew up a joint recovery program, "agreed to by a number of if not all European nations," the United States would offer support.[47] Seizing on this offer, Bevin and his French counterpart, Georges Bidault, convened a conference in Paris at the end of June.

Marshall and his European allies had no intention of allowing Stalin to stall yet another initiative for European recovery. But no one was explicitly excluded from the Paris conference. In fact, Soviet Foreign Minister Vyach-eslav Molotov proposed to the Central Committee that not only the Russians but also the Czechs and Poles should attend, and he arrived in Paris with a delegation of over one hundred. Behind the scenes, Stalin weighed the pros and cons. On the one hand, the démarche could be interpreted as a sign that the predicted crisis of American overproduction was taking hold. At the very least there was a chance of useful economic aid for the Soviet Union and its satellites. On the other hand, the Russians wanted bilateral aid without strings, on the model of Lend-Lease. They rejected the idea of a joint European program run by multinational institutions under American aegis. Nor would they accept any reduction in German reparations or any acceleration of German recovery. At root, Stalin perceived a challenge to his own sphere of influence: American economic aid would weaken Soviet political control in eastern Europe. Before walking out of the conference on July 3, Molotov predicted that the plan "would split Europe into two groups of states."[48] The Czechs, Poles, and other interested East European countries were warned against participation, and so the European Recovery Program that emerged over the next few months encompassed only the western half of the conti-nent.

It was in March 1946 that Winston Churchill, the former British prime minister, made his famous claim that an "iron curtain had descended across the Continent."[49] But, as Molotov implied, the curtain really came down in the summer of 1947. Although it took months to push the Marshall Plan through Congress, over the next four years $13 billion in American aid would flow into Western Europe, particularly Britain, France, and West Germany. Over the same period, the Soviet Union *extracted* about an equal amount from Eastern Europe in continued reparations. As Western Europe moved into the American orbit and into prosperity, most of Eastern Europe be-came an exploited Soviet colony. Only Yugoslavia, where the communist takeover owed little to the Red Army, was able to break away from Soviet control in 1948.

The divide became political as well as economic. May 1947 saw new coali-tions formed in France, Italy, and Belgium—*without* the communists. Al-though it was known that these moves would increase the chances of American aid, they were responses to internal paralysis more than to outside pressure, because the existing broad coalitions were deadlocked over how to deal with the economic crisis. Over the next year, union movements in the West also split into communist and noncommunist groups. As West Euro-pean politics swung to the right, so Eastern Europe was Stalinized. Within the existing popular-front coalitions, socialists were fused with communists, other parties were driven out, and only Moscow loyalists retained office. In September 1947 the Soviet Union established Cominform, a new organization to manage international communist parties and avoid the confusion that had occurred over the Marshall Plan. At the founding conference, its architect, Andrei Zhdanov, spoke of a world divided into "two camps"—a phrase probably added at Stalin's behest.[50] Here was a mirror image of the Truman Doctrine. Under new instructions from Moscow, the French communist party mounted a wave of strikes that autumn, and its Italian counterparts made an all-out bid to win the elections in April 1948. Against them, Italian moderates, well funded by the CIA, campaigned explicitly on the "American way of life." The communist takeover in Czechoslovakia in February 1948 caused particular alarm in France and Italy because this was a democracy that had done its best to propitiate Russia. It seemed there was no longer any hope of a middle way in the cold war.

Two Blocs, Two Germanies, Two Bombs

The clearest sign of this was the reorientation of French foreign policy. Although Soviet power was a concern in 1945, the French were more anxious about the revival of Germany, which had attacked them three times in seventy-five years. Georges Bidault, foreign minister from 1944 until July 1948, initially tried to revive the pre-1914 tradition of French diplomacy— "control of Germany thanks to alliance with Russia."[51] Bidault also demanded the amputation of the Ruhr and the Saar, heartlands of German industry, and opposed any new central German administration. In 1945–1946, therefore, France was as much an obstacle as Russia to German recovery. But by the spring of 1947, the deepening crisis in Europe and America's readiness to help transformed Bidault's thinking. He recognized that France could no longer avoid a stark choice between Soviets and "Anglo-Saxons." The French dropped their opposition to German economic recovery in return for guarantees that, as Ruhr coal output rose, coal exports to France would increase proportionately. It was now accepted that France must work with American and Britain to resolve the future of *Western* Germany alone.[52] By the spring of 1948 the French had reached agreement on fusing their zone with the Anglo-American Bizone and on creating a unified West German government, albeit on federal lines and with limited powers.

This latter decision turned what had been an economic and political confrontation into a military crisis. When the Western powers introduced a separate currency in their own zones and in West Berlin as a precursor to the new government, Stalin struck back. Berlin was deep inside the Soviet zone of Germany and on June 24, 1948, the Russians imposed a blockade on all road, rail, and river access from the West into Berlin and cut off the city's electricity. "Only Stalin's conviction that this was a negligible risk could have possibly justified his taking it."[53] But London and Washington did not back down. The next day, the two governments began sending in food and supplies by air. "We are in Berlin," announced Marshall on June 30, "and we intend to stay." That same day, the British press announced that the United States was sending two bomber groups of B-29s (sixty planes) to Britain. The B-29s constituted America's strategic strike force. It was left studiously vague whether the planes coming to Britain were capable of dropping atomic bombs.[54] Europe seemed on the verge of war.[*]

Berlin needed a daily minimum of twelve thousand tons. The first sporadic planeloads became a round-the-clock airlift. By October the city's Gatow Airport was handling three times the traffic of La Guardia in New York, formerly the busiest in the world. Planes were flying into Berlin, on average, every three minutes, day and night. They had to cross Soviet-controlled airspace and could easily have been shot down, but Stalin was not willing to risk war. As the *Luftbrücke*, or air bridge, continued throughout the winter—fortunately, much milder than feared—so Berlin followed Germany itself in becoming divided. From December there were two separate city governments. A "Free University" had started, with American funding, in the southwest suburb of Dahlem, because the historic University of Berlin was part of the Soviet sector. Meanwhile, the currency and governmental reforms went ahead. May 12, 1949—when Stalin finally admitted defeat and lifted the blockade—was also the day on which the Western military governors approved the *Grundgesetz*, or "basic law," for the new Federal Republic of Germany. In September, the new state came into operation, followed by the German Democratic Republic in the Soviet zone.

The Berlin airlift boosted America's popularity throughout Germany. It also prompted an unprecedented American commitment to European security. Back in March 1948, the governments of Britain, France, Belgium, Luxembourg, and the Netherlands had formed a security alliance among themselves—the Brussels Pact. But this was always intended as the basis of a transatlantic alliance, and the Berlin crisis gave impetus to these larger negotiations. As with earlier démarches, the Truman administration had to battle for months with Congress, but the North Atlantic Treaty was signed on April 4, 1949, and ratified the following July. Its signatories were America, Canada, and ten European states, including Italy but not Germany (Map 8). The treaty has been described as "a latter-day American Revolution"—a sign

---

[*]Naturally the crisis preoccupied the U.S. media. In its issue of July 1, the *New York Times* relegated to page 46, under "The News of Radio," a brief mention of a press conference the previous day announcing a new solid-state amplifier called "the Transistor."

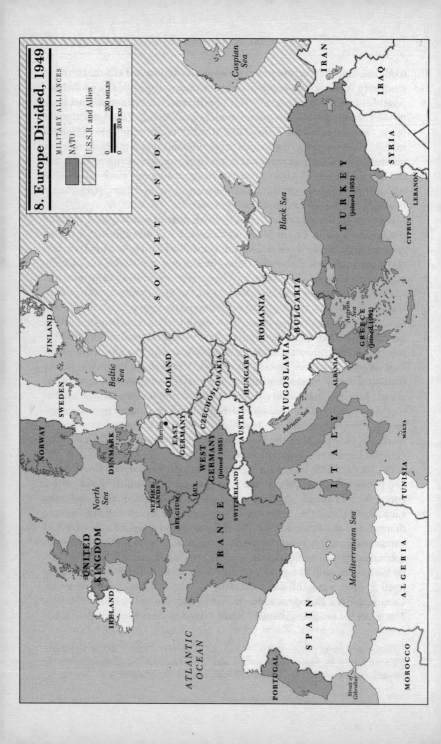

8. Europe Divided, 1949

MILITARY ALLIANCES

NATO

U.S.S.R. and Allies

0   200 MILES
0   200 KM

ATLANTIC OCEAN

IRELAND

UNITED KINGDOM

North Sea

NORWAY

SWEDEN

FINLAND

Baltic Sea

DENMARK

NETHERLANDS

BELGIUM

lux.

EAST GERMANY

Berlin

WEST GERMANY (joined 1955)

POLAND

SOVIET UNION

Caspian Sea

SWITZERLAND

FRANCE

CZECHOSLOVAKIA

AUSTRIA

HUNGARY

ROMANIA

Black Sea

ITALY

YUGOSLAVIA

BULGARIA

Adriatic Sea

ALBANIA

GREECE (joined 1952)

Aegean Sea

TURKEY (joined 1952)

IRAN

IRAQ

SYRIA

LEBANON

CYPRUS

PORTUGAL

SPAIN

Strait of Gibraltar

MOROCCO

ALGERIA

TUNISIA

Mediterranean Sea

MALTA

of just how far U.S. foreign policy had shifted in a decade.[55] The heart of the treaty was a mutual commitment that an attack on one was an attack on all. This was aimed primarily at deterring Soviet attack, but it would also apply to German aggression. A further solace to the French was the provision for U.S. military assistance to help build up their armed forces. These American guarantees were part of reconciling France to Germany's revival.[56]

The North Atlantic Treaty was formulated in accord with the United Nations Charter, specifically the right of individual or collective self-defense recognized in Article 51. But in fact the treaty showed how far the world had moved from the hopes entertained in San Francisco in April 1945, when the charter was signed. The UN resembled the interwar League of Nations, with an assembly of all member states (51 in 1945) and a smaller Security Council of eleven to take the lead on issues of peace and security. But it was also an attempt by the major Allies to cure the League's impotence. Consequently, five great powers were given permanent seats on the Security Council—the United States, the Soviet Union, Great Britain, China (at Roosevelt's behest), and France (at Churchill's). The permanent members could not block discussion of any issue, but they all had to agree before any substantive action could be taken. This right of veto, instituted to satisfy Stalin, was a significant exception to the general principle of majority voting. It meant that the UN could operate effectively on security issues *only if* wartime cooperation among the great powers continued into peacetime. This did not occur. By 1952 the United Nations was accommodated in splendid new buildings along the East River in midtown New York, and it was doing important relief and welfare work. UN programs such as UNICEF (its children's fund) and related agencies such as the Food and Agricultural Organization (FAO) were valuable, if unsung, forces for improvement in the postwar era. But the cold war froze the UN out of the crucial terrain of international security. It was seen as "a battle-ground," not "a peace chamber: as a means of scoring points rather than of securing settlements."[57]

In particular, the United Nations became sidelined over control of atomic weapons. In June 1946 the Americans proposed that a UN agency should take charge of all nuclear research, plants, and raw materials, with sweeping powers of international inspection to prevent violations. Until this plan was implemented, however, the United States would retain its own weapons. The proposals for international supervision were rejected by Stalin, and work continued on the Soviet bomb. One of the major obstacles was the lack of uranium, but here the Soviets were greatly helped in the 1940s by mines in East Germany and Czechoslovakia. Even more important was the intelligence gleaned by agents within the wartime U.S. project, notably the physicist Klaus Fuchs, which probably saved one to two years. Using his information, the Soviet constructed a copy of the plutonium bomb tested by the Americans in July 1945. Nevertheless, its development was also a tribute to Soviet science and to the command economy, which ruthlessly marshalled the necessary resources. Much of the labor to mine uranium and construct installations came from the notorious Stalinist *gulag* of prisons, labor camps, and settlements for internal exiles, whose population Stalin had expanded remorselessly since the war to perhaps 5.5 million people by 1953—double the figure in 1937.[58] Many of the inmates were wartime soldiers: anyone who had been captured by the Germans and lived to tell the tale was, by definition, a traitor in Stalin's eyes. Camp labor was deemed expendable—little attention was paid to the radioactive dangers of mining uranium—but health and safety were neglected even among scientists and skilled workers in the race to build the bomb. Around nuclear installations such as Cheliabinsk-40, near Sverdlovsk in the Urals, land and water were contaminated for decades to come.

The Americans were poorly informed of Soviet progress. On July 1, 1949, the director of the CIA advised Truman that the Soviets would probably not test a bomb until mid-1953. In fact, the first Soviet test took place in the steppes of Kazakhstan less than two months later, on August 29. To the immense relief of the scientists, led by Igor Kurchatov, it was a complete success. Lavrenti Beria composed the honors list, working on the principle that those slated for execution if the test had failed should become Heroes of Socialist Labor, those who would have received maximum prison sentences merited Orders of Lenin, and so on.[59] The news was kept secret by Moscow, but the Americans detected the telltale atmospheric radiation. On September 23, 1949, President Truman informed America and the world of the Soviet atomic test. The United States had lost its atomic monopoly and, at the end of January 1950, Truman gave a well-publicized go-ahead to develop a far more powerful "hydrogen or super bomb," using an atomic explosion to generate a runaway thermonuclear reaction.

The leading architect of the "Super" was the physicist Edward Teller. The principle was successfully proved on November 1, 1952, vaporizing Eniwetok Atoll in the U.S. testing area in the southern Pacific. At eighty-two tons and packed in a vast refrigeration unit, this was not a deliverable weapon, and the first genuine U.S. hydrogen bomb was not tested until March 1954. The Soviets were not far behind. Whereas the first Soviet atomic bomb had essentially copied the first American atomic bomb, the Soviet hydrogen bomb was an original design. Although the Americans tested first, with a more powerful device, the Soviet explosion on August 12, 1953 detonated something that could be termed a deliverable hydrogen bomb, six months ahead of the United States.[60] A full-scale test, using a bomb dropped from an aircraft, followed in November 1955.

Stalin had not lived to see the achievement. He had ailed considerably since his seventieth birthday in 1949, and, mistrustful of everyone, kept medical men at arm's length. Indeed, his last months saw a new purge against the supposed menace from "Jewish doctors." On March 1, 1953, he suffered a massive stroke. When fearful staff finally broke into his apartment late that night, they found him on the floor, in undershirt and pajama bottoms, unable to move. His eyes were full of fear, his mouth uttered only incoherent noises. On the 5th, Stalin finally died. Privately, many were relieved—not least his terrified Politburo. There were a few public displays of delight, particularly in the camps, where some prisoners threw their caps into the air. But such was the cult of personality, the power of propaganda, that the grief displayed by most Russians was probably spontaneous and genuine. Over a hundred mourners were crushed to death in Moscow in the vast crowds that watched his funeral.[61] Among his colleagues, a bitter power struggle ensued. The new leadership, initially headed by Georgi Malenkov, began to relax Stalinist tyranny (Chapter 4). But none of Stalin's successors could escape the system he had created. That was partly because of the enormity of his crimes. But it was also because Stalinism was the successor of Leninism and of tsarist autocracy. The efforts by Khrushchev and Gorbachev to blame everything on Stalin were a denial of Russian history.

Here, then, is a pattern for the cold war and after—one that will be explored in subsequent chapters in explanation of Russia past, present and future. But the Soviet era had another side, one that is equally important if we want to understand the postwar world. The Soviet system rested on fear, yes, but also on faith—on enthusiasm as well as on coercion. Consider, for a moment, Andrei Sakharov, the brilliant young physicist, barely in his thirties, who was "father" of the Soviet hydrogen bomb. In the 1970s and 1980s Sakharov won international renown as the Soviet Union's leading dissident. But in the early 1950s he was a true believer, as he worked round the clock in the weapons laboratory Arzamas-16, some two hundred fifty miles east of Moscow. Every morning the prisoners from the neighboring camp, on which the lab depended, would pass his window—"long gray lines of men in quilted jackets, guard dogs at their heels." As he admitted much later in his memoirs, "I knew quite enough about the horrible crimes that had been committed . . . to pass judgment on those responsible." But Sakharov, too, was overcome by Stalin's death. And even when that emotion had passed, "the state, the nation, and the ideals of communism remained intact for me."[62] At home and abroad, the positive image of the Soviet Union owed much to nuclear scientists such as Sakharov, whose achievements suggested that their country was more or less in the same technological league as the United States. As we shall see in Chapter 14, reality was increasingly at odds with appearance,* but to many around the world in the 1940s and 1950s the Soviet Union offered a model for the future. The cold war was a struggle of ideals as well as interest.

Above all, however, it was about power. The Eniwetok test had inaugurated the thermonuclear age. By splitting a nucleus (fission) and generating enough energy to fuse hydrogen into helium, physicists had created a weapon one thousand times more powerful than the bomb dropped on Hiroshima. Privately, leading U.S. scientists including J. Robert Oppenheimer, "father" of the atomic bomb, warned that this was "a weapon of genocide" whose power was too vast to be targeted on specific military installations. "Its use therefore carries much further than the atomic bomb itself the policy of extermination of civilian populations."[63] Winston Churchill said that the H-bomb was as far from the A-bomb as the "atomic bomb itself from the bow and arrow."[64] The question now was, What to do with it? And even if one superpower decided to do nothing, relying on nuclear weapons as a form of deterrence, could it be sure that the other would adopt the same policy?

The Iron Curtain under the Mushroom Cloud. Since 1945, international relations had moved from a concert of powers to a balance of power, constructed around a Europe divided between America and Russia. By 1949 both superpowers had atomic capability; within another five years they had tested hydrogen bombs. Stalin, the immediate cause of the cold war, was dead. But the Stalinist system, endowed with vast new destructive power, had a life of its own. And the confrontation became more intense and extensive because the United States had emerged from the war with a enlarged definition of its security, interests, and mission. The accelerating nuclear arms race showed how fragile the new balance of power really was: each superpower defined security as superiority. And outside Europe, the aftershocks of war and decolonization allowed the superpower rivalry to ripple across the world.

---

*Seven weeks after Stalin's death, the British scientific journal *Nature* published a paper by James Watson and Francis Crick that set out the double-helix model of DNA and established its importance as "the chemical of life." The genetic revolution was to pass by the Soviet Union almost completely.

2

Communist Revolutions, Asian Style

On October 1, 1949, eight days after President Truman had announced the Soviet atomic test, a small man in a plain, high-collared jacket reviewed the assembled thousands from a balcony on the Gate of Heavenly Peace, Tian An Men, in Beijing (Plate 5). *Mao Zedong wan shui!* they shouted. "May Mao Zedong live for ten thousand years!" Suddenly, there was silence as the new national flag climbed up the immense flagpole in the center of the square. At the top it cracked open in the chill wind—thirty feet broad, blood red, with five yellow stars in the top left corner—to inaugurate the People's Republic of China. The symbolism was carefully nuanced. The red flag was, of course, a banner of revolution, and the largest of the five stars represented the dominant position of the Communist party in China's "New Democracy." Yet five was a number beloved of China's philosophers—the five virtues, the five rules—and red was the historic color of the Han people of China. This revolution was both communist and nationalist.

The fact that the world's most populous country had "fallen" to communism was momentous enough. But the Chinese revolution of 1949 takes on its full significance only against the backdrop of the war. Consider two other transfers of power earlier in the decade. On the evening of February 15, 1942, General Arthur Percival, the British commander of Singapore, marched out to the Japanese lines to surrender. One hundred thirty thousand *agrarian - concerning the land and its ownership, cultivation and tenure*

British and empire forces succumbed to an attacking force half their number, with barely a fight. Winston Churchill later called it "the worst disaster and largest capitulation in British history."[1] Percival's motives were honorable: the Japanese controlled the island's water supply, and a prolonged siege would result in the deaths of thousands of soldiers and civilians. But the image that went around the world was of Percival and his officers, in their long baggy shorts, walking out with Union Jack and white flag to make their surrender. The British Empire had not only been defeated; far worse, it had been rendered ridiculous.

Percival spent the rest of the war in a Japanese prison camp. But at 9:00 A.M. on September 2, 1945, he was a guest of honor on the American battleship *Missouri* in Tokyo Bay when the Japanese surrendered. He stood next to the American commander, General Douglas MacArthur, and after the signing ceremony, MacArthur handed one of the fountain pens he had used to Percival. Now it was the turn of the Japanese to feel the anguish of defeat (Plate 4). Allied officers watched in savage satisfaction as Foreign Minister Shigemitsu Mamoru, burdened with a wooden leg, struggled to mount the steep steps. His secretary, Toshikazu Kase, had never realized before that "the glance of glaring eyes could hurt so much," like "a million shafts of a rattling storm of arrows barbed with fire." Yet he was then delighted by the magnanimity of MacArthur's words. Instead of preaching "distrust, malice or hatred," the American victor expressed the hope that "a better world shall emerge" characterized by "freedom, tolerance and justice."[2]

By 1945 the tables had been turned on the Japanese. Surrender brought to an abrupt end their empire in China, Korea, and southeast Asia, and the "white" colonial powers were able to recover the possessions they had lost in 1941–1942. In 1945–1946 the British returned to Malaya and Hong Kong, the Dutch to the East Indies, and the French to Indochina. Yet the memory of those earlier humiliations could not be wiped out. Japan's dramatic successes had fatally undermined the prestige of the white man, especially the Europeans, across east and southeast Asia. Over the ensuing decade, the Dutch and the French would discover that the empires they had regained were now untenable, while the British hung on only at considerable cost in Malaya. The vacuums created by the contraction of Japanese and European imperialism had been filled, in varying degrees and forms, by a complex blend of nationalism and communism—of which the most important exemplar was China. Communist success there in unifying and modernizing a vast agrarian society seemed the harbinger of revolution all over Asia. Only the United States, propelled into Asia by the Pacific War, had the potential to contain that expansion. The cold war gave it the will and reason to do so, particularly in Korea and Vietnam. And a remarkable new alliance with

Japan, crafted by MacArthur, was to prove America's main bulwark of containment in Asia.

Japan under U.S. Occupation

In 1940 Japan had a population of seventy-three million. Unique among the countries of Asia, it had become a major industrial power, comparable at this stage to France, and had also developed a system of parliamentary democracy on the British model, with adult male suffrage since 1925. Yet capitalism and democracy both rested on shaky foundations. The country was poorly endowed with raw materials, its main asset was cheap labor, and population growth pressed on the limited arable land available in a largely mountainous country. Over 40 percent of the work force was still in agriculture, and they were devastated by the 1930s depression. As in Weimar Germany, factional party politicians were ill equipped to cope with economic crisis. In the 1930s the Japanese military gained effective control of politics and pushed the country into colonial wars as an answer to its economic problems. The bid to build a "Greater East Asia Co-Prosperity Sphere" in China, Korea, and Southeast Asia ended in disaster, because Japan lacked the economic resources to sustain a full-scale war against the United States. From August 1945 the Japanese experienced what they, unlike much of Asia, had hitherto escaped—Western occupation.

Officially, eleven powers participated in the occupation government, but 90 percent of the forces in Japan were American and the occupation was dominated by the United States. MacArthur, as Supreme Commander of the Allied Powers (SCAP), was endowed with almost absolute powers, which he exercised in a proconsular manner. The surrender document made clear that "the authority of the Emperor and the Japanese Government will be subject to the Supreme Commander."[3] Here, then, is one important contrast with Germany, the other main defeated power: Japan was not divided among the Allies, but administered largely by the United States. Yet, second, MacArthur chose to govern *indirectly* through the Japanese government and bureaucracy, rather than setting up direct military government as in Germany. Both of these features of the occupation had considerable significance.

In 1945–1947, MacArthur oversaw a dramatic series of reforms. Most important was the new constitution of May 1947, which set out unequivocally the principles of responsible democratic government under the law. SCAP grafted American features onto the existing parliamentary system, notably popular sovereignty, judicial review, and guaranteed civil rights. The cabinet now enjoyed executive authority and was responsible to the legislature, or Diet. The constitutional principle of local government autonomy was reflected in new legal codes and in the abolition of the autocratic Home Ministry, which had controlled local government and police. And Article 9 of the constitution renounced war "as a sovereign right of the nation" and forbade the maintenance of "land, sea and air forces." This "peace clause" was one of the most controversial articles of the constitution.

Another far-reaching change was land reform, implemented through two new laws in 1945–1946. Japan's rural population consisted largely of poor peasants. The new laws addressed the serious problems of poverty and absentee landlordism. In consequence, the proportion of farm households that were owner-cultivators rose from 37 percent in 1947 to 62 percent in 1950, by which time 90 percent of the total arable land was cultivated by its owners.[4] SCAP also pushed through three new labor laws in 1945–1947, legalizing for the first time both unionization and collective bargaining. By 1949, nearly half the urban work force was unionized. Education was reformed on American lines, and women were given the vote. The constitution even guaranteed them equal rights in public life *and* marriage—provisions in advance of much of Western Europe and certainly of the United States (where the Equal Rights Amendment of 1972 was never ratified by sufficient states).[5]

The U.S. occupation of Japan has been described by one historian, with little exaggeration, as "perhaps the single most exhaustively planned operation of massive and externally directed political change in world history."[6] The new constitution, for instance, was a SCAP invention, drafted in a week in February 1946 after the Japanese had failed to come up with something MacArthur deemed adequate. In such matters of high policy the general was closely involved, personally writing the basis of the "peace clause," for instance. But on lesser issues, vast authority devolved on relatively junior members of the SCAP bureaucracy. The second and third labor laws, for instance, were largely the work of twenty-eight-year-old Ted Cohen from New York. The equal rights provisions were prepared by Beate Sirota, age twenty-two, after research in a few Tokyo libraries to check out constitutional practice elsewhere.

Yet the indirect character of the occupation must not be forgotten: SCAP worked through the Japanese government, whose politicians and bureaucrats exercised considerable influence on the reforms. SCAP's purges of war criminals and ultranationalists in 1945–1947 removed over two hundred thousand of Japan's former leaders. The first postwar elections, in April 1946, produced a Diet 80 percent of whose members had never served before. "New" politicians, and those from the 1920s who were now rehabilitated, represented reformist traditions that had been suppressed under military rule. Socialists, who led a coalition government in 1947–1948, were particularly supportive of MacArthur's vision of a demilitarized Japan. An even more important Japanese contribution came from the professional civil service, largely untouched by the purges, whose authority was enhanced during the occupation years. In some cases, they presented draft reforms to preempt American initiatives, as with the election law, but land reform was itself a long-standing goal of the Ministry of Agriculture and Forestry. Most pieces of legislation represented a dialogue between Americans and Japanese. But certain essential reforms were American impositions (notably the purges and the Constitution) and "not one of the basic reforms carried out under the Occupation could have been achieved without the best efforts of SCAP." For instance, almost no developing *capitalist* country (except for Taiwan) has carried out a smooth program of land reform. This would have been impossible in Japan "without the force exerted by the Occupation."[7]

By 1948, however, American priorities were changing. The occupation never intended to remake Japan, only to democratize and demilitarize the country so it would never again threaten international peace. Most of MacArthur's reforms were intended to do this, by liberalizing politics and society and dismantling "feudal" concentrations of power in land and industry. Although he was still trying to break up the big industrial holding companies, the *zaibatsu,* by 1948 much of his initial agenda had been accomplished. At the same time, Washington was taking a greater interest in Japan as the deepening cold war forced it to develop a global perspective. Policy makers began to see Japan as the Asian analogue to Germany in Europe—a country of great economic and military potential whose loss to communism would imperial America's influence over a whole continent. State Department planners observed in September 1947: "Idea of eliminating Japan as a military power for all time is changing. Now, because of Russia's conduct, tendency is to develop Hirohito's islands as a buffer state."[8] Guided particularly by George Kennan, Washington increasingly sought the economic recovery of Japan and even its limited rearmament. But both of these strategies would upset relations with the countries of East and Southeast Asia. Japan needed their food, raw materials, and markets for its industrial recovery. And any increase in Japanese military power would reawaken memories of past imperialism. In early 1950 Thailand's chief trade negotiator told an American official: "apparently it is United States policy to secure through political pressure what the Japanese Army failed to secure in Asia."[9]

America's policy shift on Japan was therefore partial and confused—vitiated not only by feuding among MacArthur, the Pentagon, and the State Department but also by the difficulty of drawing the rest of Asia into a new framework of containment. Meanwhile, conditions in Japan deteriorated. From 1946 wholesale prices doubled annually and in 1949–1950 inflation

was curbed only by a Washington-imposed austerity program that led to recession, bankruptcies, and increased unemployment. Labor militancy became so acute that MacArthur gradually restricted the right to strike.
Economic crisis increased political polarization. The 1949 elections decimated the socialists, boosted the right-wing Liberals to majority status in
the Diet, and gave the Japanese Communist party (JCP) its first significant
representation, with 7.5 percent of the seats. The CIA warned that the political center was being wiped out. In January 1950, the one hundred fifty
thousand-strong JCP, under pressure from Moscow, abandoned its policy of
peaceful revolution and mounted a campaign of strikes, demonstrations, and
even industrial sabotage. The Joint Chiefs of Staff told Truman that, if Japan
fell under communist influence, "Russia would gain, thereby, an additional
war-making potential equal to 25% of her capacity."[10] At the back of their
minds was the question, Might Japan go the way of China?

China and the Endgame of Civil War

In 1945 China was the world's most populous country, with nearly five
hundred million people—triple the number in the United States. Superim-
posed on a map of North America, it would extend from Atlantic to Pacific
and from Hudson Bay to Puerto Rico. It was also a civilization of great antiquity, which had pioneered the technologies of paper and print long before
Europe, and it had resisted or absorbed foreign incursions for centuries. Yet
in the half-century following defeat by Japan in 1895, China seemed in terminal decline—the "sick man of Asia" whose fate would likely emulate that
of the Ottoman empire, the "sick man of Europe" in the decades before it finally expired during World War I.

Since the collapse of the Qing dynasty in 1911, the country had been ravaged by civil war. Consolidation of power by the victorious Guomindang
(GMD) after 1928 was frustrated first by their former allies, the Chinese
communists, and then by war with Japan from 1937. With the Japanese controlling much of the northeast and east, from Manchuria down to Canton, the
communists, now led by Mao Zedong, held on in the north from their capital at Yan'an while Chiang Kai-shek (Jiang Jeishi) and the GMD tried to control south and central China from Chongqing. In the winter of 1945–1946,
after the sudden Japanese surrender, the Americans pressed both sides to
reach a negotiated settlement. But the GMD would not share political power,
and the CCP would not reduce its military power without at least a coalition
government. "Never in my experience with human beings," observed U.S.

ambassador John Leighton Stuart, "have I encountered anything like the suspicion on both sides, especially among the communists."[11] Hostilities resumed in July 1946, with Chiang determined to destroy the communist guerrilla strongholds. As U.S. military analysts predicted, he lacked the means to do so. But they also had little doubt that "the Communists cannot win either in attack or defense in a toe-to-toe slugging match with National Gov[ernmen]t forces."[12] A bloody stalemate seemed likely. Even Zhou Enlai, Mao's principal diplomatist, reckoned in 1946 that ultimate CCP success would take up to twenty years of war.[13]

And yet, by the end of 1949, the communists were in full control of the country, except for the island of Taiwan, to which Chiang and the Guomindang had retreated (Map 5). Their astounding defeat was largely self-inflicted. For all its professions of democracy and reform, the GMD had degenerated into a corrupt, faction-ridden oligarchy whose demands for conscripts and resources had alienated peasants throughout its rural base areas. In the spring of 1944, for instance, fifty thousand GMD soldiers retreating before the Japanese Ichigo offensive were killed by resentful local farmers—some soldiers even being buried alive. In the cities, home to a tenth of China's population, the biggest solvent of GMD support was rampant inflation. Chiang paid for the war by printing banknotes, with the result that average prices rose over two thousand times in 1937–1945. Postwar attempts at wage and price controls or rationing were half hearted and ineffectual: in the year from mid-1947, for instance, the cost-of-living index in Shanghai went up fiftyfold. Peasants hoarded their grain, consumers bought up scarce goods—in both cases accelerating the inflationary spiral. "Like leukaemic blood," writes the historian Lloyd Eastman, "the depreciated currency of the National Government flowed through the body politic, enfeebling the entire organism—the army, government, economy, and society generally."[14]

Of course, the CCP was hardly a benevolent taskmaster, and most peasants would doubtless have preferred to be left in peace by both sides. But the communists, despite their antecedents as displaced urban revolutionaries, did a much better job of mobilizing rural support. Indeed, that was the basis of their strategy—"setting the masses in motion" through a locally run program of land redistribution at the expense of "landlords" and rich peasants. These methods were pioneered before and during the Sino-Japanese war in CCP base areas, which Mao graphically called "the buttocks of the revolution," supporting the whole body.[15] After 1945 they were applied with great success in the northeast, in Manchuria—the decisive battleground of the civil war. Whereas the GMD "civilian bureaucracy and armies were grafted onto Northeast China," with little effort to secure local support, the CCP's restructuring of rural Manchuria enabled it "to tap the sources of manpower and supplies which they needed to wage conventional war against the Nationalist armies."[16] Yet conventional war was not the same as the guerrilla operations ("sparrow warfare") that the CCP had waged previously and which Mao still preferred. Gradually they developed the tactics and logistics to take the offensive against an enemy that still had superior firepower and commanded the main cities and railroads. After weathering the GMD advances of 1946–1947, including the loss of Yenan, the commanders of the People's Liberation Army (PLA) refined their techniques of "mobile warfare" using light infantry in rapid, surprise attacks.

This distinctive blend of peasant struggle and conventional warfare was the basis of the smashing victories won by the PLA in 1948–1949, as Lin Biao, its leading general, drove south through Manchuria to take the port of Tianjin and then Beijing itself in January 1949. The value of rural bases was dramatically shown in the Xuzhou campaign in central China in the last two months of 1948. In regular troops the two sides were evenly matched, about half a million each, but the CCP could draw on the logistic support of up to two million peasants in four surrounding provinces, coordinated by the young Deng Xiaoping. These victories transformed the military situation. The GMD opened peace negotiations in January but, following their breakdown in April, the PLA's reorganized armies moved across the Yangtze River and swept south and west to consolidate their hold with a speed unparalleled since the Manchu conquests three centuries before.[17]

Both superpowers had been wrong footed by the events of 1948–1949. Although the CCP was a member of Comintern, Stalin was always suspicious of communist leaders who took an independent line. In any case he doubted Mao's chances of vanquishing the Guomindang. In August 1945 he concluded a "treaty of friendship and alliance" with Chiang, along lines prefigured at Yalta. The Chinese acknowledged Soviet control of Outer Mongolia and accepted its claims, dating back to tsarist times, to port and railroad interests in Manchuria. In return, the Russians recognized the GMD as the national government of China and pledged it their exclusive support and aid. In 1945–1946, Stalin urged Mao to enter a coalition with the GMD. Stalin's China policy was typical of his thinking immediately after the war: secure Soviet interests in buffer regions, but avoid conflict with the Western allies and restrain local communist pressures for revolution. Although the Red Army occupied Manchuria rapidly in August 1945, allowing large quantities of Japanese arms to fall into CCP hands, the Russians did not intervene overtly in the civil war. Having looted Manchuria of most enemy industrial equipment—again emulating their practice in Europe—they withdrew their troops completely from the region in the spring of 1946. Throughout the ensuing struggle, Stalin kept his distance from Mao. In early 1949 he advised the CCP leaders not to cross the Yangtze, for fear of triggering a clash with the United States into which the Soviet Union would be drawn; the Soviet ambassador was, ironically, the last to leave Chiang. Little wonder Mao later insisted that "the Chinese revolution achieved its victory against the will of Stalin."[18]

In contrast with Soviet reserve, the Americans were perpetual meddlers in the affairs of China—though with no greater success by 1949. During the war, American aid had flowed to Chiang and Roosevelt had built him up as one of the four Allied "policemen" who would maintain world peace. In an effort to ensure a "strong, unified and democratic" China, General George C. Marshall spent much of 1946 trying to promote an agreement between Chiang and Mao. But when he failed, American policy makers refused to be drawn into the civil war. They had no illusions by now about the corruption and ineptitude of the GMD. U.S. aid to Chiang, totaling $3.5 billion by 1949, seemed like money poured down a drain. In February 1948, Marshall (by then secretary of state) told congressmen that to eliminate Chinese communism would require the United States "to be prepared virtually to take over the Chinese government and administer its economic, military, and governmental affairs."[19] The Truman administration already had its hands full with Europe, finding it hard enough to extract money from Congress for the Marshall Plan. An open-ended commitment to help Chiang destroy the CCP was inconceivable. But the administration, like the Soviets, realized only very late in the day that Mao would actually be able to destroy the Guomindang regime.

Thus, both superpowers had to redefine their China policies hurriedly in 1949–1950. Stalin shifted allegiance to the new communist government, signing a treaty of friendship and alliance with Mao in Moscow in February 1950. Mao affirmed the territorial concessions agreed to by Chiang in 1945 and secured a pledge of economic aid and a mutual military commitment if either country was attacked by another. Soviet help in these areas was essential for Mao, to rebuild the country and to help deter American aggression. He regarded the latter as a real possibility in 1949—paralleling imperialist intervention against the Bolsheviks in 1918–1921. In June 1949 he made clear that "help from the international revolutionary forces" was essential: "in order to win the victory and consolidate it we must lean to one side."[20] Yet the recent checkered history of relations with Stalin had not been forgotten or forgiven. Mao had no intention of losing China's hard-won unity and independence to Moscow, and his larger object was to restore China's place in world affairs as "the Central Kingdom." The very word *lean* implied a temporary posture. As Zhou Enlai, the new foreign minister, told American representatives, "We shall have to lean to one side, but how far we lean depends on you."[21]

Around Christmas 1949 Truman's National Security Council undertook a major review of U.S. policy in Asia. It called the CCP's victory "a grievous political defeat for us" which the USSR, already "an Asiatic power of the first magnitude," would try to exploit. But it played down any real threat to American interests, noting China's immense social and economic problems, which had "contributed to the downfall of every Chinese regime in recent history." The NSC also thought it "quite possible that serious frictions would develop between the Chinese communist regime and Moscow" if Stalin tried to exert control. In deference to Pentagon pressure, it advised a continued attempt by diplomacy and "modest" economic aid to deny Taiwan to the communists but ruled out "overt military action" to save Chiang.[22] In line with this wait-and-see policy, minimizing Sino-American friction while hoping for a Sino-Soviet rift, Truman stated publicly on January 5, 1950, that the United States would "not provide military aid or advice" to Chiang's forces on Taiwan. Nor did it have "any intention of utilizing its armed foces to interfere in the present situation." A week later Secretary of State Dean Acheson declared that in Asia, America's "defensive perimeter runs from the Ryukus to the Philippine Islands," centering on Japan. Acheson did not write off the Asian mainland, adding that in the event of aggression outside the perimeter "the initial reliance must be on the people attacked to resist it and then upon . . . the United Nations, which so far has not proved a weak reed."[23] But what was noted in Moscow and Beijing was what he had omitted. Korea and Taiwan lay outside America's guaranteed Asian defense line.

Korea: The Cold War Turns Hot

On the evening of Saturday June 24, 1950, President Harry Truman was enjoying a rare weekend with his wife and daughter at their home in Independence, Missouri. At 9:20 P.M., just as they had finished a leisurely dinner, the telephone rang. It was Dean Acheson from Washington. "Mr. President, I have very serious news," said the Secretary of State. "The North Koreans have invaded South Korea."[24] In mid-1950 this small country—roughly the size of Minnesota or the United Kingdom—was where the cold war turned hot.

By 1900, the Korean peninsula had existed as a single polity for a millennium (arguably as far back as the late seventh century). Yet it is surrounded by Asia's three major powers. Having always been under the cultural influence of China, its main northern neighbor, at the turn of this century Korea fell victim to the expansionary ambitions of Russia and Japan; after the Russo-Japanese war of 1904–1905, it fell completely under Japanese control. In the 1930s, Japan set about the economic development of Korea (and neighboring Manchuria). The result was a nascent industrial state with a vigorous bureaucracy. At the end of the Pacific War, Korea, a country smaller than most Chinese provinces, had 30 percent of China's total railroad mileage and carried half as many passengers. Equally important was the effect of the forced mobilization of Korean soldiers and workers for the Japanese war effort at home and abroad. By 1944, perhaps 20 percent of Koreans were either abroad or in provinces other than those in which they had been born—a powerful solvent of traditional attitudes. Yet this was "abortive, fractured 'development' "—partial in its effect on peasant society and aborted by the sudden Japanese surrender in August 1945.[25] Into the chaos stepped the new superpowers.

Korea was partitioned because the Americans were determined to prevent total Soviet control of the peninsula. The Truman administration wanted American forces to take the Japanese surrender in the south, and in the early hours of August 11, 1945, two days after the second atomic bomb had been dropped, U.S. planners were told at short notice to find a dividing line as far north as was militarily feasible. With only a small wall map of the Far East at their disposal, the planners, among them Dean Rusk of the State Department, latched on to the thirty-eighth parallel, which passed north of the capital, Seoul, and divided the peninsula almost equally (Map 9). Stalin accepted this plan without debate, and adhered to it even though Soviet forces occupied the north almost immediately and U.S. forces did not arrive from the island of Okinawa until September 8. Evidence from Soviet archives strengthens earlier suppositions that Stalin was not bothered about total control of the whole peninsula. His approach "was in keeping with the general aim of Russia's pre-1905 strategy, to maintain a balance of power in Korea."[26] The tacit spheres-of-influence arrangement struck with the Americans mirrored similar deals in Europe, and the 38th parallel was in fact the line around which Russia and Japan had negotiated at the turn of the century. But, as in Europe, Stalin understood "his" sphere to be Soviet property: the Russians promptly sealed off the zone and exploited its resources. They also helped local communists organize Soviet-style structures in the north but refrained from similar activities in the south. There, in a cauldron of social and political ferment, the U.S. military worked to create a right-center coalition against communism.

In principle, both the United States and the Soviet Union were committed to establishing a provisional, democratic government for the whole country, but, as cold war animosities intensified, neither was willing to move in that direction for fear of Korea's falling under the influence of the other side. In fact, the division suited both superpowers, preoccupied with European crises in 1947–1948. Following dubious elections in south and north in the summer of 1948, Soviet troops were withdrawn at the end of the year and

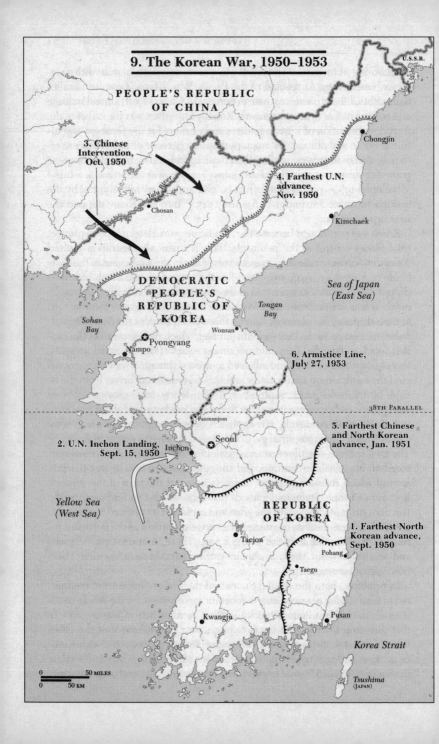

9. The Korean War, 1950–1953

U.S.S.R.

PEOPLE'S REPUBLIC OF CHINA

Chongjin

3. Chinese Intervention, Oct. 1950

Yalu River

4. Farthest U.N. advance, Nov. 1950

Chosan

Kimchaek

DEMOCRATIC PEOPLE'S REPUBLIC OF KOREA

Sea of Japan (East Sea)

Sohan Bay

Tongan Bay

Wonsan

Pyongyang

Nampo

6. Armistice Line, July 27, 1953

38TH PARALLEL

Panmunjom

Seoul

5. Farthest Chinese and North Korean advance, Jan. 1951

2. U.N. Inchon Landing, Sept. 15, 1950

Inchon

Yellow Sea (West Sea)

REPUBLIC OF KOREA

1. Farthest North Korean advance, Sept. 1950

Taejon

Pohang

Taegu

Kwangju

Pusan

Korea Strait

0   50 MILES
0   50 KM

Tsushima (JAPAN)

American troops by the following June. Each side hoped that continued military aid would maintain its client regime—in the north the left-communist alliance under Kim Il Sung, a former communist guerrilla against the Japanese; in the unstable south a government led by the veteran conservative nationalist Syngman Rhee, who had returned in 1945 from lengthy exile in the United States. But although the superpowers might have viewed this as a satisfactory solution, division at the 38th parallel made no economic sense. It left the north with most of the country's minerals and heavy industry, while the bulk of the agricultural land lay in the south, together with two-thirds of the twenty-four million population. In any case, Rhee and Kim were ardent nationalists, each determined to unify the country under his control. Neither accepted partition as permanent. It has been estimated that about one hundred thousand people were killed in political disturbances, guerrilla war, and border clashes before the formal outbreak of civil war in June 1950.[27]

Despite concern about the political and economic weakness of Rhee's regime, however, the State Department remained confident that he could survive. To quote the historian James Matray, they assumed that "local Communist parties, rather than organized military forces, acted as the primary vehicles of Soviet expansion" and that, in any case, South Korea "would be able to defend itself without extensive American aid or advice."[28] Both of these assumptions lay behind Acheson's speech of January 12; both proved mistaken. In April 1950 Kim visited Stalin in Moscow and wore down his doubts about all-out military attack, arguing that it would not provoke the United States. Kim was reassured by Acheson's defensive perimeter speech, but in any case, he insisted this would be a surprise attack, coordinated with a major communist uprising in the south, and that victory would be won in three days—before the Americans had time to intervene. Once Stalin had approved, the Soviets provided substantial support in the form of arms, ammunition, and advisers. Soviet military planners even drafted the "Preemptive Strike Operations Plan." On his way home from Moscow, Kim visited Beijing and obtained Chinese acquiescence. The failure of the Americans to intervene in China and the speeches by Truman and Acheson left Mao, like Stalin, complacent about U.S. reaction. Communism had been contained in Europe, but in Asia it seemed to be on the move.[29]

For Truman, however, this was the great test of the cold war. Before the end of June he had ordered American air, naval, and ground forces into the Korean battle and had moved the U.S. Seventh Fleet into the Taiwan Straits, effectively blocking a PRC invasion. These major shifts in America's Asian policy reflected global rather than regional considerations. Truman and his advisers had no doubt that Kim was acting at Stalin's behest. "The attack on Korea," declared the president on June 27, "makes it plain beyond all doubt that Communism has passed beyond the use of subversion to conquer independent nations and will now use armed invasion and war."[30] A "domino" mentality also prevailed in Washington. If Korea fell, Truman claimed, the Soviets would "keep right on going and swallow up one piece of Asia after another. . . . If we were to let Asia go, the Near East would collapse and no telling what would happen in Europe."[31] Truman, a history buff, was also keen to draw lessons from the past. Communism, he reflected, "was acting in Korea just as Hitler, Mussolini, and the Japanese had acted ten, fifteen, and twenty years earlier. . . . If this was allowed to go unchallenged it would mean a third world war."[32] The Americans also secured United Nations support. This was the first time that the UN had used force to defend a member state under attack.[33] Since 1945 the organization had been frozen by the cold war. Of the fifty-one founder states, twenty-two came from the Americas and another fifteen from Europe, giving the Americans a substantial majority in the Assembly. In retaliation, the Soviets repeatedly used their veto in the Security Council. Only the Soviet boycott of the Council in 1950, in protest against the PRC being denied China's seat, allowed the Korean war to be a UN operation.

Eventually sixteen nations contributed troops to the UN command in Korea, but 40 percent were South Korean and about 50 percent American. It was under the domineering U.S. command of General Douglas MacArthur that the war was run. By the end of July North Korean troops had occupied most of the peninsula. In response, MacArthur planned an amphibious landing behind enemy lines at the western port of Inchon, near Seoul. Most of his staff opposed the risky assault, but MacArthur grandly assured them that its very impracticality ensured complete surprise. He was right. The landings on September 15, 1950, were virtually unopposed. Within two weeks Seoul was in UN hands, and a jubilant Truman administration authorized MacArthur to cross the 38th parallel into North Korea. Unification was UN policy, but the Americans saw it in the context of the cold war. To quote one State Department official, "the resultant defeat to the Soviet Union and to the Communist world will be of momentous significance."[34]

MacArthur was told to draw back if there was any danger of Soviet or Chinese intervention but, confident that this would not occur, he pushed north toward the Yalu river, Korea's northern border with China. MacArthur was correct about Stalin. As soon as the Americans committed themselves in Korea, the Soviet leader distanced himself from the conflict, rejecting all Kim's pleas for Russian intervention. He had never intended a confrontation with the United States. Many of China's Politburo also wanted to stay out, including Zhou Enlai and Lin Biao. But Mao feared that China would be next on America's list and, in any case, UN successes had emboldened the CCP's opponents at home—counterrevolution threatened from within, if not from without. Like Truman, Mao saw Korea in an international context. Stalin had offered the PRC air cover if they did intervene, but the Chinese have claimed that he tried to wriggle out of his promise in early October. Whether he did or not, when Chinese "volunteers" started crossing the Yalu on October 19, Mao must have felt dangerously exposed. Certainly he was well aware of the limits of the Sino-Soviet alliance.[35]

Fortunately for Mao, the initial Chinese incursions were dismissed as insignificant by American commanders. Some three hundred thousand Chinese troops were in North Korea by November 25, when they began a full-scale offensive. Most were hardened veterans of the civil war, who quickly routed the U.S. Eighth Army. One American officer termed it "a sight that hasn't been seen for hundreds of years: the men of a whole United States Army fleeing from a battlefield, abandoning their wounded, running for their lives."[36] By January 1951, Seoul had fallen and most of North Korea was in communist hands again. In a panicky Washington, there was talk of total evacuation or of using the atomic bomb—alarming European allies such as the British. Not until March did the Americans regain the initiative. After the bloody failure of China's spring offensives, the fighting settled into a war of attrition. It took two more years to achieve a formal armistice, eventually signed at Panmunjom in July 1953. The new demarcation line snaked around the thirty-eighth parallel, where the war had started.

On all the belligerents, the effects were profound—especially for the Koreans. Thanks to Truman's restraint of MacArthur, they were spared the use of atomic weapons, but the alternative—known as "limited war"—was little more agreeable. Dead and wounded are estimated at 1.3 million in the south and 1.5 million in the north—roughly a tenth of Korea's population.[37] Developing their tactics of World War II, the Americans prefaced every assault with intense air and artillery bombardment. Seoul, for instance, changed hands four times in nine months. By the time it was "liberated" by the UN in March 1951 only the Capitol and the railway station stood amid the rubble of the major buildings. Even MacArthur, no stranger to carnage, said in 1951 that "the war in Korea has almost destroyed that nation . . . I have never seen such devastation. . . . After I looked at that wreckage and those thousands of women and children and everything, I vomited."[38]

Nor had the conflict achieved its original aim of unifying the country. On the contrary, it confirmed Korea's partition for the foreseeable future. In the south, Rhee clung on to power until 1960, rigging elections and coercing the opposition, but the economy was in ruins and recovery was minimal in the 1950s. In the north, Kim eliminated his rivals with ruthless brutality and set about Stalinizing his country. Agriculture was collectivized and a six-year plan promoted the development of heavy industry. Whereas South Korea was now dependent on the United States, Soviet influence in the north had been weakened by Stalin's failure to assist the war effort. Although needing Chinese help, Kim tried to keep a balance between his two great communist neighbors—enunciating the concept of self-reliance, *juche*, as a model for Third World communism.

American losses were small by comparison—only thirty-three thousand dead—but they were evidence that the cold war had become a hot war in Asia and might do so in Europe as well. The Korean War also inflamed antileftist feeling in a country that had no experience of left-of-center politics on European models. Senator Joseph McCarthy had started his notorious accusations about communists in high places in February 1950, but what became known as McCarthyism was part of a general assault by right-wing Republicans, mainly from middle America, on the Truman administration, especially Acheson, for being "soft" on communism, which prospered with the shambles in Korea in 1950–1951. Although McCarthy's power waned after the end of the war, his legacy was a lasting climate of fear in which all public criticism of rigid anticommunism was suspect.

In diplomacy, the main casualty of this mood was America's policy toward China. There was now a powerful pro-Chiang lobby in Congress. Its leader, Senator William Knowland, considered war with the "Chinese Reds" almost inevitable: "If we don't fight them in China and Formosa, we will be fighting them in San Francisco." Truman had interposed the U.S. Navy to prevent a communist invasion of Taiwan; his Republican successor, Dwight D. Eisenhower, indicated in February 1953 that he would do nothing to stop a Nationalist reconquest of the mainland as China's legitimate government. The Republicans intensified their blockade of the PRC and committed themselves in December 1954 to defending Taiwan and the other Guomindang offshore islands from communist attack. Secretary of State John Foster Dulles was looking for a Sino-Soviet split. But he argued that "the way to get that is to make the going tough, not easy" by keeping the PRC "under pressures which would, in turn, keep the Communists pressuring Russia for more than Russia would give."[39] NATO allies feared that such intransigence in Asia would distract the United States from European security. The British, with major interests in Hong Kong, had recognized the PRC in January 1950 and advocated a more conciliatory line to woo Beijing away from Moscow. Neither Washington nor London shifted ground, but the disagreement was symptomatic of growing concern in Europe that the Americans were now taking the cold war too seriously.

The Korean War had a profound effect on Japan. Exports soared 50 percent in the first two years of war, and GNP grew at an annual rate of 10 percent. Much of the benefit stemmed from some $3 billion that the Americans spent in Japan in 1950–1954 on war or war-related orders. The governor of the Bank of Japan called these procurement orders "divine aid"; they were "Toyota's salvation," according to the president of that company, which had

Abrogate -

been on the verge of bankruptcy in 1949.[40] As well as aiding Japan's economic recovery, the Korean War also ushered in a new security relationship with America. In August 1950, the Pentagon dropped its objections to a peace treaty with Japan, as long as U.S. bases remained. At the same time, MacArthur cracked down on Japanese communists and started training a paramilitary police reserve of seventy-five thousand. Tough negotiations followed with the Liberal premier, Yoshida Shigemuru, about the form of the new American-Japanese relationship. In the peace treaty of September 1951, Japan regained full sovereignty, but simultaneously signed a security pact accepting the continued presence of U.S. troops and promising not to offer bases to any other power. On rearmament, however, Yoshida dragged his feet, accepting only a secret paper commitment to a fifty-thousand-strong military; and a bill creating "Self-Defense Forces" was not approved by the Diet until March 1954. To smooth ratification of the security treaty by the U.S. Senate, Yoshida reluctantly agreed to sign a peace treaty normalizing relations with the Guomindang on Taiwan. He also stated that Japan had no intention of concluding a treaty with "the Communist regime of China," which, he said, was probably "backing the Japan Communist Party in its program of seeking violently to overthrow the constitutional system and the present Government of Japan."[41]

The Korean War helped, therefore, to further American aims for the economic and military recovery of Japan within a new American alliance, but Japan's prospects did not look impressive in the mid-1950s. Although Yoshida and the Liberals controlled the coalitions of 1948–1954, politics remained factional as socialist parties revived in the early 1950s and the other conservative party, the Democrats, was rent by feuding. Yoshida accepted the need, at least temporarily, for an American alliance, but he did not share the general Democratic enthusiasm for rearmament, while the socialists condemned both the security treaty and remilitarization. In any case, the inequality of the relationship with America was widely resented: the 1951 security treaty included no Japanese right to abrogate nor any formal American commitment to defend Japan (because the Japanese refusal to rearm suggested they were not willing to help themselves).[42] The unequal security pact and the enforced treaty with Taiwan were, for many Japanese, "humiliating symbols of a fraudulent independence under U.S. hegemony."[43]

Moreover, economic recovery seemed superficial. Renewed inflation was only checked in 1954 by tighter monetary controls and another recession. Earnings from procurement orders encouraged increased imports, pushing the trade deficit to $1.1 billion in 1954, when Japan's trade was still under half its prewar level. To most Western observers at this time, Japan remained an essentially "backward" country. In 1955 its GNP was one-fifteenth of America's and only half that of West Germany's. Nearly 40 percent of its work force was still engaged in agriculture, and the country was the second largest borrower from the World Bank. No less an authority than Edwin O. Reischauer, the eminent American Japanologist, wrote in 1957: "The economic situation in Japan may be so fundamentally unsound that no policies, no matter how wise, can save her from slow economic starvation and all the concomitant political and social ills that situation would produce."[44]

Consolidating Unity and Revolution in China

Internationally, the biggest beneficiary of the Korean War was the People's Republic of China. After a century of defeats by the Europeans and Japan, the Chinese had held their own against the world's leading superpower. Their soldiers were celebrated as heroes in Chinese films and books; American imperialists were likewise excoriated. In fact, the conflict was not referred to as the Korean War but as *kangmei yuanchao* ("Resist America, Aid Korea") and both of these words became popular, patriotic first names for children of the period.[45]

Yet the price had been appalling. The Chinese had suffered nine hundred thousand casualties in the war: one of Mao's sons, Anying, was among the dead. The war confirmed Sino-American enmity until the 1970s; it also forced Mao completely into the Soviet camp, even though Stalin had proved to be an unreliable ally. Because of the American embargo, trade with the USSR soared from 8 percent of China's total commerce in 1949 to 70 percent in 1952. Leaning to one side had become, at least for the moment, virtual dependence. China's international position after 1950 also had a marked effect on its internal revolution. In 1949 Mao proposed continuance of the "united front" policies that had proved so successful in the civil war. (The CCP was only one of the five stars in the new five-star flag, albeit the largest; the other stars represented peasants, workers, petty capitalists, and national capitalists.) Eleven of the twenty-four ministries went to noncommunists, and Mao's "New Democracy" was tailored to the realities of a semicolonial country in which the working class was weak and disorganized. He stated in June 1949: "Our present policy is to regulate capitalism, not to destroy it."[46] Of course, he intended in due course to establish a truly socialist state—the united front was a means, not the end. But the pace and extent of China's "socialist transformation" in the early 1950s owed much to the crisis caused by the Korean War.

In 1949 the Communist party amounted to 4.5 million members—less than 1 percent of China's population. For two decades its base had been largely rural; now it had to take control of the cities and mobilize their inhabitants. The Korean War justified and accelerated that process. A series of mass campaigns were orchestrated by the party, identifying particular enemies of the community and exposing them through public indictment. They were backed by police investigation, intimidation, and violence. The first campaign succeeded in driving out almost all foreigners by the end of 1950. Their businesses were forced to sell up, their Chinese associates scared off, and the Christian churches brought under firm state oversight. War fever encouraged a second campaign from February 1951 against "counterrevolutionaries," characterized by particular violence as old scores were settled in a flurry of arrests, trials, and summary executions. Not only suspected GMD members, but anyone with alleged ties to "foreign cultural aggressors" became targets in this two-year Terror. In Guangdong province alone, according to Zhou Enlai, 28,332 people were executed; he deplored the fact that too many counterrevolutionaries had escaped.[47] Less bloody, but equally important, were the "Three Antis" campaign of 1951–1952, to crack down on corruption in party and government, and its successor, the "Five Antis" to break business leaders, the so-called national bourgeoisie. Using the well-tried techniques of group mobilization, class antagonism, and enforced self-confession, CCP personnel obliged businessmen to admit corruption, pay massive fines, and submit to state control. By the end of the Korean War, the cities were cowed and political pluralism in China almost extinguished.

But the decisive battleground of the Chinese revolution was the countryside, where about 85 percent of the population lived. Rural life had been dominated by an elite of landlords and rich peasants, who owned much of the land, managed moneylending, and dominated village government and religious charities. Resentment against their rule was constrained by traditional ties of kinship and village solidarity. Goods were sold, loans contracted, and marriages arranged within these networks. The challenge facing the CCP was so to arouse horizontal, class antagonisms that they would sever these customary vertical ties that held together rural society. The CCP's methods had been pioneered in the old bases around Yan'an during the civil war. A "work team" of trained communists would move into a village and gradually classify the status of its households, often aided by a "Poor Peasants' Association" that they set up. The team's classifications would then be posted at the central meeting place, whereupon the "struggle phase" would begin. Victims of those identified as landlords or rich peasants were urged to denounce their oppressors in special "speak bitterness" meetings. They were often reluctant to do so, as the rural elite played on traditional ties, while the communists tried to arouse class hostility among people who had never been politicized before. Weeks of meetings and agitation might be required before poorer peasants were willing to speak out. Once sufficient numbers had done so and the accused had been coerced into confessing, the way was open to take away his property and redistribute it to poor or landless peasants.

For a glimpse of what this meant in practice, take the case of Changchuang, a former Japanese-occupied village in Shanxi province, some four hundred miles southwest of Peking, where land reform took hold in 1946 in the wake of the chaotic Anti-Traitor movement to identify collaborators. The richest man in this village of some two hundred households had been Sheng Ching-ho, a landlord whose long fingernails and long gown proclaimed that he was above manual work. He owned the largest landholding and also a liquor distillery, loaning out part of his profits at interest rates of up to 50 percent a month to desperate peasants whose defaults then served to enlarge his property. Sheng Ching-ho also managed the affairs of the local Buddhist and Confucian religious charities, which enabled him to cream off healthy commissions from regular offerings, spirit talking, the annual fair, and so on. As village head under the provincial governor, he also took a substantial cut from local taxes. When the peasants were mobilized in 1946, Sheng Ching-ho found that half the village families had scores to settle. Once one dared to accuse him, the floodgates opened. Old women who had never spoken in public before rose to denounce him. Li Mao's wife shook her fist under his nose and shouted: "Once I went to glean wheat on your land. But you cursed me and drove me away." A total of 180 accusations were made. Sheng Ching-ho stood with head bowed. When asked, he admitted them all and was judged to owe four hundred bags of milled grain. Having found less than that in his store, they beat him up and kept on doing so until he confessed, one by one, the locations of his various hoards of silver coin—the equivalent of $500. That night, villagers sated themselves on the New Year's feast he had prepared, while Ching-ho and his wife escaped and were never heard of again. As a result of the campaign to "settle accounts" with landlords, about half the people of Changchuang were the beneficiaries of land and property redistribution.[48]

During the civil war period land reform in the north was particularly radical and bloody. In the newer liberated areas to the south the pace was more measured. In 1949 only about a fifth of China's villages had been touched. When the program resumed with the Agrarian Reform Law of June 1950, its tempo and tone were affected by the tense atmosphere of the Korean War. It has been estimated that in the process "between 400,000 and 800,000 people were killed officially after 1949" and perhaps as many again unofficially.[49] Yet the government's target had been deliberately narrow, focusing mainly on "landlords" to maximize support among the richer and most productive peasants, whose output was vital to satisfy food needs. Wide differences of wealth and landownership still existed. For the CCP the point of the campaign had never been land redistribution itself, though this was the bait to attract the peasantry, but to break the traditional power structure of rural China and mobilize support for the party by fomenting class conflict. As Mao put it back in in 1927: "A revolution is not a dinner party. . . . it is necessary to create terror for a while in every rural area."[50]

The Korean War reforms in city and countryside gave the government both the foundation and the confidence to proceed with more radical socialization. The government's first five-year plan for 1953–1957 borrowed heavily from Soviet precedents, concentrating on the development of heavy industry under tight central controls. By the time it was approved in July 1955, Mao was more worried about lagging production and continued class divisions in the countryside. His speech of July 31, 1955, on collectivizing agriculture, signaled a swing away from gradualism. Poorer peasants were now mobilized against their middling counterparts, who had hitherto been courted by government reforms. By May 1956 agricultural production cooperatives encompassed over 90 percent of peasant households, compared with 14 percent in March 1955. And more than 60 percent of these APCs were now fully socialist, with all land, animals and large equipment under collective control, compared with the voluntary and partial arrangements hitherto.[51] The "socialist high tide" also engulfed the cities. By 1956 state-owned companies accounted for two-thirds of the value of total industrial output (compared with one-third in 1949). The rest of industry was in the hands of state-private partnerships, which had accounted for less than 10 percent of output in 1949. In 1955–1956 most handicraft producers—making everyday goods, tools, and utensils—were organized into cooperatives.[52]

Terror had been the instrument of revolution, of course. And worse was to come, for Mao saw revolution as an ongoing process, always in danger of being reversed. As we shall see, his doctrine of continuing revolution was to shape China for the next twenty years. But in the decade since Japan surrendered, China had already been transformed. The Chinese word was *fan-shen*—literally, turning over one's body. By 1956, most agricultural and industrial activity was under the control of the state. For those who survived the violence of war and revolution, conditions were better than before. Life expectancy in 1957 was fifty-seven years, compared with thirty-six in 1950, and real wages had increased by almost one-third.[53] Land reform had narrowed the inequalities of village life and sharply reduced the number on the edge of starvation. The lot of women was also changing. The Marriage Law of May 1950 fixed a new minimum age of eighteen for women, banned concubinage and bigamy, and allowed divorce by mutual consent. Although enforcement was patchy, the law did represent a challenge to traditional practices of arranged marriages, child weddings, and general female subordination.

All this seemed evidence of how an agrarian society could be transformed by revolution. And at mid-century, much of Southeast Asia seemed ready to "turn over" as well. In Indochina, Malaya, Indonesia, and the Philippines, communism was on the march.

Nationalism and Communism in Southeast Asia

The most significant of these revolutions occurred in Vietnam, that part of Indochina where French colonial rule had been particularly exploitative and where it had ended abruptly with Japan's occupation. The nature and outcome of the revolution reflected a mix of internal and international circumstances.

The first was Vietnam's unique and potent blend of nationalism and communism. The French had split the country into three, but 90 percent of the nineteen million inhabitants were ethnically Vietnamese whose sense of identity had been sharpened by centuries of struggle against Chinese imperialism and sustained by the distinctive practice of ancestor worship. During the French era, the development of a romanized script, *quoc ngu,* for the essentially Chinese language and its use to propagate Vietnamese traditions helped promote national consciousness among intellectuals. By the 1930s a variety of political and religious groups were agitating against colonial rule. The political success of communism in Vietnam was due largely to adroit identification with Vietnamese patriotism.[54] In 1941 the Indochina Communist Party (ICP) under Ho Chi Minh (see Plate 6) established a Vietnam Independence League, the Vietminh, in which all classes and groups would be represented in a structure right down to village level under discreet ICP leadership. The party also developed its own rural strategy, drawing on the Chinese communist example but evolving independently, and it played on the grievances of peasants whose communal life had been disrupted by the especially vigorous French economic exploitation of Vietnam. The Vietminh gained massively from the indifference of both the Japanese and their French puppet government to the appalling famine in the first half of 1945, during which over one million people probably died. Indeed, the famine may have been caused by Japan's ruthless diversion of Vietnamese rice for its own use.[55]

However, the communist strategy of national liberation and rural revolution would have had little chance but for the power vacuum in 1945. On March 9 the Japanese dispensed with French puppet rule entirely. By the summer the Vietminh had built up a powerful guerrilla base area in the hill provinces north of Hanoi, and support was spreading in center of the country. Ho bided his time until the Allies invaded. Suddenly, on August 15, came news of the Japanese surrender. The Allies hastily prepared to send Chinese Guomindang troops into the north and British forces into the south, but the Vietnamese beat them to it. In the next few days, mass demonstrations in Hanoi, Hue, and other cities, led by local Vietminh representatives, prompted the Japanese to hand over power. On September 2 Ho proclaimed the Democratic Republic of Vietnam (DRV). Despite the role of Vietminh organizers, the August Revolution was testimony to the strength of grassroots national feeling, especially after the famine. It was "in the first instance a spontaneous outpouring of emotion, and secondarily a well-organized Leninist seizure of power."[56] Moreover, the seizure of power was improvised by local urban communists, with Ho still waiting in the north. He and his lieutenants had planned a rural revolution, based on a strategy of "people's war." Instead, they were brought to power in a classical revolution akin to that in Russia in 1917.[57]

Yet Ho's rural strategy did prove vital to keep the revolution going after 1945. British forces helped the French move back into the south and, when the GMD finally withdrew in February 1946 (after extensive looting), the French returned to the north as well. They agreed to recognize the DRV as a free state within the French Union, but it became clear that this "freedom" did not guarantee full independence, let alone the unity of all Vietnam. After bloody incidents in Haiphong and Hanoi at the end of 1946, all-out war began. Although the French soon took control of most cities and towns, they were unable to pacify the villages or penetrate the forests. The breathing space of 1945–1946 had enabled Ho's principal general, Vo Nguyen Giap, to increase the DRV's military forces from perhaps three thousand to one hundred thousand.

Ho could avoid defeat, but alone he could not win victory. What decided the outcome of the Franco-Vietnamese struggle was its interaction with the deepening cold war. In 1945 no country recognized the Democratic Republic of Vietnam. Stalin was conciliating the West, Mao was still fighting civil war, and initially the Vietnamese struggle was largely ignored outside France. But by the end of the decade, the Soviet Union was encouraging revolution and China was a unified communist state. In January 1950 the new People's Republic recognized the DRV, followed by the Soviet Union, and arms and supplies were infiltrated south across the Chinese border. In the campaign of October 1950, Vietminh victory, under guidance from Chinese advisers, forced the French to abandon their blockade line along the border and ensured full Vietminh access to Chinese resources. This "changed the balance of power in the Indo-China battlefield."[58]

These developments accelerated the marked shift in American policy since the mid-1940s, when Roosevelt had opposed continued French rule in Indochina and the Vietmin's nationalist foliage had seemed more evident than its communist roots. But in May 1949 Secretary of State Dean Acheson ruled that the question of whether Ho was "as much nationalist as Commie is irrelevant. All Stalinists in colonial areas are nationalists." Once in power, their "objective necessarily becomes subordination [of the] state to Commie purpose."[59] And when in February 1950 the French created a token autonomous Vietnamese government within the French Union and led by the former emperor, Bao Dai, the Truman administration extended formal recognition. U.S. planners warned that "if Indochina falls, very likely all of Southeast Asia will come under communist domination," thereby jeopardizing food and raw materials that were vital to Japan and Western Europe.[60] By 1953 American economic aid was covering about 60 percent of French military expenditure in Vietnam, but total victory remained elusive. The ebbing French will to fight was finally drained by the disaster at Dienbienphu in the spring of 1954, when sixteen thousand troops were surrounded and shelled into surrender. Any thought of U.S. air strikes to save the beleaguered French was ruled out when congressional leaders told Dulles that "there must be no more Koreas with the United States furnishing 90 percent of the manpower" and when Britain, America's main potential ally, rejected intervention as a "great mistake."[61]

French rule ended in 1954. Yet the outcome was not total victory for Ho, but partition of the country between a communist-led north and an American-dominated south. Once more, the cold war context proved decisive. After Korea, the Chinese had no desire to fight the United States again, while the Russians wanted to minimize Mao's influence in Vietnam. Both communist powers forced partition on a bitter Ho. Similar pressure was exerted on the Americans by British premier Anthony Eden, concerned at U.S. bellicosity and "more than ever convinced of [the] dangers of [a] third world war" if an armistice were not signed.[62] Partition at the seventeenth parallel between two Vietnamese governments was intended as temporary expedient that would provide a breathing space before free elections for a unified Vietnam in July 1956. Instead, it proved an interval before a second and far more brutal Indochina war.

In the mid-1950s, however, that war was still in the future. Despite American fears, the rest of Southeast Asia had not "fallen," even partially, to communism. Comparisons with Vietnam are instructive.

The Dutch East Indies had also been under exploitative colonial rule. There, too, Japanese occupation had shattered European power and Japan's surrender in August 1945 had created the opportunity to proclaim independence. Again as in Vietnam, a bloody war of liberation followed as the colonial power, returning in the wake of British forces, fought to regain full control after negotiations with the new Republic of Indonesia collapsed in 1946. But the contrasts with Vietnam were ultimately more striking than the similarities. For the Indonesian struggle ended with total independence in December 1949, and the communists played only a minor role in the process. The orientation of the new government was Western and even pro-American.

The Dutch East Indies were a vast archipelago of some thirteen thousand islands which, on a map of Europe, would stretch from Dublin to Moscow. Over half its seventy million people in 1939 lived on the central island of Java, comparable in size to Ireland. Many of the islands had their own separate languages and cultures; most of the "outer islands" were deeply suspicious of the Javanese. The populace had, consequently, no equivalent to the long history of coherent Vietnamese nationalism; indeed, the concept of Indonesia was a twentieth-century invention. Despite anticolonial outbursts, the mobilization of nationalist feeling, particularly on Java, was in large part the result of the Japanese. They made use of urban nationalists, notably Sukarno and Mohammad Hatta, and also of rural Islamic leaders, helping to consolidate the two main political parties of the post-1945 era: the Nationalist PNI and the Islamic Masjumi. The Japanese also promoted the use of the Indonesian language, which had been discouraged by the Dutch; they mobilized the youth (*pemuda*) into militaristic civil defense units; and they trained an elite to lead the embryonic Indonesian army (PETA). Although all this was done to aid the Japanese war effort, the legacies were profound—PETA officers, for instance, became the basis of the powerful Indonesian army. More immediately, it was the younger, *pemuda* nationalists who pushed Sukarno to proclaim independence when the Japanese suddenly surrendered in August 1945. For the next few years Sukarno fought a two-front struggle—to hold the republic's central Javanese base against the Dutch and to coordinate the varied religious, political, and regional interests that vied for control of its government. To reduce communal tensions, he insisted on a religiously neutral definition of nationalism—the philosophy of *pancasila*—in which Islam would enjoy no special place. Even so, a separate Islamic state existed in western Java until 1962.

In this improvised revolution, the Indonesian communist party (PKI) played only a minor role, having been marginalized since its abortive revolts of 1926–1927. The size and ethnic diversity of the East Indies militated against class consciousness, as did the pervasiveness of Islam, albeit in syncretistic forms. In the East Indies, the PKI lacked a rural base among the peasantry, who had been less disrupted than in China and Vietnam by economic change. The push for independence in 1945 came from nonleftist revolts in key Javanese cities such as Jakarta and Surabaya. Struggling to catch up with the onrush of events, the party tried to influence the national revolution from within a coalition. When that failed and it was forced out of the government, the PKI slid into support for a *pemuda*-led revolt in Madiun, in eastern Java, in September 1948. As in 1926–1927, most of the leadership was eliminated and the party shattered. It had been "prematurely stampeded" into a revolt for which it was not prepared; even more important, it was attacking leaders like Sukarno, "who had become the very symbol of the Republic and of Indonesian independence."[63] When the PKI recovered in the early 1950s, it was taken over by D. N. Aidit and others of the *pemuda* generation, who eschewed revolutionary action and urged (at least for the moment) a political route to power. Their platform, significantly, was to complete the national revolution.

The Vietnamese symbiosis of nationalism and communism was not, therefore, replicated in Indonesia. In fact, both ideologies were much much weaker there, and national consciousness itself was as much consequence as cause of the bloody war of 1946–1949. Moreover, international circumstances were very different. The Madiun revolt of 1948 took place before the Chinese revolution was complete, and Indonesia was hundreds of miles away from Chinese support, unlike Vietnam. Those same fundamentals of time and space affected U.S. policy as well: in Indonesia the communist threat was less urgent and less proximate than in Vietnam in 1950. And in American eyes, Madiun enhanced the credentials of the republic government as the only one in the Far East "to have met and crushed an all-out Communist rebellion," in the words of Undersecretary of State Robert Lovett.[64] The aggressive Dutch "police action" in central Java in December 1948 and the outcry it produced in Congress prompted the Truman administration to press the Dutch to concede independence, warning that otherwise economic and military aid to the Netherlands might be jeopardized. This was not perhaps the decisive argument for the Dutch government, which was already moving in that direction, having secured full recognition for Dutch economic interests in an independent Indonesia.[65] But the American pressure was symptomatic of the basic differences between the Vietnamese and Indonesian revolutionary crises of mid-century.

Elsewhere in Southeast Asia, the Philippines and Malaya experienced major rural uprisings under communist leadership in the early 1950s. Both, however, were contained.

In the Philippine archipelago, independence did not require a revolution. The Americans, who had controlled this former Spanish colony since 1898, had set a timetable in the 1930s and the new republic was declared on July 4, 1946 (Plate 15). The Japanese occupation, though brutal, did not disrupt the fundamentals of Filipino society. The Americans simply transferred power to the pro-American landed elite that they had been cultivating for years and which would guarantee American economic rights and military bases. In his independence speech, President Manuel Roxas declared: "Our safest course, and I believe it is true for the rest of the world as well, is in the glittering wake of America whose sure advance with mighty prow breaks for small craft the waves we fear."[66]

Only the Huk rebellion threatened to upset the boat, but this was limited in both geographical scope and communist direction. It was confined to the rice and sugar areas of central Luzon, where, as in Vietnam, the old landlord-tenant relationship had been particularly upset by cash-crop agriculture, and the peasants had been militarized in guerrilla struggle against the Japanese. Abortive postwar protests about the land system spiraled into rural revolt from 1946. But even at its peak, in 1950, the Huks numbered only about twelve thousand, and their strength ebbed before a two-pronged government campaign of military action and economic reform. In the decade from 1946 the United States poured $1.2 billion of economic and military aid into the Philippines, concerned to protect American interests and convinced that the Huks were a communist front. In fact, the Philippine Communist Party (PKP), "as an organization, moved back and forth between alliance and non-alliance with the peasants of Central Luzon."[67] Up to 1947–1948, it followed the then Kremlin orthodoxy in advocating a political route to power. When it then took up "armed struggle," it remained an essentially working-class movement without a firm rural base and exerted only patchy influence over the Huk insurgency. Peasant aims were reformist, not revolutionary; their ethos was as much Christian as Marxist.

The Philippines, therefore, experienced no real national revolution, and communism was of peripheral significance. The corollary of all that, however, was that though this was one of the first Asian countries to declare political independence, it was one of the last to sever the ties of dependence to its former colonial masters. Economic control by the Americans and their Filipino clients continued for most of the century.

Malaya, likewise, became independent through a peaceful transfer of power, but this occurred more than a decade after the war ended and only once a major communist insurrection had been suppressed. The Malay peninsula, roughly the size of England or New York State, had a population of about five million in 1945. The Japanese occupation caused considerable disruption—including large-scale banditry and acute rice shortages—but, unlike Vietnam or Indonesia, Malaya had no nationalist movement ready and able to seize power in 1945. The power structure of the local sultans had not been destroyed in the war, and nationalist feeling was dissipated by ethnic enmity among Malays and Chinese (each about 40 percent of the population) and Indians. Moreover, the British were anxious to retain their position in Malaya, since its rubber and tin were major dollar-earning exports. They returned quickly and in force in 1945. Political mobilization really got going as a consequence of botched British plans for a Malayan Union, bringing together the patchwork of Crown colonies and princely states that made up the peninsula. This threatened the political and religious authority of the sultans; it also aroused communal anger by promising citizenship rights to the Chinese and Indians. Mass protests by the Malays forced a British U-turn in mid-1946. In 1948 Britain unveiled a looser Federation of Malaya with minimal concessions on non-Malay citizenship, thereby alienating the Chinese, who also mobilized in strikes and boycotts.

Within the aroused Chinese community, the Malayan Communist party (MCP) enjoyed considerable support, dating back to its wartime role as the main guerrilla opposition to the Japanese. In 1948, MCP policy shifted toward armed struggle, following the new Kremlin line, though the initial violence was as much the work of local cadres, aroused by the worsening economic and political situation for the Chinese. The British declared a state of emergency in June 1948, but it took until the mid-1950s to suppress the insurgency and required, at its peak in 1952, some forty thousand outside troops as well as twenty-eight thousand Malay soldiers and police and thirty-nine thousand special constables. The British were, however, better off than the French in Vietnam, because the nationalist-communist symbiosis did not materialize in Malaya. Support for the communist insurgency came almost entirely from the Chinese community. The British were also more successful at denying the insurgents a rural base. At great expense they resettled over five hundred thousand Chinese from squatter communities into New Villages. At the same time, aided by the fortuitous boom in tin and rubber prices during the Korean War, they ploughed investment into village improvements, recognizing that, in the words of the high commissioner of 1952, Sir Gerald Templer, "the shooting side of the business is only 25% of the trouble and the other 75% lies in getting the people of this country behind us."[68] The British also worked on the Malay community, because "gradual steps being taken towards giving Malay self-government kept the moderate Malayan nationalist politicians on our side."[69] This sensitivity to what Templer popularized as the "hearts and minds" dimension of counterinsurgency stood in marked contrast to French and Dutch policy elsewhere in southeast Asia. In August 1957 the Federation of Malaya gained independence, but under a conservative alliance of Malay and Chinese leaders who were committed to cooperate with Britain on security questions and to remain within the sterling area of countries whose currencies were pegged to the British pound. As in the Philippines, the former rulers believed they had engineered a favorable transfer of power to conservative leaders who would respect their continued economic and military interests. "For the British," comments historian John Darwin, "this was independence as it ought to be."[70]

The Limits of "Independence"

Clearly, the word *independence* covered a multitude of sins. In the decade after 1945, most of Asia threw off formal colonial rule (mainly European or Japanese), but that turning over, though momentous historically, tells us little about what happened to the newly independent states. The stories examined in this chapter suggest a few other important themes.

It mattered, for instance, whether independence took place through *revolutionary* or *evolutionary* means. Did it involve the violent overthrow of previous rulers, as in China, Indonesia, or, partially, in Vietnam? If so, did this presage more radical change in the political and social structure? Yes, in China and Vietnam, but less so in Indonesia. Or did independence result from a transfer of power to existing elites, as happened in Malaya and the Philippines? This gave greater scope for the ex-colonial powers to secure their interests through *informal* rather than *formal* empire, in other words, without bearing the burdens of government. The Philippines, Malaya, even Indonesia are reminders that imperialism did not end in the 1940s. The old rulers were still anxious to control the resources and policies of former possessions. *Political independence* therefore did not necessarily mean *economic independence.* Even Japan, one of the few Asian countries to avoid colonial rule and itself a former empire, became part of the American imperium after 1945.

Another problem was that the new *states* were not usually congruent with clearly defined *nations*, bound together by ties of ethnicity, language, and culture. China and Japan were rare exceptions. Vietnam was another, but there one embryonic nation was divided, for the moment, into two separate states. Most new Asian countries lacked a sharp sense of *ethnic nationalism*; instead, theirs was a *territorial nationalism*,[71] defined by the anticolonial struggle to gain control of a governmental structure created by the ruling power—as in Indonesia or Malaya. And that struggle usually involved delicate intercommunal relations among rival ethnic, religious, and sectional interests, such as the Malay-Chinese tension or the strains in Indonesia between Java and the outer islands and between orthodox and reformist Islam. The viability of the old colonial territory as a separate state and the degree to which it would be controlled by a dominant ethnic group were to be fundamental issues for the future of most "new nations."

The battles of nation building were fuel for the cold war. Around mid-century, both the Soviet Union and China supported armed struggles for communist-led national revolution, a phase beginning with the new militancy of cominform and Mao's victory in China. In Asia, still mainly a continent of impoverished farmers, success turned on the communists' ability to mobilize *peasant revolution,* notably in China and Vietnam, by a mixture of incentives and coercion. This phase abated with Stalin's death, the Korean armistice, and the partition of Vietnam. By the mid-1950s, the cold war map of Asia, like that of Europe, had been set. The new Soviet philosophy was "peaceful coexistence"—meaning continued struggle, but using political means. By now, the United States was committed to the philosophy of containment, having concluded that colonialism was often a lesser evil than communism. In the ensuing struggle, a central arena was the economic development of the new states—all of which, even Japan, felt themselves "backward" by Western standards. *Land reform* and *industrial modernization* were essential to their own prosperity and cohesion. But the form of their development, capitalist or socialist, would help determine alignments in the cold war.

3

Legacies of Empire

In East and Southeast Asia the postcolonial transition was exacerbated by cold war confrontations and often accompanied by violent revolutions. Elsewhere decolonization was more orderly, and the new superpowers were less engaged. More significant problems for many postcolonial states were their own regional and religious differences, which in turn were intertwined with the legacies of imperial rule. How colonial power was exercised and how it was relinquished were equally important in the stories of South Asia, the Middle East, and Africa, with which this chapter is principally concerned. The partition of two British possessions—India and Palestine—in 1947–1948 created fault lines in South Asia and the Middle East that would outlast Europe's cold war divide. In Africa, the conflicts between colonial governments, settler minorities, and indigenous elites produced a mosaic of unstable states. But even the most developed postcolonial countries had problems of national identity, as can be seen in Australia, New Zealand, and Canada. And states that had long been politically independent often lacked economic independence, as the postwar history of Latin America reveals. Around the globe, the legacies of empire were complicated and pervasive.

The Partition of India

The Indian subcontinent enjoys a natural unity, protected to the north by the world's highest mountains and on the other three sides by vast oceans. Over the centuries, this geographical framework has proved a distinctive "Indianizing" force, not least in confirming the Hindu religion and the caste relationships that set India apart from the modern Western world of secularism and class. Yet India was never a static or monochrome society, even in religion where Islam and Christianity both made their mark in syncretist forms. And the size of the subcontinent—half the area of the United States—reinforced its pluralism because centralized government was almost impossible. "Imperial rule" therefore meant the imposition of an India-wide administration on top of layers of regional and village authority. Influence over local life depended not so much on brute force (though this was used) but on a network of collaborators who acted as intermediaries between top and bottom. This was true for the Mughals, the paramount power in India in the sixteenth and seventeenth centuries, who consolidated the position of Islam and left behind notable monuments such as the Taj Mahal and the Red Fort in Delhi. It was also true of their successors, the British raj, which also acted through collaborators, both the Indian princes and the indigenous civil service. The British were not so much conquerors of India as intruders at the higher levels of political power.[1]

Over time, the British were obliged to concede more autonomy to their clients and more influence to their opponents, notably the Congress party, which became the main political force in India between the wars as it campaigned for independence. British rule was never an end in itself but a means to secure commercial and military benefits. In 1914 India had been the most valuable market for British exports; Britain's income from Indian trade and investments covered one-third of its payments deficit with the rest of the world. The low-cost Indian army constituted half of Britain's global fighting strength. By 1945 the cost-benefit analysis of the raj had shifted dramatically, as Indian tariffs emasculated British exports and the charges for using the Indian army in two world wars left Britain in debt to India to the tune of almost one-fifth of British GNP.[2] Although Churchill allowed sentiment to obscure these realities, his Labour successors in 1945 felt that national interest as well as socialist idealism dictated an early transfer of power before nationalist unrest proved uncontrollable.

But transfer to whom? India remained a pluralist, fragmented society. No agreement could be reached about the structure of a successor government and especially its degree of centralization. At the end of 1946 the British prime minister, Clement Attlee, concluded that "two things were necessary: one was to make the Indians feel their responsibility by announcing that we were clearing out within a definite period, the other was to find the man to put this through." On March 22, 1947, the last British viceroy of India, Lord Louis Mountbatten, arrived in Delhi. His brief was clearly publicized. If the Indians had not agreed a new constitution by the end of June 1948, the British would arrange whatever handover "may seem most reasonable and in the best interests of the Indian people."[3]

At this stage the Attlee government was not engaged in a policy of "scuttle," whatever critics such as Churchill might say. Their timetable was intended to concentrate Indian minds. And Mountbatten, although vain, quickly convinced Congress of his good faith, particularly Jawaharlal Nehru, the party's principal leader. The complication was Muhammad Ali Jinnah, leader of the Muslim League, who claimed to speak for all of India's ninety-five million Muslims, nearly a quarter of the total. Most Muslims were in the north, particularly in the provinces of Bengal and Punjab, where they constituted more than half the population. But they were also spread throughout the country and had coexisted with Hindus for centuries, more or less easily. Sharper communal self-consciousness as Hindus and Muslims was, in part, fostered by the British, whose devolution measures had allocated Muslims and other groups separate electorates in provincial assemblies. But a bigger stimulus to a Muslim political identity came in the late 1930s, when Jinnah took over the feeble Muslim League and reoriented it around the voguish slogan of *Pakistan*—"land of the pure." This was intended to win support in Bengal and the Punjab, where Muslim leaders were currently content with the benefits of their majority status and provincial autonomy.

Jinnah's ultimate aims remain a matter of controversy, but it seems likely that his espousal of Muslim politics was a matter of tactical calculation more than theocractic principle. One plausible interpretation is that he wanted to make the Muslim League the sole spokesman for Indian Muslims—a position he had largely achieved after the provincial elections of winter 1945–1946—and that he intended the threat of an independent Pakistan as leverage to secure an equal federation of Muslim provinces and Hindu provinces (Hindustan) within a loose Indian confederation.[4] Pakistan was his equivalent of Britain's timetable—to concentrate the minds of the Congress party and the British. But Congress was intent on a unified state with centralized powers, fearing that otherwise India would totally disintegrate. And the British were equally set on an early exit; indeed, Mountbatten brought the date forward to August 1947 as part of his pressure tactics and because he was convinced that anarchy would ensue if a settlement were not reached quickly. It was therefore Jinnah's bluff that was called: if he really wanted Pakistan, said Mountbatten, then that would mean partition. Even when the agreement was confirmed on June 3, 1947, there were still hopes, particularly by Nehru, that partition would be temporary. All reckoned without the communal violence now unleashed.

Under Mountbatten's timetable, the bureaucrats had seventy-two days to invent two new countries. Government property had to be redistributed. Typewriters, refrigerators, cars, even office furniture were inventoried, valued, and distributed, with 17.5 percent going to Pakistan. Reallocating 925,000 railway employees meant that 73,000 were moved from Pakistan to India and 83,500 in the opposite direction. Contrary to Jinnah's expectations, partition also meant dividing the two great provinces of Bengal in the northeast and the Punjab in the northwest, where the Muslims were a bare majority. Even in normal times this would have been difficult. But the subcontinent was now contorted by spasms of communal violence, as the ideologies of Hindustan and Pakistan—pure Hindu and Muslim states—added new frenzy to ancient tensions. Unarmed women and children were among the victims. Even trainloads of refugees crossing the border were stopped and massacred in cold blood. Just how many died in 1947–1948 is unknown—anywhere between 250,000 and one million. The seventeen million refugees constituted one of the largest population movements in history.

The political leaders, Nehru and Jinnah, were almost impotent before the whirlwind they had helped to unleash. Nehru had even predicted in late 1946 that "when the British go, there will be no more communal trouble in India."[5] One of the few to offer a constructive response was the veteran nationalist Mohandas K. Gandhi. In the 1920s, Gandhi's nonviolent protest movement had helped mobilize opposition to the raj and undermined the moral prestige of British rule. By the 1940s, however, his political influence had waned. He preached the power of powerlessness—a philosophy attractive to those in impotent opposition but less appealing to Congress leaders when office was within their grasp. Gandhi believed that *swaraj,* self-rule for India, would be complete only when Indians ruled their inner selves. He remarked in April 1946: "The foreign power will be withdrawn before long, but for me real freedom will come only when we free ourselves of the dominance of Western education, Western culture and [the] Western way of living which have been ingrained in us."[6] His distinctive dress—spectacles, loincloth and sandals—was symbolic, representing a personal reaction against his past as a London-trained barrister. As the whirlwind of communal violence mounted, Gandhi, though nearing eighty, went straight into the eye of the storm. In Calcutta in September 1947 he announced a fast until death unless the killing ended. Such was still his charisma that he succeeded in less than a week. Gandhi was engaged in a similar fast in Delhi in January 1948 when he was shot dead by a Hindu fanatic. Although his political impact on the new India was limited, his philosophy of nonviolent protest was to attract disciples across the world.

Despite the bloodbath, two independent countries were born on schedule on August 14–15, 1947 (Map 3). Of the two, Pakistan was the more unfortunate. Jinnah, already dying of cancer, was left with what he had railed against in 1944—"a maimed, mutilated and moth-eaten Pakistan."[7] His new state had two wings, in the northeast and the northwest of the subcontinent, separated by one thousand miles of Indian territory. Moreover, those wings had been savagely clipped. The Punjab lost its fertile eastern districts to India, while Bengal surrendered its western hinterland, including the great city of Calcutta. What remained were largely agricultural areas—jute in the east, cotton in the west—and an industrial base had to be created almost from nothing. The migration of Hindus also removed much of the commercial class, especially in the Punjab—the moneylenders who provided farmers with credit, the wholesalers who bought their crops, and the clerks and accountants who staffed the local banks.[8] The new government concentrated on building up a heavy-industrial base and on import substitution. The consequent neglect of agriculture and social services stored up problems for the future. The leadership also created a secular state, but communal frenzy had strengthened the hand of the religious leaders, who wanted an Islamic theocracy. Here was another fundamental tension.

But the most immediate and potent threats to Pakistan's stability were regional and ethnic conflicts. The leaders of the new state were mostly Muslim League refugees from India as well as the Punjab elite. Their rule was bitterly resented in the other western provinces. It was even more oppressive in East Bengal, which accounted for 54 percent of Pakistan's population. The Pakistan government's decision in 1952 that Urdu would be Pakistan's national language provoked riots in Bengali-speaking East Bengal. The new government delayed formulating a constitution and holding democratic elections because East Pakistanis would constitute a majority of voters and it had virtually no political base there. In 1954, Punjabis railroaded the other western provinces into a single unit, West Pakistan, to balance the power of the cohesive East where the Bengali United Party had become the dominant political force. This enabled the government to proceed with a constitution in 1956, but at the cost of further regional resentment. By this time, the Muslim League was disintegrating as a viable political party, and power in Pakistan passed to the civil service and increasingly the army, which seized power under Ayub Khan in October 1958. Elections, scheduled for the following year, were canceled and martial law imposed—in part to forestall Bengali political dominance. The pattern was thus set. "First, parliamentary democracy would not be allowed to function in Pakistan. Second, a strong central executive would dominate the provinces."[9]

The contrast with India was profound. There a new constitution came into force in January 1950. Although it incorporated some American features, notably a list of "Fundamental Rights of the People" and a Supreme Court with powers of judicial review, the constitution owed most to British patterns, particularly the division of federal and state powers established back in 1935. India also adapted the Westminster parliamentary system, with a Council of States elected by state legislatures and a House of the People (*Lok Sabha*) chosen by adult suffrage. In March 1952, the country completed its first democratic national elections. It should be emphasized how bold a step this was at the time.[10] No less than 173 million people in 3,772 constituencies were eligible to vote. The electoral roll had to be drawn up by house-to-house visitation. Since three-quarters of the electorate was illiterate, the seventy-seven parties employed symbols: yoked bullocks for the Congress Party, the sickle and grain for the communists, and so on. At each of the 133,000 polling stations the voter selected the ballot paper of the chosen party, marked it and placed it in the party's box. Then the voter's finger was itself marked with indelible ink, to prevent double voting. Such cumbersome procedures require two and half million ballot boxes and one million government officials, and they took six months to complete. Voter turnout was 45.7 percent (but the figure in the U.S. presidential election of 1948 was only 52 percent). The result was a triumph for Congress, which won 45 percent of the vote—a share that remained stable in 1957 and 1962.[11] Thus began its career, until the 1990s, as India's dominant political party, usually in power in Delhi. Equally, 1952 marked the start of a five-yearly pattern of democratic elections that was only temporarily interrupted in the mid-1970s. In both respects, India differed markedly from Pakistan.

The appeal of Congress grew partly from its leading role in winning independence—which gave it legitimacy for a generation—combined with the status of Nehru himself. But Congress also developed the natural attractions of patronage and influence that accrue to all ruling parties. Increasingly it became a party of "ins," especially at state and local levels, where its leading supporters were members of the elite castes who dominated landowning. Opposition parties often tried to mobilize middle and lower castes, usually the poorer sections of the population, for instance the socialists in parts of north India in the 1950s and the communists in Kerala and West Bengal. Linguistic and regional groupings also proved bases for opposition parties, such as the Sikhs' Akali Dal in the Punjab and the Tamil DMK party in Madras Province. The depth of caste, communal, and regional differences were reminders of the basic facts of Indian life—its ethnic, religious and social heterogeneity, which impeded the growth of unified class consciousness at least in rural areas (where three-quarters of the population lived). At state and local levels, politics were largely about power and patronage based on competition among coalitions of propertied groups mainly derived from the leading castes. At elections, especially in the countryside, caste solidarity was often the most important factor in voting behavior.

The local diversity of India was also a barrier against Nehru's larger goals. Whereas his main Congress rival, Vallabhbhai Patel, envisaged a loose national federation that respected existing traditions, Nehru had a radical, modernizing vision. In part, this stemmed from his acquaintance with Britain, where his wealthy father had sent him to school and university (Cambridge) in preparation for a career in law. Nehru's redistributive, democratic socialism owed much to the contemporary British Labour party. But it also reflected his acquaintance with the theory and practice of communism. Since his first, eye-opening visit to Russia in 1927, Nehru had no doubt that the planned expansion of heavy industry was the key to India's future as a strong state. Equally important, he believed that the development of the country's vast internal market, behind protective barriers, would give it true economic independence.

During the second and third plans (1956–1961 and 1961–1966), India established its heavy-industrial base. GDP grew at an annual rate of 3.8 percent. But this was slower than predicted and, because of concentration on import substitution, India's share of world exports was halved during the 1950s to only 1 percent.[12] Agricultural development, in particular, was unimpressive. This was partly because the planners concentrated on industry and assumed a trickle-down effect for agriculture. But Nehru's efforts, inspired by Mao's China, to promote agricultural cooperatives and village councils were frustrated by local landowners. Unlike China's, India's structures of village wealth and power remained largely intact, and agricultural policy remained the constitutional preserve of the states. Like the British before them, India's new rulers relied primarily on established local leaders to organize peasant participation in national economic and social policies.[13]

In the localities, therefore, life remained much the same. Charlotte Wiser, an American missionary, had lived in the village of Karimpur, east of Agra, from 1925 to 1930. When she came back in 1962, water supplies and medical care had improved and, in the words of one younger farmer, "we have more to eat and more to sell." But the essentials were unchanged. The village elders were often the sons and nephews of those in charge three decades before. The "houses" were still partially covered courtyards behind mud walls. Life continued to revolve around the extended family, in which the older, fit males were dominant, and the women spent much of their time in the preparation of meals. Larger loyalties were to caste and village, rather than to nebulous concepts such as nation. Wiser discerned no fundamental change in attitudes to the lowest castes, who did the most menial tasks while remaining segregated and often literally untouchable—such as the *dhobis* who did the washing and the *bhangis* who cleaned the houses and removed excrement from the privies of the rich.[14]

Untouchability had been officially abolished in the 1950 Constitution, and a program of positive discrimination was established for its victims. This included allocating some 15 percent of seats in national and state assemblies for candidates from what were now called the "scheduled castes." But such reforms again collided with the slow-changing realities of village life. "For touchable, and particularly landholding, villagers," the one-sixth of the population that was untouchable "provided the economic services of an exploitable labor pool, and the social and psychological services of *untermenschen:* people to be better than, to look down on, despise, humiliate, ridicule . . ."[15]

Despite Nehru's hopes, therefore, India was not transformed, and the underlying problems of poverty, localism, and unbalanced industrialization were to become critical in the 1960s. But in the first decade of independence the advances seemed impressive, the failures but temporary setbacks. At last India was developing its potential as a major state and, as befitted Nehru's avowed policy of nonalignment in the cold war, its modernization seemed to offer what he called "a third way which takes the best from all existing systems—the Russian, the American and others—and seeks to create something suited to one's own history and philosophy."[16] What also stands out from the 1950s, especially in retrospect, was the government's success in holding together such a vast and varied country—361 million people in 1951, 439 million a decade later—which lacked the ethnic unity of China or the Russian backbone of the Soviet Union. Moreover, it did so without military rule or a single-party state.

The achievements were considerable. In 1947–1950, some 560 principalities—a few as big as European countries, many little more than a large estate—were pressured to join either Pakistan or India. Only in a few cases, notably Hyderabad, the biggest and richest, was military force employed. The problems of linguistic pluralism were also addressed. Even Hindi was spoken by only one-third of the population; in the south, particularly, its pretensions as the official Indian language were abhorrent. Despite being the language of the raj, English became attractive not only as an international tongue but also as a defence against Hindi imperialism. A bilingual compromise therefore emerged allowing English to coexist with Hindi as the national language—temporarily in 1950, indefinitely after 1967—and English remained the lingua franca of the elite.

At the subnational level, Nehru's government accepted reorganization of most of the states on linguistic lines, for instance splitting the old southeastern province of Madras into Tamil- and Telugu-speaking states. Only where there seemed a real threat of separatism were such demands resisted, notably in the Punjab where Sikh pressures were a reminder of the religious problems underlying the new state. Although 85 percent of the population was Hindu, Muslims still constituted one-tenth. But the horrors of 1947 sobered a generation, and in the 1950s Muslims generally supported Congress, not least because of its tolerance of Islamic laws and institutions. In the decade or so after independence, India seemed to be coping with its regional, linguistic and religious diversity.

Yet India, like Pakistan, could not transcend the legacy of partition. Since 1947, antipathy between these two successor states has remained fundamental to the international politics of South Asia. At its heart has been the conflict over Jammu and Kashmir, geographically trapped between the two new states and in 1947 a Muslim principality ruled by a Hindu maharaja. When he acceded to the Indian Union, troops from the two countries—only recently part of the same army—fought a year-long struggle for control. A UN-brokered ceasefire in January 1949 left India with two-thirds of the territory, but the related agreement for a plebiscite has never been implemented by India for fear that the Muslim majority would vote to join Pakistan. Not only would this give a hostile government control of the headwaters of the Indus River, it would also damage the credibility of India as a "secular" pluralist state and encourage communal agitation within. Kashmir has been at the heart of Indo-Pakistan antagonism since 1947.

In the 1950s this in turn became part of the growing cold war bipolarity. Immediately after partition, the Americans were happy to treat South Asia as a continuing British sphere of influence, and Britain kept a balance between Pakistan and India, encouraging both to remain within the Commonwealth. In the early 1950s, however, British influence was on the wane. The Americans were increasingly concerned about the instability of the Middle East, which Pakistan, as a well-armed, Muslim but pro-Western state, might help offset. In May 1954 the Eisenhower administration extended military aid to Pakistan. Although the Pakistan government had played on U.S. fears of communist subversion and Soviet power, it wanted arms and support mainly to protect itself against India.[17] Nehru, for his part, considered the American decision "an unfriendly act" toward his own country.[18] This helped push him toward the Soviet camp at a time when Khrushchev was keen to cultivate noncommunist but left-leaning countries. In the decade 1955–1965, aid from Moscow played a significant part in building up Indian heavy industry. Yet during this period Nehru also secured substantial food aid from the United States, particularly grain. India was by no means alone in using the cold war for its own advantage, but Nehru's exploitation of both sides was a diplomatic balancing act that few other developing states managed with such success. It seemed further vindication for India's third way of nonalignment.

Palestine: One Land, Two Peoples

In the 1950s, the Middle East displayed a similar mix of imperial legacies and regional conflicts, which also became entangled in cold war politics. Again the starting point was a postcolonial war of partition with ethnicity and religion at its heart—this time to create the Jewish state of Israel. Here, too, Britain was the colonial power in retreat.

During World War I, the British had encouraged the breakup of the Ottoman empire by expansive territorial promises to Arab leaders. At the Paris peace conference in 1919 Britain secured Palestine from the League of Nations, though not as a colony but in preparation for eventual independence. A major condition was that Britain should honor its wartime promise to promote "the establishment in Palestine of a national home for the Jewish people" without prejudice to "the civil and religious rights of existing non-Jewish communities"—the so-called Balfour Declaration of 1917.[19] The two parts of that pledge proved incompatible as migration from Hitler's Europe in the 1930s pushed the Jewish proportion of the population to 29 percent by 1939. The consequent Arab backlash led to full-scale revolt in 1936–1939. In May 1939 the British government changed its tack, anxious for support from the Arab oil states in a future war, and restricted further Jewish immigration. They maintained this policy throughout the war.

For Zionists, a Jewish homeland in Palestine would roll back two millennia of dispersion and persecution. One Zionist slogan spoke of "a land without a people for a people without a land." Yet those words betrayed a pervasive Jewish indifference to the rights of the indigenous Palestinian Arabs. In reality, this was a collision of two peoples over one land—and a holy land at that because the city of Jerusalem was venerated by Jews, Muslims, and Christians alike. In this struggle of right against right, what shifted the moral weight of the argument decisively in favor of the Zionists was the Holocaust. That term was not popularized until the 1960s, when the systematic genocide of Nazi policy became clear to the wider world through trials and books. Even so, in 1945 the horrors of the Nazi camps in Germany and Poland had considerable impact. The continued presence of thousands of survivors in UN refugee camps in Central and Eastern Europe was a source of concern and embarrassment to Britain and America, especially given those governments' inaction about the genocide in the later stages of the war.

Migration to Palestine was not the only possible answer to the refugee problem—many Polish Jews, for instance, wanted to recover their homelands—and in the camps Zionist and anti-Zionist groups vied for influence. But the Zionists persuaded many British and American observers that they spoke for the vast majority. The most important convert was Harry Truman—not a convinced Zionist or very knowledgable about the intricacies of the Middle East. "From his first days in office, he had regarded the problem of Palestine as a practical matter of finding homes for miserable people ravaged by war."[20] In addition to humanitarian concern, Truman was acutely sensitive to Jewish opinion in key states at home, fearful that they might swing to the Republicans in the elections of 1946 and 1948. Although refusing to assume any direct U.S. responsibility for Palestine, his confused and erratic Zionism was a major constraint on the British in 1945–1946. The Foreign Office, under Ernest Bevin, was convinced that partition would be unworkable and continued to explore the chances of a binational solution—Jews and Arabs in one state.

Meanwhile, the Yishuv, the Jewish settlement in Palestine, saw renewed migration as a way to save the Jewish refugees *and* to force the British to concede immediate Jewish statehood. But the British still tried to stop "illegal" immigrants from Europe, shipping some fifty thousand to camps in Cyprus in 1945–1947, often with considerable brutality. In October 1945, David Ben-Gurion, the leader of the Jewish Agency in Palestine, authorized a Hebrew revolt against the British. The Haganah, the agency's military arm, sabotaged British installations, cooperating uneasily with overt terrorist groups such as the Irgun under Menachem Begin, a Polish Jew who had survived Stalinist camps, and Yitzhak Shamir, the leader of the more extreme Lehi, or Stern Gang. Both of these men were future prime ministers of Israel. By 1947, one-tenth of the armed forces of the British empire, one hundred thousand men, occupied a territory the size of Wales—one soldier for every eighteen inhabitants.[21] In July the Irgun hanged two British soldiers, as retaliation for the execution of some their men, and booby-trapped the bodies. "In cold terms of political impact," the historian Michael Cohen has observed, "it was the single most effective act of Jewish resistance."[22] In September, under intense domestic pressure, the British government announced that it would withdraw from Palestine the following summer. This was not entirely throwing in the towel. Attlee was trying the tactics applied in India, hoping that the British announcement would have "salutary results" in forcing Jews and Arabs to work out their own salvation.[23] As in India, however, this was done by blood and not by words.

At the end of November 1947, two-thirds of the UN formally approved partition, swung by intensive Jewish lobbying and last-minute support from Truman. The plan would have carved Palestine into two separate states coiled around each other, each comprising three interlinked segments. Civil war now broke out as Arabs and Jews tried to maximize their territorial positions in advance of the British departure. At this point the fundamental difference between the two societies became apparent. The six hundred fifty thousand Jews, mostly Europeans, were highly organized and dedicated to Zionism. The departments of the Jewish Agency were smoothly converted into government ministries; the Haganah became the basis of the Israeli Defense Forces, with their own command structure. In contrast, the Palestinian Arabs, though 1.25 million, were "backward, disunited and often apathetic, a community only just entering the modern age politically and administratively."[24] Two-thirds were peasants living in self-contained villages. Power belonged to the large landowning families, based in the cities, and politics revolved around the dominant el-Husayni clan and its rivals, which paralleled a regional split between Jerusalem and the coastal plain. The armed forces were a patchwork of local militias and fighting societies, capable of disrupting Jewish communications but not of large-scale operations. Haganah offensives in April 1948 left the Jews in a strong position when formal British withdrawal took place on May 15, 1948—the only time in the history of the British Empire when there was no one to whom Britain transferred power.

Immediately Ben-Gurion declared independence, and the state of Israel was born. Within days, five Arab neighbors had invaded—Egypt, Lebanon, Syria, Iraq, and Transjordan. At this desperate moment, Israel was helped by an unholy alliance between America and Russia. Anxious to steal a march on the Soviets and to secure the Jewish vote at home, Truman ignored State Department advice and extended *de facto* recognition eleven minutes after the mandate expired. The Russians, for their part, saw recognition and support of Israel as a good way to damage Britain and its Arab allies, still influential in the Middle East. Soviet arms and training helped the Yishuv circumvent the Anglo-American arms embargo and played "a key role in saving Israel from military defeat in the initial stages of the war."[25] This convergence of U.S. and Soviet policy was brief, but it ensured that Palestine did not become a superpower flash point like Germany or Korea.

In what therefore became an essentially regional struggle between Israel and its neighbors, the Jews were also helped by the disunity and halfheartedness of the Arab states. Forced to intervene because of domestic opinion, their rulers were ill prepared for a serious war. Most were concerned for internal stability and not for the fate of Palestine. Only King Abdullah of Transjordan was deeply involved, and his interests would have been satisfied by a direct partition of the mandate with Israel at the expense of the Palestinians—which was, in fact, what ensued. After intermittent but bloody fighting in 1948, armistice agreements during 1949 left Israel with four-fifths of the old mandate and Abdullah's kingdom, renamed Jordan, holding most of the rest, in the form of a large bulge across the west bank of the Jordan River.

Even so, the security of Israel was only assured by the flight or expulsion of most Palestinians—who, under the original partition plan, would have constituted 40 percent of Israel's population. This story, the darker side of the Zionist achievement, has only recently been examined by Israeli historians.[26] As soon as the civil war began, Palestinian society began to disintegrate as the upper and middle classes fled the big cities of Haifa, Jaffa, and West Jerusalem, forcing schools, businesses, clinics, and administrative offices to close. In April 1948 the flow turned into a flood as the Jews implemented Plan D, intended to consolidate territory by rooting out Palestinian irregulars from local villages.[27] Periodic atrocities, notably the revenge killings at Deir Yassin in April and Lydda in July, hastened the exodus. Deliberate expulsion also became the policy of some local commanders, notably General Yigal Allon in the south, with tacit approval from Ben-Gurion. After 1948, Israeli opinion hardened against any return. Some three hundred fifty Arab villages were destroyed, abandoned lands were leased to Jewish farmers, and new immigrants were installed in Arab houses in the cities. Only about one hundred fifty thousand Palestinians remained in Israel, nominally equal to Jews in religious and political rights but in practice regarded as a subversive minority. Between six hundred thousand and seven hundred sixty thousand Palestinians became refugees.[28] The neighboring Arab states could not cope; indeed, they had no reason to try because that would relieve the pressure on Israel to take back the Palestinians. The result was squalid refugee camps in the West Bank territory of Transjordan and along the coastal Gaza Strip. The latter, only twenty-eight miles by five, contained two hundred thousand refugees. Here was the seedbed of the future Palestine Liberation Organization.

As Palestinians fled, Jews flooded in—encouraged by the 1950 Law of Return, which promised citizenship for all members of the diaspora. Between May 1948 and December 1951 638,000 Jews arrived, almost equal to the previous Jewish population.[29] They were desperately needed to farm the new lands and swell the armed forces. But many had to be housed in tented camps. So bad were conditions that forty thousand of the newcomers had left Israel by 1952. Moreover, the Jewish nation was encircled by hostile states, blockaded by them at sea, and infiltrated by Palestinian guerrillas. Only 8,000 square miles in area, it had no defence in depth: at its waist there were only nine miles between Jordan and the Mediterranean sea. "The entire country, in short, was a frontier," geographically and psychologically, from which the fear of attack, indeed annihilation, was never absent.[30] What decided Israel's fate in the 1950s was the interplay of European decolonization, Arab nationalism, and superpower confrontation.

The Middle East after Britain and France

In the Middle East, as in Asia, the defeats of the Second World War undermined European imperialism but did not demolish it completely. The first postwar decade saw a tenacious rearguard action by Britain and France, the paramount powers in the region since 1918. The French were more seriously damaged, having lost control of Syria and Lebanon before the end of the war. But they retained their possessions in the Maghreb—Morocco, Tunisia, and Algeria. The British Labour government, guided by Ernest Bevin, hoped to transform its unequal relationship with the Arabs into an effective partnership, whereby Britain retained its economic interests and military bases while assisting the economic and political development of the client countries. Particularly important allies were the Hashemite rulers of Iraq and Jordan. What undermined the policy were the scarcity of British resources and Britain's reliance on what was known as the "old gang" in these Arab countries. Like Arab Palestine, most of these countries were creations of the post-1918 settlement—often tribal states whose borders lacked ethnic or territorial rationales. Their leaders were doubly damned by radical political groups as domestic autocrats and imperial collaborators. The trauma of defeat by Israel was often the catalyst for revolt.

Even before that war was over, in March 1949, a military coup in Syria overthrew the corrupt civilian government, which was blamed for the country's role in the Palestine debacle. The regime of Colonel Husni Zaim lasted only four months, but it began a pattern of coup and countercoup that characterized Syrian politics for the next decade. In Jordan, one-third of the population was now Palestinian refugees, many of whom despised the indigenous Jordanians and blamed King Abdullah for their fate. Although Jordan was the only Arab state to offer the Palestinians full citizenship, Abdullah's efforts to integrate them had limited success and the country teetered on the edge of collapse when he was assassinated by a Muslim extremist in July 1951. With his son mentally unstable, the succession soon devolved on Abdullah's teenage grandson, Hussein, whose future seemed uncertain in the face of internal feuds and the expansionist ambitions of Syria and Iraq.

Even more significant was the turmoil in Egypt. Unlike most of the Arab states, this was a populous country—nineteen million people in 1947. In further contrast, it was not a creation of the Paris peace conference and had a much greater sense of national identity, fostered by centuries of Islamic religion and Arabic language and focused by the valley of the Nile. Egypt, it should be remembered, is as large as France and Spain combined, yet its cultivable area is only 4 percent of the total, equivalent in size to the Netherlands.[31] The concentration of population and the importance of the annual Nile flood for national life fostered a degree of political centralization that again was unusual in the Middle East. Cairo became a metropolis on a scale unique for the region. By the same token, however, it was a hothouse for urban political radicalism that was deeply destabilizing. This was the arena for the autocratic populism of Gamal Abdel Nasser, Egypt's leader from 1952 until his death in 1970, who was the most charismatic figure in the Arab world in the 1950s.

Egypt had become a British protectorate in 1882, largely to secure Britain's interests in the Suez Canal. In 1922 the British conceded formal independence, but retained control (with the French) over the canal and also rights over the vast complex of military bases known as the Canal Zone, roughly the size of Wales. The reality of British domination was dramatized in February 1942, during the darkest days of the war, when the British ambassador, flanked by tanks, drove up to the royal palace and obliged King Farouk to appoint an anti-Axis administration. This humiliation became part of the folklore of the many Islamic and radical groups spawned during the depression and the war, for whom real independence was the panacea. Among them were a younger group of officers, lower middle-class beneficiaries of the abolition of fees for entry into the military academy, who had been born around 1918. Their "Free Officers" conspiracy included Nasser, his eventual successor Anwar Sadat (who ruled from 1970 to 1981), and Abdel Hakim Amir, head of the armed forces from 1953 to 1967.[32] Their opportunity came in 1952. On January 25, British troops fired on a recalcitrant police barracks at Ismailiya, killing fifty Egyptians. The next day, riots in Cairo caused £50 million in damage. Farouk sacked the government. Four others followed over the next six months as Egypt disintegrated. When the Free Officers learned that they were scheduled for arrest, they accelerated their own plans and mounted a bloodless coup on the night of July 22–23, using a senior general, Mohammed Neguib, as figurehead. The corpulent Farouk was swiftly despatched into exile aboard his yacht.

Effecting a British withdrawal was less easy, and took two years of hard negotiation with the Conservative government, which replaced Labour in 1951. Nasser was aided by the British foreign secretary, Anthony Eden, who argued that it was no longer possible to maintain a British presence by force against local opposition. Churchill, again prime minister, was reluctantly persuaded by the costs of the Canal Zone and by the argument that Britain's strategic needs in the Middle East had been transformed by thermonuclear weapons, which made large bases vulnerable and irrelevant.[33] The agreement signed in October 1954 gave Britain twenty months to withdraw but allowed a right of reentry until 1961 in the event of an attack on the Arab states or Turkey by a country other than Israel. By this time, Nasser had consolidated his own position. Neguib, the titular prime minister, was finally displaced in April 1954 and Nasser took over; elections for a constituent assembly were postponed indefinitely. A failed assassination attempt that autumn enhanced Nasser's domestic popularity and justified a crackdown on the main Islamic group, the Muslim Brethren. Its leaders were arrested, the organization broken, and Islamic militancy driven underground for a generation.

Although Nasser's instincts were socialist, he still looked to the West, hopeful that the 1954 agreement would facilitate assistance from Britain and the United States. Nor was he initially much concerned about Israel. But his attitudes changed in February 1955. On the 24th Turkey and Iraq, concerned about the Soviet Union, signed a defense pact in Baghdad, urged on by Britain, which also joined in April. The British saw the Baghdad Pact as a potential force for order in the Middle East, but to Nasser the strengthening of Hashemite Iraq, Egypt's main regional rival, was a hostile act. Four days later, Israeli defense forces raided an Egyptian army camp in the Gaza Strip, killing thirty-eight Egyptians. Although part of a long cycle of infiltration and retaliation by Palestinian guerrillas, Egyptian intelligence, and Israeli security forces, the Gaza raid—sponsored personally by David Ben-Gurion—was much larger in scale. Nasser, who visited Gaza for the first time since the 1948 war, was shaken and angry. The infiltrators were now dubbed *fedayeen* ("men of sacrifice"), and the Egyptian army unleashed a continuous campaign of sabotage and murder along the Gaza Strip.[34] Israel responded in kind.

One casualty of the spiraling violence was an Anglo-American effort in 1955–1956, code-named Project Alpha, to engineer a peace settlement between Israel and its neighbors. Another was the Anglo-American-French policy of trying to control arms sales to the region. In April 1955 Nasser attended the conference of nonaligned independent states at Bandung in Indonesia. Not only was this the first time the thirty-seven-year-old leader had traveled beyond Palestine and the Sudan, it also gave him new stature as an international figure and new contacts with the non-Western world. Through the Chinese, Nasser secured a commitment of arms from the Soviet bloc. The deal, announced in September, came as a bombshell in London and Washington. Their response was to stall and finally suspend their financing for the Aswan High Dam, the centerpiece of Nasser's program of state-sponsored modernization. The British had hoped to let the offer "wither on the vine" but pressure from Congress and determination to teach Nasser a lesson led John Foster Dulles, the U.S. secretary of state, to end it publicly and bluntly on July 19, 1956.[35]

This sequence of events indicated that the superpowers were now moving to center stage in the Middle East. In the Soviet case, support for Israel in 1948 had been an act of expediency; Moscow's aid waned once the Jewish state had been established and the British had left.[36] Promoting Arab nationalism was a more useful way of damaging the West and, after Stalin's death, the new leadership was ideologically prepared to help noncommunist but left-leaning regimes such as those in India and Egypt. The Egyptian arms deal was a dramatic coup for the Soviet Union, trumpeting its emergence as a serious Middle East actor. America's involvement in the region had been developing during the 1950s but again a change of administration in 1953, from Truman to Eisenhower, accelerated the process, not least because of a new readiness to use the CIA in covert operations. In August 1953, American and British intelligence sponsored a coup that toppled Mohammed Mossadeq, the Iranian premier, and secured the shah on his throne. In May 1951 Mossadeq had nationalized the Anglo-Iranian oil company (the world's third-largest oil producer). The British had not been able to get rid of him without American help and funding—one sign of growing reliance on their superpower ally.

The Iranian crisis also highlighted the growing importance of Middle Eastern oil to the Western alliance. In 1950, coal and other solid fuels accounted for 83 percent of Western Europe's energy consumption and oil only 14 percent. A decade later, the proportions were 61 percent and 33 percent.[37] As a consequence of growing demand, the sources of oil supply also changed dramatically. In 1945, two-thirds of world oil came from North America but, as U.S. demand soared after the war, it became necessary and profitable to develop new sources of supply in the Middle East, particularly Saudi Arabia and Kuwait. U.S. companies increasingly became the dominant force in the region, another facet of the gradual waning of British power. And whereas domestic supplies were still sufficient for American needs, Western Europe had become dependent on the Middle East for 80 percent of its oil by 1951. Only five years before, 77 percent had come from the Western Hemisphere.[38] Secure access to Middle Eastern oil therefore became a prime foreign-policy goal for Western Europeans and, by extension, for the United States. As Eisenhower noted in March 1956: "The economy of Europe would collapse if those oil supplies were cut off" and then "the United States would be in a situation of which the difficulty could scarcely be exaggerated."[39] Two-thirds of Western Europe's oil imports came by tanker through the Suez Canal. On July 26, 1956, Nasser announced that the canal was to be nationalized.

In part, this was retaliation for Dulles' rebuff over the Aswan Dam a week before. Revenues from the canal would help pay for the Dam. But the act also reflected Nasser's growing sense that political independence had to be buttressed by economic independence, and meticulous contingency plans had been in place for months. Success depended, in Nasser's view, on maintaining international legitimacy by compensating shareholders and preserving freedom of navigation by reliable Egyptian operation of the Canal. Both of these goals were achieved. On September 15, the canal reopened under Egyptian management. Frustrated, the British reluctantly took the matter to the UN. By mid-October negotiations were in train for an agreement between Egypt and an association of user nations about the future Egyptian operation of the canal. It seemed that, despite early fears of Anglo-French military action, the crisis would be resolved peacefully.

At this very moment, however, the military option was secretly revived. For both Britain and France, nationalization of the canal, humiliating in itself, was entangled with larger issues. The French believed Nasser was behind the rebellion against them in Algeria, which, as we shall see, dominated their attention for much of the 1950s. The British regarded him as the main threat to the Baghdad Pact, centerpiece of their security policy in the region. Both governments were under strong domestic pressure to be tough, with the lessons of 1930s appeasement regularly cited. During late summer they prepared military expeditions to recover the canal and topple Nasser. The problem was that successful Egyptian operation of the canal denied them a pretext. This was where the Israelis came in.

In December 1955 the Israeli cabinet had rejected military proposals for a preemptive war against Egypt. Prime Minister Ben-Gurion insisted that the result would be international isolation, unless Israel enjoyed great-power support. In the summer of 1956, that support was forthcoming because of the shift in French policy. Guy Mollet, the head of the socialist-led coalition government since January 1956, was a keen supporter of Israel who had been covertly sending it arms even before the canal company was nationalized. In the second half of October he drew Anthony Eden, Churchill's successor as prime minister, into a three-sided conspiracy. The Israelis would drive into Sinai to satisfy their aims of destroying the Palestinian guerrillas and the Egyptian military machine. Their thrust would threaten the canal and allow Britain and France to intervene, ostensibly to separate the belligerents and save their property.

Not only was the cover plan specious in the extreme. It rested, to say the least, on some unlikely alliances. Eden, a consistent Arabist all his life, was now conniving with the Arabs' greatest enemy. France, desperate for Britain's support, was willing to suspend cherished national tradition and place its troops under British command. And, gravest of all, in turning to France, the

British were going against their cardinal postwar precept of keeping in step with the United States. This proved the fatal mistake. Eisenhower had little doubt that Nasser was a threat to Western interests and wanted to see him overthrown. But he and Dulles were equally clear that the canal "was not the issue upon which to try to downgrade Nasser" because it smacked too much of old-style European imperialism.[40] Repeatedly he made this clear to Eden. The British ignored his warnings and went ahead with the conspiracy, keeping Washington totally in the dark.

On October 29—the day Britain, France, and Egypt were scheduled to open discussions about the canal in Geneva—the Israeli Defense Forces invaded Sinai. Despite numerical inferiority, they enjoyed total surprise. Their armored columns, parachute drops behind enemy lines, and tactical air superiority brought rapid gains. On the 30th the British and French delivered their ultimatum to the belligerents, and on the following day their planes started bombing Egyptian bases.

Nasser was totally wrong footed. On July 26, he had reckoned that the chances of war would diminish every week: "If we succeed in gaining two months by politics, we shall be safe."[41] Now, it was clear, Anglo-French invasion was imminent. He ordered his forces to extricate themselves from Sinai, which they did—though retreat turned into rout and the Israelis captured six thousand prisoners and a mass of equipment. As the bombs continued to fall, some of his circle lost their nerve: Amir, the chief of staff, urged a ceasefire. Nasser vowed to put himself at the head of his troops but his mood was fatalistic as the Anglo-French forces started to land around Port Said, first paratroops on November 5 and then amphibious units the following day. The plan was not merely to regain the canal but also to topple the Egyptian government.

Ironically, Nasser was saved by the Americans. Eisenhower was incensed at the Anglo-French deception. He was also embarrassed by its timing—just before the presidential election on November 6 and at the height of the Soviet suppression of Hungary's revolt. "I've just never seen great powers make such a complete *mess* and *botch* of things," he fumed. The United States therefore took the lead in sponsoring a ceasefire resolution at the UN. Eisenhower instructed Dulles that "at all costs the Soviets must be prevented from seizing the mantle of world leadership through a false but convincing exhibition of concern for smaller nations."[42] Britain and France were virtually isolated at the UN—an unprecedented shock for two of the organization's founders. In Britain, public opinion was deeply and bitterly divided. The Soviets threatened retaliation against all the belligerents unless the fighting stopped. Most serious of all, the Americans refused to help staunch the wartime run on sterling until a ceasefire was agreed. Britain's chancellor of the exchequer, Harold Macmillan, changed from ferocious hawk into flapping dove in what has been described as "a sensational loss of nerve."[43] On November 7 cabinet unity crumbled; Eden—ill, overwrought, and isolated—accepted an immediate ceasefire. A bitter Mollet was forced to do the same. Ben-Gurion, himself sick and strained, also agreed to pull back from Sinai: the Soviet buildup in Syria was alarming and, as he wrote in his diary, the "rampage" of their tanks in Hungary showed "what these Communist Nazis are capable of doing."[44] All three powers still hoped to use their territorial gains as diplomatic leverage, but Eisenhower kept up the pressure until they had made complete and unconditional withdrawals.

Despite its pullout from Sinai, Israel was the biggest gainer of the three from the war. The fedayeen bases along the border had been destroyed, ending the threat of raids, and the United States agreed to uphold freedom of navigation in the Gulf of Aqaba, thus breaking the Arab maritime blockade. UN forces were stationed in Gaza and Sharm el-Sheikh to guarantee these two developments. Above all, the Egyptian defeat and "the display of Israel's military prowess altered the balance between the parties—in the direction of Israeli security and Egyptian acquiescence," for a decade.[45]

For Britain and France, however, the Suez crisis was an unmitigated disaster. By January 1957 Eden was out of office, succeeded, ironically, by Macmillan, who did his best to restore relations with Washington. In France, where opinion had been less divided by Suez and the burning issue was Algeria, Mollet soldiered on until May. But both countries found their prestige severely damaged. Egypt, effectively a British protectorate only five years before, had humiliated two of the great powers of Europe. Egyptian propaganda glossed over the defeat in Sinai and the effect of superpower pressure on the belligerents. Instead, Nasser was represented as triumphant champion of Egypt and the Arabs against the European imperialists. To buttress his populist authoritarianism, he created a mass official party, the National Union, to mobilize consent and exert control. Preparations were accelerated for the country's first five-year plan, unveiled in 1960, and, after complex negotiations, the Soviet Union agreed in November 1958 to provide most of the finance for the Aswan High Dam. Abroad, Nasser was now emboldened in his bid to lead the Arab world. His rhetoric of Pan-Arabism enjoyed particular support among urban Sunni Muslims in Iraq, Syria, Jordan, and Lebanon, where it played into communal struggles. His principal target was the Hashemite regime in Iraq, Britain's last substantial ally in the Middle East.

The United States moved hurriedly to fill the vacuum created by the Anglo-French collapse and the Soviet Union's increasing influence in Egypt and Syria. In January 1957 Eisenhower asked Congress for economic aid and military assistance to protect states in the Middle East that requested such help against "overt armed aggression from any nation controlled by International Communism."[46] The Eisenhower Doctrine was, however, of limited efficacy in the internal politics of the unstable Arab states, on which the struggle now turned. In February, 1958 the Syrian socialist Ba'ath party, fearful of growing communist strength, pressed Nasser for an immediate union of the two countries, in the hope that he would rule through them. Nasser agreed to form the United Arab Republic (UAR) but took complete power, extending his one-party National Union to Syria. In response, Feisal II and Hussein, the two Hashemite cousins who ruled Iraq and Jordan, formed their own "Arab Union." It was shortlived. Iraq in the late 1950s exhibited many of the same problems as Egypt at the beginning of the decade—a corrupt monarchy that collaborated with the British through the veteran prime minister Nuri Said, who ruled an agrarian country in which landlord oppression was offset by growing urban discontent. As in Egypt earlier, there was a widespread belief in Iraq "that if they could only liberate their country everything else would somehow fall naturally into place"[47] but, given the repressive regime, the key to any change was Iraq's army command. Here Nasser's Pan-Arabism won support among junior commanders. They formed their own "Free Officers" movement, which eventually seized power on July 14, 1958, in a bloody coup. Among the officers, Brigadier Abdul Karim Qassim emerged as "sole leader."

Qassim proved to be a reforming nationalist rather than a revolutionary, and in 1959–1960 he destroyed communist strength in Iraq. But the dramatic collapse of the old pro-British regime in July 1958 was an enormous shock to London and Washington. The British blamed Nasser, the Americans blamed the Kremlin. Within days U.S. Marines entered Lebanon to shore up the Christian government against growing Muslim unrest, and British paratroops were dropped in Jordan after another plot was unearthed against Hussein. In both cases, the crises were somewhat artificial, and there was little resistance to the brief Western interventions. The marines stormed ashore in Beirut unopposed: the main obstacle was local sunbathers. In reality, the Americans intervened in Lebanon "largely in order to make a credibility-building point to the Soviets about the resolve to defend their friends in the Middle East and, indeed, worldwide."[48] The British, more concerned about Nasser himself, hoped to rebuild their regional authority and reassert the transatlantic special relationship. For both powers, Lebanon and Jordan were pawns in a larger game.

The interventions served their purpose as international gestures—attempts, as Dulles put it, to "put up sandbags" around key positions against the "flood" of Arab nationalism.[49] The British effort to create reformist partnerships with local elites had failed. The Americans tried to distance themselves from colonialism—dramatically so during the Suez crisis. But their own attempts at influence had encouraged Arab states to play both sides in the cold war. Furthermore, Arab bids for full economic independence had prompted nationalization measures inimical to Western interests, especially in regard to oil. America's growing support of the conservative monarchy of Saudi Arabia as the main Western bastion against Nasserism after 1958 indicated that, whatever the rhetoric about democracy, it was adopting the same policy as Britain. Its Middle Eastern allies were mostly fragile agrarian states that rested on clan politics and the military. The flabby parliamentarianism of the interwar period usually expired soon after independence. Only Israel was a credible democracy.

Africa and the Persistence of Imperialism

Unlike the Middle East, Africa in 1945 was largely the preserve of formal rather than informal empire.[50] Even the ancient Christian kingdom of Ethiopia had been conquered by Italy in 1935. In 1940 only two countries were not under European rule: the small west coast state of Liberia, created in 1847, where an elite descended from black American settlers ruled a "tribal" hinterland; and South Africa, since 1910 a dominion within the British Commonwealth, where white-settler control rested on the economic exploitation of the nonwhite communities. Moreover, the colonial powers were well entrenched. The autocratic Portuguese government of Antonio Salazar regarded its colonies of Angola, Mozambique, and Guinea as provinces of Portugal—vital to sustain the country's declining wealth and fading status. Belgian rule in central Africa was almost equally intransigent. Algeria was a department of metropolitan France, and the declared French goal in their federations of West Africa and Equatorial Africa was also eventual "assimilation." Whereas they, in effect, were promising that "when you grow up you will be French," the official British line throughout its empire was that "when you grow up you will be free." But although the British practiced devolution and informal empire wherever possible, the general view in London during the war was that only a few African colonies, such as the Gold Coast and Nigeria, were sufficiently "advanced" to imagine independence within thirty years. Herbert Morrison, Labour's foreign secretary in 1951, asserted that to grant most African colonies independence would be "like giving a child of ten a latch-key, a bank account and a shotgun."[51]

Unlike the case in European colonies in South and Southeast Asia, African reaction against imperial rule was in the 1940s less precocious, organized, or effective. The erosive forces of capitalism—cash crops, trading networks, and industrial growth—were less advanced; outside Johannesburg and Cairo,

Africa lacked large conurbations that were the womb of mass politics elsewhere. In addition, the lack of educational provision retarded the emergence of political leaders and politically conscious followers. And the impact of the Second World War—so damaging to European rule in the areas of Japanese conquest—was less dramatic in Africa. Its effect was seen most directly in the case of the Italian empire, which collapsed in 1940–1941: Ethiopia regained its independence immediately; the provinces of Cyrenaica, Tripolitania, and Fezzan became independent in 1951 (after British efforts to secure European trusteeship were frustrated by Cold War politics in the UN); and the Italians were only allowed a ten-year trusteeship in their part of Somali territory, which then gained independence in 1960. The other direct casualty of the war was French rule in northwest Africa, where the Vichy governments collapsed during the Allied invasion of 1942. Although France eventually regained control, the damage to its credibility was reflected in the emergence of the Istiqlal (independence) party in Morocco and the radicalization of Algerian politics, culminating in bloody riots and even bloodier reprisals in May 1945. The French island of Madagascar, where the Vichy regime was blockaded and then invaded by the Allies in 1942, experienced a similar wartime radicalization, which culminated in the disastrous uprising of March 1947, when perhaps eighty thousand died.

Nevertheless, the 1940s were a decade of momentous change in Africa. Wartime crisis had obliged the British, French, and Belgians to exploit the resources of empire as never before, and Africa was rich in foodstuffs, minerals, and essential raw materials. The pressure to do so continued after 1945 because of economic need and the shortage of hard currency for foreign trade. As the London *Daily Express* observed in June 1947: "If dollars are scarce, Africa is ample."[52] Colonial development therefore seemed economic sense—hence the British Colonial Development and Welfare Act of 1945; the French FIDES program, initiated in 1946; and the Belgian Ten-Year Plan for investment in the colonies. Such sustained intervention brought many more Africans within the framework of international capitalism—as producers of export crops, food growers for the export zones, or suppliers of migrant labor to the other two—thereby accelerating the erosion of traditional societies and the growth of cities in which group consciousness (class or ethnic) became more pronounced. In Algeria, the proportion of the population living in cities of over one hundred thousand rose from 6.6 percent in 1948 to 16.4 percent in 1960; in the Gold Coast (named Ghana after independence) it almost tripled to 9.5 percent over the same period.[53] This did not compare with Egypt or South Africa, where the urban population was over one-quarter of the national total, but the pattern and pace of change were still significant. African cities (particularly the capitals) became the foci of growing political discontent, urban and rural, at the more intensive colonial rule.

Conscious of this, and of the growing international criticism of empire (especially from America), policy makers in Britain and France (though not in Belgium or Portugal) started devolving political power to Africans, particularly in the west. Previously the British had tried to rule indirectly, generally using "tribal" leaders (exisiting or invented) but, after a policy review in 1947, the strategy of the Colonial Office was to cultivate urban African political leaders as "partners" in development and devolution. Partnership was revealingly likened by one Rhodesian politician to that between a horse and its rider, but the British found that the horse, once spurred into motion, was not always easy to control. The precedent was set in the Gold Coast, previously regarded as a "model colony," where the British were severely shaken by unprecedented riots in Accra in March 1948, in which twenty-nine died. Here they were dealing with two phenomena as yet unusual in black Africa—a mass political party (the Convention People's party) and a charismatic populist leader, Kwame Nkrumah (who had lived for more than a decade in America and Britain). Nkrumah's 1950 campaign of "Positive Action," including a general strike, landed him in prison, but after the CPP's overwhelming election victory the following year, he was released to form a cabinet with substantial powers of self-government. Nkrumah's supremacy was confirmed in the 1956 elections, admittedly on a low turnout, and the state of Ghana was born in March 1957. For many Africans it was a sensational and inspiring example.

The French were moving in a similar direction in West and Central Africa. At the end of the war trade unions were legalized and forced-labor obligations abolished. The 1946 Constitution gave all colonial subjects citizenship; over the next few years, an increasing number were granted the vote and allowed to exercise it repeatedly. In French West Africa from 1945 to 1958 Africans voted on four referenda, two constitutions, three national assemblies, and three territorial assemblies.[54] Although this was usually done through separate electoral colleges in which white votes counted for at least ten nonwhite votes, the taste of democracy was addictive. Growing unionization often provided a base for urban political parties—that of Ahmed Sekou Touré of Guinea being a notable example. And October 1946 saw the creation of the Rassemblement démocratique africain (RDA), an intercolony alliance of parties in which Félix Houphouët-Boigny of the Ivory Coast, a rich African planter, emerged as the leading figure. In 1956 the French conceded universal suffrage and a single electoral college—two long-standing African demands—and allowed self-government to the colonies except in defense, finance, and external affairs. Mass parties, rather than those based on territorial leaders, became the norm but, as in British Africa, the process was still not seen as a headlong rush to independence. Houphouët-Boigny was one of many African politicians who favored autonomy within the French Union.

In western Africa the colonies were largely rural African socities in which white interests were mostly commercial. Elsewhere on the continent, however, there were substantial mineral resources and significant white settler communities. An extreme example of both was South Africa, largely self-governing since 1910 though still with some links to the British Crown. This was the wealthiest, most industrialized country in Africa, with one of the largest white communities—21 percent of the 12.35 million population in 1950. (Africans accounted for 68 percent, "coloreds" 8 percent, and Asians 2 percent.)[55] Since the 1870s its superb natural endowment of gold, diamonds, and other minerals had been ruthlessly exploited by the whites—the Afrikaners (of Dutch descent), who had started arriving in the seventeenth century, and the more recent British, who subjugated the Afrikaners and blacks around the turn of the century. African labor was essential to extract the mineral resources; on the other hand, whites did not want to create an urban black proleteriat. Nor did rural whites welcome competition from the growing number of cash-crop black farmers. Legislation in the 1910s and 1920s therefore abolished African landowning except in native "reserves" (roughly 14 percent of the country's area by 1936) and tried to "re-tribalize" Africans there. It also fostered residential segregation in the cities and permitted blacks to live there only as migrant labor when economically needed.[56]

This system broke down, however, in the new industrial revolution of the 1940s, when many of the rural poor (both black and white) moved permanently to the cities as whole families, driven by drought and attracted by war-boom jobs. By 1946 the urban black population of 1.8 million exceeded the white, having increased 57 percent over the previous decade. Even in official figures, more than one million of them were squatters living in huts of sacking, wood, or corrugated iron in settlements around the urban centers—such as Hout Bay outside Cape Town.[57] In consequence, black protest intensified. Johannesburg, the largest city, witnessed a powerful squatters' movement (1944–1947). In 1946 a general strike of mine workers was ruthlessly suppressed.

White response to the crisis was spearheaded by the Afrikaner National Party, founded in 1934. Like other national identities, white Afrikaner nationalism was not innate and unchanging but grew dialectically out of past experiences and current politics. During the 1930s the National party deliberately promoted Afrikaner capitalism, played up historic conflicts with the British, such as the Boer War of 1899–1902, and wooed Akrikaner workers away from the English-dominated unions and the Labour party.[58] Its success enabled the National Party to win a narrow victory in the 1948 elections, whereupon it quickly consolidated earlier segregation measures into the system of apartheid. The "races" were formally categorized and sexual relations between them banned. Segregation was reaffirmed and extended to all social activities including transport, restaurants, and education. Residual political rights for coloreds and Asians were extinguished. The Suppression of Communism Act of 1950 allowed the government to ban any person or organization it labeled "communist." In an effort to regain control over black labor, illegal squatting was prohibited and African urban residence restricted. All Africans, now including females, were obliged to carry a "pass book" authorizing them to be in a particular area. Despite its harshness, this system was termed "practical apartheid"—a compromise between racist ideology and economic necessity. Prime Minister D. F. Malan insisted in 1950 that "total territorial segregation was impossible under present circumstances in South Africa," because the economic structure was based on "native labour."[59] The National party consolidated its position in elections in 1953 and 1958, winning support from many English-speakers.

During the 1950s, black protest became more determined. African women mounted a series of protests against the pass laws, including a silent demonstration by twenty thousand of them outside the Union Building in Pretoria in August 1956. Bus boycotts, strikes, and rural revolts were also recurrent. As in other parts of the continent, black political structures were in transition from elite to mass movements. The African National Congress, founded in 1912, favored a multiracial strategy of reform based on organized national campaigns rather than local community action. Its Freedom Charter of June 1955 stated that "South Africa belongs to all who live in it, black and white" and pledged equal status for "all national groups." More radical "Africanist" elements broke away to form the Pan-Africanist Congress in 1959 with the slogan "Africa for the Africans." Their grass-roots protests against the pass laws in 1960 led to a confrontation with panicky police at the township of Sharpeville, near Johannesburg, on March 21 in which sixty-nine Africans were shot dead. Strikes spread around the country. The government declared the ANC and PAC to be illegal organizations, imprisoning thousands of their leaders. For South Africa, the Sharpeville crisis marked "a turning point in the history of African nationalism, when protest finally hardened into resistance" and even strategies for revolution.[60] The international outcry also left the country isolated in world affairs, and in 1961 it withdrew from the commonwealth to preempt being evicted on grounds of its racial policies.

White settlement was also entrenched in the British colonies of East and Central Africa. Officially only Kenya, plus Northern and Southern Rhodesia were termed "colonies of settlement." Uganda, Tangyanika, and Nyasaland, each with a tiny settler presence, were "colonies of administration." The first two, at least, were slated for eventual African rule; Tanganyika, a German colony until 1914, was held as a UN trusteeship. In practice, however, the settler presence dominated the region's politics and prevented easy adoption of the West African solution. British interests were also more significant. East

African bases were important strategically for Britain's continued role east of Suez; the resources of the Northern Rhodesian copper belt and Southern Rhodesian farms were economically valuable. Moreover, small but significant Asian commercial communities added a further sensitivity in Uganda, Kenya, and Tanganyika. In both East and Central Africa, the British therefore inclined in the early 1950s toward regional federations as the best way to maintain their national interests and to balance their multiracial responsibilities.

In British Central Africa the dominant country was Southern Rhodesia, where the white settler population was larger than elsewhere (5 percent compared with less than 1 percent even in Kenya) and had enjoyed internal self-government since 1923. By the early 1950s the British government was seriously alarmed about the growing power of South Africa and about its racial policies. Afrikaners now constituted 13.5 percent of the Southern Rhodesian white population and maybe a quarter in Northern Rhodesia. The British feared that these countries would become "appendages" of South Africa, in fact and even in name.[61] A Central African Federation seemed the best way to contain South Africa *and* control Southern Rhodesia. It meant that in Northern Rhodesia and Nyasaland substantial powers over Africans were devolved from Britain to white settler governments, but London hoped was that "liberally-minded British settlers could offer Africans a middle course between the conflicting nationalisms of Nkrumah and Malan."[62] The federation of the two Rhodesias and Nyasaland lasted for a decade from 1953, but black advancement proved limited.

In East Africa, however, Kenyan settlers totally blocked a federal solution. In any case, the colony's politics were deadlocked from 1952 to 1959 by the state of emergency imposed to contain the Mau Mau uprising among the Kikuyu peoples. This was not merely a struggle of African against white, peasant against settler, but also "a Kikuyu civil war between rich and poor"[63] arising from the pressure on land as the cash-crop economy advanced. Not only did the uprising change British perceptions of African strength but the cost and brutality of its repression also helped erode political and moral support at home for continued colonial rule. In the other two East African colonies, politics revolved around different patterns of African nationalism. In Uganda, politics remained tribal, with the dominant Buganda (17 percent of the population) set against a variety of non-Ganda tribes. In Tanganyika, where there were a plethora of African groupings and Swahili constituted a common language, a unified mass party (TANU) on the Gold Coast model developed earlier under a former teacher, Julius Nyerere. But in both of these colonies, substantial change awaited resolution of Kenya's crisis.

It was in the French settler colonies of North Africa that the most momentous upheavals occurred, with vast implications for France itself as well as for Africa. Morocco, Tunisia, and Algeria were distinguished by their geographical proximity to France and by the prevalence of reformist Sunni Islam among most of the Muslim population. Although the bulk of the population was peasantry, all three had large, volatile cities where political discontent could be mobilized. What differentiated the three, however, was the length and intensity of occupation. French rule dated back to 1830 in Algeria, to 1881 in Tunisia, but only to 1912 in Morocco. Its intensity also differed. In Algeria, after a long and brutal pacification, land was appropriated, the tribal structure destroyed, and Muslim rights repressed. The settlers, from France and other European countries, were known as *pieds noirs* (black feet) and amounted to 11 percent of the population by 1955—a proportion exceeded only in South Africa. In Morocco, by contrast, the French exercised a protectorate, leaving social and political institutions largely intact and ruling through the sultan. In Tunisia—in the middle figuratively if not geographically—France exerted greater economic and political control, but the settler presence was never more than 7 percent, and there was no significant land appropriation or detribalization.

In Morocco and Tunisia, the French presence was therefore less deeply entrenched, and Muslim opposition intensified after 1945. The Istiqlal in Morocco and the Neo-Destourians in Tunisia developed into something like mass parties by the early 1950s, and their hopes were fanned by the French collapse in Indochina in 1954. But whereas Habib Bourguiba in Tunisia led a republican nationalist party, Morocco was "unique in the Middle East and North Africa in that the struggle for independence centered around the capture, revival, and renovation of a traditional institution, the monarchy."[64] This was largely thanks to French ineptitude in deposing and deporting the pro-Istiqlal sultan in August 1953, making him a national symbol and also a rallying point for secular politicians and rural peasants alike. In 1954–1955 both countries were engulfed by guerrilla warfare, but French readiness to cut their losses after Indochina and the relative unimportance of both protectorates facilitated the rapid concession of independence in March 1956.

Algeria was altogether different.[65] French rule remained repressive, although many of the one million *pieds noirs* had moved to urban areas (more than half to Algiers and Oran). But nearly one-fifth of the Muslim population was also urbanized by 1954—many in shanty towns *(bidonvilles)* on city outskirts. Here were potential centers of protest akin to the South African townships. For much of the decade after 1945, settler repression prevented the political mobilization that occurred in Tunisia and Morocco, and Algerian opposition groups were divided among assimilationist reformers, religious traditionalists, and populist elements. Galvanized by the Indochina disaster in 1954, however, radicals founded the Front de Libération Nationale (FLN) and began an armed struggle on 1 November. In August 1955, the FLN mounted terrorist attacks on European settlements around Philippeville.

Grenades were lobbed into cafes, motorists knived in their automobiles, and women and children hacked to death in their homes. The army responded with equally indiscriminate shootings of rebels and civilians, causing 1,273 deaths (ten times the original atrocities). Muslim and settler opinion was now polarized.[66]

The "Republican Front" coalition under Guy Mollet had come to power in January 1956 ready to recognize some kind of "Algerian identity" and to reverse the policy of integration with France. But Mollet changed his mind after a visit to Algiers, when settlers pelted him with tomatoes and clods of earth in a well-organized demonstration of feeling. Crushing the rebellion now took priority over political reform. In January 1957, General Jacques Massu's Tenth Parachute Division, fresh from the Suez debacle, was given responsibility for order in Algiers. The army was determined to reverse the run of French defeats: "seven years in Indo[china], two years in Algeria, three weeks in Egypt. Result: nothing!" to quote one embittered soldier.[67]

The "battle of Algiers" lasted until September. The French paras were victorious, but the violence and torture they employed irreparably tarnished France's international image. Border incidents to stop FLN support from outside provoked conflict with Tunisia and exacerbated world concern. As with Libya in 1949 and Egypt in 1956, the Algerian conflict became internationalized, prompting UN debates and U.S. pressure for a negotiated solution. Negotiation was stigmatized by the settlers, the army, and rightist parties in Paris as another Munich. It could only have been pushed through, if at all, had the socialists brought the communists into a coalition—an expedient resisted since 1947 and itself anathema to the United States.[68] A power vacuum therefore emerged in Paris as well as in Algiers in May 1958. There were even plans for the military to seize power, with Massu's paratroops dropping on Paris. The army command, however, threw its weight behind General Charles de Gaulle, the wartime Free French leader and president in 1944–1946, who had been preparing the ground for his recall and who cannily represented himself as the alternative to both political paralysis and a military coup. On May 29, 1958, de Gaulle formed a government by parliamentary consent; four days later the Assembly granted him sweeping executive powers.

May 1958 was the climax of France's colonial crisis. The war in Algeria, coupled with the centrifugal forces of French politics, had "set in motion mechanisms strong enough to bring France to the verge of civil war."[69] In Britain, not even Suez had the same domestic impact. No British settler community was as close or powerful as Algeria, nor did any of them enjoy political representation in the metropolitan parliament. In London a strong bipolar party system, with the Conservative right in power and favoring devolution, facilitated the process of decolonization and avoided the stigma of treachery.[70] But after 1958 the similarities between Britain and France were more striking than the differences, as the governments of both Charles de Gaulle and Harold Macmillan found themselves unable to dictate events. Each found the other's confusion more and more unsettling.

Up to a point, both leaders had a clear inclination to extricate their countries from the worst colonial entanglements so they could concentrate on great-power politics. Economic considerations also helped: the recovery of Western Europe in the early 1950s made empire less important economically than just after the war. It was assumed that "if the colonies were liberated quickly and good relations established with the successor regimes, there would be little or no economic loss to the metropolises."[71] This was the strategy of neocolonialism, entailing continued control of the key economic levers. But the pressures of precedent and international opinion were now intense. What was intended as strategic withdrawal quickly became precipitate retreat.

The independence of Ghana in 1957 prompted de Gaulle to offer French West Africa the choice between total independence or autonomy (and aid) within what he called the "French Community". Only Sekou Touré of Guinea took the first option, gambling mistakenly on Ghanaian and even Soviet support. Having told de Gaulle to his face "we prefer poverty in liberty to riches in slavery," he got the former with a vengeance. The French removed everything when they left in October 1958, even ripping telephones off the walls.[72] At that point de Gaulle was still envisaging African federations under French aegis—aware that most of the French colonies were too small and poor to form viable states and anxious to offset the regional dominance of Nigeria, which the British were preparing for independence under a federal constitution in 1960. But by now the momentum of nationalist politics had become too strong. Even Houphouët-Boigny of the Ivory Coast chose independence rather than subsidizing his impoverished neighbors within a federation. During 1960, fourteen of France's African colonies became independent. Their combined population was only two-thirds of Nigeria's (forty-two million)—hardly a hopeful portent. Yet their freedom en masse had a dramatic international impact.

In similar vein, de Gaulle zigzagged toward independence for Algeria, talking of "self-determination" in September 1959, "an Algerian Algeria" in November 1960, and then in April 1961, as he began negotiations with the FLN, "a sovereign Algeria." This, of course, defied the army expectations that had brought him to power, but de Gaulle told a furious Massu in September 1959 that "all the colonized peoples of the world were throwing off the yoke," adding: "You are not the Army for its own sake. You are the Army of France. You exist only through her, for her and in her service."[73] After a failed putsch in April 1961, some disgruntled army leaders went underground, trying to assassinate de Gaulle. But Algeria became independent in July 1962. In the final weeks, thousands of *pieds noirs,* with all they could carry, lined up for flights out of the Algiers airport. They included almost all the country's teachers, doctors, and engineers. The city of Oran was left without any firemen.

In London, Macmillan feared a repetition of France's agony. He told Eisenhower gloomily in August 1959: "We have our Algerias coming to us—Kenya and Central Africa."[74] Highly publicized reports of British brutality in the treatment of African detainees in Kenya and Nyasaland added to domestic and international disquiet. The Commonwealth Relations Office warned that Britain could not sustain much longer the contradictions between "one person, one vote" in West Africa, and a multiracial balance weighted against blacks elsewhere.[75] In November 1959 a vigorous new colonial secretary, Iain Macleod, ended the seven-year state of emergency in Kenya and accelerated plans to widen the franchise throughout East and Central Africa. Macmillan warned the South African parliament in February 1960: "The wind of change is blowing through this continent, and, whether we like it or not, this growth of national consciousness is a political fact. . . . [O]ur national policies must take account of it."[76] Between 1961 and 1965, all six British possessions in the region became independent, starting with Tanganyika. The big difference among them was that Southern Rhodesia made a unilateral declaration of independence in 1965 under white minority rule. In Kenya, the other key settler colony, the whites were not sufficiently numerous or entrenched to go it alone. In 1952 London had backed the Kenyan settlers; a decade later it sided with the blacks. The wind of change had blown its policies full circle.

Devolution had become decolonization; settler interests were sacrificed to majority rights. Even so, Britain and France did maintain the appearance of an orderly transfer of power. What happened if the rider completely lost control of the horse was tragically illustrated in the Congo.

Until 1959 the Belgian colony remained an island of autocratic stability—with few political rights and little education for blacks. On the other hand, the colony enjoyed a mineral-led boom for most of the 1950s, and health and welfare standards were quite high. But when the boom petered out in the late 1950s, growing rural unemployment and urban migration started a process already well advanced elsewhere in Africa. De Gaulle's concessions in French Africa spurred the minority of educated Congolese, though they talked of independence in thirty years. Then, in January 1959, riots in the capital, Léopoldville, prompted fears of another Algeria. Within days the Belgian government announced its intention "to organize in the Congo a democracy capable of exercising the prerogatives of sovereignty and of deciding upon its own independence."[77] The plan was for a gradual transition, starting with local elections in December 1959. But, as the Congolese now rushed to form credible parties to which power might be transferred, they warned that only immediate independence would ensure friendly relations and thus maintenance of Belgian economic interests. Accordingly, Belgium committed itself to independence by June 30, 1960. Within days of the Belgian departure, the Congo dissolved into ethnic and regional violence.

At this stage, two general points should be made about the process of decolonization in Africa. First, by the early 1960s, the complexities of colonial rule had been resolved, at least on the surface, into a black-white struggle. Only a few states—notably South Africa and Rhodesia, plus the obdurate Portuguese colonies—remained under white control. The conflicts, internal and external, that this generated will be discussed as part of the global politics of race in Chapter 7. The other observation is that the Congo civil war is only the most egregious case of precipitous imperial withdrawal. The British and French had also forced the pace and shape of decolonization. Determined to transfer power to politicians who had proved their legitimacy at the ballot box, they helped invent political parties that were often only loose fronts embracing a multitude of ethnic and regional groups. The states they created were usually colonial polities that lacked ethnic coherence or independent viability. "In 1964, for example, some 24 African states had populations of less than five million (four had populations of less than one million)."[78] Few had sufficient educated personnel to staff the bureaucracies, and the frenzied decolonization of the late 1950s allowed scant experience of government before independence. The legacy of accelerated decolonization was arrested development. Most significant, political independence did not signify economic independence. European companies still controlled much of Africa's trade, mining and industry. In a famous phrase, Kwame Nkrumah had declared: "Seek ye first the political kingdom, and all things shall be added to it." Subsequent African history, according to Ali Mazrui, suggests a different aphorism: "Seek ye first the political kingdom—and all else will be subtracted from it."[79]

The "White Commonwealth" between Britain and America

In Africa, as in South Asia and the Middle East, the legacies of empire were recent and dramatic. But problems of national identity and economic dependence were also apparent in countries that had gained political freedom decades before. One group was constituted by Canada, Australia, and New Zealand. By the 1970s all three would face mounting claims from long-suppressed native minorities. But in the 1950s their postimperial dilemmas were those of countries positioned at different points along a spectrum from a British imperial past toward a regional identity in which American influences were becoming ever more important.

What gives the story added significance is the matter of size—Canada was the third-largest country in the world in 1950 (following the USSR and China), while Australia was the sixth (after Brazil and the United States). And all three were developed countries in which the agricultural sector was in sharp decline as manufacturing and particularly services accounted for most of GDP. Perhaps their basic problem was that population bore no relationship to size: Canada had 12.9 million people in 1948, Australia 7.6 million, and New Zealand 1.8 million. During the postwar era, population did grow rapidly. In large part, this reflected natural increase following patterns typical of most of the developed world. But in both Australia and New Zealand, immigration (restricted to whites) accounted for more than one-third of the increase, encouraged by government promotions such as the £10 assisted-passage scheme for anyone promising to stay at least two years. Nevertheless, 2 percent annual population growth did not alter the basic demographic weakness of any of the three countries. Here were the roots of dependency.

New Zealand remained most closely identified with Britain. By 1961 it still had only 2.4 million people, and the land area of its two main islands was less than 4 percent of that of Australia. The major economic center, Auckland, accounted for around one-fifth of the population. The country had pioneered the welfare state in the 1890s, and its Labour government reinforced the pattern while in office in 1935–1949, but in many respects its economy remained a colony of Britain. Wool, meat, and dairy products accounted for well over 80 percent of the value of its exports in the 1950s; 60 percent of exports went to Britain, from which New Zealand obtained around half its imports.[80] Much of the export trade was conducted under Empire Preference and Sterling Area arrangements dating from the depression and wartime. This commonwealth economic grouping was a way of "keeping New Zealand at one remove from the American-dominated international economy."[81] Culturally, the population remained overwhelmingly of British stock; 55 percent of immigrants in 1948–1957 were from Britain (compared with only 34 percent for Australia and 28 percent in the case of Canada).[82] "How are things at Home?" was a frequent inquiry to British visitors, and Sidney Holland's national government of 1949–1957 made the phrase "where Britain goes we go" almost its motto.

Australia was bigger, more heterogeneous, and less tied to Britain. As a result of postwar migration, 20 percent of its 10.4 million population in 1961 was foreign born (double the proportion in 1947), and only 8 percent had come from Britain. Other European immigrants, particularly Greeks and Italians, now constituted significant urban minorities. Even more than New Zealand (and much more than Canada), Australia was an urbanized country, with Sydney and Melbourne dominant. Although wool still accounted for half Australia's exports in the 1950s, its trade was becoming more diversified both in composition and direction. In the early 1960s the UK took 21 percent of Australian exports and provided 31 percent of its imports, compared with 36 percent and 47 percent respectively a decade before. By this time Japan took 16 percent of Australian exports, and America supplied 20 percent of its imports—trends that were to become more pronounced over subsequent decades.[83]

The economic pattern reflected a growing consciousness in Australia of its Pacific identity. This had been brought sharply into focus in 1941–1942 by the Japanese conquests and Britain's inability to defend Australasia. The Labour prime minister, John Curtin, declared that "Australia looks to America, free of any pangs as to our traditional links or kinship with the United Kingdom."[84] By 1944–1945, admittedly, the Japanese threat had receded, and it had always been less alarming in New Zealand—twelve hundred miles east across the Tasman Sea from Australia. But it was now axiomatic that the United States was the only significant friendly power in the Pacific, and both countries, with Australia in the lead, sought to draw Washington into closer commitments. The ANZUS pact of 1951 represented America's first clear, if limited, acknowledgment of collective security among the three: Britain was not included, to Churchill's indignation. On the other hand, during the Suez crisis of 1956, Australia and New Zealand were the only countries to support Britain, France, and Israel in the UN. In New Zealand, there was little dissent from this. In Australia, it caused a cabinet rift, with the passionately anglophile Prime Minister Robert Menzies overruling his minister of external affairs, Richard Casey. Menzies publicly praised British action as "practical and courageous," and derided claims of collusion with Israel as "fantastic."[85] Both Australia and New Zealand were therefore maintaining ties with Britain *and* America in the 1950s. As we shall see, a more decisive tilt was to occur during the 1960s, with Britain's applications to join the European Economic Community and the Southeast Asian security crises over Indonesia and Vietnam.

Canada had moved closer to the United States much earlier, mainly as a result of simple geography. Indeed, Canada originated in territories that did not wish to be part of the United States in 1776. Ethnic ties with Britain were also weaker because of Canada's origins as part of the French empire. In the late 1940s only half the population was of British or Irish descent, and 31 percent were of French extraction. Most of the latter lived in Quebec—after Ontario the second most significant province—as part of a fiercely francophone culture. And Canada's loose federal structure, less centralized than Australia's, allowed the provinces greater control over finance and resources. In other words, it was harder in Canada to shape a coherent national identity as an alternative to the British connection.

In any case, the pull of the giant southern neighbor was almost irresistible. Most of Canada's population clustered near the border, well within range of American radio and later TV stations. Canada's economy had long been dominated by the United States, which provided 71 percent of its imports in 1957 and took 59 percent of its exports. (The contribution of Britain was 9 percent of imports and 15 percent of exports.)[86] Since the war, Americans had been buying up Canadian businesses, and by 1957 they accounted for 84 percent of total direct foreign investment. Americans controlled 70 percent of the capital invested in Canadian petroleum and natural gas, for instance, and 43 percent in manufacturing industry.[87]

The American connection was fostered by the Liberal governments that ran Canada from 1935 to 1957. This was true in diplomacy as well: during Suez the Canadian government abstained from supporting Britain in the United Nations, and Foreign Minister Lester Pearson won the Nobel Peace Prize for his work in creating a UN Emergency Force to help separate the belligerents. Such "disloyalty" to Britain, however, intensified Tory resentment, already acute because of the controversy that summer when U.S. companies acquired three-quarters of the Trans-Canada Pipe Lines corporation. The Liberals' alleged subservience to Washington was a factor in the Tory election victory of 1957. But John Diefenbaker, the new premier, did little to back up his rhetoric about ending "the Pearson pattern." Economic realities were too compelling, and he was not helped by either the late 1950s recession or Britain's EEC application. His ineffectual posturing about keeping U.S. nuclear warheads off Canadian soil was a major reason for his electoral defeat in April 1963.

The journalist Pierre Berton claimed this election proved that "anti-Americanism is finished as a political issue. We have cast our lot with this continent for better or worse and the people know it."[88] This was an exaggeration, as the protests over the Vietnam War were to show, but Berton was basically right. In the 1960s Canada's identity crisis was internal, not external—the new assertiveness of French Canadians in the framework of ever-weakening federal authority—which grew out of earlier legacies of empire.

Latin America: "Our" Hemisphere and "Their" Island

In most of Latin America the age of formal imperialism had passed even earlier. Although the smaller Caribbean islands remained under European rule, political independence had been achieved everywhere else by the 1830s. There were, however, abiding legacies of the imperial era. One was language: the official tongue of most of independent Latin America was Spanish, except for Portuguese in Brazil and French in Haiti. Another legacy was racial. Since the sixteenth century, South America had been populated through a complex interaction of European, native "Indians," and Africans—the latter descended from imported slaves. This was also the story in the United States, but there the Indians had been largely exterminated and white-black interbreeding restricted. The result was a highly polarized biracial society. In South America, racial prejudice was marked but interracial mixing had been the norm. The dominant ethnic component were the mestizos, those of mixed European and Indian descent. In Brazil, where the majority of black slaves had been concentrated, there was far more marriage across color lines than in the United States, and mulattos had greater opportunity to rise up the social ladder.

In 1945, twenty of the fifty-one founding members of the United Nations Organization were Latin American states. The largest, Brazil, was bigger in size than the United States (before Alaska became a state in 1959), and its 52 million people equaled about two-fifths of the U.S. population. Yet formal independence of some longevity could not conceal continued economic dependence. Since the sixteenth century, these countries had been part of a thriving Atlantic economy. From the late nineteenth century they had also experienced impressive growth rates. But theirs was "externally-oriented development" based on foreign demand for South American primary products which helped finance imports of manufactured goods from Europe and the United States.[89] Many countries relied on one or two commodities—coffee in Brazil, copper in Chile, sugar in Cuba, beef and wheat in Argentina. Although plantations were largely in domestic hands in Brazil and Argentina, foreign ownership was widespread in mining, and most of Central American production was dominated by U.S. corporations, particularly the giant United Fruit Company. Equally significant was the degree of foreign investment. Although British capital remained important in Argentina, the United States had become the largest single investor in South America as a whole by 1930.

During the early decades of the twentieth century, local industry and in consequence larger cities had developed, often sustained by massive immigration from Europe, notably in Argentina. Industrialization and urbanization were destabilizing forces. But they were usually confined to coastal areas, for example Lima in Peru or the São Paulo/Rio de Janeiro region of Brazil, leaving the hinterland undeveloped and resentful. Few countries had a big commercial middle class, unlike Western Europe or the United States, and political power usually remained with the agricultural elite, often in league with the armed forces. The growing urban working class became increasingly restive, especially when the depression of the 1930s slashed commodity prices and stunted economic growth.

Between 1930 and 1950, the triple shocks of depression, world war, and cold war set the pattern of postwar Latin American development. In external policy, the period saw the Western Hemisphere drawn unequivocally into the American orbit. With Germany controlling continental Europe and the British blockading Latin American ports, the region's commerce turned even more to the United States, anxious to control the hemisphere's strategic raw materials. By 1941 the United States accounted for over half of Latin America's trade. After Pearl Harbor the United States persuaded the Latin American republics to break off diplomatic relations with the Axis powers. All of them eventually entered the war on the Allied side, although Argentina waited until March 1945 and only Brazil made a major military contribution by sending a division to fight in Italy. Once victory was achieved, U.S. interference in the region abated. Washington's security concerns were satisfied by the Rio mutual-defense treaty of August 1947 and the formation of the Organization of American States (OAS) the following May. Both confirmed American leadership and ruled out intervention by other great powers. Compared with Europe or East Asia, Latin America offered no real military danger; consequently, U.S. officials rejected any Marshall Plan for Latin America. Between 1945 and 1950, Belgium and tiny Luxembourg obtained more direct aid from the United States than all of Latin America combined.[90]

The immediate postwar years did see a marked "swing to the left" in the region, akin to that in Western Europe in 1945–1947.[91] In Peru and Venezuela, for instance, center-left coalitions came to power for the first time, and the communists made significant gains, picking up 10 percent of the vote in the Brazilian assembly elections of January 1947 and 17 percent in Chile's municipal elections the following April. Unionization of the work force also increased—in Argentina, from 450,000 in 1941 to nearly 2 million by 1949—and unions became increasingly centralized. Politics in several states became more open and democratic, inspired ideologically by the Allied victory over fascism. The years 1944–1945 saw more democratic changes in Latin America than in almost any comparable period since the wars of independence.[92]

Yet the shift leftward was only temporary. In 1946–1948 labor unions throughout most of Latin America were brought under strict government control and the communist parties proscribed. As in Western Europe, this was a response to the new Cominform's increasingly militant line in 1947–1948 and to U.S. concerns about possible subversion. At the Bogotá conference of May 1948, from which the OAS emerged, a resolution was passed declaring that "the political activity of international communism" was "incompatible with the concept of American freedom."[93] At the same time, democratic practices were abridged, and in late 1948 military coups overturned democratic governments in both Peru and Venezuela. By the end of 1954 only four countries in Latin America could be described as democratic. Most were dictatorships based on military rule, although Chile retained a lively party system and Uruguay remained a pluralist democracy until 1973.

The United States—a champion of democratization during the war—broadly welcomed these developments. The imperatives behind the reverse course in Japan and Germany applied also to Latin America. As George Kennan of the State Department observed in 1950: "It is better to have a strong regime in power than a liberal government if it is indulgent and relaxed and penetrated by Communists."[94] American desires were made clear at Rio, Bogotá and other conferences, so there was no need for overt intervention.

The big exception in the 1950s was Guatemala. Since 1944 the country had been under military-led rulers of socialist persuasion. The president from 1950, confirmed in elections that year, was Colonel Jacobo Arbenz Guzmán, whose agenda for modernizing the country including a large public-works program and, crucially, land reform. The 1952 law expropriating uncultivated plantations struck at the interests of the American United Fruit Company, 85 percent of whose holdings were unused. Washington was also alarmed by Arbenz's (limited) association with the Guatemalan communists. Although the party numbered less than one thousand members, even on CIA estimates, President Eisenhower saw Arbenz as "openly playing ball with communists."[95] Eisenhower, unlike Truman, was ready to use the CIA in covert operations, and the agency started stirring up Arbenz's military opponents. When Eisenhower stopped arms sales to Guatemala and Arbenz turned instead to the Soviet bloc, the administration saw this as final proof that he was a communist tool. In June 1954 a small band of CIA-trained rebels "invaded" the country. They were barely two hundred strong, but CIA radio broadcasts and its bombing of the capital gave the impression of a major assault. Arbenz's nerve cracked and he fled into exile, leaving power in the hands of an American-approved military junta, Thanking the CIA afterward, Eisenhower told them: "You've averted a Soviet beachhead in our hemisphere."[96]

Nevertheless, what was left in "our hemisphere" was not America's kind of political economy. Where military rule was not overt, power often lay in the hands of a dominant party in league with the main socioeconomic groups—

a reflection of the corporatist philosophy that had lurked behind European fascism. The most durable example was the single-party state of Mexico, where the Partido Revolucionario Institucional (PRI) comprised three sectors: peasant, worker, and popular (covering the rest of society). The most flamboyant example was Argentina under Juan Perón, a career army officer whose populist presidency from 1946 to 1955 rested on an unlikely alliance of urban workers, industrialists, and the army—the latter eventually toppled him. These corporatist features testified to the often sharply divided nature of Latin American societies, as the old hegemony of the landowners was challenged by the new forces of urban industry, both capital and labor. Alliances between the latter rarely proved durable, as we shall see.

Corporatism also envisioned a major role for the state in the direction of the economy. After commodity prices collapsed during the depression, Latin American leaders of whatever political color tended to favor a strategy of import-substituting industrialization (ISI). Development of local industries would, they argued, increase employment and reduce economic dependence on foreign powers. The main mechanisms were tariffs, cartels, and other protectionist policies to aid nascent industries, and government-run companies into which investment was specially channeled. This was the philosophy, for instance, of Getúlio Vargas's *estado nôvo* in Brazil during World War II, and he continued economic nationalism in modified form during his postwar presidency of 1950–1954. Vargas established a new state-owned petroleum corporation, PETROBRAS, emulating Mexico's PEMEX of the 1930s, whose products were boycotted by the United States for three decades. In Argentina Perón claimed that he was creating neither capitalism nor communism but *justicialismo,* which he defined as "the organized society."[97] We shall see that such corporatism eventually spawned its own economic problems, but it satisfied nationalist sentiments and economic interests while the unprecedented growth of the 1950s continued.

Yet corporatism and import substitution failed to address the underlying problems of poverty and underdevelopment. In the poorest countries of Latin America—Bolivia, Ecuador, Haiti—per capita income was less than 5 percent of that in the United States. U.S. complacency about the region was dented by the rough reception for Vice President Richard Nixon during his tour in May 1958, culminating in a mob assault while he was visiting Caracas. Nixon advocated a more nuanced regional policy—a "hug" for democratic governments, a "hand shake" for dictators. Although this approach was privately described by the State Department as "essentially a matter of emphasis rather than a real change in policy,"[98] it did result in more supportive initiatives such as the Inter-American Development Bank. Under Eisenhower's successor, the young and energetic John F. Kennedy, this policy evolved into the "Alliance for Progress" to promote development, health, and literacy in the hemisphere. But the sums involved were small, and the Kennedy administration avoided fundamental issues such as land reform. In any case, Kennedy's main concern was anticommunism, and that meant Cuba.

January 1959 saw the end of the Batista military government, which had run Cuba for most of the previous quarter-century. The United States had wrested the island, only ninety miles off the Florida coast, from Spain's feeble grip in 1898. Until 1934, Cuba was an American protectorate; thereafter it remained an economic colony. In 1959 Americans dominated Cuba's main industries and refined more than one-third of its sugarcane—the main crop on which the economy depended. The United States took three-quarters of the island's exports and supplied two-thirds of its imports. Cuban monetary policy was set by the Federal Reserve Bank of Atlanta. On the other hand, the sugar monoculture had created a rural proletariat of seasonal laborers in the fields and mills, migrating to and from the cities, which accounted for 40 percent of the population. Moreover, the Catholic Church did not dominate Cuban society. These unusual features gave Cuba potential for a class-based social movement rarely found in Latin America. The guerrillas who toppled Batista were largely middle class in origin, not least their leader, Fidel Castro—the son of a wealthy Spanish immigrant who had been radicalized as a law student. But it was to rural and urban workers that Castro increasingly appealed.

Redistributing national wealth was his priority in 1959, in order to build support. The Agrarian Reform Law of June expropriated holdings of over one thousand acres, with compensation paid in Cuban currency bonds. The government effectively took over the Cuban sugar industry. Nationalization of other industries followed during 1960. Castro, it should be noted, was not a communist when he assumed power. But his revolutionary nationalism was inevitably anti-American because of Cuba's colonial predicament, and any tilt away from the United States could only be toward the Soviet Union. The February 1960 trade agreement with Moscow, under which the Russians would buy one-sixth of the Cuban sugar crop, was the first evidence of this. And in the bitter internal struggle to consolidate power, Castro drew increasingly on support from the Communist party—the only thing in Cuba close to a mass political organization. Castro's leftward march was therefore unsurprising in the circumstances.

Equally predictable was the ferocity of America's response. In 1959–1960 Castro had expropriated nearly $1 billion of American direct investment and had given the Soviets a base only eight minutes' flying time from Florida. In the cold war atmosphere of the time that was seen as an intolerable threat as well as a spectacular humiliation. U.S. officials feared that Castro would incite revolution elsewhere in Latin America. "He is your Nasser," wrote Macmillan to Eisenhower in a painful analogy.[99]

During Eisenhower's last months in office, the CIA formulated plans for an invasion by Cuban exiles in the United States, coordinated with uprisings in Cuba itself. This was inherited in January 1961 by John F. Kennedy, who had himself focused on Cuba during the election campaign, claiming, "Today the Iron Curtain is 90 miles off the coast of the United States."[100] Though Kennedyites later blamed their predecessors for the ensuing fiasco, the new president had adopted the plans over the doubts of his inner circle. For Eisenhower and Kennedy, the Guatemalan precedent seemed compelling: America could remove potential troublemakers without much effort or direct responsibility. In Castro's case, however, this was wishful thinking: "only overt military intervention by the United States could have succeeded—and Kennedy made it clear from the outset that he would never consent to that."[101] The predicted uprisings failed to materialize, and the fourteen hundred Cuban exiles who landed on the beach around the Bay of Pigs on April 17, 1961, were quickly surrounded by Cuban troops. Without support from U.S. naval and air units, they had little choice but to surrender.

For Kennedy, it was the worst possible outcome—a failure with his fingerprints all over it. Like Nasser in 1956, Castro had survived and had humbled a great power. Worse still, he had humiliated John F. Kennedy. Eliminating Castro was now top priority in the White House. The president approved a series of covert operations under the code name Mongoose, intended to "to help Cuba overthrow the Communist regime." One official on the task force noted, "We are at war with Cuba."[102]

Castro's revolution and the Bay of Pigs had transformed Washington's "mental map" of Latin America. Unlike that of South Asia, the Middle East, or Africa, the region's cartography had not been redrawn in the 1940s and 1950s. Political independence had come much earlier, most boundaries were accepted (or at least were not grounds for war), and Latin America's economic dependence on the United States seemed assured. Then suddenly, the cold war penetrated "our" hemisphere. During the 1960s, "their" island became a source of near paranoia in Washington. In 1962, it was nearly the detonator for nuclear war.

4

Two Europes, Two Germanies

Across the postwar world, the erosion of empires, the emergence of new states, and the imperatives of development allowed the superpowers to extend their influence. Bipolarity and state building developed symbiotically. In Europe, the cold war confrontation was direct and acute. In Chapter 1 we saw how the two blocs were created. This chapter looks more closely at the countries themselves. In the East, agrarian societies were driven through forced industrialization on the Soviet model, their nationalism subordinated to Moscow's "proletarian internationalism," as events in Hungary made clear in 1956. In the West, where American control was looser, capitalism revived under the new philosophies of growth, welfare, and the "mixed economy." Six Western European countries embarked on a project in transnational integration that would have far-reaching consequences. By the late 1950s, Europe's new balance of power seemed stable, partly because the two nuclear superpowers had achieved a balance of terror but also because they had apparently solved the great problem of European history in the first half of the century—the German Question.

The Socialist Transformation of Eastern Europe

During the cold war it was customary to speak simply of Eastern Europe. Yet that label covered considerable diversity. Although much of the region was still agrarian, eastern Germany and the Czech lands each had a significant industrial base. These areas, like Hungary, were also linguistically distinct from the Slavic countries to the east and south. Moving southeast through the Balkans, the religious predominance of the Roman Catholic Church gave way to Eastern Orthodoxy—a divide that cut through the federal state of Yugoslavia. The strength of Islam in Albania and Bosnia was a legacy of Ottoman rule. And during the cold war, Greece was included in "Western Europe," because the communists lost the civil war of 1944–1949 and the country joined NATO in 1952, even though its history, culture, and economy marked Greece as inextricably part of the Balkans.

These national contrasts, never totally obscured, were to assume salient importance after the cold war ended. But for most of the postwar period, similarities were greater than differences and these justify use of the term *Eastern Europe*. First of all, Europe east of the Elbe River was less developed than the western part of the continent. Nation-states had been slower to emerge: until 1918 the region was largely controlled by the Ottoman, Habsburg, and Romanov empires. Here, too, serfdom persisted until the mid-nineteenth century (having been abolished in the West some four hundred years before)—with consequences that have been likened to "the impact of slavery in the West Indies, in the Southern States of America or in Brazil."[1] Most of the area (except for Serbia and Bulgaria) remained polarized between impoverished peasants and large landowners, often of alien nationality. As a further result, urban capitalism came later than in the West, and the commercial classes tended to be unpopular foreigners, particularly Germans and Jews, but also Greeks and Armenians in the Balkans. Even after the great empires collapsed in 1914–1918 and parliamentary democracies were established, the new states generally rested on the continued dominance of landowners, who also provided most of the bureaucracy and officer corps. Except for Czechoslovakia, all ended up as military dictatorships in the depression. Consequently, in Eastern Europe (and, even more, Russia), the state was far more dominant than in the West, both politically and economically. Civil rights were limited, legislatures were less powerful, and social institutions lacked autonomy against the government. The communists eagerly exploited this political tradition.[2]

But—and this is the second similarity—all these countries went through a distinctive experience of war and revolution in the mid-1940s, even before the communists gained total power. The principal battlefields of World War II lay between the Elbe and Dnieper rivers. The disruption caused as the German empire first expanded and then contracted left much of Eastern Europe ripe for revolution. In 1945–1946 the postwar governments—often coalitions of socialist, communist, and peasant parties—took over the large estates and distributed them to the peasants. In Poland, nearly half the agricultural area changed hands; in Hungary about one-third. Land reform was nationalist as well as socialist in inspiration, since much of the property affected had been in German hands (or Italian in Albania). Similarly, the fact that the Axis occupiers had taken over most heavy industry during the war facilitated its nationalization after 1945. The new governments quickly secured the so-called commanding heights of the economy, amounting to two-thirds of industrial capacity in Poland and Yugoslavia. In short, across Eastern Europe, the years 1945–1949 marked a clear transition from capitalism to socialism.[3]

By 1949, however, these countries had fallen under complete communist control. This was the third and most significant common feature. Yugoslavia and Albania achieved this in 1944–1945 with little Soviet help, as the communists suppressed their rivals in the feuding resistance movements and in the national fronts that followed. In Yugoslavia, under Josip Broz (better known as Tito), the communists dominated the elections of November 1945 and proudly proclaimed the world's second communist state the following January. In Albania, at this time little more than a Yugosolav client state, Enver Hoxha followed suit with his own "Socialist People's Republic." Tito and Hoxha dominated their countries until the 1980s. Elsewhere, notably in Poland and eastern Germany, communists consolidated their power more slowly, with the backing of the Red Army. Stalin's policy in the region was not initially monolithic. In both Czechoslovakia, where communists had been strong before the war, and in Hungary, where they had been weak, he instructed the local parties (as in France and Italy) to eschew revolution and seek power by political means. This may have been merely a temporary tactical ploy—though Stalin kept his promise to Churchill in 1944 and stayed out of the Greek civil war.[4] In any event, two international developments certainly forced his hand. Most significant, as we saw in Chapter 1, was the announcement of America's Marshall Plan in June 1947, which Stalin considered a threat to his influence in eastern Europe. Cominform was established in September to keep foreign communists in line. The other was the growing independence of Tito's Yugoslavia, both in foreign and domestic policy. A wartime resistance hero, Tito had not spent the war in Moscow (unlike most postwar communist leaders), and he had no intention of allowing the Soviets to dominate his economy or restrain his ambitions to be the dominant influence in the Balkans. Yugoslavia was ostracized from Cominform in June 1948 on the grounds that it had broken with the "internationalist traditions" of communism, "taken the road to nationalism," and was in danger of degenerating into "an ordinary bourgeois republic" and "a colony of the imperialist countries."[5]

The Marshall Plan and the challenge of Titoism prompted Stalinization of the other Soviet satellites in the name of "proletarian internationalism." The impetus was maintained in the early 1950s by the war scare caused by the conflict in Korea. Noncommunist groups were suppressed or fused into the ruling party. Communist parties, which had expanded in the 1940s during the political bid for power, were now purged of those not deemed totally loyal. It has been estimated that one in four members were ousted.[6] Those at the very top were not immune, particularly if they had come to power not as imports from Moscow but as indigenous leaders—such as László Rajk in Hungary and Wladyslaw Gomulka in Poland. A series of rigged show trials, modeled on those in Russia in the 1930s, played up the Titoist threat and warned off potential opponents. These trials were scripted on the basis of forced confessions. In the words of George Hodos, victim turned historian: "It took only a few weeks of physical and psychological torture for communist leaders, at the height of their power, to be transformed into helpless clumps of human flesh."[7] Rajk, though a ruthless Stalinist, was one of those tried and executed, but the technique was also applied to critics of the regimes, such as Joseph Cardinal Mindszenty, the Catholic primate of Hungary, who was imprisoned after his trial at the end of 1948.

In economic terms, Stalinization meant replacing the market with the party as the determining mechanism. The party set production targets—for the economy as a whole and for individual enterprises—and also established price and wage levels. Although foreign trade continued, it was now largely within the Soviet bloc and was insulated from the domestic economy as a separate hard-currency sector. All this planning naturally led to a proliferation of bureaucracy. At the peak of Stalinization, Poland had no less than twenty-six economic ministries; in Czechoslovakia in the mid-1960s, over 11 percent of the population was employed in the state administration. The new command economy was based rigidly on the interwar Soviet model and concentrated on the rapid development of heavy industry, with scant attention to other sectors, notably agriculture. Production targets were aggregate figures: criteria of quality, cost efficiency, and consumer preference rarely applied. Before 1939, for instance, eighty different types of shoes were produced in Hungary; by the early 1950s there were only sixteen. Similarly, shops were full of large (and unwanted) items of crockery, because the plan was expressed by weight and it was easier to produce a small number of big items than a greater number of small ones.[8]

None of the East Europe communist economies ever freed itself from the rigidities of Stalinism. But the heyday of the command economy was brief. Stalin's death in March 1953 began a wrenching power struggle in Moscow, in which the fundamentals of policy were at stake as well. The suspicious Stalin had not groomed a successor, and power was shared by a collective troika headed by Georgi Malenkov, Lavrenti Beria, and—initially as the junior—Nikita Khrushchev. All were protegés of Stalin—men from the political generation *after* the 1917 Revolution. All agreed that the excesses of Stalinism had to stop—if only because they were counterproductive at home and abroad. Political prisoners were soon being released from the Gulag; Malenkov spoke of "peaceful coexistence" with the United States. But differences among the three were as important as similarities. Khrushchev and Vyacheslav Molotov—restored as foreign minister after being purged during Stalin's last years—seem to have accepted the essentials of Stalin's foreign policy. They took pride in the empire, won at huge cost in a brutal war, and believed in the revolutionary struggle against American capitalism. But Beria, the brutal secret-police chief, and Malenkov, a technocrat who had run much of the Soviet military-industrial complex during the war, had both been closely involved in the Soviet nuclear project. They understood its potential, judging, like many in the West, that the H-bomb had rendered war obsolete as an instrument of policy. The implications of their thinking remain contentious, but it seems likely that they favored a less ideological foreign policy, concentrating on consolidating the essentials of the Soviet empire rather than expanding further—safe in the possession of thermonuclear deterrence. In consequence, as we shall see, they were ready to be flexible about Germany.[9]

But the troika did not survive for long. Malenkov and Khrushchev first turned on Beria, convinced he was about to seize total power. He was arrested as a Western agent, tried, found guilty, and duly executed in December 1953. Malenkov was soon sidelined as well, though not exterminated. He lacked the skill and stomach for political infighting, unlike the pugnacious Khrushchev, who also controlled the levers of patronage as party secretary. Malenkov's claims that there were "no objective grounds for a collision" between the two superpowers and that, "given modern weapons," a new world war "would mean the destruction of world civilization" also damaged him politically, because they questioned the doctrine of revolution that justified the regime at home and abroad.[10]

The victor in the power struggle was therefore Khrushchev—like Stalin thirty years earlier, the underrated administrator who outwitted his bettereducated rivals. Beria was an architect by training, Malenkov an engineer and a graduate of the prestigious Advanced Technological School in Moscow. Khrushchev's background was very different. Born in 1894 to a family of illiterate Russian peasants near Kursk, he moved with his father to the Don-bass coal mines at the age of fourteen. He worked as a metal fitter, acted as a miners' spokesman during the Revolution, and served in the Red Army in 1919–1921. Attracting Stalin's attention in the late 1920s, he acted as Moscow party boss in 1935–1938 and as first secretary of the Ukraine for much of the war. In short, Khrushchev was no armchair revolutionary: he had worked and fought, he had seen tsarism and fascism, he believed in communism, and his own rise was a tribute to its transforming power. Under him, the revolutionary struggle would go on—in the Soviet bloc and in the wider world (Chapter 6). For Khrushchev, deStalinization and peaceful coexistence did not mean the end of the cold war but its prosecution by more skillful and effective means.

One of Malenkov's claims had been that Soviet thermonuclear capability permitted less emphasis on the military-industrial complex and more on light industry and food "in the interests of securing a faster rise in the living standards and cultural levels of the people."[11] Having criticized such ideas in the struggle for power, Khrushchev quietly appropriated them once he was secure, to help build up support for communism. The Soviet "New Course" in economics was emulated in Eastern Europe, with increased consumer production and a relaxation in agricultural collectivization. Foreign policy within the bloc changed as well. In June 1955 Khrushchev made a public apology to Tito (blaming the rift on groundless charges by Beria and other "contemptible agents of imperialism") and enunciated the principle of "mutual respect and noninterference in one another's internal affairs" because socialism could take different forms in different countries. The process of de-Stalinization reached its apogee in February 1956 when details leaked out regarding Khrushchev's secret speech to the USSR's twentieth party congress, in which he denounced Stalin for multifarious crimes and for the "cult of personality."[12]

The ideological U-turn of 1955–1956 had a devastating effect on eastern Europe. If Stalinism was relaxed, where should a line be drawn against reform? If "Titoism" was a fabrication, what of the purges imposed at Stalin's behest against the menace of Tito? Previous victims of Stalinization (however Stalinist they might have been) now became symbolic heroes of destalinization. In Poland, following serious riots in Poznan in June 1956, Gomulka, ousted in 1948, was restored to power. Although his promises of reform were generally not honored, he did reduce the Red Army's hated control over Polish life.

In Hungary, however, reform boiled over into revolution. The Stalinist leader, Mátyás Rákosi, was forced to resign in July 1956 and, as student and worker protest mounted in October, his old rival, the national communist Imre Nagy, was restored to the premiership. Eyewitnesses, such as the British communist Dora Scarlett, who had lived in Budapest for over three years, were astonished by the suddenness with which the established order fell apart.[13] A prime symbol was the huge bronze statue of Stalin in front of the City Park, which was toppled on October 23 and then gradually hacked to pieces. The head ended up near the National Theater surmounted by a road sign indicating "Dead End" (Plate 11).[14] The reformers' aims were, in part, socialist. Nagy restored the political situation to the party pluralism of the immediate postwar period, while across the country some 2,100 workers' councils were established to run local enterprises. These were to play a leading role in the resistance and symbolized the proleteriat's abhorrence of the proleterian state! But the immediate object was nationalist, and the heroes of Hungary's struggle of 1848–1849 against Austrian imperialism were repeatedly invoked in the struggle against Russian domination. Emboldened by the initial withdrawal of Soviet troops, Nagy proclaimed neutrality on November 1, 1956, because the Hungarian people desired "the consolidation and further development of its national revolution without joining any power blocs."[15] That was too much for Khrushchev, initially reluctant to intervene despite the urgings of Yuri Andropov, his hard-line ambassador to Hungary. On November 4, Soviet tanks rolled back into Budapest and, over the next week, the revolution was suppressed across the country at the cost of some four thousand Hungarian dead.

The autumn of 1956 confirmed the limits of post-Stalinism. Security was still defined in territorial terms—it depended on the bloc as much as on the bomb. Even if there were "many roads to socialism," the route maps would be provided by the Soviet Union. Reform must not threaten communist party rule or adherence to the Soviet way.

In domestic terms, the late 1950s saw renewed collectivization of agriculture, albeit with more inducements and less compulsion. In Romania, state or cooperative farms covered under 31 percent of agricultural land in 1956, but nearly 84 percent in 1960; in Czechoslovakia the growth was from 48 percent to 87 percent. Only Poland and Yugoslavia stood out against the trend, with less than one-eighth of farmland collectivized by 1960.[16] These two countries are reminders that the Soviet bloc was still not a monolith. Indeed, Tito's reforms of the early 1950s constituted an example for the whole region. Two Yugoslav expedients were widely, if partially, emulated: devolution within the planned economy to give local enterprises more discretion and, related to this, a greater role for "workers' self-management."

Yet this was mostly tinkering. Even in Yugoslavia, theoreticians of radical reform, notably Milovan Djilas with his talk of the "withering away" of the Leninist state, were reined in once the thaw with Moscow began—indicating that Tito's revisionism was largely a bid for Western financial aid (to the tune of $1.2 billion between 1949 and 1955) during his own cold war with

Moscow. In most of these communist states, the basic problems of the command economy persisted, political liberties were still denied, and agriculture remained a disaster area. Moreover, some of the trumpeted achievements of communist rule were legacies of earlier times. Only Bulgaria had a free national health service, instituted in 1951. Elsewhere, health care was based on prewar contributory systems for employees. These systems were under serious strain by 1960, when most of the population was drawn in following the collectivization of agriculture.

The deficiencies of communism in Eastern Europe stand out starkly in the wake of the 1989 revolutions. It should therefore be emphasized that in the 1950s its achievements were more apparent. Most of Eastern Europe had undergone a dramatic industrial revolution, drawing people from farm to factory and from country to city. By 1965, only in Albania, Romania, and Yugoslavia were more than half the economically active population still engaged in agriculture or forestry. In Hungary, the proportion had fallen from 50 percent in 1950 to under 30 percent by 1965; in Bulgaria the decline was even steeper, from nearly 80 percent to 45 percent.[17] Steady employment in factories and the amenities of urban living represented marked gains for those who remembered peasant poverty and Nazi oppression. Diet improved—less cereals and potatoes, more meat and sugar—and mortality rates declined. By 1960 the statistics for infant deaths in Czechoslovakia were almost comparable to those in Britain. With a party card, the opportunities were even better: "the Party provided the chance of education and of rapid social advancement—the chance, in fact, to cease being peasants."[18] Women also gained from the communist-led industrial revolution, as legal equality was conferred in state constitutions. Women were drawn into full-time, paid employment to a far greater degree than in capitalist states (constituting around half the work force in the USSR and Czechoslovakia by the 1970s). Provision of maternity leave and child-care facilities were also greater than in "the West," and there tended to be a higher proportion of women in professional occupations.[19]

When these social improvements were taken in conjunction with the high growth rates in the USSR and Eastern Europe in the late 1950s, it appeared that communism worked. Hence Khrushchev's famous boast to the West—"We will bury you"—meaning, he said in 1959, that "capitalism would be buried and that Communism would come to replace it."[20]

Communism seemed to be burying religion as well. In most of Eastern Europe in the late 1940s, church lands were expropriated and clergy brought under state supervision through a ministry of religious affairs. Religious education was banned in schools and the state tried to deter the young by making religious affiliation an impediment to career advancement and higher education. The severest intimidation occurred during the Stalinist era of the early 1950s, but the Soviet Union saw a renewed period of repression from 1959 to 1964, when perhaps ten thousand churches were closed (equivalent to half those existing in the immediate postwar period). Orthodox and Protestant leaders were most ready to reach a modus vivendi with the communist state. Metropolitans Alexei of Russia and Justinian of Romania protected their churches by providing verbal support for the regimes. In Czechoslovakia, the Protestant theologian Josef Hromádka became internationally known for his exploration of Christian-Marxist dialogue. He argued that Western capitalist civilization was now morally bankrupt and that "the Soviet people are the bearer and tool of those living and creative motives which are overcoming the problems of the present and forming the structure of future society."[21] It was the Roman Catholic Church, whose antipathy to communism had been reiterated by Pope Pius XII in 1949, that tended to be the most confrontational. Prelates such as Mindszenty in Hungary and Stefan Cardinal Wyszynski in Poland openly criticized the regime and spent years in confinement. But after 1956, most communist governments in Eastern Europe (though not the USSR) were less aggressive. With church power sapped and the young intimidated, the state was usually content to play a waiting game, assuming that religious belief would wither away.

In the 1950s Eastern Europe's endemic nationality problem also seemed on its way to resolution. The successor states created after World War I had been ethnically unstable, with one dominant national group oppressing several others—notably in Yugoslavia, Czechoslovakia, and Poland. But the 1940s saw brutal waves of what would now be called "ethnic cleansing," as the Nazis exterminated the Jews and then the Russians helped evict the Germans. Most of the Jewish populations of Central and Eastern Europe (some six million) were killed in the war. In 1945–1950 perhaps 11.7 million Germans fled or were expelled into the two Germanies—particularly from Poland and Czechoslovakia.[22] These population transfers and the concomitant redrawing of borders, especially Poland's (Map 7), resulted in states that were far more ethnically homogeneous than before 1939. Only 70 percent of the prewar Poland population was Polish; after 1945 only 2 percent was not.[23] Under communist rule the aim was "national homogenization," reflecting a genuine desire to transcend the ruinous "bourgeois nationalism" of the past. In Yugoslavia, the most polyglot state, Tito (the son of a Croat father and a Slovene mother) created a new federal structure to offset traditional Serb dominance. In 1952 he said that the creation of "a single Yugoslav nation, in which our five peoples would become a single nation" was his "greatest aspiration."[24] Even in Germany, it seemed that the national question was finally being solved, albeit by division and not unification.

Germany: East and West

East Germany (the German Democratic Republic, or GDR) was a special case within the Soviet bloc. Although the GDR was established in 1949, Stalin's government equivocated as to whether it was a former enemy or a budding ally.[25] Eastern Germany was the main target for Soviet reparations, amounting to perhaps seven-eights of the total extracted from Europe as a whole. Immediately after 1945 the Soviets dismantled about a quarter of eastern Germany's prewar industrial capacity. Thereafter they secured deliveries from current production equivalent to 20 or 30 percent of East German GNP. This drain had a devastating effect on growth and living standards in the GDR, leading to a major balance of payments crisis in 1952–1953. At the same time, although the Socialist Unity Party (SED) was in full control by 1948, communism was only slowly implemented in the GDR. In 1950, private production still accounted for 43 percent of East German output; in 1953, barely 30 percent of agricultural land was under state or collective farms. Part of the problem was that eastern Germany was not a viable state. Before the war it had thrived as part of a unified German economy but now lacked essentials such as hard coal and iron and steel capacity. Even its border was not secure: by the end of 1951 nearly five hundred thousand people had moved west, out of a population of nineteen million. Nor had the Soviet leadership decided firmly whether it considered the GDR a new socialist state or a staging post to a reunified Germany on the right terms. Its German policy was reactive to that of the West.

The crucial stimulus was the U.S. decision to rearm the Federal Republic of Germany (FRG). The Pentagon (like the British military) had advocated this in the late 1940s, but what made the idea practical politics was the outbreak of the Korean War in June 1950. The fear throughout NATO was that Western Europe might be next on Stalin's list. With only twelve active divisions and no credible war plan, NATO expected to pull back quickly to the Pyrenees. In panicky Bonn, the FRG capital, plans were made to evacuate the government; members of the German parliament cornered local supplies of cyanide capsules. In these circumstances, the rearmament of West Germany seemed essential. The Truman administration made it the condition of America's readiness to turn NATO into a real military alliance, with a U.S. commander and four new American combat divisions. The British Labour government consented, though privately admitting "no enthusiasm,"[26] but the real obstacle was France, still terrified of German aggression. Out of Franco-American deliberations emerged the compromise idea of a European Defense Community (EDC), in which a new German army would exist only as part of an integrated European force. The details took months to thrash out (and the idea eventually collapsed in 1954), but by the spring of 1952 NATO appeared to have agreed on the essentials as part of plans for a one-hundred-division army (twelve of them West German) in Western Europe by the end of 1954. It was in an effort to head off ratification of the EDC and West German rearmament that the Soviets reopened the question of German reunification.

In March and April 1952, Stalin's government addressed diplomatic notes to the Western allies, calling for a German peace treaty. This would create a united Germany that was rearmed but neutral. Although probably not a "missed opportunity" for reunification, as some German scholars and pundits argued during the cold war, it was certainly a serious offer from Stalin and had much appeal within West Germany.[27] The Allied governments concurred that this was a tactical ploy "intended solely to obstruct the building of the new Europe," to quote Dean Acheson, the U.S. secretary of state,[28] and they pushed ahead with the EDC treaty, which was signed on May 27. Significantly, the day before this happened, the GDR government announced its intent to seal the inner German border with what became a real iron curtain of barbed wire and minefields. In some cases, this cut right through existing settlements: in Mödlareuth, near the Bavarian border, the village green was in the FRG and the duck pond in the GDR. The SED party congress in July 1952 proclaimed unequivocally that "the construction of socialism has become the fundamental mission in the GDR."[29]

Even then, the door had not completely closed on reunification. The new program only exacerbated the GDR's economic crisis, and in 1953 emigration increased to 331,000 (mostly via Berlin). During the thaw after Stalin's death in March 1953, Beria and Malenkov unilaterally reversed the GDR's Sovietization campaign as part of the "New Course" reforms. Indeed, Beria was apparently willing to allow German unification in return for neutrality, because of his concern about the long-term cost of propping up the rickety GDR, particularly now the H-bomb made Eastern Europe seem less important for Soviet security.[30] He was also secretly encouraging opponents of the hard-line German leader, Walter Ulbricht, whose precipitate socialism was, he believed, destabilizing East Germany. "All we want is a peaceful Germany," he insisted, "and it makes no difference whether or not it is socialist."[31] Khrushchev and Molotov took a more conventional view of Germany's importance, not least because of the price paid to defeat it in 1945. They were also more ideological. The claim that Beria favored "handing over 18 million Germans to the rule of American imperialists" was one of the main charges at his trial.[32]

The debate in Moscow remains unclear. What is evident is that the "New Course" that it had imposed on East Germany took the lid off popular disaffection. In riots and protests in three hundred fifty towns and villages in mid-June 1953, half a million people (about 3 percent of the population) took to the streets. The SED leaders panicked—"this is not a Politburo but a madhouse," wrote one German minister—and the Soviets had to impose martial law in East Berlin.[33] Fearful that East Germany might go West, the Kremlin leaders decided they had no choice but to shore up Ulbricht and his regime. By March 1954, the Soviet Union had recognized the GDR as a sovereign state. At the same time, reparations were phased out, occupation costs were scaled down, and the Soviets started to pour substantial aid into the GDR. Wages and living standards began to improve significantly. In the late 1950s further socialist measures, notably the collectivization of agriculture, were belatedly accomplished.

Having come close to losing their part of Germany in 1953, the Soviets concluded that division (however costly) was the best course, even though re-unification remained the ostensible goal. This was also the view in Washington, London, and Paris. As British Foreign Office Minister Selwyn Lloyd noted privately in June 1953:

> To unite Germany while Europe is divided, if practical, is fraught with danger for all. Therefore everyone—Dr. Adenauer, the Russians, the Americans, the French and ourselves—feel in our hearts that a divided Germany is safer for the time being. But none of us dare say so openly because of the effect upon German public opinion. Therefore we all publicly support a united Germany, each on his own terms.[34]

None of the powers was obliged to practice what it preached until 1989–1990. Only then did German reunification occur, on West German terms.

The success of that policy owed much to the founding work of Konrad Adenauer, the Federal Republic's first chancellor, from 1949 to 1963. Initially, however, Adenauer seemed like a caretaker. In the 1949 elections his Christian Democratic Party (CDU) won only 31 percent of the vote, less than 2 percent ahead of the other main party, the Social Democrats (SPD), and Adenauer was elected chancellor in the Bundestag by only one vote—his own! (Asked later whether he had voted for himself, he replied, "Naturally—anything else would have been hypocrisy.")[35] Adenauer had made his name back in the 1920s as a reforming mayor of Cologne who was then sacked by the Nazis. He was already seventy-three years old when he assumed the chancellorship, and his doctor advised that his health could probably sustain only a year or two in office. In early 1951, with Adenauer's approval rating under 30 percent in the opinion polls, many felt his hold on power was tenuous.

Much of his weakness was due to the artificial and precarious character of the Federal Republic itself at this time. Nearly one-fifth of the country's population in 1950 were expellees (*Vertriebenen*) from the territories lost to Poland in 1945 and from countries like Czechoslovakia that had evicted them after the war. The expellees formed a powerful and embittered bloc in West German politics, especially within Adenauer's own CDU party. And they contributed to West Germany's economic and social problems. Even though the economy had improved from the days of ruin, famine, and barter in 1945–1947, unemployment was running at over 12 percent in early 1950. (Of the unemployed, nearly one-third were expellees.) Twenty percent of housing units had been destroyed in the war and these losses had not been made good by 1950. Even people who had roofs over their heads scarcely lived in luxury: two-thirds of households had no living room and less than half had access to a bath. The Federal Republic's economic problems were exacerbated by Allied controls over German industry, originally imposed as part of the demilitarization program after the war. The dismantling of major German industrial plants continued in 1949–1950 to appease French fears: in November 1949 the vast Hermann Göring steel works, a wartime showpiece, were closed at the cost of over three thousand jobs. Removing these and other constraints on German sovereignty was one of Adenauer's prime objectives.

The Korean War boom played a vital part in West Germany's transformation. The United States, and NATO in general, needed the FRG's steel, chemicals, and industrial machinery. Much of this was for export, turning a trade deficit of one billion dollars in 1949 into a surplus of two hundred million dollars by 1953. At home, wages began to rise, and the increase in national income and tax revenues helped fund a vast housing program in the 1950s. The expellees contributed significantly to this recovery, both as labor and consumers. During the 1950s, the economy was growing at 7 or 8 percent each year. By 1959 West Germany was producing nearly one-fifth of world exports of manufactured goods. This was trumpeted as the German "economic miracle," but in fact the years 1945–1950 were the real aberration, when zonal divisions and ruined transport networks had strangled commerce. Once communications were restored, the FRG could utilize its substantial spare capacity, both in plant and manpower. In 1959, Adenauer's Germany was occupying roughly the same position in the world economy as that of the kaiser's Germany in 1913—once more the powerhouse of Europe.

NATO's security crisis during the early 1950s also helped West Germany throw off Allied restrictions. Adenauer used the American desire to rearm Germany as a way of extracting concessions on the issue of sovereignty. The 1954 German Treaty, signed in parallel with agreements on admitting the FRG to NATO, made the FRG almost a sovereign state. Almost, but not quite. The Western Allies still enjoyed residual military rights, including bases and training areas on German soil, and the FRG's armed forces were committed entirely to NATO. The government also renounced so-called ABC weapons—atomic, biological, and chemical. Nevertheless, on May 5, 1955, almost exactly ten years since the Third Reich collapsed, Adenauer could proclaim that the Allied occupation was at an end.

Recovery of Germany's prosperity and status transformed Adenauer's political position. He won greatly increased majorities over the SPD in 1953 and 1957, gaining over 50 percent of the vote in the latter election. Between 1956 and 1961 he was able to rule without his former coalition partners, the Free Democrats (FDP). Despite the decline of the SPD and the FDP, overall the 1950s saw the consolidation of democracy in Germany. In 1949, ten parties won seats in the Bundestag, evoking worrying memories of the splinter politics that had undermined the Weimar Republic. Gradually, however, the small parties were absorbed, and by 1961 there were only three main groupings in the Bundestag—the CDU and its Bavarian ally, the Christian Social Union (CSU), the SPD, and the FDP. Political stability had been achieved.

Adenauer never formally accepted the division of his country or the loss of territory, but his priority was binding the free part of Germany into the Western Alliance (*Westbindung*). Whereas Kurt Schumacher and the SPD insisted on following up any chance to recover German unity, such as the Soviet proposals of 1952–1953, Adenauer was adamant that "the reunification of Germany could not be attained with Soviet help," but only "through the Western Allies."[36] A vehement anticommunist, Adenauer also saw the Soviet Union as a racial threat. "Asia stands on the Elbe," he warned in 1946.[37] Alliance with the only other superpower, America, and détente with the old enemy, France, were therefore vital to guarantee Germany's peace and liberty. As a Catholic and a Rhinelander, it was natural for him to look west; whereas Schumacher was a Prussian, for whom Germany's dismemberment was a personal tragedy. Adenauer, in fact, saw "Prussianism" as the root of what had been wrong with Germany before—"excessive nationalism, militarism and political centralization"—and he considered Schumacher's SPD as essentially a "Prussian" party.[38] As the postwar Germany sought to recover its strength and also transcend its past, Adenauer was convinced that nationalism had to be suffused with internationalism. "One must give the people a new ideology," he told his cabinet in February 1952, and "that can only be a European one."[39]

West Germany's ideological vacuum was exceptional. But all the FRG's neighbors found answers to their economic and political needs in European integration. The European Economic Community (EEC), created in January 1958, was no federalist pipe dream, but a calculated response to the postwar challenges of capitalism, nationalism, and interdependence.

Western Europe: Capitalism, Welfare, and Integration

Between 1948 and 1971, world industrial production increased by an average of 5.6 percent each year. Nothing of the sort had been seen before in history.[40] Despite major exceptions, such as sub-Saharan Africa, this was truly a global phenomenon whose vast and varied impacts will be a central theme of subsequent chapters. But although East Asia and the Soviet bloc in Eastern Europe were part of this boom, its center were the developed capitalist economies of "the West." Among these, America's growth rates were consistently slower, and Japan's boom started later. In the 1950s, noncommunist Europe surged ahead, with the six countries that formed the EEC in the vanguard. Explanations for their vitality remain controversial—not least because the debate has implications for understanding the sluggishness of the 1970s. In the broadest sense, however, Western Europe was "catching up" with the United States, both in general industrialization and in the creation of a consumer society sustained by rising incomes. This process had been delayed and disrupted by the depression and two world wars. But from the early 1950s to the mid-1970s, demand seemed insatiable, first for housing, then for consumer goods such as automobiles, refrigerators, and TVs.

The distinguishing features of this quarter-century, compared with previous decades, were high rates of investment, unparalleled growth in international trade, and very little unemployment. The latter was the most striking for ordinary people, especially those old enough to remember the 1930s depression. The average unemployment rate in Western Europe during the 1950s was 2.9 percent; in the following decade it was only 1.5 percent.[41] This was effectively "full employment." The main structural consequences were the decline of agriculture as a percentage of the work force, increased industrial productivity through new technology and more efficient use of labor, and the growth of a service sector to accommodate rising consumer aspirations. (The number employed in hairdressing salons in France tripled between 1952 and 1958.) Considerable national variations were apparent, of course. More agrarian countries on the European periphery, such as Greece or Ireland, saw a substantial shift to industrial as well as service employment during this period because their own industrialization was only now taking off. Even within the Six, patterns varied. In 1955, Belgium was already highly industrialized, with agriculture accounting for under one-tenth of the work force. In contrast, French agriculture employed over 25 percent (the EEC average) and Italy's 39 percent in 1955, respectively double and triple the percentages remaining in 1970.[42] Timings differed as well, with Germany's "miracle" starting around 1950 and Italy's only in 1958. Nevertheless, the long-term trend was everywhere the same: rural depopulation, greater productivity, and a consumer boom.

What this meant in the lives of ordinary people will be examined in Chapters 5 and 9. My concern here is with the political and economic structures of developed Western Europe, because the patterns laid down in the 1950s were decisive for subsequent decades.

First of all, these were unequivocally *capitalist* societies. That outcome had been by no means certain in the chaotic mid-1940s, when Europe's lurch to the left was at its most pronounced. Britain and France saw substantial nationalization of industry in 1945–1948, with banking, energy, and transport the main targets. The French also experimented with economic planning in 1946, under the aegis of Jean Monnet, targeting key sectors of heavy industry for investment, raw materials and growth. The Dutch established their own Central Planning Bureau in 1947. In Scandinavia, the theme was "socialization of consumption, not production."[43] Here the Social Democrats concentrated on expanding social services in a pattern that became familiar across Western Europe. Underlying all these efforts was a widespread expectation that the prize of war would at least be a significant redistribution of wealth. By the late 1940s, however, the focus had changed. Communists had been driven out of government and socialists were on the defensive because of the cold war. Governments and the middle classes also became seriously concerned over the consequences of postwar inflation; tough policies to restrict the money supply and balance the budgets were pushed through by finance ministers such as René Mayer in France and Luigi Einaudi in Italy. A series of devaluations in late 1949, starting with Britain, also helped stabilize exchange rates at more realistic levels. These deflationary policies, though the work of centrist European governments, were encouraged by the United States. And they reflected growing endorsement of what has been called "the politics of productivity," namely the American conviction that economic growth was a better way than redistribution to promote social and political harmony.[44] Put simply: instead of haggling over shares of the cake, bake a bigger cake and then everyone will gain.

Although capitalism was the name of the game, it was a capitalism significantly different in character from that of the United States. Not in the degree of concentration, because on both sides of the Atlantic large corporations now dominated national economies. But in Western Europe corporate capitalism was part of mixed economies. In these, the state sector played a significant role, such as the postwar nationalized industries in France (where the government employed one-tenth of the work force) or the "special agencies" that were a legacy of fascist Italy, notably the Institute for Industrial Reconstruction (IRI), which employed over two hundred thousand people in steel, engineering, shipbuilding and other state industries.

Even where "social ownership" was not widely practiced, as in West Germany, there was a commitment to social justice. For the German CDU, the slogan was the "Social Market Economy." The market would be regulated to avoid monopolies and cartels; equally, the people would be cushioned against market forces through social insurance against accident, illness, unemployment, and old age.

This so-called welfare state became a characteristic of postwar industrial societies, but it had been well established in Western Europe before 1914 except in France and Italy (where the Catholic Church still played a major role in caring for the sick and the aged). In North America, however, it originated during the Great Depression. Moreover, most West European states that had not already done so introduced health insurance systems immediately after 1945; in Canada this did not happen until 1972, while the United States consistently rejected the idea.[45]

In general, the United States and Canada (like Australia) followed the "liberal" model of welfare, emphasizing private insurance programs, with state benefits means tested to reach only the poor. At the other extreme was the social-democratic pattern of Scandinavia, characterized by universal benefits at fairly high levels. Here the state was replacing the family as well as the market in welfare provision. In between were so-called corporatist systems, notably France, Italy, and West Germany, which replaced the market but not the family. In these countries, status differentials were preserved, and voluntary organizations, especially the Catholic Church, assisted the family and the state.[46] These are, of course, broad patterns, and many states did not conform to a single model. Britain, for example, combined market features such as means-tested benefits with universal access to a National Health Service.[47] But overall, the welfare state, as part of managed capitalism, was a feature of postwar Western Europe.

Another theme was social continuity. The campaigns initiated in the mid-1940s to punish Nazis and their collaborators petered out within a few years. One reason was the cold war, which shifted attention to the threat from the left. But denazification, like the campaigns for national "cleansing" in France and Italy, ran into two basic problems: the significant culprits had the wealth and clout to protect themselves, and their continued tenure in administrative or commercial posts was deemed essential for the smooth running of the country. In Hitler's Germany, for instance, one person in every six (twelve million in all) had been a member of the Nazi party. For many, such as teachers or postmen, it was a condition of holding their job. Even the Americans, the most zealous denazifiers among the Allied powers, confessed defeat by 1948. They had caught mostly small fry, while the big fish had dived to safety, or even resurfaced. Hans Globke, an official of the Reich Interior Ministry in the 1930s, became Adenauer's principal aide. Likewise in Italy, in 1960 all but two of sixty-four regional prefects and every one of the 135 local police chiefs had been fascist functionaries.[48] In all these countries, the continuity of wartime personnel was to become an acrimonious issue in the 1960s, as part of a radical critique of the structural conservatism of Germany, Italy, and France.

Not merely social continuity but political convergence was the trend of the 1950s. In Germany and, even more, Italy, the dominant political force was Christian Democracy—also influential in the first postwar decade in France through the Mouvement Républicain Populaire. Since the French Revolution, Catholics had been widely identified with conservatism and even authoritarianism; this remained true in Franco's Spain. Christian Democracy, however, was a sign that "after a century and a half of indecision," Catholics had "reconciled themselves to political democracy."[49] From the other side, their old enemies, the socialists, gradually threw off their narrow class identity as workers' parties wedded to the dictatorship of the proletariat, albeit by peaceful means. By the late 1950s, particularly in Scandinavia, West Germany, Austria, and Holland, they had become social democratic parties "from which all the axioms of working-class socialism had been expunged."[50] More was involved than mere convergence, however. Both Catholic conservatives and socialist workers were emerging from their sectional, almost ghettolike politics of the interwar years to become mass parties with broad appeal. Increasingly, left and right found a modus vivendi around the doctrines of managed capitalism and the welfare state. In Austria, social democrats and Christian socialists even formed a "grand coalition" that lasted from 1949 to 1966. Their attempt to avoid repeating the Catholic-socialist rift of the 1930s included a sharing of jobs in government and state industries. This was "consociational democracy"—based on a formalized pact between social groups.

Out of an economic and social consensus unknown to interwar Europe grew a new political stability—linked to a remarkable renaissance of the democratic nation-state. After World War I, democracy had been on the defensive. European governments had found it hard to win the support of their newly enfranchised masses, seduced in an era of economic and political turmoil by the authoritarianisms of right and left. Such democracies often collapsed from within—Germany in 1930–1933 or France between 1936 and 1940. The 1950s, however, saw the democratic nation-state win new popularity in Western Europe. In part, admittedly, it was a product of undemocratic means. The combination of social continuity and state interventionism created vast opportunities for political corruption, exploited especially by the Christian Democrats in Italy. Stability was also sometimes hard won. Whereas West Germany quickly transcended the Weimar-like factionalism of 1949, the French Fourth Republic (1947–1958) was a replay of the last decade of the Third, with eighteen different cabinets and a total of 348 days without any government.[51] Such was the havoc wrought by weak executive power and a profusion of feuding parties sustained by extreme proportional representation. Only after May 1958, when the Algerian crisis enabled de Gaulle to set his own terms for a return to power, was France able to establish strong executive government.

Despite corruption, confusion, and autocracy, however, the democratic nation-states of Western Europe really earned their new legitimacy by responding far more successfully than in the depression decade to the economic aspirations of their citizens.[52] The "right to welfare" became for the postwar generation what the right to vote had been for their parents or grandparents. Social spending, broadly conceived (including education and housing), rose from 25 percent of GNP in 1950 to 45 percent in the mid-1970s. "Economic growth" became the other great slogan of the era, and often the touchstone of electoral success. Even if some countries, like Germany, adopted explicit Keynesianism only slowly, the underlying axiom of managed capitalism was that government could and should manipulate the market by using its regulatory and spending powers.

This axiom was called into question in the 1980s (Chapter 13). What matters here are some basic assumptions. First, welfare and growth were reciprocally related: growth paid for welfare, welfare justified growth. Both in turn, depended on "full employment." This made growth possible and welfare affordable. Once growth slowed and unemployment increased, from the early 1970s on, the welfare state also came into question. Secondly, although national governments were both the ostensible guides of the economy and also the political beneficiaries of its success, they could not operate alone in conditions of growing economic and political interdependence. This is why the reassertion of the nation-state was closely linked with progress in European integration.

At the heart of that integration was the continuing "German problem." Could West Germany act as the engine of European recovery without becoming, again, a menace to the continent's peace? For France, this dilemma was particularly acute. The shift in France's German policy from repression to integration had begun when Georges Bidault was foreign minister (Chapter 1), but it was dramatically signaled by his successor, Robert Schuman, in his call on May 9, 1950 for France and West Germany to pool their coal and steel production in a supranational community that other European states could join. The architect of the Schuman Plan was Jean Monnet, who had had masterminded the French modernization scheme of 1947. Access to German raw materials was critical for France's industrial recovery: 70 percent of the coke used by the French steel industry, for instance, was imported, mostly from Germany and, in effect, "the Schuman Plan was invented to save the Monnet Plan."[53] Adenauer—like his Italian counterpart, Alcide de Gasperi—saw all proposals for European integration as ways of binding their countries into the West and regaining equal international rights after wartime defeat. Both therefore responded rapidly to Schuman's initiative. Belgium, Luxembourg, and the Netherlands could not afford to be left outside such a group. In any case, having been caught in the jaws of Franco-German antagonism twice in thirty years, they welcomed any proposal, to quote the Dutch Foreign Ministry, "for Europe to profit by Germany's strength without being threatened by it."[54] There were also straightforward economic benefits. Subsidies for Belgium's declining coal mines and for Italy's emerging steel industry were features of the ensuing negotiations.

The European Coal and Steel Community, which came into operation in July 1952, therefore reflected calculations of national interest on all sides. Integration was a hard-headed decision by individual governments. They all subsequently succeeded in whittling down international control over their own industries. Yet underlying the ECSC was a genuine internationalism, particularly for Adenauer, Schuman, and de Gasperi, who all came from long-contested borderlands of Western Europe. De Gasperi's youth was spent in the Trentino, in the extreme northeast of Italy, when it was still under Austrian control. He attended university in Vienna and had been a deputy in the Austrian parliament before the First World War. Similarly, both Adenauer (a Rhinelander) and Schuman (whose home was Lorraine) came from border regions bitterly contested by France and Germany. Lorraine was under German control between 1870 and 1918 and Schuman had been obliged to fight in the *German* army in World War I. None of this made Adenauer, Schuman, or de Gasperi any less patriotic, but it did make them acutely aware of the plasticity of national boundaries. For all three, German was their lingua franca. Moreover, as Catholics they shared a sense of the historic unity of Catholic Christendom, which antedated the era of nation-states. Their Europeanism was therefore an expression of conviction and culture as well as calculation.

In retrospect, the movement for European integration seems like a juggernaut, carrying all before it to the Treaty of Rome in March 1957, which formed the European Economic Community. In reality, the momentum was faltering, the direction erratic. In 1953 both Schuman and de Gasperi were supplanted by less Europeanist successors. Monnet's hasty attempt to apply his integrationist formula to Germany's military revival—the European Defense Community—was overturned in 1954 by a French Assembly increasingly dominated by Gaullists and communists. Even the Coal and Steel Community proved a failure. Monnet had feared a steel glut and a coal shortage: in fact, German industrial recovery absorbed the steel capacity of France and its other neighbors, while cheap U.S. imports filled the anticipated coal gap. By the end of the 1950s, the ECSC had virtually collapsed as a regulatory force. Moreover, coal was losing its central importance in peace and war, because of the growing use of oil and atomic power. In 1960 solid fuel accounted for only 48 percent of the ECSC's primary energy consumption, compared with 82 percent in 1950. Significantly, by 1955 Monnet's enthusiasm had shifted toward creating a European atomic energy authority. In short, to quote the historian John Gillingham, "the once feared coal weapon was now fit only for a heraldic museum." But, he added, the ECSC "was nonetheless a latter-day equivalent to the American Articles of Confederation—a forerunner to a far stronger and more permanent union."[55]

If 1957 was Europe's 1787, that was in large measure due to the determination of the Belgian, Dutch, and Luxembourg governments. Their three foreign ministers—Paul-Henri Spaak, Johan Willem Beyen, and Joseph Bech—had drawn up the Benelux customs union of 1948; in the mid-1950s they applied similar ideas to Western Europe as a whole. Initially, Beyen was the real enthusiast for a common market—Dutch agriculture and industry were anxious to break into protected neighboring markets—whereas Spaak was at first keener about an integrated transport network. But they shared the conviction that renewed integration was the key to peace and prosperity, and in June 1955 they persuaded the foreign ministers of the Six to establish a committee under Spaak "to make further progress towards building Europe . . . first of all in the economic field."[56] National bargaining was, as ever, much in evidence. To keep the French happy, the Spaak committee took up Monnet's Euratom proposals as well as the idea of a common market. The German Economics Ministry, under Ludwig Erhard, disliked the idea of a tight bond with protectionist France, envisaging Germany's economic future in a larger free-trade area including Britain and Scandinavia, and it feared the Six would become "an island of disintegration in a world that had in the meantime become free."[57] But for Adenauer, European integration was a political, not an economic, issue: the means were secondary to the end. And, since Euratom attracted no one but the French, the chancellor put his weight behind the common market idea.

To get France on board, however, significant concessions had to be made—much to Dutch dismay. The supranational authority was played down, the five agreed to upgrade their welfare measures to French levels (to reduce competitive advantage), and France's overseas territories were included on equal terms. But these concessions were not the only reasons for growing French enthusiasm. The way that the Americans stopped the Suez operation in its tracks dramatized the limits of France's national power. "Europe will be your revenge," Adenauer supposedly told French premier Guy Mollet the day the operation was halted.[58] Mollet acknowledged that it was necessary "to develop relations between Europe and America on a basis of equality," and his ministers told critics that a united Europe was the only guarantee against similar humiliations in the future.[59] In July 1957, Maurice Faure, one of France's EEC negotiators, warned the French Assembly bluntly that it was a "fiction" to talk of Britain and France as members of the Big Four. "There are," he said, "not four Great Powers, there are two: America and Russia. There will be a third by the end of the century: China. It depends on you whether there will be a fourth: Europe."[60]

Although these geopolitical arguments were compelling, the EEC also embodied a genuine and growing economic unity among the Six. In the 1950s Germany resumed its prewar role as the main supplier of capital goods, such as steel, machinery, and transport equipment, to the rest of Europe—a role temporarily played by America just after the war. Germany's booming economy was also a major market for its neighbors, attracting at least 10 percent of their exports (20 percent in the case of the Dutch). Thus "German manufactured exports grew in a modernizing symbiosis with the exports of other western European economies,"[61] of which the Benelux countries and, later in the 1950s, Italy were particularly important. It was to avoid isolation from this nexus that the French agreed to modify their traditional protectionism. But the effect of the concessions made to them was to create a dynamic yet distinctly protectionist bloc *among the Six*, who rapidly abolished their own internal tariffs while raising a common tariff barrier against the outside world. In 1960, the EEC generated a quarter of world industrial production and two-fifths of world trade.

Within a few years the EEC had become the focal point of Western Europe. Those states left outside the Six were peripheral, both metaphorically and literally.

This was particularly true of Spain and Portugal. Economic isolation had been the deliberate policy of General Francisco Franco (1892–1976) since he seized power in 1939 at the end of the Spanish Civil War, but it also reflected Spain's loss of export markets and foreign exchange during World War II. In 1950 national income was still below the level of 1935, while prices had risen sixfold.[62] Although some American aid in the 50s—the payoff for Cold War bases—helped alleviate food shortages, inflation remained serious, and attempts at liberalization were only piecemeal for most of the decade. Moreover, Franco's dictatorship was ostracized from NATO and from the EEC, as he discovered when reluctantly applying for membership in 1962. Portugal was also an authoritarian regime, ruled since 1933 by a former economics professor, Antonio Salazar (1889–1970). But he managed to avoid the extreme isolation of Spain by retaining a form of parliamentary government and by cooperating with the Allies in World War II. Consequently, Portugal was a recipient of Marshall aid and a founder member of NATO. But it, too, was politically unacceptable to the EEC. Both Spain and Portugal remained on the margins of Europe until their economic miracles in the 1960s and their political conversions in the 1970s.

Britain's reaction to the Six was particularly significant. In retrospect, it is tempting to write the history of postwar Britain as one of steady decline. Yet the country had recovered dramatically at mid-century, assisted by the devaluation of 1949. By 1952 British trade with the dollar area was balanced, in contrast with the dollar gap that had made Britain so reliant on American loans during the 1940s. Growth rate was 3 percent and in 1951 British industry produced more than France and Germany combined. There was, however, a darker side to this impressive picture. British strength was largely a reflection of others' weakness: Germany and Japan were barely beginning to recover in 1950. Britain's export performance was particularly strong in markets protected by imperial preference or within the sterling area—in other words, with countries tied to Britain by special commercial or exchange arrangements. Although some sectors of British industry were dynamic, such as chemicals and electronics, success in the war discouraged radical efforts at modernization and consolidation, particularly in traditional industries such as shipbuilding and textiles. And invisible earnings, which had paid for one-third of Britain's imports in the 1930s, were now only half as significant because of the sale of foreign assets during the war.[63]

In other words, Britain's competitive advantage was temporary. As Germany recovered, it faced the same economic challenge as France. But the British response was very different. The Labour government declined the invitation to discuss the Schuman Plan in 1950; the Conservatives sent only an "observer" to the Spaak committee in 1955, and he was soon withdrawn. In part, the reasoning was economic. Half Britain's trade was with the Sterling Area, only one-quarter with the Six. The government's growth strategy for the 1950s was to develop the dollar-earning capacity of its overseas possessions, calculating (wrongly) that the Korean War boom in commodity prices would continue while European industry was sluggish. Britain's political imperatives were also very different. Detached from the continent, it lacked the Six's interest in resolving the German question. Victorious in war, it was less ready to sacrifice sovereignty for the sake of security than those countries which had been invaded and occupied. Federalism was therefore anathema: in the inimitable mixed metaphor of Ernest Bevin, Labour's foreign secretary, "if you open that Pandora's box you never never know what Trojen [sic] 'orses will jump out."[64] Wartime experience also strengthened the sense of alignment with America and the Commonwealth, reducing Europe to the "third circle" of British interests. Churchill, prime minister again in 1951–1955, believed in a united Europe "for them, but not for us"—as a way of bringing France and Germany together.[65] And whereas Suez made French policy more European, the British worked to rebuild what they called their "special relationship" with the United States.

Thus, there seemed many compelling reasons for Britain to go its own way. In any case, the British doubted that the French and Germans would reach agreement in 1956, underestimating Adenauer's readiness to make economic concessions for political gain. British attempts to create a larger European Free Trade Area (EFTA) including the Six had also fallen foul of this new Franco-German axis by the end of 1958, and the British prime minister, Harold Macmillan, had no doubt that de Gaulle was "bidding high for the hegemony of Europe."[66] Eventually, a rump EFTA was created in 1960 as a loose free-trade area in industrial goods, excluding agriculture and with no pretensions to political union. The seven members were disparate in character: Portugal was a dictatorship with a small industrial base, Austria maintained its tradition of high tariffs. Switzerland and Sweden were, like Britain, low-tariff industrial economies that relied heavily on imports, but Denmark and Norway, though similar, retained some nontariff barriers to protect their own industries. Holding the seven together were trading links to Britain and, most of all, a common belief that they needed to form a united opposition to the EEC. By 1960 Western Europe, in the contemporary joke, was truly at Sixes and Sevens.

The Bomb and the Wall

German recovery and the creation of the EEC were signs of the resurgence of Western Europe. In other ways, too, not all of Europe was submerged in the cold war divide. Switzerland, for instance, though in the heart of Europe, remained studiously neutral—as ready to profit from Europe's new peace as it had from its earlier war. In May 1955, the four occupying powers agreed to withdraw from Austria, as part of a deal to make it independent but nonaligned. The Austrian State Treaty was the residue of the Beria plan for Germany. For Austria, like Sweden, neutrality did not preclude EFTA membership. In the Balkans, Tito was playing both sides in the cold war; Finland, formerly part of the Tsarist empire, managed to maintain the independence it had secured at great cost in the war with Russia in 1941–1944. Even NATO membership did not bring equal commitments: Norway and Denmark avoided having U.S. bases on their soil for fear of antagonizing the Soviet Union.

In these and other ways, Europe blurred the harsh lines of bipolarity. But, when all is said and done, in strategic terms there remained only two Europes—West and East—and superpower dominance of each bloc increased as the 1950s went on.

In the East, this took the form of the Warsaw Pact—the Western name for the treaty organization formed in May 1955 in antithesis to NATO. The immediate reasons for the Soviet Union's pulling its satellites into a more coordinated structure were two international developments that same month—West Germany's admission to NATO, which the USSR saw as a threatening act, and the Austrian State Treaty, which removed the justification for keeping Soviet troops in Hungary and Romania (to protect its line of communications). But it also satisfied Molotov's old-fashioned definition of territorial security and Khrushchev's aspirations for more effective management of the bloc. In fact, the Warsaw Pact—whatever its image in the West—was, at this stage at least, more a political instrument than a military weapon. Even joint exercises did not start until the 1960s. With several national armies deeply suspect, notably the GDR and also Hungary after 1956, the Soviets' main aim was to enhance political control and justify their own military presence.[67]

NATO was not a coerced alliance. If it constituted an American empire, this was "empire by invitation."[68] Moreover, Washington had not envisaged a permanent military commitment when the North Atlantic Treaty was signed in 1949. Dwight D. Eisenhower, NATO commander in 1951–1953 and then U.S. president until 1961, kept insisting that the American troop presence in Europe was "a stop-gap operation to bring confidence and security to our friends overseas."[69] NATO rearmament, especially in Germany, was intended to replace U.S. troops by the late 1950s. But that strategy was undercut by the growing importance of nuclear weapons after the U.S. and Soviet H-bomb tests of 1952–1954. The world's new fragility inspired Winston Churchill, again British premier though nearing eighty, to press in 1953–1954 for a new international summit to end the Cold War. But his efforts were regarded as appeasement in Washington and Bonn. In any case, the defense of Western Europe was now dependent on nuclear weapons. Only the United States was in a position to match the Soviet Union's conventional strength and its capacity for nuclear blackmail.

As a democracy with a booming consumer sector, the United States could not devote the same proportion of GNP as the Soviets to military expenditure—perhaps 15–20 percent in the Soviet case. After the Korean War, Eisenhower was anxious to rein in military spending, and U.S. strategy was therefore predicated on the threat of "massive retaliation" by nuclear weapons against any Soviet attack on NATO. Moreover, in October 1953 Eisenhower accepted as official doctrine that "in the event of hostilities, the

United States will consider nuclear weapons to be as available for use as other munitions."[70]

Henceforth, NATO's strategy was that a European war would be a nuclear war. In November 1953 the first battlefield nuclear weapons were introduced in Germany, as 280-millimeter nuclear-capable cannon were transported down the Rhine in a blaze of publicity. Additional artillery and aircraft followed in 1954–1955. Britain and, later, Italy were also major bases for American nuclear weaponry. This "nuclearization" of warfare—both at the strategic and tactical levels—helped frustrate American efforts to promote European self-defense: now only the superpowers had the requisite military and economic capability. Britain became a nuclear power in 1952 but by March 1960 the escalating costs of new technology had forced it to abandon its own weapons system and buy American. That decision might have been taken some two years earlier, thus saving many millions of pounds, but for the political and status appeal of retaining an "independent deterrent."[71] The French did develop their own deterrent following their first test in February 1960, but there was never any doubt in private that the defense of France (like that of Western Europe as a whole) depended on the American umbrella.

No doubt in government circles, that is; European public opinion was not so sure. In Britain the Campaign for Nuclear Disarmament (CND), founded in 1958, was the largest spontaneous popular movement in postwar Britain.[72] Its call for unilateral nuclear disarmament split the Labour party and won the support of one-third of the population according to polls in April 1960. The nuclear issue became even more divisive in Germany. When Adenauer told a press conference in April 1957 that tactical nuclear weapons were "nothing more than the further development of artillery," in effect "normal weapons,"[73] he started a row that polarized the German Protestant churches, pushed the SPD and FDP into open opposition to nuclear weapons, and prompted a German version of CND, the Campaign against Atomic Death (*Kampf dem Atomtod*). Some one hundred fifty thousand people attended an antinuclear rally in Hamburg in April 1958.

The prospect of a nuclear-armed West Germany also alarmed the Soviet Union and helped start a new crisis over Berlin. On November 27, 1958, Khrushchev gave the West six months to negotiate a German peace treaty and transform West Berlin into a free city. If not, he warned, the Soviet Union would hand over all its rights in the city, including access, to the GDR government. Khrushchev's ultimatum injected new urgency into great-power discussions about Germany that had continued in a desultory way throughout the 1950s. Although deadlines came and went, in keeping with Khrushchev's erratic nature, the thrust of Soviet diplomacy did not change over the next three years. At stake was the fundamental imbalance between an ever-stronger Federal Republic and the still-weak GDR. Khrushchev genuinely feared a nuclear West Germany; he, and the GDR leader Walter Ulbricht, were also increasingly concerned about the flood of East Germans (particularly the young and educated) through the open border into West Berlin and thence by plane to the Federal Republic. From September 1949 to August 1961 nearly 2.7 million East Germans went west, equivalent to the whole population of Israel or Ireland. The GDR was the only country in the eastern bloc to experience a net decline in population over this period, from 19 million to 17 million.[74] As in 1953, Ulbricht played adroitly on Soviet fears that the GDR regime might collapse and with it the prestige of Khrushchev and the entire socialist camp.[75]

For Khrushchev, Berlin was a lever to force a German settlement that would ensure the security and prosperity of the eastern bloc. (Or, as he once put it, "Berlin is the testicles of the West. Every time I want to make the West scream, I squeeze on Berlin."[76]) For Ulbricht, West Berlin was a prize in itself which he hoped to annex. That would remove the Western cancer within his state and enhance the GDR's prestige. But neither leader got what he wanted. In June 1961, the tension reached new heights as Khrushchev and Kennedy made Berlin the test case of their diplomatic virility. When Ulbricht announced that no one intended to build a wall, the exodus reached new heights—over thirty thousand in July (half of them under twenty-five) and nearly twenty-two thousand in the first twelve days of August.[77] Finally, Khrushchev implemented long-standing plans to seal off East Berlin. As Kennedy admitted, the stakes had become very high: "Khrushchev is losing East Germany. He cannot let that happen. If East Germany goes, so will Poland and all of eastern Europe."[78] For Khrushchev, the wall was the only way to save the bloc.

In the early hours of August 13, GDR troops began erecting barricades and barbed wire along the sector boundary that snaked through the middle of the city. Throughout that hot Sunday crowds on both sides looked on, angry but impotent. The historic Brandenburg Gate, astride Berlin's main east-west axis, became a no man's land (Plate 12). The divide ran just yards east of the still-ruined Reichstag. What the Allied bombers had left of Potsdamerplatz— one of the busiest intersections in Europe in the 1930s—was razed to the ground, to give a clear line of fire. Soon the authorities replaced the barbed wire with a twelve-foot-high concrete wall, flanked by nearly three hundred watchtowers and a maze of ancillary fences.

The SPD mayor of West Berlin, Willy Brandt, condemned the wall as "an outrageous injustice" that turned East Berlin into "a concentration camp."[79] In a letter to Kennedy he warned that West Berlin would become a demoralized ghetto and that "instead of the flight to Berlin, we could experience the beginning of a flight from Berlin."[80] But his appeals were unavailing. The president made clear his determination to defend West Berlin but he would not risk war to reopen East Berlin. "It's not a very nice solution, "he told aides, "but a wall is a hell of a lot better than a war."[81] Within NATO, there was general relief that the crisis had been resolved. As with Germany, so with Berlin: division meant stability. In the bon mot of French writer François Mauriac: "I love Germany so much that I'm glad there are two of them."[82]

For Brandt, the wall was a defining moment. The hope that the West would help reunify Germany had proved an illusion. He said later that "in August 1961 a curtain was drawn aside to reveal an empty stage. . . . [I]t was against this background that my so-called Ostpolitik—the beginning of dé-tente—took shape."[83] That meant coming to terms with the reality of the East German state. For the GDR, the wall was also a turning point. Now that the flood of refugees had slowed to a trickle, Ulbricht felt secure enough to meet Khrushchev's demand for some de-Stalinization. It was the start of the modernization of the GDR into the Soviet bloc's shop window during the 1960s.

Yet the wall was a standing reminder that this was coerced modernization, particularly as the fugitives kept on coming—jumping from windows, cutting the wire, tunneling beneath the wall, even ballooning above it. Those who died making the attempt won immortality, if not freedom. One was eighteen-year-old Peter Fechter, who was left to bleed to death under the wall after being shot by GDR guards in August 1962. Even more than Hungary, the wall symbolized the ideological divide between the two blocs. On June 26, 1963, Kennedy finally visited Berlin, in part to commemorate the fifteenth anniversary of the 1948 Airlift. To a huge crowd at the city hall, looking out over the wall, he recalled the old Roman boast—*Civis romanus sum*—and announced that "today, in the world of freedom, the proudest boast is *Ich bin ein Berliner.*° To those around the world who didn't understand "what is the great issue between the Free World and the Communist world," he re-sponded: "Let them come to Berlin."[84]

°The roar of applause from the crowd was mostly in appreciation of his sentiments, but there was also some amusement because Kennedy should have said *Ich bin Berliner. Ein Berliner* was the local name for a doughnut.

5

Cities and Consumers

Political and military events can usually be described and explained within a short time frame. Most of them, however explosive in impact, have a short fuse and visible fallout. But changes in social and economic life usually follow a slower, less discernible rhythm, so that not merely their significance but their occurrence is clear only much later. Often it takes a sudden social rupture, such as the student and worker protests of 1968, to reveal forces that had been building up under the surface. For this reason, any account of socio-economic change in the postwar world cannot begin simply in 1945. Moreover, many of these changes have barely touched the world's population as a whole; even in North America, Western Europe, and Japan, the impact of modern technologies has been mediated by local geography, history and culture. We must therefore be sensitive to variations of space as well as time.

This chapter is the first of four (Chapters 5, 9, 14, and 17) looking at some of the changes in social life that have occurred since World War II. The focus is on shifts in the fundamentals of human existence, those that distinguish the recent past from previous eras of history. The major themes in this chapter are the demographic revolution— falling death rates and (not so quickly or generally) falling birth dates; the growth of cities and the modernist revolution in architecture; and the automobile suburbs of modern America, which spawned postwar consumer culture. My time frame is roughly the third quarter of the century, and the themes explored here will be incorporated in the subsequent narrative.

Births and Deaths

The most striking demographic fact about the postwar era is sheer numbers. In autumn 1999 the world's population passed six billion. This was unprecedented in history and called into question the earth's "carrying capacity" to sustain so many people. Equally important was the rate of growth. It had taken about a century for the world's population to double from one to two billion by the mid-1920s. But it took only half a century to double again to four billion in 1976, and the five billion mark was exceeded in 1987. Predictions were for nine or ten billion by 2050.

The other important factor was geography. Since the 1960s, most of the population growth has been outside the developed countries. In 1950, Africa's population was half the size of Europe's, by 1985 it had drawn level (480 million), and it was expected to be three times as large by 2025 (1.58 billion to 512 million). Hence the particular concern about a population explosion in the developing world, where states and economies were often less able to cope.[1]

But these familiar statistics are only part of the story. For the period 1950–2000 is, on closer examination, part of a long and complex "demographic transition."[2]

Speaking very broadly, the world has been moving from a pattern of high death rates and high birth rates to one of low death rates and low birth rates. And it has accomplished this, in large part, over the last fifty years. When completed, the result is stable, or even declining, national populations. But mortality rates usually start to decline before the fall in birth rates. In the interim, populations expand substantially until smaller numbers of children become the new norm. Hence the population explosion in the short term.

The demographic transition started first in Western Europe and North America and, despite a postwar "baby boom," was largely complete by 1950. Eastern Europe followed, as well as European Russia and Europeanized parts of Latin America, before the pattern spread to East and Southeast Asia and the rest of the Americas. In South Asia, the transition has been slower and more uneven; in the Middle East and sub-Saharan Africa fertility decline only began in earnest in the 1990s. As significant as the geography of transition is its accelerating pace: what took over a century in Western Europe has happened in two or three decades in Japan, Indonesia, and China. Reasons for the transition also vary, with medical innovations and government policy playing a greater role in the developing world, whereas rising living standards were more important in Europe and North America.[3]

These are broad themes. What do they mean in human terms? Let us begin with the basics—birth and death. Stated simply, children born in the later twentieth century had a far greater chance of living a long and healthy life than their parents, let alone their grandparents. Life expectancy at birth in 1900 was around forty years for continental western Europe and fifty in England, Sweden and the United States, compared with around seventy for all these countries by 1960. In Latin America over the same period, life expectancy doubled from twenty-seven to fifty-six years.[4] The more developed countries of East Asia showed a particularly marked improvement in the postwar period—Japanese life expectancy rose from sixty in 1950 to seventy-six in 1980, South Korea's from fifty-two to sixty-six in 1960–1980.[5] On the other hand, both South Asia and sub-Saharan Africa lagged behind. In Africa, life expectation at birth was around forty-five to forty-seven years in the mid-1970s, comparable with Bangladesh (forty-six), Indonesia (forty-eight) and India (forty-nine).[6] Much of this gain has been achieved by reducing infant mortality, that is deaths among children less than one year old. Table 5.1 gives some selected examples, showing both the rapid general decline and the geographical differences mentioned earlier. In India and Brazil, for instance, in 1975 roughly one child in ten still died before its first birthday, whereas such infant mortality in Western Europe, North America and Japan had become statistically negligible.

The decline in mortality rates has been accompanied by a shift in causes of death. First to be controlled have been the mortality crises caused by famine or epidemics of particularly dangerous diseases such as smallpox, cholera, and typhus. It took longer to curb the respiratory and airborne infectious killers, notably tuberculosis, pneumonia, and influenza (responsible for thirty million deaths in a pandemic after World War I), and childhood diseases, such as measles and meningitis. As contagious diseases were brought under control, circulatory diseases and cancers became the main killers. These now account for 60 to 70 percent of all deaths in the developed world and some 30 percent in those Asian countries where life expectancy exceeds sixty years. Mortality from these diseases reflects the elimination of other killers, but the increase in cancer-related deaths is also due to the commercial promotion of smoking, especially among young men, since World War I.[7]

How has the mortality transition been accomplished? Acute famine mortality caused solely by drought has largely been eliminated by improved distribution of grain. Since 1945, grave food crises have usually been the result of government ineptitude (as in China around 1960) or persistent war (as in

TABLE 5.1 SELECTED INFANT MORTALITY RATES PER ONE THOUSAND LIVE BIRTHS			
	1925	1950	1975
Germany (West)	109	57.0	19.3
United Kingdom	72	32.3	15.6
United States	71	29.9	15.0
Sweden	59	21.8	8.8
Poland	163	107.0	24.7
Soviet Union	178	81.0	35.0
Mexico	213	98.0	52.0
Argentina	114	67.0	44.6
Brazil	172	149.0	92.0
India	241	164.0	110–120
Japan	148	58.0	10.0

SOURCE: Jean-Claude Chesnais, *The Demographic Transition: Stages, Patterns, and Economic Implications,* translated by Elizabeth and Philip Kreager (Oxford: Clarendon, 1992), pp. 58–61.

the Horn of Africa since the 1970s). To date, increasing food supply has kept pace with the rise in population. World output of cereals rose on average by 2.7 percent each year from 1950 to 1990, and cereal yields (that is, output per unit of land under cultivation) grew by 2.25 percent. Annual population growth over this period was 1.9 percent. The main exception to this story was sub-Saharan Africa, where population grew at 3 percent and food production by 2 percent.[8] Serious food shortages in India in the mid-1960s and the steep rise in cereal prices in the mid-1970s, following the first oil crisis, were cause for alarm but did not affect the basic trend. Perhaps the most celebrated explanation is the "green revolution"—the introduction of high-yielding varieties (HYVs) of wheat and rice starting in the mid-1960s. Their short, sturdy stems were able to carry the increased heads of grain resulting from intensive application of fertilizer and water. As this account implies, however, new crops were only part of a more systematic approach to farming. This included the land reform that transformed many Asian countries after World War II, as tenants became small landowners. It also involved the subsequent effects of intensive farming for local business,—providing facilities for storage, milling, transport, and credit.[9] The way cash-crop agriculture mobilized local and then national politics is central to the history of India and many developing countries.

In explaining the decline in killer diseases, demographers differ as to the relative importance of health and wealth—in other words, how much should be ascribed to breakthroughs in medical technologies and how much to improvements in living standards. In Western Europe, smallpox vaccination was vital in the nineteenth century, as were improvements in sanitation and sewerage to help eliminate cholera, but, because of the limits of medical knowledge and practice, simple progress in nutrition, housing, and cleanliness were of perhaps greater value. The developing world has gained from Western experience and from further innovations since the Second World War. Rapid improvements in health could sometimes occur simply with determined imposition of new technologies, such as the measles vaccine first licensed in the United States in 1963 and promoted globally by the World Health Organization (WHO) since 1974. Where there is no vaccination, measles is endemic among young children, with epidemics occurring every two to five years. Historically, the virus has been most potent in previously unexposed populations, decimating Mexico and Peru in the 1530s, for instance, in the wake of the Spanish invaders. In Hawaii in 1848 and Fiji in 1874 it killed a quarter of the population. Although measles still accounted for over 1.5 million deaths a year in the 1990s, the WHO program covered half the children under the age of one and probably saved one million lives. Likewise, global eradication of smallpox was made possible by freeze drying, which prevented the vaccine from losing its potency in the tropical heat. In 1967, when WHO began its campaign, ten to fifteen million people contracted the disease each year; only Europe and North America were spared. But by 1972 it had been eliminated from Latin America and by 1975 from India, with the last natural case occurring in Somalia in October 1977.

Yet the story of malaria reminds us that technology alone is rarely enough. Spraying mosquito breeding grounds with the insecticide DDT had some dramatic effects: in Sri Lanka (Ceylon),[10] for instance, the spraying campaign immediately after World War II accounted for nearly a quarter of the country's rapid decline in mortality rates.* But even here, success depended on improved health and living standards, such as the increased number of doctors. And by the late 1970s, the WHO acknowledged that malaria control had to be coordinated with primary health care if the disease was to be fully eradicated.

---

*But the damaging side effects of DDT (and of other innovations such as fertilizers) became a rallying point for the new environmental movement in the West in the 1960s and 1970s (see Chapter 14).

For much of the world, the fundamental problem has been water. The provision of clean water and the sanitary removal of sewage, taken for granted by most readers of this book, were global luxuries in the middle of the century. Without them, diarrhea was endemic in tropical countries in Latin America, Africa, and South Asia. This was a far more serious cause of infant mortality than headline-hitting epidemics such as cholera. When a child tries to defecate six or seven times a day, its small body is drained of water and salts, causing dehydration, malnutrition, and reduced immunity. For much of the world's population, clean water was one of the most important changes of the late twentieth century (Plate 27). In Iran, only 35 percent of the population had access to safe drinking water in 1970; by 1990 the proportion was 89 percent. For Brazil, the figures were 55 percent and 87 percent.[11] Yet people also had to be educated about basic human cleanliness, such as washing food brought from fields manured by human excrement. Even the simplest technologies, such as pumps and latrines, could not succeed without changes in attitudes.

The importance of basic health education is exemplified by the prevalence of neonatal tetanus. In the late 1970s roughly one child in every ten died within the first twenty-eight days of life in Somalia and parts of rural India. (By the early 1960s the figure in the United States was one in one hundred thousand.) Many of these neonatal deaths occurred from tetanus. How this happened can be readily seen from the case of the Sereer people of Senegal, in West Africa. For a Sereer woman, delivery of a child is a momentous rite of passage from spouse to mother, to be endured alone and in silence. Half of the women give birth outside the hut, on the ground, often in an area regularly traversed by household animals. The umbilical cord is cut with the edge of a reed, or perhaps a razor, often using a piece of broken pottery as a cutting board. The cord is then tied with a band of cloth from the mother's garment or some homespun thread. Little wonder that tetanus quickly developed.[12] Those babies who survived the first month often succumbed later from measles or diarrhea in their insanitary surroundings. In many parts of West Africa in the 1950s, it was common for three or four children out of ten to die before the age of five. The figure for Sierra Leone was still close to four out of ten in 1969. By then, however, the African norm was closer to two.[13]

Even in Africa, therefore, mortality rates were declining in the third quarter of the twentieth century. But this global trend was not paralleled at the same time by a commensurate fall in fertility. Although a fairly small nuclear family (averaging five) had been the pattern in northwestern Europe even before the industrial revolution, large and extended families had been more normal in eastern and southern Europe, let alone much of Asia and Africa. In agricultural society, children were a double asset for parents—as extra labor on the land and, later, carers during their old age. In addition, a surviving male heir was often a social or even legal necessity; in communities where life expectancy was, say, only thirty, ensuring an adult son required statistically at least four children. It took time before the mortality transition changed the accepted imperatives of rural life in much of the less-developed world. And in the more developed areas, particularly Europe and the Soviet Union, varying degrees of "baby boom" in the late 1940s were a response to the human losses of the war and, in the Soviet case, the famine of the early 1930s. Even though the increase in fertility rates was only temporary in developed countries, it contributed to the postwar surge of global numbers. The population of the United States, for instance, grew by nineteen million in the 1940s (more than double the increase during the depression decade) and by twenty-eight million in the 1950s.

The consequences of population growth can be seen most strikingly in China, home of roughly one-fifth of the world's people. After 1949, the country benefited from an end to decades of war and anarchy, as well as the government's public-health measures and more efficient control of grain markets. Although the demographic trends were not clear at the time because of underreporting and official secrecy, it now seems likely that life expectancy in the People's Republic rose from forty to sixty years between 1953 and 1968. Over the same period, infant mortality was halved—from 175 deaths under age one for every one thousand live births to eighty-one. This was despite the famine caused by the Great Leap Forward in the early 1960s (Chapter 8), when infant mortality soared to 284 per one thousand. In consequence, China's population, which had grown from six hundred to seven hundred million in the decade 1954–1964, surged to eight hundred million by 1969 and nine hundred million by 1974. Apart from brief and ineffectual official campaigns for family limitation after the first national census in 1953 and again in the early 1960s, official Maoist dogma was to encourage fertility or at least to assume that economic development would match demographic growth.[14]

In contrast, India was the first country to adopt family planning as an integral component of government policy, in 1952. But it took years to develop a local infrastructure of clinics, and the widespread Hindu practice of child marriages was difficult to control. Even though the minimum female age for marriage was raised to fifteen in 1955, the law was only loosely enforced. As smallpox, cholera, and malaria were brought under control without comparable restraint on births, the population therefore boomed—from 361 million in 1951 to 439 million a decade later, and 547 million in 1971. By then India had become the second most populous country in the world after China, with 15 percent of the total, even though it occupied only 2.4 percent of the world's land area. Even an official policy of population control had made little difference in the short term.[15]

In the mid-1960s, the fertility transition had occurred only in Europe,

North America, and Australasia. In 1968 the total fertility rate for all these regions was around 2.5 children per woman, although until the early 1960s the longer North American and Australasian baby boom had kept the figure there well over three.[16] In Latin America, the more developed countries of Argentina and Uruguay had rates around three by the mid-1960s, but Brazil's was over six—still the Latin American norm.[17] In East Asia there were early signs of fertility decline in Sri Lanka and South Korea, but these were small states. The sole major exception to the generalization that fertility transition had been completed only in Europe or areas of European settlement was Japan. Here the total fertility rate had dropped from 4.5 in 1947 to 2.0 a decade later—the fastest and most precipitous decline hitherto recorded. Moreover, the average remained at two children per woman—the level required to keep the total population stable—all through the 1960s, before resuming its downward path after 1973.[18]

The Japanese story had interesting implications, both about the methods and motives for fertility control. The steep decline in the 1950s occurred primarily through a sharp rise in abortions to 1.1 million a year in the mid-1950s. Instead of a ratio of one abortion for every ten live births in 1949, the proportion was between two and three in the years 1954–1961. Alarmed at the rising incidence of illegal abortions, the government had legalized the practice in 1948, initially on health or financial grounds, but after 1952 no official permission was needed.[19] The use by Japanese women of induced abortion to control fertility is far from unique. After the restrictions of the Stalin era, abortion was relegalized in 1955 in the Soviet Union. Again the immediate reason was to reduce back-street abortions, but it soon became, *faute de mieux,* the principal family-planning method, rising to a peak of 8.3 million in 1965 and then stabilizing at around seven million each year through the 1970s and 1980s.[20] In both of these countries, the age of marriage remained relatively low during this period—around twenty for women—unlike Western Europe where a higher and fluctuating age of marriage had been a major way of controlling fertility since preindustrial times.

The general point is clear: the fertility transition in much of the developed world had been accomplished before and without the contraceptive pill, employing traditional methods of abstinence, withdrawal and, in extremis, abortion, along with increased use of condoms and diaphragms. Although, as we shall see, the pill has subsequently been a significant means of reducing Third World fertility, especially in Indonesia, its importance lies equally in sexual ethics and gender relations; I discuss it within that context in Chapter 9.

Behind all the demographic jargon are, of course, the decisions of millions of couples, particularly the women. What, then, are the motives for having fewer children? Demographers usually explain it as a facet of modernization. In industrial society, unlike the farm, the family is rarely a unit of production, and so a large number of children is not an economic advantage. Indeed, they are difficult to house in cramped urban conditions and often become an economic liability, because of the cost of the education needed to compete in industrial society. Moreover, modern states often make communal provision for old age, rendering children less necessary because social security replaces family security.[21]

At a very broad level of generality, this argument is clearly plausible. Most of the fertility transitions accomplished by the mid-1960s had occurred in relatively industrial societies, where urban fertility rates were much lower than rural. Couples living in city apartments who covet cars and TVs do not usually produce eight children. Hence the fashionable 1950s slogan, "development is the best contraceptive." But, as the distinguished demographer Ansley Coale has observed, "culture, religion, and traditions complicate any simple statement of the transition in fertility. In Kuwait in 1975, per capita income was the highest in the world, and female life expectancy at birth was about 70 years. Yet the total fertility rate was 6.2, about the same as in Pakistan with an expectation of life of less than 50 years and much lower per capita income."[22] Kuwait and Pakistan were both patriarchal Islamic cultures and, as we shall see in Chapter 11, this shaped a whole range of family values regardless of economic circumstances. And the rapidity of the Asian fertility transitions in the 1970s and 1980s, particularly in China and Indonesia, demonstrated another factor less evident in the European case, namely the role of government intervention. Clearly, the demographic shift to low death and birth rates was not a mere symptom of modernization. When all is said and done, however, this shift occurred most rapidly in urban areas—but not as fast as their populations were mushrooming through migration from the countryside. The population boom exacerbated the crisis of the cities.

Cities and Buildings

Between 1950 and 1970 global population grew from about 2.5 billion to 3.6 billion. During that time the proportion of people living in urban areas rose from 28 percent to 38 percent, and in cities of over one hundred thousand from 16 percent to nearly 24 percent.* These crude statistics give some

---

*These are rough indicators, of course. Data are problematic in many parts of the world, and there is no agreed-on figure to mark the divide between rural and urban areas (itself an artificial construct). The norm in most countries is somewhere between twenty-five hundred and seventy-five hundred people.

sense of the scale and pace of urbanization in the third quarter of the twentieth century.

What must also be noted is the significant geographical variation. In North America and northern and Western Europe, the urban population constituted about three-quarters of national totals in 1950–1970. In Australia, New Zealand, and Japan, the figure was over 80 percent. Japan's urban population had increased from 37 percent in 1950 to 83 percent in 1970 (56 percent in cities of over one hundred thousand)—the most staggering international transformation, about which more in due course. Second only to Japan's was the experience of the Soviet Union, where the urban population grew from 42 percent to 62 percent in these two decades, particularly west of the Urals. Among developing countries, Latin America, especially the temperate south, was more urbanized than most of Asia. Argentina's population, for instance, was over 70 percent urbanized in 1970, with nearly 40 percent living in cities larger than one million. In contrast, over three-quarters of the huge populations of China, India, and Indonesia were defined as rural at this date. The picture was much the same in sub-Saharan Africa, with an extreme of under 10 percent urbanized in East Africa in 1970. But South Africa was around 50 percent, the norm for southern and Eastern Europe, and North Africa was over one-third urbanized.[23]

Postwar urbanization was an acceleration of prewar patterns. Particularly striking after 1945 was the growth of the megalopolis, or giant city, where finance, industry, and government were concentrated and which dominated the surrounding area and indeed the whole country. In the developed West, the numerical growth of the megalopolis was rapid, but their weight within the nation remained much the same. The Paris agglomeration, for instance, continued to account for roughly one-sixth of France's people, New York for around 8 percent of Americans. The significant change was in Japan. While the population of the New York–eastern New Jersey conurbation had grown from thirteen million to over sixteen million between 1950 and 1970, that of the Tokyo-Yokohama metropolitan area had risen from nine million to almost twenty-four million. This accounted for 23 percent of Japan's population, as against 11 percent only two decades before. Add to this the Kyoto-Osaka-Kobe conurbation to the west (12.3 million, or nearly 12 percent of Japanese in 1968), and one can see why most of the southern middle of Japan's main island of Honshu had become an urban strip by the 1970s.[24]

Tokyo's story provides an extreme illustration of the global problems posed by such frenetic urbanization. Over half of Tokyo's housing stock had been destroyed by American bombing during the war, and nearly three million homes were built between 1945 and 1967. But even these were simply not enough to cope with the massive in-migration of the 1950s; land and house prices soared, and families were forced farther into the suburbs. Much of the housing was cramped and substandard. In 1968 nearly half of Tokyo's families were living in tenement buildings, usually wooden, often sharing toilets and kitchens. Services were also deficient. In the metropolitan area, more than one-third of the population in 1968 lacked piped water. In 1974, half the population of the central Tokyo area had no sewerage. Their excrement was collected by night gangs; much of it was then simply dumped in Tokyo Bay by the "honey fleet." The other great problem was transport. Around 1.8 million people commuted into central Tokyo daily in 1970, but the subway system had hardly expanded since the 1930s. Since most of the western commuter lines ended by law at the Yamanote circle line, four miles outside the main business district, passengers had to transfer to a subway or bus to reach their place of work. Postwar Tokyo was hardly the City Beautiful.

These basic problems of housing, services, and transport were common to most of the world's great cities in the 1950s and 1960s. One kind of response was that of London, where the metropolitan population grew only a little in this period, from 11.4 million (1950) to 12 million (1970) because of government restraint. Britain had developed one of the most rigorous systems of land-use planning anywhere in the world, culminating in the 1947 Town and Country Planning Act, which not only made nearly all new building subject to planning permission but also required development plans for every area of the country. The strategy for London, laid down at the end of the war, had three elements: rebuilding the bombed East End; checking suburban sprawl by maintaining the prewar "green belt," about fifteen to twenty miles from the city center; and moving urban overspill well beyond it into "new towns." This pattern was tried elsewhere, for instance around Tokyo and outside the Moscow ring motorway opened in 1962. But the green belt had foundered in Tokyo by 1965 because of insufficiently draconian planning controls, and both Moscow and Tokyo created mostly satellites of existing settlements or even commuter dormitories, such as Tama to the west of Tokyo. By contrast, the eight London-area new towns of the 1950s, such as Harlow and Basildon, were balanced, autonomous communities of maybe eighty thousand people—with industry, housing, shops, and services—close to the countryside. In themselves, the new towns were a success, but they did not offset the magnetic attraction of London for employers and employees. Blocked by the green belt, the commuter population moved to regional towns such as Reading and Maidstone, further burdening the rail network. The official response in the 1960s was essentially the same: more new towns, but farther out and on a larger scale, of which the best known was Milton Keynes, fifty miles to the northwest. By 1974, there were twenty-nine postwar new towns across Britain, housing over 1.8 million people.[25]

Whereas London tried containment and dispersion, Paris opted for controlled expansion. Few major cities in Europe had worse problems in the

1950s than the French capital. Housing density in the inner city was three times that of London, reflecting the prevalence of apartment blocks rather than the single-family homes favored in Britain or indeed Germany. In 1962, nearly two-thirds of all dwellings in the Paris region lacked a bath or shower, and half the sewage went untreated into the River Seine. Expansion into the suburbs had been anarchic, creating grave shortages of schools, hospitals, and other "social capital." Transport was a nightmare, not least because the Métro stopped at the city limits and (unlike London) had been built on a different gauge from the surface lines. But in 1965 government planners elaborated a new *schéma directeur* to address the congestion of the center and the underdevelopment of the suburbs by creating two new east-west axes of development—one to the north of the Seine, the other to the south. These would include eight new towns and additional suburban nodes, each with employment, housing, and facilities, such as La Défense, an urban complex northwest of the city. New express Métro lines (RER) would link these developments with the heart of Paris. The plan was grand in the extreme. Only a country with a messianic leader, a booming economy, and a *dirigiste* tradition could have carried it through. The *schéma* was pruned in the 1970s, but five of the Paris new towns were eventually built and the idea was applied to other French cities, such as Lille and Lyon.[26]

Whatever the response to the crisis of the megalopolis, it depended on effective governmental action. But often urban growth had created a monster that sprawled far beyond the original limits of the city government. In the face of such a problem, larger metropolitan authorities were created, such as the Greater London Council in 1965. The city of Moscow simply doubled the area under its jurisdiction on August 18, 1960, increasing its population overnight by one million people. But that was Soviet absolutism at work. In the United States—with its jealous, not to say myopic, democratic federalism—such autocratic solutions were impossible. In the mid-1970s, the New York metropolitan region boasted nearly fifteen hundred governmental authorities, each with the power to raise and spend money. Conflict between them over policies and federal funds was ferocious. Only in the 1970s, with the creation of the Metropolitan Transit Authority, was there even hope of a unified approach to the deficiencies of public transportation, neglected since the war as the highway network spread. New York also confronted a decline of jobs and population at its inner core, thereby reducing the tax base for essential services, as did most major U.S. cities in the 1960s. But its problem was exacerbated by the racial divide, as not only Harlem but also other old urban neighborhoods in the Bronx and Brooklyn became impoverished black and Hispanic ghettos as whites moved to the suburbs. By 1975 the combination of diminished revenue, increased welfare rolls, and pork-barrel politics had brought the city to the edge of bankruptcy.

In most cities, systematic planning was a belated 1960s response to urban growth. But ever since the war, architects had offered their own, more confident answers to how the modern city should be built. Of all the arts in the postwar period, architecture was probably the most significant in terms of global impact. Unlike literature, even in English, it was not fragmented by barriers of language. Unlike music or painting, it created the essential physical framework for daily living, rather than its ancillary pleasures. Above all, architects of the 1950s had a clear, assured gospel to preach, in marked contrast to the introspection, even nihilism, of the visual arts. Their gospel was modernism, or the international style. Their work, for good or ill, was evident in cities across the world during the 1950s and 1960s.[27]

Architectural modernism had matured in the 1920s. Its leading lights were the Germans Walter Gropius and Ludwig Mies van der Rohe, and the Swiss engraver turned Paris architect, Charles Edouard Jeanneret—all men of the 1880s who lived until the 1960s. Reacting to the Gothic revivalism of the late nineteenth century, they wanted to create a modern language of architecture appropriate to industrial society. In his 1923 classic, *Towards a New Architecture*, Jeanneret (who worked under the name of Le Corbusier) claimed that "in the last fifty years steel and concrete" had made possible "a greater capacity for construction" and "an architecture in which the old codes have been overturned."[28] The hallmarks of this modern, international style were simple rectangular volumes, flat roofs, sharply delineated strip windows, and a total absence of ornamentation. Established in France and Germany before World War II, modernism spread thereafter across the developed world, particularly in the United States, where Gropius and Mies fled from Nazism in the late 1930s. There it was harnessed to American technological skill, which had pioneered the steel and concrete construction of skyscrapers since the late nineteenth century.

The modernist answer to the teeming slums was to build high and clear the surroundings. The result would be greater local density but less overall congestion, not to mention broad vistas. Mies's early 1950s work, such as the Lake Shore Drive apartments in Chicago and the Seagram Building on Manhattan's Park Avenue, established the glass tower as a dominant motif. Le Corbusier's even more influential housing development on the edge of Marseilles, Unité d'Habitation, popularized the vertical-slab approach to apartment housing. Tower and slab became the basic shapes of postwar modernist architecture.

The glass tower, in particular, became the preferred form for corporate headquarters and international hotels. Before 1950, skyscrapers scarcely existed outside North America, with most confined to Chicago and New York. They made sense there because the concentration of offices and the prosperity of the cities drove land costs skyward and, with them, buildings. The same economic imperative governed the growth of other American cities in the postwar boom. It affected major European cities such as London and Paris, but here custom and law prevented the churches of God being dwarfed by the temples of Mammon. Paris, for instance, retained a thirty-meter restriction for new building until 1967, close to London's limit of one hundred feet. When the defenses finally came down in the late 1960s, European skylines were transformed with a suddenness not seen in North America, where height restrictions had been relaxed gradually. The seven hundred-foot Tour Montparnasse, begun in 1969, was the tallest building in Europe at the time. Although historic city cores were usually spared, they were often overshadowed by the new buildings nearby, as in the case of the Altstadt of Frankfurt. Tokyo began to grow upward as well, now that earthquake-resistant technologies rendered obsolete the city's thirty-one-meter limit. First signs were the redevelopment of Shinjuku, west of the center, as a high-rise complex of shops and offices.[29]

Residential accommodation rarely went as high as office buildings, where corporate rivalry increasingly replaced cost effectiveness as the dominant impulse. But millions of people were rehoused in tower blocks, and millions more in elongated slabs. In many European cities, wartime bombing was the immediate catalyst. The port of Rotterdam was one example: the architectural critic Lewis Mumford judged in 1963 that only London rivaled Rotterdam "for the quality of its thinking and the extent of its postwar reconstruction of a devastated area."[30] But at a deeper level, wartime destruction had literally exposed the general problem of urban slums. Part of the modernist impulse was a genuine, often messianic, belief that decent housing was a basic human right that could at last be realized in modern industrial society. New, affordable housing was one of the major goals of the postwar boom across the developed world, and in many cases the results, for all their deficiencies, were an undoubted improvement on the unsanitary and smoke-blackened slums that disappeared. One of the biggest campaigns was in Khrushchev's Russia, where 3.8 million Muscovites were rehoused in new apartments in the decade 1961–1971. With their tight space and poor detailing, these blocks came in for plenty of criticism, but by 1971 over half the city's families lived in housing completed after 1960.[31]

During the 1960s, however, a reaction set in against excesses of urban redevelopment and modernist architecture. A classic American case was the row over bulldozing Boston's West End, where a tight-knit if rundown Italian neighborhood was replaced by shops, offices, and the vast, windswept Government Plaza. The community and political battles fought in Boston were repeated across the Atlantic in the early 1970s over the old food markets of Paris and London—Les Halles and Covent Garden—and in the Lower Norrmalm area of Stockholm. In Europe, too, it seemed, urban renewal was destroying viable neighborhoods as well as rundown slums, usually for the benefit of commercial developers. There was also a reaction against the monotony of modernist architecture—box shapes, featureless glass, concrete wastelands. The most famous horror story was the Pruitt-Igoe apartment complex in St. Louis, Missouri, completed to considerable acclaim in the mid-1950s but by 1970 a verminous ruin, stinking of urine, two-thirds empty. In 1972 it was dynamited to the ground on live TV.

On closer inspection, Pruitt-Igoe was not simply the fault of the architect. Space and detailing had been cut to the bone by the city authorities to save money: in return tenants got doorknobs that came off on first use. The apartments had been designed for lower middle-class nuclear families; they became home for large, single-parent black families from rural areas, many of whom were quite unused to urban living. And, because of Federal housing policy, maintenance costs had to be found from rental income. Consequently, when rents were not paid, maintenance ceased, accelerating the spiral of decay.

In the end, however, disasters like Pruitt-Igoe did reflect the shortcomings of modernist architecture, especially as bowdlerized in architectural schools where Mies, "Grope" and "Corb" became patron saints for a generation of students. In these schools, design mattered more than detailing, a brilliant concept was esteemed above sensitivity to the client. And since most architects were male, they had little idea of basic housing functions, such as how a kitchen really worked, and gave minimal thought to the needs of children, imprisoned three hundred feet up on a rainy day. (It is not irrelevant that Le Corbusier was childless.) At his best, "Corb" was a subtle designer with a keen sense of history, who cannot be blamed for all the follies of his followers. But it is little wonder that one critic, adapting Shakespeare's Mark Antony, observed in 1988: "the evil that Le Corbusier did lives after him; the good is perhaps interred with his books."[32]

The late-1960s reaction to modernism took various forms. Among practitioners, there was renewed interest, apparent in Le Corbusier's own later work, in natural rhythms and historical traditions to ease the linear harshness of internationalism. The Tokyo architect Kenzo Tange blended modernist and national motifs in what became known as the Japan style—best seen in the curving, tensile steel roofs of his 1964 Olympic stadia in Yoyogi Park.[33] Even more celebrated was the Sydney Opera House, based on late-1950s designs by the Danish architect Jørn Utzon and opened in 1973 after numerous technical problems. The huge, vaulted shells of its auditoria mirrored the sails and waves of the adjacent harbor, and also suggested the rhythmic flow of music.

Outside the profession, and within it, there was growing support for what became known as community architecture, in which the public's relationship to the planning and design process became that of participant, not pawn. Planning itself focused more on saving the past than hastening the future. France's Loi Malraux, in 1962, established the concept of the *secteur sauve-gardé*, which was applied with early success to the Marais district of central Paris.[34] Similar laws were passed in the United States and Britain in 1966 and 1967. In the 1980s, the attack on modernist architecture and planning was taken up, to great controversy, by Prince Charles—Britain's "professional" heir to the throne (his adjective, not mine). He lambasted one recent design for central London as a "monstrous carbuncle" and another for causing more desecration than Hitler's Luftwaffe. This may be the age of the computer, he exclaimed, but "why on earth do we have to be surrounded by buildings that look like such machines?"[35]

Among theorists, the new vogue was "vernacular" architecture rather than the formalized international vocabulary of modernism. Here the classic text was Robert Venturi's *Complexity and Contradiction in Architecture* (1966), which denounced "the puritanically moral language of orthodox Modernist architecture" and espoused "messy vitality over obvious unity."[36] Venturi's claim that Main Street and the commercial strip were "almost all right" was carried to an iconoclastic conclusion in *Learning from Las Vegas* (1972) which lauded the roadside architecture of billboards and neon lights and asserted that "the A & P parking lot is a current phase in the evolution of vast space since Versailles."[37] Aptly this book was published almost fifty years after Le Corbusier's *Towards a New Architecture*. On the level of major texts, at least, modernism had given way to postmodernism—a studiously ambiguous term which "specified the departure point, but left open the final destination," thereby indicating both "the continuation of Modernism *and* its transcendence" by patterns that as yet could not (and perhaps should not) be defined.[38] The ambiguities and obsessions of postmodernism, not merely in the arts but for Western culture as a whole, will be explored in the final chapter.

Architectural modernism certainly persisted across the developing world, where buildings in the international style were desired by elites to symbol-ize the country's dawning modernity. Le Corbusier himself was invited to de-sign the government complex for the new Indian province of Punjab at Chandigarh. Significantly, Nehru viewed the city as a symbol of the New India, "free from existing encumbrances of old towns and old traditions."[39] But the most monumental expression of the modernist impulse was in Brazil. There were good social reasons why the country needed a new capital: Rio de Janeiro, where the mountains climb out of the sea, enjoys one of the most spectacular settings in the world, but that same geography made for a cramped city choked with traffic and overshadowed by hillside squatter set-tlements, the *favelas* (Plate 10) A new capital in the interior had been bruited for years. Yet the dynamic Brazilian president Juscelino Kubitschek also envisaged Brasília, nearly six hundred miles inland, as *the* national symbol of modernization. The city and its radiating transport network would stimulate development of Brazil's vast highland interior. And, in contrast to the anarchic sprawl of Rio, it would be a planned metropolis "that would ignore the contemporary reality and would be turned, with all its constitutive elements, toward the future."[40] The outline plan was conceived by a Corbusier disciple, Lúcio Costa, who called it "a deliberate act of conquest. We have to finish in five years," he declared, "or the forest will come back."[41]

The detailed designs, by another Brazilian modernist, Oscar Niemeyer, featured standardized apartment blocks and city spaces separated from the traffic and built around two axes—one residential, the other leading to the government buildings (Plate 9). To cut through budgetary and constructional obstacles, the official opening was simply set for April 21, 1960—little over three years from the plan's approval. Brasília was four hundred miles from the nearest paved highway, 120 miles from the closest airport, so basic communications had to be established before construction could begin. During the final year, work went on around the clock, by daylight or floodlight; even so, only four of the eleven ministerial buildings were complete by April 1960. But the idea of the project, and its bravura realization, seized the world's imagination, attracting foreign VIPs ranging from Eisenhower to Sukarno to visit what was billed as "the capital of the twenty-first century."

In Brazil, as elsewhere, there was, however, a postmodernist backlash. During construction, a squatter settlement, Taguantinga, proliferated around the workers' housing. After dedication, the authorities tried to bulldoze it, only to provoke a riot. By the late 1960s over half the population of the Federal District lived in Taguantinga rather than Brasília, although they were carefully screened from the Corbusian City Beautiful.[42] By this time, however, the negative image of the *favelados* as feckless and often criminal was being revised. In Rio, where one-third of the population lived in *favelas* by the late 1960s, one study argued that "they have the aspirations of the bourgeoisie, the perseverance of pioneers, and the values of patriots. What they do not have is an opportunity to fulfill their aspirations."[43]

Such squatter settlements were a feature of booming Third World cities from Turkey to the Philippines. But they were most evident in South America, because of its relatively high level of urbanization. Equivalents of the *favela* were the Peruvian *barriada*, the Venezuelan *rancho*, or the *colonia proleteria* of Mexico. In the Peruvian capital of Lima, over one-sixth of the three million inhabitants lived in such settlements by 1969. The Pérez family of the Benavides *barriada* typified the story of such "squatters" and their "vernacular architecture." The hillside settlement started in 1954, when about a hundred families mounted a well-planned nighttime invasion of land owned by the government. Bernardo and Dolores Pérez, with their seven children and a nephew, were one of the founding families, arriving by taxi and bringing straw walls ready to erect a temporary dwelling. Such was the speed and scale of the occupation that the police did not try to evict them, for fear of the serious violence that had occurred elsewhere. Within a few years, local pressure and unsanitary conditions had obliged the authorities to provide sewerage and water supply. Like most *barriada* residents, the Pérez family were not new rural migrants. Instead, they were escaping from a run-down, high-rent, three-room apartment in a *callejón* tenement in central Lima, where they shared communal facilities. As soon as funds permitted, their new lot was walled off. Inside the courtyard was the original straw dwelling, successively rebuilt in wood, adobe, and eventually brick, with space for additional rooms and also for rearing chickens, or even sheep and goats. This was a classic example of self-help by an extended family. The eldest Pérez son, Max, was a construction worker. His earnings and skills were vital for consolidation of the family dwelling. His mother worked as a cook on his construction site, while Max's wife looked after the children, and Bernardo guarded the lot. Across the *barriadas,* levels of employment, wages, and literacy exceeded the national average and that of the inner city. In contrast to the *callejónes*, these were "slums of hope," in which local people, acting illegally, were pulling themselves out of a culture of poverty.[44]

The *barriadas* are one reminder that most of the world's population still created their own living spaces, unaffected by trends in formal architecture. Although a few relatively affluent and intensively governed cities, such as Singapore and Hong Kong, developed successful programs of public high-rise housing, they were the exception. Increasingly in the 1960s, governments adopted a "sites and services" approach to the urban housing crisis. In other words, the authorities divided land, confirmed tenancy arrangements, and provided basic water and sanitation. Families then built what they wanted, in their own way, on individual plots. The system was applied both to developing new land and to upgrading existing settlements. For instance, the Calcutta development plan of 1966 adopted this approach for some two million people in the city's *bustees*, or shanty slums. By the end of 1972, it had been possible to improve environmental conditions for over half of them—no mean effort. The result was, in effect, planned slums, but this was the best most cities could immediately envisage, especially in Asia, which, in 1960, accounted for nearly 40 percent of the world's population living in towns of over twenty thousand people.[45]

"Self-build" was even more the norm for the three-fifths of the world's population who in 1970 still lived in rural areas. There, styles and materials had often changed little in the course of the century. But this chapter is concerned more with change than continuity. To conclude, we need to look at a new style of living—neither urban nor rural—that was established in postwar America and would spread from there in the last third of the century. This was suburbanization.

Suburbs and Automobiles

Suburbs in themselves were nothing new, being features of cities of the ancient world. They flourished in the nineteenth century thanks to the development of public transport—train, bus, and tram—which made it possible to live more spaciously outside the central city and commute in for work. Suburbanization in the United States started later than in Britain or France but, between 1950 and 1970, America's suburban population doubled from thirty-six million to seventy-four million, or 36 percent of the total, thereby exceeding either city or rural areas. Definitions of suburbia are, of course, notoriously inexact, but these figures give some index of this latter-day American revolution. By 1980 about two-thirds of dwellings in the United States consisted of separate single-family homes in their own "yard" or garden. The proportion for Sweden, a country of comparable affluence, was one-third.[46]

The low density of American housing and the passion for home ownership obviously reflected distinctive features of American society, notably its per capita wealth and the relative availability of land. But, contrary to the national mythology of free enterprise, it was also testimony to deliberate government policy. Before 1932, home mortgages had typically run for three to five years and had required up to half the total price as down payment. House purchase therefore necessitated several costly loans, often at sharply varying rates. The rash of mortgage failures and the collapse of thousands of banks in the depression resulted in a system of low-cost private mortgages with small down payments and twenty-year terms, insured by the federal government. By 1972 the New Deal's Federal Housing Authority had helped eleven million families to buy their homes and another twenty-two million to improve theirs. After World War II the Veterans' Administration was authorized to provide even more generous loans, for up to thirty years, to returning GIs. In short, it became cheaper to buy than to rent—especially when one included special tax deductions for mortgage indebtedness. At the same time, however, Congress offered only limited support for public housing, tying it closely to local initiatives and to slum clearance.[47] Thus, the suburbanization of America (and the related crisis of its inner cities) owed much to federal policy—state socialism, if you like, for the middle classes.

But even more important in explaining the distinctive American version of suburbia is the motorcar, which, it has been observed, "had a greater spatial and social impact on cities than any other technological innovation since the development of the wheel."[48] Adaptation of the internal combustion engine to road transport was pioneered in Germany and France in the 1890s. Indeed much of the terminology, even in English, comes from the French: *garage, chassis, chauffeur,* and *automobile* itself—a word, sniffed the *New York Times* in 1899, that "being half Greek and half Latin is so near indecent that we print it with hesitation."[49] Decent or not, the term was apt, for the essence of the motorcar was self-mobility. Its owners no longer needed trains, buses and other forms of *public* transport to move around. It was no accident that suburban home ownership and motor car ownership both surged in the 1920s and boomed in the 1950s. For the automobile was the engine of modern suburbia. Equally important, though less noticed, was the production of trucks and vans. These permitted a comparably flexible pattern for the distribution of goods and raw materials, enabling business to relocate out of the old industrial centers. Thus, place of work and place of residence no longer depended on public transport linked to the old inner-city core.

But this only occurred in a largely automobile society. In the 1900s, the United States had taken the lead in mass-producing cars; by 1927 the average was 5.3 Americans to every one automobile. Only the new, sparsely populated frontier societies of Canada, Australia, and New Zealand had a proportion remotely comparable. In France and Britain, there was one car to forty-four people, in Germany almost two hundred. In the postwar period, American dominance of motor-vehicle output was gradually eroded. The U.S. share of world production was 82 percent in 1950, 50 percent in 1961, and 35 percent in 1973—by which time Japan become the world leader in commercial vehicles. But most of this was for export: America still remained preeminent in both the production and consumption of *private* motorcars. By the mid-1970s there was one car for every two people in the United States, compared with one for every four in 1950. In 1973 France, Britain, and West Germany were just reaching America's 1950 figure. In Japan, car ownership soared in the 1960s, from five for every one thousand people in 1960 to 185 per thousand in 1973. In 1969, the Soviet Union was still at Japan's 1960 level, with most cars going to the party elite. It took the equivalent of fifteen years of the national average wage to buy even a two-year-old used car—and there were barely fifty repair garages in the whole of Moscow. Across the noncommunist Third World, the average was nine motor vehicles of every type per one thousand people in 1968. In the People's Republic of China, home to nearly one-fifth of the world's people, the ratio was less than one car per thousand people in 1979.[50]

What do all these figures signify? First, that in 1970 most of the communist and developing areas of the world were as yet virtually unaffected by the automobile revolution. As we shall see in Chapter 17, that was to come over the next twenty-five years, in tandem with a population boom and increased urbanization that together would bring many Third World cities close to collapse. Second, it is also evident that by 1970 Western Europe and Australasia were experiencing American-style suburbanization in the wake of increased automobility. There was a growing tendency for big employers as well as rich homeowners to suburbanize, thus inverting the historic pattern of urban life whereby the city center was the heart of its wealth. Signs of this could be seen, for example, in London in the 1950s and 1960s. Yet—and this is the third point—the automobilized suburbia of the United States was ultimately unique. This was partly because of the prevalence of car ownership and the impact of the American race crisis in accentuating suburb-city polarization. But again the federal government assisted the trend. In other developed countries, public transport remained important and continued to receive government subsidies. Cities like Stockholm in the 1950s, Paris in the 1960s, and Tokyo in the 1970s invested heavily in new subway systems. In contrast, many U.S. railroads rusted away after World War II, whereas roads received a vast subsidy via the Interstate Highway Act of 1956. Some forty-one thousand miles of express highway were constructed at the cost to the taxpayer of about one million dollars per mile. More state socialism for the middle classes.

The archetypal American city of the suburban era was Los Angeles whose war and postwar growth had made it the fourth largest in the world by 1970, with nearly 9.5 million people. In the 1900s, L.A. had both a thriving downtown and an efficient system of public transport, but suburbanization was promoted by the discovery of new oil fields and confirmed by the spread of freeways. These roads originated around New York in the 1910s and 1920s, but came into their own in southern California in the 1940s. By the 1960s L.A. boasted a few blocks of skyscrapers around Pershing Square but, to quote the architectural historian Reyner Banham, the freeways had "shrivelled the heart out of downtown" and facilitated the "unfocused ubiquity that has made Los Angeles what it is."[51] The resulting lifestyle was summed up by one woman: "I live in Garden Grove, work in Irvine, shop in Santa Ana, go to the dentist in Anaheim, my husband works in Long Beach, and I used to be the president of the League of Women Voters in Fullerton."[52]

With the automobile and the freeway came the distinctive American "strip" architecture celebrated by Robert Venturi in *Learning from Las Vegas*. The supermarket, for instance, was pioneered by Ralphs Grocery Store in L.A. in the late 1920s. The early 1950s Lakewood Center near Long Beach was one of the first regional shopping malls in the United States (rivaled only by Northgate in Seattle and Shopper's World in the Massachusetts town of Framingham). The first drive-in movie theater opened in Camden, New Jersey, in 1933. By 1958 there were over four thousand across the United States. And in 1954 Richard and Maurice McDonald, owners of a fast-food emporium in San Bernadino, California, teamed up with Ray Kroc, a milkshake-machine salesman from Chicago. The first of Kroc's "McDonald's" outlets was opened the following year in the Chicago suburb of Des Plaines, followed by two more in California. Kroc bought out the brothers in 1961, but kept their name and made his fortune. With their golden-arched "M" sign, free parking, drive-in access, and basic menu (hamburgers at fifteen cents, french fries at ten cents, milkshakes for twenty), McDonald's spread across the country—and thence the world.[53] They epitomized consumer culture.

The Culture of Consumption

For most of history, human beings have expended the bulk of their labor and income on food, shelter, and clothing. Most food was cereal based. A clear sign of material development has been the shift to a more varied diet and the acquisition of luxury goods. Encouraging consumption has been central to urban economies. The modern "consumer society" has been dated back to Britain in the mid-eighteenth century. But it was only with industrialization and the spread of mass production from capital industries such as machine tools to the output of domestic goods that the consumer revolution took hold. Again Britain was the pioneer, in the later nineteenth century, but the most dramatic changes in ordinary living have occurred in the postwar period, with the United States as the world's model, for good or ill.

Two basic technologies have been indispensable, one derived from chemistry, the other from physics. Polymer chemistry—the science of large molecules—dates back to Germany before World War I. But its potential to produce synthetic materials was systematically exploited in the United States, where nylon (replacing silk in stockings) proved an enormous money spinner for the DuPont company in the 1930s. During World War II, advanced chemistry helped produce vital substances such as synthetic rubber and penicillin—the first of the antibiotics. Since the war, the developed world has come to depend on the products of polymer chemistry, from man-made fibers to quick-drying paints, from pharmaceuticals to plastics. Plastics, in particular, have transformed the packaging of food and drink, the portability of household goods, and the durability of equipment hitherto made of iron or steel. The development of synthetic materials has also made the developed world less reliant on the raw materials that have been the main assets of developing countries.[54]

The second great technological change was the electrical revolution—in other words, the installation of electrically powered appliances to reduce labor-intensive household chores and transform leisure activities. This began in the United States in the 1900s and spread to Western Europe after World War I, but the revolution really took off only after 1945. It depended partly on the mass production of cheap, reliable equipment using small electric devices (for irons or toasters) and small electric motors (for washing machines and vacuum cleaners). It also required the extension of electrical supply to most houses, using standardized wiring. Although this was accomplished in much of urban America by 1929, rural electrification lagged behind that in Germany, France, and Scandinavia (where it took place under government aegis) and was only achieved through the New Deal in the 1930s. By 1940 America was wired up for the domestic revolution; the postwar economic surge, the baby boom, and suburbanization did the rest.

In 1945 only 40 percent of American families owned their homes; in 1960 the proportion was 60 percent. By then 75 percent of American families owned a washing machine, and 98 percent of homes with electrical wiring had refrigerators—compared with under 1 percent in 1925.[55] In fact, in the 1950s Americans purchased three-quarters of all household appliances manufactured in the world.[56] These gadgets, many of them utilizing plastic parts, revolutionized domestic chores. Much of humanity still cooked over an open fire, collecting fuel and water daily, and relied on lamps for illumination, whereas Americans had instant electricity for cooking, heat, and light. Much of humanity had to wash clothes and utensils laboriously by hand, often in cold running water; washing machines and dryers, let alone dishwashers, were inconceivable.

The "humanity" referred to here was, of course, predominantly female: around the world domestic chores have generally been regarded as "women's work." Consequently, the kitchen revolution emanating from America had profound effects on the position and attitudes of women, as we shall see in Chapter 9. At the same time, shopping was transformed by the spread of supermarkets to command 70 percent of America's retail food trade by the early 1960s.[57] There the suburban housewife, using the family automobile, could buy in bulk for several days and store her purchases in fridge or freezer, unlike her counterparts across the world for whom food acquisition and preparation required hours of hard physical work each and every day.

A society with increasing wealth and diminishing chores could spend more time and money on leisure. In the 1950s, the preeminent consumer symbol of leisure was television. As with electrification, America shared its development with Europe: the first TV service began in Germany in March 1935, but it lasted only four months, The "London Television Service" inaugurated in

November 1936 began regular programing, including "outside broadcasts," and by September 1939 over twenty thousand TV sets were in use in the London area. But with the outbreak of war, the whole service was suspended. The Americans had begun a regular service that spring but it, too, was largely closed down following Pearl Harbor.[58]

After the war, however, the United States surged into a dominant position, accounting for two-thirds of the seventy-five million TV sets in use in the world by the end of the 1950s.[59] At that time, 87.5 percent of American homes had a TV; the proportion was 95.5 percent a decade later, by which time 40 percent of all American households had a color set. Ratings suggested that the average viewer watched five hours of TV a week in 1960 and six in 1970, but the figure was higher in the case of women, blacks, the poor, and the less educated. During this period, TV replaced newspapers as the preferred news medium, especially for those with only grade-school education. Analysts also found that even the more educated, who claimed they watched TV for information rather than enjoyment, did not choose their viewing with information in mind.[60] For many Americans, in fact, TV became their leading leisure activity. Initially it was a family affair: the first "TV dinners" were introduced in 1953. In the mid-1950s many families geared eating, homework, and social life around programs such as Walt Disney's *Disneyland*.[61] In the fifties, the TV set, like the car and the suburban house, consolidated the American family, while helping to isolate it from other social groups. Not until the 1960s, as we shall see in Chapter 9, were the disintegrative effects of consumerism to be seen on family as well as social life.

Related to this electrically powered consumer revolution, another revolution was also underway—in communications. The car made Americans self-mobile; the TV brought the world into their living rooms. Likewise, the telephone put them in contact with the world—assuming the world could speak back, for 55 percent of the 130 million telephones in use in 1960 were located in the United States. By then, there were four phones for every ten Americans, double the proportion in 1945.[62] During the 1950s, airlines captured a greater proportion of U.S. intercity passenger traffic than railroads. The advent of the Boeing 707 in 1958 introduced Americans to the comfort and pace of jet travel. The expansion of horizons that all these new technologies made possible would amount in due course to a communications revolution. But even in America, this revolution was still in its infancy in the 1960s. Computers, for instance, were first marketed in 1950. There were 1,250 in existence in the United States in 1957 and over thirty-five thousand a decade later, but these were huge, free-standing machines for use by government and business.[63] Only with the advent of the microprocessor in the 1970s and the global telecommunication networks of the 1980s was the computer both domesticated and internationalized. The postwar communications revolution is therefore best viewed from the vantage point of the 1980s (in Chapter 14).

Before we turn to the global impact of America's consumer society, two other features of this society should be mentioned. First, it depended on credit and, increasingly, on the credit card. Credit itself dates back to antiquity; American retail stores, like Bloomingdale's of New York, had operated their own charge cards since World War I. But one historical novelty of the postwar period was the rapid extension of credit to consumers rather than business: consumer credit in the United States spiraled from $5.7 billion in 1945 to $143.1 billion in 1970 and $375 billion a decade later. Another innovation was the development of universal third-party credit cards (rather than those specific to a particular store) by a firm selling simply credit and not goods. This was pioneered by Diners Club in 1949, but after 1958 its dominance was broken by rival travel and entertainment cards, notably American Express, and by credit cards issued by banks, particularly the BankAmericard (renamed Visa in 1976) and its main rival, known after 1969 as MasterCharge. Competition was intense: in the late 1960s companies indulged in unsolicited mailings of cards, until banned by the federal government in 1970. By 1984, it was estimated, 71 percent of American families possessed at least one credit card. Equally remarkable were the losses. It was reckoned that in 1973 alone some thirty-five million American credit cards were left behind in stores or gas stations![64]

Consumer credit and plastic money made it easier to buy, but why spend in the first place? To overcome consumer resistance, advertising reached new heights (or depths) in postwar America. In his influential book *The Affluent Society* (1958), the Harvard economist John Kenneth Galbraith examined the growing divorce between consumption and need. American society, he observed, "sets great store by ability to produce a high living standard, it evaluates people by the products they possess." Ever greater consumption became an economic necessity for the country's producers and a social necessity for status-conscious individuals. In other words, said Galbraith, "the production of goods creates the wants that the goods are presumed to satisfy."[65] By the late 1950s, however, most American homes had a car and basic household appliances: the market was saturated. Producers resorted to obsolescence by design—in other words, making style rather than substance a prime selling point. Nowhere was this more evident than in new-car sales, which accounted for 20 percent of America's GNP in 1955. Slogans like "You Auto Buy" were not enough when, on average, almost every American family already owned a car. Significantly, the number of models on sale to U.S. consumers remained almost static in the 1950s (243 in 1950, 244 in 1960) but surged to 370 in 1967.[66] Marketing these and other nonessentials was the job of advertising executives, who exploited to the full the subliminal images of television.

Advertising skills were deployed most perniciously in selling cigarettes. Tobacco had been sniffed, smoked, or chewed for centuries, but only from the late nineteenth century did it become big business, with the technique of flue-curing (indoors in dry air, rather than in the open) and the growing popularity of cigarettes, which facilitated mass production and marketing. Cigarettes accounted for over half of tobacco consumption in Britain by 1920 and in the United States and France before the end of World War II, though that point was not reached in Germany and Spain until 1955 or in Belgium and Denmark until 1961. Although a study by the American Cancer Society linked smoking with lung cancer as early as 1954, the industry promoted filter tips as a "safe" alternative.[67] In 1962 nearly 60 percent of cigarette commercials on American TV appeared before 9:00 P.M., many targeted at teenagers.[68] In another fifties classic, *The Hidden Persuaders* (1957), Vance Packard explored the marketing of Marlboros, originally a filter tip aimed at women, as a cigarette for macho males through ads featuring rugged outdoorsmen, particularly cowboys. Marlboro ads, one researcher noted, summed up "some core meanings of smoking: masculinity, adulthood, vigor, and potency."[69]

Here, then, were the ingredients of the consumer society: mass-produced domestic goods, a growing population with soaring incomes, extended credit, and aggressive advertising. The United States was undoubtedly in a league of its own, but the 1950s saw consumer culture spread to much of Western Europe as wartime destruction and postwar austerity were finally overcome. In Britain, for instance, rationing continued until 1954, but thereafter living standards improved markedly, prompting the British premier Harold Macmillan to state accurately in 1957: "most of our people have never had it so good."[70] In 1956 only 8 percent of British households had refrigerators; in 1971 the proportion was 69 percent. By then 91 percent of families had a TV set and 64 percent a washing machine.[71] In Italy, the late 1950s boom was even more dramatic, though from a lower base. The proportion of Italian families owning a TV rose from 12 percent in 1958 to 49 percent in 1965; for fridges, the growth was from 13 percent to 55 percent. Instead of only 3 percent of families with washing machines in 1958, the figure in 1965 was 23 percent.[72]

France, to take another example, followed suit in the 1960s—a decade in which average wages doubled. Whereas food accounted for nearly 38 percent of the average family budget in 1959, the proportion was only 25 percent in 1975. Likewise, clothing fell from 12 percent to 10 percent. Some of the money left over was spent on travel and leisure: in 1973, 62 percent of French families went away on vacation, double the proportion fifteen years before, taking advantage of the increase in the statutory holiday, first to three weeks in 1956 and then four in 1963. Even more striking, they spent their disposable income on consumer goods. By 1975, 90 percent of French homes had a fridge, 75 percent had washing machines, and 70 percent had cars. The French were even losing their taste for small-scale food shops: in 1963 Marcel Fournier opened his first Carrefour "hypermarket." Six years later there were over two hundred fifty hypermarkets in the Paris suburbs alone.[73]

What propagated the consumer society was not simply industrial production but international trade. This was another big contrast with the interwar period. In the 1920s and especially the protectionist 1930s, world trade had lagged behind world production. In the 1950s and 1960s, it grew much faster, both in value and in volume.[74] The six countries that formed the European Economic Community were at the heart of that boom. A genuinely international trading system was, in some ways, simply a throwback to the era before World War I, with the United States as its manager rather than Britain. But volume and composition were both very different. Between 1950 and 1975 the tonnage of seaborne freight per head of of the world's population tripled to over 1,650 pounds per person. And, whereas in the early twentieth century about three-fifths of world exports were primary products, by 1984 three-fifths were manufactured goods.[75] This surge in the international trade of manufactures was at the heart of the consumer boom.

The opening up of world trade was made possible in part by postwar liberalization. The General Agreement on Tariffs and Trade (GATT) was drawn up in 1947. Pressed by the United States, which often used aid as a lever, the Europeans gradually reduced their protectionist barriers. Five rounds of GATT negotiations between 1947 and 1961 cut tariffs by 73 percent; in the Kennedy round of 1962–1967 the reduction was 35 percent. Most of the cuts affected manufactured trade, agriculture remained problematic. Whereas the 1960–1961 negotiations had involved twenty-six countries, sixty-two participated in the Kennedy round—a sign that deregulation was spreading to the developing world, even though many states, especially in Latin America, still favored a policy of self-contained import substitution.[76]

Equally important to world trade was new technology. In the 1980s cargo liners were not much quicker than the 1960s—it still took about a month, for instance, to get from London to Sydney. But bulk carriers, such as those used for oil and grain, permitted much larger loads, and, even more significant, containerization transformed the efficiency and speed with which all kinds of goods could be moved (Plate 7).

Containers had been used in U.S. trade with Alaska and Hawaii in the 1950s, but the big international breakthrough was agreement in 1965 on a standardized box, eight feet square at each end and twenty feet long (or sometimes multiples of twenty). The Twenty-Foot Equivalent Unit (or TEU) became the staple of the container trade, making possible cellular ships built to accommodate huge numbers of TEUs stacked together. The U.S. company Sea-Land and the rival British consortium Overseas Containers Limited (OCL) took the lead, but communist countries like the USSR and Poland followed, then some of the Persian Gulf oil states and, by the 1980s, Asian competitors like C. Y. Tung in Hong Kong and Evergreen in Taiwan. Between 1975 and 1985, the world's container ship fleet grew from 8.4 million tons to nearly forty million, by which time trade between Europe, America, and East Asia was almost all containerized. Containers were also penetrating the developing world—for instance, transporting about 60 percent of the trade between Argentina, Brazil, and Mexico and the developed world.[77] Containers dramatically reduced theft; they facilitated temperature-controlled movement of fruit and food; and, above all, they speeded up loading and unloading.[78] Traditional docks handled about thirty tons of freight per man per week, according to one British estimate in the 1960s, whereas containerized berths managed six hundred tons. This was one reason for the demise of older ports like London, and the rise of new containerized ports like Harwich and Felixstowe, on the east coast, which were not dominated by London's militant dock unions. Employment in the Port of London fell from thirty thousand in the mid-1950s (when one thousand ships were docking a week) to two thousand by 1981.[79] More slowly, containerization also transformed road haulage with the spread of "juggernauts" moving containers to and from ports.

Falling tariffs and improved transportation were in large part responsible for the fourfold increase in the volume of world exports between 1953 and 1977. But even so, the consumer revolution had not spread much beyond North America, Australasia, and Europe by the early 1970s—plus Japan, as we shall see in Chapter 12. One indicator, already noted, was automobile ownership; another was the spread of television. As late as 1979, 80 percent of the world's TV sets were located in Europe, Australasia, and North America. At this time there were sixty TV sets for every hundred people in North America, and thirty per hundred in Australasia and Europe (including the USSR). But in Latin America and sub-Saharan Africa the figure was about ten sets for every hundred people, in the Arab states four, and the rest of Asia three. The Indian figure was little over two sets.[80] In China, some cities had TV stations by 1960, but even in the 1970s most people had not entered the *radio* age: under 8 percent of homes in the PRC had a radio set in 1978. Many of those that did had difficulty understanding the Chinese equivalent of "BBC English"—Mandarin with a distinct Beijing accent.[81]

Another measure of the slow spread of consumerism was that most of the world was still not turned on. Full and reliable statistics for electrification are difficult to obtain, but as recently as 1984 only around half the households in India, Iran, or Egypt had electricity. In Indonesia, Sri Lanka, and Malawi the figure was about 15 percent.[82] This was not always a matter of economics. South Africa, for example, boasted by the far the highest living standard in that continent, but that was largely a reflection of white wealth. By the 1970s the country operated an effective national grid, and electricity was cheaper than coal or paraffin. But the initial charges were prohibitive: to wire a house and connect it to the main supply cost more than £50—a year or two's wages for many natives. And in any case, the national government was none too keen to encourage the electrification of the black townships: although this would increase sales for South African manufacturers, it would also exacerbate migration from the countryside. Consequently by 1974 only 28 percent of township houses were electrified, mostly around the capital, Pretoria.[83]

For whatever reasons, economic or political, much of the world was not wired up even in the 1970s, and therefore could not turn on to the consumer society. Indeed, for a majority of humanity, consumption still meant a daily battle for the basics, for food and drink. In 1970, only 3 percent of Indonesia's 120 million people were estimated to have access to safe drinking water. In India the proportion was 17 percent; in Brazil and Mexico, little over half.[84] Such grim statistics—with all they imply about malnutrition, disease, and mortality—remind us again that the consumer society was still geographically limited in the 1960s. During the last quarter of the twentieth century it would spread much more widely across the developing world, bringing grave environmental problems in its wake—a theme of the last chapter of this book.

But during the 1960s, the consumer revolution was already beginning to change lifestyles in Eastern Europe. The economics of consumerism, communist style, were naturally very different, since the state, not the market, largely dictated output and prices. But in the 1960s most East European governments responded to popular discontent by increasing consumer production. The effects were mixed. Housing costs were kept low, but quality was poor. Food was expensive and often scarce, accounting for a third of the income of worker families in Czechoslovakia or Hungary in 1970, for instance, compared with a quarter in Britain. The Polish proportion was nearly half. On the other hand, by this date, annual meat consumption (a ubiquitous indicator of "better" living standards) for all these countries was around that of Britain (150 pounds per person in 1973). Output and purchases of consumer durables also surged in the 1960s. By 1970, half the families in Bulgaria had a washing machine and 29 percent a fridge; in Czechoslovakia the proportions were 86 percent and 56 percent, respectively. (About two-thirds of British homes had these goods at this time.)[85] In general, the Czechs and East Germans were the most advanced of the eastern bloc. By 1975, in fact, the GDR roughly rivaled its western neighbor in fridges (90 percent of households), TVs (84 percent), and washing machines (76 percent), although car ownership lagged well behind at 29 percent, compared with 55 percent in West Germany.[86] These figures tell us nothing about quality, of course—the East German Trabant hardly compared with the VW Beetle as a "people's car"—but they show that the revolution in basic lifestyles was spreading beyond the capitalist bloc. Equally significant, they proved that a capitalist economy was not necessary to advance material living standards. By the 1960s, the culture of consumption had become a weapon in the cold war.

6

Eyeball to Eyeball, Shoulder to Shoulder

Moscow, July 24, 1959: the great ideological debate of the cold war took place, unintentionally but appropriately, at an exhibition featuring mock-ups of the latest American ideal home. The exhibition was one of the cultural exchanges made possible by Stalin's death. The leader of the Soviet Union and the vice president of the United States traded invective in front of a model kitchen resplendent with washing machine, electric range, and all the latest consumer durables. Nikita Khrushchev refused to be impressed. How long has America been in existence? he asked. "One hundred and fifty years," replied Richard Nixon (a lawyer by training, not a historian). Well, said Khrushchev, "we have existed not quite forty-two years, and in another seven years we shall be on the same level as America. When we catch you up, as we pass by, we will wave to you." Nixon gave as good as he got. In his speech opening the exhibition, he stressed the freedoms of American life in religion, politics, and travel. And he reeled off statistics about the ownership of cars, homes and TVs to prove that the United States had "come closest to the ideal of prosperity for all in a classless society."[1]

Both men were playing to the gallery, of course. But their "kitchen debate" made clear that the cold war had become a competition between two ways of life, in which the "commodity gap" mattered as much as the "missile gap."[2] In the Khrushchev era, the competition between the two systems reached a climax with the space race and the crisis over Cuba—discussed in the first two sections of this chapter. In October 1962, the two superpowers came eyeball to eyeball in nuclear confrontation. But as they pulled back and began searching for ways to relax the tension (what became known as détente), so their alliance structures in Europe came under strain. In the West, the principal challenge came from Charles de Gaulle, leader of a resurgent France; in the East, from Czechoslovakia under the reformer Alexander Dubček. But the upheavals of 1968–1969 in both of these countries brought dissent to an end. By the end of the 1960s, both blocs were shoulder to shoulder once again.

Eisenhower, Khrushchev, and the Space Race

From the vantage point of the 1990s, there is little doubt that Nixon came closer to the truth in the kitchen debate. By the mid-1950s, the United States, with only 6 percent of the earth's population, was producing and consuming over one-third of its goods and services. GNP rose by half in real terms during the decade. Even America's poor were rich in the world's eyes. In the rundown mining area of Harlan County, Kentucky—one of America's poorest counties—67 percent of homes had a TV and 59 percent had a car.[3] But this was not merely a tribute to private enterprise, as Nixon implied. Whereas federal spending amounted to only 1 percent of GNP in 1929, the proportion was 17 percent a quarter of a century later. Much of that spending went to underwrite America's position as a global superpower. Federal money for bases, weapons, and related industries such as electronics had become an essential part of local economies, making permanent the "garrison state" of World War II. The cold war as much as consumerism lay at the heart of the American economy.

Take, for instance, the American West, in the vanguard of the country's postwar boom. One-fifth of the population growth of the 1950s occurred in California, which had outstripped New York as the most populous state in the nation by 1963. Symbolic of the trend was the move of Brooklyn's baseball team, the Dodgers, from Flatbush to Los Angeles in 1958. Uncle Sam was responsible for much of the West's boom. (Even in the 1990s almost half the land area west of the Rockies remained under federal ownership or administration, including 86 percent of Nevada.) Life in Los Angeles and much of California would have been impossible but for the vast federal dam projects of the 1930s and 1940s that harnessed the Colorado and Columbia rivers, ensured household supplies of water, and literally made the desert bloom. Likewise, the economy of the West since 1941 relied heavily on defense-related federal funding, particularly in southern California, the Bay Area around San Francisco, and the environs of Puget Sound in the Pacific Northwest. By the mid-1950s aircraft production (particularly Boeing) employed more people in Washington State than lumber or logging. In 1957 alone the U.S. Navy was responsible for adding 215,000 people to the population of San Diego. Stanford Industrial Park (1951) was not just the precursor of Silicon Valley. It epitomized the symbiosis of business, defense, and education that was a hallmark of America's "military-industrial complex."[4]

Nixon was a Californian, but nothing of this emerged in his kitchen debate with Khrushchev. He attributed America's national wealth simply to private enterprise. Nor did he voice the undercurrent of self-criticism that was swelling in the late 1950s. From theologians like Paul Tillich to novelists such as Jack Kerouac came cries of concern about the supposedly dehumanizing effects of commuter, consumer society. And what of those on the margins—especially the poor and the blacks? Adlai Stevenson, the conscience of the Democratic party and its presidential candidate in 1952 and 1956, lamented the mixture of "private opulence and public squalor" and asked: "With the supermarket as our temple and the singing commercial as our litany, are we likely to fire the world with an irresistible vision of America's exalted purposes and inspiring way of life?"[5] Increasingly, the criticism was directed at Dwight D. Eisenhower, who was president from 1953 to 1961. His affable manner, love of golf, and frequent heart attacks were savagely lampooned as the decade neared its end. Ike's spectacular wartime career was now ancient history: he seemed complacent and ill suited to the strenuous competition of the cold war. In 1960 the columnist James Reston penned an interview with his friend "Uniquack" about the merits of various incumbents of the White House. "What about Eisenhower?" Reston inquired. "Wasn't he President?" Uniquack responded: "We must await the judgment of history on that."[6]

Although history can confirm that Ike *was* president and that Nixon was right about America's economic superiority, this was not how it looked to many in America and across the world in 1960—thanks in good measure to Nikita Khrushchev. By 1955 he was the principal Soviet leader, having won his power struggle with Beria and Malenkov (see Chapter 4). But his position within the party was never uncontested: he survived one attempt to depose him in June 1957 and succumbed to another in October 1964. His successes and failures were bound up with the problem of Stalinism. How could he admit the horrors of the past thirty years without casting doubt on the legitimacy of the Soviet system? After 1953 "the remaining four decades of Soviet history would be dominated by one overriding problem: How to bury Stalin."[7] Khrushchev's response was clear and distinctive. It shaped the climax of the cold war around 1960; as adapted by Mikhail Gorbachev, it also contributed to the Soviet Union's dénouement thirty years later.

Khrushchev genuinely believed in communism. He was the last (maybe the first) Soviet leader to be a utopian socialist. That was part of his rather unlikely global appeal. Of course, like Stalin in the 1920s, he could twist and turn ideologically to remove opposition—at first posing as a defender of orthodoxy against Malenkov in 1955 and then using anti-Stalinism to denounce Molotov in 1957. But at root, Khrushchev still believed in Lenin's revolution and wanted the Soviet system to realize its potential for human advancement. Once in power he adopted some of Malenkov's ideas for a shift from heavy industry to consumer goods to satisfy mounting domestic discontent. He also gave high priority to Soviet agriculture, the sacrificial victim of a quarter-century of frenzied industrialization. But this agenda meant reducing the arms burden on an economy that already found it hard to produce guns, let alone butter: hence Khrushchev's reiteration that war was not inevitable and that the struggle between capitalism and communism could be played out through "peaceful coexistence." Stalin, that "man of steel," had been the ideologue of heavy industry, the scourage of the peasantry, the paranoid promoter of the arms race. Reform therefore meant burying Stalin and resurrecting Lenin. This was the coded message of Khrushchev's celebrated "secret speech" to the twentieth party congress on February 25, 1956—a four-hour documentation of Stalin's personal responsibility for the terror. By blaming all on Stalin and his "gang," Khrushchev tried to safeguard the legitimacy of most of Soviet history.

Khrushchev was an emotional, impulsive man, notorious for mercurial judgments. But his rise from the bottom had left him with a keener sense of local realities than most Soviet leaders, and also a genuine concern for agriculture. The development of the "virgin lands" in the 1950s typified his approach. Whereas Malenkov (an engineer) insisted that USSR's food problems could only be solved by more intensive farming (using fertilizers and the like), Khrushchev argued that the country must bring new areas into grain cultivation, notably in southern Siberia and north Kazakhstan. This, in turn, would allow him to turn parts of the Ukraine and northern Caucasus from wheat to maize—an animal foodstuff—thereby addressing consumer demand for meat. After initial success in 1954, the virgin lands campaign was expanded. Between 1953 and 1956, 89 million acres were brought into cultivation. This was an area equal to all the cultivated land in Canada.[8]

Even such bald statistics suggest an epic story. No less than in the United States, heroic accounts of the frontier have inspired Russian national mythology. And, if anything, Siberia is more inhospitable than the Dakota plains or the Nevada desert. Rather as it had in the early stages of collectivization a quarter-century before, the party sought to fire the imagination of young communists with the challenge of the virgin lands. More than a million young men and women volunteered to go east as a result of the party's appeal in early 1954. Most were from Ukraine and European Russia. They faced temperatures that could soar to over 100 degrees Fahrenheit in summer and plummet to forty below in winter. Often they built houses and farms from scratch. On December 5, 1954, F. T. Morgun, the thirty-year-old director of a new state farm in northern Kazakhstan, issued his first order from a stable by the light of an oil lamp. He and his group spent their first winter in tents and railroad cars before building the farm out of stone trucked from a quarry over sixty miles away.[9]

The early years of the virgin lands program were a striking success. In 1953 the Soviet grain harvest was 82.5 million tons; in 1958 134.7 million. Agricultural production overall was up 50 percent. Similar improvements were recorded in many other sectors, ranging from housing construction (a 150 percent increase) to the number of hospital beds (which rose from 1.5 million to 2.2 million between 1958 and 1965). But Khrushchev was making enemies at every turn. By championing consumer goods (requiring chemicals, not steel), he was challenging the "metal eaters" that dominated Soviet industry. By abolishing many of the bloated government ministries in 1957 and turning over their powers to one hundred fifty regional economic councils, he outraged vested interests at the center and at the top of the party. And by trying to control military spending, he offended the armed forces, including allies like Marshal Zhukov, who had helped keep him in power in 1957.

In response, Khrushchev intensified de-Stalinization. A renewed campaign at the twenty-second party congress in October 1961 expunged Stalin's name from towns and monuments across the country and, with careful symbolism, had his body removed from the Lenin Mausoleum. Unlike that of 1956, this was a public campaign, emphasizing crimes against the people as well as the party, questioning even Stalin's war record, and also indicting living politicians such as Molotov and Malenkov. Somewhat casually, Khrushchev also approved publication of Alexander Solzhenitsyn's novella, *One Day in the Life of Ivan Denisovich,* which released a flood of articles about the labor camps and the terror. Khrushchev's aim was clear. "Some people are waiting for me to croak in order to resuscitate Stalin and his methods," he warned in 1962. "That is why, before I die, I want to destroy Stalin and destroy those people, so as to make it impossible to put the clock back."[10]

But destalinization made new enemies, inside and outside the party. Increasingly, the success of Khrushchev's domestic reforms turned on foreign policy. If he could represent the Soviet Union as winning the cold war by peaceful means, then he could hold his critics at bay and reduce the crippling defense burden. Yet, in the past, defense had been the Achilles heel of the

Soviet system. Despite keeping up, more or less, with the United States in testing nuclear weapons, the Soviets lagged far behind in delivery systems. By the late 1950s, the USSR was threatened not only by the B-52 intercontinental bombers of America's Strategic Air Command but also by aircraft and medium-range missiles located in Britain, Germany, and other allied countries. In contrast, the United States seemed immune from attack. That is, until *Sputnik*.

The Soviets had concentrated on developing missiles, not bombers, as a delivery system. Even so, there were several rival missile programs. Sergei P. Korolev knew in August 1957 that if the fourth test of his R-7 rocket failed, his program faced liquidation. That was better than in the Stalinist era—Igor Kurchatov would have faced *personal* liquidation in August 1949 if his A-bomb had not worked (see Chapter 1)—but it was little consolation to Korolev, himself a survivor of the Arctic camps. "Things are very, very bad," he wrote his wife back in Moscow from the test center (Tashkent-50) in the Kazakh desert.[11] But on August 21, an R-7 was launched successfully four thousand miles into the Pacific. Five days later, the news was made public. On September 7 Khrushchev personally witnessed a second successful test. Although Korolev was a missile scientist, his passion since boyhood had been space flight. He now persuaded a jubilant Khrushchev to go for another record and use an R-7 to launch the world's first artificial earth satellite. *Sputnik* duly went into orbit on October 4, 1957, and its eerie "ping-ping" became familiar to radio listeners around the world. Korolev then put a dog into space on November 3. Laika survived for ten days. While animal lovers across America agonized over her fate, U.S. policy makers grimly pondered Russia's latest technological achievement. On the fortieth anniversary of the Bolshevik Revolution, a few days after this second launch, Khrushchev proclaimed that the Soviet Union would surpass the United States in per capita output within fifteen years.

The first intercontinental ballistic missile (ICBM) and the first satellite represented a double triumph for the Soviet Union. They called into question America's military security *and* its technological superiority. They implied that communism was beating capitalism across the board. Khrushchev seized on Korolev's breakthrough to help solve his domestic problems, using it to justify his plan in January 1960 to cut the size of the armed forces by one-third. He told the Supreme Soviet that, because the country now had powerful missiles, conventional weapons like bombers and warships had lost their former importance. "In our country," he claimed, "the armed forces have to a considerable extent been transformed into rocket forces."[12] Likewise, Korolev's space program gave Khrushchev repeated and well-timed propaganda triumphs over America—the first satellite to orbit the moon was launched on the second anniversary of *Sputnik* in October 1959. Such successes left their mark not merely on Third World perceptions of the super-powers, but even on Western Europe. By August 1960, the Soviets were judged superior to the United States in military strength by 59 to 15 percent in Britain and by 47 to 22 percent in West Germany.[13]

Sputnik spelled panic in the United States. More exactly, American media and pressure groups hyped a "missile gap" and a "space race" between the two superpowers to promote their own agenda. The military and the aero-space lobby pressed the claims of their pet projects, while educators de-manded federal funding to improve the teaching of science, mathematics, and foreign languages. Politicians also seized the chance. Lyndon B. Johnson, the Senate majority leader and a Democratic aspirant for 1960, was told by one aide that *Sputnik* could "blast the Republicans out of the water, unify the Democratic party, and elect you President."[14] For two months from late No-vember 1957, LBJ's Senate Subcommittee on Preparedness kept the issue on the front pages and gave a forum to all manner of lobbyists. "We meet today in the atmosphere of another Pearl Harbor," Johnson told the hearings. "We are in a race for survival, and we intend to win that race."[15] The administra-tion's discomfiture was made worse by Ike's stroke on November 25, his third illness in two years, which strengthened accusations that he was not up to the job, and by the highly publicized failure of America's satellite launch on December 6. The world's press, specially invited to Florida's Cape Canaveral, had ringside seats as the U.S. Navy's giant Vanguard rocket climbed four feet off the pad and then subsided in a ball of fire. Pictures of "Flopnik" were beamed around the world.

Eisenhower was forced to respond. In his New Year State of the Union Address he spoke of the "all-inclusiveness" of the Soviet threat, involving weapons and trade, science and education. "The Soviets are, in short, wag-ing total Cold War."[16] On January 31, 1958, the U.S. Army finally put a satellite, *Explorer I*, into space. Two more launches followed in March. Con-gress passed a bill to create a civilian National Aeronautics and Space Ad-ministration (NASA), effective October 1. And in September 1958, the National Defense Education Act authorized $1 billion over seven years in loans, fellowships, and grants to address the "educational emergency" and "help develop as rapidly as possible those skills essential to the national de-fense."

Undoubtedly, Eisenhower's initial response to *Sputnik* had been slow and fumbling. He had failed to appreciate the symbolism of space as a metaphor for the cold war. But Ike was guided by two clear principles. First, he de-plored getting into a "pathetic race,"[17] fearful of the effect on government spending and on cold war tensions. He had become increasingly concerned about America's defense commitments and the pressure they imposed on the economy and the balance of payments. In July 1957 he told his advisers "he had no idea that there were over a million Americans stationed or resident abroad"[18] and his farewell address as president in January 1961 was a prescient if ineffectual warning against the "military-industrial complex" spawned by the "permanent armaments industry" of the cold war whose influence was felt "in every city, every statehouse, every office of the federal government." It could, he added, also corrode the independence of universities and "mortgage the material assets of our grandchildren" through taxation and debt.[19] In short, Eisenhower feared that the defense of freedom abroad might undermine freedom at home.

This was one reason why the president tried to restrain the American response to *Sputnik*. The other was his knowledge that the "gap" between the two superpowers was actually in America's favor. Losing the race into space in 1957 had more to do with rivalry between the army and the navy than between America and Russia. Once resources and energies were focused, America's space program took off. By January 1962 the United States had launched sixty-three payloads into space, the Soviet Union only fifteen.[20] With missiles, too, the Soviets could boast the world's first ICBM, but they did not have the economic and technological base to match American development in depth. At the end of 1960 the United States possessed forty-two intercontinental missiles; little more than a year later it had 224. During this time the Soviet ICBM arsenal was static at four R-7s.[21] American superiority was also qualitative. They soon moved beyond their first ICBMs, Titan and Atlas, to produce lightweight missiles using the latest aerospace designs, and to make operational the first solid-fuel nuclear missile, Polaris, in November 1960. Polaris was followed by Minuteman in 1962. The warheads were available for instant launching, unlike liquid-fuel missiles, which took time to prepare and were exceedingly dangerous. Not until 1962 did the USSR deploy ICBMs in large numbers and even this, the R-16, was liquid fueled.

Furthermore, the U.S. government had penetrated Khrushchev's missile bluff almost before it began. This was largely due to Ike himself, whose wartime commands in Europe in 1942–1945 had given him a keen appreciation of aerial intelligence. In 1954 he quickly grasped the combined potential of high-altitude flight and breakthroughs in photography. With great secrecy he pushed through construction of the U-2 reconnaissance plane and personally authorized each of its missions from their inception on July 4, 1956. During 1957 the U-2s located the Soviet missile test centers, and CIA analysts were broadly right about the size of the Kremlin's ICBM arsenal. This confidence enabled Ike to ride out the panic of 1957–1958. U-2 overflights were abruptly halted in May 1960, however, when a plane was shot down over the Urals and its pilot, Francis Gary Powers, captured. Again Ike fumbled in public—first denying the mission, and then, when Powers was exhibited, taking responsibility and allowing Khrushchev to wreck their Paris summit. But, as with *Sputnik,* he was losing the propaganda battle yet winning the cold war. Although U-2 overflights came to an end, from August 1960 the Discoverer satellite program started to provide even better intelligence. The first twenty-pound roll of film took in over one million square miles of the USSR. This, said one CIA analyst later, was "more coverage in one capsule than the combined four years of U-2 coverage."[22] Such was the value of satellite intelligence that the U.S. government was determined to exclude all weapons from space. This made good propaganda but it was also a vital tool in the cold war. The principle of what Ike called "open skies" was the only way to find out what was happening in a closed society.

When Eisenhower's second term ended in January 1961 the real "gap" in the cold war was between appearance and reality. In reality, the United States was moving ahead in missile and space technologies, as befitted a far more advanced economy with three times the GNP. In appearance, however, much of the world (and many Americans) had been taken in by Soviet space spectaculars and by Khrushchev's bluster. Missiles were "being churned out like sausages from a machine" he boasted in October 1960.[23] And on April 12, 1961, Yuri Gagarin became the first human to orbit the earth. The handsome young cosmonaut, with his telegenic smile, became a national and international hero, used as a Soviet emissary across the developing world. It was ten months before John Glenn evened the score.°

Moreover, Khrushchev's vigorous diplomacy enhanced the image of Soviet dynamism. Whereas Stalin had been a recluse, terrified of air travel, Khrushchev jetted to India, China, and even the United States (more than a decade before any U.S. president visited Moscow). In September 1959 he arrived in New York on a Tu-114, the world's largest aircraft (Americans, please note) and then toured the country, meeting film stars in Hollywood and inspecting the corn in Iowa. "Who would have guessed, twenty years ago," Khrushchev told his aides, "that the most powerful capitalist country would invite a Communist to visit? This is incredible. Today they *have* to take us into account. It is our strength that led to this."[24]

For Khrushchev the competition was real; he felt it personally. Yet Ike would still not rise to the challenge. He played down the technological race between the two systems and avoided personalizing the cold war. His successor, John F. Kennedy, was, however, very different.

°Sir Frank Roberts, a veteran British diplomat, was then ambassador to Moscow. The day after Gagarin was received in triumph at the Kremlin, Roberts had to drive to Leningrad, over 430 miles away. There were only two filling stations en route and, at the one where Roberts stopped, the automatic pumps had failed. The staff filled his Rolls Royce by hand. While waiting, Roberts savored the irony.

Kennedy, Khrushchev, and Cuba

Like all the Democrats, Kennedy had played missile politics in 1960, even though he knew the "gap" was myth. (His new secretary of defense, Robert McNamara, admitted as much within weeks of taking office.) But, more than Eisenhower, Kennedy grasped the symbolism of missiles and space and his inaugural address dispelled the ennui of Eisenhower's last years. The words and the images of that frozen, sunlit January day left an indelible mark. The handsome young president—aged forty-three, bare headed, without a topcoat—enjoined his fellow Americans, "ask not what your country can do for you; ask what you can do for your country." His predecessor, sitting behind—old enough to be his father, muffled against the cold—listening in silence as Kennedy announced that "the torch has been passed to a new generation of Americans, born in this century" and promised, in language that Ike had sedulously avoided, that the country would "pay any price, bear any burden" to "assure the survival and the success of liberty."[25]

In another of the contrapuntal phrases that were a trademark of his speech writer, Ted Sorensen, Kennedy also declared, "Let us never negotiate out of fear, but let us never fear to negotiate." But for most of his brief presidency, he never judged himself in a position to negotiate. Part of his problem was situational: Ike had used his age, his credibility as a five-star general, and his base in the more anticommunist Republican party to justify a measured approach to the cold war. Kennedy enjoyed none of these advantages, and was soon on the defensive about his youth and inexperience, especially after the botched invasion of Cuba in April—the Bay of Pigs (see Chapter 3). Politically, he needed to play it tough.

But his determination to turn the cold war into a competition between two societies and two leaders was also rooted in personality. Kennedy was bookish, shy, and dogged by ill health throughout his life, due particularly to a damaged back and to a disease of the adrenal glands that made him reliant on daily doses of cortisone and other drugs. Yet he was also fun loving, gregarious, and an inveterate womanizer whose sexual liaisons continued throughout his presidency. What pushed him into an unlikely political career was the voracious ambition of his father, Joseph P. Kennedy—a ruthless tycoon and himself a notorious philanderer—who was determined that a Kennedy would make it to the White House. When Jack's eldest brother, an accomplished all-rounder, was killed in the war, Jack inherited his role. Joe used all his cunning, wealth, and contacts to promote his son, even pulling strings to help get Jack a Pulitzer Prize for a book that was largely Sorensen's work. On Jack and all his siblings, Joe imposed a macho ethic: "Finish First" was the unofficial family motto. Everything was a test of will: school, sport, politics and, now, running the world.[26]

Kennedy met Khrushchev for the first time as president at Vienna in June 1961 (see Plate 14). The Soviet leader, nearly a quarter-century his senior, treated Kennedy like "a prima donna meeting a first-time starlet."[27] He lectured him on geopolitics, needled him about Cuba, and was openly threatening over Berlin. "I want peace," said Khrushchev. "But if you want war, that is your problem." Some of this was the usual bluster, turned on and off as required to intimidate his audience. But Kennedy was totally unprepared for the brutality of the encounter and pondered it for weeks afterwards. He saw the Bay of Pigs fiasco as its root. "I've got a terrible problem," mused Kennedy. "If he thinks I'm inexperienced and have no guts, until we remove those ideas we won't get anywhere with him. So we have to act."[28]

Even before Vienna, in May 1961, Kennedy had committed America to putting a man on the moon by the end of the decade—a policy Ike had explicitly rejected six months before. After Vienna, the president was speaking of Vietnam as another arena for action. But there the crisis built slowly. Berlin, the most likely place for a face off that summer, became less tense after the wall went up in August, though Soviet and American tanks faced each other for a couple of days across Checkpoint Charlie in October. The trial of strength came not in Europe, but ninety miles off the Florida coast. It centered around Kennedy's albatross, Fidel Castro, and Khrushchev's boomerang, the missile gap.

Ever since the Bay of Pigs, Castro's removal had been an obsession for Jack Kennedy and his brother Robert, on whose advice and passionate loyalty the president increasingly relied. The presence of this Soviet satellite so close to the United States was an ideological embarrassment, its survival after April 1961 a personal humiliation for the Kennedy clan. Constantly badgered by Bobby Kennedy, the CIA developed plans to eliminate Castro, some of which bordered on the farcical, such as poisoned cigars and exploding seashells. The CIA also enlisted the support of the Mafia, which hated Castro for closing down its lucrative gambling and drugs operations on the island. No evidence directly implicates the White House in these projects, but plausible denial is the essence of authority. As the biographer Herbert Parmet concludes, "it is impossible to absolve the Kennedys of responsibility for the attempts on Castro's life."[29] What was clearly on the record, however, was Operation Mongoose—directly authorized and coordinated by the White House. Inaugurated in November 1961, this had the aim of stirring up "a revolt which can take place in Cuba by October 1962" involving "overthrow of the communist regime" and "establishment of a new government."[30] In February 1962 Cuba was expelled from the Organization of American States, which then imposed an economic embargo upon it. During the spring and summer the Pentagon staged a series of highly publicized amphibious exercises around the Caribbean, the last of them—on the Puerto Rican island of Vieques—publicly billed to simulate the overthrow of a dictator called "Ortsac." That code word could be cracked by anyone able to read backward. Defense Secretary McNamara has continued to insist that this was just psychological warfare to back up Mongoose and that there was no intention of invading. But he admitted in 1989 that "if I was a Cuban and read the covert evidence of American action against their government, I would be quite ready to believe that the U.S. intended to mount an invasion."[31]

That was certainly how events *were* read, not only in Havana but also in Moscow. As he pondered the threat to his communist outpost in the New World, Khrushchev had other worries. Despite the Berlin Wall, he still hoped to remove the Western troops from West Berlin. And, closer to home, in April 1962 fifteen U.S. Jupiter nuclear missiles became operational in Turkey. Their deployment had been agreed to back in 1959, but Eisenhower stalled, afraid they would be seen as provocation in Moscow. Kennedy went ahead with them in the autumn of 1961, probably because he did not wish to seem weak after Vienna.[32] Although these outmoded missiles were of limited importance in the overall strategic balance, their proximity dramatized the threat to the USSR. While vacationing in the Crimea in the spring of 1962, just across the Black Sea from Turkey, Khrushchev found an answer to all his problems: "Let us launch a hedgehog into the pants of those next door," he told Defense Minister Rodion Malinovsky in a typically earthy phrase.[33] Although the Soviets lacked ICBMs, if they could place shorter-range missiles in Cuba they could deter attack on the island, regain the initiative over Berlin, *and* reduce the missile gap, as well as making a symmetrical response to the U.S. Jupiters.

Khrushchev's action was therefore an understandable reaction to American policies. Yet it was also a gambler's throw. Castro wanted a public deployment and a formal defense pact, but Khrushchev chose to proceed surreptitiously. He may have hoped to conceal the buildup until it was complete; he apparently assumed that Kennedy would have to tolerate nuclear weapons on his doorstep just as the Russians did in Turkey. His language to U.S. visitors in September betrayed his belief that the Soviet Union was the coming power. "It's been a long time since you could spank us like a little boy," he told Interior Secretary Stewart Udall. "Now we can swat your ass." To the poet Robert Frost, he was even blunter about the fading power of the West, quoting Tolstoy's aphorism about old age and sex: "The desire is the same, it's the performance that's different."[34]

Khrushchev's first step was to construct an anti-aircraft defense system in Cuba. By the end of August 1962 the CIA had hard evidence of this development. It monitored the buildup of troops and equipment through September, while advising that a emplacement of offensive nuclear missiles "would be incompatible with Soviet practice to date and with Soviet policy as we presently know it."[35] On September 4 and 13, Kennedy uttered public warnings against any such action and received private assurances from the Soviets that nothing of the sort was intended. But on October 14, a U-2 brought back nearly one thousand pictures showing clearly that medium-range missile bases were under construction around San Cristobal, on the west of the island. The evidence was placed before the president as he breakfasted on October 16.

The crisis was the result of Khrushchev's reckless gamble. But Kennedy's own macho diplomacy had helped back him into a corner. The president immediately convened a secret group of key military, diplomatic, and intelligence advisers who met regularly through the crisis: the Executive Committee, or ExComm. Contrary to early accounts, however, ExComm's function was less decision making than consensus building. Many of the vital moves were planned outside the committee, particularly by the two Kennedys, and ExComm was increasingly used to mobilize support. In particular, JFK was anxious to ensure that the senior military, generally hawkish advocates of air strikes or even invasion, could not complain about lack of consultation. With midterm elections only weeks away and the Republicans talking publicly about a missile threat from Cuba, Kennedy wanted to keep the Pentagon on board.[36]

His own policy, agreed within days, was to impose a blockade or "quarantine" of Cuba to prevent further missile deployment. This he announced in a TV address at 7:00 P.M. on October 22—the first public intimation of the crisis. He made it clear that if any missiles were launched from Cuba against any target in the Western Hemisphere, the United States would regard it "as an attack by the Soviet Union on the United States, requiring a full retaliatory response upon the Soviet Union."[37] U.S. nuclear forces were placed on Defense Condition (Defcon) 2—only one step away from Defcon 1, which meant war.

Within hours, the president's speech was being shown on TV screens around the world. Across America, fall-out shelters were made ready, hoarding expeditions were mounted to local supermarkets; everywhere people waited, prayed, and watched their TVs. But the nuclear dimension of the crisis was never made clear to the Soviet public. Russians were told only of an imperialist threat to their socialist brothers in Cuba (about whom there was much unfraternal feeling because food and goods were being diverted from Russian shops). Yet Khrushchev, his bluff called, had no doubt of the danger. "We were not going to unleash war," he told his colleagues defiantly. "We just wanted to intimidate them." But now, he added, "this may end in a big war."

On the night of October 22–23 the Kremlin gave its commander in Cuba authorization to launch his tactical nuclear weapons if the Americans attempted a landing.[38]

At two moments, the crisis teetered on the brink. The American blockade of Cuba came into force at 10:00 on the morning of Wednesday, October 24. ExComm was told that Soviet ships showed no signs of stopping, and that two were within a few miles of the line. A few minutes later the committee learned that a Soviet submarine had positioned itself between the ships. The aircraft carrier U.S.S. *Essex* was ready to intercept them. "I think these few minutes were the time of gravest concern for the President," wrote Bobby Kennedy later. "His hand went up to his face and covered his mouth. He opened and closed his fist. His face seemed drawn, his eyes pained, almost gray."[39] Then, at 10:25 A.M., the CIA reported that some of the Russian ships had stopped dead in the water. A short time later ExComm heard that twenty ships had stopped or turned round. Secretary of State Dean Rusk murmured, "We're eyeball to eyeball, and I think the other fellow just blinked."[40]

But one blink did not end the face off. Even if no more missiles reached Cuba, the existing ones were still a challenge that Kennedy could not tolerate—for reasons of national security, domestic politics, and international prestige. How to get them out? By the weekend, ExComm and even the president were leaning towards military action. Contingency plans for air strikes and/or invasion were finalized. Some eighteen thousand casualties were predicted in the first ten days of fighting. Saturday, October 27, was the second crunch point. That morning a U-2 was shot down by a SAM missile over Cuba and its pilot killed. As we now know, local Soviet commanders took the decision to open fire, but ExComm assumed it had been done on orders from Moscow. In the afternoon, Cuban anti-aircraft guns hit a low-level American reconnaissance plane, but it managed to limp home. Had it been downed as well, pressure for retaliation might have become irresistible. The Joint Chiefs were demanding an air strike on Monday or Tuesday.

But the Soviets were now backing off. Khrushchev did not think Kennedy would invade, but most of his colleagues were not so sure.[41] Even if there were no invasion, the incidents on October 27 showed how governments could easily lose control of events. If it came to a nuclear exchange, Khrushchev knew that the USSR would be the loser. (Estimates in the 1990s suggest that the Americans could have launched some four thousand nuclear warheads at the Soviet Union with considerable accuracy from ICBMs, submarines, and bombers, whereas the Soviets could respond with only 220, many of which had little chance of reaching their targets.[42]) On October 26, Khrushchev told Kennedy in a long and rambling letter that they were both pulling on a rope "in which you have tied the knot of war" and that "the harder you and I pull, the tighter the knot will become." Rather than one side cutting the knot with horrendous consequences, he suggested, it could be un-tied if the Americans pledged not to invade Cuba, enabling the Soviets to withdraw their missiles.[43] This was the basis on which the crisis was formally resolved over the next two days, though it took another month of hard bar-gaining to get Soviet bombers out of Cuba. Moscow was also assured that the Jupiters would be removed from Turkey, though not within any public deal. In this way the Americans came out as clear-cut victors. But it is now clear that Kennedy was also seeking a peaceful outcome. Having proved his tough-ness, he, too, feared the horror of nuclear war. If Khrushchev had rejected a private accord about the Jupiters, the president was preparing for an *ex-plicit* Cuba-Turkey missile trade arranged by the United Nations.[44]

Just how close the superpowers came to a nuclear conflict remains a mat-ter of debate.[45] But having stared into the abyss, both Kennedy and Khrushchev were anxious to reduce mutual tension. The president, in par-ticular, felt that success over Cuba finally gave him the strength from which to negotiate, and the second half of 1963 saw a series of unprecedented su-perpower agreements on how to control the cold war. During the crisis, for instance, both leaders had been appalled at the slowness of communication, as messages were transmitted to embassies, telegraphed around the world, and then laboriously translated. By the end Khrushchev was using American journalists and even Radio Moscow to relay his proposals. In June 1963, they therefore agreed to establish a twenty-four-hour "direct communications link" between White House and Kremlin—known as the "hot line" to Amer-icans and the "red line" to the Russians. Two months later they concluded a partial test ban treaty, eliminating all but underground nuclear tests (be-cause of deadlock about on-site inspections). The British were cosignatories; the other nuclear power, France, refused. And in October 1963 both super-powers endorsed a UN resolution banning from space nuclear weapons or any other weapons of mass destruction. The Soviets dropped their long-standing opposition to spy satellites in space, now that their own Kosmos pro-gram was bearing fruit and they could see the value of such intelligence for monitoring the test ban and assessing American capabilities. Forestalling an arms race in space was a major achievement for the superpowers: "the cold reaches of the universe," in Kennedy's words, would "not become the new arena of an even colder war."[46] Their agreements held until the "Star Wars" furor of the 1980s.

The year 1963 therefore saw first steps toward what became the détente of the early 1970s. But that was still years away, and the crisis of October 1962 also had harsher, more immediate legacies. Contrary to public impressions, the issue of Cuba had not been resolved. Soviet troops and conventional weapons remained, and the island continued as Moscow's base for communism and subversion in the Western Hemisphere, to the fury of many in Washington. Equally, because Castro would not agree to international inspections, Kennedy never made a commitment formalizing his promise not to invade Cuba once the missiles had indubitably gone. This left the administration free to resume its campaign of sabotage and attempted assassination in early 1963, though on a smaller scale and with more discretion than before.

It is possible that all this rebounded directly on Kennedy on November 22, 1963, when he was gunned down in Dallas, Texas. Perhaps Lee Harvey Oswald acted alone; perhaps Jack Ruby shot Oswald in a fit of patriotic anger.[47] But there are many candidates as possible accomplices. Castro had warned American leaders in September that "they themselves would not be safe" if attempts to remove him continued. Anti-Castro exiles in the United States may have wanted revenge for their betrayal on the beaches of the Bay of Pigs. Several mobsters had vowed to kill Kennedy because of his war on organized crime, and the CIA could have covered up the story to avoid revelations about its use of the Mafia against Castro. "Through the available evidence favors a conspiracy," observes the Kennedy scholar James N. Giglio, "it would be difficult—if not foolhardy—to define its specific nature."[48] In one way or another, Cuba may well have proved Kennedy's nemesis, not merely his albatross.

For Khrushchev, too, the Cuban missile crisis had fateful consequences. Throughout, he had masterminded Soviet foreign policy: deployment had been his gamble; withdrawal was his failure. Although only one of the indictments against him, it was the most dramatic example of his adventurism. By now the euphoria of the late 1950s had evaporated. The missile bluff was exposed, the conventional military buildup had been resumed, and the virgin lands were turning into a barren dustbowl. After the disastrous 1963 harvest, the Soviet Union was even forced to purchase grain from the United States—a huge symbolic humiliation for a communist system supposedly about to bury capitalism without trace. Khrushchev also learned that if you decentralize a command economy lacking market mechanisms, the result is chaos, and he was forced to turn the clock back in 1962–1963. Even more confusing was his decision to split the party into agricultural and industrial sections. As the historian Werner Hahn observes, "reorganizations were in many respects a substitute for resources."[49] They also alienated most of the party, now 11.75 million strong (compared with 6.9 million in 1953) and no longer numbed by fear of Stalinist terror.

In 1964 the vultures gathered around the carcass of Khrushchev's reforms. Chief among them was a former protegé, Leonid Brezhnev. At the Central Committee on October 14, 1964, a weary Khrushchev, now seventy, was stripped of his powers. But he was allowed to keep his dacha, his Moscow house, his staff, his car, his pension and, most important, his life. He told Anastas Mikoyan, a Politburo member but also an old friend:

> Relations among us, the style of leadership, has changed drastically. Could anyone have dreamed of telling Stalin that he didn't suit us anymore, and suggesting that he retire? Not even a wet spot would have remained where we had been standing. Now everything is different. The fear's gone and we can talk as equals. That's my contribution.[50]

In this respect, at least, the Soviet Union had moved on from the Stalin era. But Brezhnev, the new party secretary, soon stopped destalinization, recentralized government, and pledged an end to party upheavals. He and his colleagues also acted on what they judged the basic lesson of the Cuban crisis, namely that superpower equality required nuclear parity. Khrushchev had tried the diplomacy of bluff; in October 1962 his bluff had been called. For the rest of the 1960s, the Soviet leadership turned the economy once again to military production, determined to keep up in the arms race whatever the cost.

De Gaulle and the Travails of Western Europe

In October 1962, most of the world could only watch and wait. West European governments drew varying lessons from their relative impotence in a crisis that could, nevertheless, have left them as the front line of a resulting war. In public and private, British premier Harold Macmillan talked up his limited role as Kennedy's sounding board to prove their special relationship. He even claimed Britain "took full part in (and almost responsibility) for every American move."[51] The octogenarian German chancellor, Konrad Adenauer, whose relations with Kennedy were cool and who already doubted his commitment to Berlin, was sure the crisis could have been avoided had Washington been more vigilant and less naive in its early stages. "It's incredible that the American government didn't react more quickly," he complained in private.[52] Ironically, it was Charles de Gaulle who proved Kennedy's most loyal ally in the immediate crisis. The French president did not doubt America's right to defend its own interests in the Western Hemisphere. But the lack of real consultation strengthened his determination to regain French autonomy and reshape cold war Europe. The next few years of transatlantic relations were the Gaullist era.

De Gaulle was a cartoonist's dream, with his towering frame, bald dome, and large Gallic nose. Yet such had been his role in France's recent past that for many Frenchmen and Frenchwomen he was above caricature and even criticism. Born in 1890 and a career soldier, he had been catapulted to international fame as the leader of the Free French forces in World War II and, briefly, as France's first postwar leader. De Gaulle was by nature a deeply private man—aloof, philosophical, quietly devoted to his disabled daughter Anne, who died in 1948. But he also developed his natural reserve into the public persona of a leader above politics, waiting until 1958 for the call to serve his country again and then ruling it more as monarch than politician. For de Gaulle, 1962 was a momentous year. The cease-fire in Algeria in March meant that, for the first time since 1939, France was not at war somewhere in the world. The following month he appointed an obscure but loyal banker, Georges Pompidou, as his new prime minister—a clear signal that he intended to rule as well as reign. And after a dramatic assassination attempt by embittered partisans of Algérie française in August, which left his Citroën riddled with bullets, de Gaulle capitalized on the outpouring of emotion to strengthen his power. In a referendum on October 28, he secured a three-fifths majority for an elected presidency—one chosen directly by the people rather than through an unwieldly electoral college. The missile crisis served conveniently to reinforce his argument for strong government in a dangerous world. In legislative elections the following month, the Gaullists gained close to an absolute majority of seats in the National Assembly, ensuring them and their allies an effective working majority.

The consolidation of de Gaulle's power coincided with a turning point in transatlantic relations. Britain had now decided to apply for entry into the European Economic Community (EEC), formed in 1958. In part this reflected changed economic realities—for the first time in 1961 Britain's exports to the Six exceeded those to the Commonwealth. But international politics were probably more important. Now that the EEC had been successfully launched, Macmillan feared that it would become the main European pillar of the Atlantic alliance. To shore up the special relationship, Britain therefore needed to be in Europe and not outside it. Hence the application to join in August 1961. Negotiations were complicated and tortuous, with the position of British agriculture and that of the Commonwealth particularly at issue. As they entered a final phase in late 1962, relations with Washington were rocked first by Cuba and then by the Pentagon's announcement in November that it was canceling the U.S. Air Force's Skybolt missile, on which Britain's nuclear deterrent now depended. The decision was taken on grounds of cost and obsolescence, but preoccupation with the Cuban crisis and the heady confidence that it generated made Defense Secretary Robert McNamara insensitive to Skybolt's importance in alliance pol-

itics. Some senior administration officials saw this as their chance to remove
Britain from the nuclear club, thereby making it easier to manage international politics. But as the *Economist* weekly observed, "the independent nuclear deterrent had become a symbol of Britain's greatness which the
Conservative backbenches refused to do without."[53] Belatedly the State Department warned Kennedy that Macmillan's political survival was at stake and
that an alternative Labour government might well allow Britain "to drift toward the Scandinavian position of part-participant, part-spectator with regard
to the Atlantic community."[54] In December Kennedy agreed to let Britain
buy the new Polaris submarine-launched system in place of Skybolt. No
other American ally was given this preferential access to American nuclear
technology. For Macmillan the special relationship had been preserved.

But at the price of his European ambitions. The Polaris agreement only fu-
elled de Gaulle's suspicions of an Anglo-Saxon conspiracy. On January 14,
1963, in a typically regal press conference at the Elysée Palace, he indicated
that he would veto Britain's application to join the EEC. He cited Britain's
special relationship as evidence that it was insufficiently European, warning
that British entry would lead to "a colossal Atlantic community under American dependence." He also pointed to lessons of the Cuban crisis. Had that
come to nuclear war, "the game would necessarily be played out in Europe,"
whatever the wishes of the Europeans. Conversely, now that both superpowers could destroy each other, no one could be sure "if, where, when,
how and to what extent the American nuclear weapons would be employed
to defend Europe" if a crisis erupted there. Hence the need for independent
national deterrents and greater European autonomy.[55]

Eight days later de Gaulle and Adenauer signed a Franco-German treaty
of friendship in Paris. This cemented the rapprochement between old enemies and affirmed the accord between their two leaders. Among its offshoots
were new initiatives in language education and youth exchange, to ensure
that the next generation of French and Germans would not go to war like
their fathers and grandfathers. De Gaulle also saw the treaty as part of his bid
to offset American dominance of the alliance. But its importance was soon
negated by Bundestag approval in May of a preamble setting the treaty
within the Federal Republic's governing aims, "especially [that] of a close
partnership between Europe and the United States."[56] This reflected the
priority attached by Adenauer's Christian Democratic colleagues, led by Foreign Minister Gerhard Schröder, to relations with America and Britain. And
after Adenauer's reluctant resignation in October, his successor, Ludwig Erhard, sustained these efforts to rebuild transatlantic relations. For most Germans, America was more important than France. NATO was both a symbol
of their postwar international rehabilitation and a guarantee of their security
against the Soviet Union. Some 260,000 American troops were based in West

Germany in the early 1960s—over three-quarters of the total U.S. presence in Europe.[57] From 1961 the Germans started contributing to their cost. These "offset" payments were initially made by purchasing American military equipment, which further tied the German army to the United States.

For de Gaulle, in contrast, NATO had become an instrument of subordination. His predecessors had already set in motion France's nuclear program, with the first atomic test taking place in February 1960. France's nuclear strike force (*force de frappe*) was initially air based; the first squadron of Mirage IV bombers became operational in 1964. De Gaulle also established programs for ground- and submarine-launched missiles, which came to fruition in 1971. Although France's nuclear force was not entirely autonomous—depending, for instance, on NATO's early-warning system—it did enhance the country's capacity for independent defense. At the same time, de Gaulle gradually extricated France from NATO commands, beginning in 1959 with its Mediterranean fleet. The process reached its climax in March 1966, with notes to all allied capitals demanding a complete break. By July 1966 all French forces had been withdrawn from NATO commands; by April 1967 all American and Canadian troops had left French soil and NATO's headquarters had been moved into Belgium or the Netherlands. De Gaulle insisted that France had not abrogated its obligations under the North Atlantic Treaty; it simply felt that the American-dominated NATO was no longer the appropriate structure for this purpose. But to the other partners, France's departure from the integrated command system made the French unreliable allies, and their piecemeal cooperation in some NATO programs prompted the accusation that France wanted "NATO à la carte."[58]

At the same time, de Gaulle was also reshaping the European Economic Community. He did not share Jean Monnet's vision of a federal Europe but, by the time of his return to power in 1958, the EEC was a fact of life. De Gaulle therefore sought to turn it into a *Europe des patries,* made up of sovereign nation-states. In this confederation, France would play the leading role, hence his opposition to British membership, both in 1963 and at the time of a second application in 1967. In the chauvinist words of one French minister to his British counterpart: "At present in the Six there are five hens and one cock. If you join, with the other countries, there will be perhaps seven or eight hens. But there will be *two* cocks. Well—that's not so pleasant."[59] With Britain excluded, de Gaulle was able to shape the future development of the EEC. By 1965, progress on formulating common tariff and agricultural policies was well advanced. The French were particularly keen on the latter, since farm-price supports would benefit their large and politically vocal agricultural sector. But bureaucrats in the European Commission, led by Walter Hallstein, wanted to secure an independent EEC budget, using revenue from the external tariff rather than contributions by member states. And the Dutch led those demanding greater powers for the European Parliament, not least over the new budget. The commission, following previous EEC practice, therefore tried to construct a package deal: de Gaulle could have his common agricultural policy (CAP) in return for agreement on the budget and the parliament. But the French president rejected any concession to supranationalism. From June 1965 France simply refused to attend EEC meetings.

This policy of the "empty chair" was also aimed at the plan, under the 1957 Treaty of Rome, to impose majority voting on most issues in 1966. De Gaulle had no intention of allowing the hens to dominate the cock, and his obduracy eventually secured the Luxembourg Compromise of January 1966, under which member states could exercise a veto where "very important interests" were at stake. Each state was also allowed to determine when such interests *were* at stake.[60] Consequently, majority voting became the exception, not the rule, and the proposals for the budget and the parliament were also dropped. The crisis of 1965–1966 was a watershed in the evolution of the EEC. For the next two decades at least, it would be more of an intergovernmental than a supranational body—a confederation of states, not a federal union, in which national governments reasserted their power over the officials in the commission.

In the mid-1960s, therefore, de Gaulle had effected the greatest changes to NATO and the EEC in the history of either organization. To many, he seemed an outdated nationalist, resentful of his country's decline and steeped in its past. When criticized by Paul Reynaud for his 1963 veto of Britain, de Gaulle sent the former premier a hand-addressed envelope, with nothing inside, on the back of which he wrote: "If absent, forward to Agincourt or Waterloo."[61] Anti-Americanism was his obsession. The veteran U.S. diplomat Chip Bohlen, who was the ambassador in Paris in the mid-1960s, judged that de Gaulle did not regard the United States as a genuine nation: "We were immigrants from dozens of countries—in his eyes, a somewhat messy collection of tribes that had come together to exploit a continent. He felt we were materialistic without a solid, civilizing tradition of, say, France."[62]

Yet de Gaulle's nationalism was not mere nostalgia or instinct. In such actions as his visit to Moscow in June 1966, he can be seen as an early exponent of détente. He judged that the cold war was waning and wanted to advance the rights of smaller states in a world less dominated by the "Yalta system" of the superpowers. His assertive foreign policy was also intended to promote a new national consciousness that would support state building at home.[63] And that was his great achievement, despite criticism of his personal rule, notably in François Mitterrand's challenge for the presidency in 1965. The political stability he imposed for a decade from 1958 provided the framework for rapid economic growth, as France belatedly emulated the modernization of its European neighbors in the 1950s. This was the decade when the flight from the land took hold, when many of France's traditional small farms and businesses were rationalized or merged, and when investment levels surged to historic highs. Because of the delay in modernization, in fact, France's 5.8 percent annual growth rate between 1959 and 1970 exceeded that of Italy or West Germany. Those two countries had undergone their democratic stabilization around 1950, under the comparably strong leadership of de Gasperi and Adenauer, and this had facilitated earlier economic advance.

Gaullist France was consequently somewhat out of step with the political trend of developed Western Europe, where the 1960s saw a gradual swing to the left. Socialist parties, which had shed their dogmatic Marxism in the late 1950s and assumed a social democratic character, capitalized on the electorate's readiness for change and its growing preoccupation with the politics of welfare. In Germany, the Social Democrats under Willy Brandt became partners in a Great Coalition in October 1966, before gaining power in their own right three years later and holding it until 1982. In neighboring Austria, the collapse of the long-standing Grand Coalition in 1966 led only briefly to conservative rule before the socialists began a long period in power from 1970 to 1986, mostly under the leadership of Bruno Kreisky. For the British, thirteen years of Conservative rule gave way in October 1964 to the Labour party of Harold Wilson. Labour remained in power until 1979, apart from four more Conservative years from 1970 to 1974. And although the Christian Democrats remained the leading party in Italy, the years 1962–1963 saw a historic "opening to the left" as first social democrats and then socialists were drawn into coalition governments.

There were exceptions to this sixties trend. As we shall see in Chapter 10, Spain and Portugal remained autocracies, and Greece collapsed into military rule from 1967 to 1974. In Norway and Sweden, where the left had been in power throughout the 1950s, the pendulum swung in the opposite direction, bringing nonsocialist coalitions to power in 1965 and 1970. And the politics of many small countries, particularly with proportional representation, still revolved around a plethora of parties representing specific religious, ethnic, or class groups who formed fluctuating coalitions—so-called consociational democracy. The most intricate yet most stable was Switzerland, a tiny federal republic of twenty-two cantons and four languages (though two-thirds of the people were German speakers), whose party balance in the Nationalrat had changed little between the 1920s and the 1960s.[64] In Belgium, in contrast, the language divide between Flemish-speakers and French-speakers (Walloons) polarized national politics. This situation was exacerbated in the 1960s by the economic stagnation of Walloonia as the coal industry declined. Ministries fell over the language issue in 1965 and 1968. But despite national variety, several of these coalitions had a persistent center-left bias, as in

Denmark and Finland, and in the 1960s all of them had accepted the leftish verities of postwar politics: managed growth, full employment, and an expanding welfare state. Across Western Europe, these policies won the socialists converts in the middle class, while their working-class base was being enlarged by industrialization.

During the 1960s, therefore, the politics of convergence persisted throughout much of industrial Western Europe, with social democrats most often the beneficiaries. Yet structural problems were beginning to emerge. Especially important was the slowdown in growth rates experienced outside France. Britain's case was particularly striking. Its per capita growth rate of 2.2 percent over the 1950s and 1960s was much lower than the average for industrial Western Europe (3.9 percent) and well under half that of major rivals such as West Germany, Italy, and France.[65] The causes of this poor performance have been much debated. Some have blamed the economic burdens of the welfare state created after World War II, but this was a general European development. In fact Britain spent a smaller proportion of GDP on health and social services by the 1970s than almost all the developed countries of Western Europe.[66] More significant were the external burdens of Britain's world role. Britain's retreat from empire was less dramatic and bloody than that of France—with no equivalents of Indochina or Algeria—but it was also longer and more expensive. Although African decolonization was largely complete by the early 1960s, and imperial anachronisms in the Mediterranean such as Cyprus and Malta became independent in 1960 and 1964, Britain was slow to liquidate its commitments "east of Suez"—from Aden to Singapore. In the 1960s British defense spending averaged 6 percent of GDP, nearly double the proportion in Germany and Italy. The country's persistent payment deficit was caused not by private transactions (in surplus every year except 1964) but by government spending overseas.[67]

This spending was partly because of the expensive counterinsurgency operation to protect Malaysia in 1963–1966, but it was also tied up with the other, quite distinctive feature of British imperialism, namely the world role of sterling as a reserve currency. British economic policy still gave priority to financial rather than industrial interests—to the income from investment, shipping, insurance, and banking that accrued to the City of London, especially among countries that held significant reserves in sterling. The use of sterling depended on international confidence: in an era of fixed exchange rates that meant defending the value of the pound ($2.80 to £1 since 1949) during repeated crises, despite the drain on reserves and deflation at home. Although Harold Wilson's Labour government espoused economic modernization and wanted to reduce Britain's world role, the need to sustain foreign confidence precluded devaluation of the pound and rapid withdrawal from Asia. Moreover, from 1964 the Americans provided secret support for sterling, both to protect the dollar and to keep Britain in the Persian Gulf and Southeast Asia at a time when the United States was becoming embroiled in Vietnam.[68] Not until November 1967, after spending £3 billion to defend sterling, did Wilson devalue the pound (to $2.40) and then announce withdrawal from east of Suez (except for Hong Kong) by the end of 1971.

Relatively poor British economic performance therefore owes much to the special circumstances of Britain's overseas role. Yet the country's industrial problems also prefigured those that its neighbors were beginning to face. In the first place, Britain had long been the most urbanized and industrial country in Europe, and so had little scope to realize the vast gains in productive use of labour caused by the flight from the land across much of the Continent after the war. Between 1950 and 1965 the proportion of the labor force employed in agriculture in Western Europe fell from 30 percent to 15 percent, but by the mid-1960s this pool had been almost drained.[69] Migration from southern Europe and then from North Africa could not compensate (especially given the racial backlash). By the late 1960s, labor shortages were becoming a general constraint on European expansion as well as a lever for inflationary wage demands. A second disadvantage for postwar Britain was, paradoxically, its wartime success. All its continental rivals had been defeated and occupied at some point between 1940 and 1945. The ravages of war gave opportunities for postwar reconstruction; the shock of defeat often helped shake up older structures in politics, management, and unions. Britain lacked those incentives: it "mistook being on the winning side for having won the war."[70] But by the 1960s, those gains had been exhausted on the industrialized Continent, except for France's delayed modernization: another stimulus for growth was on the wane. And the same was true of Britain's third disadvantage—being outside the new trading networks of Western Europe. Having bet wrongly on the Commonwealth and the sterling area, Britain watched the Europe of the Six become the growth area of the 1950s and 1960s. The British predicament was exacerbated by de Gaulle's vetoes in 1963 and 1967. But by the late 1960s, the benefits of a larger trading framework had been largely realized for the EEC, and further integration, particularly monetary, was blocked by de Gaulle. Thus, by the late 1960s, the Six were reaching the limits of growth within the postwar framework.

Slower growth threatened the social consensus on which postwar recovery and stability depended. It was harder to balance the competing goals of full employment, high welfare, and low inflation. The Swedes were perhaps the most successful, using nationwide wage bargaining under the aegis of a labor market board to avoid the rigidities of a government prices and income policy. What happened when the consensus came apart was evident in Italy. The remarkable economic growth of the 1950s and early 1960s depended on low-cost labor moving from the rural south to the industrial northwest and on the weakness of the Italian labor movement—suppressed under Mussolini and divided by political party. In the 1960s, however, the Milan-Turin-Genoa industrial triangle was nearing full employment, and workers began striking for higher wages. This new militancy and the economic recession of 1963–1965 prompted employers to increase efficiency, for instance by speeding up production lines, which heightened worker discontent. But the protestors also had more general concerns. Recent migrants from the south had often seen little gain in income and conditions. Moreover, their housing conditions were often appalling, and social services had not kept pace with booming urbanization. These young men, unlike the millions of guest workers (many from Italy) who had found temporary jobs in France, West Germany, and Switzerland, enjoyed full civic rights and had also moved with their families. They therefore had additional leverage for protest. Their hopes of reform from the new center-left coalition were soon dashed, because the socialists were cramped by political opposition and economic recession. The triennial round of contract bargaining in 1969 therefore saw an explosion of discontent—the so-called hot autumn—which began several years of worker militancy that fundamentally changed Italy's economy and politics.[71]

Italian disillusionment with the center-left coalition exemplified the more general problem of political alienation. This was in large measure the result of convergence politics. As the left moved into the political center, disgruntled supporters were pushed to the sidelines. The Italian socialist party, the PSI, split after it joined the government in December 1963. Increasingly important was the New Left, usually young, educated, and middle class, which denounced the dilution of leftist ideology and, increasingly, the whole capitalist system. Its crucible was the universities, where numbers had expanded dramatically in the 1960s without commensurate improvements in housing, facilities, and staff. Most were also run in hierarchical manner with strict controls on male-female relations. The social aspects of the student revolt will be discussed in Chapter 9, but its political significance is of importance here. In Italy, for instance, the center-left government passed a law in 1962 raising the school-leaving age to fourteen. The number of secondary school students nearly doubled between 1959 and 1969, and many went on to university. Italy's student population rose from 268,000 in 1960 to 450,000 in 1968. Student protests exploded in the winter of 1967–1968 at universities from Trento to Rome—some of the earliest mass student disturbances in Western Europe. Italian students were also distinctive in forging close links with the factory workers, unlike their counterparts elsewhere. In the violent protests at Fiat's Mirafiori factory in Turin in July 1969, they coined the notorious slogan: *Che cosa vogliamo? Tutto!* ("What do we want? Everything!").[72]

It was in West Germany, however, that political alienation was most profound. As in Italy, there was the volatile cocktail of slower growth, rising aspirations, and a critical mass of discontented students centered initially on the Free University in West Berlin, where an East German refugee, Rudi Dutschke, starting organizing demonstrations in 1966. But German protest took on a distinctive character because of the country's politics, both present and past. The formation of the Great Coalition between the Christian Democrats and Social Democrats in November 1966 brought socialists into government in Germany for the first time since 1930. But it also meant that there was virtually no parliamentary opposition in the Bundestag—only forty-nine Free Democrats against 447 members of the ruling parties. To many, not only those on the extreme left, this was a threat to democracy. Dutschke used it to justify the formation of an Extra-Parliamentary Opposition. At the same time the neo-Nazi National Democratic Party made gains in state elections, culminating in nearly 10 percent of the vote in Baden-Württemberg in April 1968.

This growing extremism on left and right while the center atrophied evoked disturbing memories of the early 1930s. All the more so, since Germany's young were now reacting against the "silent generation" of their parents who had tried to forget the Hitler era without explaining it. The trial of guards from the Auschwitz death camp in 1963–1965 had stimulated discussion; likewise the appointment as chancellor in 1966 of Kurt Georg Kiesinger, a former Nazi party member who had worked in Reich propaganda during the war. The debate about past and present politics came to a head in 1967–1968 over new emergency laws. The government wanted to enact these provisions for special powers in a crisis in order to remove a constitutional loophole under which the wartime allies might resume control in Germany. But the left likened them to the Enabling Acts under which Hitler consolidated power. In April 1968, the emergency laws sparked the biggest and most violent protests in postwar German history. Increasingly moderates denounced "left-fascism": Helmut Schmidt, the leader of the SPD caucus in the Bundestag, claimed that attacks on university property or political offices were "in no way different from the conduct of the SA troops of 30 or 35 years ago." Germany's continuing struggle to overcome its past accentuated the political alienation of the 1960s.[73]

Slower growth, industrial unrest, political alienation—these were common problems across Western Europe. But nowhere did they explode more dramatically than in France. And although the French upheavals of 1968 were shorter lived than those of, say, Italy, they had the most spectacular of consequences—undermining the presidential monarchy of Charles de Gaulle.

France's economic miracle of the 1960s spawned its problems. It was still a country of small farms and small firms, with the weakness of its modern export industries reflected in persistent trade deficits. Inflation was also more pronounced than elsewhere throughout the 1960s, because of strong unions that secured wage indexation and higher social security payments. By the later 1960s, too, political opposition was mounting. François Mitterrand's strong showing in 1965 was followed in the assembly elections of March 1967 by a communist-socialist pact that left de Gaulle with only a knife-edge majority in Parliament. The government was forced to rule by ordinance in economic matters during the summer of 1967. The autumn saw a series of debilitating strikes.

Yet none of these signs prepared contemporaries for the spring of 1968. The catalyst was student protest at the cramped new University of Nanterre, on the western edge of Paris, against living conditions and the Vietnam War. When the authorities closed down the university, protest spread to the Sorbonne in central Paris, where police intervention on May 3 started a week of clashes across the Latin Quarter culminating in the "Night of the Barricades" on May 10–11. As some students ignited cars and threw paving stones at the police, others occupied the national theater, draping themselves in bizarre costumes and practicing "free love" around the clock in "les Orgies dans l'Odéon." Many other cities in France were affected, notably Nantes and Strasbourg, but until mid-May the student protests were self-contained. Then industrial workers across the country came out on strike and often occupied their factories. Largely spontaneous in origin, these strikes escalated into a general strike on May 22. Although Georges Pompidou's government conceded large pay increases to the unions, this did not quell grass-roots anger. Eight million people were on strike, public transport was paralyzed, and petroleum stocks ran low.[74]

At the height of the crisis, de Gaulle lost his grip. His TV address on May 24 contained grandiloquent but vague promises about participation. In the words of one graffito, "He took 3 weeks to announce in 5 minutes that he was going to undertake in 1 month what he had failed to do in 10 years."[75] The cry in the streets that evening was "Adieu, de Gaulle." On May 29, as Mitterrand called for a new presidential election and the communists demanded "a government of the people," de Gaulle suddenly disappeared from Paris. He had flown to Baden-Baden to visit General Jacques Massu, commander of the French forces in West Germany. Gaullists claimed that he had gone to ensure military backing, but even his official biographer suspects a temporary loss of nerve by the exhausted seventy-eight-year-old president, always a man of moods.[76] Apparently Massu, who had helped de Gaulle to power in 1958, persuaded him to fight rather than flee. After an hour or so, de Gaulle flew back to rumor-ridden Paris. In a forceful radio address next day, he dramatized the crisis as a would-be communist coup against the republic and announced new Assembly elections to confirm Pompidou in power. That evening Gaullists mobilized several hundred thousand of their own supporters down the Champs Elysées. By late June most strikers were back at work, the students were exhausted and fragmented, and the country weary of strife. France's politically divided union movement lacked the unity to capitalize on the crisis.[77] On June 30, the Gaullists won a crushing victory in the elections. De Gaulle celebrated by sacking Pompidou, even though (or perhaps because) the prime minister was one of the few to keep his head during the crisis.

Yet June 1968 was a pyrrhic victory. The "parliament of the scared," as de Gaulle called it, was testimony to a widespread fear of anarchy. But once order had been restored, the same old problems recurred with sporadic strikes and student unrest. De Gaulle had promised participation; he wanted a referendum to confirm his personal authority. But, balking at more substantive issues such as industrial participation, he proposed reforms of the Senate and the regions. These proposals aroused few crusading passions but did affront numerous interest groups. Obstinately, perhaps with a political death wish, he ignored his advisers and pushed on with the referendum, making clear in public that its fate was also his. On April 27, 1969, 53 percent of mainland France voted "no." De Gaulle resigned the next day, to be succeeded by Georges Pompidou after presidential elections in June.

When Charles de Gaulle died in November 1970, he left behind a mixed legacy. Unquestionably he had restored France's national pride, after decades of drift and defeat, and brought it stable democratic government. He had also reshaped the EEC and rejected NATO. But the economic modernization over which he presided had begun before he assumed power and, as shown by the events of May 1968, it had not solved the structural problems of what became known as the "blocked society." These were to dog France and, in different ways, all Western Europe in the 1970s. Nor had de Gaulle snapped open the cold war straitjacket. His vision of a Europe stretching from the Atlantic to the Urals remained a pipe dream. It required changes in American policy and German politics for any progress to be made.[78] Admittedly, the countries of Eastern Europe evolved more flexible relations with the Soviet Union during the 1960s, with some embarking on their own liberalization. But they faced far graver economic problems than the West. The fate of France's eastern analogue, Czechoslovakia, in 1968 made clear the acceptable limits of reform.[79]

Dubček and the Taming of Eastern Europe

One general problem in Eastern Europe, as in the West, was the slowing down of economic growth rates in the 1960s. This was less true in Balkan states such as Romania and Bulgaria, where the industrial revolution was still in progress, but was apparent in the more advanced countries of east-central Europe. In the GDR, for instance, annual growth averaged 3.4 percent in 1961–1965, compared with 10.1 percent during the 1950s; Hungary's rate was 4.1 percent instead of 5.8 percent.[80] This highlighted the need to achieve real gains in productivity and efficiency, rather than simply building more factories and employing more peasants. But instead of reforming the planned command economy, most governments contented themselves with greater emphasis on agriculture and consumer goods and with "decentralization through concentration," whereby a smaller number of economic units were allowed greater autonomy. This was the extent of reform in East Germany, for instance, and also in Poland, where agricultural collectivization was never pushed through after the crisis of 1956. On the other hand, Tito's Yugoslavia continued its aberrant course towards "market socialism." Major reforms in 1965 included the end of price controls. In 1967 foreign investment was allowed, up to 49 percent of any enterprise, with investors able to repatriate their profits. In between was the case of Hungary, whose New Economic Mechanism was phased in between 1966 and 1968. The state retained a long-term planning role but abandoned many centralized controls and permitted enterprises to make profits. Although about half of consumer goods and services were still under price controls, producer prices were greatly liberalized, especially on manufactures. The aim was total price freedom within a decade or so.[81]

Another general pattern across much of the Soviet bloc, apart from Albania and Romania, was the easing of ideological orthodoxy in the early 1960s. This followed Khrushchev's second and public denunciation of Stalinism at the twenty-second Soviet party congress in October 1961. The general loosening of controls on the arts, media, and universities was not altruism. Most regimes recognized the need to win the support of intellectuals, both to generate reform ideas and to legitimize the party in the postrevolutionary period. But this often provoked conflicts with party functionaries, whose position was thereby challenged. They reimposed many controls when Soviet policy changed after Khrushchev's political demise in 1964, and so the reform era was generally brief. In Hungary the thaw did continue, because Moscow did not want a repetition of the 1956 revolt, and the words of party leader János Kádár became an official slogan: "those who are not against us are with us."[82]

Again Yugoslavia was an extreme case. Here foreign books and foreign tourists could circulate with little hindrance and, from 1963, Yugoslav citizens were allowed to travel to the West. By 1975 one worker in every six was employed outside the country.[83]

The 1960s also saw greater Soviet tolerance of national independence, at least on the Balkan periphery of the bloc, formalized in the new doctrine of "polycentrism." This was partly the result of reactions against Soviet economic planning in the early 1960s. In the cold war campaign to develop the Soviet economy, Khrushchev tried to turn the Eastern bloc's economic organization, Comecon, into a regional plan, whereby the Balkans would be largely primary producers for the benefit of the industrialized core of east-central Europe. Albania and resource-rich Romania would have none of this. What allowed them the chance of greater independence without going outside the communist bloc, as Tito had done, was the Sino-Soviet split. As Moscow's relations with Yugoslavia (Albania's old enemy) improved in the late 1950s, Enver Hoxha, the Albanian leader, sided with China quite openly. Khrushchev severed diplomatic relations with Albania in December 1961. Romania took a middle ground, playing off both sides in the dispute and also cultivating the West. Under Nicolae Ceaușescu (1965–1989) the country's national culture was highlighted, both against Russia and against the Hungarian minority, whose rights were eroded. These ethnic impulses in Albanian and Romanian policy were signs that nationality problems had been resolved less completely in the Balkans during the 1940s than in the rest of east-central Europe. This was most obvious in federal Yugoslavia, where 1950s expectations of a new national identity proved vain. Devolution in the economy and constitutional changes in 1963 and 1968 allowed the various national groups greater autonomy. The result was more vocal protest against Serbian dominance of the state, particularly from Croats and from Albanians in the province of Kosovo.

The Balkans lay on the edge of the Warsaw Pact. Strategically and economically, they were far less important to the Soviet Union than the advanced countries of east-central Europe, on the direct axis between Germany and Russia. Here the stakes were higher and the tolerance of deviation much less. Hungary and Poland had each achieved a modus vivendi with the Soviet Union after 1956; East Germany was gradually stabilized between the crises of 1953 and 1961. But Czechoslovakia, the most industrialized country of the region, had been largely untouched by the upheavals of destalinization. This was to change in the 1960s, as the general problems that afflicted the whole bloc—economic, political, and national—fused into a major crisis in 1968.

Khrushchev's destalinization campaign of 1961 was a particular embarrassment to the hardline Czech leader, Antonín Novotný (1953–1968). Unlike those of Hungary or Poland, the Czechoslovak party had made no previous acknowledgment of the purges of the early 1950s. When the twelfth Czech party congress agreed in December 1962 to investigate these, it was a major defeat for Novotný and the party establishment. It also set in motion a long and controversial liberalization of cultural life throughout the 1960s, precipitating a growing debate about the role of the Communist party in society. The country also experienced an acute economic crisis in the early 1960s. In 1962 industrial production actually *declined* by 0.4 percent. Food shortages were so severe that restaurants resorted to one "meatless" day a week.[84] The party was humiliatingly forced to abandon its third five-year plan and set in motion economic reforms similar to, though less radical than, those in Hungary. But what made political and economic reforms in Czechoslovakia distinctive, and helped maintain their momentum throughout the 1960s, was the country's acute national question—Slovakia—which set it apart from neighboring Hungary, Poland, and the GDR.

The Slovaks had suffered Hungarian rule before 1918, followed by Czech domination except for a period as a Nazi puppet state in World War II. The Slovak Communist party, representing some 30 percent of the country's fourteen million people, therefore used political and economic reforms as issues to advance their own cause. Novotný berated "bourgeois nationalism in Slovakia," which he accused of being a front for "sinister aims of Western imperialists," but he was increasingly on the defensive.[85] In December 1967, Brezhnev made clear he would not shore up Novotný—"This is your affair!" he told Czech leaders[86]—and the following month Novotný was forced to resign as party secretary. His successor was Alexander Dubček, the Slovak party leader since 1963.

During 1967, Dubček had come out clearly in favor of political reform, economic liberalization, and Slovak nationalism, thereby appealing to the three main anti-Novotný elements in the party. But he was a compromise candidate, scarcely known in the Czech lands. As a rising apparatchik, in the mid-1950s he had spent three years at the Higher Party School in Moscow, where one of his fellow students was Mikhail Gorbachev. His personal sympathies were with Khrushchev's program of destalinization, but during the 1960s he moved cautiously, securing his position in Slovakia before coming out openly against Novotný. Though not devoid of tactical skill, Dubček was an unlikely leader—shy, no orator, somewhat naive in judgment. Above all, he was a sincere communist who believed not only in the system but also in the Soviet Union. Born in 1921, he had lived in the USSR with his family between the ages of four and seventeen, first on an international commune in bleak Kirghizia, on the Chinese border, and then in the town of Gorky, near Moscow. Shielded in those years from the realities of Stalinism by a happy family life, Dubček retained from his childhood a faith in the Russians that was shared by few of his East European counterparts.

Yet even a craftier leader than Dubček would have been tested in the crisis of 1968. He had to maintain a balancing act between the long-suppressed demand for reforms, and the need to maintain party unity and Soviet support. As Dubček promised Brezhnev after taking power as party leader, there was no purge of Novotný and the remaining hard-liners, but criticism of them mounted during early 1968 as the press was liberalized. Revelations of corruption finally forced Novotný to resign as president on March 21. His successor was General Ludvik Svoboda, a septuagenarian with reformist credentials but also commander of the Czech forces in the Red Army in World War II. The appointment of Svoboda (whose name meant "freedom") marked the beginning of what became known as the "Prague spring." In early April the party published its Action Program, which Dubček called "a first step toward a new democratic model of socialist society."[87] Social and economic freedoms were extended during the summer, including worker councils, and recognition for Slovaks and other national minorities. As the press kept exposing the iniquities of the Novotný era, pressure mounted for a fundamental reform of the party itself. A special congress was scheduled for September.

Czechoslovakia was a member of the Warsaw Pact but, unlike the GDR, Hungary, and Poland, it had managed to avoid having Soviet troops stationed on its soil—to the annoyance of Red Army commanders. The Kremlin used the Warsaw Pact maneuvers in Czechoslovakia in June as a thinly disguised warning to Prague. But the stratagem backfired. On June 27, a statement entitled "2,000 Words" appeared in the Prague newspapers. Authored by the writer Ludvik Vaculik and supported by many leading intellectuals, it warned that reform was threatened by the "revenge of the old forces" and possibly by foreign intervention and assured the government "that we will back it—with weapons if necessary." This convinced Kremlin leaders that the counterrevolutionary threat was real.[88] They began contingency plans for military intervention unless the leadership called off the special congress, now scheduled for August 26, and permitted a permanent Soviet troop presence. Their fears were shared, not only by the military and the KGB, but also by the hardline leaderships in Poland, Bulgaria, and East Germany, afraid that "uncontrolled reformism" would infect the whole bloc.[89]

At the end of July, Brezhnev gave Dubček one last chance. In face-to-face meetings between the two leaderships, Dubček responded to Soviet abuse with studied equivocation. He told a friend: "I just try to smile at Brezhnev as he shouts at me. I say, 'yes, yes, I agree,' and then I come home and do nothing."[90] When those agreements were not honored, the Politburo met on

August 17 to confirm its decision to invade. Although some members continued to have reservations—notably Premier Alexei Kosygin, who feared the effect on moves toward détente with the United States—Brezhnev came off the fence because of his fears about the spreading contagion and perhaps because of the threat to his own position from hard-liners.

During the night of August 20–21, Warsaw Pact troops invaded Czechoslovakia. Most were Soviet, with token contingents from the GDR, Poland, Bulgaria, and Hungary. No resistance was offered—the Czech army was not even mobilized—and by mid-morning Dubček and the entire executive committee of the Praesidium were on their way to KGB camps in the Carpathians. It was probably wise that Czechoslovakia did not fight back, for a bloodbath would have ensued, but remarkably Dubček never seems to have believed that the Soviets would execute their threats. As news came through of the invasion, a shattered Dubček, tears streaming down his face, exclaimed to colleagues, "I have devoted my whole life to cooperation with the Soviet Union, and they have done this to me. It is my personal tragedy."[91]

Yet the Soviets also misread the situation fundamentally. The military side of the invasion went perfectly, but politically it was a disaster. The Kremlin had expected that conservatives, led by the Slovak party chief Vasil Bilak, would mobilize support and issue a call for help, thereby legitimizing the invasion. But Bilak could not deliver. Most of the leadership, including President Svoboda, would not deal with the Soviets until Dubček and his colleagues had been released. Meanwhile, a general strike was declared, and passive resistance spread across the country. On the streets, Czech students used their schoolbook Russian to remonstrate with young Red Army conscripts, while others daubed Soviet tanks with swastikas and messages like "Ivan, go home."

Eventually, Moscow was compelled to deal with Dubček and his colleagues. Browbeaten, they signed a protocol endorsing the invasion and were then sent home to reverse their reforms. Dubček fought a courageous rearguard action, hoping that each concession would finally end the occupation, but the Soviets were now grimly determined. They also used the new Slovak party chief, Gustáv Husák—a nationalist but also a pragmatist—to drive a wedge into the leadership. Yet two acts of defiance illuminated Prague's bitter winter. On January 16, 1969, a protesting student, Jan Palach, set fire to himself in Wenceslas Square, under the statue of Bohemia's patron saint. Hundreds of thousands attended his funeral. And on March 28 the victory of the country's ice hockey team over the Soviet Union sent crowds into the streets, some of them sacking the Aeroflot offices in celebration. This only fueled Brezhnev's anger. In April 1969, Husak became Czechoslovak party leader; in June 1970 Dubček was stripped even of his party membership. He spent the next nineteen years as an obscure forestry official in Bratislava.

August 1968 sent shock waves through the communist world, much as France's May Events had shaken Western Europe. Moscow had now spelled out the limits of polycentrism. What became known in America as the "Brezhnev Doctrine" was enunciated in *Pravda* on September 26, 1968. Although national leaders could determine their country's path of development, they "must damage neither socialism in their own country nor the worldwide workers movement." Equally clear was the doctrine's implicit corollary: the Soviet Union would decide when those obligations had been broken.[92] Dissident Balkan leaders were particularly alarmed: Ceauşescu refused to join the invasion, and Hoxha withdrew Albania completely from the Warsaw Pact. In Beijing, as we shall see in Chapter 10, Soviet conduct prompted a fundamental reconsideration of who was the worse enemy, America or Russia.

The Soviet invasion also dealt a grave blow to communist ideology. Dubček, one might say, was the last true believer—hopeful of reformed, popular communism. After 1968, it was transparent that the Soviet bloc was held together by force rather than faith. For Andrei Sakharov, the now-repentant "father" of the Soviet H-bomb, that summer marked the end of his lingering hopes for "reformed socialism" and the start of his career as Russia's best-known dissident.[93]

Disenchantment was also evident on the left in France and Italy, already shaken by destalinization. For the first time the French Communist party openly censured the conduct of the Soviet Union.[94] With the Old Left of unions and parties now on the defensive against the New Left of students and radicals, August 1968 signaled the end of the Moscow-centered international communist movement. What Germans called the *Panzerkommunismus* of 1968 cast long shadows.

April 1969 saw the demise of both Dubček and de Gaulle. In very different ways, each had stood for reform of their two blocs. Again in very different ways, each had found that task impossible, trapped as they were between superpower pressure and domestic upheaval. In the West, May 1968 had underlined the fragility of order; in the East, August 1968 had demonstrated the elusiveness of freedom. Cold war divisions had hardened again: within each bloc allies shuffled into line, shoulder to shoulder. As even de Gaulle had to recognize, a reduction in tension in the cold war would depend on the superpowers. Although their confrontation had softened since the face off over Cuba in 1962, the path to détente was slow. We shall see in Chapter 10 that its pace was set by events in Asia, not Europe.

7

Color, Creed, and Coups

The Cuban missile crisis of 1962 showed that nuclear-charged bipolarity could threaten the whole globe. But the cold war divide of power and ideology did not define the totality of world affairs in the 1960s. "Race" was in the news just as much—meaning particularly a clash between "black" and "white." Southern Africa was at its heart, but "race relations" also assumed central importance in American politics and, through immigration, in the politics of many West European countries.

Equally significant were religious differences. As structures of belief and, in many places, structures of authority, religion maintained its power. The Roman Catholic Church was in ferment, Hindus and Muslims were at war again in South Asia, likewise Israel and its Muslim neighbors in 1967. This chapter looks beyond the 1960s cold war to explores these other global divides.

From one perspective, "racism" and "religion" were huge, almost natural forces—regarded as innate or premodern, depending on your point of view. Yet they were in many ways political constructs that were utilized, and sometimes invented, in struggles for power. This was particularly apparent in the American South and apartheid South Africa. It was even more true in the developing world, where the politics of color and creed became tied up with the challenges of state building. In Africa, the Middle East and South Asia, new states were struggling with their postcolonial legacies of electoral politics and economic dependence. Those struggles were also entwined with rivalries among internal elites for power and wealth. With many states so fragile, both externally and internally, government was often assumed by military officers. Not only did they control the armed forces on which state power rests, they often constituted the most educated and cohesive modernizing element in society. In states that were weak or contorted, the military formed the backbone—from Africa to Latin America. The pervasiveness of military rule in the developing world (with notable exceptions such as India) stands in contrast to the superpowers and their European clients, where the armed forces were firmly under civilian control. No less than the cold war, therefore, the sixties were about color, creed, and coups.

The Politics of Race in Black and White

In the English language, the word "race" originated in the sixteenth century and was used then to denote a common ancestry, as in the biblical expression "the race of Abraham." By the mid-nineteenth century it signified distinct types of human beings differentiated by skin pigment, head shape, and so on. In the early twentieth century, notions about separate racial groups with inherited characteristics became popular in Europe and America both as folk ideas and as official policies—reaching their nadir in the anti-Semitism of Hitler's Third Reich. These race policies had been justified on the basis of science, particularly bowdlerized versions of Darwinism. But the interwar period saw a growing critique of "scientific racism" by figures such as Julian Huxley, the eminent British biologist, which was reinforced by revulsion at Nazi Germany. After the war, this critique became the new orthodoxy. In July 1950, UNESCO—the new United Nations Educational, Scientific and Cultural Organization—issued a major report stating that race was "not so much a biological phenomenon as a social myth."[1] However, in parts of the world, myth had been institutionalized as political reality. The assault on white "racism" became a feature of the 1960s. Mounted in the name of another invented category, "blackness," this attack had the ironic effect of entrenching racial conceptions still further.[2]

"Racism" entered the international vocabulary during this decade.[3] Its connotations could never be separated from Nazi Germany. Although the death camps had been exposed in 1945, most accounts simply portrayed them as one of the multitudinous barbarisms of the Third Reich. Only in the 1960s did it became common knowledge that the Nazis had mounted a systematic campaign to exterminate the Jews to preserve the purity of the "Aryan race." This was partly the result of publicity by the Israeli government, who used the trial in Jerusalem of Adolf Eichmann, the organizer of the "Final Solution," in 1960–1961 as an extended history lesson. "We want the nations of the world to know," said Prime Minister David Ben-Gurion.[4] The issues were aired further at a similar trial in Frankfurt in 1963–1965 of former SS members accused of torture and mass murder at Auschwitz. Through these events—and through influential books, particularly by the scholar Hannah Arendt—the enormity of Nazi racism finally became clear to the wider world. In Israel itself, no one could forget—or was allowed to forget. One of the country's most sacred shrines is Yad Vashem, a mixture of museum, monuments, and archives started in 1954 just outside Jerusalem's old city walls. Conveying both Israeli "pride in heroism and shame in victimization," the museum takes visitors from the degradation of the ghetto to redemption in the promised land—each meaningful only in the light of the other. The racism memorialized at Yad Vashem was central to Israel's new "civic religion."[5]

But most of the world focused on the present, not the past. The big "race" stories in the 1960s concerned the American South, southern Africa, and Western Europe's new immigrants.

Racial discrimination was the Achilles heel of the world's leading superpower. In the United States, the postwar decade had seen incremental changes, such as the signing of Jackie Robinson, the first black (the term increasingly preferred over "negro" or "colored") in major-league baseball in 1947, and integration of the nation's armed forces during the Korean War. Less dramatically, for two decades the black middle-class pressure group, the National Association for the Advancement of Colored People (NAACP), had been chipping away at racial discrimination through test cases in the courts. On May 17, 1954, the Supreme Court issued a brief but momentous ruling that so-called "separate but equal" facilities were discriminatory. Although this decision only applied to education, it undercut the whole edifice of "Jim Crow" laws and customs across the South. But the Court, anxious to avoid a political crisis, left enforcement up to Southern judges, with the result that in 1964, a decade after the original decision, only 2 percent of Southern blacks were enrolled in desegregated schools.[6] Often schools were closed or funds cut off as white resistance stiffened. The federal government was unwilling to trespass on cherished principles of democratic localism except where public order was jeopardized, as at Little Rock, Arkansas, in the autumn of 1957. And although blacks in Montgomery, Alabama, mounted a year-long bus boycott from December 1955, which, in tandem with another NAACP test case, forced desegregation of the city's bus system, few other cities followed suit. The Supreme Court had unlocked the door, but it still had to be pushed open.

One important outcome of the Montgomery campaign was the creation of the Southern Christian Leadership Conference (SCLC) in January 1957, bringing together activist black ministers, traditionally the elite of their communities. Its importance in the early civil rights movement is another reminder of the continued power of religious belief and authority. Heading the SCLC was the Reverend Dr. Martin Luther King, Jr., who had been catapulted to prominence by his leadership of the Montgomery boycott. Born in 1929, King was a studious yet emotional young pastor who was aroused by the brutal white supremacism of Alabama. His philosophy of nonresistance was rooted in Christian pacificism—"we must meet the forces of hate with the power of love"[7]—but during and after the boycott it became systematized through closer study of Gandhi. A visit to India (he called it a pilgrimage) in February 1959 deepened his understanding of nonviolent resistance, as did the more private influence of committed pacifists such as Bayard Rustin and Glenn Smiley of the Fellowship of Reconciliation (FOR). Gandhi's tactics became the philosophy of the SCLC. Smiley helped spread them among students across the South in a series of campus workshops in 1958–1960.

In doing so, the SCLC was appealing to a new generation of blacks—babyboom offspring of parents who had climbed into the middle-class during postwar prosperity. Equally important, these families were part of articulate, urban communities: between 1940 and 1960 the proportion of Southern blacks working in agriculture fell from 40 percent to 10 percent. The parents were often politically quiescent, particularly during the viscerally anticommunist 1950s, content with the real economic gains won during their lifetimes and anxious to pass them on to their children. But their children, born since 1940, had more ambitious goals. Most knew of King and the Montgomery boycott—FOR distributed two hundred thousand copies of a "comic book" telling how "50,000 negroes found a new way to end racial discrimination"—and many had attended the campus workshops about nonviolence. In 1960 the frustration of black students finally boiled over.

The initial targets were "whites-only" restaurants and lunch counters. On February 1, 1960, four students staged a sit-in at the Woolworth's store in Greensboro, North Carolina, after they were denied food service. Protests quickly spread across the South to cities such as Nashville, Tennessee, where a campaign had already been planned. It required considerable moral and physical courage to sit at the counters, backs turned to a torrent of verbal and physical abuse. But the students had been well trained. They endured in silence and, as one group was carried away in police wagons, another group was ready to take their places. By the autumn of 1960, sit-in campaigns had been organized in more than one hundred cities, and some had already borne fruit as white businesses capitulated because of lost earnings. The Student Nonviolent Coordinating Committee (SNCC) was formed in April 1960 with the goal of rapid racial equality.

In May 1961, nonviolence took to the buses as the Congress of Racial Equality (CORE) tried to make real the 1947 Supreme Court decision that segregation on interstate transport was unconstitutional. This had never been enforced by the federal government; now CORE's "freedom riders" hoped to force the government's hand by bringing violence on themselves. In Alabama one bus was firebombed by white racists; riders from another were beaten up as local police stayed conspicuously away. The Kennedy administration was reluctantly drawn in, supportive in principle of civil rights yet wary of powerful Southern Democrats. When Attorney General Robert Kennedy appealed for a "cooling-off" period, freedom rider James Farmer told a reporter that "we had been cooling off for 100 years. If we got any cooler we'd be in a deep freeze."[8] Some three hundred freedom riders rode the buses that summer in the cause of integration. Behind the scenes, Bobby Kennedy struck a deal with Southern governors. If there was no more mob violence, he would not use federal forces to enforce federal law. That left Southern courts free to imprison freedom riders for trespass and other breaches of state law.

King was forced to move rapidly to keep up with events. The civil rights movement was in danger of fragmenting into a mosaic of rival groupings, from the litigious NAACP to the activists of SNCC. But in 1963 he reasserted his leadership and finally forced the Kennedy administration to act. Birmingham, the largest industrial city in Alabama, was a notorious stronghold of white supremacism and police brutality. Here the sit-ins, as intended, prompted a violent response from police chief T. Eugene "Bull" Connor and his men. After King was again thrown in jail, his associates, in what some regarded as a cynical act, organized a march of some six thousand black children, aged six to sixteen, on May 2. Connor used firehoses, clubs, and even dogs on them—all in front of the TV cameras. Humiliated nationally and internationally, Kennedy finally climbed off the fence. He made it clear that federal troops would be used, if necessary, to enforce desegregation in Birmingham. And in June 1963 he announced a new civil rights bill. To keep up the pressure, black leaders organized a massive March on Washington. On August 28, 1963, some two hundred fifty thousand people filled the Mall from the Lincoln Memorial to the Washington Monument (Plate 20) to hear King rhetorically unfold his dream that one day the United States would live out its creed that all men are created equal, and his children would "not be judged by the color of their skin, but the content of their character."[9] In December King journeyed to Oslo to receive the Nobel Peace Prize. But it took Kennedy's assassination and all of his success on Lyndon Johnson's legislative skills to force the civil rights bill into law in July 1964, after the longest filibuster in Senate history—taking up eighty-two working days, sixty-three thousand pages of the *Congressional Record,* and ten million words.[10] Nevertheless, racial discrimination was now illegal in public accommodation throughout the United States.

Although "whites-only" toilets, dressing rooms, and lunch counters were emotive symbols, the fundamental issue for blacks was the vote. For thirty years, the NAACP and other black civil rights groups had been quietly trying to increase black voter registration. But in 1964 barely one-third of eligible southern blacks were registered, thanks to Southern harassment and federal indifference. In mid-1964 the SNCC mounted a major effort in Mississippi ("Freedom Summer") to get out the vote for the November elections. King targeted the registration campaign in Selma, Alabama, where just 156 of fifteen thousand eligible blacks could vote in 1963. On March 7, police used clubs and tear gas to turn back marchers crossing Selma's Edmund Pettus bridge. Pictures of "Bloody Sunday" were beamed across the nation and around the world. Now Johnson's aides cut through the legal intricacies to prepare a voting rights bill. Blacks noted cynically that the deaths of two white civil rights workers in Selma in March had far more effect on national opinion than years of beatings and lynchings perpetrated on blacks. On March 15, an emotional Johnson presented his bill to the Congress. The previous November, LBJ had won a landslide electoral victory, confirming the man who had inherited Kennedy's mantle as president in his own right. The product of a poor family in eastern Texas, Johnson had a gut sympathy for blacks—unlike Kennedy (a wealthy Bostonian). He also wanted to make his own mark on the statute book. But he could not have succeeded in passing his bill without the new two-to-one Democratic majorities in House and Senate, which negated the power of conservative Southerners.

The Voting Rights Act of August 1965 was a milestone in American race relations. For the first time, federal personnel would enforce registration in recalcitrant counties. At last the voter registration campaigns took off. In Alabama the proportion of blacks registered rose from 19 percent in 1964 to over 61 percent in 1969; in Mississippi the increase was even more dramatic, from under 7 percent to over 66 percent—roughly the 1969 average throughout the South.[11] The Southern black was transformed from political object into political participant. Blacks were being elected to political office themselves, particularly at local and state levels, drawing on people and networks mobilized during civil rights campaigns. And the black vote was now substantial enough to matter to white politicians. Andrew Young, a King aide who became a U.S. Congressman from Georgia in 1974, recalled the days when "Southern politics were just 'nigger' politics"—won by the white politician who could "outnigger" the rest in his vilification of blacks. Then, said Young,

> you get 35 to 40 percent registered and it's amazing how quick they learned how to say "Nee-grow," and now that we've got 50, 60, 70 percent of the black votes registered in the South, everybody's proud to be associated with their black brothers and sisters.

The most striking example was George Wallace, the populist governor of Alabama, who in 1963 proclaimed "Segregation today! Segregation tomorrow! Segregation forever!" and physically tried to stop the first black student entering the University of Alabama. A decade later, in November 1973, Wallace crowned a black homecoming queen at the university and told a conference of black mayors: "We're all God's children. All God's children are equal."[12]

Guaranteed political rights at last allowed Southern blacks to enter the political process and use it, as had other minority groups before them, to improve their status. Yet progress was slow: even in 1975, 98 percent of elected officials in the South were white, though blacks made up one-fifth of the voting-age population. And like newly independent nations of Africa, American blacks discovered that political freedom did not mean economic equality. Five days after President Johnson signed the Voting Rights Act into law in August 1965, the deprived black ghetto of Los Angeles went up in flames. The Watts riot, in which thirty-four died and damage to property totalled $40 million, was certainly not the first disturbance in non-Southern cities. But it marked a dramatic escalation in civil disorder. Equally significant was the impotence of the civil rights movement outside the South. When King visited Watts after the riots, his conciliation efforts were resented. Many black residents had never even heard of him.

The race crisis had now shifted to the urban north. In 1940 more than half of American blacks lived in rural areas, by 1960 just over one-quarter. Over the same period the proportion of American blacks who lived in the South declined from three-quarters to a half. In the cities of the North and Midwest, blacks did not face the overt, formal segregation of the Jim Crow South. But tight residential segregation had the same effect. In the urban North and Midwest, blacks clustered in inner-city ghettos, where most of them were destined to remain because of discrimination in housing, education, and employment, while the whites and the wealth moved to the suburbs. When King tried to highlight their problems in Chicago in 1966, he got nowhere. These insidious forms of discrimination did not provide clear targets for marches and sit-ins, unlike the segregated buses or restaurants of the South.

The sign held aloft by one black picket in New York in 1963 summed up the problem: "I'd eat at your lunch counter—if only I had a job."[13]

Yet the unemployed underclass of the black ghettos had been aroused by the revolution in the South, viewing much of it on their TV screens. This, and persistent harassment by white police forces, were the fuel for the urban violence of the mid-1960s. Often the spark was spontaneous—a clash with police kindled by the summer heat—but TV pictures fanned the flames of emulation. By the end of 1968, fifty thousand had been arrested and eight thousand hurt in more than three hundred race riots since 1965. In mid-July 1967, the city of Newark, New Jersey exploded; twenty-five blacks were killed as the National Guard restored order. A few days later, downtown Detroit was destroyed in a week-long orgy of arson and vandalism. Deaths totaled forty-three, damage ran to $250 million, and fourteen square miles of the inner city were reduced to smoking ruins. But whereas Newark was the most rundown city in the nation, many Detroit blacks had jobs, cars and homes in a prosperous, progressive city. Much of the property consumed in the inferno was black, not white. The climactic spasm of violence occurred in April 1968, after King was killed by a white gunman in Memphis, Tennessee. Over one hundred cities were ravaged, and forty-six people died. TV screens around the world showed soldiers in full combat gear taking up positions around the U.S. Capitol, only a few blocks from Washington's burning black ghetto.

King did not create the civil rights movement, which grew from the grassroots mobilization of blacks, male and female, across the South. But he held it together and attracted white liberal support by his strategy of nonviolent provocation of white violence. The emotional pressures on him were enormous—he found some release in sexual promiscuity that he abhorred yet could not control—but, even before his death, he knew that the fragile civil rights consensus of the mid-1960s had broken asunder. White liberals were shocked by the violence; Johnson had turned against King because of his opposition to the Vietnam War. And King was widely denounced by his own people, many of whom took up the slogan "Black Power" and chanted "we shall overrun," not "we shall overcome." In October 1966 the Black Panthers were founded in Oakland, California, as an armed self-defense movement with a Marxist philosophy.

The most passionate spokesman of the new black nationalism was Malcolm Little, or Malcolm X, who transcended his ghetto origins as a drug dealer and petty criminal to become a hypnotic orator. After he was shot in February 1965, his words lived on in the posthumous *Autobiography*. The differences with King were fundamental. Instead of integration, Malcolm preached black separateness; he urged pride in blackness, not conformity to white values. Whereas King's leadership had been inspired by evangelical Christianity,

Malcolm X espoused Islam. And where King talked of bringing blacks within the American dream, he pointed them to their African heritage. The growing appeal of the label "Afro-American" suggested the ambivalence felt by many blacks about the idea of assimilation. It also highlighted links between the liberation struggle in the United States and that on the African continent.

In 1960, sixteen African states became independent; ten more followed over the next four years. The effect on the United Nations was profound. In 1945, only three of its fifty-one founder members were African; by 1970, African states made up a third of the 127-strong organization. Together, African and Asian postcolonial states constituted about half the UN membership.[14] By the 1960s, the early American dominance of the General Assembly was a thing of the past. And a new sense of African identity was reflected in the Organization of African Unity (OAU), established in 1963. This bore little resemblance to grander dreams of a United States of Africa, entertained by Ghana's Kwame Nkrumah and other ardent Pan-Africanists. It was a group of independent African states, dedicated to the peaceful resolution of mutual disputes and especially to total decolonization of the African continent.

By the mid-1960s, when the dust had settled from the precipitate European retreat, only a few African countries were not under black rule—mostly in the south and all of them with strong settler communities. These were South Africa, Rhodesia, and the Portuguese colonies of Guiné, in West Africa, and Angola and Mozambique, flanking South Africa on the southwest and southeast coasts.

In South Africa, the National Party tightened the apparatus of apartheid after the 1960 riots that followed the shootings at Sharpeville (see Chapter 3). Helping to legitimize it was the authority of the Dutch Reformed Church—a bedrock of white Afrikaner society. Premier Hendrik Verwoerd—austere, almost messianic in his conviction—insisted that the party would stand by its racial policies "like walls of granite."[15] Black political organizations were banned, police powers were extended, and a determined effort was made under the Separate Development Laws to force Africans into eight (later ten) Bantustans. Some of these so-called homelands did reflect tribal identities (such as Zululand), but Bophuthatswana, for instance, was an amalgam of seven widely scattered areas in the north. The aim was that Africans, though comprising 68 percent of the population, would have rights of residence in only 13 percent of the country. The Bantustans were allowed some political autonomy, but industry was restricted, and their main function was as controlled labor reservoirs of migrant male workers and commuters into nearby cities such as Pretoria and Durban. They also served as convenient disposal grounds for the economically useless—the sick, aged and disabled. The government was also elaborating its divide-and-rule philosophy by giving some Africans a vested interest in apartheid through Bantustan autonomy and development and also by allowing the Asian and "colored" populations greater civil and political rights. The government thereby hoped to serve its two goals—racial control of nonwhites, who were four-fifths of the population, and also their economic exploitation by the whites.

The autocratic Portuguese government of Antonio Salazar was the only European power still resisting the ebb tide of empire. It continued to develop the colonies, by investment and emigration, as an alternative source of wealth and status to offset Portugal's marginality in the new Europe. Some 10.5 million Africans lived under Portuguese rule. Only 1 percent of them were *assimilados* (nonwhites admitted to the status of "civilized persons," mostly because they were of "mixed blood"). A quarter of adult males were engaged in some form of forced labor, and the Portuguese showed no inclination, unlike the British or French, to concede even token political rights to African collaborators. "We will not surrender, we will not share . . . the smallest item of our sovereignty," declaimed Salazar, who had no doubt that "there are decadent or—if you prefer—backward races whom we feel we have a duty to lead to civilization."[16] In Guiné and Angola, liberation movements were formed during 1956, in Mozambique in 1962. By 1964 all of them were engaged in armed struggle against the Portuguese. The latter were forced on to the defensive by hit-and-run tactics, but the guerrillas were not numerous (perhaps eleven thousand by 1974 in Mozambique, a country double the area of California).[17] In 1969 Henry Kissinger, the U.S. National Security Adviser, judged that "the outlook for the rebellions is continued stalemate: the rebels cannot oust the Portuguese and the Portuguese can contain but not eliminate the rebels."[18]

In Southern Rhodesia, the whites, led by Ian Smith, a former wartime fighter pilot in Britain, had declared independence in November 1965 rather than accept British proposals for black majority rule (see Chapter 3). Black organizations were banned, and guerrilla activity remained ineffectual until the early 1970s. The British Labour government of Harold Wilson (1964–1970) decided not to use force to subdue Smith: the logistical problems were huge, Suez in 1956 was not an encouraging precedent, and no potential African government was waiting in the wings. Wilson therefore opted for economic sanctions, predicting in January 1966 that these "might well bring the rebellion to an end within weeks rather than months,"[19] but sanctions were hard to enforce as long as outlets existed through South Africa and Mozambique. The three white regimes were well aware that their fates interlocked—they provided mutual aid and coordinated their anti-insurgent operations—and in the late 1960s, all three looked fairly secure. As we shall see, it took a revolution in Portugal in 1974 to change the balance of power in southern Africa.

The 1960s were, however, notable for the development of African organization and ideology. In origin, the popular fronts were largely the work of educated leaders, such as Agostinho Neto of Angola, who were politicized during their time at Portuguese universities. But their followers were mostly drawn from the rural populations that they strove to mobilize. Like the Chinese communists two decades earlier, they therefore focused on local issues—crippling taxes, forced labor, poor sanitation. Unlike the Chinese, however, they were also trying to create a national consciousness out of these local aspirations, using the Portuguese and their headmen collaborators as the combined targets. Neto (a former doctor) said that the aim was "to free and modernise our people by a dual revolution—against their traditional structures which can no longer serve them, and against colonial rule."[20] Not surprisingly, the popular fronts took on an increasingly Marxist hue: Frelimo in Mozambique lurched sharply to the left under the leadership of Samora Machel after internal bloodletting in 1969. And they received much of their material aid from Soviet and Chinese sources, while the West, more discreetly, supplied Portugal, a NATO ally.

In Rhodesia and South Africa, too, there was significant rural protest. Guerrillas operating in Rhodesia played on tribal resentment about "stolen lands," not merely an economic issue but also entailing loss of ancestral holy places.[21] Likewise, in South Africa, the long-standing policy of pushing the Africans onto the most marginal lands had provoked a series of rural revolts, the most organized being the Mpondo rebellion that lasted most of 1960. But these rural protests had little connection with the urban discontent fostered by organizations such as the ANC in South Africa. And in neither of these countries, unlike the Portuguese colonies, were there indigenous liberation movements in the 1960s with their own rural base areas where political education could occur. The most significant developments during this decade, particularly in South Africa, were in black attitudes rather than actions.

In the wake of the 1960 Sharpeville uprisings, the main African political organizations, the African National Congress (ANC) and the Pan-African Congress (PAC) both formed military wings to conduct an armed struggle. The ANC began with a program of sabotage; the more radical PAC planned armed insurrection. But by 1964 both organizations had been banned and their leaders exiled or imprisoned. The ANC's Nelson Mandela, a lawyer by training, used his trial "not as a test of the law but as a platform for our beliefs" by admitting the campaign of sabotage but justifying the resort to violence. As he had hoped, his four-hour statement on April 20, 1964, was reported in newspapers across the world and even in South Africa. After setting out in detail his belief in equal political rights within a multiracial South Africa, he ended with the peroration, "It is an ideal which I hope to live for and achieve. But if needs be, it is an ideal for which I am prepared

LEGACIES OF WORLD WAR TWO — THE CLOUD AND THE RUINS

1: Atomic bomb test at Bikini Atoll in the Pacific, July 1946.

2: The Brandenburg Gate in Berlin, March 1945.

3: The Allied "Big Three"—Churchill, Truman, and Stalin—meet at Potsdam, July 23, 1945, for the final wartime summit.

4: On September 2, 1945, the Japanese delegation stands on the deck of the USS *Missouri* waiting to sign the instrument of surrender.

5: Mao Zedong proclaims the People's Republic of China from Tiananmen, the Gate of Heavenly Peace, in Beijing, October 1, 1949.

6: In October 1959, Ho Chi Minh of North Vietnam (left) and Sukarno of Indonesia confer at Cipanas in western Java.

7: One reason for the postwar trade boom was containerization. Here a container from Manchester, England, is unloaded at the Cyprus port of Famagusta, for road transportation to Nicosia.

8: Urban living—the center of the Indian city of Calcutta in 1977.

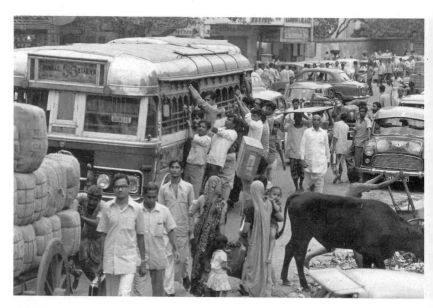

Two Styles of Architecture: Modernism and Vernacular

: Brazil's new capital, Brasília, in 1971.

0: *Favela* shanties stacked up the hillsides of Rio de Janeiro in 1968.

11: Budapest's huge statue of Stalin was decapitated during the Hungarian revolt of November 1956.

12: The Berlin Wall cut off the Brandenburg Gate from the ruined Reichstag, from where this photograph was taken.

13: NATO's Big Four—Harold Macmillan (United Kingdom), Dwight D. Eisenhower (United States), Charles de Gaulle (France), and Konrad Adenauer (West Germany)—meet in Paris, December 19, 1959.

14: The superpower Big Two—Kennedy and Khrushchev—lock horns in Vienna in June 1961.

15: As the Stars and Stripes are lowered, the new Philippine flag is raised on Independence Day, July 4, 1946—a scene repeated across the postwar world.

16: Many former colonial subjects migrated to the West. Here immigrants from Pakistan are working in an English textile factory in Shipley, Yorkshire (May 1969).

to die."[22] Contrary to expectations, Mandela and his associates were spared, but they were sentenced to life imprisonment in the grim prison on Robben Island, off Cape Town. His words made him an international celebrity and a continuing inspiration for the ANC, but for the next quarter-century he had no active role to play in the freedom struggle.

The removal of the existing black leaders left a political vacuum. No one and nothing filled it until after the Soweto disturbances in 1976, but behind the scenes a new generation of wealthier, more educated urban blacks was being politicized, akin to the one growing up in the American South in the late 1950s. These were the children of the black clerical classes, an important adjunct of apartheid, and the beneficiaries of the controlled expansion of African education intended to service the Bantustan communities. During the 1960s the number of Africans in secondary schools more than doubled to 127,000; the number of university students quadrupled. Students were taught on segregated campuses that fostered a sense both of African solidarity and of alienation from a white-dominated education system. These campuses were the seedbed for the black consciousness movement. In South Africa, as in the American South, students were the vanguard of protest—signs of a deeper youth movement that I shall examine in the next chapter.

In July 1969 African students founded the South African Students Organization (SASO) by breaking away from the National Union of South African Students. White liberals who controlled NUSAS were considered unreceptive to their goals and problems. "We are Black students not black Students," was one early slogan. Around SASO—in which the leading figures were Steve Biko and Barney Pityana—there developed a network of black self-help groups engaged in community projects to promote literacy, health and welfare. SASO's deeper goal was to instill a new pride in being black, not merely in superficial ways such as abandoning bleaching cream or hot-oil combs to straighten hair, but because, in Biko's words, "the most potent weapon in the hands of the oppressor is the *mind* of the oppressed."[23] He believed that the precondition of any political struggle was "to make the black man come to himself; to pump back life into his empty shell; to infuse him with pride and dignity."[24] SASO workshops drew on black power writings from the United States and from African exponents of Negritude such as Léopold Senghor (president of Senegal from 1960 to 1981), which took traits that European writers had condemned in Africans and revalued them positively. After intense debate, SASO also made the radical move of defining as "black" all Africans, coloureds, and Asians who felt committed to the liberation process. This transcended the South African state's racial categories and also resisted the implicit equation of "nonwhite" with nonperson. The campus workshops and discussions raised the consciousness of a generation of young blacks, who would go on to influential positions as teachers, doctors, and journalists and who often became political activists after 1976.

In the 1960s, "race relations" were an issue not only in the United States and southern Africa but also in Western Europe. In Britain the postwar years saw a growing number of immigrants from the "New Commonwealth" (a euphemism for nonwhite), especially the West Indies in the 1950s and the Indian subcontinent in the 1960s. As British subjects, they enjoyed unrestricted rights to enter, work, and live in Britain. The numbers involved were not huge, peaking at 136,000 in 1961, before the first controls were imposed. In most postwar years, Britain had more emigrants than immigrants, and even in 1971 New Commonwealth immigrants and their children constituted only 1.34 million (2.7 percent of the total population). But as nonwhites, their presence was visible and, in certain cities, substantial. The Conservative party started to control colored immigration in 1962; the Labour party, more reluctantly, followed suit while in power from 1964 to 1970. After 1968, the criterion of "patriality" became standard, in other words restricting free immigration to those with a UK parent or grandparent. On the other hand, legislation in 1965 and 1968 officially outlawed discrimination and established a Race Relations Board to try to enforce it. But the tacit bipartisan consensus was fractured by Enoch Powell, a romantic British nationalist and maverick Tory politician with leadership aspirations, who warned in April 1968 that Britain was "heaping up its own funeral pyre" by allowing fifty thousand immigrants to enter each year. He added luridly: "Like the Roman, I seem to see 'the River Tiber foaming with much blood!' "[25] Powell's populist attempt to play the race card did not succeed: British politics were more party dominated than the democratic localism of America, in which a George Wallace could prosper as long as he cultivated his local base. Powell was ostracized from his party. But his rhetoric made him a celebrity with a large following and brought race into mainstream British politics.

Immigration was substantial across Western Europe in the 1960s, because of economic growth and labor shortages. But much of it was European in origin, particularly the surge of Italians into Switzerland and Germany and of Spaniards and Portuguese into France. Britain was unusual in that, although immigration was small scale relative to the continent (over 7 percent of the German and French populations were foreign by the late 1970s), immigrants were largely nonwhites seeking permanent residence rather than whites with guest-worker status, as in Germany. Equally distinctive was the British apparatus of race-relations legislation, which reflected the country's close attention to American problems and remedies. A Labour party report in 1967 observed, "The American experience not only warns us of the dangers of racial discrimination but also indicates that legislation can contribute to the solution, if only it is enacted in time."[26] Antiracism was being used to fight racism, both helping to entrench racial stereotypes.[27]

By the 1970s most European countries were restricting migration, from whatever source, as their economies contracted and as they woke up to the socioeconomic problems of guest workers who did not, as expected, return home. Even a noncolonial country like West Germany began to experience communal tensions by the 1970s, revolving around its Turkish population (already around a quarter of total foreigners). And several other European states also found that, on the ebb tide of empire, the colonized were colonizing the former colonizers. That was Belgium's fate in the 1960s, following its rapid and chaotic departure from Central Africa. The Netherlands also experienced substantial nonwhite immigration in the early 1950s and again in the 1970s as legacies of decolonization and continued instability in what had been the Dutch East Indies. Immigration increased in France during the 1960s, reaching a peak of 174,000 in 1970, with the growth mainly from former French North Africa, which accounted for 28 percent of immigrants by this date. As in Britain, they faced discrimination in jobs and housing and also a growing backlash against their presence. In France the term "immigrant," used pejoratively, was applied particularly to Algerians, even though the Portuguese were more numerous (eight hundred fifty thousand as against eight hundred thousand). In the summer of 1973 the campaign against *immigration sauvage* by the neofascist New Order party sparked racial violence in which eleven Algerians were killed. The following year President Valéry Giscard d'Estaing banned immigration from outside the EEC and promised welfare programs for existing immigrants to create a place for them in France that would be "dignified, humane, and equitable."[28] Little was achieved, however. Henceforth, much of Western Europe would have to wrestle with the politics of race and the challenges of multiculturalism that had already emerged across the Atlantic.

Ethnicity and Conflict in Black Africa

In the 1960s, therefore, the United States, Southern Africa and Western Europe all seemed, in different ways, to reflect a new polarity in world affairs—black versus white. But although white racism was a reality, to define human conflicts entirely in this way was to gloss over the bitter divisions lurking within the term *black*. Britain's 1967–1968 crisis over immigration, for instance, had been prompted by the Kenyan decision to expel its Asian business community, mostly British passport holders of Indian origin. Uganda followed suit in 1972. Africans themselves were fragmented by ethnic rivalries. In Rhodesia, for instance, the guerrillas were split between ZANU, representing the majority Shona peoples, and ZAPU, with its largely Ndebele base. In the Central African states of Rwanda and Burundi, the seesaw struggle of Hutu and Tutsi has characterized national politics ever since the Belgians departed. Nor can one forget the bloody north-south divide between Muslim and Christian in the Sudan—a country on the historic frontier of Arab expansion into Africa. The ferocity of such ethnic and religious feuds was evident above all in two devastating African civil wars with which this section is particularly concerned—in the Congo in 1960–1964 and in Nigeria in 1966–1970.

In the Congo, as we saw in Chapter 3, the Belgians had done virtually nothing to prepare the fifteen million Africans for self-rule, which came with precipitate speed in 1959–1960. The new political parties were mostly regional and also had sharp differences over the pace of change. These tensions were personalized in rivalry between the fiery radical nationalist Patrice Lumumba, who became prime minister, and the cautious, calculating Bakongo leader Joseph Kasavubu, the Congo's first president. Within days of independence on June 30, 1960, order collapsed when the army mutinied because the senior posts remained in white hands.[29] At the same time, the copper-belt southeastern province of Katanga declared independence under its leader, Moshe Tshombe; the diamond-rich South Kasai region in the center of the country also broke away. In breach of the independence agreements, the Belgians sent troops back in to protect their nationals. The soldiers became a main prop for the Katangan regime. By the end of 1960, the Congo was split in four—the two secessionist regimens in Katanga and South Kasai, plus two rival national governments under Kasavubu and Lumumba in, respectively, Léopoldville (Kinshasa) and Stanleyville (Kisangani). And Lumumba's decision to seek Soviet logistical help pushed the Americans, already suspicious of his radicalism, into supporting plots to remove him. When Lumumba was murdered in Katanga in February 1961, he became a martyr among radical African nationalists.

Fears that the Congo would become a cold war battleground prompted novel action by the United Nations. During the Suez crisis of 1956 it had engaged in peacekeeping; now, under the energetic leadership of Secretary General Dag Hammarskjöld of Sweden, UN troops moved in as peacemakers. Although Hammarskjöld himself died in September 1961 when his plane crashed (or was shot down) in Katanga, a new if tenuous federal government was by then in operation, and decisive UN military action ended the Katanga secession in January 1963. By now the Congo had been fragmented from six provinces to twenty-one, following ethnic boundaries or old colonial districts. The compromise premier, Cyrille Adoula, lost his grip; in July 1964 Kasavuba invited Tshombe to form a government. But the army, reorganized and unified with U.S. encouragement under General Joseph Mobutu, had become the main pillar of national unity, putting down renewed rebellions in late 1964 and seizing power itself in November 1965. Mobutu, aged thirty-five, began a dictatorial presidency that was to last for more than three decades. As part of his "return to African authenticity" (often invented), in the early 1970s he renamed the country Zaire and himself Sésé Séko, meaning "all-powerful warrior."

The fate of Nigeria—by far the most populous country in Africa, with forty-two million people in 1960—was even more tragic. Although political parties there had a longer history than in the Congo and the British had tried to give Nigerians administrative experience (the Congo had only thirty university graduates to fill over four thousand senior bureaucratic posts in 1960), at root, the Nigerian republic was also a colonial administrative unit that lacked national coherence. Nigerians spoke nearly two hundred fifty languages, but two-thirds of the population fell into three groups: the Hausa-Fulani peoples of the north, mostly Islamic and ruled by autocratic emirs; the Yoruba in the southwest; and the Igbo in the southeast. Both of the latter were more Anglicized and developed. Each of these groupings was tenuous, with many internal ethnic rivalries, but increasingly Nigerian politics, before and after independence in 1960, followed these main fault lines. Yoruba and Igbo each constituted about a quarter of the population; the Hausa north, if it held together, embraced more than half and was determined to dominate the new federal government. Every political issue—be it elections, the census, or the composition of the army and bureaucracy—became a cause for ethnic-regional dispute. Confidence in the new government was also sapped by political corruption and economic failure. Fears in the army leadership (particularly Igbos) that they would be used by the north to repress the west prompted General Aguiyi Ironsi, an Igbo, to lead a coup in January 1966.[30]

The north now feared an Igbo bid for domination. Amid mounting panic on all sides, northern junior officers toppled Ironsi in July and unleashed a wave of pogroms against Igbos in the army, business, and the bureaucracy. Perhaps two million Igbos fled to the east in a bloodbath reminiscent of India in 1947–1948. The last train to arrive from the north bearing Igbo refugees in October 1966 included a woman passenger whose only possession in her suitcase was the head of her child. Such incidents were highlighted in the eastern press, sparking reprisals against Hausas and fueling popular demands for secession. During the following winter the military governor of the east, Colonel Odumegwu Ojukwu, built up the armed forces and then declared the independence of the region as the state of Biafra in May 1967. The federal government invaded on July 6, promising to end the secession in two days. In fact it took thirty months of attrition, in which 2.5 million died (mostly from hunger), before the Biafran state was squeezed into surrender in January 1970.[31] The ravaged east was left to reconstruct itself, while Nigeria continued to be governed by a military rulers except for the short-lived "Second Republic" of 1979–1983.

The bloodbaths in the Congo and Nigeria were extreme, but their underlying causes typified tensions in much of black Africa. By 1970, the OAU's early ideals of pan-African unity and prosperity seemed like preposterous delusions. In the words of Davidson Abioseh Nicol, a doctor, diplomat, and poet from Sierra Leone,

> You are not a country, Africa,
> You are a concept,
> Fashioned in our minds, each to each,
> To hide our separate fears,
> To dream our separate dreams.[32]

The most obvious sign of separateness was ethnic and territorial rivalry—what Europeans called tribalism. Although often considered "premodern," tribal distinctions had, in many cases, been sharpened as tools of colonial administration. After independence, they were then used as weapons by opposition politicians to mobilize support against ruling elites.[33] Tanzania was one of the few states without serious ethnic conflict, but neighboring Uganda was wracked by tensions between the Buganda people and the rest. In many places, as in Nigeria and the Congo, the problems were exacerbated by the perpetuation of colonial administrative units as the borders of the new state. In the case of the continent's longest-running regional conflict, in the Horn of Africa, however, the British and Italian colonial imprint had been superficial and European economic interests, such as mining, were weak. This was an essentially indigenous struggle. The coastal Somali Republic was unusual in its strong sense of nationhood based on culture, language, and Islam. Its bid to bring the remaining Somalis under its rule after independence in 1960 brought it into direct conflict with its neighbor, the hinterland Christian state of Ethiopia, under the autocratic Haile Selassie. While fighting with Somalia over the intervening Ogaden region, he was also trying to absorb the northern region of Eritrea against the resistance of a guerrilla liberation front. Thus, the early 1960s saw the beginnings of a three-cornered struggle that was to ravage the Horn of Africa for thirty years, drawing in the superpowers in the 1970s and consigning millions of people to starvation and death.

Along the way, both the Somali Republic and Haile Selassie had been swept aside by their armies in 1969 and 1974. In the 1960s, in fact, African coups became almost an international joke. In the dismissive words of George Ball, an adviser to presidents Kennedy and Johnson, "During the years I was in the State Department, I was awakened once or twice a month by a telephone call in the middle of the night announcing a coup d'état in some distant capital with a name like a typographical error."[34] Only a few countries were spared, notably Kenya under Jomo Kenyatta (1963–1978) and Tanzania, ruled by Julius Nyerere (1962–1990). However, both required British help to suppress army mutinies in 1964, and in any case electoral politics soon gave way to authoritarian one-party rule backed by the army. In neighboring Uganda, General Idi Amin seized power in 1971, beginning eight years of terror until he was toppled by a Tanzanian invasion. Even some governments with a strong political base were not immune: in Ghana, Kwame Nkrumah was overthrown in February 1966. Thereafter military rule became the norm. As in Nigeria, coup often bred coup, lower down the ranks. The most extreme mimetic example was Sierra Leone, where the majors who took power in 1967 were themselves displaced by their own subordinates the following year. More striking still, the numbers involved were usually small. Mobutu seized Léopoldville in 1965 with two hundred men; five hundred troops toppled Nkrumah's regime the following year; in 1968, the triumphant Sierra Leone army comprised one battalion with fifty officers.

"Tribalism" and coups were, however, only the superficial signs of deeper flaws in the political and economic structure. In most postcolonial countries, the bureaucracy and the army were the most coherent and effective organizational structures—the former ultimately depending on the latter. By contrast, political parties were fragmented, labor unions weak, and other social groupings inchoate. It was therefore relatively easy for small groups of resolute soldiers to seize the levers of power, notably government buildings, the airport, and the radio station. Key actors were frequently colonels, who directly controlled the regiments and also had ready access to weapons. Often the military moved to protect their own jobs, perks or ethnic interests. But increasingly they also tried to cut through the corruption and stalemate that had characterized postindependence party politics. Mobutu, for instance, began by abolishing political parties and centralizing provincial government in the interests of national unity and development. Nevertheless, most military rulers quickly became enmired in their own swamp of corruption. For the power of army and bureaucracy in postindependence countries itself pointed to a more basic problem: the dominance of state over society.

In countries without a developed economy and where most of the population were rural poor, the government was not only the main means of coercion but also of production. The road to riches was not through private enterprise but through government jobs (paid at the going rates for Europeans before independence and therefore greatly in excess of normal African wages) and by controlling government patronage, contracts, and development projects. If a nation was poor but the state was rich, office became the main avenue to wealth. Until a more developed, diversified society and economy emerged, it was a matter of the "political class" versus the rest. Military men who survived, like Mobutu, quickly shed their uniforms. And they had as much reason as the politicians (as well as greater capacity) to enforce the unity of the often artificial countries that were the source of their power and wealth. Nor did they have any incentive to restrain the growth of state expenditure, financed by internal taxation and foreign debt. By 1972 over 17 percent of black Africa's GDP was absorbed in central government spending.[35]

The military usually secured order, at least for a while, but they were no more able than the politicians to generate national (as distinct from personal) wealth. Corruption, mismanagement and indebtedness were major reasons. So, too, was the weight imposed on the economy by bureaucratic structures of planning and an obsession with heavy industry. In Ghana, Kwame Nkrumah insisted that "the vicious cycle of poverty" could "only be broken by a massively planned industrial undertaking" modeled on Stalin's Russia and Nehru's India. He was also sure that development must be "jet-propelled" because "what other countries have taken three hundred years to accomplish, a once dependant territory must try to accomplish in a generation if it is to survive."[36] Nkrumah was toppled in 1966, but his successors, civilian and military, did not change the big industry strategy until Jerry Rawlings in the 1980s.

Julius Nyerere in Tanzania was one of the few African leaders who did not succumb to heavy metal. His Arusha Declaration of February 1967 spoke of agriculture as "the basis of development" for his "socialist state."[37] Nyerere looked to a rural revolution on the Chinese model through the creation of efficient "socialist villages"—at first voluntarily, then by coercion. As a result, the proportion of the rural population living in villages rose from 16 percent in 1973 to 80 percent in 1976, though many people also fled to the overcrowded cities.[38]

Not all states adopted socialist programs. In Kenya, the majorities of the rival political parties, KANU and KADU, favored democratic capitalism open to the West. And because of the traumatic land wars of the Mau Mau period (see Chapter 3), a top priority for Jomo Kenyatta after independence in 1963 was to resettle African farmers on European farms, often using British government loans to buy out the whites. By 1971 over fifty thousand Africans had been settled on one million acres of land, and an African rural middle class was emerging.[39]

But whatever their policies, most African countries had not escaped their economic subordination to the developed economies of Europe and North

America. In the 1950s most had sailed towards independence on a wave of rising commodity prices; during the 1960s the tide turned, grounding many African countries in the economic shallows. Between 1957 and 1965, for instance, Ghana experienced a 50 percent drop in the price of cocoa, which generated nearly two-thirds of the country's export income. Some small countries were even more dependent on one crop: groundnuts accounted for 80 percent of Niger's export earnings and over 90 percent in the case of the Gambia.[40] Even where diversification occurred, it meant dependence on a handful of primary products rather than industrial development. Outside a few countries such as Nigeria, manufacturing was limited. It usually took the form of light industry, such as textiles and foodstuffs; the engineering and heavy-metal sectors (developed as the key to growth in Eastern Europe) were negligible. Of the twenty-five "least developed" countries in the world in 1975, eighteen were African.[41]

Africa therefore relied heavily on imported manufactures from Europe and, as the terms of trade turned against primary producers in the 1960s, large payments deficits became the norm. Western development aid did little to help: by the late 1960s, new loans were worth less than the interest payments on old ones.[42] Pressure mounted for a change in the fundamentals of the world economic system, indicated, for instance, by successful agitation for the establishment of the UN Conference on Trade and Development (UNCTAD) in 1964. Although this achieved little, the trend was significant. For many African countries, as for black Americans, as the 1960s continued the focus shifted from overt white racism to more insidious structures of economic discrimination.

Development and the Military in Latin America

In many respects, Latin America was much better off than Africa in the 1960s. Political independence was more than a century old. Of the twenty-six countries, twenty were sovereign republics with established presidential systems, and only Cuba was formally communist. Most territorial boundaries were uncontentious: even the border war between Honduras and El Salvador in July 1969 lasted only a few days. Treatment of the native inhabitants was an issue in some places—notably Peru, where "Indians" constituted nearly half the population in the 1940s—raising acute problems about national identity. But in general Latin America was spared the ethnic bitterness that characterized contemporary Africa or, indeed, Europe in the first half of the century. Nor was the continent wracked by racial violence. In

Brazil, where the legacy of African slavery was most apparent, complex racial gradations contrasted with the stark black-white polarity of U.S. society. In the 1950s and 1960s, in fact, Brazil was often held up as an object lesson for the United States. The Brazilian sociologist Gilberto Freyre claimed in 1959, "With respect to race relations, the Brazilian situation is probably the nearest approach to paradise to be found anywhere in the world."[43] That was hyperbole, as we shall see, but the broad contrast with the United States and with Africa seemed telling.

Socially and economically, Latin America was also regarded in the 1960s as much more "modernized" than black Africa. There were, of course, vast regional differences, both between the more developed "southern cone" of Argentina, Chile, and Uruguay and the small, agrarian countries of Central America and also, within countries, between the thriving coastal areas and the undeveloped hinterland. Yet, in broad terms, it can be said that Latin America was and is the most urbanized of the world's developing areas. Already 41 percent of its population was classified as "urban" in 1950, rising to 65 percent by 1980, putting it close to Europe or North America, where the proportion was nearly three-quarters. In contrast, even in 1980, only 30 percent of Africa's population and 24 percent of South Asia's were described as urban. Urbanization was, of course, partly a function of industrialization. Latin America's agricultural population fell from 66 percent in 1950 to 40 percent by 1970. In Argentina and Uruguay the figure by then was well under 20 percent.[44] In these more developed countries, there was also a large measure of social organization and political participation, unlike the case in much of black Africa. In 1960 over a third of the urban work force was unionized; in Argentina, for instance, the unions had mobilized as a major political force under the aegis of Juan Perón.

In the late 1950s, Latin America's prospects looked rosy. In 1959 only four of the twenty sovereign republics were still under military rule. Most were energetically prosecuting the policy of import-substituting industrialization (ISI) that had become the Latin American way to free the continent from economic colonialism. Still haunted by the collapse of the world market for their primary products in 1929, most states tried to reduce their reliance on imported manufactures (and therefore on agricultural export earnings) by developing indigenous industries, starting with foodstuffs, energy, and consumer goods. To this end, foreign investment was encouraged but tariffs were high to protect nascent industries. The theory was that the industrial sector would be the locomotive of internally led economic growth. ISI therefore placed Latin America at odds with the prevailing development strategy of the 1950s, particularly in Western Europe, of export-led growth. Latin America's consequent neglect of agriculture also stood in marked contrast to the massive subsidization of the (reduced) farm sector characteristic of Western Europe, the United States, and Japan.

At first, the results generally seemed impressive. Manufacturing output expanded at 6 percent per year in the 1950s and 1960s; GDP doubled in the period 1960–1973. Among the "big three," Argentina's slower growth rate meant that it slid from being Latin America's largest economy in 1950 (with a quarter of total GDP) to a position behind Brazil and Mexico, both of whom also performed much better than India or China. In Brazil—the world's fifth largest country, covering nearly half of Latin America—GDP grew at nearly 8 percent each year between 1956 and 1962 under its dynamic president, Juscelino Kubitschek. The symbol of Brazil's modernization, as we saw in Chapter 5, was its new capital, Brasília.

By the 1960s, however, the flaws in ISI-style policies were becoming apparent. The neglect of agriculture meant that feeding the growing urban population posed severe strains on food production and transportation. Economic dependence had not been eliminated, only altered, because the new domestic industries, such as engineering and textiles, required increasing imports of capital goods as well as mounting foreign investment. The decline of agriculture meant a fall in export earnings to pay for these imports. These various strains led to chronic inflation, growing payments deficits and periodic currency devaluations.

During the 1960s, most governments tried to address these problems by reducing tariffs and diversifying exports. In 1970, manufactured goods accounted for 15 percent of Latin America's export earnings, compared with 9 percent in 1955. There were also attempts to enlarge markets by European-style integration: 1960 saw a treaty commitment to create a Latin American Free Trade Area by 1972 and the foundation of a Central American Common Market. But LAFTA never came into existence and the trade liberalization achieved within CACM, like the reforms by individual governments, did not change the basic relationship of the Latin American economies to those of North America and Western Europe. By the mid-1960s a new school of "dependency theory" was superseding the optimistic apostles of modernization. Analysts such as André Gunder Frank warned that the monopoly position of the "metropole" countries would keep the "satellites" in a permanent state of underdevelopment, and talked of revolution as the only remedy.

Nor could impressive growth rates mask the vast disparities of income among different groups and regions. The Brazilian case was both typical and significant. By the mid-1960s, complacency about the country's superior race relations had been shaken by African independence and the American civil rights movement. New statistical evidence showed that, despite the absence of a sharp color line, the black population was largely at the bottom of society. In Rio, for instance, nearly all the *favelados* were black; nationally, 21 percent of them were black and 30 percent mulatto.[45] Regional differences were also marked. In 1970 the urbanized southeast (including Rio and São Paulo) contained 42.7 percent of the population but accounted for 64.5 percent of national income. In the country as a whole, the top 20 percent of the population increased its share of national income from 51.4 percent in 1960 to 63.3 percent a decade later. This meant that 22 million people each enjoyed an average annual income worth twelve hundred U.S. dollars, whereas the remaining 85 million received less than three hundred dollars. Some economists noted that this was like putting "Belgium in India" and asked how long such a dualism could persist without an explosion.[46]

Castro's revolution in Cuba seemed like the first big bang. The seizure of power in 1959 by rural guerrillas, followed by wholesale expropriation of land, nationalization of industry, and rapid transition to a communist state, captured the attention of Latin America. On the political left, it called into question the claim of reformers that bourgeois modernization and political action were the only viable avenues to change. In several countries, guerrilla movements sprang up, emulating Castro's rural based revolution, particularly in Colombia, Venezuela, Peru, and Guatemala. Cuba offered arms and training. Castro's aide, the Argentine physician Ernesto "Che" Guevara, became the leading theorist and instigator of guerrilla warfare. These campaigns had limited success—Guevara himself was killed in Bolivia in October 1967—but by the late 1960s the revolutionary focus had shifted to urban areas in the more developed south, notably the Montoneros guerrillas in Argentina and the Tupamaros in Uruguay. And the threat of revolutionary action, capitalizing on rural or urban discontent and backed by Castro or communism, was now a nightmare for most governments.

They responded with some reforms. During the 1960s, twelve Latin American states enacted further measures to expropriate large estates and promote cooperatives among smaller farmers. In some countries, particularly Venezuela under Rómulo Betancourt (1958–1963) and Chile during the presidency of Eduardo Frei (1964–1970), this was part of a determined bid by left-of-center parties at democratic reform within the political system. Betancourt followed a decade of military rule. More than one hundred thousand landless families in Venezuela received land, largely from unexploited estates; investment in education, water, and health had some impact on rural poverty. To help pay for all this, the state's share of profits from the increasingly lucrative but foreign-owned oil industry was raised to 65 percent. In Chile, Frei, an austere but inspiring Catholic reformer, won the 1964 election on a program called "Revolution in Liberty." Steering an intricate course between right and left, he embarked on "Chileanization" of the American-owned copper mines (which generated 75 percent of Chile's export income but at little gain to the country itself). This meant not outright nationalization but government purchase of a 51 percent stake in the mines (at prices its critics denounced as excessive). Land reform, another intricate compromise, focused on the vast estates *(latifundios)* in the middle of the country. By the end of the decade, 6 percent of the country's arable land had been redistributed, to the benefit of some twenty-eight thousand families. By past standards, these were radical reforms, alarming the right, but to mounting anger on the center-left, they did not match the expectations aroused in the euphoria of 1964. As we shall see in Chapter 10, Chile's polarization was to have momentous national and international consequences in the years 1970–1973.[47]

More common as a response to the specter of Castroism than democratic reform, however, was renewed military intervention. Between March 1962 and June 1966 nine coups took place in Latin America, usually against governments deemed too weak to stop the left or who were left leaning themselves. Military intervention in politics was not new in many Latin American states. Of Argentina's twenty-three presidents between 1930 and 1983, fifteen had been military officers; the only two to complete their legal term of office were generals who became presidents in the first place through coups. Previously, the Latin American coup *(golpe)* had usually been a temporary corrective when politicians failed. The Brazilian coup of March 1964, however, began twenty-one years of military rule and set a pattern for much of Latin America. Argentina went the same way in 1966–1973 and 1976–1983, likewise Peru from 1968 to 1980. In 1973 the military seized power in Uruguay and Chile, previously the region's two most vigorous democracies, and did not relinquish it until 1984 and 1990, respectively.

The lurch toward permanent military rule was partly a response to the Castro threat and to economic crisis. But it also reflected changes in the position and philosophy of the military itself. In weakly organized societies, the military had always been a distinct and powerful group that controlled armed force and also inculcated national sentiment. But the relative absence of war in Latin America since the 1930s gave it little to do. The consequent emphasis placed on military education (partly as a time filler) created a professionalized officer elite that was usually more informed and better trained than most of society. Moreover, by the 1960s, the most senior military schools, such as the Brazilian Superior War College, were developing a concept of "national security" that embraced political and economic problems as well as purely military ones. In short, the generals had the opportunity, training, and outlook to be governors and not merely soldiers.[48] As in parts of Africa and Europe (such as France in 1958), military elites saw themselves as the nation's answer to the politicians' failure.

This did not make all military regimes identical, however. In Peru, General

Juan Velasco and his fellow officers took power in October 1968 with radical aims. The brutal repression of the rural guerrillas in the mid-1960s—in which some eight thousand peasants died and huge areas were napalmed—had the paradoxical effect of making the army more aware of rural problems. Under military rule, virtually all large estates were broken up; by the mid-1970s, about three-quarters of the country's productive land was under cooperative management. The junta also transplanted many of the squatters in shantytowns around Lima and other big cities into state-chartered "young towns" (*pueblos jóvenes*). Velasco aimed to integrate the volatile rural and urban poor into a controlled national society; soldier-rulers elsewhere usually tried to repress them as part of a general program of closing down political parties and labor unions. Either way, the basic object of military regimes was to stabilize society and politics in order to deepen economic development. In approach, they had more in common with the preceding technocratic politicians than might seem the case at first glance. For example, the Argentine equivalent of Kubitschek was Doctor Arturo Frondisi (1958–1962), an ambitious modernizer whose efforts were ruined by the abiding political animosity between Peronists and their opponents. The army that toppled him and eventually took power itself in June 1966 replaced democratic politics with a bureaucratic-authoritarian state. But the latter was a different means to the same end: modernization without politics rather than modernization through politics. The first proclamation by General Juan Oganía's regime in 1966 called its coup "the instrument for a substantial transformation aimed at providing the country with modern elements of culture, science and technology."[49]

But Oganía, like Velasco, soon encountered resistance. Latin American society may have been too weak, incoherent, or fragmented for democratic politics, but it was still organized enough to frustrate autocratic modernization. The result in most cases was the same: economic malaise and political deadlock, punctuated by spasms of violence such as the riots in the Argentine provincial city of Córdoba in 1969 and 1971, or the urban guerrilla incidents in Brazil between 1969 and 1973. Whatever their initial reformist intentions, most military governments (though not Peru's) resorted to systematic state terror in order to retain power. In Brazil, the repressive security apparatus devised to combat the guerrillas became a permanency, with imprisonment, torture, and the murder of opponents commonplace. Argentina's junta of 1976–1983 proved as brutal, and more secretive, in eliminating "subversives."

Since 1960, in fact, only four Latin American states have entirely avoided military rule, usually because they have a weak military and a strong party system, linked to mass organizations in society. One of these is the central American republic of Costa Rica—often dubbed Latin America's "model democracy"—which officially abolished its armed forces after the civil war of 1948. But parliamentary politics and high welfare standards could not mask the fundamental polarization between large banana and coffee planters and poor peasant workers. Another country that has avoided coups is Mexico, a one-party state where the army, though important, has been under firm PRI control since the 1920s. The unions were similarly tied to the regime, in marked contrast to their powerful opposition role in Argentina. Under Mexico's President Adolfo López Mateos (1958–1964), nationalization was extended and land reform resumed. Although the economy grew at 6 percent per annum in the 1960s, income disparities also widened, leaving the richest tenth of the population with over half the national income by 1969. In the early 1970s even Mexico, previously immune, was wracked by major guerrilla insurgencies. In short, no Latin American government—be it coalition, one party, or military—could resolve the underlying problems of growth, inequality, and dependency.

Whereas Africa was dependent on the former colonial powers of Europe, Latin America was unequivocally in the economic and military orbit of the United States—that is, except for Cuba, the great affront, challenge, and obsession for Washington throughout the 1960s. Largely in response to the danger of Castroism, President John F. Kennedy launched the Alliance for Progress in 1961, promising twenty billion dollars for Latin America over the next decade. But the eventual figure was less than five billion dollars; in any case, little trickled down to the rural and urban poor. In El Salvador, for instance, which received more Alliance funds than any other state in Central America as a reward for its political stability, the funds served to strengthen the coffee and sugar oligarchs, who evicted peasants and tenants to turn over more land to commercial agriculture. During the 1960s, three hundred thousand Salvadoreans—one-eighth of the population—fled to neighboring Honduras, causing tensions that erupted in the 1969 border war. Under Lyndon Johnson, government aid was scaled back and emphasis placed on other elements of the Kennedy program, notably private investment, which often aggravated structural dependence, and military aid, which encouraged some of the 1960s coups. The Brazilian military was closely linked with its U.S. counterparts; the Johnson administration quietly approved and supported the 1964 coup.

The following year, Johnson intervened directly in the Dominican Republic, which had been in political confusion since Rafael Trujillo, the country's dictator for thirty years, was gunned down in 1961. His elected successor, the reforming journalist Juan Bosch, was toppled by a coup in 1963, and, as civil war developed between the pro-Bosch forces and the junta, LBJ sent in twenty-two thousand troops in April 1965. Although few in the CIA or the State Department shared Johnson's conviction that a Castroist, communist takeover was imminent, the president kept the troops in the Dominican Republic for eighteen months until an acceptable government was secure. He insisted that "the American nations . . . will not permit the establishment of another Communist government in the Western Hemisphere." Although LBJ was happy to invoke "the American nations" as cover for U.S. action, his private opinion of the Organization of American States was that it "couldn't pour piss out of a boot if the instructions were written on the heel."[50]

The crisis was a reminder of how much the Caribbean and, to a lesser extent, all of Latin America was under U.S. hegemony. When tension emerged between its goals of development and order, the United States usually opted for the latter because of the global imperatives of cold war. Secretary of State Dean Rusk admitted in 1968 that "the defense budget of the United States this year is roughly equal to the gross national product of all of Latin America."[51]

Christianity between Church and State

Aroused racial consciousness was one feature of the 1960s. So was the resort to military rule in countries beset by political conflict and economic underdevelopment. Equally evident was the potency of religious beliefs that, supposedly, should have been swept away by the secularizing tide of modernity. This was particularly evident in the early 1960s within Christianity (which officially accounted for about one billion of the world's population in 1960, compared with half that number of Muslims and four hundred million Hindus). Around 55 percent of Christians were Roman Catholics. It was here that the ferment of the 1960s was most intense, as the church made a determined effort to come to terms with modernity.

The papacy symbolized this change. In October 1958 a new pope was elected: Angelo Cardinal Roncalli, who took the name John XXIII. Roncalli came from a poor peasant family in the Po valley and, despite years as a papal envoy abroad, retained the common touch. It was hard to imagine the grandly austere Pius XII (1939–1958) as the "holy father" except in the nominal sense, whereas John XXIII—portly, talkative, and genial—seemed like everyone's grandpa. His final struggle against stomach cancer caught the imagination of the world. Giovanni Cardinal Montini, Paul VI (1963–1978) lacked John's warmth and charisma, but his intellect, mysticism, and pained concern for humanity had an international impact. He also ranged far beyond the Vatican, which was still emerging from a long struggle to define its relationship with the Italian state. Paul became the first pontiff of the air age, flying to both Israel and India in 1964 and addressing the United Nations in New York the following year. By personality and action, therefore, these two men raised the profile of the papacy.

The most significant development of the 1960s for the Catholic Church was the Second Vatican Council (1962–1965). The last assembly of bishops from the whole church had convened in 1870–1871. A new one was John's grand idea. He wanted to bring the church up to date (*aggiornamento,* which became a cult word in many languages, as would *perestroika* in the 1980s). But it took nearly four years to prepare the ground and combat the objections from Vatican conservatives, led by Alfredo Cardinal Ottaviani (whose motto was *semper idem,* always the same). The ailing Pope John came to see his mission as that of launching a big and heavy ship. "Another will have the task of taking it out to sea," he observed philosophically.[52] After John opened the council in autumn 1962, Paul VI steered it through three more stormy sessions to its conclusion in December 1965.

Vatican II was a positive acknowledgment of religious pluralism. Instead of traditional statements that "dissidents" must simply return to the fold, the council affirmed religious liberty, praised what is "true and holy" in other faiths, and encouraged "dialogue" with them and with the world at large. It also welcomed greater lay participation in the life of the church and authorized liturgies in national languages rather than Latin. As part of a new interest in social problems, the council spoke of reading "the signs of the times" and affirmed the church's concern for the poor, especially in the developing world. As important as its words, however, was the fact of the council itself. Simply assembling twenty-four hundred bishops from all over the world (three hundred of them African) demonstrated that European predominance in the church was waning. The council broke the stranglehold of Italians who dominated the Curia, the Vatican's bureaucracy. Henceforth the church was to be run more "collegially," with bishops meeting in national conferences and a worldwide synod. Both John XXIII and Paul VI promoted the appointment of cardinals from outside Europe and North America.

Although it became customary to depict Vatican II as a watershed, the church had already moved beyond the "closed Catholicism" of the interwar years. In those days, explicitly Catholic political parties had rested on Catholic social organizations—both under close supervision of the clergy—and the overriding issue had been the struggle against atheistic Marxism. A striking sign of the new times, mentioned in Chapter 4, was the upsurge of Christian Democratic parties, through which Catholics emerged from their religious cocoon and were pulled by lay leadership into the era of mass democracy. Christian Democracy was most evident in Western Europe—particularly West Germany and Italy—yet it was also found in Latin America in the 1960s, in Venezuela, El Salvador, Peru, and especially Chile.[53]

Although pre-Vatican II Catholicism was therefore not moribund, the change of outlook and impetus was nevertheless dramatic. Nowhere was the Council's impact greater than in Latin America, already home to 35 percent of the world's Catholics, compared with Europe's 33 percent.

Latin American bishops meeting at Medillín, Colombia, in August 1968 took up the themes of Vatican II in a continent that was sliding under renewed and brutal military rule. In addition to promoting vernacular liturgies, lay training, and other ecclesiastical reforms, the bishops discerned the signs of the times in trenchant language: much of Latin America, they said, found itself "in a situation of injustice that can be called institutionalized violence."[54] The "final document" of the conference was a manifesto for radical priests, monks, nuns, and laity committed to the struggle for justice. It created the climate for several major initiatives, in which Brazil (the most populous Catholic country in the world) took the lead. One was the proliferation of thousands of "basic Christian communities" (*comunidades eclesiales de base* in Spanish). These were small groups of lay people, meeting regularly in private homes for Bible study and prayer. As with black consciousness in South Africa, the underlying aims were to foster self-awareness and communal action. Not only were these groups often politically radical in outlook, they constituted a "church of the poor" independent of clerical guidance. On an intellectual plane, the late 1960s also saw emergence of the "theology of liberation." Liberation theology grew out of the experiences of worker-priests in countries like Argentina and Brazil. Its ideas were systematized by theologians such as Gustavo Gutiérrez and Hugo Assman. These writers reiterated the prophetic mission of the church to denounce social injustice and analyzed the world through the categories of economic dependence and class struggle, already promulgated by dependency theorists.[55] Both the basic Christian communities and liberation theology were to have great impact in Latin America and, by the 1980s, the wider world.

Yet Vatican II unsettled as well as invigorated the church. The reforms often generated a fierce conservative backlash. For instance, in France where defenders of the traditional Latin mass eventually formed a breakaway church in 1974 under the leadership of Archbishop Marcel Lefebvre. Conservatives everywhere feared that the erosion of traditional clerical dominance and of the Catholic monopoly of truth could undermine the whole fabric of authority. The air of mounting religious uncertainty was intensified by the fact that the papacy, while socially reformist, remained adamantly traditional on sexual issues. The principle of a celibate clergy was vigorously reaffirmed by Paul VI in an encyclical of 1967, sparking vehement protests, particularly among Dutch bishops. Marriage remained sacrosanct: when the Italian government at last passed a divorce law in 1970, the papacy demanded a referendum, which was soundly defeated in 1974. Female priests, now being accepted in parts of the Anglican communion such as Hong Kong (1971) and Canada (1975), were anathema. Most of all, Paul VI came out firmly against artificial birth control (and against the advice of his own commission). His 1968 encyclical *Humanae Vitae* ("On Human Life") was simply ignored by numerous Catholics, as we shall see in Chapter 9. For many, this cast doubt on the infallibility of the pope, or at least on his awareness of the modern age.

The reforms associated with Vatican II brought the Roman Catholic Church into closer contact with other churches. In December 1965, Paul VI and the Orthodox patriarch, Athenagoras, lifted the mutual excommunications pronounced by Rome and Constantinople during their Great Schism of 1054. Ecumenical discussions proliferated, though the Catholic Church remained outside the World Council of Churches, founded in 1948. The promotion of vernacular liturgies paralleled attempts in many Protestant traditions to modernize religious language and patterns of worship, using pop music, drama, and even dance. On the theological level, Protestants were even more concerned to confront modernity. A phrase of the German theologian Dietrich Bonhoeffer—a martyr of the resistance to Hitler whose prison writings were discovered in the English-speaking world in the 1960s—became a kind of watchword: "How can we reclaim for Christ a world which has come of age?"[56] By this Bonhoeffer meant that much of the West now had little time for formal religion or for the supernatural metaphysics in which the Christian message had hitherto been packaged. In Britain, the ideas of Bonhoeffer and other modern theologians were mingled and popularized by the Bishop of Woolwich, John Robinson, in *Honest to God,* published in 1963. Two years later the American academic Harvey Cox tried to relate Bonhoeffer's musings about "religionless" Christianity to the new urban environment in *The Secular City.* Both of these books sold over half a million copies and fueled debate among Protestants. But although such writings were often intellectually liberating to some of the doubting faithful, outside the church their main impact was to convey a sense that even the bishops and the professors had lost their faith.

In fact, the late 1960s saw a sharp drop in religious allegiance throughout Western Europe—whether measured by clergy resignations, weekly church attendance, or even the occasional use of church for marriage and baptism. In the Netherlands, for instance, votes for the Catholic People's party fell by a quarter between 1963 and 1967. Between 1966 and 1974 regular church attendance dropped from 64 percent of Dutch Catholics to 35 percent.[57] Such patterns, mirrored across Western Europe, were largely due to the social emancipation of the 1960s. But they were also testimony to the way church reform had shaken intellectual foundations without erecting new structures. For many conservatives, Catholic or Protestant, this was proof that reform was an agent of secularization.

Secularization is a slippery term. It is probably true that there have been no "ages of faith," meaning whole societies oriented around religious values, even in medieval Christendom. In this sense, "most history, including most religious history, was secular."[58] What *was* nearing completion in Western Europe in the late 1960s was the centuries-long collapse of Christianity as a set of structures of authority. At the intellectual level, religious literalism based on the Bible and the traditions of the church had been undermined by the scientific world-view and by historical criticism. The bitter battles of the nineteenth century, such as over church control of education, were now largely finished. As a source of political authority, the wealth and influence of the church had also waned. The gradual loss of church lands and the lengthy struggles to separate church and state were central to that process— symbolized in the emasculation of the once-vast papal states in Italy to a mere one hundred square miles around the Vatican. Nor was religion now so important as a mark of social identity. Just as nonconformists had finally won full civil rights in late nineteenth century England and lost their cohesion as a result, so the emergence of continental Catholics from social isolation in the mid-twentieth century had a similar effect, as exemplified by the Netherlands.

In much of Western Europe by 1970, therefore, religion no longer defined intellectual, political, or social authority. But the demise of institutional religion in these senses did not mark the end of religious belief. The so-called post-Christian era in Western Europe signified "not so much the disappearance of Christianity as its return instead to the socially and politically marginal position it occupied before Constantine elevated it into the official religion of the Roman Empire one-and-a-half millennia ago."[59] The emerging pattern could be seen clearly in the United States, where religious pluralism and toleration were enshrined in the first amendment to the Constitution, thereby sparing the country Europe's bitter feuds over church-state relations. By the 1960s religious differences—once significant in defining social identity and political allegiance, especially through anti-Catholicism—had lost much of their potency. The election of America's first Catholic president, John F. Kennedy, in 1960 was a symbolic catharsis. Yet the United States remained a vigorously religious society, in which regular church attendance held at around 40 percent of the population, better than in Western Europe. But American religion was fragmented—with more than two hundred different denominations, mostly Christian—and also highly individualistic, characterized by personal choice more than accepted authority.[60]

Significantly, the growth area in Christianity in the late 1960s was in evangelical Protestant sects, particularly the house-based Pentacostals, who began to spread from America to Western Europe in the 1970s. And religious belief would still intrude into political debate in the developed West, not via old issues such as anticlericalism or education, but as the politics of morals. As we shall see, issues such as abortion, contraception, and homosexuality would generate passionate religious arguments in the 1970s and 1980s.

American-style religion—fragmented, privatized, for a part of the population, rather than structures of authority defining much of national life—was to be a pattern for "secular society" in the future. But it should also be emphasized that, in parts of Europe and North America, official religion had still not lost its potency as a source of identity in the 1960s. In most cases the embattled groups were Catholic, fearful of an alien power or ideology. Ireland, Canada, and Eastern Europe provide three striking examples.

For centuries the Catholic Church in Ireland had been a nationalist bulwark against English Protestant rule. In January 1922, the Irish parliament had (narrowly) accepted the British terms for independence with partition. This created an "Irish Free State" based in Dublin but also left the six Protestant-dominated counties of Ulster in the north within the United Kingdom. The new state used Catholicism as well as the Gaelic language to define its independence from Britain. The "special position" of the Catholic Church as "guardian of the faith professed by the great majority of citizens" remained an article of the constitution until the referendum of 1972; the Church's insistence on a Catholic education system was respected, and the constitutional ban on divorce lasted until 1995.[61]

In consequence, fear of being subsumed in a reactionary "papist" state was central to the official ideology of Northern Ireland, where the bulk of the island's Protestants now lived. Thereafter, London turned a blind eye as Ulster's Unionist leaders reduced the Catholics in Northern Ireland, though one-third of the population, to the status of second-class citizens by discrimination in politics, jobs, and housing. Catholics, for their part, clung to their religion as a social and cultural defense. Ireland, therefore, represented confessional politics par excellence. Although the Irish Republican Army (IRA) mounted sporadic campaigns of violence, the catalyst for change, as in so many revolutionary situations, was token reforms by the Unionist leadership in housing and education. These emboldened middle-class Catholics who founded the Northern Ireland Civil Rights Movement in 1967, modeled on the techniques of Martin Luther King, Jr., in the United States. Equally, they antagonized many Protestants, for whom the demagogic Ian Paisley, an evangelical clergymen, became the spokesman. In 1969, Northern Ireland exploded as Catholic protestors clashed repeatedly with the Protestant police and the Ulster government became immobilized by the Unionist backlash. The British government introduced troops to keep order, but this only served to rally Catholics to the revitalized IRA, especially after soldiers shot dead thirteen marchers at a banned rally in Londonderry on January 30, 1972—which was dubbed "Bloody Sunday." In March the British government suspended the Ulster parliament and began "direct rule" from London. That year 467 people were killed in sectarian shootings and bombings, or by security forces.[62] "The Troubles" would last for another quarter-century.

The story of Quebec was less bloody but more momentous because the fate of one of the world's largest countries was at stake. The full extent of the crisis did not emerge until 1976. In the mid-1960s Canada seemed to be entering an era of quiet national self-confidence with its new maple-leaf flag and its centennial celebrations, especially the Expo '67 world's fair in Montréal, which attracted international publicity. But the country's foundations remained shaky: a loose federal structure that reinforced provincial autonomy and the resentful French Catholic presence, some 30 percent of the population, in a country dominated by anglophone Protestants. The fact that most French Canadians lived in Quebec fused these two postimperial problems of provincialism and biculturalism.

In the 1960s, Québécois were energized by a technocratic new Liberal premier, Jean Lesage. He implemented educational reform, reduced clerical influence, and promoted nationalization as part of general modernization. His victory reflected the "quiet revolution" in society that was occurring under the surface. During the 1960s, regular church attenders in Quebec fell precipitately from 80 percent of the population to 25 percent.[63] This was partly due to rapid urbanization: by 1971 over three-quarters of French-speaking Québécois lived in urban areas.[64] As in Detroit or Cape Town, so in Quebec City or Montréal, propinquity fostered a sense of inequity. The defensive Catholicism of rural French Quebec gave way to a new political activism. Lesage demanded equality for Francophones in national life. His Union Nationale rival, Daniel Johnson, went further: the choice was equality or independence, he argued in a best-selling book. In July 1967, French president Charles de Gaulle, always keen to embarrass the "Anglo-Saxons," increased the temperature when he declared before a delighted crowd in Montréal, "Vive le Québec. Vive le Québec libre." In 1969–1970 the extremist Front de Libération de Québec mounted a series of bombings and abductions, culminating in October 1970 in the murder of a senior Liberal minister and the imposition of martial law throughout the province by the federal government. Pierre Vallières, the ideologist for the FLQ, dubbed Québécois "the white niggers of America."[65]

The new assertiveness of Québécois politicians was rooted in a recognition that the old, religious pillars of French identity were weakening and additional supports were required. Language laws became the symbolic crux, with campaigns to accelerate the "francization" of Quebec and to establish French as the coequal national language. Also important was the abiding controversy about the balance between provincial and federal control of resources. On both of these issues, "special status" for Quebec would only intensify the anger of Anglophone provinces. Pierre Trudeau, Canada's flamboyant, bilingual Liberal premier from 1968 to 1984, tried to engineer a compromise with his Liberal colleagues in Quebec. But his proposal for a Canadian Constitutional Charter were deemed insufficient by them in June 1971. And in 1976 his attempt to impose bilingualism on air traffic controllers in Quebec provoked a strike by Canadian airline pilots and vehement denunciation from Anglophones. The backlash among French Canadians helped bring the separatist Parti Québécois to power in November 1976, led by René Lévesque. His main aim was a provincial referendum on steps toward independence. Canada was now set for years of chronic constitutional crisis.

It was in Eastern Europe, most of all in the developed world, that religion, culture, and nationalism were intertwined. By the 1960s, it was clear that religion had not withered away, as predicted, under communist rule. Some regimes substituted new rituals for old. In 1959 the Soviet government opened its first Palace of Weddings in an old chateau on the Neva River in Leningrad. The East German government, with some success, promoted the *Jugendweihe,* in which young people dedicated themselves to the service of socialism as an alternative to religious confirmation. There were also periodic spasms of persecution, notably in Khrushchev's Russia between 1959 and 1964, when perhaps half the churches were closed. In 1967 the Albanian government of Enver Hoxha took the unique step of formally abolishing all religions on the grounds that Islam, Catholicism, and Orthodoxy had all been "brought to Albania by foreign invaders, and served them and the ruling classes of the country." Henceforth, Hoxha announced, the only religion would be "Albanianism."[66] Hoxha was using nationalism as a weapon in his struggle to break out of the Soviet bloc. To the same end but with different results for religion, Nikolai Ceausescu of Romania (1965–1989), coopted the Orthodox Church in his campaign to steer a more independent path of Moscow, enlarging its rights in return for political support. But these were minor countries on the periphery of the Soviet empire. In the center of Eastern Europe, Moscow's hold remained firm. Religion often constituted the main bastion of national independence against Soviet imposition of socialist internationalism.

In East Germany, the Evangelische Kirche (a union of Lutheran and Reformed churches) remained strong, with half the GDR's population on its membership rolls. The level of active participation was much less, however, and, by the 1960s, to be a practicing Christian meant also being a second-class citizen, denied access to higher education and to senior positions in industry and administration. But many East German Christians were willing to pay that price, keeping alive an alternative structure to the state for a significant minority of the population.

This was even more true in Poland, where 90 percent of the population remained Catholic and clerical authority was deeply rooted. Moreover, in a country that had long been Eastern Europe's great battleground, the Catholic Church had historically acted as "the mainstay of Polishness, because by defending the religion of the Catholic peasants against the pressures imposed on them by the Orthodox and Protestant churches, it defended them at the same time against Russification and Germanization."[67] The fight to preserve Polish language, culture, and religion against Russian Marxism was simply another chapter in that saga. The Church's nine-year program of study and preaching to prepare for the millennium of the Polish church and nation in 1966 was a source of new solidarity and strength. At its center was the oath sworn by John Casimir, king of Poland, before his victory over the Swedes in 1655, to serve God, the Virgin Mary, and the Polish people and to free the country from foreign invaders. This oath was sworn anew by priests and people during the campaign. Few could mistake its contemporary implications.

Even in Europe and North America, therefore, the process of secularization was uneven, with some churches remaining important foci of political influence and social identity. Elsewhere, in Latin America for instance, the erosive forces of modernity were less advanced. And in both the developed and developing world, the decline of institutionalized religious authority was often accompanied, as we have seen, by new waves of vigorous, privatized religiosity. Moreover, Christianity was distinctive among the three major world religions in its tendency to separate church and state. This had been an agent of secularization. Both Islam and Hinduism adopted a more unified, theocratic view of religion, embracing the whole of social life—as we shall see in a moment. This was also the pattern in Israel because of the centrality of Judaism to the Zionist state. In the late 1960s the intertwined confrontations between Judaism and Islam, modernization and traditionalism, entered a new and more volatile phase.

Holy War in the Middle East

For the state of Israel, the decade after its victory in the Sinai campaign of 1956 had been one of steady prosperity. The country's population increased from 1.7 million to nearly 2.4 million by 1967, most of it urban, and per capita GNP grew at 6.5 percent each year as industry expanded to satisfy consumer demand. Particularly impressive was the development of the Negev Desert—the southern triangle running down to the Gulf of Aqaba—including the creation of planned new towns such as Beersheba and Eilat. The Negev depended on a national irrigation scheme to carry the waters of Lake Galilee over a hundred miles by pipe and conduit.

Yet growing prosperity could not mask underlying problems. Politics remained intensely factional. Although the veteran premier David Ben-Gurion finally retired in 1963, he harried his successor, Levi Eshkol, from the sidelines. The chronic trade deficit was covered only by gifts from world Jewry and reparations from West Germany, and inflation was endemic in a society that spent more than one-tenth of its resources on defense. A policy of fiscal restraint in 1965–1966 had some effect, but at the cost of severe unemployment. In 1966 emigration exceeded immigration for only the second time in Israel's history. Moreover, immigration had changed the ethnic balance of Israeli society as non-European Jews, especially from North Africa, became a majority by the late 1960s. They constituted a resentful underclass in a country still dominated by Jews of European descent. An even more serious source of social tension were the Palestinian Arabs, 12 percent of the population, who remained under military government until 1966. Although the Israeli government pumped considerable money into Arab education in the 1960s, this only created a disaffected intelligentsia voicing communal discontent.[68]

Above all, Israel remained an encircled Zionist enclave whose very existence remained intolerable to neighboring Arab states. Of these, the most important was Egypt—with over thirty million people by 1965, one-fifth of them jammed into Cairo. Under Nasser's rule, the country could boast its own socioeconomic triumphs in the 1960s, such as completion (with Soviet help) of the Aswan High Dam to harness the flood waters of the Nile. But the pressure of surging population on limited resources was unremitting: the government did not begin a family-planning policy until 1965. And Nasser's socialist revolution failed to generate either sustained growth or significant redistribution. Land reform, for instance, had been "mainly a negative political act," to destroy the old ruling class, rather than to resolve Egypt's agricultural problems.[69] Only about 10 percent of the total area was expropriated. Nasser also pursued an erratic program of nationalization which, by 1963, had been extended to all banks, public utilities, transportation, hotels, and larger industries. But its concomitant was a sprawling, inefficient, corrupt bureaucracy employing one million people—one-tenth of the work force—by 1970. The burgeoning military budget, 20 percent of national expenditure by the mid-1960s, was a consequence of Nasser's repeated foreign-policy failures after the heady days of 1956–1958. In September 1961, the

Union with Syria broke up after an army coup there. The Saudi Arabian monarchy assumed Hashemite Iraq's mantle as Egypt's main conservative opponent in the region. Egypt and Saudi Arabia became committed to rival sides in the Yemeni civil war of 1964–1967. At its peak, this guerrilla struggle embroiled half the Egyptian army, earning it the nickname "Nasser's Vietnam." By 1966, in fact, Egypt was close to bankruptcy and joined Cuba and Indonesia as the only countries to date that had defaulted on their IMF loans. United Arab Airlines, the country's hard-currency-earning national carrier, had four of its seven Comet jets grounded because of shortage of foreign exchange to acquire spare parts.

Most humiliating of all were the taunts of the Arab world that Nasser had failed to deal with Israel. Palestinian refugees from 1948 continued to press on Israel's borders, bitter that the front-line states did nothing to recover their land. Their guerrillas found a supportive base in Syria, where the socialist Ba'ath party turned the country into the second Soviet client state in the region—like Egypt, receiving substantial arms and aid. Syria was already waging its own artillery war with Israel to obstruct the Lake Galilee diversion project. From 1965 on, Palestinian raids from Syria into Israeli territory escalated. The Israeli army retaliated against refugee camps in Jordan, increasing pressure on King Hussein to strike back. Both Syria and Jordan derided Nasser for being more interested in a Yemeni empire than in Palestinian liberty. He was also accused of hiding behind the UN Emergency Force (UNEF), introduced in 1956, which was still located on the Egyptian side of the Sinai border with Israel.

In 1967, tension mounted after six Syrian fighters were shot down by the Israelis in a border dogfight on April 7. In retrospect, it is tempting to see the June 1967 Arab-Israeli war as Nasser's deliberate effort to pull himself out of the deepening morass at home and abroad. But, on current evidence, it seems more likely that he stumbled into full-scale war unintentionally.[70] The stimulus was a Soviet intelligence report, passed to Egypt on 12–13 May, stating that Israel was massing its army for an attack on Syria. This was incorrect, and may have derived from Israeli disinformation.[71] But on May 14, Nasser, responding to his patron's prodding, mobilized the Egyptian army and sent reinforcements into Sinai. Two days later, stung by Arab taunts, he demanded that the UNEF pull out from parts of Sinai and then, on the 18th, he called for a total withdrawal. Lacking the mandate, resources, or will for a fight, the UNEF departed on the 21st. Nasser took up positions along the Gulf of Aqaba and blockaded Israel's crucial southern port of Eilat. For Israel, this was a return to the grim days of 1948–1956. The government mobilized army reserves and began planning a preemptive strike into Sinai.

In February 1960 Nasser had sent troops into Sinai, only to withdraw them a month later after a display of force. He could have done the same in mid-

May 1967, claiming he had forestalled an Israeli attack. But by then the pressures on Nasser were much more intense, not only from Syria, Jordan, and the Palestinians, but also within Egypt. It is probable that General Abdel Hakim Amir, head of the armed forces and now almost a rival, was pushing to escalate the crisis, insisting the army could win a war. "On my own head be it, boss!" he told Nasser. "Everything's in tiptop shape."[72] After the shambles in the Yemen, Nasser should have known better, but he pressed on—perhaps unbalanced by severe diabetes, probably gambling that war would cut through his political coils. Syria and Iraq were already mobilizing.

Initially, Israeli intelligence believed Nasser was repeating the 1960 bluff. After the blockade and the Arab mobilization, however, most of the cabinet saw war as inevitable. But Foreign Minister Abba Eban was anxious about the reaction of the United States, both to keep the Soviets at bay and also to ensure that this time, unlike 1956, Israel would not be forced to relinquish territorial gains without diplomatic benefits. The Johnson administration, preoccupied by Vietnam, had also assumed at first that Nasser was bluffing. But as the threat to Israel mounted, American signals became more encouraging under the influence of such Zionists as Supreme Court Justice Abe Fortas. Fortas told the Israeli Ambassador on June 2, "If you are going to save yourselves, do it yourselves." As historian William Quandt has observed, the red light turned yellow. That meant "be careful," and "don't count on the United States if you get into trouble." But, added Quandt, for Israel, "as for most motorists, the yellow light was tantamount to a green one."[73]

It was certainly enough for Eban, who now backed military action. On May 30, King Hussein of Jordan threw in his lot with Nasser, signing a military alliance that placed his forces under Egyptian command. Two days later, Israeli prime minister Eshkol enlarged his cabinet to form a government of national unity and relinquished the defense portfolio, hitherto in his hands, to Moshe Dayan, hero of the 1956 Sinai campaign. Dayan pulled together plans for a preemptive attack; on June 4, the cabinet gave its unanimous assent. It recorded its belief that the Arab armies were "deployed for immediate multi-front aggression, threatening the very existence of the state." Haunted by history, like most Israelis, senior cabinet minister Yigal Allon declared that had the Arabs won, "they would have committed genocide."[74]

At 7:45 on the morning of Monday, June 5, most of Israel's air force converged on Egypt's airfields, from Sinai to Cairo. To Dayan's relief, they achieved total surprise. In three hours, all but twenty of Egypt's 340 planes were destroyed, mostly on the ground as attacks deliberately coincided with the midmorning coffee break. By the evening of June 5, most of the Syrian and Jordanian air forces were also in ruins. Over the next three days, enjoying total air superiority, Israel crushed seven Egyptian divisions in Sinai and also drove Jordanian forces from the West Bank of the Jordan, taking complete control of the city of Jerusalem—previously divided between Israel and Jordan. A new ballad, "Jerusalem the Golden," became the Israeli national anthem of the war. By June 8, both Egypt and Jordan had accepted cease-fire agreements. The Israelis then turned on Syria, which was still shelling settlements in Galilee from the Golan Heights. On June 9–10 the heights and all the surrounding plateau overlooking northeast Israel were secured in bloody fighting. A third cease-fire, with Syria, brought the Six-Day War to an end on the evening of Saturday, June 10.

In one week, Israel's regional position had been transformed from strangulation to dominance, at the cost of 759 Israeli lives. Some twenty-eight thousand square miles of territory had been gained, including the Sinai Peninsula, the Golan Heights, the West Bank of the Jordan, and East Jerusalem (Map 10). Although the Israeli government had no intention of being squeezed out of its gains as in 1956–1957, it did not initially intend to hang on to everything. The government envisaged a settlement based on the borders of the old British mandate (though policy on the West Bank, Gaza, and Jerusalem remained unclear). But hopes that Israel could now negotiate from a position of strength were quickly dashed. From the Arab summit in Khartoum at the end of August 1967 came the resounding "three no's"—no negotiations, no peace, and no recognition of Israel's right to exist. Abba Eban, the Israeli foreign minister, later observed, "It was the first time in the history of war that the victor had sued for peace while the vanquished demanded unconditional surrender."[75]

So the struggle went on, by other means. In 1967–1970, the Arab states waged their "war of attrition" by guerrilla raids and artillery attacks along Israel's borders. On their side, the Israelis settled down to administer the land they had acquired and, on it, more than one million Arabs. Roughly one-third were impoverished refugees from the war of 1948, who had spent twenty years in squalid camps. Across the Israeli political spectrum support grew for permanent annexation of the occupied territories. Although this was not an official policy of the Labor-led coalition, Jewish settlement of the occupied areas was quietly encouraged. As after 1948, so after 1967: for a state that was fighting to exist, greater security seemed synonymous with more territory.

As the battle lines hardened, so did their cold war parameters. The Soviets, who had probably not intended war but only wanted to draw Egypt into greater support of their Syrian ally, now struggled to recoup their losses. On June 10, they announced a severing of diplomatic relations with Israel. The rest of the communist world followed suit, except for Romania. Moscow also rapidly rearmed Syria and Egypt; in the latter, thousands of military advisers intensified the country's client position. On the other side, France had been Israel's main military supplier prior to the war. But de Gaulle imposed an arms embargo when fighting began, anxious to keep in with the Arabs and

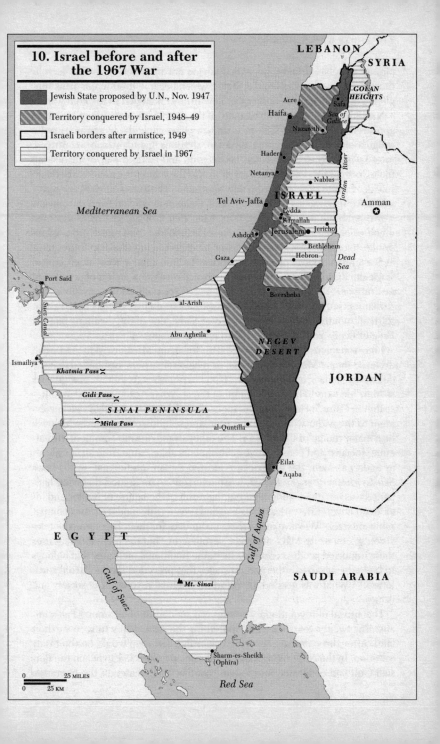

10. Israel before and after the 1967 War

- **Jewish State proposed by U.N., Nov. 1947**
- **Territory conquered by Israel, 1948–49**
- **Israeli borders after armistice, 1949**
- **Territory conquered by Israel in 1967**

LEBANON

SYRIA

GOLAN HEIGHTS

Acre

Haifa

Safad

Sea of Galilee

Nazareth

Hadera

Jordan River

Netanya

Nablus

Tel Aviv-Jaffa

ISRAEL

Amman

Mediterranean Sea

Lydda

Ramallah

Jericho

Ashdod

Jerusalem

Bethlehem

Gaza

Hebron

Dead Sea

Beersheba

Port Said

Suez Canal

al-Arish

Abu Agheila

NEGEV DESERT

Ismailiya

Khatmia Pass

JORDAN

Gidi Pass

SINAI PENINSULA

Mitla Pass

al-Quntilla

Eilat

Aqaba

EGYPT

Gulf of Suez

Gulf of Aqaba

SAUDI ARABIA

▲ Mt. Sinai

0   25 MILES

0   25 KM

Sharm-es-Sheikh (Ophira)

Red Sea

piqued that Israel had ignored his advice not to attack first. The Israelis therefore turned to the United States, which became their major arms supplier. The Arab-Israeli conflict was now firmly entangled in the cold war.

Nasser was the main Arab casualty of the war. On the evening of June 9 he appeared on Egyptian TV—face drawn, voice choked—to stammer out a resignation speech. After popular demonstrations that night, some contrived, most spontaneous, he reversed his decision and made the army leadership the scapegoat for defeat. General Amir was forced to resign and harried into suicide. Egypt's problems were now enormous. The Suez Canal was closed— a massive revenue loss—and the country depended on aid from the conservative Arab oil states. In particular, King Feisal of Saudi Arabia assumed much of Nasser's role as the principal Arab leader, obliging Egypt, for instance, to end the Yemeni war. Nasser struggled on but died of a heart attack in September 1970. For many Egyptians he remained a hero, albeit now of tragic dimensions. Yet his was a very personal revolution, bereft of permanent institutions. "During his rule he produced three political organisations, five parliaments of two years each, six constitutions, and his cabinets lasted about thirteen months."[76] His successor Anwar Sadat, one of the shrinking band of Free Officers from 1952, was left to pick up the pieces.

June 1967 constituted a crisis of faith for many Muslims. Why had Allah deserted them? Many of the *ulama*, or religious teachers, responded that the defeat was, in fact, a religious test. "God has punished us that we may go back to him," declared Hasan Ma'amum of the al-Azhar Academy of Islamic Research in Cairo.[77] Here were the roots of the Islamic revival that became evident to the wider world with the Iranian revolution of 1979 and which will be a major theme of Chapter 11. The other strand of Arab comment, threatening socialist and conservative governments alike, came from such radicals as Sadeq al-Azm, the American-educated Syrian intellectual, in his book *Self-Criticism after the Defeat,* written in 1968. Azm argued that what happened was not divine judgment but the result of the failure of Nasser and his ilk to go beyond rhetorical socialism and create truly modern states comparable to Israel. "We have made room in our lives for the refrigerator, the television set, oil wells, MIG airplanes," wrote Azm, "but the mentality that uses these imported products remains the same traditional mentality that belongs to bedouin, agrarian supernatural stages that preceded the industrial revolution."[78] What was needed, therefore, was a total revolution of society and values.

The appeal of revolutionary politics was seen most of all among Palestinians. For twenty years they had waited for the Arab states to recover their land. After three defeats, it seemed clear that self-help would be their only salvation. In the early 1960s, various Palestinian groups in Egypt and the Persian Gulf had congealed into Fatah ("conflict"), dedicated to the liberation of historic Palestine by armed struggle.[79] In response, Nasser and the Arab states tried to keep the movement under their control by sponsoring the Palestine Liberation Organization in 1964. After the Six-Day War, however, that aim was unrealizable. The front-line states had failed the Palestinians once again. Thousands flocked to Fatah, which was strong enough to take over the PLO in 1969. Its new chairman was Yasser Arafat, aged forty. Arafat grew up in Gaza and studied engineering in Cairo, but his real trade was politics. Inspired by theorists such as Frantz Fanon, he saw in these new circumstances the potential for radical, guerrilla-led revolution, comparable to those in Algeria or Vietnam. Once the Israelis established their rule over the Gaza camps, Fatah's main based moved to Jordan, where Palestinian exiles constituted over half the population and Fatah guerrillas almost a rival government—wearing their own uniforms, collecting their own taxes, poaching youths from the Hashemite royal army. Palestinian radicals started agitating for the removal of King Hussein, another failed leader from 1967. During 1970 there were several attempts on his life and repeated skirmishes between guerrillas and Jordanian troops.

The crisis came to a head in the late summer of 1970. Egypt, Jordan, and Israel finally agreed to a cease-fire in their war of attrition. Brokered by Washington, this came into effect on August 7. But it was denounced by Syria and provoked violent demonstrations by Palestinians in Jordan. On September 6, Palestinian terrorists from George Habash's Popular Front highjacked three international airliners and brought some three hundred passengers, including many Americans and Israelis, as hostages to a landing strip in the Jordanian desert. At last Hussein turned on the guerrillas. His Bedouin troops attacked their positions in refugee camps throughout Jordan. In ten days of civil war nearly two thousand guerrillas were killed, together with hundreds of innocent refugees. Of the Arab states, only Syria intervened to help the guerrillas, sending an armored column into Jordan. Assured of U.S. support, Hussein counterattacked; the Soviets, anxious to avoid an international crisis, induced the Syrians to withdraw. For Palestinians, "Black September" had shown once again that they could not rely on the Arab states. Evicted completely from Jordan by July 1971, the PLO moved its main base to Lebanon. From there it would plague Israel throughout the 1970s.

Of the three front-line leaders of the 1967 war, Hussein alone survived. Nasser's fatal heart attack was brought on by his efforts to defuse the September 1970 crisis. In Ba'athist Syria, the furor following the Black September debacle gave the defense minister, Hafez al-Assad, his chance to seize power in a bloodless coup in November. Military rule was now a feature of the region, the socialist patina of Nasserism and Ba'athism having been stripped away. In Iraq, the Ba'ath had also come to power in a coup of

July 1968, but this was basically a military government controlled by a regional clan—Sunni Muslims from Takrit led by General Ahmed Hassan al-Bakr and Saddam Hussein—just as in Syria Ba'athism was now a cover for military rule dominated by Assad's Alawite community.[80] In September 1969 another army coup, in Libya, overthrew the aging King Idris and brought to power a twenty-seven-year-old officer, Muammar al-Qaddafi, who nationalized the foreign oil companies and closed U.S. and British bases. An admirer of Nasser, Qaddafi turned his country around psychologically, toward the Middle East rather than North Africa. After his hero's death, he assumed the mantle of Pan-Arab leader, albeit with an un-Nasserite commitment to strict Islam. In Qaddafi, both strands of the Arab reaction to 1967 were personified—radical revolution and Islamic purity. As we shall see in Chapter 11, both would be features of the decade to come.

Politics, Religion, and Nationalism in South Asia

Africa was a continent, maybe just "a concept," in the phrase of Davidson Abioseh Nicol (page 216). Pan-Africanism, even when invigorated by antiracism, had little impact on the history of Africa in the 1950s and 1960s. Likewise in the Middle East: after the brief apogee of Nasserism in the late 1950s, Pan-Arabism could not paper over the territorial and ideological divisions among the Arab states. What gave them a superficial unity was the unacceptable presence of a Jewish state on Palestinian soil.

If we move to South Asia, however, the pattern is somewhat different. A broad historic civilization existed here, over which the British had exercised paramountcy until 1947. Nehru's goal was to maintain the unity of India, which he described in 1946 as "a geographical and economic entity, a cultural unity amidst diversity, a bundle of contradictions held together by strong but invisible threads."[81] It was as if one vast state encompassed most of Europe—another ancient civilization. Nehru almost succeeded in 1947 but, against the vast bulk of independent India—predominantly Hindu, with Muslim, Christian, and Sikh minorities—emerged the two-winged, largely Muslim Pakistan (see Chapter 2). Nehru's subsequent task was to maintain a pluralist unity that already existed, whereas in Africa and the Middle East, like Western Europe, unity was a goal—of doubtful plausibility.

This "idea" of India has been one of the great postwar experiments, whose outcome is still unclear. Was India indeed a natural unity, or was it an old empire gradually breaking apart? The 1950s had been a decade of success for Nehru (see Chapter 3). But in the 1960s, the Indian state and South Asia in general entered a new period of turmoil, in which power politics, religion, and ethnicity all played a part.

An essential part of Nehru's project was to maintain India's credibility as a major power. In doing so, he collided with a far more powerful neighbor—China. In the late 1950s the Chinese began to develop the Aksai Chin desert plateau, where Kashmir bulges into their territory between the provinces of Xinjiang and Tibet (Map 4). The exact frontier was a matter of dispute. As the Chinese pushed their de facto border westward and incidents multiplied in 1959–1962, Nehru decided to hit back. He assumed that China was maneuvering for advantage in the border negotiations and that there was no danger of serious war. These were fatal misconceptions.[82] After Indian troops evicted the Chinese from a strategic ridge in the Himalayas, the Chinese mounted a major offensive in October 1962 (during the Cuban missile crisis), which drove the Indian troops back in confusion. In mid-November, the Chinese also routed Indian forces in other disputed territory in the northeast. A full-scale invasion of India now seemed likely; the government was in panic. Nehru wrote secretly to President Kennedy, stating that the situation was "really desperate" and requesting at least fourteen squadrons of U.S. fighters and bombers to provide air cover for a near-defenseless India.[83] This was a humiliating breach in Nehru's cherished policy of nonalignment.

On November 21, however, China unilaterally announced that it would cease operations and pull back to the effective border of 1959. The operation had served its purpose: to protect China's position in the Aksai Chin, and to teach India a lesson about Chinese power. Not only nonalignment but also India's pretensions as a major regional power had been mocked. Nehru admitted publicly that "we were getting out of touch with reality in the modern world and we were living in an artificial atmosphere of our own creation. We have been shocked out of it, all of us."[84]

He was referring primarily to the realities of regional politics: strenuous efforts were now made to improve India's defense forces. Yet defeat also shocked the government out of its complacency in other policy areas. India's mix of partial socialism and import-substituting industrialization had run into the same problems as elsewhere. Growth rates were poor, agriculture had been neglected, and a sprawling, corrupt bureaucracy was strangling national life. Although agriculture was given new priority in the 1960s, the neglect of land reform—which would have offended local Congress leaders—frustrated radical improvements. And in focusing on industrialization, the government had ignored serious family planning (in any case anathema to many disciples of Gandhi). During the third national plan (1961–1966), population growth of 2.3 percent per year (nearly double what was anticipated) played havoc with all projections. Increased output was swallowed up by more mouths.

The ailing Nehru never fully recovered from the crisis of late 1962. He died in his sleep in May 1964 and was cremated amid an outpouring of national grief reminiscent of that at Gandhi's death sixteen years before. Congress bosses, known as "the Syndicate," chose an aging party loyalist, Lal Bahadur Shastri, to replace him.

The uncertain situation in India emboldened the Pakistan military government, under General Ayub Khan, to intensify the conflict over the disputed northwest borders of India (see Map 3). In the spring of 1965 the two governments contested the Rann of Kutch, on the Gujarat-Sind frontier. Despite rumors of possible mineral wealth, these were really desolate mud flats; principle, not profit, was at stake. "Whether there is oil or no oil, our territory is our territory," the Indian foreign minister told Parliament. "It is our territory," replied his Pakistani counterpart, "and whether barren or not it is sacred and valuable, and we have to defend it."[85] That summer the contest shifted north to Kashmir, the predominantly Muslim state that had been divided between India and Pakistan in the war of 1947–1948, prior to a plebiscite that the Indians never allowed. Pakistani raids and Indian reprisals in August turned into a large-scale tank and air war between the two countries in early September. China made threatening noises against India. Only in late September was the UN able to broker a cease-fire. The Soviet Union now moved to bolster its diplomatic position, unsettled by growing Indian links with America and China's support of Pakistan. At Tashkent in January 1966, Ayub and Shastri were induced to sign a declaration promising to restore "normal and peaceful relations" and to withdraw to prewar positions. Although not resolved, the Kashmir dispute had been defused.

For both governments, albeit in different ways, the Tashkent meeting was a watershed. Hours after signing the declaration, Shastri succumbed to a heart attack. His death helped sanctify the agreement, but it also deepened India's political crisis. As the new prime minister, the Congress "Syndicate" selected Nehru's forty-eight-year-old daughter, Indira Gandhi (no relation to the Mahatma). Although Nehru's confidante for years and a cabinet member under Shastri, she was expected to be a compliant puppet—*goongi goodia* ("dumb doll"). Her hesitant early months in office seemed confirmation of this role. But Indira's lonely and insecure childhood had forged a dominant will, intolerant of criticism. She gradually established her political hegemony, though at the cost of splitting the Congress party in 1969. The ruling element eventually became known as Congress (I). The "I" stood for Indira—aptly enough, for, although remaining a network of local factions, the essential cement of the party became loyalty to the Nehru family. Indira also dropped the idealistic language in which her father had articulated his visions of India's future. "I am less romantic and emotional than he was," she remarked in 1971. "Women are more down-to-earth than men." Her arch opponent,

Morarji Desai, was blunter: "She would ally herself with the Devil if she thought it served her purpose."[86] In March 1971 her party won over two-thirds of the seats in elections for the lower house of parliament. The long succession crisis was at an end.

In Pakistan, however, the fighting of 1965–1966 set in motion a train of events that would destroy not only Ayub Khan but also the unity of the artificial, two-winged state.[87] Despite Pakistan's official propaganda about being a Muslim homeland, in 1971 ethnicity proved stronger than religion as the Bengali east and the Punjabi west split apart.

The Tashkent Declaration sparked off riots in much of West Pakistan, where Ayub was felt to have sold out. One of the keenest critics was his thirty-eight-year-old foreign minister, Zulfikar Ali Bhutto, who resigned in the summer of 1966 and began mobilizing opposition against his former patron. Bhutto was a suave, wealthy, British-trained lawyer from a landlord family in Sind. Much of his support came from other Sindhi landlords, who felt marginalized by the Punjabi national elite, and from army factions discontented with the 1966 agreement. But Bhutto was a magnetic speaker who also capitalized on the growing mass discontent with Ayub's economic policies, which had placed growth before equality. Real wages of industrial workers in West Pakistan fell by nearly 12 percent between 1954 and 1967. Twenty-two families controlled two-thirds of industry, four-fifths of banking, and nearly all insurance companies. Ayub's chief planner dismissed ideas of equitable distribution as "luxuries which only developed countries can afford."[88]

Ayub's economic policies had also increased the poverty of Bengali East Pakistan, the other wing of this artificial state, one thousand miles away across India from its Punjabi-dominated heartland. The difference in per capita incomes between the two parts of Pakistan rose from 30 percent in 1958 to 61 percent in 1969. The 1965 war with India had also underlined the vulnerability of East Pakistan to Indian attack. Although more than half of Pakistan's population, Bengalis were poorly represented in the army and bureaucracy. In March 1966 the Bengali leader, Sheikh Mujibur Rahman of the Awami League, put forward a six-point plan to make the country a confederation, with East Pakistan controlling its own economy and militia. Ayub's response was to arrest the leaders of the Awami League but Bengali protests escalated at the same time as Bhutto was mobilizing protest in the west. In the winter of 1968–1969 strikes and riots in cities across both wings of Pakistan paralyzed the economy and forced Ayub's resignation in March 1969. His successor, General Yahya Khan, conceded democratic parliamentary elections in December 1970—the first since independence. These resulted in the Awami League's winning all but two of the 153 seats in the east and Bhutto's Pakistan People's Party winning over half the 148 seats in the west, with the rest of the vote fragmented among ten other parties.

The elections had therefore produced two dominant, regional parties. They were now on collision course, because Bhutto shared the army's commitment to national unity and its contempt for Bengalis as degenerate Muslims speaking a foreign language. Mujib was also opinionated and inflexible. When talks broke down, the Pakistan army was ready. On March 25, 1971, it moved against Bengali troops, police, and political opponents in what became a pogrom. At Dacca University, an Awami League stronghold, students and teachers were lined up and then shot or bayoneted. Bengali atrocities followed as rebellion spread. From India, surviving Awami League leaders proclaimed the independence of Bangladesh: "Pakistan is now dead and buried under a mountain of corpses."[89]

Nothing—not even the Congo or Biafra—matched the misery of the Bengali people in 1970–1971. This was one of the most densely populated areas of the world: seventy million people in an area equivalent to the U.S. state of Wisconsin. It was also one of the poorest, with a GNP per head of eighty dollars per annum (in the United States the figure was $5,780). On November 12–13, 1970, a huge cyclone-driven tidal wave from the Bay of Bengal had pounded the Ganges delta. The official death toll in what the press billed as the greatest natural disaster of the century was at least two hundred thousand, maybe double. Not even a developed country could have coped; the limited assistance from West Pakistan only fueled the Awami League's charges of colonialism. Hundreds of thousands of refugees flocked south into the Indian state of West Bengal. Once the war began in March, the efflux was greater. Perhaps ten million refugees surged into India, seven million of them Hindus bearing tales of Pakistan genocide. Conditions in the camps were appalling. By the end of September 1971, six thousand had died from cholera alone. The death toll from the fighting itself may not have been three million (the Indian figure) but was probably close to five hundred thousand.

The refugees were a huge burden on India's scarce resources. By June the state of Tripura (population 1.5 million) was hosting nine hundred thousand refugees, who exacerbated the political instability of West Bengal, where the Congress party was trying to suppress the communist-led Naxalite terrorists. But as hawks in New Delhi insisted, the crisis was also a golden opportunity for India to emasculate Pakistan. India's army, from the start, was supplying and training the Bengali guerrillas to fight the Pakistan army, while Calcutta was home to the Bangladesh government in exile. By the summer, it was clear that the great powers would do little to relieve the refugee crisis or to secure a political solution: America and China in particular did not want to jeopardize their relations with Pakistan. After Indira Gandhi had bolstered herself against Chinese retaliation by a treaty of friendship with Russia in August, she gradually increased the military pressure. From November 21 the army started moving into East Pakistan, poised to attack Dacca. Yahya Khan's air strikes on Indian airfields on December 3 provided a convenient reason to declare war. Indian forces surged forward, overwhelming Pakistani troops, who had to be supplied by sea around southern India. By December 16, all Pakistani forces in the east had surrendered. The Bangladeshi government in exile returned in triumph. In the west, Yahya Khan gave way to Bhutto, who formed Pakistan's first civilian government since 1958.[90]

December 1971 redefined the politics of South Asia. In Pakistan, the military-bureaucratic state had tried to control ethnic and regional fragmentation by closing down democratic politics. It had also concentrated on economic growth, whatever the social costs, to build up national defense in a hostile environment.[91] The pressures generated by these policies eventually split the state apart. The loss of Pakistan's eastern wing more than halved its population, reducing it from one-fifth of India's size to one-tenth, and eliminated the country's vital jute industry. Eastern secession also undercut the official ideology that Pakistan was home for all the subcontinent's Muslims and intensified separatist feeling against Punjabi dominance, especially in Baluchistan. The rump of Pakistan was left more fragile than before. The events of 1971 were, in many ways, a replay of 1947.[92] Like Jinnah, Sheikh Mujibur had sought an equitable sharing of power in a confederal state. Denied this, he made a bid for statehood—this time using ethnicity, not religion, as justification. The breakup of Pakistan replicated its creation. Moreover, partition was becoming a "recurrent motif" in the history of this diverse subcontinent.[93] As we shall see (Chapter 12) both religion and ethnicity became potent political weapons in India during the 1980s.

In Bangladesh, the old bureaucracy remained intact in the hope that it would help the Awami League government to grapple with the appalling social and economic problems of reconstruction. Such hopes were vain. Bengali nationalism had been a 1960s reaction to Punjabi discrimination in economics, politics and language. Like most nationalisms, it was stirred up by the educated elite and then became a mass cause during Ayub's repression. But it was largely a negative force—anti-Pakistan—and provided an inadequate basis for a new national identity. The ailing and autocratic Sheikh Mujibur Rahman offered only the ideology of "Mujibism," a thinly disguised cult of personality. He failed to disarm the guerrillas or check the rampant corruption, and the country soon degenerated into anarchy. After the army murdered Mujib in August 1975, Bangladesh was ruled by a succession of military-dominated governments. This slide from a negative nationalism via bureaucratic rule into military dominance was another analogy with the earlier history of Pakistan after 1947.[94]

South Asian history in the decade to 1971 encapsulates some of the major themes of this chapter: the politicization of religion, ethnicity, and military power in fragile states undergoing rapid industrialization. Much of what happened in the 1960s in South Asia—as in Africa, Latin America, and the Middle East—had nothing to do with the cold war. South Asia and the Middle East were still coping with the partition of 1947 and 1948. In Africa, the legacies of accelerated decolonization were still crippling; in Latin America, the effects of a development strategy designed to minimize American economic imperialism were the obstacle. But we have also seen that, repeatedly, superpower rivalries compounded local crises, from the Congo to the Caribbean. And as the decade progressed, both superpowers faced a new and alarming challenge across southeast Asia from a great power that mixed nationalism and communism in frenzied volatility. The 1960s saw the high tide of China's revolution.

8

East Wind, West Wind

In November 1957, Mao Zedong made his second visit to the Soviet Union. It was also only the second time he had left China. He told students in Moscow: "The direction of the wind in the world has changed. . . . At present, it is not the West wind that prevails over the East wind but the East wind that prevails over the West wind."[1] Over the next decade, the East Wind would reach hurricane force in China, with the Great Leap Forward of 1959–1961 and the Cultural Revolution of 1966–1969. These were upheavals on a titanic scale: the famine caused by the Great Leap has been judged "the largest in human history."[2] The East Wind also surged across Southeast Asia. In Indonesia, the fifth most populous country in the world, an abortive communist bid for power in 1965 ended in a bloodbath that cost at least half a million lives. But the West Wind was also blowing strongly. U.S. leaders were determined to contain communist expansion and assert their international authority. The unhappy country of Vietnam became their proving ground. Here the East and West winds met, typhoon-like, in the most destructive storm of the cold war.

The winds were blown by individual leaders. To a frightening degree, the Asian crises of the 1960s were the product of personality politics, of ego and power. Mao Zedong in China, Sukarno in Indonesia, and Lyndon Johnson in the United States bulk large in these stories. But these leaders perceived a larger struggle, to decide the fate of Asia—and much more besides. "The world today is a revolutionary ammunition dump," Sukarno declaimed in 1960.[3] Mao and LBJ would have agreed, though each drew very different conclusions. To a large extent, the peoples of China, Indonesia, and Vietnam were the victims of explosions that others had caused. But they were not totally passive. Revolution was played out in the lives of peasants and farmers. At the rice roots, it was about land and local power. And the initiators of political turmoil—from Beijing to Washington—were often student protesters. This recurrent theme points us to a deeper youth revolution that will be central to Chapter 9.

The Great Leap and the Cultural Revolution

By the mid-1950s, communism was firmly established in the world's most populous country (630 million people). The Chinese state controlled the means of production, farming had been organized into collectives, and the Soviet model of centrally planned, heavy-industrial development had been enshrined in the first five-year plan of 1952–1957 (see Chapter 2). But it was not inevitable that the People's Republic of China would surge on to ever-more doctrinaire communism. The liberalization of Eastern Europe and the Soviet attack on Stalinism had an effect in China as well, where the leadership was all too aware of the limits of support for the Chinese Communist Party (CCP) and the backwardness of the agrarian economy. Mao was particularly concerned to enlist intellectuals (most of whom were at best lukewarm about the CCP) in the educational and technological development of the country. During the summer and autumn of 1956, he encouraged them to speak out about the needs of China in the so-called Hundred Flowers Campaign. This took its name from Mao's slogans encouraging cultural and intellectual debate: "Let a hundred flowers bloom; let a hundred schools [of thought] contend."[4] In 1956, Mao also gave his support to measures by the finance and agriculture ministries to introduce some market mechanisms into the planned economy and to offset the obsession with heavy industry. Mao was no economist, but he shared the growing concern about China's ability to feed its expanding population under the new system of state control. Whether or not 1956–1957 was "one of the great turning points" in the PRC's history,[5] offering a real chance of a more pluralistic socialist economy, remains debatable, but Mao's own ideas were probably in flux at this time.

The Hundred Flowers bore bitter fruit, however. It produced intense criticism of the party and its bureaucracy, seen most strikingly in the posters along "Democracy Wall" near Beijing University. Party functionaries hit back to save their jobs, and an angry Mao authorized the June 1957 Anti-Rightist campaign to restore political control. Between four hundred thousand and seven hundred thousand intellectuals branded "rightists" lost their positions and were sent to farm or factory for "labor reform." The campaign marked the end of Mao's belief that intellectuals might be the key to economic development and revived his conviction, forged in the long civil war, that mobilizing the masses was the essence of effective revolution.

The other casualties of the party backlash were the economic reforms. These had failed to produce quick results in 1957, partly because of a poor harvest, and were easily denigrated as capitalist in the new antirightist frenzy. By August all the rural free markets had been closed. The spectacular launch of *Sputnik* in October also gave new credibility to the Soviet model of industrialization. Behind the scenes, the heavy-industry ministries and the central planners also counterattacked vigorously. They conceded the need for some decentralization but argued that the food problem could be solved by capital-intensive projects such as water control. They also proposed a rapid growth strategy concentrating on steel production by both urbanization and "backyard" enterprises in the countryside.

What fused Mao's rekindled enthusiasm for mass mobilization with the planners' new development strategy was the concept of the "people's communes." This became, for Mao, the key to China's future.[6] Following Politburo approval in August 1958, almost all China's cooperative farms were subsumed into units maybe fifty or one hundred times larger, comprising five thousand to ten thousand households. Astonishingly, this was accomplished in two or three months. The economic gain, supposedly, was that rural labor could thereby be redeployed for large capital projects, for example, mines, steelworks, dams, or irrigation. But the communes were also a huge social leap into communism, with communal eating halls and nurseries, "happiness homes" for the aged, and abolition of private plots. Traditional notions of family responsibility were under attack: women in particular were to be liberated for outside work instead of preparing food and caring for the old and young. At the same time, huge numbers of peasants were being pulled into the urban industrial work force. Between 1957 and 1960, China's urban population grew by one-third from 100 million to 130 million, mostly in 1958.[7] In both country and town, the national obsession became iron and steel production, geared to increasingly fantastic targets. In November 1957, Mao had announced that China would overtake Britain in steel production within fifteen years; in September 1958 he predicted that this would happen the following year.[8] On the communes, cooking utensils were commandeered: who needed their own pots and pans in the new communist utopia? By the end of 1958 hundreds of thousands of small, ramshackled blast furnaces dotted the countryside as nearly one-tenth of the population was frantically smelting iron or mining and transporting ore.[9]

The results were spectacular—both good and ill. China's growth rate was more than 40 percent in 1958, over 20 percent in 1959, figures that eclipsed the achievements of the First Five-Year Plan. The output of steel—still an international virility symbol—doubled in one year.[10] But much of the steel was poor quality, the communes proved too large for administrative efficiency, and the damage to food production was severe. By June 1959, Mao and his colleagues were ready to rein in the experiment with lower targets, smaller communes, and greater attention to agriculture. This was the mood as the Central Committee convened in the southern mountain resort of Lushan for its annual work conference. But there he faced an outspoken critique of the Great Leap's failings by Peng Dehuai, the blunt, bulldog-faced defense minister, who had been touring some of the provinces. Mao felt cornered and he counterattacked. Peng was driven into retirement, literally left to cultivate his own garden in a rundown house in suburban Beijing. The new defense minister was Lin Biao, a taciturn, hard-working war hero. The Lushan conference was a decisive moment. The Great Leap had been reaffirmed, not restrained.

Having sown the wind, Mao now reaped the whirlwind. The farm labor force fell from 192 million in 1957 to 151 million in 1958, thanks to the steel mania and the obsession with hydraulic projects. Cereal planting was down; in many areas the crops were left to rot in the fields. Even worse were the new commune structure and the fanaticism it generated. Chen village, near Canton in southeastern China, was brought into a commune run from a local market town. The party officials there issued senseless orders, such as crushing water jars in a futile effort to produce fertilizer or excessive planting of rice seedlings, which only starved each other out. In the meantime, the peasants gorged themselves at the free commune canteens.[11] The Great Leap became known as the "Eat-It-All-Up Period" because people were taking five or six meals a day. But there was no harvest, and no grain was stored. Nor was there any incentive to plant for the next season because most of Chen's produce would be sent into a common stock for eight villages. Two summers of such folly, 1958 and 1959, left no reserves to face some of the worst climatic disasters of the century as typhoon-driven floods ravaged the coast and severe droughts afflicted the wheat belt of east central China.

The government was slow to appreciate the magnitude of the problem. Its blindness was partly ideological—after Lushan, failure could not be admitted—but it was also statistical. The decentralization of the economy and what became known as the "exaggeration wind"—gross inflation by communes and enterprises of their output figures—made it impossible to get reliable information. The results were catastrophic. It is estimated by demographers that in 1959–1961 the "excess deaths" (in other words, above normal mortality levels) were at least fifteen million and perhaps thirty million.[12] These figures represent around 2 to 4 percent of China's population.

Perhaps. Around. It is estimated . . . The most chilling aspect of what was probably the worst famine of the twentieth century is how little we still know about it.[13] The authorities kept it quiet for a couple of years until refugees spilling from southern China into Hong Kong in 1962 revealed some details. Another telltale sign was the massive increase in China's cereal imports, which in 1961–1964 accounted for more than half the hard currency leaving the PRC. But the scale of the famine was successfully concealed for twenty years; even today, its human realities are hard to uncover.°

Most of the Chinese diet was still rice or other grains, supplemented by some vegetables. As cereals became scarce, people killed their pigs and then draft animals, further undermining farm life. They resorted to berries, plants, and leaves; in extreme cases they cannibalized the dead, even their own children. Many wandered around the countryside scavenging for food, leaving their villages to the old and the dying. Although some provinces were placed under martial law to stop looting of state granaries, for the most part this was slow, orderly death, unlike the squalor and chaos of African refugee camps in more recent times. People literally shrank, then swelled as protein deficiency allowed fluids to escape into their tissues. Hacking coughs, acute diarrhea, and total lethargy gradually prevailed. Whole villages became silent as people sat or lay, waiting for death. Some killed themselves from constipation by eating grass, bark, or even soil. Others succumbed when food finally arrived and they destroyed their digestive systems by overeating.[14]

The famine mostly affected rural areas, falling hardest on east central China, in the area between Beijing to the north, Wuhan to the south, and Shanghai on the coast. Anhui province was probably worst hit, with 20 percent (two million) of China's famine deaths in 1960. No one who lived though China's great starvation would ever forget it. Yet it is also clear that economic recovery was relatively quick. In 1959–1962, China's per capita national income had fallen by 35 percent. In the United States during the

---

°Here is a graphic reminder of the difficulties of studying the history of the world's most populous country. Data on America and most "Western" countries—about social life, the economy, or policy making—are available in profusion from the press and, up to the late 1960s, from archives. But the People's Republic was effectively closed to researchers until 1979, and it did not publish any reliable statistical series over the two decades before that—the result of the Great Leap and the Cultural Revolution. This has made historians heavily reliant on the reports of refugees (naturally somewhat biased about the regime) and on revealing but partial published sources (such as hearings to discredit former leaders). Consequently, all generalizations about China must be read with caution.

depths of the Great Depression (1929–1932), the fall had been 32 percent. But in China, output was back to 1957 levels by 1964, only two years after the nadir, whereas America did not regain 1929 output levels until 1940.[15] The speedy recovery highlights the basic dynamism of the Chinese economy and the hubristic policy failures that had turned the Great Leap into the great fall.

As China's leaders took stock, they also faced another policy crisis—the growing rift with Moscow, on which they had been dependent since the Korean War. During the 1950s, mutual need kept the two great communist powers in step, as exemplified by Soviet collaboration in China's nuclear weapons program. The decision to build a bomb was taken in January 1955. China's "Project 02" got going that autumn under the direction of Nie Rongzhen, a field commander during the civil war. But it was only possible because the Soviets agreed at the same time to supply prototypes of a nuclear reactor and a cyclotron and to set up a joint organization to prospect for uranium in China, with surpluses going to the USSR. In October 1957, Moscow agreed to provide a prototype atomic bomb and related data. But then the Kremlin began to get cold feet. Finally, on June 20, 1959, Khrushchev sent Mao a letter explaining that because of the current test-ban talks with the United States, the USSR would not be honoring the agreement.

The nuclear issue was, in reality, symptom rather than cause. It reflected Khrushchev's search for détente with the United States—seen dramatically in his American visit in September 1959—at a time when the People's Republic still feared an American-backed invasion by Chiang Kai-shek's Nationalist forces on Taiwan. At a theoretical level, Khrushchev's talk of "peaceful coexistence" jarred with Mao's continued rhetoric about "armed struggle" against capitalism and his apparent readiness to countenance even nuclear war because the communist bloc had a much larger population. In May 1958 Mao told party leaders that, even if "900 million are left out of 2.9 billion, several Five Year Plans can be developed for the total elimination of capitalism and for permanent peace. It is not a bad thing."[16] Khrushchev found such talk chilling.

Domestic policy also became an issue between the two governments. Khrushchev was scathing about the ineptitude of the Great Leap Forward and its philosophy of mass mobilization, much to Mao's fury. A suspected link between Peng Dehuai's critique at Lushan and his recent visit to Moscow may have fueled the vehemence of Mao's counterattack in 1959.

Sino-Soviet rivalry also had a personal dimension. Both Khrushchev and Mao were arrogant, erratic autocrats, intolerant of rivals and ill suited to the consulatation and compromise needed to keep an alliance afloat. Their meetings in Beijing in 1958 and 1959 were stormy; as the split widened in 1960, Khrushchev personalized the dispute, likening Mao to Stalin. In mid-July, he served notice that all Soviet advisers would leave China by early September.

In the autumn Khrushchev gained the support of most of the world's eighty-one communist parties against China's line on foreign policy and war. Only Albania openly denounced the Soviet view.

Ideological ostracism had less effect than technological isolation. For predominantly agrarian China, Soviet technical assistance had been vital to establish major new industries such as aircraft, automobiles, and electronics. The challenge to prove Chinese self-reliance was now immense; indeed it had been a major incentive for continuing the Great Leap. Nowhere was the quest for independence more important to the leadership than in nuclear weapons, the hallmark of international power in the postwar world. Chen Yi told his Politburo colleagues in mid-1961 that a Chinese bomb was essential "even if the Chinese had to pawn their trousers for this purpose . . . As China's minister of foreign affairs, at present I still do not have adequate back-up. If you succeed in producing the atomic bomb and guided missiles, then I can straighten my back." Such support at the highest level helped ensure that Nie's nuclear program was not starved of funds or too greatly troubled by the mass disturbances of the Great Leap. After the Soviet pullout, much depended on trial and error. Chen Nengkuan, a young physicist with an American doctorate, was in charge of producing explosives to detonate the bomb. On a wind-blown test range near the Great Wall, he and his men started work by melting and mixing possible chemicals in cast-off army buckets over an open fire. Luck and determination also helped. Two Russian weapons scientists had torn their papers to shreds before departing. Laboriously, the documents were reconstructed, giving the Chinese vital clues to the processes of atomic implosion. Gradually, Project 02 neared fruition, mostly at plants in the remote Gobi Desert in northwest China. On October 16, 1964, on its vast test site in a desert valley in the Lop Nur marshes, China exploded its first atomic device, equivalent in power blast to the Hiroshima bomb. Success was all the sweeter because, on the same day, the world heard of Khrushchev's enforced resignation.[17]

For China, the early 1960s were a time to take stock politically. It was isolated from the communist bloc, still at odds with America, and had just undergone a major domestic disaster. What had gone wrong? Mao insisted the problems of the Great Leap were mostly caused by the weather and the end of Soviet aid, but colleagues blamed mistaken policies. Mao was increasingly sidelined. He had already allowed Liu Shaoqi to become head of state in 1959 and, though remaining party chairman, he convened only one meeting of its Central Committee between 1961 and 1966. In the Politburo he was often quietly ignored as Liu and Deng Xiaoping, the party general secretary, set their course for recovery. Under their aegis, the communes were dismantled, some market incentives restored, and agriculture given belated priority. They judged that the Great Leap had shown the folly of mass mobilization and also the need to conduct all reforms under party control. Liu was now spoken of, even by Mao, as his successor. Liu's little book *How to Be a Good Communist* sold fifteen million copies between 1962 and 1966, eclipsing Mao's sales figures in that period. References to Mao became fewer and fewer in the party press.

In December 1963, Mao Zedong turned seventy. Stiffness and trembling—early signs of fatal motor neuron disease—were beginning to afflict him. His teeth were stained green because he never used a toothbrush and rinsed his mouth, peasant style, with tea. Waited on hand and foot, he spent much of his time in bed. He had leisure for writing poetry and reading books, especially on China's past. He compared himself with successful emperors and talked of going soon "to see Marx." But the philosopher king was not yet finished. His appetite for spicy Hunanese food, dripping with oil, remained voracious, likewise his sexual desire for young women—as those attending his twice-weekly dances could observe. Personally, he remained callous and unpredictable. He said he had "graduated from the University of Outlaws" and considered himself "subject to the laws of neither god nor man."[18] Reflection on the setbacks of recent years eventually galvanized him for renewed struggle.

The motivation was partly personal: like other ailing potentates, Mao hated to retire, and he wanted revenge on his critics. "They treated me like a dead ancestor," he complained later of Liu and Deng.[19] But he also had a deeper fear that the revolution was being betrayed. The party, supposedly the people's vanguard, was becoming corrupt, self-perpetuating, even capitalist. The way China might be going was dramatized for Mao by the shock of Soviet "revisionism" since Stalin. There, it seemed, the bourgeoisie was being "born anew" even in a socialist society. How, then, could the revolution be saved from "capitalist roaders"? Not by the intellectuals—Mao had tried that in 1956. As he resharpened the language of class struggle, Mao harked back to the mass mobilization of the civil war. That had energized a generation and taught them the meaning of class struggle. The new generation, post-1949, needed to be forged in its own crucible of revolution.[20]

China's predicament was not unique. It was the Yugoslav communist Milovan Djilas who noted a general tendency, in supposedly classless communist societies, for the party to become "the new class." What was unusual about the People's Republic was that the regime deliberately turned the masses on the government. Here again, Mao was the critical factor: without him, there would have been no Cultural Revolution, just as there would have been no Great Leap Forward. But nothing is the work of one man, not even someone with Mao's megalomania. He needed allies, and his allies used him. Pressures for cultural reform came from radical intellectuals who congregated around Mao's third wife, Jiang Qing. She was a former actress from

Shanghai; many of those known as the Cultural Revolution group, such as Kang Sheng, came from there. They used her vendetta against the Chinese cultural establishment to mount a broader attack on the party elite, with Mao's support. Equally important were Lin Biao and the People's Liberation Army, whose prestige had been enhanced by the 1962 border war with India and the successful atomic test two years later. It was in the army that the "little red book" of Chairman Mao's quotations began to be disseminated in 1964. Mao in turn encouraged the campaign to "Learn from the People's Army." In 1965 Lin assumed control over the public security apparatus; he also forged links with Jiang Qing's group by appointing her cultural adviser to the army in February 1966. The Mao-Jiang-Lin axis was the foundation of the Cultural Revolution.

Since the autumn of 1965, Mao and Jiang had been living in Shanghai; by May 1966 rumors were circulating about his illness or death. Now Mao returned to the capital, announcing his comeback with a spectacularly publicized one-hour swim in the Yangtze River on July 16. In Beijing in August he convened the first formal party plenum since 1962, packed with his own men, where he orchestrated Liu's demotion and replacement by Lin Biao as heir apparent. The plenum also approved a sixteen-point program to promote the Great Proletarian Cultural Revolution in the arts, education and the party. The aim was to "change the mental outlook of the whole of society" by mobilizing the masses to "overthrow those persons in authority who are taking the capitalist road." Despite such inflammatory language, the document warned against force and called for cultural revolution committees, under party control, to oversee the process.[21] But these committees were quickly supplanted by radical teachers and students—the Red Guards.

China's universities were insulated, self-sufficient units, with staff and students living and eating within the compound. Many were clustered together: ten of Beijing's fifty-odd universities were located in the Haidian district. This made for an intense, hothouse atmosphere, even in normal times. In the mid-1960s, the pressures on the educational system were especially intense. It was trying simultaneously to create skilled personnel for a modernizing society, to expand educational opportunities for workers and peasants, and to instill socialist values throughout the population. The result was conflicting criteria for advancement: academic achievement versus class origins versus political performance. Hitherto, the first had been given most weight: most of China's 3.5 million teachers had been educated before 1949 in Confucian or Western elitist traditions. Often they implemented ideological directives mechanically, for instance turning political education into mere memorizing of texts. Tension between older and younger teachers was therefore rife; so was friction between those with party credentials and mere "intellectuals." Debate about the relative merits of being "red" or "expert" also afflicted the student body in universities and "middle schools" (the secondary or high-school level). These schools were the critical proving ground for entrance to university (only 1 percent of China's population were university graduates) and the key to good jobs. As part of the Great Leap retrenchment, places in senior high schools and universities were cut back; as part of the 1964 Socialist Education movement and other rectification campaigns, class background and political correctness became more significant criteria. China's high schools and universities were already on edge in the spring of 1966; Mao's support of the Cultural Revolution tipped them into anarchy.[22]

At the end of May, Nie Yuanzi, a philosophy professor at the prestigious Beijing University (Beida) put up a wall poster criticizing the university administration's lack of support for cultural revolution. This was part of a long-running campaign by Nie for greater practical and ideological education. But this time she had the support of Kang Sheng, Jiang Qing's aide; at Mao's behest, Nie's poster was read over the radio on June 2. In response to this clear signal, wall posters spread across China's universities and into the middle schools. Educational administrators were defenseless; many were displaced. In July regular classes were suspended and the annual exams postponed. It was announced that new enrollments would be delayed for one semester to allow schools to implement cultural revolution. Students started traveling from campus to campus to promote their campaigns. Cultural revolutionaries at the national level mobilized them as a political force.

On August 18, 1966, some fifty thousand Red Guards paraded through the center of Beijing. At Tienanmen, the "gate of heavenly peace," where Mao had proclaimed the triumph of the revolution in 1949, he stood again, Lin Biao right behind him, to review the new revolutionaries. Waving their little red books, they marched past the high crimson gate singing their new song:

> The East is red,
> The sun is rising
> Mao Zedong has appeared in China . . .

A few chosen students from Qinghua University joined the leaders on the balcony of the gate and pinned an armband with the characters "red guard" on to the "Great Helmsman."[23] This was the first of eight such rallies over the next three months, involving about one million people. During the final one on November 26, about two hundred fifty thousand Red Guards, on six thousand trucks, were driven past their leader. Mao was becoming a deity; pictures, badges, even statues were produced by the thousand. The little red books were brandished in demonstrations, discussed on street corners, cited ostentatiously in ordinary conversation. The pressure to conform was stifling. As one teacher observed years later, "Who would not form a Red Guard unit those days? Everyone around you was doing it. If you did not, you would be criticized for being not revolutionary."[24]

As this remark suggests, the Mao cult, for all its collective hysteria, was rooted in political calculation on all sides. The army promoted the October press campaign; they also organized free rail transport to bring the students to Beijing. Mao's name and support gave the Red Guards legitimacy and prestige. Mao was radicalizing the new generation to perpetuate his revolution.

Or so he hoped. In fact, the Red Guards proved a brittle political weapon. Much of their wrath against capitalist culture was directed at trivial targets such as long hair or "rocket-shaped" shoes. They enjoyed humiliating senior teachers, making them wear dunce caps or "jet-planing" them (head bowed, arms stretched behind) to endure public criticism. In the city of Chengdu in Sichuan Province, young Red Guards reduced traffic to chaos for several days because they insisted that it was counterrevolutionary for vehicles to drive on the *right* and to stop at *red* lights.[25] Once the university and school administrations had been overthrown, many indulged in "revolutionary tourism" around the country or factional violence on the campuses as the Red Guards fragmented into warring groups. The patterns were kaleidoscopic—at Beida there were over 70 Red Guard units—and yesterday's revolutionaries were routinely denounced as today's revisionists. But often the children of the party and military elite, such as the Red Flag faction in Canton, were more conservative than those of intellectual and "middle class" parents (Canton's East Wind), who had more to gain from toppling CCP cadres. Thus, one of the many ironies of Mao's Great Proleterian Cultural Revolution was that its shock troops were not workers but students, often of "bad class" lineage.

By the end of 1966, the revolution had spread from the campuses into factories and government offices throughout the country. Red Guards, often from Beijing, were in the van, but workers and low-level officials were also mobilized in Cultural Revolution committees against their superiors. The latter, in turn, organized their own forces, and as party authority dissolved across the country the Cultural Revolution degenerated into local struggles for power. Shanghai led the way. The conflict between the Workers Headquarters and the more radical Scarlet Guards brought the city to the brink of economic collapse and toppled the CCP government in January 1967. Similar eruptions occurred elsewhere. Mao tried to insist on a "three-in-one" combination: new "revolutionary committees" should involve the revolutionary masses, but also local military and suitably "revolutionary" officials. But in only a few cities, such as Shanghai and Shantung, were revolutionary committees easily established. The party lost effective control of many central government ministries and provincial administrations. Discreetly, Premier Zhou Enlai tried to maintain orderly government and, in particular, to protect China's diplomacy and nuclear program from the ravages of insurgents. But in January 1967 Beijing militants rampaged for a time over the Lop Nur test site; in July, they invaded the Foreign Ministry itself. Officials were beaten up, files ransacked, and diplomacy became polarized between conservatives and radicals. All but one of China's ambassadors were recalled as the embassies fell into radical hands. In neighboring Burma and in British Hong Kong, overt efforts were made to overturn the governments. The British embassy in Beijing was sacked.

The events of July and August 1967 marked the nadir of the revolution. Mao, Zhou, and Lin were now agreed on the need to rein in its excesses. Leaders of the Cultural Revolution group were removed, and Jiang Qing distanced herself from "ultra leftists." Gradually provincial revolutionary committees were established across the country, but in some provinces, notably Fujian on the east coast and Guangxi in the south, armed conflicts continued well into 1968. Despite government calls, most universities and many high schools were still closed, and using the army against the students would be too dangerous politically. In the end, Mao turned to the proleteriat to subdue the hardcore Red Guards. At the end of July 1968, some thirty thousand workers from Beijing moved into Qinghua University to remove some three hundred radicals. The same thing happened in another 136 universities over the next month, nearly half of them in Beijing. In October, worker and peasant "proletarian propaganda teams" were sent in to get the schools going again. Their main medium was lengthy criticism sessions, but confinement and beatings were also frequent. At the end of the year, the classes of 1966, 1967, and 1968 were belatedly given job assignments. Perhaps four million students were dispatched to the countryside. Some never returned; most lost any chance of further education and thus, attractive careers. Children of the party and the military had some chance to escape "rustification"; those from intellectual or "bad class" families, virtually none. Perhaps three-quarters of Canton's former high school students were sent into internal exile in 1968–1969—equivalent to 5 percent of the city's total population.[26] Their bitterness was private but intense. One former Red Guard leader remarked in 1982: "First the government turned against the intellectuals, then the party members, and then the students. We were all being used."[27]

Unlike the Great Leap Forward, the Cultural Revolution was largely an urban and suburban phenomenon. Its human cost was far smaller than that of the Great Leap (perhaps five hundred thousand dead) and its disruption to the economy also much less. But the cultural and political effects were enormous. Most of China's universities were closed for four years from the summer of 1966; many of the middle schools were shut for two years. Buildings were damaged, libraries destroyed, teachers persecuted, and a generation of skilled youngsters eventually marginalized. Among China's politicians, about two-thirds of the party elite were purged, including fourteen of the Politburo's twenty-three members. Liu Shaoqi died in detention in 1969; Deng Xiaoping was stripped of office but retained his party membership. The Ninth Party Congress in April 1969 confirmed Lin Biao's place as Mao's deputy and the enhanced influence of the PLA in Chinese politics: 45 percent of members of the new Central Committee were military, compared with 19 percent in 1956. Although the Congress marked the end of extreme turbulence, the Chinese date the Cultural Revolution to a whole decade, from 1966 to 1976 when Mao finally died. For most of the 1970s, in fact, Chinese politics revolved around the long succession struggle from which, eventually, Deng, not Lin, emerged as Mao's heir.

Southeast Asia and Indonesia's Turning Point

For Mao, the revolution had an external dimension as well. The ancient empire of Han China was still not reunified, with Tibet incompletely subdued and the Guomindang in control of Taiwan. Not only was Mao determined to reestablish China as a great power (the "Central Kingdom"), he also saw the promotion of Asian revolution as a goal in itself and a way of mobilizing opinion at home. As in the Korean War era (see Chapter 2), his policy was a cocktail of nationalism and communism; unlike in the 1950s, however, when he was dependent on Moscow, he was now able to play the two superpowers against each other.

The People's Republic was ethnically far more coherent than the Soviet Union, with non-Han ethnic groups constituting less than 10 percent of the population. But they occupied about half the territory, especially the sensitive border regions of Inner Mongolia in the north, Xinjiang in the northwest, and Tibet in the southwest (see Map 5). Of these, Tibet, covering one-eighth of China, was the most contentious. The country had been invaded by the People's Liberation Army in 1950–1951. Tibet's revolution was then advanced through land reform, control of nomadic peoples, and restrictions on the powerful Buddhist monasteries. This was intensified after an abortive rising in March 1959. Between 1959 and 1966 the number of monasteries was cut from two thousand seven hundred to 550, leaving only seven thousand monks out of one hundred thousand.[28] In the past, Tibet, though a separate country, had often acknowledged Chinese influence, but first the British raj and then the Indian government encouraged Tibetan autonomy as a buffer between them and China. This policy led to the Sino-Indian border wars of

1959 and 1962. After 1959 the Indians gave sanctuary to the leader of Tibetan Buddhism, the Dalai Lama, while the CIA helped train and supply Tibetan insurgents. Internationally and internally, Tibet would remain a headache for China's leaders.

An even more explosive problem was the island of Taiwan, where Chiang Kai-shek, the defeated Guomindang (GMD) leader, had established himself after 1949, still asserting that he was the rightful ruler of all China. Beijing claimed just as forcefully that Taiwan and the offshore islands it controlled (some of them only a few miles from mainland China) were PRC territory. Skirmishes between the two governments escalated into major international crises in 1954–1955 and again in the late summer of 1958. What alarmed Beijing was the formal U.S. support for Chiang's claims, backed up by military muscle. In September 1958, the Pentagon deployed an armada of six carriers, three heavy cruisers and forty destroyers off the China coast. Almost as disturbing for Beijing was Moscow's insistence that the dispute was a purely internal Chinese matter, implying they would not intervene to save the PRC. In 1962, the aging Chiang saw the Sino-Soviet split and China's domestic crisis as his last chance. "There is no doubt that we can annihilate the Communists, reunify our country, and restore freedom to the people on the mainland in the nearest future," he announced.[29] When the crisis bubbled over in June, it took firm U.S. warnings to both sides—no American support for a GMD invasion of the mainland, firm American resistance against a PRC attack on Taiwan—to defuse the tension.

For China, the Taiwan issue was a matter of international status as well as national unity. The GMD government in Taipei still occupied China's seat at the United Nations, including its position as a permanent member of the Security Council. For most of the 1950s, America's public support of Taipei remained firm, backed by the powerful "China Lobby" in Congress and fueled by bitter memories of the Korean War. In secret, however, the Eisenhower administration was moving toward a "two-China" policy that would recognize both governments in their own territories. This shift became more pronounced under Kennedy. Chiang's repressive rule over resentful native Taiwanese was an increasing embarrassment for the Americans, and the GMD's claims to be on the verge of regaining all China had become completely implausible. Like the concept of two Germanies after the Berlin Wall, the "two-China" idea suited Kennedy's aspirations for détente based on international realities. He was also responding to the shifting balance of power in the United Nations. In November 1965, the UN vote on seating the PRC was tied, 47 to 47.[30]

The vote reflected China's cultivation of African and Asian states against both superpowers. After the Nuclear Test Ban Treaty of July 1963—which the *People's Daily* called "a US-Soviet alliance against China pure and simple," intended to deny the PRC a nuclear capability[31]—the PRC broke formally with the old socialist camp and set itself up as putative leader of a new "intermediate zone" of African, Asian and Latin American countries ranged against American and Soviet imperialisms. In the words of the Politburo member Peng Zhen in May 1965, these areas were "the lifelines on which imperialism depends for the maintenance of its rule, and they are the areas where imperialist rule is most vulnerable."[32] With rhetoric, aid, and diplomacy, the PRC tried to detach socialists and communists from Moscow and mobilize them against the West.

But this effort, directed by Zhou Enlai, collapsed in 1965. One indication was China's failure in June to convene an Afro-Asian summit in Algiers from which the Soviets were excluded. Many of these states had more to gain from links with Moscow; several, including Egypt, resented PRC aid to their own communist parties. Even more damaging in October 1965 was the army's seizure of power in Indonesia, Asia's most populous state after China and India. The Indonesian communist party (third largest in the world) was destroyed; China's main regional ally, President Sukarno, was neutralized and then toppled. To understand the failure of Beijing's hopes of regional revolution we need to look generally at developments in Southeast Asia during the 1950s and 1960s.

China's strategy and diplomacy in Southeast Asia centered on the concept of a "people's war" drawn from the struggle against Japan—in other words, guerrilla conflict in which the communists led a "united front" of nationalist groups. But U.S. imperialism was more complex and covert than Japan's wartime presence; only South Vietnam was simply an American client state. Moreover, even though communism could still play on local discontent, especially in the Indonesian heartland of Java, across most of Southeast Asia it was an alien ideology that had to contend against two fundamental trends in most of the region—intense, politicized nationalism and the related growth of state power. Although the prevailing economic philosophy (except in Burma after 1962) was capitalist in the sense of a commitment to private property, in most countries the state took a leading role in the economy and gradually dismantled liberal political institutions. Regional nationalism was evident in import substitution policies, in discrimination against alien entrepreneurs (often Chinese), and in military campaigns to subdue peripheral ethnic groups and expand territorial boundaries. Increasingly, the armed forces became the focus of both state and nation. As we have seen, these are patterns familiar from other developing parts of the world in the 1960s—patterns that militated against simple success for either Western or communist models. But, unlike the case in, say, Latin America, in Southeast Asia the colonial imprint was more recent and the superpower rivalry much more intense.

The regional trend towards a nationalistic, military-led state was most apparent in Thailand.[33] The country had a keen sense of core identity, based on reverence for the monarchy and the pervasiveness of Buddhism. Despite Western penetration, Thailand was the only country in Southeast Asia to have escaped both European colonial rule and Japanese wartime occupation. Thus, 1945 did not mark a profound break in Thai history. Modern Thailand dates back to the army seizure of power in 1932, which began a persistent pattern of military rule, punctuated by periodic coups. The army, police, and bureaucracy—rivals but also interdependent—managed the modernization of this largely peasant country behind the unifying slogan of "nation, religion, king." During the 1950s, Thailand was formally a constitutional monarchy, with a patina of corrupt party politics overlying military rule. But Field Marshal Sarit Thanarat seized power in September 1957, imposed martial law, and abolished parties and unions. According to his foreign minister, Thanat Khoman, the root cause of political instability was "the sudden transplantation of alien institutions onto our soil." History showed, he said, that Thailand worked best under "a unifying authority around which all elements of the nation can rally."[34] Even after the charismatic Sarit died in 1963, a military triumvirate led by General Thanom Kittachon perpetuated his policies, in close alliance with the United States, which had fifty thousand troops in the country by 1968. During the 1960s the country saw steady economic growth, both in import-substituting industry and in the output of rice, rubber, and other agricultural commodities. Population also grew rapidly over the decade, from twenty-seven million to thirty-four million. Throughout the postwar period the communists were a marginal force, associated particularly with the Chinese community. It was only in the late 1960s that they began to capitalize on ethnic and regional discontent, at the same time as the social and economic inequalities of modernization were creating unrest. For most of the 1950s and 1960s, however, the Thai-Buddhist core of the nation remained stable, under firm military rule.

In Thailand's northwestern neighbor, Burma, the trend toward a strong, nationalistic state was also evident. But military rule was not imposed until 1962 and here it assumed a socialist and neutral form, in accordance with the country's traditions since independence. Burma was a more fragmented country than Thailand, not only because of its colonial legacy and the ravages of the war but also because Buddhism was less dominant and ethnic diversity more apparent. The end of British rule in January 1948 was followed by several years of civil war, and throughout the 1950s the parliamentary government of U Nu was unable to enforce central control. U Nu's goal was a unitary state with Buddhism as the official religion—unlike the federal, pluralist philosophy of his friend and mentor, Aung San, the wartime nationalist leader who had been assassinated in 1947. U Nu's centralization increased regional insurgency and exacerbated factional politics. The unrest paved the way for the military coup of March 1962, which brought General Ne Win to power for the next twenty-six years. Ne Win did not make Buddhism a state religion and he reined in the political activities of Buddhist monks, one of the main sources of opposition. He also attacked the autonomy of the frontier peoples, such as the Shan, by removing their hereditary chiefs and establishing local councils under army control. His Revolutionary Council of generals promulgated a "Burmese Way to Socialism," which would complete the 1940s struggle for independence in which most of them had participated. Instead of leaving the existing mixed economy in place, the government seized control of all trade, business, and industry. Its new agricultural laws also eliminated the remaining powers of landlords. These hasty and ill-prepared reforms seriously reduced output and exports. Ne Win also nationalized Western companies, such as Burma Oil, and drove out most of the Indian middle class. In 1966–1967 shortages and inflation brought the population of Rangoon and other urban areas close to revolt. But China's revolutionary propaganda against Burma in 1967 helped Ne Win's government to deflect popular anger against the Chinese commercial community, until better harvests in 1968–1971 and improved distribution eased the food crisis.[35]

The stories of Thailand's pro-American capitalism and Burma's neutralist socialism reveal the deeper problems underlying economic development of any form in southeast Asia, particularly the difficulty of establishing sovereign control over the national territory and its subordinate ethnic groups. Nowhere was this problem more evident in the 1960s than Malaya, Thailand's southern neighbor. In 1961 its population was 7.2 million (less than one-third of Burma's), of whom Malays constituted only half. Thirty-seven percent were Chinese, and 11 percent Indians and Pakistanis. Against the Muslim majority were also set substantial Buddhist and Hindu minorities. Politics therefore revolved around communal issues; stability both before and after independence from Britain in 1957 depended on an alliance structure between the three ethnic political parties—Malay, Chinese, and Indian. At its heart was mutual recognition of Malay political predominance and Chinese economic predominance. This delicate arrangement was adroitly managed by Tunku Abdul Rahman—a Malay prince and leader of the United Malays National Organization (UMNO)—who was prime minister from 1957 to 1970.

But its continuance was threatened by the problem of Singapore, Malaya's tiny island neighbor to the south, three quarters of whose 1.7 million people were Chinese. The British had hung on to Singapore as a Crown colony because of its strategic significance as a naval base, but had conceded full autonomy in domestic affairs by 1959. The dominant People's Action Party (PAP) in Singapore, led by the autocratic Lee Kuan Yew (born 1923), campaigned for "independence through merger" with Malaya—a move vigorously resisted by the tunku until the summer of 1961. What changed his mind was the danger that the PAP might fall under control of its radical, nationalist left wing, raising the specter of Malaya's neighbor as an Asian Cuba, in thrall to Beijing. Although Lee forced out the left, which formed its own Socialist Front in June 1961, the tunku was now ready to contemplate a Malaya-Singapore federation. But to offset the inevitable Chinese majority, he wanted to include the Malay-dominated territories of northern Borneo, four hundred miles away, which were still under British rule. Both Sarawak and Sabah decided to join, but the sultan of Brunei pulled out at the last minute. Meanwhile, in Singapore, Lee Kuan Yew secured a 70 percent referendum majority. In September 1963 the Federation of Malaysia came into existence.

Communal harmony was hard to sustain under the new arrangements. The socialist, urban Chinese politicians of Singapore were not compatible with the landed Malay leaders of the peninsula, and previous understandings about mutual nonintervention were not honored. UMNO presented itself as champion of the Malays in Singapore (14 percent of the population), sparking racial riots there in July 1964 on the occasion of the Prophet Muhammad's birthday. Likewise, the PAP started campaigning among Chinese in Malaya and, by the spring of 1965, it was demanding a democratic "Malaysian Malaysia." This was an attack on Malay dominance of politics, society, and culture, as well as a call to the poor of all racial groups against the Malay elite. But Lee Kuan Yew had now overplayed his hand. The tunku rallied moderate Malay, Chinese, and Indian opinion around the traditional alliance and forced Singapore out of the federation in August 1965. This was a devastating blow to Lee, who broke down before the cameras when announcing the end of his dream. His tiny island state soon faced high tariffs and immigration controls on all movement across the narrow causeway linking Singapore and Malaya. In the longer term, however (as we shall see in Chapter 12), exclusion forced Singapore into a new and dynamic relationship with the world economy.[36]

But Singapore was not the greatest challenge to Malaysia in its early years. More threatening was the guerrilla war waged by President Sukarno of Indonesia against Sabah and Sarawak in 1963–1965 during his campaign to destroy the Malaysian federation.[37] In part, Confrontation (Konfrontasi), as Sukarno termed the war, reflected the artificiality of the colonial boundaries. Indonesia and Malaya both used essentially the same official language, which reflected the ebb and flow of peoples across the Straits of Malacca and the Java Sea for centuries. Sukarno also saw Confrontation as a continuance of the campaign for national independence and integrity across this huge archipelago, in which Javanese hegemony was still tenuous and resented. In the spring of 1958, the government put down an army rebellion in Sumatra, which had backing from Malaya. In August 1962, the Dutch agreed to surrender West Irian, over which they had continued to rule, after a vigorous military campaign. The British protectorates of north Borneo were next on Sukarno's list: the Indonesians had inherited the southern part, Kalimantan, from the Dutch in 1949 and aspired to control the whole island. Malaysia was viewed as a neocolonial creation by the British to perpetuate their rule.

Indonesian foreign policy was also intertwined with cold war politics. In the late 1950s, the Eisenhower administration, anxious about growing communist influence in Jakarta, favored a breakup of Indonesia. The Sumatran rebellion had been backed ineptly by the CIA; this became embarrassingly clear when an American pilot was shot down after accidentally bombing a church. The Soviets quickly exploited the situation; the massive expansion of Soviet arms and aid in 1960–1961 enabled Sukarno to mount his West Irian campaign. The Kennedy administration then tried to revive American influence, offering economic aid and pressing the Dutch to withdraw from West Irian. At this stage, Indonesian-Chinese relations were in tatters, following the Indonesian government's 1959–1960 campaign against Chinese traders. As in other parts of southeast Asia, this campaign reflected communal resentment against Chinese wealth and official doubts about their loyalty. (Until the mid-1950s, the People's Republic, following imperial practice, still insisted that all overseas Chinese descendants through the male line were its subjects, regardless of birthplace or domicile.) Despite these tensions, however, when it became clear that neither Washington nor Moscow approved of the campaign against Malaysia, Sukarno turned to Beijing for help.[38]

For all its regional and international origins, however, Confrontation was rooted above all in a power struggle within Indonesia itself.[39] The vast archipelago (population ninety seven million by 1961) had not settled well into electoral democracy. Between the confirmation of independence from the Dutch in December 1949 and the proclamation of martial law in March 1957, there had been seven ministries, none of them lasting more than two years. Hostility was still intense between the outer islands and Java, where 60 percent of the population lived. There was related tension between the stricter Islamic practices of the islands and the more syncretic Hindu-Muslim religion of Java. Java itself had its own divisions between *santri* purists and and the nominal *abangan* Muslims, while western Java was a stronghold of the separatist Darul Islam movement until 1962. The main unifying force in Indonesia was the army, some two hundred thousand strong in the 1950s. Although its commander, General Abdul Haris Nasution, was a devout Muslim from Sumatra, the bulk of the officer corps was Javanese. Nasution's efforts to increase central control over the regional army commanders (many of whom were engaged in smuggling and other profitable business activities) was a major cause of the revolts in Sumatra (Indonesia's richest island) and Sulawesi in 1956–1958. The failure of the politicians to check the breakup of the country paved the way for martial law in 1957 and strengthened the army's political position as Nasution put down the revolts and purged the officer corps.[40]

The other main beneficiary of the national crisis of 1957–1958 was Sukarno (1901–1970), the country's president since 1945 (Plate 6). Although he had founded Indonesian nationalism in the 1920s, Sukarno lacked his own power base and had been sidelined by younger revolutionaries since the war. For most of the 1950s he was a figurehead president, feted abroad by the so-called nonaligned states but largely impotent at home (except in the bedchamber, with which he became increasingly obsessed). Yet he remained a national figure, a magnetic orator, and a wily politician. In the late 1950s the failure of parliamentarianism gave Sukarno his chance to proclaim "guided democracy"—with himself as guide. Henceforth, political representation would be by functional groups (such as peasants, workers, religions, and regions). With Nasution's help, he used martial law to squeeze out the political parties. In July 1959, Indonesia reverted to the 1945 constitution, which gave the president extensive power. But Sukarno feared that he would end up as simply the army's figurehead. So he also cultivated the Partai Komunis Indonesia (PKI) which, under the youthful leadership of D. N. Aidit (1923–1965), had devoted itself in the 1950s to the political route to power. Sukarno now hoped to domesticate the PKI and use it to balance the army. He would be like the *dalang*, or puppet master, of the celebrated Javanese *wayang* dramas to which he loved to allude in his speeches.

"Guided democracy" was more a slogan than a program, however. Like Mao, Sukarno wanted national rejuvenation—"Revolution is only truly Revolution if it is a continuous struggle," he declaimed on Independence Day in 1957—yet, as one one of his biographers has observed, Sukarno had "a feeling for movement, but not for direction." He also knew nothing about economics. The country was brought to the brink of ruin as foreign companies were driven out and an inefficient state capitalism took over completely. Another of Sukarno's slogans was that "a nation always needs an enemy." The campaign against the Dutch over West Irian served such a purpose by arousing nationalist sentiment and diverting domestic discontent. Malaysia became his next target.[41]

The formal proclamation of Malaysia in September 1963 prompted a week of rioting in Jakarta—partly spontaneous, partly contrived—in which the British embassy was burned and British property looted. Sukarno issued his call to "crush Malaysia."[42] But Malaysia was a much tougher nut to crack than West Irian. The British government was ready to honor its defense obliga-

tions to the new federation, putting fifty thousand troops into effective counterinsurgency operations in Borneo at the height of the crisis. And the U.S.
government, after trying to retain influence in Jakarta as long as possible, suspended aid in 1964 and gave substantial support to Malaysia. Sukarno was
now pushed by the force of his own rhetoric into intensified Confrontation.
He began raids on Malaya itself from August 1964. After the UN General Assembly had condemned Indonesian aggression and elected Malaysia to the
Security Council, Sukarno withdraw his country from the UN in January
1965. "This is good for our nation to stand on its own feet," Sukarno declared.
"Go to Hell with your aid."[43]

Indonesia's only major ally was China, which used the crisis to increase military aid to Sukarno and to cultivate the PKI. But the unfolding drama was
not stage managed by Beijing: Sukarno and the army would take aid from
anyone; Aidit and the PKI were no Maoist advocates of people's war. They
used the crisis not to foment revolution but to strengthen their case for inclusion within government.[44] Within the party, grass-roots resentment was
growing about its role as a rent-a-crowd agency of Sukarnoism and the economic dislocation of "guided democracy." The bad harvest in Java in 1963
had also produced widespread rural famine. By late 1963, these pressures
helped push the PKI leadership into a move they had long favored, namely
a campaign for land reform to reduce rents and to give peasants, not landlords, a greater share of the crop. What ensued, however, was a spiral of
rural violence, especially in central and eastern Java, as landowners—often
santri and sometimes Muslim religious institutions—mobilized their supporters against "the atheists," often using black-shirted "flying squads" from
the Muslim youth organizations in terror raids of their own.[45]

Aidit was forced to scale down the land reform campaign by the end of
1964. But by then it had boosted his rural support. In the summer of 1965
perhaps twenty million Indonesians were members of the party or of its as-
sociate unions and organizations—one-fifth of the population.[46] The PKI's
weakness was that, as a mass party, it had no military capability and its membership might simply melt away if the army was unleashed, hence the PKI's
continued reliance on Sukarno's authority. Meanwhile, it pressed for greater
political control of the armed forces, while, covertly, its Special Bureau *(Biro
Chisus)* was cultivating "progressive" elements in the air force, traditionally
antipathetic to army hegemony. Publicly Sukarno was apparently moving
leftward: "I love the PKI as my brother," he declared in May 1965.[47] By the
summer he was talking of a Beijing-Jakarta axis. Nasution (whose authority
as defense minister had been reduced) and his military allies watched the
trend of events with alarm. There was discussion about a "Council of Generals" to take power from Sukarno and the communists. As reports of
Sukarno's ill health mounted in the summer of 1965, many wondered how

long the president would be around to protect his PKI allies. Both right and left seemed ready to move; Jakarta was rife with rumors of conspiracy.

The dénouement came on September 30–October 1, 1965. What exactly happened remains controversial, not surprisingly since this was the origin of the contemporary Indonesian state. The subsequent military government claimed that it had foiled a communist coup, fronted by a few dissident officers. This is unlikely: the PKI still lacked the means to seize and hold power themselves; the Revolutionary Council that was briefly proclaimed on October 1 contained only three communists among its forty-five members. The principal plotters were junior officers with roots in the Diponegoro division from central Java, who were disgruntled at the corruption of the army leadership and who were acting with air force support. They claimed to be forestalling a generals' coup that was backed by the CIA. But the communists *were* central to the story. Aidit and the PKI's Special Bureau were in league with the plotters. Fearing Nasution and his allies, yet lacking military power, they needed some military help to resist a junta. Supporting a plot to remove the leading generals would help tip the political balance further in favor of the communist party.[48]

In any event, the move on September 30 was botched. Six generals were killed, either resisting arrest or in captivity next morning. Their bodies were dumped down a well on Halim Air Force Base, the plotters' Jakarta headquarters. Nasution's five-year-old daughter was fatally wounded, but her father escaped by vaulting the garden wall into the grounds of the Iraqi embassy, breaking his ankle in the process. Absent from the arrest list was General Suharto, commander of the army's strategic reserve, Kostrad—possibly because he was known to be at odds with Nasution, perhaps (as some have speculated) because he had previously intimated neutrality or even sympathy for the plot.[49] Such speculation has been fueled by the fact that, when the plotters sent two battalions of troops to secure Freedom Square—location of the presidential palace, the radio station, and the main telephone exchange—they did not occupy the east side of the square, where Kostrad had its headquarters. Suharto was able to reach his office that morning, phone around to ascertain the situation, then enter the square and gradually persuade the troops to withdraw. At 9:00 P.M. Suharto broadcast that a coup had been averted and that he had taken over the army leadership.

In twenty-four hours, this taciturn general officer had jumped from military obscurity to the political center—a position that he was to occupy for the next three decades. Although Sukarno had probably given tacit support to the plot, once it failed, he tried to retrieve his position. But the veteran puppet master was no longer pulling the strings. Using massed student demonstrators and eventually army units, Suharto forced Sukarno to surrender effective power in March 1966, though Suharto did not assume the presidency formally until a year later. The crisis also gave Suharto the opportunity and pretext to move against the PKI, playing on emotions inflamed by retrieval of the generals' bodies from the well and the funeral of Nasution's daughter. In central Java, the cleanup of remaining plotters by elite paracommandos degenerated into massacres of whole villages suspected of being PKI. The army also encouraged and armed Muslim youth gangs to carry on the work. Across central and eastern Java, and also in neighboring Bali, rural progroms settled scores left over from the land-reform campaign or from older religious animosities between *santri* and *abangan* villages. The hated Chinese were also singled out. Bodies were hurled into rivers, sometimes clogging irrigation ditches. At Cirebon, in west Java, a guillotine was constructed to speed up the executions. In some areas, severed heads were displayed in the streets for weeks after. No one knows how many died, but at least five hundred thousand is the customary estimate.[50]

Until the end of September 1965, it had seemed that Asia's third-largest country was sliding toward communism, with the backing of Beijing. After Suharto's consolidation of power, however, Indonesia lurched toward the West, with enthusiastic support from Washington (though there is no clear evidence of American involvement in the coup itself).[51] In September 1966, the country rejoined the UN, having recognized Malaysia the previous month. In August 1967 it joined Malaysia, Singapore, Thailand, and the Philippines as founder members of ASEAN (the Association of South East Asian Nations). For China, the Indonesian crisis of autumn 1965 was one sign that the west wind was blowing strongly. Even more striking was America's dramatic escalation of the war in Indochina.

America's Anguish, Vietnam's Tragedy

Three-quarters of a century of French rule over Indochina, punctuated briefly and brutally by Japanese wartime occupation, ended with the Geneva conference of July 1954 (see Chapter 2). The three successor states were, however, very different in form and character (Map 11). The most stable in the first postindependence decade was Cambodia, where the former king, Prince Norodom Sihanouk, dominated national politics. Sihanouk was a charming yet ruthless politician who squeezed out the parliamentary parties and ran the country after 1955 through his mass movement, the Popular Socialist Community. His "Khmer Socialism" was, in reality, only skin deep: it perpetuated the hierarchical Khmer society while justifying increased state intervention. He was determined to protect his country from reverting to a

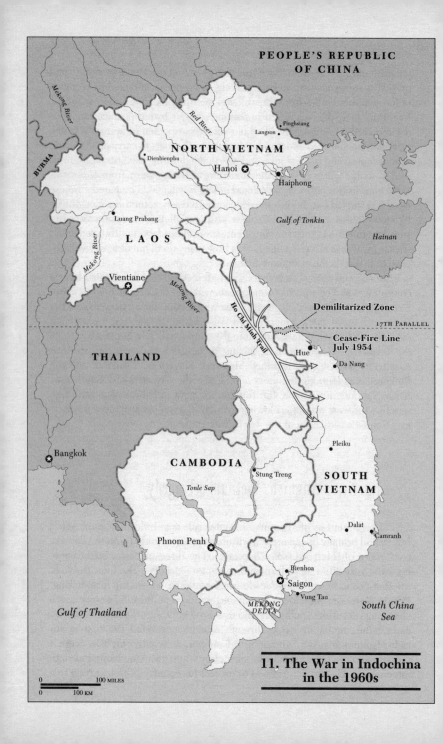

PEOPLE'S REPUBLIC
OF CHINA

Mekong River

BURMA

Red River

NORTH VIETNAM

• Langson   • Pinghsiang

• Dienbienphu

Hanoi ✪   • Haiphong

Gulf of Tonkin

• Luang Prabang

Hainan

LAOS

Mekong River

Vientiane ✪

Mekong River

Ho Chi Minh Trail

Demilitarized Zone

17TH PARALLEL

Cease-Fire Line
July 1954

Hue •   • Da Nang

THAILAND

CAMBODIA

Tonle Sap   • Stung Treng

• Pleiku

SOUTH
VIETNAM

Bangkok ✪

• Dalat
• Camranh

Phnom Penh ✪

• Bienhoa

✪ Saigon
• Vung Tau

Gulf of Thailand

*MEKONG
DELTA*

*South China
Sea*

11. The War in Indochina
in the 1960s

0 _____ 100 MILES
0 _____ 100 KM

battleground between the Thais and the Vietnamese, as had happened before the French arrived, and he harked back to the heyday of the great Angkor empire of the tenth to fourteenth centuries. Sihanouk's neutralist nationalism was resented by the Americans, who supported plots against him in the late 1950s, but he remained in power. During the decade 1954–1964 the country enjoyed greater prosperity and stability than for years before and certainly afterward.[52]

Laos, to the north of Cambodia, was less able to maintain its independence and unity once France pulled out. It was trapped between China and Burma as well as Thailand, Vietnam, and Cambodia. It also had a smaller population (about 2.5 million in 1960, half Cambodia's) and its politics revolved around feuds between various interrelated members of the royal family. There was also a sharp division between the Lao peoples, mostly Buddhist, and the animist mountain tribes, who blurred ethnically into the Montagnard peoples of Vietnam on the other side of the Truong Son range. This division was reflected to some extent in the endemic civil war between the royal Lao government and the Pathet Lao, which was patched up temporarily in November 1957 in a coalition government, only to resume soon after. The Pathet Lao, under Prince Souphanouvong, was also allied to the communists in Vietnam. The Americans had built up the Laotian army after 1954 and had also connived in coups that brought down the coalition government in 1958–1959. By late 1960, the Soviets were providing aid to the Pathet Lao. When Kennedy was inaugurated in January 1961, it looked as if Laos was going to become a superpower battleground—the Berlin of Southeast Asia.[53]

Unlike its neighbors, Vietnam had been formally divided at Geneva in 1954. The British, Russians, and Chinese had imposed partition at the seventeenth parallel, between the communist-led Democratic Republic of Vietnam (DRV) in the north and the American-backed Republic of Vietnam in the south. This was supposed to be a temporary arrangement until national elections in 1956, but Ngo Dinh Diem, the South Vietnamese leader, and the Eisenhower administration ensured that elections were never held. With American backing, Diem cracked down on political rivals, reimposed the authority of rural landlords, and gradually rooted out the communist cadres left in the south. The northern government was led by Ho Chi Minh (1890–1969), a veteran revolutionary who had left his homeland before World War I to spend a decade in Britain, France and Russia, and twenty more years in China until Vietnam's August Revolution of 1945. After another decade of war against the French, Ho concentrated in the mid-1950s on establishing a socialist society in the north, imposing agricultural collectivization and promoting heavy industry. However, national unity remained his aim. With pressure mounting from southern communists, his ruling Vietnamese Workers Party (VWP) committed itself in January 1959 to a revolutionary struggle in the south, though it sought approval from Moscow and Beijing before going ahead. During 1959–1960, rural uprisings against Diem, largely spontaneous, broke out in the central highlands and the Mekong delta. In December 1960, the National Liberation Front (NLF) was formed in the south. Modeled on the anti-French Vietminh, this was a coalition of anti-Diem groups under communist leadership. The conflict in South Vietnam was therefore "an insurgent movement inspired by local conditions in the south but guided and directed from Hanoi."[54]

In January 1961, Kennedy inherited an international confrontation in Laos and a looming crisis in Vietnam. But in 1961–1962 the great powers brokered a neutral, unified government in Laos that lasted for several years until engulfed by the war in Vietnam. In contrast, Kennedy became more and more committed to the government of South Vietnam, paving the way for full military involvement under Lyndon Johnson. One reason for the contrast lay in local differences. Laos was small and unimportant. Its government was inept and controlled a fraction of the terrain. Military aid would be hard to distribute in a land-locked country of mountains and jungle, with few usable roads and railroads. By contrast, South Vietnam had some fourteen million people; American planners envisaged it once again as a major rice bowl of Asia. It was easier to supply, being a coastal state, and its army and leader both seemed credible. Diem was a Catholic (like Kennedy) and his country received over $1 billion from the United States between 1955 and 1961 (three-quarters of it for the army), making South Vietnam fifth among all recipients of American foreign aid.

As a senator, Kennedy had made clear his personal commitment, proclaiming in July 1956: "Vietnam represents the cornerstone of the Free World in Southeast Asia. . . . It is our offspring, we cannot abandon it."[55] Moreover, the neutralization of Laos, like the Cuban fiasco, gave ammunition to Kennedy's critics on the Republican right. For this new president, determined to stand up to the Soviets and prove his virility, another foreign-policy setback was inconceivable. Convinced that "we have to act" to counter Khrushchev's apparent belief that "I'm inexperienced and have no guts," Kennedy concluded in June 1961 that "we have a problem in making our power credible, and Vietnam looks like the place."[56]

Apart from global credibility, Kennedy also worried about regional security. Sharing the fashionable domino theory of the 1950s, he and his advisers pondered the psychological effect elsewhere in Asia if an American client collapsed. The most important regional ally of the United States was Japan. In retrospect, its economic strength and Western orientation may seem axiomatic, but that was by no means so clear in 1961. Japan's celebrated "high growth" era was a feature of the 1960s, not the 1950s. In 1960, the country's gross domestic product was still less than that of either Britain, France, or West Germany (in the latter case three-fifths).[57] Among Japanese, America's political base was shaky. It relied on the ruling Liberal Democratic party, which was still divided over the postwar reforms imposed on Japan, whereas the Socialist party, which surged to one-third of Diet seats in the 1958 election, opposed Japan's alliance with America and favored a neutralist position. In January 1960 Prime Minister Kishi Nobusuke (a former member of Japan's wartime cabinet) secured a revision of the unequal 1951 security treaty, which removed America's right to intervene in Japan's internal affairs and included a commitment to defend Japan if attacked. But this did not appease the left. The debate over ratification in the Diet that spring prompted huge demonstrations and the use of police to eject protesting Socialist MPs. After Eisenhower's press aide was mobbed at Tokyo airport, Kishi was humiliatingly obliged to ask the president to cancel his June 1960 visit. Four days after the treaty was finally passed, Kishi resigned in expiation.[58] None of this encouraged confidence in America in the early 1960s about the stability of its main Asian ally.

Nor was the situation propitious in neighboring South Korea, on whose defense the United States had expended vast amounts of money and blood in the war of 1950–1953. While Kim Il Sung's regime turned the north into a communist state with Soviet and Chinese assistance, American aid was pumped into the south, still under the control of the aging Syngman Rhee. Foreign assistance covered over half of the government's budget, and Rhee's crude economic management fueled inflation. As economic growth stagnated in the late 1950s, Rhee and his Liberal party struggled to retain their grip on power, resorting to a rigged election in March 1960. The following month two hundred student protestors were shot dead by troops outside the presidential palace. The nationwide demonstrations that ensued, and American pressure, forced Rhee to resign. But factional infighting and street protests continued. An estimated one million people were involved in some two thousand demonstrations.[59] Student calls for reunification with the north were the final straw for the army: General Park Chung Hee mounted a coup in May 1961, despite American disapproval. Although military government fostered political stability and economic growth during the 1960s, Korea's future looked far from assured to Kennedy in 1961.

For all these reasons—local, regional, and global—Kennedy was determined to make a stand in Vietnam, dismissing suggestions that the Laotian settlement might be the basis for a more general neutralization of Southeast Asia. But equally, he resisted Pentagon pressure to introduce U.S. combat troops. The symbolic impact would soon be forgotten, he reflected in November 1961, and then more would be required: "It's like taking a drink. The effect wears off, and you have to take another."[60] Instead, as was to become the pattern regarding Vietnam, Kennedy sought middle ground between the contending bureaucrats. In November 1961 he decided to increase American aid and "military advisers" but also to press Diem to ease his repression and promote social change. Neither policy proved effective. By 1963, South Vietnam's basic problem, the lack of "rice roots" support for Diem, reached crisis proportions.[61]

Ngo Dinh Diem was a devout, celibate Catholic. But his principal advisers were his arrogant brother, Ngo Dinh Nhu, and Nhu's beautiful yet vicious wife, both of whom flaunted their wealth and power. Not only was this an authoritarian family dynasty, it was also perceived in South Vietnam as indelibly foreign. Many of Diem's cabinet had collaborated with the French, and key posts in government and the bureaucracy went to Catholics, although they constituted under 10 percent of South Vietnam's fifteen million population. In contrast, there were four million active Buddhists. Although not a formal religion, Buddhism served as a symbol of Vietnamese nationalism against the Diem regime. The Buddhist crisis became an international issue on June 11, 1963, because of the actions of a seventy-three-year-old monk, Quang Duc. He sat down in the middle of a major intersection in Saigon and was doused with gasoline by fellow monks. He then set fire to himself with a match. The scene was recorded by an American press photographer, alerted by the Buddhists. An agitated Kennedy observed that "no news picture in history has generated as much emotion around the world as that one has."[62] While Quang Duc's ashes were distributed to pagodas all over the country, Madame Nhu demanded more "barbecues" and invited critical American journalists to immolate themselves. "Let them burn," she sneered, "and we shall clap our hands."[63] On August 21, Nhu sent army units into Buddhist pagodas in major cities—in breach of promises by Diem—killing and wounding many monks. New waves of protest surged through Vietnam, even within the elite. Among those who resigned were South Vietnam's ambassador to the United States and its representative at the UN, respectively the father and mother of Madame Nhu.

This was the last straw for Diem's critics in Washington, led by Averell Harriman and Roger Hilsman in the State Department. On August 24 they cabled to the new U.S. ambassador in Saigon, Henry Cabot Lodge their clear support of an army coup if Diem would not remove the Nhus. Within days Kennedy was backtracking as other advisers counterattacked. But he never rejected the idea, being mainly concerned that there was "no point in trying a coup unless there was a chance of its success."[64] In Saigon the army plotters grew hot and cold in the changing breezes from Washington, but Ambassador Lodge egged them on. They finally seized power on November 1. Diem and Nhu were killed the next day in the back of an armored personnel carrier.[65] Three weeks later, John F. Kennedy himself was shot dead.

The coup settled nothing. Six governments came and went between November 1963 and June 1965 as the military situation deteriorated and Hanoi's Vietcong insurgents gained effective control of more than half the country. North Vietnam now stepped up the pressure. On one side of a long-running debate in Hanoi were those like the ailing Ho Chi Minh and General Vo Nguyen Giap—the architect of victory over the French in 1954—who anticipated another long war that would turn on the political struggle in the south. Less cautious elements led by Le Duan, the party first secretary, argued that South Vietnam was nearing collapse and that the time was ripe for a major military offensive by the north linked to a general uprising in the south. Le Duan won the argument in December 1963. By late 1964 regular units of the People's Army of North Vietnam (PAVN) were infiltrating into the south. On February 7, 1965, the Vietcong attacked a U.S. base at Pleiku, in the central highlands. Eight Americans were killed and over one hundred injured—the first large-scale U.S. casualties.

Pleiku brought on a similar great debate in Washington. In the first year of his presidency, Lyndon Baines Johnson had tried to downplay Vietnam. He was building up his own political base after winning election in his own right in November 1964 with 61 percent of the popular vote, the greatest presidential margin to date. With two-to-one majorities in both houses of Congress, LBJ believed he had both the electoral mandate and the legislative support for his Great Society programs against poverty and racism. In fact, he was forced to leave what he called "the woman I really loved" for "that bitch of a war on the other side of the world."[66] Johnson's inner circle, notably Defense Secretary Robert McNamara and National Security Adviser McGeorge Bundy—both holdovers from Kennedy—told him that he had to escalate the American commitment or South Vietnam would collapse. Pleiku became the pretext for a policy that had been mooted for months, namely to start bombing military and industrial targets in the north. Reluctantly, Johnson agreed; the bombing, code-named Rolling Thunder, began on March 2, 1965. The military commander in South Vietnam, General William Westmoreland, immediately demanded two battalions of U.S. Marines to guard Danang and other bases from which the attacks were launched. During April, the marines were permitted to engage in counterinsurgency operations as well as mere defense, and their numbers were augmented. And in July, Johnson succumbed to pressure from McNamara and the Joint Chiefs of Staff to introduce American troops into large-scale combat. On this schedule, 175,000 U.S. troops would be in the country by the end of 1965, with the possibility of another one hundred thousand during the following year.

The situation in South Vietnam did not improve, however. In June 1965, several months of shaky civilian government came to an end as the military regained power. The new head of state, Nguyen Van Thieu, was an ambitious and ruthless general; the prime minister, Nguyen Cao Ky, a playboy airman who boasted Hitler was his hero—"because he pulled his country together." But, said Ky, the situation was now so desperate that "we need four or five Hitlers in Vietnam." Bill Bundy, the Assistant Secretary of State, said that Thieu and Ky were "absolutely the bottom of the barrel."[67]

The chronic political chaos in Saigon and the feeble performance of the ARVN (Army of the Republic of Vietnam) forces cast doubt on the original justification for American involvement, namely, to help South Vietnam defend itself. But U.S. policy makers rejected the counterargument—advanced by a State Department "dove," George Ball, and others—that America should cut its losses, withdraw and seek a neutralized Vietnam. They believed that, whether or not the country was viable, it could not be allowed to fall, because the United States had invested too much in its survival. "Why are we in South Vietnam?" Johnson asked—and answered again and again. First, there were the promises, made repeatedly to South Vietnam by successive presidents since 1954, which raised the issue of American credibility. "If we are driven from the field in Viet-Nam, then no nation can ever again have the same confidence in American promise, or in American protection." Nor could one forget the so-called lessons of appeasement: "we learned from Hitler at Munich that success only feeds the appetite of aggression." There was also the underlying issue of "national security." North Vietnam, declared Johnson, was "spurred on by Communist China. Its goal is to conquer the South, to defeat American power, and to extend the Asiatic boundaries of communism."[68] Beijing, he said in April 1965, was "helping the forces of violence in almost every continent."[69] In short, the tiny country of South Vietnam (far less important intrinsically than Indonesia) had become the test case of America's cold war credibility as a superpower. On the other hand, Johnson and his civilian advisers were fearful that cold war might become hot war. For this reason, the president personally supervised the bombing targets, keeping the centers of Hanoi and the port of Haiphong off limits lest diplomatic and support personnel from Russia or China be hit. Nor would he allow ground operations in North Vietnam itself. Recalling how the Korean War had escalated disastrously in 1950, he worried that such action might trigger a "secret treaty" between Hanoi and Beijing and bring China into the war.

Ironically, the Russians may have held an almost mirror image view of the stakes in Vietnam. In the decade after 1954, they viewed the conflict as a local quarrel to which it was enough to give propaganda support and token aid. As Hanoi and Washington began to escalate in 1964–1965, the Soviets had two contrasting concerns. On the one hand, an intensified war could only damage Soviet-American relations and play into the hands of China, currently Hanoi's main patron. On the other hand, failure to assist the DRV would damage Moscow's stature in the Sino-Soviet struggle for support in the communist world. The Soviet ambassador in Washington, Anatoly Dobrynin, told an American journalist, "A Socialist country—a very small country—is being bombed by you. We have to respond. The Socialist world is looking to us to respond. We know how dangerous this is, but we have to do it."[70] Consequently, the increased aid, signaled by Prime Minister Alexei Kosygin's visit in February 1965, was intended both to cover the Soviets in the propaganda battle with Beijing and also to increase their leverage over Hanoi, in the hope of brokering a negotiated settlement.

Even in China, there were clear limits on the desired escalation. Several Chinese army regiments were sent as "volunteers" to the DRV in mid-1965, but these were engineers and anti-aircraft units, not combat troops. Beijing, like Washington, did not want another Korean War—though it did hint strongly that an American invasion of the DRV would make China fight.[71] Nor did it favor a smashing DRV victory that might herald renewed Vietnamese expansion in Southeast Asia at China's expense. Zhou Enlai believed the conflict could be controlled if the PRC regulated the flow of supplies, restricting Hanoi to a "people's war" without heavy weapons. This would aid China's anti-American strategy throughout the region in 1965. Domestic motives also influenced China's policy. Mao saw the crisis atmosphere created by the Vietnam war as a way of promoting continued revolution at home.[72]

So America, Russia, and China each had a stake in limiting the Vietnam war but also in not losing it. The state of Sino-American relations in early 1965 made it difficult to imagine either of these governments pulling out. The Americans had several causes for concern: China had just tested an atomic device, Sukarno had left the UN, and the crisis within Indonesia was building to a climax. The critical decisions on bombing and troop commitments were taken against this disconcerting regional background. It is therefore probable that any U.S. president would have been pushed to escalate the Vietnam war in 1965. Eisenhower publicly urged Johnson on and, despite the assertions of Kennedy intimates that he would have pulled the country out of Vietnam in his second term,[73] he had made the original commitments (including over fifteen thousand military "advisers") and shared the general world-view.

The critical difference between LBJ and his predecessors was probably over the politics of the policy rather than its principles. Bundy and McNamara coupled their calls for escalation with requests that the president mobilize consent at home by securing full Congressional support and by raising taxes to pay for the war. Kennedy might well have taken that route: his passion was foreign affairs, his self-image was bound up with the cold war, and he had the charisma and oratory to rouse public opinion for a new crusade.[74]

But Johnson's heart was in domestic affairs. His legislative priorities for 1965 were public housing, voting rights for blacks, and Medicare for the elderly. Pushing these through Congress required the cooperation of conservatives of both parties, who dominated the key committees. The president feared that if he dramatized Vietnam, his conservative critics would "take the war as their weapon." He believed they would say, "beat the Communists first, then we can look around and maybe give something to the poor."[75]

Consequently, Johnson played down the escalation. The bombing campaign, he said, was "not a change of purpose" but "a change in what we believe that purpose requires."[76] The troop commitments were announced in a midday press conference rather than in a special message to Congress. Instead of full political debate, he took refuge behind a congressional resolution, passed in August 1964 at the time of minor naval incidents in the Gulf of Tonkin, supporting the president in taking "all necessary measures to repel any armed attack against the forces of the United States and to prevent further aggression."[77] The Gulf of Tonkin Resolution became his pretext for ever larger troop commitments without further congressional endorsement. The costs of war were financed by government borrowing. In 1965 and 1966 he refused to ask Congress for tax increases, fearful that this would "kill" his legislative program.[78]

Yet LBJ's domestic bias did not betoken lack of conviction about the basic issues at stake in Vietnam. On the contrary, a man of vast self-confidence who had spent two decades wheeling and dealing with great success on Capitol Hill, he believed that he could sort out poverty and Vietnam simultaneously. "I was determined to be a leader of war *and* a leader of peace," he admitted later. "I wanted both, I believed in both, and I believed America had the resources to provide for both."[79] As biographer Robert Dallek has remarked: "Losing was never a word in Lyndon Johnson's vocabulary."[80] For LBJ's deception and for his hubris, America was to pay an enormous price.

But it was not, of course, the intent or expectation of LBJ and his advisers that America's undeclared war in Vietnam would last another seven years. Having seen how controlled U.S. escalation obliged a nuclear superpower to pull back humiliatingly from Cuba in 1962, they could not imagine the leaders of an agrarian Asian statelet being able to tough it out. The bombing was supposed to "interdict" the supply routes into the south and force the DRV to negotiate. The troops were supposed to stabilize the situation in the south and then root out the Vietcong insurgency by the end of 1966.

Neither assumption proved correct. Strategic bombing had not been decisive in World War II, even against a highly industrialized, urban enemy such as Germany. Much of North Vietnam's munitions were imported from Russia and China, factories were moved out of urban centers, and fuel stocks quickly dispersed across the country. Using the network of trails along the jungle-clad mountain range inside Laos, the North could transport supplies slowly but surely into South Vietnam, increasingly by truck but often by bicycle. American B-52s bombed what they called the Ho Chi Minh Trail incessantly, but it was never closed. As for the ground war in the south, American firepower was often irrelevant against an unconventional and elusive enemy who fought without tanks or fighter cover. Indeed, it was usually counterproductive, because it sacrificed the advantage of surprise. According to a National Security Memorandum in December 1968: "Three-fourths of the battles are at the enemy's choice of time, place, type, and duration. CIA notes that less than one percent of nearly two million Allied small unit operations conducted in the last two years resulted in contact with the enemy."[81]

In such a war without clear fronts, how could you tell you were winning? The prime criterion became the "body count." But how to know whether you had hit the enemy? Or whether the peasants you killed were actually hostile? Every officer had an interest in boosting his unit's body count. The rule of thumb was well known: "If it's dead and it's Vietnamese, it's Vietcong." In Vietnam, American "technowar" proved a very inexact science.

The main victims of that inexactitude were, of course, the Vietnamese. American bombing may not have brought the DRV to its knees, but no one who survived a B-52 raid could forget the explosions, the shock waves, or the enormous craters. Hanoi claimed it had constructed thirty thousand miles of trenches to help people moved around safely and twenty million bomb shelters—usually prestressed concrete tubes set vertically five feet into the ground for individuals to stand in. "Call the shelter your second home," one slogan urged. Although central Hanoi was not heavily bombed, deliberately, some smaller towns were virtually wiped off the map. At the height of the bombing campaign, the Americans were dropping an annual average of three hundred pounds of explosive for each inhabitant of the DRV.[82]

The inhabitants of the south suffered even more. U.S. troops were mostly young draftees on a one-year tour of duty for whom DEROS (Date of Estimated Return from Overseas) was the most important acronym in the book. Few of these "grunts" knew the country or language, and most despised the locals, variously known as "gooks," "slants," or "dinks." Their fear and hatred was understandable, since many villagers relayed information for Viet Cong ambushes or helped lay vicious Soviet antipersonnel landmines. "To us," one grunt recalled, "there were no friendly civilians, only ones who posed no immediate threat." Another observed, "When you are trying to survive, there is no such thing as too much firepower."[83] Many Vietnamese therefore became refugees from their villages, crowding into bigger towns and their shanty suburbs. Between 1960 and 1968 the urban population of South Vietnam grew from 20 percent to 36 percent, an urbanization rate far in excess of any other developing country. There they were drawn into the war's service economy, satisfying the material and sexual desires of U.S. troops. The government of South Vietnam had no real economic policy of its own, and by 1966 perhaps 85 percent of its budget stemmed from U.S. aid.[84] In the words of one historian, "South Vietnam, as a legitimate national entity, existed only on the balance sheets of the U.S. Treasury."[85]

The human experience of the war can be sensed from the story of My Thuy Phuong ("Place of Beautiful Waters"), a village of some 7,000 people seven miles southwest of Hue, the old imperial capital in central Vietnam. For a while after 1954, Diem's regime had been welcomed because the French had gone. Soon, however, it was clear little had changed: the same families ran the village in the same corrupt way. In the early 1960s, the new NLF won many sympathizers. By 1965 about 80 to 85 percent of the villagers supported the Front and 5 percent the government, with the rest uncommitted. Over half the supporters were active helpers, running messages, providing food, even aiding guerrilla operations. Undoubtedly, coercion played a part. But compared with a corrupt governing elite, the NLF offered positive policies such as land reform.

The situation in My Thuy Phuoung changed dramatically at the beginning of 1968, when elements of the 101st Airborne Division constructed Camp Eagle on the edge of the village. With its films, camp sports, and steak and chicken barbecues this high-tech Americanized cocoon was like a different world. Every morning hundreds of villagers lined up outside the gates in the hope of being hired for menial jobs in the laundry and mess, or cleaning the latrines. Others picked over the garbage dump outside the camp. But the Americans never won the battle for "hearts and minds." Their Civic Action Programs, such as education and medical care, made little impact. People remembered the bulldozing of family graves to clear land for the camp. They recalled the gratuitous violence of many American soldiers who used water buffalo for target practice or threw cans of C-rations at gooks as they passed in trucks. NLF meetings may have ceased, and all the guerrillas disappeared, but probably half the village still supported the Front. It was at this "rice roots" level that America lost the war.[86]

And so the struggle dragged on through 1966 and 1967. The DRV, sensing victory, had no incentive to negotiate seriously. Periodic American peace bids got nowhere. Johnson and the civilians at the Pentagon also ruled out dramatic escalation, still wary of provoking China and perhaps Russia into all-out war. They also rejected calls from the Joint Chiefs of Staff to invade part of the DRV or to attack bases and supply lines in Laos and Cambodia. Instead, LBJ kept trying a little more of the same attrition strategy, acceding to periodic requests from the U.S. commander, General William Westmoreland, for more troops. The American military presence rose from 184,000 in December 1965 to 485,000 two years later. By then, nearly sixteen thousand Americans had died.[87] Nevertheless, this remained an undeclared war, with Johnson still fighting it under the cover of the Gulf of Tonkin Resolution. He was also slow to acknowledge the limits of his guns-and-butter economic policy. Because of his determination to fund the war by borrowing, not taxes, the government deficit rose from $1.6 billion in 1965 to $25.2 billion in 1968. Not until in January 1967 did LBJ ask Congress for a modest tax surcharge, but the bill took eighteen months to pass because of his reluctance to cut domestic programs, causing soaring inflation and a falling dollar.[88] These were also the years when racial violence in American cities reached its peak. By 1967 Johnson faced a crisis of confidence in his presidency. His overall approval rating dropped to 39 percent in August; 54 percent of those polled disapproved of how he was handling Vietnam.[89]

A large and vocal antiwar movement was now centered on students who did not want to be cannon fodder for Vietnam. Draft calls were running at thirty thousand a month. Most days, a tired and fractious Johnson could hear demonstrators outside the White House chanting, "Hey, hey, LBJ, how many kids did you kill today?" On October 21, 1967 some thirty thousand marched on the Pentagon itself. Liberals who had lauded Johnson in 1964–1965 for his Great Society legislation now denounced him. Particularly infuriating for LBJ was the vocal opposition of Martin Luther King, Jr., who came out publicly against "the madness of Vietnam" in the spring of 1967.

Mounting liberal opposition did not mean, however, that most of the country was against the war in principle. The press still took its cue from official statements, while TV portrayed the war as a moral struggle between American goodies and North Vietnamese baddies. Less than a quarter of film reports from Southeast Asia in 1965–1967 showed actual combat, or even clips of American dead or wounded. As in any war, the media did not want to seem blatantly unpatriotic; in the debate about Vietnam, "television was a follower rather than a leader."[90] What legitimized dissent was the growing debate among the political elite, expressed by senators such as J. William Fulbright. The media began reflecting this debate at the top. But even in November 1967, 65 percent of Americans felt that "in Vietnam the military has been handicapped by civilians who won't let them go all out."[91] When the anguished McNamara dug in his heels against further escalation in November 1967, Johnson replaced him with Clark Clifford, then a firm supporter of the war, and took personal charge of a campaign to sell the war to the public. "Overall, we are making progress," the president declared on November 17.

"The end has begun to come into view," claimed Westmoreland four days later.[92] The public was therefore ill prepared for what happened in February 1968.

In North Vietnam, too, advocates of an attrition strategy were on the defensive. During 1967 those pushing for an all-out offensive won out. A reluctant General Giap was obliged to design a strategy for a massive civilian uprising in the south, drawing on all Vietcong and NLF manpower. To mask his intentions, however, Giap organized a major conventional buildup in the central highlands, in particular besieging the U.S. Marine base at Khe Sanh, a remote border outpost, starting on January 21. Relieved to be conducting a major conventional engagement, yet fearful of a repeat of Giap's famous victory over the French at Dienbienphu in 1954, Westmoreland and Johnson became obsessed about Khe Sanh. The president had a model of the battle constructed in his situation room in the basement of the White House, and would prowl around it in his dressing gown during his frequent sleepless nights. For Giap, however, Khe Sanh was a diversion from the main operations in the south, scheduled for the new year holiday of Tet on January 30. That day, Vietcong and North Vietnamese units struck five of the six main southern cities, thirty-six of the forty-four provincial capitals, and scores of small towns. The aim was to eliminate South Vietnamese officials and prompt a general uprising by the local populace. In the old imperial capital of Hue, several thousand citizens were killed and thrown into mass graves.

The Tet offensive took American and South Vietnamese units completely by surprise. Although expecting a renewed assault, they had not anticipated its timing or strength, and had assumed that the main thrust would be around Khe Sanh. But Giap won strategic surprise at the cost of tactical effectiveness. Too many forces had been diverted to the central highlands, leaving operations in the south without sufficient punch. Worse still, the civilian uprising did not materialize. Within weeks the Americans and the ARVN had the situation largely under control.[93] During Tet, the Vietcong suffered about thirty thousand casualties, most of them members of the local apparatus that had been painfully built up over many years. Henceforth, the war would have to be waged much more by the North Vietnamese army. Tet, in short, was a major military setback for Hanoi.

Yet it was also a diplomatic triumph. The Johnson administration had been insisting that things were going well. So why was there fighting all across South Vietnam, even briefly in the grounds of the U.S. embassy in Saigon? For the first time, the war was both urban and active, and therefore easily portrayed on TV screens. The protracted battles at Hue and Khe Sanh—not relieved until April 15—kept Vietnam in people's living rooms for a couple of months. Moreover, this was not the sanitized war of earlier days. Pictures of the South Vietnamese police chief calmly putting his gun to the head of a Vietcong captive and pulling the trigger were featured around the world. In the ruins of Ben Tre, a U.S. major delivered the notorious sentence: "It became necessary to destroy the town in order to save it." In February 1968, less than one-third of Americans believed the U.S. was making progress in Vietnam; by late March, LBJ's approval rating on the war had dropped thirteen points to 26 percent.[94]

Like the country, official Washington was initially shaken by the surprise onslaught. General Earle Wheeler, the Army Chief of Staff, demanded another two hundred thousand troops in an effort to make the president fight something closer to all-out war. During March, however, the new defense secretary, Clark Clifford, became persuaded that the Pentagon had no convincing strategy for military victory; so did the "Wise Men"—an advisory panel of veteran policy makers led by former Secretary of State Dean Acheson. "The establishment bastards have bailed out," Johnson reportedly snarled after a fateful meeting on March 26.[95] Meanwhile, opposition to the war achieved new legitimacy because of the success of Eugene McCarthy in the New Hampshire presidential primary on March 12. There he gained over 42 percent of the vote compared with Johnson's 49 percent. Although many of his campaigners were students, McCarthy was a cerebral and aloof U.S. senator—no long-haired radical. McCarthy's success prompted Bobby Kennedy, another critic of the war, to announce his own challenge.

By now LBJ was demoralized and exhausted. On March 31, he announced that he would restrict the bombing to the southern part of the DRV, providing the North Vietnamese agreed to negotiate. He also stated that he would not run for reelection in November. Instead, he would dedicate the remainder of his presidency to a diplomatic solution. A week after the speech, Hanoi, shaken by the Tet disaster, agreed to peace talks in Paris.

But 1968 brought no peace to Vietnam. And as spring lengthened into summer, America's domestic conflicts deepened. On April 4, Martin Luther King, Jr. was shot dead. From coast to coast, the ghettos burned with new fury. On June 5, Bobby Kennedy was gunned down in Los Angeles. This time the nation was numbed, not violent. And in Chicago on August 28, as Democrats affirmed Vice President Hubert Humphrey as their candidate for November, outside the convention hall the city police were beating and gassing peaceful antiwar demonstrators, many of them local and middle class.[96] Again the images went around the world. To many, it seemed that Vietnam had brought America to the brink of a civil war. In the scholarly words of Eugene McCarthy, "It's the old Roman problem—their policing of the Mediterranean world as Rome decayed at home."[97] Could even the great Pax Americana cope with crises at home and abroad simultaneously?

The Vietnam War and America's Allies

The Asian hurricane unsettled America's allies as well. Johnson had done his best to draw them into Vietnam, to prove that the struggle was vital to all democracies and to reassure Americans that they were not bearing all the burdens. But the administration's "more flags" campaign, started in 1964, had limited success. The war was becoming controversial in many allied countries. Most sent only token support—hospital units or supplies—and even those who made major contributions did so for their own reasons.

The largest contributor was South Korea, whose peak troop strength in South Vietnam, including two combat divisions, was nearly fifty thousand men, about 7 percent of the country's armed forces. The Park government sent these forces because of a direct request from Washington, on whom its security and economy still depended. The commitment helped strengthen the Korean-American alliance: the Americans promised in 1965 not to withdraw their troops from South Korea without prior consultation, and they provided substantial military aid to modernize the Korean armed forces. As time went on, South Korea also gained substantial economic benefits. The Americans agreed to buy clothes, gasoline, and other war supplies there and also covered the extra costs of sending Korean troops overseas, including substantial overseas allowances. This meant, for instance, that a Korean private in Vietnam received thirty-two dollars instead of two dollars each month. This was still much cheaper than supporting a U.S. soldier in Vietnam—five thousand dollars a year compared with thirteen thousand dollars—but the total bill for subsidizing South Korea's war effort came to over $1 billion in 1965–1973. South Korea's military presence in Vietnam accounted for 20 percent of the country's foreign currency earnings during this period.[98]

Thailand, with a peak commitment of eleven thousand troops, and the Philippines (fifteen hundred) were the other significant Asian allies. Both of these governments had similar military and economic motives to those of South Korea. "Strictly speaking," said one sardonic American diplomat, "the only non-mercenary third country allies we had in Vietnam were Australia and New Zealand."[99] But their peak commitments were small—eight thousand and five hundred, respectively—and, although self-financed, their involvement was no less self-interested. In 1964–1965, the Australian government was deeply concerned about Southeast Asian instability both in Vietnam and in Indonesia, their near neighbor to the north. Consequently, they were willing to support both Malaysia and South Vietnam. Announcing the first commitment of Australian combat troops in April 1965, Prime Minister Sir Robert Menzies insisted that the threat to South Vietnam "must be seen as part of a thrust by Communist China between the Indian and Pacific Oceans." In 1965, the Australian government, particularly Paul Hasluck, the minister for external affairs, was actively encouraging U.S. escalation of the war. His object was to draw the Americans more fully into regional security; token Australian troop commitments were deemed the necessary quid pro quo. As Harold Holt, Menzies' successor after January 1966, observed, "The USA are there [in South Vietnam] to stay. We will win there and get protection in the South Pacific for a very small insurance premium."[100]

In the mid-1960s the Americans seemed to be filling a vacuum in Southeast Asia created by the continued contraction of British power. For Australia, the period 1965–1967 marked a turning point in the country's relations with Britain. By the late 1960s, only 20 percent of the country's imports came from Britain (half the figure of two decades earlier) and only 10 percent of its exports went to the mother country (compared with 40 percent in 1948–1949). In imports, exports, and investment, Britain now came in second to the United States as a force in the Australian economy. In February 1966, as if symbolically, the country adopted a new decimal currency denominated in dollars and cents.[101] Britain was also pulling back from its commitments east of Suez. Australian aid to Britain in Malaysia in 1963–1965 had been given in the hope of slowing that process, for the same reasons as its involvement in Vietnam. Once Confrontation waned in 1965–1966, the British made clear their determination to accelerate withdrawal. For Australia and, less dramatically, New Zealand these crises of the mid-1960s were part of their redefinition as American allies and, more slowly, as Asian powers.

The lack of even token British support in South Vietnam irked Johnson, particularly once the excuse of the Malaysian crisis was over. In July 1966 he told Prime Minister Harold Wilson that "a platoon of bagpipers would be sufficient; it was the British flag that was wanted."[102] But Wilson's Labour party, with its strong antiwar traditions, was deeply divided about the war. To critics of Johnson such as Cabinet Minister Richard Crossman, Vietnam was "a great moral issue on which depends the whole future of American leadership in the Western world."[103] Wilson rode out the American pressure to send troops to Vietnam in return for support of sterling, and kept his criticism muted. De Gaulle, less dependent, was more outspoken. Drawing on France's own bitter experience, he urged the neutralization of Indochina and indeed all of Southeast Asia. In September 1966, at a huge rally in the Cambodian capital, Phnom Penh, he called on the Americans to renounce "a distant expedition in a distant land, once it appears to be without benefit or justification."[104] And when LBJ announced his readiness to talk in March 1968, de Gaulle was quick and vocal with his praise. His reward was that

Paris became the venue for the Vietnam peace talks. Despite Johnson's animosity toward de Gaulle, the French capital was less unacceptable than Hanoi's other preferences, Phnom Penh or Warsaw.

The Vietnam peace talks opened near the Arc de Triomphe on May 13, 1968. That same day, however, on the opposite bank of the Seine, French students were pulling up paving stones and occupying the Sorbonne. The Vietnam war was "a fundamental reference point for the movement of 1968 . . . a symbol of oppression and of resistance."[105] For many of the youthful left across Europe, images of napalmed Vietnamese and burning black ghettos epitomized the institutionalized violence of cold war capitalism abroad and at home. Yet, as we saw in Chapter 6, the student New Left revolt ranged far beyond Vietnam: it was directed against political and educational systems, the Old Left, and the old in general. And student protest was not merely confined to Washington, Paris, or even Prague. It has run like a thread through this whole chapter—from Seoul and Tokyo in 1960, through Saigon in 1963, to Jakarta and spectacularly, Beijing in 1966. Such protest transcended differences of communism and capitalism, of Asia and the West. It reflected deeper pressures of cultural and generational change.

9

Cultures and Families

The 1960s have become known in the West as years of liberation from antiquated cultural values and from the tyranny of the patriarchal family. Among the emblems of change were rock music, student revolt and the women's movement; these are three central themes of this chapter. To some, these changes were liberating, to others signs of decadence. In 1985, the right-wing British politician Norman Tebbit derided "the insufferable, smug, sanctimonious, naive, guilt-ridden, wet, pink orthodoxy . . . of that third-rate decade, the Sixties."[1]

But historical developments rarely fit neatly into ten-year boxes. The sixties were a complex period, with much that ran counter to subsequent stereotypes. Forget the Beatles for a moment—this was an era in which more people than ever before were listening to Brahms and Beethoven. In any case, headline stories about hysterical rock fans, revolting students, and bra-burning women were only the spray from deeper waves of cultural change. An educational revolution was transforming the lives of children worldwide; together with urbanization, it was also reshaping the experience of women. Similarly, rock music was part of a larger challenge to traditional concepts of classical art and Eurocentric culture that was spawned by the consumer society and by what many regarded as the demon of Americanization.

The Consumption of Culture

During the 1960s and 1970s the consumerism of postwar America (see Chapter 5) spread to Western Europe and beyond. With it came goods, music, and fashions that appalled defenders of high culture in the Old World. For them, the "American invasion" became an obsession during the 1960s. Yet the culture of consumption proved double edged. It also made possible the consumption of "culture" on a hitherto unprecedented scale. This was just one of the ambiguities of "the sixties."

Nowhere was criticism of American-style materialism more strident than among the guardians of high culture in France. In the early 1950s, an unholy cabal of cultural nationalists, communist politicians, and capitalist beverage manufacturers tried in vain to prevent Coca-Cola from setting up in France, as it had done in much of postwar Western Europe. (One peeved U.S. congressman said that drinking Coke would give the French just what they'd needed since the war: "a good belch.") During the 1950s French intellectuals inveighed against America, the "civilization of bathtubs and Frigidaires," to quote the poet Louis Aragon. Under de Gaulle, the government tried to resist growing American ownership of French companies—what journalist Jacques Servan-Schreiber called *The American Challenge* in his 1967 best seller. But de Gaulle had to allow General Electric to take a 20 percent stake in the struggling French computer company Machines Bull in 1964, after failing to construct a consortium of French investors. As France was flooded during the 1960s with Levi's jeans, Marlboro cigarettes, Scotch tape, Tupperware, and Tampax, concern was growing about the purity of the French language itself. In his 1964 polemic, *Parlez-vous Franglais?* the Sorbonne professor René Etiemble cited a journalist's report during the Algerian war, packed with English words: "J'étais au snack bar! Je venais de prendre au self-service, un bel ice cream; la musique d'un juke-box m'endormait quand un flash de radio annonça qu'un clash risquait d'éclater à Alger. Je sortis, repris ma voiture au parking et ouvris mon transistor. Le premier ministre venait de réunir son brain-trust."[2] The problem, as the statistics showed, was that for most Frenchmen and women, civilization did mean bathtubs and Frigidaires, rather than Molière and Monet.

Although the French were particularly sensitive, concern about American economic and cultural penetration was widespread across Europe. Because of the common language and commercial contacts, in the mid-1960s Britain attracted one-third of America's corporate investment in Europe and a greater amount than any other country except Canada. Although British investment overseas was still double that of foreign investment in Britain, the

American takeover of household names like Smith's Crisps and Gallaher's to-bacco hit the headlines.[3] Mimicking the "American invasion" literature of the 1900s, journalists claimed that Britons were becoming so dependent on American money and goods that they were "American-orientated from the cradle to the grave," giving a new and sinister meaning to the slogan "all the way with LBJ."[4] There was also a furor about the "brain drain" of scientists and engineers across the Atlantic: the British prime minister Harold Wilson warned in 1967 that Europe would become "an industrial helotry" while America produced the sophisticated technology of the future.[5] Although Britain was particularly open to American influences, the concern about creeping consumerism could even be found across the Iron Curtain. One Hungarian newspaper in 1965 attacked "refrigerator socialism" and lamented how "we marvel indiscriminately at everything" from the West. "Why do we crawl on our bellies before cars and trinkets, nylon lace and refrigerators, so that the mud splatters all our faces?"[6]

A prime vehicle for consumerism was television. In the United States this was the preserve of commercial stations under minimal government control that derived their revenue from screen advertising of consumer goods. West European states did not go to the opposite extreme of the Soviet Union, where TV was rigidly controlled by a special state committee, but most exercised tighter official supervision. One model was that of Britain's BBC (British Broadcasting Corporation), a public broadcasting system with significant autonomy. This pattern was followed in France and West Germany. On the other hand, Italy, like Sweden and Switzerland, established a private corporation in which the state had a commercial stake. Either way the results were much the same. French TV steered clear of controversies such as Algeria in the late 1950s or the 1968 riots; RAI in Italy was slavishly Christian Democratic in politics and piously Catholic on cultural issues, with sex under wraps and divorce unmentioned. Only after RAI's monopoly was declared illegal by the Constitutional Court in 1976 did stations proliferate and Italian TV become a mass medium. In part because of this stifling conformity, the 1950s and 1960s were the heyday of Italy's cinema, on which Italians spent more in 1970 than on radio, TV, theater, and sports combined.[7]

The threat from commercial television was widely regarded by cultural conservatives as of decisive importance. The argument was particularly intense in Britain, then the European leader in TV, in the early 1950s. The BBC's own attitude was summed up in the warning of its first Director General, the puritanical John Reith, in 1952 that "somebody introduced small-pox, bubonic plague and the Black Death" into England and "somebody is minded now to introduce sponsored broadcasting." In America, claimed a senior BBC executive, competition "has driven advertisers to play down to what they believe is the majority taste for crime, cheap sex, appeals to avarice and worse." In 1953, the debate about commercial television spawned rival pressure groups to influence public and politicians—a novel development in British life. Although the Television Bill eventually became law in July 1954, the opposition won important safeguards. The government rejected the American system whereby advertisers directly sponsored individual programs and could therefore control their content, and an Independent Television Authority, akin to the BBC's Board of Governors, was established to oversee standards and prevent bias. Commercial TV in Britain took to the air on September 22, 1955, with its first commercials attracting more attention than the evening's entertainment.[8]

Not only was Europe being debased by American low culture, critics warned, but European high culture was now going west. One sign of this was the boom in art prices beginning in the late 1950s, after three flat decades since the depression. The purchasing power of American private and institutional collectors was accentuated by changes in U.S. tax law that allowed collectors to write off part of the value of their art against income tax if it were left to a museum on the owner's death. In November 1961, Rembrandt's painting of Aristotle contemplating a bust of Homer was bought by New York's Metropolitan Museum of Art for $2.3 million, double the previous world record for a picture. Acknowledging where the money now was, the premier London auction house, Christie's, opened a New York office in 1963. As aggressive salesmanship inflated the price of all forms of art, one English critic claimed in 1974 that the art market "embraces anything and everything and caters for every taste and no taste."[9]

Not only art but also artists were deserting Europe, it seemed. The exodus to escape Hitler, which rejuvenated American architecture (see Chapter 5), also included composers such as Arnold Schoenberg, Paul Hindemith, and Béla Bartók. In the visual arts, New York became the center for a diverse group of abstract expressionists, including Mark Rothko and Willem de Kooning, immigrants from Russia and Holland respectively, who had settled in Manhattan in the 1920s. Jackson Pollock from Wyoming became their best-known exponent in the postwar decade, until he was killed in a car crash in 1956, because of his technique of dripping paint across a canvas on the floor. Although widely derided at home—President Truman called it "dribble art" produced by "lazy, nutty moderns"[10]—Pollock's work was lauded by critics for affirming the autonomy of the artist and the act of painting in a way that went far beyond European cubism or surrealism. "Compared to Pollock," wrote Bruno Alfieri, "poor Pablo Picasso . . . becomes a quiet conformist, a painter of the past." The American critic Clement Greenberg claimed in 1948 that "the main premises of Western art have at last migrated to the United States, along with the center of gravity of industrial production and political power."[11] Abstract expressionism became something of a cult in

Western Europe in the 1950s, where it was known as action painting or *tachisme*, from the French word for "spot." But this cult status owed less to artistic merit than to media hype and cold war propaganda, as the State Department exhibited action painting across Europe. In their hands, its "abstracted anxiety" about living in the nuclear age "was translated, ironically, into a symbol of uniquely American freedom"—the unfettered, dynamic artist.[12]

The wave of abstract expressionism was therefore both a derivative of prewar artistic trends and a product of cold war consumer culture. As such, it embodies two important themes in the history of postwar high culture. In the arts, Western Europe was still recovering from the destructive impact of two world wars and of the cultural repressions by Hitler and Stalin. Artistic creativity usually requires both the assertion of individual novelty and the support of group solidarity, as the impressionists or the cubists had shown; the "breakthrough period" in which an artist makes his mark and forms his style is usually brief, perhaps five or ten years.[13] These delicate preconditions were largely absent in Europe in the 1930s and 1940s because of war and persecution, with Vienna, Berlin, and Paris—hitherto cultural capitals—as the prime casualties. New York constituted an alternative after 1945 but, in general, high culture in the 1950s and 1960s was working through the intellectual capital created in the decades before 1914, when the cubists upset criteria of perspective and representation observed since the Renaissance, and Schoenberg mounted a parallel, though less complete, assault on the musical discipline of key that had ruled for four centuries. The implications of these revolutions were still being explored in the second half of the twentieth century, after the delays and disruptions of the era of two world wars.

What was novel about the period after 1945 was less the *creativity* of high culture, therefore, than its unprecedented *dissemination*. The culture of consumption also promoted the consumption of culture. No one embodied this better than Pablo Picasso, the Spanish exile resident in France, who towered over the visual arts in the 1950s and 1960s, mocking Alfieri's 1948 obituary. Picasso's achievement was partly a function of age: he was in his ninety-second year when he died in April 1973, having produced some twenty thousand works. Cubist friends and rivals had faded long before: Henri Matisse died in 1954, a mere seventy-four; Georges Braque was eighty-one when he expired in 1963. Nor did either show the prodigious creativity of Picasso's final years—347 etchings in less than seven months in 1968, for instance, or the 167 paintings, mostly in brilliant reds and yellows, that he produced in thirteen months after January 1969. So much for another critic who scoffed in 1965: "he became a national monument and produced trivia."[14] But Picasso's fame was that of the artist as much as his art. Matisse was an invalid for more than a decade before he died, Braque a hermit who worked in seclusion either in Paris or Normandy. Picasso, in contrast, was a public figure of conspicuous notoriety, because of his association with Resistance leaders during the war, his membership in the Communist party after 1949 and, most of all, his sexual appetite—seven serious liaisons, each decisive for a phase of his art, plus innumerable brief affairs and paid encounters. His ex-mistress Françoise Gilot's 1965 revelations of *Life with Picasso* served only to enhance his reputation. Picasso, a consummate businessman, used the media to promote himself and the value of his art. When he died, his estate was worth one billion French francs (around $250 million today) and it included two castles, three houses, a superb art collection, and hundreds of works of his own. Longevity, creativity, productivity, and notoriety all contributed to the apotheosis of his final years. The spectacular Hommage à Picasso in Paris in the winter of 1966–1967 attracted 850,000 people to view not merely paintings and drawings, but also ceramics and sculptures hitherto largely unknown. For his ninetieth birthday in 1971 eight Picassos were exhibited in the Grande Galerie of the Louvre, an honor never before bestowed on a living artist.[15]

Classical music was also a beneficiary of consumer society and its associated technologies. In America, concertgoing attracted only around 1 percent of the adult public in the 1960s, overwhelmingly wealthy, professional, and middle aged. Although most major symphony orchestras reported increased attendance during the 1950s, the growth rate of 1.1 percent was less than that of the population as a whole.[16] In other words, live classical music was becoming an increasingly minority taste. Its survival was due partly to public subsidies but, even more, to the recording industry. It has been justly observed that "recorded sound probably has been the most significant development in musical life in the West since the development of music writing during the ninth century," when techniques of notation first separated performers from composers.[17] Thomas Edison's phonograph dated from 1877, Emile Berliner's flat disc gramophone from 1888; recording had become big business in America and Europe by the 1920s, when electric microphones replaced the original acoustic collecting horns. The technology for further advance was available in the 1930s, but depression and then war delayed its marketing. By using a tougher coating of vinyl rather than shellac, it was possible to cut around two hundred fifty grooves per inch of disc (three or four times those on the old 78-rpm records). The result on a twelve-inch disc was a groove nearly half a mile long, enough for thirty minutes of music per side.[18]

The eventual advent of the long-playing record (LP) in 1948 and stereophonic sound nine years later were of particular benefit for classical music, with its lengthy scores and large orchestras. Companies moved fast. The popular favorites of leading composers were re-recorded; so too were their minor works. By 1952 329 sides of Beethoven were on LP; that year alone nearly four hundred more were issued.[19] Led by Deutsche Grammophon, record companies embarked on vast and comprehensive recording programs. Baroque music started reaching a large audience, likewise the works of modern composers such as Gustav Mahler. Recording in turn had an effect on the live repertoire, in quantity and also quality because of the more demanding standards now required of orchestras. And the consumption of classics was also encouraged by the celebrity of postwar conductors. The pioneer was the Italian-American Arturo Toscanini, who presided over the NBC Radio Symphony Orchestra from 1937 until 1954. When he died three years later, *Newsweek* wrote: "More than any other single cultural influence, he made classical music a part of popular American culture," doing for Verdi, Wagner, and Beethoven "what Broadway song pluggers do for the Hit Parade."[20]

Toscanini's postwar successors prospered even more through the dual media of records and television. Notable among them was the New Yorker Leonard Bernstein (1918–1990), a glamorous composer-conductor, equally at home with classics and jazz, and a natural showman off the podium and on it. One critic observed, "he is a specialist in the clenched fist, the hip swivel, the pelvic thrust, the levitation effect . . . the uppercut, the haymaker."[21] Bernstein's European equivalent was the Austrian conductor Herbert von Karajan, who took over the Berlin Philarmonic in 1954. Karajan was perhaps the most accomplished postwar conductor, renowned for his imagination, discipline, and technique. But he was also a cult media figure—slim and handsome, with striking blue eyes—who loved skiing and fast cars and owned his own jet plane. Whereas his predecessor, Otto Klemperer, claimed that "listening to a recording is like going to bed with a *photograph* of Marilyn Monroe," Karajan was infatuated with new technologies and had produced over nine hundred recordings by his death in 1989. Sales of his boxed set of the Beethoven symphonies ran to over eight million. He recorded the cycle four times—on LP, video, CD, and laserdisc.[22]

Yet classical music, even Karajan style, amounted to a tiny percentage of record sales. In 1976 Americans purchased 273 million LPs, 190 million singles, and 127 million music tapes—the equivalent of nearly three records or tapes for every man, woman and child.[23] In the consumer age the mass production of music was geared above all to mass markets, and the explosion of rock among the postwar baby boomers was the most spectacular example.

The technology to reach this audience was made possible by the transistor, developed by Bell Laboratories and announced, to general indifference, at the start of the Berlin airlift in 1948 (see page 31). Its enormous significance will be examined more fully in Chapter 14. Suffice it to say here that, by using a semiconductor in the form of a germanium crystal to amplify electric current, it was possible to replace the large, expensive and fragile vacuum tubes (or valves) previously used in electronic equipment. By 1954 transistorized radios were being marketed in the United States. Twelve million were in use by 1959; in the 1960s there were more radios than households. The transistorized phonograph for the home hit the U.S. market beginning in 1961; this was a small, square box containing turntable, amplifier, and tuner. These modern radios and record players were made largely of plastic for portability as well as cheapness. Prewar models, made of finished wood, had often been designed as articles of living-room furniture, for listening by all the family. By the 1950s TV had taken over as the family leisure instrument, but small modern radios and record players were ideal for individual use by the young, and radio listening and record buying began to surge again starting in the mid-1950s.

Changes in the structure of the radio and recording industries were also important. As the TV era dawned and the old radio networks declined, so radio had to find specialist niches, both geographically and socially. Local radio stations sprang up in the 1950s, with recorded music as their main programming. At the same time, with the cost of record production dropping in the era of magnetic tape, small, independent record companies were able to challenge the monopoly of the major companies like Columbia and RCA.[24]

If they had a sound to sell, that is. They found that in rock and roll—a blend of black blues music and white country music emanating from the American South. There in the 1950s the color line was still stark, but the airwaves were integrated. White adolescents developed a taste for black music, and singers in the South became more eclectic in their repertoire. Early exponents were Chuck Berry and Bill Haley. The latter's "Rock Around the Clock" took America by storm in 1955. But Haley was too old for stardom, and Berry was black. "If I could find a white boy who could sing like a nigger, I could make a million dollars," lamented Sam Phillips of Sun Records in Memphis, Tennessee.[25] His prayer was answered in the form of a young, music-mad truck driver whose family had moved from Mississippi in 1948. Phillips launched Elvis Presley in 1954, then sold him to RCA. The Elvis phenomenon was visual as much as audial. TV and film popularized the greased hair, curled lip, upturned collar, and gyrating pelvis. Just as thousands of teenage girls had been driven into screaming frenzy by his live performances, so his movies touched off riots from London to Oslo and generated clones such as Masaki Hirao in Japan and Hungary's László Komar. After two years in the U.S. Army in 1958–1960, Elvis devoted most of his time to movies, making twenty-one in the years 1961–1968.[26] The 1973 TV spectacular "Aloha from Elvis in Hawaii" was estimated to reach one-sixth of the world's population.[27] After he died in 1977, bloated by food and drugs, his Memphis mansion, Graceland, became a place of pilgrimage, attracting seven hundred thousand people a year by the 1990s, more than any other private residence in the United States except the White House. On the wall outside, devotees of "the King" scrawled messages of adoration:

> Elvis, we believe, always and forever.
> Elvis is a God.
> Elvis, I'm having your baby. 29 Sept. 1991.[28]

In the early 1960s, it seemed that rock and roll might have peaked. American record sales in 1960 were down slightly on 1959, in 1963 barely above those for 1962. But then came the Beatles. The British group from Liverpool—the guitarists John Lennon, Paul McCartney, George Harrison, and the drummer Ringo Starr [Richard Starkey]—stormed the British charts in 1963 and the Western world the following year. In a triumphant American tour in February 1964, they attracted an audience of seventy-three million (one-third of the American population) for their televised appearance on the *Ed Sullivan Show*. Clean cut, with collarless suits, they seemed less threatening to the older generation than Elvis. Their zany wit also appealed. (Ringo Starr was asked by reporters what he thought of Beethoven. "I love him," he replied, "especially his poems." [29]) And the composers McCartney and Lennon had real musical ability, evident as the group progressed from the simple lyrics and rhythms of "Please, Please Me" (1963) to the intricate artistry of *Sergeant Pepper's Lonely Hearts Club Band* (1967). The cumulative effect of looks, wit, and music made Beatlemania even headier among the young than Elvis worship. Every Beatles single and LP sold at least one million copies worldwide; "I Want To Hold Your Hand" notched up three million in America, 1.5 million in Britain, and another five million elsewhere. By January 1969, world sales for the Beatles ran to an estimated 260 million.[30] Although the Beatles split up in 1970 and Lennon was shot dead in 1980, they spawned imitators across the world from the Monkees in America to the Czech group Olympic and left an indelible mark on popular music. Alexander Gradsky, later a leading Soviet rock star, heard Beatles music for the first time in 1963: "I went into a state of shock, total hysteria. They put everything in focus. All the music I'd heard until that time was just a prelude."[31]

But rock music posed particular problems in the Soviet bloc as an American product with broad appeal among the young. After Stalin's death in 1953, restrictions on jazz and other Western influences were relaxed. This was particularly true in Poland and Hungary, whose governments offered cultural sweeteners to offset the bitterness left by 1956. However, throughout Eastern Europe, governments still controlled the record industry, with most emulating East Germany's notorious 60/40 law of 1958, whereby no more than 40 percent of a concert could be music from capitalist countries. Most rock was played illicitly in underground clubs by bands regularly broken up by the police. In the Soviet Union, thousands of pirated versions of Haley and Presley circulated on old hospital X-ray plates—a process dubbed *roentgenizdat,* or recordings on bones. During the 1960s, however, it became harder to control the rock scene, or to channel youthful energies into updated ballroom dancing. If records were still in short supply, the growing availability of radio plus the music programs of Voice of America and Radio Free Europe brought Western hits to the ears of millions of Eastern bloc adolescents. By the end of the 1960s, Leninism was losing the battle against Lennonism: official policy became cooption rather than coercion. Governments would license and sponsor "vocal instrumental ensembles" if the performers cut their hair, reduced the decibels, and purged their repertoire of objectionable Western songs. In the 1970s most countries had tame (and rich) socialist rock groups such as the Puhdys in the GDR and Olympic in Czechoslovakia. In Moscow, Tsvety (Flowers) was led by Stas Namin—real name Anastas Mikoyan—the namesake and grandson of the former Soviet Politburo member.

Capitalist or communist, rock music was now big business. In the late 1960s cassette tapes appeared, though they were not to rival records until well into the 1970s. In 1973 U.S. sales of records and tapes amounted to over $2 billion—close to the revenue from movies and sports combined. Japan was the next biggest market, at $555 million, followed by West Germany with $454 million.[32] Recorded music was still subject to the same geographical constraints as the rest of the consumer culture: even in the late 1970s three-quarters of world sales were in the United States, Japan, West Germany, France, and Britain, with America alone accounting for 40 percent.[33] Notwithstanding the success of the Swedish group Abba in the mid-1970s, international rock music was mainly a product of American and British groups, trading on the globalism of the English language. However, thanks to radio, rock was already reaching the developing world—embryonically a global popular culture.

But, many critics asked, what kind of culture was this? Rock music seemed like the next stage in a creeping debasement of cultural values that went back through commercial TV and Coca-colonization, to Hollywood and jazz in the 1920s. This was not merely the view of West European defenders of high culture such as Louis Aragon or Lord Reith. Soviet leader Nikita Khrushchev made the same point in 1962 when attacking the new Soviet craze for the twist and other Western dances: "Some of them are completely improper. You wiggle a certain section of the anatomy, if you'll pardon the expression. It's indecent." Music and art, said Khrushchev, "should ennoble the individual and arouse him to action."[34] The most internationally influential critique of rock music came from members of the Frankfurt School of Marxism, which had found a haven in New York during the war. One of them,

Theodor Adorno, developed the thesis that, for modern capitalism, culture was simply another commodity, like cars or fridges, and that "the culture industry" was now mass producing music for mass markets to satisfy false needs. It became conventional to contrast this "mass culture" with the authentic "popular culture" of the lower classes. The American critic Dwight Macdonald popularized the term *midcult*, a "middlebrow compromise" whose peculiar danger was "that it exploits the discoveries of the avant-garde."[35] The combination of cultural elitism and anticommercialism underpinning such criticisms, from Adorno to the English literary critic F. R. Leavis, is graphically expressed in a diatribe by British journalist Paul Johnson against "The Menace of Beatlism" in 1964. This was provoked by pictures of teenage audiences in TV studios watching record programs such as *Juke Box Jury:*

> What a bottomless chasm of vacuity they reveal. The huge faces, bloated with cheap confectionery and smeared with chain-store make-up, the open, sagging mouths and glazed eyes, the hands mindlessly drumming in time to the music, the broken stiletto heels, the shoddy, stereotyped, "with-it" clothes: here, apparently, is a collective portrait of a generation enslaved by a commercial machine.[36]

The cultural significance of rock music remains hard to assess. After all, "high culture" also depended on consumers, as Michelangelo and Mozart were acutely aware. The difference was that their patrons were the rich few in church and state rather than the affluent many of consumer society. Most classical art had also been shaped by the technology of the time (Liszt's pianistic pyrotechnics would have been impossible on the clavier of Bach's day) and by its stylistic forms (the impressionists were in part a revolt against the tyranny of the Académie Royale). The purist reaction to mass culture therefore pulled art out of its historical context, elevated certain forms to special status, and closed off the artistic canon. Museums, in the words of one critic, "became shelters for art of the past . . . cemeteries of art."[37] The case for rock music, then, was that it was authentic art for its time, using new technologies to create new forms rather than being imprisoned in those of the past. To quote the Canadian academic Marshall McLuhan, one of the most celebrated cultural theorists of the 1960s, the "electronic age" had established radically new media of communication and ended "the mechanical age that had gone into high gear with Gutenberg."[38]

In principle, the electronic revolution was not incompatible with the classical orchestra, as the young German composer Karlheinz Stockhausen showed in the 1950s. But much of the creative talent of the day (as well as many hacks) was drawn into the new media of TV and rock. In Britain, in fact, numerous rock musicians, from John Lennon to David Bowie, came to the business via a disenchanting experience of art school.[39] They saw themselves as bringing the arts back from a sanitized sanctuary into the mainstream of daily life. This was especially evident in the related vogue for pop art, which updated dada without the satirical bite, using the graphic techniques of TV. Andy Warhol's representation of a Campbell's soup can was reproduced in posters throughout the West. In other ways, too, the triumph of rock reflected a challenge to classical European conceptions of art. Like jazz, but far more powerfully, it embodied African-American codes of music in which rhythm rather than tonality was all important.[40] It also renewed the symbiosis of music and dance—normal in much of human history, but severed by European classicism: Chuck Berry was making a serious historical point with his 1956 hit "Roll Over Beethoven."[41]

Although rock might be art, sales figures also confirmed Adorno's thesis that it was an industry. Most records had a shelf life of 60–120 days as far as manufacturers were concerned: success or failure was instant. The aim, it seemed, was to sell records, not make music—"We're Only In It For the Money" to quote the title of Frank Zappa's stab at the Beatles. In the late 1960s it became fashionable to distinguish the artistic quality of "rock" from the commercialized "pop" music peddled to the mass market. That distinction proved hard to maintain, but there were other rejoinders to Adorno's line of argument. One was that the 1960s, at least, were the heyday of independent record companies. Whereas America's Big Four produced at least three-quarters of the country's weekly top ten in the early 1950s, their share dropped to between a quarter and two-fifths for most of the 1960s.[42] Yet the consequent diversity still had to flourish within the constraints of money-making. The most compelling response to Adorno was that he had neglected musical consumers, who were not the undifferentiated "mass" of conventional caricature. Indeed, many were not passive consumers at all, because rock music encouraged both participation (through dance) and also production of its own, in the thousands of amateur bands who made no records but simply made music.

The common factor in this musical culture was that the consumers were predominantly young. Rock music, pop music—call it what you will—was mainly the preserve of those in their teens and early twenties. "Youth culture," like "teenagers," was in part a concept created by the consumer society in order to increase sales. But in multiple ways, overt or implicit, young people also used the youth culture, especially rock music, to differentiate themselves from their parents. Student politics was one example; another was sexual mores. This leads us into one of the most profound social developments of the 1950s and 1960s—again centered on the United States and Western Europe but spreading out from there in the last third of the century—namely, challenges to the patriarchal family through radical changes in the positions and attitudes of children and women.

Educational Revolutions

Underlying the changing lifestyle of children are the educational revolutions of the second half of the twentieth century. These were not merely "Western" but affected much of the developing world as well. A few crude statistics illustrate what happened. Between 1950 and 1970, the number of pupils enrolled in primary education worldwide almost doubled to 343 million, those in secondary education tripled to 113 million, and those in higher education quadrupled to 26 million (Table 9.1). In all of these sectors, growth outstripped that of the world's population, which increased by 45 percent to 3.6 billion. These figures are crude and in some ways misleading, but they hint at the upheavals under way. Although students hit the headlines, we shall see that, in many ways, schoolchildren were more important.

TABLE 9.1 WORLD ENROLLMENTS BY LEVELS OF EDUCATION
(Figures in millions)

Year	Total	Primary	Secondary	Tertiary
1950	221.5	177.2	38.0	6.3
1960	323.6	248.5	63.9	11.2
1970	482.5	343.2	113.2	26.1

SOURCE: UNESCO, *Statistical Yearbook, 1970* (Paris: UNESCO, 1971), Table 2.2, and *Statistical Yearbook, 1973* (1974), Table 2.1.

The educational revolution, like most postwar changes, was an acceleration of earlier trends. In the broadest sense, we are talking about a shift in the role of children from producers to consumers.[43] Except in northwest Europe, large families have been the norm in most agrarian societies, where children are valued as extra labor and sons, in particular, as status symbols. This remains true in the early stages of industrialization, when child labor is still important for family incomes, but as this process advances, a need also grows for education to enable children to accomplish more complex industrial tasks. In due course, the service sector also expands, both reflecting and enlarging consumer demand. Children become one of its prime targets—not only for clothes and goods, but also for education, which becomes a status symbol as well as a job qualification.

Increased emphasis on education is not merely a response to economic change, of course. In Western Europe and North America, at least, it has also reflected changing patterns of child rearing, with parents tending to lavish greater attention for a longer time on fewer children. Together, these changes in education and parenting have fostered the notion of "adolescence." In part this concept stems from the falling age of puberty as nutrition has improved: in Western Europe its onset has dropped about four months every decade during the twentieth century, with boys on average reaching full growth at age seventeen in the 1960s, compared with twenty-three as in the 1900s.[44] But the onset of puberty varies enormously with class and income: adolescence is as much a social construct as a biological event. The educated child, though near physical maturity, remained dependent for years longer on the increasingly intense atmosphere of the home. Yet these children were spending much of their time in the company of people of the same age, thereby promoting a distinctive youth culture in reaction to the parental ethos. Of course, youth gangs had long been a feature of working-class society in Europe, likewise rowdy student clubs an integral part of university life. But the extent and intensity of post-1945 youth culture constituted a historical novelty, tied to the consumer and education revolutions and expressed particularly in rock music.

This pattern was most evident in North America and Western Europe in the 1960s. Leading the way, as with most aspects of the consumer society, the United States boasted one-third of the world's college students in 1970: 8.5 million. There were another four million in Europe and 4.5 million in the Soviet Union. Student conduct depended a great deal on the nature of the political system, of course: the Soviet Union saw little student protest in the late 1960s. But even rigorous communist rule was no insurance against trouble—as shown by Czechoslovakia in 1968—and Moscow, as we have seen, had its own subterranean rock culture. In fact, student protest was evident across much of the world in the late 1960s, from Tunis to Beijing. In Mexico City in October 1968, police shot dead fifty demonstrators and wounded hundreds more after two months of protests that threatened to upset the imminent opening of the Olympic Games. The common denominator was not politics—though Vietnam was a unifying cause for many in the West—but the effect of exploding student numbers on educational institutions and on society at large.

Universities were the fastest-growing sector of education in the 1960s, with numbers rising by around 10 percent a year. In extreme cases, the increase was much more. In France there were 202,000 registered university students in 1959 and 615,000 in 1969; in West Germany, growth was from 196,000 to 376,000.[45] In most countries, existing institutions were unable to cope: staff-to-student ratios deteriorated, buildings were inadequate, housing was hard to find. Moreover, students were intolerant of the rigid, hierarchical administrative structures of the past. Here they often made common cause with junior faculty who shared their animosity toward the senior professorial elite. Another source of anger were restrictions on male-female relations, particularly separate halls of residence. This was a burning issue, for instance, in Paris in the spring of 1968. In North America and Western Europe, new students flooded into the humanities and social sciences. These were less costly for universities than experimental science, but they introduced thousands of young people not only to Marx but also to theorists less favored by the Old Left, such as Antonio Gramsci and Louis Althusser. In many countries, of course, choice of subject as well as right of entry was officially determined, so that became another grievance. The Cairo newspaper *Al-Ahram* observed that "if Picasso were born in our country we would offer him a place in the Faculty of Commerce."[46] And action against protesters by the police or right-wing activists often proved the final straw, especially where a martyr resulted, as when the student leader Rudi Dutschke was wounded in Berlin in April 1968.

In the West, much student revolt was unabashedly hedonistic. From Herbert Marcuse, a second-generation philosopher of the Frankfurt School, young people derived a critique of late capitalism as inherently brutal and puritanical, forging a society dedicated to achievement rather than pleasure. In a similar vein at the end of the 1960s, Theodor Roszak popularized the term "counterculture" to sum up the multifaceted youth assault on the spurious objectivity of the "scientific consciousness" and the "technocratic totalitarianism" that it had produced.[47] In America, the celebration of feelings over reason could be seen in the popularity of Eastern mysticism, drug experimentation, and hippie communes—for all of which the Haight-Ashbury district ("Hashbury") of San Francisco became internationally renowned. In Germany, New Left ideas had a similar effect, inducing *Bürgerschreck,* or bourgeois horror, in a country where Marxism had been so thoroughly banished, to quote one student leader, that "you could terrify the middle-class simply by carrying around a copy of [Marx's] *Capital.*"[48] Yet the students were also predominantly middle class, privileged products of the consumer society they denounced. A Western cliché pointed up a global moral—these were the children of Marx and Coca-Cola.

In the Soviet bloc, Pepsi-Cola was the social lubricant—the company won the exclusive franchise in an agreement signed during Nixon's visit to Moscow in 1959[49]—but the essential point was the same. Russian students were also a privileged elite, questioning the system that had produced them.

In the USSR there was no student explosion—only subterranean rumbles from the underground rock clubs—but the sixties did not leave Soviet society untouched. The products of Khrushchev's thaw became politically conscious in the university boom of the 1960s. They read reformist journals like *Novy Mir* ("New World") and, mostly in secret, discussed the prospects for liberal socialism. During these years, the Soviet Union created an educated middle class, necessarily party members but skeptical of old verities. Among these *shestidesyatniki* ("people of the sixties") was a rising provincial politician, born in 1931, named Mikhail Gorbachev.[50]

In the Soviet Union, the sixties generation did not become a political force until the 1980s. In the People's Republic of China, in contrast, it was given its head by Mao and the radicals—and then brutally rusticated. The fact that China experienced revolution in the 1960s and the Soviet Union did not would profoundly affect each country's capacity and tolerance for reform twenty years later (Chapter 15). But in both countries, a generational divide was emerging, as it was in the West. Of course, the concept of generations must be used with circumspection; like adolescence, it is a social construct, not a biological event. "What is essential to the formation of a generational consciousness," writes historian Robert Wohl, "is some common frame of reference that provides a sense of rupture with the past."[51] Wohl was examining the "generation of 1914" but a similar point could be made of the 1940s, those years of war and revolution that scarred Europe and much of Asia. Whether it was the "silent generation" of Germans that had lived with Nazism, the Britons who now cherished "the Dunkirk spirit" or the Chinese communists who had won the civil war, the 1940s defined the experience of millions. Likewise in the Soviet Union, when Andrei Sakharov "came out" as a dissident in 1968, he was told by his political boss that Stalinism, for its faults, had won a great war, rebuilt the economy, and matched the U.S. arms race. "You have no moral right to judge our generation—Stalin's generation—for its mistakes, for its brutality; you're now enjoying the fruits of our labor and our sacrifices."[52] Elsewhere, the words would be different, but the sentiments the same. The children of the sixties had not experienced the great rupture of the 1940s. They were ready to make their own breaks with postwar patterns and values.

The student revolt was spectacular, but a more profound educational revolution was taking place in the world's primary schools. In 1950 only 25 percent of Algerian children aged six to eleven were enrolled in school; the proportion was 70 percent in 1968. Over the same period, the Indian enrollment rate doubled to 56 percent; in Indonesia it rose from 57 percent to 72 percent. Even the African state of Niger, perhaps the most impoverished in the world, showed an increase from 2 percent to 14 percent.[53] With four years of schooling needed for basic literacy, the results were dramatic. In

1950 the United Nations estimated that about 55 percent of the world's population over the age of fifteen could read and write in their own language. In 1970 the figure was 66 percent.[54]

Of course, the statistics must be read with caution. South Africa boasted a primary school enrollment rate of 92 percent by 1970, yet that tells little about the quality of education, especially for blacks. Under the Bantu Education Act of 1953, the national government had devolved the costs of education on the Bantu homelands, to help create "a sense of responsibility," as Dr Henrik Verwoerd put it. Given black poverty, that meant a widening racial divide; in real terms expenditure on black education did not reach the white level of 1949 until 1974. Although the government did meet its target for doubling school enrollment, the provision of teachers did not keep pace. Staff-to-pupil ratios for blacks rose from 1:43 in 1949 to 1:59 in 1970. Most black children in the first two years of school were educated in the "double-session" system—forty-five to fifty pupils for three hours in the morning before the teacher took a similar-sized group for the afternoon.[55]

South African blacks were discriminated against by government policy, but similar patterns were evident elsewhere. In Egypt, for instance, the increase in primary school enrollment from 1.5 million in 1952 to 3.6 million in 1969 masked the fact that over half the children were taught on a dual-shift basis and that almost a fifth of primary school teachers were untrained. Like the leaders of most developing countries after independence, Nasser saw education as a primary national goal. But too much emphasis was placed on secondary and university education, in the belief that these were the key to economic development. The managerial and government elite also wanted education for their children because university degrees conferred status and opened doors to government employment.[56] This neglect of the primary sector because of national and elite priorities was a theme in many developing countries in the 1960s.

Along the Mediterranean coast, Tunisia had a better record: in 1971–1972, 73 percent of children aged six to fourteen were in school compared with 29 percent on the eve of independence from France in 1956. By then the Bourguiba government was spending over one-third of its budget on education— double the average for developing countries. But 1971–1972 also saw marked cutbacks in educational provision, in both funding and places. The proportion of children passing the high school entrance exam was deliberately cut from 40 percent to 25 percent. Tunisia had found that the provision of education had outstripped the economy's demand for educated manpower. In 1966 40 percent of boys between fifteen and nineteen were unemployed, with an acute shortage of places at vocational training centers. Education was no panacea. Without sensitive policies, its fruits were not economic development but politicized frustration.[57]

In Europe and the Americas literacy rose in both proportions and absolute numbers. But in Africa, the increase in literacy from 15 percent to 26 percent was accompanied, due to population growth, by an increase in illiterates from around one hundred million to over one hundred fifty million. The Asian story was similar: a marked increase in literacy rates from around 37 percent to 53 percent but also in total illiterates from around 520 million to 580 million.[58] China is not included in these UN statistics because of its closed society and the chaos of the 1960s. After the 1982 census, the government claimed that 68 percent of China's population was literate, but this was based on minimal definitions such as attendance in school and the ability to write one's name. One study suggests that during the Great Leap Forward and the Cultural Revolution (1958–1962 and 1966–1975)—when schools were shut for years by famine or politics—virtually all school-age children (over 99 percent) failed to achieve functional literacy. In 1975, only a tenth of China's adult population was functionally literate, compared with one-third in 1955.[59]

Leaving China aside, by 1970 a marked contrast had emerged between the educational development of Eastern Asia and that of South Asia. As Table 9.2 shows, the contrast has proved enduring. With the small but significant exception of Sri Lanka (formerly Ceylon), the countries of South Asia started from a lower base and made slower progress than those of East and Southeast Asia, among whom Japan boasted almost total adult literacy even in 1960.

TABLE 9.2 ADULT LITERACY IN SELECTED COUNTRIES OF ASIA
(figures indicate percentages)

Country	1960	1975	1990
Pakistan	15	21	35
Bangladesh	22	26	35
India	28	36	48
Sri Lanka	75	78	89
Indonesia	39	62	77
Malaysia	53	60	79
South Korea	71	93	97
Japan	98	99	99

SOURCE: Data from Jandhyala B. G. Tilak, *Education for Development in Asia* (New Delhi: Sage, 1994), p. 194.

Part of the problem was money. South Asia invested less per head on education than East and Southeast Asia: the Indian figure was the equivalent of U.S.$40 in 1970, South Korea's was $127. But educational priorities were equally important. For countries at the early stages of development, primary education has the lowest unit costs and highest rates of economic return. In other words, it costs much less to educate a schoolchild than a university student (anything between one-fifth and one-fifteenth the amount), and the economic gains are substantially greater. Despite a general commitment to universal primary education, however, most South Asian governments (backed by self-interested elites) invested disproportionly in higher education: India had one of the highest growth rates in Asia for university students and the lowest for primary enrollments. In the 1970s, Bangladesh and Pakistan were increasing spending on higher education at the expense of primary schools, whose share in Bangladesh fell from 60 percent in 1973 to 44 percent in 1981. In contrast, the developing countries of East Asia in the mid-1960s (and Sri Lanka in South Asia) were allocating two-thirds of educational spending to the primary sector and less than a tenth to higher education. All across Asia, of course, most of the money went to teacher salaries, very little to classroom resources. But in qualititative terms, India's schools were some of the most rudimentary. In the early 1980s, nearly half its primary schools did not have all-weather buildings (14 percent were in the open, in tents, or in thatched huts), and half did not have drinking water facilities. Over 40 percent had no chalkboards; three-quarters lacked any kind of library resources.[60] As we shall see (Chapter 12), the contrasts in educational performance between East and South Asia were part of a deeper socio-economic divide.

Another global pattern was also important. Across the world and at every age level, females enjoyed less access to education than males. The UN's crude global estimate for adult male literacy in 1970 was 72 percent, for women 60 percent. In most developing countries, the statistic for female educational enrollment was usually about two-thirds that of males at the same level. Discrepancies were particularly marked in higher education: in 1970 women were 23 percent of West German students and 20 percent in Mexico. Even in the United States the proportion had only risen from 37 percent to 41 percent during the 1960s.[61] But the educational revolution underway in the 1960s was to have a disproportionate effect on women. It helped revive and reshape organized feminism into a movement that could no longer be ignored. And it was part of a larger transformation of women's lives—unprecedented in human history—that was spreading beyond the developed world.

Women on the Move

Female protest has a long history, including medieval monasticism and early modern witchcraft. Some classic statements of the rights of women are centuries old, such as those by Olympe de Gouges and Mary Wollstonecraft in the 1790s. But movements of women concerned specifically to improve the status of women are a phenomenon of the last century or so. They have generally emerged in more industrialized countries with a substantial middle class where women, especially married women, play a significant role in the paid labor force.[62] In the first half of this century, most, though not all, women's movements cohered around demands for the vote. New Zealand was the first country to concede full female suffrage, in 1893; Australia followed in 1901. In Europe, Finland led the way in 1906, followed by the rest of Scandinavia, revolutionary Russia, Germany, and the United States by 1920. Full female suffrage was delayed in Britain until 1928, only six years before Turkey. Some Latin American countries gave women the vote during the depression, including Brazil and Uruguay in 1932, but most waited until the decade after World War II, and Paraguay held out until 1961. In eastern and southern Europe, only Czechoslovakia took action between the wars, but after 1945 female suffrage was enshrined in the constitutions of the postwar communist governments of Europe and also of China, and in those of most newly independent states from India to Tunisia. In both cases, "votes for women" was a hallmark of progressive politics.

Yet suffrage did not transform the social position of women. For one thing, women voted within existing party structures, often very conservatively. This was particularly true in Catholic countries, where liberals and the left (usually advocates of woman suffrage) had feared that, to quote one Mexican deputy in the 1930s, if women got the vote "we shall have a Bishop as President."[63] Such anxieties were one reason why female suffrage was not enacted in France, Italy, Portugal, and Belgium until the years 1944–1948. In postwar Italy, for instance, newly enfranchised Catholic women proved critical to the success of the Christian Democratic party. In 1953, two-thirds of its voters were female. The proportion started dropping below 60 percent only after 1983 as secularization took hold.[64]

In Italy and elsewhere in the West, women were grossly underrepresented in party leadership positions. Britain and France were near the bottom of the list, averaging 4 or 5 percent female representation in their lower houses in the postwar era. Scandinavia was at the top, with Sweden surging to over 20 percent by the mid-1970s.[65] In Japan, on which the Americans imposed female suffrage in 1945, 8 percent of the lower house were women in 1946, but the proportion then fell sharply and averaged 1.3 percent (seven or eight women) for most of the 1960s and 1970s. In the Soviet bloc, the picture was somewhat better, with over 30 percent of deputies in the Soviet and GDR national legislatures and 25 percent in Czechoslovakia in 1970 being women.[66] But prior to the 1980s, male domination of the Soviet Politburo was broken only by Ekaterina Furtseva (a close ally of Khrushchev) in 1957–1961; no communist state ever boasted a female head of government. In Argentina, the former nightclub singer Isabel Perón was president in 1974–1976 simply because she was her husband's wife and heir. Sirimavo Bandaranaike, prime minister of Ceylon/Sri Lanka in 1960–1965 and 1970–1977, and Indira Gandhi, the premier of India from 1966 to 1977 and 1980 to 1984, were skilled politicians, but they, too, stepped into dead men's shoes. Bandaranaike took over party leadership from her assassinated husband; Gandhi from her revered father, Jawaharlal Nehru. By the mid-1970s, only Golda Meir, who led Israel between 1969 and 1974, could be said to have made it to the top without any family advantage—though, of course, nepotism is hardly unknown in the history of male politics![67]

A contrast is often made between the "first wave" of feminism earlier in the twentieth century and a "second wave" starting in the late 1960s. The former focused on educational, legal and political rights, especially the vote; the latter raised broader social and economic issues, particularly employment, and also attacked conventions about sexuality and family life. This sharp distinction has been widely qualified.[68] Women did not simply retreat into the kitchen after winning the vote; often their organizations became more fragmented as they lost an overriding cause (suffrage) and diversified into issues such as marriage laws or health care. In the new communist states and in developing countries such as Egypt, feminist organizations had generally been small and socially exclusive: once suffrage was enacted from above as an act of policy, the organizations were closed down as independent actors. Nevertheless, the first- then second-wave pattern does have some validity for the developed world. The vote was widely, if wrongly, seen as a panacea for women's problems. In any case, Europe and North America were preoccupied from the 1930s to 1950s with depression, war and, recovery—all challenges where the good of the whole society was felt to take precedence over the rights of specific groups. In this sense, second-wave feminism can be seen as another product of the consumer society: it developed first in countries that had crossed a threshold of wealth and stability. The United States exemplified this story and also set precedents for the world.[69]

After the American women's movement became established in the late 1960s, it was customary to depict the 1950s as the nadir of female enslavement to suburban domesticity. Although this has been shown to be a caricature rather than a snapshot,[70] like most caricatures it exaggerates an underlying reality. Women constituted little more than one-third of U.S. college students in 1958, compared with nearly half in 1920; less than one Ph.D. in ten went to women, instead of one in six. In fact, only 37 percent of women entering college in the 1950s completed their degrees: "We married what we wanted to be," said the wife of a university administrator years later. "If we wanted to be a lawyer or doctor we married one." Women constituted less than one-third of the employed work force in 1960; most were in traditionally "female" jobs, such as nursing, teaching, or clerical work. About 95 percent of all doctors, lawyers, architects, and natural scientists in the United States were male; most large law firms refused even to interview women.[71] A few women were public figures, notably Eleanor Roosevelt, the widow of the former president, whom Truman made ambassador to the UN: "I told her she was the First Lady of the World."[72] But even she combined forthright public speeches and articles with a conventional role as mother and grandmother. There was little organized protest among American women, let alone the passionate anger of the late 1960s. An intensive Gallup survey in 1962 concluded that "apparently the American woman has all the rights she wants" and that "few people are as happy as a housewife."[73]

Yet the fifties also nurtured the feminism of the sixties. In the age of fridges and washing machines, of automobiles and supermarkets, being a housewife consumed less time and energy. In a country where life expectancy at birth had increased from sixty-one years in 1930 to seventy-one in 1960, women also faced many years of active life after child rearing was over. Although the female proportion of the employed work force grew only slowly, its composition changed dramatically as the social barriers against married women gradually fell away. By 1970, 40 percent of all married women were in paid employment, compared with 17 percent in 1940. An increasing proportion were mothers: half those with children between six and seventeen worked, compared with a quarter in 1948.[74] Black mothers had always worked in larger proportions: this new growth was mainly white middle-income mothers coming into the work force, often part-time. Many were doing so for family ends rather than self-advancement—to pay for vacations, children's education, and the like. But they acted as role models for their daughters, and also experienced first hand the discrimination in pay and prospects that working mothers lower down on the social scale had long endured. Their clarion call was Betty Friedan's *Feminine Mystique* (1963), which articulated the author's disillusionment as an educated wife and mother and that of wartime classmates she surveyed. Being "just a housewife" was like being in a "comfortable concentration camp," fumed Friedan. "American women are not, of course, being readied for mass extermination, but they are suffering a slow death of mind and spirit."[75] Her impassioned plea for education and a career outside the home sold more than a million copies.

All these factors were preconditions of revolt, but what turned frustration into action was the black protest movement of the early 1960s. This put human rights in general on the American political agenda—the 1964 Civil Rights Act banned discrimination on grounds of sex as well as race—and also established new models for political organization and direct action, not least through black female leaders such as Ella Baker and Fannie Lou Hamer. By the mid-1960s, the movement was also generating its own feminism as black and white women activists were radicalized by the condescension of male colleagues, for whom they were often mere cooks, secretaries, and camp followers. The response by Stokely Carmichael to a 1964 paper on "The Position of Women in SNCC" became notorious: "The only position for women in SNCC is prone."[76] The experience of male chauvinism in the New Left movements of the late 1960s had a similar effect on many women students.

The result of this arousal, however, was not one movement but several. Friedan was a moving force behind the National Organization of Women (NOW) in 1966, and became its first president. By 1974 NOW boasted a membership of forty thousand, a few thousand more than the National Women's Political Caucus (NWPC), founded in 1971. These and other organizations formed the liberal wing of the feminist movement, whose membership was largely middle class and college educated and which focused on economic and political issues. In 1970 the Women's Equity Action League (WEAL) started filing class actions in the courts against graduate and professional schools. As a result, women entrants to medical school rose from 9 percent in 1969 to over 20 percent in 1975.[77]

Like those of the early civil rights movement, the aims of liberal feminists were integrationist and egalitarian: women should enjoy equal rights with men in public life. In contrast, younger and more radical women became increasingly exercised during the sixties by the conventions of private life and particularly by sexual mores. They captured national media attention for the first time on September 7, 1968, when a hundred women in jeans and miniskirts disrupted the annual Miss America pageant in Atlantic City, New Jersey, singing lyrics like "Ain't she sweet? Makin' profit off her meat," and throwing dishcloths, bras and high-heeled shoes into the "Freedom Trash Can." That evening a few protesters managed to penetrate the pageant itself and unfurled a white sheet carrying the words WOMEN'S LIBERATION.[78]

Unlike the liberals, many radical feminists inclined toward separatism rather than egalitarianism. They saw men as the problem and demanded distinctive female institutions to avoid cooption into the male-dominated structures of society, of which sex was the cornerstone. Kate Millett developed the theme that "sex is a status category with political implications" in a classic piece of early feminist literary criticism, *Sexual Politics* (1970).[79] Many radicals went on to conclude that lesbianism was the only appropriate sexual orientation. After a major battle, NOW endorsed lesbianism the following year, and Friedan was shunted aside. By now the movements for civil rights and women's rights had spawned one for homosexuals as well, though gay rights were not to become a major issue until the 1980s.

By the 1970s, a plethora of feminist groups were arguing against each other as much as against men. Taken as a whole, feminist organizations embraced only 2 or 3 percent of American women, mostly white and middle class. The indifference of most black women to the movement was a source of special dismay: talk of careers and sexual liberation seemed a luxury to women struggling to hold down a job and hold together a family, often as a lone parent. Even for wealthier white women, changes in employment and educational opportunity were slow to take effect. In fact, in the judgment of two recent historians, "for the majority of American women, life at the end of the sixties was not markedly different from what it was at the beginning." But, they add, "the real legacy" of the decade was "the internalization of feminism" by many who did not join NOW, let alone identify with the radicals.[80] In 1962 a Gallup poll indicated that two-thirds of American women did not feel themselves victims of discrimination; by 1974 two-thirds said they did.[81] During the decade, feminist issues were also taken up by traditional women's groups, such as the American Association of University Women, and by labor unions, churches, and other broad social organizations. By the 1970s, the status of women had entered mainstream politics.

Two legal landmarks testified to this development. In the late 1960s most feminist organizations put their weight behind the Equal Rights Amendment, first proposed in 1923 but frozen in Congress for decades. Reintroduced in August 1970, the fiftieth anniversary of woman suffrage, the ERA passed through Congress in 1971–1972 and then went to the states for approval. At that stage, its ratification seemed inevitable.° The other great legal issue was the decriminalization of abortion. The campaign for reform began in the late 1950s largely as a medical issue—to curtail back-street abortions—but during the 1960s it became a touchstone of whether women had control over their bodies. Beginning in 1967, test cases in the courts forced many states to modify their laws. In January 1973 the Supreme Court's decision in *Roe v. Wade* legalized abortion on demand in the first three months of pregnancy. Although a backlash was to follow against this decision and against the

---

°In fact, a well-organized conservative backlash in the late 1970s prevented it from being approved by three-quarters of the states, as the Constitution required to ensure ratification.

ERA, at the time these two events were major triumphs for the women's movement.

Probably the most important single development of the 1960s for American women was "the pill." In 1951 Margaret Sanger, a pioneer of birth control, and Katharine D. McCormick, the heiress to part of the International Harvester empire, started to fund research by Dr. Gregory Pincus, a Massachusetts researcher, to develop a physiological contraceptive that could be "swallowed like an aspirin."[82] Pincus worked with progesterone, the female "pregnancy" hormone produced when a matured egg was released, using it to trick the body into believing fertilization had already occurred and therefore to stop further ovulation. He was aided by development of a synthetic form, progestin, in the early 1950s. Collaborating with Dr. John Rock, a Harvard gynecologist, Pincus tested the pill in the mid-1950s, mostly on Latin American women. It was licensed initially in 1957 for menstrual disorders, but the drug company G. D. Searle received formal approval in May 1960 to market it as a contraceptive. Other companies joined in. In 1964 the Johnson administration launched a birth-control program for the American poor; the following year the Supreme Court struck down Connecticut's state law banning the *use* of contraceptives, though the last law against their *sale* (in Massachusetts) was not repealed until 1972.

Some black militants claimed official "pill-pushing" was a form of "genocide."[83] Also opposed was the Catholic hierarchy, which continued to insist on "natural" methods, but many of its flock took no notice. By 1967 an estimated seven million American women out of 39 million capable of motherhood had used the pill, particularly the more educated. One month's supply cost about two dollars. The only problem was remembering to take one daily: many women kept them with the toothpaste in the bathroom. By April 1967 *Time* magazine was announcing in a cover story that the pill had "changed and liberated the sex and family life of a large and still growing segment of the U.S. population: eventually, it promises to do the same for much of the world."[84]

Sixties America was therefore the epicenter of a feminist earthquake: equal rights, women's lib, overt lesbianism, and the pill. The shock waves were not instantaneous but were certainly evident in Western Europe by the early 1970s. These countries came closest to American patterns: a well-educated consumer society with growing participation of married women in the work force as the service sector expanded.[85] National stories varied, of course. In France, women had traditionally formed a larger proportion of the work force than in Britain because of the persistence of small farms and shops; the 1950s and 1960s saw a shift from agriculture to service work rather than a real increase in female participation.[86] Movements also varied in their achievements: abortion was legalized in Britain in 1967, but remained a criminal offense throughout the history of West Germany. And nowhere were there mass movements on the American scale, rather myriad local groups. Feminists mostly came out of the socialist tradition, more deeply rooted in Western Europe than across the Atlantic, and were often radicalized by the experiences of 1968. Despite these differences, however, the American example was pervasive, in both principles and methods. Employment rights were one major strand, the other was reproductive issues, with abortion rights often a unifying cause.

France illustrates the general West European pattern. Perhaps the most influential work of postwar feminism came from a French author, Simone de Beauvoir, in 1949. *The Second Sex* appeared in English in 1953, eventually selling two million copies in that language, as well as thousands more in other translations from Arabic to Tamil. By the 1970s it was being called the feminist equivalent of *Das Kapital*.[87] But that was a quarter-century later. In the 1950s, *The Second Sex* caused only a minor storm. This was partly because, like Marx, de Beauvoir had written a scholarly tome, not an incisive polemic. It was also because her feminism was rooted in socialism: she insisted that women's work made no sense if "they get economic independence only as members of a class which is economically oppressed."[88] Above all, the book was ahead of its time and only had real effect when adopted by the American women's movement and then relayed back to Europe in the 1960s.

Active French feminism grew out of the New Left movements of 1968, which revealed the potential for revolutionary action and also the chauvinism of the male leadership. Its birthday was widely said to be August 26, 1970, when a dozen French women showed solidarity with ERA supporters in the United States by demonstrating at the Tomb of the Unknown Soldier at the Arc de Triomphe. In front of forewarned pressmen, they unveiled banners proclaiming "There's someone more unknown than the soldier: his wife," and, as they were taken away by police, they shouted, "We're the mothers of future veterans."[89] The following April, 343 leading women, including de Beauvoir, signed a press release stating that they had had illegal abortions and demanding decriminalization. This became the unifying issue of the early 1970s, leading to the 1975 law that permitted abortion on medical grounds in the first ten weeks (extended to four months in 1979). But after 1975, French feminists, like their American counterparts, broke into feuding groups—separatist versus integrationist, heterosexual versus lesbian, socialist against feminist.[90]

In Western Europe, as in the United States, the pill became a symbol of women's liberation and the "permissive society," yet its precise effects remain a matter of debate. Birth rates had been declining long before women starting taking the pill, as we saw in Chapter 5. In France, the pill was not fully legalized until 1975, by which time fertility had already sunk below the population replacement level, mainly due to the practices of male withdrawal and female douching. Finland and Denmark reached the same point in the late 1960s, with the condom as the preferred method of contraception; withdrawal remained prevalent in southern Europe. All this is a reminder that birth control is not simply a matter of technology: "when people have wished to control their fertility they have done so."[91] That said, the pill was a more effective contraceptive. In the United Kingdom it became available on prescription in 1961; sales increased rapidly in the late 1960s. By 1975 some 2.25 million British women were on the pill, or about two-thirds of those aged fifteen to forty-four. Such widespread use may well account for the sharp decline in fertility in the early 1970s.[92] Furthermore, the pill was a *female* method of contraception: it gave women a sense of control over their bodies (even though they were actually putting them in the hands of pharmaceutical companies, as subsequent scares about side effects made clear).

Did the pill encourage permissiveness? On that, reliable evidence is even harder to find and evaluate. In the 1960s, American and British surveys suggested that the incidence of premarital sex was not much greater than before the war and that, where it occurred, the partner was often the future spouse. By the later 1970s, among another generation, what stood out was not the use but nonuse of the Pill by teenage girls who took risks and paid the price. The consequences of mounting single parenthood and illegitimacy will be a theme of Chapter 17. The point here, however, is that "the sexual revolution, such as it was, was not principally driven by the sudden availability of the Pill" but by wider cultural and social changes, especially those arising from growing consumerism and the youth revolt.[93]

Outside North America, Western Europe and Australasia the Pill was just a word, with not even the flickerings of "second wave" feminism apparent until the late 1970s. The year 1979, for instance, saw the appearance of women's magazines like *Manushi* in India and the underground *Almanac* in Russia; China's first National Women's Conference in two decades was held in 1978. In Latin America, there were some women's organizations in the late 1950s and early 1960s, but most were suppressed after military rule took hold. Indeed, the women's "pots and pans" marches against inflation in Brazil in 1964 helped legitimize the ensuing army coup. Nor were the guerrilla movements of the late 1960s a force for women's liberation. Although women participated, especially in the urban groups, the dominant ethos of the revolutionary left, like that of the New Left in Europe, was chauvinistic. Che Guevara's widely read handbook on *Guerrilla Warfare* paid tribute to women's "extraordinary importance" but also made clear that this was in a supporting role. He stressed the value of good cooking. "One of the great tortures of the [Cuban] war was eating a cold, sticky, tasteless mess. Further-more, it is easier to keep her in these domestic tasks; one of the problems in guerrilla bands is that they [the men] are constantly trying to get out of these tasks."[94]

Yet the absence of a feminist movement does not mean that women's lives remained unaffected. In the Soviet bloc, official doctrine claimed that the communist revolution had led directly to women's liberation. To some extent this was true: the American furor about the ERA was inconceivable in most communist states, where equality was a constitutional right. Soviet bloc states also had a larger proportion of elected women politicians than in the West and of women professionals, such as doctors. A combination of socialist prin-ciples and economic necessity meant that a much greater proportion of women were in paid employment. In the Soviet Union, around 43 percent of the work force was female in the 1950s, a figure that rose sharply to 51 percent by 1970.[95] The GDR figure was 50 percent, Hungary's 41 percent.[96] By this date, most Soviet bloc states were facing a serious labor shortage as birthrates declined. On the one hand, they needed more women as workers; on the other, they wanted more women to be mothers. Most sought to bal-ance the production versus reproduction dilemma by raising pay and pen-sions for those at work and by improving maternity leave and allowances for those having children. The GDR, with the lowest birthrate of the communist world, created one of the most comprehensive public childcare systems any-where, covering 82 percent of preschoolers by 1975.[97]

But by the late 1960s it was also clear that the genuine egalitarian virtues of the Soviet bloc covered a multitude of Western-style sins. The nature of women's employment, for instance, was much the same. Women formed the overwhelming bulk of nurses, teachers, and stenographers, and of low-skilled industrial workers in areas such as textiles and food processing. They were grossly underrepresented at the higher levels of management and business. At all levels, they suffered discrimination in pay. Contraception, though widely available, was hazardous. The more advanced East European states were emulating Western methods: the Czech government started producing its own version of the Pill and the intrauterine device in 1966. But in 1970 they probably were used by only about 6 percent of fertile women, and male withdrawal and female abortion remained the principal methods of birth control.[98] Abortion was most prevalent in the Soviet Union itself, where the pill was virtually nonexistent, IUDs were in short supply until the 1980s, and Russian condoms were nicknamed "galoshes." Abortion was relegalized in 1955 after Stalin's death. Abortions peaked at 8.3 million in 1965 and ran at around seven million throughout the 1970s—statistics that reveal little of the crude methods and intense suffering endured.[99]

It was wryly observed that the three main methods of contraception in the Soviet Union were the housing shortage, the lack of double beds, and the exhaustion of working wives. This joke points up the most basic similarity with the West, indeed with humanity as a whole, namely the unequal division of domestic labor. Women still did the bulk of work in the home—cleaning, cooking, child rearing—whether or not they had paid employment as well. And since consumer goods were less available in communist states, more work had to be done laboriously by hand. In 1970, for instance, only half of Soviet households had a washing machine, one-third had a fridge, and a bare 12 percent boasted a vacuum cleaner.[100] Soviet data suggested that women devoted an additional twenty-eight hours a week to housework, compared with twelve for men, giving the latter over 50 percent more leisure time.[101] One Russian divorcée complained bitterly, "Having a husband is like having another baby in the apartment."[102] Many women the world over would still agree.

In China, the communist takeover in 1949 also prompted a major improvement in women's legal rights. The 1950 marriage law established the principle of "free-choice" marriage and raised the minimum age to eighteen. In urban areas, women's participation in higher education and in the employed work force grew in the 1950s and 1960s. But as elsewhere, women mostly performed lower-paid, less skilled jobs, making up the majority of cooperative factory workers rather than those in the elite mechanized state sectors of the economy. Further, China, unlike most of the Soviet bloc, was still overwhelmingly rural, so traditional attitudes remained strong. Woman's prime function was reproductive, to breed male heirs. Why bother to invest in a girl's education, especially when any economic benefits would accrue to the husband's family and not one's own? It remained axiomatic that she would be obedient to her father, then to her husband, and finally, in widowhood, to her eldest son. With the state only slowly enlarging welfare provision, large families were still seen as insurance against sickness and old age. Moreover, women did much of the agricultural labor, and domestic work remained time consuming: China's modernization concentrated on heavy industry, not consumer goods. Mao himself decreed that "to liberate women is not to manufacture washing machines."[103] Yet China's traumatic 1960s did not leave women unchanged. Mass mobilization, both geographical and political, and the ubiquitous ideology of equality had an impact, particularly on the young and urban. Even in rural areas, the widespread use of political study groups later in the Cultural Revolution helped to promote women's confidence and self-expression.[104]

India, also a deeply traditional rural society, underwent no similar internal revolutions. After independence, the Congress party had legislated female suffrage and, more slowly and controversially, new Hindu personal laws. Their provisions included strict monogamy, legitimization of intercaste marriages, and equal rights of inheritance for widows and daughters, not merely sons. The minimum age of marriage was set at eighteen for boys and fifteen for girls. The practice of exorbitant dowry demands was banned in 1961.

All these changes existed mainly on paper, however. In practice, traditional attitudes remained strong, even among women. One survey of rural wives around Bangalore in 1978 showed almost total ignorance of these laws along with marked opposition to the free choice of partners and to divorce for women. Only on matters of dowry and inheritance were their attitudes in tune with the new law.[105] As in rural China, the preconditions for general social change in the position of women were absent: female adult literacy was under 19 percent in 1971 (half that of men), and only 12 percent of women were in the paid work force. Not until 1976, for instance, did India have its first woman police officer.[106]

Caste was a further complication. Traditionally, the upper two castes had regimented women most closely, in part to prove their own superiority over the impure hordes below. In the 1960s, the practice of *purdah* could still impose claustrophobic confinement, or it might mean little more than the Western cult of domesticity. Either way, the idea of keeping women in the home as a mark of social status was appealing to many upwardly mobile Indians. Nevertheless, some women from more emancipated upper-caste families were given extensive opportunities for education and career. The practice of sexual segregation offered them a major role in areas such as teaching and health. Over 21 percent of India's doctors were female by 1973. Yet even for these professionals, traditional attitudes often prevailed at home. One women civil servant at the top of the Home Ministry still wore a veil in her own house in deference to her in-laws.[107]

In the Middle East, Israel was a Western enclave with legal equality for women, universal suffrage and universal military service at age eighteen, and a few women in parliament—eight out of 120 in April 1967, for instance.[108] But in the Arab world, the patriarchal family remained the basic unit of social and economic life, with female subordination clearly defined. Whether this subordination was inherent in Islam from the beginning, or whether it represents a perversion by "feudal" rulers and the religious establishment has been a vexatious issue among Islamic scholars since the 1970s,[109] as will be discussed more fully in Chapter 11. The basic point here, however, is that after 1945, most Islamic states divided into two groups: those sticking rigidly to the *shari'ah*, or Islamic law, and those blending it with secular law. Most of the former were in the Arabian peninsula, plus Afghanistan; often they did not allow men or women to vote. The reformers were usually postcolonial societies in North Africa and the Near East in which granting some measure of women's rights was part of proving national independence. Of these, Tunisia after 1956 was the most radical, setting minimum ages for marriage, giving men and women equal rights to divorce, and even banning polygyny. Nevertheless, the government of Habib Bourguiba faced strong opposition from the Islamic authorities; Tunisia did not follow Albania or Turkey into complete secularization. No other government in the 1950s and 1960s abolished the *talaq*, the unilateral male right of divorce, let alone outlawing polygyny.

Socioeconomic change in the Arab world remained slow. In many villages, resistance to mixing the sexes and the cost of building *two* schools meant that girls were often not educated, even at the primary level. Egypt, Iraq, Jordan, and Syria were among the few states to accept primary coeducation. Only a few elite women went right through secondary and university education, although, as in India, sex segregation gave those who did considerable opportunities in teaching and medicine. In general, women's participation in the paid work force was low, even when compared with countries at similar stages of development—6 percent of Egyptian women at the late 1970s, or instance, and 9 percent of Syria's.[110] But a more meaningful distinction may be drawn between rural areas and the cities. In the latter, especially in urban Egypt, patterns of employment, marriage, and fertility paralleled those in the developed world. The importance of this contrast is underlined by the case of Turkey, where Islamic law was abolished in the 1920s but where the population was still three-fifths rural in the 1970s. In country areas, traditional attitudes to women persisted and the practice of polygyny remained widespread.[111]

The implication of this evidence is, of course, that modernization brought progress for women, whereas tradition meant repression. An extreme example would be the persistent practice of killing baby girls. In China, the communists had managed to curtail female infanticide but, even so, in 1982, men outnumbered women by a ratio of 106 to 100, and girl deaths increased after the government introduced its one-child policy in 1979.[112] In India, the statistics were even more telling. The proportion of women in that country's population steadily declined from 972 per thousand males in 1901 to 929 in 1991.[113]

Yet the equation of economic modernization with women's liberation is by no means absolute, as can be seen in sub-Saharan Africa—one of the most "backward" parts of the world in developmental terms. The Basa peoples of Cameroon, for example, established independent nuclear households on marriage; for Yoruba women in Nigeria, marriage came relatively late, when they had attained a measure of economic independence. Nor did many African women experience the same tensions as those in the West between child rearing and wage earning, because care of children was deemed a communal responsibility, not the sole and intense duty of the biological mother. Further, even though polygyny was most common in this region of the world, it did not necessarily mean women were devoid of rights or power. Usually a woman had sole charge over the household and its economic management. And older women, beyond child-bearing age, enjoyed particular authority and respect.[114] Both of these last statements are, in fact, valid for most rural societies. More generally, it is obvious that all marriages are relationships whose balance depends on the personalities of the man and women. Although patriarchy may have been the global norm (with exceptions, such as southern India), in practice most marriages were (and are) a matter of negotiation as much as domination.

After entering these qualifications, it is nevertheless true that the principal catalyst for women's liberation was economic development. Women's education was one of its most important elements. Not only was this a solvent of traditional attitudes to marriage and employment. It also led directly to better health, hygiene, and nutrition within the family. Demographers reckoned that one additional year of female education was associated with a 9 percent drop in child mortality. In consequence, increased women's education often assisted initially in population growth, but in the longer term it had the effect of reducing fertility through changing attitudes to birth control and encouraging a later age of marriage.[115] The second major implication of development was the growing involvement of women in the cash economy.[116] Sometimes this occurred in rural areas, as women worked on big estates in Asia, Latin America and, increasingly, in Africa, growing commodities such as tea, coffee, and sugar for the world market. Especially in Asia, many entered industrial employment in factories or "cottage" industries, sewing garments or processing foodstuffs. In 1974, an estimated 2.5 million women in India were engaged in the production of cigarettes. But increasingly women entered the cash economy by migrating to big cities, where they found casual work as domestic servants or small retailers, often supplemented by prostitution. In Kampala, the capital of Uganda, the first step was often home brewing of native beers, starting with pineapple and graduating to banana skins and eventually maize.[117] Whatever the work, it was usually arduous and unremunerative. Women who ran their own market stalls in Lima, the capital of Peru, were up by 4:00 A.M. to prepare midday meals for children going to school, before trudging off with the younger ones to buy produce from wholesalers in time to set up their stalls by 6:30. The selling day did not end until 5:00 P.M., and then they went home to cook food and wash clothes before collapsing into bed.[118] Some prospered, many did not. But for them, and for their daughters, it was a very different lifestyle from that of the rural peasantry.

In the developed world by 1970, a revolution in women's conditions had also helped launch vocal women's movements, with the United States leading the way. In the regimented communist world, and in less developed

Latin America, economic changes were slower to take effect. In the developing world they had barely begun, except in the cities. But 1975 was an important milestone. The UN, pressed by various women's organizations and prominent Americans such as the anthropologist Margaret Mead, designated 1975 "International Women's Year." In June, a two-week conference was convened in Mexico City. The formal meetings were attended by delegates (half of them men) from 133 countries, but they agreed an action plan for a UN Decade of Women, with events and conferences through 1985. The plan went ahead despite pressure from Soviet bloc countries and some developing states to subsume "women's issues" in a traditional Marxist insistence on the egalitarian effects of revolutionary change. Equally important at Mexico City were the informal sessions, involving some six thousand women—mostly from North and South America—who discussed practical issues such health, nutrition, and education.

These and many other women's gatherings, such as the mid-decade conference in Copenhagen in 1980, had a huge effect. They spread information, raised consciousness, and created international networks. Moreover, they placed "women's issues" on the global map and encouraged Western aid donors to support women's organizations concerned with development.[119] This was drip-feed change, not radical revolution, but it had long-term effects. Although the UN was often impotent when faced with the big issues of peace and security, it played a major role, through high-profile gatherings like 1975, in shifting the international agenda.*

In the early 1970s, of course, this remained very much a man's world. But, as we resume the history of male follies, we must not forget that "her-story" had now entered the domain of high politics. Gender issues will crop up more frequently in the narrative that follows—for instance, in the discussion of Islam in Chapter 11. And the growth of women's organizations would contribute to bottom-up political change in the 1980s—Latin America being a notable example (Chapter 13). When we take a final Braudelian glance at underlying social trends in the 1990s (Chapter 17), we shall see how all the changes described in Chapters 5 and 9—demography and urbanization, consumerism and education, youth protest and female mobilization—shook the foundations of the patriarchal family around the world.

*Likewise for environmental issues—see Chapters 14 and 17.

10

Superpower Détente, Communist Confrontation

"You saved 1968," read the telegram, from someone Colonel Frank Borman had never met.[1] After a year of violence and tragedy—from January in Saigon to August in Prague, from springtime in Paris to summer in Chicago—Christmas brought something to celebrate. The American *Apollo 8* spacecraft, under Borman's command, had been the first to orbit the moon. He and his crew, Bill Anders and Jim Lovell, broadcast live to millions back on earth on Christmas Eve, reading the opening verses of the book of Genesis: "In the beginning, God created the heavens and the earth. . . ." *Earthrise,* an image of their home planet seen as *Apollo* emerged from behind the moon, was beamed around the globe. President Lyndon Johnson sent copies to every head of state, including Ho Chi Minh.

Only seven months later, *Apollo 11* launched its lunar module, *Eagle,* down to the dusty surface of the Sea of Tranquillity. On July 20, 1969, while Michael Collins piloted the command module in orbit above, Neil Armstrong and Edwin "Buzz" Aldrin prepared to set foot on the moon. The official timetable called for seven hours sleep after landing but that, said Aldrin later, "was like telling kids on Christmas morning they had to stay in bed until noon."[2] He took Holy Communion before climbing out; Armstrong, who would be first to leave the module, had a specially prepared sentence for a billion TV viewers watching from earth: "That's one small step for a man, one giant leap for mankind."° After more than two hours on the moon's surface, conducting experiments and planting a U.S. flag, the two men rejoined the command module for the flight home. President Richard Nixon told them jubilantly, "This is the greatest week in the history of the world since the Creation" (for which he was sternly rebuked by the Christian evangelist Billy Graham). "As a result of what you have done," Nixon added, "the world has never been closer together."[3]

True, yet false. The TV drama on the moon excited millions the world over; the pictures from space evoked awe and poetry, expressed in different ways by Aldrin and Armstrong before they took their first steps on the moon (Plates 17 and 18). From start to finish, however, the $25 billion project had been a weapon in the cold war. Stung by the Soviets' success in putting the first man into space, Kennedy had pledged in 1961 to put a man on the moon and bring him back safely by the end of the decade. For much of the 1960s, the Russians seemed ahead: in March 1965, the cosmonaut Alexei Leonov made the first walk in space, and in January 1967, the three-man crew for the first Apollo mission died in a cockpit fire during routine testing. But the triumph of *Apollo 8* transformed the situation. In February and July 1969 two Soviet test rockets exploded on the launch pad, and the unmanned *Luna 15* crashed into the moon while Armstrong and Aldrin were actually there. Nor, despite Nixon's hyperbole, was humanity closer together. America was still fighting a brutal war in Indochina. The Soviets were catching up in the arms race. And in July 1969, even as Armstrong and Aldrin looked back in wonder, the world again seemed close to nuclear war—this time with communist ranged against communist.

A New Strategic Triangle: America, Russia, China

China and the Soviet Union shared one of the longest land borders in the world. Much of it was in dispute because the Chinese protested the "unequal treaties" extracted by the tsars in the nineteenth century as well as the status of Mongolia, formerly a Chinese province, as an independent state under Soviet protection. These long-standing animosities were exacerbated by the Sino-Soviet split in the 1960s. The Kremlin had been particularly alarmed by the Chinese nuclear test of October 1966, in which a live warhead

---

°Like most great moments in history, this did not go exactly according to plan. On the recording of Armstrong's voice, the indefinite article "a" is missing—probably forgotten in the excitement, possibly lost in transmission. Either way, earth got the message.

was fired five hundred miles into the northwestern border region of Xinjiang. China's first H-bomb test followed in June 1967. The Soviets were also concerned about long-term security, as China's population (three times that of the USSR) continue to soar. With typical black humor, one Moscow joke imagined the party secretary, Leonid Brezhnev, calling President Nixon over the phone: "I've heard you have a new super-computer that can predict events in the year 2000." Nixon proudly confirms this, whereupon Brezhnev asks who would be the members of the Soviet Politburo at that date. A long silence ensues. "So," Brezhnev crows, "your computer isn't so sophisticated after all." "Oh, no," replies Nixon, "the names came up all right. But I can't read Chinese."[4]

During 1967, the USSR built up a large military presence in Mongolia, which brought Soviet troops within a few hundred miles of Beijing. China's leaders feared that Moscow might intervene during the turmoil of the Cultural Revolution. Border incidents increased in 1967–1968. When the Soviets invaded Czechoslovakia in August 1968, claiming that "proletarian internationalism" must override national sovereignty, Beijing was determined to deter any similar move against China. On March 2 and 15, 1969, there were clashes on the disputed island of Zhenbao/Damansky in the Ussuri river along the eastern border. The second encounter was a minor battle in which the Russians suffered sixty casualties, the Chinese eight hundred. When the Soviet prime minister, Alexei Kosygin, tried to speak directly on the telephone hotline with Mao or Foreign Minister Zhou Enlai, he was instructed to send a note through normal diplomatic channels. "You are a revisionist," said the Chinese operator, "and therefore I will not connect you."[5]

During the summer of 1969, the Soviets themselves engineered a series of border incidents, trying to push the Chinese to reopen talks. They even encouraged the impression that they were ready to mount a preemptive strike on Chinese nuclear facilities. While this was probably part of a war of nerves by the Politburo, some military circles were in favor of such a move, and practice exercises were conducted in Siberia and Mongolia in June. At the same time, Soviet forces in the Far East were reinforced, rising from twenty-two divisions in 1968 to thirty-seven by 1970. With the Soviets enjoying a massive nuclear superiority—3,700 missiles, planes and other delivery vehicles to China's 150—the Beijing leadership backed down and agreed to reopen talks on the border issue on October 20.[6] But so fearful was it that the arrival of the Soviet delegation might be a diversion from a full-scale attack that in the middle of October most senior leaders were instructed to leave the capital and the army was placed on combat alert. About one million troops were redeployed.[7]

In Washington, the U.S. government was engaged in similar brinksmanship. For Richard Nixon, inaugurated in January 1969, the top problem was

Vietnam, where Americans were dying at the rate of two hundred a week in an unpopular war that was costing about $30 billion every year. "I'm not going to end up like LBJ," Nixon told an aide, "holed up in the White House, afraid to show my face on the street. I'm going to stop that war. Fast." In March 1969 he sanctioned secret bombing raids on Vietcong sanctuaries in neighboring Cambodia. Over the next fourteen months, 3,630 sorties were flown and 110,000 tons of bombs dropped (50 percent more than the tonnage on Britain in 1939–45).[8] Amazingly, word did not leak out at home. Nixon also developed his "madman" theory to close staff. "I want the North Vietnamese to believe I've reached the point where I might *do* anything to stop the war." Let them know "Nixon is obsessed about communism. . . . and he has his hand on the nuclear button." Then, said Nixon, "Ho Chi Minh will be in Paris in two days begging for peace."[9] But when Ho died in September 1969, the Paris peace talks were still deadlocked and North Vietnam was hunkering down for a war of attrition.

Meanwhile, the superpowers' arms race had entered a new phase. Soviet leaders were determined that they would never again be humiliated as over Cuba in 1962, when Khrushchev's diplomacy of bluster and bluff had been exposed. It was in the 1960s that the Soviet Union settled down to a real arms race, devoting around a quarter of its GNP and the same proportion of its work force to this goal, while the Pentagon was preoccupied with Vietnam. In these years the USSR "did not *have* a military-industrial complex," as Eisenhower had complained about the USA, "it *was* a military-industrial complex."[10] In July 1964, the United States had three times the Soviet number of nuclear launchers of all types; by November 1969 its advantage was only 50 percent. In fact, the Soviet arsenal of intercontinental ballistic missiles (ICBMs) exceeded America's by 1,140 to 1,054. Admittedly, on the other two legs of what was known as the strategic triad—submarine-launched ballistic missiles (SLBMs) and nuclear-capable bombers—the United States still enjoyed superiority of more than three to one, but the trend toward parity was clear.[11] Would that content the Kremlin, or would it push for superiority?

Equally important were new technological twists to the arms spiral. One was the development of antiballistic missile systems (ABMs), which, if successful, might encourage the possessor to mount a nuclear strike with impunity, confident that its victim could not hit back. The Soviets started building a system around Moscow in the mid-1960s; Congress gave the go-ahead for an American program in August 1969. The other problem was MIRVs—multiple, independently targetable reentry vehicles—or, in plain language, missiles with several warheads, each of which could be aimed at a separate target. The Pentagon began testing these in 1968. If developed and deployed, MIRVs could greatly increase a superpower arsenal and perhaps encourage a preemptive first strike. Controlling the arms race, and the new challenges of ABMs and MIRVs, was therefore of critical importance, but action was delayed by Nixon's desire to make talks conditional on progress in Vietnam.

These looming crises—between China and Russia, America and Vietnam, and Russia and America—were known only to a few. But, for much of 1969, they threatened the peace of the world. In the autumn, however, some movement occurred. On October 19, Nixon abandoned plans for escalation of the war against North Vietnam. He was dissuaded partly by the Pentagon and State Department, but even more by the nationwide moratorium four days before, when millions of Americans stopped work or school in dignified protest against the continuing war. The son of the defense secretary, Melvin Laird, and the daughter of Vice President Spiro Agnew were among the moratorium's supporters.[12] Next day, Nixon set a date for talks on a strategic arms limitation treaty (SALT), dropping any linkage with Vietnam. The first round began in November, alternating between Helsinki and Vienna. Also on October 20, China and Russia began their talks in Beijing. Although these made limited progress, the feared Soviet attack did not occur and border incidents abated.

These developments in October 1969 defused some of the tension, but the underlying problems had not been resolved. The astonishing changes of the next three years—what became known in the west as détente, or relaxation of tension—depended on a remarkable conjunction of shifts in policy and politics in Washington, Beijing, and Moscow. These climaxed in Nixon's visits to both communist capitals in 1972 and a peace agreement for Indochina in January 1973.

The opening moves came from Nixon and Henry Kissinger, his national security adviser. They were an unlikely pair—the reclusive, driven son of a California grocer, the gregarious, sparkling Jewish intellectual, a childhood refugee from Hitler's Germany. Nixon (1913–1994) was almost a career politician who made his name as an anticommunist in the McCarthy era, served two terms as Eisenhower's vice president, and then clawed his way back from humiliating defeat in the 1960 election. Kissinger, ten years younger, climbed to power as a Harvard professor and foreign-policy consultant, positioning himself adroitly to serve either a Republican or a Democratic president after the 1968 election. But both men shared certain traits: they were loners, often paranoid about rivals; they were hard-headed practitioners of realpolitik; and, above all, they were capable of thinking big, new ideas about America's place in the world.

Nixon, and more gradually Kissinger, believed that U.S. policy "must come urgently to grips with the reality of China," instead of continuing the policy of hostile isolation, and slowly "pull China back into the family of nations."[13]

Both also saw the need to bring Soviet-American competition under control. Kissinger, particularly, advocated a tactic of linkage, whereby all problems in the relationship were used as leverage, one on the other. Both men hoped that improved relations with Russia and China might help extricate the United States from Vietnam by adding diplomatic pressure to America's military might. But they were sure that success in all these areas depended on bypassing the normal conduits of diplomacy. In August 1969 Kissinger opened his own secret talks in Paris with envoys from Hanoi; by then he had a secret link to Moscow, "the Channel," via regular meetings with Soviet ambassador Anatoly Dobrynin. None of this was known to William Rogers, Nixon's courtly secretary of state, who was treated with contempt by the president and with vitriolic hatred by Kissinger.

But what really transformed international politics were events in China. Although border incidents diminished in 1970–1971, the sense of Soviet threat had not disappeared. On the contrary, the Chinese responded to the Kremlin's troop buildup by sending thousands of disgraced Red Guards to colonize the frontier regions and by increasing its troop strength along the border from forty-seven divisions in 1969 to seventy by 1973. Even more striking was the "third front" *(san xian)*. This was a massive development of industry in border and mountain regions, less vulnerable than the urbanized coast or central cities such as Wuhan. The program began in the southwest after the Vietnam war scare of 1964–1965, but gathered momentum in the crisis of 1969. Old factories were moved from the coast and massive new complexes constructed for steel, machinery, and chemicals, backed by huge hydroelectric programs. The aim was to create an entire inland industrial base that could survive a long war. As with so much of China's history, the details remain vague. But between 1965 and 1971 half the government's construction expenditure went to the ten third-front provinces, which had accounted for under one-fifth of national output in 1965. In these years, it has been justly said, China's industrialization policy *"was* the Third Front."[14]

These were preparations for *two* possible wars, because the the new threat from Russia stood alongside the old threat from U.S. bases in Japan, Korea, and above all Taiwan, whose leaders the United States still officially recognized as the rightful government of mainland China. Yet Mao and Zhou saw Vietnam and Czechoslovakia as signs that America was in decline and the Soviets on the march. By 1971, with China emerging from the frenzy of the Cultural Revolution, they were ready to respond to Nixon's feelers and reduce the pressure from one of the superpowers. On both sides, the diplomatic minuet was conducted in secret, behind the backs of foreign-policy professionals, initially via Warsaw and Paris. Few anticipated Kissinger's clandestine visit to Beijing in July 1971 (concealed by diplomatic "illness" during a trip to Pakistan). Kissinger hammered out arrangements for a visit by Nixon the following February, which was announced to an astonished world on his return. Kissinger told Nixon: "We have laid the groundwork for you and Mao to turn a page in history."[15]

But first, a chapter in China's turbulent annals also had to be closed. Exactly how and why Mao's designated heir, Defense Minister Lin Biao, met his death in September 1971 remain a mystery. The official story had it that Lin, his ambitious wife Ye Qun, and their clique opposed the tilt toward America, maybe even arguing for compromise with the Soviet Union. They also tried to consolidate Lin's position by having him named state chairman (head of state) at the plenum in Lushan in August 1970. Blocked by an angry Mao, Lin reportedly told an ally: "Doing things in the civilian manner doesn't work, using armed force will work."[16] His son Lin Liguo, abetted by fellow air force officers, tried to organize Mao's assassination during a regional tour in September. When Mao evaded them, the plotters panicked and tried to flee, but their plane ran out of fuel and crashed in Mongolia, killing Lin Biao, Ye Qun, and all those aboard. This is the party line, though many Chinese intellectuals still believe that Lin met his end in an officially sponsored rocket attack on his car in Beijing.[17] But much of our evidence about Lin's "plot" depends on trials and "confessions" of his associates afterward, which cannot be taken at face value. The man himself was not an obvious conspirator. Severely wounded by the Japanese in 1938, he was by some accounts a hypochondriac, so terrified of light, wind, and water that he rarely went outdoors. Unable or unwilling to read, he only worked for one or two thirty-minute periods a day, when selected documents were read to him by aides.[18] It is possible, therefore, that Lin was more schemed against than scheming, manipulated by his wife and son. Ultimately, however, the man who mattered in this drama was not Lin but Mao. The Great Helmsman had become alarmed at the growing power of the army—the bastion of order after the Cultural Revolution and of defense against the Soviet threat. During 1971 he began to rein in military power. Who really moved first, Mao or Lin, remains unclear. But by the end of September 1971 Mao had destroyed a second heir, and the road to the summit lay open.

On February 21, 1972, Richard Nixon became the first U.S. president to visit China. Zhou Enlai was at Beijing airport ready to greet him. Remembering that at Geneva in 1954 Zhou had been insulted by John Foster Dulles's refusal to shake hands, Nixon thrust out his arm as he descended the aircraft steps. Zhou said later, "Your handshake came over the vastest ocean in the world—twenty-five years of no communication."[19] Equally significant, Nixon and Zhou stood there alone. This was TV prime time back in the United States, and Nixon was adamant that no one (especially Kissinger) was to leave the plane until he had greeted Zhou. Just to be sure, a burly Secret Service man blocked the aisle of Air Force One. In many ways, the picture of Zhou and Nixon summed up the visit—more symbol than substance. But only two decades after a savage and bloody war between the two countries, the image spoke volumes. And the beleaguered Nixon hoped it would pay dividends in the November election campaign. As he had written ten years earlier, "where voters are concerned . . . one TV picture is worth 10,000 words."[20] Exact details of what was agreed on remain unclear, but there appears to have been some trade-off between Taiwan and Vietnam. In the final communiqué, the United States committed itself to total military withdrawal from Taiwan as an "ultimate objective", and promised, in the interim, to "progressively reduce its forces" there "as the tension in the area diminishes." This last phrase gave China a direct stake in helping America extricate itself from Vietnam.[21] On the eve of his departure, the jubilant president indulged in typical hyperbole: "This was the week that changed the world."[22]

The Soviet leaders, particularly Prime Minister Alexei Kosygin, could also see many reasons for détente. It would enable them to concentrate on the threat from China; it would facilitate progress on European problems such as Germany and Berlin; it would confirm nuclear parity with the United States and thus equality of status between the two superpowers. Kosygin also hoped for economic benefits, in a country where defense needs and consumer demands were increasingly at odds, where nondefense technology was lagging behind that of Eastern Europe let alone the West, and where the harvest was exceedingly bad again in 1969. The case for détente was pressed in 1971 by a potent new axis between Foreign Minister Andrei Gromyko and the energetic KGB chief, Yuri Andropov. But the benefits were by no means assured and, in any case, cozying up to the capitalists remained anathema to many ideologues and military men, not to mention Brezhnev himself in the mid-1960s.

This is where politics came in. For several years after Khrushchev's demise, power within the collective leadership remained both dispersed and balanced: Nikolai Podgorny, the hard-line head of state, dominated relations with Third World countries; Prime Minister Kosygin handled the economy and urged détente with the West; Brezhnev, the party secretary, looked after Eastern Europe, harping on the threat from Germany and the United States. Gradually, in the late 1960s, Brezhnev maneuvered his way into preeminence. Partly, like Stalin and Khrushchev before him, he used his control of the party apparatus to promote allies and topple enemies. But he also raised his profile by moving into the foreign-policy arena, stealing some of Kosygin's ideas while retaining his own reputation as a hard-liner on security.[23] It was Brezhnev who put the new "peace program" to the twenty-fourth party congress in April 1971. During the summer, Gromyko indicated that in future Nixon should write to Brezhnev, and not Kosygin, about foreign policy. Even after 1971, the Soviet leadership remained collective: Brezhnev was first among equals and never achieved the dominance of Khrushchev, let alone Stalin. Yet his emergence from the domestic power struggle was critical not only for arms control but also for any Soviet-American summit.[24]

During 1971, therefore, the Soviets inched toward détente. But they were still dragging their feet about a Moscow summit, hoping that Nixon's electoral imperatives would force him to make further concessions on Berlin. After the bombshell news in July that Nixon was going to Beijing, the Kremlin dropped most of its conditions, fearful that it was being isolated by a new Sino-American axis. Nixon and his party arrived in Moscow on May 22, 1972, also the first visit by a U.S. president, though Nixon had been there as vice president in 1959 (see Chapter 6).

As in Beijing, the emphasis was on symbols and atmospherics. Nixon was anxious to develop a working relationship with the Soviet leaders. Kosygin, he judged, was "by Communist terms an aristocrat; while Podgorny is more like a Midwestern senator; and Brezhnev like a big Irish labor boss." He was struck by the latter's drive, deep voice, and "animal magnetism"—Brezhnev would often jump up and march around the room during their meetings.[25] Learning of the general secretary's liking for fast, flashy cars, Nixon presented him with a Cadillac. Brezhnev had more of a problem reciprocating, since even Gromyko's American specialists did not know whether the workaholic Nixon had any hobbies. "I think what he'd really like," remarked Gromyko drily, "is a guarantee to stay in the White House for ever." In the end, the Russians gave Nixon a hydrofoil, on the grounds that Brezhnev liked them.[26] Overall, the mood was very positive. "You can do business with Nixon," said Brezhnev.[27]

The business transacted at Moscow was more substantial than in Beijing. In all, ten agreements were signed, of which the Russians attached most importance to the declaration of "Basic Principles," which affirmed "peaceful coexistence" and indicated the new equality of the two superpowers. The Americans gave prominence to the SALT agreements limiting ABM systems and imposing a five-year freeze on missile launchers (where the two sides were now equal), but here they had lost out through Kissinger's lack of mastery of the details in earlier backchannel talks. He had belatedly been able to bring submarine-launched missiles into the equation, but only by limiting these to a level far above current Soviet building programs. And he could not pin down the Soviets to wording that would prevent them from modernizing their missiles with multiple warheads at a later date. Because the president, as usual, wanted all credit, the U.S. arms control experts were left in Helsinki while Nixon and Kissinger tried to handle the arcane yet vital detail. Their main leverage in tying up the deal were the still-secret economic agreements on trade, credits, and grain, on which Brezhnev and Kosygin were especially keen. These permitted the Russians quietly to buy up most of the American grain reserve.[28] What became known to the press as "the great grain robbery" was a huge embarrassment to the administration.

In all these ways, the specifics of the Moscow summit were not favorable to the United States. On the other hand, both superpowers had shown for the first time a willingness to limit their arms race. And Nixon and Kissinger were probably more interested in the appearance of success than in success itself. A peace summit in Moscow would help calm the nation and boost Nixon's chances for reelection, after which they hoped to construct a more advantageous SALT agreement and "reinstitutionalize a favorable balance of power."[29] All this was a gamble, however. Success depended, above all, on two factors—a second term and peace in Vietnam.

On the latter, détente with China and Russia undoubtedly eased America's path out of Indochina, where Nixon had become more deeply involved than Johnson during 1970–1971. March 1970 saw the end of Prince Norodom Sihanouk's long neutralist balancing act to keep Cambodia from falling completely into the cauldron of war (see Chapter 8). While out of the country for medical treatment, Sihanouk was deposed. The new government, headed by General Lon Nol, demanded withdrawal of the hated North Vietnamese troops and asked for American aid. On May 1, 1970, thirty-one thousand Americans joined forty-three thousand South Vietnamese soldiers in a massive "incursion" into Cambodia. In the campus protests that followed, four students (two of them women) were shot dead at Kent State University in Ohio. Tens of thousands now descended on Washington, putting the White House under siege. Nixon was obliged to pull U.S. forces out of Cambodia by the end of June without a decisive victory and with that country spiraling into a long and bloody civil war.

In February 1971, mindful of the furor over Cambodia, Nixon had sent South Vietnamese forces and not U.S. troops into Laos against communist sanctuaries. But they were driven back in heavy fighting. Film of South Vietnamese troops clinging to the skids of American helicopters again cast doubt on the success of the Pentagon's program of "Vietnamization"—turning the war over the army of South Vietnam (ARVN). On the other hand, domestic protest was defused by the continued exodus of U.S. troops—down to nearly 150,000 by the end of 1971, compared with over five hundred thousand when Nixon took office.[30] And Nixon's overtures to Beijing and Moscow were now paying off. Both urged North Vietnam to reach a compromise agreement leaving the Saigon regime in place, on the grounds that victory would eventually follow a U.S. withdrawal. In Mao's words, "as our broom is too short to sweep the Americans out of Taiwan, so yours is too short to do the same in South Vietnam."[31]

To Hanoi, this seemed reminiscent of its betrayal at Geneva in 1954, when China and Russia imposed a "temporary" partition. The Politburo pushed ahead with plans for an all-out offensive in March 1972, its first since Tet in 1968, but this time avoiding the cities and using most of North Vietnam's conventional troops. Against the demoralized ARVN, they achieved dramatic early success; only massive American firepower turned the tide. Surveying the ruins of Quang Tri, a provincial capital, one U.S. officer observed, "We'd like to pound a place until there's nothing standing and we can walk in without a fight."[32] The pounding also extended to North Vietnam. "Those bastards have never been bombed like they're going to be bombed this time," Nixon vowed privately, after his May announcement of sustained attacks on Hanoi and Haiphong and the mining of major harbors.[33] Again the protests from Beijing and Moscow were relatively mild; despite Washington's fears, the Soviets did not postpone the Moscow summit. Once more, détente was giving Nixon diplomatic room for tactical escalations to permit a strategic withdrawal.

Its offensive having failed, Hanoi decided that it was better to reach a settlement before Nixon's likely reelection toughened his stance. On its side, Saigon was now anxious to extract the best possible terms. Although peace was not achieved by the November election, as Nixon had hoped, the eventual outcome no longer seemed in doubt. In a last effort to force concessions from Hanoi, Nixon and Kissinger resumed their bombing of the North during the Christmas period. There was an outcry at home and abroad, this time including Moscow and Beijing, and the bombing stopped on December 30 without forcing any major change in the DRV position. At the same time, Nixon pumped another $1 billion of arms into South Vietnam, while telling Thieu that, if there was more delay, he would "explain publicly that your government obstructs peace. The result will be an inevitable and immediate termination of U.S. economic and military assistance."[34] The Saigon leader finally succumbed.

On January 23, 1973, Kissinger and Hanoi's principal negotiator, Le Duc Tho, initialed the peace agreement in Paris, just hours after the death of Lyndon Johnson, who had done so much to get America into Vietnam. The cease-fire came into effect five days later. Fifty-eight thousand Americans had died in the conflict, as well as perhaps two million Vietnamese. About one million tons of bombs had been dropped on North Vietnam—far less, ironically, than the four million tons that fell on South Vietnam. (For comparison, the United States had dropped two million tons of bombs on Germany, Italy, and Japan in the whole of World War II.)[35] But three days after his inauguration for a second term on January 20th, Nixon could announce that "we have concluded an agreement to end the war and bring peace with honor in Vietnam and in Southeast Asia."[36] The last part was blatantly untrue: the Paris accords did not resolve the continuing conflicts in Laos and Cambodia. And the first part was dubious at best: although Thieu remained in the south, so did 100,000 North Vietnamese troops. But these were problems for the future. What mattered now was that U.S. troops were no longer engaged. Nixon's approval rating of 68 percent, rivaled that in the early months of his presidency. As his second term began, without the incubus of Vietnam, Nixon seemed free to reshape world affairs from a position of strength.

West Germany Looks East

The early 1970s also saw dramatic changes in the patterns of power in Europe. The most momentous concerned Germany. Although the basic division between East and West remained, détente agreements centering on Germany built bridges between the two blocs.

The German Democratic Republic (GDR) now seemed a fact of life. The Berlin wall had sealed off its citizens from escape. In the mid-1960s, they prospered economically while political freedoms were reined in. Although there was a good deal of popular unrest in 1968, particularly among the young, it was largely spontaneous and (unlike in Czechoslovakia) enjoyed no support from the unified, hard-line leadership.[37] It was difficult for many in the Federal Republic (FRG) to accept the situation. The Christian Democrats (CDU) and their Christian Socialist allies (CSU) in Bavaria, supported by millions who had been expelled from postwar Poland and Czechoslovakia, refused to acknowledge the new borders or to recognize the GDR. There was some change in the CDU's position after Adenauer's retirement in 1963, including increased economic contacts. But throughout the 1966–1969 Great Coalition between the CDU/CSU and the Social Democrats (SPD), the majority CDU rejected substantive negotiations with the GDR or the Soviet Union.

By the late 1960s, the international situation made such intransigence difficult to sustain. The superpowers were moving toward détente, the Russians were keen to improve trade with West Germany, and the Americans had tired of Bonn's obduracy about Berlin. But, as with relations within the Big Three triangle of America, Russia, and China, so German détente required shifts in domestic politics to facilitate changes in foreign policy. In Bonn, the turning point was the Bundestag elections of September 1969. Although these left the CDU as the largest single party, the SPD gained just enough seats to forge a coalition with the Free Democrats (FDP), whose swing to the left in the late 1960s precluded alliance with the CDU. Despite doubts within the SPD, its leader, Willy Brandt (1913–1992), moved decisively to negotiate with the FDP. On October 21, he was elected German's first Social

Democratic chancellor since 1928. One day earlier, Nixon had agreed to start SALT talks with the Russians.

Brandt signified a new era. He was relaxed and charismatic—sometimes described as the German version of John F. Kennedy (with all that this implied). The illegitimate son of a Lübeck salesgirl, he became an ardent socialist and sought refuge in Norway after Hitler came to power. He did not take up German citizenship again until 1947. Unlike many in the CDU, he therefore had an unblemished record during the Third Reich. Further, as an easterner, he shared little of the emotional commitment of Catholic Rhinelanders like Adenauer (and later Helmut Kohl) to links with France. Indeed, as the SPD mayor of Berlin when the wall was erected, Brandt felt passionately about the fate of his countrymen in the GDR. Instead of insisting, like CDU diehards, that détente must follow reunification, he gave priority to the former, as part of a new European Peace Order. The object, said Egon Bahr, Brandt's Kissinger, was "change through rapprochement," on the grounds that "small steps are better than none" (a pun in German—"kleine Schritte sind besser als keine"). This meant grasping the nettle and talking to both Moscow and East Berlin, in other words, recognizing the hard reality of an East German state with borders that excluded a quarter of the prewar Reich.[38] In the words of Walter Scheel, the FDP leader and Brandt's foreign minister, their policy started with "the situation as it is . . . It does not say whether something is good or not."[39]

The first phase of Brandt's diplomacy was addressed mainly to the GDR's eastern allies. In February 1970 Soviet and West German negotiators concluded a complex deal to build a natural gas pipeline from the USSR, using German technology and German credits. Bahr and Scheel then hammered out the basis of a political settlement. In the Moscow treaty of August 12, 1970, both governments renounced the use of force and declared the existing borders in Europe to be "inviolable" (unverletzlich)—the Germans having rejected the adjective "unalterable" (unveränderbar) which would have precluded eventual peaceful change.[40] Whatever the words, however, they were accepting the reality of the 1945 Oder-Neisse border between Poland and the GDR and thus the loss of most of old Prussia and Pomerania (map 7). In December 1970, Brandt signed a similar agreement with Poland. His visit to Warsaw movingly illustrated how facing the future meant coming to terms with the past, as many young Germans had been insisting against the "silent generation" of their parents. Six million Poles, including almost all of Polish Jewry, had died at Nazi hands. At the memorial to the Warsaw Ghetto, Brandt dropped to his knees. In the words of one reporter: "Then he knelt, he who has no need to, on behalf of all who ought to kneel but don't." It was a photo of silent eloquence (Plate 32), like the Nixon-Zhou handshake in Beijing fourteen months later, which sped round the world. Yet many German conservatives were angry and ashamed. To them Brandt spoke on TV that evening. The treaty, he said, "surrenders nothing that was not gambled away long ago—gambled away not by us . . . but by a criminal regime."[41]

In Bonn's diplomatic lexicon, Ostpolitik, or eastern policy, was distinct from Deutschlandpolitik, or relations with the East Berlin regime. But in practice, the two could not be separated, and progress on both issues required a political shift in the GDR as well as in the FRG.[42] East Germany's veteran leader, Walter Ulbricht (aged seventy-six by the time Brandt came to power), continued to take a hard line on any talks with Bonn. He demanded full diplomatic recognition, which would have violated the FRG's commitment to eventual reunification—to the growing displeasure of Moscow, as moves toward superpower détente gathered speed. After disturbances in Poland in December 1970 that threatened to spill over into the GDR, Ulbricht's colleagues, with Moscow's undisguised backing, began to ease him from power. In May 1971, after nearly eighteen years in power, he was replaced as party secretary by Erich Honecker (1912–1994). Like Brandt, though in a different way, Honecker had suffered for his left-wing principles, spending a decade in Berlin prisons as a young communist until freed by the Russians in 1945. Unlike Brandt, however, his image was that of a colorless functionary. Although the new government still anticipated "the victory of socialism in all countries and also in the Federal Republic," Honecker dropped Ulbricht's oposition to détente and talked mostly about East Germany as a fully independent "socialist nation."[43]

Ulbricht's departure eased negotiations on Berlin, and the Soviets accelerated the pace after news of Kissinger's visit to China in July 1971. In September an agreement on the Berlin question was signed by the four Allied occupying powers—the USA, the USSR, Britain, and France—which still had responsibility for the city in the absence of a postwar peace treaty. The West implicitly acknowledged East Berlin as the GDR's capital and agreed to play down the FRG's presence in the city (for example, by not holding the election of the federal president there). But the quid pro quo was substantially improved access rights from West Germany to West Berlin and for West Berliners into East Berlin and the GDR. These were fleshed out in detailed agreements between the two German states in December 1971. Brezhnev, however, insisted that Soviet ratification of the Berlin agreements would depend on prior approval by the FRG Bundestag of the unpopular Moscow treaty on the German-Polish border. This created a storm in Bonn, where the SPD/FDP's narrow ten-seat majority was fast eroding. The CDU/CSU leader, Rainer Barzel, calculated that he had secured enough FDP votes to replace the chancellor in a "constructive vote of no confidence." But on April 27, 1972, he fell two votes short. In the welter of bribery and arm twisting on both sides, the SPD had won back an FDP defector and detached four members of the CDU.[44] The affair poisoned Bonn politics for years, but Brandt had survived. On May 17, 1972, most of the divided CDU/CSU abstained in votes on the treaties about Poland, allowing them to be ratified comfortably. Nine days later the SALT treaty was signed in Moscow, and on June 3 the Berlin agreements were confirmed. And in elections in November 1972, Brandt exploited the popularity of Ostpolitik to win himself a substantial Bundestag majority.

Having seen off his domestic critics, Brandt was able to conclude the greatest prize—agreement with East Germany. This was initialed on November 8, eleven days before the elections, with Brandt rushing for a political coup and the GDR leaders anxious to avoid tougher terms if the CDU won. The "Treaty on the Basis of Relations" (*Grundlagenvertrag*) fudged many of the big issues. The FRG did not extend *de jure* recognition, exchanging "permanent representatives" instead of ambassadors. By maintaining his policy of "two states, one nation," Brandt kept open the goal of eventual reunification. But the Soviets and the GDR had gained *de facto* recognition of the East German state as well as acknowledgment of its eastern borders. The treaty was ratified over the votes of most of the CDU/CSU and Brezhnev paid the first visit by any Soviet leader to West Germany in May 1973. There he made clear the USSR's keenness for Western trade and technology, telling astonished business leaders, "We are looking for new cooperation agreements for 30, 40 and 50 years." As an example of West German technology, Brezhnev was given a Mercedes sports car to enhance his automobile collection. Delighted, he roared off for a test drive, to the consternation of his security guards.[45]

The German treaties were hard to negotiate and even harder to implement. "Previously we had no relations," said Egon Bahr in 1973. Now "we will have bad ones, and this is progress. It will be a long time before we have better ones."[46] In line with Bahr's goal of change through rapprochement, the hope was that greater east-west contacts would ameliorate life for East Germans and gradually undermine the GDR. A web of small agreements was intended to span the two parts of the German *Kulturnation*—from mail and phones to operation of West Berlin's S-Bahn railways, still run by an authority in the east. Above all, people could move to and fro with less harassment. In 1969, there were one million visits from West Germany to the GDR; by 1975 the figure was four million. Another four million visits were made between West and East Berlin, where the wall had previously blocked all contact.[47] Each visit chipped away at the GDR policy of *Abgrenzung*, or strict segregation of East Germany from the west. In the short term, however, détente stabilized the GDR. The new credits and trade from the FRG, gifts such as those to Protestant churches in the GDR, not to mention the "welcome money" extracted in hard currency from all visitors—in these and many other ways, West Germany helped keep East Germany going.

Détente had a similar effect throughout the Soviet bloc, especially in Poland, where the government of Wladyslaw Gomulka had failed to develop even the limited consumer socialism of Kádár's Hungary. The ailing Polish leader was deposed during the strikes of December 1970. His successor, Edward Gierek, made a determined effort to quell persistent worker unrest through consumer-led economic growth. In this task, Gierek naturally looked west: his father had migrated there and Gierek spent his early years in France and Belgium as a coal miner and union official. Starting in 1971, massive imports of capitalist technology, financed by credits from the FRG and other Western countries, enabled Poland to modernize its plant and expand consumer industries. By the mid-1970s it had the third fastest growing economy in the world. But it also had a foreign debt of $6.4 billion, nine times that of 1971.[48] The pattern was similar, if less extreme, in other parts of Eastern Europe—import—led growth funded by the debts of détente.

Détente facilitated a larger European settlement.[49] Since the mid-1960s, the Warsaw Pact countries had been demanding a European Security Conference. Its focus would be political; its aim to recognize the two Germanies, dissolve the two alliances, and thus force the United States out of Europe. The West was more concerned about the military balance. Since 1967, NATO had been pushing for talks about the reduction of forces in Europe, in part to head off growing pressure in the U.S. Congress, orchestrated by Senator Mike Mansfield, for unilateral American withdrawals. At the Moscow summit in May 1972, the two superpowers agreed to proceed on both the political and military fronts. A preparatory Conference on Security and Cooperation in Europe (CSCE) opened in Helsinki that November, while exploratory talks about Mutual and Balanced Force Reductions (MBFR) in Europe started in Vienna the following January. The latter plodded on throughout the 1970s, plagued by mutual distrust and disputed data. But the CSCE talks resulted in agreements signed by thirty-five nations at Helsinki at the end of July 1975. The various proposals had been placed in three "baskets." The first two contained commitments to the "inviolability" of all European frontiers plus a collection of agreements on economic and technological cooperation. These confirmed the Soviet position in Eastern Europe and enlarged the access to capitalism by which communism could be sustained. But in return, the Soviets had to accept the contents of Basket Three—commitments on freedom of speech, information, and travel, which, as communist leaders feared, would offer limited but vital protection for dissidents. Like the intra-German agreements and Eastern Europe's foreign debts, Helsinki's Basket Three was another time bomb ticking away under the shored-up Soviet bloc (see Chapter 15).

Western Europe Looks North and South

While Central and Eastern Europe were reshaped, Western Europe was also in flux. The European Community began a more dynamic phase with new northern members (including Britain) and plans for deeper integration. In 1974–1975, the demise of autocratic regimes in Greece, Portugal, and Spain ushered in the democratization of southern Europe.

Again, 1969 was a decisive year. The logjams within the European Community broke after de Gaulle's resignation in April. His successor as president was Georges Pompidou, the former prime minister whom de Gaulle had made the scapegoat for the troubles of May 1968. Pompidou took the initiative to "relaunch" the community at a summit of the Six in The Hague in December 1969. With some justice, the European Commission called this "a turning point in its history."[50] Pompidou, with warm support from Brandt— always anxious to show that "our Ostpolitik is based on our Westpolitik"[51]— secured agreement in three main areas, known in EC jargon as completion, deepening, and enlargement. The first referred particularly to the community's budget, previously funded by ad hoc contributions from the member states. By 1970 it had been agreed that levies on food imports and certain other national revenues would constitute the EC's "own resources," accruing automatically to Brussels. "Deepening" signified further integration among the Six. Committees set up at the Hague summit drew up plans for cooperation on foreign policy and for monetary union by 1980. Most important, however, was enlargement. This meant reopening the issue of British membership, blocked by de Gaulle throughout the 1960s (see Chapter 6).

Pompidou did not share de Gaulle's visceral suspicion of the British. In fact, he saw Britain as a balance to a strong West Germany that was tilting, perhaps alarmingly, to the east. But that did not make it easy to resolve issues such as Britain's budget contribution and its agricultural ties with the Commonwealth. What mattered in these negotiations, as in others in the early 1970s, was a change of political leadership. In the election of June 1970 Edward Heath's Conservatives defeated Harold Wilson and the incumbent Labour party. Heath was unique among postwar British premiers in being fervently committed to Europe. At a summit in Paris in May 1971, he satisfied Pompidou of his European credentials, and French negotiators were told to be more accommodating about the remaining obstacles.[52] By the end of June terms for British entry had been agreed. To convince domestic opinion, Heath's government played up the geopolitical arguments for entry: saying "no" would mean that "in a single generation we should have renounced an Imperial past and rejected a European future."[53] The probable economic costs of membership through higher food prices and heavy budget contributions were glossed over: Heath hoped that, once Britain was inside, he could redress the community's dominance by agricultural interests. In October 1971, Heath won a Commons majority of 112 for British entry, with most of the Labour party voting against. Following in Britain's wake were two close trading partners, Ireland and Denmark. The Norwegian government, which had also negotiated entry terms, was narrowly repudiated by its own voters in a referendum in September 1972, after a passionate debate that scarred Norwegian politics for years to come. On January 1, 1973, Britain, Denmark, and Ireland joined the European Community. The Six had become the Nine.

The mood in Brussels in the early 1970s was therefore one of heady optimism. Europe (or at least the EC's part of it) seemed on the move again. But the euphoria was short lived. The main reason was the oil crisis and ensuing inflation, which crippled the European economies for the rest of the decade. (Their impact will be examined in Chapter 12.) Nor did Britain's entry have the desired galvanic effects. Heath fell in February 1974, and Wilson was once again preoccupied with holding together his feuding party. To appease the left, he engaged in cosmetic renegotiation of Britain's terms of entry and then put the issue to a referendum in June 1975. This won him a two-to-one majority but, since only 64 percent of the electorate voted, it meant that a mere 43 percent of British voters had given positive support. Britain remained a lukewarm and marginal "European." And although a European monetary system did come into existence in 1979 (without Britain), this was mainly a framework for keeping exchange rates in line. It was a far cry from full monetary union.

The most significant démarches were in European political cooperation, where twice-yearly summits of heads of government became the norm. Increasingly, these meetings (known as the European Council) set policy for the community over the heads of bureaucrats in the European Commission. From the mid-1970s, the council also became the framework for a new Franco-German axis. Pompidou lost the presidential election in May 1974, just weeks after an embattled Brandt resigned as chancellor following revelations that a close aide was an East German spy. The two new leaders in Paris and Bonn, Valéry Giscard d'Estaing and Helmut Schmidt, struck up a warm personal relationship. This was maintained by phone calls and informal visits as well as regular summitry, though ironically their lingua franca was English.[54] After de Gaulle's isolation and Brandt's preoccupation with the East, Giscard and Schmidt were keen to make Paris and Bonn the main axis of West European politics.

The mid-1970s also saw winds of change blowing across southern Europe. In northwest Europe and also Italy, multiparty democracies were the norm by 1970; the Eastern European pattern was stable one-party states with the army firmly under political control. But in southeast and southwest Europe, like much of Africa and Latin America, democracy was either fragile or nonexistent, and the military played a decisive role in politics. The 1970s proved a critical decade in the transition to stable democracy for Turkey, Greece, Spain, and Portugal.[55]

Modern Turkey did not fit most of the normal categories of international affairs. Its population was overwhelmingly Muslim, yet it had been a secular republic since Mustafa Kemal Atatürk saved the remnants of the Ottoman empire from partition after World War I. Although geographically in Asia, not Europe, Turkey had been a member of NATO since 1952. Its army, over three hundred thousand, was the second largest in the alliance, playing a vital role on NATO's southern flank. And although Atatürk established the foundations of a liberal democracy, the army remained close to power, befitting an institution that had often run the Ottoman empire and had also been the main instigator of reform, as in 1876 and 1908. Until his death in 1938, Atatürk ran the country autocratically through his Republican People's party (RPP). After the Second World War, in which Turkey remained neutral, President Ismet Inönü acknowledged the demise of fascism by permitting other parties to operate. In 1950 the Democracy party won power on a wave of resentment at twenty-seven years of RPP rule. But the DP simply used the same repressive political system to advance economic modernization and also its own gain. In May 1960, dissident junior officers toppled the government; its leaders, including premier Adnan Menderes, were hanged. A new, liberalized constitution was approved in 1961. But when the Justice party, successor to the DP, failed to control the wave of strikes and student militancy that nearly paralyzed the country by the end of the 1960s, the army intervened again. In March 1971, prime minister Süleiman Demirel was forced to resign, a new government was installed, and the constitution made less liberal. During the 1970s, Turkish politics became polarized between the resurgent Demirel, a former engineer from a peasant family, and Bülent Ecevit, the charismatic, American-educated journalist who took over the RPP in 1973. With spiraling terrorism from political extremists as well as regional minorities, the army deposed Demirel again in September 1980 and ruled until elections in 1983.[56]

The pattern, it seemed, was clear, even neat: military intervention once every decade (1960, 1971, 1980) because Turkish democracy was still feeble. There had been one prime minister between 1950 and 1960, three from 1961 to 1971, and eight ministries in the years 1971–1975.[57] Yet beneath the periodic upheavals, democracy was putting down roots. Some of Turkey's problems were institutional: the autocracy of RPP and DP rule reflected a winner-take-all voting system that, like the U.S. electoral college, translated narrow popular majorities into a vast superiority in parliamentary seats. An extreme form of proportional representation was imposed as a corrective in the constitution of 1961, but this helped produced the ensuing paralysis.[58] Moreover, the decadal military interventions were not the same, as implied by the tags "colonels' coup" for 1960 and "generals' coup" for 1980. After the first, reminiscent of the Young Turks of 1908, senior commanders took tighter hold of the army. Subsequent interventions were mounted from the very top by generals who retained operational control.[59] Above all, these interventions were not full-scale coups but corrective actions that were followed by renewed civilian rule. This reflected the fact that by the late 1970s Turkey was "too complex a society to function without politics."[60] Economic development and social change had created a profusion of competing groups in a country where, by 1973, industry contributed more than agriculture to GNP and the urban populace (40 percent in all) were mostly Westernized consumers. Turkey's problems were profound, but they were being addressed within a political framework.

Even in the 1960s, Greece was still haunted by the savage civil war of 1946–1949, when communist guerrillas were defeated with U.S. and British help. Greece, like Turkey, joined NATO in 1952. Anticommunism became the foundation of Greek foreign policy and the talisman of the conservative political establishment, which ran the country through shifting coalitions into the 1960s. The February 1964 election was therefore a milestone in postwar Greek politics. The large majority won by George Papandreou's Progressive Center Union party (EK) ushered in Greece's first postwar government of the left. The EK was, however, an unstable coalition; both the army and the new, assertive monarch, twenty-three-year-old Constantine II, feared a lurch to the left. The king dismissed Papandreou in July 1965, but five alternative premiers failed to form stable governments in 1965–1967. With elections scheduled for May 1967 and victory likely for the increasingly radical EK, a group of junior army officers seized power on April 21.[61]

The new government was reluctantly sworn in by the king, conferring legitimacy on men who were soon trimming his own powers. After an abortive attempt to raise loyal army units against the junta, Constantine fled the country in December. Thereafter the patina of civilian rule was stripped away. The colonels, headed by George Papadopoulos, drew up a new constitution, suspending most civil liberties and allowing only a token parliament. Long hair for men and miniskirts for women were banned; in secret, dissidents were imprisoned and often tortured. Economic growth was accompanied by soaring inflation, over 30 percent during 1973. Growing student unrest resulted in at least twenty deaths when army tanks ended a sit-in at Athens Polytechnic that November. Junta colleagues used the wave of revulsion to remove the increasingly autocratic Papadopoulos, who had abolished the monarchy and named himself president earlier in the year. But, although shaky, the junta was still in command—until it committed suicide over Cyprus.

Although Greece and Turkey were officially allies in NATO, the Greeks had never forgiven their years within the Turkish empire. Both governments had rival territorial claims in the eastern Mediterranean. The island of Cyprus was a microcosm of these problems. Its population of six hundred thousand was four-fifths Greek and one-fifth Turkish. The Greek-Cypriot leadership, headed by Archbishop Makarios, had long espoused *enosis,* or union with Greece, for which its military arm, EOKA, had fought a vicious terrorist campaign against British rule in the 1950s. In the end, Makarios was persuaded that the Turks would not allow *enosis.* He accepted simple independence in 1960, with two British base areas remaining in perpetuity and substantial autonomy for both communities. Plans for a loose national government soon proved unworkable and after communal violence in 1963–1964 a UN presence was introduced to help keep the peace. A decade later, the embattled Athens junta turned again to *enosis* to boost its popularity. But the coup in Cyprus on July 15, 1974, using Greek-Cypriot units, misfired and Makarios escaped. Five days later Ecevit sent in troops to protect the Turkish people. The junta, totally unprepared, ordered military mobilization but then reversed itself a day later, admitting the army was not ready for war. Even if it had been, Greece's nine million people had little chance against a country of thirty-five million, with a far larger army only one hundred miles from the Cyprus coast.

The Cyprus fiasco was the immediate cause of the junta's demise. The humiliation was transparent, popular anger intense. But the transition to civilian rule was orchestrated by the military itself.[62] On July 23, the president, General Phaedon Gizikis, invited Constantine Karamanlis, the premier for most of the period 1955–1963, to return from exile in Paris and form a new civilian government. That night Athens was a cacaphony of car horns, and thousands of people descended on the airport to greet their new leader. But in the absence of any settlement in Cyprus, the Turks mounted a full-scale invasion on August 14, occupying the northeastern third of the island before a U.S. brokered ceasefire was imposed. The so-called Green Line, drawn in colored pen across the map from northwest to southeast, bisected the capital, Nicosia, where sandbags, barbed wire and no man's land evoked in miniature the division of Berlin. Talks got nowhere, mainly because, after Ecevit's fall in September 1974, no Turkish government enjoyed the power and popularity to be flexible about such a national triumph.[63] The crisis also aggravated other Greco-Turkish feuds, notably over oil exploration rights in the Aegean, and both sides strengthened their garrisons on key coasts and islands.[64] July 1974 confirmed another durable and dangerous partition line in international politics.

Greece's democratic transition was in large part the achievement of Constantine Karamanlis, premier from 1974 to 1980 and then president until 1985. Once back in Athens, he immediately revoked the 1968 constitution and ended martial law, preparing the way for democratic elections, which his New Democracy party won handily. His strategy was to neutralize the anti-Democratic right—both by purging the army and abolishing the monarchy through a plebiscite—and to domesticate the left through a new constitution that removed most of the restrictions dating from the civil war era.[65] But Karamanlis could never decide whether he was a national or a party leader: his New Democracy, like most previous Greek political parties, was an alliance of regional magnates, with a vague ideology, under a charismatic leader. Support for it in 1974 reflected a simple choice articulated by the composer Mikis Theodorakis: "It's Karamanlis or the tanks."[66]

It was through the new socialist party, PASOK, that Greek democracy came of age. PASOK not only brought the left into mainstream politics, it was also Greece's first noncommunist mass party with extensive grass-roots organization and support. New Democracy was forced to follow suit at its party congress in 1979. Clientage networks still mattered, of course, and the fact that PASOK's leader was Andreas Papandreou, son of George, testified to the continued cult of personality. But even before PASOK surged to power in the 1981 election, democracy in Greece had a new and much surer foundation.

Portugal's democratic transition also followed disaster abroad in 1974. Previously, Portugal had been a byword for stability.[67] It was the oldest nation-state in Europe, with borders almost unchanged since the thirteenth century, and it had no significant linguistic, racial, or religious minorities. After Salazar took complete control in 1933, Portugal had experienced four decades of political autocracy, continued after his stroke in 1968 under Marcello Caetano. But, as we saw in Chapter 6, Salazar's Portugal was also the most obstinate European defender of empire, fighting a rearguard action against insurgency in Guiné, Angola, and Mozambique for most of the 1960s. It was a debilitating struggle. A country the area of Scotland, with a population comparable to that of greater London (nine million), was trying to hold down an African empire twenty times its size. By 1968 the wars absorbed 40 percent of the national budget, and the conscript army was demoralized. Many soldiers had become infected by their captured enemies with leftist ideas about national revolution. Beginning in 1968, General António de Spínola had some success in Guiné, initiating local reforms and boosting army morale, but when he publicly expressed support for a political solution, blasting the "old hermits" in government who had ruined the country with "an eternal prolongation of the war," Caetano sacked him in March 1974.[68] Spínola became a rallying point for the Armed Forces Movement (MFA), a disparate group of perhaps three hundred junior officers, some anxious to restore the army's self-respect, others hopeful of reforming Portugal.

Headed by Major Otelo de Carvalho, the MFA removed Caetano on April 25, 1974 in an almost bloodless coup and installed their superiors, headed by Spínola, as a "Junta of National Salvation." As a symbol of their peaceful intentions, troops handed out carnations in the streets. In the days following the Carnation Revolution, exiled politicians flocked back to Lisbon. The first cabinet spanned the political spectrum, including two communists. The Portuguese Communist party (PCP), which had existed as an underground opposition since the 1920s, spread rapidly after the coup and claimed a membership of 115,000 by the end of 1976. Against ill-organized rivals, it was well placed to exploit the political confusion.[69]

The turmoil that ensued over the next eighteen months had several causes. One was a power struggle between junior officers in the MFA and the army command, headed by Spínola, whose underlying conservatism was typified by his monocle and riding crop. The MFA, allied with the communists, espoused increasingly radical policies, including the destruction of capitalism and immediate decolonization. Spínola was obliged to concede immediate independence for the African colonies in July 1974 and, after an abortive attempt to seize full power in March 1975, he fled the country. But the radicalism of the MFA and its communist allies was now polarizing the country. In the poor Alentejo region of the south, the PCP encouraged tenants to seize the large estates. Several million acres changed hands during 1975 in one of the biggest agrarian reforms of postwar Western Europe. New land laws that summer legitimized what had happened.[70] Such an upheaval was anathema to the more conservative north, where small holdings, not large estates, predominated. Encouraged by the Catholic Church, northern farmers mobilized during 1975 against the PCP and the MFA, and there was growing popular violence.

Out of this crisis, two forces for democratic stability emerged. One was the Socialist party (PS) under Mário Soares, who broke his initial alliance with the PCP and campaigned in the April 1975 elections on the platform "Socialism, yes! Dictatorship, no!" While other parties polarized around the right-left, north-south divide, the Socialists came out on top with 38 percent of the vote spread fairly evenly across the country. This set a pattern, and the PS emerged as both the most popular single party and the one occupying an acceptable middle ground. The other critical development, as in Turkey and Greece, was restored army discipline. With Lisbon almost ungovernable in November 1975, moderate army officers finally moved against the MFA, disbanding its organizations. Their leader, Colonel Ramalho Eanes, quickly

rose to be army chief of staff. In June 1976 Eanes became Portugal's first democratically elected president for half a century. He invited Soares to form
a coalition government; the PS leader remained premier for the next two
years.

In the words of one historian, "What started as a coup became a revolution
which was stopped by a reaction before it became an anarchy. Out of the tu-
mult a democracy was born."[71] Admittedly, democratic politics remained
febrile. Portugal had fifteen governments between April 1974 and the summer of 1983. Opinion polls indicated continued public ignorance and growing apathy. Yet the fluid coalitions after 1976 allowed much of the new
political elite, except the communists, to experience office. And the firm but
constitutional use of presidential power by Eanes, who was reelected for a
second five-year term in 1980, checked the centrifugalism of Assembly politics.[72] Although the party system was less mature than in Greece, Portugal
had accomplished its democratic transition.

Alarm at the turmoil in Portugal was one reason that neighboring Spain
moved peacefully out of the Franco era following the death of the old dictator on November 20, 1975.[73] But the potential for violence was considerable,
with labor militancy, popular protest, and the Basque region close to open revolt. That it was avoided was due, in part, to the skill of two men, the thirty-
seven-year-old king, Juan Carlos, and his chosen premier after July 1976,
Adolfo Suarez. Since Juan Carlos was Franco's designated heir and Suarez
the secretary general of the Francoist National Movement, they seemed unlikely reformers. But the new monarch had no intention of going the way of
his brother-in-law, the deposed king Constantine of Greece. He backed
Suarez's policy of reform from above, as the premier used Francoist institutions to dismantle Francoism while persuading the left to abandon its calls
for a total break with the past in favor of a negotiated rupture (ruptura
pactada). Suarez's proposals for a Constituent Assembly elected by universal suffrage were overwhelmingly approved in the referendum of December
1976; other political parties, including socialists and communists, were legalized over the next few months; and Spain's first free elections for forty
years passed off peacefully in June 1977. Suarez served as premier until January 1981. Only then did parts of the army make a move, when Colonel Antonio Tejero took over the lower house of parliament on February 23. His
coup failed when Juan Carlos, as commander in chief, appealed to loyal army
officers.

Yet the combination of Juan Carlos and Suarez—like Eanes and Soares in
Portugal—is only part of the story. The Spanish army was a very different animal from its neighbor. After its triumph in the civil war, it had not fought
again in earnest, because Franco allowed Spain's African empire to go without a fight in the 1950s. The army was therefore not radicalized by defeat,

unlike Portugal's. In contrast to the military in Turkey or Brazil, it was not a modernizing force but a lethargic garrison soldiery with neither incentive nor will to intervene politically. Furthermore, behind the Francoist facade, Spain had been radically changed by the economic modernization of the 1950s and 1960s. It was the tenth largest capitalist economy in the world; two-thirds of the population was urban. Unions were already legitimate, universities had become a haven for critical thought, and the post–Vatican II Catholic Church was a far cry from the crusading National Catholicism of the 1930s.[74] When Juan Carlos became head of state, the primate of Spain, Cardinal Vicente Tarancon, made clear that "the Christian faith is not a political ideology, nor can it be identified with any political ideology."[75]

Spain, in the contemporary cliché, remained a conditional democracy *(democracia vigilada):* legal reform from above meant that authoritarians remained entrenched within institutions like the civil service and the judiciary, and the weakness of the democratic right reflected the weakness of the commercial middle class in a country where modernization had also been imposed from above. Regional separatism remained acute, in contrast with more unified Portugal. But the unchallenged election of a socialist government in October 1982 showed how far Spain had moved in less than a decade.

There were many differences in the experience of these four countries. Greece and Turkey followed a longer path to democracy; in Portugal and Spain the rupture was more sudden and dramatic. In Greece and especially Portugal, the end of authoritarian rule followed bitter national humiliation, whereas in Spain the catalyst was the death of Franco, icon of the old order. But in all these countries, a dual underlying pattern was evident: gradual economic development had created the conditions for political pluralism, however precarious the multiparty systems might be.

In all four, there was also a larger aspiration—to become part of the larger West European world. Greece had had an association agreement with the EEC since 1962, but this had been denied to Spain and Portugal because of their autocracy. Full EC membership became a goal of all three, and later Turkey, for political as much as economic reasons. Karamanlis's main avowed aim as premier was "Europeanizing the Greeks," to restrain their obsessive nationalism. Likewise, Spaniards often quoted the dictum of the philosopher José Ortega y Gasset: "Spain is the problem, Europe is the solution."[76] (Twenty-five years earlier, Adenauer, Schuman, and de Gasperi had said much the same about Germany, France, and Italy.) In the 1970s, Karamanlis was the most successful at Europeanizing his country. Although the European Commission worried about the economic costs of Greek entry and about the backlash in Turkey, it was overruled by the Council of Ministers on political grounds: membership would consolidate Greece's transition to democracy. Many Socialists denounced the EC as "the other face of NATO" and campaigned on the slogan "Greece belongs to the Greeks," but New Democracy insisted "We belong to the West." Terms of entry were agreed in April 1979, and Greece joined the EC in January 1981.[77] Portugal and Spain applied in 1977 but their applications took much longer to settle, as we shall see, while Turkey's application was delayed for another decade because of the generals' coup in 1980. For all these states, however, becoming democracies and joining "Europe" were closely linked. The southern periphery was coming in from the cold.

America in Retreat, Détente in Decline

The reshaping of Europe was made possible by superpower détente. But that process continued even when Soviet-American relations deteriorated during the 1970s. At the same time, relations between Moscow and Beijing worsened as the two powers vied for influence in Southeast Asia in the wake of America's retreat. The late 1970s exposed the conflicting understandings of détente by all three major powers. It also highlighted the contrast in domestic politics: the Soviet leadership apparently stronger and more secure than in two decades; the People's Republic emerging at long last from the turmoil of Mao's endgame; the United States severely shaken by the aftershocks of Vietnam and, especially, Watergate.

As Nixon's biographer Stephen Ambrose has observed, the president did not directly order the break-in and bugging of the Democratic party's national headquarters on June 17, 1972, and "he almost certainly did not know of the operation in advance."[78] But Nixon created the atmosphere that encouraged his reelection campaigners to take such action: the relentless secrecy, the propensity for backchannel operations, the obsessive concern about press and political criticism that was reflected in vituperative comments scrawled on the daily news summaries—"freeze him," or "fight him," or "dump him."[79] And there is no doubt of the President's early involvement in the cover-up that followed the arrests at Watergate. On June 23 he agreed that aides should warn the FBI, "don't go any further into this case, period" on the spurious grounds that it involved the CIA and could prejudice U.S. foreign policy.[80] Managed by Nixon's special counsel, John W. Dean, the cover-up portrayed Watergate as a maverick act by overzealous operators on the fringe of the reelection campaign. Dean successfully kept the lid on the case until after the November 1972 election, but by March 1973 the Watergate defendants were ready to talk in return for lighter sentences. The White

House tried to buy them off. "How much money do you need?" the president asked Dean on March 21. "A million dollars over the next two years," was the reply. "We could get that," said Nixon.[81] But by the end of the month the press was claiming that culpability lay much higher; Dean, seeing that he would become the scapegoat, started talking secretly to Watergate prosecutors. To save himself, Nixon sacrificed his closest aides, Bob Haldeman and John Ehrlichman, on April 29. But privately he recognized the writing on the wall: "I've trapped myself," he told Haldeman on April 17, only three months after his second inaugural. As Dean observed, it was "a domino situation."[82]

Yet it was another fifteen months before the final domino, Nixon himself, would fall. A fighter all his life, he conducted a dogged rearguard action on two fronts—against the Democratic-controlled Congress, now in full cry with televised hearings, and Archibald Cox, the independent special prosecutor that Nixon had been forced to concede because of indications that the Justice Department itself was implicated in Watergate.

Ironically, though, it was Nixon who sealed his own fate. In July an aide admitted to Congress that Nixon had installed a voice-activated taping system to record all his conversations. This most secretive of presidents was apparently anxious to document his every word, in preparation for eventual memoirs. The tapes then became the prime issue between the president and his adversaries, especially the indefatigable Cox. On October 20, 1973, the attorney general and his deputy resigned rather than follow Nixon's order and fire the special prosecutor. Cox was eventually dismissed by the solicitor general, but the public outcry at this "Saturday Night Massacre" obliged Nixon to accept a new special prosecutor with wider powers, and to surrender nine tapes. This only fueled further demands. In April 1974, he released another forty-two tapes and made public edited (but still embarrassing) transcripts. Within a week, two best-selling paperback versions had appeared, with damning effect on Nixon's popularity. Using this evidence, the staff of the House Judiciary Committee prepared the case for impeachment (among them a young Yale Law School graduate named Hillary Rodham). This constitutional provision for trying a president for "treason, bribery or other high crimes and misdemeanors" had only been used once before, unsuccessfully, in 1868. But at the end of July the Judiciary Committee approved the articles of impeachment, and the Supreme Court rejected Nixon's final effort to withhold subpoenaed tapes. Release of the June 23, 1972, transcript—the so-called smoking gun—sealed Nixon's fate. With Republican support in Congress collapsing, he resigned on August 9 to avoid the inevitable. In a final, tearful speech to loyal staff, he told them, "Always remember, others may hate you, but those who hate you don't win unless you hate them, and then you destroy yourself."[83] If Nixon had followed his own precepts, he might have avoided self-destruction.

Most of the world watched in bemusement as the Watergate drama unfolded. It seemed incredible that the world's most powerful leader could be toppled by what seemed like a minor burglary and its concealment. Certainly it made no sense in either Beijing or Moscow, where far graver breaches of civil liberty were routine and any political backlash inconceivable. "Too much freedom of expression," muttered Mao, who blamed Nixon's downfall on American "warmongers."[84] The Kremlin, likewise, assumed that the furor was part of a counterattack against détente by American hardliners. Brezhnev, an impulsive man, sent several messages of encouragement to the beleaguered president, in marked contrast to the silence of most West European leaders.[85]

The standard defense of Nixon is that bypassing Congress, the bureaucracy, and the media was necessary for foreign policy success, because the U.S. political system, in which power is deliberately packaged out, frustrates vigorous executive leadership. As Kissinger put it, "His administrative approach was weird and its human cost unattractive, yet history must also record the fundamental fact that major successes were achieved that had proved unattainable by conventional procedures."[86] There is some truth in this contention, but one could equally say that, through their secrecy and deception, Nixon and Kissinger failed to establish a strong domestic consensus behind their policies. Had their undoubted successes "been attained through more conventional procedures and less sleight of hand," writes one historian, "they might have enjoyed greater staying power."[87]

This was particularly true in Indochina. Neither side in Vietnam had any intention of honoring the 1973 Paris accords, and fighting soon resumed. Nixon and Kissinger hoped to keep Thieu going through massive economic aid and the threat of U.S. air power in neighboring Thailand and the China seas. But a tide of press revelations about how Congress and the public had been deceived by Johnson and Nixon, plus the mounting anger at Watergate, prompted a backlash on Capitol Hill against what historian Arthur Schlesinger dubbed "the imperial presidency." As of August 15, 1973, Congress banned any U.S. military operations on or over Indochina. In November the War Powers Act placed a sixty-day limit on troop deployment overseas without Congressional consent. And military aid to South Vietnam was trimmed from $2.3 billion in 1973 to $1 billion in 1974. Lacking U.S. air power, and starved of fuel and ammunition, Thieu's high-tech army was virtually paralyzed.

Yet sustained American help would not have altered the basic fact that South Vietnam was a corrupt and demoralized state, held together by military rule—"not a country with an army but an army with a country," in the words of one U.S. officer.[88] By 1974 one-fifth of the civilian work force was unemployed, inflation was running at 65 percent, and desertion from the army was rife. The North Vietnamese offensive in March 1975 succeeded beyond their wildest dreams. When Thieu ordered evacuation of the central highlands, retreat turned into rout. DRV troops drove south, through places like Pleiku and Hué that, seven years before, had been described as vital for the survival of the free world, and raced toward Saigon. Thousands of South Vietnamese, Thieu among them, fled the country. The last U.S. helicopter took off from the roof of the U.S. embassy just before 8:00 A.M. on April 30, 1975. Beneath it, would-be evacuees tried to break through the barricaded stairwell, while other Vietnamese looted the building. Around noon, DRV tanks bulldozed the gates of the presidential palace; within minutes the National Liberation Front flag flew from the flagpole.

The rest of Indochina soon followed. In Laos, a fragile cease-fire had held in early 1973, allowing the rival factions to form a coalition government. But in the wake of the DRV victory in Vietnam, the communist Pathet Lao resumed its offensive and took control of the country by the end of August 1975. Cambodia's agony was far worse. There was no cease-fire after the Paris accords: although the Cambodian government army was falling apart, the communist PCK had now turned on the Vietnamese. Nixon continued bombing until the deadline of August 15, 1973, imposed by Congress. Over 250,000 tons of bombs fell on Cambodia in 1973, *after* he had declared peace in Indochina—more than the United States dropped on Japan in 1941–1945.[89] The main effect of the bombing was to accelerate the flood of refugees into Phnom Penh, the capital. In January 1975, the communists began their final offensive, with weeks of indiscriminate rocket attacks, before the city fell on April 17. Since the end of Cambodia's tenuous neutrality in 1970—with Sihanouk's overthrow and Nixon's intervention—half a million Cambodians had died. Although Nixon could legitimately claim that Vietnam was Johnson's war, Cambodia was all his own.

By mid-1975, therefore, communist governments were in power in all three countries of Indochina. Thailand—under factional civilian rule since October 1973—seemed to be going the same way, until the military installed its own government again in October 1976. As we shall see later, communist Indochina proved to be no monolith, but the fall of regimes on which the United States had expended so much money and blood was a devastating blow to its credibility as an ally. It called in question the "Nixon Doctrine" articulated in 1969 to justify U.S. retrenchment on the grounds that America would still offer its allies finance and hardware while they provided the troops. In 1971 the president had characterized Cambodia as "the Nixon Doctrine in its purest form."[90] He and Kissinger argued that the subsequent debacle was the fault of Congress, but that was hardly reassuring to allies across the world from Japan to Western Europe, already unsettled by the unheralded revolutions in U.S. diplomacy in 1972. After Saigon fell, the *Frank-*

furter Allgemeine Zeitung, a leading German paper, printed a front-page editorial headlined AMERICA—A HELPLESS GIANT.[91]

The debacles of Vietnam and Watergate also helped weaken the American presidency. From the spring of 1973, Nixon was preoccupied with political survival and had little left for foreign affairs. In June 1973 Brezhnev visited America, but returned with nothing of substance beyond an agreement on preventing nuclear war (and another automobile, this time a Lincoln Continental). Nixon's final trip to the Soviet Union the following summer made little progress on arms control, now a minor priority for the White House and consequently more vulnerable to Pentagon hawks. Nixon's successor was Gerald R. Ford, a long-time congressional politician who had only made it to the vice presidency because Spiro Agnew had resigned in October 1973 to avoid being prosecuted for accepting bribes. The full pardon Ford gave to Nixon damaged Ford's popularity, fueled suspicion of a prior deal, and may have contributed to the election victory of Jimmy Carter in November 1976.

Carter was an evangelical Christian and former governor of Georgia who had never served in Congress or the executive branch. Much of his success came from running as a self-professed outsider, untainted by Washington politics and intrigue. Carter made "human rights" a diplomatic priority, using it to judge ally and adversary alike. This was a matter of personal conviction, but it also acknowledged the public desire for a new morality in U.S. foreign policy. It also aspired to reunite his fragmented Democratic party by appealing to liberals disgusted by Vietnam and conservatives worried by détente.[92]

In contrast, the Soviet leadership seemed strong and coherent. Brezhnev had removed his main Politburo critic, Pyotr Shelest, before the May 1972 summit—partly for his obstreperous Ukrainian nationalism but mainly because of his opposition to détente. The following spring he brought his key allies Yuri Andropov, Andrei Gromyko, and Andrei Grechko into the Politburo—the first time in twenty years that the KGB chief plus the foreign and defense ministers had all been members. Yet Brezhnev remained first among equals, still working through consensus. He had sold détente to colleagues as an economic and political gain without significant loss. By the end of 1974 that argument was harder to sustain. In the U.S. Congress, a loose coalition of the Jewish lobby and anti détente conservatives successfully tied approval of the 1972 trade agreements to Soviet commitments on Jewish emigration in an early example of the "human rights" lever. No Soviet leader could countenance that kind of interference in domestic affairs, and the treaty lapsed. In November 1974 Ford and Brezhnev agreed on guidelines for a SALT II agreement, but the Americans refused to include in the equation their forward-bases systems in Europe (aircraft and shorter-range missiles). This was an issue on which the military, led by Marshal Grechko, had been emphatic. To appease them, Brezhnev approved a modernization program for Soviet intermediate-range missiles in Europe. At the top of the list was what the Americans called the SS-20.[93]

Both superpowers, then, had shaky internal support for their foreign policies. But the root problem was divergence in American and Soviet conceptions of détente. Kissinger believed that "the problem of our age is to manage the emergence of the Soviet Union as a superpower,"[94] which old-fashioned containment had failed to prevent. His answer was to enmesh the USSR in a new international order to restrain and eventually transform the Soviet system. For their part, Brezhnev and his colleagues never understood "peaceful coexistence" to mean acceptance of the status quo. Rather, by reducing the danger of nuclear war, it would allow the class struggle to continue more safely and swiftly toward the triumph of Marxism-Leninism. The apparent American concession of parity in nuclear weapons and international status, coupled with Watergate and Vietnam, were read as signs that U.S. power was on the wane. Both governments, therefore, saw détente as a continuation of the cold war by safer means. But the American public was encouraged to understand détente as entente—not a mere relaxation of tension but Soviet conversion to American norms. And the Politburo and its constituencies were alert for signs that they were not being treated as equals.[95]

On both sides, the touchstone for détente was how the other reacted to local crises in the developing world. The Soviets believed they now had an "equal right to meddle in Third Areas"[96] while Kissinger insisted that, even if the world was becoming more diverse, "we set the limits of diversity."[97] This divergence of view recurred through the 1970s. The rest of this section looks at three crises that were particularly significant in the decline of détente: Chile in 1973, Angola in 1974–1976, and the Horn of Africa in 1977–1978. The last section of the chapter will examine the deathblow to détente—Afghanistan in 1979–1980.

In September 1970, Dr. Salvador Allende's socialist-communist alliance in Chile became the first Marxist government to gain power through free elections in any major country. Three years later Allende was toppled and killed in the most violent coup in postwar Latin American history, which occurred in a country renowned for its democratic politics. Exactly what happened is still disputed, but the basic points are clear. Allende never enjoyed majority support, winning only 36 percent of the vote in 1970, yet he tried to use that as the basis of revolution by constitutional means. He made two critical mistakes: not reaching a consensus with the Christian Democratic center-left, and pushing through a program of nationalization and redistribution that disrupted the economy and alienated the productive middle-class.[98] Inflation spiraled and strikes mounted, that of the independent truck owners, vital for moving fuel and food in a country that is 80 percent mountains, being particularly important. In 1973 the military intervened to save the country from total collapse, though it took leftist threats among junior officers in the navy to push the leadership finally into action.[99] It remains unclear whether Allende died in a hail of army bullets or blew off his own head with an automatic rifle given him by Castro. But politically, his fall was suicide as much as murder.

American involvement in the Allende saga was deep and extensive. In 1970, Nixon and Kissinger had done their best to stop Allende's election from being ratified by the Chilean Congress. Neither wanted to see "another Cuba" in the Western Hemisphere; Nixon was also pressed by powerful supporters in U.S. corporations who faced likely nationalization. The Nixon administration encouraged a putsch and, after that failed, it imposed a credit squeeze on Allende and funneled about six million dollars to opposition groups, while keeping in close touch with the military opposition. The precise U.S. role in the 1973 coup remains unclear. The plotters were anxious to avoid an obvious American liaison, while Washington, for its part, maintained a "correct outward posture" so as not to give Allende, like Castro in the 1960s, a foreign target against which he could rally support at home and abroad.[100] In 1975 a Senate committee "found no evidence" that the USA "was *directly* involved, covertly, in the 1973 coup in Chile" but added that its actions and attitude "probably gave the impression that it would not look with disfavor on a military coup."[101]

Few outsiders doubted American complicity. For the Soviets, certainly, it was sobering evidence that the United States was not going to let the class struggle take its course. The following year, however, in Angola, Washington learned just how far the Soviets would go to promote Marxism-Leninism.

The army takeover in Lisbon signaled the end of Portugal's empire, with profound consequences for southern Africa as a whole, as we shall see in Chapter 13. In Guiné and Mozambique, independence was relatively peaceful, because the guerrilla movements in both were largely united. Angola, by contrast, had three rival factions, each with tribal roots, and it also boasted large mineral resources, including oil. In January 1975 agreement was reached on a transitional coalition, which would assume full power from Portugal after independence in November. Long before that, however, factional fighting had broken out, with growing great-power involvement. What alarmed Ford and Kissinger was the role of Cuban troops and Soviet arms in turning the tide in the autumn for the Marxist-led Movement for the Liberation of Angola. By the time the MPLA won the war in March 1976, seventeen thousand Cuban troops were in Angola. The administration was deeply concerned at this use of "proxies" and the precedent it could set. Kissinger warned that détente could not "survive any more Angolas."[102] Ford even banned the word détente from his lexicon, after claims by his rival for the Republican presidential nomination, Ronald Reagan, that "this nation has become Number Two in a world where it is dangerous—if not fatal—to be second best."[103]

In Moscow, however, the situation seemed very different. In 1974, many countries were funneling aid into Angola. Soviet support was stepped up initially to rival China's: as in Vietnam, the USSR must not seem lukewarm in the revolutionary struggle. The Soviets also feared that a Sino-American axis was backing the MPLA's rivals, the FNLA and UNITA. Moscow's lurking nightmare in the 1970s was that China and America would make common cause against it. At home, Brezhnev was under pressure following the fall of Allende and the defeat of the Portuguese communists. According to Politburo critics, these events showed how the United States was waging class war under cover of détente and how the Soviets must do the same. Even the story of Cuban proxies was more complex than American opinion believed. Castro had a long and independent interest in helping African revolutions. There was feeling as well as calculation in his claim that "African blood flows in our veins,"[104] and he would have responded to the MPLA's call for help in 1975 whatever the Soviet attitude (the two governments in fact favored different leaders within the MPLA).[105]

That said, the Cuban presence would not have been so potent without Soviet arms and air transport. But both Cuba and Russia were, in their view, responding to an *American* proxy, namely South Africa, which was funding UNITA and whose troops made a major raid into Angola in October 1975. In fact, the Pretoria government was also acting semi-independently: it had large investments in Angola and feared a regional security crisis if the MPLA came to power. But it moved only in parallel with the U.S. government; when CIA funding stopped, the South Africans, bitterly, backed off. Asked later whether the United States had "solicited South Africa's help to turn the tide against the Russians and Cubans," the South African premier replied, "I won't call you a liar."[106] Thus each superpower, unwilling to lose in a crisis that was not of its making, used a proxy state already partly involved. What neither fully grasped was how repugnant its proxy was to the other camp—revolutionary Cuba, racist South Africa.

In 1977–1978, détente was further strained by another Soviet-Cuban success, this time in the Horn of Africa. Here Ethiopia continued its struggle to put down Eritrean separatists in the north and repulse the efforts of Somalia, to the east, to regain the Ogaden, home of one million Somalis (Chapter 3). For years, Washington had provided modest aid to the repressive

Ethiopian emperor, Haile Selassie, while the Soviets built up Somalia following an opportune coup there in 1969. In September 1974, however, Haile Selassie was overthrown after months of unrest as the country's economy was dragged down by drought and famine. By mid-1976, the Soviet-leaning Colonel Mengistu Haile Mariam was firmly in control. His remaining enemies within the country's military committee, the Derg, were eliminated in a shootout the following February. The Soviets seized the chance to build up influence in Ethiopia as well, but the Somali leader, Colonel Mohammed Siad Barre, invaded the Ogaden in July 1977 before Ethiopia could become too strong. After his initial success, the Soviets mounted a massive airlift in December 1977, involving a quarter of their air transport fleet, to fly a billion dollars of military hardware into Ethiopia. This included five hundred tanks and eighty modern jet fighters, together with twelve thousand Cuban troops. The Cuban-Ethiopian offensive rolled the Somalis out of the Ogaden by March 1978. It also enabled Mengistu to turn on the Eritreans with new ferocity.

To Washington, this was alarming Soviet empire building. Once again, however, the story is more complex than it seems. Getting a foot into Ethiopia was a natural move for the Soviets: the country, though poor, had the second largest population in black Africa (thirty-four million, about seven times that of Somalia). But Moscow underestimated the force of ethnic rivalries and assumed that the leftist governments in both countries could be brought into a Marxist federation for the whole region. Siad Barre's rejection of this idea came as a rude shock in March 1977. By the end of the year, Moscow had lost all influence in Somalia and was in danger of seeing its new ally, Ethiopia, crumble as well. Although failure was then redeemed spectacularly, Mengistu proved no Soviet pawn. He resisted demands for a Soviet naval base at Massawa and opposed a negotiated settlement for Eritrea. Even though the economy was nationalized and, under pressure, he formed a Soviet-style vanguard party in 1984, his regime remained a personal despotism, akin to Haile Selassie's.[107]

But the West saw the Horn as another highly visible success by the Soviets and their Cuban proxies. Indeed, visibility was as important to Brezhnev as success itself. The scale of Soviet intervention far exceeded Ethiopia's needs; it was reported that some of the huge Antonov transports flying from Moscow to Addis Ababa were actually empty.[108] Angola and Ethiopia were dual and public humiliations for the United States. One elderly Cuban boasted: "We have done twice what the Yankees could not do once in Vietnam."[109] Having kept its balance between Moscow and Beijing for most of the 1970s, Washington was now ready to play "the China card"—with fateful consequences in Indochina.

New Indochina Wars—Communist against Communist

China's leadership crisis in the 1970s was even more profound than America's.[110] For most of the decade, court politics over the succession to Mao were exacerbated by continued fallout from the Cultural Revolution. The immediate beneficiary of Lin Biao's death in September 1971 was Premier Zhou Enlai, who had kept daily administration going through domestic turmoil and who managed the tilt toward Washington. But Zhou's attack on the extreme left in 1972, to rehabilitate those purged and boost production, prompted a counterattack from remnants of the Cultural Revolutionaries, notably the Gang of Four led by Jiang Qing, Mao's estranged but still powerful wife. At the August 1973 party congress the radicals strengthened their position in the Politburo; in 1974, they mounted a massive media campaign to "Criticize Lin and Confucius"—an attack on conservatism and, by implication, Zhou himself. Mao was now ailing fast—he needed oxygen before his increasingly rare public appearances—but his mind remained clear and he continued to balance between the two factions, suspicious of Zhou yet aware that without him the government might grind to a halt. In May 1972, medical tests revealed that Zhou was suffering from incurable stomach cancer. With mixed feelings Mao turned again to Deng Xiaoping.

Deng was born in Sichuan province, in southwest China, in 1904, making him eleven years younger than Mao. An even more important difference was the five-year period he spent as a worker-student in France in the 1920s. For Deng, like his mentor, Zhou Enlai, this created an awareness of the outside world that the sinocentric Mao always lacked. During the wars against Japan and the Nationalists, Deng was a political commissar with the army, rising to prominence as the logistics supremo for the vast 1948–1949 campaigns. Such administrative skill won him Politburo preferment in the 1950s, but his pragmatic emphasis on economic recovery after the disasters of the Great Leap Forward marked him out as a "Capitalist Roader" in the Cultural Revolution. Deng lost his posts but, unlike Liu Shaoqi, not his life. After two years under house arrest in Beijing, he was moved during the October 1969 war scare to Nanchang, the capital of Jiangxi province in the southeast. There the former secretary general of China's Communist party lived, together with his wife and stepmother, in four rooms of an army building—growing vegetables, chopping wood, and working part-time in a tractor factory. He still had access to books, however, both Chinese and foreign, and in 1971 he was joined by his elder son, Deng Pufang, who had been crippled for life when thrown from the window of a university building by Red Guards. Despite increasing deafness, Deng was still fit and well—full of the impatient, often angry, energy that compensated for his diminutive size (he was under five feet). But since he was nearly seventy, it seemed that his political career was over—that is, until Mao brought him back to Beijing in 1973. At first, he handled foreign affairs, but in October, with Zhou hospitalized, Mao gave him charge of the government with the title of first vice premier. In January 1975, despite the Gang of Four, the ailing Zhou Enlai was able to secure Deng's elevation to vice chairman of the party as well. It was an astonishing rehabilitation.[111]

Yet Mao's endgame was not yet over. By now the chairman was virtually blind; his speech was incomprehensible to all but his latest young confidante, Zhang Yufeng. Doctors discerned the symptoms of motor neuron disease. Yet the bedridden Mao maintained his balancing act, backing Deng's attacks on the bloated PLA and labor unrest while still voicing support for cultural revolution. When Zhou finally died in January 1976, Mao promoted another unknown, Hua Guofeng, aged forty-five, to be the acting premier and first vice chairman of the party. But the death of Zhou, an immensely popular figure, prompted an outpouring of feeling that was genuine, if manipulated by Deng. Thousands of mourners placed wreaths and poems in Zhou's memory around the Heroes Monument in the center of Tiananmen Square. On April 4, 1976, traditionally Ancestors' Day, around two million people came to pay their respects and, often, to denounce the Gang of Four. Such evident support for Deng alarmed Hua, Jiang Qing, and other enemies of Deng in the Politburo. With Mao's assent—his words that Deng had "never been a Marxist" became their imprimatur[112]—police removed the wreaths the following day and drove demonstrators from the square. One hundred, reportedly, were killed. Outside Mao's room, Jiang Qing toasted her success: "Bottoms up. I will become a bludgeon, ready to strike."[113] On April 7, Deng was relieved of his posts and Hua promoted to premier. After Liu Shaoqi and Lin Biao, he was Mao's third, and final, heir.

As if these shocks were not enough, August 1976 saw a disastrous earthquake in the northern coal-mining city of Tangshan, in which perhaps 250,000 people died. As unrest mounted across the country and Hua and the Gang of Four feuded in the Forbidden City, Mao's life gradually ebbed away. He died soon after midnight on September 9. Party veterans and senior PLA marshals persuaded Hua to arrest Jiang Qing and her allies. But they also knew that the man to pull the country out of its troubles was not Hua, widely dubbed a country bumpkin, but Deng, whose supporters had quickly flown him down to the south after his purge. By July 1977 he had been reinstated in all his offices and, using his stronger base in party and army, he proceeded to winkle Hua's supporters out of prominent positions.[114] It was not until 1980 that Hua lost his post as premier and the Gang of Four was put on trial, but Deng's decisive policy battles over economic modernization and closer links with America were fought and won in 1978. As in 1971–1972, coincidence was critical: this was also the year when America was ready to play what it called the China card.

Sino-American relations had not progressed with the speed anticipated in 1972 when Nixon visited China. The collapse of his presidency and the power struggle in Beijing were part of the explanation, but there was also the serious obstacle of America's cold war alliance with the Nationalists on Taiwan. For Beijing, this was another lost province (like Hong Kong), whereas the Nationalist regime still claimed to be the rightful rulers of the mainland. Although Chiang Kai-shek had died in 1975, his son and heir Chiang Ching-kuo insisted he would have nothing to do with the Communists "except for battlefield contact in the shape of a bullet."[115] Taiwan's active and well-financed lobby in the United States was backed by many conservative congressmen, and Carter initially had no desire to push the issue when he was already battling Congress over his proposed surrender of the Panama Canal.

America's China policy was part of a larger calculus about the strategic triangle with Russia. Kissinger saw the United States as pivoting between the two communist states, moving toward one and then the other to maintain a balance of power. Thus, it was important not to give the impression of exclusive commitment to either side. This was also the view of Carter's secretary of state, Cyrus Vance, who wanted to advance superpower détente through a new arms control treaty.[116] But the national security adviser, Zbigniew Brzezinski, was a brash Polish-American academic who took a more hostile view of the Soviet Union (and of Vance). When Carter had appointed them, his line was that "Zbig would be the thinker, Cy would be the doer, and Jimmy Carter would be the decider."[117] But Carter failed to decide or to stop the feuding encouraged by his indecision. In August 1977, Vance visited Beijing but proceeded cautiously on normalizing relations, anxious to avoid disrupting the SALT talks with Russia. In March 1978, after the Soviet escapade in Ethiopia, however, Carter agreed to send Brzezinski, not Vance, on another visit to Beijing. By choosing his more hawkish adviser, the president wanted to send a warning to Moscow and a message to Beijing that "the United States has made up its mind" on normalization.[118] This entailed accepting the PRC's demand for a formal break with Taiwan. Brzezinski made the tilt overt. *Time* magazine reported that, racing his hosts up a section of the Great Wall, he joked: "Last one to the top fights the Russians in Ethiopia!"[119] All this was encouragement to Deng; it also aggravated Soviet paranoia about a Sino-American alliance. For both governments, it fed into their power struggle in Indochina.

By then, it was clear that, although communists now ruled both Vietnam and Kampuchea (their new name for Cambodia), ideology was subordinate to history. The Kampucheans still harked back to the days of the Angkor empire, when much of southern Vietnam was a Khmer province, whereas Vietnam made little secret of its continuing desire to control Indochina. The battleground was their long-contested frontier. Both governments chose to fan the flames because of domestic problems caused by their breakneck attempt to impose communism. The Kampuchean government escalated border skirmishes into major conflict in 1977, as part of its purge in the eastern zone, but this was probably encouraged by evidence of Vietnamese assistance to dissident cadres.[120] Fighting intensified in 1978, to the alarm of Moscow and Beijing.

After 1975, the Chinese had rapidly lost influence in Hanoi under its Soviet-leaning party secretary, Le Duan. Beijing could not match the aid offered by its more developed rival. Moreover, Vietnamese nationalism played on a legacy of popular resentment against earlier Chinese overlordship. The two were still at odds over their mutual border and over the Hoa, Vietnam's Chinese minority, some 1.2 million in a population of forty-five million, who were mainly small traders in the capitalist south. In February 1978, the Vietnamese Politburo decided to prepare an invasion of Kampuchea, and to abolish capitalist trade in the south as part of accelerated socialism. By July some 160,000 Hoa had fled into China; another one hundred thousand "boat people" had left by sea. Beijing responded by canceling aid projects, staging military exercises in the Gulf of Tonkin, and building up troops on the border. It is worth noting, however, that during the period 1975–1979, about half the Chinese in Kampuchea were also killed, some two hundred thousand people, with little protest from Beijing.[121] The difference was that Kampuchea was China's one remaining ally in Indochina, whereas Vietnam had moved firmly into the Soviet camp. Hence Beijing's downplaying of Sino-Kampuchean differences and its search for other allies. The American tilt toward China in May came at an opportune moment for Beijing, and in August China concluded a long-delayed peace treaty with Japan. Ratifying the treaty in October, Deng denounced Vietnam as "the Cuba of the East," a junior partner in Moscow's bid for hegemony.[122]

The Vietnamese army was six hundred thousand strong—three times larger than Kampuchea's. It was also battle hardened and well equipped with modern Soviet weaponry. But it could not risk a full-scale war with China as well. Consequently, Hanoi signed a formal alliance with Moscow, something it had previously avoided on grounds of national independence and diplomatic flexibility.[123] The Soviets exacted a high price for their support, including use of the superb base at Cam Ranh Bay, which had been built by the Americans at the cost of nearly $250 million. They also ensured that the Treaty of Friendship and Cooperation signed in November 1978 did not pledge "mutual assistance" or "immediate military aid" if either party were attacked but only said that each "shall take appropriate and effective measures to safeguard the peace and security" of the other.[124] This minimized the danger of Vietnam's being drawn into war against China. On December 25, more than one hundred thousand Vietnamese troops crossed the border in a Blitzkrieg-style attack so unusual in Indochina wars that many suspected Soviet involvement in its planning. Within a couple of weeks, Phnom Penh, the Kampuchean capital, had fallen, and Vietnam had installed an alternative government.

What was soon dubbed "the third Indochina war"—after those against the French and the Americans—was therefore a mixture of old regional rivalries and great-power machinations. With some justice, Brzezinski dubbed the border conflict "the first case of a proxy war between China and the Soviet Union." Early in his administration, Carter had called the Kampuchean regime "the worst violator of human rights in the world today," but this did not dictate his stance in 1978–1979 now that American policy was reverting to containment of Moscow.[125] On December 15, Carter announced that full diplomatic relations between Beijing and Washington would be established on January 1, 1979. The Chinese had at last conceded that the United States could maintain unofficial relations with Taiwan—Congress later established the American Institute in Taiwan for this purpose—in order to reach agreement and expedite Brzezinski's promised sweetener, a state visit to the U.S. When Deng Xiaoping arrived in Washington at the end of January 1979, he disclosed plans for a Chinese punitive strike into northern Vietnam. Carter offered words of discouragement but Brzezinski was anxious not to upset the new rapprochement. The final communiqué expressed shared opposition to "hegemony"—the familiar Chinese code for the Soviet threat.

Just as Vietnam had insured itself in Moscow, so Beijing had done the same in Washington. Despite party disagreement, Deng personally pushed the idea of a brief punitive strike into Vietnam—akin to that against India in 1962—to maintain China's credibility.[126] He may also have seen it as a way to resolve the long-running debate about whether or not the army's strategy and weaponry were outmoded, a key issue in his general modernization campaign.[127] The Chinese incursion began on February 17, 1979. It was deliberately confined to the northern mountains above the Red River delta, and neither side used air power. Once the Chinese had captured the strategic town of Lang Son on March 5, they pulled back. Losses were heavy, at least ten thousand Chinese dead, and the Vietnamese remained in Kampuchea, but China had been seen to act decisively.

Vietnam's invasion of Kampuchea exposed for the first time the enormity of what the communists had done. Their notorious interrogation center, S-21, located in a former school in Phnom Penh, became a "genocide museum" commemorating nearly twenty thousand people tortured and murdered in its rooms. From mass graves like that at Ta Mon, thousands of skulls were excavated and piled into pyramids. Survivors told how in the days immediately after the communist takeover on April 17, 1975, two to three million people (one-third of the population) were driven from cities and towns amid warnings of epidemics or U.S. bombing. Vast shuffling files of humanity clogged the roads out of Phnom Penh—young and old, male and female, even sick and wounded being pushed along in their hospital beds until they died and then were tipped into ditches. Within a few days, the capital was deserted. From the countryside came stories of day-long labor gangs and evening criticism sessions; of the abolition of Western medicines and pesticides, including DDT, which made thousands vulnerable to malaria; of roundups, massacres, and civil war in the east.

Subsequent research has qualified some early blanket judgments. In many rural areas, life was probably not much worse in 1975–1976 than during the civil war. The area of worst suffering was probably the northwest, where one million people were resettled in another forced migration in 1976–1977. The east was more tolerable until the war of 1977–1978.[128] But these are only nuances. Most estimates concur that nearly one million people died in Kampuchea in 1975–1978—about one person in eight.[129] This was perhaps "the greatest per capita loss of life in a single nation in the twentieth century."[130] The country was an international horror story, captured vividly in the 1985 movie *The Killing Fields*.

It became customary to depict the regime's secretive leader, Pol Pot (1927–1998), as another Hitler. Yet all those who knew him in earlier life— as Saloth Sar, a landowner's son, as a student in France in the early 1950s, a Phnom Penh teacher a few years later, or the leader of Cambodia's underground communist party after 1963—remarked on his smooth face, unruffled manner and genial personality. Undoubtedly the man was obsessed about enemies: the "microbes" in the party, the cooks trying to poison his food, the would-be assassins who could only be foiled by strip searching all who attended party meetings. He personally approved most of the executions carried out in S-21. But although one would need to dig deep into a textbook on abnormal psychology to make sense of all that Pol Pot did, he is ultimately a recognizable historical type. One ex-colleague applied to him the words used about Lenin in 1910 by a pre-war Menshevik: "He was a revolutionary twenty-four hours a day, and when he slept, he dreamt of revolution."[131]

Pol Pot's regime represented the ultimate in intellectual-led peasant revolution. Despite professions of national uniqueness, it drew heavily on past models, including Stalin's purges and particularly Mao's China, where Pol Pot had spent several months in 1966, early in the Cultural Revolution. There was frequent talk of conducting a "Super Great Leap Forward"—in other words one better than Chinas. When the party ideologue Khieu Samphan visited Beijing in 1975, the dying Zhou Enlai advised him to "take things slowly" and move "step by step." But Khieu Samphan just smiled an incredulous, superior smile. Back home he insisted, "We will be the first nation to create a completely communist society without wasting time on intermediate steps."[132] This was the method behind the madness. Keeping the communist party secret and hiding behind Sihanouk's figurehead until the constitution and arranged elections of 1976 prevented an early backlash. Emptying the towns pulled up capitalists from their roots at a stroke—from money, banks, employment, property. The new work gangs striving for two rice crops a year and building vast irrigation projects were designed to make Kampuchea self-sufficient in food. The illiterate teenage peasants who were the government's ubiquitous agents represented a dual revolutionary force—the young versus their elders, the Khmer countryside against the Westernized cities. As one party official exclaimed while emptying Phnom Penh, "There are money and trade in cities and both have a corrupting influence. People are good, but cities are evil. That is why we shall do away with cities."[133] Pol Pot was the heir to Stalin and Mao. From the logic of instant revolution came the madness of national suicide.

Afghanistan, the Olympics, and the Demise of Détente

As communist fought communist in Indochina, superpower relations fell apart. Angola and Ethiopia still rankled Washington; the Soviets were deeply suspicious of Carter's tilt toward Beijing, which Brezhnev publicly called "playing with fire."[134] There was also ill feeling about the way Carter had pushed aside the guidelines for the SALT II arms limitation treaty agreed to by Brezhnev and Ford in November 1974. Carter, a zealot about nuclear weapons, sought more radical cuts, but as one Soviet policy maker remarked privately, Brezhnev "had to spill political blood" to secure the acceptance by the Soviet military of the 1974 deal. He was therefore furious when the issue was reopened by Carter in the spring of 1977.[135] Establishing new guidelines and then negotiating the details took more than two years, and Moscow made a treaty the precondition for a summit. It was therefore not until June 1979, over halfway into the Carter presidency, that the two leaders met for the first time (and the last). Although protocol dictated a U.S. venue, Carter agreed to Vienna because of Brezhnev's ill health.

The president was an enthusiast for personal diplomacy, often remarking on what good would follow "if only I could get my hands" on Brezhnev.[136] Their meeting *was* a breakthrough in human terms: Brezhnev observed that the American was "quite a nice guy, after all" while Carter, on day three of the summit, toasted "my new friend, President Brezhnev."[137] But the summit had been too long delayed to reverse the decline of détente, particularly given the weakness of the two leaders by 1979. Brezhnev was now visibly failing, and the unpopular Carter was embarking on a difficult reelection campaign.

The SALT II treaty signed in Vienna was an advance on the 1974 framework, restricting each side to 2,250 nuclear launchers. Overall, the Americans retained a 50 percent advantage in the total number of strategic-range nuclear warheads. But this contrasted with a three-to-one advantage back in 1974, and the Pentagon was particularly concerned about the potency of Soviet heavy ICBMs, in which Moscow had a substantial advantage.[138] One leading critic, Senator Henry Jackson, likened the Vienna summit to the Munich conference of 1938, calling it "appeasement in its purest form."[139] The treaty's deficiencies, together with growing anti-Soviet feeling on Capitol Hill, presaged a hard fight to secure Senate ratification of the treaty. Carter promised a 5 percent real increase in defense spending to help win right-wing support. Senate ratification of the SALT II treaty was in doubt—even before Moscow's Christmas invasion of Afghanistan.

This remote, mountainous country had long been an international arena because of its strategic position. During the nineteenth century it was a battered buffer between the Russian empire and British India. Ethnically, Afghanistan was hard to distinguish clearly from its neighbors: nationalists demanded a Pushtunistan state embracing Pushtun peoples in Pakistan; one-fifth of the population were Shia Muslims with close ties to Iran to the southwest; and one-third were of the same ethnic groups as the Soviet republics to the north—Tajiks, Uzbeks, and Turkmen. Not only did Pushtuns constitute less than half the population (estimated at fifteen million in 1979), but allegiances also remained tribal and familial in a country where one-sixth were still nomads. Nevertheless, in Afghanistan as elsewhere, urbanization and education proved powerful solvents of the old order, especially in the capital, Kabul. The Durrani family, rulers since the eighteenth century, conceded some press and political freedoms in the 1960s, but the result was greater instability. A junior family member, Sardar Daoud, seized power in July 1973 with the support of leftist officers and politicians whom he then purged. They, in turn, took over in April 1978, gunning down Daoud and eighteen family members in a room in the presidential palace. This brought the People's Democratic party of Afghanistan (PDPA) to power.[140]

In the West, what hit the headlines was that the PDPA was a communist party and that its links with Moscow intensified following the April revolution. But feuding was soon apparent within the PDPA between the Khalq and Parcham factions, who took their names from their rival newspapers (respectively, *The People* and *The Banner*). The Parchamis, led by Babrak Karmal, were mostly Tajiks and other non-Pushtuns, frequently from the towns, who favored gradualist reform. The Khalqs were radicals, largely Pushtun, from rural areas. Many were teachers who had been politicized at college, notably their charismatic leader Hafizullah Amin (who had a master's degree from Columbia University in New York). Amin and Karmal, both aged fifty in 1979, were bitter foes, but the PDPA's head was an older Khalq, Nur Mohammad Taraki, a self-educated writer with nomadic roots who was celebrated, ruthless, but often drunk.

From the PDPA's unholy alliance the Parchamis were quickly purged, with Karmal sent into exile in Moscow. The Khalqs, whom Taraki dubbed "the children of history" to indicate their mission to modernize Afghanistan, then embarked on a frenzied campaign of reform, with land redistribution, secularized education, and female emancipation at the top of the list. Like the Khmer Rouge, they were "vulgar Marxists"—knowing the texts but not understanding their contexts. Soon they had alienated much of the country, including tribal and religious leaders. Serious uprisings ensued, notably at Herat in March 1979, when thousands died. The Khalqs were also at war among themselves as the fading Taraki battled Amin for supremacy. From Moscow, Soviet leaders watched with mounting anxiety the civil war on their borders. They urged Taraki to moderate the reforms and broaden his government. But after a shootout on September 14 between their bodyguards, Amin had Taraki imprisoned and later suffocated with a pillow. By now, the Politburo was moving toward direct intervention.

During the uprising of March 1979, Taraki had requested Soviet combat troops, but the Politburo firmly declined. Some of the comments proved prescient in the light of subsequent events. "I do not think we can uphold the revolution in Afghanistan with the help of our bayonets," said KGB chief Yuri Andropov, while Foreign Minister Andrei Gromyko warned, "The SALT II talks would be ruined."[141] What, then, had changed by the autumn? The U.S. backlash against SALT II and NATO's plans to deploy Cruise and Pershing missiles in Europe suggested that détente was on the rocks. The Afghan civil war had worsened, with all the dangers of ethnic fallout for the Soviet Central Asian republics. And Taraki had been publicly fêted by Brezhnev in Moscow as a key Soviet ally only days before his overthrow. Brezhnev regarded Taraki's murder as a personal affront, asking angrily "how should the world be able to believe what Brezhnev says, if his words do not count in Afghanistan?"[142] There were also hints, played up by Karmal in Moscow, that Amin was tilting toward Washington. Soviet security and credibility were therefore the main motives for intervention. Even so, the decision to intervene was taken reluctantly on December 12, as the hawks, notably Defense Minister Dmitri Ustinov, sidelined doves like Alexei Kosygin and a skeptical General Staff.

During December 25, 26, and 27, nearly eight thousand Soviet troops were airlifted into Kabul. This was done with Amin's agreement, to help in the civil war. But on the evening of the 27th, Soviet special units assaulted the presidential palace, killing Amin. Babrak Karmal, the exiled Parchami leader, was flown in from Moscow to head a new government. Moscow's dual hopes were that Parchamis and "good" Khalqs in the Taraki tradition would form a broader and stable coalition, and that Soviet troops, scheduled to reach seventy-five thousand in early 1980, would help the Afghan army suppress the insurgency. Both hopes proved illusory. Political feuding continued in Kabul, and the Afghan army fell apart. Within weeks the government had lost control of the countryside; riots broke out in Herat, Kabul, and other cities. Unprepared Soviet troops were left to prop up Karmal's regime in an all-out guerrilla war. Like the Americans in Vietnam, they found it hard to distinguish friend from foe, civilian from combatant, and atrocities were commonplace. Their notorious helicopter gunships tended to treat any assembly as threatening: numerous wedding parties were decimated. Villages were razed in retaliation for Soviet casualties, and there were "fun" shootings into passing buses or private homes. Much of Logar province, between Kabul and the rebel supply zones in Pakistan, "looks like an archaeological site," reported a Swedish journalist in 1982. "The most common sight except for ruins are graves."[143] By the end of 1982 one-fifth of the population had fled abroad, mostly to Pakistan.

The magnitude of the Afghan tragedy was not, of course, apparent in early 1980. But within days of the Christmas coup, the U.S. government's response was clear. Carter withdrew the SALT II treaty from Senate consideration. He announced an embargo on new grain exports to the USSR and a ban on sale of high-tech goods. He suspended most cultural exchanges and called on U.S. athletes to boycott the 1980 Olympic Games in Moscow. Reversing previous nonproliferation policies, he sanctioned weapons for Afghan rebels and military aid to to their backer, Pakistan. And the "Carter Doctrine" of January 1980, modeled on Truman's speech of 1947, articulated U.S. determination to prevent outside control of the Persian Gulf. The centerpiece of the new policy was the Rapid Deployment Force, enabling prompt U.S. intervention anywhere in what was now dubbed the "arc of crisis" from the gulf to the Horn of Africa.

This string of measures represented a victory for the hawkish Brzezinski over the pro-détente Vance, who resigned in April 1980. The president now seemed to have accepted his national security adviser's dictum that "you first have to be a Truman before you are a Wilson"—in other words proving

America's toughness before making peace.[144] If anything, Carter became more ardent than Brzezinski in his denunciations of Moscow. Having, as he believed, established a direct rapport with Brezhnev at Vienna, he now felt personally betrayed. Electoral politics also required tough talk and firm actions. He told an interviewer on December 31 that the Soviet action "has made a more dramatic change in my own opinion of what the Soviets' ultimate goals are than anything they've done in the previous time I've been in office"—a comment that sounded so naive that the White House kept it out of the public record.[145] On January 8 he told congressmen that "our own nation's security was directly threatened" and that, if unchecked, the Soviets might push on to the Persian Gulf and control "a major portion of the world's oil supplies." Repeatedly he insisted that this crisis "was the greatest threat to world peace since the Second World War."[146]

All this talk was hyperbole. Unquestionably the Politburo's brutal action required a response. But as declassified documents confirm, it was essentially defensive in motivation and certainly did not presage a drive southwest to the gulf. Carter's exaggerated rhetoric, the extent of his sanctions, and his ill-advised linkage of them to total Soviet withdrawal from Afghanistan were counterproductive. The grain embargo, for instance, cost the United States $4 billion and had no effect on Soviet policy. The Soviets struck back in kind, calling the Carter Doctrine "an overt U.S. claim to world domination."[147] During 1980, U.S. policy reverted to something close to cold war containment. This echoed public feeling. Polls in early 1980 indicated over 70 percent support for the grain embargo and the Olympic boycott; for the first time since 1973, a majority favored increased defense spending."[148]

Of all Carter's sanctions, it was the Olympic boycott that brought the end of détente to worldwide attention. This was not the first time, of course, that international sports had been entangled in international diplomacy. Since the Olympics had been revived in 1896, "almost every celebration of the Olympics has been fraught with politics."[149] In 1916, 1940 and 1944 the games had not been held at all because of world wars. In the postwar era, West Germany and Japan were excluded until 1952. There were long-running arguments about the status of the two Chinas and the two Germanies. East Germany had to wait until 1968 to enter a separate team. The September 1972 games in Munich were overshadowed by the shooting of eleven Israeli athletes by Palestinian kidnappers. Four years later, twenty-eight black African states boycotted Montréal to protest New Zealand's continued sporting links with South Africa. Despite these precedents, however, the Olympics were different in 1980. "No longer were they simply a sideshow of international politics but instead were elevated to the main event."[150]

Even before the Aghanistan crisis, the idea of boycotting the Moscow Olympics was popular in the United States. The venue had always been controversial, especially since Moscow had beaten Los Angeles (which had already hosted the Olympics in 1932). For the U.S. government, a boycott would cost little but gain vast publicity, and Carter espoused it like a crusade. Pressed by overwhelming majorities in House and Senate and threatened by possible funding cuts and new tax liabilities, a reluctant U.S. Olympic Committee complied in April. Vice President Walter Mondale told delegates before they voted, "History holds its breath, for what is at stake is nothing less than the future security of the civilized world."[151] After the U.S. ice hockey team beat the USSR in the semifinal of the Winter Olympics at Lake Placid, New York, Carter fêted them at the White House as "modern day American heroes." He wrote later that their victory was "one of the high spots of my year."[152]

The administration also twisted the arms of its allies. Canada and Japan, both particularly vulnerable, succumbed. In West Germany, Chancellor Helmut Schmidt tried to balance between old NATO loyalties and new Ostpolitik ties before following suit. The German Olympic Committee eventually voted 59–40 to stay away, after a four-hour debate shown live on German television.[153] But most of Europe went to Moscow—the British team despite (or perhaps because of) firm instructions from Prime Minister Margaret Thatcher. Carter had more success in Asia and among Muslim countries, but his use of the black American boxer Muhammad Ali as an emissary to black Africa was regarded as insulting by several African leaders and ended with Ali returning home a critic of the boycott. In the end, eighty-one countries participated—far less than the 122 in 1972 but close to the eighty-eight at boycott-ridden Montréal in 1976. Although thirty-six world records were broken, the spectacular success of the Soviet and East German teams (with respectively eighty and forty-seven gold medals) testified to the hollowness of many contests.

The boycott did little for Afghanistan or for Carter's reelection. The main sufferers, as in earlier cases, were the athletes who had wasted years of training. The U.S. team, competing in alternative events back home, attracted most attention, but spare a thought for Youssef Nagui Assad, a physical education teacher from Cairo, who was also a keen shot-putter. In 1968, aged twenty-three, he just missed qualifying for the Egyptian Olympic team—by two centimeters. In 1972, he went with the team to Munich, only to be withdrawn by his government in solidarity with the PLO. In 1976, Assad traveled to Montréal, only to be pulled out again as part of the antiapartheid boycott. And in 1980, when he was thirty-five and nearing retirement, his dreams of Olympic gold were dashed when Egypt shunned the Moscow Games.[154]

Afghanistan destroyed what remained of détente, and in January 1981 a new right-wing president, Ronald Reagan, made explicit the renewed cold war. The acrimonious end of détente was in part the result of superpower actions—Soviet involvement in Angola, Ethiopia, and Afghanistan, the U.S. tilt toward China. It also reflected the misplaced assumptions on which détente had been based: Moscow believed that nuclear parity made it safe to back socialist revolutions, Washington expected that the Soviets would now behave according to American norms. But the Afghan crisis cannot be understood simply by reference to the dynamic of Soviet-American relations. Fully to explain the fateful overreaction by both sides—Moscow to events in Kabul, Washington to the Soviet aggression—we have to remember what was happening in neighboring southwest Asia (Map 4).

The Iranian revolution of February 1979, following the overthrow of the Shah, threatened to inflame the Muslim peoples of Soviet Central Asia.[155] The Politburo was also sensitive to signs that the United States might try to build an alternative regional base in Afghanistan to replace its long-time ally in Iran. Likewise, Carter's hyperactive crusade about Afghanistan was in part an expression of his impotence over the fifty-two U.S. diplomats held in Teheran since November 1979, whose fate haunted the rest of his presidency. And his fixation with the Persian Gulf as a target of Soviet policy only makes sense in the light of the oil crises that had enervated the West since the Arab-Israeli war of 1973.

11

Israel, Oil, and Islam

Of the four Arab-Israeli wars, the conflict of October 1973 was the greatest. Over twenty-five hundred Israeli soldiers were killed, as well as some five thousand from Egypt and Syria. The fighting involved the biggest tank battles since World War II. Yet this was also the last full-scale Arab-Israeli war, for it pushed Israel and Egypt to a negotiated settlement and convinced the other front-line Arab states surrounding Israel that Zionism could not be destroyed by military means. The Palestinians were left to wage their own struggle, resorting to the terrorist tactics that the Zionists had used against the British after World War II. The 1970s, therefore, saw a consolidation of the Israeli state that had been created in 1948 and extended in 1967, especially after the shift of power from Labor to the more intransigent Likud coalition in 1977.

Among Israel's neighbors, this was a decade of dramatic change—at least for states that were well oiled. Starting with the 1973 war, a cohesive oil cartel—the Organization of Petroleum-Exporting Countries, or OPEC—pushed up prices on the world market. The sudden crisis helped tip the Western economies, now dependent on cheap petroleum products, into extended recession. At the same time, the oil boom began to transform living standards in states around the Persian Gulf while imposing severe strains on their political systems. These came to a head in the Iranian revolution of

1979, when the shah's autocracy was displaced by an Islamic theocracy. The politicization of Islam, in part a reaction to rapid, oil-fired "Westernization," became a feature of the Muslim world during the 1980s. This caused acute alarm in the United States, the shah's patron, which was stigmatized by Islamic radicals as the "Great Satan." But Islam was not the monolith caricatured in the American media. Like Christianity, it took many different forms, each rooted in politics, society, and history. The struggle for Israel, the omnipotence of oil, and the varieties of resurgent Islam are central themes of this chapter on Southwest Asia in the decade after 1973.

October 1973: Arab Gamble, Superpower Crisis

Israel's preemptive strike in June 1967 had enlarged its territory more than threefold, bringing Jerusalem, the Golan Heights, and the Sinai peninsula under Israeli rule (Map 10). No Arab government could accept that situation. In Syria, it obsessed the defense minister, Hafez al-Assad, prompting his successful bid for full power in November 1970. But Syria had only seven million people; it could not move without Egypt, thirty-five million strong, which now faced Israeli troops across the Suez Canal. Anwar Sadat (1918–1981), who assumed the presidency on Nasser's death in September 1970, was seen at home and abroad as a stopgap leader. Although one of the Free Officers who seized power in 1952, he had been a marginal figure, widely regarded as a toady ("Colonel Yes-Yes" as Nasser called him). Sadat's half-Sudanese ancestry (and, thus, dark skin) did not help. Nothing came of his rhetoric that 1971 would be the "Year of Decision" against Israel. Student demonstrators in Cairo openly mocked Nasser's successor: *Rah al-Wahsh, Gaa al-Gahsh* ("Gone is the giant, the donkey has taken his place").

Sadat's government teetered on the brink of financial collapse, bereft of revenue from the Suez Canal and unable to raise taxes for fear of popular protest. The Soviet presence also inflamed nationalist feeling. In July 1972 Sadat suddenly evicted Soviet military advisers. This has been seen as a shrewd bid to extract more aid from Moscow,[1] but Sadat was probably more concerned with placating domestic opinion and winning greater financial support from the conservative Arab states, led by Saudi Arabia. He also hoped that Washington would add its weight to the peace process, once he had shown some independence from Moscow.[2] But Nixon was now immersed in Watergate. Frustrated, Sadat became quite open in his warnings, telling *Newsweek* in April 1973, "[T]he situation is hopeless and—mark my words—highly explosive. . . . Everything in this country is now being mobi- lized for the resumption of the battle—which is now inevitable." But Kissinger had heard such words too often before. He dismissed Sadat as a "bombastic clown."[3]

The Egyptian leader was now planning a new war. Its code name was Op- eration Badr, after the first of the Prophet Muhammad's great battles on the road to Mecca. Despite such grandiloquence, however, this was to be a lim- ited war for political ends. Sadat's chief of staff, General Saad el-Shazly, made clear that Egypt could not venture far into the Sinai for fear of Israeli air power, which had been so devastating in 1967. The object, therefore, was to recover the Suez Canal and use it as a bargaining chip in new negotiations. But to satisfy the Syrians, who were not likely to attack if Egypt intended to advance only a few miles, more ambitious plans were shown to Assad for an offensive into Sinai. In April 1973, these were enough to forge an alliance be- tween Egypt and Syria, but the divergence in goals was to have fatal conse- quences once war began.[4]

Meanwhile, in October 1972, Moscow had resumed relations with Egypt because the Kremlin could not afford to lose its major Middle Eastern ally. A new military aid package was worked out, which was vital for modernizing Egypt's armed forces and completing its SAM missile system against Israeli air attack. But the Soviets advised repeatedly against war, doubting Egypt's chances and fearful of jeopardizing détente with Washington. They even warned the Americans that the situation was critical; Brezhnev gave Nixon a late-night harangue during their June 1973 summit. When apprised of the Arabs' date for war, Moscow made no effort to conceal the airlift of its citi- zens from Cairo and Damascus. This may well have been a calculated wink to U.S. intelligence.[5]

If so, Washington closed its eyes. Domestic politics took most of Nixon's at- tention as he battled Congress over the Watergate tapes and tried to replace his discredited vice president. Kissinger assumed that any serious threat to Israel would be transmitted in good time by that country's intelligence ser- vice, Mossad. In fact, the data were not in short supply: as with many intel- ligence failures, the fault lay in analysis, not evidence.[6] The very visible Syrian and Egyptian preparations were dismissed as maneuvers or provocation; Is- rael had mobilized its reserves at considerable expense and political embar- rassment during a war scare in May. And the 1967 war had bred complacency, not least in its architect, Moshe Dayan, now the defense min- ister, who was spending more time on occupation policy than on military readiness. It was assumed that the Arabs would not attack without air supe- riority and that, if they did, the Israeli Defense Forces (IDF) would mop them up. One Israeli joke imagined this exchange between Dayan and Chief of Staff General David Elazar:

> Dayan: There's nothing to do.
> Elazar: How about invading another Arab country?
> Dayan: What would we do in the afternoon?

October 6, 1973, came as a rude awakening. Egypt and Syria attacked on Yom Kippur, the day of atonement, when even secular Jews fasted and prayed. That afternoon, some seven hundred of Syria's Soviet tanks rolled onto the Golan Plateau behind a massive artillery barrage, outnumbering the Israeli armor there by nearly four to one. The southern Golan had fallen by nightfall. Meanwhile, a daring helicopter raid by Syrian commandos seized Israel's radar post on Mount Hermon to the north, from which the IDF had surveyed the road to Damascus. On the Suez front, three hundred miles to the southwest, Arab gains were even more spectacular. Egyptian forces had to cross a two hundred-yard waterway with steep concrete banks, backed by a huge sand wall forty feet high, along which ran a road linking some thirty forts located at likely crossing points. Oil reservoirs near the forts would allow the Israelis to flood the canal with fuel and turn it into a blazing inferno. Some miles to the east, an Israeli armored division was ready to destroy any successful incursion. At least that was the theory. Instead, eight thousand Egyptian infantry, hidden behind their own sandbanks, suddenly rushed across the canal in small boats. Special units, armed with West German high-pressure firehoses, blasted gaps in the sand walls. Engineers used twelve bridges and thirty-one ferries to move men and vehicles across the canal. The Israeli reservists in the forts were stunned and outnumbered; some fought bravely, many eventually surrendered. Above them, the Israeli air force was held at bay by the Egyptian SAM batteries. And the tank counterattack was ineffectual. That was partly because the armor was widely dispersed, but, to Israeli astonishment, the despised Egyptian infantry also countered with devastating effect, using Russian bazookas and hand-fired rockets. Within twenty-four hours, Egypt had one hundred thousand men and one thousand tanks across the canal and several miles into Israeli territory. Instead of ten thousand expected casualties, they lost only 280 men.[7]

In Western eyes, these events are usually viewed as a brief prelude to ensuing Egyptian humiliation. It is therefore important to emphasize that, for Arabs, they were regarded as a spectacular and lasting victory. This was partly because the subsequent debacle was hushed up, especially in Egypt. But the sense of triumph was justified. After 1948, 1956, and especially 1967, the Israeli had assumed superman status in the eyes of many Arabs. Now they watched TV pictures of bedraggled Jewish soldiers shuffling into captivity and stared at Israeli tanks, guns, and equipment displayed in the squares of Cairo and Damascus. The humiliation and self-doubt of 1967 had been erased. As one Muslim newspaper in Beirut exclaimed early in the war: "In forty-eight hours how many victories we have won over ourselves!"[8] On October 16, when Sadat addressed the National Assembly, hundreds of thousands packed the streets of Cairo to cheer "the hero of the crossing." Assad of Syria was more circumspect, but he also gained from the early victories. Two shaky leaders were confirmed in power; the boost to Arab pride was immense.

Meanwhile, in Tel-Aviv, the normally inspirational Dayan was unnerved. "We are heading toward a catastrophe," he told Prime Minister Golda Meir late on October 7, advising her to pull back to the edge of the Golan and to the Sinai passes.[9] In this critical phase it was General Elazar, the chief of staff, who took control, rather as Dayan had eclipsed Rabin in 1967. Elazar ensured that, unlike 1956 and 1967, the bulk of Israeli forces were shifted to the Syrian front, where the threat to Israel itself was now grave and where Jordan and possibly Iraq seemed likely to intervene. He also opted for a war of movement, unlike the static defense that had just failed so dismally. After bitter fighting on October 8–10, Israeli tanks and aircraft destroyed the Syrian armor on the Golan and prepared to move toward Damascus. Meanwhile, against army advice, Sadat insisted on an offensive beyond the canal toward the Sinai mountain passes. This was mainly to relieve Assad, but it is possible that Sadat, like many victorious leaders, was carried away by success. The Egyptian offensive on October 14 saw the biggest armored battle since Kursk in 1943, involving some two thousand tanks. It petered out with heavy Egyptian losses against well-prepared Israeli positions. Worse, it opened a gap between the Egyptian Second and Third armies, which a daring counterattack by General Ariel Sharon exploited on the 15th. Exceeding his orders, Sharon threw a raiding party across the canal just north of the Great Bitter Lake. This created a bridgehead through which Israeli forces could spread behind Egyptian lines. By October 16, the day of Sadat's Cairo triumph, the war hung in the balance. That balance would be decided by the superpowers.

Fearful of Arab defeat, the Politburo mounted a major airlift of supplies to Syria and Egypt from October 9. This preserved Moscow's credibility as a reliable ally and protected Brezhnev against such hawks as Marshal Grechko. But to the Americans, sure that the Soviets had prompted the war, this was provocative in the extreme and required U.S. aid to Israel. Kissinger hoped to keep the aid small and secret. But the beleagured Nixon ordered a full-scale airlift, anxious to demonstrate his resolve at home as well as abroad, and the first huge C-5 transports landed in Israel on October 14. Soviet and U.S. aid may have hardened their respective clients against a cease-fire—Egypt and Syria early in the war, Israel in its later stages.[10]

Moscow had been pushing for a cease-fire from the start; Washington was resistant until Israel's position had improved. But on October 19, following a backchannel hint from Kissinger, Brezhnev invited the U.S. secretary of state to Moscow. There they drafted a joint call for a cease-fire and for immediate negotiations "under appropriate auspices aimed at establishing a just and durable peace settlement in the Middle East." This became UN Security Council Resolution 338, approved on October 22. Privately, Kissinger and Gromyko agreed that the phrase "under appropriate auspices" signified "the active participation" of both superpowers throughout the negotiations. Kissinger flew home via Tel Aviv to sell the idea to the Israelis but found them unwilling to accept an ultimatum. They had now pushed south from their canal bridgehead, surrounding Egypt's Third Army, in reality only two reinforced divisions whose destruction would be disastrous for Egypt. Brezhnev cabled Nixon suggesting they "urgently dispatch Soviet and American military contingents to Egypt to ensure implementation of the Security Council decision." He concluded: "I will say it straight that if you find it impossible to act jointly with us in this matter, we should be faced with the necessity urgently to consider taking appropriate steps unilaterally."[11]

Brezhnev and most of his colleagues, it is now clear, had no plan to enter the fighting. What they had in mind was a joint force of some two hundred fifty military observers from each side to supervise the cease-fire. But given the need to avoid Egypt's humiliation, the last sentence was added, probably by the angry Brezhnev himself, as bluff in the hope of forcing America's compliance.[12] The effect of the message was quite the opposite, however. Kissinger learned of it during the evening of Wednesday October 24, just as the latest cease-fire was taking hold. He understood Brezhnev to mean: "send in forces together or he will send them in alone."[13] A meeting of the National Security Council was hastily convened. Just before midnight, U.S. forces worldwide were placed on Defense Condition III, the highest state of readiness short of imminent attack. The meeting was chaired by Kissinger. Nixon, though commander in chief, was in his quarters, exhausted (some say drunk) after the furor caused by his "Saturday Night Massacre" of senior staff to protect the Watergate tapes.[14] He did not approve the alert until next morning.

The motives behind the U.S. action remain in dispute. The Soviet ambassador states that Kissinger told him the next day the alert was mostly determined by "domestic considerations." But others argue that "with or without Watergate, the same course almost certainly would have been taken" because of the perceived need to show American resolve.[15] Kissinger claimed in his memoirs that "the Soviets subsided as soon as we showed our teeth."[16] But the Politburo never seriously envisaged Soviet intervention and was, in fact, puzzled by the U.S. alert. Although Marshal Grechko and KGB chief Yuri Andropov favored comparable mobilization to show that the USSR could not be pushed around, the Politburo eventually followed a suggestion from

Brezhnev: "What about not responding at all to the American nuclear alert? Nixon is too nervous—let's cool him down."[17] It was a wise move. Despite some bluster from Nixon, the crisis subsided with the end of the fighting.

Over the next few days, Kissinger forced Israel to allow food, water, and medicine to reach the Egyptian Third Army by threatening that otherwise the Soviets or even the Americans would do so themselves. On October 27, at a marker indicating kilometer 101 on the road from Cairo to Suez, uneasy Egyptian and Israeli officers began talking about the details of the cease-fire. It was the first direct discussion between the two governments since Israel came into existence twenty-five years before.

Israel now controlled even more Arab territory than before the war. But at immense cost: $7 billion in equipment, property, and lost output—equivalent to one year's GNP.[18] Israel had learned the hard way that neither territory nor weapons guaranteed security and that the Arabs were no longer risible foes. It had also become dependent on economic and military assistance from Washington, in marked contrast with the 1950s and 1960s. In 1970 U.S. aid amounted to $71 million, in 1973 $467 million, the next year nearly $2.6 billion.[19] This helped to win victory in 1973 and rebuild defenses afterward, but Israel was left vulnerable to U.S. peacemaking. For Washington was now bent on resolving the Middle East conflict. The threat it posed to détente and even world peace seemed too great. Here Sadat succeeded, though not in the way he had intended. As we shall see, the road to peace proved long and tortuous. But it began at Kilometer 101 between Cairo and Suez at the end of October 1973.

It is unlikely, however, that the Middle East would have become so central to U.S. diplomacy in the 1970s but for the oil crisis. Although Sadat's grand strategy was poorly executed, its goals were astute—diplomatic negotiation forced by limited war *and* economic leverage. The leverage depended above all on King Feisal of Saudi Arabia, the largest Arab oil producer and effective leader of the Organization of Petroleum Exporting Countries (OPEC). Sadat courted the Saudis assiduously in 1972–1973. Feisal's pledge of support in August 1973 was crucial in the decision for war. On October 16–17, in the middle of the conflict, Arab oil ministers meeting in Kuwait City took two crucial decisions. After protracted haggling with Western oil companies, they unilaterally raised oil prices by 70 percent. They also agreed on a rolling embargo against supporters of Israel, cutting supplies by 5 percent a month. After Nixon publicly pledged a $2.2 billion package of aid to Israel on the 19th, Feisal imposed a total oil embargo on the United States. The Arab's vigorous, coherent use of economic warfare was, if anything, more of a shock than their military attack on Israel. As we shall see, it had deep and lasting effects on the Western economies. And it constituted a further reason for the intensive American peacemaking that followed.

Partial Peace: Israel, Egypt, and the Palestinians

Among the outside powers, the United States was the principal beneficiary of the conflict. The Soviets had neither been able to restrain their allies from war nor bring them victory over Israel. Sadat and Assad were therefore ready to cooperate with Kissinger's attempt to turn the tenuous cease-fires into durable disengagements. The Israeli government wanted its prisoners of war repatriated, which gave Kissinger leverage with them. Shuttling between Cairo and Tel Aviv, Kissinger secured a disengagement agreement in Sinai on January 18, 1974. After intense haggling, Assad signed a similar deal for the Golan at the end of May. One Kissinger aide recorded that in the previous month his boss had held 130 hours of face-to-face talks with Assad and had been through Damascus Airport twenty-six times.[20] It was a triumph for Kissinger's shuttle diplomacy, earning him the nickname "Henry the Navigator." In consequence, the Arab oil embargo was lifted.

Kissinger encouraged the Arabs to believe that the disengagement agreements were steps toward a comprehensive peace, whereas he told the Israelis that he was merely trying to reduce the pressures on Washington and Tel Aviv. Whatever Kissinger's real goals, Nixon's collapse and Ford's weakness reduced his leverage. Unwilling or unable to confront the Palestinian issue, he kept up some momentum in 1975 by engineering a second Sinai disengagement in September by which Israel withdraw to the Mitla and Gidi passes, some thirty miles from the canal, and relinquished valuable oil fields along the Gulf of Suez. In return, Yitzhak Rabin—who had replaced Golda Meir as Israeli prime minister in April 1974—extracted more U.S. aid. Among the Arabs, Egypt's unilateral diplomacy was condemned for its neglect of Syria and the Palestinians. The other Arab countries cut back financial aid to Egypt, exacerbating the country's economic crisis.

Because of domestic discontent, Sadat had ruled out higher taxes to pay for war and rearmament. Egypt's foreign debt therefore soared: whereas 22 percent of the government's budget was covered by borrowing in 1966, the proportion was 53 percent in 1975. But as Arab aid declined after 1975, Sadat found that American and IMF loans came with their own price tag of stabilization measures, including cuts in food subsidies. Bread prices, held constant since the early 1960s, were doubled at a stroke in January 1977, prompting riots on a scale not seen since the British occupation. After seventy had died, the price rise was canceled, but that made it even more urgent to reduce the need for heavy defense spending.

Israel faced similar economic pressures. Nearly half of GDP was being siphoned off in taxation by 1976. Additional defense expenditure was therefore covered by American aid (mostly tied to U.S. weapons). Israel's external debt soared from $1.4 billion in 1967 to $8.1 billion a decade later. By 1977 the foreign debt amounted to 24 percent of national income compared with 10 percent in 1973. For both Israel and Egypt, in short, peace had become an economic imperative.[21]

In 1977 the new U.S. president, Jimmy Carter, was ready to capitalize on the situation. As an evangelical Christian, he had a special interest in the Holy Land and a moral commitment to peacemaking. Carter sought a comprehensive settlement whereby Israel would withdraw to its 1967 borders in return for pledges of peace and security. But Carter's hopes seemed dashed by the election of Menachem Begin as the Israeli prime minister in June 1977, displacing the Labor politicians who had led Israel since independence. Begin owed the victory of his Likud (Unity) coalition in part to disenchantment with Labor's inefficiency and corruption, symbolized by revelations about the Rabins' illegal U.S. bank account. But he was also the beneficiary of underlying demographic changes, picking up disproportionately the votes of the young and poor Sephardic Jews. Although the early Jewish immigrants to Israel had come from Europe (the Ashkenazim), the "ingathering" of the 1950s had been mostly from the Mediterranean region, particularly North Africa. Despised by many Ashkenazim and treated as second-class citizens, these Sephardic Jews had become a majority by 1965 and their birthrate was double those of European extraction. Their antagonism toward Labor's European elite helped push Likud narrowly into power in 1977.

Begin seemed an unlikely leader—small, in poor health, peering through thick spectacles. Rabin, a charismatic ex-general, derided him as an "archaeological specimen."[22] This was also a reference to Begin's politics. During the British mandate, Begin had commanded the Irgun—an underground army in his view, terrorists to the British. A Polish Jew, he was preoccupied by the Holocaust—he called Israel's pre-1967 frontier the "Auschwitzborder" and denounced the PLO as "the Arab S.S."[23] He made no distinction between moderate and extreme Arab states and damned the strategem of land for peace as madness, insisting that Israel should include all the old Palestine mandate, Greater Israel, what he termed the biblical lands of Judaea and Samaria. Yet in June 1977, the sixty-four-year-old Begin had to foresake the intellectual luxuries of opposition and face up to the hard choices of power. A first sign of this was the appointment of Moshe Dayan, a Labor defector, as foreign minister, to broaden his base and appeal to world opinion. Forced to sound constructive about the West Bank, he suggested limited Palestinian autonomy under permanent Israeli sovereignty. He also went along with Carter's plans for a peace conference at Geneva under American and Soviet chairmanship. Nevertheless, the prospects for real progress seemed small—until Sadat's bombshell.

On November 9, 1977, the Egyptian president announced that he was willing to go "to the ends of the earth" for peace, even to the Israeli parliament itself. His motives remain unclear: perhaps to keep the Soviets out of the arena, perhaps to break the diplomatic deadlock.[24] In any event, it was a gamble akin to the crossing in 1973 and an offer that the initially incredulous Begin could not refuse. Yet Sadat's visit to Jerusalem would not have exerted such an impact but for the news media in the new era of satellite broadcasting. TV cameras covered Sadat's plane touching down on Israeli soil on November 19. "President Sadat is now reviewing a guard of honour of the Israeli Defense Forces," gasped one Jewish reporter. "I'm seeing it but I don't believe it." Over the next week, Sadat gave more than one hundred media interviews: indeed, he had talked to all the three main American TV networks on the thirty-minute flight from Sinai. In the battle for U.S. public opinion, Begin had to play to the gallery as well. "Never mind the Nobel Peace Prize," exclaimed Golda Meir later, "give them both Oscars."[25] Sadat's two-day visit personalized the peace process. It also developed a momentum of its own. "Egypt and Israel became hostage to each other. The failure of the peace process was liable to inflict heavy damage on one, or both, of them."[26] Although Sadat was taking the greater risks, Begin had now been sucked in.

But not sucked down. The Israeli leader rejected Sadat's demands for withdrawal to the 1967 borders and a separate Palestinian state. He also accelerated the construction of new Jewish settlements in Gaza and the West Bank, pushing the number of settlers up from 3,200 in 1977 to 28,400 by 1983.[27] Carter therefore took his own gamble, inviting both Begin and Sadat to Camp David, the presidential retreat in Maryland, in September 1978. Once they were there, cut off from the media, Carter hoped to pressure both leaders into a settlement (Plate 33). Begin seems to have underestimated the danger: his delegation was divided and unprepared for definitive talks. By the time the twelve days of talks had ended, he had accepted two frameworks for negotiation—on an agreement between Egypt and Israel, and on a period of self-rule for the West Bank and Gaza.

Back home in the Knesset, many Likud supporters were outraged about losing Sinai. The Camp David agreement was approved only with Labor votes. Begin then dragged his feet on concluding a treaty, forcing Carter to commit his authority again by visiting Egypt and Israel in March 1979 in what he later called "an act of desperation."[28] As at Camp David, Foreign Minister Dayan and Ezer Weizmann, the defense minister, overcame Begin's resistance. Carter returned home in triumph.

The Egypt-Israel peace treaty was signed in Washington on March 26 and the phased evacuation of Sinai was completed three years later. Yet Begin had avoided any direct linkage with progress on the Palestinian question: he had relinquished Sinai in the hope of retaining Gaza and the West Bank. The outcome, whatever Sadat claimed, was a separate peace, and the Arab states severed relations and aid to Egypt after March 1979. Although Carter regarded agreement between Egypt and Israel as a major achievement of his presidency, it had not brought peace to the Middle East. If anything, it made the Palestinian problem even harder to resolve.

The 1973 war had shown again that the front-line Arab states were unable or unwilling to evict the Jews from Palestine. The Palestine Liberation Organization (PLO) under Yasser Arafat therefore escalated its terrorist operations against Israeli civilians. At the same time, it was gaining new international status. In November 1974, Arafat was invited to address the UN General Assembly, which was now dominated by African and Asian states opposed to America and Israel. Yet Arafat's movement was fragmented, its base small: three-quarters of Palestinians lived under Israeli or Jordanian rule. After King Hussein evicted the PLO from Jordan in 1970, it turned the Lebanese refugee camps into a state within a state. In the decade after 1973, Lebanon became the crucible of the Palestinian struggle.

Lebanon is a mountainous country half the size of Wales, about 135 miles long and nowhere more than thirty-five miles wide, with around 2.5 million people in the mid-1970s. In the 1920s the French had carved a separate Lebanese state out of Syria. Lebanon gained full independence, like Syria, after World War II. Its coastal cities became havens of bustling capitalism and the metropolis, Beirut, was known as the Paris of the Middle East. About a quarter of the population was Sunni Muslim, a quarter Shia Muslim, and another quarter Maronite Christian. As France's clients and heirs, the Maronites remained politically dominant. But a delicate balance had been created to minimize communal friction: under the National Pact of 1943 the president would be a Maronite, the prime minister a Sunni, and the Speaker of the House a Shia, while parliamentary seats were divided between Christians and Muslims in a six-to-five ratio. Politics revolved around deals between the dynastic leaders of the various communities, including the Druze, a mystical Shia offshoot whose small numbers (some 7 percent of the population) were offset by its warlord tradition. By the 1970s, however, the country's fragile stability was proving hard to maintain. The original political balance had been upset by rapid Muslim population growth and by increased communal tension in the expanding cities, notably Beirut, where rival militias had been formed. Then the PLO base, in a country sandwiched between Syria and Israel, turned Lebanon into a regional battleground.[29]

By 1975 Palestinians amounted to around one-fifth of the population. The PLO presence frightened Maronites and alarmed Sunni leaders, anxious to maintain communal cooperation and prosperity, but it was applauded by many younger Muslims. The Druze, under Khalid Jumblatt, forged a coalition of leftist Arab groups in support of the PLO. The shooting of twenty-seven Palestinians in Beirut in April 1975 sparked off eighteen months of civil war. Jumblatt saw his chance to destroy the old political system and take power himself. His forces advanced on the Maronite mountain heartland and were stopped only by Syrian intervention in June 1976. By the time the Saudis brokered a cease-fire in October, Assad controlled much of the country. A new government was installed in September on the old principles of communal power sharing and Maronite primacy. But thirty thousand had died, and Beirut was now partitioned between Christian east and Muslim west along the so-called Green Line. Moreover, the new government existed only because of Syria. Assad had no desire to see a strong Lebanese government, allied to the PLO, on his doorstep. Apart from probably provoking Israeli intervention, it threatened his own regional ambitions.

In the 1920s Lebanon had been created at the expense of Syria: Assad regarded it as rightful Syrian territory. "Our history is one, our future is one and our destiny is one," he declaimed in July 1976. He said the same thing about other neighbors, calling Palestine "a principal part of Southern Syria" and asserting that "Syria and Jordan are one people and one country."[30] Assad was reviving the myth of "Greater Syria," a country extending from Turkey to the Nile, which supposedly had been fractured by European mandates and Israeli wars. Personal conviction was one reason for his stance, but political calculation was more important. There had been twenty-one changes of government in Syria between 1946 and 1970, and many outsiders assumed that Assad would soon join the list. Sunnis constituted two-thirds of the population, his minority Alawi sect a mere tenth. For an Alawi to rule Syria was as shocking to Sunnis as "an untouchable becoming maharajah in India or a Jew becoming tsar in Russia."[31] Assad secured his position by a repressive security apparatus and by adroit alliances with Christians, Druze, and other minorities. He also kept a token Sunni presence in positions of power. "Greater Syria" served as another unifying force in his fractious country.

For Israel, the outcome of the Lebanon civil war was doubly alarming. Syria was now entrenched in Lebanon, and PLO raids into Israel intensified. In March 1978, guerrillas from Arafat's Fatah organization highjacked a bus en route to Tel Aviv; in the ensuing shoot-out, thirty-four Israelis were killed. In retaliation, twenty-five thousand Israeli troops, backed by planes and warships, invaded southern Lebanon. Some 140,000 Shia villagers fled north to the refugee camps of Beirut. Although Israel ceded most of the land it gained to a UN force, a border zone three to six miles wide was handed over to the Christian militia leader, Saad Haddad. Israel's alliance with Haddad and other extreme Maronites was an attempt to offset Druze, PLO, and Syrian dominance. Its most important partner was Bashir Gemayel, scion of a major Maronite dynasty and the leader of a Beirut militia. Like Jumblatt before him, Gemayel was ready to overturn the balance of Lebanese politics, this time to gain complete Christian dominance. But he was too weak to act alone. That was where the Israelis came in.

Begin had long been contemplating another strike into Lebanon. PLO rockets were regularly shelling northern Israel; in the spring of 1981 the Syrians moved missiles into the southern Bekaa Valley. The threat seemed akin to that from the Golan Heights in 1967. Israeli domestic politics were also conducive to military action. The election of August 1981 had enabled Begin to form a more right-wing coalition, including General Ariel Sharon as defense minister. Sharon was a maverick ex-officer whose war record from Sinai in 1956 to the recrossing of the canal in 1973 had been marked by daring, insubordination, and brutality. "Brilliant general, vicious man," said Begin later.[32] It was Sharon who drew up the detailed war plans. By the spring of 1982, diplomatic restraint was no longer necessary, since the final stages of the Israel-Egypt peace had been completed. The assassination of Israel's ambassador in London (though not Arafat's work) gave Begin the pretext he needed. On June 6, 1982, Israeli forces invaded southern Lebanon. Unlike in 1978, however, they did not stop. Within a week they had driven north up the coast to Beirut. Their goals were far reaching—to install a client Lebanese government and destroy the PLO, thereby leaving the West Bank no hope of an alternative to Israeli rule.[33]

Sharon and Begin had deceived the cabinet about their true intentions, but at first the gamble paid off. After a bloody air battle over Beirut, the Syrians withdrew their forces from western Lebanon. On June 13, Israeli forces linked up with Gemayel's militia in Beirut, surrounding fifteen thousand PLO fighters and about five hundred thousand Palestinians in the west of the city. But Gemayel, with his eye on the presidency, would not wage war in West Beirut, so Israel could not destroy the PLO by proxy. It was only after relentless Israeli bombardment, in defiance of American and world opinion, that the PLO evacuated West Beirut at the end of August. Tunisia alone would let them in. It was the nadir of Arafat's career.

On August 23, the Lebanese parliament elected the thirty-three-year-old Bashir Gemayel as the next president. As in 1976, the parliament session was ringed by tanks—but this time they were Israeli, not Syrian. On September 12, Sharon and Gemayel secretly agreed that the Lebanese army would enter West Beirut, in defiance of the evacuation agreement, to root out remaining PLO fighters. But two days later Gemayel was assassinated by a Syrian bomb. On the 15th, with the approval of Begin but not the cabinet, Israeli forces secured strategic positions in West Beirut and allowed the Christian militias to enter the Palestinian refugee camps. As many Israeli officers predicted, they wanted revenge for Gemayel's death: instead of weeding out PLO remnants, the militias indiscriminately massacred civilians. While Israel celebrated the Jewish New Year, the world's media screened appalling pictures of what had happened in the Sabra and Shatilla camps. Mounds of corpses, hastily dug mass graves, countless thousands of flies. One Norwegian reporter tried to record his story clinically on tape: "I have come to another body, that of a woman and her baby. They are dead. There are three other women. They are dead. . . ." From time to time he would push the "pause" button and vomit before continuing his grisly inventory.[34]

Estimates of the dead ranged from seven hundred to over a thousand. It was clear that Israeli commanders had authorized entry into the camps and had done nothing to stop the massacre. Many in the army were furious at Sharon for blackening its good name. An estimated four hundred thousand Israelis joined a "Peace Now" rally in Tel Aviv. As usual, Begin started by meeting criticism with vehement, self-righteous denial. "*Goyim* [non-Jews] are killing *goyim*," he reputedly told the Cabinet, "and the whole world is trying to hang Jews for the crime." In an earlier letter to President Reagan, he had likened the assault on Arafat and the PLO in Beirut to sending "an army to Berlin to annihilate Hitler in the bunker."[35] But as the evidence piled up, and with it uproar from Jews at home and abroad, Begin recognized the damage done to Israel's reputation. After a damning official inquiry, Sharon was forced to resign from the Defense Ministry: like Dayan before him, the hero of the last war brought down by the next. Begin, always volatile, slid into a deep depression, and he retired from the premiership in September 1983, a broken man. For Israel, too, it was a turning point. Since the horrors of World War II, the Jewish homeland had commanded the moral high ground of international opinion, especially in the United States. Now Sharon's brutal realpolitik had undermined Israel's unique moral authority.

The Gulf States and the Oil Boom

At Christmas 1970 a forty-two-gallon barrel of oil cost around two dollars. Ten years later the spot price was over forty dollars. Even allowing for inflation, the real increase was more than tenfold. Between October and December 1973 alone the oil price quadrupled to $11.65 because of OPEC's actions. The second great surge, from late 1978 into 1981, was prompted by the Iranian revolution and the Iran-Iraq war. In 1981, according to one estimate, it would take the Saudis only nineteen hours' oil output to buy Harrods, the prestigious London department store, and under three days' pumping to acquire Buckingham Palace—in the unlikely event that Queen Elizabeth wished to sell.[36] How could such a transformation occur? Why did the Arab oil producers, hitherto ignored or despised, suddenly have the developed world over a barrel?

The basic reason was the West's rapid shift from coal to imported oil as the prime sources of energy. In 1972 Western Europe relied on oil for 60 percent of its energy consumption, compared with under 38 percent in 1962. Japan's dependence was even more acute: 73 percent, compared with 44 percent a decade before. In both cases, virtually all the oil was imported. The United States was less exposed: oil accounted for only 46 percent of energy consumption in 1972—little changed from 1962—and only 30 percent of that oil was imported.[37] But that was a sharp increase over the 20 percent level of 1962. In absolute terms the amount was massive, given that American motorists consumed one in every seven barrels of oil used in the world each day.

Growing U.S. imports also reflected a second major change, namely the displacement of the United States by the Middle East as the swing factor in world oil production. In 1945 North America accounted for two-thirds of world oil output, the Middle East a mere 7 percent. In 1973 North America produced 21 percent and the Middle East 38 percent.[38] By the 1970s, existing U.S. reserves were running out; import quotas, imposed since 1958 for strategic reasons, had been abolished even before the oil crisis in 1973. Roughly two-thirds of the extra demand for oil in the 1960s had been satisfied by Middle East producers. Saudi Arabia, with a quarter of the world's proven reserves, had become the world's largest oil exporter. Logically, it was only a matter of time before the Middle East had a greater say in setting its price.

At this same time, Western influence over the "Persian Gulf" region was in decline. In 1974, more than one-third of Middle East oil production came from the small princely states running down the eastern coast of the Arabian peninsula—Kuwait (the third-largest regional producer after Saudi Arabia and Iran), the United Arab Emirates (UAE), Bahrain, Qatar, and Oman (Map 4). All had been coveted by their large neighbors: Iraq considered Kuwait a renegade province, the Saudis and/or Iran had claims over the rest. Some are tiny in the extreme: Bahrain is a group of islands totaling only two hundred fifty square miles. What had saved them from absorption in the past was the protection of Britain, whose trading interests required friendly states along the gulf. But in 1968, Britain's Labour government announced a complete withdrawal of troops from east of Suez (except for Hong Kong). The local rulers and the United States offered to bear some of the costs, but the collapse of the pound and fears of nationalist unrest were overriding concerns in London. Having taken a few steps to promote stability, such as encouraging a federation of the seven Trucial States into the UAE, Britain pulled out in 1971. Within two years, the West would have cause to rue its loss of leverage over the gulf oil producers.

Increasing Western dependence on oil from a region over which it exerted decreasing influence laid it open to "oil shocks." But what turned potential into reality was the new assertiveness and coherence of the producer states. Earlier in the century, Western oil companies paid desert rulers for concessions to drill for oil and then pocketed most of the profits. Iran had nationalized its oil industry in 1951 but could not run it without Western expertise. Starting in the 1950s, profits were shared on a fifty-fifty basis as Western companies were forced into partnership with new national oil companies. But it was not until Muammar al-Qaddafi seized power in Libya in 1969 that the balance really shifted. Western Europe relied on Libya for a quarter of its oil after closure of the Suez Canal in the 1967 Arab-Israeli war. Exploiting this need and threatening nationalization, Qaddafi forced increases in profit shares and oil prices in 1970, with other producers following suit. Libya and Iraq began nationalizing the oil companies before the 1973 war, Kuwait and Saudi Arabia did so thereafter. What mattered as much as control over their own oil industries was cooperation with fellow producers. The Organization of Petroleum-Exporting Countries had been founded by Venezuela, Saudi Arabia, Iran, Iraq, and Kuwait in 1960. But it made little impact until the Saudis assumed their "swing" role in the early 1970s. Even then, much depended on the skill of Ahmed Zaki Yamani, an American-educated Saudi lawyer who became his country's oil minister at the age of thirty-two in 1962 and who steered the OPEC cartel. With his big eyes, goatee beard, and dapper attire (be it Arab or Western), Yamani became a media celebrity. But his real forte was patient, logical negotiation that wore down opposition and held OPEC in line for most of the 1970s to a policy of moderate but not excessive price rises.

These were the reasons for the Middle East's new wealth, wealth that gave Kuwait a per capita GDP 50 percent higher than that of the United States by 1981. And Kuwait provided striking visual evidence of the revolution wrought by oil. In the 1950s about half its population of two hundred thousand lived within the confines of Kuwait town, a pearl-diving port on a promontory, bounded on the landward side by a mud wall. But oil-powered growth was already having an effect in the 1960s. Guided by British planners, Kuwait renovated much of the old city and developed a new town outside its walls. During the oil boom of the 1970s, the Kuwaiti royal family commissioned top international architects to refashion its waterfront with some of the most innovative buildings in the world. Kenzo Tange of Japan designed the airport; Arne Jacobsen of Denmark produced the gold-domed Central Bank; another "great Dane," Jørn Utzon (of Sydney Opera House fame), was responsible for the new parliament; TAC from Cambridge, Massachusetts, did the Al-Safat shopping development; and so it went on. From sleepy

fishing port to jet-set metropolis in less than two decades—it was a staggering transformation.[39]

Yet Kuwait boasted only a million people in 1975. Its gulf neighbors were
even smaller. The countries that mattered in the Middle Eastern oil boom
were Saudi Arabia, Iran, and Iraq. It is on them that we must focus in particular.

The kingdom of Saudi Arabia occupies most of the Arabian peninsula and
is about three-quarters the size of India. In 1974 it had a population of about
seven million, of whom more than one-quarter were nomadic. Less than 1
percent of the land area was cultivated and there was little industry. In 1972
the whole country boasted only fifty-seven thousand telephones. Not until
the 1960s did it develop a national paper currency. But it was sitting on one-
quarter of the world's proven oil reserves, and the price boom of the 1970s
transformed its prospects. The government's second five-year plan, for
1975–1980, was free of any foreign-exchange constraints: it had a budget of
$149 billion (nine times that of the first plan in real terms). The centerpiece
was the creation of two massive new industrial conuburbations at Jubail on
the east coast and Yanbu on the west, to expand the kingdom's manufacturing base. The third plan, for 1980–1985, with a budget of $235 billion, main-
tained the goal of economic diversification but also emphasized education
and training, to reduce dependence on foreign personnel.

The oil boom and government policy changed ordinary life in three main
ways. First, urbanization accelerated. Between the early 1970s and 1984,
the proportion of the population living in urban areas increased from 26
percent to 70 percent. The population of royal capital, Riyadh, more than
doubled from seven hundred thousand to 1.8 million.[40] Second, the number
of Saudis enrolled in some form of education rose from 669,000 in 1972 to
nearly 1.7 million a decade later—over 20 percent of the population.[41] Third,
average living standards improved dramatically. Saudi citizens paid no income tax, the sales tax was abolished because of surging government oil revenues, and food and other essentials were heavily subsidized. The extension
of free health care was a major government objective. As we have seen, urbanization, education, and welfare have been general themes of world history in the later twentieth century. But for the oil boomers, the revolution
was especially rapid. In February 1980, the Red Sea port of Jeddah was
billed as the most expensive city in the world, with a cost of living double that
of New York or London. Yet in the same month its municipal authorities
rounded up 4,350 sheep and goats that had been left to stray on the streets
by their owners.[42]

Tensions between growth and backwardness were evident throughout the
oil-rich Arabian peninsula. Spectacular growth rates in GDP were largely

generated by oil income, which in turn was used to purchase foreign imports: it would be years before development programs could diversify the economic base. Dependence on oil (and thus on the oil price) remained acute: in Saudi Arabia and the gulf states in 1980, oil constituted about two-thirds of national production, over 85 percent of government revenues, and at least 90 percent of export earnings.[43] Even to run the oil industries, let alone to diversify, the peninsula depended on foreign workers because, again, it would be years before the education boom would produce skilled native-born personnel. By 1981, citizens made up only 14 percent of the UAE work force, in Kuwait 22 percent. Even in Saudi Arabia the proportion was around 57 percent. Foreign workers were mostly Muslim, but increasingly from Pakistan, the Philippines, and other parts of Asia. The domestic beneficiaries of education mostly went not into productive industry but into the proliferating administrative sector—the so-called petrobureaucracy, which, at the extreme, employed an astonishing 60 percent of Kuwaitis of working age by 1981.[44] With government jobs and welfare services, the family dynasties of the region could coopt potential opponents and placate the populace. In the process, they weakened their traditional rivals from regional tribes, religious sects, or—in gulf states like Kuwait and Qatar—merchant families on whom they had previously relied for revenue.[45] In short, oil royalties kept the royals on their thrones—the Sabah family in Kuwait, the Khalifahs in Bahrein, the Thani clan in Qatar, and most of all the house of Saud.

Often perceived from outside as a tribal despotism, Saudi Arabia was in fact an oligarchy whose pillars were the populous Saudi royal house, the religious leaders, or *ulama,* and the leaders of the provincial and tribal dynasties, the emirs. The deposition of the corrupt King Saud in 1964 was a consensual act by all three elements, even though his brothers took the lead. Thereafter, the dominant figures were Feisal, who was king from 1964 until his assassination by a deranged nephew in March 1975, and then his half brother Fahd, the leading figure during the reign of the ailing King Khalid from 1975, who then ruled in his own right from 1982. Feisal was an austere and methodical man who promoted cautious modernization; Fahd was less restrained and more overtly pro-American. Both used modernization and bureaucracy to buy off opposition, particularly from the urban western coast, the Hijaz. Yamani, Feisal's protegé and oil minister, came from a Hijazi commoner family. In this way, nationalist opposition was diverted without the house of Saud (unlike the Sabahs in Kuwait) having to honor periodic promises to establish some form of assembly. But the family never ignored its traditional supporters, especially the leaders of the puritanical Wahhabi sect with which it had been allied for two centuries. Although the *ulama* failed to prevent innovations like television and higher education, especially for women, they were allowed to control the content of both. TV broadcasts were mostly religion and sanitized news; women's education (a strong if discreet interest of Feisal's wife Iffat) was strictly segregated, with any men teaching only by closed-circuit TV. Saudi rulers were mindful that they not only sat on a quarter of the world's oil reserves; they were also guardians of Islam's two holiest places, the cities of Mecca and Medina, to which all Muslims are enjoined to make a pilgrimage once in their lives.[46]

The Saud family's political adroitness stood in marked contrast to the mismanagement of the oil boom by Mohammad Reza Pahlavi, the shah of Iran, who had succeeded his father in 1941 at the age of twenty-two. In 1978, Iran's agricultural and industrial output constituted only about one-fifth of GNP, compared with oil and services, which each amounted to one-third. Medical improvements centered on prestige projects such as city hospitals, rather than rural health care: about half the doctors and hospital beds in the country were located in Teheran.[47] The shah was less careful than the house of Saud to tailor spending to what the economy could absorb, bidding to make his country "the Japan of the Middle East." The result was soaring inflation and, as oil revenues stabilized, a budget deficit of over $7 billion in 1978, which then required austerity measures that produced a sharp recession. The shah also entertained grandiose political ambitions, encouraged by the Nixon administration, which built him up as the Gulf policeman after the British withdrawal and gave him carte blanche to purchase nonnuclear weaponry from the United States. By 1975 Iran was the world's top importer of military equipment and the seventh largest arms spender in the world. For many at home and abroad, the shah's hubris was dramatized in October 1971, when he invited world leaders to the desert ruins of Persepolis to celebrate the twenty-five-hundredth anniversary of the Persian empire founded by Cyrus the Great. A tent city was erected, complete with marble bathrooms; food and wine were flown in by Maxim's and other French caterers. At the high point of the ceremonies, which cost at least $100 million, nine kings, thirteen presidents, and a clutch of other VIPs saw the shah stand before the tomb of Cyrus to greet his predecessor "at this moment when Iran renews its pledge to History . . . to watch over your glorious heritage."[48]

Not only did the shah, unlike the house of Saud, alienate most major groups in his country. Iran was also a more complex, less manageable society, four times larger than Saudi Arabia (thirty-eight million in 1979). The burgeoning new middle class of intellectuals, professionals, and students was regarded as a nationalist threat and not coopted into the regime. The traditional middle class of the bazaars—ranging from big merchants and moneylenders down through the well-organized guilds of shopkeepers to salesmen and street vendors—were threatened by the shah's urban development program of highways and supermarkets. He offended religious leaders by eroding their endowments and schools, imposing the forcible unveiling of women, and establishing a Religious Corps to promote a statist version of Islam. And, although industrial workers had been bought off by better wages and housing, the recession of 1978 bit hard, and there was unrest among the very poor. Teheran, in particular, was polarized between the rich suburbs north of the old city and the shantytowns to the south.

Even so, economic protest and political opposition were kept under control by Savak, the shah's feared secret police, and by the four hundred thousand-strong armed forces. When President Carter lauded Iran as "an island of stability," his diplomatic hyperbole reflected the perception of official Washington.[49] The turning point came in early 1977, when the shah began a limited liberalization. This was partly a response to the Carter administration's new pressure on human rights. But it stemmed as much from the shah's own dynastic concerns: already seriously ill with leukemia, he wanted to prepare political institutions that would survive him and buttress his teenage son. During 1977, writers, intellectuals, and professionals, particularly in Teheran, held protest meetings and created reformist organizations, starting a process not easily controlled. Despite his autocratic image, the shah was reserved and indecisive. He oscillated between reform and repression, as did the signals he was getting from Washington, where the Vance-Brzezinski battle (see Chapter 10) muddied this area of U.S. policy as well. The shah was also cut off from reality: unlike the vast Saudi royal family, whose tentacles reached across society, the Pahlavi dynasty was small and out of touch. Yet even the failures of leadership might not have been critical but for the underestimation by both the shah and the Americans of the revolutionary power of religion.

In understanding the place of Islam in Iran, two points are fundamental. First, Iran is not an Arab country. The native language is Farsi (though it uses the Arabic script), and the shah's harking back to Cyrus the Great was part of his effort to free the country from Islamic traditions imposed by its seventh-century Arab conquerors. Second, Iran is the main home of the minority Shi'ite tradition within Islam. The split between Sunnis and Shi'ites dates back to the bloody struggle soon after the death of the Prophet Muhammad as to who was his true successor *(caliph)*, in which Shiat Ali (the party of Ali, his son-in-law) was eventually defeated. The climactic event, in 680, was the battle of Karbala in what is now central Iraq, when Ali's son, Hussein, and seventy followers were killed after epic resistance. Thereafter the caliphate was handed down through the dominant *Sunna* tradition (the "trodden path" of the prophet and his early followers), first from Damascus, then Baghdad, and finally Istanbul, as Middle Eastern empires waxed and waned. Meanwhile, the Shia tradition became the official religion of Persian dynasties from the sixteenth century, thereby sharpening the distinction between Persia and its Sunni Arab neighbors. In many respects, of course, the two traditions differed little. For devout followers of either, daily life centered on the Qur'an, or scriptures, and the sharia, their codification into Islamic law. But Shia's embattled history fostered a keener commitment to social justice, a more critical view of temporal states, and a strong millenarian tradition as they awaited the *mahdi,* or messiah. The martyrdom of Hussein was held up as allegory of their own sufferings, until the mahdi's eventual victory.

That in itself was not necessarily a revolutionary doctrine. Hussein (like Christ) could be a model for patient suffering *or* violent resistance, and in fact the dominant strain in Iranian Shiism until the 1970s was quietist.[50] Its transformation into a militant ideology was supremely the work of Ayatollah Ruhollah Khomeini (1902–1989). A leading critic of the shah's reforms and the U.S. connection in the protests of 1963, Khomeini was exiled to Turkey and then Iraq. From there he moved from criticism of modernization in the name of Islamic values to a denunciation of monarchy itself as un-Islamic (especially after the 1971 jamboree at Persepolis). Here was a powerful critique of pietistic Shia and its identification with the Iranian state. It was spread through Iran by transcripts of Khomeini's prolific writings and cassettes of his lectures, using the network of mosques and Islamic associations controlled by his followers. In a country lacking strong secular traditions of opposition, Khomeini's calls for the Islamic community *(ummat)* to unite in struggle against a boundless tyrant *(taghut)* in league with Western, anti-Islamic forces provided the only unifying language of protest.[51] When the shah persuaded the Iraqi government to evict Khomeini in October 1978, he moved to a Paris suburb. There he had much greater access to the Western media, to whom he gave 120 interviews in the next four months. Thanks to improved air service and the new direct-dial phone system installed by the shah, he was also in closer touch with opposition groups in Iran.[52] It is ironic that, from his Iraqi cassettes to his Paris phone calls, the great opponent of modernization was helped inestimably by the technologies of modernity.

The shah's last months as ruler saw "one of the greatest populist explosions in human history."[53] In August 1978, four hundred had died when an Abadan cinema was torched; next month hundreds more were killed when the police opened fire on demonstrators in Teheran's Jaleh Square. Across the city, hundreds of thousands were on the march—students in jeans, workers in overalls, clerics in ecclesiastical robes, women in veils (now a symbol of protest), and suited professionals—visual testimony to the extent of opposition. The shah had not been driven by car through his capital for years because of security fears, but a helicopter ride over the crowds made him aware (apparently for the first time) of the scale of protest and left him deeply shaken. October and November saw nationwide strikes against the austerity program, stopping factories and squeezing oil revenues. The shah installed a military government in November, but then spoiled the effect by apologizing on TV for past mistakes and arresting the hated former boss of Savak. Early December coincided with the holy month of Moharram, when the faithful reenact Hussein's death in emotional passion plays. Khomeini skillfully turned past into present: the battle of Karbala became the motif of Iran's contemporary martyrdom. In defiance of the evening curfew, thousands across Teheran shouted "Allah is great" in a deafening rooftop chorus. Between five hundred thousand and one million marched peacefully on December 10, nearly two million the next day. These were some of largest mass protests of the twentieth century. The shah, zigzagging again, appointed a civilian government, which persuaded him to leave the country, at least for the moment. On January 16, 1979, he bade farewell to ministers and generals on the windswept tarmac of Mehrabad Airport, his Boeing 707 surrounded by rows of planes grounded by the strikes. He wrote later: "A harrowing silence was broken only by sobs."[54]

Teheran, however, exploded in a cacaphony of car horns on hearing the news. On February 1, Khomeini flew home in triumph after more than fourteen years of exile and set up an alternative government under Mehdi Barzagan, a reformist Shia politician. The power struggle between the rival governments now turned on the loyalty of the military, whose ranks were depleted by desertions, its leadership riven by the Shah's indecision. Backstairs negotiation helped neutralize the commanders, but peaceful confrontation was even more effective. "Face the soldier with a flower," Khomeini told protesters. He also warned the troops (mostly Shia) that if they fired on their brothers and sisters, "it is just as though you are firing at the Qur'an."[55] Despite a brief but bloody battle between air force units and the Imperial Guard, the end of the Pahlavi dynasty was surprisingly peaceful. The shah's civilian government fell on February 11.

Khomeini had returned as "spiritual leader." Some in Washington still hoped that progressive nationalists and pro-Western officers could form a moderate government in which the Ayatollah would play only a "Gandhi-like" role.[56] This was also the expectation of Iranian politicians like Barzagan. In short, an even greater surprise than the fall of the shah was the emergence of a cleric-dominated Islamic republic that galvanized militancy across the Muslim world.

The Iranian Revolution and Islamic Resurgence

It took all Khomeini's spiritual authority and tactical skill to manage the disparate forces unleashed in Iran's revolution. His root advantages were the loyal mosques and local committees, and the quickly formed Islamic Republican party, which mobilized support from the bazaars and urban workers under ulama direction. By the autumn of 1979 his Pasradan, or Revolutionary Guards, constituted the largest militia in Iran, some twelve thousand strong.[57] Yet, like most successful leaders, Khomeini was also lucky. He consolidated power thanks to his opportunistic use of three related crises in 1979–1980: the American hostages seized in November 1979, the war with Iraq from September 1980, and the struggle over a new, Islamic constitution.

The immediate pretext for occupying the U.S. embassy in Teheran was the shah's admission to the United States for medical treatment. But the move had been planned for some months by a select group of militant Muslim students under the supervision of Khomeini's son, Ahmed. When the embassy was seized on November 4, 1979, few in Teheran or Washington imagined that the fifty-two American diplomatic staff would be held until January 1981. But the hostages became pawns in a larger game. What the radicals initially wanted was paper, not people. From captured American documents, some of them painstakingly reconstructed after being shredded, they accumulated evidence that was used over the ensuing months to discredit political opponents. Carter's vehement reaction, including a freeze on Iranian assets in the United States, also enabled Khomeini's supporters to whip up anger against the "Great Satan" and use it to build support at home. A breakthrough in the hostage crisis came only when Khomeini decided, after Iraq's assault in September 1980, that Iran did not need two major enemies, but it then took months to resolve the question of Iranian assets. The hostages were released on January 20, 1981, at the moment when Ronald Reagan was inaugurated as Carter's successor.

On the American side, the real significance of the hostage crisis is the way it preoccupied the public throughout 1980. This was partly because the administration, from both guilt and calculation, made release of the hostages its prime foreign-policy goal and identified Carter personally with their fate. But it probably had little choice because, in the words of one White House staffer, "the crisis was the longest-running human interest story in the history of television."[58] The networks spliced shots of Iranian students chanting "death to America" and interviews with anxious relatives back home against the backdrop of calendars showing each passing day of the 444-day crisis. Carter's failure to get them out, including a botched rescue mission, played a significant part in his election defeat on November 4, 1980—the anniversary of their seizure. In a country where, before 1979, few knew much about Iran or Islam, Khomeini's stern, bearded face became as familiar as Carter's, "experts" on Iranian society appeared on every news bulletin, and Shi'ite became a household word (and a disguised expletive). The hostage crisis created a new American image of fanatical Islamic "fundamentalism."

That image hardened with the Iran-Iraq war. The conflict was rooted in the old enmity of Persians and Arabs and in long-standing disputes over access to the gulf—labeled as "Persian" or "Arabian" depending on one's nationality. It is also likely that war would not have broken out but for the determination of the new Iraqi leader, Saddam Hussein, to exploit the chaos and weakness of Iran and make himself the dominant regional power. Nevertheless, what stood out to Western observers was the religious dimension of the conflict. As soon as he gained power, Khomeini declared, "We will export our revolution to the four corners of the world." Such rhetoric had a catalytic effect in Iraq, where the socialist Ba'ath party, nominally Sunni, ruled over a populace at least 55 percent Shia. Protests by Iraqi Shi'ites against official discrimination and secularization intensified. As part of his campaign of repression, Saddam executed a leading Shia cleric, who was a personal friend of Khomeini, in April 1980. When news reached Teheran, Khomeini called on Iraqis to overthrow their government "because the regime is attacking Iran, attacking Islam and the Qur'an."[59] Iran became a base for Iraqi militants; border incidents escalated during the summer. Saddam's decision for war in September was therefore an act of both domestic and foreign policy.

It was also a reckless gamble. Iraq had only one-third the population of Iran, the army was trained on Soviet lines for defensive war, and the loyalty of its largely Shia soldiery was far from certain. Moreover, the Iranian army was imbued with the idea that this was a holy war against the infidel, and that the dead were martyrs in the service of God. The government's Martyrs Foundation ensured the welfare of widows and children on a generous scale. In the first year of war, thirty-eight thousand Iranians died, compared with twenty-two thousand Iraqis. By the summer of 1982, Iraqi troops had been cleared from Iranian soil, and the Supreme Defense Council in Teheran, defying professional military advice, decided to invade Iraq and proclaim a rising against Saddam Hussein.

Their failure to achieve their goal, despite substantial advances, was partly due to the priority given to piety over professionalism in the army command. But it also reflected the support now being given to Iraq by states anxious to contain Khomeini. Although Iraq was formally a Soviet ally, both Saudi Arabia and Kuwait provided substantial logistic and financial aid to Saddam, as did France. More striking, alarm at the prospect of Iranian victory prompted the Reagan administration to move from official neutrality and tilt heavily toward Iraq in 1983–1984, providing intelligence and equipment for Saddam on a scale that dwarfed Soviet aid. Evidence linking Iran with the car bomb attack on the U.S. Marine base in Beirut in October 1983, in which 241 died, was also a powerful impetus. By terrorism and war, it seemed, Khomeini was exporting his revolution.

Meanwhile, the ayatollah had used the crises with America and Iraq to consolidate his position at home. This involved removing opponents—both pro-Western reformers and clerical conservatives—and rewriting the constitution to establish "an Islamic republic." The draft constitution drawn up by Barzagan's government in June 1979, though paying lip service to the idea, proposed a Gaullist-style presidency with no special role for the ulama. Ironically, it was opposition from secular parties and the left to a strong executive that led to reconsideration of the constitution in an Assembly of Experts. There, however, middle-level clerics pushed the idea of a theocratic government headed by a pre-eminent Islamic jurist (velayat-e-faqih), modeled on Khomeini's writings. This proposal outraged not only the secular parties but also conservative clerics. "We seem to be moving from one monarchy to another," warned Ayatollah Kazem Shariatmadari, their main spokesman.[60] But the anti-American furor whipped up after the embassy seizure enabled Khomeini's supporters to push through a referendum approving the constitution in December. After riots in Tabriz and other cities, Shariatmadari's political party was suppressed in January 1980 and he was put under house arrest.

Elected that month, Iran's first president was Abolhassan Bani Sadr, a suave, French-educated economist. He came to power determined to wrest the revolution back from "a fistful of fascist clerics."[61] But American sanctions crippled his government, and he could not extricate the hostages without offending the militants. The war with Iraq strengthened the militants both ideologically and politically, through the role of mosques and local committees in wartime rationing. In June 1981, U.S. embassy documents revealing 1978–1979 overtures to Bani Sadr from the CIA were used to vote him from power. The remaining opposition was snuffed out in 1981–1983. First were the mojahedin, urban terrorists inspired by an Islamicized Marxism, whose high command was discovered and killed in February 1982, then the Tudeh, or Iranian communist party, which was suppressed in 1983 when its (tactical) support of Khomeini was no longer needed by the Islamic leadership. By 1983, with the war against Iraq turning in Iran's favor, Khomeini's position was secure.

What was the nature of the new Islamic republic? Its basic principle was governance by a supreme religious leader who would interpret Islamic law, act as commander in chief, and exercise vast powers of appointment and dismissal. Decisions of the National Consultative Assembly (majiles) were subject to approval by a clerical Council of Guardians. Clerical domination extended through society. All schools had reopened on a single-sex basis by the end of 1981. Forty thousand teachers were purged. Higher education was in the hands of a seven-man Council for Cultural Revolution; when the universities reopened in 1982–1983, students and curricula were closely vetted, and the proportion of women enrolled was reduced to 10 percent, compared with 40 percent before the revolution. At all levels of education, Islam and the Arabic language were encouraged; in contrast with education in the shah's day, the pre-Islamic era of Iranian history was played down. The economy saw a large-scale nationalization of industry, banks, and trade, with confiscated properties placed in the hands of a religious foundation. In 1981, the Islamic Dress Law imposed compulsory veiling and loose-fitting clothes on women to conceal their features and shape. In 1983 laws were passed to establish interest-free banking.

Not surprisingly, these changes reinforced the Western image of Islamic revolution. But, as we shall see in Chapter 16, there were clear limits on radical traditionalism in a complex, increasingly urbanized society. In the same way, Khomeini's regional impact requires careful analysis. Islamic militancy was most apparent in Shia communities, which overall constituted only about one-tenth of Muslims. Even among them, the Iranian example was attractive only in situations of extreme social crisis. The main instance apart from Iraq was Lebanon, where fundamentalism helped radicalize the Shia communities as the country disintegrated in 1982. Iran served as inspiration and banker for the Hizbullah, or party of God, which was responsible for many of the bomb attacks in Beirut. Iran's example also stirred up the downtrodden Shia workers of Saudi Arabia's Eastern Province, where there were serious disturbances in 1979–1980. But even among Shia clerics, Khomeini's concept of the Islamic republic as a personal theocracy was controversial. And the widespread animus among Arabs toward the Shia tradition as a Persian heresy militated against any general acceptance of his teachings as a model.

More loosely, the Iranian example did act as inspiration for Muslim radicals in the region. On November 19, 1979, virtually the eve of the Islamic year 1400—at a time when millenarian expectations were high—Juhayman al-Utaybi, a former soldier, and some four hundred Islamic students seized the Grand Mosque in Mecca and proclaimed the overthrow of the house of Saud. Although their revolt failed to ignite, it took three weeks to stamp out. The government's failure to protect Islam's holiest shrine was a damaging blow. Juhayman was connected with the Saudi branch of the Muslim Brotherhood (Ikhwan), a movement that enjoyed considerable support in Syria among the majority Sunnis, who were alienated by Alawite rule. Its stronghold was in the northern cities of Aleppo and Hama, whose Sunnis, unlike those in Damascus, had not been coopted into the Assad regime. Growing guerrilla war led to a bloody siege of Hama by the government in February 1982 in which thirty thousand may have died. The Ikhwan had originated in Egypt; it was here that an offshoot, Jihad, in league with dissident officers, gunned down President Sadat in September 1981. The shock felt across the world was evident at his funeral, attended by three former U.S. presidents

(Nixon, Ford, and Carter) and other heads of state, as well as seven hundred journalists. It confirmed the impression, to quote one Cairo academic, that "Islam has replaced Arab nationalism as the ideology of dissent."[62]

Although that was also a widespread view in the West—suddenly aware of Islam after years of ignorance or stereotyping[63]—Sadat's death was largely the result of his own ill-judged manipulation of the Islamic issue. He had made religious concessions to help ease the country away from Nasserite socialism. In 1971 the constitution was amended to make the sharia a major source of national law; in 1980 it was designated *the* major source. These changes and the relaxation of Nasser's controls on Islamic groups alarmed Egypt's Christian minority, the Copts. Although less than 10 percent of the population, they were prominent in business and in the cities. Mounting Christian-Muslim tensions in the 1970s intensified the fervor of Islamic militants. After extreme communal violence in the summer of 1981, Sadat began to arrest extremists on both sides—but too late to save himself.

The temptations and dangers of playing the Islamic card were also evident in Egypt's southern neighbor, Sudan, Africa's largest state. There the military government of Jafar Muhammad Nimeiri, in power since 1969, succeeded in ending a seventeen-year civil war in 1972. This had pitted the largely Muslim north against the south, where the Christian minority (some 10 percent of the population) was concentrated. Despite this success, however, Nimeiri found neither state socialism nor pragmatic capitalism a panacea for his country. In the late 1970s he became increasingly reliant on support from the Muslim Brotherhood. His initial reaction to the Iranian revolution was blunt—"We do not want any Khomeinism in the Sudan"[64]—but his faltering regime could not ignore its challenge nor the lesson of Sadat's demise. To head off Islamic militants and to distract attention from government failure and corruption, he therefore announced in September 1983 the rigid imposition of Islamic law. Not only did this self-proclaimed "Islamic Revolution" alarm the non-Muslim south, playing a major part in reopening the civil war, but its traditional content and barbaric implementation also upset many Muslims. Growing disorder led to Nimeiri's overthrow by the military in April 1985.

The stories of Sadat and Nimeiri demonstrate that the politics of Islam were far more volatile by the early 1980s. Yet this does not negate the basic point that Islam remained the ideology of government more than of dissent. Most rulers used religion to legitimize and stabilize their regimes at a time of rapid socioeconomic change. These rulers could be radical or traditional, as shown by the examples of Libya and Pakistan, on the African and Asian edges of the Islamic world.

Qaddafi and his Libyan Free Officers seized power in 1969 from a monarchy based on the Sanusi religious order. At first he was therefore keen to erode Sanusi privileges and win support from the non-Sanusi ulama. Alcohol consumption was banned, nightclubs were closed, and Islamic punishments decreed for various crimes—such as hand amputation for theft. In fact, the harsher punishments were rarely applied and, by the late 1970s, Qaddafi felt strong enough to move against the ulama. He restricted their endowments and announced that the Qur'an but not necessarily the Sunna was binding on Libyan Muslims. By this time, Qaddafi was publishing Mao-style "green books" to promulgate his "Third Universal Theory," a new way between capitalism and communism that he called "the comprehensive solution to the problems of human society."[65] The theory was an idiosyncratic blend of state socialism and guided democracy, using grass-roots "Basic People's Congresses." Yet, although Qaddafi apparently became more secular and socialist over time, not to say increasingly eccentric and even psychotic as far as most Westerners were concerned, Islam remained at the heart of his rule. For one thing, it animated his foreign policy, which was dedicated to the overthrow of Israel and its Western backers by any and every means. Substantial oil revenues gave him the freedom to try this with relative impunity. Qaddafi also needed Islam for domestic reasons. Libya was a sprawling state (the fifteenth largest in the world), with a weak sense of national identity and, as Qaddafi often complained, a marked political passivity. It was also a classic *rentier* state, made rich by oil revenues rather than economic development, whose populace, through no exertion of their own, had seen per capita income quadruple during the 1970s to exceed that of Britain.[66] Because it was hard to motivate people whose wealth bore little relation to their work, revolutionary discipline had to be instilled by religious zeal.[67] Hence Qaddafi's insistence that Libya practised "Islamic socialism."

This was also the refrain of Zulfikar Ali Bhutto, who became president of Pakistan in December 1971 when Ayub Khan's military government collapsed in the wake of Bangladesh's secession. Bhutto's Pakistan People's Party (PPP) was a diverse coalition of antigovernment groups. During the 1960s he had used Islam as a unifying force, insisting that "Islam preaches equality, and socialism is the modern technique of attaining it."[68] Yet, once he was in power, Bhutto's energetic but erratic state socialism proved deeply divisive. It appealed to large landowners and industrialists, who benefited from his nationalization programs, and to the poor, who were electrified by his oratory and bolstered by his welfare measures. But it alienated much of the productive middle class—middling farmers, small merchants, and industrialists, many of whom were also devout Muslims offended by the arrogant Bhutto's Western manners, sybaritic lifestyle, and heavy drinking. The Muslim concept of "proper conduct" therefore became a rallying point for all concerned about his assault on Islamic values and private property. A coalition of religious and secular opponents fought the March 1977 election under the banner of the Pakistan National Alliance (PNA) and, after winning only a quarter of the seats in a manipulated poll, took their battle into the streets. Bhutto imposed martial law but, after troops rebelled against firing on their own people, the chief of staff, General Mohammed Zia-ul-Haq, arrested Bhutto on July 5, 1977.

Zia's proclaimed intention was simply to ensure "free and fair" elections within ninety days, but he also stated that "I consider the introduction of [the] Islamic system as an essential pre-requisite for the country."[69] The strength of the PPP and the charisma of Bhutto sucked Zia ever deeper into politics. The clash between the two men seemed symbolic: the rich, Westernized landlord versus the austere, religious soldier, a product of the middle class that Bhutto had so outraged. Zia subjected Bhutto to a show trial, after which he was hanged on April 4, 1979. Backed by the principal Muslim party, Jamaat-i-Islami, Zia had already taken the presidency in September 1978 and tightened martial law. A new legal code in June 1980, based on the sharia, provoked protest from non-Muslims and from women, as well as from the Shia minority, who wanted their own code. Zia adroitly cultivated both the ulama establishment and Islamic populists, and used the emotive issues of chador (the veil) and chardivari (literally, the "four walls of the house") to appeal to middle-class concerns about women's honor and private property. He insisted that the Western party system was corrupt and that unfettered elections were inappropriate in a society with limited literacy. What was needed was "Islamic democracy" run by practicing Muslims of unquestioned integrity. "I believe one hundred per cent in democracy as it is enshrined in Islam," he claimed in 1980. "Islam is most democratic. It gives you the most democratic system."[70]

Yet this did not imply any change in Pakistan's strongly pro-American foreign policy. During the 1980s, the top security issue for Zia was the war between guerrillas and the Soviets in neighboring Afghanistan. As a "front-line" state, Pakistan was able to extract more aid from Washington, and the crisis also justified retention of martial law. Pakistan became the main supply base for Afghan guerrillas, not to mention the reluctant host to over three million refugees by 1984. But although the war was depicted in the West as a straightforward struggle between "freedom fighters" and Soviet imperialism, it epitomized the complexities of the region. There were at least nine hundred guerrilla groups—some under traditional leaders, others led by younger commanders from the educated middle class. One of the latter, Ahmad Shah Massoud, won considerable fame in the West but, as a Tajik, he was resented by leaders from the Pushtun ethnic majority.[71] Religious divisions were also significant. The majority of Afghans are Sunni; many of the mojaheddin guerrilla groups had close links to Pakistan. But the country also has a sizeable Shia minority and is adjacent to Iran. Several Shia groups were trained and funded by Khomeini's government—the so-called Iran Eight. Thus, Afghanistan in the 1980s was a multilayered battleground. Beneath the superpowers' proxy war was a kaleidoscopic local struggle that was linked to a regional contest between Khomeini's Iran and Zia's Pakistan—both fiercely Islamic yet representing rival religious traditions and political ideologies.[72]

Bangladesh had broken away from Pakistan in 1971 (see Chapter 7), but its politics followed a similar pattern. Parliamentary democracy under the "father" of Bangladesh, Sheikh Mujibur Rahman, survived only three years before he imposed a one-party dictatorship. Mujib and twenty-one members of his family were killed in August 1975 by dissident officers. Over the next fifteen years two senior military held power, General Ziaur Rahman (1975–1981) and General Hussain Ershad (1981–1990). Each followed the same pattern of progressively loosening military control only to be toppled themselves. Bangladesh's political problems were not unusual but they were extreme. Unlike Pakistan, the army was fragmented as well as politicized. There were twenty-six coup attempts against Ziaur Rahman alone.[73] Parties were acutely factional: one survey in 1986 found 161 political organizations.[74]

Bangladesh's successive rulers justified martial law as the only way to address the country's developmental problems. These, too, were extreme. The population grew from seventy million in 1972 to one hundred million in 1986, by which time per capita GNP was $160 per year (one of the lowest in the world). Secondary school enrollment was only 18 percent; four-fifths of women were illiterate.[75] And the country was still overshadowed by India, which controlled the headwaters of the Ganges, whose floods were critical for Bangladesh's agriculture.

Yet a Bangladeshi sense of identity was emerging. The unifying force in 1971 had been the Bengali language. This distinguished the country from West Pakistan, which was also predominantly Muslim, but during the 1970s and 1980s, Bangladeshi leaders played up Islam to confirm their control. For Ziaur Rahman, Islam was a way of distancing Bangladesh from India. When Ershad made it the state religion in 1988, he was trying maintain control as civilian politics were restored. At the village level, local elites often used the criteria for being a "good Muslim," particularly strict seclusion of their womenfolk, to reinforce their status as community leaders.[76]

Islam could therefore be used to justify Libya's populist socialism *and* Bangladesh's conservative authoritarianism; it was compatible with the anti-Americanism of Iran *and* the pro-American stance of Pakistan and Saudi Arabia. All this shows just how simplistic it was to equate Islam with revolution or indeed with any one political ideology.

In fact, the proper relationship of Islam and politics became a matter of intense debate among Muslims after the Iranian revolution. Against Khomeini's conservative theocracy one should set the influential Ali Shariati, a

Paris-educated Iranian who died in 1977. Trained in Western sociology, Shariati abandoned traditional, text-based "Islamic studies" and applied the classic writings to contemporary society. His aim was a new "practical Islam" freer from ulama control. The thrust of Shariati's argument points to another great divide, between scriptural literalists and Islamic liberals. The former, exemplified by the Pakistani jurist Abdul al-Ala Mawdudi (1903–1979) harked back to the supposed golden age of the first four caliphs, Mohammad's immediate successors. Mawdudi insisted that the sharia constituted "a complete scheme of life and an all embracing social order where nothing is superfluous and nothing is lacking."[77] Against him stood liberals such as Mohammad Iqbal (1875–1938)—poet, philosopher, and apostle of Pakistan—whose education at Cambridge and Munich led him to build bridges between Islam and Western thought. Iqbal argued that Islam was not a closed book but dynamic and evolving. He was one of the best-known advocates of *ijtihad,* independent reasoning from first principles, which is of cardinal importance for all reformist Muslims.

Yet outside Iran, the dynamic element in so-called fundamentalism was not the senior religious scholars but Islamic students or graduates in their twenties. These were the men who plotted the death of Sadat or seized the Grand Mosque in Mecca. Educated and urbanized, they were products of modernization. But they were also its principal victims, denied appropriate jobs because of flawed development and clotted bureaucracies, denied political avenues of protest by the authoritarian state. It has been aptly observed that "the Islamists are not angry because the aeroplane has replaced the camel; they are angry because they could not get on the aeroplane."[78] This "intellectual proleteriat" of students and minor functionaries constituted the core of Islamic militancy (and, indeed, of *all* opposition politics, left or right, religious or secular).[79] But Islamic student associations were particularly potent in the crowded and faceless Middle Eastern universities of the 1970s. They often became a focus of identity for the lonely or alienated young, especially rural migrants, from whom many of the militants were recruited. In fact, Middle Eastern fundamentalism had "much in common with the youth revolution of the 1960s" in the West,[80] with Muhammad playing an analogous role to Marx.

Yet to focus on the politicized few does not explain why so many governments felt it necessary or desirable to Islamicize their polities in the late 1970s and 1980s. Here we move from minority activists to broader public attitudes, particularly among the educated middle class. This period saw renewed observance of religious duties, such as the regular daily prayer calls, attendance at Friday corporate prayers, and fasting during the holy month of Ramadan. There was greater use of Islamic dress by men and women, and avoidance of un-Islamic practices such as drinking alcohol and going to nightclubs. Not all of this can be attributed to official sanctions or to new cultural nationalist pride in the Islamic past. It was also a response to the strains on traditional social values because of rapid urbanization. In the cities, the patriarchal family was breaking down, with students and workers separated from their parents and women moving around in defiance of conventional segregation and seclusion. The practice of delayed marriage (because of education and work) posed acute frustration in a culture that totally condemned premarital sex. The widespread support for some (re)imposition of Islamic social values testifies to concern about urban social breakdown and to the failure of the state in response.

This broader, social Islamic revival was particularly concerned with the position of women. In the West, the revival of "veiling" after years of decline was widely seen as a sign of reaction and repression. But this overlooks the fact that *hejab,* or modest dress, was often adopted voluntarily in the 1980s by young, educated women. Instead of the dour black coverings of their grandmothers, they wore turbans or head scarves and fitted dresses that combined style and decorum. Sometimes this was a coded rebuff to their Westernized parents, a form of youth rebellion. But it was also a practical response to mixed urban living. One Egyptian medical student described Islamic dress as "a kind of uniform. It means I am serious about myself and my religion but also about my studies. I can sit in class with men and there is no question of attraction and so on—we are all involved in the same business of learning, and these garments make that clear." Veiling might even be a means to liberation. Another young Egyptian woman remarked that now that she wore Islamic dress, her parents were "not worried if I stay out later that usual or mingle with friends they do not always approve of. In this dress, my reputation remains intact."[81] It remains true that for many Muslim women, particularly the rural and less educated, veiling was part of traditional patriarchalism. But the *adoption* of veiling by young women illustrates the danger of treating Islamic revival simply as a form of reaction.

The 1970s witnessed a ferment of Islamic debate about gender as well as politics. At one extreme was Maulana Mawdudi, the Pakistan Islamic militant, who insisted, "Harem is the last place of refuge where Islam guards its civilization and culture." Near the other was Ali Shariati, whose widely read book *Fatima is Fatima* (1971) used the story of the Prophet's daughter to argue that each Muslim woman must "create" her own identity.[82] Textual criticism was central to these arguments: did the Qur'an and the early Islamic traditions, the *hadith,* stipulate veiling for all women or simply for the wives of the Prophet? Female scholars, influenced by the women's movement in the West, increasingly distinguished between Islamic traditions and the "feudal" societies in which they had become embedded. In this way, a return to sacred texts could be an instrument of liberation for women, too. For instance, the late 1970s saw a growing campaign by women, especially doctors, in the Sudan and Upper Egypt against the continued practice of female circumcision, whose crude implementation by village midwives and female elders left many young women with chronic pelvic infections and impaired reproductive organs. Campaigners argued that this was not an Islamic practice, but one dating from ancient Egypt that Islam had simply condoned.

In short, for women as well as men, Khomeini's Iran was not the epitome of Islam in the 1980s. A religion that commanded allegiance, at least nominally, from nearly a fifth of the world's people could not be stereotyped, whatever parts of the Western media implied. As this brief survey from Libya to Bangladesh has shown, much depended on the social and political context of each state. This can be underlined, in conclusion, by reference to the persistent claim that Islamic doctrines explained the high birth rates of the Arab world.

On the face of it, the figures seem suggestive: across the Arab states of North Africa and the Middle East during the late 1980s, women had an average of 5.6 children, compared with 3.9 in less-developed countries as a whole. In explanation, critics often cited Islam's approval of sexual enjoyment in marriage and its legitimization of women's domestic dependence—"poor, powerless, and pregnant." Yet Islam has traditionally condoned contraception and, on close examination, the regional demographic pattern was variegated. Apart from familiar differences—noted in Chapter 5—between urban and rural areas and between educated and less educated women, national interest was also important. In the fractious states of this unstable region, the old equation of numbers and power remained compelling. Minorities wanted to be majorities, small states feared bigger neighbors. These arguments help explain the persistently high fertility of Iraq, Jordan, Syria, and the Palestinians. Iraq in fact tried to *increase* fertility; so did its tiny neighbor, Kuwait, albeit unsuccessfully. By contrast, North African states felt less threatened and were therefore readier to advocate birth control. Domestic stability also mattered. As one scholar has observed, "The ambivalence of many Arab/Muslim leaders toward female emancipation stems from their need to address two conflicting demands in their societies: prosperity, which means modernization; and identity, which is partly rooted in tradition."[83] These leaders differed sharply in the precise balance they struck between modernization and tradition, but specific policies, whether on the constitution or on women, were always conceived as part of a larger social equilibrium.

The oil shocks, the related modernization of the Middle East, and the politicization of Islam that was both result of and reaction to social change all posed a serious challenge to the international dominance of North America and Western Europe in the 1970s. At the same time, another challenge had emerged from the economies of East Asia. This challenge was even more potent because these were not societies suddenly made rich by the oil boom but ones whose wealth was sustained by economic development. Furthermore, this was capitalism of a different sort from the versions in the United States or West Europe. It transformed East Asia even more profoundly than had the upheavals of decolonization and communism after World War II.

12

Capitalist Revolutions, Asian Style

For North America, Western Europe, and Australasia, the oil crisis of 1973–1974 marked a postwar divide, separating the long boom of the 1950s and 1960s from a slump and then much slower growth in the years to follow. What caught the eye in the late 1960s was the dynamism of Japan, which emerged as one of the world's most developed and competitive economies. It also survived the oil shocks better than most of the West to become a leading manager of the world economy by the 1980s.

Other Asian "tigers" emulated Japanese methods in the 1970s, followed by several Southeast Asian "cubs" as the 1980s progressed. Most important was the sudden economic growth of communist China, the world's most populous country, as it began market reforms after 1978. The cumulative effect was a shift of productive capacity away from North America and Western Europe to Japan and the Pacific Rim. There was also talk of a new form of capitalism, expressive of "Asian values," in contrast with those of the West.

But the Asian states were no monolith: in each case, development had distinctive features rooted in politics, society, and history. The contrast between the dynamism of most of East and Southeast Asia, on the one hand, and the more elephantine growth of South Asia, on the other, is highlighted by the story of India in the two decades after Nehru's death in 1964.

The West and Stagflation

The West's postwar boom had been running out of steam well before the oil crisis of 1973. In continental Europe, the rapid growth in the 1950s and 1960s was largely a matter of catching up with the United States after fifteen years of depression and war. Growth was not as fast in the United States and Great Britain, where wartime damage had been much less, although there was scope for regional catch-up even within the United States as the South was drawn out of its agrarian past. But high growth rates could not be sustained indefinitely. By the late 1960s, demand for housing and consumer durables was nearing saturation, the postwar flow of cheap labor—refugee or immigrant—was trailing off, and the productivity gains from new technologies had mostly been realized. The 1970s slowdown was, in part, the predictable sequel to earlier catch-up.[1]

There were structural changes as well, because the world economy was now less easily controlled by individual nation-states. The 1960s spread of multinational corporations (MNCs)—firms that produced in several countries—posed a serious challenge to national control. The sales of each of the top ten multinationals in 1976 was over $16 billion—more than the GNP of a hundred countries. Those of the world leader, Exxon, exceeded all but twenty-two nation-states, including developed countries such as Austria. By 1974, more than half of Canada's manufacturing industry was in foreign hands, mostly American. Canada was an extreme case, but multinationals also accounted for about one-fifth of the industrial output of France and West Germany in the late 1970s.[2] At this stage, most of the MNCs were American (with a few notable exceptions such as ICI and Royal Dutch Shell), but they became a global phenomenon in the 1970s and 1980s with the emergence of Japanese and other Asian multinationals.

Another, related sign of the erosion of the nation-state as an economic unit was in international finance. By the end of 1958, most of North America and Western Europe had achieved full currency convertibility, so that dollars could be changed into pounds, francs into deutschmarks, and so on. One unanticipated consequence was the rapid growth of the Eurocurrency market. This started in the late 1950s, using dollars kept in Europe for investment, which were bought and sold by banks. Other currencies were also traded, including sterling, deutschmarks and the Swiss franc, but the dollar predominated. To manage this lucrative business, banks expanded their foreign operations and opened new overseas branches; international banking eclipsed the old imperial banking systems of Britain, France, and the Netherlands. By 1970, the total pool of Eurodollar deposits ($57 billion) far exceeded the dollar reserves held by governments ($37 billion).[3] Since this was speculative capital—highly mobile and highly volatile—its potential for instability was considerable.

Not even the United States was immune. Since World War II the dollar, unique among currencies, had been convertible on demand into gold. This, and the postwar demand for dollars, were the bases of the Bretton Woods monetary system created in 1944. With America producing half the world's manufactured goods and holding half its reserves, the burdens of international management were not onerous at first. Throughout the 1950s Washington sustained a balance of payments deficit in order to finance loans, aid, and troops for allied states. But during the 1960s the costs of doing so became less tolerable. By 1970 the United States held under 16 percent of international reserves. Its share of global exports had fallen from 16.7 percent in 1950 to 13.7 percent twenty years later, whereas the EEC's share had almost doubled to 28.8 percent.[4] Adjustment to these changed realities was impeded by the commitment to fixed exchange rates and by America's obligation to convert dollars into gold on demand.

In the late 1960s, both the dollar and the pound were overvalued compared with the current trading positions of their two countries, while the deutschmark and the yen were undervalued. Naturally, the Germans and Japanese had no desire to revalue and thereby make their exports more expensive, whereas America and Britain sought to maintain their international credibility by avoiding devaluation. The pressure on governmental reserves was intensified by the new international currency markets, with their vast pools of speculative capital sloshing around in search of quick profits. Washington saw sterling as the front line for the dollar but, despite substantial American help in the mid-1960s, the Labour government was forced to devalue in November 1967. By 1971, as the Vietnam War accelerated inflation, the United States was running not merely a payments deficit but also a trade deficit (for the first time in the twentieth century). On August 15, 1971, the Nixon administration unilaterally suspended convertibility of gold into dollars and imposed a 10 percent surcharge on all imports. Treasury Secretary John Connally shrugged off European anger: "We had a problem and we're sharing it with the world—just like we shared our prosperity. That's what friends are for."[5]

The surcharge was dropped in December 1971 as part of a general revaluation of major currencies, which were henceforth allowed 2 1/4 percent deviations from the agreed exchange rate. But even the more flexible official rates could not be defended against the speculators. By March 1973, all the world's major currencies were floating—in other words, their exchange rates were not set by governments but depended on demand across the international currency markets.

The next decade saw attempts at intergovernmental coordination. One landmark was the inauguration of the European Monetary System (EMS) in March 1979. This was a looser arrangement than the 1970 plan for European monetary union, which foundered in the financial crisis. It established an Exchange Rate Mechanism (ERM) that sanctioned 2 1/4 percent deviations around the norm. Member states also contributed 20 percent of their reserves to a stabilization fund. Although this signaled a revival of European cooperation, several major states—notably the United Kingdom—remained outside the ERM, while Italy secured 6 percent deviations for the lira. The renewed decline of the dollar in the mid-1980s prompted action by central bankers of the leading industrial countries. Agreements in New York and Paris in September 1985 and February 1987 (the so-called Plaza and Louvre accords) were signs of government cooperation, as well as marking the emergence of Japan as a major actor in international management. Yet neither had a decisive effect on the dollar's value, a further sign that private, not public, capital was now dominating the world's currency markets.

Another shift of economic power was evident by this time in most developed states, especially West European ones, namely the growing power of labor against employers. This reflected the tightness of labor markets, particularly in Italy and West Germany, after years in which workers were abundant and cheap thanks to population growth, the exodus from the land, and foreign immigration. This tightness made wage demands hard to resist, and the new generation of workers also lacked their parents' restraining memories of interwar unemployment and (in Germany and Austria) hyperinflation. The 1970s were the heyday of the labor movement in Western Europe. Unions capitalized on the swollen industrial proleteriats of postwar Europe and also on the growth of public-sector employment through nationalization and the welfare state. In 1980, about half the employed workers in Italy and Britain were unionized; the figure was nearly 40 percent in West Germany. Scandinavia was the most unionized region of the world, led by Sweden with 80 percent membership, whereas the figure for the United States in 1980 was 23 percent, for Canada 35 percent.[6]

In the mid-1960s, some governments, such as the Dutch and the British, tried to contain the inflationary consequences of wage demands by a formal prices and incomes policy. Others, notably Sweden, favored a corporatist structure in which centralized unions regulated wage claims in return for government promotion of growth and welfare. But the late 1960s saw a general wage explosion across Western Europe, reacting against earlier government restraint and the efforts of employers to protect their contracting profit margins through workplace rationalization. France in the spring of 1968 and Italy's "hot autumn" of 1969 were the most spectacular examples (see Chapter 6). Particularly alarming for employers was the increasingly anarchic nature of labor relations, with plant-level strikes a feature in Britain and France and rivalry between workers about pay differentials evident, notably in Italy and Britain. In all these ways, the balance within capitalism between employers and workers had shifted markedly by the 1970s, just when the growth era was coming to an end.

That era had also depended on cheap supplies of raw materials. Here, too, the balance tilted dramatically in the 1970s. Since the end of the Korean War boom, commodity prices had been low and stable. The harbinger of change was the grain market, dominated by four big producers (the United States, Canada, Australia, and Argentina, of which America accounted for around half of world exports), and by a handful of multinational corporations. During the 1960s, producers were cutting back on production and stocks because of a world surplus, but between 1971 and 1975 world grain trade increased 50 percent in volume. This was partly caused by Russian demand for foreign wheat, but the larger cause was new and massive speculation in wheat futures. Just when opportunities for gambling on the price of gold waned with the end of the Bretton Woods era, the Russian food crisis focused speculators' attention on grain and other commodities. It was another sign of the growing power of markets compared with that of governments. In 1972–1973 commodity prices rose at double the rate for manufactures—a pattern previously unknown in peacetime.[7]

The oil crisis (see Chapter 11) cannot, therefore, be understood in isolation. It was one of several changes in the Western and world economies that brought the previous boom to an end. But the interruption of oil supplies in 1973–1974, and the substantial price rises, were a particular shock. The cumulative effect of rising inflation, falling share values, and soaring oil prices finally took their toll on confidence when Germany's largest private bank, the Herstatt, collapsed on June 26, 1974, from speculative foreign exchange losses. Trading on currency markets halved, and there was a run on smaller banks. The damage to confidence, investment and profits was lasting.

The oil shocks of 1973–1974 and 1979–1980 led to a transfer of real resources to oil producers equivalent to about 2 percent of world GNP. Such a shift was almost unprecedented both in speed and scale. By 1983 the foreign holdings of the Saudi Arabian public sector equaled the total assets of Citicorp or Bank of America, the world's largest banks. The foreign holdings of Kuwait and the United Arab Emirates ranked alongside the world's top ten banks. Yet the shift in wealth did not cause a general international collapse, as happened in the early 1930s when U.S. lending declined so catastrophically. This was partly because the Federal Reserve did not repeat the deflationary policies it adopted then. But it was also because much of this capital flowed back into the Western economies. By 1982, OPEC holdings accounted for about 12 percent of the Eurocurrency market. OPEC investment strategy proved conservative and stabilizing. Saudi Arabia, which generated half the OPEC's current account surplus, and Kuwait, with a quarter, invested much of their new wealth via Western banks and governments—the United States and Britain initially, later Germany and Japan. The Saudi government's concern for the health of the world economy was evident in its agreement in May 1981 to loan the IMF nearly $9.5 billion. This gave it the sixth largest voting power in the organization.[8]

But although Western capitalism did not collapse, it suffered something almost as dangerous—stagflation. This neologism summed up the bizarre mix of stagnant growth and soaring inflation that afflicted most developed economies. The combination of wage rises, higher commodity prices, and expansion in the money supply during the early 1970s all fueled inflation and squeezed profits. Governments imposed deflationary measures that only exacerbated the effects of the oil crisis and the 1974 collapse of confidence. But, unlike the 1930s, radical deflation was politically impossible. Unions and workers, far more powerful than forty years ago, would not accept wage cuts; indeed, they pressed harder for pay rises to offset the inflation. At the same time, governments sustained, even extended, welfare programs to cushion the pain of economic downturn, which usually meant increased borrowing, since tax revenues were declining. Their aim was to "squeeze" inflation out of the system with minimum pain; the result was to deflate enough to exacerbate the slump but not enough to restrain the price spiral. Limited recovery in the late 1970s was halted by the second oil shock of 1979–1980, which drove up prices and wages and prompted further deflation. In the developed countries as a whole, the inflation rate was 9.7 percent in 1973–1981, compared with 4.4 percent in 1960–1973, while their 1973–1981 growth rate averaged 2.4 percent—half that of the preceding period. Unemployment in the EEC nearly doubled to 5.4 percent.[9]

This is the broad picture; there were, of course, marked national variations. Overall, the United States survived the 1970s as well as any developed state. Despite 7 percent unemployment, it kept inflation below 8 percent in the period 1973–1981 and growth was a steady if unspectacular 2.3 percent. Unlike most of Western Europe and Japan, which imported nearly all their oil, its own supplies could satisfy two-thirds of domestic need, and these were priced below world levels. The sharp fall in the dollar's value in the second half of the 1970s enabled the United States to undercut foreign exporters and thereby sustain production.[10] The dollar also remained the prime reserve currency. In 1979, 90 percent of official government reserves were held in foreign currency, and of these 75 percent were in dollars.[11] All this testified to the underlying strength of the U.S. economy.

Stagflation was most evident in the developed countries of Western and northern Europe. Overall, West Germany was most successful, keeping inflation below 5 percent and unemployment at 3.4 percent in the period 1973–1981, while sustaining 2 percent growth. But no one escaped the energy crisis. Most European economies were heavily dependent on imported oil (though the Netherlands was a major producer of natural gas, and significant revenues from North Sea oil began to flow into Britain's coffers after 1975.) Italy was in the most desperate position, with no oil, gas, or even coal (unlike France and Germany). What caused the gravest problems was a combination of high rates of unionization and decentralized wage bargaining, as in Britain and Italy. Both also practiced annual bargaining, unlike the United States where plant settlements were hard fought but usually lasted three years. In Italy wage settlements were also often indexed against inflation.[12] Britain had the worst growth rate (0.5 percent in 1973–1981) and one of the highest inflation rates (15.8 percent) among developed countries; Italy had worse inflation (17.6 percent) but also an average growth rate. Both countries experienced nearly 7 percent unemployment. Not surprisingly, it was in Britain and Italy that the social fabric was most under strain.

In Britain, in 1973, the powerful National Union of Mineworkers used the oil crisis to stage a ban on overtime, seeking a pay rise above rates approved in the Conservative government's new prices and incomes policy. The prime minister, Edward Heath, called a state of emergency and rationed industry to three days' electricity per week. With the miners ready for a national strike, he held a snap election in February 1974 on the slogan "Who governs Britain?" Heath narrowly lost, but the new Labour government was no more successful in curbing industrial unrest. Although it abandoned a formal incomes policy for a continental-style "social contract"—wage restraint in return for secure living standards—union leaders could not control unofficial strikes, and the government could not control inflation. The workers' refusal to accept official pay targets led to a rash of disputes in the "winter of discontent" early in 1979. TV films of garbage uncollected, hospitals picketed, and the dead unburied contributed to Labour's election defeat in May 1979.

Italian politics were even more volatile. In the June 1976 elections, the communists, capitalizing on economic discontent, polled 34 percent of the vote. Rather than try to topple the ruling Christian Democrats, their leader, Enrico Berlinguer, tried a corporatist pact with employers, regulating wages and strikes in return for growth and jobs.[13] Although this curbed inflation, it disillusioned many workers, who saw little reduction in unemployment. Berlinguer's compromise also alienated students and radical groups, products of the mobilization of Italian society that had occurred over the previous decade. Spring 1977 saw violent clashes between students and police in Bologna, a communist stronghold. The Red Brigades, modeled on Latin American urban guerrillas, also embarked on a new "strategy of annihilation," intended to kill and terrorize the governing elite. Its most spectacular coup was the kidnapping of Aldo Moro, the godfather of the Christian Democrats, on a Rome street in March 1978. After much debate, his party refused any deal and Moro was murdered two months later. The killings continued in 1979 and 1980, in what Italians called "the years of the bullet," until the government broke the Red Brigade. For a while, terrorism had threatened the fragile foundations of the Italian state.

Italy had no oil, by 1980 Britain's oil output exceeded that of Iran or Kuwait[14]—their stories remind us that the oil shocks were part of a larger crisis whose relative severity depended on economic and political conditions within each state. This was equally true in Australasia,[15] where Australia and New Zealand elected Labour governments at the end of 1972. The ensuing inflationary expansion of public services made both countries more vulnerable to the unexpected oil shock the following year. In Australia, the efforts of Gough Whitlam's government to secure Arab oil money through unofficial channels provoked political scandal and eventually a constitutional crisis when the governor general, Sir John Kerr, dismissed Whitlam in November 1975 and asked Malcolm Fraser to form a Liberal-Country coalition. Kerr's action aggravated nationalist discontent about the connection with the British crown. Fraser duly won a landslide election victory, as did Robert Muldoon's National party in New Zealand. In both countries, the socialists paid the price of incumbent governments elsewhere amid acute economic crisis. Although Fraser and Muldoon survived the 1970s, neither could control stagflation, which was particularly severe in New Zealand after the second oil shock: increased prices for wool and meat did not match the surging cost of imported oil and manufactures. Economic contraction also exacerbated racial tensions, as Australian aborigines and New Zealand Maoris pressed claims about the loss of their ancestral lands. The thirty-day Maori Land March in 1975 across North Island to Wellington, led by the activist Whina Cooper in her eightieth year, was particularly dramatic.

In Canada, the economic downturn further weakened the fragile federal structure. In November 1976 the Francophone separatist Parti Québécois had won power in Quebec. But in a referendum in May 1980, nearly 60 percent of Quebec voters rejected the PQ's proposals for a new "sovereignty-association" agreement with the rest of Canada "based on the equality of nations." Quebec was, in fact, only the most vocal protagonist in a centrifugal struggle between the provinces and the Ottawa government, a struggle exacerbated by the energy crisis. Oil-rich Alberta wanted to keep control of its production and raise prices to world levels, whereas the consuming eastern provinces were naturally opposed. The Maritimes and the western provinces shared the desire to control more of their own resources. Economic crisis in the 1970s therefore aggravated the structural weaknesses of Canada's federal system, unbalanced by the demographic predominance of

Ontario and Quebec (respectively one-third and one-quarter of the population), by the resource wealth of the peripheries, and by the magnetic attraction of Canada's powerful southern neighbor. In consequence, national integration was weak: Canada was a collection of regional economies, more closely linked to the United States than to each other.[16] By the spring of 1982, the Trudeau government in Ottawa had wooed the other provincial premiers from Quebec's hard-line position, but at cost of further devolution. Few observers expected the new Canada Act to be the last word.

Stagflation was therefore a feature of the developed countries of North America, Western Europe, and Australasia for most of the 1970s and early 1980s—exacerbating deeper political and social problems. The long era of Western economic supremacy seemed to have come to an end. Economic power seemed to be shifting to the dynamic economies of Asia.

The Japanese "Miracle"

When Japan penetrated the American psyche in the 1980s, it became fashionable to ascribe the country's economic success to historic cultural traits, for example, the ethics of group loyalty rooted in Confucianism. Such concepts are, however, notoriously slippery: in the 1950s, Confucianism had often been cited to explain Japan's economic *stagnation*.[17] Moreover, these cultural explanations often betray an underlying Western stereotype of inscrutable, even devious, Orientals. In fact, up to a point, there is nothing mysterious about Japan's development. Despite its mid-1950s fragility, noted in Chapter 8, this was a country with a firm industrial base. The so-called high-growth period of the 1960s can, in part, be ascribed to the familiar features of catch-up economies. In consequence of rapid migration from the countryside to cities, labor shifted from small-scale peasant farming to commercial agriculture, industry, and services—an automatic boost to productivity—while wages remained low by international standards. Educational enrollments surged, increasing skills and enlarging female aspirations. This, in turn, helped to push up the age of marriage and thus push down fertility rates. Recovering from wartime devastation, like the Germans, the Japanese also had a high propensity to save and invest; later, consumer demand help drive economic growth. None of this is very surprising; indeed, in the 1960s almost equally impressive growth rates were recorded by Italy, a country hardly renowned for its Confucian values. In short, "the latecomer effect accounts for much of the Japanese economic expansion."[18]

Much, but not all, and this is where the story becomes interesting. In the first place, the pace of change in Japan was unprecedented. Across much of Western Europe the demographic transition of industrialization had taken the best part of a century; in Japan, it was accomplished in less than two decades. Within this period Japan moved from a rural society with low levels of literacy and high birth and death rates to an urban, well-educated society with low birth and death rates. The reduction in Japan's farm workers from 38 percent of the labor force in 1955 to 12.6 percent in 1975 was "the most rapid decline in the agricultural population that the world had ever seen." By 1970 the three great conurbations of Tokyo-Yokohama, Kyoto-Osaka-Kobe, and Nagoya housed 46 percent of Japan's population, having grown in size by half during the 1960s.[19] Even more dramatic was the drop in the fertility rate over the decade 1947–1957 from 4.54 births per woman to 2.04. It stayed around this level until 1973, when a further fall began. As noted in Chapter 5, the 1950s decline was due largely to abortions. Thereafter, contraception was widely practiced but because Japan (uniquely among industrialized countries) banned the pill on health grounds until 1999, it also had the highest rate of condom use in the world.[20]

In common with most developing countries, heavy manufacturing and large corporations were characteristic of Japan's growth, but its enterprise groups *(keiretsu)* were unusual. These were conglomerates of firms in various industries that held each other's shares, borrowed mainly from banks within the group, and operated in strategic alliance. Thus, the giant Mitsui group included Toshiba electronics, Toyota vehicles, Taisho insurance, and Onoda cement. In 1975, the six biggest groups accounted for 5 percent of Japan's employees, 15 percent of sales, and 18.5 percent of net profits.[21] With some exceptions, notably Mitsui and Mitsubishi, most keiretsus developed after the war. Thanks to interlocking share ownership and reliance on bank capital (rather than on equity finance in a country whose stock market was still rudimentary), they were insulated from the mergers and acquisitions that became a feature of Anglo-American capitalism. Also less susceptible to demand from shareholders for annual profits, the keiretsus concentrated on building market share through superior production. And the diversity of the group provided opportunities for the sharing of products and research, as well as preferential access to capital.[22]

In the 1960s, Japanese companies also operated in a more congenial economic and political atmosphere than their West European rivals. The industrial militancy of the occupation period, stimulated by the permissive U.S. labor laws of 1945–1947, was soon suppressed by MacArthur's anticommunist backlash and the obduracy of Japanese employers. Union membership fell sharply from 55 percent of the work force in 1949 to under 43 percent in 1951, then leveled off at around one-third in the 1960s—lower than in any major developed country except the United States.[23] Moreover, most unions were company unions, in other words one union for all the workers in that firm, rather than being part of industry-wide unions, several of which would be represented in one company. The commitment of workers to the firm was also encouraged, at least in large companies, by principles like "lifetime employment" and seniority-related pay. In return, Japanese workers accepted lower pay than their foreign counterparts. Big companies, for their part, were seeking employees who could do a variety of jobs throughout their career rather than, as in the West, a worker with particular skills who might do the same job in several different companies.[24] (This philosophy also implied a high commitment to retraining by employers and employees.)

These cooperative labor relations were reinforced by the country's political stability. After the right-wing parties coalesced in 1955 into the Liberal Democratic party, the LDP *(Jiminto)* remained in power nationally until 1993. The only analogous Western country was Italy, but here Christian Democratic supremacy was diluted by coalitions with the socialists from the 1960s. Yet the Italian analogy is helpful, because the LDP was also a catchall party—a highly factional coalition of local patronage groups—facing the more ideological and fragmented parties of the left.[25] The LDP also benefited from Japan's multimember constituency system (three, four, or five MPs per seat rather than one as in Britain) and from the failure of the apportionment system to keep pace with urbanization. Although a problem in most urban countries, this was acute in Japan where, by 1979, the most populous urban constituencies had up to four times the electors of their rural counterparts, where the LDP still had a strangehold.[26] LDP predominance also owed much to its cultivation of business through favorable tax and credit policies. And in the high-growth period of LDP rule, the top levels of government were dominated by former bureaucrats. The three premiers of this era were all ex–civil servants: Kishi Nobusuke (1957–1960), Ikeda Hayato (1960–1964), and Satō Eisaku (1964–1972). The influence of bureaucrats in the LDP owed much to the discrediting of politicians during the 1930s and to the Americans' postwar purge.[27] It also encouraged policies that looked beyond purely partisan interests.

Economic policy was another notable feature of Japanese high growth. The government combined macroeconomic orthodoxy in fiscal and financial matters with an interventionist microeconomic policy in key sectors.[28] In other words, as a relatively small economy, reliant on imported raw materials, Japan was anxious to avoid payments deficits. It restricted the inflow of foreign capital, kept taxes low, and minimized government borrowing. These measures followed the dictates of classical economics. On the other hand, in its bid for growth, the government promoted key industries, particularly steel in the 1950s and cars in the 1960s. This was done not by the command methods of the Soviet bloc but through a mixture of legislation and "administrative guidance" by the Ministry of Finance and the Ministry of International Trade and Technology (MITI). Methods included tax concessions, directed investment, controls on new companies, and especially protective tariffs and quotas to exclude foreign competition. In many developing countries, of course, the result was cosseted, high-cost industries. But Japan was unusual in having a large domestic market (the population was 83 million in 1950, 93 million in 1960, and 103 million in 1970[29]) and government promoted what has been called "compartmentalized competition" so that each major industry was not a monopoly but a "competitive polyopoly."[30] In other words, it had a controlled number of players operating under tight rules, but within that framework, the battle for market share was fierce.

The transformation of the Japanese automobile industry illustrates the national story in microcosm. Japan's total output in 1950 was 30,000 vehicles—about one and a half days' worth of American production. Thirty years later it displaced the United States as the world's leading auto manufacturer.[31] There was a small base in the truck manufacturers promoted by government during the war, but it took huge government loans to keep them going during the occupation, when U.S. vehicles flooded the country. The real difference came, therefore, with the protective framework established after 1952, which allowed Japanese companies to move into car manufacture and expand domestic sales without foreign competition. Equally important was their acquisition and development of foreign technology either through temporary foreign tie-ins, such as Nissan and the British manufacturer Austin in the 1950s, or via Toyota's more eclectic imitation and modification.

But, again, catch-up does not explain everything, for the Japanese also revolutionized production methods. In the 1950s, the two biggest companies, Nissan and Toyota, which together generated two-thirds of production, made the radical decision to subcontract more and more components, in contrast with the U.S. practice of in-house centralization. This cut the costs of personnel, capital, and inventories, not least because small subcontractors could be coerced into the *keiretsu* and squeezed on their profit margins. Both companies also developed methods of quality control—ironically, originating in America—and made this the responsibility of shop-floor personnel rather than specialist inspection teams. Japan's Quality Circles of workers attracted worldwide attention in the 1970s. Most of all, Toyota revolutionized production management, thanks to the ferocious determination of Ōno Taiichi, a thirty-year-old textile engineer with no college education, who moved into automobile management in 1943. Ōno noted that American mass production of a few basic models produced large inventories and numerous defective parts. Instead, he moved toward small-lot production of a variety of models and developed a highly synchronized system where each stage of the assembly line would pull in the parts it needed "just in time." Ōno's "Toyota Revolution" was widely copied at home and abroad in the cost-conscious 1970s.

Yet to focus exclusively on the big companies and their "salary men" as the explanation of Japan's "miracle" would be misleading. Unlike many developing countries, particularly with communist regimes, Japan had increased food production *and* shifted labor into industry. The solution was small-scale rural mechanization through mini tractors, transplanting machines, and small combines, to reduce the intense but seasonal need for labor in traditional rice production. In consequence, Japan had become self-sufficient in grain for human consumption by the late 1960s, yet farming was increasingly part-time work for women and older men. Mechanization also transformed productivity in small-scale industry and services in the 1950s and 1960s, with commensurate effects on productivity. Contrary to the big business image of "Japan, Inc." current in the West, 55 percent of the manufacturing work force was in units of under one hundred in 1966.[32] The mechanization of farms, small industry, and services was critical for Japan's 1960s growth: this was balanced economic development, unlike the skewed "heavy-metal" ideologies of many socialist states. And, in further contrast to foreign stereotypes, much of Japan's high growth in the 1960s was due to the consequent surge in domestic demand as incomes in all sectors grew. This was the deliberate focus of Prime Minister Ikeda's "Income Doubling" plan of 1960.

It was in the 1960s that most Japanese moved suddenly into consumer society. Between 1957 and 1965 the proportion of nonfarm households with fridges rose from under 3 percent to nearly 69 percent, those with washing machines from 20 percent to 78 percent. Japan also entered the TV age with a vengeance. Between 1960 and 1965 the proportion of nonfarm households with black-and-white sets jumped from 44 percent to 95 percent. A decade later the figures for color TVs rose from 30 percent in 1970 to 90 percent in 1975. Only automobile ownership lagged behind that in other developed states: despite the obsession with owning "my car," only 37 percent of nonfarm households had an automobile by 1975.[33] The proliferation of new *mai* words in the Japanese lexicon—such as *maika, maikara* ("my color TV"), and later, *maikon[pyuta]*—suggests the growing penetration of what has been called Western "hardware individualism" and its erosion of Japan's traditional group and family values.[34]

This argument cannot be pushed too far, however. In society as well as the economy, Japan modernized in its own national style. It is true that legal and economic change sounded the death knell of the old *ie* family—a household of several generations ruled by its patriarch. Between 1955 and 1985 the proportion of extended-kin households fell from over one-third to under one-fifth. In urban areas, it became acceptable to start married life in a separate household. Yet this was not so true in the countryside and, in general, both Japan's rural population and its urban middle class had a much higher incidence than in the West of aged parents living with their children. This reflected, on the one hand, Japan's uniquely high cost of housing (because of land prices), which impeded young couples setting up alone and, on the other, the limitations of its welfare system, which left the old vulnerable in their (increasingly long) retirement. For these reasons, the tradition of living with the oldest son and his family gained a new lease of life in modern Japan. The parents provided the home, the son provided the care.[35]

In 1955 and in 1985 women formed around 39 percent of Japan's work force but, at the first date, only one-third were employees, whereas thirty years later the proportion was 70 percent.[36] This reflected the demise of family farms and businesses. As in other industrializing countries, increased female opportunity for education and employment was seen in women's higher average age at marriage, which rose from about twenty-three and a half in 1951 to twenty-five in 1960.[37] Yet, once married, Japanese women were more likely to stay at home than their Western counterparts, while their salaried spouses spent long weekdays, and often Saturday mornings, at work or with colleagues. There was even less division of domestic labor than in the West; on the other hand, many Japanese women jealously guarded their separate sphere of authority and, as one American sociologist noted, they developed complex skills of "husband management" to help "equalize the power of husband and wife without upsetting the superior position of the husband."[38] One of the prime duties of motherhood, second only to childbirth for many aspiring Japanese families, was helping the offspring to pass Japan's notorious entrance exams into the best universities, which in turn secured employment in the best companies. In the 1980s, three of Japan's 5,453 high schools supplied about 10 percent of successful candidates for the elite Tokyo University.[39]

These are a few examples of how Japan modernized in its own way, not simply as a clone of the United States. Yet the American connection was absolutely vital for Japan's high-growth era. Although industrial structures and government policies owed much to the military *dirigisme* of 1931–1945, the effect of the occupation had been enormous. American-imposed land reform was the prerequisite for Japan's agricultural revolution; U.S. military procurements during the Korean War had been the first big stimulus to Japan's postwar recovery. In the postoccupation era, the alliance with the United States—however unpopular it remained on the Japanese left—freed the country from most of the costs of its own security. Until the mid-1980s Japan was spending no more than 1 percent of GDP on defense, compared with more than 7 percent for the United States in the 1960s and well over 5 percent for Britain.[40] A "free ride" in defense allowed Japan to concentrate on economic development; the U.S. war effort in Vietnam led to more lucrative procurements for Japan in the 1960s. In the interests of cold war security, the Americans also tolerated Japan's trade protectionism until well into the 1960s and, for similar reasons, fixed the exchange rate at a generous one dollar to 360 yen in 1949. This undervaluation gave Japan a huge price advantage in export markets. Not surprisingly, Japanese policy makers fought strenuously to preserve the rate, so it was not until December 1971 that the yen was revalued at 308 to one dollar, a huge 17 percent appreciation.[41] And, overall, the stability of the American-led Western economy and its prodigious trading growth, after the protectionism of the 1930s, was ideal for a fast-developing country.

Between 1966 and 1969, Japan surpassed Italy, Britain, France, and then West Germany in total GDP. By the 1970s, however, catch-up gains had largely been exhausted, and international conditions were less propitious. What is more striking, therefore, is Japan's continued if less spectacular success in the oil-shock era.

In 1972 Japan relied on oil for nearly three-quarters of its energy consumption, virtually all the oil was imported, and nearly 80 percent of oil imports came from the Middle East. A Swedish journalist likened it to "an enormous, fat sumō wrestler dancing in tiny, tiny ballet shoes."[42] The quadrupling of oil prices in late 1973 was therefore bound to have inflationary consequences, but these were exacerbated by compensatory union demands and by the Bank of Japan's expansionary monetary policy in 1971–1973. Overall, consumer prices rose by 23 percent; in 1974 the economy actually contracted in real terms.[43]

Japan's adjustment to the economic crisis was complicated by growing opposition to its low-cost methods of high growth. Part of this came from abroad: the enforced appreciation of the yen, the liberalization of tariff barriers, and the new American pressure in the 1970s to eliminate Japanese capital controls. All these changes presaged an economy more open to international competition. But resentment was also growing at home about the impact of probusiness policies on the quality of life. Japan's labor force worked longer hours for lower wages than their international counterparts. They also lived in significantly smaller houses; even in 1983, under 60 percent had flush toilets (in West Germany the proportion was 97 percent).[44] Although housing was Japan's greatest problem, the environment was also a topic of mounting public concern in the 1970s. One economist observed that in Japan, the abbreviation "GNP" could stand for "Gross National Pollution."[45] The cause célèbre was the case of mercury poisoning in Minamata Bay on the western island of Kyushu, which occurred when effluent from a chemical plant was absorbed by fish and entered the food chain. The disease was evident by 1953, but it took twenty years for the victims to achieve redress in the courts.[46]

Politicians began to address the social fallout from economic growth. The early 1970s saw left-wing governments in control of many major cities. In Yokohama, the socialist mayor Asukata Ichio developed pollution controls that became a model for other urban areas. At a national level, there was a major extension of Japan's welfare laws in 1973. Old-age pensions, for instance, were substantially increased and partly indexed against inflation. Consequently, government spending on social security rose from 5 percent of GNP in 1970 to 11 percent by 1980. Quality of life is, of course, a many-sided concept: for instance, Japan's social cohesion and strict controls on handguns helped keep robberies at 2 per one hundred thousand population compared with the American figure of 250 in 1981. The homicide rate was 1.5 per one hundred thousand as against nearly 10 in the United States.[47] But the welfare net for the very poor remained skimpy, pollution was not seriously checked, and government housing programs were inadequate.

There was little doubt that public goods had not kept pace with corporate wealth. Moreover, redressing the balance was harder in an era of slower growth. Government spending rose from 12.7 percent of GNP in 1973 to 17.7 percent in 1980, bringing Japan closer to the United States, where the rise was only from 19.2 percent to 22.1 percent. Since revenue growth did not grow commensurately, Japan resorted for the first time to substantial government borrowing. The deficit increased from 1.5 percent of GNP in 1973 to 5.8 percent in 1980; the U.S. figures were 1.2 percent and 2.8 percent.[48] Slower growth, plus the increases in public expenditure and government deficit, all suggested in the 1970s that the miracle was over and Japan was becoming a "normal country."

Yet Japanese unemployment remained much lower than the West's. The rate of under 3 percent in 1980, for instance, was half that of the United States.[49] Companies absorbed the shocks through reduced profits; the tradition of job security held firm. And Japan's economy continued to expand healthily throughout the oil-shock era. Admittedly 3.6 percent growth in 1973–1981 looked pathetic against 10.4 percent in 1960–1973, but it was far better than the performance of Japan's main rivals: U.S. growth was 2.3 percent in 1973–1981, West Germany's only 2 percent. The United Kingdom managed only 0.5 percent.[50] Japan's contrast with Britain owed much to the way in which lessons from the first oil shock were applied to the second. For instance, in 1979–1981, the Japanese government kept the money supply under strict control, and unions restrained wage demands.

At a structural level, the 1970s were when Japan really shifted into export-led growth as its huge domestic market, the basis of its 1960s expansion, became saturated. Whereas only 20 percent of Japanese car production was for export in 1970, the figure in 1980 was 54 percent. Half the export sales were in North America, another 20 percent in Western Europe. Japan's superior production methods and lower labor costs were part of the explanation: it was estimated that Japanese manufacturers could produce and ship an automobile to the United States for around fifteen hundred dollars less than it cost American firms to market a similar vehicle.[51] Japan also gained from the depreciation of the yen after it floated in 1973, which helped keep prices competitive.

Although MITI was less potent in the liberalized 1970s than before, it still mattered. Recognizing that Japan was being undercut in some areas, such as shipping or TVs, by the even lower-cost economies of such developing neighbors as South Korea and Taiwan, the government identified new growth opportunities. Major MITI reports in 1971 targeted high-tech industries to develop a "knowledge-intensive" industrial structure for the future, with computers, robots and computerized machine tools at the top of the list. Although formal tariff barriers were now taboo internationally, these nascent industries could still be protected by other means, such as complex customs procedures, exacting product standards, and substantial government investment in basic research. By 1986 40 percent of the so-called make anything machines (computerized machine tools) were located in Japan. The country also had more industrial robots than anywhere else—thirty-six for every ten thousand workers, six times the rate for Western Europe and even better when compared with the American average.[52] Thus, strategic government policy enabled Japan to move not merely into export-led growth but into new kinds of exports as well. Many of its rivals, particularly in Western Europe, were much slower to adapt to the decline of traditional heavy industry.

In other ways, too, the patterns of the high-growth era remained in place. Of particular importance was the continuance of very high rates of domestic savings. These ran at 30 percent of GDP every year from 1973 into the mid-1980s, whereas no other major industrial country achieved that rate in any year. Couples saved to cover the huge costs of housing, to pay for higher education for their children, and to offset the skimpiness of government social security in old age. Although saving rates remained high, in an era of slower growth the opportunities for domestic investment were reduced. On the other hand, barriers to investment abroad were gradually being liberalized under American pressure, culminating in the Foreign Exchange Law of 1980. The stage was therefore set for Japan's emergence as a major financial as well as industrial power in the 1980s. Some of the new foreign investment was the result of manufacturers' creating factories in rival countries to jump over Western protective barriers or to take advantage of lower wage costs in other parts of Asia. Japan's direct investment increased tenfold in 1975–1987 to a total of $33.3 billion. But little more than 3 percent of Japan's production was done overseas, compared with 20 percent in the American case. The real change was in Japanese portfolio investment, in overseas stocks, shares and bonds, which grew spectacularly from $8 billion in 1980 to $117 billion six years later.[53]

Here, as in earlier decades of Japanese growth, American policy played a facilitating role. As we noted, the U.S. government deficit and debts compared favorably with Japan's in the late 1970s, but the situation changed radically in the 1980s. A combination of the tight monetary policy of the Federal Reserve and the loose fiscal policy of the Reagan administration allowed the dollar to rise sharply. In contrast to the rate of around two hundred yen to one dollar in 1980, the exchange was around 260 in 1985.[54] The high price of American exports created a huge trade deficit, while the scale of Reagan's budget deficit and consequent government debt drove up U.S. interest rates.

Japan gained commercially and financially. Weak American competition enhanced its trade surplus, while the attraction of U.S. capital markets turned Japan into a major foreign investor. By 1985 Japan was the world's leading creditor nation (and the United States its largest debtor). The following year Japan became the top earner of foreign investment income, and in 1987 Tokyo overtook New York as the leading stock market measured in the total value of listed stocks.[55] Some of these changes reflected the appreciating value of the yen after Japan agreed in September 1985 to help drive up the dollar. But the signing of that agreement was evidence of Japan's new role in international monetary management. And, at root, its place in the global hierarchy was based on its productive strength, with a large internal market and highly competitive exports. By the mid-1980s, Japan's total GNP was second only to the much more populous United States. Japan now boasted the largest per capita GNP in the world.[56] The talk in the United States was of "Japan as Number One."[57]

The Asian Tigers

Japan was not alone. The four "tigers"—South Korea, Taiwan, Singapore, and Hong Kong—crossed the threshold of modernity even more rapidly. Within twenty years, they completed the industrial transition to an urbanized work force with a preponderance of labor in the high-productivity sectors of manufacturing and services. At the same time, they effected the demographic transition to societies with low death and birth rates, and the educational transition to high rates of literacy and secondary school enrollment. The interrelationship among these three transitions was critical. Improved education, for instance, produced a skilled work force and promoted birth control; opportunities for workers with greater skills made education more attractive and delayed the age of marriage and childbirth. In all these areas, the shifting role of women (spending longer as pupils and workers rather than mothers and homemakers) was vital.

The results were evident in growth rates of 8 to 11 percent in the 1960s and 1970s. Even more striking, the tigers outstripped the most developed countries of Latin America. In 1963, all four had lagged well behind the income levels of Argentina, Chile, and Mexico; by 1988 they were all much wealthier, Hong Kong and Singapore by a factor of more than three. Like Japan, they practiced a mix of prudent macroeconomic policies, including low inflation and debts, with interventionist microeconomic policies to foster selected growth industries. Whereas much of Latin America remained committed to a policy of import substitution—building up domestic industry for local demand—the tigers soon moved to the promotion of manufactured exports. They also generally avoided too many heavy industrial projects in favor of light industry such as textiles and, later, electronics. The transformation of their trading position was dramatic. In 1963 the four tigers accounted for only 1.6 percent of the world's total exports; by 1988 the proportion was 8.1 percent—not much less than Japan's 9.6 percent and almost double the share of the whole of Latin America (4.2 percent).[58]

The Asian tigers' spectacular leap to economic prominence attracted much comment. Some Western economists, notably at the World Bank, depicted it as vindication of free-market principles; others focused on the ways in which the tigers could be said to "govern" the market.[59] But their transformation cannot be understood without reference to the larger political framework. All four benefited economically from previous foreign rule or influence, whether it was British commerce in Hong Kong and Singapore, or Japanese industrialization and then American land reform in Korea and Taiwan.[60] Furthermore, each of the tigers was an artificial polity severed from powerful neighbors—communist China in the case of Taiwan and Hong Kong, Malayasia for Singapore. Likewise, South Korea was the product of postwar division and bloody civil war. Each therefore felt acute insecurity, which was translated into political structures that restricted civil liberties and social well-being for the sake of economic growth. Politics as much as economics explain the East Asian "miracle."

The Republic of Korea was the most important. It covered less than one hundred thousand square kilometers (little larger than the U.S. state of Indiana). Its population by the mid-1980s was around 40 million (having doubled since the end of the war). In 1960, agriculture accounted for nearly 40 percent of GDP and employed two-thirds of the work force; the country's per capita income was lower than that of Liberia or El Salvador.[61] By the 1980s, however, average incomes exceeded those in all Latin American countries, and Korean brands were household names in the West. In the early 1970s, Samsung was turning out a few hundred microwave ovens each year from one cramped, old laboratory. Two decades later it was the world's leading manufacturer of microwave ovens, producing eighty thousand a week.[62]

In South Korea, unlike Japan, the essential political stability was provided by military rule. General Park Chung Hee's coup in May 1961 was a turning point (see Chapter 8). Park dissolved the National Assembly, banned political parties and existing unions, and took control of the press. A Korean Central Intelligence Agency (KCIA) was established, and it maintained internal security with ruthless efficiency. Pressed by the Americans, Park conceded elections in 1963, but widespread corruption ensured his victory. After another narrow victory in 1971, he used the growing protests to justify a state of national emergency and a new autocratic constitution, which in 1972 effectively made him president for life. Although Park was assassinated in October 1979, sparking new upheavals, General Chun Doo Hwan seized power in July 1980. He established an ostensibly new republic but on terms similar to Park's.[63]

Within this iron political framework, South Korean leaders pushed through forced industrialization. Park—a diminutive career officer, aged forty-four in 1961—had been trained by the Japanese and served in their army during World War II. He took Japan's early industrialization as a model.[64] The Korean government controlled most of the major banks for two decades starting in 1961. It established powerful state bodies, notably the Economic Planning Board. Most automobile imports were banned until 1988: in the latter year only 305 foreign cars were sold in South Korea, in contrast with the five hundred thousand cars that the country sold abroad (half its total output).[65] In South Korea, business concentration was even more pronounced than in Japan. Park encouraged Korean conglomerates (the *chaebol*) during the 1970s. These were usually headed by family firms—the Chung Ju-Yung family in the case of Hyundai or that of Lee Byung-Chull, the founder of Samsung. In 1974, sales of the top ten *chaebol* represented 15 percent of GNP; a decade later the proportion was 67 percent.[66] These family-run *chaebol* were also a convenient conduit for raising political funds. Their massive kickbacks helped keep the regime in power.

Political control and astute emulation would not have been sufficient, however, but for continued patronage from Washington and Tokyo. Because of South Korea's importance as a front line of the cold war, the United States kept open its markets for Korean exports and pumped in economic aid to the tune of $6 billion between 1946 and 1978 (compared with $6.89 billion for the whole of Africa and $14.8 billion for all Latin America). The quid pro quo in the 1960s was the Korean commitment of troops to the Vietnam War (see Chapter 8). Huge soft loans were also provided by Japan, anxious to recreate informally their imperial position in Korea. These loans were particularly important in helping the country overcome its debt crisis during the second oil shock. In return, Japanese companies were able to set up joint ventures in Korea, using cheaper Korean labor and duty-free imports of Japanese capital goods. Much of Korea's early development was as an assembly plant for Japanese products. As late as 1986, 90 percent of South Korean imports from Japan went into export industries. Roughly one-third of earnings from a Korean VCR or merchant ship went to Japan to pay for components. Consequently, South Korea's export surplus to the United States was offset by its import deficit with Japan, and the country's massive export-led growth did not generate a trade surplus until 1986. Korea's technological deficiencies were a major reason for the push into information technology in the 1980s.[67]

The social costs of such rapid development were even more burdensome than in Japan. South Korea was one of the most densely populated countries in the world, with around one-fifth of its forty million population packed in the capital, Seoul—some two million in slum accommodations. Worker cooperation was bought by secure jobs and rising wages, but there was no unemployment benefit and welfare spending in general was very low. By the 1980s air and water pollution in Seoul were appalling, and political protest at the lack of civil liberties had become more organized and sophisticated, involving students, the churches, and unions. Here, then, was a mixed achievement by the mid-1980s—remarkable economic success, won at great political and social cost by a country still reliant on foreign backers and facing an implacably hostile neighbor whose threat helped justify continued military rule.

For Taiwan, as well, insecurity was both a fact of life and a spur to industrialization. Threatened by invasion from the People's Republic, Chiang Kaishek's island republic could not have survived the crises of the 1950s without the U.S. security guarantee. Nor could its economy, wrenched in quick succession from Japan's orbit and then China's, have developed without American aid, which constituted more than 30 percent of domestic investment every year from 1951 to 1962.[68] Although American aid was cut back in the 1970s, when Washington wooed Beijing, and President Carter broke formal diplomatic ties in 1979 on recognizing the People's Republic, the economic and security links were maintained. But uncertainty about the U.S. commitment accelerated the country's shift from subsidized import-substitution in the 1950s to export-led growth. Like Korea, Taiwan moved from cheap, labor-intensive manufactures, such as textiles and toys, into an expansion of heavy industry and infrastructure in the 1970s, and then to advanced electronics in the ensuing decade. Taiwan also had a similar trading pattern, exporting to the United States while importing materials and components from

Japan, which were then worked up in special duty-free export zones such as the southern port of Kiaohung. By 1980, Taiwan was the twentieth-largest trading state in the world,[69] a remarkable achievement for a country smaller than Estonia, with a population of under eighteen million.

Taiwan was an authoritarian state, but the military never had the same political dominance as in Korea after 1961. Control was exerted through the dominance of the Guomindang under the Mandarin leadership of Chiang Kai-shek up to his death in 1975 and then of his more informal son Chiang Ching-kuo until he died in 1988. In further distinction with homogeneous South Korea, there was a sharp ethnic divide in Taiwan. The Guomindang was a party of refugee mainlanders who imposed their rule on the native Taiwanese. Resentment at mainland rule sparked off riots in 1947, but it was mitigated thereafter by land reform, access to education and the civil service, and opportunities in local and provincial politics. In 1969, Taiwanese were allowed to contest national elections. It also helped that the country had one of the most equitable income distributions of developing Asia: by 1980 the richest fifth of the population accounted for 37 percent of national income, the poorest fifth nearly 9 percent. This four-to-one ratio contrasted with twenty to one in 1953 (61 percent against 3 percent).[70]

Taiwan also had less industrial concentration than *chaebol*-dominated South Korea. Hyundai of Korea's gross receipts in 1981 were three times those of Taiwan's top ten conglomerates. In 1976, the average manufacturing firm on the island had thirty-five employees, half as many as its Korean counterpart.[71] On the other hand, the state sector was one of the largest in the world outside the communist bloc and black Africa—an interesting gloss on the tigers' free-market image. Public enterprises accounted for 13.5 percent of GDP by 1980, double the share in Korea.[72] But public enterprises were tightly controlled and efficiently run. Substantial investment was made in the 1970s in vital infrastructure projects such as the North-South Expressway and Taipei's new international airport, and in the 1980s on industrial parks and advanced technology. Overall, although Taiwan's growth was driven by similar motives and instruments to Korea's, it was more equitable and less corrupt, and created less political and social turmoil.

Singapore and Hong Kong, the most spectacularly successful of Asian tigers, were similar in many ways. Both of these city-states originated as British colonies acting as entrepôts, or trans-shipment ports, for their surrounding regions. An additional boost came from British military bases and facilities, especially in Singapore. Demographically, both were dominated by Chinese immigrant populations, though in Singapore around a quarter of the inhabitants were Malay or Indian. In the postwar era, their catch-up industrial growth was distinctive from that of the rest of Asia in two respects. First, because of their minuscule agricultural sectors, growth resulted from a shift of labor and capital from commerce to manufacturing, not from farming to industry as in most other industrializing countries in the world. Second, growth was based unequivocally on free trade, with none of the barriers against imports of goods and capital apparent elsewhere in East Asia. These cramped statelets, with little food or raw materials of their own and small domestic markets, had no alternative to laissez faire. Well-tuned British connections and the prevalence of the English language helped plug them into global networks of trade and communications. By the 1980s, both had become major financial centers. Their success—measured by high growth rates and income levels at least double those of Korea and Taiwan—was noted the world over.

On closer inspection, however, there were sharp contrasts between the two city-states. And as elsewhere, political structures as much as economic policies shaped their growth.[73]

Singapore was the smaller of the two, an island of 240 square miles (about the size of St. Lucia in the Caribbean), with a population that rose from one million in 1950 to 2.5 million in 1983. In the interwar years Singapore grew by shipping and financing the commodity exports of the Malay states, a mile across the water to the north. The two critical dates in its postwar development were 1959, when Britain conceded independence to the dominant People's Action Party (PAP), and 1965, when (as noted in Chapter 8) the two-year federation with Malaysia collapsed and Singapore struck out alone. Barred from Malaysia's protected domestic market, the government turned to export-led growth. At the same time, the break with Malaya saved Singapore from becoming a mecca for unemployed rural workers. Had Singapore remained tied to Malaya, its growth would have been much slower.[74] The artificiality of this city-state as much as its free-trade policies accounted for Singapore's success.

Free trade abroad was also combined with state socialism at home, a point often forgotten in appraisals of Singapore. The PAP was led by the dynamic Lee Kuan Yew (born 1923), who had become the world's longest-serving premier by the time he retired in 1990. He used the crisis of the mid-1960s to depoliticize the unions and impose internationally competitive wages. But the government also addressed Singapore's proliferating slums. By the mid-1980s, 80 percent of the population lived in subsidized public housing, a proportion unknown in the democratic world. Coupled with firm control over the media and opposition, it constituted a major reason for the PAP's recurrent success at the polls. Unlike the East Asian tigers, Singapore exercised little microeconomic intervention to promote individual firms, but the government did fund infrastructure projects, such as the new mass transit system built during the 1980s. By tax cuts and other incentives, it also made Singapore the center of a new Asian dollar market after 1968, modeled on the Eurodollar boom. And the PAP was also ready to intervene in social life, preaching a policy of abstinence that helped give Singapore one of the highest savings rates in the world, then promoting population growth in the 1980s after the birth rate had fallen below replacement levels.

Two other unique features of Singapore's growth sum up this combination of free trade abroad and government direction at home. Because there were virtually no restrictions on capital movements, Singapore's manufacturing growth was dominated by large foreign firms. By 1980 companies under total or majority foreign ownership accounted for 58 percent of employment and 74 percent of output in the manufacturing sector. This situation was unparalleled among the Asian tigers.[75] In contrast, the formal state sector was small, accounting for about 10 percent of GDP. But less visibly, key areas of the country were run by state boards such as those for housing and development, and the Port of Singapore. Through their monopoly position and efficient management, these generated vast surpluses in the 1970s and 1980s. In this period the public sector accounted for about two-thirds of national savings, twice that of Korea and five times the figure for Taiwan—both supposedly much more statist.[76]

Like Singapore, Hong Kong was an artificial city-state, but its political situation differed in two important respects. First, it remained a British Crown colony through the period of high growth, ruled by a succession of governors and their officials, with a Legislative Council to make laws. Since all members of Legco were appointed until 1984 and full direct elections did not occur until 1991, this was an administrative state par excellence, in which officials ruled with minimal political interference. Secondly, Hong Kong was not merely artificial but temporary. Hong Kong Island itself had been extracted from the Chinese under a forced treaty in 1843. The tip of the Kowloon Peninsula across the superb natural harbor to the north (Plate 41) was acquired in similar fashion in 1860. But most of the 406-square-mile colony was made up of the New Territories farther into southern China from Kowloon, which were held on a ninety-nine-year lease signed on July 1, 1898. Without them, the colony was not viable. After lengthy negotiations, the British Government agreed to return the whole of Hong Kong when the lease expired. Under the Sino-British Agreement of 1984, Hong Kong was to be a special administrative region with a high degree of autonomy under the rubric "one country, two systems." In short, Hong Kong was "a borrowed place in a span of borrowed time."[77]

The colony had grown rich as an entrepôt for southern China. It therefore lost its raison d'être when the new communist leadership closed off China to the West. On the other hand, China's civil war created a vast flow of refugees into Hong Kong, particularly from the great port of Shanghai. This influx of capital, labor, and skills was vital for Hong Kong's postwar growth. Like South Korea, Hong Kong ran a persistent trade deficit because "it exports to live, but lives on imports" to supply the necessary raw materials.[78] Its deficit was covered by services and especially direct investment abroad, in which Hong Kong outstripped most developing nations. Although, like Singapore, Hong Kong moved "upstream" from textiles into electronics and then high tech, its economic structure was very different. Hong Kong firms were usually small and flexible, often family owned. In 1977, 92 percent of firms employed less than 50 people.[79] Hong Kong's notorious sweatshop economy flourished in the absence of government regulation of hours and conditions.

Although less dirigiste than Singapore, Hong Kong was not completely laissez-faire. The government employed only 6 percent of the work force, compared with 20 percent in Singapore, but it set key prices, such as for rice and rents. Subsidized public apartments housed 40 percent of the populace by the 1980s, a smaller proportion than in Singapore but still dwarfing Western Europe. The government imposed heavy taxes on cars and fuel, so that only 12 percent of households owned an automobile in the mid-1980s.[80] It also constructed and ran the mass-transit system built in the 1970s. By the end of that decade, the government accounted for about a quarter of gross domestic capital formation. In short, Hong Kong was a mixed economy operating in a free-trade framework.[81]

The success of the Asian tigers was therefore a combination of catch-up growth, favorable demography, export-led policies, and, not least, controlled political structures. Reaction against the latter would create problems in the late 1980s. By then, however, other countries in Southeast Asia were emulating the tigers' example.

The Tiger Cubs

The most successful cubs were Thailand and Malaysia, followed by Indonesia. At the other end of the spectrum was the disaster of the Philippines under the Marcos regime. Their stories highlight not merely the importance of export-led growth but also, for good and ill, of political structures and, especially in the Philippine case, of political leaders.

By the mid-1980s, Malaysia and Thailand began to figure in the list of newly industrialized economies. In 1985, Malaysia's manufactures generated 32 percent of export earnings, compared with 6 percent in 1965. Its old staples, rubber and tin, had fallen from 62 percent to a mere 12 percent.[82]

Here the crucial agent was not the armed forces (unlike in South Korea) but civilian politicians, in an adroit display of authoritarian populism tailored to Malaysia's delicate ethnic situation.[83]

The exit of Singapore from the Malaysian federation and the end of the war with Sukarno's Indonesia in 1965–1956 (see Chapter 8) did not solve Malaysia's internal problems. The Alliance coalition of Malays, Chinese, and Indians (respectively about one-half, one-third and one-tenth of the peninsula's population) collapsed in the elections of May 1969. After riots against the Chinese and Indians in May–June 1969, in which at least two hundred were killed, a state of emergency was declared. Younger Malay politicians consolidated their hold in a new political structure. For two years the country was run by a National Operations Council that pushed through a New Economic Policy to increase Malay participation in government and the economy by quotas and special rights. The Sedition Ordinance was extended to prohibit discussion of "sensitive issues" such as Malay rights, the status of Islam as the official religion, and the position of Malay as the national language. Having ensured Malay predominance, the Alliance was enlarged into a new *Barisan National* (BN) ethnic coalition on Malay terms. The BN won 60 percent of the vote and 88 percent of the seats in 1974.

During the 1970s, the governments of Tun Abdul Razak and Hussein Onn mixed import substitution and export promotion to good effect: by 1985 manufacturing generated 19 percent of GDP, compared with 8 percent in 1960.[84] But it was the advent of Dr. Mahathir Mohammad in July 1981 that galvanized Malaysia and put it on the economic map. Mahathir, a physician by training, was the first commoner to hold the premiership, and he was soon challenging the residual powers of the Malay princes. He was also a combative Malay nationalist who urged his countrymen to "Buy British last" and to "Look east" by modeling their economy on those of Japan and South Korea. In a joint venture with Mitsubishi in 1985, the country started producing the first Malaysian car, the Proton Saga backed by massive government subsidies. Islam was used to legitimize the BN's rule, through promoting food and fasting laws, greater TV time for Islam, and more mosque building. The Proton was billed as an Islamic car, marked with the star and crescent. Mahathir's vehement criticism of Western democracy as both hypocritical and unsuitable led him to champion "Asian values."

Thailand was a much larger country (fifty-one million people in 1985, compared with Malaysia's fifteen million). It was also much more cohesive: Chinese constituted only about 7 percent of the population and Malays roughly 3 percent. The Chinese had been assimilated into Thai culture, in which Buddhism still acted as a unifying force. After an interlude of frenetic party factionalism in 1973–1976, Thai politics reverted to the long-standing pattern of military-based bureaucratic rule, punctuated by periodic coups. The monarchy also remained a stabilizing force. After King Bhumiphol Adulyadej had ascended to the throne in 1946 at the age of eighteen, he matured from an American-educated, jazz-loving playboy into a sober, revered ruler.[85]

Within this firm framework and despite continued communist insurgency, Thailand's economy developed rapidly. In the 1950s and 1960s, its exports had been mainly commodities such as tin and rice (in which it was a world leader). Industrial development in the 1970s had concentrated on import substitution behind high tariff barriers. But after the second oil shock and the collapse of world rice prices in 1980–1981, the emphasis shifted to manufacturing exports, which rose from a quarter of total exports to over half between 1981 and 1987.[86] The main industrial center was the capital, Bangkok, but the eastern seaboard became a location for textiles, petrochemicals, and electronics. Thailand was now benefiting from its low labor costs and large population, attracting substantial investment from the more developed and expensive Asian tigers.

Indonesia was the fifth most populous country in the world (164 million by 1985). But this sprawling archipelago, some three thousand miles across, played only a bit part in the world economy until the 1980s, accounting for under 1 percent of global trade. The most important feature of its history in the 1970s was political stability, based on military support for a strong political leader.[87] After the chaos of the Sukarno years and the pogroms surrounding the failed 1965 "coup" (see Chapter 8), President Suharto stayed at the helm for three decades. The bureaucracy was transformed from feuding fiefdoms into an instrument of government; the fractious regionalism was controlled by a combination of firm military rule and generous transfer payments from the center; and although the state was still based on the armed forces, these were trimmed in size and independence. Suharto squeezed Islam out of politics during the 1980s. The government party, Golkar, dominated national elections.

Stability did not mean harmony, of course. An enduring problem was East Timor, on one of the ragged edges of this Javanese imperium, which the Indonesian army invaded in December 1975 after the Portuguese colonial rulers had pulled out. In guerrilla warfare over the next fifteen years, at least 170,000 died.[88] But because Suharto shifted his vast country into the Western orbit, the Americans turned a blind eye to events in East Timor, and growing U.S. arms sales to Suharto were used illicitly against the rebels.

The unprecedented political stability of Suharto's "New Order" was the key to economic growth.[89] But also important was Suharto's reliance on a group of economists from the University of Indonesia—trained in and well connected to the West—who were to shape policy for two decades. They brought inflation under control, opened the country again to Western investment, and moved the state toward balanced budgets. During the 1970s, real GDP grew at an annual average of nearly 8 percent, with the country becoming an economic entity for the first time. One major success was the transformation of Indonesia from the world's largest rice importer in the late 1970s, taking up to one-third of the globe's traded rice, to rice self-sufficiency by 1985, thanks to high-yield grains and government guidance.

Indonesia also mounted one of the world's most successful population programs. The fertility rate fell from six children per woman in 1965 to 3.3 two decades later. Whereas Sukarno had opposed birth control, Suharto made it a priority; a powerful Family Planning Board, with effective local networks, was established in 1970. By 1987, nearly 48 percent of currently married women were using some form of contraception (16 percent were on the pill and 13 percent used IUDs), against only 18 percent in 1976 (Plate 25). The average age of marriage also began to rise. There were fewer arranged matches and, despite Muslim traditionalists, the Marriage Law of 1974 set minimum ages of sixteen for women and nineteen for men.

Notwithstanding these improvements, Indonesia's development was more problematic than that of its neighbors. A few provinces generated nearly all its primary products, notably Riau and Aceh on Sumatra and East Kalimantan, with oil and timber by far the most profitable exports. Most of the country's manufacturing was located in Jakarta, by 1985 a metropolis of 7.8 million, with a population density exceeding that of Singapore or New York.[90] The official "transmigration" program to resettle Javanese on the outer islands, involving perhaps 1.8 million people at its peak in the period 1979–1984,[91] caused great human suffering as well as ecological damage through clearance and soil erosion. Private business was dominated by a few Chinese tycoons, notably Liem Sioe Liong and the logging king, Bob Hasan, both of whom began by servicing Suharto's army command in Java in the 1950s. Animosity to these "crony capitalists" and their partners among the president's children became intense during the 1980s. The predominant state industrial sector was a buttress against foreign capital, but it worked hand in glove with the army and was riddled with corruption. This became clear in 1976 when the national oil company, Pertamina, nearly collapsed with debts equal to 30 percent of GDP.

Oil was, in fact, at the root of Indonesia's successes and problems in the 1970s and 1980s. The surges in the oil prices in 1973–1974 and 1979–1980 transformed the nation's finances. Net energy exports soared from $1 billion in 1973 to over $13 billion in 1980. Corporate oil taxes generated 70 percent of government revenue in 1981–1982, compared with 20 percent in 1969–1970.[92] This new income accrued automatically, rather than being extracted through politically contentious taxation, and it gave Suharto's economists undreamed-of freedom to maneuver. Oil revenues made possible massive aid to poorer regions and the promotion of rural infrastructure—in contrast, say, with the appropriation of such income by urban elites in Nigeria.[93] Oil revenues were also important for Suharto politically. They enabled him to address the serious rice shortages of 1973, and also to see off elite and student criticism in the late 1970s after the Pertamina scandal. It was in this period that Indonesia began moving to the export-led growth strategy of the Asian tigers. Between 1983 and 1991 manufactures grew from 6 percent to over 40 percent of total exports,[94] as Indonesian textiles, clothing, and footwear began to spread around the Asia-Pacific region. But what would happen after the oil boom and after Suharto was far from clear.

In most of Southeast Asia, economic performance and material living standards were far better in the mid-1980s than twenty years before. But two major countries were egregious exceptions—Burma and the Philippines.

Burma remained locked in the neutralist, state-socialist mode it had adopted after the coup of 1962 (see Chapter 8). Ne Win's military government continued to spend roughly one-third of the budget on defense, trying to control the communist and ethnic insurgencies that plagued the Burmese majority. Economic growth was sluggish and official policies regressive. Due to government opposition to birth control, the population doubled between 1962 and 1988 to 40 million. Moreover, no real agrarian reform had occurred. Indeed, Burma declined from the leading rice exporter of the world before World War II to a mere 2 percent market share by 1970, partly because of population increase but also because farmers were deterred by insecurity of tenure and the exceptionally low price paid by the government for their rice (so as to maximize revenue from export sales).[95] In 1960, Burma's per capita GDP was comparable to Indonesia's; by 1987 it was under half the figure (two hundred U.S. dollars), making the country one of the poorest in the world.[96] In short, "Burma under Ne Win had hardly begun to address the economic issues that neighbouring Southeast Asian countries had tackled years before."[97]

Given its postindependence past, Burma's problems were hardly surprising. But the same cannot be said of the Philippines, which had been one of the most advanced economies in eastern Asia. In 1963, per capita GDP was larger than South Korea's and equal to Taiwan's; twenty-five years later it was one-third of their size, less than Thailand's, and nearly equaled by that of Indonesia.[98] What had gone wrong?

Like Indonesia, the Philippines was a sprawling archipelago—with some seven thousand islands and, by 1985, fifty-five million people, half of them on the main islands of Luzon and Mindanao. Unlike Indonesia, however, the Philippines lacked reserves of oil to lubricate its way through the 1970s. It was also a victim of history: Spanish and American colonial rule had fostered an entrenched plantation economy. Moreover, the Americans did not engineer land reform before they left in 1946, in contrast with their achievements in Japan, Taiwan, and South Korea. The Philippines therefore lacked the thriving, independent peasantry that was the backbone of Thailand's postwar growth. The dominance of the Roman Catholic church—another product of three centuries of Spanish rule—militated against artificial contraception. Policy failures were also responsible for the Philippines' problems. Unlike its neighbors, it remained committed to heavy industry and domestic-led growth. Governments neglected agriculture, expanded the state sector, and ran up crippling foreign debts. But such policies were not irreversible. The Philippines' decline was in large measure attributable to two people—Ferdinand Marcos and his wife, Imelda. Their story is a reminder that, in a world apparently shaped by impersonal economic and social forces, individuals still matter.

Ferdinand, born in 1917, was an Ilocan from the north of the Philippines. Athletic, intelligent, and a superb orator, he rose rapidly in postwar Filipino politics. Imelda, twelve years younger, came from a prominent Leyte family, but her real assets were beauty, charm, and, as with Ferdinand, ruthless ambition. Ferdinand and Imelda married in 1954 after an eleven-day courtship and then harnessed their formidable talents to advancing his career. Filipino politics were rooted in the country's entrenched clan system, with national parties acting as loose coalitions of "ins" and "outs." In 1965 the Marcoses and their allies displaced the incumbent president, using all their skills of oratory, charm, patronage, and corruption. Marcos's reelection was engineered by similar means in 1969. Denied a third term by the constitution, Marcos used growing political violence (some of which he stirred up) to justify imposing martial law in September 1972.

Marcos claimed that authoritarian rule would enable him to create the "New Society" that the Philippines desperately needed. At first, there were signs that a Suharto-style technocratic government was taking shape. Inflation was cut from 40 percent in 1974 to 10 percent in 1975; the country achieved self-sufficiency in rice by 1977. Over the decade from the first oil shock it reduced dependence on imported oil by one-fifth. But land reform was neglected, except where it could weaken the president's opponents, and development aid was diverted into the pockets of the Marcos family and their crony capitalists—far more even than in Suharto's Indonesia. In contrast to other states in the region, such as Thailand or South Korea, where authoritarianism rested on the institutions of the military and/or the bureaucracy, the Marcoses ran an essential personal dictatorship.

Just how much the two of them looted will probably never be known for sure. Initial estimates of $5 to 10 billion were soon raised to $15 billion, over half the country's national debt. Imelda's conspicuous consumption was notorious. She accumulated clothes, jewels, property, and paintings with remorseless determination. She was equally celebrated for conspicuous construction, what Filipinos (quietly) called her "edifice complex." The Cultural Center in Manila was followed by a Population Center, an Arts Center, a Convention Center, and so on, not to mention more than a dozen luxury hotels.[99]

The persistence of the Marcos regime and the extent of its financial aid from the West would not have been possible without the U.S. Government. The Carter administration's human rights agenda took second place to concern for the U.S. bases at Clark Field and Subic Bay, two of the largest outside the United States. Carter secured their continuance, on a reduced scale, in 1979 at a cost of five hundred million dollars over five years. His successor, Ronald Reagan, struck a new deal in 1984 for $900 million. The Reagans were old friends of the Marcoses, and Reagan's administration was even readier to turn a blind eye to the internal situation. Marcos suspended martial law in January 1981, just before a papal visit, but his enlarged decree powers covered most of what had been lost. After a sham presidential election in June, Vice President George Bush toasted the Marcoses: "We love your adherence to democratic principle and to the democratic processes."[100]

By now, however, the regime was unstable as well as corrupt. Although Marcos had made peace with Muslim rebels in Mindanao in 1975, after years of bloody fighting, and then undermined them through skillful patronage, the communist NPA insurgency in central Luzon spread to other provinces in the early 1980s. In the cities, student protest was growing, radical priests espoused liberation theology from Latin America, and the Catholic hierarchy adopted a stance of "critical collaboration" that became ever more critical as the 1980s progressed. Its leader was Jaime Sin, the archbishop of Manila, a man of courage, skill, and humor—who rejoiced after his elevation in the title of Cardinal Sin.

The turning point came in August 1983. Ferdinand Marcos was by then suffering from a terminal disease of the immune system and went into seclusion for a kidney transplant. Knowing of Marcos's ill health, his long-time political rival Benigno Aquino returned from America to build support for a democratic transition. But he was shot dead on the airport tarmac as he landed on August 21, probably on the orders of Imelda and the head of the palace guard, General Fabian Ver. Like Marcos, Aquino had started his political life as an ambitious clan politician. He even dated Imelda for a while until marrying a sugar heiress, Corazon (Cory) Cojuangco. But seven years in jail under martial law gave Aquino a new moral zeal, and murder sanctified him as a martyr. One million people followed his funeral procession, new opposition groups proliferated, and a reform movement emerged within the army. After a huge flight of capital, the regime was obliged to halt its debt repayments from October 1983 to May 1985, and in 1984 GNP *declined* by 5 percent, the first fall since the war. The crisis also began to erode support for

Marcos in Washington, which was now fearful of communist-led revolution. As one State Department official remarked: "They didn't ease him out because he was corrupt. They eased him out because he lost control of the country."[101]

Desperate, Marcos called a snap presidential election for February 7, 1986, hoping to extort a new mandate that would shore up his position abroad. At least five hundred million dollars was allocated to vote buying; about 10 percent of the potential electorate was probably disenfranchised by various dirty tricks. But Marcos's political victory proved a moral defeat. A combination of citizens' organizations and international observers exposed his methods quite clearly, as even Reagan had to admit. The feuding opposition had been pushed into a unified campaign, brokered by Cardinal Sin and led by Aquino's widow, Cory. Despite her wealth, she cast herself as a simple housewife, pledged to democracy. When Marcos accused her of political inexperience, she turned the gibe back on him: "I admit I have no experience in cheating, stealing, lying, or assassinating political opponents."[102]

After the election, Cory Aquino mounted a campaign of civil disobedience, attracting huge crowds to her rallies. But on February 22, Marcos moved against plotters in the army, where the reformers, headed by General Fidel Ramos, had been in contact for some time with General Juan Ponce Enrile, the defense minister who had profited handsomely from the Marcos years but who was now alienated by the growing influence of General Ver. When their plot was discovered, Enrile and Ramos fled to a suburban army base with only a few hundred lightly armed soldiers. Although Marcos controlled the mass media, the church's network, Radio Veritas, broadcast calls from Cardinal Sin for "people power" to protect them. Directed by continuing radio bulletins, the regime's opponents moved to key points, festooned with yellow ribbons (the Aquino campaign color), often with nuns in the front line to deter the troops from attack. The Reagan administration warned Marcos against a bloodbath and the demoralized duo, with their entourage, flew to asylum in Hawaii on February 26.

The Filipino public were then allowed to visit Malacañang Palace, where Imelda had left three thousand pairs of shoes, two thousand ball gowns, five hundred bras, and gallons of anti-wrinkle cream. "Compared to her," said U.S. Congressman Stephen Solarz, "Marie Antoinette was a bag lady." Yet signs of decay were as evident as those of opulence. Despite the air conditioning, the palace reeked with the stench of the polluted River Pasig. The family quarters looked more like a hospital ward than a presidential palace, full of Ferdinand's dialysis machines, medicines, and oxygen tanks.[103] Malacañang was not merely good propaganda for the Aquino government; it was a symbol of the Marcos years, perhaps even a sermon.

17: The Shot Seen Round the World. On a huge TV screen set up on a hillside in Seoul, South Koreans watch the launch of the *Apollo 11* moonshot, July 1969.

18: One World Half Visible. The *Apollo 11* lunar landing craft returning to the command ship as Earth rises in the background.

19: Reverend Dr. Martin Luther King, Jr., and President Lyndon B. Johnson in December 1964.

20: The March on Washington on August 28, 1963, was a prototype for mass protests across the world.

ASIAN TURMOIL IN THE 1960S

21: A mass rally during the early stages of China's Cultural Revolution in the northeastern province of Heilongjiang.

22: A South Vietnamese soldier leads a family to safety in war-torn Saigon during North Vietnam's Tet offensive of February 1968.

BETTER HEALTH AND EDUCATION IN THE POSTWAR WORLD

23: In a Calcutta neighborhood in 1977, an Indian female doctor conducts health checks.

24: Older children attend the primary school.

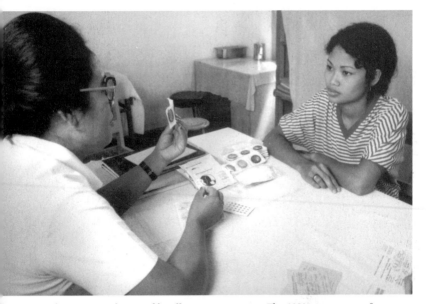

25: Women's lives were revolutionized by effective contraception. This 1980 picture comes from an Indonesian clinic.

26: Women reached the top politically. Here two Iron Ladies, Indira Gandhi and Margaret Thatcher, are seen in a softer mood in Delhi in November 1983.

THE BASICS—WATER

27: Clean water transformed health. African villagers in Burkina Faso make use of a new artesian well in 1974.

28: Water also meant power—with World Bank help, the Mangla Dam in Pakistan nears completion in 1965.

29: In May 1983 a fisherman's home on a remote Philippine island finally received electricity.

30: Phone networks were a prime indicator of economic development. This is the Colombian capital, Bogotá, in 1974.

DÉTENTE IN THE 1970S

31: Leonid Brezhnev, the Soviet party leader, and President Richard Nixon toast the agreements reached at their summit in Washington, D.C., June 19, 1973.

32: As part of détente with Poland, West German Chancellor Willy Brandt expresses contrition for Nazi crimes at the memorial to the Jewish ghetto in Warsaw, December 7, 1970.

Ferdinand Marcos died in 1989. Back in 1970, he had confided to his diary: "I often wonder what I will be remembered in history for? . . . Reorganization of government? Builder of roads, schools? The green revolution?" After his death, Marcos *did* make it into *The Guinness Book of World Records,* but not as he would have wished. You will find him in the section on the world's greatest robbers.[104]

The Chinese Dragon

Although impressive, the Asian tigers were almost unimportant in global terms compared with the transformation of the People's Republic of China in the decade after Deng Xiaoping won effective power in 1978 (see Chapter 10). China was the world's most populous country, with more than one billion people by the early 1980s. It therefore contained double the population of the rest of East and Southeast Asia, and more than Latin America and sub-Saharan Africa combined.

Despite China's new openness to the outside world, reliable statistics remain problematic. Nevertheless, it seems likely China achieved a growth rate of around 7 percent in the decade 1978–1987, which was comparable to that of Japan and South Korea in the fastest phases of their postwar boom. In this decade, per capita income doubled—a gain matched in so short a time only by South Korea between 1966 and 1976.[105] During this period the PRC also rose in the world ranking of exporters from thirty-second place to sixteenth.[106] And between 1978 and 1988, the proportion of the work force in agriculture fell from 71 percent to 59 percent.[107] Yet what made China's industrial revolution unique, compared with those of other Asian countries in the postwar era, was that, at the same time, it was also beginning a painful and confused transition away from a command economy toward the market.

Much of the growth in this decade can be ascribed to catch-up after the distortions and backwardness created in the previous twenty years. Econometricians reckon, for instance, that China's per capita output and consumption in 1992 would have been nearly three times as large as the actual figures but for the devastating impacts of the Great Leap Forward in the early 1960s and the Cultural Revolution decade.[108] Moreover, communist China had been largely cut off from Western technology, products, and ideas. One econometric analysis concluded that there was *no* positive technological change in China in the period 1950–1980.[109] Likewise, the growth in China's trade under Deng must be set against the autarky that had prevailed for most of the Mao era. By the mid-1980s, China was simply getting back to the trading position one would expect of a country of its size and income, with foreign trade around 17 percent of national product.[110]

Yet the economic legacies of Mao were not all negative. The decentralization of the Cultural Revolution meant that the economy was less tightly directed from Beijing. The "Third Front" program, begun as a security response to the Vietnam War, had a similar effect by dispersing the industrial base. Autarky meant that there was no history of foreign debt and defaults to burden the economy and sour relations with Western creditors, as East European communist governments faced when they began market reforms.[111] Moreover, in an overwhelmingly agrarian country, the "Plan" never had the same hold over the economy as it did in the more urbanized and industrialized Soviet Union. In 1978, factories with over one thousand workers generated 74 percent of Soviet industrial output, compared with only 40 percent from Chinese factories of over five hundred workers. In the USSR, some sixty thousand commodities were allocated by the plan, compared with about six hundred in China.[112] Also, isolation had never been total because of the vast Chinese diaspora across East and Southeast Asia. The success of Asian tigers like Taiwan suggested a model for market reform under authoritarian control, and the wealth of emigré Chinese there and in Hong Kong constituted potential foreign investment of a sort unavailable to the USSR.

By the early 1980s, China had also accomplished "one of the most dramatic fertility reductions in the historical demographic record."[113] In 1963 the fertility rate for women of childbearing age was 7.5. That reflected the efforts of many families to recover from decimation by the famine, but a rate of around six children per women persisted for much of the 1960s. By 1980, however, the figure had dropped to 2.2 and by 1985 to 2.0. There were, of course, variations around this average: rates were lower in urban areas than in the countryside; the east coast in general saw a sharper decline than the remote northwest, where the non-Han minorities were less coerced by the government. But the overall trend was clear, and it was largely due to intensive family planning, particularly the *wan xi shao* program of 1971. These three Chinese characters indicated the priorities: *later* marriages, *longer* intervals between children, and *fewer* children. The campaigns of the early Deng years built on this program, notably the "one child" policy of 1979 and the 1981 marriage law that raised the legal age of first marriage from twenty to twenty-two for men and eighteen to twenty for women.

Initially, the main instrument of birth control was abortion, as in other developing countries, such as Japan in the 1950s. The national rate rose from one abortion for every five live births in the early 1970s to a ratio of one to two by 1980 (nearly double the American average). In urban areas, the incidence was even higher: in Shanghai between 1975 and 1981, there were more abortions than live births. But more modern methods of birth control were also spreading. A fertility survey in 1982 suggested that over two-thirds of married women between the ages of fifteen and forty-nine were using some form of contraception, much the same as in Japan and the United States. Use of the pill was low by Western standards, amounting to only 8 percent of all married women in this age bracket, but it was estimated that China had 70 percent of IUD users in the world.[114] Aside from such coercive methods as abortion and IUD insertion, birth quotas were imposed right down to local factories and communes, and peer pressure was encouraged (even sometimes publicizing records of women's menstrual cycles). Those who had a second child might face wage cuts and medical charges.[115] Although there was a backlash against these policies during the 1980s, they had transformed China's fertility in just one decade.

The People's Republic therefore entered the post-Mao era of peace and stability with much potential for development, *if* appropriate policies were applied. Yet there was no consensus on policy or politics. The Ten-Year Plan promulgated by Mao's heir, Chairman Hua Guofeng, in February 1978 was "more a political wish than an economic blueprint."[116] It combined Stalinist gigantomania about massive heavy-industry projects and Brezhnevite fascination with imported foreign technology, to be financed by China's burgeoning oil industry. As oil output slipped during 1978 and as the planners' crudities were exposed, the plan collapsed. With Hua becoming the scapegoat, Deng was able to consolidate his power and the party plenum of December 1978 saw the rehabilitation of his old ally Chen Yun. Instead of following whatever Chairman Mao had ordered, Deng's new maxim was to "seek truth through facts." The plenum turned the party toward a new strategy to modernize China and rebuild legitimacy. Agricultural output would be increased by individual incentives, not massive investment. Instead of the heavy-industry obsession, more attention would be given to consumer goods. This would reduce energy use, soothe the populace, and mop up the surplus labor returning from the countryside now that Mao's rustication program had ended. The urban labor force (ninety-five million in 1978) expanded by some eleven million in the late 1970s as former Red Guards returned to the cities and as those labeled "landlords" or "capitalists" during the Cultural Revolution reentered the productive economy.[117]

What was the place of Deng Xiaoping in China's economic reform? Clearly, he set the general direction. Five years in France in the early 1920s had given him a window on the West that Mao conspicuously lacked. Even more important, four days in New York in 1974 (to address the UN) showed him more clearly than any amount of reading how far China lagged behind in the attributes of modernity.[118] But although Deng is rightly regarded as "the architect of the reform era," that is not the same as being "the architect of reform."[119] The great survivor had celebrated his seventy-fifth birthday in August 1979 and now husbanded his energy. Moreover, his leadership style was more collegial than Mao's: he readily delegated to trusted lieutenants. Although some economic policies, notably the Open Door to the West, bore his mark, Deng was more involved in foreign policy and political reform.

Beneath him, economic policy polarized across a generational divide between Chen Yun (born, like Deng, in the 1900s) and rising stars from the post–World War I era. In economic affairs, Zhao Ziyang (born 1919) was the notable reformer, becoming premier in 1980. However, all through the 1980s Chen and his allies controlled the important State Planning Commission.[120] In December 1982 Chen insisted that the economy had to remain within a plan, like a bird in a cage. "Without a cage it will fly away. The cage has to be the right size, and the cage itself has to be adjusted regularly. But no matter what, there has to be a cage."[121] Yet Zhao was taking increasing control of daily management. In 1984–1985 he crafted a deal among conservatives, planners, and heavy industry whereby the planned sector of the economy was safeguarded but the rest would expand. China would literally grow out of the plan.[122] The three growth areas were household agriculture, rural industry, and foreign trade.

Four-fifths of China's population still lived in the countryside. In 1978, the commune structure established during the Great Leap was still largely in force. Communes of several thousand households were divided into production brigades and then into work teams. Each layer was subject to government plans and quotas; produce not contracted for by state agencies was strictly limited. This meant acute shortages of poultry, fish, pigs, vegetables, and fruit—made worse by the closure of tens of thousands of rural markets.[123] In Gansu, one of the poorer provinces of west-central China, a 1980 survey found that production had changed little since 1949, with cultivation still depending on draft animals. Two-thirds of the people between the ages of sixteen and forty-five were illiterate: among other things, this meant that many local cadres could not manage collective production or handle bookkeeping. Some party leaders embezzled funds while commune members went hungry; many more refused to work in the fields, becoming an extra burden on working peasants.[124] Some communes were efficient and successful, but many were not. In 1978–1980 average grain consumption by the rural populace was several percentage points *lower* than it had been in 1955–1957.[125]

By the end of 1983, however, China's agriculture was almost completely decollectivized. The new "Household Responsibility System" had originally been intended for poorer areas where the commune system had completely failed. But it spread rapidly from pioneer provinces such as Anhui, pushed by the government and pulled by the peasants as the benefits became evident. This change reflected deep hostility to the commune system dating back to the famine of the early 1960s (chapter eight).[126] The breakdown of the commune was not an unalloyed benefit: with the decline of collective obligations, rural infrastructure such as paths and irrigation ditches was often neglected. Renewed reliance on family resources made the one-child policy even less attractive, with the result that the fertility rate crept up during the 1980s. But the immediate gains were enormous. Each household was allocated several plots from which it was contracted to produce a set amount of grain or some other crop. Once the quota had been fulfilled, the land could be used to grow other crops and to sell them at the relegalized local markets. During the early 1980s, agricultural output grew at nearly 10 percent per annum. Most households enjoyed a substantial rise in incomes and in savings. At a time when state revenues were falling, the latter were vital to sustain China's growth.

The introduction of some market mechanisms was another dramatic change. Factories and other state enterprises were allowed to retain some of their profits and, once their quotas were fulfilled, to sell their goods at market prices. Younger, educated managers were gradually introduced, and direction from party officials reduced. The scope of the plan was also relaxed: nominally it covered 256 items of machinery, for instance, in 1980 but only sixty in practice.[127]

For ordinary people, the biggest change was the revival of rural and urban markets—like peasant plots, a practice familiar to older Chinese. Almost as important was the promotion of small industries in rural areas and on the fringes of towns and cities. These absorbed surplus labor freed by the end of the commune—up a third of the work force in some areas, which showed how inefficient many communes had become. Nearly a third of rural industrial employment was in building materials, particularly brick making for the housing boom. Kilns sprang up across the country; roads were filled with carts carrying loads of bricks. Many towns set up textile workshops, others created rudimentary (and hazardous) mines to join in the "coal rush" caused by China's energy shortage.

The new "rural industries" were usually under the control of the town or village, but private enterprise was becoming a feature of rural China. In early 1982, a British journalist visited a village in Anhui province, where, amid the mud-walled, thatch-covered dwellings, Mr. Yang had built a new two-story stone house roofed with brick tiles. Yang made so much money from "sideline production"—selling pigs, tobacco, or vegetables above his grain quota—that he was known locally as "Mr Five Dollars Every Time He Opens His Door." Next to that door was posted a couplet:

> Better live among men than in paradise dream,
> Better farm my own patch than work in a Team.

Outside another stone house, newly built for his daughter and her husband, was mounted another verse:

> My new tiled house is bright and clean,
> Here comes the cart with our sewing machine!

Inside, eight young women working at eight sewing machines were jammed into one room, where Mr. Yang's daughter was teaching them how to make clothes.[128]

Land reform and rural enterprise had been vital for Japan's postwar growth; likewise in other Asian tigers (apart from the city-states). Where 1980s China was unusual, given its stage of development, was in also opening up to foreign trade and investment. This had not occurred in Japan and Korea until their agricultural and industrial revolutions were well advanced.[129] As with domestic development, the Chinese state relaxed, rather than relinquished, control. Overseas trade was still licensed, but instead of about a dozen foreign trading companies to conduct all of it, there were about 800 by the mid-1980s and over 5,000 in 1990. The Bank of China's monopoly of foreign exchange was also loosened, with ninety banks and institutions acting as dealers by 1988. Enterprises were allowed to keep a proportion of foreign earnings. Perhaps most important, the government devalued the currency by nearly a half in January 1981. This applied only to trade—tourists, for instance, were ripped off at the old, overvalued rate—but it helped bring Chinese prices closer to world values.[130]

At the same time, Special Economic Zones were established in coastal areas, with tax breaks and other incentives for foreign investors, most of whom were Chinese businessmen from nearby Hong Kong, Macao and Taiwan. Four such zones were created in 1979 and a fifth (Hainan Island) in 1988. Although modeled on export-processing zones elsewhere in Asia, these were often larger and also had substantial tourist facilities. Extending the procedure, fourteen "open cities" were created along the east coast. Most of these areas were havens for labor-intensive light industry of the sort the government wanted to promote. The most successful SEZ—Shenzen, next to Hong Kong—had displaced Shanghai as the most important export center in China by 1990.[131]

Rising incomes, increased production, and a new opening to trade all made the 1980s the decade of China's consumer revolution. By 1990, the standard of living of the average citizen was more than double that of 1978. Some 38 percent of Chinese households had a washing machine and 12 percent a refrigerator. Rural areas lagged far behind the eastern "gold coast," of course, and overall living standards were only comparable to those of Japan in the late 1950s. Even so, only 39 percent of homes had a toilet (compared with

88 percent in Japan around 1960).[132] And only 1 percent of dwellings had a phone in 1990. But the media revolution was perhaps the most profound sign of China opening up. Whereas in 1978 less than 8 percent of households had a radio and TV ownership was negligible, by 1990 most families had a radio, and there was an average of one TV for every eight people (one to three or four in the cities).[133]

Television was a double-edged weapon. On the one hand, it was under tight government control via the Central China TV network established in the mid-1970s. Thanks to satellite broadcasting, the network could reach about three-quarters of the country by 1990. Using Mandarin (the Beijing dialect), it acted as an agent of nation building. Television also played a role in the party's modernization campaign. By the late 1980s about one million students were enrolled in the TV university—nearly double the total attendance at China's campus universities. On the other hand, the new Open Door allowed the entry of foreign values as well as goods. American movies such as *Love Story* or *Rambo* were now shown. Like Hong Kong TV, which could be picked up in parts of southern China, these depicted countries with higher living standards and looser hierarchical values. The same ideas were insinuated by the foreign commercials with which TV programs from abroad were interwoven. Although many rural folk had still never seen a train, let alone a TV, for urban Chinese, these glimpses into an outside world, from a country largely isolated for thirty years, encouraged a keen awareness of contrasts. One woman in Shanghai observed in 1986:

> Western people come home from work, go into the kitchen, open this and that, and cook dinner. In my family we have to put the refrigerator in the bedroom! Western people take a shower and go to bed. We don't have a shower in the house. Western people go to the supermarket to pick up food, pay for it, and go home. . . . We still have to wait in lines to get food sometimes. We cannot compare China with the West.[134]

As we shall see, this growing discontent and the demands for radical reform became politically explosive in 1989.

The Indian Elephant

In the 1970s and 1980s, India performed far worse than East and Southeast Asia on most developmental indicators. This section looks at the reasons for its elephantine growth, with a glance southeast at the embattled island of Sri Lanka. Again we shall see the importance of politics as well as economics.

India was the second most populous state in the world (eight hundred million by 1987). Regional variation was therefore considerable: per capita income in the most prosperous state, the Punjab, was more than double that in Bihar, one of the poorest (see Map 3). Overall, whereas in 1960 India had an average per capita income about equal to that of Indonesia or Thailand, the former's was 50 percent more than India's by 1987 and Thailand's nearly three times as large.[135]

In part, this can be explained by differences in policy. Under Nehru and his daughter, Indira Gandhi, India remained committed to state-run industrialization for much longer than the countries of the Pacific Rim. These policies helped to build a major, self-sufficient military power. In May 1974 the country tested its own atomic device, a decade after China. In consequence, however, the Indian economy became enmeshed in administrative controls—the so-called permit-license-quota raj—in which a multitude of bureaucrats and businessmen developed vested interests. The potential for export-led growth was neglected in favor of a protected home market. India's share of world trade fell from 2.5 percent in 1938 to 0.9 percent in 1968 and only 0.5 percent in 1988, despite having one-sixth of the world's people. China's share also fell from 2.3 percent to 0.9 percent between 1938 and 1968 but then rose to 1.6 percent by 1988.[136] Rajiv Gandhi effected some piecemeal deregulation in the mid-1980s, but fundamental changes in policy did not begin until 1991.

The obsession with heavy industry meant that agriculture was marginalized, in further contrast to its importance in most of eastern Asia. Land reform was neglected, with some exceptions such as the southern state of Kerala during periods of communist rule. And although roads, irrigation, and other infrastructure were improved, there was nothing comparable to the vigorous programs of rural development that transformed agricultural productivity in East and then Southeast Asia. In 1960, 74 percent of the work force was in agriculture; the proportion had fallen only 4 percent by 1985. During that same quarter-century, the Indonesian figure had dropped from 75 percent to 57 percent, in South Korea from from 66 percent to 36 percent. Government population programs were belated and erratic, unlike in Indonesia under Suharto. There the total fertility rate had fallen from an average of 5.4 births per woman to 3.3 between 1960–1965 and 1985–1990; India declined only from 5.8 to 4.3. Over the same period, South Korea pushed the figure down from 5.4 to 2, while, as we have seen, China, although even more agrarian than India, accomplished a similar fertility transition.[137] Moreover, India's poor educational record at the primary level (see Chapter 9) was an obstacle to both development and birth control. Not until the 1990s was a bare majority of the population literate: most of India's limited spending on education (2 percent of GDP in 1986, compared with 18 percent on defense) went to high schools and universities for children of the elites. In fact, "few countries in Latin America or Asia have expended less effort on eradicating illiteracy."[138]

Low literacy and high fertility were evidence of India's general failure to mobilize its female population. In the developing "tiger" economies at least a third of the labor force was female by the mid-1980s; in India the proportion was 26 percent—a slight *fall* from the 1960 figure.[139] Across Asia, women were the tigers' teeth. They dominated the labor-intensive, light-manufacturing industries that attracted foreign investment and generated export earnings; women often constituted four-fifths of workers in the special export-processing zones. "It was the ready and seemingly endless supply of young, malleable, and cheap female labor that was (and still is) the cornerstone of industrial success and the magnet for foreign investments."[140] Of course, employers' motives were hard headed: women could be paid less than men; they were usually more docile and less likely to join unions. But even under sweatshop regimes, young women were "liberated" by urban employment from rural poverty and domestic incarceration. India's lower levels of development, urbanization, and literacy retarded this social revolution.

Some observers have discerned deeper cultural traits that impeded growth and development. Talk of "the Hindu rate of growth" became a cliché. As we have seen, however, reference to cultural values—be they Hindu, Islamic, or Confucian—is of limited utility. We shall learn much more about the nature and problems of India's development by examining its *politics* in the 1960s, 1970s, and 1980s. For India was unique in the developing world as a vigorous but fragile democracy in a country the size of a continent.

India covers 1.25 million square miles, comparable in area to the fifteen-member European Union after 1995, but far more diverse. The 1971 census listed thirty-three languages with more than one million speakers; even Hindi was the mother tongue of only about one-third of the country's population.[141] Although most states had been reorganized along lines of language by the mid-1960s, all had significant linguistic, religious, and tribal minorities. Over 11 percent of the populace was Muslim. Not only Hindus, but also Muslims, Sikhs, and Christians were divided by caste into a myriad of *jatis* (birth groups). Each *jati* had, in principle, strict rules against marrying, eating with, or even working with outsiders, especially other orders of society (*varnas*), of whom one-sixth remained literally "untouchable." Such diversity of language, religion, and caste has led one scholar to call India "a mosaic of mosaics."[142]

Of necessity, then, India's government was a federal system, in which the power of the states was growing. This lack of central control vitiated programs of national development, such as land reform or birth control. And because India's diversity was that of the subcontinent as a whole, its problems also had an international dimension. In the 1970s, there were more Muslims in India than in the "Islamic" state of Pakistan. Major language groups were split between rival states: Punjabis between India and Pakistan, Bengalis across India and Bangladesh, and Tamils between India and Sri Lanka. Even though sensitive northern borders stabilized after the wars of 1965 and 1971 (see Chapter 7), Kashmir remained a flash point between India and Pakistan; Sikh extremists fought for independence from the Punjab; Assam was in turmoil over Bengali immigration. In such a fractured polity, state building was a very different task than in, say, South Korea.

For the first two decades after independence in 1947, what held the country together was the dominance of the Indian National Congress, a catch-all political party that under Jawaharlal Nehru combined firm but flexible leadership with the cooption of significant economic, local and communal elites. After Nehru's death in 1964, however, Congress's hold weakened at both the union and state levels.

Nationally, the critical figure was Nehru's ruthless daughter and political heir, Indira Gandhi—"the only man in a cabinet of old women,"[143] to quote a contemporary joke.° At all levels, she substituted loyal cronies for the old Congress leadership, whose plotting against her climaxed in the decision of the Allahabad High Court in June 1975 to invalidate her 1971 election to parliament on grounds of malpractice. Bolstered by her favorite son, the brash and ruthless Sanjay, Indira responded by arresting her opponents, suspending the constitution, and imposing a dictatorial "state of emergency." Then, equally suddenly, in January 1977 Mrs. Gandhi ended the emergency and announced new elections in March. Insulated from criticism, she underestimated the depths of hostility to her and the ability of her diverse opponents to forge an alliance. Yet her decision also testified to the strength of India's democratic tradition: elections had become the touchstone of legitimacy.

In March 1977, Congress (I)—"I" for Indira—was routed, with mother and son both losing their seats in the party's first national defeat since independence. But the Janata coalition that replaced her soon fell apart, and she was returned triumphantly to power in January 1980. After Sanjay was killed

---

°When she visited Washington in April 1966, Lyndon Johnson learned that she disliked being styled "Madam Prime Minister" and phoned the Indian ambassador to ask what he should call her. "Anything he wants," Mrs. Gandhi told the ambassador, and then added, "You can also tell him that some of my cabinet ministers call me 'sir.' He can do so too, if he likes." (LBJ did not.)

stunt flying a few months later, his elder brother, Rajiv, became crown prince, assuming the premiership when his mother was killed by Sikh bodyguards in October 1984. He, too, was soon enmired in corruption scandals and was ousted in 1989 by another unholy alliance of opponents, the Janata Dal coalition, which also soon fell apart. By the end of the 1980s, therefore, Congress had lost its monopoly of power at the center, but it remained the only nationwide party in India. The result was chronic political instability.

The weakening of Congress's hold over national politics reflected its collapse at the state level. For two decades after independence, the party was in continuous control of every state government except, briefly, Kerala. The watershed election was 1967, when Congress lost half the states, mostly to unstable coalitions paralleling Janata at the national level. Locally, Congress had lost its catch-all role as the party of the economically and politically potent. State governments and their supporters gradually wrested greater control over policies and funds from the Congress elite in New Delhi. The trend of the new federalism seemed clear: India was "becoming a multi-nation state of nation-provinces."[144]

The erosion of Congress's power at the center and in the states demonstrated the growing democratization of Indian politics. In Nehru' time, elections were still dominated by national and local elites, but by the 1960s other groups in India's cellular society had organized to advance their own interests. A simple indicator is the rising turnout figures for general elections: 46 percent of the potential electorate voted in 1952, but over 61 percent in the critical election of 1967.[145] Political mobilization sharpened social divisions. Democracy, after all, is a numbers game: power depends on the quantity, not the quality, of your support. Historically, India had been "a world of minorities, because this world was not governed by a form of politics which would make statistical majority a vital principle of advantage."[146] By the 1960s, opposition minorities saw the need to construct majorities, at state and national levels, to supplant Congress. This exacerbated the politicization of both caste and religion.

The early Congress leadership was largely drawn from elite Hindu castes, particularly Brahmans. But the "green revolution" (see Chapter 5) helped create a new rural middle class that sought its share of the benefits. In Uttar Pradesh, in 1967, Charan Singh, a defector from Congress, mobilized middling peasant proprietor castes to wrest power from Congress. Over the next decade, networks of local and regional alliances were built up to oppose the Congress elites. The enlargement of these alliances into national politics created the Janata coalition that toppled Mrs. Gandhi in the election of 1977. Janata then politicized positive discrimination. The 1950 constitution had singled out the "Scheduled Castes and Tribes" at the very bottom of society—about 20 percent of the population—for special education and welfare programs and "reserved" for them a quota of bureaucratic posts and parliamentary seats. Pressed by its own supporters to expand the beneficiaries, Janata established the Mandal Commission in 1978. This proposed that a further 27 percent of the population be given positive discrimination. The report became a political football: Mrs. Gandhi kicked it off the field on her return to power in 1980, but it was thrown back into play when Janata Dal took over in 1989. In August 1990, Prime Minister V. P. Singh issued an order reserving 27 percent of federal government and public sector jobs for "Other Backward Classes," thereby enlarging positive discrimination to cover about half the population. Since the 1970s, state governments had also been enacting their own OBC laws. Little wonder that caste politics and caste violence proliferated. With jobs, subsidies, political seats, and university places all at stake, the consequences for winners and losers were immense.[147]

A similar pattern can be discerned in religious politics, where diversity is again a fact of Indian life. But diversity does not automatically entail hostility among Hindus, Muslims, Christians, Sikhs, and the like, who often live cheek by jowl with each other in a religious culture that is highly syncretistic and also fragmented along caste lines. And although four-fifths of the population could be termed Hindu, their religion lacks the ecclesiastical structure and doctrinal orthodoxy of, say, Roman Catholicism. For all these reasons, Hindu nationalism was not potent in India's early postindependence decades.

By the 1980s, however, the situation was very different. Congress, with its secular ideology, was no longer dominant, memories of the communal bloodbath in 1947 had faded, and India's social groups were becoming more politicized. Mobilization along religious lines seemed an attractive strategy. Indira Gandhi started to play on Hindu feeling in the early 1980s, notably by her toughness against Sikh extremists in the Punjab. Her politically motivated decision in June 1984 to storm rather than besiege the terrorists occupying the Sikhs' Golden Temple in Amritsar inflamed communal feeling and led directly to her own assassination. Hindu groups such as the RSS (Rashtraiya Swayamsevak Sangh), a militarized Hindu brotherhood, highlighted Sikh atrocities, Hindu conversions to Islam in the south, and the "threat" from the pope's forthcoming visit in 1986. In 1984, they also revived the dormant issue of the Babari Masjid mosque in the Uttar Pradesh city of Ayodhya, which Hindus claimed had been built on top of a temple commemorating the birthplace of Ram, one of their greatest gods. Ayodhya became the centerpiece of a campaign about hundreds of such contested sites across India, which helped the RSS to build support in the south.

Most important, leaders of the new Bharatiya Janata party (BJP) took up the Hinduization theme. The party had been formed after Janata's collapse in 1980; the BJP's initial strategy was to build a Janata-style broad coalition, even with Muslims. But after winning only two seats in the 1984 elections, the BJP decided that Hindu nationalism was the key to success. Allying with groups like the RSS, it organized marches and protests across the country. In the elections of 1989, the BJP was rewarded with 11.4 percent of the vote, eighty-eight seats, and a major place in the Janata Dal coalition government. When Prime Minister V. P. Singh implemented the Mandal Commission report in 1990, the BJP leader, L. K. Advani, judged that the communalism card could trump the caste card. He began a sixty-two-hundred-mile journey across north India toward Ayodhya in a vehicle decked out as Ram's chariot. With riots escalating, the government arrested Advani in October 1990. This ended the BJP compact with Janata Dal, brought down V. P. Singh, and led to new elections in 1991 that returned Congress to power. The BJP's campaign at Ayodhya climaxed in December 1992, when extremists pulled the mosque to the ground. Over the next few weeks at least a thousand people died across the country in the worst Hindu-Muslim violence since partition.[148]

Against the Nehru tradition, therefore, regionalism, caste, and communalism had become the fuel of politics. In such a diverse yet democratic country all aspects of economic development were enormously contentious. This can be seen from a glance at two central issues in development—birth control and women's rights.

Although the 1961 census focused attention on India's population growth, the sensitivity of birth rates for rival communities led the government to adopt a voluntary policy, with payments to those who volunteered. After initial success—over three million sterilizations in fiscal year 1972–1973—numbers fell away sharply. One problem was use of payments to those who acted as "motivators" of the volunteers, which caused widespread cases of coercion and blackmail. India also lacked a basic health service to support contraceptive techniques. Women were given little explanation about IUDs and often removed them at the first pain or bleeding. Taking advantage of the Emergency, in April 1976 the government mounted a National Population Program under the aegis of Sanjay Gandhi. This raised the age of marriage by three years, to eighteen for women and twenty-one for men, and allowed states to impose sterilization on parents with three children. Only one state enacted such legislation before the Emergency ended, but many local bureaucrats and politicians, freed from legal restraints and enticed by the financial inducements, operated a quasi-compulsory policy. Government employees were given quotas to fill. A certificate of sterilization was often required to obtain a phone, a driver's license, or a new house. With Sanjay Gandhi so closely associated with this hated policy, sterilization became a major issue for voters in 1977. This was "the first election in the world in which family planning was a—if not the—deciding factor."[149] The climate of fear that had been created set back India's birth control program for years to come.

The issue of what in the West was called women's rights was also caught up in the maelstrom of Indian politics. The 1970s saw a proliferation of women's groups, encouraged by the UN Decade of Women (1976–1985) and by the shock of an official report, *Toward Equality* (1974), which suggested that the status of women had actually declined since independence. One success of the activists was a campaign against "dowry murders"—the killing of young wives in domestic fires started by their in-laws for financial gain—which resulted in a tightening of the law in 1986. And in September 1987, the case of Roop Kanwar, an eighteen-year-old widow burned to death in ritual *sati* with her husband's corpse on a site then consecrated by thousands of Hindus, prompted a feminist outcry and a law reiterating the ban on *sati* and outlawing its "glorification." But women's groups were themselves usually structured on lines of caste or religion, and in the 1980s gender questions were often eclipsed by these controversies. In April 1985 the Indian Supreme Court delivered a favorable judgment in the Shah Bano case, a long-running appeal by a divorced Muslim woman for maintenance from her husband. It argued that Muslims were not exempt from India's criminal code. This judgment brought Muslim men onto the streets to protest in unprecedented numbers. In this way a gender issue had been redefined as a communal issue.[150]

Those who believed that India's communalism was not merely economically damaging but potentially suicidal pointed to Sri Lanka as a salutary warning. This island country was only twenty-five miles from southeastern India at the narrowest point of the Palk Strait (see Map 3). In 1981, about 74 percent of population (fifteen million in all) were Sinhalese; 18 percent were Tamils of Indian descent. Two-thirds were Buddhists (mostly Sinhalese), but there were also Hindus (predominantly Tamils), some Muslims, and a Christian element, especially among the English-speaking elite.

After independence in 1948, the island (called Ceylon until 1972) was initially run by the Anglophone elite in the United Nationalist Party (UNP). In its secular, tolerant, socialist ethos and its rule by one family, the Senanyakes, it resembled the Indian National Congress in the Nehru era. By the early 1950s, however, Sinhalese agitation against English as the official language (and thus the passport to jobs and advancement) fused with campaigns to make Buddhism the official religion. The political opportunity was seized by Solomon Bandaranaike, an Oxford-educated Christian, who left the UNP, converted to Buddhism, and created the "Sinhala Only" Sri Lanka Freedom Party (SLFP), which swept to power in the elections of 1956. After his assassination, his widow Sirima continued his policies as premier from 1960 to

1965 and again in 1970–1977, before a new period of UNP predominance until 1994. But this was a very different UNP from that of the 1940s—now as ready as its rival to cultivate Sinhalese and Buddhist causes. With Tamils living in a few constituencies in the north and east and no system of proportional representation, the electoral arithmetic left both main parties free to engage in "competitive chauvinism" for the Sinhalese vote.[151]

In response, Tamils became more organized and militant, supported from India by their fellows in Tamil Nadu. In 1983 the Tamil Tigers began an open insurrection, gaining control of the Jaffna peninsula at the top of the island. After the failure of the government offensive in 1987, Rajiv Gandhi tried to defuse the crisis by imposing a peace accord. The Sri Lankan government agreed to merge the northern and eastern provinces, paving the way for a Tamil-majority government there, and Indian troops were introduced to suppress the Tigers. But the latter retreated to the hills and, by the time Gandhi withdrew the troops ignominiously in March 1990, the Indians had lost eleven hundred dead. In May 1991, Rajiv was killed by one of the Tigers' suicide bombers, as was the Sri Lanka president two years later. Despite government successes, the civil war dragged on through the 1990s.

In the 1950s, Sri Lanka had been the Philippines of South Asia, a growing economy with high levels of welfare and literacy. Its descent into civil war was a grim warning to its Indian neighbor. There were, however, notable contrasts. Sri Lanka's polarization had been exacerbated by persistent use of emergency powers, whereas, in India, these had been applied nationwide only in 1975–1957. Sri Lanka was also a small island gripped by the single-issue politics of language and religion. India was far larger; its fractures and therefore its politics were more diverse. "Better a gigantic muddle than a single divide!" in the words of one analyst.[152] And in India, unlike Sri Lanka, the English-speaking middle class retained its role as a unifying if often exploitative force.

This brings us back to an essential point about India's economy. The persistence of poverty, the absence of radical land reform, the weight of bureaucratic socialism, the intensification of caste and communal politics—all these should not distract from the considerable growth of the Indian economy in the 1970s and 1980s. Thanks to the green revolution, India had become self-sufficient in food grains, with no major famine since that in the eastern state of Bihar in 1966. The policy of industrial self-sufficiency may have eroded India's position in international trade, but it did create a large, diverse industrial economy that pushed the country into the world's top twenty in terms of GNP.[153] Despite the state sector, this was essentially a capitalist economy, with many large as well as small private firms. Unlike the "managerial capitalism" of the West, Indian big business was also family business: of the top twenty commercial groups, nineteen were family owned in the 1980s, headed by the Tatas and the Birlas. And even if the Indian "middle class" was only 15 to 20 percent of the population, this was a huge number in absolute terms, given the population of eight hundred million. By 1990 India had the largest pool of English-speaking scientific talent in the world outside the United States, including over one hundred thousand software engineers and technicians.[154] Rajiv Gandhi's limited liberalization of the mid-1980s boosted the output of consumer goods. Motorbikes and scooters soared from 417,000 in 1980 to 1.55 million in 1988; TV production jumped from 710,000 in 1983 to 5.7 million in 1988.[155]

In India, as in China, the TV revolution was complex in its effects. Television broadcasting was introduced into India in 1959, but the real breakthrough came in 1975, when the INSAT satellite was launched. This gave the government's Doordarshan TV network a truly national reach. By the late 1980s, 70 percent of the population could receive TV signals, though less than 10 percent of Indians, mostly in urban areas, had convenient access to a TV set.[156] In the 1980s, the government opened the TV network to India's movie industry, the biggest producer of feature films in the world. Such was the fame of film stars that two of them, M. G. Ramachandran (known as MGR) became the chief minister of Tamil Nadu from 1977 to 1987, and N. T. Rao (NTR) swept to power in Andhra Pradesh in 1983, having never before run in an election.

TV had its greatest effect on young people, spreading consumer values. "The movies are like a teacher to us," commented one rural West Bengali; "they tell us what to do and what not to do."[157] But across the whole family, even in rural areas, TV had a solvent effect. A study of one north Indian village in the mid-1980s showed how acquisition of a TV eroded traditional hierarchies of age and gender in the extended family. Its purchase and viewing often occurred over the objections of the patriarch. The set was located in a room in the women's quarters, encouraging more mixing between men and women. Women organized work and cooking around peak viewing times and began to adopt movie standards of appearance and dress.[158]

Lest this suggest a simple process of "modernization," we should note that TV was also an agent of communal mobilization in the 1980s. In 1987–1988 Doordarshan broadcast an adaptation of the Hindu epic, the *Ramayana* ("Romance of Ram") in seventy-eight half-hour episodes aired on Sundays. The project had the backing of Rajiv Gandhi, seeking to woo Hindu opinion. It was "a mixture of soap opera and national mythology, designed to appeal to everyone, from teen-agers to old people."[159] The authorities followed up with another Hindu epic, the *Mahabharata,* in ninety-one episodes in 1988–1990, whose average audience was estimated at nine out of every ten people with TV sets. In these series, Ram was a masculine, warlike figure—

equivalent to the heroes of Hollywood epics like *Ben Hur.* These broadcasts helped create a *national* Hindu identity for the first time.[160]

India's problems in the 1970s and 1980s highlight the successes of the Asian tigers. Vital preconditions for economic development were land reform, population control, export-led growth, high literacy rates, and female labor in industry or services. In all these areas, India lagged behind its Asian neighbors. Equally important was political stability, whether imposed by one-party dominance (as in Taiwan), military rule (as in South Korea), or communist control (as in China). In India, by contrast, the years of Congress hegemony had come to an end. India also lacked the compactness and homogeneity of many Asian states. And its uniquely democratic politics allowed, indeed encouraged, the politicization of social divisions. On the other hand, electoral politics in a federal polity acted as a safety valve. The social pressures that built up in many controlled Asian states would eventually become explosive—as we shall see with China in 1989 and Indonesia in 1998.

13

Challenges for the West

To anyone looking back, the revolutions of 1989 seem to dominate the 1980s. The collapse of communism in Eastern Europe, followed by the disintegration of the Soviet Union two years later, were so spectacular and so complete that we can easily forget how precarious the West seemed in the first half of the decade. The long economic boom in North America and Western Europe had been followed by inflation, stagnation, and protest; attempts at reform (Thatcherism and Reaganomics) were creating new problems without curing old ills. By the mid-1980s, the United States had become the world's greatest debtor, reversing the capital flows on which the postwar economy had depended. An acute debt crisis undermined the economies and polities of major states in Latin America and threatened to bring down the Western banking system. In both Central America and southern Africa, revolutionary struggles against landowning elites became the battle fronts of the new cold war. In Europe, America's new missile deployments in Europe and its "Star Wars" program for space-based defense brought arms control talks to a halt and provoked a popular backlash that shook the NATO alliance to its foundations. In the early 1980s, in short, challenges for the West seemed top of the international agenda.

Thatcherism, Reaganomics, and the Crisis of Capitalism

Stagflation was a feature of the developed economies for most of the 1970s (see Chapter 12). The crisis called in question the verities of postwar economic policy. Were the West's mixed economies and welfare states, sustained by Keynesian policies, still appropriate? In 1981, victorious French socialists said yes, but soon had to change their tune. From the United States and Britain came powerful calls for a return to the maxims of classical economic liberalism.

One such maxim was the importance of private enterprise, reiterated by a guru of this neoliberal New Right, Friedrich von Hayek, the Austrian economist and 1974 Nobel Prize winner, who spent most of his professional life teaching in London and Chicago. In his 1944 book damning socialism as *The Road to Serfdom,* Hayek insisted that "in the ordering of our affairs we should make as much use as possible of the spontaneous forces of society, and resort as little as possible to coercion."[1] The New Right questioned the burden of regulation imposed on modern capitalism. They denounced public ownership as inefficient and expensive. Above all, they castigated the growing burden of taxation as an obstacle to growth. In 1950 public expenditure in North America and Western Europe constituted around 25 to 30 percent of GDP, though Denmark was under 20 percent and Sweden over 37 percent. By 1975, the norm was at least 40 percent in most states, with Sweden and the Netherlands over half. In West Germany and the United Kingdom the proportion had risen from 30 percent to 46 percent, in the United States from 27 percent to 36 percent.[2]

Only in the United Kingdom and the United States did defense take more than 10 percent of public spending. Most of the increase was in subsidies and transfer payments for social welfare, and this constituted a second target for the neoliberals. During the period 1965–1981, welfare spending had risen in the United States from 12 percent of GDP to 21 percent, in the United Kingdom from 16 percent to 24 percent, and in West Germany from 22 percent to 31 percent. Sweden allowed the proportion to jump from 19 percent to 33 percent. Much of the rise came from pension payments; health and especially education grew much less.[3] Critics argued that such extensive welfare provision was unsustainable without economic growth. Indeed they saw the welfare state as an impediment to growth, both through its burden of taxation and bureaucracy and through what many considered its corrosive effect on individual responsibility. "It corrupts the virtuous, and pays equal benefits to those who spurn virtue. . . . it makes passive clients of them all."[4]

Big government and flabby welfare, neoliberals argued, were both maintained by the pernicious dogmas of Keynesianism. Just as the latter had gained credibility by apparently explaining and remedying the depression of the 1930s, so it was undermined by the stagflation of the 1970s. For many, the new panacea was the monetarism advocated by Milton Friedman, another Chicago economist and Nobel laureate, who backed calls for a return to the "golden age" of nineteenth-century laissez faire with an insistence that firm control of the money supply was the key to a sound economy. Monetarism was to replace Keynesian demand management and deficit spending.[5] Monetary targeting had been practiced by most Western governments during the 1970s, but in conjunction with other policy instruments. In the United States, the appointment of Paul Volcker as chairman of the Board of Governors of the Federal Reserve System in August 1979 signaled a single-minded tight-money policy. Then, with the election of Margaret Thatcher as the British prime minister in May 1979 and the inauguration of Ronald Reagan as the U.S. president in January 1981, the assault on the Keynesian welfare state began in earnest.

Margaret Thatcher, born in 1925, was an Oxford-educated research chemist whose marriage to a wealthy businessman allowed her to pursue first law and then politics as a career. In 1975 she won an audacious bid for the Conservative party leadership, after Edward Heath had lost two general elections the previous year. Her unlikely position as the first woman leader of a patronizingly male party strengthened her "them and us" mentality—solicitous of those within her circle, antagonistic toward all outside. Despite an upbringing of bourgeois thrift as the daughter of a provincial shopkeeper, her early years as a government minister had not been distinguished by markedly right-wing views. These developed only after her election as party leader, under the tutelage of Sir Keith Joseph. "Each time you go further along the Socialist road, nearer and nearer to the Communist state, then the consequences of the Communist State will follow," she warned in 1977.[6] In foreign affairs, she was also a vehement anticommunist, earning (and relishing) the sobriquet "Iron Lady" from Moscow. She portrayed the 1979 election as a chance to arrest the story of Britain's postwar decline at home and abroad: "Unless we change our ways and our direction, our greatness as a nation will soon be a footnote in the history books."[7]

Within the first year, her government had reduced the rates of income tax, imposed monetary targets, and set strict rules for government borrowing. She also attacked the power of trades unions. Legislation in 1980 and 1982 restricted intimidatory picketing, reduced unions' legal immunities, and weakened their ability to draw all workers in a factory into a union (the "closed shop"). As protests mounted, old-style paternalists in her cabinet advocated a U-turn. But Thatcher was unmoved. "You turn if you want to," she declared in October 1980. "The lady's not for turning."[8]

Thatcher and Reagan were an unlikely pair. She was small, clever, and assertive; he was tall, affable, and easygoing. Born in 1911, he grew up in small-town Illinois before making his name as a sports announcer, movie actor, and TV host, which he and his ambitious wife, Nancy, used as the platform for a two-term governorship of California. In the 1980 presidential election, he overwhelmed Jimmy Carter.

Reagan came to power as the standard bearer of the right, speaking out against high taxes and the Soviet threat, but he was no Thatcherite ideologue. "He probably spends two or three hours a day on real work," an aide admitted. "All he wants is to tell stories about his movie days." Journalist Anthony Lewis complained of the "vacuum at the center . . . a President with a seven-minute attention span, a President interested not in reality but in appearance, in slogans."[9] Later it became known that his schedule was choreographed by his wife, after consultation with her astrologer. Chief of Staff Donald Regan was obliged to keep a color-coded calendar on his desk, with green for "good days," red for "bad days," and yellow for "iffy days."[10]

Reagan was mocked by intellectuals, but his success as a politician could not be denied. Tip O'Neill, the Democratic Speaker of the House, acknowledged that "with a prepared text he's the best public speaker I've ever seen," eclipsing even Roosevelt and Kennedy.[11] Reagan's skills as the "Great Communicator" were vital to enact the legislative agenda of 1981. The president was also helped by Republican victory in the Senate and a narrowing of the Democratic margin in the House. Income tax rates were cut by 25 percent over three years, and the new budget mandated a 10 percent annual increase in defense spending from 1982 to 1986. In a political system designed to impede radical change, these congressional victories evoked comparisons with the early New Deal and became known as the Reagan Revolution.

The dangers of bucking the new rightward trend in Western capitalism were exemplified by the case of France. On May 10, 1981, less than four months after Reagan's inauguration, the French elected their first socialist president since the Second World War, François Mitterrand (1916–1996). To some extent, the avowed "break with capitalism" was rhetoric, not reality—needed to woo the communist PCF into Mitterrand's alliance. The "real" Mitterrand remains opaque[12]—a devout Catholic who converted late to socialism, a tainted servant of Vichy *and* a courageous *résistant* during the war, a vehement critic of Gaullist "dictatorship" who proved a consummate autocrat.* Nevertheless, 1981 saw a clear determination to promote "socialism

---

*His predecessor, Valéry Giscard d'Estaing, had respectfully refrained from occupying de Gaulle's office in the Elysée Palace. Mitterrand occupied the office and even used the general's desk. "De Gaulle is not the only one in the history of France," he stated firmly.

in one country" whatever the international climate, with new public-sector jobs, an increased minimum wage, and extensive nationalization.

But the socialist victory also started a massive run on the franc, forcing the Bank of France to spend a third of the country's reserves in the ten days between Mitterrand's election and inauguration. The new president, however, refused to devalue, believing that this would reward speculators, damage the socialists electorally, and undermine France's international standing. As Mitterrand later confessed, it was a major error. Over the next three years he was forced to emasculate socialist programs as budget and trade deficits widened, inflation soared to 14 percent, and unemployment rose to over 10 percent by 1985. In March 1983 Mitterrand did consider regaining France's independence by abandoning the European Monetary System, devaluing the franc, and then expanding behind protectionist barriers. But he was told that the franc would collapse completely. "Leaving the EMS would put us in the hands of the IMF," warned one adviser starkly.[13]

Thereafter, Mitterrand made virtue out of necessity. Unable to escape from Europe's Exchange Rate Mechanism, he sought to avoid it being simply a deutschmark zone. As for earlier French leaders, European integration became his answer: "France is our country, but Europe is our future."[14] This change of policy was evident in renewed partnership with West Germany within the European Community and in Mitterrand's enthusiasm for eventual monetary union to offset the power of the deutschmark. These goals were advanced in Brussels by Jacques Delors, Mitterrand's finance minister in 1981–1984, who was chosen as president of the European Commission (the EC's top bureaucrat) in January 1985. Although the integrationist agenda found little favor in London, Thatcher had been mollified by settlement in 1984 of her long-running battle to reduce Britain's contribution to the EC's budget. With her market ideology, she was attracted to the idea of completely dismantling all the community's internal obstacles to the free movement of goods and people. Visible barriers created by tariffs and quotas had already disappeared, but a true "single market" depended on common standards for products and employment and open access to investment and ownership. This project was supported by other member states and by national business organizations concerned about American and Japanese competition. For Thatcher, the Single European Act, ratified in 1986 and targeted for completion by the end of 1992, was an end in itself. For Mitterrand and Delors, it was an essential step to eventual monetary union.[15]

Another sign of Mitterrand's *grand tournant* was his new use of Reaganite language. "I am not an enemy of profit when profit is fairly earned," he announced in September 1983, adding, "Too much tax means no tax. It suffocates the economy."[16] When Prime Minister Pierre Mauroy resigned in July 1984, the president appointed Laurent Fabius as his successor. Fabius was thirty-seven, a brilliant, pushy Paris technocrat—far different in image from Mauroy, an old-style socialist and the former mayor of Lille. Fabius's slogans in 1985 included "Computers for everyone." At the end of that year, the government announced that a European Disneyland would be built on the outskirts of Paris. De Gaulle would have turned in his grave, but it was good for jobs, tourism, and political popularity. In 1986–1988 the political balance of the Assembly forced Mitterrand into "cohabitation" with a right-wing prime minister, Jacques Chirac, whose avowedly Reaganite agenda included denationalization and tax cuts. Although in 1988 Mitterrand became the first president of the Fifth Republic to win a second seven-year term, the socialists were now an essentially presidential party headed by a centrist leader. After the elections two commentators wrote that "the Left no longer has hope, the Right no longer has fear."[17]

Yet, if socialism had failed in France, this did not mean that capitalism had been rejuvenated in Britain and America. On the contrary, the early Thatcher and Reagan years were also marked by spectacular disasters. In 1979–1981, Thatcher tried to restrain spending and borrowing just as the second oil crisis began to bite. The result was a rise in unemployment to 11 percent and an 18 percent fall in industrial production (compared with 10 percent in the slump of 1929–1932). Inflation was still around 20 percent. To cover growing unemployment and poverty, social spending increased, as did government spending as a proportion of GDP. The overall tax burden also grew because, although income tax rates had been cut, the government had nearly doubled the rate of sales tax. Despite monetarist targets, the money supply also rose during this period. The period 1979–1981 was therefore richly ironic for Margaret Thatcher, the vitriolic critic of socialist mismanagement: monetarism had failed, government spending had risen, and Britain was in its worst recession for forty years.[18] Early in 1982, the opinion polls suggested that it was Thatcherism, not communism, that was headed for the scrap heap of history.

Salvation came from the South Atlantic. In April 1982 the Argentine junta invaded the Falkland Islands, one of Britain's last imperial outposts. Thatcher responded with relish and resolution, dispatching a substantial task force and using victory over the demoralized Argentine conscripts as a metaphor for national renewal: "We have ceased to be a nation in retreat. . . . Great Britain is great again."[19] Calling an early general election to exploit the national mood, she surged to victory in June 1983 over the feuding, ineptly led Labour party. In her second term she was able to start privatizing major state utilities, such as electricity and gas. In 1984–1985, she won a decisive victory over the coal miners, using large stockpiles and new antiunion legislation to break their year-long strike. The years 1985–1987 saw the high tide of Thatcherism, but the price of dogma at the start of her administration had been lasting deindustrialization. Economic recovery came only later in the decade, after tax cuts and, ironically, a looser monetary policy.

The early 1980s also saw even more spectacular setbacks for Reagonomics. The 1981 economic legislation in the United States was a mishmash of rival recipes, hastily thrown together and forced down the throat of Congress while its appetite for the Reagan Revolution was still keen. The result was a half-baked mess. Monetarists were placated by tight controls on the money supply; cold warriors won large increases in the defense budget; and the advocates of low taxation gained substantial cuts. But how could taxes be reduced *and* defense spending enhanced without increasing the deficit? Advocates of supply-side economics argued that low taxes encouraged extra enterprise, which generated additional revenue. Even if that were true, however, Budget Director David Stockman had no doubt that spending cuts were also needed. Yet Reagan declared the social security budget, almost half of government spending, off limits for fear of middle-class opposition to cuts in pensions and entitlements. Racing to get his budget to Congress within the administration's deadline of only forty days, Stockman slashed programs across the board and, when the figures still did not add up, resorted to "the magic asterisk"—which signified "future savings to be identified." Reagan presided genially and unknowingly over the shambles.

Despite anxiety on Wall Street, a patently unbalanced budget was pushed through Congress. By 1982, wrote Stockman later, "I knew the Reagan Revolution was impossible—it was a metaphor with no anchor in political and economic reality."[20] Instead of monetarism or supply-side economics, Reagan was actually practicing Keynesianism on a scale not seen since the Democratic sixties, but this time the spending was not on welfare but defense.

Thatcher had been consistent: a tight monetary policy and a tight fiscal policy. But the price was deflation in the midst of depression. Reagan's America combined the Fed's tight-money regime with an expansionary fiscal policy. In the short term, its price was soaring interest rates (briefly touching 20 percent) and a serious recession with 10 percent unemployment in 1982. Thereafter, fiscal stimulation produced steady growth (4.2 percent per year in the period 1982–1988), which compared favorably with the more restrictive regimes in Western Europe. Yet the medium-term effect of Reaganomics was a soaring budget deficit as spending exceeded revenue year on year. The deficit rose from $60 billion in 1980 to a peak of $220 billion in 1986 (well over 5 percent of GDP). Over this period, the national debt more than doubled from $749 billion to $1,746 billion.[21] Since American savings rates were very low (roughly one-third of Japan's), the deficit was mostly covered by borrowing from abroad, turning the United States within a few years from the world's greatest creditor nation into its largest debtor. Not only was this damaging to America's status, it was also a profound shift in the postwar international financial system, which had relied on the export of American capital. As the dollar soared in value, so American exports became increasingly uncompetitive, with Japan as the leading beneficiary. This also fueled American anxiety about Japan as the emerging "Number One."

By the mid-1980s, therefore, monetarism was being quietly downgraded in America and Britain. Both adopted essentially Keynesian policies to pull out of recession; the Reagan Revolution fizzled after 1981.[22] In neither country was it clear that capitalism had been renewed. On the contrary, Reaganomics seemed actually to be undermining the international hegemony of the United States on which the Western economies depended. Moreover, the American debt crisis was only the tip of the iceberg. Across Latin America and Africa, Western clients were facing an even graver debt burden that threatened to pull down the whole international banking system in ruins.

Latin America: Debt, Democracy, and Revolution

In Latin America, the debt crisis coincided in several countries with the end of military rule. The conjunction of economic and political upheavals was particularly hazardous. Moreover, some regions, notably Central America, were wracked by revolutionary wars. For Latin America, the 1980s were the decade of debt, democracy, and revolution.

We saw in the previous chapter that OPEC's reinvestment of its oil profits sustained international liquidity during the 1970s. This was done largely via Western banks, whose loans helped the non-Western world to maintain growth. Developing countries also benefited from the continued rise of commodity prices during the 1970s. In 1980, they accounted for nearly 28 percent of world exports, 11 percent up on 1970.[23] Many emerging economies became dependent on a continuation of both the flow of loans and the rise in commodity prices.

The most attractive area for bank lending in the 1970s was Latin America, much of which boasted growth rates equal to those of East Asia. By 1981, 63 percent of bank debt in the developing world was in Latin America. The region's foreign debt doubled in the period 1978–1982 to $330 billion. Some 80 percent was owed to private banks—unlike during the 1960s, when Western governments or the World Bank had been the main lenders. Indebtedness became self-perpetuating because new loans were vital to cover interest payments. By 1982, Latin America's debt equaled 41 percent of its export earnings. If Western banks changed their credit policies, crisis would ensue.[24]

Since this seems so obvious in retrospect, it might be asked why Latin American states ran up such huge private debts. The conventional answer is to blame government errors, and, as we shall see, these were blatantly obvious. It should therefore be emphasized that the banks also bear a massive share of responsibility. Foreign earnings had become a major component of the total profits of big U.S. banks—two-thirds in the case of Citicorp during the period 1973–1982. Moreover, the Eurocurrency market had stagnated with the slump in the developed world. Latin America therefore became the new frontier of the 1970s, at a time when other Western banks were challenging the established American giants in the business of foreign loans. In this competitive situation, the result was low interest rates, long maturity dates, and little risk evaluation. "All the banks in the U.S. and Europe and Japan stepped forward," recalled a senior Mexican financial official. "They didn't do any credit analysis. It was wild." Peru, for instance, saw no new foreign lenders between 1969 and 1971. Then, after rumors of large oil deposits, forty-three new lenders entered the Peruvian market in 1972, and another thirty-eight the following year—all offering very good terms.[25] A few countries, notably Colombia, resisted bank overtures. Most did not look a gift horse in the mouth.

Servicing the loans depended on a continued rise in commodity prices. For many developing countries, the oil boom of the 1970s was particularly important. Yet, in the 1980s, the oil price fell steadily. By 1986 it was at about the level of the mid-1970s in real terms. The Middle Eastern states were prime casualties of this fall, but others were also affected, of which Mexico and Nigeria figure in the present chapter.

Why did oil prices collapse? Largely because OPEC was the victim of its own success. The rise in oil prices had made it profitable to develop hitherto uneconomic fields, such as the North Sea, where the costs of offshore drilling in appalling weather were enormous. Even more important was the Prudhoe Bay field on the north coast of Alaska, discovered in 1967. After the first oil crisis, Congress gave the go-ahead for an eight-hundred-mile Trans-Alaskan Pipeline to carry oil to the southern coast. By the early 1980s, Alaska contributed a quarter of U.S. oil production. Consequently, OPEC no longer dominated the market. In 1977 it produced two-thirds of the noncommunist world's crude oil; by 1982 non-OPEC producers accounted for over half, and they forced down the price.

Moreover, Western countries developed alternative sources of energy. Coal revived in popularity, countries like France extended their nuclear programs, and gas became increasingly important. In 1978 oil constituted 53 percent of energy use in industrialized countries; by 1985 the proportion was 43 percent. Western governments also encouraged conservation measures—better insulation, fuel-efficient vehicles, or simply switching off unneeded lights and appliances. Americans remained the world's most prodigal energy users: during the crisis of 1979 it was estimated that panicky motorists were wasting one hundred fifty thousand barrels a day by waiting in line outside U.S. gas stations to fill their tanks! Legislation in 1975 requiring automobile manufacturers to double average fuel efficiency over ten years would raise it only to 27.5 miles per gallon. But even America's far-from-draconian measures made the country 25 percent more energy efficient in 1985 than in 1973. In 1983 oil consumption in the noncommunist world was 45.7 million barrels a day, compared with 51.6 million in 1979.[26]

In the 1980s, countries that were heavy foreign debtors *and* big oil producers proved particularly vulnerable to the new international economy. Mexico was the prime example, and also the catalyst for the debt crisis as a whole.

Although not under military rule, Mexico was a one-party state run by the Partido Revolucionario Institucional (PRI), a pyramid of local client groups.[27] By the late 1960s, postwar growth was running down (see Chapter 7) and urban discontent was manifest in the riots of October 1968. Luis Echeverría Álvarez, the new president from December 1970, tried to buy support through increased government spending on education and health, but the first oil shock left Mexico with a massive balance of payments crisis. José López Portillo, Echeverría's successor from 1976, initially adopted a more conservative economic policy, but confirmation in 1978 of a huge oil field in southeastern Mexico, coupled with the soaring oil price, revolutionized the fiscal arithmetic—just as it did for Suharto in Indonesia. "There are two kinds of countries in the world today," the president proclaimed, "those that don't have oil and those that do. We have it."[28] The spending spree resumed, with deficits largely covered by the foreign investment now pouring into Mexico in the early 1980s, as recession bit in the United States and Western Europe. "You've got to be in Mexico," said one American banker in December 1980. "This is where the action is."[29] Mexico's foreign debt more than doubled between 1978 and 1981, from U.S. $35 billion to $75 billion. Over the same period the share of oil in total export earnings rose from 31 percent to 73 percent. Mexico's ability to service its soaring debt depended largely on its oil revenues.

Most of López Portillo's advisers, like the World Bank, anticipated a steady rise in oil prices throughout the 1980s. But in mid-1981 prices started to fall, just when the U.S. recession and budget deficit started pushing up American interest rates. Suddenly Mexico faced a crisis: the cost of debt servicing rose, while the country's oil earnings fell. Wealthy Mexicans moved their assets abroad, to the tune of U.S. $11.6 billion in 1981. In February 1982 the peso was allowed to float and the government imposed austerity measures, but capital flight continued, and foreign loans dried up. By August the country's reserves were exhausted. Mexico suspended interest repayments on its debt and, on September 1, López Portillo announced that all banks would be nationalized. He claimed histrionically that "in a few, recent years, a group of Mexicans . . . headed, counseled and aided by the private banks, have withdrawn more money from this country than all of the empires that have exploited us from the beginnings of our history."[30]

Thus began an international panic greater even than that of mid-1974, after the first oil shock. Within weeks the media were asking whether the world financial system was teetering on the brink of another Wall Street crash. The crisis was aggravated by the sudden contraction of lending to Latin America when Western bankers belatedly realized what a house of cards they had built. In 1981 nearly $40 billion in new loans flowed into Latin America, but only $20 billion in 1982, and under $3 billion in 1983—a reduction that the World Bank termed "brutal."[31] It was also counterproductive. Even countries without serious payments problems, such as Colombia, were undermined; by early 1983 no fewer than seventeen Latin American countries were in trouble over debt repayment. Heading the list were Brazil ($98 billion) and Mexico ($94 billion), the developing world's biggest debtors.[32] Loans to these two were equivalent to over 90 percent of the total capital of America's nine largest banks.[33] As a proportion of these banks' total loans, Latin American debts were less significant (because banks might loan up to twenty times their capital), but with two-thirds of the Latin American debt vulnerable in 1982–1983, the overhang was potentially very dangerous.

The Latin American debt crisis was the first big test of the post-1973 world monetary system, in which commercial banks matched national governments and international bodies such as the IMF as the main creditors. In Mexico's case, an IMF rescue package of $3.9 billion was linked, unprecedentedly, to the commercial banks' coming up with their own rescue plan. This was the first of many "forced lending" arrangements, in which banks were bailed in rather than bailing out.[34] The combination of speedy action by official bodies, notably the IMF, and new loans from commercial banks prevented Latin American defaults and Western bank failures. But the crisis had not been solved. The rescue packages simply helped service the rescheduled payments. The *Economist* called it a "system of resuscitating pork by paying it to look like pig."[35]

Creditors were worried, but Latin American debt caused a far greater crisis for the debtors. Between 1976 and 1981, at the peak of the loan boom, the net transfer of resources to Latin America amounted to $76 billion. Between 1982 and 1987, however, the net transfer of resources *from* Latin America *to* the West totaled $148 billion.[36] This was equivalent in real terms to two Marshall Plans—but with the United States as *recipient* rather than donor.

In large part, the collapse of foreign lending after 1982 was to blame, coupled with the insistence by creditors that interest payments be maintained. This placed most of the cost of the crisis on the debtors. But the problem was compounded by the policies of Latin American governments. Spending cuts—amounting to over 20 percent in Mexico, Uruguay, and Venezuela between 1982 and 1986—produced a sharp fall in public investment. High tariffs and other import barriers, imposed to reduce the payments deficits, added to domestic hardship. And heavy borrowing at home, to replace foreign loans, forced up interest rates and fueled inflation. The latter averaged around 300 percent per year in Mexico and Argentina in the period 1982–1986, and a massive 776 percent in Bolivia. Where countries accepted IMF aid on inevitably neoliberal terms, the costs were equally hard, as government spending was decimated and protection for domestic industries dismantled. At the end of 1987, per capita income across Latin America was nearly 6 percent lower in real terms than in 1980.[37] The 1980s became known as the continent's "lost decade."

What did this mean in human terms? Again, the Mexican case is illustrative. In the late 1970s over 40 percent of households had earnings below the accepted poverty line of U.S. $120 per month; 45 percent of the population lacked access to private or public health care. The 1980 census indicated that half the households had no running water, a third used the kitchen as a bedroom, and a quarter lacked electricity. In this impoverished society of 70 million people, real incomes then proceeded to *fall* by 40 percent between 1983 and 1988. With prices soaring and subsidies cut back on staples such as tortillas and beans, the cost of a basic basket of food rose from 30 percent of the minimum wage in 1982 to over 50 percent in 1986. These were draconian cuts in the standard of living. During 1983, government officials held their breaths, fearing a social explosion.[38]

Why did that not occur? In part, because of the control exerted by the one-party state over unions and peasant organizations. But also because of the resilience of ordinary Mexicans. Home-grown crops cushioned the rise in food prices; nonwage income substituted for the fall in wages so that by 1987 the average Mexican derived only 30 percent of income from wages. Studies of working class households in the Mexican city of Guadalajara offer a glimpse of how people coped. Newlyweds tended to move in with the husband's parents. Adolescents stopped school at an earlier age to take up paid work or, especially for girls, domestic labor at home. By redistributing child care to older or younger members of the household, mothers were more able to take outside jobs. Families cut back on meat, fish, and dairy products, lowering nutrition, and used traditional or homeopathic medicines to avoid doctors' fees. Most family members earned part-time, informal incomes, from street vending to clothes making.[39]

Across Latin America, it was a similar story. People survived by falling back on networks of kin, clientage, and contractual friendship (*compradrazgo*), of the sort that still flourished across much of the region. They also compensated for the collapse of formal wage income by improvising in the informal sector. As in Mexico, most of the improvisation was done by women—traditional defenders of family and community. In 1986, an unprecedented 49 percent of the female population of Lima, the capital of Peru, was economically active. Women also intensified their voluntary work. The city's emergency program to distribute daily milk to one million children was possible only through the work of one hundred thousand women.[40]

The 1980s also saw an explosion of "New Social Movements" protesting at the failure of government to address social ills. The Mexico City earthquake of September 1985, in which at least six thousand lost their lives, was a catalyst for local self-help groups, angered at the government's inept relief efforts. These coalesced into a citywide Victims Network (*Coordinadora Unida de Damnificados*). This political mobilization helps explain the election results in July 1988, when, even on official tallies, the PRI won only 55 percent of the vote.[41]

New Social Movements were particularly evident in Brazil, the sixth most populous country in the world (136 million in 1985). In major cities, neighborhood groups led campaigns about basic needs such as clean water or paved roads. São Paulo had nine hundred such groups in 1982. New trade unions were formed to circumvent the corporatist unions created by the state. One result was a new political party, the *Partido Trabalhista*, in 1980, which campaigned on the slogan "Vote PT, a party without bosses."[42] The PT also owed much to religious activists from the Catholic base communities that had grown up since the 1960s. The urban middle class was also mobilizing, particularly among professionals alienated by political corruption. And Brazil had a flourishing feminist movement by the late 1970s, stimulated by International Women's Year in 1975.[43] For the moment, divisive gender issues such as abortion were downplayed. The goal for most feminists, and for Brazil's new social movements in general, in the early 1980s can be summed up in one word—democracy.

What made the debt crisis so sensitive was its conjunction in several major South American states with the transition from military rule. The Pinochet regime in Chile held on until 1989, but the early 1980s saw the onset of democratization in Peru (1980), Argentina (1983), and Brazil (1985). In each case, the transitions had two main elements: pressure from the new social movements and concessions from at least part of the military leadership, both prompted by economic crisis and the erosion of the regime's support. The speed and extent, however, varied from country to country.

In Peru, the junta that had ruled since 1968 was an early victim of economic crisis. After the country's foreign debt became vulnerable in the first oil shock, the IMF imposed austerity measures. Between 1973 and 1978 the real value of the minimum wage was almost halved. Social and political groups mobilized; July 19, 1977, saw the country's first general strike since 1919. Nine days later, the junta announced plans for a transition to democracy. Presidential elections in May 1980 brought back to power Fernando Belaúnde Terry, whom the military had deposed in 1968.

In Brazil, the transition was slower, and the junta did not collapse. Instead, there was a Spanish-style "negotiated rupture." Although the Brazilian military had been in power since 1964, acting brutally in its early years, it had ruled "by distorting rather than disbanding the basic institutions of political democracy."[44] General Ernest Geisel, who was president from 1974 to 1978, began a policy of *distensão,* or decompression. He gradually allowed competitive elections while trying to fragment opposition against the government party. But the debt crisis and mounting popular mobilization made it harder for the regime to control the process. In the November 1982 elections, the government lost its absolute majority in the lower house. And in the presidential elections of January 1985, the opposition Popular Front swept to power, headed by Tancredo Neves, the seventy-four-year-old governor of the southeastern state of Minas Gerais. After Neves collapsed and died on the eve of his inauguration, he was succeeded by Vice President José Sarney.[45]

The most dramatic collapse occurred in Argentina. In 1976, a junta led by General Jorge Rafael Videla had seized power. Hard-liners were determined to destroy not merely the urban guerrillas but also all forms of leftism, including the union power on which Peronism had been based. The army was imbued with American cold war ideology: "Argentina is one of the battlefields of World War III—the war against subversion," the Argentine Joint Chiefs of Staff declared in March 1976. According to one middle-ranking officer, "The struggle we engage in does not recognize moral limits; it is beyond good and evil."[46] During its "dirty war" of 1975–1978, between eleven thousand and thirty thousand people joined the ranks of "the disappeared." Most were young men and women in their twenties. Torture was commonplace, the electric cattle prod being a favored instrument, the anus a preferred target. Afterward most were shot, then buried in graves marked only with a date and the legend NN (for "no name"). In the short term, the dirty war was successful. By 1980, opposition was cowed and social movements like those in Brazil had been largely snuffed out. Except, that is, for the women who congregated in the main square of Buenos Aires every Thursday afternoon. The Mothers of the Plaza de Mayo, as they became known, began their silent processions around the central obelisk in April 1977 and, with only a brief hiatus in late 1979, continued each week to bear witness to the disappeared.[47]

Despite its enforced stability, however, Argentina was already exhibiting the problems of debt-financed growth that afflicted Mexico, with an over-valued peso prompting speculative spasms and capital flight. In December 1981, the army commander, General Leopoldo Galtieri, took over the junta, backed by hard-liners opposed to a return to civilian rule. Galtieri was known for bombast: "We do not want just a country, but a great country; not just a nation, but a great nation."[48] To divert popular discontent, he revived his country's claim to the nearby Malvinas, settled by the British since 1833 and ruled as the Falkland Islands. British reinforcement of the garrison in March 1982 was one reason for Galtieri to speed up his invasion plan. Another was the vast demonstration in the Plaza de Mayo on March 30 for "peace, bread and work"—the first open protest since 1976. On April 2, Argentine forces raised their flag over the Malvinas. Next day, the Plaza de Mayo was again full of demonstrators, but this time Galtieri was acknowledging their rapturous applause from the presidential balcony.

The ensuing war was a classic of misperceptions. The Thatcher govern-ment had underestimated Argentine resolve to recover the islands; now the junta assumed the British would abandon them without a fight. Galtieri later admitted, "I judged any response from the English scarcely possible."[49] But the imperatives of national pride and political survival were as potent in Lon-don as in Buenos Aires. By the time Thatcher's task force regained the islands on June 14, the junta was totally discredited. Galtieri was quickly displaced by General Reynaldo Bignone, who promised elections in 1983, but the army's defeat had forced into the open its once-taboo "dirty war." The deci-sive turn in the election campaign was the accusation by the Radicals that the Peronists had collaborated with the military. This helped the Radical candi-date, Raúl Alfonsín, to victory in October 1983 on a simple slogan of "Democracy or Anti-Democracy."

Yet in Argentina and elsewhere, democracy was no panacea. For one thing, the new governments took power just as the bottom fell out of the economy. In 1982, Brazil had the largest debt in Latin America, with Argentina in third place and Peru in sixth. For Peru, interest payments were equivalent to a quarter of its exports; for Argentina and Brazil, well over half.[50] None of the new democratic governments was anxious to impose IMF austerity on their citizens; when forced to do so, Brazil and Argentina sugared the pill with half-baked stabilization plans, while Peru embarked in 1985–1986 on a ruinous Keynesian expansion.

A second problem was the fragility of the new civil society that had emerged with the contraction of military rule. In Argentina, the armed forces remained powerful and unrepentant, mounting three abortive coups in 1987–1988.[51] Argentina's transition to democracy was so abrupt in 1982–1983 that new social movements had not had time to take root. Where they did, the focus was on human rights, and this retarded broader mobilization: the Mothers of the Plaza de Mayo politicized motherhood, for instance, but at the expense of wider feminist and women's issues. Even Brazil, where the transition was long and mobilization extensive, found that many of the new social movements were ephemeral. After the emotional high of 1985, some grass-roots organizations withered, disillusioned with the Sarney government. Others faced the dilemmas of subsumption in the new political parties or survival in impotent independence. The "shallowness" of Brazil's democracy—its lack of social groups autonomous of the state—would be slow to remedy.

Third, all of these new democracies were riven by social fissures, especially class in Argentina and race in Brazil. Perhaps the poorest and most fractured polity in South America was Peru, where divisions of class, ethnicity, and region were mutually reinforcing. Here the whites—some 12 percent of the population, centered in Lima and descended from the Spanish conquerors—dominated an indigenous, largely Indian people living mainly in the Andean mountains. Not surprisingly, the highlands were the traditional base for rebel movements and in 1980 a new armed struggle was mounted by the Maoist "Shining Path" (Sendero Luminoso)—the offspring of peasants radicalized at universities. Belaúnde's new government was slow to react, but when it did, in 1983, the result was armed repression, which only strengthened Sendero's support in the highlands.[52]

Yet in South America as whole, whatever the instability, revolutionary insurgency no longer posed the challenge it had in the 1960s. By contrast, in Central America and the Caribbean, the early 1980s saw political conflict reach a new peak, bringing death and misery to millions. In March 1979, a small group of Marxist insurgents, the New Jewel Movement, took over the tiny east Caribbean island of Grenada, toppling the corrupt autocracy of Eric Gairy. The following July, the brutal Somoza dynasty in Nicaragua was overthrown by the Sandinista National Liberation Front under a largely Marxist leadership. The U.S. response to these two events helped make the region (see Map 1) a front line in the new cold war.

Radical takeovers were hardly surprising, given the dominance of the region by repressive elites that were sustained by the United States. The economies remained agrarian: even in 1980 coffee, bananas, and cotton still constituted half of Central America's exports, usually produced by a rural proletariat on large plantations for trade dominated by big U.S. companies. The vulnerability of these states was accentuated by their smallness—Guatemala, the most populous of the six states on the Central American isthmus, had only seven million people in an area the size of Kentucky. The Caribbean countries were even more fragile. Some islands remained under French, Dutch, or British colonial rule; those that became independent were scarcely viable. Britain's attempt in 1958 to create a federation of the West Indies lasted just a few years, leaving as its only relic a common cricket team. The weakness of these "microstates" was transparent in the eastern Caribbean. Grenada (with 109,000 people in 1983) was comparable in population and area to the Isle of Wight, yet it had been a fully independent member of the UN since 1974. Bananas, cocoa, and nutmeg generated two-thirds of its export earnings.[53]

In 1977, Jimmy Carter negotiated a treaty with Panama, under which America would relinquish control of the canal completely by the end of 1999. But this did not change the basic geopolitics of the region. The most egregious pro-American despotism was Haiti, whose six million people were the poorest in the Western Hemisphere, thanks to systematic looting by the Duvalier family between 1957 and 1986. The Somoza dynasty, which ruled Nicaragua from 1936, was even more brutal, sustained by its infamous National Guard and by U.S. aid. In a country with no proper representative institutions, armed resistance was the only option, and the country degenerated into civil war from the autumn of 1977. By the time Anastasio Somoza fled in July 1979, at least fifty thousand Nicaraguans had died, and one-fifth of the population was homeless. Several regional governments extended aid to the Sandinistas. In fact, Latin America provided more aid to Nicaragua than did the Soviet bloc.[54] Once in power, the Sandinistas gave their country its first proper health care programs.

But Reaganites, preoccupied with the cold war, were mainly interested in two points. First, the Sandinistas' nine-man directorate (like the New Jewel Movement in Grenada) were Marxists bent on establishing a one-party vanguard state. Second, Cuba was the principal backer of both regimes. The takeovers occurred when the Soviet-Cuban axis was exploiting other regional crises, as Angola and Ethiopia had shown (see Chapter 10).[55] The buildup of the Nicaraguan armed forces, from ten thousand to sixty-two thousand by 1986, was largely due to Cuban and Soviet aid. In 1980–1982 the Sandinista government also sent arms to insurgents in neighboring El Salvador, where a weak government under the thumb of the military did nothing to stop right-wing terror.[56]

Thus, American conservatives were right in that the events of 1979 did constitute a significant (if still limited) shift in the regional balance of power, whereas liberals were equally correct that the roots of Central America's problems lay in economic dependency and political repression. In principle, the Reagan administration recognized that the situation required a dual approach, "military assistance combined with effective social reform," but a balanced, low-key policy was sacrificed to the Reaganites' determination that, in the words of incoming Secretary of State Alexander Haig, El Salvador was where they would "draw the line" in the new cold war.[57] The president told a joint session of Congress in April 1983, "The national security of all the Americas is at stake in Central America. If we cannot defend ourselves there, we cannot expect to prevail elsewhere. Our credibility would collapse, our alliances would crumble, and the safety of our homeland would be put in jeopardy."[58]

It sounded like Lyndon Johnson all over again. And that was part of the problem. As a senior State Department official put it: "There are two things the American people do not want. . . . another Cuba . . . and another Vietnam."[59] In other words, fear of communism was balanced by fear of another divisive war. As Congress tried to limit U.S. involvement, so Reagan followed Nixon down the path of covert and illegal operations. CIA financing of operations by the anti-Sandinista Contra guerrillas was reined in by Congress after revelations in 1984 of the agency's complicity in mining Nicaraguan harbors, but the administration created its own secret funding network. Managed by Colonel Oliver North, a senior official on the National Security Council, the network involved private American donors and aid from other countries. Reagan personally met King Fahd of Saudi Arabia in February 1985, who agreed to double Contra aid to $2 million a month.[60] To suspicious members of Congress, National Security Adviser Robert McFarlane insisted in October 1985, "There is no official or unofficial relationship with any member of the NSC staff regarding fund raising for the Nicaraguan democratic opposition." Although Reagan was notoriously uninterested in details, North noted privately in May 1986 that "the President obviously knows why he has been meeting with several select people to thank them for their 'support for Democracy' in Cent[ral] Am[erica]."[61]

In this increasingly messy situation, the president enjoyed one clear-cut success—his brief intervention in Grenada, after an intraparty coup led to the execution of the New Jewel leader Maurice Bishop and close aides on October 19, 1983. Reagan had long made a rhetorical issue of developments like the new Grenadan airfield, built with Cuban help, but the Pentagon had no contingency plans to intervene until after the October coup. And although Castro inclined to his friend Bishop, whereas Moscow was probably more comfortable with his rival, Bernard Coard, neither ally was well informed about the party feud, let alone involved in its bloody outcome.[62] What tipped the balance in Washington, as so often, were global imperatives. With nearly one thousand Americans on the island, Reagan feared another hostage crisis, like that in Iran. "I'm no better off than Jimmy Carter," he groaned at one point.[63] Four days after the Grenadan coup, on October 23, two hundred forty U.S. Marines were killed by a car bomber in Lebanon. The need to demonstrate American power became overwhelming. On the 25th, U.S. troops, with token eastern Caribbean contingents, invaded Grenada and secured the island within days.

By this time, the United States had contained the spread of Marxism in Central America. Nicaragua and Cuba recognized that the Salvadoran insurgency was not likely to succeed. Moscow, always a tentative prober in the region, was drawing back from further commitments. But the price of containment had been high. To avoid another Vietnam, the Reagan administration had deceived the U.S. Congress. To forestall another Cuba, it had turned Central America into a battleground. In addition to conflict-ridden Nicaragua and El Salvador, their northern neighbor, Honduras, became a network of U.S. bases, swamped by American aid. To the west, Guatemala was also coopted, exacerbating the long-running civil war and throwing up a particularly brutal military regime in 1982–1983. Even democratic Costa Rica was being undermined, as Reagan made cooperation against the Sandanistas the price of U.S. help for its debt crisis, prompting guerrilla violence as well as public protests.

Even more than in South America, the 1980s were Central America's "lost decade." Out of a population of twenty-three million, some one hundred fifty thousand (mostly civilians) were killed between 1978 and 1986. By 1983, perhaps five hundred thousand Guatemalans had fled their homes (about 6 percent of the population); in El Salvador UN estimates suggested up to one million (or 20 percent). These two countries were among the foremost violators of human rights in the world.[64] Some of the casualties were famous, such as Oscar Romero, the Catholic archbishop of San Salvador and an outspoken advocate of the poor—shot dead in March 1980 at the altar while celebrating mass. Most were anonymous, like the six hundred refugees massacred by Salvadoran troops near the Sampul river while trying to flee into Honduras—including children tossed into the air for target practice.[65] Guerrillas, for their part, also engaged in assassinations, kidnappings, and reprisal killings, though, international observers judged, "to a lesser extent" than "the military death squad apparatus."[66] Meanwhile, America's five "allies" in Central America—Guatemala, Honduras, El Salvador, Costa Rica and Panama—received nearly $3.9 billion in U.S. aid between 1980 and 1985, or roughly $180 per person (about three months' per capita income in El Salvador).[67] Yet it made very little difference to their quality of life. In 1985, the average cat in the United States consumed more beef than the average person in Central America.[68]

Although events in the region incensed some liberals and church groups, most Americans remained oblivious. But in two respects, the United States was being profoundly affected in 1980s by the instability of Central and Southern America.

One was the surge in immigration as millions fled their poor and troubled countries for "El Norte"—the promised land of the United States. The decade 1981–1990 saw 7.3 million official immigrants entering the United

States (nearly a quarter of them Mexican), a figure only exceeded by the 8.8 million immigrants (overwhelmingly European) between 1900 and 1910. By 1990, "Hispanics" constituted 9 percent of the U.S. population—even in official figures, which seriously underestimated the level of illegal immigration.[69]

The other way in which Latin America's problems literally came home to the United States in the 1980s was through narcotics. Of two hundred fifty million Americans, around twenty million used marijuana. Between eight and twenty-two million were regular cocaine users. Latin America produced all the cocaine on the U.S. market and four-fifths of the marijuana.[70] Colombia was the hub of the drug trade; the leading producer states were Bolivia and Peru. Often the drugs were smuggled across the porous Mexican border. Most of the Caribbean, not least Cuba, was involved in money laundering. Not just poorly paid police but also political leaders were often hand in glove with the traffickers. The Bolivian coup of July 1980 (the country's 189th since independence in 1825) was funded by drug barons. General Manuel Noriega, who took control of Panama in 1983, was reckoned to be one of the top traffickers in the Western Hemisphere—an embarrassment to Washington since he was also a major ally against Nicaragua. But political leaders were not alone. In some countries, involvement in the drug trade became the main way to survive the "lost decade." Perhaps half a million Colombians (out of thirty million) were employed in some way by the drug trade in the early 1980s. When the price of tin, Bolivia's main export, collapsed in 1985, thousands of jobless miners moved to Beni and Santa Cruz, centers of the coca agrobusiness. In Jamaica, marijuana had become the largest cash crop by the 1980s, helping to cover essential imports and maintain jobs. For Latin America, drugs were one way to repay its debt to Uncle Sam.

Sub-Saharan Africa: The Collapse of the State

Along with Latin America, sub-Saharan Africa was the principal victim of the debt crisis of 1980s. And southern Africa, like Central America, was the other great arc of revolutionary war, where regional conflict entwined with superpower rivalry. But black Africa was far less developed than Latin America, both economically and politically. In the 1980s, the state structure of many countries collapsed in the face of debt, drought, and civil war. In southern Africa, the decade after 1975 saw the end of white rule in Rhodesia and its death knell in South Africa.

For both these regimes, the collapse of Portuguese rule in Mozambique and Angola in 1974–1975 was of decisive importance. A glance at Map 2 shows their strategic significance in protecting the northern flanks of South Africa. Mozambique also gave Ian Smith's besieged white government in Rhodesia vital access to the sea. When the Frelimo rebels gained power in Mozambique in 1975, they stepped up the guerrilla war against Rhodesia. Smith's main patron, the South African premier John Vorster, acknowledged that the settler regime was no longer viable and that South Africa itself was at "the crossroads" between "peace and escalating strife."[71] Pressed by Vorster, Smith negotiated an internal settlement. This produced a black-led government for "Zimbabwe-Rhodesia" under Bishop Abel Muzorewa, but left whites in control of administration and the security services, and of enough reserved parliamentary seats to block a constitutional amendment. This new arrangement took effect in April 1979. Since it was unacceptable to the guerrillas, the war carried on. It was now costing Rhodesia at least half a million pounds a day.

The new Conservative government in London, elected in May, then tried its hand. Pressed by the black Commonwealth and persuaded by her foreign secretary, Peter Carrington, Margaret Thatcher convened a new constitutional conference in London that autumn. Because Smith's regime had declared unilateral independence, Britain remained the "legal" colonial ruler. Lord Carrington was determined to secure an orderly, face-saving transfer of power. Step by step he secured agreement on a new constitution, then transition arrangements, and finally procedures for cease-fires and troop withdrawals so that elections could take place. Although campaigning for the elections in February 1980 saw intimidation on all sides, the Marxist Zimbabwe African National Union (ZANU), under Robert Mugabe, was particularly culpable. But, Carrington noted, to debar Mugabe would have placed "at probably fatal risk the international endorsement we had tenuously procured."[72] Most analysts, including the British government and Rhodesian whites, expected a balance among Muzorewa, Mugabe, and ZANU's rival Zimbabwe African People's Union (ZAPU) under Joshua Nkomo. In the event, Smith's party won all twenty seats reserved for whites, but fifty-seven of the eighty black seats went to Mugabe and only twenty to Nkomo, with Muzorewa reduced to three.

Some whites pressed General Peter Walls, Chief of Staff of the Rhodesian Security Forces, to mount a coup, but he recognized that "a white military victory is not on at all."[73] Instead, many whites left (Walls among them), reducing the white population from 232,000 in mid-1979 to eighty thousand (out of 10.8 million) in 1990.[74] After the 1985 elections, white-reserved seats were eliminated, though whites continued to dominate business and industry. As Mugabe moved toward a one-party state, the coalition with Nkomo collapsed in 1982 and ZAPU retreated into its tribal base among the Ndebele.

The collapse of Portuguese colonialism and of white Rhodesia was a serious threat to white South Africa. By the early 1980s, the South African government was engaged in three local wars—in Namibia, Angola and Mozambique. Its occupation of uranium-rich Namibia, a former German colony seized in 1915, had been condemned by the International Court of Justice in 1971. Here the South West African People's Organization (SWAPO) enjoyed strong support in Ovamboland, with major bases across the border in Angola. This was one reason to draw South Africa into the Angolan civil war, supporting the Unita rebels against the tenuous MPLA government that took control after the Portuguese collapse (see Chapter 10). Another reason was the role of Cuban troops and Soviet equipment in sustaining the MPLA, which also prompted U.S. aid for Unita. The third threat came from Mozambique, South Africa's northeastern neighbor, where, unlike in Angola, the Portuguese departure had left a relatively clear-cut victor in the form of Samora Machel's Frelimo. The Rhodesian security forces had fostered a guerrilla opposition, Renamo, which South Africa took over after 1980 and built up into a major insurgency contesting much of the country. In Mozambique, as in Tanzania, Marxist dogma was imposed crudely and abruptly by forcing peasant farmers into villages in order to erode traditional attitudes and extend state control. The reaction to "villagization" gave Renamo a popular base.[75]

Thus, southern Africa in the early 1980s, like Central America, became a battleground for local, regional, and international forces. Without arms from communist states, it is likely that Frelimo and the MPLA would have succumbed. On the other hand, the Soviets backed the wrong horse in Zimbabwe—Nkomo's ZAPU—and their limited economic assistance did not detach Angola and Mozambique from reliance on Western outlets for, respectively, oil and agricultural exports.[76] To Reagan, the situation had no nuances—"the African problem is a Russian weapon aimed at us"[77]—but, unlike in Central America, here a clear moral issue was at stake, literally in black and white, which made it impossible to back South Africa and its proxies unequivocally. The limitations on both superpowers therefore helped to prevent clear-cut victory for either side. The result was persistent civil conflicts that engulfed most of Mozambique, Angola, and northern Namibia, bringing misery to millions. Between 1980 and 1988, in UN estimates, 325,000 Mozambicans and Angolans were killed in war (out of populations of about fifteen million and nine million, respectively), and another 350,000 died from war-related famine or disease. About 1.9 million people (two-thirds from Mozambique) fled these countries to become about one-seventh of the world's total refugees in 1989. Six million more were displaced within their own countries. Thousands were disabled by land mines. This level of civilian casualties was not accidental: all sides targeted villagers and crops in their bid to undermine enemy support.[78]

As South Africa's security deteriorated to the north, it was also under-mined at home. After 1973, the economy followed the Western world into re-cession, prompting a rash of strikes among black workers. Many blacks were inspired by the collapse of white rule further north. The black consciousness movement among students at school and university (see Chapter 7) also proved a powerful mobilizing force. The explosion occurred in Soweto, the vast black township on the edge of Johannesburg, where each house aver-aged seventeen people and most had no toilets or running water. Half the population was under 25.[79] On June 16, 1976, police fired on some fifteen thousand pupils protesting the imposition of Afrikaans as the teaching medium. This sparked a rebellion that spread from Soweto across most of the black townships in the next year, drawing in angry black parents as well. At least one thousand died, including Steve Biko, the black consciousness leader, who was beaten to death in police custody. Hundreds of young refugees provided new recruits for nationalist organizations exiled in neigh-boring countries.

In September 1978, after a corruption scandal, Vorster was replaced by P. W. Botha. The new state president modified apartheid to safeguard white su-premacy. In 1977, whites still received 64 percent of national income, while constituting only 16 percent of the population. The "African" populace had grown to 72 percent of the total, but its share of income was only 26 percent. The remaining 10 percent was divided between mixed-race "coloreds" (9 percent of the people) and "Asians" (nearly 3 percent). Despite the black homelands, 60 percent of blacks were living in "white areas," playing an in-dispensable part in the industrial economy yet living in appalling slums.[80] This is why Botha called apartheid "a recipe for permanent conflict" and in-sisted that whites must "adapt or die."[81] He argued that, under siege from without, South Africa needed to develop its internal market (twenty-eight million in 1980). This meant raising black living standards to create skilled workers and prosperous consumers. Botha therefore legalized black trade unions in 1979 and created black local authorities in the townships. He also tried to mobilize support among "coloreds" and "Asians" by giving them sep-arate chambers in the national parliament, with some responsibility for ed-ucation, health, and culture. This measure was approved in a whites-only referendum in 1983. Meanwhile, Reagan's America and Thatcher's Britain—respectively South Africa's leading trading partner and foreign investor—protected the country from the imposition of international economic sanctions.

But Botha's optimism was short lived. Exclusion from the new constitution enraged blacks, while their new, if limited, freedom to organize produced a flood of "civic associations," student groups, and independent unions (with some nine hundred thousand members by 1986). In August 1983 a United

Democratic Front (UDF) had been formed to oppose the constitutional reforms. As in Latin America, this combination of new social movements and a clear democratic agenda proved explosive. On September 3, 1984, the day the new constitution took effect, about 60 percent of workers and most pupils stayed at home in the Johannesburg area. Protests soon spread across the country. Unlike in 1976, they involved rural areas as well as townships and were orchestrated by grass-roots black organizations.

Matters came to a head in the summer of 1985. On July 20, the government imposed a state of emergency in thirty-six of South Africa's 266 magisterial districts. On July 31, the Chase Manhattan Bank stopped "rolling over" short-term loans to South African borrowers. "We felt that the risk attached to political unrest and economic stability became too high for our investors," explained one executive.[82] Two weeks later, Botha gave an intransigent speech on international TV, flatly rejecting both the principle of one person, one vote, and the idea of a fourth, black chamber in parliament.[83] Share prices tumbled, the rand fell sharply on currency markets, and other banks joined Chase Manhattan in what became a massive currency flight. Within days, South Africa was unable to service its loans. The debt crisis had now engulfed Africa's most advanced economy.

Although rescheduling was eventually arranged, a net capital inflow of $1.3 billion in 1984 turned into a net outflow of $7.2 billion in 1985 and $8.4 billion in 1986.[84] In June 1986, Botha extended the state of emergency to cover the whole country. Reagan was no longer able to stem demands, now even from many Republicans, for economic sanctions. In October 1986 Congress overrode his veto to pass the Comprehensive Anti-Apartheid Act.

Despite the emergency, disorder continued. Consumer boycotts and rent strikes became routine as did police violence. Many townships became no-go areas for the authorities. In places, street committees took over: "We have made ourselves ungovernable by the apartheid regime, and now we are starting to implement people's power" announced one activist on the eastern cape.[85] More often, however, order disintegrated completely, with gang violence commonplace as rival groups of blacks vied for power. In one resettlement camp, the housing sites were only twenty feet by fifteen. "The people are crowded like sardines," noted a resident. There was also no electricity. "The result is that after dark you cannot just walk in the streets." And "out of every ten people, eight have guns."[86] Emblematic of the anarchy was the practice of "necklacing," whereby a car tire was rammed round the victim's neck, doused with gasoline, and then set on fire. At least six hundred died in this way up to 1988, often from group frenzy in the search for informers.[87]

In short, order had disintegrated across much of South Africa in the mid-1980s. Even countries not directly gripped by civil war were destabilized by guerrilla bases and thousands of refugees, Zambia (a neighbor to Angola,

Mozambique and Zimbabwe) being particularly afflicted. This collapse of state authority was, in fact, the predominant pattern across most of sub-Saharan Africa in the late 1970s and early 1980s.

Many African states were still contested domains. In some cases, their borders had been inherited from the colonial era and bore little resemblance to ethnic boundaries. In some regions, notably the Horn of Africa (see Chapter 10), these borders became the source of bitter conflict. Elsewhere the new state was itself the arena of struggle, as in the long-running civil wars in Chad and the Sudan, which, like Nigeria, straddled the continent's fault line between Muslim and Christian. Like caste and religion in India, tribal and ethnic identities, though often colonial constructs, became politicized after independence because they were potential conduits to secure state resources. The complexity and cost of such ethnic struggles can be seen in Uganda, to which the British gave independence in 1962 as a delicately balanced federation. Despite a profusion of ethnic groups, the country exhibited a fundamental divide between the Bantu tribes (two-thirds of the population) in the south, where most of the cash crops were grown, and the north, from which most of the colonial army had been recruited. The military regime of Idi Amin (1971–1979) began as northern, Muslim rule over the more developed Protestant south, but Amin's terror became indiscriminate. After Amin had been deposed by Tanzanian troops, the former president, Milton Obote, regained power with the backing of the northern army, only to impose his own autocracy. Southern guerrilla groups led by Yoweri Museveni waged a bloody three-year war before Obote fled in July 1985.[88]

Apart from territorial or ethnic instability, many states were, by Western standards, perniciously corrupt. As we saw in Chapter 7, across much of Africa, government was not merely the locus of power but also the fount of wealth. Between 1967 and 1982 the proportion of GDP consumed by black African states doubled to an average of 30 percent. In Congo-Brazzaville, the agricultural extension staff increased tenfold between 1960 and 1972, by which time their combined salaries exceeded the income of the six hundred thousand peasants they supposedly served.[89] This was one sign of a new "Afropean" ruling class, whose members arrogated the posts and status of the European elite whom they had once denounced. One-party rule protected their power, while plebiscitary democracy offered a patina of legitimacy. In some cases, the result was personal despotism. Perhaps the most gruesome example was Jean-Bédel Bokassa, a career African officer in the French army, who seized power in the Central African Republic in 1966. As greed and paranoia took over, he had himself crowned emperor in 1977 in a Hollywood-style evocation of Napoleon Bonaparte. Schoolchildren who protested at the introduction of compulsory school uniforms (obtainable only from a company controlled by his wife) were tortured and killed, some by Bokassa himself. When he was finally ousted in 1979, human corpses stuffed with rice were found in the presidential freezer.[90]

Many of these states were sustained only by cold war rivalries. Oil in West Africa and minerals in the center were among the prizes at stake. Competition intensified as détente cooled in the late 1970s. Some countries were Soviet clients, such as Ethiopia or Bénin. Most were backed by western countries, of which France—with extensive postcolonial interests—remained the most intrusive. French aid to sub-Saharan Africa totaled nearly $2 billion in 1987 (50 percent more than from the World Bank). Personal links between French presidents and African leaders were strong. Giscard was closely associated with Bokassa and Joseph Mobutu, who ruled Zaire from 1965 and 1997. His successor, Mitterrand, soon abandoned socialist principles and used the intricate business networks of companies like Elf-Aquitaine, the oil giant, to maintain neocolonial influence. By comparison, the United States was less involved in black Africa, providing only 5 percent of the region's total aid in 1989 against France's 21 percent. But U.S. assistance helped keep several regimes in power during the new cold war—notably those of Mobutu in Zaire, Nimeiri in the Sudan, and Samuel Doe in Liberia. In 1989 President George Bush was still calling Mobutu "one of our most valued friends [on] the entire continent of Africa."[91]

Most African states were therefore both authoritarian and fragile. They were ill equipped to cope with the economic and social crises of the 1980s.

One pressure was demographic. In the period 1970–1990, Africa had the highest population growth rate in the world. (Latin America came second, reversing the pattern of the previous two decades.) Mortality had fallen rapidly, as improvements in public health and living standards alleviated malnutrition and reduced deaths from diseases such as measles. Between the early 1950s and the early 1980s, average life expectancy across black Africa rose fourteen years, to around fifty. Moreover, in black Africa, almost uniquely, there was no sign of an accompanying fall in fertility until the 1990s and then in just a few countries such as Kenya, Zimbabwe, and Senegal. Before 1974, the only countries in sub-Saharan Africa that had serious population policies were Ghana, Kenya, and Mauritius. In the mid-1980s the average woman in Nigeria, Africa's most populous country (over one hundred million), would bear seven children in her lifetime. As a result, Africa's total population grew from 222 million in 1950 to 642 million in 1990. In most countries of black Africa, nearly half the people in 1990 were under the age of fifteen. In North America and Western Europe the proportion was around one-fifth; in Latin America and Asia around one-third.[92]

This combination of rapid population growth and a huge proportion of children to feed, house, and educate would have strained an advanced economy. But most of sub-Saharan Africa (outside South Africa) was in the early stages of development. In the 1980s, only Nigeria's GDP was larger than that of tiny Hong Kong.[93] In sub-Saharan Africa per capita GDP *fell* in real terms by one percent each year.[94]

Economies remained skewed by patterns established in the colonial era, being heavily reliant on a few key commodities produced for the developed world. In 1990, Burundi and Uganda still received around three-quarters of their export earnings from coffee; Nigeria and Angola were 90 percent dependent on oil.[95] During the 1970s, generally buoyant world commodity prices had encouraged the growth of cash-crop agriculture, mining, and related industries, and had offset the effects of the two oil shocks. But then the terms of trade turned dramatically against much of sub-Saharan Africa. Nonoil commodity prices fell by nearly a quarter between 1980 and 1986, partly because of recession in the developed world but also because of growing use of synthetic materials. Liberia's export earnings (largely from iron ore and rubber) fell by 40 percent between 1980 and 1985; Zambia's were more than halved.[96] Even oil-rich Nigeria did not escape. This was "peripheral capitalism"—a highly developed oil sector whose benefits did not percolate through the economy. Indeed, by forcing up the value of the currency, the oil boom undermined exports of Nigeria's cash crops. The country's military rulers (and the brief Second Republic of 1979–1983) funneled most of the oil revenues into the cities, neglecting rural development. When oil prices collapsed in 1983, government revenues were almost halved, and state spending was decimated.[97]

As in Latin America, the economic downturn of the early 1980s made Africa's foreign debt insupportable. The result was a series of rescheduling agreements and reluctant acceptance of IMF restructuring programs. But total borrowing was relatively insignificant—the foreign debt of all of black Africa in 1983 was smaller than Brazil's—and much less of it was to commercial banks because Africa had never been an attractive investment opportunity. In consequence, African debt never threatened the stability of the international banking system, and individual countries received less sympathetic treatment than Latin America. Western adjustment programs often ignored the political imperatives that drove African economic policies. The market was not an automatic mechanism but a "political arena" that ruling groups structured to favor their allies. These were usually urban (despite exceptions such as Kenyan farmers and the planters of the Côte d'Ivoire).[98] Cutting bloated bureaucracies or opening up protected industries therefore weakened the regimes that held these precarious states together.

Smaller export earnings and government revenues, larger import bills and debt repayments—all these spelled cuts in state expenditure on ordinary people. As in Latin America, this was a lost decade, reversing social progress made over the previous twenty years. During the 1980s, primary school enrollment *fell* across Africa, from 77 percent of the age group to 70 percent. In Ghana, per capita spending on health dropped by 60 percent in real terms between 1974 and 1984.[99] The result was the recurrence of diseases eradicated years before, such as yaws, and the intensification of others such as tuberculosis and cholera. With sanitary conditions and water supply often critical factors, Africa's burgeoning urban population was particularly at risk. During the 1980s, cities grew at twice the rate of the population as a whole, often in response to rural insurgencies or the crisis of commercial agriculture. The Nigerian capital, Lagos, was Africa's second largest conurbation (after Cairo). Numbers exploded from two million to 7.7 million in two decades from 1970. In 1980, three-quarters of Lagos households lived in only one room; the average household comprised three people.[100]

In the 1980s, more and more Africans pulled out of the formal economy. This had long been the case in the cities, where selling one's wares or even one's body on the streets had become a way of life for many. Now it was spreading into rural areas, because farmers stopped selling to government marketing boards as prices fell. One response was smuggling: in 1985 over half of Senegal's peanut harvest was illicitly moved into neighboring states, losing the government two hundred million francs in taxes.[101] Others responded by moving out of cash crops into staples such as cassava; working in trade or farm labor, often on a barter basis; or falling back on the complex networks of lineage and clan that still constituted the most profound loyalties for many.[102] In one sense, these were strategies of survival, as in Latin America. But they were also reminders that, *unlike* Latin America, the state was a shallower and much more recent implant in Africa, whose most distinctive contribution to human history, it has been claimed, was in fact "the civilized art of living fairly peaceably together *not* in states."[103] In some countries—such as Chad, Niger, or Burkina Faso—most of the populace could not disengage from the state because they had never been engaged in the first place. Yet they had no safe retreat into traditional ways because the old social networks had been eroded by markets and governments.

In short, this was a crisis of state *and* society. For many people, its meaning could be spelled out in one word—food. To quote the scholar Jean-François Bayart, "south of the Sahara 'to eat' is a matter of life and death" and therefore all politics are "the politics of the belly."[104]

Although Africa was largely a continent of small farmers, there had been no East Asian–style agricultural revolution to increase productivity. Whereas in the United States, by the 1980s, 2 percent of the labor force was sufficient to feed the population and to sell or donate large amounts of food abroad, in Africa more than two-thirds of the population was in agriculture but could not supply even domestic needs.[105] Some of the problems stemmed from neglect of farming in the early postindependence years and the failure to diversify from a few commodities. But Africans were not totally to blame. The green revolution made little impact, mainly because the best-researched crops—wheat and rice—were not central to the traditional African diet. A third of the continent's soils are too arid to permit any cultivation, and almost another half is completely unsuited to rain-fed production of millet, sorghum, and maize—the staple food crops. Moreover, Africa is sparsely populated, with a much lower population density than Asia. Sudan, for instance, is three-quarters the size of India, but it had only twenty million people in 1981 (compared with India's seven hundred million). Aside from the relative shortage of labor, such a scattered population makes it more expensive to provide roads, schools, and other services. For all these reasons, Africa's food crisis became acute. In the period 1970–1982, annual food production increased at only half the rate of population growth, and by the early 1980s one in five people in Africa were reliant on imported food aid.[106]

The 1970s and 1980s even saw the return of mass famines, not seen in Africa since the 1920s (Plate 47). Aside from the general agricultural crisis, these famines had two basic causes. One was natural—the drought that set in from 1968 to 1985, spreading east from the Sahel. The other was human—the distribution failures and mass migrations caused by war. When the two came together, tragedy ensued, notably in the Horn of Africa, where Sudan's civil war waxed and waned and the struggle between Ethiopia and the neighboring Somalians, Eritreans, and Tigreans had not abated (see Chapters 10 and 11). What demographers call "excess mortality" (that is, above normal causes) was about five hundred thousand in Ethiopia in 1980–1985 and in Sudan perhaps two hundred fifty thousand.[107]

More than anything else, it was the Ethiopian famine that brought Africa's crisis into the living rooms of the developed world. The cue was a vivid BBC-TV piece reported by Michael Buerk in October 1984 that depicted "a biblical famine, now, in the twentieth century." The BBC said later that this footage had been shown by 425 of the world's broadcasting organizations with a potential audience of 470 million. From then on the publicity spiraled, climaxing in the "Live Aid" charity concert arranged by the rock star Bob Geldof on July 13, 1985, which linked London and Philadelphia in sixteen hours of music. This was seen on TV in 152 countries by an estimated 1.5 billion people. The money raised was in excess of $50 billion. Although modern technology was essential to provide the oxygen of publicity, it proved a mixed blessing. "The freelance photographers are the worst," fumed one aid worker in the Sudan. "We had one bastard here, a Japanese, who spent three hours crouching by an old woman, so he could get a picture of her death." Moreover, the graphic media reporting of Ethiopia often obsured the fact that mass starvation was now the exception not the rule in Africa. The basic food and health problem was widespread malnutrition, which required long-running and sensitive programs of rural development. These, however, did not make dramatic TV footage.[108]

Hardly had the fuss about aid died down when AIDS hit the headlines. Acquired immune deficiency syndrome was first postulated in 1981, to explain why some people's immune systems collapsed against normally curable diseases. In 1983 U.S. and French researchers identified the infectious agent as a human immunodeficiency virus (HIV). Transmission was usually by sexual contact or through infected blood. Since HIV infection often displays no symptoms and the development of AIDS can be delayed by up to a decade, the origins and scale of the epidemic were hard to define. But it was estimated that, of eight hundred thousand probable AIDS cases in 1990, two-thirds were in Africa. It is likely that the virus had been present for many years in isolated groups in central Africa. By the late 1970s it had spread through urbanization, especially in societies with few restrictions on pre-marital sex. Uganda was probably worst affected: estimates in 1987 suggested that a quarter of the urban population there was infected. Zaire and Zambia were also badly hit. The sexually active portion of the population also provided most of the productive workers and homemakers, on whom the burden of supporting Africa's young (half the population) would fall.[109]

By the 1980s, AIDS was no longer an African disease. How it spread to the Western Hemisphere remains controversial, but the prime suspects are Cuban mercenaries or Haitian guest workers. Port-au-Prince was the prostitution capital of the Caribbean.[110] From there, Americans were the transmitters. By the end of 1988 the best estimates suggested that between five and ten million people worldwide, in nearly 140 countries, were HIV-infected. Perhaps one-fifth of them were in the United States, where eighty thousand AIDS cases had developed and fifty thousand people had died. Unlike in Africa, the disease spread initially among American homosexual men but, as precautions increased, the main means of transmission was by use of infected needles among the intravenous drug users.[111] Western media seized on the disease in hyperbolic terms, making AIDS into a modern Black Death. Like Latin American drugs, it seemed, this was Africa's revenge on the West.

The "New Cold War" and Transatlantic Turmoil

In various ways, then, the upheavals in Latin America and Africa damaged the Western world. The debt crisis shook its financial system. Drugs and AIDS began sapping its health. Growing poverty and hunger in Africa and Latin America during the "lost decade" called into question its claims of moral superiority over communism. The greatest crisis for the West occurred in the NATO alliance itself. The "new cold war" intensified after the Afghanistan crisis of 1979–1980 (see Chapter 10), especially once Reagan became president in January 1981. At the same time, the alliance seemed to be tearing itself apart from top to bottom. The first half of the 1980s saw a recurrent pattern—the United States at odds with the Soviets *and* with its European allies as well.

One of these dual crises occurred over Poland, where eighteen months of political turmoil ended with the imposition of martial law in December 1981.

In addition to the rigidity of the command economy, Poland had two distinctive problems. One was its inefficient peasant agriculture. Collectivization had been suspended in the disturbances of 1956, and so the government had the worst of both worlds—private agriculture that obstinately resisted modernization. Food subsidies cost one-eighth of GDP.[112] The country had also accumulated a crippling foreign debt, because Edward Gierek's headlong expansion of the early 1970s had been funded by Western loans. As the debt burden became oppressive, the government tried to raise consumer prices. Each time, in 1970 and 1976, it backed down in the face of massive strikes. When it tried again in July 1980, the strikes escalated in a political crisis.

One reason was the resurgence of Polish nationalism after the election of Karol Cardinal Wojtyła, the archbishop of Cracow, as Pope John Paul II in October 1978. At fifty-eight, he was the youngest pope in a century and a half, and also the first non-Italian in 455 years—a result of the internationalizing of the College of Cardinals after Vatican II (see Chapter 7). John Paul was conservative on ethical issues like birth control but a forthright defender of religious freedom.[113] When the Polish government allowed him to visit his homeland in June 1979, the crowds were vast and euphoric. He told worshipers in Cracow, "The future of Poland will depend on how many people are mature enough to be nonconformist."[114] In a country where most people were Catholic and the church had been a beacon of nationalism for centuries, his visit was dubbed "Our Nine Days of Freedom."

New organization as well as new nationalism also helps account for the upheaval of 1980. After 1976, a Workers' Defense Committee (KOR), had been created. This drew intellectuals and political activists into the strike movement and formed the nucleus of a thriving opposition counterculture. In 1980, KOR helped coordinate the various strike demands and give them a political focus. At the vast Lenin shipyard in Gdansk, strike leaders and KOR representatives negotiated with party bosses, their every word relayed to workers and journalists. On August 31 the government conceded their demand for an independent trade union. Over the next few weeks, hundreds more unions were formed across the country, taking the collective name of

Solidarity. Its head was Lech Wałęsa (b. 1943), a sparky electrician and devout Catholic, who had led the Gdansk protest. Wałęsa's stocky figure and drooping moustache were to become familiar sights on the world's TV screens in the 1980s.

Gierek suffered a heart attack in September 1980, allowing the party to retire him and his faction. Stanislaw Kania, a cautious centrist, was elected general secretary. For the next year the struggle ebbed and flowed, amid deepening economic crisis, as Solidarity (which boasted a membership of 80 percent of the work force) mounted periodic general strikes.[115] In December 1980, Russian, Czech, and East German troops massed on Poland's borders. But the Soviet Politburo was in a quandary. On the one hand, Poland occupied a vital strategic position en route to Germany, and the collapse of communist power there would send shock waves through the whole Soviet bloc. On the other hand, the crisis came only a year after the Politburo had blundered into a disastrous war in Afghanistan. To quote the ideologist Mikhail Suslov, the use of Soviet troops would be "a catastrophe" and "world public opinion will not permit us to do so."[116] In December 1980, the Politburo drew back.

In the end, the crisis turned on the battle between hard-liners and reformers within the Polish leadership. In October 1981, Kania himself was toppled, but his successor was General Wojciech Jaruzelski (b. 1923), another centrist. Jaruzelski was the son of landed gentry who had fought in the USSR's Polish army during World War II and had been defense minister since 1968. Jaruzelski's motives remain unclear. How far was he Moscow's willing agent? How far was he worn down by its relentless pressure? At all events, on December 13, 1981, he finally did what the Soviets wanted, imposing a state of martial law that enabled him to round up Solidarity leaders and suspend civil liberties. Poland was now ruled by a military council. Martial law remained in place for nearly two years. The country's prospects were bleak.

As over Afghanistan two years before, NATO's response to Polish martial law seriously strained the Western alliance. The Europeans, led by West Germany, were not anxious to jeopardize the fabric of détente, especially the East-West trade that, they hoped, would gradually open up the Soviet bloc. In any case, the Soviets themselves had not invaded (unlike in Afghanistan), and so the Europeans confined themselves to a ban on new credits to the Polish government. Washington, however, went much further. Administration hawks seized the opportunity to sabotage the economic centerpiece of European détente—the Siberian gas pipeline.

The development of Siberia under Brezhnev was one of the quiet revolutions of Soviet history. In 1965, the region accounted for a mere 1 percent of Soviet output of oil and natural gas. Twenty years later, the proportions had risen to about 63 percent and 57 percent respectively.[117] To develop Siberia, the Kremlin needed equipment and credits from Western European states, which were seeking to diversify their energy supplies after the Middle Eastern oil crises. By 1977, eleven contracts had been signed with EC nations, basically trading gas for technology. In November 1981, just weeks before martial law in Poland, Brezhnev visited Bonn and concluded a deal for a new pipeline. This would bring Siberian natural gas over three thousand miles to the Czech border, where it would be fed into the German and Austrian systems. Later, France, Italy, and Switzerland also signed on.

The pipeline was the USSR's biggest-ever construction project, to be driven through miles of permafrost, over the Ural mountains, and across scores of broad rivers. It would require six million tons of large-diameter steel pipe, not to mention 125 turbines and forty-one compressor stations. In return for construction, lubricated by credits of nearly $6 billion, the European participants would be guaranteed gas supplies for twenty-five years. Major European companies were involved, including Deutsche Bank, the French construction giant Creusot-Loire, and Nuovo Pignone of Italy for the turbines.

A long campaign against the project had been waged by hawks in the Reagan administration, notably Defense Secretary Caspar Weinberger and his assistant, Richard Perle. This was part of their larger struggle to wrest control of U.S. foreign policy from Secretary of State Alexander Haig. Isolated for most of 1981, the hawks seized on Jaruzelski's crackdown as a pretext for dramatic action. Their line was "shall we be like Carter and waffle or shall we lead the world?"[118] Although America's role in the pipeline was relatively small, it included items vital to the European companies, notably turbine components. When the administration banned the export of oil and gas equipment to the USSR, the European consortia were thrown into turmoil. Their confusion was made worse as hawks and moderates in Washington haggled over how the ban was to be interpreted. Haig tried to stitch up a compromise with the Europeans, but he was outmaneuvered by the hawks. In June 1982, the president enlarged the ban to include equipment produced by subsidiaries of U.S. companies abroad and equipment manufactured under American license. Even equipment already shipped to Europe was covered.

There was fury across the Atlantic. The French foreign minister told the press that America had declared "economic warfare on her allies" and warned that this could be "the beginning of the end of the Atlantic Alliance."[119] Even Margaret Thatcher, usually a staunch ally of Reagan, was incensed. The British company John Brown stood to lose £200 million in turbine orders. Moreover, a government that preached the virtues of the free market was striking at the law of contract, on which all market dealing was based. When Reagan, honoring a campaign promise to American farmers, went on to sign a new grain deal with Moscow a month later, the incensed Europeans decided to tough it out. Pipeline suppliers such as John Brown were ordered to honor their contracts, whereupon they were blacklisted by the U.S. government.

The alliance crisis took months to resolve. Gradually, Washington backed off as it became clear that sanctions would not stop the pipeline and that European dependence on Moscow would amount to only 6 percent of energy supplies, equivalent to its use of Libyan oil.[120] When the Europeans agreed to an anodyne review of East-West trade, George Shultz, Haig's successor as secretary of state, was able to get the sanctions dropped in November 1982 without grave loss of face. But as Thatcher observed, the whole affair was "a lesson in how not to conduct alliance business."[121]

Even more serious for NATO was the controversy over introducing new intermediate-range missiles into Western Europe. In this case the rift was not so much between the Reagan administration and its counterparts across the Atlantic as between the NATO governments and their own publics.

The controversy had its roots in 1974, when Brezhnev and Ford agreed to guidelines for a SALT II strategic arms treaty based on an equal number of U.S. and Soviet missile launchers. Brezhnev was obliged to drop his demand that British and French nuclear forces be included in the arithmetic. But to placate his military, he started testing a new, mobile intermediate-range missile, known in the West as the SS-20. This could replace outdated SS-4s and SS-5s, which were solid fueled and mostly located on fixed, open launchers. It would also serve as a bargaining chip for future arms control talks, not least against possible U.S. development of Cruise missiles, which could creep in low under Soviet radar. The Americans decided to develop Cruise in early 1977. Later that year, after Carter asked to renegotiate the 1974 accords, the Soviets started to deploy SS-20s in Western Europe.[122]

From Moscow's angle, therefore, these moves were a natural response to the arms race. In Western Europe, however, they were seen as a serious threat to the strategic balance at a time when America's attention seemed to be moving away from Europe toward the hot spots of Asia, Africa, and the Middle East. In Bonn, Chancellor Helmut Schmidt was particularly concerned, since most of the SS-20s were aimed at West Germany. He saw America's nuclear guarantee of Western Europe as the essential complement of détente. To strengthen the credibility of deterrence, the Carter administration decided in 1977 to develop an enhanced radiation weapon, the so-called neutron bomb. The problem with all such battlefield nuclear weapons was that Germany would be the battlefield. The German left dubbed the neutron bomb a capitalist weapon that would "kill people but not property." While administration officials pushed Schmidt toward accepting deployment, the president began to back away. In March 1978, confessing he had "a queasy feeling about the whole thing," Carter decided not to deploy.[123] Schmidt, who had invested considerable political capital in the business, was furious. It confirmed his impression of Carter as both "idealistic and fickle."[124] The neutron bomb fiasco had fateful consequences for NATO and for Moscow.

On the Western side, it became even more necessary for Carter to dispel European skepticism about American reliability. On December 12, 1979, NATO agreed to deploy 572 Cruise and Pershing II theater nuclear missiles in Germany, Britain, Italy, and the Netherlands. But to appease the left, particularly in Germany, it also agreed to press ahead with new talks with the Soviets about arms control in Europe. December 1979 therefore became known as the "dual track" decision, based on the principle of negotiation from a position of renewed strength.

So concerned were the Americans to square the Europeans that little attention was given to likely Soviet reaction. In Moscow, however, the December 12 decision was seen as destabilizing—just as the SS-20 deployment had been viewed in the West. Indeed, some Russian sources now claim that it helped tip the Politburo into the invasion of Afghanistan.[125] Be that as it may, the Kremlin drew its own lesson from the neutron bomb affair. It saw the public reaction against that weapon as a success for the propaganda campaign Moscow had orchestrated in the West. In 1980, the Kremlin was confident that the new missile deployment could be blocked in the same way.[126] For NATO and the Warsaw Pact, therefore, the Cruise and Pershing deployment became a battle for the hearts and minds of Western Europeans.

The early 1980s saw a renaissance of the antinuclear movements of the 1960s, especially in Britain and West Germany. In Britain, the intended base for 160 Cruise missiles, the Campaign for Nuclear Disarmament (CND) jumped in membership between 1979 and 1985 from five thousand to one hundred thousand; and the women's "peace camp" around the U.S. base at Greenham Common gained an international reputation. In the 1983 election, the Labour party campaigned for a nonnuclear Britain, stripped of U.S. bases and of the British nuclear force. In West Germany, where 108 Pershing II missiles were to be located, the peace movement rallied around the "Krefeld Appeal" of November 1980 by leaders of opposition and church groups, under the slogan: "atomic death threatens us all—no atomic weapons in Europe".[127] Within eighteen months, the appeal had attracted over 2.5 million signatures. In October 1981 and again in July 1982, crowds estimated at two hundred thousand to three hundred thousand demonstrated in Bonn. In October 1982, the Free Democrats (FDP) defected from Schmidt's SPD-led coalition, forging a new alliance with the CDU/CSU, led by Helmut Kohl. Although Kohl's coalition was confirmed in power by elections in March 1983, the SPD had now turned against Schmidt and repudiated the INF deployment completely. The Green Party also became a political force, with 5.6 percent of the vote (little less than the FDP) and 27 Bundestag seats. Greens wanted to abolish nuclear weapons and the two alliance blocs.

Despite this opposition, Kohl's victory proved a turning point in the Euromissile debate in Germany, ensuring that the deployment would go ahead. Thatcher's reelection in June 1983 was likewise decisive in British politics. When Cruise and Pershing missiles started arriving in Europe, in November 1983, the Soviets walked out of the talks in Geneva on both intermediate forces and strategic missiles. Soviet hopes that they could repeat their success over the neutron bomb had proved misplaced; NATO had neutralized public opposition. "For the first time in nearly fifteen years, the Americans and Soviets were no longer negotiating in any forum."[128]

This deadlock on arms control also reflected another row that had arisen in 1983—over what was known as Reagan's "Star Wars" program. The pipeline had incensed West European governments; the Euromissiles had alarmed their publics. But Star Wars upset governments and publics alike. It also became Moscow's deepest fear of the mid-1980s, helping provoke a real war scare in the Soviet Union in 1983–1984.

In March 1983, the president delivered what were probably the two most celebrated speeches of his first term. On March 8, he told an audience of evangelical Christians in Florida that Soviet leaders were "the focus of evil in the modern world" and that no one should ignore "the aggressive impulses of an evil empire." This speech reiterated his Manichean view of the world and made the term "evil empire" a global catch phrase.° On March 23, however, in a TV address on the defense budget, the president offered his remedy for the arms race. He claimed that it was now technologically feasible to develop a strategic defense against nuclear missiles, which could replace the policy of massive retaliation. "Wouldn't it be better", he asked, "to save lives than to avenge them?" Although it would "take years, probably decades, of effort on many fronts," the United States was starting a long-term research program to that end, and Reagan called on "the scientific community in our country, those who gave us nuclear weapons," now "to give us the means of rendering these nuclear weapons impotent and obsolete."[129]

To America's allies, and to many in the administration, the speech came out of the blue. It reflected secret pressure from the "High Frontier" group of researchers, including Edward Teller, father of the American H-bomb, and from the Joint Chiefs of Staff, seeking an alternative to the problematic MX missile and a bargaining chip in future arms control talks. But the critical fig-

---

°Less often noted is this sentence: "I believe that communism is another sad, bizarre chapter in human history, whose last pages even now are being written."

ure was Reagan himself. The president was anxious to outflank the American nuclear freeze movement, which was mobilizing huge demonstrations and also commanded widespread support in the churches, even among the normally apolitical Catholic bishops. In addition, Reagan had long felt deep abhorrence for the MAD doctrine of mutual assured destruction. He never forgot his July 1979 visit to the NORAD command center at Cheyenne Mountain in Colorado, which would coordinate U.S. defenses in a nuclear war. This was a vast underground city carved into the mountain and protected by steel doors several feet thick. Yet when its commander was asked what would happen if a Soviet SS-18 landed nearby, he replied: "It would blow us away." Reagan was shocked that even the nerve center of America's defenses was defenseless against nuclear missiles. Hence the appeal of assured survival instead of assured destruction.[130]

During 1983, specialist panels evaluated the High Frontier proposals—officially labeled the Strategic Defense Initiative—and in April 1984 an SDI Office was established in the Pentagon. Its slick propaganda campaign took Reagan's conception at face value. TV commercials depicted an astrodome suspended over the United States against which incoming missiles bounced and burst. It was on that basis that SDI was sold to the American public and to Congress. But most analysts concluded that a total shield against missiles was technically impossible. At best, warned the former Kennedy policy makers McGeorge Bundy and Robert McNamara, SDI would defend "some of our weapons," not "all our people."[131] It was as a local, "point defense" of America's missiles that the Pentagon privately backed the program. And from this perspective, it was deeply alarming to the Soviets, because it would make U.S. nuclear missiles "potent and modern rather than impotent and obsolete" as Reagan had promised.[132]

In September 1983, Soviet-American relations reached a new low when a Russian fighter shot down a Korean Airlines jumbo jet that had strayed persistently into Soviet airspace. All 269 people on board were killed, including a U.S. congressman and sixty other Americans. The incident was probably the result of panic and incompetence by local commanders, who claimed that they believed it was a military spy plane. But the brutal act caused widespread anger in the United States, and this was compounded by Moscow's subsequent bluster and evasion. The administration seized on the episode as vindication of the "evil empire" thesis. Reagan called it "an act of barbarism, born of a society which wantonly disregards individual rights and the value of human life."[133]

The crisis prompted the most sombre Soviet message in years from Yuri Andropov, who had succeeded Brezhnev as party leader in November 1982. At the end of September 1983, in a special statement read over Soviet TV and radio, he warned that the U.S. administration was following "a militarist course that represents a serious threat to peace," aimed at ensuring "a dominating position in the world for the United States."[134] Bluster aside, the Politburo was genuinely unsure about Reagan's intentions. Since 1981, it had conducted a major intelligence operation in NATO countries to detect early signs of a surprise American nuclear strike. Monitoring included blood-donor drives and even slaughterhouse activity (as a clue to food stockpiling). Just how jittery Moscow had become by late 1983 is shown by its warning on November 8–9 to Soviet missions that U.S. bases had been placed on alert.[135] This was a false alarm—caused by misreading a major NATO exercise in Europe, code-named Able Archer—but it testified to Moscow's continued fear of surprise attack (in a nuclear version of Hitler in 1941, with whom Reagan was often compared at this time). During the winter of 1983–1984, the combination of Andropov's speech, the collapse of arms control talks, and the Soviet campaign against SDI set off a serious war scare among the Soviet populace as a whole.[136]

Although both superpowers made private overtures during the next year, the public barometer in 1984, as in 1980, was Olympic politics. In May 1984, the Soviet Union announced that it would not attend the 1984 Games in Los Angeles. Many suspected that this had been planned all along as retaliation for the U.S. boycott of Moscow in 1980. However, the Soviet justification—the security of its athletes—was not completely specious in view of public plans by right-wing groups in the United States to induce defections and spread anti-Soviet propaganda. The president of the International Olympic Committee, Juan Antonio Samaranch, judged that Soviet policy shifted suddenly after February 1984 because of Andrei Gromyko's influence over Konstantin Chernenko, who became the Soviet leader in February. "If Andropov had survived," said Samaranch, "I think we would have been OK in 1984."[137] Be that as it may, the result was an Olympics as one sided as Moscow in 1980, but this time a triumph for American athletes and commercialism. Held in Reagan's home state and opened by the president, it did nothing to harm his reelection campaign.

In late 1984, with the SDI appropriations and then Reagan's reelection, it became clear in Western Europe that Star Wars could no longer be dismissed as "castles in the air" (*Zukunftmusik*) or "a Maginot Line in space."[138] Even if the president's seductive dream were realized and nuclear weapons abolished, a French spokesman observed, the prospect of "making the world safe for conventional war is not at all appealing for Europeans."[139] But if the result were successful defense of U.S. missiles, that could encourage the United States to decouple its security from Western Europe—an equally alarming prospect. And the vast sums that the federal government was promising for SDI research in the United States suggested that a new high-tech gulf might develop across the Atlantic in some of the vital civilian technologies of the future. In March 1985, to avoid a transatlantic row, the Pentagon formally invited Western European participation. Rightly suspecting that this was tokenism, President Mitterrand announced a rival European high-tech program, Eureka, which, he said, "would establish without delay technological Europe."[140] But the British and German governments agreed to participate in SDI research in the (misguided) hope of large and lucrative contracts. The British Ministry of Defence talked of $1.5 billion; by 1991 the actual value was $92 million.[141]

Not surprisingly, the transatlantic rows of the early 1980s—over the Siberian pipeline, the Euromissiles, and Star Wars—provoked a larger debate about the future of the NATO. Some argued that the division of Europe between the two superpowers constituted "an enduring balance" that would probably survive into the twenty-first century. Others believed that the Atlantic Alliance was "visibly crumbling" and suggested that "an increasingly post-Atlantic Europe" might emerge under "a new, radical socialism" inspired by the activism of the peace movement.[142]

The mood of introspection was especially profound in West Germany. In 1984, Bonn was excluded from commemorations of the fortieth anniversary of D-Day. Chancellor Kohl, like many of his countrymen, considered it time for Germany to overcome its Nazi past (Vergangenheitsbewältigung). He seized on the fortieth anniversary of the end of the war, May 1985, as an opportunity to celebrate the Western alliance, in which post-Hitler Germany had played a leading and positive part. But his invitation to Reagan to lay a wreath at a cemetery near the south German town of Bitburg backfired when it became known just beforehand that the cemetery included the graves of soldiers from Himmler's Waffen-SS. Jewish groups were outraged, but Kohl was sure that cancellation would be politically fatal. Grimly, Reagan went ahead with the ceremony, balancing it with a visit to the Bergen-Belsen concentration camp, but the episode remained a disaster. As Reagan admitted, "old wounds have been reopened" at what should have been "a time of healing."[143]

Bitburg strengthened calls by German conservatives (and by many of the young) to develop a new pride in being German. But this could only be done by throwing off the burden of collective guilt for the Nazi past. In June 1986, Ernst Nolte, a controversial historian of fascism, published an article entitled "The Past That Will Not Pass Away." In this, he suggested that Hitler's atrocities merely emulated Stalin's and were a defensive response to the threat of such "Asiatic" barbarism. Nolte was accused by the philosopher Jürgen Habermas of a "strategy of moral relativization" designed to excuse the Holocaust, and, by celebrating the continuity of German history, to play down the "opening of the Federal Republic to the political culture of the West" which, Habermas claimed, was "the great intellectual achievement of our postwar period."[144] Other academics weighed in and this *Historikerstreit,* or historians' feud, dominated West German debate through 1986 and 1987. The journalist Josef Joffe noted shrewdly that "the Battle of the German Historians and the War against the American Missiles" were "clearly related." For conservative scholars and leftist students alike "the real object of conquest was the past that would not pass away"—be it the burden of Nazi guilt or the U.S. occupation imposed as postwar punishment. Both groups, Joffe said, sought "national reassertion and the reclamation of moral worth."[145]

By this time, a mood of self-doubt afflicted even the United States. In November 1986 the American media reported that the administration had been secretly shipping arms to Iran in the hope of securing the release of seven U.S. hostages held by pro-Iranian guerrillas in Lebanon. The administration denied that it had been trading arms for hostages but, to many, the shipments seemed a clear breach of Reagan's avowed antiterrorist policy. The previous April, for instance, he had bombed targets in Libya, on the grounds that it was behind a terrorist bomb that had injured Americans in a Berlin disco. (This caused another transatlantic row because only Britain allowed its bases to be used for the raid.) When news of the Iranian arms deals surfaced, the administration therefore stood accused of practicing a double standard—bombing some "terrorists," arming others. Worse, it was also revealed that some of the proceeds from the Iranian arms sale had been diverted to Contra guerrillas in Nicaragua, despite congressional legislation. The Iran-Contra operations were, in large part, run by Colonel Oliver North, a buccaneering Vietnam veteran on the NSC staff, with the backing of the CIA director, William Casey. Because George Shultz and Casper Weinberger, the secretaries of state and defense, opposed the deals, they were excluded from decision making. Once the operations became known, however, North and Admiral John Poindexter, the National Security Adviser, lost their jobs, as did Donald Regan, the abrasive White House chief of staff—scapegoat for Nancy Reagan's ire at the mess her husband was now in. The columnist Charles Krauthammer summed up the Washington mood in late 1986: "This presidency is over: 1987 will be a Watergate year—and the following an election year."[146]

Most damaging of all for the administration was the effect of "Irangate" on Reagan's reputation. In his first term, he had been the "Teflon president," on whom no dirt had stuck. Despite his verbal gaffes and inattention to detail, astute media management by his aides had kept him above criticism. But now he was revealed as an incompetent and possibly a liar. When he told the American people in November 1986 that "we did not—repeat—did not trade weapons or anything for hostages" only 14 percent believed him.[147] Reagan's authorization of the arms sales to Iran was on the record; direct evidence of his complicity in what North called the "Contrabutions" was harder to find but, given his close and enthusiastic involvement in the Contras' cause, it "seems implausible that Reagan had no knowledge of the diversion of funds from arms sales."[148] What saved him from the threat of impeachment was the insistence by Poindexter—in total contradiction to President Truman's famous dictum—that "the buck stops here with me."[149] Even so, the Iran-Contra story ran for a full year, including televised congressional hearings that made North into a national hero for some and a hypocritical villain for others. In the process, the flaws in Reagan's "management style" were laid bare—not to mention the president's reliance on his wife, and hers on astrologers.

Then in October 1987, doubt turned to panic. On Friday the 16th, the Dow Jones industrial average suffered a record one-day decline of 108 points. The following Monday, markets from Tokyo to London all took their cue, posting substantial falls; the mood in Britain was not helped by a devastating hurricane the previous Friday. When Wall Street opened a few hours later, the market collapsed on a scale that eclipsed even the Crash of 1929. By the end of "Black Monday," 604 million shares had been traded, and the Dow had dropped 508 points (over 22 percent) from 2,247 to 1,739—all unwelcome Wall Street records. "Some $500 billion in paper value, a sum equal to the entire gross national product of France, vanished into thin air."[150] Although the Dow rallied in the next few days, there was renewed selling the following week, both in the United States and around the Western world. Most global equity markets lost between 30 and 50 percent of their share value during October, with the Mexico City index falling 75 percent in two weeks.[151]

The shock of Black Monday was immense, particularly in the United States. Despite assertions by Reagan that "the underlying economy remains sound," there was general anxiety, at home and abroad, about the size of the U.S. budget deficit, expected to reach $170 billion in fiscal year 1987. *Time* magazine, a bellwether of national moods and a staunch supporter of Reagan in the first term, warned, "What crashed was more than just the market. It was the Reagan Illusion: the idea that there could be a defense buildup and tax cuts without a price, that the country could live beyond its means indefinitely."[152] "Indulging in escapist fantasies," said *Time,* Americans had ignored "global realities. They have lived on credit cards, while the Japanese and other foreign investors have been buying up their assets."[153]

A book published a few weeks after the 1987 crash touched this nerve acutely. *The Rise and Fall of the Great Powers* by Paul Kennedy—a British historian teaching at Yale—was a long and scholarly history of imperial overstretch since Habsburg Spain in the sixteenth century. His final chapter, on the era since 1945, was something of an afterthought, but it made the book a best seller with its theses that power ultimately depends on wealth, that no state could "remain *permanently* ahead of all the others," and that the emergence of Japan as the world's leading creditor and of America as the leading debtor showed that the United States now faced "the problem of number one in relative decline." Kennedy provocatively updated the playwright George Bernard Shaw: "Rome fell; Babylon fell; Scarsdale's turn will come."[154] In its first six months the book sold over two hundred thousand copies. Its author became a globe-trotting celebrity, addressing politicians, businessmen and the media across America and around the world. His theme became an obsession in a country waking up to the idea of Japan as number one and, with it perhaps, an early end to what the news magnate Henry Luce had predicted in 1941 would be "the American Century." Instead, a *Newsweek* cover story talked of "The Pacific Century: Is America in Decline?"[155]

This chapter has spotlighted a series of problems in the United States, Western Europe, and what were still economic dependencies of the West—Africa and Latin America—that came to a head in the first half of the 1980s. They revealed serious problems in Western capitalism, particularly the costs of the Keynesian welfare state and the burden of international debt. Western society also seemed in grave danger, particularly from drugs and AIDS. Moreover, this sense of crisis occurred at a time when the United States and the Soviets were locked in a new cold war that strained the NATO alliance and threatened an accelerating arms race.

Some of the problems analyzed in this chapter were enduring; we shall return to them at the end of the book. But whatever the challenges to the West in the early 1980s, it became clear as the decade lengthened that the crisis of communism was far worse. Under the surface of international politics, vast changes had been taking place in science and technology. These rejuvenated international capitalism, and helped to open up autarkic economies and closed societies.

14

Chips and Genes

In the 1980s, much of the developing world was still moving from agrarian society to industrialization, driven by the dynamics of coal and steel, of cities and cars. But the developed countries, led by the United States, were entering what became known as the information age. At its heart were revolutions in telecommunications and data processing, both of them entwined with the cold war. Much of this chapter will be devoted to satellites and computers, to transistors and integrated circuits. By the 1980s these technologies were also being used to start another information revolution—in human genetics—which had vast potential for the production of food, the treatment of disease, and the manipulation of life itself.

The icons of late-twentieth-century technology were chips and genes. In contrast, despite mid-century predictions, nuclear physics failed to become *the* science of the future. In fact, by the 1970s, it was the main target of a backlash against technology in general, because of the damage being done to humanity, nature, and the ecology of the planet itself.

Science, Business, and Government

"When history looks at the twentieth century," wrote the American physicist Alvin Weinberg in 1961, "she will see science and technology as its theme; she will find in the monuments of Big Science," such as huge rockets and particle accelerators, "symbols of our time just as surely as she finds in Notre Dame a symbol of the Middle Ages."[1]

Weinberg helped popularize "Big Science" as a catchphrase of the 1960s. Although hard to define precisely, the term connoted a combination of big money, big equipment, and big teams, focused on a few key areas and involving a fusion of pure science, technology, and engineering. Big science was not totally a postwar phenomenon—in the 1930s, some German and American companies already had large industrial research departments—but it took World War II and the cold war to introduce the crucial element of big government. The state became the preeminent patron of scientific research largely because of the new imperatives of national security. This was particularly true in America and Russia. But there was also a persistent if contested belief in the benefits of "basic research" for the economic well-being of the country. This shaped science in countries that eschewed large military establishments, such as Germany and Japan. The locus of research varied: Germany, France and the USSR favored specialist institutes, whereas the United States and Britain kept research mostly within government laboratories and universities (thereby encouraging a symbiosis with teaching). In these various forms, the government-industrial-academic complex was the motor of Big Science across the world for most of the cold war era.

The story centers on the United States. By World War II, the age of the "heroic inventor"—men such as Thomas Edison—had long passed. In 1940, over two thousand U.S. companies had research and development (R&D) departments, employing some seventy thousand people, of which the biggest were Bell Labs in telephony, followed by General Electric and the chemical giant Du Pont. Basic research in such universities as the Massachusetts Institute of Technology (MIT) and its West Coast rival, Caltech, was largely funded by business or by philanthropic foundations such as Rockefeller and Carnegie. Federal R&D funding was small, and mostly for agriculture. All this changed with World War II when the U.S. government mobilized the nation's universities and R&D labs on a contract basis. The massive projects for radar and the atomic bomb (see Chapter 1), costing maybe $3 billion and $2 billion respectively, were only the best known. By the end of 1945, the Office of Scientific Research and Development, headed by Vannevar Bush, formerly the vice president of MIT, had signed two thousand three hundred contracts worth nearly half a billion dollars.[2]

Although the OSRD was wound up at the end of the war, Bush's valedictory report, *Science: The Endless Frontier*, established the idea that "basic research" was "the pacemaker of technological progress" and that much of its future funding had to come from Uncle Sam.[3] The U.S. military were totally converted: "the laboratories of America have now become our first line of defense," Secretary of War Robert Patterson declared in October 1945. Each service sponsored a plethora of big R&D projects in universities and industry, even before the Soviet atomic test and the Korean War in 1949–1950 made the cold war a real issue of national security. By 1956, defense projects constituted more than half of all spending on industrial R&D in the United States.[4] The humiliation of the Soviet *Sputnik* launch in 1957 (see Chapter 6) pushed funding to new levels. Aeronautics and electronics were the prime beneficiaries, but many areas of science were transformed or even invented, in the case of oceanography or materials science. Although direct military sponsorship of R&D became relatively less important after 1960, it remained at roughly the same level in real terms through the 1970s and 1980s. What was new was the emergence of other federal funders such as the National Science Foundation (NSF), the National Aeronautics and Space Administration (NASA), and especially the National Institutes of Health (NIH), which accounted for about half of federal R&D by the 1970s. Most of their sponsorship was concerned with national security and status in a broad sense, and it resulted in other vast programs in the 1980s such as the Human Genome Project and the $2 billion Hubble Space Telescope.

But although government funding has shaped whole areas of scientific research, several qualifications must be made. First, scientists were not mere slaves of the military. Shrewd scientist-politicians such as Frederick Terman at Stanford and John Slater at MIT were able to advance their own research goals by packaging them attractively for military-industrial sponsors.[5] The Hubble Telescope and the Genome Project are both recent examples of this pattern on an even larger scale. Second, there was extensive, if erratic, civilian spinoff from military-funded research. Cooperation between scientists and business on government projects spawned the Stanford Industrial Park (1951), precursor of "Silicon Valley," and the network of high-tech companies around MIT's labs along Route 128 near Boston. By the 1960s, the federal government was also spreading its funding more widely, to start-up companies as well as to established giants like Lockheed or IBM. Third, as business-academic links became established and as defense funding waned, physics lost its position at the center of revolutionary research. By the 1980s, biotechnology was becoming a serious competitor, with academic research fed by business dollars in the hope of lucrative pharmaceutical applications. Government subsidies helped, but not to the same degree as in electronics at the height of the cold war.

The United States dominated scientific and technological innovation in the postwar period. But the pattern of big science was replicated, on a smaller scale, across the developed world. This was particularly true of states with great-power pretensions. In Britain, government funding rose from 44 percent of total R&D in the mid-1930s to 57 percent by the early 1960s. During that period R&D increased from 0.3 percent of GDP to about 2.5 percent.[6] France led continental Western Europe in state funding for R&D, with high priority given to the nuclear weapons program in the 1950s and 1960s, and then to the conversion to nuclear power generation in the 1970s and 1980s. Most of the basic research was conducted through state agencies, notably the Centre National de Recherche Scientifique (CNRS).[7] Britain and France were nuclear powers; elsewhere in Europe the military was less dominant, but big science proliferated just the same. During the early post-war era Japan was unusual in the small amount it devoted to R&D—around 1.5 percent of GDP in the 1960s compared with 2.5 percent among its European rivals. But the oil shocks of the 1970s and the challenge from the Asian tigers fostered a new interest in research. Japan's R&D spending rose to around 3 percent of GDP during the 1980s, and the Ministry of International Trade and Industry set up advanced technology projects in computers, lasers, and superconductors.[8] Even so, R&D remained mainly private, with the government's share only 22 percent in 1983 (less than half the U.S. figure).[9] And Japan remained resistant to the concept of basic research.

In the developing world, big science—especially big physics—was also seen as a mark of progress. During the 1970s, for instance, India tested its own nuclear device and embarked on its own space program. The People's Republic of China, like India obsessed with security and status, devoted almost all its scientific resources to the nuclear program until the first atomic test in 1964. But the most enormous military-industrial-academic complex was in the Soviet Union.

State control of science was not invented by the Bolsheviks; they built on tsarist precedent. Their structure of research institutes also drew on elitist German practice. What was novel, however, about Stalinist big science was the *extent* of official control and of elite isolation. The regime needed scientific innovation to enhance national wealth and security; yet such innovation depended on critical discussion of a potentially subversive character. This was Stalin's dilemma, and it helps explain why so many Soviet scientists and engineers were purged and imprisoned. It also explains the deliberate physical isolation of Soviet science in institutes and special, closed cities. In consequence, Soviet physics was "an island of intellectual autonomy in the totalitarian state . . . the closest thing to civil society in the Stalinist regime." From its ranks dissidents like Andrei Sakharov were to spring.[10]

Centralized Soviet control of manpower and resources facilitated their concentration on major projects such as nuclear weapons, the space program, and hydroelectric power. In these areas, the Soviet Union was able to match the United States. But the Soviets paid a double price for segregating scientists. First, they were cut off from university teaching, with the result that Soviet science had to live off the intellectual capital of men educated in the years of relative international openness before the Revolution. Those scientists retired and died in the 1960s and 1970s, to be replaced by juniors formed in a Stalinist mold that excluded whole areas of science as bourgeois, cosmopolitan fallacies. Genetics was the most notorious example—destroyed for a generation after 1948 in deference to the fraudulent theories of Trofim Lysenko—but quantum physics was also under a cloud in the late Stalin years. Second, scientists were also isolated from ordinary industry. In 1982, only 3 percent of Soviet research scientists with the *kandidat* degree (roughly equivalent to an American Ph.D.) were employed by industrial plants. Moreover, the country lacked a thriving consumer economy full of opportunities for entrepreneurship. All these factors reduced the scope for commercial development of military-funded innovations such as computers.[11]

At the height of the cold war during the McCarthyite fifties, big science in the United States had many similar features. Major government institutions like Los Alamos were also tightly insulated. But overall, the United States was a more complex economy and a more open society. There was far more civilian spinoff from military-funded research, and most new technologies gradually freed themselves from the handcuffs of Uncle Sam. The computer and the transistor are notable examples. In short, the technologies that have shaped the late twentieth century, though derived from cold war big science, are emphatically the products of capitalism, not communism.

Telecommunications and the Satellite Revolution

Satellites were one spectacular spinoff from cold war big science. Since the 1960s, they have transformed national and international communications in conjunction with related innovations such as coaxial and fiber-optic cables. Equally important for telecommunications has been the opening up of national TV and phone systems, which for much of their history were monopolies under government control. Deregulation began in the United States in the late 1970s and spread across the globe in the 1980s and 1990s. Some analysts argue that deregulation was the simply the result of technological innovation.[12] For others, "new policies came from new ideas"—notably the neoliberal economics of the Reagan-Thatcher era.[13] But neither materialist nor idealist explanations are sufficient. Also important were pressures from business, consumers, and politicians who exploited new technologies and new ideas for their own benefit.

As we saw in Chapter 6, the successful Soviet launch in October 1957 of the first artificial earth satellite, the grapefruit-size *Sputnik,* started a space race between the two superpowers. Although the international media became obsessed with manned flight to the moon, the satellite revolution was far more significant for life on earth. Between 1957 and 1989, a total of 3,196 satellites and space vehicles were launched. Of these, 2,147 were Soviet and 773 were American; Japan was in third place with a mere 38. About 60 percent of the launches were military; one-third were "spy satellites" for photographic reconnaissance.[14] The superbly detailed intelligence thereby gained enabled each superpower to keep watch on the other, and provided essential reassurance for their more stable relationship after the Cuban missile crisis of 1962. In January 1967 the superpowers signed the Outer Space Treaty, which banned "nuclear weapons or any other kinds of weapons of mass destruction" from space, the moon, and "other celestial bodies."[15] Although both governments continued research into antisatellite weapons as a safeguard, their consensus on the peaceful use of space was not breached during the cold war.

Because space was not a battleground, satellite technology could be used for civilian benefit.[16] Again, the military pioneered the way. The U.S. Army's Tiros series of weather satellites, begun in 1960, transformed meteorological information and prediction. An early indication was the evacuation program mounted before Hurricane Camille hit Florida in August 1969. This was one of America's strongest hurricanes, causing $1.5 billion in property damage, but only 260 lives were lost because of satellite early warning. The Soviets had their own metereological system operating by the end of the 1960s. Cartography was also transformed. Satellite surveys of Brazil in the 1980s revealed serious errors in the mapping of Amazonia. In some cases the world's longest river had been drawn twenty miles out of place, and several dozen bridges designed for the Amazon superhighway were found to be superfluous. One of the biggest benefits of satellites was in navigation systems. These were pioneered in the 1960s for military use; full development awaited the waning of the Cold War. But in December 1993 the first Global Positioning System became fully operational, using twenty-four satellites. Those with a few hundred dollars to spare for a GPS receiver can determine their location to within a meter or two. The users are countless, ranging from motorists on unfamiliar roads to freight companies tracking their cargoes.

Perhaps the greatest effect of satellites, however, was on communications. Back in October 1945 a young British officer, Arthur C. Clarke, published an article in the journal *Wireless World* suggesting that versions of the V-2 rockets that Germany had rained down on London could be used to launch "artificial satellites" into orbit. Three such repeater stations, 120 degrees apart in stationary orbit at the right height, could relay radio and TV coverage to the whole planet.[17] Clarke was already writing science fiction and would later make his name with classics such as the story on which *2001: A Space Odyssey* was based, but he had also done war service on radar. Clarke's visionary predictions were essentially correct, but even he did not expect them to be realized for at least fifty years. In fact, the first communications satellite, *Score 1*, was launched by the U.S. Army Signal Corps in December 1958. As Clarke admitted in the early 1990s, "the political accident of the Cold War is really what powered our drive into space. If it had been a peaceful world, we might not even have the airplane, let alone landed on the moon."[18]

In 1960, the National Aeronautics and Space Agency (NASA), the civil arm of America's space program, offered to launch private satellites at cost, provided clients shared their results. The communications giant AT&T quickly applied for permission to build its own satellite, and on July 10, 1962, *Telstar 1*, a mere thirty-five inches in diameter, accomplished the first transatlantic TV transmission from a ground station in Maine to stations in Britain and France. On July 23, an estimated two hundred million viewers in the United States, Canada and sixteen European countries were treated to a kaleidoscope of pictures from Seattle to Rome. This "monster show" made Telstar famous overnight. November 22, 1963, saw the first live TV broadcast from the United States to Japan. It had been intended that President Kennedy would transmit a message; instead the test carried the dramatic news of his death. Three days later Kennedy's funeral was beamed as it happened to Europe, Japan, and parts of North Africa. August 1964 saw live trans-Pacific broadcasts from the Olympic Games in Tokyo. In that same month the International Communications Consortium (Intelsat) was established by fourteen countries. A year later Intelsat had forty-five members, in 1975 a total of eighty-three.

Television news was profoundly affected by satellite broadcasting. As we saw in earlier chapters, such historical turning points as the first moon walk in 1969 (Plates 17 and 18), Nixon's China odyssey in 1972, and Sadat's pilgrimage to Jerusalem in 1977 derived their international impact from TV images. In 1979, after the capture of the U.S. diplomats in Teheran, the ABC network began a nightly program on the crisis, entitled *America Held Hostage*. The title also summed up how the televised drama had paralyzed the nation in ways unimaginable during the radio or newspaper age. By the

1980s, news was being gathered as well as received by satellites, as reporters were dispatched around the world with vans carrying their own "flyaway up-link" equipment.

International sports were also transformed by satellites. Instead of flying film across the world, networks could now air events live. In the 1970s ABC turned itself from the third-place American network into the equal of CBS and NBC through intensive sports broadcasting. The centerpiece of its strategy was the Olympic Games, for which it bought the exclusive U.S. TV rights in 1968, 1972, and 1976. Using close-ups, replays, and interviews, ABC put the spotlight on telegenic sports and athletes with advertising potential. The attention it lavished, for instance, on the teenage Russian gymnast Olga Korbut in 1972 made her an international celebrity and turned gymnastics into a prime TV sport. The ABC treatment—sports as entertainment, with the focus on personalities—obliged the other networks to compete. Their rivalry vastly increased the TV revenues for major sports, notably American football.[19] Following the same philosophy, the Australian media magnate Kerry Packer used one-day international cricket to raise the ratings for his Nine Network. Starting in 1977, his "World Series Cricket"—with its colored uniforms, nighttime games and new rules to promote high scoring—not only boosted revenues but also jazzed up cricket's sedate image.[20]

But if satellites added an international dimension to television, they often made it more intensely national by opening up all areas of a vast country to official television. The Soviet Union was the first to grasp the potential. By the mid-1970s, its Ekran satellites, combined with some three thousand ground stations, spread national TV across Siberia and the Soviet Far East. Over 90 percent of the population could receive at least one channel by the mid-1980s.[21] As we saw in Chapter 12, national satellites also enabled some of Asia's huge developing countries—Indonesia, China, and India—to enlarge their national TV networks. Although satellites served a similar function in large Western countries—Telesat Canada opened up the country's remote north—it was particularly in authoritarian developing states that its role in nation building was significant. Television was a potent medium for educating the populace and a way of disseminating an official national language. TV also became the favored "transmission belt" for conveying government propaganda to the masses, though most became inured to yet more programs about the heroism of labor or the latest five-year plan. (Adapting Marshall McLuhan's famous dictum, it was said that "the tedium is the message.") In the United States, by contrast, the message was business. Although there was, unusually, no government broadcasting system, the three big American networks imposed increasingly monochromatic programming determined by the ratings war and its effect on advertising revenue.

What really undermined dominant national systems, both official and commercial, was the linkup between cable TV and satellite broadcasting. In the United States, cable had been used mainly for transmission to mountainous areas, where broadcast reception was poor. In 1965, only 2.4 percent of homes with TV were connected by cable and most of the thirteen hundred stations were "mom and pop" outfits. By 1995, however, 62 percent of TV homes were connected. Although there were now thirteen thousand stations, over half them owed allegiance to the ten largest operators, in whose hands most of cable broadcasting became concentrated. During this time, the big three networks saw their share of prime-time audiences fall from over 90 percent to 60 percent.[22] The pioneer of the new-look cable TV was Home Box Office, which in 1975 started renting satellite capacity to broadcast new movies, without commercials, to participating stations that then relayed them to subscribers for a fee. Like radio in the 1950s (see Chapter 9), the new stations aimed at specialist niches, particularly sports. Ted Turner, owner of a struggling Atlanta baseball team and a struggling local TV station, used satellite to beam his programs and his team across the country. By 1984 the Atlanta Braves could be viewed by 28 million people on four thousand stations.[23] In 1980 Turner started the first twenty-four-hour cable news station, CNN, which soon established itself as a prime national and global current-affairs channel.

New stations like CNN would not have been possible without fundamental changes in the regulatory environment for American television. This was controlled by the Federal Communications Commission, whose philosophy until the late 1960s had been to preserve the national predominance of the big networks. Demand for change came partly from the bigger cable operators, but also from those on the political left who saw cable as a way to provide minority-interest programs and community-service television. Under pressure from this unholy alliance, restrictions on cable companies were eased in 1972, allowing Turner and others to set up their own superstations. Most remaining restrictions on entry were abolished over the next few years; the Reagan administration then loosened controls on the content of broadcasting. Reagan's chairman of the FCC, Mark Fowler, called television "just another appliance. It's a toaster with pictures."[24]

Few European governments would go that far. They still clung to the old ideal of broadcasting as a public service, maintaining a duopoly of a few government and commercial stations under tight rules. But they did ease entry for cable and satellite operations in the late 1980s. By 1995, 21 percent of TV homes in Britain and 13 percent in France had a satellite dish. In Germany by this time, half the population had cable and two-thirds satellite reception. In the flatlands of Holland and Belgium, coverage was almost total. Among major West European countries, only Italy remained largely untouched by cable and satellite TV during the 1990s.[25] As in the United States, sports were the main way to gain new subscribers: Rupert Murdoch's Sky channel and the German media giant Bertelsmann used this to establish their new satellite channels in Europe in the late 1980s. In 1988, satellite TV broke open the BBC-ITV cartel that had monopolized soccer on British television, quadrupling the game's TV receipts to £20 million a year. The new money helped produce a Premier League of the top twenty-two clubs in 1992, which Sky then scooped with a five-year contract worth £300 million. Top British soccer was finally going the big-money way of American football.[26]

The cable-satellite revolution eroded monolithic TV in developing countries. Numerous small stations began international broadcasting; the cost of a reception dish for an individual home fell to the equivalent of a few hundred U.S. dollars. By the early 1990s, Malaysians could receive twenty-nine different international channels, even though it was strictly illegal to own a satellite dish. In urban China, tens of thousands of informal cable stations had been created by this time, often by the owner of a satellite dish who then distributed the programs via cable to his neighbors. In form, the stations were like the "mom and pop" stations of America in the 1960s, except that the content was now potentially global.[27]

Satellites have therefore exerted a variety of impacts on television—internationalizing the mass medium but also nationalizing it and then latterly helping to break up national networks. But satellites were only part of a larger revolution in telecommunications in the postwar world.

In most European countries, post, telephone and telegraph (PTT) services were under the control of a government department. This model had been exported to the developing world. PTT services, even more than television, were essential to national communications and vital for national security. Control of them also enabled governments to play "Big Brother" through mail censorship and phone tapping. Such surveillance was routine in communist or authoritarian states, but most Western governments during the Cold War also kept PTT services under close control. The FBI under J. Edgar Hoover was notorious for its extensive phone tapping.

The United States did not have a government-run phone network, but the American Telephone and Telegraph Company had enjoyed an effective monopoly since the 1930s. It operated the only long-distance network; its subsidiary Western Electric made most of the phones and equipment. AT&T's research arm, Bell Telephone Laboratories, developed the essential technologies. The survival of this monopoly, despite antitrust actions by the U.S. Justice Department, was due to the Pentagon's need for a single organization with all these capabilities that was at the beck and call of the U.S. Government. In the late 1940s, the U.S. military accounted directly for 15 percent of Bell Labs' budget.[28] In 1970, AT&T was the largest corporation in the world. It had $53 billion in assets, generated $2.5 billion in net income, and employed over one million workers. The American company next in size, Standard Oil of New Jersey, had $19 billion in assets, $1.3 billion in net income, and a mere 143,000 employees.[29]

Throughout the postwar world, therefore, it was axiomatic that PTT services should be in the hands of a monopoly provider that was closely linked to the government. Economies of scale reinforced the imperatives of national security. Within that framework, however, several developed countries worked energetically to maximize services. As usual, the United States led the way: half the households in the country had a phone in 1946, 90 percent in 1970. In West Germany the proportion rose from 12 percent to 75 percent between 1960 and 1980.[30] Extending service meant spreading the costs and increasing revenue but, once something close to universal service had been achieved, other ways had to be found to boost income, such as persuading customers to upgrade equipment or purchase additional services.

Particularly important among such services was the demand for international communication as world trade and travel soared. In 1956 the first transatlantic telephone cable (TAT1) was inaugurated. Two cables ran two thousand miles from Scotland to Newfoundland, providing thirty-five phone circuits in each direction. Three years later TAT2 linked Newfoundland with France. These coaxial cables were a vast improvement on shortwave radio for international phone calls, but they in turn were overtaken by satellites. *Intelsat I* ("Early Bird"), launched in 1965, had circuits for 240 simultaneous calls; *Intelsat IV* (1971) boasted two thousand. Over this period, the cost of each circuit fell from around twenty thousand dollars a year to seven hundred dollars.[31]

Technology changed again with the development of optical fibers during the 1980s. Concentrated light offered almost unlimited communication capacity because of its huge frequency and therefore vast bandwith. It also provided complete freedom from electromagnetic interference from power lines, radio waves, and the like. But it took nearly two decades of work, particularly by Corning Glass Works in the United States, to develop glass fiber with sufficiently low light loss. During the mid-1970s both Bell Labs and British Telecom mounted successful field tests; by 1983 optical fiber systems linked New York with Washington and London with Birmingham. The first transatlantic optical cable, TAT8, was opened in December 1988, connecting the AT&T system in New Jersey with Britain and France. Capable of forty thousand simultaneous phone conversations, TAT8 doubled the existing transatlantic cable capacity and constituted a serious rival to international satellites.[32] The result was also a steep drop in the price of a transatlantic phone call. Dialing from Britain cost about £1.50 for three minutes in 1992, compared with £40 (in 1992 money) in 1945, and £241 when the service was inaugurated in 1927.[33]

Not all Western countries invested heavily in their domestic phone systems. In France, for instance, only half the households had a phone in 1983. Overall, the United States, Britain, and Japan constituted the telecommunications Big Three, with more than half the world's 341 million access lines in 1985.[34] But the biggest contrast was between the capitalist and communist worlds. In 1985, the Soviet Union boasted only about one-sixth of the number of household phones in the United States (although it had an 18 percent larger population). Only 1.7 billion intercity calls were made, compared with 37 billion in America. Two-thirds of the transmission network was cable, none of it fiber optic, and not much coaxial. Unlike in the West, communication satellites carried very little civilian phone traffic. They were used mainly for Soviet TV and, from the late 1970s, to transmit copies of Moscow newspapers across the country for local printing and distribution. This again illustrated the priorities of the regime.[35] The pattern was similar across the Soviet bloc, where phone penetration averaged about twelve lines per one hundred people in the late 1980s, compared with the European Community average of thirty-seven.[36] As in the USSR, equipment was outmoded, reception poor, and waiting lists long. Whereas in the West, the emphasis was increasingly on consumerism, the communist bloc's philosophy remained one of control.

In much of the developing world, phone networks had also been neglected. Postwar economists identified energy and transport as the vital infrastructure networks for economic development. Investment in telecoms in the developing world averaged only 0.5 percent of GNP in the 1970s and 1980s, though, significantly, Asian tigers did much better: in Singapore 1.1 percent and Malaysia 2.3 percent.[37] In general, most of the world's people lived in communities without even a pay phone. Even in the cities, where networks were extensive, traffic was congested and connections poor. Heavy rain could literally swamp a city's phone service. The demand for phones could be gauged by long waiting lists and by the readiness to pay bribes for connections. Few governments could generate the investment needed to meet soaring demand.

As with television, the decisive change was the precedent set by deregulation in the United States. To end a persistent antitrust action by the U.S. Justice Department, in 1982 AT&T agreed to break up the world's leading corporation, effective from January 1, 1984. This meant divesting itself of all local interests: the twenty-two Bell operating companies would be grouped into seven independent regional holding companies. AT&T could retain its long-distance market, but in competition with several hundred other carriers. By the end of the 1980s it still had over 60 percent of that market, with the nearest rivals MCI (17 percent) and Sprint (12 percent), but the U.S. telecommunications industry had been placed on a totally new footing.[38]

The antitrust action, which had been rumbling along since 1974, reflected long-standing opposition to AT&T's near monopoly of services and equipment, particularly by large users. They resented the fact that, as in most countries, long-distance charges were used to subsidize cheap local calls, and looked to satellite and microwave technologies to bypass the AT&T network. At the same time, rival suppliers of equipment and services, such as Motorola and MCI, chipped away at AT&T's position through legal loopholes. Thus "new technologies and new economic players emerged together." They mattered as much as the new Reaganite economic philosophy.[39]

As in television, other developed countries followed the lead of U.S. telecommunications, albeit in their own ways. When British Telecom was sold off in 1984, a duopoly was established between it and a new private company, Mercury. In 1985, new Japanese legislation opened up the national domestic phone company, NTT, to competition; one-third of NTT was sold in 1987–1988. These changes in telecom's Big Three set a pattern, which Western Europe and some Latin American countries followed in the late 1980s (led by Chile) and parts of Asia and the old Soviet bloc in the 1990s. Although many shied away from full privatization, telecoms were usually removed from control of a government ministry and established as money-making enterprises. Private-sector cooperation was encouraged, if not by share issues then by joint ventures or sale of some parts of the business. Competition was permitted in long-distance and specialist services, though usually not at the local level. A looser legal framework was adopted, usually under American-style regulators.[40]

The motivation for these changes was complex. There was general awareness that governments were not providing sufficient investment to modernize the systems. As in America, coalitions of big users and rival suppliers pressed for deregulation. And in many developing countries, particularly those with democratic systems, governments were responding to public dissatisfaction about poor service. But in all economies, developed and emerging, the language of telecommunications was changing. The emphasis was no longer on providing a basic public service but in meeting the needs of the new "information society." Improved communications were deemed essential to transmit the vast amounts of data being generated by modern computers.

Computers and the Electronics Revolution

Although an electromechanical automatic calculator was being constructed by IBM at Harvard as early as 1937, electronic computers were largely another technological spinoff of World War II. They were made possible by expertise and technology from the vast British and American radar projects; they were made necessary by the massive and speedy mathematical calculations required in technowar. By the end of 1943 the British government was using an electronic calculator, Colossus, to crack German cyphers at its Bletchley Park code-breaking center. Ten other machines were in operation there by the end of the war.[41] At the same time, an even more elaborate American counterpart, the ENIAC, was under construction to calculate trajectory tables for the U.S. Army's artillery. ENIAC cost $750,000 to build and did not become operational until November 1945, but a proposed design for its successor, the EDVAC, incorporated the idea of a storage device to hold the program instructions and the data. This eliminated the need for rewiring the vacuum tubes before running each new problem. The stored-program concept was developed by a group headed by John von Neumann, the Princeton mathematician. His unpublished but widely disseminated *Report on the EDVAC* of June 1945 made "the von Neumann architecture" the logical and technological foundation of the computer industry. Drawing heavily on it, and also on wartime expertise from Colossus and radar, researchers built and tested the first stored-program computers in England at Manchester University in June 1948 and at Cambridge University the following May (Plate 43).[42]

These early computers were essentially mathematical instruments, designed for complicated calculations. During the 1950s, however, their successors were developed as data-processing machines to replace desk calculators or punched-card systems. The first marketed computer was also British, based on the Manchester model and delivered in February 1951, but the British computer industry was quickly eclipsed by the American and it was in the United States that the decisive developments took place. Here several companies in either business machines (IBM and Remington Rand) or electronics (RCA and General Electric) began to test the market, but the real stimulus came from Remington's UNIVAC, developed by ENIAC veterans John Mauchly and J. Presper Eckert, and handed over to the U.S. Census Bureau in March 1951. UNIVAC became a household name in November 1952 as the centerpiece of CBS's election coverage, when it rightly predicted an Eisenhower landslide on the basis of early results although opinion polls all suggested a close race. A dummy console covered with flashing Christmas tree lights heightened the effect.[43]

This stunt generated enormous publicity for UNIVAC and introduced Americans to the computer age. It also spurred IBM into serious competition. The first of its 701 models was installed at IBM headquarters on New York City's Madison Avenue in December 1952. Intending to match UNIVAC, the company planned the occasion to be a big photo opportunity—until light from press flashbulbs started erasing the memory that was stored in the electrostatically charged surfaces of the vacuum tubes.[44] Although the 701 (now with opaque doors to protect the tubes) was formally unveiled the following spring, Remington Rand maintained its lead in business computers. Indeed, many Americans in the mid-1950s spoke of "the Univac" rather than "the computer." Yet within a few years IBM dominated the computer industry. By 1964, IBM machines accounted for 70 percent of the worldwide inventory of computers, totaling $10 billion. Five years later, IBM's seven main rivals accounted for only $9 billion of the $33 billion total. The media called them Snow White and the seven dwarfs.[45]

In part, IBM won out through its tradition of superior customer support and service, developed over years of marketing business machines. In addition, unlike Remington Rand, it invested heavily in R&D. Thomas J. Watson, Jr., who took control of the company after the death of his father in 1956, was convinced that IBM's future lay in computers and not in the typewriters and punched card machines on which its early success had been based. But there is little doubt that government contracts, particularly for the military, played a critical part in establishing IBM as the industry's giant for the first quarter-century. Over half IBM's revenues from electronic data processing in the 1950s came from its analog guidance computer for the B-52 bomber and from the SAGE air defense system, built for the air force. SAGE, in particular, was enormously important: at around $8 billion, it was the largest, costliest military project of the 1950s. In 1955, about 20 percent of IBM's thirty-nine thousand American employees were working on it.[46]

After the Soviet nuclear test in 1949, USAF planners were alarmed at the vulnerability of the United States to Soviet air attack. To coordinate information from radar all over North America a vast computing system was needed that could operate in real time—often a few seconds. (Data processing, say, for the Census Bureau or a corporate accounts department, did not have these time-sharing and real-time constraints.) In addition, the system had to be extremely reliable as well as operational round the clock, whatever the need for servicing. The USAF turned first to MIT, establishing a special research program there in 1951, which became the famous Lincoln Laboratory near Route 128. This program also salvaged work being done at MIT's computer lab by Jay W. Forrester to develop a real-time computer. Once MIT had designed a feasible system and tested a prototype on Cape Cod, south of Boston, IBM won the contract to build and run the computers for the whole system. The first SAGE direction center became operational in July 1958, but the whole system was not fully deployed until 1963. SAGE involved twenty-four separate centers, each with two identical computers to permit servicing and prevent any system collapse. Each computer had sixty thousand vacuum tubes and occupied an acre of floor space. Later,

Forrester replaced the vacuum tubes with magnetic cores, vastly enhancing speed and reliability. SAGE therefore pioneered the random-access core memory that within a few years was routine in all commercial computers. Not only did SAGE generate about half IBM's profits in the 1950s, it also gave thousands of IBM engineers and programmers basic training in the business. The experience they gained was fully utilized when IBM was asked in 1957 to design a computerized reservations system for American Airlines. Little wonder that Watson claimed, "It was the Cold War that helped IBM make itself the king of the computer business."[47]

Not until 1959 did IBM's revenues from commercial electronic computers exceed those from SAGE and other military computing projects. By 1964, however, the commercial business had quadrupled in value from $300 million to $1.3 billion and accounted for 57 percent of the company's product revenue as IBM finally moved from punched-card products to computers.[48] Its great innovation of the 1960s was the System 360, unveiled with triumphant fanfare in April 1964. This was a "family" of six computers and forty-four peripherals such as printers, all using the same software. This helped eliminate internal IBM rivalry over models and also checked the spiraling costs of writing software for myriad separate programs. The name implied universal applicability—covering, as it were, all points of the compass. System 360 was developed in great secrecy after perhaps the largest civilian R&D projects in history. One journalist called it "IBM's $5 billion gamble," eclipsing the U.S. atomic bomb project of World War II.[49] But the gamble paid off. At a stroke, IBM had rendered existing computers obsolete. By the end of the 1960s, the company controlled three-quarters of the world market for mainframe computers.

System 360 was a set of third-generation computers, light-years away from ENIAC or UNIVAC. The generational change was partly the result of applying and refining the magnetic core memory developed for SAGE. But even more important was the revolution in electronics that made possible first the transistor and then integrated circuits.

Electronics is the design of devices that conduct electricity. The initial phase, pioneered in the first decade of the century, involved passing electricity through vacuum tubes (or valves, the British term) from hot to cold filaments. These amplifying devices were fundamental to the radio industry of the interwar years, to early television sets, and to the first computers. But vacuum tubes were large, fragile, and expensive, they consumed large amounts of energy, and they had a short working life. Hence the appeal of semiconductors, materials that partly conduct and partly resist electricity. Research into their properties had generated a new field, known as solid-state physics. In the late 1930s, Bell Labs was energetically trying to develop a solid-state amplifier for use in telephony. While the theoretical physics was well advanced, the technology and knowledge of materials were not. In both of these areas, World War II research into radar made a decisive contribution because electronic tubes could not be used for microwave detection. Crystals could be, however, and wartime experience in using germanium and silicon as semiconductors was essential for subsequent breakthroughs. Equally important, the massive radar program coordinated by MIT's Rad Lab introduced hundreds of physicists and engineers to the field and promoted interchange between them in the so-called crystal meetings.[50]

After the war many of these men were drawn into Bell Labs, which utilized their wartime knowledge in a renewed search for a solid-state amplifier. Two of the scientists were Walter Brattain, an experimentalist, and William Shockley, a theorist; both had experimented with copper oxide during the 1930s. Turning now to germanium, they were joined by John Bardeen, a specialist on the theory of metals. This interdisciplinary combination was typical of Bell Labs and an important reason for eventual success. The first demonstration of a point-contact transistor, in December 1947, was the unforeseen byproduct of other work by Brattain and Bardeen, and it could not initially be explained. Nevertheless, evidence that two electrodes placed close together on a germanium crystal proved an effective amplifier was a major breakthrough. Bell announced it to the world in June 1948.[51] In 1949–1950 Shockley developed a more sophisticated junction transistor by sandwiching a positive semiconductor between two negatives. Because the junctions were buried within the crystal, they were less vulnerable to their surroundings. Brattain, Bardeen, and Shockley were jointly awarded the Nobel Prize for their work in 1956.

But theoretical significance was not the same as commercial viability. Although Western Electric, Bell's manufacturing cousin within the AT&T family, started marketing transistors in late 1951 and the first transistor radios were on sale three years later, the new technology took time to catch on. Early transistors were much more expensive than tubes and considerably less reliable. This was mainly because they were produced by ad hoc, craft arrangements—usually by rows of women workers manipulating components under microscopes using tweezers. It was only during the mid-1950s that production became more sophisticated. In May 1954 Texas Instruments of Dallas pioneered a transistor using silicon, a more robust material than germanium. In 1959–1960 another small company, Fairchild Semiconductor, developed a planar process for their manufacture. Components with a flat (planar) surface were much easier to mass produce. Because the technique was less suited to germanium, it made the silicon transistor the norm.

By 1960, therefore, the basis for a commercial industry had been achieved. But it would not have reached that point without military assistance. The transistor was hugely attractive to the armed forces because of their need for reliable, lightweight communications systems in ships, planes, or guided missiles. By 1953 the U.S. military was funding half of Bell Labs R&D into transistors. Even more important, the military provided large, secure markets. The proportion of U.S. semiconductor production for military use rose from 35 percent in 1955 to a peak of nearly 48 percent in 1960. In 1963 transistor sales to the military were worth $119 million, those to industry $92 million, and those to the consumer only $40 million (nearly all for radios).[52]

Military backing was therefore vital for the transistor's success, but it was not the whole story. Much of the R&D money in the 1950s went to established enterprises like Bell Labs and RCA, who saw the transistor mainly as a substitute for the vacuum tube in electronic communications. But by the 1960s, the military was spreading its money more widely, to smaller, specialist semiconductor firms like Fairchild and Texas, who took a more imaginative view of the new technology. These companies were another sign of the fluidity of the military-industrial-academic complex in the United States (unlike that in the Soviet Union). Although AT&T earned a large amount of licensing income, it relinquished the basic transistor patents to avoid an antitrust action to break up the conglomerate.[53] At the same time, scientists who had worked at Bell Labs were moving on: Shockley, for instance, set up on his own at Stanford in 1955, and dissidents from his company started Fairchild Semiconductor two years later. In this way, the new technology was diffused and its potential exploited outside telecommunications.

These new companies were the motor for the next phase in solid-state technology. Instead of linking separate transistorized components in circuits, in 1959 Jack Kilby of Texas Instruments developed a single integrated circuit in one piece (or chip) of germanium. About the same time, Robert Noyce of Fairchild adapted the existing planar technology to chip manufacture. Although the two firms haggled for years over patents, by eventually combining their work they made integrated circuits a commercial proposition. The race then began to see how many components could be etched by photolithographic techniques onto each silicon wafer, or chip. On average the number doubled every eighteen months or so—what became known in the trade as Moore's Law. The first chips were marketed in March 1961. Again the military helped at the crucial start-up stage, taking over 50 percent of production until 1967. But by the end of the decade integrated circuits had become the norm in electronic components. Their potential was evident during the 1970s in vogue consumer goods like digital watches and electronic calculators, both of which soared in sales and slumped in price as the decade progressed.

It was in the computer that the chip found its real home. Computer technology had benefited from the electronics revolution, first replacing tubes with transistors (the second-generation machines) and then substituting chips in third-generation computers like the IBM 360. By 1963, the computer industry spent more on transistors than all consumer sales put together. In consequence, prices fell and sales rose: between 1964 and 1968 the number of computers in the United States trebled to seventy thousand. But these were business or government machines. And transistorization was still being used conventionally, to modernize and miniaturize the circuitry. What made computers personal was the application of chips to the memory in the form of a microprocessor. This application originated with Robert Noyce, Gordon Moore, and their colleagues at Intel, a new company set up in 1968 by defectors from Fairchild. Intel's 4004 microprocessor was initially designed for a calculator, but promotional literature in November 1971 billed it as the "computer on a chip." It took several years, however, to move from rhetoric to reality, and in *this* technological revolution the military played no part.[54]

It was, in fact, a very antiestablishment revolution, born in the Californian youth culture of the Vietnam War era. Its prophets and practitioners were mostly young computer enthusiasts who worked in the industry or in electronics and had played around with computers since their schooldays. Many were also influenced by the computer liberation ideology trumpeted by Californians such as Ted Nelson, who wanted to wrest communications from the corporations. To these computer buffs, the Altair 8800, unveiled in January 1975, was a godsend—a primitive microprocessor computer that could be built from a kit for less than four hundred dollars. The Homebrew Computer Club, established at Menlo Park, on the edge of Silicon Valley, became a mecca for enthusiasts. Soon dozens of new computer firms were competing for the hobbyist market, but one of them managed to turn the personal computer into a consumer product. This was the achievement of Apple Computer, founded in their hometown of Cupertino, California, by Stephen Wozniak and Steve Jobs, two college dropouts with complementary talents. Woz was a brilliant engineer, Jobs a charismatic salesman. Their first Apple computers—not much more than crude circuit boards—were assembled in the Jobs's family garage. But Jobs had the vision to imagine an Apple II with far greater appeal: a self-contained unit in a plastic case, with keyboard, screen, and printer, which could be used for correspondence, accounts, and other household requirements. This Wozniak designed and Jobs launched in the spring of 1977, aided by the software packages for word processing and spreadsheets that were now coming onto the market.

Apple's motto was "one person—one computer," in line with Jobs' counterculture philosophy of democratizing computer power. But spreadsheet software suggested that the future of the PC lay in the office as much as the home. Belatedly, IBM decided to enter the market. Its PC, launched in August 1981, "both 'legitimized' the personal computer and changed the course of the revolution it was supposed to engender."[55]

The IBM PC was the brainchild of William C. Lowe, the lab director of the company's site at Boca Raton, Florida. In the summer of 1980 Lowe persuaded his superiors that there was a vast untapped business market for personal computers, noting for instance that fewer than 10 percent of the nation's fourteen million small businesses were using them. Lowe insisted that the PC market could not be tapped by IBM's skilled but expensive sales and service systems. Hardware and software would have be developed from outside sources, with the product marketed through regular retail channels. In short, he said, "we can't do this within the culture of IBM."[56]

Put in charge of what became known as Project Chess, Lowe selected appropriate firms for components. Two, in particular, made their reputations on the IBM PC. The 8088 chip came from Intel, setting the company on course for dominance in the market for computer integrated circuits. The software operating system came from a small Seattle firm called Microsoft, whose cofounders Bill Gates and Paul Allen were also computer fanatics who got started in the business by designing the BASIC operating systems for Altair and then the Apple II. Picked by IBM for Project Chess, Microsoft's new MS-DOS operating system was sold with every machine.

IBM's PC put the imprimatur of one of the world's greatest corporations on the personal computer. It was no longer a hobbyist's toy. Other companies rushed to produce "IBM-compatible" machines. Most of them were sold with MS-DOS, which, by the mid-1980s, was the dominant operating system in the business and the source of half of Microsoft's annual revenue.[57] PC sales doubled from 724,000 in 1980 to 1.4 million in 1981 and doubled again to 2.8 million in 1982.[58] In consequence, the U.S. computer market was transformed. In 1978, computer sales were worth $10 billion, of which about three-quarters was large mainframe. By 1984, the figure was over $22 billion, of which less than half was mainframe. The computer was moving from government and corporations into small businesses and the home. In the process, the industry became much less reliant on government patronage. The federal share of computer-related R&D expenditure fell from two-thirds in the 1950s to one-fifth by the 1980s.[59]

In January 1983, *Time* magazine gave the PC its "Man of the Year" accolade—the first time in fifty-five years that a nonhuman had been chosen. According to *Time:* "The 'information revolution' that futurists have long predicted has arrived, bringing with it the promise of dramatic changes in the way people live and work, perhaps even in the way they think. America will never be the same again." *Time* also quoted a remark from the Austrian chancellor, Bruno Kreisky: "What networks of railroads, highways and canals were in another age, networks of telecommunications, information and computerization . . . are today."[60]

As Kreisky indicated, the "information network" was a product of the revolution in telecommunications as much as of that in computing, because data had to be transmitted as well as managed. A precursor of such a network was bar coding. By 1970, U.S. supermarkets commanded three-quarters of grocery business, but profit margins were eroding. The supermarkets had strong incentives to improve productivity at the checkout, which accounted for nearly a quarter of operating costs. In 1969 the National Association of Food Chains commissioned investigations of a universal product code system. Each product would have a ten-digit number—the first five for the manufacturer, the other five for the specific product. Electronic scanners would read in the data at the checkout. A computer network would alert stores, chains, and suppliers to inventory levels. Various coding methods were proposed—RCA, for instance, suggested a bull's-eye pattern—but IBM won out with its distinctive pattern of vertical bars. The large food manufacturers and retailers developed the system, then forced it on their smaller brethren. Deliveries of scanners and bar-coded goods began in 1974 and most food-store chains had adopted the system by the 1980s. Coding then spread to other packaged retail goods.[61]

Bar coding was a very limited network, however. Once again, it was from a military system that networking really stemmed. The Pentagon's Advanced Research Projects Agency (ARPA) was established after the *Sputnik* furor of 1957 to generate long-term technological programs. One of these projects was to connect the computers of ARPA's participating institutions all over the United States. The challenges were enormous. Linking each computer to all the others by dedicated long-distance phone lines could produce astronomic bills. And their various software systems were horrendously incompatible. So the Arpanet designer, Lawrence G. Roberts, developed the "packet switching" method, whereby each message was broken up into small packets and sent along the best available route to be reassembled at the destination. The network was a series of nodes, each with a minicomputer to receive and transmit, and also to harmonize the software. By the end of 1969, four nodes were operational, but in September 1973 forty nodes were handling 2.9 million packets a day. A public demonstration of the system at an international computer conference in Washington, D.C., in October 1972 put computer networking on the map.[62]

During the 1980s, other networks were developed by government organizations such as NASA, consortia of colleges, and commercial providers. In 1983 ARPA established a set of "protocols" enabling the various networks to interact, and this marked the beginning of the Internet. But even in 1984 the Net had only about one thousand "hosts" or connected computers. Not until the late 1980s, with the dissemination of the PC, did use grow exponentially. For many people, speedy communication was the main attraction. E-mail (electronic mail) seemed far superior to "snail mail" (the postal service) both for private citizens and business users. The Net also became a treasure trove of information as thousands of individuals and groups used it to publish documents. It took time to make this uncatalogued mass of electronic data accessible. Perhaps the most important innovation was the World Wide Web, spun off by a British researcher, Tim Berners-Lee, from the system he developed in 1989 for CERN, the High-Energy Physics Laboratory in Geneva. This allowed users to move from a word or phrase highlighted on the screen (hypertext) to related information on computers all over the world. The Web made the Net user friendly. During 1992 the number of hosts exceeded one million.[63]

The "Information Society" and International Rivalries

By the 1980s, therefore, the revolutions in computing and telecommunications were fusing. This prompted talk of an information revolution that could transform human existence. The Harvard sociologist Daniel Bell, who had popularized the concept of a postindustrial society in the early 1970s, now updated it by identifying information as the core service industry. Others envisaged the "information society" that would make real McLuhan's 1960s prophecy of the global village.

I shall return to the idea of an information revolution in the final chapter, but two comments should be made here. First, for all their novelties, computers were another instance of a persistent correlation in history between knowledge and power. In other words, the capacity of governments has grown in proportion to the information at their command—about both their citizens and their enemies. Indeed, one could say with sociologist Anthony Giddens, "*all* states have been information societies."[64] The impetus given to communications and computing by America's national security state during the cold war fits this pattern. Second, the information society was, in large part, an offshoot of capitalism. Information became a commodity, to be packaged and sold like toothpaste or automobiles—whether to big corporations in the early days of mainframe computing, or to the ordinary consumer when the PC came of age. Whatever the talk of global implications, the information revolution had most effect on the rich world and on its richer citizens. In other words, it sharpened differences of wealth and class.

Thus, the information society was, on closer examination, one fragmented by nationalism and capitalism.[65] These are points to which I shall return in Chapter 17. But they are also relevant to grasping the effect of the information revolution on international relations in the 1970s and 1980s.

On one level, the development of computers and semiconductors is a story of national commercial rivalries, as the United States fought off early European challenges and maintained a dominant position, especially in computers, until Japanese competition became acute in the 1980s. Britain's pioneering computer industry held its own during the 1950s, with government support targeted at defense use and scientific calculations, but it was overwhelmed by the growth in business computing in the 1960s. By 1966, American machines had taken half the British and French markets; in West Germany their share was nearly three-quarters. This lead was maintained: in 1987 U.S. firms took almost 60 percent of the West European market; IBM's share of that was over one-third. Japan fared somewhat better. Unlike Britain and France, which tried and failed to support a single national "champion," it encouraged competition among a small cartel of computer manufacturers. But it also protected them from foreign competition, once the industry had been established under licensing arrangements with U.S. firms. Consequently, Japanese manufacturers increased their share of the domestic market from 25 percent in 1961 to 80 percent in 1986. By this time, their IBM-compatible machines were also surging into export markets.[66]

In semiconductors, too, the United States sustained a huge lead. Its share of the world market was 61 percent in 1979. Among the also-rans, Japan's share was 26 percent—double that of all Western Europe.[67] The Japanese blend of protectionism and promotion sustained a national semiconductor industry of international dimensions. Initially, the Japanese had concentrated on consumer electronics. Their first transistor radio appeared in August 1955, less than a year after Texas Instruments launched theirs in the United States. In 1959 the Japanese took half the American market for portable radios. They were then wrong-footed, first by the silicon revolution in the United States and later by the marriage of chips and computers. In 1978 only 9 percent (by value) of U.S. semiconductors went into consumer goods; in Japan the figure was 63 percent. In the mid-1970s, the Japanese Ministry of International Trade and Industry set out to address this problem, much as it had promoted computers a decade before. Heavy government investment in Large- and Very Large-Scale Integration (to the tune of some $250 million) enabled Japan to build up a huge lead in large-memory devices by the mid-1980s and created a major trade crisis with Washington. In 1986, for the first time Japan had a bigger share of the world semiconductor market than the United States.[68]

From the point of view of *production,* therefore, computers and semiconductors were part of the familiar story of national industrial rivalry among the world's advanced states. From the perspective of *application,* however, these new technologies connected rather than divided. Together with innovations in telecommunications, such as satellites and optical fibers, they advanced the integration of the world's leading developed nations, giving capitalism a new dynamic and internationalism. Nowhere was this more evident in the mid-1980s than in financial services.

Information is "both the process and the product of financial services."[69] Their raw material is data about markets, risks, rates, and returns; their output comes from adding value to that data, especially by the speed and range of dissemination. Since the days of the telegraph and the telephone, bankers have eagerly exploited the latest information technologies. This was no less true in the era of PCs, satellites, and fiber optics. Between 1972 and 1985 the one thousand largest U.S. banks increased the proportion of their operating expenses dedicated to telecommunications from 5 percent to 13 percent. Many installed their own global networks. At the forefront was Citicorp, which ran the largest private network in the world, linking offices in ninety-four countries, transmitting eight hundred thousand phone calls a month by 1985, and allowing the company to trade $200 billion each day in foreign exchange markets.[70] Walter Wriston, Citicorp's dynamic chairman between 1970 and 1984, liked to say that "the information standard has replaced the gold standard as the basis of world finance."[71]

Traditionally, trading was conducted by personal deals. This practice became institutionalized in the great stock exchanges and currency markets of the world's leading cities. But the information revolution began to challenge the practice of face-to-face capitalism. Take, for instance, the New York Stock Exchange, where the volume of trading tripled during the 1960s, with the the the result that, between 1967 and 1970, the Exchange closed on Wednesday afternoons to allow firms to catch up on the paperwork. One response, in 1971, was the National Association of Securities Dealers Automated Quotations. NASDAQ used twenty thousand miles of leased phone lines to link subscriber terminals to a central computing system that recorded prices, deals, and other information. By 1985, 120,000 terminals were connected. With sixteen billion shares listed at a total value of around $200 billion, NASDAQ had become the third-largest stock exchange in the world, behind New York and Tokyo. Starting in 1983 NASDAQ replaced the phone with computerized trading.[72] This practice spread to foreign exchange, futures, and other financial markets. In order to stay in business, the old stock exchanges had to automate their transactions. Even so, they were hard pressed to compete as computers and fiber optics reduced the need for physical proximity. At the same time, these technologies opened up the potential for twenty-four hour markets, with the three major centers—Tokyo, London, New York—occupying time zones that, among them, conveniently straddled the whole day.

As with the telecommunications revolution, these innovations were not simply the result of technology but also required related changes in deregulation. Again New York took the lead. The "May Day Revolution" of 1975, eliminating fixed brokerage commissions, was intended to make the stock exchange more attractive now that markets could be made in other ways. The result was a major shakeout of uncompetitive firms, followed by a wave of consolidation in the early 1980s as brokerage companies were bought up by corporate giants like Sears Roebuck or American Express. The growing world demand for capital and the greater capitalization of American houses in turn put pressure on London merchant banks, such as Morgan Grenfell or S. G. Warburg. At the same time, the London Stock Exchange was also losing business and faced criticism for its restrictive practices. In 1983, after five years of wrangling, the exchange reached agreement with the government to abolish minimum commissions, end the demarcation between brokers (who acted for clients) and jobbers (who dealt in stocks), and open up the exchange to outsiders, including foreign firms. This would take effect in October 1986. Prior to the so-called big bang there was a wave of mergers and acquisitions similar to that in Wall Street, from which vast new financial combines emerged.

The revolutions in technology and regulation were preconditions of the "globalization" of national economies. This became a buzzword of the 1990s, as we shall see later. Here, however, the focus is specifically on the information revolution and the effect it had on the cold war. If it was now axiomatic that "money is an information product,"[73] then lack of information diminished national wealth. By the 1980s, this had become the Achilles' heel of the Soviet bloc.

In 1950, S. A. Lebedev produced MESM, the first electronic stored-program digital computer in continental Europe. By the early 1960s, the USSR had produced about two hundred fifty second-generation versions.[74] Like Western Europe, it was thereafter unable to keep up technically with the Americans; unlike them, however, it did not enjoy easy access to U.S. high technology, most of which was tightly controlled under cold war legislation. Industrial espionage helped, but the result was a derivative technology, and one that lagged well behind the United States. Most Soviet mainframe designs since the 1960s were modeled on pirated IBM 360 architecture. In line with other Soviet innovations, moreover, the priority was military applications, followed by computer systems for government ministries. Networks, modeled on the Arpanet, were also developed, both for the government and, in the case of the Akademset, for Soviet R&D work.[75] But the weakness of the consumer economy militated against PC development. And the West Coast computer hobby culture that nurtured entrepreneurs such as Steve Jobs and Bill Gates was inconceivable in the USSR.

In microcomputers and microelectronics generally, the Soviets lagged behind European clients such as Czechoslovakia and the GDR. Yet even their pirated products did not compare with authentic Western versions. In 1986, the creator of the Czech Ondra micro lamented the growing penetration of Western PCs:

> With these computers comes not only technology but also ideology. . . . Children might soon begin to believe that Western technology represents the peak and our technology is obsolete and bad. . . . [I]n 10 years' time it will be too late to change our children. By then they will want to change us.[76]

Thus, the PC and communications revolutions posed a double challenge to the Soviet bloc—economic and ideological. One historian has described the East German economy in the late 1980s as being in "a race between computers and collapse."[77] Moscow's twelfth five-year plan of 1985 envisaged 1.3 million PCs in Soviet schoolrooms by 1995. But the Americans already had three million in 1985 and, in any case, the main Soviet PC, the Agat, was an inferior version of the outdated Apple II.[78] Mikhail Gorbachev, the new Soviet leader from 1985, was keenly sensitive to these problems. *Informatizatsiya* (crudely, informationization) became a buzzword of his new era. His American counterpart, Secretary of State George Shultz, played on this concern by periodically giving him minatory tutorials about how the rest of the world was moving from "the industrial age to the information age."[79] At the same time, the communications revolution in phones and faxes, TV and radio, made it ever harder to insulate Soviet-bloc citizens from evidence of the failure of their regimes and of the lifestyles of the West. As we shall see in the next chapter, the information and communications revolutions were at the heart of the crisis of communism in 1989.

Molecular Biology and the Revolution in Genetics

By the 1980s there was talk of another kind of information revolution—about the nature of life. After "cracking the genetic code" in the 1950s and 1960s, scientists were able to manipulate its contents through biotechnology. The idea that biology was engineering in which humans could now engage grew out of an intellectual revolution that had been going on, for the most part quietly, since the late 1930s. Its product was a novel discipline, molecular biology, which ranks with the earlier development of atomic physics as one of the century's two great scientific revolutions. Not merely did molecular biology follow the new physics chronologically, it depended on it in a technical sense. Methods such X-ray crystallography and mass spectroscopy, tools such as electron microscopes and personal computers, were indispensable. Much of the challenge and significance of molecular biology lay in its interdisciplinary character. One of its leading exemplars, Francis Crick, claimed that he adopted the title because "I got tired of explaining that I was a mixture of crystallographer, biophysicist, biochemist, and geneticist."[80]

The decisive conceptual breakthrough in modern human genetics was the double-helix model of DNA, created in 1953. This represented the confluence of several streams of research. One was the work being done on bacterial viruses (or phages) in the United States by the so-called Phage Group clustered around the Italian microbiologist Salvador Luria and the German physicist Max Delbrück—both of whom had fled fascist Europe before Pearl Harbor. Capitalizing on electron microscopes, invented just before the war, they and their colleagues were able to examine the reproductive behavior of viruses, widely suspected to be "a form of naked genes."[81] At the same time, important work was being done by biochemists who had steadily exposed the makeup of chromosomes. Early in the century it was clear that they contained both proteins and DNA (deoxyribonucleic acid). But DNA seemed relatively simple, whereas proteins were huge molecules, comprising many amino acids. As Delbrück later admitted, "at that time it was believed that DNA was a *stupid* substance"[82] and, consequently, that only proteins had the capacity to carry life's genetic code. Suggestions to the contrary by the American biochemist Oswald Avery and his colleagues, published in 1944, were not seen as definitive: like many scientists, Avery pulled his punches in print and did not hammer home the implications of his research.

In the 1940s the "protein paradigm" was central to the new molecular biology.[83] In Britain, the techniques of X-ray crystallography were now being applied to the problem. At the Cavendish Laboratory at Cambridge, Max Perutz and John Kendrew undertook the lengthy crystallographic work from which they eventually determined the molecular structure of hemoglobin and myoglobin during the 1950s. At King's College, London, Maurice Wilkins—a renegade physicist from the atomic bomb project—was beginning to apply X-ray methods to DNA. But all this work was upstaged in 1951 by Linus Pauling at Caltech, who discovered the basic structure of the protein molecule. This he accomplished not so much by experiment as by inspired model building, using his expertise as a physical chemist. Pauling's success was galling for the Cavendish researchers, but it was to stimulate a fertile fusion of British and American methods.

In the autumn of 1951, James D. Watson arrived at the Cavendish. He was a brash, clever American postdoctoral student, aged twenty-three, who had done his Ph.D. with Luria on bacterial phages. Unlike that group, however, he was fascinated by DNA and anxious to learn X-ray crystallography: hence his arrival in Cambridge. There he met Francis Crick, a physicist twelve years his senior, who had spent his war designing magnetic mines before eventually deciding to work with Perutz and Kendrew on protein structures. Watson and Crick quickly hit it off, partly, as Crick put it later, "because a certain youthful arrogance, a ruthlessness, and an impatience with sloppy thinking came naturally to both of us."[84] Both also shared an obsession with DNA (though not officially working on it). Their skills were complementary—Watson coming from bacterial genetics, while Crick's background lay in crystallography and proteins. Above all, both saw the potential of Pauling's model-building approach and sought to apply it to DNA. According to Watson's memoir, "Within a few days after my arrival, we knew what we had to do: imitate Linus Pauling and beat him at his own game."[85]

Beat him they did, after several false starts. Their model of DNA as a double-helix structure—shaped like a spiral staircase formed of sugars and phosophates, with pairs of so-called base molecules as the steps—was published in the scientific journal *Nature* on April 25, 1953. But "all the evidence . . . was from other people's work."[86] In particular, from X-ray photographs taken at King's College, London, by Maurice Wilkins and Rosalind Franklin. Franklin was a superb crystallographer, brought in to complement Wilkins, but the two soon became bitter rivals, and he was progressively denied access to her data. Yet Franklin lacked the biological background to interpret her pictures. For much of 1952, she was obstinately convinced that the structure of DNA could not be a double helix. As her subsequent colleague, Aaron Klug, remarked, "She needed a collaborator, and she didn't have one. Somebody to break the pattern of her thinking, to show her what was right in front of her, to push her up and over."[87] Thus, the symbiotic pairing of Watson and Crick was not replicated in London. Wilkins, however, was a friend of Crick's, and they talked frequently about their work, giving the Cambridge duo insights into what was happening in London. Pauling's erroneous structure for DNA, published in January 1953, and glimpses of Franklin's data (which they read quite differently from her) spurred Crick and Watson into another frenzy of modeling in March. Shown the result, both Wilkins and Franklin readily assented, and they published their data alongside Watson and Crick's paper in April 1953.[88] Subsequently, Watson, Crick, and Wilkins were awarded the Nobel Prize for Medicine in 1962. A Nobel Prize can only be shared three ways. Franklin's untimely death from leukemia in 1958 had spared the judges an invidious choice.

There were murmurs of disquiet about the methods that Watson and Crick had used. But there was no denying both the brilliance of their insight and the elegance of their model. In other papers during 1953, they developed the detail and spelled out the genetic implications. DNA was now confirmed as the gene, displacing the protein paradigm. Over the next decade or so experimentalists confirmed and clarified the Watson-Crick model. The larger task was to explain how DNA did its work as "the chemical of life," and this brought together the research on proteins and enzymes as well as on DNA. It took more than a decade of experimental work, particularly in France, Britain, and the United States, to clarify the exact process. Progress was erratic and uncertain; in mid-1959 "we were completely lost," Crick recalled later. "Nothing fitted."[89] But by the late 1960s the "genetic code" relating the sequence of nucleic acids in a DNA molecule to the sequence of amino acids in a protein molecule had been firmly established, together with the processes of "transcription" and "translation" by which protein synthesis occurs inside cells.

Two points should be made about this transformation. First, the move from hypothesis to confirmation had occurred with astounding rapidity, at least when measured by the past history of science. This owed much to the impact of the physics revolution on experimental biology, for example in the use of radioactive isotopes to label pieces of DNA. Second, in the process, the paradigm of genetics as information had been firmly established. By 1953 Watson and Crick were talking of the sequence of bases in DNA molecules as "the code which carries the genetic information." Within another decade the language of "codes" and "dictionaries" formed the conceptual framework for molecular biology.[90] Had the vocabulary remained essentially biochemical, this work might have had little popular impact. Instead, it resonated powerfully with the contemporary "information revolution." The public could be told, "Just six million millionths of a gram of DNA carries as much information as ten volumes of the *Complete Oxford English Dictionary*."[91] And the former could now be read almost as easily as the latter.

Knowledge was power. And power was money. In the 1970s, the potential of genetic information became apparent. In November 1972 two California scientists—Herbert Boyer, a geneticist, and Stanley Cohen, a biochemist—were chatting about their work after a conference session in Hawaii. Over corned-beef sandwiches, they forged a Watson-and-Crick-style collaboration and within months had developed the technique of "gene splicing." This used a so-called restriction enzyme to cut DNA at precise points and thereby permit one fragment to be spliced with DNA fragments from a different organism, producing "recombinant DNA" (rDNA). Their results, published in November 1973, were the foundation of genetic engineering.

In 1976 Boyer set up his own company, Genentech (short for Genetic Engineering Technology), with a young venture capitalist and former biochemist named Robert Swanson. The Silicon Valley phenomenon—small-scale, high-tech spinoffs—was spreading from chips to genes. And on August

24, 1978, Genentech accomplished the successful genetic engineering of human insulin—vital for the treatment of diabetes. Two weeks later, its results were announced, together with news that the company had signed a deal with Eli Lilly, the pharmaceutical giant, for mass manufacture. In October 1980 Genentech was floated on Wall Street. Its starting price was $35, high for an untested, small company, but in thirty minutes underwriters had sold all their million shares and Genentech closed the day at $70. A few months later Boyer's chubby, moustached face adorned the cover of *Time* magazine, which claimed that "gene splicing is the most powerful and awesome skill acquired by man since the splitting of the atom" and predicted that it was "a new alchemy that may one day turn the basest of creatures into genetic gold." What became known as biotechnology was dubbed by the *Economist,* a British weekly, as "one of the biggest industrial opportunities of the late twentieth century."[92]

"Biotechnology—the very word was invented on Wall Street," claimed one American historian of the genetic mania.[93] This was a widespread assumption but, in fact, the term had been around for decades. It probably originated in 1917 with an Hungarian agricultural engineer, Karl Ereky, who used it to describe systematic, large-scale farming. It had a long history of use by microbiologists interested in the production of nutrients (such as single-cell proteins) and energy alternatives (such as biogas and gasohol). Symbiosis with the new genetics occurred only in the late 1970s.[94] Even then, the techniques of genetic engineering might have been pioneered in traditional biotechnology areas such as food and chemicals. So why did they become spliced first with drugs?

By the 1980s, the market for antibiotics, which had sustained the pharmaceutical industry since the advent of penicillin, had reached saturation. In 1983 Congress lowered regulatory hurdles, enabling companies to produce nonpatent "generic" drugs and starting a price war at a time when hospitals faced intense pressure to cut costs. So the pharmaceutical giants moved into biotechnology as a hedge to protect themselves against possible rivals and to capture the spoils if media predictions proved accurate.[95] During the 1980s most of the leading American biotech companies were swallowed up, including Genentech by Hoffmann-La Roche in 1990, leaving just Amgen and Biogen as big independents. Only huge and wealthy corporations could sustain the costs of research and testing. Only the obsession with health in the developed world could generate sufficient return. Walter Gilbert, a Harvard professor and a founder of Biogen, had begun with high hopes of many applications for genetic engineering. But by 1984, he admitted the need to concentrate on drugs because this, rather than food or chemicals, was the field in which the technology would be "most commercially rewarding over the next ten to fifteen years."[96]

The language of biotechnology had turned from revolution to evolution. Genes, it seemed, were not going to be the chips of the 1980s. There were several major differences.[97] In the case of transistors and chips, the interval between scientific invention and commercial production was only a few years. But biotechnology companies went public before they had viable products and therefore became dependent on outside finance. This difference reflected the more complex nature of the products, stiffer regulatory hurdles because human health was involved, and also the contrasting roles of government finance. For defense reasons, the U.S. government sustained the electronics and computer industries during expensive product development phases in the 1950s and early 1960s. Most of all, electronics was building on developments dating back over a century to the telegraph and telephone. The basic physics underlying it was well established. Biotechnology, on the other hand, had been invented only in the 1970s, and the sciences of molecular biology and human genetics were still in their infancy. A far deeper foundation of basic science was needed. This the Human Genome Project promised to provide.

The human genome, or total complement of genes, is probably about one hundred thousand genes. The DNA in each gene contains chemical instructions for a distinct function, such as producing insulin or making eyes brown. The genes are arranged along twenty-three pairs of chromosomes (twenty-two plus the X or Y chromosome that determines sex)—identical copies of which exist in every cell of the body (except in red blood). If genes are the words of our genetic code, the four chemicals, or bases, of which they consist may be compared with letters (known as G, A, T and C). Long runs of these bases form "sentences" that can be read by a cell and translated into proteins. But genes consist of anything from ten thousand to one hundred fifty thousand code letters; the total number in a human being may be three billion base pairs. And although it had been possible to link a few genes to specific diseases, such as cystic fibrosis, this still told scientists nothing about how a gene actually triggered the disease. For that, a full sequencing of the bases would be required. Techniques for this were developed by Walter Gilbert at Harvard and Fred Sanger at Cambridge, both of whom published their work in 1977.

But sequencing genes was laborious work. In the 1970s, a scientist might complete one hundred base pairs a year; in the mid-1980s, ten thousand to twenty thousand. By 1985, only 0.06 percent of base pairs in the human genome had been sequenced, and only 4 percent of its genes located.[98] Discussions began about collaborative projects: in 1980–1981 the European Molecular Biological Laboratory (EMBL) in Heidelberg explored the idea of a consortium to sequence the genome of the *E. coli* bacterium (a mere 4.5

million base pairs). Then in the mid-1980s, the Human Genome Project (HGP) took off. Its goal was nothing less than an international division of labor to "map" the positions of all one hundred thousand genes on the human chromosomes and to determine the precise sequence of all three billion base pairs. The estimated cost was $3 billion over a decade and a half.

Like other examples of big science described in this chapter, the HGP was born of a marriage between research and politics.[99] Scientists saw it as a headline-catching program that could secure long-term funding for their work. The vocal support of Nobel laureates such as Walter Gilbert and James Watson helped ensure interest at an early stage. Equally vital was bureaucratic rivalry between the National Institutes of Health and the Department of Energy (whose interest in genetic mutations dated back to research on Japanese A-bomb victims). This attracted attention in Washington. Both the DOE and NIH had established genome research in their budgets by 1988. Political patronage was offered by several leading congressmen who saw advantages for their constituents. Senator Lawton Chiles of Florida was captivated by the idea of genetically enhancing the resistance of fruit to frost—of vital interest to local orange-growers. Senator Pete Domenici of New Mexico was anxious about the future of the state's national laboratories, such as Los Alamos, as the cold war waned. "What happens if peace breaks out?" he asked bluntly in 1987.[100]

So scientists, bureaucrats, and congressmen all hyped the project, especially its promise for eradicating disease and maintaining America's edge in biotechnology. Metaphors such as reading "the Book of Man" or finding biology's "Holy Grail" abounded. The media was primed to talk about "a monumental effort that could rival in scope both the Manhattan Project, which created the A-bomb, and the Apollo moon-landing program—and may exceed them in importance."[101]

Although the Human Genome Project was coordinated from within the NIH in Bethesda, Maryland, it involved extensive international collaboration. One of the biggest single contributors was the Sanger Centre at Hinxton, near Cambridge, England, opened in 1993 with the ambitious goal of sequencing one-sixth of the human genome by 2002. The dynamics behind the center were similar to those in the United States—concern of leading molecular biologists such as Sydney Brenner and Walter Bodmer to maintain the momentum of British research, the interest of the British government in the economic and social benefits of biotechnology, and the support of a big-science patron, the Wellcome Trust, which funded the Genome Campus at Hinxton.[102] In addition to the Sanger Centre, the campus was also home to EMBL's Bioinformatics Institute. This was the world's first sequencing database—a reminder that the genome project would have been inconceivable without the advances in computing, especially PCs, that had occurred over previous decades (Plate 44). One information revolution depended on another—chips were needed to decode genes.

A full account of the human genome would provide the basic science that molecular genetics and biotechnology had hitherto lacked. But, even in the 1980s, the new genetics was already making an impact. Polymerase chain reaction (PCR)—invented by a Californian researcher, Kary Mullis, in 1983—permitted the manufacture of millions of copies of DNA in a few hours, using only a test tube, a few simple reagents, and a source of heat. No longer was it necessary, as in the era of Boyer and Cohen, to rely on bacteria like *E. coli* to do limited DNA replication over several days. In Britain a year later, Alec Jeffreys of Leicester University pioneered techniques of "DNA fingerprinting"—using restriction enzymes and radioactive labels to create an image rather like a personal bar code. These techniques were soon commercialized and used to adjudicate paternity or maternity cases and to detect perpetrators of rape or murder. In September 1990, four-year-old Ashanthi DeSilva made history as the first human to undergo gene therapy. She was suffering from ADA deficiency, a devastating genetic illness that crippled her immune system and required a hermitlike existence to avoid infection. After researchers at the NIH had removed some of her blood cells, modified them with a correct version of the ADA gene, and injected them back into her body, her immunity was enhanced and she could live a normal life.[103]

Here, then, were further signs that the new understanding of human genetics, however fragmentary, had the potential to transform existence. Genes, like chips, were symbols of revolution. But revolutions are often threatening, especially where they tamper with life itself—as in the case of biotechnology. The tabloid press fanned lurid speculation about deadly viruses escaping from the laboratory. In several cities near American universities, local governments moved to restrict such research. Some scientists were also concerned about the implications of rDNA experiments, even after NIH guidelines were published in 1976. George Wald of Harvard, a Nobel laureate, called this biotechnology "probably the largest ethical problem that science has ever had to face." He was worried about the potential for "restructuring nature" by creating new organisms that moved across the "species boundaries" between lower and higher levels. "Once created," Wald warned, "they cannot be recalled."[104] A California biologist, Robert Sinsheimer, put it more bluntly: "Before we displace the first Creator we should reflect whether we are qualified to do as well."[105]

Such questioning was not confined to genetics. In the 1970s and 1980s, many on the left in the West believed that big science was a big mistake. It is time to look at the backlash against technological "progress," which pitted

Nature against Science and centered on what in 1945 had been the supposed harbinger of the modern era—nuclear power.

Nuclear Power and the Environmental Counterrevolution

Concern for the environment was not novel.[106] The late nineteenth century had seen the creation of organizations for the protection of nature, such as the Sierra Club in the United States (1892) and the National Trust in Britain (1895). The first national park in the world was established at Yellowstone, Wyoming, in 1872. By 1970 there were over one thousand two hundred around the world, more than a quarter of them in the United States.[107] And after 1945 a number of international organizations were formed to conserve natural resources and to protect nature and/or wildlife, such as the World Wildlife Fund (1960). But these organizations were generally the preserve of elites and specialists. The "new environmentalism" of the 1970s had broader aims and different tactics. Its concern was nothing less than the survival of humanity, and it adopted the activist, political methods of the civil rights and student movements. Indeed, its ethos was strongly antiestablishment and embodied a critique of industrial capitalism in general.

Just as the United States had pioneered so much of modern science and technology, so it led the backlash against them. A basic text was *Silent Spring* (1962) by Rachel Carson, a marine biologist turned crusader against the contamination caused by chemical pesticides and fertilizers. She denounced "the current vogue for poisons" and its underlying philosophy of ruthless "control of nature" as a hangover from "the Stone Age of science."[108] *Silent Spring* sold half a million copies in hardcover. It even stimulated a presidential commission on pesticides that led to the banning or restriction of DDT and most other toxins on her list. Over the next few years, major accidents raised environmental consciousness. In March 1967, spillage from the oil tanker *Torrey Canyon* polluted hundreds of miles of coastline in southwest England. In Norway and Sweden environmentalists began a campaign against acid rain, caused mainly by factories in Britain and Germany. By the end of the decade, the notorious cases of pollution in Minamata Bay and other parts of Japan (see Chapter 12) were reaching the courts. Huge media coverage was attracted by Earth Day in the United States on April 22, 1970, when thousands of schools and colleges held rallies and teach-ins. And a clutch of best sellers established the idea that humanity had to live in harmony with nature and must set "limits to growth."

One sign of the new mood was the UN Conference on the Human Environment in Stockholm in June 1972. Delegates from 113 countries attended, as well as over four hundred nongovernmental organizations. As a result, the UN set up a special environment program. Although vitiated by lack of funds, poor leadership, and its location (for political reasons) in the Kenyan capital, Nairobi, it helped promote regional agreements on pollution of the Mediterranean and other seas. But the conference also had to face the very different priorities of developing countries, who argued that North America and Europe were the main polluters and that restrictions on growth would hamper emerging nations. Against the North's new interest in the environment, the South emphasized the imperatives of development. Out of this clash came the idea of "sustainable development," popularized by another UN-sponsored commission on environment and development, chaired by Gro Harlem Brundtland, the Norwegian premier, which reported in 1987.

The Brundtland report, *Our Common Future,* defined sustainable development as "development that meets the needs of the present without compromising the ability of future generations to meet their own needs."[109] Skeptics argued that it was a political slogan, neatly spanning the rift between environmentalists and proponents of development, rather than a precise tool of policy making.[110] But it helped define the problems, if not the answers.

Meanwhile, the practical difficulties of harmonizing development with the environment were demonstrated in India, where, following the international trend, a Department of the Environment had been established in 1980. But in 1983–1984 its budget was a mere $16 million and it had only 237 staff members. In December 1984 at least two thousand five hundred people died after a gas leak from an American-owned pesticide factory in Bhopal. The disaster highlighted inadequate regulation, poor emergency procedures, and factory standards far below what would have been tolerated back in the United States.[111]

Environmentalism therefore ran into the North-South divide. It was also contained by the East-West confrontation. Only after the end of the cold war did it become clear how appalling had been the pollution of the Soviet Union. Two analysts of the subject suggested that an eventual autopsy on Soviet communism may well "reach the verdict of death by ecocide" because "no great civilization so systematically and so long poisoned its land, air, water and people." It was estimated in 1990, for instance, that almost three-quarters of the country's surface water was polluted, and one-quarter was totally untreated. Major rivers such as the Volga and the Don were virtually open sewers. To compensate for inefficient farming practices, the Soviets resorted to massive use of chemicals, continuing with DDT long after it was banned in the West. The biggest disaster was the Aral Sea region in Soviet Central Asia, where the frenetic expansion of the cotton monoculture had been accomplished by river diversions and saturation use of fertilizers and pesticides. Between 1960 and 1989 the volume of the sea dropped by two-thirds; its surface area (once larger than Lake Huron's) fell by 44 percent. The Aral Sea was, in fact, turning into a desert, jeopardizing the water, health, and livelihood of three or four million people in surrounding Kazakhstan and Uzbekistan.[112]

By 1985 over 140 countries had national environmental agencies; in 1971 the figure had been twelve.[113] Many laws were enacted, but their impact was limited. The 1970s saw the emergence of overtly environmentalist parties, starting with the Values Party in New Zealand in 1972. The most significant of these, the Greens in West Germany, won 5.6 percent of the vote in the Bundestag elections of 1983, making them a significant political force. Issues such as the appalling pollution of the northern Rhine had been a powerful spur. In the next few years Green parties made breakthroughs in Switzerland, Austria, Finland, and Sweden. Some were genuinely new organizations, others were small socialist parties repackaging themselves— reds in green clothing. But they indicated the attraction of environmental politics to a vocal minority. Pressure groups became more aggressive. In America, Friends of the Earth was established in 1969, after a split within the Sierra Club over activist methods. Its reach was soon international. Greenpeace was founded in 1973. Its confrontational tactics—often involving small boats blocking warships, whalers, or other large vessels—were intended to attract media attention. They also angered governments. In July 1985 the Greenpeace vessel *Rainbow Warrior* was blown up in Auckland harbor, New Zealand, by French agents, determined to stop its obstruction of French nuclear testing.

Nuclear power was, in fact, the central target of the new environmentalists. The technology that had ushered in the postwar world and apparently promised so much in its early years had become, for many, the ultimate symbol of what was wrong with modernity. Contrary to expectations, it had far less positive impact on the second half of the twentieth century than other technologies, some of them also launched in World War II, with which this chapter has been concerned. Chips and genes, computers and satellites— these have shaped our modern world more than the products of atomic physics.

Why did this happen? In large part because of the circumstances under which the "atomic age" began. Had atomic energy been developed in peacetime and inaugurated with some dramatic display of civilian benefit, the story might have been different. Instead it was used with spectacular effect as a war-winning weapon and trumpeted as such by military and political leaders for years afterward. Many of the scientists who had developed nuclear weapons became afflicted with a keen sense of guilt. As J. Robert Oppenheimer, "father" of the U.S. atomic bomb project, remarked in 1947: "the physicists have known sin; and this is a knowledge which they cannot lose."[114] (In the Soviet Union, Andrei Sakharov came to feel the same guilt about his contribution to the Soviet H-bomb.) When President Truman dubbed the atomic bomb "the greatest achievement of organized science in history," the commentator Dwight MacDonald shot back that it was "so much the worse for organized science." Moreover, most physicists knew that it would be much harder to "harness" the power of atom than to "unleash" it on an enemy. Days after Hiroshima, the *New York Herald Tribune* predicted that atomic power, if wisely used, could be "a blessing that will make it possible for the human race to create a close approach to an earthly paradise." A spate of books and articles followed, envisaging atomic automobiles and household power plants, cures for cancer, and control of the weather. But Albert Einstein, by now the avuncular face of modern science, warned, "I do not foresee that atomic energy is to be a great boon for a long time."[115]

U.S. policy makers therefore had a vested interest in playing up the potential benefits of atomic power and in accelerating their development. Yet at the same time, they were citing the awesome violence of fission and fusion as the basis of national security. Little wonder that public opinion was ambivalent. Having elevated the atom into the god of war, policy makers could not then persuade their peoples that it was also the god of peace.[116] This was seen most clearly in the debate about nuclear energy.

The first reactor designed for electrical power generation started operating at Obninsk, near Moscow, in June 1954. Commercially used production was pioneered in Britain in October 1956, when electricity generated by the Calder Hall reactor in Cumberland was connected to the national grid. In Britain, shortages of coal and the need to import oil prompted an ambitious program for nuclear power stations in the mid-1950s. America's energy position was more secure, but the Russian and British developments accelerated its civilian nuclear program. A reactor at Shippingport, Pennsylvania, near Pittsburgh, began operation in December 1957.

All three reactors were spinoffs from military projects—as we have seen, a pattern with much postwar big science. Both Obninsk and Calder Hall were dual-purpose reactors: heat from the fission reaction produced steam from which electricity was generated, while plutonium from the spent uranium fuel was reprocessed for use in nuclear weapons. Indeed the basic aim of both programs was military, not civilian, and relentless demands from the armed forces were largely to blame for serious incidents in both Britain and Russia in 1957. That October a fire in the nuclear reactor at Windscale, near

Calder Hall, was extinguished only at the cost of a serious emission of radioactive gas. The plant itself had to be shut down permanently. The immediate cause of the incident, hushed up by the government, was human error, but the mistakes occurred because training and operating standards had been neglected as staff was increased to meet the needs of the defence program.[117] In the Soviet Union, both secrecy and safety were far worse. In September 1957 there was an explosion at a nuclear waste-disposal plant at Kyshtym. Some seventy tons of radioactive material were blasted into the open. Nearly eleven thousand people were evacuated, and farming across some four hundred square miles was banned for several years.[118]

Shippingport was a military project of a rather different sort—an offshoot of one of the Pentagon's big science projects of the early cold war, the nuclear-powered warship. This was the obsession of Captain Hyman G. Rickover, who carved out for himself a vast, well-funded empire as head of the U.S. Navy's naval reactors program. Through his contracts, Westinghouse and General Electric established themselves as technological leaders in the field—much as IBM had been enabled to do in computers, or Bell Labs in solid-state technology. The world's first nuclear-powered submarine, the *Nautilus*, was launched in January 1954, the precursor of several hundred more. Rickover was placed in charge of the federal government's crash program to build Shippingport.[119] The eventual reactor that Westinghouse installed for him was an enlarged version of the pressurized water reactor they had developed for submarines. In order to operate at sea, ordinary ("light") water was used to moderate the reaction. "Heavy" water, based on deuterium rather than hydrogen, was superior but very expensive. The naval program helped establish the light water reactor (LWR) as the preferred American design, despite serious risks of a runaway reaction if the water coolant failed to operate. American-style LWRs became the staple of the nuclear power industry worldwide. To understand this, we must take cold war diplomacy into account.

Until 1953, the United States had kept its nuclear secrets to itself, cutting out even Britain, its wartime A-bomb partner, from further collaboration. It had also treated nuclear technology as essentially a military secret, with civilian uses limited by security priorities. But by 1953, both the Soviet Union and Britain had nuclear weapons. Canada, Russia, France, and Norway had also developed experimental reactors. Sweden followed in 1954.[120] Like it or not, the United States no longer had a monopoly of nuclear technology. And the new president, Dwight Eisenhower, was genuinely concerned "to find some new approach to the *dis*arming of atomic energy."[121] Although many in the Pentagon and the State Department judged him naive, there was agreement on the need for initiatives to reduce public concern about nuclear testing and to gain an ideological advantage over the Kremlin. The result of these varied motives was Ike's "atoms for peace" speech to the United Nations in December 1953. This marked a U-turn in U.S. policy, confirmed by the Atomic Energy Act of August 1954, which enabled U.S. companies to export plant and fuel as did those in Canada and Europe.

Frenetic publicity now replaced obsessive secrecy. Lewis Strauss, chairman of the Atomic Energy Commission, predicted electricity that would be "too cheap to meter."[122] In August 1955 the United Nations organized a major conference in Geneva on the peaceful uses of atomic energy, in which American, Soviet, British, and French scientists unveiled many of their nuclear secrets to hundreds of colleagues from around the world. At a nearby industrial fair, manufacturers were able to display and market their nuclear wares. In this peaceful version of the nuclear race, United States won easily. By the end of 1957 it had signed bilateral agreements for research or power generation with forty-nine countries, from Cuba to Thailand, and U.S. firms had sold twenty-three small research reactors. Yet this campaign "set down reactors in nations that lacked the economic structure and skills to exploit them, nations that had far more need for fertilizer or high school teachers."[123]

Although one objective was to show that atoms could be used for peace, commerce was equally important. Between 1941 and 1955 the U.S. government had spent some $12.3 billion on atomic energy, of which more than one-third was on plant. Expenditure by private industry was minuscule—only $8 million in 1951–1954, for instance.[124] But unlike computers or transistors, on which substantial sums of public money had also been spent, commercial utilization of nuclear power was problematic. Since the depression, America's electricity had been generated by a multitude of small utility companies. They were reluctant to enter the nuclear business because capital costs were two to five times those of conventional power generation (even though running costs were distinctly less). Moreover, nuclear plants took years to plan and build—thereby delaying any return on investment—and the risks implied serious legal bills if things went wrong. With the domestic market therefore limited, Washington was determined to promote exports and thereby gain a return on its nuclear investment.

Despite the entry of both Sweden and West Germany into nuclear energy generation in the 1960s, the United States gradually pulled back Europe's early advantage. Whereas Western Europe boasted 63 percent of the world's nuclear power capacity in 1968, in 1970 the proportion was only 39 percent; by 1975 the United States was the world leader.[125] In the late 1960s, even the nationalistic French shifted to LWRs, in order to compete in the American-shaped world market, leaving only the British sticking obstinately to gas cooling. Although in 1965 Fred Peart, the minister of power, called plans for Britain's new advanced gas-cooled reactor (AGR) the "greatest breakthrough of all time" and boasted "we have hit the jackpot with this," the prototype at

Dungeness in Kent took nearly two decades to build and cost more than twice the original estimate.[126]

By mid-1975 514 nuclear power plants were in operation, in construction, or under contract. But a mere seven of these were in Latin America and only twenty-five in Asia (excluding Japan and the USSR). Much of the Third World interest came from advanced developing countries such as Argentina, Brazil, South Korea, and Taiwan. The essential irrelevance of nuclear power can be understood if one appreciates the energy position of most of the world. In the late 1970s noncommercial fuel, notably firewood and animal dung, accounted for about one-third of China's primary energy use, a half in India, and 75 percent in Bangladesh. Only 4 percent of black Africa's rural population had access to electricity.[127] A 1947 prediction that nuclear power plants could transform Africa into "another Europe" was clearly a long way from realization.[128]

The mid-1970s saw a precipitous fall in orders for reactors across the Western world. On the face of it, this may seem surprising because the oil shock of 1973–1974 aroused panic about energy supplies and renewed interest in nuclear power. But as we saw in Chapter 12, it was also part of a prolonged economic crisis in which falling output combined with soaring inflation. This stagflation had a profound effect on the economics of nuclear power, which had assumed that electricity demand in the West would continue to grow along the exponential growth curve of the previous two decades. These estimates were radically revised in the stagflation of the mid-1970s. Also relevant to cost-benefit analysis was the public backlash against nuclear power. This meant long public inquiries, big protests, and higher safety standards. In West Germany, a camp around the reactor site at Wyhl, near Freiburg, became a symbol of resistance. In the United States, Seabrook on the coast of New Hampshire assumed a similar importance. There was also growing concern, particularly in Germany and Britain, about the reprocessing of nuclear waste and its shipment across country.[129]

The main exception to the antinuclear trend was France, where the government decided in 1974 to convert almost entirely to nuclear power (le tout nucléaire). There were vehement protests, but the country's dirigiste tradition and the absence of a federal structure (unlike the United States and West Germany) prevented the opposition from gaining a political foothold. The average lead time for completing a reactor in France (six or seven years) was nearly half that in the United States. In contrast with America's plethora of utility companies, France's electricity was provided by a government monopoly, and nuclear power plants were built to a standard design. The average generating cost of nuclear power was therefore roughly half that in America. By the late 1980s about three-quarters of France's electricity was generated by atomic energy—by far the highest proportion in the world.[130]

Global resistance to nuclear power was reinforced by two highly publicized accidents. On March 28, 1979, there was a serious leak of radioactive gas from a reactor on Three Mile Island near Harrisburg, Pennsylvania. Anxiety was heightened by the coincidental release of *The China Syndrome,* a movie about a core meltdown in a nuclear power plant. As with Windscale in 1957, operator errors were the immediate cause, but a presidential inquiry pinpointed flaws in basic training, operating procedures, and emergency drills. It noted that the industry and its regulators were "heavily equipment-oriented rather than people-oriented" and that the response to the leak was "dominated by an atmosphere of almost total confusion."[131] Advocates of nuclear power therefore argued that Three Mile Island was "a failure not of technology but of technocracy."[132] When Mount St. Helens in Washington State erupted the following May, it was noted that sixty-eight people died and damage to property and crops topped $1.8 billion. In contrast, no deaths or physical damage could be directly traced to Three Mile Island, and most of the $1 billion costs were incurred in cleaning up the reactor itself.[133] But 144,000 people fled their homes for several days. This was testimony to the fear of radiation—unlike volcanic lava, an unseen and lasting menace. In the words of a bumper sticker marketed soon after the event: "I survived Three Mile Island—I think."

The other accident was far worse, and, unlike Windscale or Three Mile Island, it caused many casualties. At 1:23 A.M. on April 26, 1986, there was an explosion at the number-four reactor at the Chernobyl nuclear power station in Ukraine. This poured "more radioactive material into the atmosphere than had been released in the atomic bombings of Hiroshima and Nagasaki."[134] It took two weeks to extinguish the fire and seven months to encase the damaged reactor in concrete. Two technicians were killed in the accident itself. Another twenty-nine died over the next four months, mostly firefighters exposed to massive doses of radiation.

But Chernobyl was no local incident. The huge plume of gas and debris drifted north and west, over the rest of the Ukraine, into Belorussia and Poland, causing contamination in Scandinavia and, to some degree, in most of Western Europe. Belorussia received 70 percent of the fallout; even in 1992, nearly a fifth of the state budget was still going toward resettlement, decontamination, and medical treatment. Some eight hundred thousand "liquidators" assisting in the cleanup across the western USSR were exposed to very high levels of radiation; many more people in East and Central Europe were affected through absorption into the food chain. Because of the long incubation time for cancers, the full extent of the disaster will not be clear until around the year 2010.[135]

Chernobyl was, in fact, "the most expensive industrial accident in modern history," costing the USSR the equivalent of $19 billion by the end of 1988.[136]

As with Windscale and Three Mile Island, human errors were the proximate cause, but the disaster exposed a profound indifference to safety throughout the Soviet nuclear program. By the end of 1990 the Kremlin, faced with the mounting environmentalist backlash, decided to suspend construction on nearly all nuclear power plants. This played havoc with its energy program, which, in view of the escalating extraction costs for Siberian oil and natural gas, had planned that nuclear power would generate half the country's electricity by the year 2000.[137]

Chernobyl also had a devastating effect on the nuclear industry across Europe. In 1980 the Swedish parliament had decided in principle to phase out nuclear power by 2010. After Chernobyl, legislation was passed in 1987–1988 to close down the first two power stations in the mid-1990s. In Italy, Chernobyl prompted a referendum on nuclear power in 1987, which produced a large, hostile majority. Subsequent legislation ended work on new power stations, despite substantial sums already spent. Defenders of nuclear power continued to insist that the dangers had been irrationally exaggerated, compared with, say, the risks entailed in air or road travel.[138] But nuclear imagery was rarely rational. The cloud escaping from Chernobyl seemed reminiscent of that above Hiroshima four decades before. As David Lilienthal, the first chairman of the Atomic Energy Commission, had remarked back in 1947, nuclear power and nuclear weapons were "two sides of the same coin."[139]

That perception was strengthened in the 1970s by alarm about Third World countries moving from civilian to military atomic capability. In 1968, the United States, the United Kingdom, and the Soviet Union signed a nonproliferation treaty. By the end of 1973, seventy-three other states had accepted it. But in May 1974, India conducted what it termed "a peaceful nuclear explosion." Even though India did not conduct more tests in the 1970s or build a nuclear arsenal, this episode called in question the effectiveness of the nonproliferation regime. India's reactor had been provided by Canada; the heavy water came from the United States. There was also concern about French and German deals to provide what could become fissionable material to South Korea, Pakistan, and Brazil.

In 1977 Jimmy Carter, a passionate opponent of nuclear power, became president. Reflecting his own concerns and also pressure from Congress, a nuclear nonproliferation act was passed in 1978. The law tightened controls, particularly on reprocessed nuclear fuel that might have military use. Carter also reinterpreted previous bilateral agreements, angering both Western allies and developing countries. The latter pointed out that America, with only 6 percent of the world's people, consumed one-third of its commercially produced energy—equal to the amount used by the whole developing world, which had two-thirds of the world's population.[140]

Although the Reagan administration (1981–1989) was more relaxed about nuclear proliferation, the underlying problem remained. It now cost a mere $50 million to design, build and test a plutonium-based nuclear device, compared with $2 billion expended by the United States between 1941 and 1945.[141] By 1980, it was estimated that forty states had the technical ability and resources to build a nuclear arsenal.[142] Several that had not signed the nonproliferation treaty were dubbed "threshold states" and were watched with particular care because of their tense regional situations. These were Argentina and Brazil, India and Pakistan, and Israel and Iraq.

The latter case was especially sensitive. Israel had been assisted in its nuclear energy program during the 1950s and 1960s by France, then a close ally, which turned a blind eye to military spinoffs. It is likely that Israeli had developed nuclear weapons by the early 1970s but kept the components unassembled in order to justify the claim, necessary to maintain U.S. aid, that Israel was not a nuclear-weapons state. As Yigor Allon, a cabinet minister, put it in 1965, "Israel will not be the first to introduce nuclear weapons into the Middle East, but it will not be the second either."[143] When Saddam Hussein in Iraq began a nuclear power program, again with help from the French—who were notably even handed whenever commercial profit was involved—the Israelis decided to preempt future weapons development. In June 1981 they mounted a daring air strike on the reactor being built at Tammuz. This set back the Iraqi program by several years.

By 1989 nuclear power generated about 17 percent of the world's commercially supplied electricity. The proportion was nearer one-third in Europe and higher still in individual states (see Table 14.1).[144] But decisions taken in the 1970s and 1980s ensured that there would be little new capacity for the rest of the century. In considering the environmental benefits of nuclear power compared with fossil fuels, its advocates argued that "the current shift is a retreat—not a demise" and that nuclear power would surge back in the next century once questions of safety and security had been addressed after its overhasty development during the early cold war.[145]

It was clear by the 1980s that nuclear power had, as yet, failed to match the promises of its early apostles. For instance, only six nuclear-powered civilian ships had been built, and plans for a nuclear-powered plane had been scrapped after costly research. On the other hand, nuclear weapons had not yet brought about the global disaster that some had predicted. For example, C. P. Snow, the British scientist and author, had warned in 1960 that "within, at most, ten years some of these bombs are going to go off. . . . That is a certainty." Three years later, President Kennedy foresaw the possibility in the 1970s of his successors "having to face a world in which fifteen or twenty or twenty-five powers may have these weapons."[146] Instead, no more atomic bombs were dropped in anger, and the nuclear club remained at five certi-

TABLE 14.1 NUCLEAR ELECTRICITY GENERATION AT THE END OF 1989

Country	Operating nuclear capacity		Nuclear as percent of electricity production
	Number of units	Gigawatt output (= 1 million kilowatts)	
United States	110	98.3	19.1
France	55	52.6	74.6
USSR	46	34.2	12.3
Japan	39	29.3	27.8
West Germany	24	22.7	34.3
Canada	18	12.2	15.6
United Kingdom	39	11.2	21.7
Sweden	12	9.8	45.1
Spain	10	7.5	38.4
South Korea	9	7.2	50.2
Belgium	7	5.5	60.8
Taiwan	6	4.9	35.2
World totals:			
Operating	426	318	
Under construction	96	79	

SOURCE: Terence Price, *Political Electricity: What Future for Nuclear Energy?* (Oxford: Oxford University Press, 1990), p. 4.

fied members until 1998. States such as Israel, India, and South Africa found an ambiguous threshold status more convenient than expensive and provocative nuclear arsenals. The atomic age therefore brought neither paradise nor perdition during the cold war era. Humanity learned to live, uneasily, with the bomb.

Although this chapter has ranged far beyond the cold war, it has also returned repeatedly to the superpower polarity. Rivalry between the two systems was the principal stimulus for big science, a major impulse for ecologically damaging heavy industries, and the prime cause of a spiraling arms race that threatened humanity with annihilation. But as we have also seen, the Soviet bloc was the recurrent loser in the high-tech contest of the 1970s and 1980s. Early successes in satellites and rocketry came to nothing. The Soviet Union could not match America's costly but creative symbiosis between the military-industrial-academic complex and the entrepreneurial consumer culture. By the 1980s, Soviet deficiencies in telecommunications, semiconductors, and computers had become alarmingly evident to a younger generation of leaders. At the same time, the ecological damage inflicted by rampant industrialization provided both focus and legitimization for growing citizen protest across the Soviet bloc. And the new technologies of communication made it ever harder to insulate the Soviet bloc from Western ideas and information. In short, the problems and promise of big science were present from the start of the cold war, and they also played a major part in its dénouement. This theme runs through the next chapter.

15

The Crisis of Communism

In April 1985, only weeks after Mikhail Gorbachev assumed power, the Soviet Union's Central Committee privately admitted that "the country finds itself on the verge of a crisis."[1] Similar analyses were circulating among Moscow's Warsaw Pact allies. This chapter is an account of how reform turned to revolt, demolishing the Soviet bloc in 1989 and the USSR itself two years later. It is about mass movements as well as high politics, because the Gorbachev thaw set off an avalanche of civic protest akin to that in Latin America. At the heart of the story is the unification of Germany, around whose division cold war Europe had taken shape forty years before.

These events were part of larger pattern. At the beginning of 1989, twenty-three states around the world could be defined as communist. Five years later the figure was only five.[2] But one of these was the People's Republic of China. While the Soviet Union disintegrated, leaving behind poverty and instability across Eurasia, the PRC reformed itself into a state-guided market economy with the potential to be the world's biggest by the early twenty-first century. These contrasting outcomes owed much to structural differences—particularly the ethnic diversity of the Soviet Union, the omnicompetence of its command economy, and its more urbanized society. But policy mattered as well, particularly contrasting judgments on whether economic liberalization required democratic politics. This is why we need to look at Russia in tandem with China, at Deng Xiaoping as well as Mikhail Gorbachev.

Gorbachev and the "New Thinking"

By the early 1980s, the Soviet economy was in a state of zero growth. There were various reasons. The population was rising by barely 1 percent each year (half the rate of the 1950s) as the fertility transition took effect in the western half of the USSR. The arms race with the United States consumed at least one-sixth of GDP, perhaps one-quarter, to the detriment of civilian production. But the root problem was the inefficiency of the command economy, which was ruled by a rigid but ineffectual plan, administered by a vast bureaucracy, and riddled with corruption at all levels. It was an economy characterized by prodigious wastage of resources and manpower, and by conspicuous shortages of goods—as the lines outside shops indicated. In TV factories, for instance, lack of parts early in the month meant hours of short-time work or tedious party lectures, followed by frenetic "storming" at the end of the month in order to meet production targets. "We never use a screwdriver in the last week," admitted one worker in a Lithuanian TV factory. "We hammer the screws in."[3]

Some of the Soviet Union's economic problems had been masked by the boom in world oil prices in the 1970s and by the country's vast Siberian reserves. Between 1972 and 1980, Soviet output of crude petroleum increased by 50 percent, and in 1975 the USSR displaced the United States as the world's biggest producer.[4] Oil and natural gas were by far the most valuable Soviet export to the West, earning essential hard currency and prompting serious concern in the Reagan administration about possible Western European dependence on Soviet energy (see Chapter 13). But the oil boom was brief. Prices started to slip after 1980 and fell precipitously in the middle of the decade, just as Gorbachev assumed power.

In any case, the average Soviet citizen saw little benefit from the oil boom. Perhaps the most striking of many grim statistics are the figures for life expectancy. A child born in 1966 could expect to live, on average, about twenty-four years longer than one born in 1938—to age sixty-five for men and seventy-three for women. But between 1966 and 1980, life expectancy at birth *fell* by 3.75 years for men and 1.74 for women.[5] This was the consequence of poor health care, environmental pollution and, especially for Slavic men, chronic alcoholism.

After he succeeded the tempestuous Khrushchev in 1964, Leonid Brezhnev had made stability his top priority. But stability increasingly became stagnation as officials at all levels (not to mention Brezhnev's own family) were left to cultivate their corrupt little enclaves while the economy atrophied.* Medically, too, Brezhnev epitomized the health of the nation. In his last years, he was frequently a basket case from arteriosclerosis, his body and brain ravaged by the effects of alcohol, cigarettes, and overeating. After his death in November 1982, it seemed briefly as if a new era had dawned. His successor, Yuri Andropov, had masterminded the crackdown on dissidents as head of the KGB since 1967. But in the early 1960s, while at the Central Committee Andropov had patronized reformist intellectuals such as Oleg Bogomolov and Georgy Arbatov, who later become heads of major research institutes. The elevation of Andropov therefore promised both "discipline *and* reform"[6]—manifest in a crackdown on corruption and alcohol, and in the promotion of energetic younger leaders. But Andropov was soon undergoing regular dialysis for kidney failure, and he spent most of his last eight months in hospital. After he died in February 1984, the old guard, led by Foreign Minister Andrei Gromyko, engineered the election of Brezhnev's right-hand man, Konstantin Chernenko, also a septuagenarian. Chernenko was seriously ill with emphysema. His occasional, wheezing appearances on TV suggested that yet another state funeral was in the offing. After attending Andropov's obsequies, Vice President George Bush told U.S. embassy staff in Moscow, "See you again, same time, next year!"[7] Bush was wrong—by one month. When Gorbachev succeeded Chernenko in March 1985, the USSR had seen four general secretaries in less than two and a half years.

Yet there was another, hidden side to what became known as "the era of stagnation." To quote one British journalist: "The country went through a social revolution while Brezhnev slept."[8] In 1960, 49 percent of the population was categorized as urban; by 1985 the proportion was 65 percent. In numerical terms, 180 million Soviet citizens lived in cities and towns, compared with fifty-six million before World War Two.[9] Peasants became workers—with all the concomitant change of world-view. Many workers rose into an educated middle class. In 1955, only 2.7 percent of the work force had a university degree; a further 3.7 percent had a technical qualification obtained after secondary schooling beyond the legal minimum. Thirty years later, the comparable figures were 11 percent and 15 percent.[10] These "spe-

---

*With typical Russian black humor, one joke imagined all the country's leaders, present and past, in a train crossing the steppes. Suddenly the train ground to a halt. Stalin jumped up and shouted, "Flog the driver." The driver was duly flogged, but nothing happened. "Rehabilitate the driver," ordered Khrushchev, but still the train did not move. Then the pudgy Brezhnev stood up, drew the curtains of the compartment and, smiling his hooded smile, said, "Let's just pretend the train is moving."

cialists" were usually party members—a card was essential for most positions of responsibility—but they became increasingly dissatisfied with the failings of the system.

As in so many other parts of the developing world, therefore, urbanization and education were powerful solvents of the old order. The media were less subversive in the USSR because of state control, but nine households in ten had a TV by the 1980s, and (when it worked) the television offered glimpses of a wider world. More important, in the words of the dissident Leonid Pinsky, was the simple fact that millions of people could now "shut their own front door."[11] The massive building program of the Khrushchev years enabled much of the urban population to move from communal apartments to single-family flats. There, around the kitchen table, families and friends could talk confidentially and critically about politics and society. Many of those gaining prominence in the 1980s were "people of the sixties" (*shestidesyatniki*)—offspring of the new urban middle class who had been awakened by Khrushchev's thaw and then silenced (but not suffocated) in Brezhnev's repression.

The Soviet Union was therefore in a volatile state by the 1980s—an economy with grave structural problems, an urban, educated society that was less easy to direct. But none of this portended sudden collapse. Most Western analysts anticipated that the system would survive into the 1990s and beyond, with sluggish growth and continued party control. The social changes made evolution likely, but not revolution. The revolution began from above, within the state or, more exactly, from "the state of mind of those running the state."[12] It began with Gorbachev and his advisers.

Mikhail Gorbachev was born in the Stavropol region of southern Russia in March 1931. Age set him apart from his predecessors—Brezhnev (born 1906), Andropov (born 1914), and Chernenko (born 1911). They had risen to power during Stalinism and had survived Germany's surprise attack in 1941 as adults. Their domestic and foreign policies never fully escaped from the paranoid concepts of stability and security engendered in those years. Moreover, Gorbachev epitomized the new middle class—five years of legal education at Moscow University—and he shared some of its aspirations. Several visits to Western Europe in the 1970s also opened his eyes to the limitations of the Soviet system. Bright and diligent, Gorbachev became secretary of his home region before the age of forty. Not surprisingly, he caught Andropov's reforming eye. The KGB chief helped bring Gorbachev to Moscow in 1978 and then, as general secretary, pushed him as heir apparent. Although this bid failed, Gorbachev was well positioned when Chernenko died on March 10, 1985. That night, walking in the garden of their Moscow home (to avoid the KGB's bugs), he told his wife that if he really wanted to change something he would have to accept the nomination. "We can't go on living like this."[13]

So Gorbachev came to power as a would-be reformer. But our understanding of what that meant in 1985 is too easily clouded by what Gorbachev later became.[14] His reformism in 1985 was that of a man determined to improve the system, not to overthrow it. His early policies were relatively cautious, with strong echoes of the Andropov interregnum. There was administrative reform, a new crackdown on alcoholism, and a drive to promote computers and high technology. Gorbachev was still working within the structure of the command economy. In June 1985 he insisted, "Not the market, not the anarchic forces of competition, but above all the plan must determine the basic features of development of the economy."[15] The buzzword in this first year was *uskorenie,* acceleration; in other words, getting things moving.

But the results were modest, even negative in the case of antialcoholism because it cost the government enormous sums in lost revenue (liquor was a state monopoly) and encouraged the sale of lethal moonshine by organized crime. It became clear that new economic programs would be vitiated without radical restructuring *(perestroika)* of management and party. And this could not be done unless the system was more open, more transparent *(glasnost),* even at the level of basic information about what was going on. These two words had been around for years, but they now became the catchwords of the Gorbachev era—indeed, the terms became internationalized.

Their importance came home to Gorbachev after the Chernobyl nuclear reactor exploded in April 1986 (see Chapter 14). Initially, the bureaucracy tried to cover up the disaster in the best Soviet tradition. But the information revolution had now taken the lid off even closed societies. U.S. satellite pictures clearly showed the reactor with its roof blown off and its graphite core on fire. Not only did the cover-up embarrass the Kremlin internationally, it also delayed effective action and aggravated human suffering. Nearly three weeks elapsed, for instance, before the authorities permitted the evacuation of children from the city of Kiev (population 2.5 million), which was little over sixty miles away.[16]

Gorbachev admitted in 1991 that Chernobyl "shook us immensely" and called it "a turning point" toward greater openness.[17] The disaster also became a rallying point for growing political agitation, most of which started as protests about the USSR's appalling environmental pollution.[18] There were implications for perestroika as well. Facing a severe drop in oil prices, the 1986 plan had called for a new reliance on nuclear power, which was scheduled to double to 22 percent of total electricity generation by 1991. That policy was now in ruins because of the antinuclear backlash among experts and public. And the international fallout from the disaster—radioactive and diplomatic—strengthened Gorbachev's awareness of an interconnected world in which nuclear catastrophe threatened communists and capitalists alike.

The three years from mid-1986 were the high point of the Gorbachev era, when reform from above gathered momentum and before it was overwhelmed by revolt from below. Impelled by his evolving ideas and those of his advisers, and buffeted by the ever more complex social and political forces his reforms had unleashed, Gorbachev gradually moved beyond piecemeal tinkering with the system to fundamental transformation. During this time he also chipped away at the old leadership. In 1985–1986, his right-hand men were two other Andropov protegés—Nikolai Ryzhkov, a technocratic manager from Sverdlovsk, who took over as prime minister, and Yegor Ligachev, the blunt, puritanical party boss of Tomsk, who became Gorbachev's deputy. At the party congress in March 1986, around 45 percent of the Central Committee was replaced.[19] It was much harder, however, to change men and mentalities at regional, district, and city levels, and among the thousands of industrial managers and farm directors. They became a basic obstacle to reform.

The most dramatic developments in the early years occurred in foreign policy, where Gorbachev was less shackled by the Soviet bureaucracy. One of his earliest personnel changes, in July 1985, had been the replacement of Andrei Gromyko, foreign minister since 1957, by the Georgian party secretary, Eduard Shevardnadze. The new man was as surprised as everyone else by his elevation, but Gorbachev dealt briskly with his objections: "No experience? Well, perhaps that's good thing. Our foreign policy needs a fresh eye, courage, dynamism, innovative approaches."[20] What mattered to Gorbachev was Shevardnadze's commitment to perestroika and the fact that, as a politician rather than a career diplomat, he would be receptive to "new thinking." This was fermenting rapidly among Gorbachev's advisers—men who had maintained their critical faculties in the research institutes created by Andropov protegés such as Arbatov and Bogomolov in the 1960s. Of these, the most influential was Alexander Yakovlev, whose decade of quasi-exile as ambassador to Canada since 1973 had exposed him deeply to Western ways.

In the three years after Gorbachev's accession, Soviet-American relations were transformed. The Reagan-Gorbachev meeting in Geneva in November 1985 was the first summit since Carter and Brezhnev had signed the ill-fated SALT II treaty in Vienna in June 1979. There were no major agreements at Geneva; indeed the two men had many spirited arguments. What mattered, to quote the White House chief of staff, was personal chemistry: Reagan and Gorbachev "discovered they could talk to each other even if they could not agree."[21] The two conferred again the following October in the Icelandic capital of Reykjavik. In December 1987, in Washington, they concluded an agreement to eliminate all intermediate-range nuclear forces. Although the INF treaty covered only about 5 percent of their warheads, it was the first time the superpowers had agreed to reduce the nuclear stockpiles (as distinct from limiting expansion). The SS-20s, Pershing IIs, and Cruise missiles—whose deployments had sparked the new cold war in the early 1980s—would disappear. Moreover, the treaty was buttressed by unprecedented Soviet agreement to on-site inspections. This solved a problem that had dogged all previous attempts at superpower arms control. At summits, Reagan parroted one of his few Russian phrases—*doveryai, no proveryai* (trust but verify). The INF treaty rested on new levels of trust *and* verification.

What had happened to transform the relationship? Most of the changes were on the Soviet side. Instead of dour rigidity, instead of reading from prepared scripts, Gorbachev and his foreign minister were lively and personable, forging bonds of respect and even affection with their opposite numbers. Even more important were changes in Soviet policy—indeed, the INF treaty is largely a story of successive and often breathtaking Gorbachev concessions. At Reykjavik, for instance, Reagan refused to agree that tests of Star Wars technology would occur in the laboratory and not in space. This seemed to jeopardize any chance of an arms control agreement. But in February 1987, Gorbachev dropped all linkage with SDI. Back in 1981, Reagan had proposed a "zero option"—if you pull out your SS-20s, we won't put in Cruise and Pershing IIs. At the time this was generally seen as a propaganda exercise to avoid real talks: no one imagined that the Soviets would agree.[22] But in 1987, Gorbachev accepted the zero option. He went on to make it "double zero" with the inclusion of short-range forces in Europe, and then turned it into a "global double zero" when he offered to include Soviet forces worldwide.

Little wonder, therefore, that many in the West saw this as a victory, citing NATO's tenacity in implementing Cruise and Pershing deployment as a major reason for Soviet concessions.[23] Others claimed that "the Strategic Defense Initiative contributed significantly to the West's triumph in the Cold War."[24] There is little doubt that, by 1985, the Soviets found themselves down a blind alley of their own construction, making a U-turn essential. But "push" factors alone cannot explain such a radical shift in Soviet policy. We must add the "pull" of the "new thinking," which produced a very different conception of Soviet security.[25] Through Yakovlev and other advisers, Gorbachev created a new vocabulary, drawn from German and Scandinavian social democrats. These ideas had been publicized in a 1982 report entitled *Common Security: A Blueprint for Survival* by an international commission under the former Swedish premier, Olof Palme.

From the nuclear threat, and other dangers such as environmental pollution, Gorbachev built the argument that "we live in a vulnerable, rather fragile but interconnected world. . . . Whatever divides us, we have the same planet to live on."[26] By 1988, this concept of interdependence was expressed in terms of "common human values" that took precedence over the values of class and nation that had animated the cold war.[27] On a practical level, he developed the idea of "reasonable defensive sufficiency." This was already gaining ground in the Soviet military because of the costs of the nuclear arms race on the one hand and, on the other, the growing efficacy of high-tech conventional deterrence.[28] These ideas, endorsed by Marshal Sergei Akhromeyev, chief of the General Staff in 1984–1988, not only justified the asymmetrical Soviet cuts in the INF agreement but also the large, unilateral reductions in troop levels in Europe that Gorbachev went on to propose in 1988.

In the 1970s, détente had been fatally flawed because of divergent basic assumptions. Under Gorbachev, Soviet conceptions of security changed fundamentally, and something approaching entente developed. But as Reagan liked to say, it takes two to tango. Had U.S. policy not shifted as well, the transformation would not have been so profound.

In part, the president himself changed, satisfied that he had now made America "walk tall" again. Second-term ambitions to go down in history as a peacemaker, encouraged by his wife, were reinforced by a new awareness of the Russians as human beings rather than communist automata. In a speech in January 1984, Reagan mused about what might happen if two ordinary couples, one Russian and one American, could sit down and chat together about family life. By 1984, he also began to appreciate the deep insecurities of a country that had been ravaged by both Napoleon and Hitler. The Soviet war scare of 1983–1984, prompted in part by NATO's Able Archer exercise (see Chapter 13), made him realize, as he put it in his memoirs, that "many people at the top of the Soviet hierarchy were genuinely afraid of Americans and America. Perhaps this shouldn't have surprised me," he added, "but it did."[29]

As important as the education of Ronald Reagan was the ascendancy of Secretary of State George Shultz. For nearly a decade, U.S. foreign policy had been plagued by feuds between the National Security Council and the State Department, driving two secretaries of state—Vance and Haig—into resignation. Shultz nearly went the same way in 1986, but the discrediting of the NSC in the Iran-Contra affair and the gradual sidelining of Weinberger at the Pentagon strengthened his influence over the president. Unlike Weinberger, the obdurate cold warrior, Shultz believed in genuine negotiation. His excellent relationship with Shevardnadze soon paid dividends. After Weinberger resigned in October 1987, Shultz worked well with Frank Carlucci as defense secretary and General Colin Powell as national security adviser. This, he wrote later, was "by far the best team, and in fact, the first genuine team, assembled in the entire Reagan presidency." When Shultz's tenure ended in January 1989, Powell told a dinner in his honor that the national security adviser and the secretary of state had not gotten on so well since the days when Henry Kissinger held both jobs simultaneously.[30]

The new entente was therefore a two-way street. Gorbachev moved more, but Reagan came to meet him. Without this change in the international climate, Gorbachev would not have sanctioned the European revolutions of 1989. Nor would he have felt able to embark on radical reforms at home.

Glasnost was always intended as a political weapon. Gorbachev and his advisers hoped that greater openness would mobilize intellectuals and the new middle class against party oligarchs. A powerful symbolic act was the release in December 1986 of the dissident physicist Andrei Sakharov, after nearly seven years under house arrest in the provincial city of Gorky. Dissidents were a tiny minority, however. More important was the growth of *neformaly,* or informal groups, akin to the New Social Movements in Latin America (see Chapter 13). By 1989 there were at least sixty thousand such groups across the country. Some were formed by young people for sports or rock music, but a significant number developed a political edge. Often the stimulus was local pollution, as for "Ecology" in Volgograd, or the group in Brateyevo, a high-rise housing estate in Moscow threatened by "dirty industries" in their backyard. A conference in Moscow in August 1987, bringing together delegates from some fifty organizations in twelve cities, helped to coordinate and politicize their activities. An independent political party, Democratic Union, was formed in May 1988.[31]

More pervasive still was the impact of glasnost on the media and cultural life. Under the aegis of Alexander Yakovlev, new editors were appointed and censorship rules loosened. Sales figures soared as Soviet newspapers and magazines became worth reading for the first time. Some issues remained taboo until the end of the decade, notably the armed forces and ethnic tension, but social problems such as crime and pollution were soon being examined, and suppressed works of art and literature made their appearance.[32] In February 1987 Gorbachev declared that "there should not be any blank pages in either our history or our literature,"[33] and in October a Politburo commission was established to investigate controversial features of the Stalin years. This reflected Gorbachev's growing use of the later Lenin as ideological legitimization for his reforms. Georgy Smirnov, Gorbachev's ideological adviser, coined the slogan: "Not back to Lenin, but forward to Lenin."[34] But Gorbachev had started a hazardous game. It would be hard to keep Lenin on his pedestal while toppling Stalin.

Conservatives in the party leadership became increasingly alarmed at the trend of events. Two celebrated "affairs" in the winter of 1987–1988 were of decisive importance in the struggle over perestroika and glasnost. These made Boris Yeltsin and Nina Andreyeva household names—the latter for a fleeting moment, the former as a major political figure and an irreconcilable foe of Gorbachev.

Yeltsin had been born in Sverdlovsk province in 1931. Like Gorbachev, he was an energetic, hard-driving meritocrat who had risen through the construction industry to become Sverdlovsk party secretary by 1976. But temperamentally, the two men were very different. Yeltsin was an instinctive rebel, rarely out of trouble. As a boy he had lost two fingers on his left hand while taking apart a grenade stolen from a local armory. Nor was he an intellectual like Gorbachev. Most of his student career was spent playing volleyball, and over the years he developed a serious alcohol problem. But in Sverdlovsk he made his name as a dynamic, honest leader who met his targets. This endeared him to Ligachev, who had him moved to Moscow in 1985. There Yeltsin took over as party secretary, with a mandate to clean up the city's administration. He threw himself into the task with characteristic populist energy, joining the queues, for instance, to investigate shortages in the shops. But the party in Moscow (over one million members) was far more tenacious than in Sverdlovsk, and Yeltsin stirred up a hornets' nest when he questioned their food, cars, and other perks. Ligachev turned against him and gradually made his position untenable.

At a Central Committee plenum in October 1987, an exhausted Yeltsin announced his resignation and lambasted Ligachev. He went on to criticize the failings of perestroika and warned of a "cult of personality" beginning to form around Gorbachev. Denounced by almost all his colleagues, including Gorbachev and Yakovlev, Yeltsin crumpled and made a lame apology. Two weeks later he was hospitalized with a heart attack. But Gorbachev ordered him from his hospital bed to be formally dismissed by the Moscow party committee. For four hours, Yeltsin sat on the podium, pumped full of drugs and barely conscious, to hear his accusers. It was like a Stalin show trial. Except, that is, for the ending. Yeltsin was sacked, not shot. And as the meeting broke up, with Yeltsin slumped over the table, head in hands, Gorbachev showed a typical touch of humanity. He returned from the door, took Yeltsin's arm, and helped him into his old office where they waited for the ambulance to arrive.[35]

Yeltsin's blunderbuss speech, spraying criticism in all directions, had left Gorbachev little choice but to side with his critics. In any case, Ligachev was still deputy leader and, contrary to his later neo-Stalinist image, he was a genuine reformer who was not just against corruption and alcoholism, but also in favor of the regulated market economy and many early glasnost measures.[36] But he parted company with Gorbachev at three points—creeping privatization, excessive democratization, and the extent of historical revisionism. The decisive battle over history was fought in March 1988. While Gorbachev and Yakovlev were out of the country, Ligachev (who shared responsibility for the media with Yakovlev) publicly endorsed a letter to the paper *Sovetskaya Rossiya* written by Nina Andreyeva, an obscure chemistry instructor from Leningrad. She urged Russians not to denigrate every aspect of the Stalin era and to uphold Marxist-Leninist principles. For three weeks no one dared to reply. Yakovlev said later: "At that time it was still possible to smother *glasnost.*"[37] Only after a two-day Politburo meeting was Gorbachev able to turn the tide. Henceforth Yakovlev was given sole charge of the press; he personally supervised a full-page rebuttal of the Andreyeva article. Journalists found their voice again, and pressed the case for greater openness.

Victory in the Andreyeva affair gave Gorbachev new momentum after the Yeltsin fiasco. A special conference of the Communist Party of the Soviet Union (CPSU), long delayed, was convened at the end of June 1988. This endorsed the principles of competitive elections and limited terms of office. The aim was not to surrender the leading role of the party, but to open it up and enlist the energies of more of the populace in public life. Gorbachev told the conference that democratization was the "principal guarantee of [the] irreversibility of perestroika."[38] Constitutional amendments in December provided for a new Congress of People's Deputies of over two thousand, meeting twice a year, from which a quarter would be elected to act as a full-time legislature (the new Supreme Soviet). Elections were held in the spring of 1989. The nomination process was tightly controlled, and over 87 percent of the deputies were party members. But even in this situation, many voters exercised their hitherto unused constitutional right to strike out unacceptable names on the ballot paper. The backlash was particularly strong in the Baltic states and in big cities such as Moscow, Leningrad, and Kiev. Overall, twenty-one out of fifty-five regional first secretaries were rejected in this way. Moreover, the fact that there was some kind of contest for 73 percent of the seats was a novelty for Soviet voters, and an education in real politics with political meetings, press interviews, and mass rallies. Many of the nominal party members elected were representative of the new middle class that Gorbachev wanted to mobilize—men such as Anatoly Sobchak, a Leningrad law professor, who quickly made a name for himself as a skillful debater.[39]

The biggest political battle occurred in the special citywide seat for Moscow, which Yeltsin had decided to contest as part of his political comeback. Now a hero for many on account of his populist policies and his widely publicized feud with Ligachev, Yeltsin surged to victory with 89 percent of the vote. In firing Yeltsin less than eighteen months before, Gorbachev told him he would never be allowed back into politics. But by March 1989, politics were no longer Gorbachev's to dictate. The votes of more than five million Muscovites had resurrected Boris Yeltsin.

The new Congress of People's Deputies convened in Moscow on May 26, 1989. No more than one-sixth could be described as real reformers; party conservatives ensured that those elected to form the new Supreme Soviet were mostly compliant hacks. But the congress, televised across the USSR to eager audiences, was the country's baptism in parliamentary politics. Its proceedings were deftly chaired by Gorbachev, who relished the cut and thrust of debate and also the discomfiture of many Politburo colleagues as they listened to the litany of complaints about party misrule. That, after all, was what he wanted democratization to achieve. But, as round two of the "Yeltsin affair" showed, Gorbachev had started a reform process that he could no longer control.

With the revolution from below gaining momentum, Gorbachev also had to respond to turmoil across the communist world. On June 4, 1989, while the congress was in session, the Chinese leadership was brutally suppressing the demonstrators in Beijing and setting its own reforms on a very different course. The same day, free elections in Poland resulted in victory for the Solidarity trade union, presaging the end of communist rule. The winds of change, which Gorbachev had fanned, were now reaching hurricane force.

The European Revolutions of 1989

In retrospect, the dramatic collapse of communist power in Eastern Europe in 1989 seems even more inevitable than the fall of the Soviet Union two years later. In many countries, especially Poland, economic problems were graver than in the USSR. Except in Yugoslavia and Albania, communist rule was an outside imposition, tainted by Russian imperialism. When it became clear that Gorbachev would not use force in an effort to hold the bloc together, in contrast with 1956 or 1968, the floodgates opened. Yet the course of events was more erratic at the time than hindsight suggests. Other factors also mattered: divisions at the top as communist elites began debating reform, pressure from below by newly mobilized people power, and especially the multiplier effect of the media. It has been aptly observed that 1989 was "as much the triumph of communication as the failure of Communism."[40]

During 1989, the communist monopoly on power crumbled in six east European countries—Poland, Hungary, East Germany, Czechoslovkia, Bulgaria and Romania. All six were by then in deep economic crisis, with GDP actually contracting. Apart from the general sclerosis of command economies, Eastern European parties faced two additional problems. Seventies growth had been funded by Western loans during détente. The result was a soaring foreign debt, exceeding $95 billion by 1988. Of this, Poland accounted for $40 billion; East Germany and Hungary each owed $20 billion.[41] Servicing the debts became a crippling burden as oil prices rose after 1973 and international bankers imposed tougher conditions following the Mexican debt crisis of 1982. Soviet subsidies never matched the soaring energy costs. To buy one million tons of Soviet oil in 1974, Hungary had to sell eight hundred Ikarus buses; by the mid-1980s the price was over four thousand buses.[42] As debt servicing absorbed most of export revenues, so less was available for Western capital goods to modernize industry and Western consumer goods to placate the masses.

This economic openness to the West was a critical factor. Had the Soviet bloc remained a closed system based on coal, steel, and heavy industry, it might have staggered on. But insulation was impossible. Committed to competition with the West, it was falling further behind as North America and Western Europe transcended their crisis of capitalism by cutting heavy industry, expanding services, and developing new technologies. As we have seen, that restructuring caused high unemployment and was politically contentious. But by the mid-1980s, it was well underway. Communism now had to face the same structural problems of outdated heavy industry in a globalizing market, within a system far more ossified in its command management and heavy-metal ideology.[43]

Politically, the East European governments faced similar problems to the CPSU. Most had septuagenarian leaders who had been around for years: János Kádár in Hungary and Todor Zhivkov in Bulgaria had come to power in the mid-1950s, Erich Honecker had ruled East Germany since 1971. Parties had lost not only the intelligentsia but also the new middle class created by urbanization and education over previous decades. They had certainly lost the young, who expressed their alienation via rock music or in protests against the appalling industrial pollution. What made things harder for the authorities was that a certain level of dissent had to be tolerated under the Helsinki accords of 1975 (see Chapter 10). Organizations such as Solidarity in Poland or Charter 77 in Czechoslovakia were the price to be paid for détente and Western loans. Worse still, the Iron Curtain was no barrier to the air waves that carried Western radio and TV across central Europe. The BBC, Voice of America, Deutsche Welle and especially Radio Free Europe were all widely heard in the East. Most of the GDR could receive West German TV, likewise Austrian TV in Hungary; the Czechs could watch programs from both. By the 1980s, TV ownership was general, and official jamming had become another casualty of détente.[44] The words and images of these programs, not to mention the commercials, delivered a damning verdict on the communist system. This was reinforced firsthand for some, especially Poles and Hungarians, by travel in the West.

But the push from the east was as vital as the pull from the West. The Soviet buzzwords *glasnost, perestroika,* and *demokratizatsiya* had entered East European lexicons by 1987–1978. "New thinking" in Soviet diplomacy and the shift to "defensive sufficiency" also had implications for the Warsaw Pact. Particularly potent was the concept of a "common European home," a term from the Brezhnev era now given new meaning. In April 1987, speaking, significantly, in Prague, Gorbachev used de Gaulle's phrase about Europe "from the Atlantic to the Urals" and said that the "common European home" entailed "recognition of a certain integrity [wholeness], although the countries involved belong to different social systems and are members of opposing military and political blocs."[45] That November he declared that "unity does not mean uniformity" and that "there is no model of socialism to be imitated by all."[46]

The new openness sounded like an abandonment of the policy of "socialist internationalism"—what the West called the Brezhnev Doctrine—under which the suppression of democracy in Czechoslovakia had been justified in 1968. Matching actions to words, in April 1988, the USSR signed the Geneva accords for a full withdrawal from Afghanistan. The withdrawal was completed on schedule the following February. In nine years of fighting, fifteen thousand Soviet troops and perhaps one million Afghans had died. The costs of the war and the domestic backlash were the main reasons for Gorbachev's U-turn, which was endorsed in principle in the Politburo back in 1985–1986. But it was also clear that, without withdrawal, few in the West would believe that the Brezhnev Doctrine was no longer official dogma.[47]

Some of Gorbachev's aides even claim that the Brezhnev Doctrine had received its "death blow" at his very first talk with Warsaw Pact leaders in March 1985.[48] But this is too simple. The issue was political dynamite in Moscow and, until July 1989, Gorbachev's statements were double edged. He was not offering total freedom of choice to the peoples of Eastern Europe but extending more autonomy to their communist leaders about what form of socialism should take.[49] And whatever Gorbachev said, the past spoke louder than his words. It was, after all, Khrushchev who had popularized the idea of "many roads to socialism"—and then sent the tanks into Budapest in 1956. Even in late 1988, informed Western analysts such as Jacques Rupnik found "little reason to believe that, with or without Gorbachev, the Soviet Union would behave any differently from how it has in the past."[50]

These uncertainties explain the tortuous progress of reform in Eastern Europe: the red light had clearly changed, but it seemed to be at amber and not green. In any case, an ironic paradox was embedded in the new thinking: leaving East European leaders to themselves meant they could not be forced to reform. Thus, what mattered initially was the debate within communist parties. Only when cracks opened at the top could pressures explode from below. That is why Poland and Hungary were so important. Their (contrasting) reforms in 1988–1989 set an example for the rest of the bloc.

In Poland, martial law in 1981–1983 (see Chapter 13) had solved nothing. Thanks to years of strife, the economy was the worst in the bloc. That meant shortages of the most basic daily goods such as meat, milk, and toilet paper. When the Jaruzelski government tried to impose price rises, Solidarity was still capable of bringing out the workers in mass strikes in May and August 1988. It seemed like the deadlock of 1981 all over again, except that the option of martial law was now impossible in the Gorbachev era. Solidarity ended the strikes only when promised round-table talks without preconditions.

It took Jaruzelski several months, including the threat of resignation, to bring party hard-liners around. Talks finally began in February 1989 in the Radziwill Palace (where the Warsaw Pact had been signed in 1955). Pictures of the huge round table were beamed by TV across the country and the bloc, becoming a symbol and an inspiration. Over the next two months, a compromise was hammered out whereby Solidarity would be legalized and elections would be held in June. In a revived upper house, or Senate, all seats could be contested, but 65 percent of seats in the lower house, the Sejm, were reserved for the communist party and its allies.

These were hardly free elections. Like those offered in the USSR in 1989, the aim was to secure support for communist-led reform. The government still dominated the media, and Solidary was a loose coalition of unions, not a political party. But even more resoundingly than in the USSR, the government's strategy backfired. In the first round, on June 4, Solidarity won ninety-two of the one hundred Senate seats and all but one of the 161 free seats in the Sejm. In the second round two weeks later, Solidarity increased its Senate tally to ninety-nine. Some of its leaders preached caution. It was unclear whether Moscow would acquiesce and, in any case, the Polish communist party still controlled the bureaucracy, the security forces, and a parliamentary majority. But Wałęsa was persuaded by others, notably the intellectual Adam Michnik, that Solidarity should bid for power by detaching the communists' allies, the Peasant and Democrat parties. This prevented the communists from forming a government, and in August Jaruzelski accepted Tadeusz Mazowiecki of Solidarity as prime minister. Mazowiecki formed a carefully crafted coalition. To avoid antagonising Moscow, communists were given the sensitive defense and interior portfolios; Solidarity leaders, to the anger of radicals, ensured that Jaruzelski was elected president. But the symbolism was clear. By election and negotiation, Poland had contrived Eastern Europe's first noncommunist government since the Czech coup of 1948.[51]

Hungary's democratic transition was also negotiated, but in a very different way.[52] Though the New Economic Mechanism (see Chapter 5) had stalled in the 1970s, it permitted a thriving private economy that, if not generating prosperity for the country's ten million people, at least avoided Polish-style shortages. Politically, Hungary was also the most open East European society. In 1985, the parliamentary elections offered voters a choice of two candidates for each seat. Both were party approved, but this introduced more of the educated middle class to national politics and ventilated provincial anger about services, infrastructure, and pollution. Such safety valves avoided a Solidarity-style explosion.

Hungary's crisis therefore developed within the ruling party. At first it centered on the challenge to the ailing first secretary János Kádár (born 1912) from younger leaders, born in the early 1930s. In June 1987, in the deepening economic crisis, Kádár appointed a new prime minister, Károly Grósz, the Budapest party boss. He became the focus for anti-Kadar reformers, of whom Imre Poszgay was the most important. Both men combined against Kádár, using Soviet perestroika as justification. At a special party conference in May 1988, the old leader was finally pushed aside and Grósz became general secretary. That autumn, the new government began limited market reforms and legalized other political groups.

But the party soon split again. Whereas Grósz sought a "controlled division of power" with noncommunists, provided they accepted "socialism" as the dominant ideological paradigm, Poszgay believed that only radical surgery could save the party. Not merely did this mean relinquishing its "leading role" but also acknowledging its betrayal of the people in 1956. As in the USSR, history was a potent weapon in Hungarian glasnost. In February 1989, the Central Committee reluctantly accepted the judgment of a historical commission, headed by Poszgay, that 1956 was a "popular rising" and not a "counterrevolution." This paved the way for rehabilitating Imre Nagy, Hungary's reformist leader in 1956 who had been executed by the Russians with Kádár's complicity. On June 16, 1989, Nagy's body was reburied with honor, after a ceremony watched in person by two hundred fifty thousand people and by millions more on television. Three days earlier, a National Round Table began its work, encouraged by the Polish example. On September 18, agreement was reached for multiparty elections the following spring.

Strife-ridden Poland, semicapitalist Hungary, but surely not Moscow's Germany? The GDR was described by one British textbook in 1988 as "apparently one of the world's most stable regimes."[53] Although hardly luxurious, living standards were the best in the bloc, with none of Poland's shortages of basic goods. In June 1989 it was officially estimated that there were only two thousand five hundred "hostile, oppositional or other negative forces" in the country.[54] Whereas the Polish Catholic church was a bastion of opposition, German Protestants had been allowed religious freedom in return for political quiescence. Even more important in controlling dissent was the state security police, the Stasi. Through official employees and paid informers it kept files on over a third of the GDR's sixteen million people, tapping phone calls and sampling the mail. It even kept a museum of "smell jars" (containing rags wiped around chairs on which suspects had sweated through interrogation) in case dogs were needed to hunt them down.[55]

Beneath the surface, as is now clear, the GDR did face serious problems. The churches provided both foci and meeting places for small but significant protest groups during the 1980s on issues such as nuclear weapons and the environment. These embryonic networks became the basis of opposition politics in 1989. Local elections in May, in which the SED claimed 98.85 percent of the vote, caused real anger, coming as they did after the multicandidate polls in the USSR. Even worse, by this time the country had accumulated a foreign debt of $26.5 billion, whose servicing alone cost over 60 percent of export earnings.[56] Only the willingness of the Federal Republic to provide credits in the early 1980s had saved the GDR from the debt crises of its neighbors.

Yet these pressures for change were largely hidden from Western observers, and none, in itself, would have caused the system to self-destruct so quickly. The catalyst for change in the GDR came from outside—from Hungary.

On May 2, 1989, world TV cameras were invited to watch as Hungarian soldiers rolled up the wire across the border with Austria. This was part of the Grósz government's policy of improving its image in the West. Removing the Iron Curtain was intended to be largely symbolic: Hungarians had been able to travel freely into Austria for years, and the government had protocols with other East bloc countries whereby illegal migrants would be deported home. But East Germans were a unique case: unlike, say, Czechs or Poles, they were legally West German citizens—if they could make it to the Federal Republic. That summer, thousands were willing to try: driving their cars to the Hungarian border and then making a dash for Austria, or camping out in the grounds of the West German embassy in Budapest to demand asylum. Hundreds more converged on the embassy in Prague.

Faced with a serious humanitarian crisis, the Bonn government took action. On September 11, Hungary dropped all its restrictions on GDR migrants. This action followed a meeting with West German Chancellor Helmut Kohl just over two weeks before at which the FRG agreed to a credit of one billion Deutsche marks. Afterward the Hungarian foreign minister, Gyula Horn, was told by a colleague that "of the two German states we are choosing the West German." No, replied Horn, "we are choosing *Europe*."[57]

The refugee drama was played out on world television, much of it watched within the GDR. These TV pictures profoundly affected both regime and citizenry. At the top, it made possible organized criticism of the party leader, Erich Honecker, whose ability to rule had already been called into question by his prolonged absence from early July to late September because of surgery for gallstones. On his return, he cracked down by closing all the GDR's borders. But by then, thirty thousand had fled via Hungary and another fourteen thousand through Czechoslovakia. In the whole of the previous year, 1988, the GDR had permitted only twenty-nine thousand legal migrants.[58]

Once East Germany's fortieth-birthday celebrations on October 7 had passed, Politburo critics came out into the open. On October 18 Honecker was forced to surrender the party leadership. His successor was Egon Krenz, twenty-five years younger, who cast himself as a Gorbachev-style reformer. But it was too late. The televised emigration crisis had also mobilized the people, with rallies and meetings in many cities and towns. The biggest occurred in the city of Leipzig, which was ravaged by pollution and denied the face-saving money pumped into Berlin.[59] Meanwhile, the language of protest was changing. Freedom of travel remained the most important demand but the cries of "We want out" (Wir wollen raus) now mingled with "We're staying here" (Wir bleiben hier). The embryo opposition also gave birth politically. On September 13, the founding summons of New Forum, for dialogue and restructuring within a socialist state, acted as stimulus for a series of neighborhood and professional groups. By the end of the month an East German Social Democratic Party had been formed. "We are the people" (Wir sind das Volk) became the shorthand for a new social contract between rulers and ruled.

In early July, Gorbachev had stated unequivocally, "What the Poles and Hungarians decide is their affair, but we will respect their decision whatever it is."[60] The Brezhnev Doctrine had now been repudiated, and the Soviet press spokesman, Gennadi Gerasimov, coined the term "Sinatra Doctrine" in its place. Citing the Frank Sinatra song "My Way," he claimed that "Hungary and Poland are doing it their way."[61] But Gorbachev still set limits, particularly in Germany. Having made clear his disapproval of Honecker during a visit in October, he saw Krenz as a belated chance to reform the GDR. While acknowledging that German unification might occur decades in the future, Gorbachev told Krenz on November 1 that this was "not a problem in current politics."[62]

Eight days later, however, the Berlin wall crumbled before people power. That was certainly not the intention of the Krenz government. It was gambling that promises of greater freedom of movement would allay popular discontent. Its new travel plan still required visas, and designated Berlin only as an exit point for permanent emigrants. And although the draft law said that the changes would take place "immediately," this meant "once the law had been approved" by the Volkskammer, the GDR parliament. But when asked about the proposals at a press conference on the evening of November 9, Günter Schabowski, a Berlin party official who had not actually attended the meeting, garbled the details and baldly stated that the new law would take effect "immediately." As confused reports of the press conference spread via East and West German media, excited Berliners flocked to the wall that Thursday evening, pressing against border guards and insisting that they now had the right to cross. The guards, massively outnumbered and bereft of official instructions, knew the crowds could not be held back by force. The barriers were lifted, and East Berliners flooded into the West.[63]

Most flocked back later that night, having enjoyed a night on the town in West Berlin, and two or three million more came as weekend tourists. They spent their time enjoying the freebies on offer—riding the subway or going to soccer matches—or using their "welcome money" from the West German government to purchase scarcities like bananas or to eat hamburgers in McDonald's. At Checkpoint Charlie, where U.S. and Soviet tanks faced off in 1961, Mstislav Rostropovich, himself an exile from Soviet communism, entertained crowds with Bach cello sonatas. Others danced on the wall, harassed now by nothing worse than GDR water cannon aimed far above their heads. Soon they were chipping holes in the masonry.

Krenz insisted that there had only been a clerical error: because of Schabowski, the wall had merely opened a day early.[64] But his intentions had been very different: an announcement of future reforms to pacify discontent while he constructed a new Council of Ministers. Instead, "one of the most colossal administrative blunders in the long history of public bureaucracy,"[65] aggravated by the multiplier effect of the media, had allowed Berliners to breach the wall, the preeminent symbol of the Iron Curtain. And, as an American observer noted a week later, in East Berlin "the idea has spread that in conquering the Wall the people seized power."[66] The GDR regime never recovered. The Volkskammer began a special session on November 13. No longer a rubber-stamp body, it elected an independent speaker, scrapped censorship, and launched an inquiry into SED corruption. When the press exposed the party's business empire and TV cameras penetrated its luxurious Wandlitz compound, the Communist party lost all credibility. The whole Politburo resigned on December 3, and a new leadership began round-table talks with opposition groups. These paved the way for elections in March 1990.

The abrupt collapse of the SED's power had literally been an "exit from communism." Unlike other alienated East Europeans, East Germans had somewhere else to go, being rightful West German citizens. In the GDR, the "pull" factor mattered as much as the "push." Watching some 2 percent of the population go West during 1989 also had a devastating effect on SED leaders. Many had persuaded themselves that the GDR was the best in the bloc and, as Schabowski put it later, this "desertion by thousands and thousands of our people day by day" produced a sense of "humiliation" and even "terror."[67] In explaining the failure to use force, the SED's own loss of will mattered as much as the demise of the Brezhnev Doctrine.

Poland, Hungary, and East Germany were the critical dominos. Once they fell, Bulgaria, Czechoslovakia, and Romania soon followed.

On November 10, 1989—the day after the Berlin wall was breached—Todor Zhivkov was forced to resign as first secretary of the Bulgarian Communist Party. He had been in power for over thirty-five years, making this former printer's apprentice the longest-serving ruler in Bulgarian history. Although Bulgaria had seen considerable turbulence in 1989, especially mass deportations of the Turkish minority and politically motivated protest by the environmental organization Ecoglasnost, his fall was largely the result of a palace coup by younger party leaders. Despite multiparty elections in 1990, the former communists remained in control of government until the autumn of 1991.[68]

Czechoslovakia was also emboldened by the German example, but here the effects were farther reaching. For most of the 1980s, the country still stifled under the "normalization" imposed by Moscow after the "Prague Spring" of 1968 (see Chapter 5). Its chosen instrument, Gustáv Husák, remained in power till December 1987, just before his seventy-fifth birthday, but the new party secretary, Miloš Jakeš, was only a decade younger and scarcely less hard line. Among the leadership, there was no Hungarian-style pressure for reform; across the country, no mass movement analogous to Solidarity. The Communist party therefore remained secure through the summer of 1989. It was the collapse of the GDR, played out around the West German embassy in Prague and on the TV screens of Czechs tuned into the West, that proved the spark for people power. Even so, the revolution would not have happened so fast but for the network of dissident groups in Prague, many of them rooted in the Charter 77 human rights organization headed by the playwright Václav Havel. As communism crumbled, they were ready to pick up the pieces and build a new polity.[69]

In the midst of what Havel called Prague's "Velvet Revolution," Timothy Garton Ash, a British commentator, joked, "In Poland it took ten years, in Hungary ten months, in East Germany ten weeks: perhaps in Czechoslovakia it will take ten days!"[70] He underestimated by two weeks but even so, the pace of events was breathtaking. Yet on day one, Friday, November 17, revolution looked unlikely and velvet revolution impossible, as security police used force to break up a peaceful protest march into the center of Prague.

Several hundred were injured; reports suggested, erroneously, that one demonstrator had died. On November 19, emboldened by people power in East Germany, Civic Forum was established in Prague under Havel's leadership to serve as an umbrella for opposition groups seeking dialogue with the government. Universities and schools closed and young people worked around the clock with pen and ink, typewriters and carbon paper, to spread word of Black Friday. (Photocopiers were still almost as carefully guarded as nuclear weapons—because knowledge was power.)

Mass demonstrations now became a daily event in Prague. On November 24, Jakeš and several of the old guard were removed by a panicky leadership, and Alexander Dubček, the leader during the Prague Spring of 1968, joined Havel to greet crowds from a balcony above Wenceslas Square. Posters developed the iconography of 89 as 68 turned upside down. The opposition called a lunchtime general strike on November 27. Czechoslovak TV, now wriggling free of the state, gave it live coverage. It was estimated that 38 percent of the population stopped work and that around three-quarters marked the event in some way.[71]

The effect on the party leadership was devastating. On the 29th, its leading role was officially abolished, and a coalition government was formed on December 10. One week later, the border wire with Austria was ceremonially cut. After mollifying Slovaks by making Dubček the chairman of the Federal Assembly, Havel was unanimously elected by it as president on December 29. For a man who had been in and out of prison for more than a decade, it was an amazing transformation. In 1983, he told a French reporter, "I am not, never have been, and have not the slightest intention of becoming, a politician."[72] Now, aged fifty-three, he had the task of guiding his country toward democratic elections.

The year of revolutions ended in Romania, with the Christmas executions of Nicolae Ceaușescu and his wife, Elena, who had ruled the country as a dynastic despotism since 1965.

Ceaușescu had broken with Moscow long before, ostensibly over the invasion of Czechoslovakia, in reality over the Kremlin's plans to keep Romania as an agrarian colony. Like Tito, he then secured his independence by aid and credits from Western governments, which also lavished on him their highest honors—a knighthood from Queen Elizabeth and the *Légion d'honneur* from Giscard d'Estaing, not to mention honorary citizenship of Disneyland. At home, however, Ceaușescu was an unreconstructed Stalinist: the text of his last national plan was over 130 feet long and covered one thousand eight hundred products. He pushed on with the heavy industrialization of Romania at an appalling cost in pollution: by 1989, it is now estimated, 40 percent of his twenty-three million people suffered from chronic bronchial or chest disorders.[73] To pay off the country's Western debt in the

1980s, he squeezed imports and boosted exports: bread was rationed, virtually all meat except offal was sold abroad, light and heat were rationed, and TV transmission was reduced to two hours a day—half of it Ceaușescu. In his own version of the edifice complex, he cleared the old quarter of Bucharest to build his palatial Casa Republicii—a complex smaller only than the Pentagon and which could have accommodated Buckingham Palace comfortably in its underground parking garage.[74]

In the combustible atmosphere of 1989, Romania's spark came from the western region of Transylvania. Here the Hungarian minority (some 8 percent of the population) had been persecuted for years under Ceaușescu's Romanian nationalist policies. In 1988 they were prime targets of his new program of rural collectivization, involving forced resettlement and destruction of homes. At least one hundred thousand fled to refugee camps across the Hungarian border.[75] Grass-roots opposition was led by László Tökés, a Calvinist pastor in the city of Timošoara, who made collectivization a rallying point for Hungarians and Romanians alike. Finally, on December 16, 1989, the authorities imposed a deportation order on him. The next day, the streets of Timošoara were cleared by the army and the country's brutal secret police, the Securitate.

What followed was, perhaps, 1989's supreme example of the multiplier effect of the mass media. Across Romania, the news of communism's collapse elsewhere had been heard on foreign radio stations and glimpsed on Bulgarian, Hungarian, and Yugoslav TV. By this roundabout route, reports of events in Timošoara on December 16–17 were disseminated, bringing out even larger demonstrations in the city on December 20 and prompting new protests elsewhere. Responding, Ceaușescu delivered a major televised speech on the morning of December 21 to a picked crowd in Palace Square in Bucharest. But over the staged applause came shouts of "Timošoara" and "murderer" from corners of the crowd. Ceaușescu stopped, bewildered, and then retreated from the balcony into the Central Committee building. Although he resumed some minutes later, the vulnerability of the dictator had suddenly been shown on TV to all his subjects. It remains a matter of controversy whether the protests were spontaneous or fomented by dissident elements within the party and army. But, even if the latter is true, the plotting was more consequence than cause of the popular turmoil. As crowds broke into the lower floors of the Central Committee building on the twenty-second, the codictators lifted off from the roof in a helicopter weighed down with booty. By 1:00 P.M. students had taken over the radio station and proclaimed that Romania was free. Across the country, crowds poured onto the streets, ransacking party offices. Meanwhile, the helicopter pilot had persuaded the Ceaușescus that they were too vulnerable a target. They highjacked a car at gunpoint and continued their flight until caught by militia.

By now communist veterans and elements of the army and Securitate had hastily announced formation of a National Salvation Front (NSF) under the leadership of Ion Iliescu. On Christmas Eve, the NSF abandoned its original plan for a formal trial of the Ceaușescus, on the grounds that a quick end would discourage further loyalist resistance. Although the total death toll was probably seven hundred to one thousand, radio reports at the time suggested much higher figures. The NSF leaders also found it politically convenient to make the pair scapegoats for a system in which they too were deeply implicated. The result was therefore "pseudo-judicial murder"[76]—a hasty show trial followed by summary execution while most of the Western world was enjoying its Christmas dinner. Edited highlights were aired next day on Romanian television, and, as part of the new anticult, viewers were shown her diamond-studded shoes and his choice of six dinner menus on a TV tour through many of the family's eighty-four separate residences.

The NSF leaders had therefore adroitly commandeered the popular bandwagon to save themselves and their system.[77] Collectivization and rationing were duly scrapped, and the NSF surged to victory in elections in May 1990. But Romania was "still a facade democracy."[78] The same could be said of most of Eastern Europe. Despite a heady year of TV revolutions, exit from communism had only just begun. And, as we shall see in the next chapter, markets and democracy proved no panaceas.

German Unification and European Union

The events of 1989 also reordered geopolitics. Over the next two years the map of Europe was redrawn more radically than at any time since the end of World War I. October 1990 saw the two German states become one. In December 1991 the European Community committed itself to fuller union, including a single currency by the end of the decade. That same month, the Soviet Union disintegrated into fifteen separate states. These three related developments established the framework for post–cold war Europe as it neared the millennium.

In retrospect, the unification of Germany° seems an inevitable outcome of the events of 1989, but this was far from clear at the time. Both the pace and the peacefulness of German unification were remarkable. This was due above all to the speedy collapse of the GDR state and the will of East Ger-

---

°Diplomats were careful to avoid the term "reunification" lest they imply that Germany wished to regain its 1937 borders, which included territory now in Polish hands (Map 7).

man people. But the West German government seized the initiative adroitly, backed by Washington and, most astonishing, not blocked to any real degree by Moscow.

In Bonn, the lead actor was Helmut Kohl, the Christian Democratic chancellor since 1982, who was often derided as an unsophisticated provincial trencherman. "I make my living by being underestimated," he joked in November 1989.[79] Kohl was a Rhinelander with Adenauer's belief in the importance of Franco-German rapprochement, but he shared the gut feeling of many Germans of his generation (he was born in 1930) that the division of their country was unnatural. His wife had come from the East; likewise Hans-Dietrich Genscher, the Free Democratic leader and foreign minister in Kohl's coalition, who had fled his native Halle in 1952. But similar instincts could not conceal tactical differences between Kohl and Genscher; nor did coalition compacts preclude partisan rivalry. Anxious to capture the high ground for the CDU, Kohl was the first to come out with a policy on the GDR, announcing a ten-point plan for "confederal structures" and eventual "state unity" on November 28, 1989. But even Kohl was at this stage imagining unity in five to ten years.[80] And Paris and London were deeply disturbed at the whole idea. François Mitterrand told Margaret Thatcher that it could be like Munich in 1938 if their two countries did not stand up to Germany.[81]

What changed these calculations was the collapse of the GDR. Many of the East German intellectuals and churchmen who led the opposition in the autumn of 1989 favored a reformed socialism in a reformed GDR. In November 1989 polls suggested that 86 percent of the population also wanted a "third way" between capitalism and communism, but by the February 1990 the proportion had dropped to 56 percent, and nearly a third endorsed capitalism.[82] Many agreed with a prominent West German industrialist who declared that the third way would prove "the way to the Third World."[83] Increasingly, *Wir sind ein Volk* (we are one people) replaced *Wir sind das Volk* (we are the people) as the most popular marching chant. As the idea of unity gained in popularity, the GDR state was falling apart. Output had collapsed, the debt crisis was acute, and people were now leaving in droves—129,000 in December, another seventy-three thousand in January.[84] On January 15, angry crowds occupied the Stasi headquarters, exposing the new impotence of the communist party, and Prime Minister Hans Modrow formed a nonparty coalition prior to elections in March.

In response to the GDR crisis, Kohl's thinking evolved rapidly. He secured support from his coalition partners for an immediate offer of currency union on the grounds that "if the DM [Deutschmark] doesn't come to Leipzig, then the Leipzigers will come to the DM."[85] This offer was made on February 6. Four days later, in Moscow, Gorbachev indicated to Kohl that it was up to the two German states to decide whether, when, and how unification would occur. And on February 13, at a NATO meeting in Ottawa, a framework was agreed for great-power involvement in unification talks. The so-called 2 + 4 formula (the two Germanys plus the four postwar occupying powers: the USA, the USSR, Britain, and France) had emerged from Washington and Moscow. Bonn agreed, as long as it was 2 + 4 and not 4 + 2—in other words, provided the Germans took the lead. When NATO allies like Italy complained about being sidelined, Genscher told them sharply, "You are not part of the game."[86]

Even with these initiatives and agreements, unification would have been much more complex and protracted but for the surprise result of the East German elections on March 18. Although the ex-communists were now a discredited remnant, it was widely expected that the new Social Democratic Party would come out on top. They favored gradual negotiations between two equal states, whereas Kohl now wanted rapid absorption of East Germany into the Federal Republic—what critics punningly dubbed *Kohlonization*. In the last few weeks of the campaign, Kohl made six personal appearances in the GDR, heard live by some one million people. His "Alliance for Germany," forged with two minor parties, picked up 48 percent of the vote, more than double the count for the SPD. "The March 18 vote ended the East German revolution."[87]

Kohl now began negotiating currency union with the new East German coalition. A treaty was signed in May 1990, and currency union took effect on July 1, after six thousand tons of banknotes and five hundred tons of coins had been distributed to ten thousand local offices across the GDR. Bonn economists and the semi-independent Bundesbank would have preferred a gradual process—one senior advisor likened rapid economic integration to trying "to climb the Eiger north face in winter"—but they were overruled.[88] Nor were they successful in arguing for a realistic exchange rate for the GDR DM, whose purchasing power was roughly a quarter of its West German counterpart. East Germans insisted that "a mark is a mark," and Kohl agreed. For him, economics were subordinate to politics: what mattered was to keep East Germans in the east by a rapid and beneficial currency union. (Kohl was mindful that currency revaluations in 1924 and 1948 had decimated the savings of millions.) The CDU also dismissed warnings of the costs of unification, with Kohl personally promising "no new taxes".[89] The chancellor had a keen sense that he had to seize the historic opportunity for unification, often repeating the adage, "We must get the hay into the barn before the storm."[90] He feared that the GDR could soon disintegrate completely and that the favorable mood in Moscow might prove ephemeral. He was also conscious that 1.5 million nuclear-armed troops of NATO and the Warsaw Pact were still facing off along the inner German border.

The 2 + 4 process was therefore extremely important in managing such breathtaking change. In these talks, which began in early May 1990, two major issues emerged. The first was Poland's western border, established by the Allies in 1945 at the expense of German territory and accepted by the Bonn government in the treaty of 1970. But Kohl, sensitive to the many exiles and their families in the CDU, refused to prejudge the attitude of a future all-German government, even though Poles like Adam Michnik warned, "Any attempt to change this border simply means war."[91] Slowly Kohl responded to pressure from his allies and from Genscher. In late June the FRG and GDR parliaments both promised to affirm the border in perpetuity through a new treaty.

The other big issue was the question of Germany's membership in NATO. This was anathema to many conservatives in the Soviet armed forces and foreign ministry: Moscow's policy since 1945 had been predicated on the possible threat posed by a revived Germany. At times in the spring, Shevardnadze returned to Stalin's formulation of 1952: Germany could unify provided it was neutral. But, when he met Bush at the end of May, Gorbachev effectively acknowledged Germany's right to choose its alliance, winning in return Bush's signature to a new trade agreement. And when Kohl visited in Russia in mid-July, the two leaders tied up the details, including a cap of 370,000 on Germany's armed forces, reaffirmation that Germany would not be a nuclear power, and arrangements for the phased removal of Soviet troops. Under heavy pressure from Gorbachev in September, Kohl doubled the amount of German aid to ease the transition, ending up with a figure of DM12 billion for the troop removal and DM3 billion in interest-free loans.

On September 12, the four powers signed away their residual rights in Germany affirming the arrangements Kohl and Gorbachev had thrashed out. On the 27th, the treaty of union between the two Germanys was concluded. As critics claimed, the West largely absorbed the East, though some issues had been hard fought: for instance, abortion was more liberal in the GDR than in the Catholic-influenced FRG, and it was agreed that, for the moment, local abortion laws would still apply. On October 2, the East German parliament dissolved itself; the GDR flag was stripped unceremoniously from public buildings. At midnight, amid fireworks and celebration, the united Germany was born with a jubilant Kohl mixing with huge crowds around the still-ruined Reichstag. Two months later, on December 2, in the first all-German election since 1932, he won a smashing victory as "Chancellor for Germany." For a leader who was trailing in the polls in the spring, it was a spectacular end to an amazing year.

Although this dénouement was largely the outcome of the GDR's self-destruction and Kohl's political agility, it could not have happened without

American support. Unlike many of his predecessors, let alone Margaret Thatcher, President Bush was not interested in history and had few hang-ups about German revanchism. So-called lessons of 1914 or 1939 seemed to him irrelevant in 1989: "[W]e don't fear the ghosts of the past; Margaret does," he told Kohl.[92] Without the support of Bush and his advisers for the unification process, Kohl could not have achieved his goals.

To a large extent the combination of the GDR collapse and U.S. support for Kohl's policy created a *fait accompli* for Gorbachev. "I fear the train has already left," he would say to skeptical advisers.[93] But it remains puzzling that he did not set tough conditions at an early stage, for example when meeting Kohl in February 1990. In part, this was because, like everyone else, he was surprised by the quick collapse of the GDR state and by the CDU victory in March 1990. But at a deeper level, he was trapped by the logic of his own "new thinking," which made it hard to justify stopping Germans doing things "their way." In addition, by 1990, Germany, however perturbing, was less important than the economic crisis at home, and Gorbachev saw the German settlement as a quid pro quo to extract economic aid. Shevardnadze was left to take most of the flak from domestic critics.[94] Gorbachev's strategy worked in 1990 but, as we shall see, resentment at the German "sellout" provoked a backlash during 1991.

France and Britain shared Soviet doubts about speedy unification but they were more easily shunted aside by the Kohl-Bush express. Thatcher's influence over Reagan was a thing of the past: her relationship with Bush was cooler, as the president made clear in May 1989 when he spoke of the West Germans as America's "partners in leadership." Thatcher had hoped to build an axis with Mitterrand but found, to quote her memoirs, that he would not "match private words with public deeds" and ultimately sided with Bonn.[95] Mitterrand had expected Moscow to block German unification—"I have no need to oppose it, the Soviets will do that for me," he observed privately in November 1989—and was therefore irate when Gorbachev later "surrendered on everything."[96]

But, at root, there was a fundamental difference of tactics between Thatcher and Mitterrand. She was a practitioner of traditional balance-of-power politics, who found in 1990 that she lacked power abroad—or even at home, where she was pushed out of the premiership by party opponents in November. Mitterrand, in contrast, resorted to the policy of successive French governments toward Germany: "If you can't beat them, join them." New initiatives in European integration were intimately bound up with the German settlement of 1990, and it is to these that we must now turn.

Renewed integration in Europe had several dimensions—military, economic, and political. Most visible in 1990 were changes in the two armed alliances that had divided Europe for four decades. At its summit in London in July 1990, NATO announced that "nuclear forces were truly weapons of last resort and that the Alliance would adopt a lower-profile, defensive strategy.[97] In November 1990, members of the two alliances signed a treaty on conventional forces in Europe that affirmed that they were "no longer adversaries" and welcomed "the end of the era of division and confrontation."[98] It also agreed to new and equal force levels in Europe, such as twenty thousand tanks and six thousand eight hundred combat aircraft. Most of the cuts were to fall on the Warsaw Pact (though these were partly evaded by pre-emptive withdrawals east of the Urals).

By this time, however, the Warsaw Pact was in terminal decline. The new Czech and Hungarian governments had quickly begun talks to remove the hated Soviet troops; Poland followed, albeit more slowly because of countervailing fears of German expansion. Gorbachev had hoped to turn the pact into an alliance of equals "formed on a democratic basis," but the burden of history was too heavy.[99] In March 1991, the Warsaw Pact was wound up; in November NATO offered its former members involvement in a new North Atlantic Cooperation Council. This established a framework for the enlargement of NATO later in the 1990s.

Contrary to some predictions in 1989, therefore, NATO remained one of two basic institutions for Europe in the 1990s. The other was the European Community, whose reform was also intimately connected with the end of the cold war. The decisive event for the EC was the Treaty of Maastricht in December 1991. This was the result of two intergovernmental conferences (IGCs) in 1990–1991—on monetary union and on political union. The treaty was the most important institutional reform of the EC since its founding in 1957.

Monetary union grew directly from previous community initiatives. The commission, energized by its French president, Jacques Delors, was keen to build on the commitment to a single market by the end of 1992, which had been agreed to back in 1985 (see Chapter 13). For Delors, the Single European Act (SEA) was part of a "Russian dolls" strategy: member states would accept one policy, only to find others contained within it.[100] Delors believed that a single market would force the EC toward a single currency, and also to greater workers' rights in order to balance the new opportunities for business. His insistence that the EC must develop a "social dimension" won wide support from continental socialists and from poorer peripheral states such as Ireland, Spain, and Greece, which stood to gain from further transfers of funds. With the support of Kohl and Mitterrand, he secured the chairmanship of a committee of central bankers who reported on monetary union in April 1989. The Delors Report set out proposals for European Monetary Union (EMU). The European Council—the biannual summit of heads of government—agreed to establish an IGC on this when they met in June 1989.

In contrast, ideas about political union were inchoate. For years, the European Parliament had been demanding increased powers to offset the authority of the commission (Brussels bureaucrats) and the member governments. This was termed the "democratic deficit." There was also a case for bringing the growing diplomatic cooperation between member states—European political cooperation (EPC)—within the competence of the EC. The French, in particular, saw this as a first step toward a common security policy independent of the U.S.–led NATO. But it is unlikely that these broad discussions about European political integration would have produced a full-scale intergovernmental conference except for the collapse of the Soviet bloc in late 1989. An effective common foreign policy was made urgent by the prospect of chaos in Eastern Europe and of new applicants banging on the EC's door. The spectre of an enlarged Germany in the center of an undivided Europe also revived the 1950s tactic of using European integration to contain German power.

Despite these prior discussions, monetary and political union came to the top of the EC's agenda mainly because of the Franco-German axis. By late 1989, Kohl was cooling on the concept of monetary union as he foresaw the vast economic problems entailed by German unification. But at the European Council meeting in December 1989, he reaffirmed his commitment to EMU in return for French acceptance of German unification. And in April 1990 Kohl and Mitterrand submitted a joint proposal "to accelerate the political construction of the Europe of the Twelve" through a conference on political union, held in parallel with the one on EMU.[101] Complex discussions followed over the next twenty months before agreement was reached at Maastricht in December 1991. But, broadly, France got monetary union as a way of mitigating the economic power of a triumphant deutschmark. In return, Germany secured further political integration to reassure its neighbors of its peaceful, democratic credentials. As Genscher said in March 1990, quoting a dictum of the novelist Thomas Mann: "We don't want a German Europe but a European Germany."[102]

Although conceding the principle of monetary union, Kohl wanted this to occur on German terms. He was under intense pressure from the Bundesbank, which was already unhappy about the currency union with the GDR. Kohl therefore insisted on a European central bank that would be fully independent of member governments and committed to monetary stability as its prime goal. He also demanded strict criteria for economic convergence before countries could join. The new currency had to be as stable as the DM, which was regarded by many Germans, mindful of the hyperinflation of the early 1920s and the mid-1940s, as the guarantor of their country's postwar economic success. Theo Waigel, the FRG's finance minister, said that EMU would "bring the German currency order to Europe."[103] Bonn also negotiated a longish timetable that was unlikely to produce monetary union before 1999.

The Franco-German bargain was central to Maastricht. But other deals were woven into this web of compromises.[104] Spain led successful pressure from poorer members for enlarged social development funds. Socialists were gratified that workers' rights were enshrined in the "social chapter," and members of the European parliament could look forward to policy "co-determination" with the Commission. Britain also had to be bought off. In October 1990, the British government had finally joined Europe's exchange rate mechanism just before Thatcher was forced out of office. Although her successor, John Major, insisted that he wanted Britain "at the heart of Europe,"[105] he shared her preference for little more than trade cooperation and, in any case, faced a growing body of "Eurosceptics" within his party. Thatcher's trade minister, Nicholas Ridley, had stigmatized monetary union as "a German racket, designed to take over the whole of Europe."[106] At Maastricht, Major agreed not to block the treaty but won two "opt-outs" in return. As a result, Britain did not sign the social chapter and could choose not to join monetary union.

The Maastricht Treaty proved problematic. In retrospect, Delors concluded, "We shouldn't have made a treaty on political union, it was too soon."[107] There was also a popular backlash when the treaty was submitted to member states for ratification. The Danish referendum in June 1992 resulted in a narrow rejection (50.7 percent); only the negotiation of British-style opt-outs enabled the Danish government to secure a 56.8 percent "yes" vote the following May. Even more alarming, the French referendum in September 1992 produced what the media called "un petit oui" of only 51.05 percent. This partly reflected the unpopularity of the socialist government, but, like the Danish vote, it also suggested that political elites had lost touch with popular sentiments about Europe. Because of the Danish problem and a constitutional challenge in Germany, the Maastricht Treaty did not come into force until November 1993, eleven months late, when the various European communities became the European Union. In some respects, it was a "driving mirror Treaty,"[108] codifying *de jure* what had happened *de facto*. But as Delors had hoped, it also looked forward by setting a timetable for monetary union by 1999. This would probably not have happened but for the Franco-German compromise to facilitate German unification.

A united Germany, a reformed NATO, a rejuvenated European Union operating as a single market and committed to a single currency—these were three of the basic structures of post–cold war Europe. The other development, and the most important of all, was that by the end of 1991 the Soviet Union had disintegrated into fifteen independent states.

Soviet Dis-Union

In the second half of 1989, Gorbachev was preoccupied with the disintegration of the Soviet bloc in Eastern Europe. As he turned anew to domestic affairs in 1990, he faced a similar meltdown at home. His aim had been reformed socialism, his tactic to erode the plan and the party by cautious encouragement of markets and political opposition. Perhaps that kind of halfway house was inevitable—Gorbachev needed support from the old order while building the new—but by 1990, it had produced a rickety and unstable structure.

Gorbachev's initial economic policies in 1985–1986 had exacerbated the country's (still secret) budget deficit. He had boosted imports of Western machine tools to help modernize Soviet industry. At the same time, revenues fell dramatically with the antialcohol drive and the collapse of oil and gas prices. The exact scale of the deficit is hard to estimate—even Gorbachev did not know—but the CIA reckoned that it jumped from seventeen billion rubles in 1985 to sixty-four billion in 1987 (roughly equivalent to $100 billion).[109] After 1988, the extra money printed and the loosening of price controls made inflation a serious problem in the USSR for the first time since World War II. The problems were made worse by the new policy in 1987–1988 of a "regulated market economy." The government permitted private cooperatives and allowed state enterprises to sell part of their production in the market. But this encouraged them to produce high-value luxuries and to cut down on basics such as soap, matches, or razor blades. Panicky consumers started stockpiling whatever they could buy. Economic crisis made it politically difficult for Gorbachev to address the root problems of prices and subsidies.[110]

If the economy was floundering between plan and market, the political system was teetering even more precariously between party, state, and democracy.[111] In January 1990, many disparate informal organizations and popular movements came together under the loose umbrella organization Democratic Russia (DemRossiya). In March 1990, the leading role of the CPSU was finally removed from the constitution and a separate USSR presidency established. Gorbachev had moved in this direction in order to loosen the tentacles of the party, but he continued to be party leader as well as state president. Looking back, Gorbachev made two fatal compromises in 1990. Although the presidency would, in future, be elective, he decided not to put himself through an election this time to avoid political turmoil. By 1991 his lack of democratic credentials would prove deeply damaging. Second, Gorbachev did not bring his conflict with conservatives to a head at the twenty-eighth congress in July 1990. Preoccupied with separating state from party—which had vast implications for property, appointments, and military power—he would not risk a total break with conservatives by creating a reformed communist party.[112] Without that, however, he lacked a firm political base by 1991, as power seeped out of his hands.

The economic and political crises came together in a crisis of the Union itself—in 1991 the real break point. Back in 1985, few (and certainly not Gorbachev) envisaged the solvent effects of perestroika and glasnost on the unity of the USSR. Nominally the country was a federation of fifteen separate republics, but there were, even by official criteria, 140 nationalities among its 286 million people.[113] Many had broken away from the tsarist empire after the First World War, only to be forced into the Union by Lenin and Stalin. Thus, the reopening of history under glasnost was as dangerous in parts of the USSR as it was in Eastern Europe. Georgians, for instance, wanted to know about the Russian invasion in 1921; likewise, the Baltic states about the Nazi-Soviet pact in 1939 under which their interwar independence was brought to an end. Perestroika also had national implications because reform implied renewed centralism after the relative autonomy of the Brezhnev years. The first major ethnic disturbances of the Gorbachev era occured in the Kazakh capital, Alma Ata, in December 1986 after the corrupt but Kazakh party boss was replaced by a Russian imposed by Moscow.

This was only the beginning. In many republics, including Russia, one ethnic group dominated several more, and glasnost opened up this problem as well. February 1988 saw the resurgence of a long-running dispute between Christian Armenia and Muslim Azerbaijan over the latter's largely Armenian enclave of Nagorno-Karabakh. Moscow was obliged to impose its own direct rule as violence spilled over into the two rival republics. In April 1989 there were independence riots in Tbilisi, the Georgian capital, in which more than twenty people were killed. In August of that year, on the fiftieth anniversary of the Nazi-Soviet pact, Baltic protestors, abetted by the governments, organized a human chain of over one million people, running some 370 miles across the three republics of Estonia, Latvia, and Lithuania. Freer elections gave nationalist fronts power in all the Baltic states. In March 1990 Lithuania's Supreme Council declared independence. Latvia and Estonia, where Russians constituted about a third of the population, were more cautious, announcing a transitional period before independence. Gorbachev imposed an economic blockade of Lithuania until the government agreed in June to freeze its declaration of independence. Delicate negotiations ensued with all three Baltic states.[114]

Although the Baltic crisis hit the Western headlines, these three states totaled only some eight million people. Less dramatic but far more significant was the political emergence of Russia. Despite denials by Soviet apologists, the USSR was effectively the tsarist Russian empire under new leadership. The Bolsheviks imposed Russian language and practices on the republics and dealt brutally with dissent. Because Russia dominated the Union, most Russians gave little thought to any distinction between the two—much as many Englishmen assumed that Great Britain and the United Kingdom were extensions of England. But the ethnic revival of the late 1980s called Russian assumptions into question. Although the Russian republic covered 80 percent of the Soviet Union, Russians now constituted barely 50 percent of the total population (145 million) compared with three-quarters in the days of Lenin. The nationalist backlash prompted many Russians to argue that they had long been subsidizing the republics, with cheap oil for example, and to express fears for the twenty-five million Russians living in other republics. Demands were also growing for Russia to have its own institutions, previously underdeveloped because of the equation of the Russian republic and the Soviet Union. As Russian nationalism became vocal in the late 1980s, what emerged was a tension between "empire savers" and "nation builders"—those who wanted to hold the Russian-dominated Union together and those who wanted to create a strong Russian state.[115] This tension became personified in the bitter power struggle between Gorbachev and Yeltsin.

Gorbachev began to focus on the national problem only in 1989. In line with his "back to Lenin" philosophy, the government's aim was to "restore . . . the original Leninist principles of a Soviet federation."[116] But, like Lenin's, Gorbachev's concessions to nationalism were essentially tactical; in his mind, the Soviet Union was a synonym for Russia. Yeltsin, by contrast, cultivated Russian nationalism, especially after he gained election as chairman of the republic's new Supreme Soviet in May 1990. The following month, Yeltsin secured legislation giving Russian laws priority over Soviet laws and withholding two-thirds of the USSR's budget.

Yeltsin's use of democracy and nationalism was largely tactical. Unlike Havel or Wałęsa, Yeltsin was an old-style party boss with no dissident background or contacts. Squeezed out of Union politics by Gorbachev in 1987, he needed an alternative platform, which he established by representing himself as a Russian nationalist and a committed democrat. For his part, "Gorbachev underestimated the importance of Russia emerging as a second power base," in the opinion of Alexander Bessmertnyk, Soviet foreign minister for part of 1991. "He was often blinded by his dislike of Yeltsin."[117]

Plan versus market; party versus state; authoritarianism versus democracy; center versus republics; the Union versus Russia; Gorbachev versus Yeltsin: such were the multiple fractures opening up in the USSR by 1990. Most of them were apparent in the controversy over the 500-Day Plan for economic reform touted that summer. The proposal originated with radical economists in the new Russian government, led by Grigory Yavlinsky, who called for immediate privatization and a rapid transition to market economics. But during the autumn, with hard-line opposition mounting, Gorbachev backed away from the idea. Exactly why remains obscure. Was he faced by "a concerted operation" from the military and the KGB? Or was such talk "hysteria" among intellectuals?[118] Whatever the reasons, Gorbachev distanced himself from the reformers, if only to ensure that he still occupied center ground. Over the next few weeks, the shift was palpable.

On November 16, Gorbachev denounced the 500-Day Plan as a threat to the Union. At the end of the month, he appointed a new head of state TV and radio, with a brief to cut off the oxygen of publicity to nationalists, radicals, and especially Yeltsin. On December 2 he sacked his embattled liberal interior minister and replaced him with the hard-line KGB General Boris Pugo. On December 20, his foreign minister, Eduard Shevardnadze, announced his own resignation, warning dramatically that "dictatorship is coming."[119] And on January 13 and 20, 1991, Soviet troops mounted what appear to have been abortive coup attempts to impose hard-line governments in Lithuania and Latvia. Thirteen died in Vilnius, another five in Riga. Domestic and foreign protests were strident. Again, Gorbachev's role remains a matter of debate. Did the military act behind his back, only to be stopped as soon as he knew? Or was he happy to let others do his dirty work to keep hold of the Union?[120] The parallels with August 1991 accentuate the importance of this controversy, but it remains unresolved.

The Baltic crisis became a further weapon in Yeltsin's battle with Gorbachev. The Russian leader gave vocal support to the Baltic states. In February, he even called for Gorbachev's resignation. Yet Yeltsin was under threat at home, with hard-line communist deputies agitating for his dismissal. That spring his main goal was legislation for an elective Russian presidency. Intense picketing by DemRossiya helped swing the vote in the Russian Congress, but equally important was Yeltsin's deal with the breakaway "Communists for Democracy" faction in return for giving their leader, Colonel Alexander Rutskoi, an Afghanistan war hero, the vice-presidential slot on his ticket. As usual, Yeltsin was mixing democratic politics and old-style patronage to gain his ends.

These shifts in the political balance prompted Gorbachev to change tack again. On April 23, 1991, he signed an agreement with the leaders of nine republics, including Yeltsin, to open negotiations on a new Union treaty.° The precise relationship between center and republics was then debated for several months. Meanwhile, Yeltsin's own position was strengthened by his landslide election on June 12 as the Russian president, giving him a democratic

°Staying out were Georgia, Armenia, Moldavia, and the three Baltic states.

legitimacy that Gorbachev conspicuously lacked. Yeltsin now intensified his "war of laws" with the center, successfully insisting that taxes to finance the Union's budget would be established "at rates determined by agreement with the republics."[121] This meant that the new Union of *Sovereign* Socialist Republics would be a loose confederation akin to the United States between 1776 and 1787. The treaty was promulgated in early August for signature on August 20, spurring hard-liners to make their final, desperate move. The key figures were probably Vladimir Kryuchkov, the head of the KGB; Boris Pugo, the interior minister; and Marshal Dmitri Yazov, the defense minister. Anatoly Lukyanov, chairman of the USSR Supreme Soviet, played a shadowy role as éminence grise.

The outline of their putsch is familiar. On August 18, the plotters sealed off Gorbachev in his vacation home in the Crimea. The next day they imposed a state of emergency and brought tanks on to the streets of Moscow, besieging Yeltsin, radical deputies, and their supporters in the "White House," the home of the Russian parliament, on the Moscow river west of the Kremlin. In Leningrad, the democratically elected mayor, Anatoly Sobchak, and masses of protesters also rallied against a military takeover. On the nights of the 19th and the 20th, assaults on the White House seemed imminent, but they did not occur. On August 21, the troops were withdrawn and the coup collapsed. One of the "Gang of Eight"—Pugo—committed suicide. The others were imprisoned, awaiting trial.[122]

The putsch was so badly botched that it has been called a "low comedy."[123] As early as September 2, *Newsweek* was writing of "the Gang of Eight whose B-movie ineptitude already is legendary."[124] It seems likely that the plotters expected Gorbachev to endorse their action: one of them told him in the Crimea, "Nothing is required of you. Stay here. We will do all the dirty work for you."[125] When he refused to cooperate, a coup was hastily arranged, even though the plotters included no obvious alternative leader. Back in October 1964, Nikita Khrushchev had also been isolated in the Crimea and then forced to surrender power. The country simply acquiesced. The plotters of 1991 probably "expected a repeat of 1964, and when that failed to materialize they were lost."[126]

The differences between 1964 and 1991 showed how much Russia had changed in the intervening quarter-century. Yeltsin in Moscow and Sobchak in Leningrad were not merely symbols of defiance. They were also elected representatives, and the people they mobilized were exercising legal rights of peaceful protest. All this showed how far political pluralism had developed in the Gorbachev years. When Khrushchev was removed, only the decision of the Central Committee, rubber-stamped by a parliament of hacks, was needed for legitimacy. Equally important, in 1991 the armed forces were unwilling to use force against their own countrymen, even though the defenses of the White House were scanty. As the air force commander, General Yevgenii Shaposhnikov, remarked later, the armed forces "reflected the immense changes since 1985. That was something that the putschists did not understand."[127]

Most important of all, to quote Yeltsin, "the middle-aged coup plotters simply could not imagine the extent and volume of the information age, which was so new to them." They "were not prepared—especially psychologically—for an atmosphere of complete publicity."[128] In 1964, a news blackout could be imposed on both the country and the world. In 1991, when Yeltsin dictated his denunciation of the coup and his daughters typed up the text early on August 19, his fax machines ensured that within an hour, it was being read in cities across Russia. All the while, CNN and other Western networks were beaming live reports from Moscow. Ordinary citizens, too, could pick up the news from Russian-language services of foreign radio stations. In the Russian parliament itself, an improvised shortwave station, Radio White House, started broadcasting from little more than a broom closet. Cutting this web of modern communications would have required organization and brutality on a scale beyond the plotters. The Soviet Union was no longer susceptible to totalitarian control.

For two days, much of the Soviet Union, together with local leaders, had sat on their hands, waiting to see how events would develop. The proportion of active protesters was miniscule. But they were sufficient. By the 21st, it was clear that the putsch leaders were either unwilling or unable to suppress the opposition. Early that morning, the defense ministry's fifteen-man collegium overrode Marshal Yazov and voted to pull their troops out of the city. Within hours the plotters had fled. Yeltsin's emissaries brought a shaken but still resilient Gorbachev back from the Crimea. On August 23 he appeared before a hostile session of the Russian Parliament, whose heroism he had been slow to praise. There, in front of the TV cameras, Yeltsin exacted sweet revenge for the humiliations inflicted on him in 1987.[129] He forced Gorbachev to read out the minutes of the State Committee meeting on August 19, which showed how a succession of his appointees supported the coup. He obliged him to ratify a series of new appointments to top USSR offices. And he presented him with a law banning the Communist party as a criminal organization. Gorbachev huffed and puffed, twisted and turned, but it was clear that his authority was now in tatters. Next day, he resigned as CPSU general secretary and dissolved its central committee. Meanwhile, in Moscow and other cities, the statues of Soviet "heroes" were peremptorily toppled, including that of Felix Dzherzinsky, founder of what became the KGB, in front of its headquarters. Moscow's statues were laid out for public viewing in Gorky Park in what was dubbed "an open-air museum of social history."

The August plotters had intended to save the party and the Union. Instead, they hastened the demise of both. Within days, all the republics had declared their independence. The Baltic states seceded immediately. Negotiations ensued to see if a loose confederation could be formed among those which remained. Some states, notably those in Central Asia, saw economic and political benefits in continued cooperation, but the centrifugal forces were now overwhelming. Meanwhile, the Russian government encroached further and further on the functions and institutions of the Union. In the last quarter of 1991, the USSR had no proper budget and survived only by printing money until Russia took over the funding. On December 1, Union negotiations were terminated when the Ukrainian referendum produced a 90 percent majority ratifying immediate independence. A week later, the leaders of Russia, Ukraine, and Belorussia—the three Slavic republics that together embraced 70 percent of the Soviet population—agreed to form their own Commonwealth of Independent States. Eight more joined in due course, but CIS was a flimsy organization, without a president, a foreign ministry, or even a flag.

On December 10–11, Yeltsin secured the agreement of military leaders to the breakup. (He had prudently announced a 90 percent pay rise for all military officers a few days earlier.)[130] Once the Russian parliament had also approved, it only remained formally to bury the Soviet Union. The obsequies were soured by the enduring Gorbachev-Yeltsin feud—as one of Gorbachev's aides noted, "magnanimity is not in the character of Yeltsin and humility is not in the character of Gorbachev."[131] The final act of passing the briefcases containing codes that would launch the Soviet nuclear arsenal was performed through an intermediary. But at 7:35 P.M. on Christmas Day 1991, the Red Flag was lowered down the Kremlin flagpole. Ten minutes later it was replaced by the red, white, and blue tricolor of the Russian Republic.

At the end of World War I, the vast empires of the Ottomans, the Habsburgs, and the Romanovs collapsed, leaving Eastern Europe and Eurasia in turmoil. Only the Russian empire was revived, under Bolshevik leadership. Stalin drove it through forced industrialization and brutal war to become a superpower apparently rivaling the United States. Yet it remained essentially an empire, held together now by party rather than tsar. The command economy proved progressively less able to cope with "postindustrial" technologies and with demands from the new industrial middle class. Yet the Soviet Union, though in serious difficulty in the early 1980s, might have staggered on for years more, but for Gorbachev. Perestroika spelled deconstruction, not reconstruction, of the economy; and glasnost allowed economic and nationalist disaffection to bubble up. When Gorbachev tried to reform the party, he dissolved the bonds that held state and union together. But even when things fell apart and Gorbachev tacked back from reformers to hard-liners, he maintained one clear reformist principle. As in Eastern Europe in 1989, so in the Soviet Union in 1991: he shied away from using force to keep the empire together and the party in power. In this he was very different from the leaders of the People's Republic of China. Backed by brutal political repression, reform communism took root in China and propelled the country to a new economic preeminence while its old rival, the Soviet Union, fell apart.

The Chinese Exception

The People's Republic was, of course, a very different command economy from that of the Soviet Union—still predominantly agricultural and less regimented from the center. Moreover, economic reform had begun back in 1978 and was well-established by the time the political crisis became intense in the late 1980s (see Chapter 12). Yet that crisis had much in common with the turmoil in other communist states. Looser political control allowed elements of a civil society to emerge outside the state, particularly student and intellectual groups. Their growing audacity was encouraged by evident splits within the party leadership over the nature and limits of reform. In China, as in the Soviet bloc, in short, pressure from below could erupt because of rifts at the top. And the explosions reverberated through the new mass media.

The most important political difference was, however, that in the late 1980s the Soviet bloc was emerging from a long "era of stagnation," whereas China was barely a decade away from the turmoil of the Cultural Revolution. This cast a shadow over the 1980s. For instance, Deng Xiaoping and the other party elders rehabilitated in 1977–1978 had suffered grievously at the hands of the Red Guards. They wanted to return to an orderly Leninist party, after a decade in which legitimacy depended on a charismatic but arbitrary leader and tidal waves of ideological fervor, backed by uncontrolled force. A show trial of the Gang of Four, including Mao's widow Jiang Qing, was mounted in the winter of 1980–1981, making them scapegoats for the mistakes of the previous decade. To the same end, Deng gave support to the "Democracy Wall" movement in Beijing in late 1978, because it also targeted Maoist excesses. But he reined it in 1979 when it became clear that this movement, with its talk of democracy, had very different roots and objectives from the party leadership.

During the Cultural Revolution about seventeen million young people were sent into rural exile, in an attempt to tame their Red Guard passions, which Mao had unleashed. About 7.6 million were still there at the end of 1977, but 6.5 million returned to the cities in 1978–1979 as restrictions were lifted. Angry at their treatment and at the loss of their university education, most were profoundly disenchanted with the system. During 1977, another one million "rightists" were also relegitimized, including most of the non-communist intelligentsia. They, too, had many grievances to articulate.[132] And in 1977 the government ended the Cultural Revolution policy of concentrating on mass education at the primary and secondary levels. National college entrance exams were reinstituted. Ten million applied in 1978, of whom five hundred thousand were successful. But it was impossible to make up years of neglect overnight. At the college and university level, China was way behind other developing countries, with only 0.1 percent of the age range enrolled (compared with nearly 0.6 percent in India and 35 percent in the United States).[133] A whole generation had lost out on higher education. Their frustrated radicalism, and the questioning that the Cultural Revolution disaster encouraged among their successors, made China's cities and universities seedbeds of discontent in the 1980s.

The story of the Democracy Wall movement of 1978–1979 set the pattern for the next decade. Spasms of political openness were followed by sharp crackdowns when protests got out of hand. Deng Xiaoping's interest was in economic, not political, change. He saw regulated market reforms as a way to strengthen party legitimacy after the Cultural Revolution disaster. Democracy was acceptable as long as it meant democratic centralism, in other words returning authority to a rule-governed party. This, in turn, was essential for a strong, modern country, able to survive and compete in the world. Deng would have no truck with "bourgeois democracy," which elevated the individual over the collective good, and derided a separation of powers between executive, legislature, and judiciary. The Americans, he liked to say, "actually have three governments."[134]

But Deng was not in full control. His generation, from the 1900s, was gradually failing in powers. Below them, younger leaders were ready and eager to take the reins. Zhao Ziyang, the premier from 1980 to 1987, was the leading advocate of economic reform; Hu Yaobang, the party secretary over that same period, was the other leading reformer, with a growing interest in the political dimension. This generational struggle, of course, paralleled that in the Soviet bloc, but there was a critical difference. China's octogenarians enjoyed special legitimacy as the Long March generation who had led China through Japanese occupation and civil war to a triumphant national revolution. Further, the disasters of the Great Leap and the Cultural Revolution made them even more determined not to relinquish power until totally sure of their successors. By contrast, Gorbachev had removed or neutralized his gerontocrats within his first year.

In 1986, political reform returned to the official agenda. Hu and Zhao persuaded Deng that economic modernization was being blocked by entrenched party officials. He set up a Political Reform Office headed by Zhao, and endorsed their preliminary report on the need for competitive party elections, greater separation of party and government, and a strengthened legal system (to clarify property and contractual rights).[135] To mobilize support for these reforms, intellectuals and academics were given freer rein. The astrophysicist Fang Lizhi became well known in the West for his advocacy of human rights. The crusading journalist Liu Binyan made the celebrated remark that China could not move forward because Deng's reforms had a very long economic leg and a very short political leg. By December 1986 the word *democracy*—its meaning hotly debated—had mobilized students, and big demonstrations were organized in Wuhan, Beijing, and Shanghai. In panic, conservative elders demanded a clampdown, and Hu, who had endorsed the idea of Deng's complete retirement, was thrown to the lions by his patron. Dissidents like Fang Lizhi were expelled from the party. A campaign against "bourgeois liberalization" was given its head during the spring. But the purges were far less draconian than in Mao's time—Hu, for instance, though replaced by Zhao as party secretary, retained his Politburo post. By the summer of 1987 Deng and Zhao reined in the campaign on the grounds that it threatened economic reform.[136]

During the party congress at the end of October 1987, Zhao was able to push through watered-down versions of the political reforms drawn up in 1986. These included separation of party and state at enterprise and local level, and the policy of more candidates than posts in intraparty elections. He also addressed the problem of the gerontocratic transition. Following a vigorous recruiting drive, bringing in nearly thirteen million new members since 1978 (two-thirds under the age of thirty-five), the party had now developed a pool of younger talent. The 1987 Congress saw a big cleanout of the old guard.[137] Nearly half the 209 Central Committee members were pushed into retirement (sweetened by big pensions and welfare benefits). Deng set the example, but he retained his post as Chairman of the Military Affairs Committee (effectively commander in chief) and secured a secret understanding that he would be consulted on all critical decisions. The Politburo's vital Standing Committee of five was balanced between the reformists Zhao Ziyang and Hu Qili and the conservatives Li Peng (now premier) and Yao Yilin. Qiao Shi straddled the two camps.[138]

Unsteadily, therefore, on its one-and-a-bit legs, the People's Republic stumbled into the crisis of communism in 1988–1989. By now the media revolution was having its effects. In the summer of 1988 national TV showed a six-part series entitled *River Elegy*. This took the Yellow River, the artery of China's once-great civilization, as a metaphor for arbitrary power and agrarian backwardness. The series provoked an intense urban debate about modernization, going far beyond intellectuals, and the elders were apoplectic yet again. In other ways, too, the cities were becoming harder to control. China's thriving "Gold Coast," gilded with foreign investment, was attracting huge transient populations in search of lucrative jobs. They came in defiance of strict laws against mobility and despite the consequent lack of papers allowing them food coupons, medical insurance, and the like. In 1989 it was estimated that Beijing and Shanghai each had around two million such illegal visitors, many of whom did not find regular work and added to the pool of urban disaffected.[139]

By this time, even those with legal jobs were also turning against the economic reforms. The mid-1980s growth had created serious inflation and frequent shortages, hitting hardest those on fixed state incomes, such as teachers and academics. Inflation was exacerbated when Deng suddenly spoke out in May 1988 for price reform, touching off a wave of panic buying. In the universities, prices for meals and heating soared, adding further to the disaffection of students crammed into dormitories, sometimes seven or eight to a room. The overcrowding was one consequence of the party's frenetic expansion of higher education in the 1980s, from 625,000 students in 404 institutions in 1977 to over two million in 1,016 by 1988.[140] In one sense China's privileged elite, the students were now increasingly frustrated at the lack of opportunities available through higher education in a get-rich-quick society. Most would be allotted work according to the plan's graduate assignment system: "We are just hammered into place," one complained.[141] And there was anger at the corruption created by market opportunities, prominent beneficiaries of which were the party elite and their children (including those of Chen Yun and Zhao Ziyang). With news of reform being relayed from Poland, Hungary, and the USSR, it was widely expected that there would be massive protests on May 4, 1989—the eightieth anniversary of China's student uprising against the humiliations of the Versailles settlement.[142]

The crisis was exacerbated by the death of Hu Yaobang, whose dismissal in 1987 had boosted his popularity among students. When he succumbed to a heart attack at a Politburo meeting on April 8, 1989—supposedly while arguing with hard-liners—he became a convenient democratic martyr. Students used the opportunity of his state funeral on April 22 to bring forward their protests, and some two hundred thousand gathered in Tiananmen Square. Similar protests occurred in Shanghai and other cities. As they subsided, the elders fanned the flames. Deng was given a lurid briefing by Li Peng and other conservatives. He responded by denouncing the protests as "a planned conspiracy," influenced by events in Poland and elsewhere, "to overthrow the leadership of the Communist party and to forfeit the future of the country and the nation." Deng added that "worker and peasant cadres support us" and "we also have several million PLA [soldiers]. What are we afraid of?" Armed with his warrant, conservatives produced a similar editorial in the *People's Daily* the next day, April 26.[143]

The attack on their patriotism incensed students. On the 27th, thousands broke through police barricades and marched to Tiananmen Square, cheered on by sympathizers. In all, an estimated five hundred thousand to one million were on the streets—the largest spontaneous demonstration in the history of the People's Republic. Students were now demanding recognition of their autonomous union and formal dialogue with the government. What made the situation particularly sensitive was that Beijing was currently welcoming several hundred foreign journalists, including American TV networks with satellite hookups, because of two major shop-window events: the annual meeting of the Asian Development Bank, which China was hosting for the first time from May 4 to 8, and a state visit by Mikhail Gorbachev from May 15 to 18. Both entailed events in the Great Hall of the People on Tiananmen Square itself. During this time, a violent clampdown was impossible.

As with the Democracy Wall affair a decade earlier, the politics of May 1989 were exceedingly complex. The students were using the occasion of Hu's sudden death to renew debate about political reform. Zhao Ziyang saw the students as a way of recovering ground against the conservatives, now that their hard-line tactics had boomeranged. For a couple of weeks, he had the initiative. Deng supposedly told him: "The most important thing you should do is stabilize the situation. . . . If the situation is under control, you can implement your plans if they prove feasible, disregarding whatever I have said."[144] Signs of official conciliation emboldened the students; on May 13, their leaders started a hunger strike in Tiananmen Square. But the only concession that would get them out of the square—effective recognition of them as political equals with the party—was one that Zhao could not deliver from the incensed elders, now pressing their views in meetings of party bodies. As the Gorbachev visit drew to a close, and with it the need to maintain appearances before the world media, so the days of a soft line were numbered.

The political crisis peaked in a series of meetings of the Politburo Standing Committee in mid-May. There Zhao was consistently outvoted in his call for a dialogue with the students and an attack on party corruption. Some of these meetings were enlarged to include Deng. At the climactic encounter, on May 17, Deng supposedly exclaimed, "I have the Army behind me." Zhao replied, "But I have the people behind me," to which Deng retorted, "Then you have nothing."[145] Around dawn on May 19, a tearful Zhao visited students camped in the square. But by now, he had lost his job. "I came too late, too late," he murmured. "We deserve your criticism." Later that day, Li Peng, now the acting party secretary, announced the imposition of martial law, warning that not merely "our nation's reforms" but "even the fate and future" of the country was "facing a serious threat."[146]

Plans for martial law had been in train for weeks. The position that Deng had retained since 1987 as formal commander in chief was of decisive importance in this crisis. As with much of the story of Chinese politics in 1989, the details of the martial law decision remain murky. Was there dissent from some military commanders? Did Deng make a special trip to the central city of Wuhan to rally their support? Both issues remain in dispute. It does seem likely that the commander of the 38th Group Army, based around Beijing, was relieved because of his opposition to martial law, but it is also clear that, by May 20, Deng had secured units from every military region. All would therefore be implicated in the imposition of martial law. At least one hundred thousand regular troops had been moved to the environs of the capital by the time the decision was announced. The leadership hoped to end the disturbances by a mere display of force. They tried to rush the troops into the center in large numbers.

It was at this point, however, that the protests of students and intellectuals developed a broader base, because residents of Beijing rallied against the imposition of troops. Even in the civil war, the capital had changed hands peacefully, and resentment at the government's action was widespread.[147] People improvised roadblocks across most of the major arteries. Troop trains were stopped by sit-ins on the tracks. Attempts to bring troops in via the labyrinth of underground passages built as air-raid precautions after the Sino-Soviet split failed when their city-center exits were blocked by students and residents. Unprepared for passive resistance on such a large scale, troops and government backed off.

Such a challenge to the party's authority was unprecedented. In addition to the action by residents, some Beijing workers were also rallying behind the protest. They established an autonomous union at the end of May. Although the hunger strike had been called off and numbers in the square had diminished, the bulk of the students there now were from outside Beijing— testimony to widening national support. Outside the luxurious government compound Zhongnonhai, on the northwest edge of the square, students were camped in protest under a banner proclaiming, "It is not the government who decides for the people but the people who decide for the government."[148] To add to the ire of the old men blockaded inside, on May 30, fine arts students erected a thirty-foot-high statue made of white plaster and styrofoam—the Goddess of Democracy—modeled on the Statue of Liberty in New York.

At the beginning of June, the government tried to infiltrate troops into the city. Some were despatched in unmarked trucks, others entered on foot, ostensibly out on training runs. Many of the troops were turned back, often after ugly scenes. On Saturday night, June 3–4, the army was given the task of clearing the square, using waves of motorized troops and armor to break through the roadblocks. They now had live ammunition and were authorized at least to fire warning shots. The government clearly expected casualties, indeed intended them, because it was convinced that the populace had to be taught a lesson if order was to restored. As opposition to the troops increased, late on Saturday night units were permitted to fire at the crowds—an order that must have been approved by Deng himself. But it does seem likely that the *scale* of the casualties and destruction was the result of army incompetence. The troops, many of them youngsters from the provinces, were untrained for crowd control or even urban warfare, and they were poorly coordinated by commanders. When blocked by residents, they frequently panicked, abandoned their vehicles, and tried to shoot their way out of trouble, further provoking the citizens. It took units of the 38th Group Army four hours to move less than four miles. According to official figures, they lost six dead and over eleven hundred wounded. In addition, sixty-five trucks and forty-seven armored personnel carriers were destroyed, and another 485 vehicles were damaged.[149]

By two o'clock on Sunday morning, the Army had fought its way to the edge of Tiananmen Square. In contrast, clearing the square itself was relatively peaceful: despite some casualties, most students were induced to leave by the threat of force. After the publicity given to the hunger strikers, the regime did not wish to stain the Square of the Gate of Heavenly Peace with the blood of China's children. Consequently, most of the dead were the ordinary people of Beijing, standing in human roadblocks across the avenues leading to the Square. How many were killed? That question may never be answered. Official figures of two hundred to three hundred dead, mostly soldiers, are hardly credible, but opposition claims of up to ten thousand also seem unlikely. The best estimates suggest between eight hundred and two thousand six hundred. But as one student exclaimed later, "It doesn't matter . . . if the total number killed was one or ten thousand. The point is that our government turned its guns on its people."[150] The blow to official legitimacy was huge and enduring. Although regaining the square physically, the party had lost it symbolically—perhaps forever. Tiananmen, a name barely known outside China before 1989, became a worldwide synonym for government brutality.

Over the next few days, the army tightened its grip on Beijing. Students and intellectuals were hunted down, their autonomous organizations disbanded. Several thousand arrests were made, and identified ringleaders were executed. At the same time, a massive disinformation campaign, including doctored videos, was mounted to persuade China and the world that "a very few thugs engineered a counterrevolutionary rebellion" but were frustrated by "the valiant struggle of the People's Liberation Army" using the minimum necessary force.[151] The power and the ambiguity of television was nowhere better seen than in the image of the lone nineteen-year-old filmed haranguing a line of tanks near the Beijing Hotel on June 5 (Plate 38). His picture went around the world as a symbol of courageous defiance. But it was also featured on Chinese government TV as a symbol of the military's restraint.[152]

On October 1, 1989, the People's Republic of China celebrated its fortieth anniversary. On that same day in 1949 Mao Zedong had addressed the adulatory crowds from the Gate of Heavenly Peace (see Chapter 2). Forty years on, the mile-wide square was again full, but the mood was very different. The city was under curfew and riot police ringed the square. In the evening, thousands of young people from sixteen universities danced for joy. It was said later that they had been promised a month's boot camp if they did not do so. So they danced—for the TV cameras of China and the world, and for a few old men sitting atop the Gate of Heavenly Peace.[153]

A hollow triumph, bought in blood. But a real one, nevertheless. Halfway round the world, in Berlin, another communist government celebrated its fortieth birthday only a few days later. As we have seen, however, there the party was soon over, in more ways than one. A little more than two years later, Mikhail Gorbachev, his party, and even his country were also consigned to the garbage heap of history.

Why did the stories of the two great communist powers, the Soviet Union and the People's Republic, diverge so dramatically? Some analysts point to basic structural differences between the two countries: China's economy "was still reformable, but the USSR had long since passed that point" because of the dominance of heavy industry and the planning bureaucracy in the economics and politics of a much more urbanized society.[154] Others argue that both countries were capable of reform, had Gorbachev looked east and not west—to Asian examples of authoritarian state capitalism rather than Western models of bourgeois liberalism. Instead, he gradually destroyed the political structures on which economy, state, and society depended.[155] The relative homogeneity of the two countries may also have been a relevant factor. Although China had its own ethnic problems, especially in Tibet and Xinjiang, these were nothing like the nationality problems in the Soviet Union.

The jury is still out on these historical debates, which have implications for postcommunist transitions as a whole. But it is also clear that in 1989 the leaders of China and Russia both faced major political crises—Deng at home, Gorbachev in Eastern Europe—and that Gorbachev faced a similar one in the USSR in 1991. The difference, in the last analysis, is that one used force, the other did not. As the judgments of history mature, that contrast is unlikely to be forgotten.

Yet history's judgments are rarely simple, and they are often tinged with irony. Consider the speech Deng gave to the martial law units on June 9, later shown on national TV. The diminutive leader had not been seen in public for over three weeks, prompting rumors that he had been killed. Now he paid tribute to the army's "martyrs" who had helped the "veteran comrades" to save country and party from "a rebellious clique and a large number of the dregs of society." These words were widely quoted by Deng's critics in the West. Less familiar is the bulk of Deng's speech—a passionate plea to continue the policies of economic reform combining plan and market, and of "opening our country to the outside world."[156] Although forced to ditch his second heir, Zhao Ziyang, Deng did not intend to abandon the goals to which he had dedicated the last decade.

This became clear over the next three years. In the short term, Li Peng and Yao Yilin, backed by Deng's old rival Chen Yun, tried to recentralize the economy and revive state planning. But the result was a sharp recession in 1989–1990, as output and demand both fell. In 1990 the new party secretary, Jiang Zemin, renewed the momentum of "growing out of the plan." Jiang had made his name as the boss of Shanghai in the 1980s, modernizing the economy while keeping the lid on student protest. Here, then, was a man in Deng's mold, who presented an acceptably Western face and was not stigmatized abroad as one of the butchers of Tienanmen Square. Deng had promoted Jiang over Li to the post of party secretary and gave him full support in the renewed push for economic reform.

Although little was seen of Deng in 1990 and 1991, he embarked on a long tour of coastal China in early 1992, targeting cities where his word would easily be picked up in Hong Kong and, thence, reported back to China and across the world. Like Mao in 1965–1966, the aged leader, now eighty-seven, was going public to outflank his foes. Particular attention was given to his remarks, reprinted in the *People's Daily*, that "both planning and market are just economic means. The nature of socialism is to emancipate the productive forces, to eliminate exploitation and polarization, and finally to achieve the goal of common affluence."[157] This helped confirm Jiang Zemin's victory over Chen Yun and his associates. In October 1992, the fourteenth party congress committed the country to a "socialist market economy with Chinese characteristics."

Foreign investment resumed in a big way, now that political stability seemed assured. By 1993 it amounted to 20 percent of domestic fixed investment, compared with no more than 6 percent all through the 1980s.[158] Per capita income had doubled between 1978 and 1987, only to double again by 1995.[159] Some analysts predicted that China would have the largest GDP in the world by 2010. Meanwhile, in Russia, output and national income fell by perhaps 50 percent between 1989 and 1994—a collapse comparable to that in America or Germany in the Great Depression, or China after Mao's Great Leap.[160] As the twentieth century fades into history, the contrasting stories of the Soviet bloc and the People's Republic in 1989–1991 will probably be regarded as one of its great turning points.

16

States, Wealth, and Order after the Cold War

In the wake of the cold war, the world seemed beautifully simple to many Americans. In 1989 the commentator Francis Fukuyama spoke of "an unabashed victory of economic and political liberalism" on the American model that marked "the end of history."[1] Two years later, President George Bush foresaw "a new world order . . . A world in which freedom and respect for human rights find a home among all nations."[2]

By mid-decade, although President Bill Clinton was still talking about "the global trend toward democracy and free markets,"[3] complexity had replaced simplicity. Capitalism was now the name of the economic game, but it took a variety of forms. Likewise, multiparty elections became more common, but this new wave of democratization[4] did not produce Western liberal democracy. Much depended on the maturity of "civil society"—the mesh of parties, unions, professional associations, and religious groups that mediated between the state and private life.[5] Above all, elections and markets were no panacea if states were unstable. This was the problem across much of the world, either because governments lacked an internal monopoly of force (as in ex-Yugoslavia or much of black Africa) or because they were at odds with each other over land and people (as in the Middle East and southern Asia). The porousness of the state was the underlying theme of the 1990s.

Iraq, Israel, and the Search for Peace in the Middle East

In the Middle East, the unprecedented international coalition that won the gulf war of 1991 and then helped expedite Israel's peace with the Palestinians and Jordan in 1993–1994 seemed striking examples of Bush's new world order. But the problems of Iraq and Palestine remained unresolved. And, overall, the state structure and political complexion of the Middle East both remained resistant to change.

August 1988 finally saw a cease-fire in the Iran-Iraq war. The conflict that Iraq had begun in September 1980 (see Chapter 11) had turned into the longest conventional war of the twentieth century. Casualties exceeded one million (of whom 262,000 Iranians and 105,000 Iraqis died). The cost, including direct damage and lost oil revenues, ran to $1.2 billion.[6] Although the fighting ended, no peace was signed. And less than two years later, on August 2, 1990, Iraq invaded and occupied its southeastern neighbor, the emirate of Kuwait.

In 1990, as in 1980, the primary cause of war was aggression by the Iraqi leader, Saddam Hussein.[7] With vast war debts and growing internal discontent, he reckoned that invading Kuwait was the best way to increase his regional power, enhance his oil revenues, and shore up domestic support. President Bush talked starkly of "Hitler revisited."[8] But we must also take account of the peculiarities of the Iraqi state.[9] Hacked by the British in 1921 out of the ruins of the Ottoman empire, Iraq was virtually landlocked, having only fifteen miles of coastline through which its exports (mostly oil) could flow into the gulf. Consequently, territorial disputes with both Iran and Kuwait were a feature of its national history. Iraq had already come close to invading Kuwait when the British finally ended their protectorate there in 1961.[10] Iraqi aggression was, therefore, the act of a fragile state as well as a megalomaniac leader. And it was possible only because the West had built up Saddam as a major power. As the conflict with Iran turned against him, America and Arab states, including Saudi Arabia and Kuwait, came to his aid to avert victory for the Khomeini revolution. In 1983–1984, Baghdad's trade with Washington was three times the value of its trade with Moscow, officially its main patron.[11] France, Germany, Britain, and other NATO states also expanded Saddam's arsenal, often using a spurious distinction between military and nonmilitary equipment to sell machine tools, computers, and other manufactures he needed to build heavy weaponry.[12] Moreover, the lack of Western condemnation of Saddam's war on Iran (including the use of chemical weapons) encouraged him to expect similar indifference when he attacked Kuwait.

The outcry that greeted Saddam's attack—from Bush in Washington to Mubarak in Cairo—was partly anger at having been deceived and surprised. But there was more at stake than *amour-propre*. Although Kuwait was an autocratic monarchy, it was also a small state brutally overwhelmed by a larger neighbor. Within hours Iraq had been unanimously condemned by the fifteen-member UN Security Council; even Cuba supported the United States. Sanctions followed within days. With Iraqi tanks moving to the Saudi border, there loomed a larger concern. By occupying Kuwait, Saddam had doubled his control over world oil reserves to 20 percent. If he moved into Saudi Arabia and the United Arab Emirates, then the proportion would rise to over half. Did he plan such moves? The verdict now is "probably not." But having been caught off guard over Kuwait, the CIA and U.S. policy makers lurched from complacency to alarm. Within days the Saudis had acceded to American pressure and asked for U.S. troops to help defend their kingdom. Thus began Operation Desert Shield. By November, Bush was convinced that sanctions alone would not evict Saddam. He approved the doubling of U.S. forces to over half a million men to provide an offensive capability, and set a deadline of January 15, 1991, after which force would be used. At that point Desert Shield became Desert Storm.

The Bush administration offered various justifications for the war, from stopping Hitlerite aggression to securing Western oil, from safeguarding American jobs to denying Saddam a nuclear arsenal. But gradually another slogan took precedence. As Bush put it in January 1991: "What is at stake is more than one small country. It is a big idea. A new world order where diverse nations are drawn together in common cause to achieve the universal aspirations of mankind."[13] Bush's "big idea" reflected the remarkable international coalition that was taking shape.[14] Only once before had the UN gone to war, in Korea in 1950, and that was only possible because Stalin had boycotted the Security Council. This time, Gorbachev was a supportive ally despite persistent carping from Politburo hard-liners about such servility to the United States. Thus, the Americans had to tolerate periodic Soviet efforts to reach a peaceful solution. The French also tried to be both allies and mediators. But in the end, the Assemblée Nationale took the decision, unprecedented since France left NATO in 1966, to place French forces in the gulf under U.S. command for the duration of the war.

Bush was equally successful at holding most Arab states, except Jordan, within the coalition, despite the enthusiasm of much of their populations for Saddam. Here Saudi support was essential, to give credibility with the Arabs, a logistical base for the buildup, and increased oil production to help avert another oil crisis with 7 percent of world output removed from the market (a proportion similar to that in 1973–1974).[15]

Saddam's last gamble was to play the Israeli card, hoping that by launching Soviet-built Scud missiles against Tel Aviv and Haifa in January he would trigger Israeli retaliation and thus start another Arab-Israeli war. But despite opposition from cabinet hawks, Prime Minister Yitzhak Shamir accepted military advice for restraint. In return, he secured more U.S. aid, plus batteries of Patriot missiles to help destroy the Scuds. This aid, and the inaccuracy of the Soviet missiles, prevented major Israeli casualties. Meanwhile, Bush had shored up support at home—crumbling after he announced an offensive buildup—by "going the extra mile" for peace in a further effort in January, and by securing resolutions from the Security Council and the U.S. Congress before using force. Fearing a long and bloody conflict, he wanted no repetition of the Vietnam controversy about undeclared war. When the UN deadline passed on January 15, the mood in America was somber. Playing on these fears, Saddam promised "a second Vietnam" and the "mother of all battles."[16]

It proved yet more bluster. On January 17, the coalition began intensive bombing of Iraq's air defense and command systems and then of similar targets in occupied Kuwait. After a last flurry of Soviet diplomacy, ground operations started on February 24. By then, the allied commander, General H. Norman Schwarzkopf, controlled 540,000 U.S. troops and two hundred fifty thousand from the allies, of whom the Saudis comprised the largest contingent. Schwarzkopf planned a classic encirclement. Feint attacks north against Kuwait City would engage the enemy, while the bulk of his U.S. armored and mechanized units, plus a British and a French division, would sweep hundreds of miles west and then east to cut off the Iraqi forces. The execution was almost perfect. The ground war lasted only one hundred hours before Bush called a halt late on the 27th to avoid what seemed on TV to be "wanton killing."[17] But the figures for Iraqi dead were soon scaled down from the 100,000 first bruited. Later estimates range from 35,000 to 82,500. The coalition lost 240 killed in action, 148 of whom were Americans. Almost a quarter of the American dead, and over half the British, were killed by "friendly fire."[18]

For Washington, the supreme fact was, as Bush put it, "We've kicked the Vietnam syndrome once and for all."[19] Combined with the sense of victory in the cold war, it imbued many Americans with new confidence and pride. Much was also made of the new techologies of warfare. The flanking attack would have been impossible without the Pentagon's Global Positioning System to provide accurate navigation. And the bombing campaign featured computerized, satellite-guided missiles capable of turning down individual streets or entering the front doors of military bunkers. Admittedly, less than

10 percent of the tonnage dropped during the gulf war was precision bombs, and their accuracy was only as good as target intelligence. Moreover, the allies were pounding a demoralized enemy in open terrain (unlike the jungles of Vietnam). But it was fair to claim that, in the gulf war, "air power was the arm of decision to an extent entirely unprecedented in the annals of warfare" and that "smart weapons" were a harbinger of technowars to come.[20]

Diplomatically, however, the significance of the war was less clear. Saddam's removal had never been an explicit war aim. The coalition would not have allowed it, and Bush hoped for a coup to establish a strong but unaggressive regime. This did not occur. Having demonized Saddam as a new Hitler to gain support, Bush created a sense that America had won the war but lost the peace.[21] Nor did the allies want Iraq to disintegrate into a civil war from which only Iran could gain. They did not, therefore, intervene in March 1991 when Saddam's defeat precipitated a Shia revolt in the south and a Kurdish uprising in the north of Iraq. The non-Arab Kurds—spread out over five different countries and denied a separate state after the resurgence of Turkey in the 1920s—were particularly bitter at the lack of Western help. When Saddam's Republican Guard put down the risings, driving over a million Kurds up to the Iranian and Turkish borders, Britain initiated a "safe havens" policy. This led to an autonomous region in northern Iraq, run by feuding Kurdish leaders under UN protection.[22] Iraqis endured the 1990s under harsh UN sanctions, imposed at Washington's behest in a futile effort to root out Saddam's "weapons of mass destruction." A four-day bombing campaign in December 1998, mounted by America with token British support, damaged some installations but left his regime unshaken. But Clinton maintained sanctions and periodic bombing in the continued hope of prompting a coup by Iraq's armed forces.

A similar pattern of dramatic change and then deadlocked continuity characterized the Israel-Palestine saga during the 1990s. The problem had been restored to the international agenda in 1987–1988 by the Palestinian uprising, or *intifada*, in Gaza and the West Bank, occupied by Israel since the war of 1967. Many of the 1.7 million people were refugees, without civil and political rights.[23] Film of beatings and shootings by Israeli soldiers seriously damaged Israel's image in the West. And by commandeering leadership of the revolt, Yasser Arafat's PLO gained a new status in regional diplomacy at the expense of Jordan, previously the main patron of the Palestinians.[24] Prodded by his arms supplier, the USSR, and cajoled by the Americans, in November 1988 Arafat announced that the PLO recognized the state of Israel. In return, he was promised direct dialogue with Washington.[25]

For the PLO to recognize Israel and, in effect, for America to recognize the PLO were major breakthroughs. But under the Likud-led coalition run by Yitzhak Shamir, Israel still would not talk to the PLO. Such was Shamir's obduracy that Bush's Secretary of State James Baker exclaimed in exasperation in June 1990, "Our number is 1-202-456-1414. When you're serious about peace, call us."[26]

The allied victory in the gulf war loosened the logjam. With enhanced leverage in the region, Baker embarked on intensive shuttle diplomacy. (Indeed, a new U.S. effort was part of the deal to win Soviet support against Iraq.) In October 1991, he managed to convene an international conference in Madrid. As he admitted, the atmosphere had "all the warmth of an arranged courtship."[27] But the symbolism was profoundly important. Israelis had sat down at the same table with Palestinians and Arab leaders. Nothing like this had happened before.

But it was another case of stop-go. After Madrid, the detailed bilateral negotiations soon bogged down. It took a change of government in Israel to give real impetus to the peace process. The June 1992 elections ended an almost unbroken fifteen-year period of Likud predominance, enabling Labor and its allies to form a coalition. Labor was committed to surrendering territory in order to make peace, unlike Shamir, who was planning to drag out the peace talks as a cover for continued Israeli settlements.[28] But June 1992 was not merely a victory for Labor, it was also a victory for Yitzhak Rabin, who had replaced Shimon Peres as party leader earlier that year. Whereas Peres was a professional politician, widely distrusted for his crafty maneuvering, Rabin was an ex-soldier whose reputation as strategist of the 1967 war and suppressor of the intifada gave him the status at home to make peace.

With official channels blocked, Rabin gave wary approval to secret contacts between Israeli academics and PLO leaders. These had been promoted by Peres, now the foreign minister, under the auspices of the Norwegian government and were held at a secluded country house near Oslo. Their modus operandi was to avoid intractable issues such as Jerusalem and the Jewish settlements, and to build a working relationship by addressing matters that could be resolved. The Israelis offered substantial Palestinian autonomy in Gaza, which many were happy to get rid of, while moving more slowly on the West Bank, though Arafat insisted on including at least Jericho in any deal. To avoid breakdown, in July Rabin was also obliged to accept recognition of the PLO—previously anathema. But as he admitted, "peace is not made with friends, peace is made with enemies."[29]

Like most of the world, Washington was astonished when informed of the agreement. But although not brokering the deal, America was vital to make it stick. To that end, the Oslo accords were formally signed before TV cameras on the White House lawn on September 13, 1993. There President Bill Clinton orchestrated a public handshake between Arafat and Rabin (Plate

39). The Israeli premier was visibly cringing, such was his residual distaste for the PLO, but the symbolism of the act mattered far more than its motivation.

Many Palestinians were irate that big issues such as Jerusalem had been pushed aside. Edward Said, the Palestinian-American intellectual, damned the deal as "an instrument of surrender, a Palestinian Versailles."[30] But Arafat argued that this was the first step to Palestinian statehood, while Rabin and Peres saw Oslo as the springboard for peace with Israel's Arab neighbors. Jordan was particularly promising. The two governments signed a formal peace agreement in October 1994, at a point on their border that had been a minefield until days before. This treaty went far beyond Israel and Egypt's "cold peace." It acknowledged Jordan's special role as protector of Islam's holy places in Jerusalem and established a broad range of cross-border cooperation, including telecommunications, policing, shared water resources, and an electricity grid. For Peres, this agreement was the prototype of a new transnational framework for the Middle East, as closed war economies were opened up in a spirit of cooperation, like that between France and Germany within the European Community. "The Middle East needs a Jean Monnet approach today," he wrote, to expedite "the transition from an economy of strife to an economy of peace."[31]

But that was still a long way off. What had been affirmed in Oslo was only a Declaration of Principles. Not until May 1994 were details of the handover in Gaza and Jericho finalized, allowing Arafat to enter the occupied territories in triumph in July and set up the headquarters of the new Palestinian National Authority (PNA) in Gaza. Further progress on the West Bank was delayed until the so-called Oslo II accords in September 1995. Under these, the PNA would gradually be given full control of major towns on the West Bank and administrative control, including policing, over seven hundred thousand Palestinians in some four hundred fifty villages, while Israel retained discretionary rights of military intervention. This would leave some three-quarters of the West Bank still under Israeli control, but over two-thirds of the Palestinian population would be under full or partial PNA authority. Agreement on the final status of the occupied territories, including Jerusalem, was to be reached by May 1999.

The two Oslo agreements had been possible because of the window of political opportunity opened up in Israel by Rabin's premiership. But the accords were vilified by militant settlers and ultra-orthodox rabbis. In this fevered climate, Rabin was shot dead by a extremist student in Tel Aviv on November 4, 1995. Peres became premier and tried to use the mood of public shock to reach an early agreement with Syria. But progress was slow, and opinion in Israel soured after sixty people were killed in a week of terrorist bombings at the end of February 1996. By the time Peres called elections in May, the opinion polls had turned against him. Israelis were voting for the first time on a split ballot, whereby the prime minister was elected directly rather than chosen after complex bargaining among the parties in the Knesset. Although Labor won more seats than Likud, Peres lost the premiership by 1 percent to the new Likud leader, Binyamin Netanyahu, who secured 50.5 percent of the popular vote. Just how much was a vote against peace, how much a vote against Peres, was unclear. But the return of a Likud-led coalition in June 1996 closed the window of opportunity in Israeli politics.

Netanyahu was a smooth political operator who had kept his options open by campaigning on a slogan of "peace with security." He ended up delivering neither. His coalition was even more beholden than Shamir's to hard-line religious parties to whom any surrender of Greater Israel was anathema, and to the soft right of secular Jews, mostly recent Russian immigrants, who had no desire to see their promised land handed over to the Arabs. When American pressure in the autumn of 1998 finally prodded Netanyahu into implementing the Oslo accords, this brought down his government in the Knesset. Elections in May 1999 produced a landslide victory for Labor's Ehud Barak—like Rabin, another general and war hero turned politician and peacemaker. His task was enormous. The Oslo process had gambled that removing molehills such as Gaza would build the trust needed to move mountains such as the Golan Heights, Palestinian statehood, and, most intractable, Jerusalem. During the 1990s, however, both Labor and Likud had been consolidating Jewish settlements in and around the holy city. Rabin and Barak, like Netanyahu, claimed that Jerusalem was not negotiable.[32] To forge a lasting peace, Barak had to square that circle, while also retaining the trust of the Palestinians during their delicate transition from Arafat's ailing monarchy toward democratic statehood.

The vicissitudes of the gulf war and the Israeli peace process were the main media stories from the Middle East in the 1990s. Together with flurries of Islamic terrorism, they confirmed the region's image of instability. But taking the Middle East as a whole, there were many contrary signs.[33]

For the most part, the political cartography of the Middle East drawn by the European powers after the First World War had endured, as had the Zionist amendments of 1948 and 1967 (apart from Sinai). Many of the borders did not accord with the divisions of ethnicity or terrain. Some borders were still vigorously contested, particularly in the gulf but also on the Saudi frontier with Yemen. Yet the Iraqi occupation of Kuwait had been repulsed, and Kurdish state building had achieved only an embattled autonomy in Iraq and a long-running insurgency in southeastern Turkey. The only other major change of the decade was the union of the two Yemens in May 1990 after the south had been undermined by the end of Soviet aid. Four years later, resentful of northern dominance, it tried to secede, only to be brought forcibly under northern control.

In some places, however, the issue was not land but water. The combination of generally low rainfall, increased urbanization, and inefficient irrigation was draining the region's resources. Moreover, some states were dependent on foreign-controlled water—almost totally in the case of Egypt (where Sudan and Ethiopia controlled the headwaters of the Nile), about two-thirds in the case of Israel and Iraq, and one-third for Jordan and Syria. The Jordan basin was at the heart of the Israeli-Jordanian treaty of 1994. President Sadat in 1979 and King Hussein in 1990 each announced that the only issue that could bring his country to war again was water.[34]

The regional balance of power had been achieved by turning the Middle East into the world's greatest arms bazaar, taking some 40 percent of global weapons imports at the cost of about three-quarters of the region's oil revenues.[35] As the oil price slid from the mid-1980s, revenues immediately fell because few states had used the income to diversify their economic base. Countries aligned to the West, like Egypt and Turkey, found that their mounting debt made them vulnerable to IMF pressure for restructuring. Those who had been Soviet clients, like Syria and Iraq, found the collapse of the USSR an equally sharp spur toward economic rethinking. In Syria, the open-door (intifah) policy that complemented Assad's new interest in an American-brokered peace in the early 1990s resulted in extensive privatization in agriculture and in industries such as textiles and food processing. In Egypt, construction and services were the main pillars of the new private sector. But these remained planned economies, with the government still controlling most heavy industry to ensure gradual economic change and political stability. Likewise, in the nonsocialist dynastic states such as Saudi Arabia and its gulf neighbors, the large state sector and, in most cases, the pervasive bureaucracy remained essential to buy off influential social groups (see Chapter 11). The economy, then, was still seen across the region as a foundation of regime power as much as of national wealth.

Overall, the regimes themselves also proved extremely durable. The egregious example was Saddam Hussein, who hung on despite the gulf war and UN sanctions. For Saddam's great foe, Assad in Syria, the gulf war was a godsend. His importance in the coalition prompted the United States to turn a blind eye as Syria consolidated its hold over Lebanon. Here the fifteen-year civil war had abated and a new pact among the religious groups, less favorable to the Maronite Christians, was hammered out in October 1989. In October 1990, Syrian forces crushed those Maronites who rejected the deal. Syrian influence over Lebanese politics was sustained through the decade as Elias Hariri, the recurrent coalition premier, began reconstructing his battered country. Both Saddam Hussein and Assad continued to rule through a mixture of clan structures, repressive security networks, and personality cults. Instability seemed most likely to occur through succession struggles after their deaths, especially in Syria, where Alawi dominance was still resented by the Sunni majority. In Saudi Arabia, likewise, politics were personalized in the ruling royal family, where King Fahd reluctantly relinquished his powers to his half-brother Crown Prince Abdullah following a stroke in 1995. Elsewhere both patrominial and socialist regimes were obliged to make some political concessions in the 1990s. These were grudging in Kuwait after the gulf war and more radical in Jordan, where freer elections in 1989 (when women voted for the first time) were followed in 1993 by legalization of political parties. But everywhere the theme was limited reform—to coopt malleable opponents, repress extremists, and maintain the hegemony of the ruling elite or party.

Yet that task was becoming ever more difficult. After Africa, the postwar Middle East had seen the most rapid population growth in the world, as well as intense movement from country to town, boosting the urban population from 27 percent in 1950 to 65 percent in 1994. Cairo's population density of over one hundred thousand per square mile was one of the highest in the world (the figure for Washington, D.C. was twenty thousand). The three most populous countries of the Middle East were Egypt and Turkey (both around sixty million in 1994) and Iran (about sixty-six million). By this date, all had family planning policies, but these would not show real results for decades. Moreover, the age structure was now highly skewed: 35 percent of Turks were less than fifteen years old. In Egypt the figure was 39 percent, in Iran 45 percent. Most major cities therefore faced shortages of jobs and housing. With regimes also engaged in deflationary policies to privatize the economies and placate international creditors, civil unrest was almost inevitable.[36]

There were fears in the United States that these problems could fuel "Islamic revolution." The scholar Samuel Huntington attracted attention with his 1993 warnings that, after the cold war, "the fault lines between civilizations will be the battle lines of the future" and that Islam, in particular, had "bloody borders."[37] The bombing of the World Trade Center in New York that February by Islamic extremists brought home his message. In 1994, the conservative commentator Charles Krauthammer asserted, "Iran is the world's new Comintern"—in other words, the headquarters of Islamic revolution. From Iran, in similar vein, Ahmed Khomeini, the ayatollah's son, declared in 1991: "After the fall of Marxism, Islam replaced it, and as long as Islam exists, U.S. hostility exists, and as long as U.S. hostility exists, the struggle exists."[38] Each side was operating with a mirror image of the other. Yet, as in the 1980s (see Chapter 11), Islamic politics were the products of particular national conditions rather than the expression of some unchanging religious essence.[39]

This is evident from Algeria, notorious in the United States and Western Europe because of the gruesome civil war that followed the military's seizure of power in January 1992 after the success of FIS (Front Islamique de Salut) in the first round of national elections. The crisis was the result of "a flawed transition from single-party to democratic politics" without prior agreement between secularists and Islamists about the future polity.[40] The Front de Libération Nationale (FLN), which had ruled since winning independence from the French in 1962, was widely hated as a corrupt, Westernized regime, backed by one of the largest armies in the region. Following riots in October 1988, President Chadli Bendjedid, the ruler since 1979, shifted abruptly to multiparty democracy, hoping to manipulate the elections and divide his opponents. Although FIS was pledged to create an Islamic republic, the details had been left vague because of party divisions. Muslim associations were popular because of their welfare work among Algeria's urban masses, and FIS's share of the vote in the December 1991 elections was more a protest against the regime than a sign of rampant Islamism. FIS was also careful to identify itself as the "son" of the original, now corrupted, national revolution—"le FIS est le fils du FLN" in the punning French slogan. In short, it was "a radical nationalist party that articulated its policies in the context of Islam, rather than a purely fundamentalist organization."[41]

Denied power by the ballot, however, Algeria's Islamist opposition resorted to the bullet. Guerrilla organizations targeted the Francophone elite in terrorist acts that prompted equally brutal army reprisals. Although General Lamine Zeroual, who became president in January 1994, moved cautiously toward democratization, the killing on both sides did not abate. By the end of 1997, an estimated eighty thousand had died.

But Algeria's agony did not imply that Islamic revolution was about to engulf North Africa. In Tunisia, society was more Westernized and the economy less ravaged. In Morocco, King Hassan had incorporated Muslim parties into a controlled pluralist politics as part of his long-running "divide and survive" strategy for maintaining the monarchy.[42] Moreover, Algeria had a long tradition of violent struggle against a weak state: indeed, the stability of the 1970s had been the exception, not the rule. Egypt, in contrast, had a much firmer nation-state identity. Moreover, successive governments had brought the mainstream Islamic clergy and their schools under official patronage and supervision, using them to help isolate radical groups.[43] Muslim welfare organizations thrived in the grim conditions of Cairo, but periodic acts of terror, such as the killing of 68 foreign tourists at Luxor in November 1997, did not mean that Egypt was going the way of Algeria.

A similar pattern can be discerned in the secular republic of Turkey, where

Turgut Özal, the dominant political figure for a decade after the military permitted elections in November 1983, had deregulated the economy and opened it up to foreign investment. This brought business prosperity and a consumer boom, but peasants and workers saw steep falls in real incomes and unemployment of over 15 percent. In these conditions, Muslim politics prospered. A new Islamic party—significantly named Refah, or Welfare—won a fifth of the vote in the December 1995 elections and entered government as part of a new coalition in June 1996. This was the first time since the establishment of the secular republic in the 1920s that an Islamic party had been in office. Refah lost power a year later when the coalition collapsed, and it was banned by Turkey's Constitutional Court in January 1998. But most of its members formed a new "Virtue party" that still constituted the largest single party in the Assembly. Muslim politics were now a factor in Turkish life. Yet, in a strong state, committed to the secular tradition and long aligned with the West, that did not mean that Turkey was going the way of Iran in the 1970s. "Turkey may be a state of Muslims, but it is far from an Islamic state."[44]

Even Iran was changing course in the 1990s. The economy had been ruined by the Iran-Iraq war of 1980–1988: per capita GDP fell by nearly 16 percent and per capita income by 45 percent.[45] The new leadership after Khomeini's death in June 1989 was more pragmatic. Sayid Ali Khameni was selected as spiritual leader *(faqih)* by the Assembly of Experts; Ali Akbar Hashemi Rafsanjani, veteran speaker of the Majlis, or parliament, won the presidential election the following month. Neither intended to abandon the clerical hold on political life. Nor were they in full control—Iran remained a polity of competing jurisdictions—and the two leaders were often at odds. Nevertheless, the early 1990s saw the Islamic populists, hitherto entrenched in the Majlis, lose out to conservatives, backed by propertied interests and *bazaari* merchants. The country's leaders revived capitalist practices, with which Iran had never fully broken, and opened up anew to the global economy, on which its oil incomes depended. Under Rafsanjani, Teheran's stock exchange was rejuvenated, many nationalized industries were privatized, and foreign investment was encouraged. The Islamic constitution was now mainly a device "to legitimate the rule of the clergy."[46]

In the presidential election in May 1997, over two-thirds of the electorate backed Sayid Mohammed Khatami, aged fifty-four, as Rafsanjani's successor. Although a cleric, Khatami was cosmopolitan in background. He spoke fluent English and German, and, as culture minister in the 1980s, had eased censorship on books and films. Khatami made clear his wish to improve relations with the United States, which still imposed sanctions on Iran because of its links with terrorists and its suspected nuclear arsenal. Tensions with Khameni, who was still the spiritual leader, intensified, and Iran faced the prospect of a long struggle between conservatives and reformers. But Khatami's Iran was clearly a far cry from Khomeini's. Here, as in Turkey, Egypt, and Algeria, Islamic politics had to be understood in national context. Despite polemicists on both sides, "Islam" was no more a unity than "the West".[47]

Poverty and Despotism in Sub-Saharan Africa

The 1980s were a disaster for most of Africa, with war across the south and the effective collapse of many states (see Chapter 13). The early 1990s, however, seemed more hopeful. South Africa's transition from white minority rule in 1994 was matched by the demise of long-standing black autocrats, from Banda in Malawi to Mobutu in Zaire. But the revival of multiparty politics did not resolve Africa's underlying social and economic crises. The 1990s also saw genocidal civil war in central Africa, famine across the Horn, and the inexorable spread of AIDs.

Nevertheless, the transformation of South Africa was, as Nelson Mandela put it, "a small miracle."[48] In January 1990 Mandela was enduring his twenty-seventh year as a political prisoner. In April 1994, aged seventy-five, he voted for the first time in his life in an election that made him the state president.

Even in the late 1980s, the government of P. W. Botha had recognized the need for a new course after the failure of the state of emergency (see Chapter 13). But real progress came after the ailing Botha was maneuvered from power by F. W. de Klerk, who became state president in August 1989. De Klerk released most of the leadership of the banned African National Congress (ANC) and began dismantling apartheid. On February 2, 1990, in his inaugural address as state president, he announced the unbanning of all political parties, including the ANC and the communists, and stated that "only a negotiated understanding among the representative leaders of the entire population is able to ensure lasting peace."[49] Nine days later, Mandela himself was freed from jail.

De Klerk was, in part, responding to economic pressures. The collapse of direct foreign investment and the imposition of trade sanctions had undermined the economy. Security spending, both against domestic insurrection and neighboring insurgencies, absorbed some 9 percent of GDP.[50] The end of the cold war also offered new opportunities. During 1988, Washington and Moscow brokered an agreement over Namibia. South Africa was persuaded to withdraw from its northern neighbor and concede independence, in return for the removal of Cuban troops. Namibian independence was declared in March 1990 after SWAPO had won the country's first election. The metamorphosis of this Marxist revolutionary front into pragmatic advocates of a mixed economy encouraged Pretoria. In the new international atmosphere, as de Klerk put it, "the risk that the ANC was being used as a Trojan Horse" by the Soviets "had drastically diminished."[51]

De Klerk seemed a far cry from his predecessor—fifty-two years old to Botha's seventy-three, exuding a pragmatic reasonableness very different from the cantankerousness of the "Great Crocodile." But the contrast was not total. Far from conceding ANC majority rule, de Klerk hoped, like Botha, to build an anti-ANC coalition with Zulus and coloreds and to protect white minority rights through veto powers. Unable to repress the armed struggle, he hoped to outwit the aged revolutionaries in the back rooms of politics.

At first, he seemed to be succeeding. Despite its popular support, the ANC faced a herculean task. It had to turn itself from a front organization in exile into a nationwide political party and to convert stale Marxist slogans, often learned in Cuba or Eastern Europe, into policies for an advanced capitalist economy. It also faced escalating domestic violence, as ANC supporters battled with those of Chief Mangosuthu Buthelezi, leader of the Inkatha Freedom Party, who wanted an independent Zulu state in Natal. In the years 1985–1989, some five thousand four hundred South Africans had died in political violence. Between January 1990 and April 1994, supposedly years of transition, the figure was 14,211, over half of them in Natal.[52] With the government's security forces implicated in some of Buthelezi's violence, relations between the ruling National Party (NP) and the ANC also deteriorated.

Meanwhile, talks about talks had finally moved into a formal Convention for a Democratic South Africa (Codesa). Involving nineteen different parties, this met in the World Trade Center in Kempton Park outside Johannesburg, from December 1991. But the gulf was too vast: "many in the 'establishment' camp assumed that the ANC had come back to join the existing order; many in the 'liberation' fold believed that the exiles and prisoners had returned to take the NP's surrender.[53] Codesa broke down in May 1992. The next few months saw a rolling campaign of "mass action" by the ANC, hoping that strikes and marches could crack the apartheid state. South Africa, however, was less vulnerable to "people power" than the Philippines or Eastern Europe. The violence only produced more massacres. Both de Klerk and Mandela were appalled by the bloodbath. They were also sobered by warnings that, as Mandela put it, "the economy is going to be so destroyed that when a democratic government comes to power, it will not be able to solve it."[54]

A new Multi-Party Negotiating Forum began work in September 1992. The venue was the same, Kempton Park, but the assumptions were very different. Instead of trying to build a coalition against the ANC, the NP was now ready to strike a bargain with it. Instead of insisting on separate "group rights" for whites and coloreds, it sought constitutional checks on a majority government, both at the center and via a federal structure. The ANC had also moved, recognizing that a successful transfer of power meant a gradual transition, not a sudden handover. Joe Slovo, the veteran communist leader, paved the way with his proposal of "sunset clauses" to protect whites during the dusk of the old order, including job security in the bureaucracy and armed forces, an amnesty on past crimes and, above all, "compulsory power sharing for a period of years."[55] The aim was agreement between the two political elites based on "sufficient consensus"—in other words, papering over the cracks lest delay produce total anarchy.[56] By November 1993 agreement had been reached on an interim constitution. This provided for elections the following spring to choose a "government of national unity." Any party with more than 5 percent of the vote would be entitled to a proportionate share of cabinet seats. This government would serve for five years, while a new constitution would be drafted and approved.

The ANC and the National Party had brokered a transition, with the former now in the ascendancy. But the deal would not work if other interested groups refused to abandon the bullet for the ballot. So Mandela negotiated feverishly with black and white extremists, persuading even Buthelezi to enter the elections. At last, the chronic violence began to subside. Over four days, April 26–29, 1994, South Africans voted in their first multiracial elections. Accusations of fraud and intimidation were rampant, especially in the new province of KwaZula/Natal, where Inkatha and the ANC battled on. But in the end, the parties made some secret deals and then accepted the electoral outcome. The alternatives were far worse—a rerun or even renewed violence—and in any case, the results gave something to all the major players. The ANC had gained 252 of the four hundred Assembly seats, but fell 4 percent short of the two-thirds majority needed to change the constitution. The National Party had crossed the 20 percent threshold required to make de Klerk one of the deputy presidents, and Inkatha picked up enough support to earn three cabinet posts. Equally important, extremists on right and left—the white Freedom Front and the Pan-African Congress—had both entered the elections, only to win minimal support. Whether or not the voting was totally "free and fair," this was a triumph of politics over violence and, as such, the crux of South Africa's "negotiated transition."[57]

Above all, it was a triumph for Nelson Mandela and the philosophy of multiracial conciliation that he had pressed on the ANC. At his inauguration on May 10, 1994, he pledged himself to create "a rainbow nation at peace with itself and the world."[58] His new cabinet included blacks, whites, coloreds, and Asians (all four of apartheid's racial groups), as well as capitalists, socialists, a communist (Joe Slovo), and three Zulu nationalists. But this was still a country with over 30 percent unemployment, in which only 20 percent of blacks had running water in their homes, and in which perhaps a quarter of the 40 million population had "no formal shelter," many of them living in squatter camps constructed of mud, sheet metal, or plywood. South Africa's per capita figures for murders and violent crime outdid even those of the United States.[59] Although the new government addressed these problems—connecting over one million blacks to running water in the first four years, for instance—it could not create an economic miracle. To gain international confidence, most of the old socialist policies were jettisoned in favor of fiscal restraint, deregulation, and privatization of several major industries. But this increased unemployment. The government was caught between the demands of international capitalism and the expectations of its domestic proleteriat.

Despite the rhetoric, the 1994 election had been largely an "ethnic census."[60] Only 3 or 4 percent of blacks and whites voted across racial lines. The same was true in the election of June 1999, after which Thabo Mbeki succeeded Mandela as ANC leader and State president. After the years of transition, the party was now clamoring for rapid transformation of South Africa's racial imbalances. The new constitution, which took effect in 1999, dropped all vestiges of power sharing. This opened the prospect of unequivocal rule by the black majority (75 percent of the population), particularly if the ANC commanded more than the two-thirds of seats needed to change the constitution. At that point, South Africa might follow the path of other African states after independence from white rule toward a one-party state. The long-term prospect for multiparty democracy depended on the ANC's fragmenting, perhaps along class lines, if richer blacks forged new alliances with reformist whites.

South Africa's political transition was not unique. The period 1990–1994 saw what has been called the "most far-reaching shifts in African political life since the time of political independence 30 years earlier." In January 1989 only five of the forty-seven states in sub-Saharan Africa could be described (using generous criteria) as having a multiparty system: Botswana, the Gambia, Mauritius, Senegal, and Zimbabwe. By the end of 1994, the figure was thirty-eight. Hitherto, only once had a political leader been displaced by an election, but eleven suffered that fate in 1990–1994, and three more were elected in contests where the incumbent did not run. Most striking, in 1995 Africa had no *de jure* one-party states; in 1989 there had been twenty-nine.[61]

How can this transformation be explained? External pressures were particularly important. One was the effect of international aid on corrupt, statist economies. In the decade 1979–1989, the World Bank established sixty-six structural adjustment programs (SAPs) in thirty African countries, mostly after 1983.[62] The condition of aid was economic liberalization: ending protectionism, pruning regulation, and cutting government spending. To the World Bank, "unleashing markets" was an economic panacea;[63] less well appreciated were the political effects. Cutting government projects and slashing state jobs hit the patronage networks created by African rulers. Reducing subsidies on food and fuel caused popular discontent when the price of essentials suddenly rose. Apart from structural adjustment, there was another important external influence. The breaching of the Berlin wall and the televised execution of Ceauşescu in Romania in 1989 had a powerful effect—as did, nearer home, Mandela's release from prison in February 1990. Across urban Africa, the potential of "people power" and the demise of one-party states were noted by rulers and ruled alike.

Frequently the democratic transition began with strikes and demonstrations by workers, students, government employees, and other disgruntled victims of structural adjustment. Some protests were on a massive scale: in Madagascar in the summer of 1991, perhaps five hundred thousand marched through the capital, Antananarivo, on several occasions. Governments responded with a mixture of coercion and concession, but their capacity for both was constrained by the crisis of the state. Gradually demands became politicized as unions and professional organizations were drawn in. Rulers conceded first greater liberalization—particularly a freer press—and then constitutional reform. The device of a "national conference," though used in South Africa, was otherwise confined to Francophone Africa. More common was a referendum, usually to approve a constitution but sometimes (as in South Africa and Malawi) to decide its content. The whole process generally climaxed in multiparty elections. As in Eastern Europe, the media had a mimetic effect. The national conference in the West African state of Benin in February 1990 was televised across the former French Africa, acting as a model for Congo, Mali, and other Francophone states.

In most cases, the critical question was whether large but random street protests could be directed into a coherent movement for political reform. And this depended less on external stimuli than on the condition of civil society within individual African states. Of particular importance were three social elements: a strong, independent trade union movement; middle-class associations of lawyers, academics, and other professionals, who codified political demands and monitored human rights; and church leaders and their national organizations who used their protected position to take a lead in speaking against the regime. As these groups opened up the political arena, they often facilitated the reentry of "old politicians"—either veteran opposition figures such as Oginga Odinga in Kenya or more recent defectors from the ruling party such as Kenneth Matiba. Both of these men were leaders of Kenya's reform movement in 1991.[64]

There were some spectacular casualties of Africa's new electoral politics.

In Zambia, President Kenneth Kaunda had last faced a competitive democratic election in 1968, four years after independence. But the Movement for Multi-Party Democracy, orchestrated by the union leader Frederick Chiluba, obliged him to legalize political opposition and permit elections in October 1991. Despite government intimidation, gerrymandering, and abuse of emergency powers, Chiluba and his party won a landslide victory. In Malawi, "President-for-Life" Hastings Banda and his Malawi Congress party suffered a similar fate. In the late 1980s, Banda's "companion" Cecilia Kadzamira and her uncle, John Tembo, extended their brutal control over Malawi as the president (who was probably as old as the century) lost his grip. But a pastoral letter from Malawi's Catholic bishops, read out in every church in March 1992, unleashed real protest, and the information revolution breached Banda's closed society. Opposition groups based in Zambia bombarded businesses and government offices in Malawi with faxes about reform in Zambia and South Africa, which were then disseminated by photocopier; and desktop publishing on PCs produced several dozen unofficial newspapers. In October 1992 Banda conceded a referendum on multiparty elections the following June. By a two-to-one vote, this ended the twenty-seven-year ban on competitive politics. Elections in May 1994 brought victory for the opposition United Democratic Front.[65]

There was another side to the story, however. Although fourteen African elections in 1990–1994 led to a change of government, another twenty-one confirmed existing leaders in power.[66] One of these was Jerry Rawlings, who had ruled Ghana since his coup in 1981. His structural adjustment program was lauded by the World Bank in 1994 as "one of the most successful in Africa.[67] Subsidies had been cut, state assets sold off, and the currency floated. Although Rawlings began to lose control in 1989–1990 as economic reform eroded his base and political opposition was emboldened by reform elsewhere, his government reckoned that it could manage the new process successfully. Creation of new district assemblies enabled him to win support from chiefs and local notables; economic liberalization allowed aspirant capitalists to make money from trade, foreign exchange, and government contracts. Mass support, particularly in the neglected north, was engineered by new roads, rural electrification, and other infrastructure projects.[68] Rawlings duly won the presidential election of December 1992, but his party was widely accused of fraud and intimidation. Four years, later, however, Ghana's first fully independent elections since independence in 1957 renewed his mandate and also created a solid opposition in parliament.

In Ghana the leadership survived, although the system seemed to be changing. More typical, however, was the case of Kenya, which also elected its president in December 1992. President Daniel arap Moi's increasingly autocratic government (*L'État, c'est Moi*) rested mainly on support from his own Kalenjin region. Opposition from unions, churches, and the dominant Kikuyu farming and commercial elites mounted in 1990–1991. Western donors made multi-party elections a condition of further aid. But Moi used local government officials to harass his opponents, adroitly exploiting their division along ethnic lines. The result was victory for Moi despite his winning little more than one-third of the vote. In Kenya, the advent of multiparty politics changed virtually nothing, and the country remained an authoritarian state.[69] This was one example of the new "big man democracy," in which the formal trappings of pluralism cloaked the old patrimonial politics.[70]

Nor was the military finished as a political force. The example with greatest significance was Nigeria, with about 120 million people Africa's most populous state, where the military had ruled from 1966 to 1979 and again since the end of 1983.[71] General Ibrahim Babangida, the army chief of staff, took charge after a bloodless coup in August 1985. After one of the longest and most complex democratic transitions in history, he created two political parties—one, in his words, "a little to the left," the other, "a little to the right." When Nigeria finally voted in June 1993, Moshood Abiola, a Muslim press magnate from the south, won an estimated 58 percent of the vote. But the results were never declared because Babangida promptly annulled the election, apparently afraid that northern military predominance was in jeopardy. After a brief interim government, a new military council was established in November 1993 under General Sani Abacha. Abacha's pledges of early civilian rule proved as empty as Babangida's. His regime became personal, corrupt, and brutally repressive. In June 1994 Abiola was imprisoned indefinitely, becoming a focus for opposition. The political deadlock was broken only when first Abacha and then Abiola died of heart attacks in the summer of 1998. The new army leader, General Abdusalam Abubakar, honored his promise of early civilian rule, and Olusegun Obasanjo, who had been Nigeria's military ruler twenty years before, won the election of February 1999. But it would take years for Nigeria to transcend its patrimonial and regional politics, which had long pitted the dominant Muslim north against the more Christian south.

Nigeria was a reminder that, in much of Africa, the military remained the backbone of the state. Some regions, in fact, were ruled by the gun. Although most of southern Africa had been pacified, civil wars ravaged two other vast areas—the Horn, and the "Great Lakes Region" of central Africa.

In the Horn, two of Africa's most durable dictators were toppled during 1991. In January, Mohammed Siad Barre, who had ruled Somalia since 1969, was overthrown by rebels of the United Somalia Congress. In May, Mengistu Haile Mariam, whose revolutionary Derg government had controlled Ethiopia since 1974, fled Addis Ababa in the face of a combined offensive by

Ethiopian and Eritrean guerrillas. The struggle in Ethiopia, Africa's third most populous state with about fifty million people, had cost an estimated one million lives since 1974. Mengistu's Marxist-Leninist regime had been undermined by declining Soviet aid during the Gorbachev era, while the United States, no longer so concerned about cold war geopolitics, had become less supportive of Siad Barre.

But 1991 did not bring peace and stability to the Horn. The United Somalia Congress, a wartime front, soon degenerated into clan conflicts—"the culmination of a struggle for territorial control" in a society where the rights of farmers and pastoralists had been crushed by land nationalization and state farms during the Barre era.[72] American TV, however, focused only on the struggle over the government in Mogadishu, representing Somalia as a warlord movie with Mohammed Farah Aydid cast as the principal bad guy. By late 1992, about a quarter of Somalia's seven million population was estimated to be facing starvation. Public pressure grew for the Bush administration to mount a "shoot-to-feed" operation. The president was sensitive to charges that his "new world order" was mere gulf war rhetoric.[73] Against Pentagon advice, he therefore committed U.S. Marines in December 1992; they became the core of a UN force that peaked at nearly forty thousand men. With them, of course, came the TV crews. CBS spent $2.5 million in the first three weeks of the U.S. presence. ABC rented a mansion from one of Mogadishu's drug dealers, outbidding the Save the Children Fund.[74] But by October 1993, as U.S. soldiers were shot and killed in a televised hunt for Aydid around the streets of Mogadishu, American opinion swung against further involvement. Bush's successor, Bill Clinton, pulled out U.S. forces, and the UN operation ran down. But the fighting went on. After Aydid died of gunshot wounds in August 1996, leadership devolved on his thirty-five-year-old son, Hussein, a former U.S. Marine reservist who had lived in America since the age of fourteen but who had returned to Somalia in 1992 with the U.S. peacekeeping force![75]

Nor was the rest of the Horn at peace. Eritrea had regained its independence in 1993, but border disputes brought it into conflict with Yemen and Djibouti in 1995–1996, and with its former ally, the new government in Ethiopia, in 1998–1999. Their western neighbor, the Sudan, was still wracked by the civil war that had been waged with only one decade of respite since independence in 1956. Conflict between the Christian and African minority in the south and their Arab, Islamic rulers in Khartoum had resumed in 1983, when President Nimeiri tore up the 1972 agreement on regional autonomy and imposed Islamic law on the whole country.[76] Southern rebel groups, of which the most significant was led by John Garang, continued the struggle against the military government that took power in 1989, in association with the National Islamic Front. The government received substantial support from Iran, to the alarm of Sudan's non-Islamic neighbors, who gave help to the rebels. After Mengistu's fall, President Museveni of Uganda became Garang's main backer, and fighting dragged on through the 1990s. An estimated one million southerners had died in the fifteen years since 1983.[77] Famine was endemic, but the world was indifferent, apart from occasional media flurries. Clearly, the end of the cold war had changed the faces but not the rhythms of politics across the Horn of Africa.

The mid-1990s also saw the implosion of central Africa as genocidal conflict engulfed Burundi and especially Rwanda in 1993–1994, with knock-on effects that finally toppled the Mobutu regime in neighboring Zaire.

Burundi and Rwanda, each little larger in area than Wales, were Belgian trust territories from the end of World War I until independence in 1962. The underlying ethnic tension was between Tutsis, the precolonial elite of cattle keepers whom the Belgians had used as agents of their rule, and the Hutu farming majority. After independence, the Tutsis had retained power in Burundi, but in Rwanda the Hutu middle class led the liberation movement and formed the new government. Some two hundred thousand Tutsi refugees fled Rwanda, half going to Uganda.[78] In the 1980s, some of them (and their descendants) helped Yoweri Museveni's National Resistance Army to gain power in Uganda in 1986 (see Chapter 13). They then formed a Rwandese Patriotic Front (RPF), backed by Museveni, which fought a three-year war until the Rwandan government of General Juvénal Habyarimana signed a peace agreement in August 1993. This provided for a broad transitional government, including the RPF, and a fusion of the army and police.

Many in the West portrayed what happened next as evidence of the irredeemable primitiveness at the heart of the Dark Continent. But as we shall also see in Yugoslavia, ethnicity is rarely a spontaneous force. It needs to be manipulated by politicians. What mattered in Rwanda was the reaction of Hutu hard-liners in the party and the army to their impending loss of power. Although details of what happened on April 6, 1994, remain murky, it seems that they shot down Habyarimana's plane to sabotage the peace agreement. They then mounted a well-planned massacre of liberal politicians and leading Tutsis. But the killing became anarchic as street boys, car washers, and the unemployed vented their fury on anyone with wealth and authority; villagers seized the chance to pillage and to settle old scores. Neither hospitals nor churches provided any sanctuary against the marauders and their machetes. In Kigali, when a few thousand Tutsis sought refuge in the sports stadium, the Rwandan army lobbed in artillery shells. Women were raped before being murdered, babies smashed against rocks or thrown alive into latrines. The death toll was probably eight hundred thousand—about 11 percent of the population and proportionately one of the worst genocides of the postwar era. Meanwhile, the world looked on. The Clinton administration desperately avoided the word *genocide,* afraid it would be sucked into another Somalia-style intervention.[79]

Instead of blocking the power-sharing agreement, the massacres ensured total victory for the RPF. With Rwanda in anarchy, RPF troops advanced on Kigali, and by July were in full control of the country. While thousands of Tutsis returned from exile in Uganda, Tanzania, and Zaire, some two million Hutu refugees fled the country, mostly to Zaire. Although the RPF established a coalition government, in which General Paul Kagame, the thin, bespectacled former army leader, was the key figure, Tutsi control became more marked, and independent Hutus were gradually squeezed out. In Burundi, a Hutu-led coalition that had won power through elections in June 1993 was toppled by a Tutsi-led coup in July 1996. This gave Tutsis control over both Rwanda and Burundi, yet the populations of the two countries were about four-fifths Hutu. Both governments depended on foreign aid, insurgencies were gaining strength, and pluralist politics were now impossible. For Tutsis after 1994, "democracy means death."[80]

Rwanda's ethnic turmoil also overwhelmed Joseph Mobutu in Zaire. Hutu refugees flooded into eastern Zaire's Kivu region. Their camps were used to attack Zaire's Tutsi minority, who organized in self-defense. The camps were also bases for raids into Rwanda and Uganda, whose governments gave their backing to the Tutsis of eastern Zaire. In autumn 1996, Tutsi forces linked up with other dissidents under the leadership of Laurent Kabila. Together they pushed westward. Kivu lies a thousand miles east of the capital, Kinshasa, with dozens of rivers in between and no decent road. But Mobutu, now gravely ill with prostate cancer, was frequently out of the country, and most of his troops melted away. Kabila's forces entered Kinshasa in May 1997; Mobutu died in exile in Morocco four months later. But the new leader proved little better than the old. Kabila was a corpulent Marxist who had been fighting Mobutu on and off for thirty years from his Kivu enclave, out of touch with Kinshasa, let alone modernity. Once in power, he renamed the country the Democratic Republic of Congo, promised a rapid transition to democracy, and began mouthing the free-market slogans necessary to endear himself to Washington. But the reality was a Mobutu-style personal rule, with state power again a form of booty. By the summer of 1998, Kabila's regime was under attack from his former allies, the Tutsis, and their backers in Rwanda and Uganda. With Angola and Zimbabwe drawn in on his side, the Congo seemed in danger of becoming, as in the early 1960s, the arena of civil war and regional conflict.

Major powers were also involved. Museveni of Uganda had become one of

America's leading African allies. In Paris, the revolutions he backed in Rwanda and Zaire, at the expense of veteran French clients, were deeply alarming. There was also growing French concern about the future of the franc zone in West and central Africa, as economic liberalization opened doors for the almighty dollar. A new "scramble for Africa" was predicted, centering on Washington and Paris.[81]

African commentators debated how to avoid renewed economic "dependency" on the West. For some, the answer was to break away from Western ideologies that, in their view, had been the neocolonial curse of the postindependence era.[82] Instead of "top-down" politics and economic individualism, they argued, Africa needed decentralized, participatory politics, rooted in indigenous traditions of kinship and communal obligation. Nigerian federalism was cited as an example. The number of states there had risen from twelve in 1967 to thirty in 1991, to mitigate the battles over resources and revenues that had helped cause the 1960s civil war.[83] The government of post-Mengistu Ethiopia also adopted a federal structure in 1995 for similar reasons.[84] But skeptics claimed that Nigerian devolution was evidence of a vast, ungovernable polity being pulled apart, and that decentralization was more likely to produce anarchy than democracy. Rural networks of kin and community had been fractured by years of violent state building and chaotic urbanization. Moreover, experience in East Asia and Latin America suggested that strong states were preconditions for capitalist growth. Without them, Africa would be marginalized in an increasingly global, knowledge-based economy. The combination of weak states and economic crisis indicated, in this view, that, for decades to come, Africa's "bedrock political form will remain weak, authoritarian, clientelist, and inefficient."[85]

Meanwhile, sub-Saharan Africa as a whole was wracked by demographic crises. It was the one region of the world in which fertility had not begun seriously to decline, outside South Africa, Botswana, Zimbabwe, Kenya, and parts of Nigeria.[86] Thus, the pressure of population on resources would be unremitting for decades to come. Africa was also the region most ravaged by AIDS, which struck hardest at working adults and parents—the economic and social linchpins of society. In Botswana and Zimbabwe one in four adults was infected with HIV by 1998; South Africa was nearing that figure. (The worldwide HIV infection rate for adults was 1 percent.) Vast long-term damage had already occurred: in East Africa, 40 percent of children under fifteen had lost at least one parent.[87] In a continent where states were weak and markets distorted, the family—that fundamental source of stability and wealth—was also being ripped apart. Africa's new politics were but a surface wave on its sea of troubles.

Latin America: Opening Up Economies, States, and Region

For Latin America, as for sub-Saharan Africa, the 1980s was a "lost decade." Debt crises, military rule, and Central America's brutal wars brought misery to millions (see Chapter 13). But Latin America was better off than black Africa. Most borders were accepted, states were firm if repressive, and extensive urbanization created the potential for a vigorous civil society, which was realized in the new social movements of the mid-1980s. Moreover, the overcommitment of international banks to Latin America and the concern of the United States about instability among its neighbors guaranteed greater outside attention than was accorded to Africa.

In consequence, the 1990s saw historic changes across much of Latin America. First, crises induced by debt and adjustment prompted a general abandonment of the import-substituting economic nationalism that had been prevalent since the trauma of the depression in the 1930s (see Chapter 3). Second, these policies were sustained by civilian governments operating within more open electoral politics. Overall, the 1990s reinforce the shaky transition to democracy that had begun in the 1980s, building on the new social movements aroused in that decade. Third, the late 1980s and early 1990s also saw the consolidation of regional peace in Central America and the isolation of Castro's Cuba as a failing Leninist state. Instead of cold war conflicts polarized around Cuba, a new pattern emerged: regional integration increased as market-driven semidemocracies sought to confirm their economic and political transitions by closer cooperation among themselves and with the United States.

The first two developments should be considered together, since it had been a widespread assumption that authoritarian regimes were best placed to push through socially painful programs of economic adjustment.[88] Party politics and freedom of expression, so the argument ran, militated against the necessary cuts in spending, subsidies, and protectionism. This claim was apparently validated by the so-called heterodox economic programs imposed in Argentina, Brazil, and Peru in the mid-1980s, which tried to cure inflation through exchange and price controls while maintaining government spending to cushion the social damage and satisfy key interest groups. These populist projects only served to boost the budget deficit while failing to eliminate inflation, which was running at 7,000 percent in Peru in 1990. In contrast, the Chilean junta of President Augusto Pinochet (1973–1990), guided by economists schooled in American neoliberalism, pushed through a program of privatization and deregulation that gave Chile average annual rates of 6 percent growth and only 20 percent inflation in the period 1985–1989. By 1990, Chile was one of the most open and diverse Latin American economies.

During the 1990s, however, it became clear that nonmilitary governments *could* sustain significant economic and political liberalizations simultaneously. But two conditions were especially important. First, states that embarked on a democratic transition after economic crisis had been resolved found the task much easier. Second, institutionalized party systems with deep social roots helped to mobilize consent for tough economic reforms.[89]

Chile's experience highlights the first point.[90] It was not until the end of the 1980s, later than most of Latin America, that political opposition to Pinochet was organized. This secured a 55 percent "no" vote in the October 1988 plebiscite on whether Pinochet should continue as president. The Democratic Coalition went on to win electoral victory in December 1989 for Patricio Aylwin, a Christian Democrat from the Allende era. Another Christian Democrat, Eduardo Frei (son of Chile's president in 1964–1970) succeeded him four years later as head of the continuing coalition. But although boosting social spending, Aylwin and Frei continued Pinochet's main economic policies, conscious that they were essential for the confidence of foreign investors and domestic business. At the same time, Pinochet shaped the political transition. The 1978 amnesty law prevented legal redress for the killings and torture of the early years of military rule, and the presence of nine appointed senators in the upper house blocked the two-thirds majority needed for constitutional change. Pinochet remained commander of the armed forces until March 1998 and then became a senator for life (giving him immunity from civil actions). His presidency therefore cast a long shadow over Chile's economy and politics.

Mexico and Argentina (the region's second and third most populous states, with eighty-four million and thirty-two million, respectively, in 1990) were contrasting examples of the second theme—the vital role of party systems in managing economic and democratic transitions.

In Mexico, the Partido Revolucionario Institucional (PRI) retained its dominance by acting as a broad coalition of economic and political elites. Under President Carlos Salinas de Gortari (1988–1994), another American-trained technocrat, the momentum of liberalization was maintained, with continued tariff cuts and privatization of sacred cows such as the national telephone company. Mexico's economy also survived another massive currency crisis in 1994–1995, when Salinas delayed an orderly devaluation of the peso. His successor, Ernesto Zedillo (another technocrat but of working-class background), was left with no choice in December 1994. The ensuing panic by foreign investors produced a major recession, including a 5 percent fall in GDP. On the other hand, Mexico's exports became more competitive, and the economy was growing strongly again by 1997.

Politics were also being liberalized. A combination of voter hostility and electoral reform made the 1988 election the closest in Mexico's modern history, with Salinas winning only 50.7 percent of the vote. He came into office acknowledging that "the era of the virtual one-party state has ended."[91] Further reform, plus opposition monitoring, helped make Mexico's 1994 contest the fairest ever, even though the PRI's patronage network and plutocrat backers still ensured victory. In July 1997 the PRI lost control of the lower house for the first time in its history. A robust party system was taking shape, with the National Action Party (PAN) building up its local support, and the charismatic politician Cuauhtémoc Cárdenas (son of the revered 1930s president) leading a breakaway faction of the PRI. Cárdenas won a third of the vote in the 1988 presidential election. Although he was less successful in 1994, his election as mayor of Mexico City in 1997 created a firm base for his campaign in the year 2000.

In Argentina, by contrast, the democratic transition preceded economic transformation. Indeed, the collapse of the junta after its defeat in the war with Britain coincided with the debt crisis of 1982–1983 (see Chapter 13). The October 1983 elections brought victory for the Radicals, one of the country's two established parties. But President Raúl Alfonsín could not resolve the economic crisis: his "heterodox" Austral Plan failed to check inflation or boost growth. Not only did the Peronists under Carlos Menem, a former provincial governor, win the presidential elections of May 1989, but the outbreak of humiliating food riots that summer also prompted Alfonsín to resign six months early.

From this unpropitious start, however, Menem was able to effect a transformation. Like Salinas in Mexico, he foreswore his statist, big-spending past and, tutored by economists from Argentina's leading multinational, Bunge y Born, he pushed through liberal economic policies despite the social costs. His ability to do so was enhanced by his Peronist credentials, which made him less vulnerable to attacks from big labor.[92] Menem won a second term in 1994; despite recession in 1995 and continued high unemployment, the economy grew strongly in the later 1990s. The political transition was also consolidated. The four minor military revolts of 1987–1990 were followed by more effective civilian control in the following decade. In the midterm elections of October 1997, the Peronists lost control of the lower house to the new alliance between the Radicals and the center-left Frepaso. Competitive politics were taking root, provided the country could maintain its stability after Menem's second term ended in 1999.

In Mexico and Argentina, the party system helped manage an orderly process of economic and political liberalization. This was not the case in

Brazil—Latin America's most populous country, with nearly one hundred fifty million people in 1990. Here political parties were weak and transitory, serving as vehicles for local elites to maintain some influence during military rule (1964–1985).[93] The presidential elections at the end of 1989 took place after the collapse of the Sarney government's Cruzado economic plan. Hyperinflation was running at nearly 3,000 percent per annum; the economy had contracted by over 4 percent during that year.[94] In these circumstances, the party system virtually fell apart. Victory was seized by Fernando Collor de Mello, the scion of a wealthy political family with large media interests, who mounted a shrewd TV campaign to promote himself as an outsider building "the New Brazil." Collor's independence allowed him to impose a draconian program of austerity and liberalization, but his lack of a political base made bribery and favors even more necessary to push through his plan. His corruption was exposed in the summer of 1992. After mass street protests and a tenacious legislative campaign, he was forced to resign in December to avoid impeachment. His fall showed that Brazilian democracy had acquired a certain stability. "For the first time in the country's history, a severe governmental crisis had been resolved without resort to extra-constitutional means."[95]

A caretaker government continued Collor's economic policies. Its finance minister, Fernando Cardoso, imposed a new currency that helped curb inflation. Cardoso used this success to win the presidency for himself in the elections of late 1994; continued price stability helped earn his broad coalition a second term in October 1998. Pushing ahead with privatization later than its neighbors, Brazil mounted a massive sell-off, including much of the electricity and telecom systems. Serious government deficits—due in part to the country's "peripheralized federalism," which left substantial revenues in local hands[96]—made Brazil vulnerable to debt-related pressure on its currency in the world financial crisis of 1998. But the country's strong growth rate and vast internal market made it the world's eighth largest economy, generating 40 percent of Latin America's GDP.

Thus South America's largest and most developed states sustained economic and political liberalization during the 1990s. The post–cold war decade also marked a new era for Central America, where the transition to political pluralism was also a passage from war to peace.[97] In 1978, only Costa Rica, Latin America's most durable democracy, had an elected civilian regime; by 1995 all six countries of the region had one. In 1982, El Salvador, Guatemala, and Nicaragua were ravaged by civil wars; by the end of 1996 all three had been terminated. In the process, however, some two hundred thousand people had died, another two million were uprooted, and the peace and prosperity of the whole isthmus was destroyed.

In the early 1980s, Central America had become one of the main arenas of the new cold war (see Chapter 13) as the Reagan administration tried to contain the 1979 Sandinista revolution in Nicaragua and the resurgent Cuban challenge. The vacuum created by the contraction of Soviet power in the later 1980s and the waning authority of the Reagan administration after the Iran-Contra scandal provided scope for local initiative. This came from Oscar Arias, the new president of Costa Rica, whose peace plan of February 1987 centered not on security issues and foreign intervention but on national reconciliation through gradual democratization. This was the basis for a set of agreements signed in August 1987 by the governments of Guatemala, El Salvador, Honduras, Nicaragua, and Costa Rica. Reagan did his best to frustrate the agreements but, once endorsed by George Bush in 1989, they served as foundations for a new order in Central America.[98]

Implementation took time. The decisive opening came in Nicaragua. The the Sandinista government of Daniel Ortega, though still unbowed in 1988, was spending half its budget on defense and presiding over hyperinflation of 33,000 percent a year. Once Gorbachev ceased arms shipments to the Sandinistas and Bush stopped aid to their Contra opponents, Ortega accepted elections in February 1990, confident that he would win. Instead, a fragile coalition headed by Violeta Chamorro gained 55 percent of the vote. Ortega accepted the electoral verdict. The handover of power in Nicaragua set a precedent. In El Salvador, a peace agreement was signed in January 1992, in Guatemala in December 1996. Thanks to war weariness, democracy had triumphed by default.

Sometimes, however, the United States intervened directly to clean up the debris of cold war. In Panama, the problem was General Manuel Noriega, the military commander and effective ruler, who had served in the past as a CIA operative and as a channel for aid to the anti-Sandinista forces in Nicaragua. By the late 1980s, however, Noriega's drug running and harassment of U.S. military personnel provoked American ire. After Noriega had annulled elections in May 1989, President Bush sent in twenty-three thousand troops in December to capture him and install the probable victor of the elections, Guillermo Endara, as president. The United States also sent another twenty thousand troops to Haiti in September 1994 to reinstate the elected president, Father Jean-Bertrand Aristide, who had been exiled after a coup in September 1991. This followed an agreement with the military regime, which had been brought to its knees by international sanctions. The return of civilian government did little, however, to relieve the poverty of Haiti's seven million people, still suffering from three decades of the Duvalier family's venal despotism (1957–1986).

Such power projections were a reminder of Washington's dominance in the region. In contrast, Fidel Castro's Cuba, feared in the 1960s as the vanguard of Soviet expansion, was now an embattled anomaly. In the mid-1980s, the

Soviet bloc accounted for 85 percent of Cuba's trade. Only Moscow's readiness to buy Cuba's sugar crop at three times the market price and to supply heavily subsidized oil kept the country afloat.[99] The collapse of Soviet economic aid, combined with the maintenance of U.S. sanctions, caused economic crisis. Castro tried to boost food self-sufficiency and cut imports through consumer rationing. To save on oil, half Havana's bus routes were eliminated, and the city suffered chronic power cuts. After mounting protests, however, in July 1993 Castro ended the official ban on holding U.S. dollars and legitimized private food markets and small businesses. Around tourism, a corrupt, parasitic capitalism sprang up. Although the economy grew by 6 percent in 1996, the collapse of state finances ruined the health and education services that had been the positive side of Castro's dictatorship.[100] Repression became more marked in the mid-1990s as hard-liners, led by Fidel's brother, Raúl, sought to shore up the regime, which became increasingly dependent on the army and security services. As long as Fidel remained in power, the system was likely to survive, but he was now over seventy and in failing health. With him or without him, Cuba's future seemed grim.

While Cuba remained isolated, the rest of South America began a new era of economic integration. The most important framework was the North American Free Trade Agreement (NAFTA) among the United States, Canada, and Mexico. When NAFTA came into effect in January 1994, it created the world's most populous free trade market, comprising 360 million people with a combined GDP of $6.5 billion. Canada and the United States had already forged a common market in 1989. The initiative for Mexico's inclusion came from President Salinas, keen to reinforce his country's conversion to export-led growth. Agreement was reached in principle in August 1992 after fourteen months of negotiations. Although the deal was generally supported in Mexico, it faced strong opposition in the United States from labor unions, concerned about the threat to jobs from the low-wage Mexican economy, and from environmental groups, worried that firms would go south to evade strict U.S. regulation. With these interests well represented in the Democratic-controlled House, it took considerable personal lobbying by President Bill Clinton to secure passage in November 1993. In Mexico the effects were seen both along the border in the *maquilladoras,* or duty-free assembly plants set up by U.S. companies, and among local industries such as automobiles and textiles, which started to gear up in quantity and quality for the North American market. The new sense of political solidarity, after decades of hostility and tension, was demonstrated by the speed with which Clinton rushed through the huge rescue package for the peso in January 1995, despite opposition from Congress.

NAFTA was the precursor of other free-trade pacts. In March 1991 agreement was reached on a South American common market (Mercosur) among Argentina, Brazil, Paraguay, and Uruguay. This followed difficult negotiations because Brazil was anxious to protect key areas of its industry, such as data processing. It reflected a very different atmosphere from a decade before when it seemed that Argentina and Brazil were on the verge of a nuclear arms race. (Both governments renounced the development and use of nuclear weapons in November 1990.) Mercosur came into effect in January 1995. That same month the five members of the Andean Pact—created in 1969 to promote integration among Bolivia, Colombia, Ecuador, Peru, and Venezuela—agreed to seek a free trade agreement with Mercosur. The overarching goal was a free-trade agreement for the whole Western Hemisphere "from Alaska to Argentina." This was proclaimed by the Summit of the Americas in December 1994, the first such gathering since 1967, at which thirty-four states (all the Western Hemisphere except Cuba) were represented. Although negotiations would take years to complete, they began formally in April 1998.[101]

The new surge of economic integration represented a vast change in the political economy of South America, highlighting the shift from economic nationalism and authoritarian rule. Spurred by the debt crisis of the early 1980s, a new technocratic elite, an emerging middle class, and grass-roots social movements had helped redirect policy and politics across much of Latin America.[102] Yet the changes were not wholesale and were often shallowly rooted.

In some countries, for instance, economic liberalization depended on authoritarian political rule. This was true of Peru under Alberto Fujimori, an outsider who won the 1990 elections at a time of deep cynicism about the established parties. Fujimori implemented a draconian program of price rises and economic liberalization to cure hyperinflation. After bitter battles with the legislature, Fujimori and the army executed the so-called *autogolpe*, or self-coup, of April 1992, whereby he suspended the legislature and ruled by decree.[103] Under a new constitution approved by referendum in October 1993, Fujimori was able to win a second term in April 1995 and to bid for a third in the year 2000.

Fujimori's rule was economically liberal but politically authoritarian because of his lack of a party base. Even where democratic politics had developed, political parties were Latin America's Achilles' heel. They often consisted of the personal followings of regional leaders. The new social movements of the 1980s had not become coherent political organizations. Yet analysts agreed that an institutionalized party system was essential for consolidating democracy by providing stability, legitimacy, and orderly representation of social groups.

Inchoate politics left space for populist politics and volatile mass movements.[104] In these circumstances, the military still saw itself as the political backbone. In some states, such as Chile, its role as the guardian of stability was institutionalized as part of the transition. In others, such as Argentina, the military enjoyed considerable freedom in matters of intelligence and internal security. And generally the extent of civilian control and legislative scrutiny was far from clear. Democratic politics depended to varying degrees on military acquiescence.[105]

Economic liberalization also had its limits. Take privatizations, for instance. Between 1990 and 1995 Latin America accounted more than half (by value) of all privatizations in the developing world, including Central and Eastern Europe.[106] But, behind the free-trade rhetoric, selling off state assets was often a way for rulers to enrich themselves and a new elite of political supporters. In Salinas's Mexico, "directed deregulation" produced a dozen or so strategic monopolies that controlled whole industries such as television or copper. The intention was that these monopolies would be strong enough to resist U.S. penetration under NAFTA, and also grateful enough to keep providing massive donations for the ruling party. Mexican capitalism in the 1990s resembled the United States' during the "robber baron" era of Andrew Carnegie and John D. Rockefeller.[107] Moreover, many of these economies remained heavily dependent on a few commodities—such as coffee for Brazil and Colombia, or oil for Mexico and Venezuela—whose price were falling on the world market. And the new openness of these economies, including international stock markets, made them acutely vulnerable to investor withdrawals like that following the 1994–1995 peso crisis in Mexico.

Above all, economic liberalization brought social costs. The result of such policies, at least in the short term, was falling real incomes and higher unemployment. For many people, the "informal economy" remained the only way of life. At its heart was narcotics, whose production, dissemination, and financing were still vital to the economies of Central America and the microstates of the Caribbean. Colombia, the center of Latin American drug production, remained mired in guerrilla wars that were financed by the trade. From this perspective, freer trade was a mixed blessing. By 1993 Mexico had become America's third largest trading partner—but also the entry point for 70 percent of its drugs and the largest source of illegal immigrants.[108]

Within Latin America, the combined effects of economic liberalization and democratic politics were particularly felt by indigenous populations. These forgotten peoples attracted international attention after the January 1994 rebellion in Chiapas, one of Mexico's wealthiest provinces in natural resources but one of its poorest in living standards. The threats to land, culture, and political rights were of particular sensitivity in Peru and Ecuador, where indigenous peoples made up 40 percent of the population.[109] Most serious, across whole societies, was the educational deficit. Civil wars and funding crises had played havoc with education across the region. Budgetary tightness in the 1990s shifted the emphasis to decentralized programs and private provision, especially at university level. Educational policy remained "contested terrain" between religious and political groups. Even in Brazil, where governments in the era of economic nationalism had created a major computer industry, the lack of educational skills among the population was a major impediment to exploiting the information revolution.[110]

For Latin America, the 1990s marked a tentative transition. The new tides of economic liberalization, democratic consolidation, and regional integration had many crosscurrents. A "reverse wave" could not be ruled out. Nevertheless, the post–cold war era was considerably easier for Latin America than it was for the old Soviet empire.

Postcommunism and the Redefinition of Europe

Nowhere was the magnitude of change in the 1990s greater than in the former Soviet bloc. These countries had been one-party states geared to command economies—both of which disintegrated in the late 1980s. The crisis was also a collapse of empire, whether Russia's in the USSR and Eastern Europe, or Serbia's in Yugoslavia. Thus, the exit from communism was a "triple transition"—political, economic, and territorial—which entailed vast human suffering.[111] Some analysts have identified a fourth transition underpinning the rest, namely the need for "civil society," not merely in the sense of associations outside the state but also the ideal of "civility"—of conduct regulated by law, not violence.[112]

On the other hand, these countries were not monolithic. Those closest to Western Europe geographically were also closest to it in political and economic form. This closeness has been reflected in the eastward enlargement of NATO and the European Community.

By the late 1990s, Russia had a system of multiparty electoral politics. But it was harder to establish representative government because of two structural problems—the struggle between president and parliament and the anarchic party system. Although Yeltsin had played the democrat to destroy Gorbachev, his conception of the presidency was highly autocratic. He either acted as his own prime minister (until June 1992) or appointed men of his choice, regardless of Parliament. This was not surprising, since the legislature was chaotic. The profusion of small parties, their aversion to coherent alliances, and voters' suspicions of any party after the communist era were all to blame.[113] During 1993, the rift with the parliamentary leadership became total; on September 21, Yeltsin took the unconstitutional step of dissolving the legislature. In defiance, some members led by the Speaker, Ruslan Khasbulatov, led a sit-in, which was joined by paramilitary elements. Fearing a coup, on October 3, Yeltsin persuaded a reluctant army command to send in the troops—but only when he issued a written order.[114] The next day, the parliament building, or White House, was shelled until its defenders surrendered. The official death toll was 145, after the bloodiest street fighting in Moscow since 1917.

Yeltsin was now free to impose a constitution with strong presidential powers, which was approved by referendum in December 1993. But the December voting also saw sweeping gains for nationalists and communists, reflecting public disenchantment with the costs of economic reform. Yeltsin's course became increasingly erratic. He had two heart attacks in 1995 and multiple bypass surgery in 1996. His propensity for alcohol became a diplomatic embarrassment, and he spent long periods "ill" or "recuperating." In the June 1996 presidential election, the communist leader, Gennady Zyuganov, posed a severe challenge. Yeltsin won only with massive support from new tycoons such as Boris Berezovsky—far beyond legal campaign contributions. Yeltsin's credibility was finally destroyed when he sacked Viktor Chernomyrdin, his premier since 1993, in March 1998, to prove his virility, only to try to restore Chernomyrdin in August amid financial crisis. This time Parliament refused to be browbeaten and bribed. It obliged Yeltsin to accept Yevgeni Primakov—the former foreign minister—as premier. But Yeltsin, manipulated by Berezovsky, dismissed him in another autocratic spasm in May 1999. Only the end of Yeltsin's term in 2000 offered the hope of a system of politics that was less presidential and more parliamentary.

Yeltsin's declining popularity was a reflection of Russia's economic woes. Between 1989 and 1992, as the command economy fell apart, the country's national income dropped by one-third, a crash as spectacular as the United States or Germany had undergone sixty years before in the depression.[115] Policy failures made things worst. In early 1992 Yeltsin endorsed Yegor Gaidar's "shock therapy" of liberalizing prices, but the political battle prevented this being balanced by action to control inflation. In July 1993 Gaidar was obliged to accept Viktor Gerashchenko as chairman of the new Central Bank of Russia. The candidate of the old Soviet managerial elite, Geraschenko handed out easy credit with devastating inflationary effect. Meanwhile, advised by Western market economists, Russia embarked on the largest and fastest privatization that the world has seen. Nearly 11 million apartments had been bought by their occupiers before the end of 1993. By mid-decade, the retail trade, services, and much small industry was in private hands. But most big enterprises were acquired by their old managers, spawning a new rich in league with criminal mafias and/or Western investors. Construction, transport, energy, and agriculture remained largely state monopolies run by powerful lobbies from the Soviet era. At the bottom, those on fixed incomes were reduced by inflation to penury, prostitution, or crime.[116] Yeltsin's inept handling of the financial crisis of summer 1998 produced another catastrophic drop in the value of the ruble. Local government collapsed in many places. Combined with harvest failure, this led to a severe food shortage.

Supporters of economic reform claimed that "however messy and imperfect, Russia is a market economy, and has been since the end of 1993." More plausibly, critics responded that half-baked reform had consolidated the "semi-criminal oligarchy" fostered by the old Soviet system into "robber-baron capitalism."[117] The central government had lost control over the localities, bureaucracy, and economic fiefdoms; its tax revenues had collapsed. Russia was a "weak state" as well as a "weak society."[118] On the other hand, reversion to a command economy seemed almost impossible. Likewise, despite the poverty and alienation of the army, Russian and Soviet traditions militated against military rule. After the financial crash and political crisis of 1998, Asian-style state capitalism under semiauthoritarian rule seemed Russia's most likely course—if the state structure survived.

Across most of the former Soviet Union, the Russian story was repeated, with variations, during the 1990s. Economies were deregulated but not stabilized; politics became plural but chaotic. Most countries saw bitter feuds between president and legislature; few had viable party systems or traditions of civil society. The majority were still led by leaders from the Soviet era who favored authoritarian rule. Economic opening to the West offered riches for a few—notably in oil-rich states around the Caspian Sea—but poverty for the many. The commanding heights of the economy were controlled by the old managers in fractious alliances with the new rich. Only in the Baltic states were there signs of Western market democracy, particularly in Estonia, which was less scarred by Russian heavy industry and more exposed to the West through Finland, whose language was much the same.[119] Elsewhere, the decisive factor was whether there had been a Russian-style collapse of state structures. This had occurred in Ukraine—the most populous of the new republics, with fifty million people (a third of Russia's)—and in much of the western USSR, where Western market reforms had been the norm. It was less true farther east. "Broadly," noted a Western journalist in 1998, "the Caucasus have strong presidents, whereas Central Asia has dictators,"[120] the most egregious being Supramurad Niyazov of Turkmenistan, who still ran a one-party police state. The "Asian path" was advocated by Islam Karimov of Uzbekistan (with over twenty million people, the next most populous former Soviet state after Ukraine). His dictum was much quoted: "You do not tear down your old house before you are finished building the new one."[121]

As the former Soviet Union carved out its political and economic future, it was also coping with the collapse of the Russian empire. This third transition greatly complicated the other two. Whereas Europe's end of empire had followed a long period of nationalist agitation or official devolution, the USSR fell apart very rapidly in 1991—an outcome that, in much of Central Asia, was not desired. Also, the Russian empire had been continental—not transoceanic like those of Britain, France, or the Dutch—with unmatched mingling of colonizers and colonized. In 1989, about 120 million Russians lived in Russia itself, and twenty-five million in the other fourteen republics.[122] The largest numbers were in eastern Ukraine and northern Kazakhstan. In the latter, the Kazakhs were actually a minority of the population (around 40 percent). There was also friction in Estonia and Latvia, where Russians, about a third of the populace, suddenly found themselves second-class citizens. Aside from Russian people, there was also the issue of Soviet property. Overnight in December 1991, Ukraine and Kazakhstan became major nuclear states—the former with 1,900 strategic warheads, the latter 1,000 (Russia had 9,500).[123] Their transfer to Russia for destruction was only completed, after lengthy wrangles, in 1996.

Even the Russian republic was a multiethnic empire, 20 percent non-Russian, with some thirty more or less autonomous units. Some tried to break away, particularly in the North Caucasus region (Map 4). In December 1994, the Kremlin decided to suppress the independence of Chechnya. The secretary of his security council observed privately: "We need a small victorious war to raise the President's ratings."[124] But the war was neither small nor victorious. Capturing the capital, Groszny, took three months of grim street fighting. Despite repeated brutality, the Russian army could not subdue the Chechen guerrillas. Under its equally brutal leader, Jokhar Dudayev, this little country, the size of Wales, became a "free-market zone"—code for Russia's biggest black market for arms, oil, and money laundering. Dudayev was killed by a Soviet missile in April 1996—targeted on the signal from his satellite phone—but Chechen forces regained Groszny that summer. Politically it was now vital for Yeltsin to end the war, his equivalent of Afghanistan. A more conciliatory Chechen leadership eased his task. The agreement negotiated in August 1996 left Chechnya autonomous but shelved the issue of formal independence for five years. Estimates of the death toll ranged from 60,000 to 100,000.

The Russian Question was not the only ethnic problem facing the new states of the former USSR. In the early 1990s, Armenia and Azerbaijan fought a bitter war over the disputed region of Nagorno-Karabakh. Secessionist movements nearly dismembered neighboring Georgia. A bloody civil war exploded in Tajikistan in 1992, rumbling on for much of the decade. In general, boundaries across Central Asia had been drawn, Africa style, with little attention to ethnicity. Potential for further conflict was acute, particularly in the Caucasus and along the contested borders of Afghanistan and Iran. These areas were likely to become the international hot spots of the early twenty-first century.

In the 1990s, signs were already evident of a new variable geometry for post-Soviet geopolitics, as the encircling Iron Curtain fell apart. Latvia, Lithuania, and Estonia were reviving their Baltic identity, linked to Scandinavia, Poland, and Germany. China's economic penetration of its neighbors Kazakhstan and Kyrgyzstan was increasingly apparent. Muslims in the south, most of them Turkic in language, were reopening links with the Middle East. In the long term, this suggested that "Turcophones will become more important in the Middle East and Arabophones less so. What used to be the Northern Tier—Turkey, Iran, Afghanistan—will stand at the heart of the Middle East."[125] But the biggest geopolitical question of all was how Russia would relate to the new Europe. That, in turn, depended on events in what used to be called Eastern Europe.

In Yugoslavia, the territorial transition was more violent than anywhere else in the former communist bloc.[126] The South Slav federation patched over deep historic enmities: against Serbs as the dominant nationality, against Muslims as descendants of the Ottoman ruling elite, and against Croats as client rulers for the Nazis during World War II. The federation had weakened even under Tito: the 1974 constitution gave the six republics and two autonomous provinces far more power. After his death in May 1980, the country lost its unifying force, while the debt crisis of the 1980s reduced the government largesse that had lubricated federal relations.[127] But bloody disintegration was not the inevitable dénouement. If ancient nationalisms were thawed out, it was because modern politicians had stoked the fires.

The flash point was Kosovo, one of Serbia's two autonomous provinces, where the population was 90 percent Albanian. After university riots in 1981, separatist agitation intensified, and thousands of Serbs were expelled. Slobodan Milošević, the leader of the Serbian communist party from 1986, made Kosovo into a crusade to advance his political career. His speeches and writings revived the cult of Prince Lazar, vanquished by the Ottoman Turks on the field of Kosovo Polje (Black Birds). Milošević made the six hundredth anniversary of the battle, June 28, 1989, into a national event. For months beforehand, Lazar's bones were paraded around towns and villages, and perhaps one million Serbs gathered on the battlefield on the day itself. In May 1989, Milošević forced Ivan Stambolic from the Serbian presidency on the grounds that he was irresolute over Kosovo. In September a new constitution annulled Kosovo's autonomy, and incorporated the province completely within Serbia.[128]

Milošević, now bidding for the Yugoslav presidency, had shown how nationalism could give new legitimacy to old communists. Others followed his example, playing on fears that Serb bellicosity had been aroused elsewhere in Yugoslavia. Notable among these were Franjo Tudjman, whose Croatian Democratic Union swept to power in the elections of April 1990. In Croatia and in Slovenia—Yugoslavia's northernmost and most developed republic—antipathy grew toward the Serb-dominated union. In June 1991, after Serbia had rejected the Croatian nominee for the rotating federal presidency, Slovenia and Croatia declared independence. The Serb-run Yugoslav National Army soon pulled back from Slovenia, but Croatia did not win its independence until January 1992, at the cost of twenty thousand dead and with one-third of the territory still in Serb hands. Worse was to come in Bosnia-Hercegovina.

Bosnia straddled the great ethnoreligious fault line of Eastern Europe.[129] Its 4.5 million population was 17 percent Croat (mostly Catholics), 30 percent Serb (mostly Orthodox), and 44 percent Muslim. For decades the intermingled populations had lived, if not in harmony, at least without serious violence. But as Yugoslavia crumbled, separate ethnic parties were formed, and an attempt at coalition government disintegrated. The Muslim leader and Bosnian president, Alija Izetbegović, pushed through a referendum on independence in March 1992. Radovan Karadžić, the leader of the Bosnian Serbs, whipped up fears that independence would mean full-scale Islamization. His paramilitary units, backed by the Yugoslav army, were soon engaged in the brutal "ethnic cleansing" of Serb-controlled areas. Croat fighters joined, helped by the Croatian army—initially against the Serbs, but soon against Muslims, as the flood of refugees swamped local communities and destroyed ethnic tolerance. By the spring of 1993 the main war was between Croats and Muslims, much to the delight of the Bosnian Serb commander, General Ratko Mladić, who remarked, "I will watch them destroy each other and then I will push them both into the sea."[130] Although ethnic cleansing became ubiquitous, the main victims were the Muslims, and the main perpetrators were Bosnian Serb militias. Half the country's population became refugees.

Most West European governments took the view that this was yet another Balkan civil war, which might engulf Europe if badly handled—as in 1914. Russian sympathies for Serbia and German support for Croatia were of particular concern to Britain and France. As with the Spanish Civil War of 1936–1939, London and Paris therefore hoped to insulate the conflict, notably by maintaining an arms embargo on all belligerents. This militated, in practice, against the poorly armed Muslims.[131] A multinational UN peacekeeping force, led by France and Britain, was introduced, but only to help with humanitarian aid. By the summer of 1993, the EU and the UN were proposing partition of Bosnia into Serb, Croat, and Muslim areas. In Washington, particularly once Clinton became president in January 1993, there was a growing tendency to blame Serbian aggression for the war. But the United States had no interests in Bosnia (an oil-free zone, unlike Kuwait), and, after Somalia, Clinton was determined not to commit ground troops.

Bosnia's agony dragged on for three and a half years. A tenuous settlement in 1995 was the result of three major changes. The first, in March 1994, was a peace treaty between the Croats and the Muslims. This created a Muslim-Croat federation in their part of Bosnia and permitted combined military operations against Serb-held territory. In August 1995 Croat forces won back part of southern Croatia, with devastating effect on Serb morale. Second, the impotence of the UN and the Europeans was dramatically exposed that summer. Peacekeepers, including French and British troops, were taken hostage by the Serbs to deter air strikes. The UN had been unable to protect the towns of Srebrenica and Žepa, which it had designated as "safe areas" for Muslims. The third, and most important, development was that the United States now stepped in as a "peace enforcer." Anti-Serb elements had gained the upper hand in Washington. There was also concern, after the hostage crisis, that the U.S. might have to help evacuate the UN force. The administration secretly encouraged the Croatian offensives, and, after a Serb mortar had killed thirty-seven people in a market in Sarajevo on August 28, NATO mounted two weeks of air strikes on Serb positions.

Seeing that the tide had turned, Milošević pushed his Bosnian Serb allies to the negotiating table as the Americans, led by diplomat Richard Holbrooke, secured a cease-fire and arranged a peace conference. To avoid the parties' grandstanding for the media, the conference was not held in Washington but on a secluded air base near Dayton, Ohio, where Izetbegović, Tudjman, and Milošević (who represented Serbia *and* the Bosnian Serbs) were virtually imprisoned for three weeks in November 1995 until they reached agreement.

The Dayton Accords were, in essence, the European idea of partition, enforced by American power, within the shell of a continued Bosnian republic. In the center was the Muslim-Croat federation formed in 1994, which covered 51 percent of the territory. The Serb Republic was wrapped around it on the north and south, these two parts being linked by a narrow corridor along the eastern border. Even on paper, the settlement seemed problematic and it was only implemented because of a sixty-thousand-strong NATO-led force, one-third American. Renewed fighting was likely if and when this implementation force was withdrawn. To the south, in Macedonia—which had also left Yugoslavia in 1991—another international force helped keep a tenuous peace between the Slavic majority and its Albanian minority (20 percent). Albania itself, Europe's poorest state, was also unstable. The disastrous collapse of investment schemes in early 1997 had sparked rebellion across much of the south. This was only put down by a multinational force led by Italy (which had been engulfed by Albanian refugees).

In Kosovo in 1998, Milošević, weakened at home by economic disaffection, played the nationalist card again, applying his familiar methods of military strikes and ethnic cleansing against Albanian separatists. A decade before, Kosovo had made his political career. Convinced now that it could also unmake him, Milošević defied Western leaders and refused to sign a new autonomy deal for Kosovo. With its own credibility also on the line, NATO began a bombing campaign against Yugoslavia's military infrastructure in March 1999. This served to accelerate the pogroms and turn the flow of Albanian refugees into a tidal wave, totaling nearly one million. NATO leaders, especially Clinton, hoped that a few days' bombing of military installations would bring Milošević to heel. In fact, the air war lasted eleven weeks, during which much of the infrastructure of Serbia was damaged (and hundreds of Serb civilians killed) in a fruitless attempt to avert a humanitarian disaster in Kosovo. Only when Clinton moved toward committing ground troops did Milošević accept a peace deal and withdraw his forces from Kosovo in mid-June. As the Kosovar refugees returned, protected by NATO troops, and many Serbs in their turn fled, so the extent of Serb brutality was revealed in plundered houses and mass graves. Stability for Kosovo, inside or outside the rump of Yugoslavia, would clearly depend for the foreseeable future on a NATO presence.

For Yugoslavia, therefore, the territorial transition eclipsed all else during the 1990s. The death toll exceeded one hundred thousand; at least 3.5 million refugees had fled their homes, many of them forever. One thing seemed probable: regardless of the erratic concern of Western leaders, and whatever the fate of Milošević, it would take years of "ethnic cleansing" and political wrangling before the Balkans achieved a stable congruence between nations and states. In the interim, several parts would be little more than Western protectorates.

In some other East European countries, ethnic tensions continued—notably over Hungarians in Romania and Turks in Bulgaria. The vicissitudes of political and economic reform in these countries tempted politicians to play the ethnic card (like Ceaușescu and Zhivkov before them). Further north, Czechoslovakia followed its "velvet revolution" of November 1989 with the "velvet divorce" of January 1993 as Slovakia broke away from the Czech Republic. This separation, too, was pushed through by opportunist politicians, notably Vladimir Meciar of Slovakia, another communist turned nationalist, even though polls showed that only a quarter of Czechs and a third of Slovaks wanted a total break (rather than a more balanced federation).[132] Slovakia was left with only one-third of the fifteen million population, the less developed economic regions, and a serious Hungarian minority problem of its own.

But at least the divorce had been peaceful. Central Europe was more ethnically stable than the Balkans and the former Soviet Union. The transitions it faced were therefore largely political and economic.

Most states experienced bitter struggles between executive and legislature, exacerbated by a fragmented party system resting on proportional representation. In 1993, President Lech Wałęsa of Poland, like Yeltsin in Russia, dissolved his obstreperous parliament and called new elections. As with Yeltsin, too, though more quickly, Wałęsa's autocratic manner damaged his reputation, and in the presidential election of December 1995 he was defeated by a former communist. With ex-communists regaining power across much of the region (though not in the Czech Republic), the Western press worried about a new "pink revolution." But the communist revival of 1993–1994 was largely a matter of protest votes picked up by one of the few well-organized parties in existence. Most of these retread leaders continued with economic reform, albeit at varying speeds.

In economic terms, as in Russia, the initial pain was considerable, compounded by the general European recession of the early 1990s and the uncompetitiveness of much of East European industry in unprotected markets. The immediate result of rapid price liberalization, notably in Poland in 1990 and Czechoslovakia the following year, was devastating inflation. Privatization, whether by vouchers and share allocations (as in Czechoslovakia) or direct sell-offs (as in Hungary) opened up the retail and service sectors but also dropped lucrative monopolies into the pockets of a few. As in Russia, ex-communists used their control of state assets and their managerial experience to "transform themselves from guardians of public property into a proprietary capitalist class."[133] It would take years to foster stock markets, commercial banking, and productive business. At the end of the 1990s, as at the beginning, it remained true that "in the ex-communist countries the most successful market is the black market."[134]

By mid-decade, however, as Europe's recession waned, several Central European countries could boast impressive growth, and falling inflation. The relative success of their economic and political transitions was indicated by the European Union's decision in July 1997 to open negotiations with five ex-communist states (plus Cyprus) with a view to membership early in the new century (Map 6). The five were Poland, with thirty-nine million people; Hungary and the Czech Republic, each with ten million; plus tiny Slovenia, the most developed offshoot of the former Yugoslavia; and Estonia, similarly advantaged among the Baltic states. That same month, Poland, Hungary, and the Czechs were invited to begin negotiations to join the NATO alliance in time for its fortieth birthday in April 1999.

The double invitations to Poland, Hungary and Czech Republic showed how the old political geography of Europe was changing. Once lumped together as part of "Eastern Europe," these states were now identified again as "Central Europe," implying closer affinities with Western Europe. "Eastern Europe" had now been pushed east to cover the western parts of the former Soviet Union, particularly the Baltics and Ukraine, whereas Russia's status as a "European" was a matter of dispute. Turkey, a member of NATO since 1952, had once again been blocked in its application for EU membership—a resented reminder that it was not regarded as truly part of "the West."

NATO and the EU were not simply enlarging, they were also being transformed. With the demise of the Warsaw Pact, the Atlantic alliance had lost its old rationale—preparing for a defensive land war in the center of Europe. The gulf war and the Bosnian crisis highlighted the need for mobile, rapid-deployment forces outside the NATO area, and so the alliance gradually evolved plans for a "Combined Joint Task Force."[135] In the United States, Congress was also pressing for NATO reform, particularly greater burden sharing and a broader geographical range: NATO would go "out of area or out of business," in the blunt words of Senator Richard Lugar.[136] This domestic pressure was one reason why Clinton advocated eastward enlargement. It also seemed important to reassure Central Europeans after Moscow became more nationalist and assertive in 1994. According to some accounts, Clinton was persuaded that this would swing the votes of immigrants in states that he had to win in the 1996 election.[137] For whatever reasons, the administration pushed NATO enlargement on reluctant European allies worried about the cost of reequipping the Polish, Czech, and Hungarian forces and, even more, about the signals that their inclusion would send to Moscow. The NATO-Russia joint council agreement in May 1997 only papered over the cracks. Was NATO redefining its identity, or redividing Europe further east? These new policies posed new problems for the future.

The same could be said of EU enlargement. The European Union had only just brought Austria, Finland, and Sweden into the fold in January 1995. (Norway had also negotiated but, as in 1972, the entry terms were narrowly rejected in a national referendum, after pressure from the farm and fishing lobbies.) This fourth round of enlargement meant that the original Six of 1958 had now become the Fifteen (see Map 6). Although there had been several difficult issues in the negotiations—such as neutrality and environmental protection—these candidates were developed states and long-standing EU trading partners whose admission would be relatively easy.[138] Brussels had been able to insist on its standard policy that applicants must eventually take on all the EU's existing rules and regulations—the *acquis*

33: Hosted by Jimmy Carter, Anwar
Sadat of Egypt shakes hands with
Menachem Begin of Israel at the U.S.
presidential retreat of Camp David,
Maryland, August 7, 1978.

34: Iranians opposed to the Shah
demonstrate under a large poster of
Ayatollah Khomeni, January 1979.

35: Economic summit of Western leaders at Williamsburg, Virginia, May 1983. From the left, Pierre Trudeau (Canada), Gaston Thorn (EC), Helmut Kohl (West Germany), François Mitterrand (France), Ronald Reagan (U.S.), Yasuhiro Nakasone (Japan), Margaret Thatcher (U.K.), Amintore Fanfani (Italy).

36: Communism's Big Two meet in Beijing, May 16, 1989: Mikhail Gorbachev is greeted by Deng Xiaoping.

37: Berlin's Brandenburg Gate, November 11, 1989: joyful East Germans hail the collapse of the Iron Curtain.

38: A lone demonstrator confronts government tanks near Tiananmen Square, Beijing, June 1989.

39: Twenty-five years after Camp David, another Arab-Israeli handshake. Prompted by Bill Clinton, Yitzhak Rabin greets Yasser Arafat after signing the Oslo accords at the White House, September 13, 1993.

40: Nelson Mandela and F. W. de Klerk—reluctant allies in the dismantling of South African apartheid—pictured in Cape Town, May 8, 1996.

41: Hong Kong, city-state and Asian tiger, was returned by Britain to Chinese rule on July 1, 1997.

42: The West prepared for the year 2000. This computer image of the Millennium Dome at Greenwich, in London, features a huge abstract sculpture of The Body at its center.

43: Cambridge University's EDSAC I, one of the first stored-program computers, in May 1949.

44: In the 1990s, DNA sequencing is highly automated. Directed by its computer operator behind the glass screen, this robot at the Sanger Centre, near Cambridge, can manage up to 384 pipetted samples of DNA simultaneously.

45: Two giants of 1990s technology and science: Bill Gates admires Stephen Hawking's computerized voice box, May 1998.

46: A familiar sight in West Africa until recently: a child leading a victim of the parasitic disease of river blindness (*onchocerciasis*) in Burkina Faso, 1974.

47: Victims of Ethiopian famine come to the town of Kobo for food in 1975.

communautaire—and that the only debate could be about the length of the transitional period.

In the case of the six candidates of 1997, however, this principle would be hard to follow. Poland, for instance, still had a quarter of its work force in agriculture. Admitting countries of this sort without modifying the *acquis* would bankrupt the common agricultural policy, impose huge strains on the social and regional funds, and anger public opinion in net contributors like Germany and Britain.[139] Furthermore, others were waiting in the queue. Including all ten Central and East European applicants would boost the EU's population by nearly one-third but its GDP by only 4 percent.[140] And in a union of twenty-six or more countries, unanimous decisions would be impossible. In short, external enlargement would necessitate major internal reforms on issues like agriculture and majority voting, for which there had been little preparation.

Most of the EU's energy in the 1990s was, in fact, devoted to implementing the 1991 Maastricht Treaty on monetary union. That was no easy task. The Danish and French referenda on Maastricht in 1992 (see Chapter 15) highlighted public scepticism. Even more damaging were the Europe-wide recession of the early 1990s and the collapse of the European Exchange Rate Mechanism (ERM) amid currency turmoil in 1992–1993. These cast doubt on the Maastricht timetable of currency union in January 1999. Under the treaty, the period 1994–1998 was to see growing economic convergence among the member states, permitting judgments about which had met the criteria for monetary union. These included low interest and inflation rates, a budget deficit of no more than 3 percent of GDP and a public debt of no more than 60 percent of GDP. But in the mid-1990s, few member states were meeting these criteria.[141]

One major problem was the cost of German unification. East Germany made a unique transition from communism by incorporation in one of the world's leading capitalist states. Overnight, the East's inefficient heavy industry entered world markets, where its uncompetitiveness led to catastrophic unemployment. So unattractive was it that the Bonn government sustained a *loss* of DM230 billion from its privatization. That sell-off was also politically contentious. The Trust Agency, or Treuhandanstalt, charged with this task was, in 1990, the world's largest industrial employer, with thirteen thousand enterprises and four million employees. Unlike the rest of the communist bloc, the assets did not go via vouchers, auctions, or sale to former socialist managers. Instead, this sell-off was "negotiated privatization" to those who had owned the property before 1945 or to "competent" private investors.[142] Despite local anger, most were West Germans. Animosity between "Ossis" and "Wessis" was two-way, evidence of the "wall in the head" that remained long after the Berlin wall had gone. West Germans resented the flood of migrants, pressing on housing and welfare resources, and the subsidies paid to East Germany to prevent social collapse. Some of the funds came from tax rises, the rest from heavy public borrowing. This meant high interest rates, which slowed German recovery from recession. And, with European currencies shadowing the omnipotent Deutschmark via the ERM, the result was high interest rates for all of Western Europe.

In the October 1994 elections, Chancellor Kohl squeaked back into office by only ten Bundestag seats. In the east, the former communists picked up nearly 20 percent of the vote.[143] But Kohl had staked too much on monetary union to give up; in any case, EMU was the international quid pro quo for German unification. Determined not to be left out of monetary union in a "two-speed" Europe, rightist governments in France and Italy imposed draconian spending cuts in 1995–1996 to keep their debts and deficits within the convergence criteria. Although they fell in the public backlash, the center-left coalition in Italy in power from June 1996 and the socialist government elected in France a year later moderated, rather than abandoned, these programs. They were helped by the general economic recovery in 1997 and by "creative accounting" such as Italy's "tax for Europe" (repayable after 1999) and French manipulation of France Telecom's pension funds. Equally important was Bonn's tolerance for these ploys (indeed, it tried them itself) in its anxiety to keep EMU on track. In May 1998 the EU summit duly announced that eleven of the fifteen members would fix their exchange rates irrevocably on January 1, 1999, and then phase in the new common currency, the Euro, over the next three years. Three countries (Britain, Denmark, and Sweden) opted out, while Greece failed to meet the convergence criteria. Thus, the European Union began what even supporters acknowledged was a political and economic gamble at the same time as it was opening up to new, far less developed members. The tensions between "deepening" and "widening" were likely to strain the EU fabric close to breaking point over the years ahead.

Aware of this, Germany, the biggest net contributor, demanded reform of the EU's finances while Britain tried to cling on to the budget rebate negotiated by Margaret Thatcher and the French to the grotesque subsidies provided under the Common Agricultural Policy (which still accounted for half of EU spending). At the heart of the EU, the Commission remained particularly resistant to reform. After a damning report exposed extensive cronyism and fraud, all twenty Commissioners resigned in March 1999. The mass walkout might have been avoided had the president of the Commission, Jacques Santer of Luxembourg, forced out the main target of criticism, Edith Cresson of France. But Santer was an ineffectual leader, and the French government backed the obdurate Cresson, treating the matter as one of national pride. Collective responsibility therefore became an excuse to avoid individual responsibility. The man chosen by the EU's leaders as Santer's successor, Romano Prodi, a recent Italian prime minister, was a respected reformer. But the unprecedented crisis in the Commission had shown again how entrenched the EU's practices had become.

The redefinition of Europe affected even the core states of the West. In fact, the triple transition outlined earlier for postcommunism—economic, political, and territorial—is in some ways applicable to Western Europe as well.

The triumph of neoliberal economics—of freer markets and privatization—sounded the death knell of postwar European socialism. Whereas in the 1950s the right had adopted many leftist principles, notably the mixed economy and the welfare state, in the 1990s the left moved right.[144] After a fourth consecutive election defeat in 1992, Britain's Labour party was bludgeoned by its new leader, Tony Blair, into renouncing state ownership, shedding its working-class image, and adopting Thatcherite policies. Blair surged to victory in May 1997, after eighteen years of Conservative rule. In Germany, the SPD followed suit under the telegenic Gerhard Schröder. The September 1998 elections brought to power an SPD-Green coalition, ending Kohl's sixteen-year tenure as the Federal Republic's longest-serving chancellor. Across the continent, the European left now accepted capitalism; the challenge was how to regulate it in a postsocialist era.

Meanwhile, the political system was under strain. One sign was the falling voter turnout figures across Western Europe, down from an average of 83 percent in the 1960s to 76 percent by the early 1990s.[145] Old ideological polarities had gone: the left suffered from the erosion of class consciousness and the right from the demise of its defining enemy, Marxism-Leninism. The role of parties as prime mediators between rulers and ruled was also undercut by the electronic media, especially TV, which allowed rich candidates to appeal directly to the voters. The most dramatic example was the Italian media tycoon Silvio Berlusconi, whose Forza Italia party, formed only two months before, won the March 1994 elections at the head of the Freedom Alliance and ruled for the rest of the year. That was a long time by Italian standards, testimony to the effects of the constitutional reforms of 1993. Whereas Italy was curbing proportional representation to enhance stability, Blair's Britain was toying with it because many voters were disenfranchised by the country's first-past-the-post system. In short, Western Europe's democracy had no cause for complacency at the turn of the century.

There was also a territorial dimension.[146] Since the 1970s, several West European states had created structures of regional government to manage economic development and/or to appease opponents of centralization. In Belgium, the bitter battles over culture and resources between the Flemish north and the Walloon south were resolved in a federal constitution approved in July 1993. This created three territorial areas—Flemish, Walloon, and Brussels, each with significant devolved powers. In Spain, the post-Franco Constitution of 1978 sanctioned "autonomous communities" where desired. Although intended to address the specific problems of Catalans and Basques, this provision was seized on by much of the country. In the mid-1990s Spain had seventeen autonomous regions, each with an elected legislature and prime minister. Attitudes were changing even in the "United Kingdom of Great Britain and Northern Ireland." When New Labour won power, it pushed ahead with plans for Welsh and Scottish parliaments, the latter having tax-varying powers. Northern Ireland also regained its own assembly in July 1998 following paramilitary cease-fires and a Good Friday peace agreement. If that agreement held, and paramilitary weapons were decommissioned, the way was open for an end to "the Troubles," which had claimed three thousand six hundred lives since 1969, and also for a more open territorial framework that would loosen Northern Ireland's bond to Britain and strengthen its links with the Irish Republic.

New regional institutions were therefore emerging in many parts of Western Europe. These did not mean the end of the nation-state, as had some predicted, but they offset the centripetal forces of European integration. Regions, states, and the EU were *all* part of the variable geometry of the continent in the 1990s. When one adds to these the "two-speed Europe" over monetary union and the "concentric circles" approach to EU/NATO enlargement, it becomes clear how complex the redefinition of Europe would be. Two geometrical principles were clear, however. If Russia felt excluded from Europe's magic circle—or worse, threatened by it—then that would jeopardize Russia's transition and Europe's peace. Second, the center of the new Europe was shifting east with EU enlargement, German unification, and the Bundestag's 1991 decision to move the federal government back to Berlin. Although Germany's economic woes slowed the timetable, they did not prevent the old Berlin wall, especially around the location of Hitler's bunker, from becoming the biggest and most lucrative building site in Europe. After a half-century of division, Germany and Berlin were back at the heart of Europe.

The Crisis of "Asian Values"?

Asia's agenda in the early 1990s was very different from Europe's. The region's political geography was relatively stable, and many countries had thriving capitalist economies. The pattern of China's transition had been set since the late 1970s—economic liberalization under firm communist party rule. The success of Japan, the emergence of the tigers and the transformation of China prompted talk of common "Asian values" based on respect for the family, order, and hard work, rather than the rampant individualism of the West. Emanating particularly from the governments of Singapore and Malaysia in the early 1990s, this was a frontal attack on the post–cold war triumphalism of the West. The Malaysian premier Mahathir Mohammad went so far as to claim that "Asian values are universal values. European values are European values."[147]

But the 1997–1998 crash of most Asian financial markets posed serious questions for the region. Was its "economic miracle" a durable product of distinctively Asian capitalism, or a transitory phase of high growth based on rickety authoritarianism? For some countries, notably Indonesia, political and territorial stability were now in question. China's less open economy escaped relatively unscathed from the crash; during the 1990s, it replaced Japan in the America psyche as the coming Asian power. But the rigidity of the country's political system, at a time of frenetic economic change, suggested interesting comparisons with the democratic values of India, the other Asian giant in demographic terms.

Japan began the 1990s with signs that a new post–cold war identity was emerging. The Liberal Democratic party (LDP), which had headed Japan's governments ever since its foundation in 1955, was wracked by internal feuds and corruption scandals. In the elections of July 1993 it lost its overall majority and was replaced by a succession of multiparty opposition coalitions. Between June 1994 and January 1996 Japan had its first socialist premier since 1948. The early 1990s also saw lively debate about a more assertive foreign policy, less subservient to Washington. A 1989 bestseller entitled *The Japan That Can Say No* attracted attention in the United States.[148] After the rape of a Japanese girl by three U.S. servicemen on the island of Okinawa in September 1995, widespread local anger forced the United States to cut its troop presence and relinquish some of its resented bases.

But none of these developments presaged a durable change in Japan's political development. In January 1996, the LDP returned to power with the same catch-all coalition of local patronage networks, hand in pocket with business. Nor did foreign policy change dramatically. Unlike Germany, the country had not become enmeshed with its neighbors through economic and political integration. Its main international tie was with the United States; that alliance remained essential, given continuing uncertainties about the giants of mainland Asia, Russia and China.

What did change, however, was Japan's economic condition. Starting in mid-1991 Japanese growth slowed sharply to an annual average of little more than 1 percent over the rest of the decade, while unemployment doubled to

4 percent by 1998. The government blamed weak domestic demand because of the suppression of domestic living standards (especially housing) in the search for export-led growth, and also the need for business restructuring.[149] Here the most serious problem was the vast losses accumulated by Japan's major banks through overinvestment in property in the late 1980s. In four years from March 1986 land prices in Japan's major cities rose over forty times more than the wholesale price index.[150] When the property bubble burst in 1991, following the collapse of share prices, the banks were left with huge amounts of bad loans and worthless collateral. This, in turn, undermined the business groups with which the banks were closely associated. The government was slow to reflate. Then, seeing signs of recovery in 1996 and concerned about the country's public debt, it imposed some of the biggest tax increases in Japanese history. These helped drive the country into full-scale recession.[151] Absorbed with its own problems, Japan did little to staunch the financial deluge that engulfed the Asian tigers after the Thai currency was allowed to float on July 2, 1997.

During the second half of 1997 most major currencies of East and Southeast Asian collapsed against the U.S. dollar. The Thai baht and the South Korean won halved in value; the Indonesian rupiah tumbled by 60 percent. While greedy speculators attacked the currencies, jittery investors dumped their newly acquired shares. Stock-market falls during 1997 ranged from 20 percent (in dollar terms) for Hong Kong to over 70 percent for Malaysia, South Korea, Indonesia, and Thailand. Despite rallies, financial markets remained in turmoil during the first half of 1998 so that by July 1—a year after the crisis began—the effective currency devaluation ranged from 20 percent for Taiwan to a horrendous 80 percent for Indonesia, with Malaysia, Korea, and the Philippines all posting falls of around one-third.[152]

The crisis was partly due to foreign speculation against currencies that, unlike those of Western Europe since the 1970s, were still pegged to the U.S. dollar. After the Thai government, its reserves nearly spent, abandoned the struggle on July 2, speculators simply moved elsewhere. But predatory speculation reflected deeper structural problems. Like Japan, most of the vulnerable economies had overinvested in fixed assets (especially the property boom or excess plant), so that banks and corporations had accumulated huge debts. Unlike Japan, most had done so by heavy reliance on foreign investment; the debt burden became crippling once their currencies depreciated against the dollar. As domestic banks got into trouble, they became less willing to "roll over" the mountain of corporate debt, much of it short term. Firms went bankrupt, laying off workers and fueling political protest. In Southeast Asia, many of the new unemployed were migrants, legal or not, who had provided cheap labor in the boom but were now a burden during the bust. Hundreds of thousands of Indonesians in Malaysia and Singapore and similar numbers of Burmese in Thailand were particular problems for communal relations. And in the countryside, soaring inflation drove many below the poverty line. The World Bank estimated that in June 1998, the number of people in Indonesia living on less than the equivalent of one U.S. dollar a day had doubled from twenty million to forty million.[153]

Stories like that in the Western press ended talk of the Asian miracle. Some Western analysts had already written it off, arguing that Asia's industrial growth was the result of "perspiration rather than inspiration," that is, heavy investment of capital and labor, not dramatic growth in productivity.[154] Also called into question was the previous acclaim for Asian values against Western individualism. There was particular schadenfreude in the West at the humiliation of Malaysia's authoritarian premier Mahathir Mohammad, whose trumpeting of "Asian values" had been, in part, a way to build national unity in his delicate Malay-Chinese-Indian state.[155] In similar vein, Mahathir initially blamed the 1997 crash on Western speculators and the Jews, but his railings accelerated the loss of foreign confidence in Malaysia.[156] A lower debt burden enabled him to escape the clutches of the IMF, and he battened down the hatches with currency controls. But now in his seventies and tarnished by charges of corruption, he faced growing opposition from younger reformers, notably Vice Premier Anwar Ibrahim, whom he sacked and jailed in September 1998. Although the prime minister was a ruthless infighter, Malaysia had probably entered the twilight of the Mahathir era.

But Western denigration of Asian capitalism could go too far. In many of these countries, basic strengths such as high savings, open trade, and an educated work force promised real, if slower, growth once the immediate crisis had been overcome. These were very different economies from those of the former Soviet Union or even Latin America. Some, in fact, weathered the financial storm relatively well, particularly Singapore and Taiwan, which had better regulated financial sectors and lighter burdens of foreign debt. Neoliberal commentators in the West, who blamed overregulation, were ignoring the fact that it was the rapid and poorly regulated opening up of Asian finance in the 1990s, under pressure from the IMF and the Western banking interests it represented, that laid these economies open to speculative flows. The financial crisis was not so much the failure of Asian capitalism, more the result of its hasty liberalization.[157] And as with the growth of the Asian tigers (see Chapter 12), politics mattered as much as economics in explaining why some of them slumped so badly in 1997–1998. A glance at Indonesia, Korea, and the Phillipines is revealing.

Indonesia was the world's fourth most populous country, with 195 million people in 1997. It was also hardest hit by the crash. In a year from July 1997 the rupiah fell 80 percent against the U.S. dollar, prices rose by 60 percent, and the economy contracted by over 10 percent. In mid-1998 the whole Indonesian stock market was valued at less than the British supermarket chain Tesco.[158] In part, Indonesia's sins were those of the region, writ very large—especially its levels of short-term foreign debt, unregulated credit growth, and politicized crony capitalism. But Indonesia's growth owed far more than the rest to the temporary boom in oil prices, which fell dramatically in the mid-1990s. This was resource-led growth, as in the gulf states in the 1970s, not true economic development. Moreover, the financial crisis hit a country caught in the endgame of an autocratic regime. The sharpest fall in the value of the rupiah occurred in December and January, after rumors about the health of the country's veteran president. Suharto, the architect of Indonesia's recovery since the crisis of the early 1960s (see Chapter 8), was elected by his packed parliament for a seventh five-year term in March 1998. Rising living standards had kept political discontent at tolerable levels during the early 1990s, but in 1998 roaring inflation wrecked the implicit social contract. Street protests in the capital, Jakarta, boiled over into full-scale riots after four students were shot on May 12. In a week of arson and looting, directed mainly at assets of the first family and Chinese businesses, one thousand two hundred died. On May 21, Suharto resigned, handing over to his protegé and vice president, B. J. Habibie. Whether or not Habibie proved the caretaker that many in the West predicted, any Indonesian government faced vast problems in economic and political reconstruction and in holding together this fractious imperial archipelago.[159]

After Indonesia, South Korea posted the worst falls in currency values and stock prices. Although its forty-five million people boasted the world's eleventh-largest market economy, South Korea was unusually dominated by its now flabby business conglomerates (chaebols), which had kept going by running up a large burden of foreign debt. Structural reform was both particularly necessary and particularly difficult. Moreover, 1997 was also politically momentous. South Korea's ruling party had allowed competitive elections in 1992, but the first real contest came in December 1997, while the economic crisis was at its height. The election campaign aggravated financial turbulence. The victor was Kim Dae Jung, a veteran opposition politician who had survived exile, imprisonment, and near assassination to win the presidency on his fourth attempt. Although a new broom, Kim was seventy-four (only two years younger than Suharto) and faced problems that would have taxed a far younger man. GDP fell by 5 percent in 1998 and unemployment nearly tripled to 7 percent, arousing the country's powerful unions. Meanwhile, the former ruling party held a majority in the National Assembly (elected separately from the president), thereby blocking many of Kim's reforms.

South Korea therefore faced economic crisis in the middle of its democratic transition—the worst possible combination, as we saw with Latin America. There was a marked contrast here with the Philippines, whose real political transition occurred in 1986 when Marcos fell (see Chapter 12). Despite several attempted coups, Corazon Aquino survived with the support of the key military leader, General Fidel Ramos, whom she endorsed as her successor in the elections of 1992. Although Ramos gained less than a quarter of the vote in the May 1992 presidential elections (a seven-horse race), clever deals with key rivals ensured his peaceful accession. The old clan networks of Philippine politics were being grafted onto new pluralist politics. Economically, too, 1986 was a turning point. The conditions imposed by the IMF bailout obliged the government to open up the economy, but U.S. interest ensured substantial economic aid. Although the country's currency and stock markets were badly shaken in 1997–1998, the seventy-three million Filipinos were therefore less vulnerable politically and economically than many Asian neighbors. The vitality of their democracy was evident when Ramos sought an unconstitutional second term, only to back off in the face of church and citizen protest, and the Philippines weathered its election of May 1998 with much less turmoil than South Korea.[160]

South Korea had another, unique political problem, which exacerbated the crisis of 1997–1998. Unlike Germany, the other great cold war fault line, it remained a divided country, officially still in a state of war. The architect of North Korea, Kim Il Sung, finally died in July 1994. His fifty-two-year-old playboy son, Kim Jong Il, was less secure politically, and his Stalinist state was on the brink of collapse. Repeated floods had destroyed the fragile agricultural sector; a substantial part of the 23 million population was near starvation. Meanwhile, the country was testing new offensive missiles and developing its nuclear capability. The depth of international concern was indicated by a remarkable 1994 deal by South Korea, Japan, and the United States to build two new lightwater reactors at the cost of $5 billion, in return for North Korea's shutting down its existing reactors, which were capable of producing weapons-grade plutonium. North Korea's future conduct was impossible to predict. "We are watching the collapse of the country," said one American official in 1997. "The only question is whether it will implode or explode."[161] Implosion would be disastrous for its own people; explosion could be devastating for South Korea and its neighbor Japan. The growing crisis aggravated South Korea's loss of confidence in 1997–1998.

North Korea was the most unreconstructed and isolated communist state in the world. In Indochina, however, the postcommunist transition had begun, albeit hesitantly. Cambodia's civil wars finally subsided with a UN-imposed cease-fire in 1991. But despite elections in 1993 and 1998, it was effectively a single-party system wracked by internal power struggles and brutalized by two decades of conflict. In Laos and Vietnam, the victorious communists of 1975 were still in power. Their policy in the 1990s was one of cautious economic liberalization combined with firm political control. Vietnam was by far the biggest country in Indochina, with some seventy-six million people by 1998, compared with ten million in Cambodia and five million in Laos. The government's goal was a "market economy under state management." Private business and foreign investment were encouraged, and in 1995 Washington normalized diplomatic relations. Once again, Vietnam became a leading grain exporter. But the party old guard retained their grip on power, the state sector remained large and protected, and growth was mostly in the ex-capitalist south. Ho Chi Minh City (formerly Saigon) received about 60 percent of foreign investment.[162] Overall, Vietnam's per capita GDP was on a par with Bangladesh, one of Asia's poorest countries.

The story was very different in China, where Deng Xiaoping had survived the political crisis of 1989 and steered the country back to economic reform (see Chapter 15). So China continued its dual revolution from agriculture to industry and from a command economy to a "socialist market" (see Chapter 12). Annual growth rates fluctuated around 7 or 8 percent over the two decades 1978–1997; per capita income doubled between 1978 and 1987, then doubled again by 1996.[163] The government also cut inflation from 24 percent in 1994 to around 6 percent in 1996. The architect of this "soft landing," Zhu Rongji, became premier in March 1998 when the conservative Li Peng was retired. Jiang Zemin, widely seen as a caretaker when he was catapulted in 1989 from Shanghai boss to party leader, had consolidated his position even before Deng's death at the age of ninety-two in February 1997 finally ended lingering questions about the succession.

China was also insulated from the full effect of the financial crisis in 1997–1998 because its currency was only partly convertible and its foreign debt less burdensome: debt servicing accounted for only 10 percent of export earnings in 1995, compared with 31 percent for Indonesia.[164] The contrast between Japan's slump and China's boom during the 1990s mesmerized some Western pundits, who predicted that, on current growth rates, China would have the world's largest GDP by 2010. But it was easy to lose perspective. In 1998 China accounted for less than 3 percent of world GDP and a similar proportion of world trade.[165] Despite frenetic growth along the coast, much of the interior remained mired in poverty. Over 20 percent of China's 1.2 billion people were living on the equivalent of one U.S. dollar a day.[166] There was simply no comparison with Japan, one of the world's strongest, most high-tech economies, where per capita GDP, even on the least favorable estimate, was eight times as large.

In reality, China's growth to date had been extensive rather than intensive, consisting of increased inputs of capital and labor (mostly from agriculture to industry), not gains from improved productivity. State enterprises still accounted for a third of industrial output and two-thirds of urban employment. The government sustained them by subsidies and cheap credit, but exercised little control over their managers, who engaged in large-scale embezzlement. Most of the credits for state enterprises came from the four big state banks, which together accounted for 90 percent of China's bank assets. By the mid-1990s it was estimated that their bad loans amounted to around a quarter of GDP. Equally important for China's development, therefore, was addressing its *internal* debt crisis and, in the longer term, creating a viable commercial banking system, reaching down into the localities. China also had a serious fiscal problem. The greater autonomy of enterprises and localities during economic reform cut budget revenues from 35 percent of GDP in 1978 to 11 percent by 1995. This fall in income, plus a desire to avoid an inflationary budget deficit, meant that government spending also fell—to 12 percent of GDP (against the average for developing countries of 32 percent). This retarded spending on infrastructure, education, and poverty relief, all vital for long-term development.

In short, China's transformation in the 1980s and 1990s was impressive, but it would take far greater miracles to maintain such growth and development for another two decades. Yet only continued high growth would enable China to absorb the millions of new unemployed created by agricultural modernization and the closure of state enterprises. As China opened further to the world, it would also be harder to insulate the economy from global turbulence like the crash of 1997–1998. Eventually, China's rulers would also have to move beyond economic reform to "reinvent government."[167] Market freedoms would generate renewed pressure for political freedoms from the urban middle class, as it had in the late 1970s and late 1980s. And although China was ethnically much more homogenous than the former Soviet Union, the non-Han minorities (a mere 6 percent of the population) occupied over 40 percent of the terrain in their autonomous areas. Two in particular—Xinjiang and Tibet—were extremely volatile (see Map 5). This problem, coupled with the de facto devolution occurring during economic reform, prompted some Western commentators to predict an increasingly federal structure for this last great empire.

But in the 1990s the leadership was still talking the language of old nationalism, not new federalism. Its goal was completing the reunification of China after the depredations of colonialism and the cold war. On July 1, 1997, Hong Kong was returned to China at the end of Britain's ninety-nine-year lease. Belatedly, during these final years, the British started developing democratic institutions, producing furious rows between the last governor, Chris Patten, and the authorities in Beijing. Patten was vilified as a "serpent," an "assassin," and "the criminal of all time."[168] Nevertheless Beijing honored the "one country, two systems" agreement made with Britain in 1984 and tolerated greater civil liberties than on the mainland. In December 1999 another piece of the postcolonial jigsaw was due to fall into place with Portugal's return of the tiny peninsula-port of Macao.

Beijing's great obsession was Taiwan, the island "tiger" still governed by successors to the Guomindang leaders who had fled the mainland in 1949. In March 1996, the GMD leader, Lee Teng-hui, was returned to power in Taiwan's first direct elections for the presidency. This evidence of democracy on its doorstep, plus Lee's attempts to ease Taiwan's international isolation, so angered Beijing that it mounted a series of live-fire military exercises near Taiwan during the election, causing panic on the island. The Americans, honoring defense ties, responded by sending a naval task force to the area. Nevertheless, this dangerous face-off prompted a shift in U.S. policy, which, since 1989, had tried to punish Beijing for its suppression of democracy. The Clinton administration moved to a policy of "constructive engagement" by downplaying human rights, bribing China to control weapons proliferation, and distancing itself again from Taiwan. Clinton's visit to Beijing in June 1998—the first by a U.S. president since before Tiananmen Square—was the climax of this shift.[169] During the 1990s, policy toward Russia had moved in the opposite direction, from cordiality to coolness.

Asia's second most populous state, India, was also in economic transition in the 1990s from an enclosed, statist economy, but this was a volatile democracy, not a repressive one-party state (see Chapter 12). In early 1991, India came close to defaulting on its foreign debt. The immediate cause was the Kuwait crisis, which meant rising oil prices and falling remittances from Indian workers in the gulf region. But the deeper problem was the fiscal folly of successive governments, which had bought local support by subsidies funded from foreign borrowing. The budget deficit rose to 9 percent of GDP and the public debt to around 60 percent.[170] An IMF bailout came with the usual conditions, at a time when events in Russia and China had cast doubt on India's tradition of economic planning. Under the minority Congress government that ruled from 1991 to 1996, technocrats changed course, cutting regulation, promoting exports, and soliciting foreign investment. In mid-decade, India was achieving annual growth of 7 percent. But politically motivated subsidies (such as cheap electricity) continued, and with them high borrowing, while state enterprises remained well protected. In 1993–1994 the public sector absorbed 42 percent of gross fixed capital investment but produced only 29 percent of GDP.[171] Like China's, India's reforms had not yet addressed core problems.

Politically, the 1990s were also momentous for India. The elections of 1989, 1991, 1996, and 1998 all resulted in hung parliaments. The Congress party's "natural" majority was a thing of the past, though in March 1998 the election as its leader of Sonia Gandhi (Rajiv's widow, but by birth an Italian Catholic) showed the abiding magic of the family name. By mid-decade the

Hindu-nationalist BJP had become the largest single party in parliament. In March 1998, after new elections, it was able to put together a coalition to form the country seventh government since 1989. In the wider world, especially Pakistan, there was alarm at the coming to power of a party whose platform included abolishing the special Muslim and Christian personal law codes and ending the constitutional autonomy of India's only Muslim-majority state, Kashmir. But the price of power was the dilution of BJP principles. To win support outside its northern strongholds and among lower castes, the party played down its goal of *hindutva*, or greater "Hinduness." It also maintained the new commitment to trade, deregulation, and foreign investment. Heading an eighteen-party coalition, the BJP government fell apart after thirteen months. Nevertheless, coalition politics were increasingly the name of the game. With most parties regional, not national, this increased the centrifugal pressures on the Indian state.[172]

Prospects for India's Muslim neighbors, Pakistan and Bangladesh, were even less encouraging. They lacked either the developmental authoritarianism of China or the vigorous democratic and civilian politics of India. By the 1990s, overt military rule had come to an end—in Pakistan after the death of General Mohammed Zia ul-Haq in a plane crash in August 1988, in Bangladesh after a combination of political and military opposition forced General Hussain Muhammad Ershad to resign in December 1990. But in both countries, the military remained in the wings, bureaucracies were swollen and unaccountable, and political parties factional and dynastic. Thus, the Pakistan People's Party, which had ruled in 1988–1990 and again in 1993–1996, was led by Benazir Bhutto, the daughter of the man whom Zia had ousted in 1977. The Bangladesh National Party, dominant in the early 1990s, was headed by the widow of General Ziaur Rahman, president from 1976 to 1981. The Awami League, which returned to power after two decades in the elections of June 1996, was led by Sheikh Hasina Wajed, the daughter of the founder of Bangladesh, Sheikh Mujibur Rahman. Although both countries opened up to foreign trade and investment, their fiscal systems, even more than India's, were political tools. State resources were used to enhance personal wealth and electoral influence, especially in the case of Bhutto's two governments in Pakistan, each dismissed by the president for mismanagement and corruption. These dismissals reflected the strong presidentialism of Pakistan's constitution. Bangladesh, in contrast, reverted to a parliamentary system after a referendum in 1991.[173]

In the medium term, population pressures were likely to be enormous in all three major South Asian states. Unlike those in East and Southeast Asia, their demographic transitions were only just beginning. In 1993 fertility rates were 3.7 children per woman in India, 4.3 in Bangladesh, and 6.1 in Pakistan. (China's figure was 2.0, Indonesia's 1.7.)[174] In managing the politics of development, all three South Asian giants suffered from the lack of a stable regional framework, unlike Latin America or especially Western Europe. Bangladesh was at loggerheads with India over borders, trade, and, above all, the waters of the Ganges. Pakistan's northern border was vulnerable because of the disintegration of Afghanistan, following the Soviet pullout, into a new chaos of warring ethnic militias.[175] Above all, Pakistan and India were still officially at war over Indian control of Kashmir and, more deeply, over the claims of Pakistan to be the Muslim homeland. Relations deteriorated sharply in 1998 when these two "threshold" nuclear states stepped dramatically into the club.

In mid-May 1998, the new BJP-led coalition in India announced that it had detonated five nuclear devices. It blamed recent Pakistani missile tests and China's nuclear assistance to Lahore. But making India an overt nuclear power had been an avowed aim of the BJP. Its critics also charged that the party was whipping up nationalist enthusiasms to bolster its fragile coalition. Pakistan responded at the end of May with six underground explosions, making it the world's seventh declared nuclear power. But international sanctions, imposed by the United States and its allies, soon cooled popular fervor in both capitals. Pakistan's economy, smaller and less self-sufficient than India's, was particularly vulnerable to the cuts in loans, and the country suspended payment on parts of its debt. "We are a nuclear country with a begging bowl," admitted one official.[176] Pressure increased for Pakistan to sign the Comprehensive Test Ban Treaty, which had been approved by the UN General Assembly in September 1996. Within a month, 129 states had signed up, including the existing five nuclear powers and Israel, the other "threshold" power. China and France consented after they had completed a further round of tests in 1995–1996, judging that sophisticated computer simulation made further formal testing unnecessary. Although fears of a South Asian nuclear arms race did not disappear, it seemed possible that India and Pakistan would follow the same course. Having entered the club, they might eschew costly nuclear arsenals and honor the treaty in deed, if not word.

Few areas of the world welcomed the test-ban treaty more than the Pacific islands, ribbons of archipelagos and atolls across a vast quadrilateral of ocean between Indonesia, Australia, New Zealand, and Hawaii. For half a century since 1946, they were the nuclear testing ground of the great powers. Between 1946 and 1958 the United States conducted sixty-six atmospheric nuclear tests in the Marshall Islands. The British used Christmas Island as well as the western Australian desert in the 1950s. The French turned to their Polynesian possessions around Tahiti after losing Algeria in 1962. Unlike the British and Americans, they continued atmospheric tests until 1975 and underground tests until 1996. The environmental and human damage caused by all these programs will take years to ascertain. In addition, the Marshall

Islands and French Polynesia became economically dependent on their patrons. The French, in particular, had resisted demands for full political independence, both in strategically vital Polynesia and in New Caledonia, where a third of the two hundred thousand people were French.

Elsewhere in the South Pacific, many larger territories had gained independence in the 1970s from Britain, Australia, and New Zealand. But most were economically dependent, and their politics were dogged by legacies of colonial rule. In Fiji (population 770,000 in 1998) there was intense communal friction between the native Fijians and the descendants of Indian workers brought in by the British to work on the sugar plantations, who were now a majority of the population. The election of a Indian-dominated government in 1987 prompted two coups and military rule until 1990. A multiracial polity was not restored until 1998. Papua New Guinea (population four million) faced a secessionist movement on the island of Bougainville from 1990. Despite Australian support for the government, the war dragged on through the decade. In part, islanders were incensed at the environmental damage caused by the vast Australian copper mines. There was also racial animosity between "black" Bougainvillians and "brown" Papuans. But this was hardly surprising, since the island was actually eight hundred kilometers away in the Solomon Islands and had only been lumped in with Papua because of earlier colonial bargains![177]

Australia and New Zealand were advanced economies and flourishing liberal democracies, but they, too, were shaped by the region's changing geopolitics. In the mid-1960s, they seemed to be changing from British dominions into American protectorates, such was their fear of Asian communism (see Chapter 8). The U.S. alliance remained particularly important to Australia, adjacent to Southeast Asia, and it did not follow the New Zealand Labor party in 1985–1986 into an antinuclear policy that prompted Washington to end its ANZUS alliance obligations. But New Zealand's estrangement from Washington encouraged closer links with Australia in defense and commerce (a free-trade agreement took effect in 1990). In fact, both countries followed similar paths in the 1980s and 1990s. Labour party victories in 1983–1984 ended long periods of conservative hegemony and began radical attacks on the protectionism and regulation behind which both economies had atrophied since the 1970s. In New Zealand, Premier David Lange's finance minister, Roger Douglas, imposed his own version of monetarism ("Rogernomics") and embarked on one of the most radical privatization programs in the developed world. Despite a serious recession in the late 1980s and Labor's defeat in 1990, the New Zealand National party continued these policies. The country began to see substantial growth after 1991.[178] In Australia, Labour followed suit in the early 1990s under Bob Hawke and his successor, Paul Keating, who was premier from 1991 to 1996.

These policies were, in part, a response to Asian example. By the late 1990s, the bulk of Australasia's trade was across the Pacific, with Japan and East Asia taking 60 percent of Australia's exports and nearly 40 percent of New Zealand's.[179] Australia's ethnic identity was shifting as well, as Hawke and Keating promoted a new philosophy of "multiculturalism." About 40 percent of immigrants in the mid-1980s were Asian; in the 1990s the "foreign-born" constituted over a fifth of the country's population.[180] As commercial and cultural links strengthened with Asia, so the ties with Britain waned. Keating, an Irish Catholic by background, pushed republicanism onto the agenda. New Zealanders were also beginning to debate the issue.

Another colonial legacy was even more acrimonious—the land rights of the original inhabitants. Legislation in 1985 by the Lange government allowed Maoris to enter claims back to the original Treaty of Waitangi in 1840, under which Britain gained the islands. In Australia in 1992 the Mabo Judgment by the High Court overturned the principle that, before the arrival of Europeans, this was *terra nullius*—unoccupied territory—and prompted Keating to push through the Native Titles Act of 1993, which created a network of compensation tribunals.[181] The shift away from a "monocultural" identity provoked a backlash against native rights and Asian immigration from New Zealand First and the One Nation party in Australia. Though they were minorities, the passions they aroused testified to the painful transition for these "orphans of the Pacific," largely European in culture, essentially Asian in geography.[182]

By the late 1990s, the prophets of the "end of history" and the "new world order" were silent. From Africa to the former Soviet Union, multiparty politics and regular elections had become more prevalent, but often the result was not political stability, let alone Western-style democracy. Constitutional forms mattered enormously. Presidentialism offered the possibility of strong leadership but also bitter confrontation, as the career of Tsar Boris demonstrated. Proportional representation gave more people a voice, but could easily create a babel of parties. In any case, there was more to liberal democracy than frequent elections. It required a political culture in which differences were resolved by compromise, not force. And it could only be sustained by a thriving civil society of autonomous groups mediating between the public and private spheres. These features could not be created overnight.

Much the same could be said for the economic transition. "From what" was clear: regulation, state ownership, and closed economies were all under attack. The example of Thatcher's Britain and Reagan's America was reinforced by the information revolution that we examined in Chapter 14. But "To what?" was harder to answer. Especially after the financial crash of

1997–1998, it was clear that there was no easy, simple leap from Marx to markets. The crash also reminded ardent neoliberals of the importance of *political* economy. In the capitalist West, the state played a vital role in setting the rules of the market (on monopolies, for instance) and in providing basic public goods such as defense, law and order, and property rights. Where states failed to provide these goods, as in Russia and much of Africa, elections and markets were almost irrelevant. In short, big bangs needed steady states. Rather than convergence on an American norm, the global economic trend was toward a *"spectrum* of capitalist social orders," with widely differing balances between the public and private sectors, between markets and government, between growth and equity.[183]

States and wealth; what about order? The dynamic of the early postwar era—the collapse of multinational empires—had been renewed with the breakup of the Soviet Union and Yugoslavia. Other large states, from Nigeria to India (not to mention little Belgium), tried to maintain coherence through a federal system. Yet this was also an era of *voluntary* aggregations of states, a new regionalism against the gales of globalization. The European Union was a pioneer, but the Americans were developing their own common markets, and much of eastern Asia was being informally integrated by investment and trade. On the other hand, in South Asia, Africa, and the Middle East, interstate relations were usually a matter of plate tectonics rather than fluid dynamics, as hard yet brittle structures kept colliding. Territorially, too, the world was in flux.

17

Goods and Values

Compared with the rest of the world, the United States seemed to be in a different league in the mid-1990s. It had emerged from the cold war era supreme in power, wealth, and values. Yet on closer inspection, it was an anxious, divided country whose vices, like its virtues, epitomized patterns in the world at large. Moving from 1990s America into a final look at deeper social and cultural trends, I shall concentrate on some of the buzzwords of the decade. Perhaps the most resonant was the so-called globalization of technology, economies, and culture. At the level of ideas, the spread of religious fundamentalism was in part a politicized reaction to global consumerism. But it was, in addition, a rejection of secular, scientistic definitions of truth. These were also questioned, from within the West, by postmodernist thinkers and radical philosophers of science. Whatever the philosophical debate, working scientists in 1990s were breaching fundamental distinctions between "man" and "nature," as test-tube babies and genetic engineering brought scientists close to creating life. How to sustain life was another vexed politico-scientific issue of the 1990s, along with controversy about environmental pollution and global warming. Social life was also under strain, particularly from urbanization and the weakening of family ties. In short, an increasingly global flow of goods posed challenges to values old and new.

Solitary Superpower, Anxious Americans

The 1990s confirmed the United States as the world's sole superpower. Bipolarity had disappeared with the Soviet Union; contrary to predictions, Germany and Japan had not yet turned economic muscle into military might to create a new era of "multipolarity." The 1990s were "the unipolar moment."[1] The gulf war of 1991 and the Bosnian pacification of 1995 showed that decisive international military action depended on the United States. Although the defense budget for 1999 was two-thirds of the 1989 figure in real terms, the United States still accounted for 35 percent of the world's defense spending (ten times Russia's share).[2] Clinton modified U.S. strategy from global containment of the Soviet Union to a capacity to fight two major regional wars "nearly simultaneously".[3]

The 1990s were also years of plenty for most Americans. After the recession of 1990–1991—which helped Bush lose the 1992 election—the economy had boomed, with 3.6 percent growth in 1997, 50 percent better than Germany and Japan. The U.S. unemployment rate of 5 percent was half that of Germany.[4] The savage "downsizing" of old industries in the 1980s had enhanced competitiveness. American business had capitalized more quickly than its rivals on new information technologies. A sign of confidence was the spectacular growth of share values. The Dow Jones Industrial Average climbed from under 2,000 after the 1987 crash to 4,000 in February 1995, to 8,000 in July 1997, and 9,000 in April 1998. Although falling back during the financial crisis of late summer, the Dow rallied to top the 10,000 mark in March 1999 and 11,000 in May.

Another set of numbers also changed dramatically. In the early 1990s, Americans had been mesmerized by the size of the budget deficit—largely the result of Reagan's supply-side follies (see Chapter 13)—which reached $290 billion by 1993. But in February 1998, Clinton presented to Congress a balanced budget for the fiscal year 1999. Compromise between president and Congress, after deadlock in 1995–1996, was one reason, but equally important were tax rate increases by Bush and Clinton and larger tax revenues from the booming economy and the stock market. A decade of budget surplus was predicted for the new century.

The 1990s also highlighted the relative success of American federalism. Compared with India or Nigeria, let alone the Soviet Union, the United States had been able to hold together a vast country in a flourishing federal polity. What happened when federalism failed were illustrated just across the northern border, where nineties Canada was still haunted by the specter of separatism. The Meech Lake Accord of 1987 proposed a constitutional amendment acknowledging Quebec, with its Francophone majority, as a "distinct society," but this was rejected by some of the Anglophone provinces. The federal government negotiated a new agreement in 1990–1992 that was designed to appease the less populous western provinces with equal representation in a new upper house, but this proposal was rejected by 54 percent of voters in a national referendum in October 1992. As these votes indicated, the issue was not simply Quebec versus the rest, but the provinces against the center in a battle for resources. In the United States, the federal government received about two-thirds of total government revenues in the late 1980s; in Canada the proportion was 46 percent.[5] Meanwhile, separatist feeling in Quebec seemed to be strengthening. In its referendum of October 1995, only 50.6 percent of voters rejected sovereignty within "a new economic and political partnership" with Canada, whereas in 1980 the majority against "separatism" had been nearly 60 percent (see Chapter 12). The Parti Québécois geared up for a new effort in 1999.[6]

Given America's successes during the cold war era, some pundits predicted that the twenty-first century would also belong to America, building on its lead in pioneering the "new frontier" of the global information economy.[7] But was America's surge in the 1990s a linear trend, or just a cyclical upturn when rivals were down? In the late 1980s, after all, Japan rode high and America low. By the late 1990s, the U.S. economy showed signs that its latest cycle was nearing a peak—such as a tight labor market, overvalued shares, and a huge burden of household debt (equal to nearly 90 percent of annual disposable income by 1997). In effect, Americans were spending almost all they earned, thanks to the soaring stock market. What would happen if the bubble burst?

Militarily, too, America's predominance in the 1990s was real, but probably exaggerated. The warning posed by Paul Kennedy in 1987 was still apt. In the twenty-first century the United States was likely to face *relative* decline as China grew, Russia recovered, and Germany and Japan gained in international power.[8] Even in the 1990s, a new insecurity was evident in American concern about "unconventional weaponry"—nuclear, chemical, and biological weapons, together with ballistic and cruise delivery systems. Their spread among developing countries, as the technologies fell in price, was highlighted by the persistent threat from Saddam Hussein in Iraq. In September 1993, Clinton said that restricting these weapons of mass destruction was one of America's "most urgent priorities." The new strategy of counterproliferation dominated administration policy toward Iraq, Iran, and North Korea, and influenced its handling of China, India, and Pakistan.[9]

Although Americans championed the virtues of democracy abroad, disillusion with their own political system was acute in the 1990s. In the 1960s, the turnout in presidential elections never fell below 60 percent of the potential electorate; for the remainder of the century, it did not rise above 55.2 percent. In 1996 it fell to 49 percent.[10] Another sign of disillusion with regular politics was the appeal of the antiparty candidate Ross Perot, who won 19 percent of the popular vote in 1992, mostly at Bush's expense. Perot was a maverick Texas billionaire without political experience, but this was the essence of his appeal to 19 million Americans, who applauded his attack on "a political nobility that is immune to the people's will."[11] Voters also reacted to the electoral system. The outdated sequence of primaries (unnecessary in a TV age) and the high cost of advertising made money the name of the game. The 1996 elections for president and Congress were the most expensive in U.S. history ($1.6 billion). Political alienation sometimes took extremist forms, notably the April 1995 bombing of a government building in Oklahoma City, in which 168 died.

For all these reasons, American politics in the 1990s were extremely volatile. In November 1992, the Democrats won the White House for the first time since the election of 1976. Bill Clinton was a professional politician—governor of Arkansas for most of the 1980s—but he ran as an anti-Washington outsider and a "new Democrat," shedding the party's big government, big welfare image. In November 1994, after Clinton failed to deliver the health-care reform on which he had staked his presidency, the midterm elections gave the Republicans control of both houses of Congress for the first time since 1953–1954. In 1995 the Republican leadership, directed by House Speaker Newt Gingrich, was acting almost as the real executive, as it started implementing its "Contract with America" to downsize the federal government. But in November 1996, after budget deadlock had closed down the government and Clinton had adroitly shifted blame on to the Republicans, he became the first Democrat since Franklin Roosevelt in 1936 to be elected for a second term.[12] Yet the "comeback kid" was also the "come-on" kid, with an adolescent urge for sexual gratification—as a series of revelations made clear. Clinton's lies and evasions in trying to conceal his sordid affair with a White House intern, Monica Lewinsky, gave the Republican majority in the House just enough pretext to impeach him for perjury and obstruction of justice in December 1998. He was only the second president to suffer the humiliation of impeachment—supposedly reserved under the U.S. Constitution for "treason, bribery, or other high crimes and misdemeanors." Although the Republicans lacked the majorities needed to convict Clinton, the president's second term had been irreparably tarnished. Truly, the 1990s were a decade of yo-yo politics.

Clinton's fate was Clinton's fault—no question. But his hero, John Kennedy, was a far worse philanderer who had been able to keep his sexual antics secret. The contrast between the two presidents illustrated profound changes in U.S. public life between the 1960s and 1990s. Watergate was a watershed. It encouraged a less deferential press, inspired by the role of the *Washington Post* in bringing down Nixon. It also infuriated Republicans: their zeal to nail Clinton was, in part, payback for 1974. Watergate also set a precedent for Congress to establish ad hoc special prosecutors with vast inquisitorial powers. Kenneth Starr (who had been Bush's Solicitor General) used these powers to the full, grubbing far beyond his original brief to investigate a shady 1978 Arkansas land deal until he dug up some dirt to justify the $40 million his office had spent. Broader social trends also explain Clinton's humiliation. The culture of women's rights and the litigation boom since the 1960s made "sexual harassment" suits routine. The Lewinsky affair was exposed during one such case. Moreover, Clinton's sins were common gossip on the Internet even before Republicans won a vote to post the whole of the salacious Starr Report there as well. This, to quote one Democrat, made "near-pornographic material available on the Internet with the imprimatur of the U.S. Congress."[13] Although his own worst enemy, Clinton was also a victim of "the immediacy, saturation and viciousness of the Information Age."[14]

Clinton's lechery, the prurience of Starr's report, and the opportunism of senior Republicans (many of whom were also adulterers who had lied about their conduct) heightened the disgust felt by many Americans for their leaders. A sense of malaise infected society as well. Pundits noted that the readiness to join local associations—from churches to unions, from the Red Cross to the Jaycees—had fallen steadily since the 1960s. This was taken as a sign of decay in America's own "civil society," which foreigners since Alexis de Tocqueville in the 1830s had deemed the wellspring of U.S. democracy.[15]

In fact, 1990s America seemed in many ways a very *uncivil* society. Moral issues such as homosexuality, abortion, and the death penalty became battle cries for the new "Christian right" that had emerged during the Reagan era. Pat Buchanan, a demagogic aspirant for the Republican nomination in 1992, claimed that the country was engaged in "a cultural war, as critical to the kind of nation we will one day be as the cold war itself."[16] The sense of conflict was accentuated by two distinctively American traits. One was the widespread ownership and use of firearms, vehemently defended by the National Rifle Association, the country's leading lobby, and justified by a selective reading of the Second Amendment to the Constitution (which affirmed the need for state militias) as an unconditional "right to bear arms." In 1996, handguns were used to murder 9,390 people, compared with 211 in Germany, 106 in Canada, and 30 in Britain. Nearly one in three murders, robberies, and aggravated assaults involved firearms—about half a million incidents a year.[17]

Grabbing a gun to settle disputes was one sign of incivility; another was hiring an attorney. America had two hundred fifty thousand lawyers in the late

1970s, and eight hundred thousand by 1991—70 percent of the world's lawyers.[18] More lawyers needed more litigation to keep themselves in business. Hence the boom in malpractice suits against anyone in positions of responsibility, from doctors to accountants, from hairdressers to sports umpires. The parasitic legal culture sharpened the divisions in American society.

Another controversial issue was immigration. By the mid-1990s, nearly one American in ten was foreign born—the highest proportion since 1930. Whereas the bulk of new immigrants then were European, in the 1990s half were from Latin America and the Caribbean, and a quarter from Asia.[19] "Hispanics" were particularly emotive for the political right. First, they had been successful since the 1960s in achieving bilingual education in many school districts, breaking the tradition that the immigrant must learn English. Second, they were concentrated in the Southwest, prompting warnings of "nationality divisions" within America.[20] The analogy of Quebec was sometimes invoked. Yet Hispanics were not a racial group, but a cluster of nationalities united only by language. Half of Mexican-Americans considered themselves "white"; and many believed bilingualism marginalized them from mainstream society.[21] In fact, because of intermarriage there was more and more need for a "mixed race" category in the U.S. census. This was highlighted by the golf star Tiger Woods, who described himself as Cablinasian—a blend of Caucasian, black, Indian, and Asian.[22] Even if America could assimilate its new immigrants as it had those in the past, however, the strains would be immense. Among major developed countries, only Australia had a larger proportion of foreign born.

African Americans remained a special case. Whereas foreign-born immigrants of Asian or Hispanic descent often married Americans outside their group—respectively, about half and a third according to the 1990 census—fewer than one-tenth of blacks intermarried.[23] In general, the 12 percent of the populace that was black remained disproportionately disadvantaged. Nearly two-thirds of black babies were born outside wedlock, over half of black families lacked a father, and almost 45 percent of black children lived below the official poverty line. (These figures were three or four times those for whites.) Thanks to their concentration in decaying inner cities, 63 percent of black youngsters still attended segregated schools. Black unemployment rates were roughly double those for whites; arrests for most forms of violent crime were at least triple.[24] For many blacks, the arrest statistics were evidence of police racism. These beliefs—and the general alienation of blacks—boiled over in Los Angeles at the end of April 1992 in America's worst race riots since the 1960s. After a jury containing no blacks had ignored videotape evidence and acquitted four white police officers of beating up Rodney King, a black motorist, riots and looting engulfed South Central Los Angeles. Damage was estimated at over $1 billion. Fifty-eight people died, and twelve thousand were arrested.

Culture wars and immigration; race, poverty, and violence—these were just a few of the problems facing America in the 1990s. To quote Sam Nunn, a veteran senator from Georgia, "It's as if our house, having survived the great earthquake we call the Cold War, is now being eaten away by termites."[25] Yet America's vices, like its virtues, were often those of the world writ large. Single mothers and teen pregnancies illustrated larger changes in family life. Culture wars and religious zealotry had parallels with fundamentalist movements elsewhere. And black poverty and unemployment reflected a general marginalization of unskilled workers in a globalizing economy. In many ways, as we shall see, America was both microcosm and model for the world in the 1990s.

"Globalization" and Its Discontents

Globalization has been called "*the* concept of the 1990s," yet its meanings are as varied as its users.[26] Usually the term has an "objective" and a "subjective" element, signifying both "the compression of the world" and greater "consciousness of the world as a whole."[27] Following this definition I shall discuss globalization as economics and then as culture.

The sources of late-twentieth-century globalization lie in the changes in technology and trading described in Chapter 14. In the 1990s those trends accelerated. For television, the big development of the 1990s was the impending shift from analogue to digital broadcasting. Digital compression allowed anything from four to sixteen channels to occupy the same space on the spectrum reserved for one analogue channel. The number of host computers connected to the Internet grew from thirty-three thousand in July 1988 to 36.7 million in July 1998. By the end of the decade over one million new hosts were being connected every month.[28] Demand for computers and software continued to soar. This and the stock-market boom made Bill Gates of Microsoft (Plate 45) the richest man in history by the late 1990s, even though his company, like IBM and AT&T before it, was being targeted by trustbusters in the U.S. Justice Department. The reliance of the developed world on computers was indicated by the costs of the "millennium bug"—the inability of older computers to recognize the two digits 00 as abbreviation for the year 2000. The global bill for correction was likely to be around $300 billion, equivalent to a fifth of the world's ordinary information technology (IT) spending in 1997–2000.[29] In America (home to a third of all computers), the

Y2K problem was taken very seriously. Predictions ranged from a minor economic blip to total disaster. Some warned that the distribution of power and food could collapse, nuclear missiles could be fired in error.

The growth area in telecommunications was in "mobile phones," in which microcomputing was applied to radio telephony via cellular systems that divided the service area into adjacent cells, each with a radio transmitter and receiver. These were pioneered by Televerket in Sweden and AT&T in America in the early 1980s. There were 17 million cell phones worldwide by the start of 1992, of which 51 percent were in the United States and 29 percent in Europe. Since 1996, more than half of all new telephone subscriptions have been for mobile phones. In developing countries the share was three-quarters because mobile systems were cheaper and quicker to develop than fixed systems. They were a substitute for basic telephony, not a supplement.[30]

As in the 1980s, new technologies could take effect because of reduced regulation. The spread of capital markets in the 1990s was possible only because much of the developing world and the old Soviet bloc had allowed currencies to float and had relaxed their capital controls. In 1990, $50 billion of private capital flowed into "emerging markets"; in 1996 the figure was $336 billion.[31] (As the crisis of 1997–1998 showed, what flowed in could also flow out.) Nor could telecoms have flourished if the old state-run monopolies had survived. In major countries of Latin America, led by Chile in 1987, the tendency was toward rapid privatization, usually to a foreign company to help modernize operations quickly. Pakistan also took that route, but much of Asia preferred to turn the nationalized industry into a commercial company and allow some private competition.[32] In global terms, too, the regulatory environment was changing. December 1993 saw completion of the Uruguay Round of GATT trade negotiations, begun in 1986. Despite its acrimony, this was the most comprehensive GATT agreement to date. It cut tariffs on manufactures by over one-third and brought agriculture and services into the world trade regime for the first time. The agreement also transformed GATT from a treaty into a permanent structure, the World Trade Organization, which began work in Geneva in January 1995.[33]

What were the effects of these changes in technology and regulation on the international economy? Some analysts of globalization predicted a "borderless economy" with nation states reduced to "little more than bit actors" as "almost every factor of production—money, technology, factories and equipment—moves effortlessly across borders."[34] Enthusiasts predicted that the home would again become a workplace—what the futurologist Alvin Toffler called "the electronic cottage"—and even suggested that, "bonded together by the invisible strands of global communications, humanity may find that peace and prosperity are fostered by the death of distance."[35] At the other extreme were those who foresaw growing international inequality—"a 20 to 80 world, a one-fifth society in which those left out will have to be pacified by tittytainment" (tits plus entertainment)—or "a deepening international anarchy" as "market forces and shrinking natural resources drag sovereign states into ever more dangerous rivalries."[36]

Much of this debate implied that globalization was a revolutionary force. In many ways, however, it continued the internationalization of commerce that had been going on for a century, except during the protectionist 1930s and World War II. The controversy over globalization therefore had echoes of the "modernization" and "dependency" debates of the 1950s and 1960s. But the 1980s and 1990s were distinctive in several respects. First in scope: Asian capitalism and the communist transitions had extended international markets far beyond the developed West. The scale was also greater: world exports were worth twice as much in real terms in 1993 than twenty years earlier, while daily turnover on the foreign exchange markets had exploded from $200 billion in the mid-1980s to $1.2 trillion in 1995, roughly 85 percent of total world reserves.[37] The causes were also different from the internationalization of the 1950s and 1960s: a steep drop in the cost of communication rather than transport; liberalization of capital and not just trade. Also evident in consequence was a "new international division of labor" both in manufacturing (Nike subcontracted its sports shoes to whichever developing countries had the cheapest labor costs) and in services (such as the Indian city of Bangalore for basic computer software). As the head of one U.S. multinational put it, "We are able to beat the foreign competition because we are the foreign competition."[38]

Globalization was distinctive, therefore, but not unprecedented. Nor was it truly global. In the early 1990s the so-called triad of North America, the European Union, and Japan accounted for about three-quarters of total investment flows, around two-thirds of world exports, and a similar proportion of global GDP.[39] Most of the world was unaffected. Where the globalizing trend mattered to the balance of the international economy was via a few major emerging countries with large consumer markets and reasonably educated populations who were able to work in both manufacturing and information services for a fraction of Western labor costs. Candidates for the "big ten" varied, but they included China and South Korea, Brazil, Mexico and Argentina, and usually India, South Africa, and Indonesia.[40] As we saw in the last chapter, many of these countries have serious question marks hanging over their economic, political, and even territorial future, so prognoses are problematic. But, *assuming* continued growth and development, it is from these emerging economies that challenges to the Triad seem likely to come.

Within the West, the impact of trade and new technologies was often exaggerated. Many person-to-person services, from retailing to health care, could not be "outsourced" abroad or "downsized" significantly by automation. The state sector was also likely to remain substantial, ranging from the armed forces to schoolteachers. The line between services and manufactures had also become increasingly blurred: McDonald's, for instance, was a service industry based on mass production; most modern cars included a range of computerized services. But even if the future would not be totally a "winner-take-all society"[41], the likely losers were already clear—older, less skilled male manual workers who lacked the education to adapt, and who were not traditionally active in the female-dominated "caring" trades and professions. Whereas in the 1960s, incomes rose as the economy grew—to use President Kennedy's phrase, "a rising tide lifts all the boats"—this no longer applied in the 1980s. High school dropouts in the United States earned 22 percent less in real terms in 1993 compared with 1979; high school graduates 12 percent less. Across the developed world (and beyond), workers in industry and basic services faced lower remuneration and a greater chance of unemployment.[42] Although labor had traditionally been more mobile in America than in Europe, both continents faced a growing structural problem of a permanent, alienated underclass. The same could be predicted for ex-communist states with antiquated heavy industry.[43]

The biggest losers from expanded world markets in finance and trade were those outside the triad and the big ten. In other words, the two-thirds of the world population who received less than one-tenth of total foreign direct investment accounted for only one-fifth of world trade and generated a mere quarter of its GDP.[44] Most of the world remained untouched by the Internet, or even by telephones. In 1995, China averaged about three phone lines for every hundred people, India little more than one. Cell phone penetration in both was far less than one per hundred. (In America the figures were 63 percent and 13 percent, respectively.)[45] Much of the world was not even wired up: well under half the dwellings in India and Indonesia had electric lights; in Bangladesh only one-seventh.[46] On the extreme margins of globalization was the "international underclass" of heavily indebted poor countries (HIPCs), constituting nearly a quarter of World Bank members. These forty-one states (thirty-two of them in sub-Saharan Africa) owed debts amounting to more than double their export earnings. For more half of them, debt servicing cost over 20 percent of government revenues. In 1996, the World Bank proposed a new HIPC initiative to reschedule debts to "sustainable" levels, but even those modest proposals were opposed on commercial grounds by major states such as Japan, Germany, and Italy.[47] In any case, this initiative did not address the basic deficiencies of the structural adjustment programs imposed at such social cost over two decades. By the 1990s, thanks to the burden of debt servicing, developing countries were transferring more money to the IMF and World Bank than they received.[48]

Therefore, a concomitant of globalization was marginalization, whether in the world economy at large or within individual states. By the end of the 1990s, it became clear that "globalization" was, in part, an ideology.[49] It had been portrayed as an irresistible force in order to justify omnivorous greed. Consider two of the decade's most spectacular examples of casino capitalism. In February 1995, Britain's most venerable merchant bank, Barings, collapsed after management allowed Nick Leeson, a trader in Singapore, to run up losses of $1.4 billion on the Asian futures market. In September 1998, Long-Term Capital Management—a leading U.S. hedge fund to which banks had loaned a trillion dollars against its $4 billion capital for betting on market trends—was resuscitated by creditors for fear that its collapse would destroy investor confidence (not to mention their own investments). Such sordid debacles showed that markets still needed regulation, both nationally and internationally, though how to do so without stifling enterprise was the great dilemma. By the late 1990s, the economics of globalization had not been resolved, but the debate had been demystified.

In culture, too, "globalization" was an accentuation of earlier trends that were discussed as modernization and Americanization in Chapter 9. As before, the prime concern was usually the perceived threats to a distinctive "national" ethos.

Some observers believed that there was now "something like a true global culture."[50] For example, about a quarter of the world's population was either fluent or competent in English by the mid-1990s.[51] The language of British colonialism and American cinema was also the lingua franca of commerce and computing. The spread of the fast-food giant McDonald's was often taken as another sign of the times. By 1995 it served some thirty million customers a day at some twenty thousand restaurants in over one hundred countries; foreign sales were set to overtake those within the United States.[52] Cultural globalization, it was claimed, was "pressing nations into one homogenous global theme park, one McWorld."[53] More insidious for the nation state was the so-called de-massifying of the media.[54] The mass media, especially government-controlled radio and TV, had been agents of nation building in the developing world and had also sustained the cold war between America and Russia. But mobile phones and satellite TV, PCs and the Internet, opened up a vast range of communications that transcended state boundaries. In the era of "niche" media, not mass media, it seemed that the individual could escape the prison of national culture.

In culture as in economics, however, sweeping rhetoric about globalization needed qualification. Most social theorists saw "little prospect of a unified global culture." Instead they identified a variety of "global cultures."[55] Such transnational identities took many forms—the immigrant and the tourist; globe-trotting professionals in international finance, law, or sports; and the enlarged horizons of those exposed to international TV, music, and film. More generally, the old debate about cultural imperialism had often revolved around crude Marxist models in which the West dominated the Rest.[56] The reality was more complex, however—as the film industry suggests. Measured by what was shown in cinemas across the world, "Hollywoodization" was an accomplished fact—except in a few big Asian countries like India and China. In the European Union, for instance, by the early 1990s, U.S. films had taken over 70 percent of the market; even the jealously guarded French film industry commanded only a third of its domestic market. But films were no longer synonymous with the cinema. Most films made as much money from TV and video; the majority of film viewing worldwide was done at home, using the plethora of TV channels in the era of satellite and cable. It was here that the diversity of the world film industry could be judged, not by reference simply to Hollywood blockbusters like *Jurassic Park* or *Titanic* that grabbed media attention and broke box-office records.[57]

In other words, the technologies of globalization could also encourage localization. On the Internet, for instance, English was the dominant language because the Net was an American invention and two-thirds of host computers were in the United States. But minority languages, such as Welsh or Galician, found that the Net gave them a louder and cheaper voice than traditional media like radio. By 1997 there were at least one hundred Usenet language groups of this sort.[58] Moreover, global tendencies could be locally adapted. Thus the novelist Salman Rushdie (born in India, domiciled in Britain) noted how the people "once colonized by the [English] language are now rapidly remaking it," just as Americans had shaped "British" English.[59] Even McDonald's, supposedly a prime mover of "McWorld," was not a global monolith. Its franchisees were all indigenous, and the company was at pains to take on local coloring. In Beijing, for example, whose first McDonald's opened in 1992, it featured birthday parties for the Little Emperors produced by the one-child policy. In East Asian McDonald's, fast food slowed down because customers lingered far longer than in America, treating these restaurants as updated teahouses rather than alien take-outs.[60]

National as well as local resistance to globalization was also evident. The majority of the world's population was still under the sway of state-controlled mass media, especially radio and television. Most developing countries were not willing to surrender that influence. (We saw at the end of Chapter 12 how television could be used in India to heighten Hindu identity.) Some governments tried to restrict citizens' access to the Net: China, for instance, developed a giant national intranet, or electronic filter, at the cost of $15 million.[61] In general, as the debate about electronic pornography in the West indicated, the almost total lack of regulation of this new medium in the 1990s was likely to be an initial phase rather than a lasting norm. Nationalization, like localization, was a prevalent response to globalization.

If national cultures were being eroded yet global culture was far from triumphant, were the fault lines of the future to be found in a "clash of civilizations"? Samuel Huntington's thesis attracted considerable attention in America and abroad, but many ruinous recent wars (such as Vietnam-Cambodia, Iran-Iraq, or Hutu-Tutsi) had occurred *within* his putative "civilizations," most of which were really extensions of American minority groups.[62] Indeed, his real target seems to have been "the divisive siren calls of multiculturalism" at home. The survival of the United States, he claimed, depended on Americans "reaffirming their commitment to Western civilization" and their ties with Europe—the argument used by East Coast WASP elites since the start of the century. For Huntington, multiculturalism was bunk: "History has shown that no country so constituted can long endure as a coherent society."[63] Yet several major countries, including India and Australia, were predicated on the opposite assumption. In a era of increasing migration and guest workers—when the new media could help sharpen ethnic identities—multiculturalism would be a central cultural issue of the new century.

Here the uses of the past mattered enormously. The "heritage industry" was in part big business, a response to the doubling of international tourists between 1980 and 1996 to six hundred million.[64] But it was also a reaffirmation of national culture in the face of globalization. The vogue for "national museums" that had been part of nation building in nineteenth-century Europe, starting with Berlin, spread across the developing world after 1945. Nigeria, for instance, opened its National Museum in Lagos in 1957, just before independence; Saudi Arabia channeled some of its oil riches of the 1970s into a similar project in Riyadh.[65] Such museums sought to define a unique historical essence for the nation by deliberate anachronism: "the present is used to explain the relics of the past, and then the meanings given to the past are used to justify aspects of the present."[66] The wider enthusiasm for preserving historic buildings, which was pervasive in the developed world by the 1980s, was often a product of "wilful nostalgia" in the face of globalized consumerism.[67] The National Trust in Britain—despite its name a private charity—soared in membership from one hundred fifty thousand in 1965 to over two million by the end of 1990 (more than Britain's three main political parties combined) and became a bigger landowner than the crown or the Church of England.[68] Behind some of its work, particularly the preservation of aristocratic mansions, one critic detected a clear ideology: "The nation is not seen as a heterogeneous society that makes its own history as it moves forward, however chaotically, into the future. Instead, it is portrayed as an already achieved and timeless historical identity which demands only appropriate reverence and protection in the present."[69] "Heritage" was therefore a bulwark against both globalization and multiculturalism.

Yet the idea of common national history and culture was breaking down at the academic level. In America, the civil rights and women's movements encouraged greater self-consciousness about past as well as present. The result was black history and feminist history, followed by those of gays, lesbians, and ethnic minorities—in short, "every group its own historian" until "the American historical profession was fragmented beyond any hope of unification."[70] The American pattern was replicated elsewhere, albeit less quickly or polemically. In Australia and New Zealand, history was rewritten to take into account the aborigines and the Maoris; Europe saw an efflorescence in histories of subordinate nations, such as Scots or Catalans. One of the most influential models was the 1980s school of "subaltern studies," which attacked both the imperialist and nationalist histories of India. The former had portrayed the country as passive object, the latter as active agent, but both assumed an abiding essence controlled by a political elite. Subaltern studies not only rescued the underlings of history (artisans, laborers, poor peasants) as autonomous actors, but also contested the underlying axiom of national unity. They served as a model for particularist, bottom-up history across the academic world.[71] Once again, the concomitant of globalization was fragmentation.[72]

Faith and Doubt

One of the most striking examples of this dialectic was the upsurge of so-called religious fundamentalist movements, largely in response to the spread of secular, consumerist values. At the same time, the scientific knowledge on which those values were based was coming under philosophical attack. This was part of a critique of truth and objectivity that afflicted the humanities as well as the sciences. We need to look more closely at these two buzzwords of the late twentieth century—fundamentalism and postmodernism.

As a religious term, "fundamentalist" originated in the American South around World War I as a call "to do battle royal for the Fundamentals" of Protestant doctrine against liberal theology and Darwinian science. It rested on a literalist belief in the authority of the Bible.[73] Many scholars have claimed that it is also possible to talk of fundamentalist movements in Judaism and Islam because they, too, are "religions of the book" with sacred texts, religious laws, and prophetic traditions.[74] As with globalization, however, a common term conceals vast differences. In Christianity, with its established tradition of separating church and state, most fundamentalist movements do not share the widespread Islamic belief in a theocracy. In many developing countries, religious radicals have a distinctively anti-imperialist motivation that is absent in the West. Religious fundamentalism is "a label of convenience"[75] but, used sensitively, it reminds us that the last quarter of the twentieth century witnessed vehement assertions of religious "fundamentals" in reaction to the corruptions of modernity and the intrusions of the state.

Consider a few late-1970s milestones noted at earlier points in the book. In 1977 the Likud coalition triumphed in the Israeli elections, thanks in part to a surge of support for religious parties. In 1978, John Paul II became pope, determined to replace the compromises of the Vatican II era with an evangelical insistence on Catholic doctrine. In 1979, Ayatollah Khomeini seized power in Iran and began to create an Islamic state. And in 1980, Ronald Reagan won the U.S. presidency, aided by evangelical Protestants such as the Moral Majority, who had been mobilized to defend "family values" against abortion, gays, and pornography. It was the conjunction of events in America and Iran, in particular, that prompted general use of the "fundamentalist" label.

Speaking very broadly, all these movements were "militant, mobilized, defensive reactions to modernity."[76] Most sought to seize the initiative from their own religious hierarchies—deemed too acquiescent—and mount a counterattack against the perceived degradation of conduct and morals. Usually this meant the assertion of patriarchal family values against sexual permissiveness and women's liberation. Given these concerns, religious revivals often entailed engagement in high politics, but equally important, they were efforts from below to reshape society, especially via schools and the media.[77]

This last observation is a reminder of the point already emphasized in Chapters 11 and 16 about Islamists: fundamentalism was not simply "orthodoxy in confrontation with modernity."[78] It also used modernity against itself. Just as Khomeini spread his message from exile via cassettes and telephones, so American evangelicals depended on television for their appeal and funds. Jerry Falwell, the independent Baptist minister who led the Moral Majority, started his ministry in a disused soda-bottling plant in Lynchburg, Virginia, in 1956. By 1981 his services were broadcast on nearly four hundred TV channels and six hundred radio stations, and Thomas Road Baptist Church had an annual income of $60 million.[79]

The "orthodoxy" that fundamentalists defended was also highly selective, be it a Shi'ite elevation of the learned jurist as a sort of philosopher-king, or the prophetic strand of biblical Christianity from books such as Daniel or Revelation. Similarly, in India, proponents of "Hinduness" within the BJP highlighted from the diverse corpus of Hindu literature the figure of the divine warrior-king figure, Ram. As we saw in Chapter 12, they also promoted him assidously through TV and other media. Tradition, in short, could be manipulated, perhaps even invented.

The precise form taken by these religious revivals depended largely on the political context in which they operated. In authoritarian states, it was possible to gain power, directly, as in Iran, or with the help of the military, as in Sudan. But even where Islamic law was made part of the public culture, as we also saw in Chapters 11 and 16, these remained plural societies. Even Iran was relaxing its monoculture in the late 1990s. In democratic polities, the constraints of pluralism were institutionalized. As we saw in Chapter 16, the Hindu BJP had to play coalition politics once it gained power in India in 1998. Likewise, the bid by the American televangelist Pat Robertson to secure the 1988 Republican presidential nomination ended in ignominious failure, having won less than 2 percent of the total number of delegates. These were illustrations of the underlying dilemma of all fundamentalist movements: if they remained religious enclaves, they would be pure but powerless; if they became political forces, they would be powerful but impure.[80] Yet democratic politics did make it easier to exercise *local* influence. After the demise of the Moral Majority in 1989, amid predictions that the New Christian Right was dying, Robertson founded the Christian Coalition to focus on issues at the local level. The group grew to 1.7 million members by late 1995.[81] Likewise, the success of Islamic parties, such as Refah ("Welfare") in Turkey, was rooted in their ability to address day-to-day material needs in the burgeoning cities.

There was a back-to-fundamentals strain in the Roman Catholic church. Under John Paul II, a liberal in politics but not dogma, the Vatican II message of "updating" the faith (Chapter 7) was abandoned in favor of "re-Christianizing" public life. An important instrument was the "Communion and Liberation" movement founded by Father Luigi Giussani in Milan in 1956, which became politicized during the 1974 Italian referendum on divorce. The movement spread to some thirty countries, from the United States to Uganda.[82]

The most dynamic elements in world Christianity in the 1980s and 1990s were charismatic movements like Pentecostalism—sect churches committed to faith healing and speaking in tongues. Strong in the United States, they were also prominent in South Korea, some African countries like Nigeria and South Africa, and especially Latin America, where they became major rivals to the Catholic church. In Brazil and Chile, the most important examples, around 20 percent of the population was Protestant by 1990. Overall, more than half of Latin America's Protestants were Pentecostal by this time. Although Pentecostalism tended to be apolitical, it usually appealed to those who considered themselves outcasts and oppressed. And simply by creating a "free space" outside the political world and critical of it, Pentecostals helped expand civil society and further erode Catholicism's hold over national cultures.[83]

Even apolitical religious movements in nontheocratic states could therefore affect the political agenda. Another example was the *haredim*, or orthodox Jews in Israel who, despite their traditional opposition to state obligations such as military service and even to Zionism itself, became decisive weights in the scales of Israeli coalition politics. They, like more assertive religious Jews such as the Gush Emunim pro-settler movement, were part of the culture wars between secular and religious (Tel Aviv versus Jerusalem, as some observers put it) that underlay the struggles about Israel's domestic politics and foreign policy. Even among Jews, therefore, Israel was a multicultural society. Moreover, a fifth of its people, *within* the pre-1967 borders, were Arabs—either Muslim or Christian. Nor was such diversity unusual. Even in the 1970s, less than 10 percent of the world's states were, like Denmark, truly homogeneous in language, religion, and ethnicity.[84] The proportion fell further with the collapse of the Soviet Union and Yugoslavia. America's multiculturalism was therefore normal, not aberrant.

Thus, the religious denominators of thought and culture remained far more potent than exponents of secularization and modernization had assumed after World War II. But religions themselves, like "orthodoxy" and "modernity," were not unchanging essences. All of them, even the monotheistic faiths, had been formed from many different traditions. This process continued in the late twentieth century; indeed, the technologies of globalization encouraged it. Syncretism flourished particularly on the borders between the major religions—along the Christian-Muslim fault line in Africa, for instance, or in the Hindu-Muslim mosaic of South Asia—and in areas where they engaged with local animist or magical cults. Religions were also in flux because of feminist challenges to their prevailing patriarchal ethos. By the mid-1980s, most Protestant denominations had accepted women priests or ministers (though at the cost of acrimonious argument in the Church of England); likewise, both Reformed and Conservative Judaism. Although the principle was still anathema in the Catholic church and Eastern Orthodoxy, and women's roles were even more circumscribed in Islam, all these traditions faced challenges from feminist theologies. The prospective feminization of religious belief and practice, however gradual and erratic, had as much historical significance as the surge of religious fundamentalisms.[85]

But most so-called fundamentalists would not accept the idea that religion is historically and culturally conditioned. What they shared, above all, was the premise that "religious truth is essentially unchanging and timeless" and that it was "knowable as an object in the external world" because of revelation in divinely inspired individuals and texts.[86] Since the European Enlightenment of the eighteenth century, skeptics had challenged revelation in the name of reason. Now many fundamentalists in the Judaeo-Christian tradition denounced the Enlightenment as the root of modern evils—particularly what Jean-Marie Lustiger, the cardinal archbishop of Paris in the 1980s, called its "divinization of human reason."[87]

By this time, however, reason, and indeed the whole "Enlightenment project" of rational knowledge, was under attack by secular philosophers. The shorthand for such skepticism was postmodernism.

The term derived its power from its vagueness. Arguably, how one defined "modernism" mattered less than one's usage of "post" (did it signify break, or continuation, or both?).[88] The term migrated into academic culture from architecture, where it had been employed since the late 1960s to connote a reaction to the strict vocabulary of the modern movement—towers and slabs, straight lines and minimal ornament (see Chapter 5). Architectural postmodernism signified both "the continuation of Modernism and its transcendence."[89] Continuation meant recognizing that we could not return to the premodern either in style or technologies. Transcendence meant employing "codes" from the past, but ironically rather than with nostalgia. One example was Charles Moore's Piazza d'Italia in New Orleans' "Little Italy," which combined theatrical fragments of classical columns with Art Deco ornament and neon lights to suggest the dislocated history of Italian-Americans. Another postmodernist "classic" from the same period was the Neue Staatsgalerie in Stuttgart (1984) by James Stirling, Michael Wilford and Associates. In the late 1960s, Stirling had inflicted a piece of gross modernism on the history faculty at Cambridge University—a glass bell-tent, innovative in design, but poorly constructed, and conceived with arrogant indifference to both users and context. The Staatsgalerie, in contrast, was a work of sensitivity and humor, blending past and present in a way that befitted a modern museum—for instance, in mounting a pseudo-Acropolis on top of a parking garage, and in using "fallen" stones to expose the steel-frame construction.[90]

The pluralism of postmodern architecture, its self-conscious juxtaposition of present and past—often in unresolved contradictions—provided the motifs for a more general, philosophic postmodernism. At its heart was a radical "deconstructionist" approach to language.

Intellectual postmodernism was developed by several French philosophers and social scientists in the late 1960s and 1970s in poststructuralist writings that were read in translation across the English-speaking world. Structuralism had posited structures of meaning underlying cultural phenomena, most notably in linguistics, which had been invented in its modern form by the Swiss professor Ferdinand de Saussure before World War I. He set out the dichotomy between words and things—between the signifier and the signi-fied—noting that the relationship between the two was not immutable but a matter of convention. In other words, the "meaning" of words changed over time. De Saussure still believed that one could discern underlying struc-tures and establish a science of linguistics. But poststructuralists pushed his ideas about language to radical, sometimes nihilistic, conclusions, encour-aged by the events of May 1968. In the words of one slogan, scrawled on the blackboard of a deserted classroom at the Sorbonne, "Structures do not take to the streets."[91]

For Jacques Derrida, the Algerian Jew who migrated to Paris to study phi-losophy, we live in "a world of signs without fault, without truth and without origin."[92] Because there is no absolute relationship of signifier to signified, no text can have a fixed meaning. For Derrida, all texts are textual in the sense that they are written by reference (conscious or not) to all previous texts that the author has encountered. By close reading—or "deconstruction," to use the term for which Derrida became famous—one can reveal the texts within the texts and the contradictions in the author's use of terms, thereby deconstructing his power over his writings. If Derrida seemed to reduce meaning to the free play of language, the psychoanalyst Jacques Lacan did the same for the concept of an autonomous subject. Lacan insisted that our sense of self was not innate or intuited but was constituted by our entry into language. There is no subject independent of language. Because the rela-tionship between signifier and signified is arbitrary and always in flux, Lacan called into question the subject-object polarity which forms the basis of all modern science, natural or human.

Deconstructionist postmodernism was greeted skeptically by many philosophers in America and Britain, not least because it appeared to reduce all concepts to metaphors and to deny the possibility of critical thought. But it had huge appeal in literary theory, influencing numerous novelists from Salman Rushdie in Britain to John Barth in the United States. They operated on the now-fuzzy borders of history and fiction, used complex techniques of narration to expose the problem of subjectivity, and engaged in frequent "in-tertextuality" by weaving past texts into their own. Perhaps the most cele-brated postmodernist novel was by Umberto Eco, an Italian professor of linguistics and literary theory—who achieved international fame with *The Name of the Rose* (1981). According to Eco: "The postmodern reply to the modern consists of recognizing that the past, since it cannot really be de-stroyed . . . must be revisited: but with irony, not innocently."[93]

The impact of postmodernism extended far beyond literature. In social studies a hugely influential figure was Michel Foucault, the philosophical his-torian who died of AIDS in 1984, at the age of fifty-seven. Foucault attacked the idea of the rational self through his studies of the archaeology, or "posi-

tive unconscious," of modern thought. *The Order of Things* (1966) argued
that the concept of "man" as autonomous subject was the product of late-
eighteenth-century rationalism. Now that the philosophical tide had turned
against the Enlightenment, Foucault predicted, "man would be erased, like
a face drawn in sand at the edge of the sea."[94] For Foucault, language was
power: definitions of truth, crime, and rationality were ways of disciplining
modern populations without the use of brute force. The philosopher Jean-
François Lyotard took a similar view. "Knowledge and power are simply two
sides of the same question," he insisted in *The Post-Modern Condition*
(1979). "Who decides what knowledge is, and who knows what needs to be
decided?" At stake was the "legitimization" of power, accomplished through
"language games"—effectively a form of conflict, though "the war is not
without rules."[95] Lyotard's work appeared to dissolve truth claims into language games, played to win the battle for power.

Postmodernists were certainly not a coherent school, and they frequently
(if inconsistently) denounced "misreadings" of their work by would-be disciples. It was possible to view postmodernism in a moderate light as an exercise in living with contradictions—accepting that terms like *truth* and
reality are problematic, while not abandoning them as concepts.[96] Derrida
spoke of defending "the most serious tradition of the university" while also
exploring "the abyss beneath the university."[97] Yet the thrust of most postmodernist work seemed deeply nihilist: "truths are illusions of which one has
forgotten that they are illusions" in Derrida's aphorism.[98] This thrust was
pushed home by the sociologist Jean Baudrillard who announced the end of
the "wager of representation" that had characterized Western intellectual history—the idea that a sign had a meaning because it represented a reality.
Now, he argued, "simulation" had totally replaced "representation": the sign
"bears no relation to any reality whatever" except itself.[99]

Postmodernism challenged natural science, as well. For Lyotard, science
was but another language game, given privileged status in Western culture
by resort to "grand narratives" about technological progress. At the same
time, philosophers were questioning the epistemology of science, prompted
by a similar concern for language and history.[100]

Most practicing scientists are realists and rationalists. That is to say, they
believe as an assumption of working life that their research represents external reality and that it proceeds by canons of rational argument ("the scientific method"). In mid-century, the history of science was in its infancy as
a discipline. The philosophy of science was still suffused with a logical posi-
tivism that reduced rationality to logicality in that scientific explanation supposedly took the form of subsuming data within "covering laws." Both
disciplines, however, were transformed by *The Structure of Scientific Revolutions* (1962). Its author was Thomas S. Kuhn, an American physicist turned

historian. Kuhn's central concept was "paradigms," a term that became as popular (and as vague) as "deconstruction". He claimed that "normal science" works within a paradigm, or exemplary model, such as Newtonian mechanics. It carries on "solving puzzles" within that framework until "anomalies" crop up to block further progress. Out of this crisis, an era of "revolutionary science" develops until a new paradigm is formed, such as Einsteinian mechanics. Kuhn insisted that rival paradigms were "incommensurable"—they were different ways of seeing the world—and that in choosing between them there was "no standard higher than the assent of the relevant community" of scientists.[101] Kuhn's approach was pushed to an extreme by the American philosopher Paul Feyerabend. *Against Method* (1974) reduced both realism and rationality to unprovable ideologies. For Feyerabend, there were no "bare facts" because all information was packaged within ideas. The anarchic history of science showed that instead of a fixed method, the "only principle that does not inhibit progress is: *anything goes.*"[102]

Critics of Kuhn and Feyerabend exposed many confusions in their work. But it helped effect a "fundamental transformation in philosophical perspective: science became an historical phenomenon."[103] Often "truth" was dropped in favor of words like "verisimilitude," greater "observational success," and increased "problem-solving capacity." This kind of "temperate rationalism"[104] seemed the only way out of the prison of historicized language in which late-twentieth-century Western thought was immured. But as the example of an electron suggested, if you could measure or manipulate a postulated entity, then it was probably real. For most scientists, experimenting, not theorizing, seemed "the best proof of scientific realism."[105]

A prime example of this axiom—and one with vast implications for science and faith—was the late-twentieth-century rethinking of cosmology. Scientific cosmology examines the universe and its origins. As "the study of a unique object and a unique event," it is therefore a problematic science, because "no physicist would happily base a theory on a single unrepeatable experiment."[106] But, through a tenuous yet powerful fusion of observation and theory, working back from new axioms in nuclear and particle physics, the discipline has been transformed since the 1960s.

The idea that the universe might have originated in some kind of original explosion emerged in modern form in the 1920s, from both Einsteinian mathematics (though Einstein himself resisted the idea) and also the observational work of the Californian astronomer Edwin Hubble, who measured how galaxies were receding from earth. But the so-called steady-state theory, propounded in 1948 by Herman Bondi, Thomas Gold, and Fred Hoyle in Britain, accommodated Hubble's evidence by postulating the continuous creation of new matter. There was little interest in what Hoyle derided as the "big bang" thesis championed during the 1940s in America by George Gamow and his collaborators. In any case, all this work was largely theoretical. Without much new empirical input, cosmology remained a backwater throughout the 1950s.

Things began to change in 1965 with what has been called "one of the most important scientific discoveries of the twentieth century."[107] Two young radio astronomers, Arno Penzias and Robert Wilson, had adapted a Bell Labs satellite antenna in New Jersey with the aim of studying radio emissions within our own galaxy. But they were unable to eliminate a persistent background hiss of microwave radiation, apparently emanating from farther afield. These findings made sense only when the pair was fortuitously put in touch with a group of physicists at Princeton University (less than thirty miles away) headed by Robert Dicke—another of the radar veterans of World War II. Although Dicke did not subscribe to the "big bang," he believed that the universe had oscillated in size and postulated that the expansionary phases of extreme heat would leave behind traces of background cosmic radiation. His group was looking for this evidence, but Penzias and Wilson had unwittingly beaten them to it. In the spring of 1965 their observational findings were published in the *Astrophysical Journal,* coupled with an interpretive essay by the Dicke group—just as, twelve years before, Crick and Watson had explained the experimental work on DNA done by Franklin and Wilkins. In the 1970s, breakthroughs in particle physics by Steven Weinberg and others, and further theoretical work, notably the "inflationary" model of Alan Guth, helped refine the big bang thesis. The Cosmic Background Explorer (COBE) satellite, launched in 1989, provided confirmatory measurements of microwave radiation from outside the earth's atmosphere.[108]

The big bang thesis was not incompatible with a Christian Doctrine of creation. Indeed, it was embraced by Pope John Paul II—with the rider that, although scientists could examine the evolution of the universe, the bang itself was off limits, being the moment of creation and thus the work of God.[109] As the American cosmologist Don Page—a devout Christian—put it, the question of whether the universe was created by God "is a question that science can neither affirm nor refute."[110] But the new cosmology had put human beings more starkly than ever in their place by representing the earth as "just a tiny part of an overwhelmingly hostile universe" made of matter far different from ourselves.[111] The cosmological debate in the 1980s and 1990s was between those who postulated an open universe that would gradually run down over billions of years or a closed universe that would eventually climax in a "big crunch" mirroring the big bang. Neither "slow refrigeration" or "dramatic cremation"[112] was an attractive ending—though they are far enough in the future not to trouble even the youngest reader of this book.

Academic astronomy was, of course, a minority pursuit. In the late 1990s there were only about fifteen thousand professional astronomers in the world, predominantly in Europe or North America.[113] But popular interest was intense, as demonstrated by the phenomenal success of *A Brief History of Time* (1988) by the British cosmologist Stephen Hawking (see Plate 45). As he remarked later, "It was in the London *Sunday Times* best seller list for 237 weeks, longer than any other book (apparently the Bible and Shakespeare aren't counted). It has been translated into something like forty languages and has sold about one copy for every 750 men, women and children in the world."[114] In part its appeal derived from Hawking's clear, often witty, explanation of complex ideas; in part from his hypothesis about the universe, in which there was no place for creation or a creator. Hawking's professed goal was a Grand Unified Theory of the universe and matter that would be tantamount, in theological language, to knowing "the mind of God."[115]

Yet Hawking was one cosmologist among several. Popular interest was aroused by the scientist as much as his science, for Hawking (born in 1942) had been incapacitated since his early twenties by motor neuron disease, from which his body gradually atrophied, although the higher functions of brain and memory were unimpaired.[116] What caught the public imagination was the image of a "crippled genius," hunched in his electronic wheelchair, mumbling incomprehensible profundities. Hawking's ability to work, indeed his very survival, depended on devoted family, nurses, and colleagues, but it was also a triumph of modern technology. After a tracheotomy in 1985, he was fitted with a new computer-generated "voice" based on a menu of some three thousand words from which he could select using a hand-held switch. A century before, someone like this would have decayed in silence in an institution. Instead, he had written a best seller about one universe that had eclipsed Wendell Willkie's *One World*.

Creating Life?

Stephen Hawking's achievement was but one example of how modern science was pushing back the boundaries of life itself. This capacity was seen most of all in the biological sciences. Transplantation surgery used the dead to give new life to the dying. In vitro fertilization simulated artificially the act of procreation. By the late 1990s, genetic engineering had created new strains of superplants and transgenic animals, most famously Dolly the sheep. Humanity's enhanced ability to shape, even create, life raised profound ethical questions as well as new technological vistas.

The first recorded transplant of a vital human organ from one unrelated person to another occurred in the Soviet Union in 1936, though the patient only lived for two days with his new kidney. The first such operation in the United States occurred in Chicago in June 1950, but the kidney failed within months.[117] As these cases indicated, the greatest challenge was not the surgery itself but the problem of rejection. Successful transplants were possible only because of breakthroughs in immunological science in the 1950s and 1960s.

Immunology has been described as the science of "self and not-self," how the body distinguishes and protects its own tissues from toxins and alien microbes.[118] The leading work was done by groups led by Peter Medawar in Britain and McFarlane Burnet in Australia. Medawar's experimental investigations of rejection and tolerance in animals had grown out of his wartime work on skin grafts for burn victims. His research complemented that of Burnet, a virologist, on how antibodies are generated to reject the invaders of the self. They were awarded a Nobel Prize jointly in 1960.[119] Subsequent work identified precisely the lymphocytes, or white blood cells, that were critical for recognition and response, determined the structure of antibodies, and mapped the complex of genes that governed the immune system. By the mid-1960s, this research had generated enough understanding to permit manufacture of basic immunosuppressant drugs that would override the body's natural defenses and avoid rejection. Kidney transplants became commonplace; surgeons now wanted to conquer the heart.

The first cardiac transplant took place on December 3, 1967, at the Groote Schuur Hospital in Cape Town. The heart of Denise Darvall, a young car-accident victim, was given to businessman Louis Washkansky. The surgeon was Christian Barnard, aged forty-five, who had entered the transplant arena fairly recently and had been badgering the hospital authorities to mount a heart program. (They agreed, so long as donor and recipient were both white.) Washkansky died of an infection of the lungs after eighteen days, but Barnard became an international superstar, boosted by a South African government anxious to polish its apartheid-stained image.

Barnard had beaten more experienced U.S. teams because the laws on death in South Africa were much looser. There a patient could be pronounced dead on the say-so of two doctors. No clinical criteria for their judgment were prescribed. Barnard could therefore go ahead as soon as brain death was pronounced, not when the heart stopped beating—the prevalent legal definition of death in America. Following a trial in Virginia in 1972, that state and many others adopted brain death as one of the legal definitions of mortality. Most Western countries followed during the 1970s, but not Japan—only one heart transplant has occurred there, in 1968.

In the years immediately after Barnard's coup, it became a test of professional and national virility to claim a heart transplant operation. Yet the immunological therapy was still crude. Because the drugs overrode the whole immune system, most patients who survived rejection succumbed to infection. During 1968, 102 heart transplants were attempted by forty-seven teams in eighteen countries, from India to Venezuela, but only twenty-four patients lived longer than six months. By the early 1970s, heart transplants had slowed to little more than a dozen a year.[120]

It was not until the 1980s that the transplant of vital organs became routine. This was largely due to the "wonder drug" cyclosporin, synthesized from a soil fungus, which inhibited rejection of foreign tissues but had less effect on resistance to infection. Cyclosporin was introduced in the United States in 1983. In conjunction with better matching of tissues between donor and recipient, it transformed success rates. Of the six thousand heart transplants that had occurred worldwide by the end of 1988, about 80 percent had taken place in the previous four years.[121] Over ten thousand kidney transplants were performed annually in the United States by the late 1990s. The survival rate at one year was about 90 percent, double that in 1967. Survival rates for heart transplants were 80 percent, for livers 70 percent.[122]

Even in its routine phase, however, transplantation was still profoundly contentious. Was this the "gift of life" from one stranger to another, or was it a commercial transaction? By the 1980s, the shortage of donors encouraged the latter view, particularly in the developing world. In India, for instance, the sale of organs was a thriving minor business until the government passed a law banning the trade in human kidneys in 1995. Because of the shortage of human organs, there was growing interest in xenotransplants from animals. Experiments on chimpanzees in the 1960s had aroused a storm of protest, so researchers turned to pigs, whose organs were the right size and whose bodies were already sacrificed daily in vast numbers for the dinner table. To circumvent the rejection problem, genetically engineered pigs were bred in Britain and America in the 1980s from eggs injected with genes that would neutralize the defense mechanisms of the human body. Because of protests by animal-rights activists, this work took place in intense secrecy.

Even if organs could be found, transplantation itself remained contentious. Was it right to spend $250,000 on one heart-lung transplant, given what that money could do in basic health care for hundreds of people? And how long should medical intervention go on? By the age of five, Laura Davies of Manchester, England, had become famous as the only person in the world whose existence depended on six transplanted organs. Her parents finally insisted in November 1993 that she be taken off a ventilator and allowed to die in peace. Such cases raised questions about whether human beings had become guinea pigs for medical experiment.[123]

"Spare parts" surgery helped keep life going. In 1978 the first "test-tube baby" prompted claims that scientists were now creating life. In vitro fertilization (IVF) involves taking eggs from a woman's uterus, fertilizing them with prepared sperm in a glass dish (in vitro), and then placing any embryo that is formed back in the uterus in the hope that a normal pregnancy may result. Although success was achieved on rabbits in France and America during the 1950s, human IVF was much slower. As with many scientific breakthroughs, it was the result of intellectual fertilization, in this case between an experimentalist and a surgeon. Robert Edwards, a geneticist at Cambridge University, had been working on the problem since the early 1950s, starting with mice and rabbits. Patrick Steptoe, a surgeon at Oldham Hospital, near Manchester, had pioneered a technique called laparoscopy, involving a tiny fiber-optic telescope to pinpoint the eggs, which could then be extracted from the ovary by a needle and suction. Their partnership was fraught with difficulties—both official (opposition from the British medical authorities) and practical (Oldham was an arduous four hours' drive from Cambridge). But after a decade of work and over a hundred unsuccessful embryo replacements, the first IVF baby, Louise Brown, was born in Oldham in July 1978. After Steptoe retired from the National Health Service, he and Edwards eventually found business collaborators and opened a private clinic at Bourn Hall, near Cambridge, in early 1981.[124]

By the spring of 1985, nearly one thousand IVF births had occurred; most big cities in Western Europe, the United States, Australia, and Japan had an IVF program.[125] As with transplant surgery, these techniques raised serious ethical questions. The Vatican convened a working party of gynaecologists and theologians in Rome in November 1984, where all but one member judged IVF to be morally acceptable. Their report was never published, however, and in February 1987 the Vatican issued an instruction condemning IVF. The U-turn was similar to that in the 1960s over the pill (see Chapter 9); indeed, the argument in both cases was the same. Intercourse and procreation were indissolubly related—you must not try to have one without the other.[126] As with the encyclical on contraception, many Catholics took no notice.

Most ethicists took a more moderate view than the Vatican. "You cannot put genies back into bottles," wrote Professor Ian Kennedy of London University. "You can, however, try to make sure that the genies do not go around granting any old wish. You can give the genies some rules."[127] Those rules varied from country to country, particularly on the questions of whether there should be voluntary or statutory regulation of IVF, and whether embryos could be used for research or just for replacement. British legislation in 1990 established a statutory body and allowed research on embryos up to fourteen days. Germany's 1990 law banned all research but did not create a regulatory authority. In America, there was no federal legislation or regulatory body, but federal funds could not be used for IVF research.[128]

The research generated by IVF also raised profound questions about how one understood the human person. Christian theology traditionally insisted that the embryo was a person from the moment that the egg was fertilized by sperm. But some ethicists now adapted the conception of "brain death" used in transplant surgery to claim that the embryo was not a person until "brain birth" had occurred, at around eight weeks. Others suggested that the dividing line should be fourteen days, by which time the "floating" embryo was implanted on the wall of the uterus, thereby obtaining nutrients from the mother to permit continued cell growth. This was an important justification for those who wished to use early embryos for research.[129]

Apart from confusing the definition of personhood, IVF also blurred the concept of parenthood. In cases where the genetic mother was unable to carry the embryo through a successful pregnancy and used a surrogate womb, who was the "real" parent? Disputes between rival mothers and controversy about "rent-a-womb" businesses cast doubt on the object of IVF. Was it to make money? Was it to advance experimental science? Or was it to alleviate infertility, which condemned millions of women around the world to misery and even ostracism because they had failed in their supposedly prime role as mothers? Once again, new technologies raised profound questions about goods and values.

IVF was insemination without intercourse. It did not tamper with the genetic equipment of sperm or egg. But such manipulation was now possible, thanks to recombinant DNA technologies (see Chapter 14) and the in vitro methods of IVF. By the 1990s, "transgenics" enabled researchers to insert individual genes into plants and embryos to alter their genetic information. It was even possible to transfer the nuclei of embryos in order to reproduce an individual animal in what was known as cloning.

In February 1997, the media trumpeted the news that an obscure agricultural research breeding station at Roslin in Scotland had cloned a sheep, to which it gave the name Dolly. The team, led by Ian Wilmut, had used a ewe's egg from which the nucleus had been extracted, and then added the nucleus of a frozen udder cell from another sheep, before transferring the embryo to a surrogate mother. After 277 attempts using this technique, Dolly* had been born in July 1996—the twin of a sheep born six years earlier who, by then, had been killed, cooked, and eaten! Technically, the work was impressive because it was the first successful use of an *adult* cell, rather than nuclei from embryos, whose cells had not yet differentiated into specialist functions such as brain or udder. Initial scientific scepticism was dis-

*Officially, she was lamb 6LL3, but Wilmut called her "Dolly" after the country music star Dolly Parton, who, he said, was also known for her mammaries.

pelled in July 1998 by news that two calves had been born in Japan from cells taken from an adult cow. That same month, researchers in Hawaii also announced mice cloned from previous clones—effectively three generations of identical twins.[130]

Media speculation ran riot, with art, as so often, shaping perceptions of reality. Stephen Spielberg's 1993 blockbuster, *Jurassic Park,* had imagined that dinosaurs could be re-created from their fossilized DNA. For scientists, however, Dolly herself was something of a red herring. The real interest of Wilmut's team, and the many others who rushed into the field, was not transgenic livestock itself but the pharmaceutical products that could be generated in large quantities from the milk, using the animals as living factories. Most of this work was funded by the so-called pharming industry of drug and biotech companies. Yet the implications for humans could not be avoided indefinitely. Even though most Western countries had laws forbidding human cloning, were there not some acceptable uses for these techniques, such as repairing damaged tissue? In the animal world, cloning might also be used to preserve endangered species. Where to draw the line poses major ethical and political dilemmas.[131]

In its early days, biotechnology concentrated on drugs because most of its investment came from the pharmaceuticals industry. But in the 1990s, biotechnology literally bore fruit. Genetically modified organisms (GMOs) were created using two main techniques—gene addition and gene inactivation. An example of the first was insect-resistant plants developed by synthesizing them with insecticides coded by cloned genes. Inactivation allows, for instance, slowing down the ripening process in fruits to allow flavor to mature before they have to be picked and shipped.[132] The American harvest of 1996 saw the first commercially successful GMOs, particularly corn and soybeans. In the next couple of years, several chemical companies hurriedly repositioned themselves as "life sciences" corporations, embracing agriculture, pharmaceuticals, and food by acquiring a strategic mesh of biotech companies, genomics laboratories, and seed suppliers. The market leaders included Du Pont and Monsanto in America and the Swiss giant Novartis (formed from a merger of Ciba and Sandoz in 1996).

There was considerable resistance to plant biotechnology in the European Union, partly because of health fears but also because of the EU's rooted agricultural protectionism. The United States was less restrictive. In 1998 GMOs accounted for about 15 percent of the U.S. corn harvest, 30 percent of the soybean crop, and over half the production of cotton. The potential implications were enormous. Monsanto, for instance, unveiled plans in 1998 for "blue cotton," made by transferring a gene from a plant with a blue flower into a cotton plant. Once commercially available, this could transform jeans production *and* eliminate the pollution caused by toxic dyes. Among other plans for environmentally friendly "biofactories" were plastics grown in plants and vaccines grown in bananas.[133]

These advances were made possible by rapid progress in gene sequencing (see Chapter 14). The international Human Genome Project was on course to make a complete sequence of human DNA publicly available by 2005. More selectively, commercial genomics companies, funded by pharmaceuticals, focused on potentially profitable proteins and on the essential genetic material amid the mass of "junk" DNA.[134] Back in 1965, Moore's Law had predicted that the number of transistors that could be placed on a silicon chip would double every eighteen to twenty-four months. In 1997 Monsanto postulated that "the amount of genetic information used in practical applications will double every year or two" and predicted that the economic effects "may be even larger" than those of Moore's Law.[135] Since genomics depended largely on computerization, Moore's Law was, in fact, a precondition for Monsanto's Law. Chips + Genes = ? This was one of the great open questions for humanity in the new millennium.

Sustaining Life

Nowhere was the potential of biotechnology more important than in demography. In the autumn of 1999 the world's population passed the six-billion mark, having doubled since 1950. About 58 percent lived in Asia, 13 percent in Africa, and 10 percent in Europe and North America. More than eighty million people were being born each year. The UN did not expect fertility rates to stabilize at population replacement levels until the mid-twenty-first century, by which time humanity would total around 9.4 billion.[136] These projections were highly tentative, of course, but they highlighted the slowness of the fertility transition in much of the developing world and the acute pressure of population on resources for at least the next half-century. Was there enough food and water available? Were they safe to consume, given the scale of pollution? Had the ecological balance of the planet itself been seriously damaged? "Environmental security" became a post–cold war battle-ground, with the use and abuse of new technologies at its heart. As we shall see, the issues were as much political as technological.

By 1984, world grain production was more than two and half times greater than in 1950, defying predictions of an impending Malthusian crisis (see Chapter 5). But beginning in the early 1980s, a different trend was perceptible. Whereas world grain production per person had risen from 550 pounds in 1950 to a peak of 763 pounds in 1984, it then fell to 690 pounds by 1996. If these trends could not be reversed, by 2030 China, Bangladesh, Pakistan and India would look to imports for at least 20 percent of their grain. On this scenario, the Worldwatch Institute in Washington predicted that "food scarcity is likely to emerge as the defining issue of the era now beginning."[137] An alternative view, however, was taken by econometricians at the World Bank and the UN Food and Agriculture Organization. They believed that grain production could keep pace with rising consumption, mainly because of increased crop yields. The green revolution had helped boost productivity in the 1960s and 1970s; they argued that the gene revolution could do likewise in the 2000s and 2010s.[138] Whereas environmentalists warned that natural limits had been reached, technologists predicted that, once again, this was only a temporary obstacle.

But such optimism assumed that the benefits of biotechnology would be made widely available to the developing world—an assumption that was not being realized in the 1990s. And some areas of agriculture were not commercially viable for biotechnology, such as subsistence crops. These would require public sector investment, as would the research, infrastructure, and education required to make all new technologies productive at the local level. These challenges were political as much as technological.[139] Also required was a redefinition of "food security" away from virtual self-sufficiency. This was particularly true of China, whose aim of keeping grain imports at only 5 percent was deemed unrealistic even by those optimistic about the country's scope for improved use of irrigation and fertilizer.[140] The government still thought of food (and fuel) imports as *dependence* rather than *interdependence*.[141] This might change as the People's Republic moved from xenophobic isolation to involvement in the world economy, much as Japan had done after World War II.

Unlike food, water is less susceptible to human manipulation through global trade or technological innovation. Nearly all the world's water takes the form of oceans. Only 2.7 percent of the total is fresh water; of that, 76.5 percent is stored in polar ice caps and another 22.9 percent in ground water. Thus, runoff from lakes and rivers constituted only 0.6 percent of the world's fresh water, of which only about one-third is "stable" enough to be used (as opposed to floods). Ecological pessimists pointed to falling water tables and the failure of irrigation to keep pace with population growth since 1979.[142] Yet technological optimists reckoned that stable runoff was sufficient in principle to cover the predicted increase in world consumption, *if* it was effectively managed. That meant reducing wastage through transmission—about a quarter in a developed country like Britain, up to one-half in poorer countries due to inefficient irrigation. (About 70 percent of world water use was for irrigating crops, compared with 23 percent for industry and 7 percent for domestic/municipal use.) It also meant pricing water as a scarce resource, rather than providing heavy subsidies that encourage waste.[143] Even in problem areas such as the Indonesian islands of Java and Bali, it was reckoned that many of the problems of water supply and use could be met by a proper system of pricing and metering.[144] These were essentially political decisions.

Politics also mattered at the international level. It was estimated that 214 river or lake basins were shared by two or more states, and that nine of these were shared by up to six countries. Of the nine, only two rivers—the Danube and the Rhine—were in the developed world.[145] We noted in Chapter 16 that the inequitable distribution of water was highly sensitive in parts of the Middle East (the Jordan Valley or the headwaters of the Tigris and the Euphrates) and in South Asia (the Ganges and the Indus). In water, even more than food, the concept of national self-sufficiency was untenable for many states. Hydropolitics would be an important theme of international relations in the new century.

Thus, in most of the world, shortages of food and water were usually a problem of distribution, not production. The big exception was sub-Saharan Africa,[146] the one region of the world where, since 1950, grain production had risen more slowly than population. This was largely because it was the only region where the fertility transition had yet to take hold. In addition, sub-Saharan Africa started out with natural disadvantages—poor soil, harsh climate, and acute water shortages (half of its total runoff was in the Congo basin). And, as we have seen, the state structure was unusually weak, making it harder to address the challenges of development and distribution.

Resource problems were a matter of quality as well as quantity. Building on the slogan of "sustainable development" in the Brundtland report of 1987 (see Chapter 14), the United Nations held a special global conference on environment and development in Rio de Janeiro in June 1992 (the "Earth Summit"). Agencies like the World Bank started incorporating environmental criteria in development programs.

The bank's statistical analysis of the problem made sobering reading.[147] For instance, an estimated one billion people in developing countries did not have access to clean water (often defined only as a standpipe serving dozens of families), and 1.7 billion lacked adequate sanitation (which could be just a communal latrine). The two problems were connected, since the principal threat to water quality—greater than industrial pollution—was human sewage. The result was three million child deaths a year from diarrhea. In the Indonesian capital of Jakarta, the equivalent of 1 percent of the city's GDP was spent on boiling water. A World Water Forum in Marrakesh in March 1997 marked the start of concerted international efforts in this area.

Air quality was also problematic. About 1.3 billion people (nearly a quarter of the global population) lived in urban areas that did not meet the World

Health Organization's standards for "suspended particulate matter" (in plain language, airborne dust and smoke). Although developed countries had imposed restrictions on vehicle emissions, lead poisoning of the atmosphere was a grave problem in many Third World cities. Often, the most polluted environment was actually the home. Between three hundred and seven hundred million people suffered severely from the indoor burning of wood, straw, and dung for fuel. In the worst cases, the effects on health were equivalent to smoking several packs of cigarettes a day.

The earth was also being polluted. One of the biggest problems was rapid deforestation, particularly of the tropical rain forests. These were disappearing at an average of around 1 percent a year in the 1980s, and much more rapidly in Indonesia, Thailand, and Brazil (home to one-third of the world's total tropical rain forest). Such deforestation was a prime cause of shrinking biodiversity, another 1990s slogan that referred to the accelerating extinction of species, not just large vertebrates like tigers and rhinos but also plants and insects on whose interactions much of the natural balance depended. Deforestation was a major cause of soil erosion, and also upset water cycles. The clearing of timber waste by fires created serious air pollution. The annual summer burnings in the Indonesian islands of Kalimantan and Sumatra got completely out of control in 1997, creating perhaps "the most pernicious man-made smog in history," which covered some seventy million people in six countries, from Malaysia to the Philippines, for several weeks.[148] TV pictures featured people walking through the poisonous red haze wearing face masks.

As these examples show, pollution was a worldwide problem. By the 1990s, it was also global in a systemic sense, with signs that humanity was now inflicting serious damage on the fragile biosphere that made life possible on this planet.

In the media, the two slogans were "the greenhouse effect" and "the hole in the ozone layer." The first of these referred to the way atmospheric pollution trapped some of the heat radiated by the earth's surface, producing "global warming." Estimates in the early 1990s suggested that average global temperatures had increased by up to 0.6° Celsius during the twentieth century. If nothing was done to control the emission of greenhouse gases, they could rise by another 2°–4° in the century to come. If sea levels rose three feet in consequence, Egypt would lose at least 12 percent of its arable land and Bangladesh about the same proportion of its total area.[149] The main culprit was carbon dioxide (CO_2), of which the main human causes were the burning of fossil fuels such as coal and oil, and deforestation. Another important greenhouse gas was methane, generated particularly by waterlogged rice paddies, livestock manure, and the burning of oil and natural gas. Also significant were emissions of nitrous oxide (for example, from fertilizers) and the chlorofluorocarbons (CFCs) used in aerosol containers and in the cooling units of refrigerators. CFCs were also the main source of the second danger, "ozone depletion" at the top of the earth's atmosphere. Scientific reports in the mid-1980s of a "hole" in the ozone layer above Antarctica focused international attention. This layer absorbs ultraviolet rays from the sun, thereby promoting convection currents that shape the world's weather. Even more important, it provides essential protection against harmful solar radiation for life at all levels, from humans to plankton. Possible dangers ranged from increased skin cancers to reduced fish stocks.

By the 1990s, the evidence for global warming and ozone depletion was largely accepted. The implications, however, were intensely controversial. Predicting long-term climatic change was an extremely inexact science. Except for the very recent past, data were nonexistent or problematic, making it difficult to assess long-term trends. Models of how the climatic conditions interacted were still extremely crude. It was, for instance, possible that the increased cloud cover created by global warming would reflect more incoming solar radiation and so lower the temperature again. This image of complex feedback was popularized particularly by the British scientist James Lovelock in 1979. His "Gaia" hypothesis (from the Greek for Mother Earth) suggested that "the biosphere is a self-regulating entity with the capacity to keep our planet healthy by controlling the chemical and physical environment."[150] This proposal for a new "geophysiology" to examine the interactions of the earth's biology, physics, and chemistry attracted growing scientific interest during the 1990s. Whereas Greens often assumed that nature was highly fragile, many scientists took a more robust view of its strength and adaptability.[151]

During the 1990s, the most authoritative climatic models, designed by a panel created by the UN and the World Meteorological Organization, reduced projections for global warming. At the end of 1995 its "best estimate" for the global mean surface temperature in 2100 was 2° higher than 1990—one-third less than its prediction in August 1990. Similarly, its best estimate for average sea level in 2100 had been cut by 25 percent between 1990 and 1995 to a rise of 50 centimeters.[152] But, whatever the numbers, there was little dispute that late twentieth-century lifestyles were changing the natural environment at an historically unprecedented rate. Estimates in 1990 suggested that half of humanity's total carbon emissions had probably occurred since 1920, half its total lead emissions since 1950, and half its phosophorus and nitrogen releases in a mere fifteen years since 1975.[153]

The *acceleration* of human impact was the critical point. Even if one accepted a Gaia-like idea of the earth's self-regulation, this concept operated on a geological, not a human, time scale.[154] The dilemma was therefore acute. Long before firm scientific knowledge was available, decisions had to be taken on how to balance this generation's prosperity against a future generation's survival.

In other words, the issues of pollution and climate change were as much political as scientific. And, as with other so-called global problems (such as "globalization" itself), the impact varied from place to place.[155] The prime users of fossil fuel were developed countries, who were now moving into the postindustrial era. Countries like China, with substantial reserves of coal, asked why they should limit their future industrialization for the benefit of the West. Only a substantial North-South transfer of funds and new technology would provide compelling inducements. But this argument was not a simple divide between the developed and the developing. The oil-exporting countries of the Middle East, for instance, would be damaged by reduced use of fossil fuels, whereas not merely Egypt and Bangladesh but low-lying European countries such as the Netherlands would be threatened if nothing was done and sea levels rose substantially. In sub-Saharan Africa, by contrast, long-term climate change was less urgent than the extension of deserts and the degradation of the soil. And whereas equatorial croplands might be significantly damaged by global warming, the combination of warmer temperatures and greater rainfall could extend agriculture into more northerly latitudes of Canada, Russia, and Japan.[156]

In the complex new environmental politics, the position of the United States was critical. On the one hand, it was the world's biggest polluter: 5 percent of the globe's population generated over 20 percent of all human CO_2 emissions. On the other, its resources would be essential in any package of inducements to persuade the developing world. On the question of ozone depletion, Washington took the lead in pushing through the Montreal Protocol of September 1987, whereby signatories would cut their CFC emissions to half the 1986 level by 1999. Strengthened at London in 1990, the protocol had over one hundred signatories by the end of 1993, including China and India. The principal U.S. negotiator called it "a paradigm for a new form of global diplomacy . . . through which nations accept common responsibility for stewardship of the planet."[157] But ozone depletion was a greater threat to countries near to polar latitudes, such as the United States. A big American media campaign had already produced legislation banning aerosol sprays in 1978. It was therefore in the interests of U.S. business to impose similar restraints on their international competitors, hence the support from the otherwise fanatically antigreen Reagan administration.

Greenhouse gases were a different story, however. The United States had grown rich on its plentiful supplies of coal and oil. It had little incentive to shift from high-intensity use of fossil fuels, which were still abundant, and it would face little economic damage from global warming because of the small contribution to GDP of both its agricultural sector and its threatened coastline. America's situation was far different from that in many developing countries, reliant on a few crops and lacking the research and governmental capabilities to monitor and manage any climate change.[158] Consequently, the United States was the main obstacle to radical action on global warming, as the summits of 1992 and 1997 made clear.

The Earth Summit in Rio in June 1992 was one of the biggest international conferences to date. A total of 178 states were represented; over one hundred heads of government put in an appearance. There were also one thousand five hundred accredited nongovernmental organizations and some seven thousand journalists. But the conference's achievements were limited. The United States blocked firm targets on greenhouse emissions; Malaysia, backed by India, opposed restrictions on deforestation in the name of national sovereignty. The developed countries had failed to offer sufficient resource transfers to forge a real bargain.

But although Rio was no triumph, it was not a disaster. The UN organizers, led by Maurice Strong of Canada, intended it as a high-profile media event that would help raise international awareness about environmental issues. And Rio produced two pioneering international treaties on climate change and biodiversity. These gained widespread support, although the United States refused to sign the latter because it might dilute America's advantage in biotechnology.[159]

At the climate conference in Kyoto in December 1997, thirty-eight industrialized countries set binding targets for human greenhouse emissions, intended to cut the world total in 2012 by 5.2 percent from 1990 levels. Japan, the United States, and the European Union respectively promised reductions of 6, 7, and 8 percent. Once again the obstacle to bigger cuts had been the United States. Although greener Democrats were now in the White House (Rio was negotiated by a Bush administration facing reelection during an economic downturn), the control of probusiness Republicans over Congress tied Clinton's hands, and the coal and oil industries mounted a huge propaganda campaign in advance of the summit. To many environmentalists, the emission targets were grossly inadequate. Nor were potential big polluters of the future, such as China and India, bound by the agreement. There was also criticism of the deal whereby countries could trade "emission credits" so that big polluters could buy unused emissions from cleaner nations. This was instituted at U.S. behest and was modeled on its domestic legislation to reduce sulfur emissions from power plants. But it did have the effect of incorporating climate damage into the cost of doing business—in other words, if you want to pollute, it will cost you. This was, potentially, an important precedent.[160]

Thus, in the last years of the century, prognoses for climate change were as murky as the Indonesian smog. The science was uncertain, the politics confused. One possible avenue of progress was that some major greenhouse emitters were also major victims of their own pollution, such as China, India, Mexico, and Brazil. This gave them a direct incentive to clean up. But meaningful change depended on a redefinition of natural assets. Forests, for instance, were both national property (as Malaysia insisted at Rio) and also a common good (because of the global effects of deforestation).[161] Developing countries would not stop exploiting the resources on which their hopes of rapid industrialization were based, unless the developed world offered alternative technologies to help them bypass the carboniferous era. Yet, as with the United States and genetic engineering, those technologies were often seen as a great national asset for postindustrial states. Thus, the new concept of "environmental security" presaged a complex process of international bargaining, of which Rio and Kyoto were but the start.

Social Life

New potential to create life, new challenges in sustaining life—in these multiple encounters between what used to be called "man" and "nature," the limits of human existence were being stretched and tested in the late twentieth century. But those challenges, though portentous for humanity in the long term, barely affected the bulk of the world's population in the 1990s. More immediate and urgent were the daily challenges of living in society. Here the big changes, building on earlier trends, were increasing urbanization and the weakening of traditional family ties.

Early in the twenty-first century more than half of humanity would live in urban areas. (Exactly when depends on definitions of urbanization, which are notoriously imprecise.) Within that generalization were marked regional differences: in North America, Europe, and Latin America, three-quarters of the population was urban, in Asia and Africa, less than two-fifths. Overall, "megacities" were less important by the year 2000 than had been anticipated. Only about 3 percent of the world's population lived in conurbations of over ten million, and most of these (even Calcutta and Mexico City) had grown in the 1980s at less than 5 percent each year. More significant were the 280 cities that boasted more than one million people. Nearly half of those living in these "million-cities" were Asians, and less than one-fifth were Europeans (compared with nearly two-fifths in 1950)—another sign of how the global center of gravity had shifted during the late twentieth century.[162] The critical point was not so much size as lifestyle. Most urban dwellers did not make their living from the soil.

Many, indeed, barely made a living at all. Most urban settlements in the developing world had grown without regulation. What urban historians call an "informal" or "illegal" city accumulated around the official core. The UN estimated in 1996 that 30 to 60 percent of the housing stock in most cities in "the South" was strictly illegal, in that the buildings contravened land ownership laws and/or planning and building codes. In time, many of the squatter families replaced their shacks with more substantial dwellings (see Chapter 5) or moved to established urban areas. But as with pollution, it was not the process itself but the pace and scale of urbanization that were alarming. In Calcutta, for instance, an estimated three million of the ten million inhabitants lived in shantytowns and refugee settlements that had no potable water or sewerage systems. Thousands of families were literally "pavement dwellers" who existed in huts of a few square feet spilling onto the street.[163]

The environmental crisis in most cities in developing countries was therefore different from that in the developed world. The prime need was usually for basic services, particularly clean water and proper waste disposal. The situation was analagous to that of many cities in Europe and North America at the beginning of the century, or to Tokyo after World War II (see Chapter 5). Those problems had been addressed in large part through the development of effective local government, elected by its citizens and armed with extensive planning powers. In many developing countries, however, local government was weak, either because government in general was fragile (as in Africa) or because central governments guarded their authority (as in much of East and Southeast Asia). In short, across the developing world, many so-called environmental problems stemmed from a failure of governance.[164]

An extreme example is Mexico City, by some definitions the world's largest city since it was a single metropolis, unlike Tokyo/Yokohama or New York/New Jersey. Its fifteen to twenty million people constituted about a fifth of the national population and possessed around four million cars. The smog hanging over the city for most of the year was far worse than in Los Angeles, its population density was double that of New York, and an estimated 50 to 60 percent of the population lived in settlements that started out illegally. Few civic administrations could have coped with the scale and speed of the conurbation's expansion since the 1950s, but Mexico City lacked an administration in all but name. Since 1928, its core, the Federal District, had been under the authority of the president, who appointed a regent and local mayors—usually outsiders who were being rewarded by the PRI's patronage machine. Only in 1997, as the PRI lost its one-party grip, was Mexico City allowed to elect its own mayor, but central government retained significant powers, and the mayor's writ did not run outside the Federal District—now home to less than half of Mexico City's population.[165]

Ineffectual and unresponsive municipal government was at heart of the crisis of the state in much of the developing world. But developed countries were not immune. The District of Columbia, for instance—site of the U.S. federal capital—was, in some ways, a microcosm of Mexico City. It had been allowed its own elected government somewhat earlier (1973). However, this remained under the thumb of the U.S. Congress and had no powers outside D.C.'s sixty-one square miles (one hundred sixty square kilometers) and 550,000 people, even though they constituted the impoverished, crime-ridden core of a metropolitan area of over three million.[166] The British capital did not even have its own municipal government in the 1990s. In 1985 Margaret Thatcher abolished the Greater London Council because it was incorrigibly Labour controlled. This left London's problems to be thrashed out by five government departments, thirty-two London boroughs, the City of London corporation, and some sixty committees and boards. The Thatcher government decided to leave the redevelopment of London's docklands in the 1980s to "market forces." The result was a surfeit of office space, skimpy transport provision, and major bankruptcies for which the taxpayer had to foot the bill. In fact, market forces had been given their freedom by vast acts of central government intervention: the docklands area was wrested from local authorities, planning regulations were suspended, and developers wooed with generous tax breaks.[167]

Thatcher's London stood in marked contrast to François Mitterrand's Paris. The president was determined to celebrate the two hundredth anniversary of the revolution of 1789 (and ensure his place in history books) by ramming through a series of *grands projets* to reverse urban decay and champion modern architectural styles. A new opera house was built near the Bastille, the disused Orsay station and hotel became a museum about the nineteenth century, and the old slaughterhouse area at La Villette was transformed into a science museum, a music center, and an imaginative urban park. The most controversial work, at least initially, was the glass pyramid designed by the Chinese-American architect I. M. Pei, to cap his underground extension to the galleries and services of France's premier museum, the Louvre.[168] These and other great buildings, such as the new Bibliothèque Nationale, were only possible because of a combination of *dirigiste* government and socialist spending.

But the collapse of East Germany in 1989–1990 allowed the German government a similar opportunity to reshape the urban geography of central Berlin. New government offices once again graced Unter den Linden. Potsdamer Platz was transformed from cold war wasteland into a glistening business hub. And the restored Reichstag, for years a wartorn ruin (see Chapter 1), became home to united Germany's new democratic Parliament.

The challenges of Paris and Berlin were very different from those of Calcutta or Mexico City. But two similarities stood out. First, municipal government acted as enabler rather than provider. Few cities were now engaged, for instance, in massive housing projects. Many had sold off their housing stock as part of the general retreat from socialism in the 1980s and 1990s, including the most assiduous builders of public housing, Singapore and Hong Kong. Government's role was to establish a planning framework, provide basic services such as infrastructure, and correct market imbalances, for example through mortgage provision. The second similarity was that all cities now faced a huge and growing problem because of the motor car. The yearning for automobility (see Chapter 5) and the neglect of public transport had spread from the United States, where western cities like Los Angeles and Phoenix had become smog-ridden gridlocks, to become the hallmark of urban living across the world from São Paulo to Kuala Lumpur, from Paris to Perth.

One answer was road pricing—making drivers pay the full social cost of using their cars, instead of subsidizing that cost through more roads and cheap fuel. The pioneer, not surprisingly, was Singapore. Since 1975, this cramped city-state has developed a mix of road, petrol, and parking taxes; since 1998, electronic tolls have been imposed automatically via a transponder in each vehicle. Road pricing was also adopted by Oslo and Trondheim in Norway; the Netherlands planned to introduce it for major cities in 2001.[169] Some "Southern" cities also found their own solutions. Curitiba, in Southeast Brazil, had grown from three hundred thousand to over two million people between 1950 and 1990, but thanks mainly to its architect-mayor during the 1970s, Jamie Lerner, it developed a public transport system that combined the cheapness and flexibility of buses with the speed and capacity of subways. The buses used dedicated tracks, passengers paid before they boarded, and hinged buses were used to accommodate greater numbers. Companies were paid according to length of journey rather than number of passengers.[170]

Curitiba became a global showcase for the "sustainable city."[171] But though three-quarters of commuters took the bus, the city still had five hundred thousand private cars that people used for pleasure. Even here, the automobile had been regulated, not eliminated. And much of the developing world was only just entering the motor age. Compared with the U.S. figure of more than one car for every two people and the European and Japanese norm of one for every three, in 1985 Argentina (the highest for Latin America) had only one car for every ten people—about the same as Malaysia.[172] Not until the 1990s did the automobile revolution even begin in the world's two most populous countries, China and India. The latter had fewer than three cars per one thousand people in 1996 (compared with 560 in the United States). All the world's big carmakers were rushing to exploit its newly opened market. Despite high taxes on cars and fuel, despite the fact that only about 20 percent of India's roads were car worthy, demand was predicted to reach two million new passenger vehicles a year by 2000.[173] For all the talk about high-tech industry and the information society, the most ubiquitous technology of the early twenty-first century was one that humanity had inherited from the nineteenth—the internal (and infernal) combustion engine.

The most lethal smoke was self-inflicted. Communicable diseases such as smallpox and cholera, and respiratory diseases such as pneumonia and tuberculosis, were all much less fatal in the developed world than a century before. In contrast, the incidence of circulatory diseases and cancers had fallen much less. They were now the main killers, accounting for 60 to 70 percent of all deaths in developed countries and in the former Soviet bloc, and at least 30 percent in those Asian countries where life expectancy at birth exceeded sixty years. A major cause of many of these deaths, particularly for men, was cigarette smoking.[174] In the United States, smoking was responsible for over four hundred thousand deaths a year in the early 1990s—more than those from drinking, driving, work, and recreation combined.[175] This figure was hardly surprising since, in the 1960s and early 1970s, consumption was the equivalent of over four thousand cigarettes a year for every American over eighteen. The average was still nearly three thousand four hundred in 1985.[176]

Since the 1960s, a wide variety of studies had identified smoking as a significant cause of lung cancer and heart disease; by the 1980s, there was also substantial evidence that nicotine was an addictive drug and that "passive smoking" harmed the health of nonsmokers. All these statements would, of course, be denied as vicious lies by the tobacco industry—though each had been echoed in private by their own researchers and executives.[177] If the industry were to admit smoking was damaging to smokers and nonsmokers, that would encourage government regulation; if they acknowledged it was addictive, that would undermine the industry's claim (supported, for instance, by civil liberties groups in the United States) that smoking was an act of free, rational choice. This would open the way for litigation against the companies for pedalling dangerous drugs, as happened in the United States in the 1990s.

The tobacco multinationals fought a skilful and ruthless rearguard action. The biggest two—Philip Morris and British American Tobacco—were respectively the fourteenth largest company in the world and the thirty-sixth (measured by sales) in the late 1980s.[178] They diversified into other industries, produced prosmoking "research" of their own, and bought goodwill by bankrolling politicians, subsidizing charities, sponsoring sports, and even endowing professorships. Their efforts varied in success. In the United States, the fragmented political system and the libertarian tradition made it harder than in Europe to restrict advertising and tax smokers. On the other hand, those same factors made it easier to enact draconian bans on smoking in public once the right of smokers to smoke could be shown to infringe the right of nonsmokers to healthy air.[179] Whatever the contrasts, however, across the developed world by the late 1990s, smoking was being confined, by law and custom, to a private vice.

The developing world was a different story, however. In 1988 the eight multinationals accounted for only 35 percent of world cigarette production; 60 percent came from state monopolies that manufactured largely for home consumption. Moreover, 60 percent of the world tobacco crop was grown in Asia (half of that in China). It was in vast developing markets like China, India, and Indonesia that the tobacco industry's future lay. The monopolies were lucrative sources of income for many governments, giving them little incentive to impose health regulations. Even where monopolies were dismantled as part of freer trade, the tax income was still enormous—worth at least 10 percent of state revenue in many developing countries in the late 1980s. Multinationals and governments around the world could look forward to a "healthy" income from tobacco for years to come.[180]

For those who survived, the age structure of society would be very different in the early twenty-first century. Consider, for a moment, the figures in Table 17.1, which suggest the likely trajectory of the demographic transition over half a century from 1975. First, there will be more older people than ever before, thanks to falling mortality rates. Those over sixty are projected to grow from under 9 percent of the world's population in 1975 to over 14 percent in 2025. Second, the fertility transition is gradually taking effect in Asia, the Middle East, and Africa. This is indicated by the steady fall in the under-fourteens from nearly 37 percent of all humanity to under 25 percent. But, third, birth rates have fallen more slowly than death rates. This is seen particularly in the proportion of young people between fifteen and twenty-four, which is scheduled to decline only slightly from 18.6 percent to 15.8 percent over the half-century. Since world population is likely to have more than doubled from the figure of four billion in 1975, the under-fourteens and the fifteen- to twenty-four-year-olds would both be far larger in absolute numbers in 2025—even though they had declined as proportions of total population.

As some of the regional statistics make clear, these patterns will vary considerably across the world. In North America and Europe, where the demographic transition to low mortality and fertility had been accomplished, the over-sixties would be around a quarter of the population in 2025. In Africa, where the transition was slowest, the proportion would have risen by

TABLE 17.1 AGE STRUCTURE OF THE WORLD POPULATION, 1975–2025

| | *Percentage of the Population in Specific Age Groups* | | | | | | | | |
| | 1975 | | | 2000 | | | 2025 | | |
	0–14	15–24	60+	0–14	15–24	60+	0–14	15–24	60+
World total	36.9	18.6	8.5	30.6	17.3	9.8	24.8	15.8	14.2
Europe	23.7	16.4	16.4	18.0	13.8	20.0	16.3	11.3	26.7
North America	25.3	19.0	14.6	21.7	13.3	16.3	19.6	12.6	24.4
Japan	24.3	15.4	11.7	15.3	12.7	22.4	13.9	10.6	31.8
China	39.5	19.1	6.9	25.3	15.4	9.9	20.4	12.8	18.0
India	39.8	18.8	6.2	33.5	18.8	7.6	23.0	16.5	12.4
Latin America	41.1	19.7	6.4	31.9	19.0	8.1	23.6	15.6	14.2
Africa (all)	44.8	19.1	4.9	43.2	19.6	5.0	35.7	19.5	6.5

SOURCE: Statistics from United Nations Centre for Human Settlements (HABITAT), *An Urbanizing World: Global Report on Human Settlements, 1996* (Oxford: Oxford University Press, 1996), Table 2, pp. 444–6.

less than 2 percent in fifty years to 6.5 percent, whereas more than one-third of the population would be under fourteen. India would be somewhere in the middle between Europe and Africa, while Latin America's profile fits the world average. Perhaps the most significant case would be China, home to a quarter of the world's population in the 1990s. China's one-child policy was projected to halve the proportion of under-fourteens between 1975 and 2025, and more than double those over sixty from 7 percent to 18 percent.

What do such data mean in human term? Answer: serious social tension. Take the soaring number of fifteen- to twenty-four-year-olds. Here the critical factors will be the availability of education, which raises expectations, and the lack of employment, which produces alienation and discontent. Both points have been underlined repeatedly in the second half of this book and need little repetition here, except to note that the scale and intensity of the problem is likely to become worse because of greater numbers and greater migration. The pressure of the discontented outsiders on southern Europe or the southern United States will be particularly insistent.

More novel, perhaps, are the implications of the aging statistics. Care of the elderly will become a major social problem as networks of both family security and social security are strained and often broken. On the one hand, migration into cities disrupted kinship groups. In many Arab countries, for instance, nuclear families accounted for more than half of all family units by the 1980s.[181] In these situations, traditional obligations to support aged parents and other family members are less readily honored. On the other hand, in the developed world, where society has taken over responsibility for the security of the old, these programs are threatened by the new demographics. Many of the pensions schemes are pay as you go (PAYG), meaning that contributions from those now at work provide the pensions for those now retired. But the ratio of those over sixty-five to those aged twenty to sixty-four was likely to increase substantially—in the extreme case, Japan, doubling between 1990 and 2020. Even Britain, with an unusually extensive system of properly funded private pensions (covering 75 percent of the work force by the mid-1990s), has decided to raise the legal retirement age for women from sixty to sixty-five during the 2010s. Other developed countries face hard decisions about reduced benefits, delayed retirement, and private programs, made all the more difficult to implement politically as the electorate became "grayer".[182]

In the developing world, the crisis of social security was often immediate and acute. In Latin America, where pension plans had often been poorly managed, the actuarial calculations were destroyed by the growth of the black economy during the debt crisis of the 1980s. An estimated 40 percent of the Brazilian work force was in the informal sector by the late 1980s; for Bolivia and Guatemala the figure was around 60 percent.[183] In China, pensions for those who had worked in state enterprises (funded by PAYG) were thrown into chaos by economic liberalization. Extraordinarily rapid urbanization upset old traditions of family responsibility. And the equally rapid fertility transition meant that by 2020 there would be six people of working age (fifteen to sixty-four) for every pensioner compared with ten in 1995.[184] Discreet relaxation of the one-child policy from the late 1980s was a recognition of this projection as much as a concession to rural protest. If the one-child program had been totally successful, 41 percent of China's population would have been over sixty-five by 2050.[185] Here was a reminder that countries could suffer from too few children as well as too many.

Even more important for family life than the changing age structure of the population was the continuing shift in gender relations. In this the formal feminist movement played a limited role. By the 1990s it had waned as a political force in Europe and the United States, as ideological differences intensified and postmodernism took its toll of cherished feminist absolutes like "patriarchy" and even "gender."[186] In retrospect, feminism's main achievement had been to overturn the cult of domesticity that had prevailed in postwar America and Western Europe as a brief middle-class aberration from the norm of women's work in both agrarian and industrial societies. It had also placed "women's rights" on the formal political agenda, both in the West and among female elites in Westernized countries like India. But for most of the world, where women worked not from choice but dire necessity, its concerns were of limited relevance.

At the end of the century, as in the middle (see Chapter 9) the main catalysts of change in women's lives were still education and contraception. By the mid-1990s, enrollment rates in primary schools were virtually the same for girls and boys in the developed world, the former Soviet bloc, East Asia, and Latin America. In Africa, the Middle East, and South Asia they were about four-fifths. This presaged greater intellectual equality in marriage and greater intellectual inequality between generations. Education also helped women to control their own fertility in conjunction with modern methods of contraception. In the mid-1990s, three-quarters of married women aged fifteen to forty-nine in the industrialized countries and East Asia were using contraception, and two-fifths in South Asia, the Middle East, and North Africa. In sub-Saharan Africa, the figure was only 13 percent,[187] but even here (particularly in the east and south) fertility was starting to fall because of later marriage and greater intervals between births.[188] This was yet another reminder that birth control was a matter of culture as much as technology. The demographic transition was "a transition in the relative value of childbearing" in an era of lower mortality and greater economic opportunity, particularly for urban society.[189]

The historical novelty of the late twentieth century for women worldwide lay, therefore, less in production than reproduction—in the control of fertility rather than in the "opportunity" to work. It was becoming clear just how culture specific Western notions of female work had been in the immediate postwar era. Notoriously, national accounting statistics made little effort to include domestic labor or to take adequate account of anything less than full-time paid employment. This was particularly true in the developing world. In Ghana, for instance, one survey of a savanna village found that women were spending over two hours a day on food preparation and cooking and another two hours in collecting water and fuel—all essential for the domestic economy. The women also produced substantial amount of money by selling home-produced charcoal to town dwellers. This income was often neglected by official statistics that equated income with cash crops marketed via official channels.[190]

The big global change in women's work in the late twentieth century was their entry into paid employment outside the household. This was particularly marked in the developed economies, as shown by the figures in Table 17.2. Female employment was highest in Scandinavian countries like Sweden, with its socialist tradition of equality and employment rights, but the figure was over 70 percent in America and Britain, and nearly two-thirds in

TABLE 17.2 WOMEN'S PARTICIPATION IN PAID EMPLOYMENT, 1973-1992

	Employed women as a percentage of women aged 25–54	
	1973	1992
West Germany	49.9	57.0 (in 1990)
France	52.8	66.4
Italy	27.5	38.3
United Kingdom	58.6	70.2
Sweden	66.8	85.2
United States	49.7	70.2
Canada	40.4	65.9
Japan	53.4	64.1

NOTE: Male employment rates in all these countries were over 90 percent.
SOURCE: Candace Howes and Ajit Singh, "Long-Term Trends in the World Economy: The Gender Dimension," *World Development*, 23 (1995), 1904–5.

Japan. A similar trend is evident in parts of the developing world, particularly the East Asian tiger economies, where women as a percentage of all those employed in industry is often higher than industrial economies. As we saw in Chapter 12, women have been the tigers' teeth in export industries such as textiles and electronics. Growing levels of manufacturing employment are evident for women in other expanding economies such as Brazil and Mexico, but in Latin America as a whole about 70 percent of women's employment is in services. In sub-Saharan Africa, over 80 percent of women's employment is agricultural—though all these figures must be taken as rough indicators, given the statistical problems and the pervasive informal economy.[191] For much of the former Soviet bloc, however, the collapse of statist economies has led to a steep rise in female unemployment and the abolition of supports like child care and maternity pay. In China, the female activism encouraged in the Cultural Revolution has been followed by a new insistence on a woman's place in the home.

Within this motley pattern of paid employment, two threads stand out. Women are generally paid less than men for comparable tasks, and they are less likely to occupy senior managerial positions. This was mainly because of the prevalence of "part timing," which many employers deemed second-class work. In the EU about one-third of employed women worked less than the standard week of thirty-five to forty hours, whereas the figure for men was about 5 percent.[192] The main reason for this was that wives still bore a disproportionate domestic burden—of both child rearing and homemaking.

One of the most striking statistics of the 1990s was that about one-fifth of the world's households had female heads—either a single mother or several generations of women. Both Africa and Latin America were close to that average—East Asia and the Pacific somewhat below it with 13 percent—and such households were most common in urban areas.[193] They indicated the growing separation of family life from the institution of marriage.

The most dramatic sign of this in the developed world was the divorce revolution of the 1960s and 1970s. During those decades, most countries in North America, Australasia, and Western Europe (except Ireland) enacted no-fault laws. This effectively left the decision to the couple rather than the state or the church. These legal changes were a response to growing marital breakdowns in the 1960s rather than their cause. Enhanced expectations of marriage (emotional or egalitarian) and increasing female work outside the home were probably important stimuli. Although divorce did not cause breakdowns, it probably facilitated the move from breakdown to divorce, as severance became easier to obtain and less of a social stigma.[194] In Britain, where the "Royal Family" had become the epitome of domesticity in the 1950s, all three of Queen Elizabeth II's married children were divorced in the 1990s, including her veteran heir, Prince Charles. Across North America and Western Europe, divorce rates rose, cohabitation became acceptable, and a substantial proportion of children were born outside marriage. By the 1990s, one marriage in every three was likely to end in divorce in Britain and Denmark. The figure was nearer to one in two in Sweden and the United States.[195]

In Britain, France, and Sweden, more than 10 percent of steady heterosexual couples were unmarried (over 20 percent in Denmark). A third of births occurred outside marriage in America, Britain, and France (and around half in Denmark and Sweden).[196] Often, cohabitation and parenting were the prelude to marriage, but that progression was by no means assured and, in any case, it testified to a more pragmatic view of the marital bond. Defenders of "family values" decried such trends; some demographers pointed to similarities with working-class life in the nineteenth century, when cohabitation, illegitimacy, and female-headed families were familiar. But whether the "bourgeois nuclear family" was a norm or an aberration, it was undoubtedly in flux.

The developed West, one might say, saw a growing divorce between having children and being married. Each was possible, indeed acceptable, without the other. This was evidence of a deeper change—the separation of sexuality from reproduction. Reliable contraception made it possible to have sex without having children. Artificial insemination made it possible to have children without having sex. And, by the 1990s, there was greater tolerance in some Western countries for homosexual relations by men and women.

In many countries, homosexuality had been decriminalized during the 1960s and 1970s, though the process was slower in federal polities like the United States, where such laws were the preserve of individual states. But only a few countries made discrimination against homosexuals a crime, and even fewer (such as Denmark since 1989) gave homosexual partnerships a status equal to marriage. The attack on the heterosexual family was pushed a stage further by some American feminists in the "lesbian baby boom" of the 1990s. What they termed "alternative insemination" from a "donor" offered the opportunity to produce children who would live with two female parents. These "gay families," with or without children, were another variation on the theme of families by choice.[197]

Much of the developing world still took a more conventional view of family life. For instance, a report in 1989 estimated that of 202 countries in the world, homosexual behavior was illegal in seventy-four of them; 144 showed no support for gay and lesbian rights. In Islamic countries and much of Africa, homosexuality remained illegal—likewise in Castro's Cuba.[198] As for marriage: in much of Africa, the Middle East, and South Asia, it remained a contract between two families, sealed by a transfer of wealth (either from the bride's parents to the groom's, as in India, or the other way round in much of Africa and the Middle East). In such cases, the bride usually became subsumed in the husband's family, though the opposite was true in a few matrilineal societies in Africa. Although divorce had long been a well-established practice in Arab societies, it usually occurred because of the wife's infertility. In much of the rural developing world, legislation liberalizing women's right to divorce was often a dead letter. Islamic societies in particular had punitive laws against premarital sex. But all of these generalizations broke down in urban areas, where nuclear families, extramarital arrangements, and female-headed households were becoming common. Here, as in the West, sexual relations were becoming matters of personal choice rather than family obligation.[199]

The debates about women and the family were part of a much broader argument about the place of human rights in international relations. That concept was, in origin, distinctively Western, going back to classical theories of natural law. It had been expressed most famously in declarations on the "Rights of Man" in the American and French Revolutions. In America, rights theory was given renewed impetus in the 1970s by political philosophers such as Robert Nozick and John Rawls. The culture wars of 1990s America were conducted almost entirely in these terms—gay rights and abortion rights, the rights of smokers versus those of nonsmokers, the right to bear arms, the rights of the unborn child. To quote the formulation of Ronald

Dworkin, rights were "political trumps"—individualist cards played to beat any assertion of collective obligations.[200] Rights were also becoming an international language, building on the Universal Declaration of Human Rights adopted by the UN in December 1948. In June 1993, delegates from more than 180 countries met in Vienna for the first World Conference on Human Rights. Like other great conferences of the 1990s, such as the Rio Earth Summit, Vienna testified both to the globalism of debate and to the divisions between the West and the Rest.

Countries facing criticism, such as the junta that had ruled Burma since 1988 or China in the wake of Tiananmen Square, responded that these were internal domestic matters. They argued, in effect, that sovereignty trumped rights. Controversy was also generated by the idea of "universal values." This was depicted by some, like Mahathir of Malaysia, as another form of neoimperialism. At Vienna, however, the U.S. secretary of state, Warren Christopher, insisted that "we cannot let cultural relativism become the last refuge of repression."[201] There was also conflict between the individual rights espoused by the West, particularly by U.S. Democrats like Carter and Clinton, and the priority given in many non-Western declarations to collective values. These included the rights of "peoples" set out in the African Banjul Charter of 1981, or those of the community of Muslims in the "Cairo Declaration on Human Rights in Islam" in 1990.[202] Debates about women and the family fell into a similar "North-South" divide. At the UN's fourth World Conference on Women in Beijing in September 1995, many of the forty thousand delegates found American concerns irrelevant. "They ask for abortion rights," remarked one Indian women's leader. "We ask for safe drinking water and basic health care."[203]

Human rights were also weapons in 1990s diplomacy. They were used to justify Western military actions in Bosnia in 1995 and Yugoslavia in 1999; in the latter case NATO was bombing a sovereign state. Western application of the concept was inconsistent, as the Somalian spasm in 1992–1993 and the Rwandan hand washing in 1994 had shown. Only the United States had the power to act, and American foreign policy during the Clinton era often seemed hostage to the president's erratic interest, political calculation, or even hormonal balance. Nevertheless, the growing use of human rights language was a feature of post–cold war diplomacy and a sign of the less rigid international order.

To use the language of rights was, of course, to make judgments of value, not statements of fact—to claim that, in some respects, all human beings should be regarded as of equal worth. Consequently, human rights were bound to be contested terrain. But, in the half-century since World War II, they had been placed firmly on the international map. The global conferences at Vienna and Beijing made that clear. Like Rio, they also served to educate politicians, public, and above all the media about some of the issues at stake. How individual rights were set against social duties was problematic; likewise the balance between a state's right to develop and its larger ecological obligations. But the megaconferences of the 1990s were signs that the world was trying to discern some shared values beyond those of the sovereign state or the global market.

Epilogue

There can be no conclusion. Contemporary historians teeter on the brink of an unknown future. Yet it is appropriate here to offer some final reflections about the last half-century.

Much depends, of course, on the time frame within which one sets the period since World War Two. In the early 1990s, it was common to talk of "the short twentieth century," framed by the Russian revolutions of 1917 and 1991. The result was a history centered on the rise and fall of communism, with the cold war as its central dynamic. The tone of such accounts, especially in the United States, was often triumphalist, with the 1990s marking "the end of history." A veteran Marxist, though, could adopt this periodization but deny its implications by depicting the years since the "golden age" of 1945–1973 as the end of everything.[1] Others have talked of a "long twentieth century" stretching back to the 1600s and built around the successive hegemonies of Dutch, British, and American capitalism in an increasingly global economy, with perhaps a shift since the 1980s toward Japan, China, and East Asia.[2] Intellectual historians might choose to set the recent past against the span of the last two hundred fifty years. Postcommunism and postmodernism could thus be seen as "Enlightenment's Wake,"[3] the fading of an era in which "man" was at the center of the universe and politics was the art of the perfectible. If one took the last three centuries, that would highlight the stories of industrialization and the fossil fuel era. A five hundred-year frame would privilege the ebb and flow of European colonialism, and make the "end of empires" the preeminent theme of our times.[4]

All these frames of reference are, in some ways, arbitrary. Yet each is suggestive. The period since 1945 has seen changes that are rightly deemed revolutionary, yet they all have roots in what has gone before.

Humanity's growing capacity to manipulate the physical world is almost a synonym for the word "history" but, since 1945, that capacity has been of a totally different order. Technologies such as televisions and telephones, plastics and synthetic fibers, have changed the texture of daily life for much of the world's population. This has also been the era of nuclear energy and genetic engineering, neither of which has begun to exhaust its potential for good and ill. These technologies have reduced human dependence on the constraints of nature—of time and space, of climate and season. Reduced, but not abolished, because recent technological change has also brought humanity up against some ultimate limits. The mushroom cloud—the specter of mass incineration or contamination—has hung over the postwar era. More recently, fears of global warming have highlighted the delicacy of the biosphere that makes life possible in this fragment of the universe. Is technology the problem, or the solution? This is hardly a new question—it has dogged the industrial age—but the last half-century has raised the stakes immeasurably.

Thanks to medical and technological innovations, the world is now home to more people than ever before, the majority of whom live longer and more comfortable lives than their grandparents. The doubling of the world's population from three billion to six billion in only four decades after 1960 is likely to be historically unique, because the fertility transition has now set in. Although total population numbers will still increase substantially in the next century, the rate of increase will not be as fast.

Better health and nutrition have dramatically enhanced longevity. In East Asia and the Pacific, life expectancy rose from forty-nine to sixty-six between 1960 and 1994; even in Africa, it grew by ten years to fifty-one.[5] The improvement in living standards depended most of all on two fundamentals—water and electricity. In Indonesia, for instance, one of the world's six most populous countries, only 3 percent of the people had access to safe drinking water in 1970; by 1990 the figure was 34 percent, while access to sanitation rose from 13 percent to 45 percent. By the mid-1990s, 44 percent of Indonesian dwellings had electricity.[6] Although those figures show that have-nots still outnumber haves in Indonesia—as they do in the world at large—it was the growth of basic services rather than the persistence of poverty that was *historically* significant. Clean water and adequate sanitation were essential for health; electricity offered the potential to transform lighting, cooking, and the safe preservation of food, as well as permitting access to television. The era since 1945 should not be remembered simply as the nuclear age; it was equally the age of water and wiring.

Despite the poverty and pollution of many cities, the improvements in living standards were, in large measure, the result of urbanization. That process had accelerated dramatically since World War II. In the early twenty-first century, more than 50 percent of the world's population would live in urban areas, compared with under 30 percent in 1950. Given the problems of defining "urban," these figures are only a rough guide. One can make the point more effectively by saying that for the first time in history, fewer than half the world's people were making a living mainly from farming, fishing, or other agricultural activity.

Social life was also in flux, as reproduction, production, and security became more detached from the family setting. These were not totally novel trends, particularly in the developed West, but they spread across the globe in the postwar era. For much of recent history (except in northwest Europe), the extended family of several generations with close kinship links had been the basic building block of society and of the agrarian economy. Where industrial work and urban living became the norm, that family structure lost its rationale as an economic unit. In countries that instituted basic health care and old-age pensions, *social* security either replaced or at least coexisted with *family* security as protection against illness and aging. Even where it did not, fewer births were needed to ensure sufficient children as carers for one's old age.

On the other hand, developed societies lavished more resources and attention on the children who were born. That was evident most of all in education, which removed the child from productive work now in the hope of enhanced earnings later on. The extension of schooling to most of the world's children and many of its teenagers was one of the great changes of the postwar era. It was a precondition of economic development and the catalyst for a less deferential society.

The belated extension of education to girls encouraged fertility control and increasing female employment. Working women were not a novelty—on the contrary, workless wives were the historical oddity—but the growth of paid employment *outside the family* was the innovation of the postwar era. Greater control over both their reproductivity and their productivity, won at considerable cost, was a feature of the late twentieth century for a significant proportion of the world's women.

Any account of the last half-century must begin in these areas, with technology, demography, and family life. But it must also acknowledge that these changes took place in, and were shaped by, political structures.

The so-called age of globalization was also the era of the nation-state. In 1945 there were fifty-one founding members of the United Nations; fifty years later the membership totaled 185. The explosion of states resulted from the destruction of empires, particularly those of Japan and the Europeans in the 1940s to 1970s, and those of Russia and Serbia in the early 1990s. In some regions, the colonial boundaries corresponded to ethnoreligious divisions. In most places they did not—at least not without a good deal of pushing and trimming. The conflicts of the postwar era have mostly been wars of postcolonial succession, from the Mekong to the Limpopo, from Bosnia to the Caucasus, from the valley of the Jordan to the frontiers of India. In some areas, such as eastern Asia, the result is tolerably stable states. In others, including much of Africa, the state is a fiction of diplomacy, lacking almost any ability to control or protect its citizens. In Europe, on the other hand, the trauma of two great wars has prompted an on-off experiment in integration that falls short of federalism but is far more than a mere alliance. Thus, the postwar state takes a variety of forms.

Given the fragility of many new states, it was hardly surprising that their armed forces often constituted the political backbone. These provided defense against external enemies, security against internal subversion, and, often, the main source of educated leaders. Communist states subordinated army to party within a ruthless security apparatus. But in much of Africa, the Middle East, Latin America, and southern Asia (despite exceptions such as India), the postwar decades were largely a story of military rule, either overt or cloaked in one-party politics.

Yet military rule was usually presented as a brief intermission in democracy. The meaning of that word has been one of the central debates of the whole century, pitting liberal democracy against people's democracy, representative government against a single-party state. But in recent decades, urbanization and education have had a erosive effect on most authoritarian regimes, from the Soviet Union to sub-Saharan Africa. By the late 1990s, most governments had conceded the principle of electoral democracy—in other words, regular and reasonably open polls, in which adult citizens (male and female) could choose their rulers. That was another historical novelty of this period. Whether governments were really accountable to their people was, however, questionable, even in the "democratic" West. Often the pattern was still one of elite politics in a more complex form. The strength of democracy depended on the vitality of "civil society," that mesh of media, social organizations, and economic groups outside the orbit of the state bureaucracy. Even in Latin America, let alone in most developing and postcommunist states, civil society was still inchoate and ineffectual.

Government legitimacy derived as much from economic performance as democratic credentials. The idea that rulers could and should manage the domestic economy was not unprecedented: across the world as a whole, industrialization had come about as much from state policy as from market forces. But the proper role of government was one of the great controversies of the postwar era. Here, the legacies of the 1930s and World War II were profound. The Great Depression and the success of the Soviet war economy together suggested that economic planning and even direct government control of the "commanding heights" were essential to promote economic growth and to smooth out the oscillations of the market. From India to Egypt, state socialism was the policy of many postcolonial states, directed against "feudal" and "bourgeois" elites and against foreign capitalists. Similarly, the rapid development of Japan and East Asia was a form of state capitalism in which the market was abridged, rigged, and protected. Even in Western Europe, some kind of mixed economy seemed desirable for growth and welfare. On the other hand, neither the West nor East Asia went the route of many big developing countries in South Asia, the Middle East, and Latin America in the 1950s and 1960s, where industrialization won out over agriculture, and the promotion of export industries was neglected in favor of a tariff-walled domestic market.

The story of the 1980s and 1990s, from Moscow to Mexico City, has been one of waning statism and protection, as governments began deregulating their economies and opening them up to the outside. But markets were no panacea. The postcommunist disaster in Russia and the Asian financial crisis of 1997–1998 made that clear. How to promote growth at acceptable social and environmental cost was the big economic question at the end of the twentieth century. The era since the Great Depression had seen the rise and fall of the statist answer, but the dilemmas of market regulation remained as acute as ever.

The reemergence of a global economy and the discrediting of protectionism has suggested to some a reversion to the free-trade internationalism of the late nineteenth century.[7] But the differences between the two periods are more important than the similarities. In the first case, the players were a few major industrialized states, with the rest of the world involved in international trade and finance largely as appendages of empire. Today, with over 180 states, the politics of the world economy are far more intricate. Added complexity is created by multinational actors—giant corporations that produce in several states, and banks and other investors who move vast sums of capital across national exchanges on a scale that dwarfs governmental reserves.

Moreover, the nature and intensity of economic interactions since 1945 was totally different from the years around 1900. In the first half of our period, the most dynamic area was trade in goods, which increased much faster than total output and population growth until the first oil shock in 1973–1974. The bulk of this trade was in manufactures, unlike the early twentieth century, when primary products predominated. Since the mid-1970s, the engine of globalization has been international finance. The Western financial crisis of the early 1970s marked the end of the postwar experiment in fixed exchange rates pegged to gold via the dollar. Floating exchange rates became the norm for developed countries, with various attempts at intergovernmental coordination, particularly in Europe. In the 1990s, flexible rates became more common elsewhere.

Global finance brought dangers and benefits. One danger was the volatility of private capital. Sudden speculative movements repeatedly unhinged national finances. In the longer term, servicing external debts often became a huge burden on society and economy. For many countries, these have been the most striking features of globalization. On the other hand, benefits stemmed from new and vast sources of investment that could transform national economies. One of the most striking examples was in telecommunications, a decisive technology for the twenty-first century.

A changing system of states in a changing international economy produced shifts in the balance of power. The immediate legacy of World War II was the ruination of Europe, the division of most of it into two superpower blocs, and the accelerated retreat from global empires (though that process lasted into the 1970s for Portugal). Western Europe eventually recovered from the disasters of depression and war, both economically and politically, but henceforth it was under the aegis of the United States, whose power, wealth, and values became the love-hate focus of European attention. Reliance on America seemed necessary because of the dominance of the nuclear-armed Soviet Union over Eastern Europe, including eastern Germany, the country at the heart of Europe's cold war. In Asia, the Middle East, and later Africa, the superpower confrontation was aggravated by decolonization. From Korea to Egypt, from Vietnam to Angola, America and Russia each sought to fill the vacuums created by the contraction of imperial power.

In Europe, bipolarity became less dangerous in the 1970s, but these were also the years when the West seemed to run out of steam. The first shock came from the oil crises of 1973 and 1979, which suggested a transfer of economic power to the Middle East. That shift, though real, did not prove lasting or substantial. Oil was just black gold, a natural resource whose price had temporarily gone through the roof. By the mid-1990s the price had fallen through the floor. A more durable challenge came from East and Southeast Asia, led by Japan, whose wealth was the result of economic development, not raw materials. Their growth was checked but not stopped by the financial crisis of the late 1990s.

The biggest losers from the oil shocks and export-led growth were most of Africa and Latin America, whose economies were stagnating by the 1970s and 1980s. They had also availed themselves of the foreign credit sloshing around as international finance opened up. The consequent debt crisis exposed them to pressure from Western creditors for structural adjustment. Whatever the long-term benefits, the immediate economic and social costs of adjustment were enormous. For Africa and Latin America the 1980s were the lost decade.

By contrast, the 1980s were the decade in which China finally returned to the international stage. The communist victory of 1949 had restored its unity, but Mao's attenuated revolution brought turmoil, disasters, and self-imposed isolation for the next quarter-century. Not until the 1980s did China begin opening itself to the dynamic Asian economies, but then it grew prolifically. A strong, united China was a marked contrast with the first half of the twentieth century and much of the nineteenth. Together with the rise of Japan (still a major actor despite its 1990s recession), these were signs that the supremacy of "the West" was no longer axiomatic. Slowly and erratically, despite the United States' "unipolar moment," the world was moving toward a more balanced and complex international system, reflecting the shift of wealth and population away from North America and Western Europe.

What, then, of the cold war itself? Undoubtedly, it stimulated many important developments of the postwar era, ranging from the technologies of satellites and transistors to the initial stages of West European integration. But overall, I have argued that it fits, albeit as a central piece, *within* many of the stories I have just told.

Into the story of empire, for instance. The Soviet Union was the tsarist Russian empire under new leadership, surviving when the Habsburgs, Ottomans, and Hohenzollerns collapsed in 1918, and even outliving the British, French, and Dutch empires in the post-1945 era. Its hegemony in Eastern Europe resulted from the rise and fall of another empire—Hitler's Third Reich. Yet, in 1991, the Soviet Union also fell apart. Like the others, its postimperial transition will be long and probably bloody.

The Soviet Union was also the exemplar of autarkic industrialization, initially as a desperate measure to ensure survival in a hostile world, later as the supposed model for developing countries. Eventually, it suffered the same fate as others that had staked all on heavy industry and domestic-led growth. As an inefficient economy obsessed with security, it had devoted a disproportionate amount of economic and human resources to defense, particularly nuclear weapons. By the 1980s, it lagged far behind in the vital new technologies of the information revolution. And despite brutal social control, its authoritarian regime, like others, was eroded by urbanization and education, which produced a skeptical, discontented populace and, even more important, a skeptical, reforming leadership.

The collapse of communism was also a crisis of faith. In that sense, it also fits into another global pattern, namely the erosion of structures of intellectual authority. Communism survived mainly by repression. But it was also sustained, certainly in early postwar Europe, by belief in the utopia it proclaimed and by the practical changes it brought to newly urbanized peasants. The loss of faith came abruptly, with Hungary in 1956, but the faith had once been real. Likewise, Mao's Great Leap Forward and Pol Pot's instant revolution were animated not merely by paranoid politics but also by social utopianism.

The other great structure of faith to rise and wane was politicized Islam. Reared as a defense against Westernization in Khomeini's Iran, it was feared by some, particularly in America, as the successor to international communism. But although it prompted an extension of Islamic law in many Muslim countries, it was not a precursor of global revolution but an instrument of social control against the forces of urbanization and education. To emphasize the political dimensions of Islam is not to deny the persistence and vitality of religious belief—in the Muslim world and beyond. In Latin America and parts of the West, the erosion of ecclesiastical authority was accompanied by rapid growth in informal, revivalist sects. But belief was becoming more personal and idiosyncratic, particularly in urban areas—an incipient democracy in values as well as politics.

Such intellectual pluralism reflected growing awareness of the wider world. Increased trade produced greater variety of food and goods. Increased tourism permitted direct, if fleeting, contact with foreign cultures, offering millions of people some glimpses of the single world that Wendell Willkie mapped out after his circumnavigation of 1943. The spread of telephones meant that distance was no barrier to conversation. The spread of radio, and especially television, enlarged people's horizons even within the home. The potency of the media was exemplified in the mimetic European revolutions of 1989, which represented the triumph of communication as well as the failure of communism.

But those events came at the end of our period. Because of the importance of these technologies, access and content were tightly regulated by most states. Telecommunications remained under government control until at least the 1980s, and TV was often a tool of propaganda and nation building. The idea of the *mass* media betokened the mass production of values, for the benefit of state policy as much as for the consumer economy. In the Soviet Union, and even in the United States, the cold war could not have been sustained without the manipulation of information and images. The eventual opening up of the media depended partly on the erosion of deference and social control, partly on changes in official attitudes to economic regulation, and also on new technologies such as computers and satellites. By the 1990s, for a privileged few there was even the World Wide Web—secreted by the Pentagon but spun out by private initiative.

From the Atom to the Net. From an icon of division and destruction to an icon of connection and creativity. Is that how we should see the global transition? Yes, but also no. We live in a world in which more people are more conscious of its interrelation—in economics, communications, or the environment. But globalization has also made people more conscious of divisions. Thanks to television, we are aware as never before, for instance, of the varieties of wealth and poverty around the world. The "20:80 world" is not new, but it is news. Often, the local has been asserted, even created, in antithesis to the global—be it nations out of empires, black against white, heritage versus consumerism, or Islamic values in the teeth of Westernization. More than ever, this is one world; more than ever, it is divisible.

The paradox is especially evident in the story of warfare. The period 1900 to 1945 was scarred by two world wars within three decades. By 1950, the two new superpowers had developed weapons of unprecedented destructive power, but, against the odds, they did not embark on World War III. By luck, design, and deterrence, the cold war did not become hot at the global level. Yet one still balks at calling the cold war era "the long peace."[8] Body counts are an inexact science, but an authoritative estimate is that eighteen million people have been killed in wars and other armed conflicts in the fifty years since 1945. Of these, ten million were East Asians, most of them from Korea, Vietnam, and Cambodia; another nearly three million died in sub-Saharan Africa.[9] The list of wounded and maimed is far larger, from the land-mine victims of Angola to those gassed in the Iran-Iraq war. This is only the beginning of an inventory of suffering. African famines flicker on and off the TV screens, but millions more starved silently in Mao's China in the early 1960s. "Structural change" may have opened up some African and Latin American states to markets and democracy, but at a social price that no amount of creative econometrics by the IMF can conceal. "Fertility transition" was a root cause of economic development; but from Russia to China, it was accomplished by abortion, not the pill, at the cost of untold pain. In history, all is change. But the mechanism of historical change is human suffering.

And yet it would be wrong to end on such a negative note. As two demographers have written of African famine: "The real lessons were not how easily man succumbed to the drought but how tenacious he was in managing his survival."[10] Across much of Africa, in fact, survival itself is a triumph in a continent so naturally hostile to life.[11] But people do not live by bread alone. Consider this little poem by a survivor of the Argentine junta's "dirty war" in the 1970s:

> I've lived through good times and bad,
> And here I am.
> Champagne at times, beer or anis at others,
> And here I am.

> I went from Triple A to Triple Z,
> Bombs and bonbons, c'est la vie. . . .
> God alone knows what I have lived through,
> Yesterday and today, and here I am.
> Look at me—here I am.[12]

Hardly Shakespeare, but one of countless attempts to distill the spirit of hope from the dregs of suffering. Human beings are uniquely capable of transcending their current predicament by thought and creativity. Turning sorrow into song, pain into poetry, anguish into art, is the essence of being human.

In its own way, writing history is also an attempt at transcendence. In English and in several other languages, the same word is used to denote both what occurred in the past and what is written about it. That is apt. We understand what happened, in the minutiae of daily life or the epics of world affairs, by constructing stories. And as we discern meaning in the momentary, so we are freed, just a little, from the tyranny of time. You may not agree with the meanings that one white, male, middle-aged English historian has discerned, but by disagreeing, you are also making history. That is the spirit in which I have written this book.

Further Reading

Detailed citations are given in the Notes section that follows. For those wishing to read further in the areas covered by each chapter, I have suggested a few introductory books.

Chapter 1: The Mushroom Cloud and the Iron Curtain

Jeremy Isaacs and Taylor Downing, *Cold War* (New York and London: Bantam, 1998), provide a lively and lavishly illustrated overview based on a TV series. A good textbook on the early years, particularly strong on Germany, is Wilfried Loth, *The Division of the World, 1941–1955* (London: Routledge, 1988). For brief introductions to U.S. and Soviet policy in the period after 1945, see Thomas G. Paterson, *On Every Front: The Making and Unmaking of the Cold War*, 2nd ed. (New York: Norton, 1992); and Vladislav Zubok and Constantine Pleshakov, *Inside the Kremlin's Cold War: From Stalin to Khrushchev* (Cambridge, Mass.: Harvard University Press, 1996). The European dimension, west and east, is examined in David Reynolds, ed., *The Origins of the Cold War in Europe: International Perspectives* (New Haven: Yale University Press, 1994); and Martin McCauley, ed., *Communist Power in Europe, 1944–1949* (London: Macmillan, 1977)—an older book that is still useful. John Lewis Gaddis, *We Now Know: Rethinking Cold War History* (Oxford: Clarendon Press, 1997), synthesizes archival material from both sides on the period up to 1962. For biographies of the American and Soviet leaders, consult Alonzo L. Hamby, *Man of the People: A Life of Harry S. Truman* (New York: Oxford University Press, 1995); and Dmitri Volkogonov, *Stalin: Triumph and Tragedy*, ed. and trans. by Harold Shukman (London: Weidenfeld & Nicolson, 1991).

Chapter 2: Communist Revolutions, Asian Style

A good overview of the region's international history is provided by Roger C. Thompson, *The Pacific Basin Since 1945* (London: Longman, 1994). Robin Jeffrey, ed., *Asia: The Winning of*

Independence (London: Macmillan, 1981), includes incisive essays on the Philippines, Indonesia, Vietnam, and Malaya. Useful introductions to the two main conflicts are Peter Lowe, *The Origins of the Korean War*, 2nd ed. (London: Longman, 1997); and Anthony Short, *The Origins of the Vietnam War* (London: Longman, 1989). For surveys of national histories see Edwin O. Reischauer, *The Japanese Today: Change and Continuity* (Cambridge, Mass.: Harvard University Press, 1988); Jonathan D. Spence, *The Search for Modern China* (New York: Norton, 1990); Donald S. MacDonald, *The Koreans: Contemporary Politics and Society*, 2nd ed. (Boulder, Colo.: Westview Press, 1990); Robert Cribb and Colin Brown, *Modern Indonesia: A History since 1945* (London: Longman, 1995); and Nicholas Tarling, ed., *The Cambridge History of Southeast Asia*, vol. 2, *The Nineteenth and Twentieth Centuries* (Cambridge: Cambridge University Press, 1992).

Chapter 3: Legacies of Empire

On some of the broad themes covered in this chapter, see R. F. Holland, *European Decolonization, 1918–1981: An Introductory Survey* (London: Macmillan, 1985); and the lively vignettes in Brian Lapping, *End of Empire* (London: Granada, 1985). On the major regions, see Sugata Bose and Ayesha Jalal, *Modern South Asia: History, Culture, Political Economy* (London: Routledge, 1998); Roger Owen, *State, Power and Politics in the Making of the Modern Middle East* (London: Routledge, 1992); J. D. Hargreaves, *Decolonization in Africa* (London: Longman, 1988); and Thomas E. Skidmore and Peter H. Smith, *Modern Latin America* (3rd ed., New York: Oxford University Press, 1992).

Chapter 4: Two Europes, Two Germanies

J. Robert Wegs, *Europe Since 1945: A Concise History*, 3rd ed. (London: Macmillan, 1991), offers a general overview; while Geoffrey Swain and Nigel Swain, *Eastern Europe since 1945* (London: Macmillan, 1993), pay particular attention to the political economy of communism. For histories of NATO and the EEC see, respectively, Lawrence S. Kaplan, *NATO and the United States: The Enduring Alliance*, 2nd ed. (New York: Twayne, 1994); and Derek W. Urwin, *The Community of Europe: A History of European Integration since 1945* (London: Longman, 1991). On the new transatlantic political economy up to 1961 see the survey by David W. Ellwood, *Rebuilding Europe: Western Europe, America and Postwar Reconstruction* (London: Longman, 1992). Owen Chadwick, *The Christian Church in the Cold War*, 2nd ed. (London: Penguin, 1993), offers a brief introduction to the place of religion in the east-west divide. For key countries, see the very detailed *History of West Germany* by Dennis L. Bark and David R. Gress, 2 vols., 2nd ed. (Oxford: Blackwell, 1993); on France, Jean-Pierre Rioux, *The Fourth Republic, 1944–1958* (Cambridge: Cambridge University Press, 1987); Paul Ginsborg's superb revisionist *History of Contemporary Italy: Society and Politics, 1943–1988* (London: Penguin, 1990); and the later parts of Keith Robbins, *The Eclipse of a Great Power: Modern Britain, 1870–1975* (London: Longman, 1983).

Chapter 5: Cities and Consumers

For introductions to the main themes of this chapter see the encyclopedic if contentious Jean-Claude Chesnais, *The Demographic Transition: Stages, Patterns, and Economic Implications*, trans. by Elizabeth and Philip Kreager (Oxford: Clarendon Press, 1992); Peter Hall, *The World Cities*, 2nd ed. (London: Weidenfeld & Nicolson, 1977); William J. R. Curtis, *Modern Architecture Since 1900* (Oxford: Phaidon, 1982); Jean-Pierre Bardou et al., *The Automobile Revo-*

lution: The Impact of an Industry, trans. James M. Laux (Chapel Hill: University of North Carolina Press, 1982); John Wyver, *The Moving Image: An International History of Film, Television and Video* (Oxford: Basil Blackwell, 1989); Kenneth T. Jackson, *Crabgrass Frontier: The Suburbanization of the United States* (New York: Oxford University Press, 1985); and Hermann van der Wee, *Prosperity and Upheaval: The World Economy, 1945–1980,* trans. Robin Hogg and Max R. Hall (London: Penguin, 1987).

Chapter 6: Eyeball to Eyeball, Shoulder to Shoulder

Two books by Michael R. Beschloss, *Mayday: Eisenhower, Khrushchev and the U-2 Affair* (New York: Harper & Row, 1986), and *The Crisis Years: Kennedy and Khrushchev, 1960–1963* (New York: HarperCollins, 1991) provide detailed narratives of Soviet-American relations in the late 1950s and early 1960s, focusing on the leaders, but his work has been overtaken at some points by new evidence, particularly on Cuba. For the latter see Aleksandr Fursenko and Timothy Naftali, *"One Hell of a Gamble": Khrushchev, Castro, and Kennedy, 1958–1964* (New York: Norton, 1997). The space race and its technocratic implications are explored in Walter A. McDougall, *The Heavens and the Earth: A Political History of the Space Age* (New York: Basic Books, 1985).

On France, Serge Berstein, *The Republic of de Gaulle, 1958–1969,* trans. Peter Morris (Cambridge and New York: Cambridge University Press, 1993), provides a good overview; likewise Hans Renner, *A History of Czechoslovakia since 1945* (London and New York: Routledge, 1989), chapters 3–6. Also relevant is Wegs, *Europe Since 1945,* listed in the bibliographical note to Chapter 4, and Derek W. Urwin, *Western Europe Since 1945: A Political History,* 4th ed. (London and New York: Longman, 1989), chapters 11–12.

Chapter 7: Color, Creed, and Coups

Ivan Hannaford, *Race: The History of an Idea in the West* (Baltimore: Johns Hopkins University Press, 1996) is substantial and stimulating. For particular areas, see Harvard Sitkoff, *The Struggle for Black Equality, 1954–1980* (New York: Hill and Wang, 1981) on the United States; Tom Lodge, *Black Politics in South Africa Since 1945* (London: Longman, 1983); and Tomas Hammar, ed., *European Immigration Policy: A Comparative Study* (Cambridge: Cambridge University Press, 1985). On democracy and the military, Ruth First, *Power in Africa: Political Power in Africa and the Coup d'Etat* (Baltimore: Penguin, 1972) remains useful; Robert Wesson, ed., *The Latin American Military Institution* (New York: Praeger, 1986) is a valuable comparative study. Gary W. Wynia, *The Politics of Latin American Development* (Cambridge: Cambridge University Press, 1978) offers a stimulating framework for thinking about that continent; likewise, Ayesha Jalal, *Democracy and Authoritarianism in South Asia: A Comparative and Historical Perspective* (Cambridge: Cambridge University Press, 1995). The regional essays in George Moyser, ed., *Politics and Religion in the Modern World* (London: Routledge, 1991), provide a useful introduction to this theme. See also Stuart Mews, ed., *Religion in Politics: A World Guide* (London: Longman, 1989).

Chapter 8: East Wind, West Wind

On China, the best detailed survey can be found in the comprehensive and well-integrated chapters of the *Cambridge History of China,* ed. Roderick MacFarquhar and John K. Fairbank (Cambridge: Cambridge University Press), vol. 14 (1987) on 1949–1965 and vol. 15 (1991) on 1965–1982. Ross Terrill, *Mao: A Biography,* 2nd ed. (New York: Touchstone, 1993) is readable and informed. On Vietnam, T. Louise Brown, *War and Aftermath in Vietnam* (New York: Routledge, 1991) offers an eclectic survey of different facets of the war; the northern side is well covered by William J. Duiker, *Sacred War: Nationalism and Revolution in a Divided Vietnam* (New York: McGraw-Hill, 1995). The standard overview of U.S. policy remains George C. Herring, *America's Longest War: The United States and Vietnam, 1950–1975*, 3rd ed. (New York: McGraw-Hill, 1995). Michael Yahuda, *The International Politics of the Asia-Pacific, 1945–1995* (London: Routledge, 1996) fills in the larger geopolitical context. Many of the general books listed for Chapter 2 remain useful, particularly Nicholas Tarling, ed., *The Cambridge History of Southeast Asia* (Cambridge: Cambridge University Press, 1992) vol. 2; and Robert Cribb and Colin Brown, *Modern Indonesia: A History Since 1945* London and New York: Longman, 1995).

Chapter 9: Cultures and Families

Richard Pells, *Not Like Us: How Europeans Have Loved, Hated, and Transformed American Culture since World War II* (New York: Basic Books, 1997) is a broad survey that goes beyond simple clichés about "Americanization." Rosemary Lambert, *The Cambridge Introduction to Art: The Twentieth Century* (Cambridge: Cambridge University Press, 1981); and Jean-Luc Duval, *History of Abstract Painting*, trans. Jane Brenton (London: Art Data, 1989) provide entrées into these fields. Andre Millard, *America on Record: A History of Recorded Sound* (Cambridge: Cambridge University Press, 1995) is excellent on technologies; Mike Jahn offers a lively overview of the performers in *Rock: From Elvis to the Rolling Stones* (New York: Quadrangle, 1973). Janet Salzmann Chafetz and Anthony Gary Dworkin, assisted by Stephanie Swanson, *Female Revolt: Women's Movement in World and Historical Perspective* (Totowa, N.J.: Rowman & Allanheld, 1986), provide useful factual comparisons; Jeanne Bisilliat and Michèle Fiéloux, *Women and the Third World: Work and Daily Life*, trans. by Enne Amann and Peter Amann (London: Associated University Presses, 1987) offer a broad and stimulating thematic essay. There are also useful chapters in Mary F. Katzenstein and Carol M. Mueller, eds., *The Women's Movements of the United States and Western Europe: Consciousness, Political Opportunity and Public Policy* (Philadelphia: Temple University Press, 1987).

Chapter 10: Superpower Détente, Communist Confrontation

Andrew Chaikin, *A Man on the Moon: The Voyages of the Apollo Astronauts* (London: Michael Joseph, 1994), provides a vivid account of the U.S. moon program. China's experience, both domestic and foreign, is best followed in Roderick McFarquhar and John K. Fairbank, eds., *The Cambridge History of China* (Cambridge: Cambridge Univ. Press, 1991), vol. 15 (1991) chapters 3–5. Raymond Garthoff, *Détente and Confrontation: American-Soviet Relations from Nixon to Reagan*, 2nd ed. (Washington, D.C.: Brookings Institution, 1994), is essential for the superpower relationship and its global ramifications; but see also the essays and documents in Odd Arne Westad, ed., *The Fall of Détente: Soviet-American Relations during the Carter Years* (Oslo: Scandinavian University Press, 1997). On European themes, see Timothy Garton Ash, *In Europe's Name: Germany and the Divided Continent* (London: Jonathan Cape, 1993), especially chapters 2–4; and the essays in Allan Williams, ed., *Southern Europe Transformed: Political and Social Change in Greece, Italy, Portugal and Spain* (London: Harper & Row, 1984). Arnold R. Isaacs, *Without Honor: Defeat in Vietnam and Cambodia* (Baltimore: Johns Hopkins University Press, 1983), covers the period 1970–1975 from a critical American angle, while David P. Chandler offers a balanced appraisal of *The Tragedy of Cambodian History: Politics, War, and Revolution Since 1945* (New Haven: Yale University Press, 1991).

Chapter 11: Israel, Oil, and Islam

Frank Aker, *October 1973: The Arab-Israeli War* (Hamden, Conn.: Archon Books, 1985), provides a succinct account of the conflict. David Hirst and Irene Beeson, *Sadat* (London: Faber & Faber, 1981) is a perceptive biography of the Egyptian leader; and Howard M. Sachar, *A History of Israel* (New York: Alfred A. Knopf, 1988), chapters 24–25, offers a useful overview of Israel in the 1970s. William B. Quandt, *Peace Process: American Diplomacy and the Arab-Israeli Conflict Since 1967* (Washington, D.C.: Brookings Institution, 1993) is the best introduction to its theme; Daniel Yergin, *The Prize: The Epic Quest for Oil, Money, and Power* (New York: Touchstone, 1992) is entertaining and insightful on the oil crisis and its consequences. Mohsen M. Milani, *The Making of Iran's Islamic Revolution: From Monarchy to Islamic Republic*, 2nd edn. (Boulder, Colo.: Westview Press, 1994) is good on both history and theory. Two stimulating essay collections expose the variety of modern Islam: Shireen T. Hunter, ed., *The Politics of Islamic Revivalism: Diversity and Unity* (Bloomington: Indiana University Press, 1988), which focuses on individual states; and John L. Esposito, ed., *Voices of Resurgent Islam* (New York: Oxford University Press, 1983), more interested in ideas and perceptions. Also useful are some of the national essays in Stuart Mews, ed., *Religion in Politics: A World Guide* (London: Longman, 1989).

Chapter 12: Capitalist Revolutions, Asian Style

Philip Armstrong, Andrew Glyn, and John Harrison, *Capitalism since 1945* (Oxford: Blackwell, 1991), set the scene. For Japan, see Reischauer, *The Japanese Today*, listed in the bibliographical note to Chapter 2. Harry T. Oshima, *Economic Growth in Monsoon Asia: A Comparative Survey* (Tokyo: University of Tokyo Press, 1987) is suggestive on national differences; Bela Balassa, *Economic Policies in the Pacific Area Developing Countries* (London: Macmillan, 1991), analyzes the national statistics. Jon Woronoff, *Asia's "Miracle" Economies* (Tokyo: Yohan, 1986), is a lively survey of Taiwan, South Korea, Singapore, and Hong Kong. Essays edited by Hal Hill explore *Indonesia's New Order: The Dynamics of Socio-Economic Transformation* (Honolulu: Univ. of Hawaii, 1994). There are useful chapters in Terry Cannon and Alan Jenkins, eds., *The Geography of Contemporary China: The Impact of Deng Xiaoping's Decade* (London: Routledge, 1990); and Barry Naughton, *Growing Out of the Plan: Chinese Economic Reform, 1979–1993* (Cambridge: Cambridge University Press, 1995) offers a major reinterpretation. Nicholas Tarling, ed., *The Cambridge History of Southeast Asia*, (Cambridge: Cambridge Univ. Press, vol. 2 (1992), part II, is valuable on comparative trends; and Robert W. Stern, *Changing India: Bourgeois Revolution on the Sub-Continent* (Cambridge: Cambridge University Press, 1993), is a stimulating and eclectic essay.

Chapter 13: Challenges for the West

John N. Smithin, *Macroeconomics after Thatcher and Reagan: The Conservative Policy Revolution in Retrospect* (Aldershot: Edward Elgar, 1990) is helpful on theory and practice. David Mervin, *Ronald Reagan and the American Presidency* (New York: Longman, 1990) is a perceptive if sometimes indulgent explanation of his successes; Hugo Young, *One of Us* (London: Macmillan, 1989) is the best of the Thatcher biographies. Duncan Green, *Faces of Latin America* (London: Latin American Bureau, 1991) is informative, impassioned and vividly illustrated; Helen Schooley, *Conflict in Central America: Keesing's International Studies* (London: Longman, 1987), provides a detailed factual account. April A. Gordon and Donald L. Gordon, eds., *Understanding Contemporary Africa*, 2nd ed. (Boulder: Lynne Rienner, 1996), offer a solid introduction, and Robert M. Price, *The Apartheid State in Crisis: Political Transformation in South Africa, 1975–1990* (New York: Oxford Univ. Press, 1991), is incisive and compelling. Raymond L. Garthoff, *The Great Transition: American-Soviet Relations and the End of the Cold War,* (Washington, D.C.: Brookings Institution, 1994) is essential; Fred Halliday, *The Making of the Second Cold War,* 2nd ed. (London: Verso, 1986) provides both analysis and a flavor of the times.

Chapter 14: Chips and Genes

John Krige and Dominique Pestre, eds., *Science in the Twentieth Century* (Amsterdam: Harwood, 1997), provide a useful collection of essays on research, applications, and social impact. John Bray, *The Communications Miracle: The Telecommunication Pioneers from Morse to the Information Superhighway* (London: Plenum Press, 1995), is a helpful introduction, featuring British examples. Joseph R. Dominick, Barry L. Sherman, and Gary Copeland, *Broadcasting/Cable and Beyond: An Introduction to Modern Electronic Media,* 2nd ed. (New York: McGraw-Hill, 1993) is an excellent textbook. Martin Campbell-Kelly and William Aspray, *Computer: A History of the Information Machine* (New York: Basic Books, 1996), weave together technology, business, and society into an outstanding book. Walter Bodmer and Robin McKie, *The Book of Man: The Human Genome Project and the Quest to Discover our Genetic Heritage* (Oxford: Oxford University Press, 1997), take a broad view of recent developments; while Horace Freeland Judson, *The Eighth Day of Creation: Makers of the Revolution in Biology* (London: Jonathan Cape, 1979), is a vivid, personalized account of the emergence of molecular biology. John McCormick, *The Global Environmental Movement: Reclaiming Paradise* (London: Belhaven Press, 1989), provides a useful introduction; and Spencer Weart, *Nuclear Fear: A History of Images* (Cambridge, Mass.: Harvard University Press, 1988) is a pioneering piece of cold war cultural history.

Chapter 15: The Crisis of Communism

John Miller, *Mikhail Gorbachev and the End of Soviet Power* (London: Macmillan, 1993), offers a succinct introduction to the period 1985–1991, while Archie Brown, *The Gorbachev Factor* (Oxford: Oxford University Press, 1996), is a full and very sympathetic biography. Patrick Brogan, *The Captive Nations: Eastern Europe, 1945–1990* (New York: Avon Books, 1990), moves from country to country in a lively account of the history of these regimes and their collapse; Elizabeth Pond, *Beyond the Wall: Germany's Road to Unification* (Washington, D.C.: Brookings Institution, 1993), is an incisive blend of high and low politics. The international dimension is covered in Philip Zelikow and Condoleezza Rice, *Germany Unified and Europe Transformed: A Study in Statecraft,* 2nd ed. (Cambridge, Mass.: Harvard University Press, 1997), which is an effective blend of memoir and documents. Peter Nolan, *China's Rise, Russia's Fall: Politics, Economics and Planning in the Transition from Stalinism* (London: Macmillan, 1995), is a stimulating comparison, emphasizing policy choices as the critical difference between the two. On Chinese politics, see Immanuel Y. Hsü, *China without Mao: The Search for a New Order,* 2nd ed. (New York: Oxford University Press, 1990), and Nan Lin, *The Struggle for Tiananmen: Anatomy of the 1989 Mass Movement* (Westport, Conn.: Praeger, 1992).

Chapter 16: States, Wealth, and Order after the Cold War

Naji Abi-Aad and Michel Grenon, *Instability and Conflict in the Middle East: People, Petroleum and Security Threats* (London: Macmillan, 1997), address larger regional issues. Useful introductions to their respective continents can be found in the companion volumes by April A. Gordon and Donald L. Gordon, eds., *Understanding Contemporary Africa* (Boulder, Colo.: Lynne Rienner, 1996), and Richard S. Hillman, ed., *Understanding Contemporary Latin America* (Boulder, Colo.: Lynne Rienner, 1997). Leslie Holmes, *Post-Communism: An Introduction* (Cambridge: Polity Press, 1997) covers politics, economics, and external policy in Eastern Europe and the former USSR with a broad but sensitive brush. Ian Bremmer and Ray Taras, eds., *New States, New Politics: Building the Post-Soviet Nations* (Cambridge: Cambridge University Press, 1997) is a detailed state-by-state guide; and the textbook by Ian Budge, Kenneth Newton, et al., *The Politics of the New Europe: Atlantic to Urals* (London: Longman, 1997), ably synthesizes material from east and west. There are some very useful essays on countries and themes in Ross H. McLeod and Ross Garnaut, eds., *East Asia in Crisis: From Being a Miracle to Needing One?* (London: Routledge, 1998).

Chapter 17: Goods and Values

The essays edited by R. J. Johnston, Peter J. Taylor, Michael J. Watts, *Geographies of Global Change: Remapping the World in the Late Twentieth Century* (Oxford: Blackwell, 1995), range widely over economics, politics, society, culture and the environment. Malcolm Waters, *Globalization* (London: Routledge, 1995), is a straightforward introduction; while Gilles Kepel, *The Revenge of God: The Resurgence of Islam, Christianity and Judaism in the Modern World*, trans. Alan Braley (Cambridge: Polity Press, 1994), presents a lively and perceptive overview of these themes. Charles Jencks, *What is Post-Modernism?*, 4th ed. (London: Academy Editions, 1996), is stimulating on the arts and architecture; Madrun Sarup, *An Introductory Guide to Post-Structuralism and Postmodernism*, 2nd ed. (New York: Harvester Wheatsheaf, 1993), looks at some of the major thinkers. Stephen Hawking, *The Illustrated A Brief History of Time* (New York: Bantam, 1996) is a more accessible version than the original 1988 text of *the* nonfiction bestseller of the late twentieth century. Tony Stark, *Knife to the Heart: The Story of Transplant Surgery* (London: Macmillan, 1996), is a readable survey. *An Urbanizing World: Global Report on Human Settlements, 1996* (Oxford: Oxford University Press, 1996), prepared for the UN's Habitat II conference, contains a mine of data and analysis about trends in demography, society and urban living.

Notes

Introduction

1. Wendell L. Willkie, *One World* (New York: Simon and Schuster, 1943), pp. 1–2. For the sales figures, see Joseph Barnes, *Willkie: The Events He Was Part Of—The Ideas He Fought For* (New York: Simon and Schuster, 1952), p. 315, and Ellsworth Barnard, *Wendell Willkie: Fighter for Freedom* (Marquette: Northern Michigan Press, 1966), pp. 411–5.

2. Adapting the image of Michael Howard, "Winning the Peace," *Times Literary Supplement,* January 8, 1993, p. 8.

3. Walter Raleigh, *The History of the World,* ed. C. A. Patrides (London: Macmillan, 1971), preface, p. 80.

4. Cf. David Carr, "Narrative and the Real World: An Argument for Continuity," *History and Theory,* 25 (1986), pp. 121–2.

5. Robert Lacey, *Ford: The Men and the Machine* (London: Heinemann, 1986), pp. 238–9; William Shakespeare, *The Tempest,* act II, scene 1, line 261.

6. *Das Treffen in Telgte,* quoted in Stuart Parkes, *Understanding Contemporary Germany* (London: Routledge, 1997), p. 158.

7. *Public Papers of the Presidents of the United States: George Bush, 1992* (Washington, D.C.: Government Printing Office, 1994), p. 157.

8. Jeremy Isaacs and Taylor Downing, *Cold War* (London: Bantam Books, 1998), title page and dustjacket.

9. Tom Bottomore, *Classes in Modern Society* (2nd ed., London: Routledge, 1992), p. 98—a salvage exercise on the 1955 classic.

10. Cf. David Cannadine, *Class in Britain* (New Haven: Yale University Press, 1998), ch. 1.

11. Peter B. Evans, Dietrich Rueschemeyer, and Theda Skocpol, eds., *Bringing the State Back In* (Cambridge: Cambridge University Press, 1985).

12. Fernand Braudel, *La Méditerranée et le Monde Méditerranéen à l'Epoque de Philippe II*, 2 vols. (Paris: Armand Colin, 1966), preface to 2nd edition.

13. Anne Michaels, *Fugitive Pieces* (London: Bloomsbury, 1997), p. 77.

Chapter 1 The Mushroom Cloud and the Iron Curtain

1. For a lively account of wartime radar and postwar applications, see Robert Buderi, *The Invention That Changed the World: The Story of Radar from War to Peace* (London: Little, Brown, 1996).

2. See John Ellis, *World War II: The Sharp End* (2nd ed., London: Windrow and Greene, 1990), p. 170.

3. *Time*, August 20, 1945, pp. 1, 78.

4. Richard Rhodes, *The Making of the Atomic Bomb* (London: Penguin, 1988), pp. 734, 740–2. See also Paul Boyer, "Exotic Resonances: Hiroshima in American Memory," *Diplomatic History*, 19 (1995): 297–318.

5. Quotations from Reinhard Rürup, ed., *Berlin 1945: A Documentation*, trans. Pamela E. Selwyn (Berlin: Willmuth Arenhövel, 1995), pp. 61, 63, 70.

6. John Barber and Mark Harrison, *The Soviet Home Front, 1941–1945* (London: Longman, 1991), p. 42.

7. Mark H. Leff, "The Politics of Sacrifice on the American Home Front in World War II," *Journal of American History*, 77 (1991): 1296.

8. These figures follow Gerhard Weinberg, *A World at Arms: A Global History of World War II* (New York: Cambridge University Press, 1994), p. 894.

9. François Bédarida, *Le nazisme et le génocide* (Paris: Nathan, 1989), pp. 58–9.

10. Jonathan R. Adelman, *Prelude to the Cold War: The Tsarist, Soviet, and U.S. Armies in the Two World Wars* (Boulder, Colo.: Lynne Rienner, 1988), p. 128.

11. See Saburo Ienaga, *The Pacific War, 1931–1945* (New York: Pantheon, 1978), esp. pp. 247–9.

12. See discussion in David Reynolds, et al., eds., *Allies at War: The Soviet, American, and British Experience, 1939–1945* (New York: St. Martin's, 1994), pp. 122, 163, 208–12.

13. William T.R. Fox, *The Super-Powers* (New York: Harcourt, Brace, 1944), p. 2. Initially Fox included Britain in this category.

14. See David Holloway, *Stalin and the Bomb: The Soviet Union and Atomic Energy, 1939–1956* (New Haven: Yale University Press, 1994), esp. pp. 129, 132–3.

15. Alan Bullock, *Hitler and Stalin: Parallel Lives* (London: HarperCollins, 1991), pp. 401–2.

16. Richard Overy, *Russia's War* (London: Allen Lane, 1998), p. 16.

17. Robert H. McNeal, *Stalin: Man and Ruler* (London: Macmillan, 1988), pp. 264–5.

18. Dmitri Volkogonov, *Stalin: Triumph and Tragedy,* ed. and trans. by Harold Shukman (London: Weidenfeld & Nicolson, 1991), pp. 552, 557.

19. Figures from Alec Nove, *An Economic History of the USSR, 1917–1991,* 3rd ed. (London: Penguin, 1992), ch. 1.

20. James T. Patterson, *America's Struggle against Poverty, 1900–1980* (Cambridge, Mass.: Harvard University Press, 1981), p. 80.

21. Henry L. Stimson, diary, vol. 37, January 17, 1942, Sterling Library, Yale University.

22. Alfred D. Chandler, Jr., *The Visible Hand: The Managerial Revolution in American Business* (Cambridge, Mass.: Harvard University Press, 1977), p. 482.

23. John M. Blum, *V Was for Victory: Politics and American Culture during World War II* (New York: Harcourt, Brace, Jovanovich, 1976), p. 115.

24. A point emphasized in Robert Higgs, "Wartime Prosperity?: A Reassessment of the U.S. Economy in the 1940s," *Journal of Economic History,* 52 (1992): 42–3.

25. Quoted in Christopher Thorne, *Allies of a Kind: The United States, Britain, and the War against Japan, 1941–1945* (London: Hamish Hamilton, 1978), p. 503.

26. As emphasized by Ernest R. May, "The U.S. Government, a Legacy of the Cold War," *Diplomatic History,* 16 (1992): 27.

27. David Brinkley, *Washington Goes to War* (New York: Ballantine Books, 1988), p. 72.

28. Walter Isaacson and Evan Thomas, *The Wise Men: Six Friends and the World They Made* (New York: Simon and Schuster, 1986), p. 338.

29. Thomas G. Paterson, *On Every Front: The Making and Unmaking of the Cold War,* 2nd ed. (New York: Norton, 1992), p. 100.

30. Melvyn P. Leffler, *A Preponderance of Power: National Security, the Truman Administration, and the Cold War* (Stanford: Stanford University Press, 1992), p. 67.

31. On Stalin's world-view, see Vladislav Zubok and Constantine Pleshakov, *Inside the Kremlin's Cold War: From Stalin to Khrushchev* (Cambridge, Mass.: Harvard University Press, 1996), ch. 1.

32. See William O. McCagg, *Stalin Embattled, 1943–1948* (Detroit: Wayne State University Press, 1978), esp. pp. 63, 151–8.

33. Robert Dallek, *Franklin D. Roosevelt and American Foreign Policy, 1932–1945* (New York: Oxford University Press, 1979), p. 508.

34. Alonzo L. Hamby, "The Mind and Character of Harry S. Truman," in Michael J. Lacey, ed., *The Truman Presidency* (Cambridge: Cambridge University Press, 1989), p. 25.

35. See discussion and documents in A. N. Bazhenov and O. A. Rzheshevsky, eds, *Yalta. 1945: Problemi Voini i Mira* (Moscow: Russian Academy of Sciences, 1992), pp. 86–94.

36. Holloway, *Stalin and the Bomb,* pp. 156, 272.

37. John L. Gaddis, *The United States and the Origins of the Cold War, 1941–1947* (New York: Columbia University Press, 1972), p. 336.

38. Thomas H. Etzold and John L. Gaddis, eds, *Containment: Documents on American Policy and Strategy, 1945–1950* (New York: Columbia University Press, 1978), pp. 61–2.

39. Letter to the War Department, March 27, 1946, in Jean Edward Smith, ed., *The Papers of General Lucius D. Clay: Germany, 1945–1949*, Vol. I (Bloomington: Indiana University Press, 1974), p. 184.

40. Leffler, *Preponderance of Power*, p. 106.

41. Alec Cairncross, *Years of Recovery: British Economic Policy, 1945–51* (London: Methuen, 1985), p. 278.

42. Sir Orme Sargent, quoted in Kenneth O. Morgan, *Labour in Power, 1945–1951* (Oxford: Oxford University Press, 1984), p. 42.

43. House of Commons, *Debates*, 5th series, vol. 437, col. 1965.

44. Alan Bullock, *Ernest Bevin, Foreign Secretary, 1945–1951* (London: Heinemann, 1983), p. 352.

45. Richard Clarke, *Anglo-American Economic Collaboration in War and Peace, 1942–1949* (Oxford: Clarendon, 1982), p. 156.

46. Robert J. Donovan, *Conflict and Crisis: The Presidency of Harry S. Truman, 1945–1948* (New York: Norton, 1977), p. 284.

47. Quotations from Forrest C. Pogue, *George C. Marshall: Statesman, 1945–1959* (New York: Viking Penguin, 1987), pp. 196, 213.

48. Scott D. Parrish, "The Turn to Confrontation: The Soviet Reaction to the Marshall Plan," Cold War International History Project, working paper no. 9 (Washington D.C.: Woodrow Wilson Center, March 1994), p. 25.

49. Martin Gilbert, *Winston S. Churchill, vol. 8, 1945–1965* (London: Heinemann, 1988), p. 200.

50. Zubok and Pleshakov, *Inside the Kremlin's Cold War*, p. 133.

51. Georges-Henri Soutou, "Georges Bidault et la construction européenne, 1944–1954," *Revue d'histoire diplomatique* 105 (1991): 268.

52. John W. Young, *France, the Cold War and the Western Alliance, 1944–1949* (Leicester: Leicester University Press, 1990), p. 146.

53. Vojtech Mastny, "Stalin and the Militarization of the Cold War," *International Security*, 9 (1984/5): 120.

54. They were not. See Forrest C. Pogue, *George C. Marshall: Statesman, 1945–1959* (New York: Penguin, 1987), pp. 304–5; Ann and John Tusa, *The Berlin Blockade* (London: Hodder and Stoughton, 1988), p. 155.

55. Lawrence S. Kaplan, *NATO and the United States: The Enduring Alliance* (Boston: Twayne, 1988), p. 1.

56. A point emphasized in Timothy P. Ireland, *Creating the Entangling Alliance: The Origins of the North Atlantic Treaty Organization* (Westport, Conn.: Greenwood, 1981), ch. 4.

57. Evan Luard, *The History of the United Nations*, vol. I (London: Macmillan, 1982), p. 382.

58. R. W. Davies, "Forced Labour under Stalin: The Archive Revelations," *New Left Review,* 214 (November–December 1995): 67.

59. Holloway, *Stalin and the Bomb,* esp. pp. 176–7, 220, 222–3.

60. Holloway, *Stalin and the Bomb,* p. 317.

61. See Vladimir Andrle, *A Social History of Twentieth-Century Russia* (London: Edward Arnold, 1994), p. 194.

62. Andrei Sakharov, *Memoirs,* trans. Richard Lourie (London: Hutchinson, 1990), quoting pp. 114, 164.

63. Reports of October 1949 quoted in Richard Rhodes, *Dark Sun: The Making of the Hydrogen Bomb* (New York: Simon and Schuster, 1995), pp. 400–1.

64. Quoted in John Colville, *The Fringes of Power: Downing Street Diaries, 1939–1955* (London: Hodder and Stoughton, 1985), p. 676.

Chapter 2 Communist Revolutions, Asian Style

1. Winston S. Churchill, *The Second World War* (6 vols, London: Cassell, 1948–1954), vol. IV, p. 81.

2. William Manchester, *American Caesar: Douglas MacArthur, 1880–1964* (New York: Dell, 1978), pp. 525–30.

3. Thomas W. Burkman, ed., *The Occupation of Japan: The International Context* (Norfolk, Va.: MacArthur Foundation, 1984), p. 4.

4. R. P. Dore, *Land Reform in Japan,* 2nd ed. (London: Athlone, 1984), pp. 175–6.

5. Susan J. Pharr, "The Politics of Women's Rights," in Robert E. Ward and Sakamoto Yoshikazu, eds., *Democratizing Japan: The Allied Occupation* (Honolulu: University of Hawaii Press, 1987), pp. 224–5.

6. Robert Ward, "Conclusion," in Ward and Sakamoto, eds., *Democratizing Japan,* p. 401.

7. Sakamoto Yoshikazu, "The International Context of the Occupation of Japan," in *Democratizing Japan,* p. 67.

8. Quoted in Michael Schaller, *The American Occupation of Japan: The Origins of the Cold War in Asia* (New York: Oxford University Press, 1985), p. 104.

9. William S. Borden, *The Pacific Alliance: United States Foreign Economic Policy and Japanese Trade Recovery, 1947–1955* (Madison: University of Wisconsin Press, 1984), p. 136.

10. Quoted in Melvyn P. Leffler, *A Preponderance of Power: National Security, the Truman Administration, and the Cold War* (Stanford: Stanford University Press, 1992), p. 339.

11. Quoted in Jacques Guillermaz, *A History of the Chinese Communist Party, 1921–1949* (London: Methuen, 1972), p. 375.

12. Military attaché, report, September 1946, in Department of State, *Foreign Relations of the United States, 1946,* vol. 10 (Washington, D.C.: Government Printing Office, 1972), p. 235.

13. Roderick MacFarquhar and John K. Fairbank, eds., *The Cambridge History of China,* vol. 14 (Cambridge: Cambridge University Press, 1987), p. 71.

14. In John K. Fairbank and Albert Feuerwerker, eds., *The Cambridge History of China,* vol. 13 (Cambridge: Cambridge University Press, 1986), p. 584.

15. Fairbank and Feuerwerker, *Cambridge History of China,* vol. 13, p. 631.

16. Steven I. Levine, *Anvil of Victory: The Communist Revolution in Manchuria, 1945–1948* (New York: Columbia University Press, 1987), pp. 88–89.

17. Jonathan D. Spence, *The Search for Modern China* (New York: Norton, 1990), p. 511.

18. Quoted in Chen Jian, "The Sino-Soviet Alliance and China's Entry into the Korean War," Cold War International History Project, Working Paper 1 (June 1992), p. 5, n. 16.

19. Forrest C. Pogue, *George C. Marshall: Statesman, 1945–1949* (New York: Penguin, 1987), p. 275.

20. *The Selected Works of Mao Tse-tung,* Vol. 4 (Oxford: Pergamon Press, 1961), pp. 415–16.

21. Quoted in Michael B. Yahuda, *China's Role in World Affairs* (London: Croom Helm, 1978), p. 44.

22. NSC 48/1 and 48/2, in Thomas H. Etzold and John L. Gaddis, eds., *Containment: Documents on American Policy and Strategy, 1945–1950* (New York: Columbia University Press, 1978), esp. pp. 253, 256–9, 273–5.

23. Truman and Acheson speeches in Dean Acheson, *Present at the Creation: My Years in the State Department* (New York: Norton, 1969), pp. 351, 357.

24. Robert J. Donovan, *Tumultuous Years: The Presidency of Harry S Truman, 1949–1953* (New York: Norton, 1982), p. 191.

25. Bruce Cumings, *The Origins of the Korean War,* 2 vols., (Princeton: Princeton University Press, 1981–90), 1: 16, 54, 67.

26. Kathryn Weathersby, "Soviet Aims in Korea and the Origins of the Korean War, 1945–1950: New Evidence from the Russian Archives," Cold War International History Project, working paper no. 8 (Nov. 1993), p. 6.

27. John Merrill, *Korea: The Peninsular Origins of the War* (Newark: University of Delaware Press, 1989), p. 181.

28. James I. Matray, *The Reluctant Crusade: American Foreign Policy in Korea, 1941–1950* (Honolulu: University of Hawaii Press, 1985), pp. 226, 231.

29. Sergei N. Goncharov, John W. Lewis, and Xue Litai, *Uncertain Partners: Stalin, Mao, and the Korean War* (Stanford: Stanford University Press, 1993), ch. 5.

30. Quoted in Peter Lowe, *The Origins of the Korean War* (London: Longman, 1986), p. 163.

31. Quoted in Leffler, *Preponderance of Power,* p. 366.

32. Quoted in Ernest R. May, *"Lessons" of the Past: The Use and Misuse of History in American Foreign Policy* (New York: Oxford University Press, 1973), pp. 81–2.

33. Evan Luard, *A History of the United Nations,* Vol. I (London: Macmillan, 1982), p. 242.

34. Freeman Matthews, quoted in James I. Matray, "Truman's Plan for Victory: National Self-Determination and the Thirty-Eighth Parallel Decision in Korea," *Journal of American History,* 66 (1979): 329.

35. Goncharov et al., *Uncertain Partners,* ch. 6; cf. documents and commentary by Alexandre Y. Mansourov in *Cold War International History Project Bulletin* 6–7 (Winter 1995–6): 94–119.

36. Quoted in Max Hastings, *The Korean War* (London: Michael Joseph, 1987), p. 194.

37. David Rees, *Korea: The Limited War* (London: Macmillan, 1964), pp. 460–1.

38. Quoted in Callum A. MacDonald, *Korea: The War before Vietnam* (London: Macmillan, 1986), p. 248.

39. Quotations from Knowland and Dulles in Richard A. Melanson and David Mayers, eds., *Reevaluating Eisenhower: American Foreign Policy in the Fifties* (Chicago: University of Illinois Press, 1989), pp. 68, 92–3.

40. Borden, *Pacific Alliance,* pp. 146–7.

41. Burkman, *Occupation of Japan,* p. 263.

42. See John Welfield, *An Empire in Eclipse: Japan in the Postwar American Alliance System* (London: Athlone, 1988), pp. 51–2.

43. Howard Schonberger, "Peacemaking in Asia: The United States, Great Britain, and the Japanese Decision to Recognize Nationalist China, 1951–52," *Diplomatic History,* 10 (1986): 73.

44. Quoted in Peter Duus, ed., *The Cambridge History of Japan,* Vol. 6 (Cambridge: Cambridge University Press, 1988), p. 15.

45. Philip West, "Confronting the West: China as David and Goliath in the Korean War," *Journal of American–East Asian Relations,* 2 (1993): 25.

46. Mao, *Selected Works,* 4: 421.

47. Jacques Guillermaz, *The Chinese Communist Party in Power, 1949–1976* (Folkestone, Kent: William Dawson, 1976), pp. 21–2.

48. William Hinton, *Fanshen: A Documentary of Revolution in a Chinese Village* (New York: Monthly Review, 1966), esp. pp. 29–33, 136–8.

49. Benedict Stavis, *The Politics of Agricultural Mechanization in China* (Ithaca, N.Y.: Cornell University Press, 1978), pp. 29–30.

50. Guillermaz, *Chinese Communist Party in Power,* p. 28.

51. Vivienne Shue, *Peasant China in Transition: The Dynamics of Development towards Socialism, 1949–1956* (Berkeley: University of California Press, 1980), pp. 285–7.

52. Carl Riskin, *China's Political Economy: The Quest for Development since 1949* (Oxford: Oxford University Press, 1987), pp. 95–8.

53. MacFarquhar and Fairbank, eds., *Cambridge History of China,* vol. 14, pp. 155–6.

54. Huỳnh Kim Khánh, *Vietnamese Communism, 1925–1945* (Ithaca, N.Y.: Cornell University Press, 1982), p. 26.

55. Bùi Minh Dũng, "Japan's Role in the Vietnamese Starvation of 1944–45," *Modern Asian Studies,* 29 (1995): 573–618.

56. David G. Marr, *Vietnamese Tradition on Trial, 1920–1945* (Berkeley: University of California Press, 1981), p. 408.

57. Stein Tønnesson, *The Vietnamese Revolution of 1945: Roosevelt, Ho Chi Minh and de Gaulle in a World at War* (London: Sage, 1991), p. 411.

58. Chen Jian, "China and the First Indo-China War, 1950–1954," *China Quarterly,* 133 (March 1993): 94.

59. Marilyn B. Young, *The Vietnam Wars, 1945–1990* (New York: HarperCollins, 1990), pp. 20, 23.

60. Leffler, *Preponderance of Power,* p. 437.

61. George C. Herring and Richard H. Immerman, "Eisenhower, Dulles, and Dien Bien Phu: 'The Day We Didn't Go to War' Revisited," in Lawrence S. Kaplan, Denise Artaud, and Mark Rubin, eds., *Dien Bien Phu and the Crisis of Franco-American Relations, 1954–1955* (Wilmington, Del.: Scholarly Resources, 1990), pp. 88, 94.

62. Kevin Ruane, "Anthony Eden, British Diplomacy and the Origins of the Geneva Conference of 1954," *Historical Journal,* 37 (1994): 171.

63. George M. Kahin, *Nationalism and Revolution in Indonesia* (Ithaca, N.Y.: Cornell University Press, 1952), pp. 300–01.

64. Robert J. McMahon, *Colonialism and Cold War: The United States and the Struggle for Indonesian Independence, 1945–1949* (Ithaca, N.Y.: Cornell University Press, 1981), p. 244.

65. Pierre van der Eng, "Marshall Aid as a Catalyst in the Decolonization of Indonesia, 1945–1949," *Journal of Southeast Asian Studies,* 19 (1988): 350.

66. Quoted by Alfred W. McCoy, "The Philippines: Independence without Decolonization," in Robin Jeffrey, ed., *Asia: The Winning of Independence* (London: Macmillan, 1981), p. 26.

67. Bernard J. Kerkvliet, *The Huk Rebellion: A Study of Peasant Revolt in the Philippines* (Berkeley: University of California Press, 1977), p. 264.

68. Richard Stubbs, *Hearts and Minds in Guerrilla Warfare: The Malayan Emergency, 1948–1960* (Singapore: Oxford University Press, 1989), p. 259.

69. Quoted in A.J. Stockwell, "Insurgency and Decolonisation during the Malayan Emergency," *Journal of Commonwealth and Comparative Politics,* 25 (1987): 78.

70. John Darwin, *Britain and Decolonisation: The Retreat from Empire in the Post-War World* (London: Macmillan, 1988), p. 204.

71. I am adapting here the distinctions in Anthony D. Smith, *National Identity* (London: Penguin, 1991), pp. 11, 110–16.

Chapter 3 Legacies of Empire

1. Judith M. Brown, *Modern India: The Origins of an Asian Democracy* (Delhi: Oxford University Press, 1985), p. 46.

2. B. R. Tomlinson, *The Political Economy of the Raj, 1914–1947: The Economics of Decolonization in India* (London: Macmillan, 1979), pp. 1–6, 106, 140.

3. Quotations from R. J. Moore, *Escape from Empire: The Attlee Government and the Problem of India* (Oxford: Clarendon, 1983), pp. 205, 221.

4. For this argument see Ayesha Jalal, *The Sole Spokesman: Jinnah, the Muslim League and the Demand for Pakistan* (Cambridge: Cambridge University Press, 1985), esp. pp. 122, 174–5. For a range of views, see Mushirul Hasan, ed., *India's Partition: Process, Strategy, Mobilization* (Delhi: Oxford University Press, 1994).

5. Sarvepalli Gopal, *Jawaharlal Nehru: A Biography*, 3 vols. (London: Jonathan Cape, 1975–1984), vol. 2, p. 14.

6. Judith M. Brown, *Gandhi: Prisoner of Hope* (New Haven: Yale University Press, 1989), p. 373.

7. Jalal, *Sole Spokesman*, p. 121.

8. Richard Symonds, *The Making of Pakistan* (London: Faber & Faber, 1950), p. 84.

9. Omar Noman, *Pakistan: Political and Economic History since 1947* (London: Kegan Paul International, 1990), p. 15.

10. See W. H. Morris-Jones, *The Government and Politics of India*, 2nd ed. (London: Hutchinson, 1967), p. 95.

11. Paul R. Brass, *The New Cambridge History of India*, Vol. IV, Part 1: *The Politics of India since Independence*, 2nd ed., (Cambridge: Cambridge University Press, 1994), pp. 101, 104. This section draws heavily on chs. 3–4.

12. Robert E. B. Lucas and Gustav F. Papanek, eds., *The Indian Economy: Recent Development and Future Prospects* (Delhi: Oxford University Press, 1988), esp. pp. 6 and 219.

13. Francine R. Frankel, *India's Political Economy, 1947–1977: The Gradual Revolution* (Princeton, N.J.: Princeton University Press, 1978), p. 23.

14. William H. Wiser and Charlotte Viall Wiser, *Behind Mud Walls, 1930–1960*, rev. ed. (Berkeley: University of California Press, 1963), chs. X–XII, quoting from pp. 159 and 224.

15. Robert W. Stern, *Changing India: Bourgeois Revolution on the Sub-Continent* (Cambridge: Cambridge University Press, 1993), p. 75.

16. Frankel, *India's Political Economy*, p. 3.

17. Robert J. McMahon, "United States Cold War Strategy in South Asia: Making a Military Commitment to Pakistan, 1947–1954," *Journal of American History*, 75 (1988): 839.

18. Gopal, *Nehru*, 2: 187.

19. T. G. Fraser, ed., *The Middle East, 1914–1979* (London: Edward Arnold, 1980), p. 18.

20. Peter Grose, "The President versus the Diplomats," in Wm. Roger Louis and Robert W. Stookey, eds., *The End of the Palestine Mandate* (Austin: University of Texas Press, 1986), pp. 55–6.

21. Wm. Roger Louis, *The British Empire in the Middle East: Arab Nationalism, The United States, and Postwar Imperialism* (Oxford: Clarendon, 1984), p. 467.

22. Michael J. Cohen, *Palestine and the Great Powers, 1945–1948* (Princeton, N.J.: Princeton University Press, 1982), p. 247.

23. Alan Bullock, *Ernest Bevin: Foreign Secretary, 1945–1951* (London: Heinemann, 1983), p. 476.

24. Benny Morris, *The Birth of the Palestine Refugee Problem, 1947–1949* (Cambridge: Cambridge University Press, 1987), p. 17.

25. Efraim Karsh, "Israel," in Yezid Sayigh and Avi Shlaim, eds., *The Cold War and the Middle East* (Oxford: Clarendon, 1997), pp. 159–60.

26. For some of the issues, see Avi Shlaim, "The Debate about 1948," *International Journal of Middle Eastern Studies*, 27 (1995): 287–304.

27. See Ilan Pappé, *The Making of the Arab-Israeli Conflict, 1947–1951* (London: I.B. Tauris, 1992), esp. pp. 87–99.

28. Morris, *Birth of the Palestinian Refugee Problem*, p. 298.

29. See figures in David Shimshoni, *Israeli Democracy: The Middle of the Journey* (New York: Free Press, 1982), p. 100.

30. Howard M. Sachar, *A History of Israel* (New York: Alfred A. Knopf, 1988), p. 429.

31. For these illuminating comparisons see Peter Mansfield, *The Arabs* (Harmondsworth: Penguin, 1978), p. 448.

32. See P. J. Vatikiotis, *Nasser and His Generation* (London: Croom Helm, 1978).

33. Wm. Roger Louis, "The Tragedy of the Anglo-Egyptian Settlement of 1954," in Wm. Roger Louis and Roger Owen, eds., *Suez 1956: The Crisis and Its Consequences* (Oxford: Clarendon, 1989), p. 69.

34. Benny Morris, *Israel's Border Wars, 1949–1956: Arab Infiltration, Israeli Retaliation, and the Countdown to the Suez War* (Oxford: Clarendon, 1993), p. 413.

35. William J. Burns, *Economic Aid and American Policy toward Egypt, 1955–1981* (Albany: State University of New York Press, 1985), pp. 95–6.

36. Galia Golan, *Soviet Policies in the Middle East: From World War II to Gorbachev* (Cambridge: Cambridge University Press, 1990), p. 41.

37. Georges Brondel, "The Sources of Energy, 1920–1970," in Carlo Cipolla, ed., *The Fontana Economic History of Europe*, vol. 5, part 1 (Brighton: Harvester Press, 1977), p. 227.

38. Daniel Yergin, *The Prize: The Epic Quest for Oil, Money, and Power* (New York: Touchstone, 1992), p. 425.

39. William Stivers, "Eisenhower and the Middle East," in Richard A. Melanson and David Mayers, eds., *Reevaluating Eisenhower: American Foreign Policy in the Fifties* (Urbana: University of Illinois Press, 1989), p. 195.

40. Quoted in W. Scott Lucas, *Divided We Stand: Britain, the U.S. and the Suez Crisis* (London: Hodder and Stoughton, 1991), p. 179.

41. Moshe Shemesh, "Egypt: From Military Defeat to Political Victory," in Selwyn Ilan Troen and Moshe Shemesh, eds., *The Suez-Sinai Crisis, 1956: Retrospective and Reappraisal* (London: Frank Cass, 1990), p. 151.

42. Stephen E. Ambrose, *Eisenhower: The President* (New York: Touchstone, 1984), pp. 360, 364.

43. Keith Kyle, *Suez* (London: Weidenfeld and Nicolson, 1991), p. 465.

44. Quoted by Netanel Lorch, "David Ben-Gurion and the Sinai Campaign, 1956," in Ronald W. Zweig, ed., *David Ben-Gurion: Politics and Leadership in Israel* (London: Frank Cass, 1991), p. 307.

45. Michael Brecher, *Decisions in Israel's Foreign Policy* (London: Oxford University Press, 1974), pp. 310–11.

46. Robert A. Divine, *Eisenhower and the Cold War* (Oxford: Oxford University Press, 1981), p. 91.

47. Marion Farouk-Sluglett and Peter Sluglett, *Iraq since 1958: From Revolution to Dictatorship* (London: I. B. Tauris, 1990), p. 47.

48. N. J. Ashton, " 'A Great New Venture'?: Anglo-American Cooperation in the Middle East and the Response to the Iraqi Revolution, July 1958," *Diplomacy and Statecraft,* 4 (1993): 84.

49. Ambrose, *Eisenhower,* p. 474.

50. For Africa in the 1940s and 1950s see in general the omnibus essays in Michael Crowder, ed., *The Cambridge History of Africa,* vol. 8 (Cambridge: Cambridge University Press, 1984), which takes a colony-centered view; and Ali Mazrui, ed, *General History of Africa,* vol. 8 (Oxford: Heinemann/UNESCO, 1993), written mostly by African authors from a Pan-African perspective.

51. Quoted in Brian Lapping, *End of Empire* (London: Granada, 1985), p. 15.

52. Quoted in R. D. Pearce, *The Turning Point in Africa: British Colonial Policy, 1938–1948* (London: Frank Cass, 1982), p. 187—generally an important source on British policy.

53. See Crowder, ed., *Cambridge History of Africa,* vol. 8, p. 149.

54. Patrick Manning, *Francophone Sub-Saharan Africa, 1880–1945* (Cambridge: Cambridge University Press, 1988), p. 143.

55. See table in James Barber and John Barratt, *South Africa's Foreign Policy: The Search for Status and Security, 1945–1988* (Cambridge: Cambridge University Press, 1990), p. 345.

56. For an overview, synthesizing recent scholarship, see Nigel Worden, *The Making of Modern South Africa: Conquest, Segregation and Apartheid* (Oxford: Blackwell, 1994), esp. chs. 3–4.

57. Statistics from Deborah Posel, *The Making of Apartheid, 1948–1961: Conflict and Compromise* (Oxford: Clarendon, 1991), pp. 24, 34.

58. See generally Dan O'Meara, *Volkskapitalisme: Class, Capital and Ideology in the Development of Afrikaner Nationalism, 1934–1948* (Cambridge: Cambridge University Press, 1983).

59. Quoted in Posel, *Making of Apartheid,* p. 62.

60. Tom Lodge, *Black Politics in South Africa since 1945* (London: Longman, 1983), p. 225, and generally chs. 2–9.

61. Ronald Hyam, "The Geopolitical Origins of the Central African Federation: Britain, Rhodesia and South Africa, 1948–1953," *Historical Journal,* 30 (1987), esp. pp. 170–1.

62. Hargreaves, *Decolonization in Africa,* p. 136.

63. David Throup, *Economic and Social Origins of Mau Mau, 1945–1953* (London: James Currey, 1987), p. 250.

64. John P. Entelis, *Comparative Politics of North Africa: Algeria, Morocco, and Tunisia* (Syracuse, N.Y.: Syracuse University Press, 1980), p. 35.

65. For an overview, see Charles-Robert Ageron, *Modern Algeria: A History from 1830 to the Present,* trans. Michael Brett (London: Hurst & Co., 1991), esp. chs. 6-8.

66. Alistair Horne, *A Savage War of Peace: Algeria, 1954-1962* (London: Penguin, 1979), remains the basic account in English.

67. Quoted in Henri Alleg et al., *La Guerre d'Algérie* (Paris: Temps Actuel, 1981), p. 418—a major study in French.

68. This argument of Alfred Grosser, *La IVe République et sa politique extérieure,* 3rd ed. (Paris: Armand Colin, 1972), p. 398, is particularly applicable to the crisis of 1958.

69. Jean-Pierre Rioux, *The Fourth Republic, 1944-1958,* trans. Godfrey Rogers (Cambridge: Cambridge University Press, 1987), p. 310.

70. On these contrasts see Miles Kahler, *Decolonization in Britain and France: The Domestic Consequences of International Relations* (Princeton, N.J.: Princeton University Press, 1984), esp. pp. 354-63.

71. David Fieldhouse, *Black Africa, 1945-80: Economic Decolonization and Arrested Development* (London: Allen & Unwin, 1986), p. 232.

72. Manning, *Francophone Sub-Saharan Africa,* p. 149.

73. Jean Lacouture, *De Gaulle: The Ruler, 1945-1970,* trans. Alan Sheridan (New York: Norton, 1993), p. 247.

74. Harold Macmillan, *Riding the Storm, 1956-1959* (London: Macmillan, 1971), p. 748.

75. See Ritchie Ovendale, "Macmillan and the Wind of Change in Africa, 1957-1960," *Historical Journal,* 38 (1995): 457.

76. Harold Macmillan, *Pointing the Way, 1959-1961* (London: Macmillan, 1972), p. 156.

77. Quoted in Jean Stengers, "Precipitous Decolonization: The Case of the Belgian Congo," in Prosser Gifford and Wm. Roger Louis, *The Transfer of Power in Africa: Decolonization, 1941-1960* (New Haven: Yale University Press, 1982), p. 330.

78. Billy J. Dudley, "Decolonisation and the Problems of Independence," in Crowder, ed., *Cambridge History of Africa,* vol. 8, pp. 85-6.

79. In Mazrui, ed., *General History of Africa,* vol. 8, p. 105.

80. W. H. Oliver, with B. R. Williams, eds., *The Oxford History of New Zealand* (Wellington: Oxford University Press, 1981), pp. 473-5, and generally chs. 13-16.

81. Malcolm McKinnon, *Independence and Foreign Policy: New Zealand in the World since 1935* (Auckland: University of Auckland Press, 1993), p. 106.

82. See table in Geoffrey Sherrington, *Australia's Immigrants, 1788-1988,* 2nd ed. (Sydney: Allen & Unwin, 1990), p. 134.

83. This paragraph draws particularly on D. J. Walmsley and A. D. Sorensen, *Contemporary Australia: Explorations in Economy, Society and Geography,* 2nd ed. (Sydney: Longman Cheshire, 1992), esp. pp. 33-4 (immigrants) and 70-1 (trade).

84. Article published on December 27, 1941, quoted in Alan Watt, *The Evolution of Australian Foreign Policy, 1938–1965* (Cambridge: Cambridge University Press, 1968), p. 55.

85. Glen St. J. Barclay, *Friends in High Places: Australian-American Diplomatic Relations since 1945* (Melbourne: Oxford University Press, 1985), p. 96.

86. Robert Bothwell, Ian Drummond, and John English, *Canada since 1945: Power, Politics, and Provincialism,* 2nd ed. (Toronto: University of Toronto Press, 1989), p. 189.

87. Donald Creighton, *The Forked Road: Canada, 1939–1957* (Toronto: McClelland and Stewart, 1976), p. 259.

88. Quoted in Bothwell et al., *Canada since 1945,* p. 235.

89. Bill Albert, *South America and the World Economy from Independence to 1930* (London: Macmillan, 1983), pp. 29–41.

90. Stephen G. Rabe, "The Elusive Conference: United States Foreign Economic Relations with Latin America, 1945–1952," *Diplomatic History* 2 (1978): 292.

91. On this see Leslie Bethell and Ian Roxborough, eds., *Latin America between the Second World War and the Cold War, 1944–1948* (New York: Cambridge University Press, 1992), esp. pp. 1–32.

92. See David Rock, ed., *Latin America in the 1940s: War and Postwar Transitions* (Berkeley: University of California Press, 1994), p. 20.

93. Quoted in Roger R. Trask, "The Impact of the Cold War on United States–Latin American Relations, 1945–1949," *Diplomatic History,* 1 (1977): 28.

94. Robert A. Pollard, *Economic Security and the Origins of the Cold War, 1945–1950* (New York: Columbia University Press, 1985), pp. 212–13.

95. Stephen G. Rabe, *Eisenhower and Latin America: The Foreign Policy of Anti-Communism* (Chapel Hill: University of North Carolina Press, 1988), p. 47.

96. John Ranelagh, *The Agency: The Rise and Decline of the CIA* (London: Sceptre, 1988), p. 268.

97. Paul H. Lewis, *The Crisis of Argentine Capitalism* (Chapel Hill: University of North Carolina Press, 1990), p. 162.

98. State Department memo, February 2, 1959, quoted in Steven F. Grover, "U.S.–Cuban Relations, 1953–1958: A Test of Eisenhower Revisionism," in Günter Bischof and Stephen E. Ambrose, eds., *Eisenhower: A Centenary Assessment* (Baton Rouge: Louisiana State University Press, 1995), p. 243.

99. Letter of July 22, 1960, quoted in Alistair Horne, *Macmillan, 1957–1986* (London: Macmillan, 1989), p. 298.

100. Quoted by Thomas G. Paterson, "Fixation with Cuba: The Bay of Pigs, Missile Crisis, and Covert War against Castro," in Thomas G. Paterson, ed., *Kennedy's Quest for Victory: American Foreign Policy, 1961–1963* (New York: Oxford University Press, 1989), p. 126.

101. Christopher Andrew, *For the President's Eyes Only: Secret Intelligence and the American Presidency from Washington to Bush* (London: HarperCollins, 1995), p. 257.

102. Quoted in Morris H. Morley, *Imperial State and Revolution: The United States and Cuba, 1952–1986* (Cambridge: Cambridge University Press, 1987), p. 149.

Chapter 4 Two Europes, Two Germanies

1. Antony Polonsky, *The Little Dictators: The History of Eastern Europe since 1918* (London: Routledge & Kegan Paul, 1975), p. 4.

2. See George Schöpflin, *Politics in Eastern Europe, 1945–1992* (Oxford: Blackwell, 1993), ch. 1.

3. See M. C. Kaser and E. A. Radice, eds, *The Economic History of Eastern Europe, 1919–1975*, vol. II (Oxford: Clarendon, 1986), ch. 22.

4. Irène Lagani, "Les communistes des Balkans et la guerre civile grecque, Mars 1946–Aout 1949," *Communisme*, 9 (1986), 60–78.

5. Duncan Wilson, *Tito's Yugoslavia* (Cambridge: Cambridge University Press, 1979), p. 58.

6. L. P. Morris, *Eastern Europe since 1945* (London: Heinemann, 1984), p. 31.

7. George Hodos, *Show Trials: Stalinist Purges in Eastern Europe, 1948–1954* (New York: Praeger, 1987), p. xii.

8. See Nigel Swain, *Hungary: The Rise and Fall of Feasible Socialism* (London: Verso, 1992), p. 72.

9. For contrasting emphases in interpreting this period see Vladislav Zubok and Constantine Pleshakov, *Inside the Kremlin's Cold War: From Stalin to Khrushchev* (Cambridge, Mass.: Harvard University Press, 1996), ch. 5; and Vojtech Mastny, *The Cold War and Soviet Insecurity: The Stalin Years* (New York: Oxford University Press, 1996), ch. 10.

10. Quotations from Zubok and Pleshakov, *Inside the Kremlin's Cold War*, pp. 164, 166.

11. Quoted in Caroline Kennedy-Pipe, *Stalin's Cold War: Soviet Strategies in Europe, 1943–1956* (Manchester: Manchester University Press, 1996), p. 182.

12. Quotations from Malenkov and Khrushchev in Joseph L. Nogee and Robert H. Donaldson, *Soviet Foreign Policy since World War II* (New York: Pergamon Press, 1981), pp. 89, 102, 203.

13. Bill Lommax, ed., *Eye-Witness in Hungary: The Soviet Invasion of 1956* (Nottingham: Spokesman, 1980), p. 52. For recent research, see the summary in *Cold War International History Project Bulletin* 2 (Fall 1992): 1–3.

14. See Miklós Molnár, *Budapest 1956: A History of the Hungarian Revolution*, (London: Allen & Unwin, 1971), p. 115.

15. Quoted in Paul Zinner, ed., *National Communism and Popular Revolt in Eastern Europe* (New York: Columbia University Press, 1956), pp. 463–4. For an overview using materials opened since 1989, see György Litván, ed., *The Hungarian Revolution of 1956: Reform, Revolt, and Repression, 1953–1963* (London: Longman, 1996).

16. W. Brus, "1957 to 1965," in M. C. Kaser, ed., *The Economic History of Eastern Europe, 1919–1975*, Vol. III (Oxford: Clarendon, 1986), pp. 79–81.

17. Statistics in this paragraph from Kaser, *Economic History of Eastern Europe*, vol. III, ch. 25.

18. Norman Davies, *Heart of Europe: A Short History of Poland* (Oxford: Oxford University Press, 1986), p. 47.

19. Alena Heitlinger, *Women and State Socialism: Sex Inequality in the Soviet Union and Czechoslovakia* (London: Macmillan, 1979), pp. 147, 193.

20. Quoted in Michael R. Beschloss, *MAYDAY: Eisenhower, Khrushchev and the U-2 Affair* (New York: Harper & Row, 1986), p. 195.

21. Essay of 1951, quoted in Milan Salajka, *Our Time: From the Ecumenical Legacy of J. L. Hromádka* (Prague: Czech Ecumenical Council of Churches, 1978), p. 31. Generally, see Trevor Beeson, *Discretion and Valour: Religious Conditions in Russia and Eastern Europe,* 2nd ed. (London: Fount, 1982).

22. Two million more are estimated to have died en route. See Rolf-Dieter Müller and Gerd R. Ueberschär, *Kriegsende 1945: Die Zerstörung des Deutschen Reiches* (Frankfurt a. M.: Fischer Tauschenbuch Verlag, 1994), p. 123.

23. R. F. Leslie, ed., *The History of Poland since 1863,* 2nd ed. (Cambridge: Cambridge University Press, 1983), pp. 285–7.

24. Ivo Banac, "Political Change and National Diversity," *Daedalus,* 119/1 (Winter 1990): 152.

25. For the following statistics see especially Ann L. Phillips, *Soviet Policy towards East Germany Reconsidered: The Postwar Decade* (New York: Greenwood Press, 1986), pp. 73, 77, 83, 202–3.

26. Foreign Secretary Ernest Bevin, quoted in Saki Dockrill, *Britain's Policy for West German Rearmament, 1950–1955* (Cambridge: Cambridge University Press, 1991), p. 41.

27. See Rolf Steininger, *The German Question: The Stalin Note of 1952 and the Problem of Reunification,* trans. by Jane T. Hedges (New York: Columbia University Press, 1990), esp. pp. 2, 20, 94.

28. Department of State, *Foreign Relations of the United States,* 1952 (Washington D.C.: Government Printing Office, 1986), vol. VII, p. 204.

29. Conclusions of the 2nd SED Party Conference, July 12, 1952, in Hermann Weber, ed., *DDR: Dokumente zur Geschichte der Deutschen Demokratischen Republik, 1945–1985* (München: Deutscher Taschenbuch Verlag, 1986), p. 188.

30. See James Richter, "Reexamining Soviet Policy towards Germany during the Beria Interregnum," Cold War International History Project, Paper 3 (June 1992), p. 14.

31. According to Vyacheslav Molotov, *Molotov Remembers: Inside Kremlin Politics. Conversations with Felix Chuev,* ed. Albert Resis (Chicago: Ivan R. Dee, 1993), p. 334.

32. D. M. Stickle, ed., *The Beria Affair: The Secret Transcripts of the Meetings Signalling the End of Stalinism,* trans. Jeanne Farrow (Commack NY: Nova Science Publishers, 1992), p. 22.

33. See the essay by Christian F. Ostermann in *Cold War International History Project Bulletin,* 10 (March 1998): 67–8.

34. Lloyd to Churchill, June 22, 1953, quoted in Rolf Steininger, "Ein vereintes, unabhängiges Deutschland?: Winston Churchill, der Kalte Krieg und die deutsche Frage im Jahre 1953," *Militärgeschichtliche Mitteilungen,* 36 (1984): 130.

35. Konrad Adenauer, *Memoirs, 1945–53* (London: Weidenfeld and Nicolson, 1966), p. 182.

36. Quoted in Josef Foschepoth, "Westintegration statt Wiedervereinigung: Adenauers Deutschlandpolitik 1949–1955," in Josef Foschepoth, ed., *Adenauer und die Deutsche Frage* (Göttingen: Vandenhoeck & Ruprecht, 1988), p. 49.

37. Konrad Adenauer, *Briefe, 1945–1947*, ed. Hans-Peter Mensing (Berlin: Siedler, 1983), p. 191.

38. Anselm Doering-Manteuffel, *Die Bundesrepublik Deutschland in der Ära Adenauer: Aussenpolitik und innere Entwicklung, 1949–1963* (Darmstadt: Wissenschaftliche Buchgesellschaft, 1988), pp. 31–2.

39. Hans-Peter Schwarz, *Adenauer, Band 1: Der Aufstieg, 1876–1952* (München: Deutscher Taschenbuch Verlag, 1986), p. 856.

40. Herman van der Wee, *Prosperity and Upheaval: The World Economy, 1945–1980* (London: Penguin, 1987), pp. 48–9.

41. Derek H. Aldcroft, *The European Economy, 1914–1970* (London: Croom Helm, 1978), p. 167.

42. Ali M. El-Agraa, ed., *The Economics of the European Community*, 3rd ed. (London: Philip Allan, 1990), pp. 188–9.

43. Lennart Jörberg and Olle Krantz, "Scandinavia, 1914–1970," in Carlo M. Cipolla, ed., *The Fontana Economic History of Europe*, vol. 6 (New York: Harper & Row, 1977), p. 441.

44. Charles S. Maier, "The Politics of Productivity: Foundations of American International Economic Policy after World War II," *International Organization*, 31 (1977), esp. 606–8.

45. See Peter Flora and Arnold J. Heidenheimer, eds., *The Development of Welfare States in Europe and America* (New Brunswick, N.J.: Transaction Books, 1981), esp. pp. 82–3.

46. See the typology in Gøsta Esping-Andersen, *The Three Worlds of Welfare Capitalism* (Cambridge: Polity Press, 1990), esp. pp. 26–9.

47. Allan Cochrane and John Clarke, eds., *Comparing Welfare States: Britain in International Context* (London: Sage, 1993), pp. 9, 23–9.

48. Ginsborg, *Contemporary Italy*, p. 92.

49. Irving, *Christian Democracy in France* (London: Allen & Unwin, 1973), p. 12.

50. Stephen Padgett and William E. Paterson, *A History of Social Democracy in Postwar Europe* (London: Longman, 1991), p. 24.

51. Rioux, *Fourth Republic*, p. 449.

52. This paragraph follows generally the argument of Alan S. Milward, *The European Rescue of the Nation State*, 2nd ed. (London: Routledge, 1994), esp. ch. 2.

53. Alan Milward, *The Reconstruction of Western Europe, 1945–51* (London: Methuen, 1984), p. 395.

54. Quoted in Klaus Schwabe, ed., *Die Anfänge des Schuman-Plans, 1950/51* (Baden-Baden: Nomos Verlag, 1988), p. 287.

55. John Gillingham, *Coal, Steel, and the Rebirth of Europe, 1945–1955: The Germans and French from Ruhr Conflict to Economic Community* (Cambridge: Cambridge University Press, 1991), pp. 360, 363.

56. Pierre Gerbet, *La Naissance du Marché Commun* (Brussels: Editions Complexe, 1987), p. 84.

57. Quoted in Clemens Wurm, ed., *Western Europe and Germany: The Beginnings of European Integration, 1945–1960* (Oxford: Berg, 1995), p. 49.

58. Maurice Vaisse, "Post-Suez France," in Wm. Roger Louis and Roger Owen, eds., *Suez 1956: The Crisis and its Consequences* (Oxford: Clarendon Press, 1989), p. 336.

59. Pierre Guillen, "L'Europe remède a l'impuissance française?: Le gouvernement Guy Mollet et la négociation des traités de Rome (1955–1957)," *Revue d'histoire diplomatique*, 102 (1988): 333.

60. Quoted in Miriam Camps, *Britain and the European Community, 1955–1963* (Princeton: Princeton University Press, 1964), p. 88.

61. Milward, *The European Rescue of the Nation State*, p. 154.

62. Josep Fontana and Jordi Nadal, "Spain 1914–1970," in Cipolla, ed., *Fontana Economic History of Europe*, 6: 512.

63. See Alec Cairncross, *Years of Recovery: British Economic Policy, 1945–1951* (London: Methuen, 1985), esp. pp. 39, 87, 276, 278.

64. Alan Bullock, *Ernest Bevin: Foreign Secretary, 1945–1951* (London: Heinemann, 1983), p. 659.

65. Quoted in David Reynolds, *Britannia Overruled: British Policy and World Power in the Twentieth Century* (London: Longman, 1991), p. 195.

66. Quoted in John W. Young, *Britain and European Unity, 1945–1992* (London: Macmillan, 1993), p. 64.

67. Paul G. Lewis, *Central Europe since 1945* (London: Longman, 1994), ch. 9.

68. Geir Lundestad, "Empire by Invitation?: The United States and Western Europe," *Journal of Peace Research*, 23 (1986): 263–77.

69. Quoted in Marc Trachtenberg, *History and Strategy* (Princeton, N.J.: Princeton University Press, 1991), pp. 163–4.

70. NSC 162/2, quoted in H.W. Brands, "The Age of Vulnerability: Eisenhower and the National Insecurity State," *American Historical Review*, 94 (1989): 972.

71. Ian Clark, *Nuclear Diplomacy and the Special Relationship: Britain's Deterrent and America, 1957–1962* (Oxford: Clarendon Press, 1994), p. 186.

72. Philip M. Williams, *Hugh Gaitskell* (Oxford: Oxford University Press, 1982), p. 336.

73. Hans-Peter Schwarz, *Adenauer, Band 2: Der Staatsmann, 1952–1967* (München: Deutscher Taschenbuch Verlag, 1993), p. 333.

74. David Childs, *The GDR: Moscow's German Ally* (London: Allen & Unwin, 1983), pp. 64 and 142.

75. Hope M. Harrison, "Ulbricht and the Concrete 'Rose': New Archival Evidence on the Dynamics of Soviet-East German Relations and the Berlin Crisis, 1958–1961," Cold War International History Project, Paper 5 (May 1993), esp. pp. 4 and 55.

76. Quoted in John Lewis Gaddis, *We Now Know: Rethinking Cold War History* (Oxford: Clarendon, 1997), p. 140.

77. Anthony Read and David Fisher, *Berlin: The Biography of a City* (London: Pimlico, 1994), p. 277.

78. Quoted in Gaddis, *We Now Know*, p. 148. On the historiography see Gerhard Wettig, "Die sowjetische Politik während der Berlinkrise 1958 bis 1962: Der Stand der Forschungen," *Deutschland Archiv*, 30 (1997): 383–98.

79. Quoted in Dennis L. Bark and David R. Gress, *History of West Germany*, 2nd ed., 2 vols. (Oxford: Blackwell, 1993), vol. 1, p. 465.

80. Brandt to Kennedy, August 18, 1961, printed in Diethelm Prowe, "Der Brief Kennedys an Brandt vom 18. August 1961: Eine zentrale Quelle zur Berliner Mauer und der Entstehung der Brandtschen Ostpolitik," *Vierteljahrshefte für Zeitgeschichte*, 33 (1985): 381.

81. Quoted in Michael R. Beschloss, *The Crisis Years: Kennedy and Khrushchev, 1960–1963* (New York: HarperCollins, 1991), p. 278.

82. Quoted in Harold James, *A German Identity, 1770–1990*, 2nd ed. (London: Weidenfeld and Nicolson, 1990), p. 208.

83. Willy Brandt, *People and Politics: The Years 1960–1975*, trans. J. Maxwell Brownjohn (London: Collins, 1978), p. 20.

84. Quoted in Beschloss, *Crisis Years*, pp. 605–6.

Chapter 5 Cities and Consumers

1. Paul Kennedy, *Preparing for the Twenty-First Century* (New York: Random House, 1993), pp. 22–4; *Times* (London), July 10, 1998, p. 18.

2. Used here despite some of its conceptual problems—on which see Simon Szreter, "The Idea of Demographic Transition and the Study of Fertility Change: A Critical Intellectual History," *Population and Development Review* 19 (1993): 659–701.

3. See generally Jean-Claude Chesnais, *The Demographic Transition: Stages, Patterns, and Economic Implications*, trans. by Elizabeth and Philip Kreager (Oxford: Clarendon, 1992).

4. Eduardo E. Arriaga and Kingsley Davis, "The Pattern of Mortality Change in Latin America," *Demography* 6 (1969), 241.

5. Andrew Mason et al., "Population Growth and Economic Development: Lessons from Selected Asian Countries," *Policy Development Studies* 10 (1986), table 2.

6. Chesnais, *Demographic Transition*, pp. 58–61.

7. Alex Mercer, *Disease Mortality and Population in Transition: Epidemiological-Demographic Change in England since the Eighteenth Century as Part of a Global Phenomenon* (Leicester and New York: Leicester University Press, 1990), pp. 136–9.

8. Figures from Donald O. Mitchell, Merlinda D. Ingco, and Ronald C. Duncan, *The World Food Outlook* (Cambridge: Cambridge University Press, 1997), pp. 1–2.

9. For a case study, see Rita Sharma and Thomas T. Poleman, *The New Economics of India's Green Revolution: Income and Employment Diffusion in Uttar Pradesh* (Ithaca, N.Y.: Cornell University Press, 1993).

10. R. H. Gray, "The Decline of Mortality in Ceylon and the Demographic Effects of Malaria Control," *Population Studies*, 28 (1974), 205–29. More generally, for this section see relevant entries in Kenneth F. Kiple, ed., *The Cambridge World History of Human Disease* (Cambridge and New York: Cambridge University Press, 1993).

11. World Bank, *World Development Report, 1994: Infrastructure for Development* (Oxford: Oxford University Press, 1994), table A.2. See also Kenneth F. Kiple, ed., *The Cambridge World History of Human Disease* (Cambridge: Cambridge University Press, 1993), esp. pp. 467, 676–80.

12. Odile Leroy and Michel Garenne, "The Two Most Dangerous Days of Life: A Study of Neonatal Tetanus in Senegal (Niakhar)," in Etienne van de Walle, Gilles Pison, and Mpembele Sala-Diakanda, eds.., *Mortality and Society in Sub-Saharan Africa* (Oxford: Clarendon, 1992), pp. 160–75.

13. Althea Hill, "Trends in Childhood Mortality in Sub-Saharan Mainland Africa," in van de Walle, et al., eds., *Mortality and Society in Sub-Saharan Africa,* esp. pp. 15–16, 20, 27.

14. See Dudley L. Poston, Jr., and David Yaukey, eds., *The Population of Modern China* (New York and London: Plenum, 1992), esp. pp. 15, 208–9, 277–85.

15. Judith M. Brown, *Modern India: The Origins of an Asian Democracy* (Oxford and New York: Oxford University Press, 1985), pp. 370–2; cf. Tim Dyson and Nigel Crook, eds., *India's Demography: Essays on the Contemporary Population* (New Delhi: South Asian Publishers, 1984), esp. pp. 1–2, 141.

16. Chesnais, *The Demographic Transition*, p. 131.

17. Leslie Bethell, ed., *The Cambridge History of Latin America*, vol. VI, part 1 (Cambridge and New York: Cambridge University Press, 1994), p. 19.

18. Naohiro Ogawa and Robert D. Retherford, "The Resumption of Fertility Decline in Japan: 1973–92," *Population and Development Review* 19 (1993), 703.

19. Noriko O. Tsuya, "The Fertility Effects of Induced Abortion in Postwar Japan," in James Lee and Osamu Saito, eds., *Abortion, Infanticide, and Reproductive Culture: Past and Present* (New York: Oxford University Press, forthcoming).

20. Alexandr Avdeev, "Contraception and Abortions: Trends and Prospects for the 1990s," in Wolfgang Lutz, Sergei Scherbov, and Andrei Volkov, eds., *Demographic Trends and Patterns in the Soviet Union before 1991* (London and New York: Routledge, 1994), esp. pp. 141–4.

21. See, e.g., George Alter, "Theories of Fertility Decline: A Non-Specialist's Guide to the Current Debate," in John R. Gillis, Louise A. Tilly, and David Levine, eds., *The European Experience of Declining Fertility, 1850–1970: The Quiet Revolution* (Oxford: Blackwell, 1992), pp. 13–27; and Peter McDonald, "Fertility Transition Hypotheses," in Richard Leete and Iqbal Alam, eds., *The Revolution in Asian Fertility: Dimensions, Causes, and Implications* (Oxford: Clarendon, 1993), pp. 3–14.

22. Ansley J. Coale, "Nuptiality and Fertility in USSR Republics and Neighboring Populations," in Lutz et al., eds., *Demographic Trends and Patters in the Soviet Union,* p. 17.

23. Statistics here and elsewhere in this section are drawn from Kingsley Davis, ed., *World Urbanization, 1950–1970,* rev. one-vol. ed. (Westport, Conn.: Greenwood Press, 1976), esp. book I, tables A and B, and book II, tables 1 and 2.

24. Peter Hall, *The World Cities,* 2nd ed. (London: Weidenfeld and Nicolson, 1977), pp. 5 and 17. Subsequent discussion of city case studies owes much to this incisive little book.

25. J. B. Cullingworth, *Town and Country Planning in Britain* (6th ed., London: Allen & Unwin, 1976), p. 199.

26. Catherine Chatin, *9 villes nouvelles: Une éxperience française d'urbanisme* (Paris: Bordas, 1975), p. 6.

27. For a good overview see William J. R. Curtis, *Modern Architecture since 1900* (Oxford: Phaidon, 1982), esp. part 3.

28. Le Corbusier, *Towards a New Architecture,* trans. Frederick Etchells (New York: Praeger, 1960), p. 250.

29. Mark Girouard, *Cities and Peoples* (New Haven: Yale University Press, 1985), pp. 329–30; Spiro Kostof, *The City Shaped: Urban Patterns and Meanings through History* (London: Thames & Hudson, 1991), pp. 311, 331–3.

30. Quoted in E. R. M. Taverne, "The Lijnbaam (Rotterdam): A Prototype of a Postwar Urban Shopping Centre," in Jeffry M. Diefendorf, ed., *Rebuilding Europe's Bombed Cities* (London: Macmillan, 1990), p. 153.

31. Hall, *The World Cities,* p. 159.

32. Peter Hall, *Cities of Tomorrow: An Intellectual History of Urban Planning and Design in the Twentieth Century* (Oxford: Basil Blackwell, 1988), p. 204, and generally ch. 7.

33. On Tange see David B. Stewart, *The Making of a Modern Japanese Architecture: 1868 to the Present* (Tokyo and New York: Kodansha International, 1987), chs. 7–8.

34. See Anthony Sutcliffe, *The Autumn of Central Paris: The Defeat of Town Planning, 1850–1970* (London: Edward Arnold, 1970), pp. 312–5.

35. Quotations from Charles Jencks, *The Prince, the Architects and the New Wave Monarchy* (London: Academy Editions, 1988), pp. 43, 47–9.

36. Robert Venturi, *Complexity and Contradiction in Architecture* (New York: Museum of Modern Art, 1966), p. 22.

37. Robert Venturi, Denise Scott Brown, and Steven Izenour, *Learning from Las Vegas* (Cambridge, Mass.: MIT Press, 1972), p. 10.

38. Charles Jencks "Introduction," in Jencks, ed., *The Post-Modern Reader* (London: Academy Editions, 1992), pp. 10–11.

39. Quoted in Sten Nilsson, *The New Capitals of India, Pakistan and Bangladesh* (Lund, Sweden: Studentlitterature, 1973), p. 89.

40. Kubitschek reflecting in 1975, quoted in James Holston, *The Modernist City: An Anthropological Critique of Brasília* (Chicago: University of Chicago Press, 1989), p. 85.

41. Quoted in Norma Evenson, *Two Brazilian Capitals: Architecture and Urbanism in Rio di Janeiro and Brasília* (New Haven: Yale University Press, 1973), p. 151—a study on which this paragraph is based.

42. See D. G. Epstein, *Brasília, Plan and Reality: A Study of Planned and Spontaneous Urban Development* (Berkeley: University of California Press, 1973).

43. Janice E. Perlman, *The Myth of Marginality: Urban Poverty and Politics in Rio de Janeiro* (Berkeley: University of California Press, 1976), pp. 1, 243.

44. William P. Mangin and John C. Turner, "Benavides and the Barrida Movement," in Paul Oliver, ed., *Shelter and Society* (London: Barrie and Jenkins, 1969), pp. 127–36.

45. See Hamish S. Murison and John P. Lea, eds., *Housing in Third World Countries: Perspectives on Policy and Practice* (London: Macmillan, 1979), esp. pp. 54, 89–99.

46. Kenneth T. Jackson, *Crabgrass Frontier: The Suburbanization of the United States* (New York and Oxford: Oxford University Press, 1985), pp. 7, 283–4—a book on which these paragraphs rely.

47. Brian J. O'Connell, "The Federal Role in the Suburban Boom," in Barbara M. Kelly, ed., *Suburbia Re-examined* (New York and London: Greenwood Press, 1989), pp. 183–92.

48. Jackson, *Crabgrass Frontier,* p. 188.

49. Quoted in Jackson, *Crabgrass Frontier,* p. 158.

50. Jean-Pierre Bardou et al., *The Automobile Revolution: The Impact of an Industry,* trans. James M. Laux (Chapel Hill: University of North Carolina Press, 1982), esp. pp. 112, 175, 178–9, 186–7, 196–202.

51. Reyner Banham, *Los Angeles: The Architecture of Four Ecologies* (New York: Penguin Books, 1973), p. 212.

52. Quoted in Jackson, *Crabgrass Frontier,* p. 265.

53. Richard Longstreth, "The Perils of a Parkless Town," in Martin Wachs and Margaret Crawford, eds., *The Car and the City: The Automobile, the Built Environment, and Daily Urban Life* (Ann Arbor: University of Michigan Press, 1992), pp. 141–53; and Jackson, *Crabgrass Frontier,* pp. 253–65.

54. See John Krige and Dominique Pestre, eds, *Science in the Twentieth Century* (Amsterdam: Harwood, 1997), ch. 27 on polymer chemistry; Penny Sparke, ed., *The Plastics Age: From Modernity to Post-Modernity* (London: Victoria & Albert Museum, 1990).

55. William H. Chafe, *The Unfinished Journey: America since World War II* (New York: Oxford University Press, 1995), pp. 111–2; William E. Leuchtenberg, *A Troubled Feast: American Society since 1945* (Boston: Little, Brown, 1973), p. 63.

56. Karal Ann Marling, *As Seen on TV: The Visual Culture of Everyday Life in the 1950s* (Cambridge, Mass., and London: Harvard University Press, 1994), p. 255.

57. Chester H. Liebs, *Main Street to Miracle Mile: American Roadside Architecture* (New York: Little, Brown, 1985), p. 133.

58. Anthony Smith, ed., *Television: An International History* (Oxford: Oxford University Press, 1995), pp. 29–32.

59. *Encyclopaedia Britannica,* 1962 ed., vol. 21, p. 911.

60. Statistics from Robert T. Bower, *The Changing Television Audience in America* (New York: Columbia University Press, 1985), esp. pp. 7, 12, 33, 35, 88–9, 96–7.

61. Marling, *As Seen on TV,* pp. 122, 232–7.

62. *Encyclopaedia Britannica,* 1962 ed., vol. 21, pp. 894–5.

63. Leuchtenburg, *A Troubled Feast*, p. 44.

64. See Lewis Mandell, *The Credit Card Industry: A History* (Boston: Twayne, 1990), esp. pp. 22, 66, 153.

65. John Kenneth Galbraith, *The Affluent Society* (Boston: Houghton Mifflin, 1958), p. 155.

66. Bardou, et al., *The Automobile Revolution*, p. 177.

67. Jordan Goodman, *Tobacco in History: The Cultures of Dependence* (London: Routledge, 1993), chs. 1 and 5.

68. Mary Ann Watson, *The Expanding Vista: American Television in the Kennedy Years* (New York and Oxford: Oxford University Press, 1990), pp. 174–7.

69. Vance Packard, *The Hidden Persuaders* (New York: David McKay, 1957), quoting from p. 97.

70. Quoted in Alistair Horne, *Harold Macmillan, 1957–1986* (London: Macmillan, 1989), p. 64.

71. Arthur Marwick, *British Society since 1945*, 2nd ed. (London: Penguin, 1990), p. 117.

72. Paul Ginsborg, *A History of Contemporary Italy: Society and Politics, 1943–1988* (London: Penguin, 1990), p. 239.

73. Serge Berstein, *The Republic of de Gaulle, 1958–1969*, trans. Peter Morris (Cambridge: Cambridge University Press, 1993), pp. 110, 146–8.

74. Hermann van der Wee, *Prosperity and Upheaval: The World Economy, 1945–1980* (London: Penguin, 1987), pp. 258–61.

75. Michael Chisholm, "The Increasing Separation of Production and Consumption," in B. L. Turner (princ. ed.), *The Earth as Transformed by Human Action: Global and Regional Changes in the Biosphere over the Past Three Hundred Years* (Cambridge: Cambridge University Press, 1990), pp. 95–6.

76. Joan Edelman Spero and Jeffrey A. Hart, *The Politics of International Economic Relations*, 5th ed. (London: Routledge, 1997), pp. 52–7, 215–21.

77. M. G. Graham and D. O. Hughes, *Containerisation in the 1980s* (London: Lloyd's of London Press, 1985), esp. pp. 31, 40–1, 196.

78. Ronald Hope, *A New History of British Shipping* (London: John Murray, 1990), p. 426.

79. Roy Porter, *London: A Social History* (London: Hamish Hamilton, 1994), pp. 348–9.

80. Rabi Narayan Acharya, *Television in India: A Sociological Study of Policies and Perspectives* (Delhi: Manas Publications, 1987), p. 16.

81. James Lull, *China Turned On: Television, Reform, and Resistance* (London and New York: Routledge, 1991), p. 20.

82. World Bank, *World Development Report, 1994: Infrastructure for Development* (Oxford: Oxford University Press, 1994), table 32.

83. Renfrew Christie, *Electricity, Industry and Class in South Africa* (Albany, NY: State University of New York Press, 1984), esp. pp. 159–61.

84. *World Development Report, 1994*, table A2.

85. L. P. Morris, *Eastern Europe since 1945* (London: Heinemann, 1984), pp. 149–57.

86. V. R. Berghahn, *Modern Germany: Society, Economy and Politics in the Twentieth Century* (Cambridge: Cambridge University Press, 1980), p. 275.

Chapter 6 Eyeball to Eyeball, Shoulder to Shoulder

1. Quotations from Stephen E. Ambrose, *Nixon: The Education of a Politician, 1913–1962* (New York: Simon and Schuster, 1987), pp. 523, 526.

2. Phraseology from Elaine Tyler May, *Homeward Bound: American Families in the Cold War Era* (New York: Basic Books, 1988), pp. 17, 164.

3. James T. Patterson, *America's Struggle against Poverty, 1900–1981* (Cambridge, Mass.: Harvard University Press, 1981), p. 80.

4. See Clyde A. Milner II, Carol A. O'Connor, and Martha A. Sandweiss, eds., *The Oxford History of the American West* (New York: Oxford University Press, 1994), esp. pp. 452–60, 482–97.

5. Quoted in William E. Leuchtenberg, *A Troubled Feast: American Society since 1945* (Boston: Little, Brown, 1973), pp. 110–1.

6. Quoted in David Halberstam, *The Best and the Brightest* (New York: Fawcett, 1972), p. 51.

7. Martin Malia, *The Soviet Tragedy: A History of Socialism in Russia, 1917–1991* (New York: Free Press, 1994), p. 315.

8. The comparison is from Alec Nove, *An Economic History of the USSR, 1917–1991*, 3rd ed. (London: Penguin, 1992), p. 340—whose chapter 12 is the source for most subsequent economic statistics.

9. Martin McCauley, *Khrushchev and the Development of Soviet Agriculture: The Virgin Lands Programme, 1953–1964* (London: Macmillan, 1976), esp. pp. 174–85.

10. Quoted by Stephen F. Cohen, *Rethinking the Soviet Experience: Politics and History since 1917* (New York: Oxford University Press, 1985), p. 111, who provides (ch. 4) an incisive account of the ideological dimension of Khrushchev's reforms.

11. Steven J. Zaloga, *Target America: The Soviet Union and the Strategic Arms Race, 1945–1964* (Novato, Calif.: Presidio, 1993), chs. 6–7, quoting from p. 145.

12. Quoted in Carl A. Linden, *Khrushchev and the Soviet Leadership*, 2nd ed. (Baltimore: Johns Hopkins University Press, 1990), pp. 92–3.

13. USIA survey cited in Walter A. McDougall, *The Heavens and the Earth: A Political History of the Space Age* (New York: Basic Books, 1985), pp. 240–1.

14. Letter from George Reedy, quoted in Robert Dallek, *Lone Star Rising: Lyndon Johnson and His Times, 1908–1960* (New York: Oxford University Press, 1991), p. 529.

15. Quoted in Barbara Barksdale Clowes, *Brainpower for the Cold War: The Sputnik Crisis and National Defense Education Act of 1958* (Westport, Conn.: Greenwood Press, 1981), p. 59.

16. Address of January 9, 1958, in *Public Papers of the Presidents of the United States: Dwight D. Eisenhower, 1958* (Washington, D.C.: Government Printing Office, 1959), p. 3.

17. Comments on February 4, 1958, in Stephen E. Ambrose, *Eisenhower: the President* (New York: Touchstone, 1985), p. 458.

18. NSC meeting 331, item 2, July 18, 1957, Ann Whitman File, NSC series, Box 9, Dwight D. Eisenhower Library, Abilene, Kansas.

19. Eisenhower, *Public Papers, 1960–1961*, pp. 1035–40.

20. McDougall, *The Heavens and the Earth*, p. 272.

21. Zaloga, *Target America*, p. 191.

22. Dino Brugioni, quoted in Christopher Andrew, *For the President's Eyes Only: Secret Intelligence and the American Presidency from Washington to Bush* (London: HarperCollins, 1995), p. 250.

23. Quoted in Zaloga, *Target America*, p. 195.

24. Sergei Khrushchev, *Khrushchev on Khrushchev: An Inside Account of the Man and His Era*, ed. and trans. William Taubman (Boston: Little, Brown, 1990), p. 356.

25. *Public Papers of the Presidents of the United States: John F. Kennedy, 1961* (Washington, D.C.: Government Printing Office, 1962), pp. 1–3.

26. Among recent biographies that go beyond the early hagiography, see Thomas C. Reeves, *A Question of Character: A Life of John F. Kennedy* (London: Arrow Books, 1992).

27. The phrase is from Vladislav Zubok and Constantine Pleshakov, *Inside the Kremlin's Cold War: From Stalin to Khrushchev* (Cambridge, Mass.: Harvard University Press, 1996), p. 243.

28. Quotations from Michael R. Beschloss, *The Crisis Years: Kennedy and Khrushchev, 1960–1963* (New York: HarperCollins, 1991), pp. 223, 225.

29. Herbert S. Parmet, *JFK: The Presidency of John F. Kennedy* (New York: Penguin, 1984), p. 221.

30. Lansdale memo, "The Cuba Project," February 20, 1962, in Laurence Chang and Peter Kornbluh, eds., *The Cuban Missile Crisis, 1962: A National Security Archive Documents Reader* (New York: New Press, 1992), pp. 24–5.

31. Quoted in James A. Blight and David A. Welch, eds., *On the Brink: Americans and Soviets Reexamine the Cuban Missile Crisis*, 2nd ed. (New York: Noonday Press, 1990), p. 329.

32. See Barton J. Bernstein, "Reconsidering the Missile Crisis: Dealing with the Problems of the American Jupiters in Turkey," in James A. Nathan, ed., *The Cuban Missile Crisis Revisited* (New York: St. Martin's, 1994), esp. pp. 58–63.

33. According to the historian Dmitri Volkogonov, as quoted in Yuri Pavlov, *Soviet-Cuban Alliance: 1959–1991* (Miami: University of Miami Press, 1994), p. 32.

34. Quotations from Ernest R. May and Phillip D. Zelikow, eds., *The Kennedy Tapes: Inside the White House during the Cuban Missile Crisis* (Cambridge, Mass.: Harvard University Press, 1997), p. 39.

35. CIA Estimate, "The Military Buildup in Cuba," Sept. 19, 1962, in Chang and Kornbluh, eds., *Cuban Missile Crisis*, p. 65. The CIA director, John A. McCone, did not share this view, however.

36. See Elizabeth Cohn's essay on ExComm in Nathan, ed., *The Cuban Missile Crisis Revisited,* ch. 7.

37. Kennedy, *Public Papers, 1962,* p. 808.

38. Aleksandr Fursenko and Timothy Naftali, *"One Hell of a Gamble": Khrushchev, Castro, and Kennedy, 1958–1964* (New York: Norton, 1997), pp. 240–3.

39. Robert F. Kennedy, *Thirteen Days: The Cuban Missile Crisis* (London: Pan, 1969), p. 71.

40. Beschloss, *Crisis Years,* p. 498.

41. Fursenko and Naftali, *"One Hell of a Gamble,"* pp. 273–7.

42. Zaloga, *Target America,* p. 213.

43. Text in Chang and Kornbluh, ed., *Cuban Missile Crisis,* pp. 185–8.

44. According to the recollections of Dean Rusk in and after 1987: see Blight and Welch, *On the Brink,* pp. 83–4.

45. See, for instance, the exchange in *Cold War International History Project Bulletin,* 3 (Fall 1993), pp. 40–50.

46. Quoted in Paul B. Stares, *The Militarization of Space: U.S. Policy, 1945–1984* (Ithaca, N.Y.: Cornell University Press, 1985), p. 236.

47. As affirmed by the journalist Seymour Hersh, otherwise a habitual conspiracy theorist, in *The Dark Side of Camelot* (London: HarperCollins, 1998), pp. 450–1.

48. James N. Giglio, *The Presidency of John F. Kennedy* (Lawrence: University of Kansas Press, 1991), p. 260—also the source for the Castro quote, above.

49. Werner G. Hahn, *The Politics of Soviet Agriculture, 1960–1970* (Baltimore: Johns Hopkins University Press, 1972), p. 84.

50. Quoted in Sergei Khrushchev, *Khrushchev on Khrushchev,* p. 154.

51. Diary entry, November 4, 1962, in Alistair Horne, *Macmillan, 1957–1986* (London: Macmillan, 1989), p. 380.

52. Quoted in Hans-Peter Schwarz, "Adenauer et la crise de Cuba," in Maurice Vaïsse, ed., *L'Europe et la crise de Cuba* (Paris: Armand Colin, 1993), p. 86.

53. *The Economist,* December 29, 1962, p. 1253.

54. State Department briefing paper, December 13, 1962, quoted in Ian Clark, *Nuclear Diplomacy and the Special Relationship: Britain's Deterrent and America, 1957–1962* (Oxford: Clarendon, 1994), p. 410.

55. Quotations from the official French translation, pp. 7, 9, and 10, copy in John F. Kennedy Library, Boston, Mass., NSF 73: France.

56. Quoted in Alfred Grosser, *The Western Alliance: European-American Relations since 1945,* trans. Michael Shaw (London: Macmillan, 1980), p. 207.

57. See table in Simon Duke, *United States Military Forces and Installations in Europe* (Oxford: Oxford University Press, 1989), p. 64.

58. See Michael M. Harrison, *The Reluctant Ally: France and Atlantic Security* (Baltimore: Johns Hopkins University Press, 1981), ch. 4.

59. Quoted in Harold Macmillan, *At the End of the Day, 1961–1963* (London: Macmillan, 1973), p. 365.

60. Stephen George, *Politics and Policy in the European Community* (Oxford: Oxford University Press, 1985), p. 11.

61. Jean Lacouture, *De Gaulle: The Ruler, 1945–1970*, trans. Alan Sheridan (New York: Norton, 1993), p. 359.

62. Quoted in Richard F. Kuisel, *Seducing the French: The Dilemma of Americanization* (Berkeley: University of California Press, 1993), p. 148.

63. For these arguments see Philip G. Cerny, *The Politics of Grandeur: Ideological Aspects of de Gaulle's Foreign Policy* (Cambridge: Cambridge University Press, 1980), p. 2ff.

64. Jonathan Steinberg, *Why Switzerland?* (Cambridge: Cambridge University Press, 1976), p. 82, table 3.2.

65. Derek Aldcroft, *The European Economy, 1914–1970* (London: Croom Helm, 1978), p. 163.

66. As discussed in Jose Harris, "Enterprise and Welfare States: A Comparative Perspective," *Transactions of the Royal Historical Society*, 5th series, vol. 40 (1990), pp. 179–84.

67. Andrew Gamble, *Britain in Decline: Economic Policy, Political Strategy and the British State*, 2nd ed. (London: Macmillan, 1985), pp. 109–11, 244.

68. See Clive Ponting, *Breach of Promise: Labour in Power, 1964–1970* (London: Hamish Hamilton, 1989), esp. chs. 3–4.

69. George, *Politics and Policy in the European Community*, pp. 57–8.

70. B. W. E. Alford, *British Economic Performance, 1945–1975* (London: Macmillan, 1988), p. 105.

71. Donald Sassoon, *Contemporary Italy: Politics, Economy, and Society since 1945* (London: Longman, 1986), pp. 42–65, 98–9, 123–31; and David Hine, *Governing Italy: The Politics of Bargained Pluralism* (Oxford: Clarendon, 1993), pp. 35–48.

72. Paul Ginsborg, *A History of Contemporary Italy: Society and Politics, 1943–1988* (London: Penguin, 1990), ch. 9, esp. pp. 299, 316.

73. Klaus Hildebrand, *Von Erhard zur Grossen Koalition, 1963–1969* (Stuttgart: Deutsche Verlags-Anstalt, 1984), pp. 365–83, quoting from p. 380.

74. See generally Keith A. Reader, with Khursheed Wadia, *The May 1968 Events in France: Reproductions and Interpretations* (New York: St Martin's, 1993), chs. 1–2.

75. Quoted in Bernard E. Brown, *Protest in Paris: Anatomy of a Revolt* (Morristown, N.J.: General Learning Press, 1974), p. 19.

76. Lacouture, *De Gaulle: The Ruler*, pp. 544–54; for the "tactical retreat" argument, see, e.g., Hugues Portelli, *La politique en France sous la Ve République* (Paris: Bernard Grasset, 1987), pp. 110–11.

77. As emphasized in Georges Lefranc, *Le Mouvement Syndical de la Libération aux Événements de mai–juin 1968* (Paris: Payot, 1969), p. 250.

78. Hans-Dieter Lucas, *Europa vom Atlantik bis zum Ural?: Europapolitik und Europadenken im Frankreich der Ära de Gaulle, 1958–1969* (Bonn: Bouvier Verlag, 1992), p. 419.

79. See generally R. J. Crampton, *Eastern Europe in the Twentieth Century* (London and New York: Routledge, 1994), chs. 17–18; Geoffrey Swain and Nigel Swain, *Eastern Europe since 1945* (London: Macmillan, 1993), ch. 6.

80. George Schöpflin, *Politics in Eastern Europe, 1945–1992* (Oxford: Blackwell, 1993), p. 138.

81. Ivan T. Berend, *The Hungarian Economic Reforms, 1953–1988* (Cambridge: Cambridge University Press, 1990), ch. 18.

82. Swain and Swain, *Eastern Europe*, p. 151.

83. Barbara Jelavich, *History of the Balkans,* vol. 2, *Twentieth Century* (Cambridge and New York: Cambridge University Press, 1983), pp. 392–3.

84. Galia Golan, *The Czechoslovak Reform Movement: Communism in Crisis, 1962–1968* (Cambridge: Cambridge University Press, 1971), pp. 12–13. This remains a useful study of the 1960s.

85. Quotations from Eugen Steiner, *The Slovak Dilemma* (Cambridge: Cambridge University Press, 1973), p. 120.

86. Gordon Skilling, *Czechoslovakia's Interrupted Revolution* (Princeton, N.J.: Princeton University Press, 1976), p. 169.

87. Skilling, *Czechoslovakia's Interrupted Revolution*, p. 219.

88. Karen Dawisha, *The Kremlin and the Prague Spring* (Berkeley and London: University of California, 1984), p. 165.

89. Jiri Valenta, *Soviet Intervention in Czechoslovakia, 1968: Anatomy of a Decision* (Baltimore and London: Johns Hopkins University Press, 1979), p. 136. Valenta and Dawisha are the basic pre-glasnost accounts of Soviet policy, albeit from different conceptual angles, but see also Mark Kramer, "The Prague Spring and the Soviet Invasion of Czechoslovakia: New Interpretations," *Cold War International History Project Bulletin,* 3 (Fall 1993), 2–13, 54–5.

90. Quoted in William Shawcross, *Dubček* (London: Weidenfeld and Nicolson, 1970), p. 175.

91. Quoted in Harry Schwartz, *Prague's Two Hundred Days: The Struggle for Democracy in Czechoslovakia* (London: Pall Mall Press, 1969), p. 217.

92. Quotations from Joseph L. Nogee and Robert H. Donaldson, *Soviet Foreign Policy since World War II* (New York and Oxford: Pergamon Press, 1981), p. 226.

93. See Andrei Sakharov, *Memoirs,* trans. Richard Lourie (London: Hutchinson, 1990), ch. 20.

94. Alfred Grosser, *The Western Alliance: European-American Relations since 1945,* trans. Michael Shaw (London: Macmillan, 1980), p. 249.

Chapter 7 Color, Creed, and Coups

1. Quoted in Elazar Barkan, *The Retreat of Scientific Racism: Changing Concepts of Race in Britain and the United States between the World Wars* (Cambridge: Cambridge University Press, 1992), p. 341.

2. A theme of the most comprehensive recent overview in English by Ivan Hannaford, *Race: The History of an Idea in the West* (Baltimore: Johns Hopkins University Press, 1996). See also Michael Banton, *Racial Theories* (Cambridge: Cambridge University Press, 1967).

3. It first appears in the *Oxford English Dictionary* in 1972. See Barkan, *Retreat of Scientific Racism*, p. 3.

4. Quoted in Michael R. Marrus, *The Holocaust in History* (London: Penguin, 1993), p. 5.

5. Quotations from James E. Young, *The Texture of Memory: Holocaust Memorials and Meaning* (New Haven: Yale University Press, 1993), ch. 9.

6. Harvie Wilkinson III, *From Brown to Bakke: The Supreme Court and School Integration: 1954–1978* (New York: Oxford University Press, 1979), p. 65.

7. Quoted in Stephen B. Oates, *Let the Trumpet Sound: The Life of Martin Luther King, Jr.* (New York: Mentor, 1985), p. 75.

8. Quoted in Arthur M. Schlesinger, Jr., *Robert Kennedy and His Times* (New York: Ballantine Books, 1978), p. 321.

9. Juan Williams, *Eyes on the Prize: America's Civil Rights Years, 1954–1965* (New York: Viking Penguin, 1987), pp. 204–5.

10. See Hugh Davis Graham, *The Civil Rights Era: Origins and Development of National Policy, 1960–1972* (New York: Oxford University Press, 1990), p. 151.

11. Steven F. Lawson, *Black Ballots: Voting Rights in the South, 1944–1969* (New York: Columbia University Press, 1976), p. 331.

12. See Jack Bass and Walter DeVries, *The Transformation of Southern Politics: Social Change and Political Consequence since 1945* (New York: Basic Books, 1976), quoting respectively from pp. 47, 62, and 68.

13. Robert Weisbrot, *Freedom Bound: A History of America's Civil Rights Movement* (New York: Norton, 1990), p. 154.

14. See figures in David Armstrong, *The Rise of the International Organization: A Short History* (London: Macmillan, 1982), pp. 60–1.

15. Quoted in James Barber and John Barratt, *South Africa's Foreign Policy: The Search for Status and Security, 1945–1988* (Cambridge: Cambridge University Press, 1990), p. 90.

16. Quoted in Michael Crowder, ed., *The Cambridge History of Africa*, vol. 8 (Cambridge: Cambridge University Press, 1984), pp. 762, 764.

17. Thomas H. Henriksen, *Revolution and Counterrevolution: Mozambique's War of Independence, 1964–1974* (London: Greenwood Press, 1983), pp. 4, 41.

18. Quoted in J. D. Hargreaves, *Decolonization in Africa* (London: Longman, 1988), p. 215.

19. Quoted in Ben Pimlott, *Harold Wilson* (London: HarperCollins, 1992), p. 377.

20. Quoted in Basil Davidson, *In the Eye of the Storm: Angola's Peoples* (London: Longman, 1972), p. 279.

21. As argued by Terence Ranger, *Peasant Consciousness and Guerrilla War in Zimbabwe: A Comparative Study* (London: James Currey, 1985), esp. chs. 4–5.

22. Quotations from Nelson Mandela, *Long Walk to Freedom* (London: Little, Brown, 1994), pp. 346, 354.

23. Quoted in Lindy Wilson, "Bantu Stephen Biko: A Life," in N. Barney Pityana et al., eds, *Bounds of Possibility: The Legacy of Steve Biko and Black Consciousness* (London: Zed Books, 1991), p. 50.

24. Quoted in Yunus Mohamed, "The Power of Consciousness: Black Politics, 1967–77," in Robin Cohen et al., eds, *Repression and Resistance: Insider Accounts of Apartheid* (London: Hans Zell, 1990), p. 267.

25. Quoted in Zig Layton-Henry, *The Politics of Immigration: Immigration, "Race," and "Race" Relations in Post-War Britain* (Oxford: Blackwell, 1992), pp. 80–1.

26. Quoted in Gary P. Freeman, *Immigrant Labor and Racial Conflict in Industrial Societies: The French and British Experience, 1945–1975* (Princeton, N.J.: Princeton University Press, 1979), p. 144.

27. Cf. Hannaford, *Race*, p. 390.

28. Quoted in Freeman, *Immigrant Labor*, p. 98.

29. Crawford Young, *Politics in the Congo: Decolonization and Independence* (Princeton, N.J.: Princeton University Press, 1965), remains essential.

30. I am following here the argument in Larry Diamond, *Class, Ethnicity and Democracy in Nigeria: The Failure of the First Republic* (London: Macmillan, 1988).

31. Detail from Herbert Ekwe-Ekwe, *The Biafra War: Nigeria and the Aftermath* (Lampeter: Edwin Mellen Press, 1990), esp. pp. 73, 98–9.

32. Abioseh Nicol, "The Meaning of Africa," in Jacob Drachler, ed., *African Heritage: Intimate Views of the Black Africans from Life, Lore, and Literature* (New York: Crowell-Collier, 1963), p. 122.

33. Richard Sandbrook, with Judith Barker, *The Politics of Africa's Economic Stagnation* (Cambridge: Cambridge University Press, 1985), pp. 76–81.

34. Quoted in Ruth First, *Power in Africa: Political Power in Africa and the Coup d'Etat* (Baltimore: Penguin, 1972), p. 1, on which this paragraph draws.

35. D. K. Fieldhouse, *Black Africa, 1945–80: Economic Decolonization and Arrested Development* (London: Allen & Unwin, 1986), p. 242.

36. Tony Killick, *Development Economics in Action: A Study of Economic Policies in Ghana* (London: Heinemann, 1978), quoting respectively from pp. 44 and 42.

37. The declaration is printed in Julius K. Nyerere, *Freedom and Socialism: A Selection from Writings and Speeches, 1965–1987* (Dar es Salaam: Oxford University Press, 1968), pp. 231–50.

38. See Fidelis Mtatifikolo, "Population Dynamics and Socioeconomic Development in Tanzania," in Moriba Touré and T. O. Fadoyomi, eds, *Migrations, Development and Urbanization in Sub-Saharan Africa* (Dakar: CODESRIA, 1992), pp. 213–36.

39. William R. Ochieng', *A Modern History of Kenya, 1895–1980* (London and Nairobi: Evans Brothers, 1989), pp. 209–10.

40. See Peter Lionel Wickins, *Africa, 1880–1980: An Economic History* (Cape Town: Oxford University Press, 1986), p. 216.

41. Crowder, ed., *Cambridge History of Africa*, vol. 8, pp. 205–6.

42. See Joan E. Spero, *The Politics of International Economic Relations*, 2nd ed. (London: Allen & Unwin, 1981), p. 163.

43. Quoted in Robert Brent Toplin, *Freedom and Prejudice: The Legacy of Slavery in the United States and Brazil* (Westport, Conn.: Greenwood Press, 1981), p. 9

44. Statistics from Leslie Bethell, ed., *The Cambridge History of Latin America*, vol. VI, part 1 (Cambridge: Cambridge University Press, 1994), pp. 29–31, 329.

45. Janice E. Perlman, *The Myth of Marginality: Urban Poverty and Politics in Rio de Janeiro* (Berkeley: University of California Press, 1976), p. 58. On general trends in racial attitudes, see Thomas E. Skidmore, *Black into White: Race and Nationality in Brazilian Thought* (New York: Oxford University Press, 1974), pp. 207–18.

46. See Werner Baer, *The Brazilian Economy: Its Growth and Development* (Columbus, Ohio: Grid Publishing Co., 1979), esp. pp. 101–3, 186–7.

47. Paul E. Sigmund, *The Overthrow of Allende and the Politics of Chile, 1964–1976* (Pittsburgh: University of Pittsburgh Press, 1978), remains essential.

48. For this argument see Wesson, *The Latin American Military Institution*, esp. pp. 197–8; also Alfred Stepan, "The New Professionalization of Internal Warfare and Military Role Expansion," in Abraham F. Lowenthal, ed., *Armies and Politics in Latin America* (New York: Holmes and Meier, 1976), pp. 244–60.

49. See Juan Carlos Portantiero, "Political and Economic Crises in Argentina," in Guido di Tella and Rudiger Dornbusch, eds., *The Political Economy of Argentina, 1946–83* (London: Macmillan, 1989), ch. 2, quoting from p. 22.

50. Quotations from Walter LaFeber, *Inevitable Revolutions: The United States in Central America* (New York: Norton, 1983), pp. 157–8.

51. Quoted in LaFeber, *Inevitable Revolutions*, p. 159.

52. Quoted in Peter Hebblethwaite, *John XXIII: Pope of the Council* (London: Geoffrey Chapman, 1984), p. 444.

53. See the comparative analysis in Michael Fleet, *The Rise and Fall of Chilean Christian Democracy* (Princeton, N.J.: Princeton University Press, 1985), ch. 6.

54. Quoted in Gustavo Gutiérrez, *A Theology of Liberation: History, Politics, and Salvation*. 2nd ed. (London: SCM Books, 1988), p. 63.

55. See discussion in Michael Dodson, "Liberation Theology and Christian Radicalism in Contemporary Latin America," *Journal of Latin American Studies*, 11 (1979): 203–22.

56. Dietrich Bonhoeffer, *Letters and Papers from Prison* (London: Fontana, 1959), p. 115.

57. Hugh McLeod, *Religion and People of Western Europe, 1789–1970* (Oxford: Oxford University Press, 1981), p. 139.

58. Quotations from David L. Edwards, *Religion and Change* (London: Hodder and Stoughton, 1969), pp. 18–19.

59. John Madeley, "Politics and Religion in Western Europe," in George Moyser, ed., *Politics and Religion in the Modern World* (London: Routledge, 1991), p. 64.

60. On American religion, see generally Kenneth D. Wald, *Religion and Politics in the United States,* 2nd ed. (New York: St. Martin's, 1992).

61. See R. F. Foster, *Modern Ireland, 1600–1972* (London: Penguin, 1989), pp. 533–4, 544.

62. David Harkness, *Northern Ireland since 1920* (Dublin: Helicon, 1983), p. 173.

63. Eric Hobsbawm, *Nations and Nationalism since 1780: Programme, Myth, Reality,* 2nd ed. (Cambridge: Cambridge University Press, 1992), p. 172.

64. Robert Bothwell, Ian Drummond, John English, *Canada since 1945: Power, Politics, and Provincialism,* 2nd ed. (Toronto: University of Toronto Press, 1989), p. 266. I have made extensive use of Chapters 23 and 28 for this section.

65. Quoted in David V. J. Bell, *The Roots of Diversity: A Study of Canadian Political Culture,* 2nd ed. (Toronto: Oxford University Press, 1992), p. 111—on whose general analysis this section also draws.

66. Quotations from Moyser, ed., *Politics and Religion in the Modern World,* p. 89.

67. Jan Jerschina, "The Catholic Church, the Communist State, and the Polish People," in Stanislaw Gomulka and Antony Polonsky, eds., *Polish Paradoxes* (London: Routledge, 1990), p. 78. In general, this section draws on Trevor Beeson, *Discretion and Valour: Religious Conditions in Russia and Eastern Europe,* 2nd ed. (London: Collins, 1982).

68. Generally see Howard M. Sachar, *A History of Israel: From the Rise of Zionism to Our Times* (New York: Alfred A. Knopf, 1988), chs. XVIII–XX.

69. P. J. Vatikiotis, *Nasser and His Generation* (London: Croom Helm, 1978), p. 206.

70. See the reconstruction using Russian and Egyptian evidence by Richard B. Parker, "The June 1967 War: Some Mysteries Explored," *The Middle East Journal,* 46/2 (Spring 1992), 177–97.

71. Galia Golan, *Soviet Policies in the Middle East: From World War II to Gorbachev* (Cambridge: Cambridge University Press, 1990), pp. 61–2.

72. According to Anwar el-Sadat, *In Search of Identity: An Autobiography* (London: Fontana, 1978), p. 210. See also Parker, "The June 1967 War," esp. pp. 192–5.

73. See William B. Quandt, *Peace Process: American Diplomacy and the Arab-Israeli Conflict since 1967* (Washington, D.C.: Brookings Institution, 1993), chs. 2–3, quoting from pp. 41, 47, 48.

74. Quotations from Michael Brecher, with Benjamin Geist, *Decisions in Crisis: Israel, 1967 and 1973* (Berkeley: University of California Press, 1980), respectively pp. 95 and 39. Chapters 2, 5, and 8 of this book provide a day-by-day policy analysis.

75. Abba Eban, "Israel's Dilemmas: An Opportunity Squandered," in Stephen J. Roth, ed., *The Impact of the Six-Day War: A Twenty-Year Assessment* (London: Macmillan, 1988), p. 25.

76. Derek Hopwood, *Egypt: Politics and Society, 1945–1981* (London: Allen & Unwin, 1982), p. 184.

77. Quoted in Yvonne Haddad, "Islamists and the 'Problem of Israel': The 1967 Awakening," *Middle East Journal* 46/2 (1992), p. 274.

78. Quoted in Fouad Ajami, *The Arab Predicament: Arab Political Thought since 1967* (Cambridge: Cambridge University Press, 1981), p. 36.

79. For this account see particularly Helena Cobban, *The Palestinian Liberation Organisation: People, Power and Politics* (Cambridge: Cambridge University Press, 1984), chs. 1–3.

80. On this point see Marion Farouk-Sluglett and Peter Sluglett, *Iraq since 1958: From Revolution to Dictatorship* (London: I. B. Tauris, 1990), p. 109.

81. Jawarharlal Nehru, *The Discovery of India* (London: Meridian Books, 1946), p. 485.

82. See Steven A. Hoffmann, *India and the China Crisis* (Berkeley: University of California, 1990), esp. pp. 123–4, 238.

83. Quoted in Sarvepalli Gopal, *Jawaharlal Nehru: A Biography*, vol. 3 (London: Jonathan Cape, 1984), pp. 228–9.

84. Speech of October 25, 1962, in Gopal, *Nehru*, vol. 3, p. 223.

85. Quotations from Swaran Singh and Zhulfikar Ali Bhutto in Denis Wright, *India-Pakistan Relations, 1962–1969* (New Delhi: Sterling Publishers, 1989), p. 59.

86. Surjit Mansingh, *India's Search for Power: Indira Gandhi's Foreign Policy, 1966–1982* (New Delhi: Sage, 1984), p. 34.

87. On this period see generally Lawrence Ziring, *The Ayub Khan Era: Politics in Pakistan, 1958–1969* (Syracuse, N.Y.: Syracuse University Press, 1971).

88. Omar Noman, *The Political Economy of Pakistan, 1947–85* (London: Kegan Paul International, 1988), pp. 41–2.

89. Tajuddin Ahmad, premier of the exile government, on April 17, 1971, quoted in G. W. Choudury, *The Last Days of United Pakistan* (London: C. Hurst & Co., 1974), p. 186.

90. See Richard Sisson and Leo E. Rose, *War and Secession: Pakistan, India, and the Creation of Bangladesh* (Berkeley: University of California, 1990), esp. chs. 9–11.

91. See the analysis in Ayesha Jalal, *The State of Martial Rule: The Origins of Pakistan's Political Economy of Defence* (Cambridge: Cambridge University Press, 1990).

92. A point emphasized by Sugata Bose and Ayesha Jalal, *Modern South Asia: History, Culture, Political Economy* (London: Routledge, 1998), p. 242.

93. Sunil Khilnani, *The Idea of India* (London: Penguin, 1998), p. 29.

94. See the discussion by Nasir Islam, "Islam and National Identity: The Case of Pakistan and Bangladesh," *International Journal of Middle East Studies*, 13 (1981): 55–72. For a general history see Lawrence Ziring, *Bangladesh: From Mujib to Ershad, An Interpretive Study* (Karachi: Oxford University Press, 1992).

Chapter 8 East Wind, West Wind

1. Quoted in John Wilson Lewis and Xue Litai, *China Builds the Bomb* (Stanford: Stanford University Press, 1988), p. 68.

2. David Arnold, *Famine: Social Crisis and Historical Change* (Oxford: Blackwell, 1988), p. 20.

3. Quoted in J. D. Legge, *Sukarno: A Political Biography* (London: Allen Lane, 1972), p. 351.

4. Stuart Schram, *The Thought of Mao Tse-Tung* (Cambridge: Cambridge University Press, 1989), p. 120.

5. David Bachman, *Bureaucracy, Economy, and Leadership in China: The Institutional Origins of the Great Leap Forward* (Cambridge: Cambridge University Press, 1991), p. 1.

6. On the Great Leap, the standard work remains Roderick MacFarquhar, *The Origins of the Cultural Revolution*, vol. 2, *The Great Leap Forward, 1958–1960* (Oxford: Oxford University Press, 1983).

7. Penny Kane, *Famine in China, 1959–1961: Demographic and Social Implications* (London: Macmillan, 1988), pp. 64, 117.

8. Dali L. Yang, *Calamity and Reform in China: State, Rural Society, and Institutional Change since the Great Leap Forward* (Stanford: Stanford University Press, 1996), p. 34.

9. Carl Riskin, *China's Political Economy: The Quest for Development since 1949* (Oxford: Oxford University Press, 1991), p. 126.

10. Willy Kraus, *Economic Development and Social Change in the People's Republic of China*, trans. E. M. Holz (Berlin: Springer-Verlag, 1982), pp. 161, 338.

11. See Anita Chan, Richard Madsen, and Jonathan Unger, *Chen Village: The Recent History of a Peasant Community in Mao's China* (Berkeley: University of California Press, 1984).

12. Yang, *Calamity and Reform in China*, pp. 37–8, surveys the various estimates.

13. For efforts at reconstruction see Kane, *Famine in China*, and Basil Ashton et al., "Famine in China, 1958–61," *Population and Development Review* 10 (1984): 613–45.

14. For reconstruction, based on oral testimony, see Jaspar Becker, *Hungry Ghosts: China's Secret Famine* (London: John Murray, 1996), esp. ch. 13.

15. Roderick MacFarquhar and John K. Fairbank, eds., *The Cambridge History of China*, vol. 14 (Cambridge: Cambridge University Press, 1987), p. 395.

16. Quoted in Michael B. Yahuda, *China's Role in World Affairs* (London: Croom Helm, 1978), p. 109.

17. For details see Lewis and Xue, *China Builds the Bomb*, esp. pp. 130 (Chen), 153–4, and 160–1.

18. Zhisui Li, *The Private Life of Chairman Mao: The Memoirs of Mao's Personal Physician* (London: Arrow Books, p. 120. See generally chapters 11 and 45.

19. Ross Terrill, *Mao: A Biography*, 2nd ed. (New York: Touchstone, 1993), p. 311. Chapter 17 provides a vivid account of this phase of his life.

20. Schram, *The Thought of Mao Tse-Tung*, pp. 158–71.

21. See Roderick MacFarquhar and John K. Fairbank, eds., *The Cambridge History of China*, vol. 15 (Cambridge: Cambridge University Press, 1991), pp. 140–1.

22. For this and subsequent paragraphs I have drawn particularly on Julia Kwong, *Cultural Revolution in China's Schools, May 1966–April 1969* (Stanford: Stanford University Press, 1988) and also Stanley Rosen, *Red Guard Factionalism and the Cultural Revolution in Guangzhou [Canton]* (Boulder, Colo.: Westview Press, 1982).

23. See the account in Jacques Guillermaz, *The Chinese Communist Party in Power, 1949–1976*, trans. Anne Destenay (Folkestone: Dawson, 1982), pp. 390–3.

24. Quoted in Kwong, *Cultural Revolution*, p. 33.

25. Jung Chang, *Wild Swans: Three Daughters of China* (London: Flamingo, 1993), p. 382.

26. Rosen, *Red Guard Factionalism*, pp. 244–7.

27. Quoted in Kwong, *Cultural Revolution*, pp. 131–2.

28. Bill Brugger and Stephen Reglar, *Politics, Economy and Society in Contemporary China* (London: Macmillan, 1994), p. 324.

29. Quoted in Roger Hilsman, *To Move a Nation: The Politics of Foreign Policy in the Administration of John F. Kennedy* (New York: Delta, 1967), p. 310.

30. See Arthur Waldron, "From Non-Existent to Almost Normal: U.S.–China Relations in the 1960s," in Diane B. Kunz, ed., *The Diplomacy of the Crucial Decade: American Foreign Relations during the 1960s* (New York: Columbia University Press, 1994), esp. pp. 223–37.

31. Quoted in Yahuda, *China's Role in World Affairs*, p. 133.

32. Quoted in Andrew Hall Wedeman, *The East Wind Subsides: Chinese Foreign Policy and the Origins of the Cultural Revolution* (Washington, D.C.: Washington Institute Press, 1987), p. 100.

33. For a useful overview, see John L. S. Girling, *Thailand: Society and Politics* (Ithaca, N.Y.: Cornell University Press, 1981).

34. Press article of March 10, 1959, quoted in David K. Wyatt, *A Short History of Thailand* (New Haven: Yale University Press, 1984), p. 280.

35. Josef Silverstein, *Burma: Military Rule and the Politics of Stagnation* (Ithaca, N.Y.: Cornell University Press, 1977), esp. pp. 161–2.

36. For an overview, see James P. Ongkili, *Nation-Building in Malaysia, 1946–1974* (Singapore: Oxford University Press, 1985), chs. 5–6.

37. The basic study remains J. A. C. Mackie's judicious *Konfrontasi: The Indonesia-Malaysia Dispute, 1963–1966* (Kuala Lumpur: Oxford University Press, 1974).

38. See generally Ide Anak Agung Gde Agung, *Twenty Years Indonesian Foreign Policy, 1945–1965* (The Hague: Mouton, 1973), esp. chs. 9–10, 14–16.

39. M. C. Ricklefs, *A History of Modern Indonesia*, 2nd ed. (London: Macmillan, 1993), chs. 18–19, provides a good overview.

40. On this theme, see Harold Crouch, *The Army and Politics in Indonesia,* 2nd ed. (Ithaca, N.Y.: Cornell University Press, 1988), esp. chs. 1–2.

41. Quotations from J. D. Legge, *Sukarno: A Political Biography* (London: Allen Lane, 1972), pp. 350, 352, and 365.

42. See the discussion in Mackie, *Konfrontasi,* pp. 179–94.

43. Agung, *Twenty Years Indonesian Foreign Policy,* p. 504.

44. David Mozingo, *Chinese Policy towards Indonesia, 1949–1967* (Ithaca, N.Y.: Cornell University Press, 1976), ch. 7, esp. p. 219.

45. Rex Mortimer, *Indonesian Communism under Sukarno: Ideology and Politics, 1959–1965* (Ithaca, N.Y.: Cornell University Press, 1974), ch. 7.

46. Mortimer, *Indonesian Communism,* pp. 366–7. Membership of the PKI itself was probably over three million.

47. Quoted in Brian May, *The Indonesian Tragedy* (London: Routledge and Kegan Paul, 1978), p. 89.

48. For detailed scholarly accounts stressing either PKI centrality or marginality, see respectively J. M. van der Kroef, "Origins of the 1965 Coup in Indonesia: Probabilities and Alternatives," *Journal of Southeast Asian Studies,* 3 (1972): 277–98, and Mortimer, *Indonesian Communism,* pp. 392–4, 413–41. What follows accords more with the argument of Crouch, *Army and Politics in Indonesia,* ch. 4.

49. Olle Törnquist, *Dilemmas of Third World Communism: The Destruction of the PKI in Indonesia* (London: Zed Books, 1984), p. 54.

50. For recent work, see Adrian Vickers, "Reopening Old Wounds: Bali and the Indonesian Killings—A Review Article," *Journal of Asian Studies,* 57 (1998): 774–85.

51. H. W. Brands, "The Limits of Manipulation: How the United States Didn't Topple Sukarno," *Journal of American History,* 76 (1989): 785–808.

52. See David P. Chandler, *The Tragedy of Cambodian History: Politics, War, and Revolution since 1945,* 2nd ed. (New Haven: Yale University Press, 1993), esp. ch. 3.

53. See Anthony Short, *The Origins of the Vietnam War* (London: Longman, 1989), pp. 227–33.

54. William J. Duiker, *Sacred War: Nationalism and Revolution in a Divided Vietnam* (New York: McGraw-Hill, 1995), p. 137.

55. Quoted in George C. Herring, *America's Longest War: The United States and Vietnam, 1950–1975,* 2nd ed. (New York: Alfred A. Knopf, 1986), p. 43.

56. Comments to James Reston, quoted in David Halberstam, *The Best and the Brightest* (New York: Fawcett, 1973), p. 97.

57. See Takashi Inoguchi and Daniel I. Okimoto, eds., *The Political Economy of Japan,* vol. II (Stanford: Stanford University Press, 1988), p. 220.

58. Tadashi Aruga, "The Security Treaty Revision of 1960," in Akira Iriye and Warren I. Cohen, eds., *The United States and Japan in the Postwar World* (Lexington: University Press of Kentucky, 1989), pp. 61–79.

59. Joungwoon Alexander Kim, *Divided Korea: The Politics of Development, 1945–1972* (Cambridge, Mass.: Harvard University Press, 1975), p. 209.

60. Arthur M. Schlesinger, Jr., *A Thousand Days: John F. Kennedy in the White House* (New York: Fawcett, 1971), p. 505.

61. For a good survey of the Kennedy period, see Lawrence J. Bassett and Stephen E. Pelz, "The Failed Search for Victory: Vietnam and the Politics of War," in Thomas G. Paterson, ed., *Kennedy's Quest for Victory: American Foreign Policy, 1961–1963* (New York: Oxford University Press, 1989), pp. 223–52.

62. Quoted by Robert D. Schulzinger, " 'It's Easy to Win a War on Paper': The United States and Vietnam, 1961–1968," in Kunz, ed., *The Diplomacy of the Crucial Decade*, p. 188.

63. Quoted in Clarence R. Wyatt, *Paper Soldiers: The American Press and the Vietnam War* (New York: Norton, 1993), p. 102.

64. Notes of White House conference, August 27, 1963, in U.S. Department of State, *Foreign Relations of the United States, 1961–1963*, vol. III (Washington, D.C.: Government Printing Office, 1991), p. 663.

65. Robert S. McNamara, with Brian VanDeMark, *In Retrospect: The Tragedy and Lessons of Vietnam* (New York: Random House, 1995), p. 84.

66. Doris Kearns, *Lyndon Johnson and the American Dream* (New York: Signet, 1977), p. 263.

67. Quotations from Brian VanDeMark, *Into the Quagmire: Lyndon Johnson and the Escalation of the Vietnam War* (New York: Oxford University Press, 1991), pp. 149–50.

68. News conference of July 28, 1965, in *Public Papers of the Presidents of the United States: Lyndon B. Johnson, 1965* (Washington, D.C.: Government Printing Office, 1966), book 2, p. 794.

69. Speech at Johns Hopkins University, April 7, 1965, in *Public Papers, 1965*, 1: 395.

70. Quoted in Illya V. Gaiduk, "Soviet Policy towards US Participation in the Vietnam War," *History* 261 (January 1996): 45. See also Douglas Pike, *Vietnam and the Soviet Union* (Boulder, Colo.: Westview Press, 1987), esp. pp. 76–89.

71. CIA report, "The Sino-Vietnamese Effort to Limited American Actions in the Vietnam War," June 9, 1965, printed in *Journal of Contemporary Asia*, 13 (1983): 261–71. See also William J. Duiker, *China and Vietnam: The Roots of Conflict* (Berkeley: University of California Press, 1986), pp. 49–50.

72. Chen Jian, "China's Involvement in the Vietnam War, 1964–1969," *China Quarterly*, 14 (1995): 386; see also Wedeman, *East Wind Subsides*, ch. 3.

73. Arthur M. Schlesinger, Jr., *Robert F. Kennedy and His Times* (New York: Ballantine Books, 1978), p. 780; McNamara, *In Retrospect*, pp. 96–7.

74. See Robert Dallek, "Lyndon Johnson and Vietnam: The Making of Tragedy," *Diplomatic History* 20 (1996): 147–62.

75. Halberstam, *The Best and the Brightest*, p. 615.

76. Johnson, *Public Papers*, 1965, vol. I, p. 395.

77. *FRUS, Vietnam, 1964*, p. 664.

78. See VanDeMark, *Into the Quagmire,* p. 180.

79. Kearns, *Lyndon Johnson,* p. 296.

80. Robert Dallek, *Flawed Giant: Lyndon Johnson and His Times, 1961–1973* (New York: Oxford University Press, 1998), p. 476.

81. Quoted in James William Gibson, *The Perfect War: Technowar in Vietnam* (Boston: The Atlantic Monthly Press, 1986), p. 109.

82. Duiker, *Sacred War,* pp. 194–203.

83. Quotations from Eric M. Bergerud, *The Dynamics of Defeat: The Vietnam War in Hau Nghia Province* (Boulder, Colo.: Westview Press, 1991), pp. 171 and 175.

84. South Vietnam statistics from Gabriel Kolko, *Anatomy of a War: Vietnam, The United States, and the Modern Historical Experience* (New York: Pantheon, 1985), pp. 201, 224–5.

85. Louise Brown, *War and Aftermath in Vietnam* (New York: Routledge, 1991), p. 236.

86. This section is based on the study by James W. Trullinger, *Village at War: An Account of Conflict in Vietnam,* 2nd ed. (Stanford: Stanford University Press, 1994), chs. 6–10.

87. Figures from McNamara, *In Retrospect,* p. 321.

88. On this see Vaughn Davis Bornet, *The Presidency of Lyndon B. Johnson* (Lawrence: University Press of Kansas, 1983), pp. 240–5.

89. Larry Berman, *Lyndon Johnson's War: The Road to Stalemate in Vietnam* (New York: Norton, 1989), p. 60.

90. Daniel G. Hallin, *The "Uncensored War": The Media and Vietnam* (New York: Oxford University Press, 1986), pp. 129–30, 163 (quotation).

91. Berman, *Lyndon Johnson's War,* p. 121.

92. Wyatt, *Paper Soldiers,* p. 179.

93. See James J. Wirtz, *The Tet Offensive: Intelligence Failure in War* (Ithaca, N.Y.: Cornell University Press, 1991), pp. 252–75.

94. Hallin, *The "Uncensored War,"* pp. 167–74.

95. Quoted in Roger Morris, *Uncertain Greatness: Henry Kissinger and American Foreign Policy* (London: Quartet Books, 1977), p. 44.

96. Lewis Chester, Godfrey Hodgson, and Bruce Page, *An American Melodrama: The Presidential Campaign of 1968* (New York: The Viking Press, 1969), pp. 582–3.

97. Quoted in Theodore A. White, *The Making of the President, 1968* (New York: Pocket Books, 1970), p. 98.

98. Chin-Ha Suk and James L. Morrison, "South Korea's Participation in the Vietnam War: A Historiographical Essay," *Korea Observer,* 18 (1987): esp. 294–301.

99. Chester Cooper, *The Lost Crusade: America in Vietnam* (New York: Dodd, Mead, 1970), p. 267.

100. Quotations from Gregory Pemberton, *All the Way: Australia's Road to Vietnam* (Sydney: Allen & Unwin, 1987), pp. 313, 316.

101. Pemberton, *All the Way*, pp. 329–31. See also Carl Bridge, *"Special Relationships": Australia, Britain and the United States since 1941* (London: Menzies Centre, 1991).

102. Harold Wilson, *The Labour Government, 1964–1970: A Personal Record* (London: Weidenfeld and Nicolson, and Michael Joseph, 1971), p. 264.

103. Richard Crossman, *The Diaries of a Cabinet Minister*, vol. 2 (London: Hamish Hamilton and Jonathan Cape, 1976), p. 530, entry for October 22, 1967.

104. Jean Lacouture, *De Gaulle: The Ruler, 1945–1970*, trans. Alan Sheridan (New York: Norton, 1993), p. 404.

105. Bruno Groppo, "Mai 68 dans le contexte internationale," in René Moriaux et al, eds, *1968: Exploration du Mai Français*, vol. I (Paris: Editions L'Harmattan, 1992), pp. 27–8.

Chapter 9 Cultures and Families

1. Quoted in Bart-Moore Gilbert and John Seed, eds., *Cultural Revolution?: The Challenge of the Arts in the 1960s* (London: Routledge, 1992), p. 2.

2. Quotations from Richard F. Kuisel, *Seducing the French: The Dilemma of Americanization* (Berkeley: University of California Press, 1993), pp. 38, 63, 192, 195.

3. John H. Dunning, "The Role of American Investment in the British Economy," *Political and Economic Planning Broadsheet* 507 (Feb. 1969): 119. .

4. James McMillan and Bernard Harris, *The American Take-Over of Britain* (London: Leslie Frewin, 1968), p. 6.

5. *The Times* (London), January 24, 1967, p. 8.

6. Ivan T. Berend, *The Hungarian Economic Reforms, 1953–1988* (Cambridge: Cambridge University Press, 1990), p. 150.

7. John Wyver, *The Moving Image: An International History of Film, Television and Video* (Oxford: Basil Blackwell, 1989), pp. 203–5; and Zygmunt G. Baranski and Robert Lumley, eds., *Culture and Conflict in Postwar Italy: Essays on Mass and Popular Culture* (London: Macmillan, 1990), esp. pp. 60–1, 199–201.

8. Asa Briggs, *The History of Broadcasting in the United Kingdom*, vol. IV, *Sound and Vision*, 2nd ed. (Oxford: Oxford University Press, 1995), ch. VII, part 1, quoting pp. 803 and 813.

9. Robert Wraight, *The Art Game Again!* (London: Leslie Frewin, 1974), p. 235. See generally Peter Watson, *From Manet to Manhattan: The Rise of the Modern Art Market* (London: Hutchison, 1992), part III.

10. Quoted in Karel Ann Marling, *As Seen on TV: The Visual Culture of Everyday Life in the 1950s* (Cambridge, Mass.: Harvard University Press, 1994), pp. 76, 80.

11. Quotations from Steven Naifeh and Gregory White Smith, *Jackson Pollock: An American Saga* (London: Barrie & Jenkins, 1989), p. 606; Serge Guilbaut, *How New York Stole the Idea of Modern Art: Abstract Impressionism, Freedom, and the Cold War*, trans. Arthur Goldhammer (Chicago: University of Chicago Press, 1983), p. 172.

12. Erika Doss, "The Art of Cultural Politics: From Regionalism to Abstract Expressionism," in Lary May, ed., *Recasting America: Culture and Politics in the Age of Cold War* (Chicago: University of Chicago Press, 1989), p. 216.

13. See the suggestive discussion in Alan Bowness, *The Conditions of Success: How the Modern Artist Rises to Fame* (London: Thames and Hudson, 1989), esp. pp. 50–7.

14. John Berger, *The Success and Failure of Picasso* (Baltimore: Penguin, 1965), p. 179. For output, see Gert Schiff, *Picasso: The Last Years* (New York: George Braziller, 1983), p. 12.

15. Generally see Patrick O'Brian, *Pablo Ruiz Picasso: A Biography* (London: Collins, 1976); and Jean-Paul Crespelle, *Picasso and His Women*, trans. Robert Baldick (London: Hodder and Stoughton, 1969).

16. Philip Hart, *Orpheus in the New World: The Symphony Orchestra as an American Cultural Institution* (New York: Norton, 1973), pp. 385–91.

17. Lance W. Brunner, "The Orchestra and Recorded Sound," in Joan Peyser, ed., *The Orchestra: Origins and Transformations* (New York: Scribner's, 1986), p. 479.

18. Andre Millard, *America on Record: A History of Recorded Sound* (Cambridge: Cambridge University Press, 1995), esp. Ch. 10.

19. Brunner, "The Orchestra and Recorded Sound," p. 506.

20. Quoted in Joseph Horowitz, *Understanding Toscanini* (London: Faber & Faber, 1987), p. 305.

21. Harold C. Schonberg, *The Great Conductors* (London: Victor Gollancz, 1968), p. 357.

22. Norman Lebrecht, *When the Music Stops . . . : Managers, Maestros and the Corporate Murder of Classical Music* (London: Simon & Schuster, 1996), p. 305 (Klemperer) and 423; and Helena Matheopoulos, *Maestro: Encounters with Conductors of Today* (London: Hutchinson, 1982), p. 269.

23. Millard, *America on Record*, p. 5.

24. Millard, *America on Record*, pp. 216–31; and Richard A. Peterson, "Why 1955? Explaining the Advent of Rock Music," *Popular Music*, 9 (1990), 97–116.

25. Quoted in Albert Goodman, *Elvis* (London: Allen Lane, 1981), p. 110. See generally Steve Chapple and Reebee Garofalo, *Rock'n'roll Is Here To Pay: The History and Politics of the Music Industry* (Chicago: Nelson-Hall, 1977), chs. 2–3.

26. See generally Robert Matthew-Walker, *Elvis Presley: A Study in Music* (Tunbridge Wells: Midas Books, 1979), pp. 1–27.

27. Peter Wicke, *Rock Music: Culture, Aesthetics and Sociology*, trans. by Rachel Fogg (Cambridge: Cambridge University Press, 1990), p. viii.

28. Ted Harrison, *Elvis People: The Cult of the King* (London: Fount, 1992), pp. 76–9.

29. *New York Times*, February 8, 1964, p. 40.

30. Counting a single as one record, an EP (extended player) as two, and an LP as five records. Statistics from Hunter Davis, *The Beatles: An Authorized Biography*, 2nd ed. (London: Granada, 1978), p. 395.

31. Quoted in Timothy W. Ryback, *Rock Around the Bloc: A History of Rock Music in Eastern Europe and the Soviet Union* (New York: Oxford University Press, 1990), p. 109. This section draws heavily on Ryback's book.

32. Chapple and Garofalo, *Rock'n'roll Is Here To Pay*, pp. xi, 187.

33. Simon Frith, *Sound Effects: Youth, Leisure, and the Politics of Rock* (London: Constable, 1983), p. 144.

34. Quoted in Sabrina Petra Ramet, ed., *Rocking the State: Rock Music and Politics in Eastern Europe and Russia* (Boulder, Colo.: Westview, 1994), pp. 182–3.

35. Dwight Macdonald, "Masscult and Midcult," *Partisan Review* (Summer 1960), pp. 589, 605.

36. Paul Johnson, "The Menace of Beatlism," *New Statesman and Nation*, February 28, 1964, p. 327.

37. Ernest van den Haag, "Art and the Mass Audience," in Brian O'Doherty, ed., *Museums in Crisis* (New York: George Braziller, 1972), p. 70.

38. Marshall McLuhan, *Understanding Media: The Extensions of Man* (New York: Signet, 1964), p. 303.

39. Wicke, *Rock Music*, p. 95.

40. Brian Longhurst, *Popular Music and Society* (Cambridge: Polity Press, 1995), p. 166.

41. A point developed by Wicke, *Rock Music*, p. 8.

42. Longhurst, *Popular Music and Society*, p. 31.

43. For this paragraph see generally Michael Mitterauer and Reinhard Sieder, *The European Family: Patriarchy to Partnership from the Middle Ages to the Present*, trans. by Karla Oosterveen and Manfred Hörzinger (Oxford: Basil Blackwell, 1982), chs. 3–5.

44. John R. Gillis, *Youth and History: Tradition and Change in European Age Relations, 1770–Present* (London: Academic Press, 1981), p. 188. See also John Demos and Virginia Demos, "Adolescence in Historical Perspective," *Journal of Marriage and the Family* 31 (1969): 632–8.

45. Donald Sassoon, *One Hundred Years of Socialism: The Western European Left in the Twentieth Century* (London: Fontana, 1997), p. 394.

46. Quoted in Bill Williamson, *Education and Social Change in Egypt and Turkey: A Study in Historical Sociology* (London: Macmillan, 1987), p. 176.

47. Theodor Roszak, *The Making of a Counter Culture: Reflections on the Technocratic Society and Its Youthful Opposition* (London: Faber & Faber, 1970), quoting p. xiii. See also Uwe Schlicht, *Vom Burschenschafter bis zum Sponti: Studentische Opposition Gestern und Heute* (Berlin: Colloquium Verlag, 1980).

48. Quoted in James F. Tent, *Freie Universität Berlin: Eine deutsche Hochschule im Zeitgeschehen* (Berlin: Colloquium Verlag, 1988), p. 353.

49. Richard Pells, *Not Like Us: How Europeans Have Loved, Hated, and Transformed American Culture since World War II* (New York: Basic Books, 1997), pp. 200–1.

50. See Archie Brown, *The Gorbachev Factor* (Oxford: Oxford University Press, 1996), pp. 19, 40.

51. Robert Wohl, *The Generation of 1914* (London: Weidenfeld and Nicolson, 1980), p. 210.

52. Efim Slavsky, quoted in Andrei Sakharov, *Memoirs,* trans. Richard Lourie (London: Hutchinson, 1990), p. 287.

53. UNESCO, *Statistical Yearbook, 1970* (Paris: Unesco, 1971), table 2.5.

54. UNESCO, *Statistical Yearbook, 1963* (Paris: Unesco, 1964), table 3; and *Statistical Yearbook, 1972* (1973), table 1.4.

55. Ken Hartshorne, *Crisis and Challenge: Black Education, 1910–1990* (Cape Town: Oxford University Press, 1992), pp. 33–42.

56. Williamson, *Education and Social Change in Egypt and Turkey,* chs. 6, 7, and 10.

57. On Tunisia, see James Allman, *Social Mobility, Education and Development in Tunisia* (Leiden: E. J. Brill, 1979), esp. ch. 3.

58. UNESCO, *Statistical Yearbook, 1963,* table 3; *Statistical Yearbook, 1972,* table 1.4.

59. Vilma Seeberg, *Literacy in China: The Effect of the National Development Context and Policy on Literacy Levels, 1949–1979* (Bochum: Brockmeyer, 1990), esp. pp. 268, 278–9.

60. Tilak, *Education for Development in Asia,* table A4.1 and chs. 3–4, esp. pp. 49–50, 64–5, 67–8.

61. Data from UNESCO, *Statistical Yearbook, 1972* (Paris: UNESCO, 1973), tables 1.4 and 4.1.

62. See the analysis by Janet Saltzmann Chafetz and Anthony Gary Dworkin, assisted by Stephanie Swanson, *Female Revolt: Women's Movements in World and Historical Perspective* (Totowa, N.J.: Rowman & Allanheld, 1986), esp. p. 218.

63. Quoted in Francesca Miller, *Latin American Women and the Search for Social Justice* (Hanover, N.H.: University Press of New England, 1991), p. 111.

64. Robert Leonardi and Douglas A. Wertmann, *Italian Christian Democracy: The Politics of Dominance* (London: Macmillan, 1989), pp. 164–7.

65. Gisbert H. Flanz, ed., *Comparative Women's Rights and Political Participation in Europe* (Epping, Essex: Bowker, 1983), pp. 126, 147.

66. Joni Lovenduski and Jill Hills, eds., *The Politics of the Second Electorate: Women and Public Participation* (London: Routledge & Kegan Paul, 1981), pp. 258–9 and 307–8.

67. For biographical sketches see Olga S. Opfell, *Women Prime Ministers and Presidents* (Jefferson, N.C.: McFarland & Co., 1993).

68. Elizabeth Sarah, "Towards a Reassessment of Feminist History," *Women's Studies International Forum* 5 (1982): 519–24.

69. For a general survey see William H. Chafe, *The Paradox of Change: American Women in the Twentieth Century* (New York: Oxford University Press, 1991), chs. 10–11.

70. Joanne Meyerowitz, "Beyond the Feminine Mystique: A Reassessment of Postwar Mass Culture, 1946–1958," *Journal of American History* 79 (1993): 1455–82. This is also a theme of Eugenia Kaledin, *Mothers and More: American Women in the Fifties* (Boston: Twayne, 1984).

71. For these details see Kaledin, *Mothers and More*, pp. 36, 43, 53, 63, 66, 217.

72. Quoted in Joseph P. Lash, *Eleanor: The Years Alone* (New York: Signet, 1973), p. 214.

73. *Saturday Evening Post*, December 22–29, 1962, pp. 26, 32.

74. Lynn Y. Weiner, *From Working Girl to Working Mother: The Female Labor Force in the United States, 1820–1980* (Chapel Hill: University of North Carolina Press, 1985), pp. 89 and 93.

75. Betty Friedan, *The Feminine Mystique* (New York: Norton, 1963), quoting from pp. 305–8.

76. Quoted in Blanche Linden-Ward and Carol Hurd Green, *Changing the Future: American Women in the 1960s* (New York: Twayne, 1993), p. 55.

77. Linden-Ward and Green, *Changing the Future*, p. 79.

78. Rosalind Rosenberg, *Divided Lives: American Women in the Twentieth Century* (New York: Hill and Wang, 1992), pp. 192–3.

79. Kate Millett, *Sexual Politics* (London: Virago, 1977), p. 24.

80. Linden-Ward and Green, *Changing the Future*, pp. xvii, 443.

81. Chafe, *Paradox of Change*, p. 211.

82. See the account in Bernard Asbell, *The Pill: A Biography of the Drug that Changed the World* (New York: Random House, 1995), quoting pp. 59–60.

83. See Mary Smith, "Birth Control and the Negro Woman," *Ebony*, March 1968, pp. 29–37.

84. See *Time*, April 7, 1967, p. 78.

85. See generally Rose-Marie Lagrave, "A Supervised Emancipation," in Françoise Thébaud, ed., *A History of Women in the West*, Vol. V (Cambridge, Mass., and London: Harvard University Press, 1994), pp. 466–77.

86. See Louise A. Tilly and Joan W. Scott, *Women, Work, and Family*, 2nd ed. (New York and London: Routledge, 1987), Ch. 9.

87. Claude Francis and Fernande Gontier, *Simone de Beauvoir*, trans. Lisa Nesselson (London: Sidgwick & Jackson, 1987), esp. pp. 254, 290, 343.

88. Simone de Beauvoir, *The Second Sex*, trans. and ed. H. M. Parshley (New York: Vintage, 1974), p. 756.

89. Françoise Picq, *Libération des Femmes: Les Années-Mouvement* (Paris: Éditions du Seuil, 1993), pp. 16–17.

90. See Claire Duchen, *Feminism in France: From May '68 to Mitterrand* (London and Boston: Routledge & Kegan Paul, 1986).

91. Gigi Santow, "Coitus Interruptus in the Twentieth Century," *Population and Development Review* 19 (1993): pp. 767–92, quoting from p. 786.

92. Michael Murphy, "The Contraceptive Pill and Women's Employment as Factors in Fertility Change in Britain, 1963–1980," *Population Studies* 47 (1993): 221–43.

93. Asbell, *The Pill*, pp. 197–207.

94. Quoted in Miller, *Latin American Women*, pp. 146–7.

95. Gail Warshofsky Lapidus, *Women in Soviet Society: Equality, Development, and Social Change* (Berkeley: University of California, 1978), p. 166.

96. Marilyn Rueschemeyer and Szonja Szelényi, "Socialist Transformation and Gender Inequality: Women in the GDR and Hungary," in David Childs, Thomas A. Baylis, and Marilyn Rueschemeyer, eds., *East Germany in Comparative Perspective* (London and New York: Routledge, 1989), pp. 89, 94.

97. Alena Heitlinger, *Women and State Socialism: Sex Inequality in the Soviet Union and Czechoslovakia* (London: Macmillan, 1979), p. 198.

98. Heitlinger, *Women and State Socialism*, p. 185.

99. Alexandr Avdev, "Contraception and Abortion Trends," in Wolfgang Lutz, Sergei Scherbov, and Andrei Volkov, eds., *Demographic Trends and Patterns in the Soviet Union before 1991* (London: Routledge, 1991), esp. pp. 132, 143.

100. Heitlinger, *Women and State Socialism*, p. 87.

101. Gail W. Lapidus, ed., *Women, Work, and Family in the Soviet Union* (Armonk, N.Y., and London: M. E. Sharpe, 1982), p. xxxv.

102. Quoted in J. Robert Wegs, *Europe since 1945: A Concise History*, 2nd ed. (London: Macmillan, 1984), p. 210.

103. Elisabeth Croll, *Chinese Women since Mao* (London: Zed Books, 1983), p. 59 and, more generally, ch. 1.

104. Points emphasized by Phyllis Andors, *The Unfinished History of Chinese Women, 1949–1980* (Bloomington: Indiana University Press, 1983), Chs. 3 and 5.

105. Mumtaz Ali Khan and Noor Ayesha, *Status of Rural Women in India: A Study of Karnataka* (New Delhi: Uppal Publishing House, 1982), esp. pp. 160–95, 204–6.

106. Neera Desai and Vibhuti Patel, *Indian Women: Change and Challenge in the International Decade, 1975–1985* (Bombay: Popular Prakashan, 1985), pp. 26, 32, 35.

107. Joanna Liddle and Rama Joshi, *Daughters of Independence: Gender, Caste and Class in India* (London: Zed Books, 1986), ch. 9, also pp. 191, 244.

108. "Women in Israel," in *The Annals of the American Academy of Political and Social Science* 375 (January 1968): 79–81.

108. See, for instance, Leila Ahmed, *Women and Gender in Islam: Historical Roots of a Modern Debate* (New Haven and London: Yale University Press, 1992).

110. On all these matters, see the good overview by Debbie J. Gerner, "Roles in Transition: The Evolving Position of Women in Arab-Islamic Countries," in Freda Hussain, ed., *Muslim Women* (London: Croom Helm, 1984), pp. 71–99.

111. Fatma Mansur Coşar, "Women in Turkish Society," in Lois Beck and Nikki Keddie, eds., *Women in the Muslim World* (Cambridge, Mass., and London: Harvard University Press, 1978), pp. 125–7.

112. Bill Brugger and Stephen Reglar, *Politics, Economy and Society in Contemporary China* (London: Macmillan, 1994), pp. 263–4, 276, 297–8.

113. Robert W. Stern, *Changing India* (Cambridge: Cambridge University Press, 1993), p. 44.

114. For all these points see the introduction to Helen Ware, ed., *Women, Education and Modernization of the Family in West Africa* (Canberra: Australian National University Press, 1981).

115. Tilak, *Education for Development in Asia,* ch. 9.

116. This theme is developed in Jeanne Bisilliat and Michèle Fiéloux, *Women and the Third World: Work and Daily Life,* trans. by Enne Amann and Peter Amann (London: Associated University Presses, 1987).

117. Christine Obbo, *African Women: Their Struggle for Economic Independence* (London: Zed Press, 1980), ch. 8.

118. Ximena Bunster B., "Market Sellers in Lima, Peru: Talking About Work," in Mayra Buvinić, Margaret A. Lycette, and William Paul McGreevey, eds., *Women and Poverty in the Third World* (Baltimore and London: Johns Hopkins University Press, 1983), pp. 92–103.

119. Miller, *Latin American Women,* ch. 7. See also Lynne B. Iglitzin and Ruth Ross, eds., *Women and the World, 1975–1985: The Women's Decade* (Santa Barbara: ABC Clio Press, 1986).

Chapter 10 Superpower Détente, Communist Confrontation

1. Andrew Chaikin, *A Man on the Moon: The Voyages of the Apollo Astronauts* (London: Michael Joseph, 1994), p. 134.

2. Buzz Aldrin and Malcolm McConnell, *Men from Earth* (London and New York: Bantam Press, 1989), p. 239.

3. *Public Papers of the Presidents of the United States: Richard Nixon, 1969* (Washington, D.C.: Government Printing Office, 1971) p. 542.

4. For a version of the Nixon joke, see Arkady N. Shevchenko, *Breaking with Moscow* (London: Jonathan Cape, 1985), p. 166.

5. According to Zhou in 1972: see *The Memoirs of Richard Nixon* (London: Arrow Books, 1979), p. 568. In general see Thomas W. Robinson, "The Sino-Soviet Border Dispute: Background, Development, and the March 1969 Clashes," *American Political Science Review* 66 (1972): 1175–1202.

6. Figures from Roderick MacFarquhar and John K. Fairbank, eds., *The Cambridge History of China,* vol. 15 (Cambridge: Cambridge University Press, 1991), pp. 299–300 (abbreviated as *CHOC*).

7. Frederick C. Teiwes and Warren Sun, *The Tragedy of Lin Biao: Riding the Tiger during the Cultural Revolution, 1966–1971* (London: Hurst & Co., 1996), pp. 111–5.

8. Seymour M. Hersh, *Kissinger: The Price of Power* (London: Faber & Faber, 1983), p. 65; cf. R. J. Overy, *The Air War, 1939–1945* (London: Macmillan, 1980), p. 120.

9. Quotations from Walter Isaacson, *Kissinger: A Biography* (New York: Simon and Schuster, 1992), pp. 160, 163–4.

10. Martin Malia, *The Soviet Tragedy: A History of Socialism in Russia, 1917–1991* (New York: Free Press, 1994), p. 371.

11. David Holloway, *The Soviet Union and the Arms Race*, 2nd ed. (New Haven: Yale University Press, 1985), pp. 58–9.

12. Melvin Small, *Johnson, Nixon and the Doves* (New Brunswick, N.J.: Rutgers University Press, 1988), pp. 182–7, 226.

13. Richard M. Nixon, "Asia after Viet Nam," *Foreign Affairs* 46/1 (October 1967): 121–2.

14. Barry Naughton, "Industrial Policy during the Cultural Revolution: Military Preparation, Decentralization, and Leaps Forward," in William A. Joseph, Christine P. W. Wong, and David Zweig, eds., *New Perspectives on the Cultural Revolution* (Cambridge, Mass.: Harvard University Press, 1991), esp. pp. 158, 161.

15. Quotations from Henry Kissinger, *The White House Years* (London: Weidenfeld & Nicolson and Michael Joseph, 1979), pp. 745, 754. See generally Lowell Dittmer, *Sino-Soviet Normalization and its International Implications, 1945–1990* (Seattle: University of Washington Press, 1992), ch. 12.

16. Quoted in *CHOC*, 15: 320. Against this account, pp. 311–34, see, for instance, Teiwes and Sun, *The Tragedy of Lin Biao*.

17. As told in Yao Ming-Le, *The Conspiracy and Murder of Mao's Heir* (London: Collins, 1983), ch. 16; but see the KGB sources cited in Peter Hannam, "Solved: The Mystery of Lin Biao's Death," *Asiaweek*, February 2, 1994, pp. 32–3.

18. See *CHOC*, 15, p. 315, and the portrait in Zhisui Li, *The Private Life of Chairman Mao: The Memoirs of Mao's Personal Physician* (London: Arrow Books, 1996), pp. 453–4.

19. Nixon, *Memoirs*, pp. 559–60.

20. Quoted in Hersh, *Kissinger*, p. 500.

21. Raymond Garthoff, *Détente and Confrontation: American-Soviet Relations from Nixon to Reagan* (2nd ed., Washington, D.C.: Brookings Institution, 1994), p. 267.

22. Toast at Shanghai banquet, February 27, 1972, in Nixon, *Public Papers, 1972*, p. 379.

23. Harry Gelman, *The Brezhnev Politburo and the Decline of Detente* (Ithaca, N.Y.: Cornell University Press, 1984), ch. 4; Richard D. Anderson, *Public Politics in an Authoritarian State: Making Foreign Policy during the Brezhnev Years* (Ithaca, N.Y.: Cornell University Press, 1993), ch. 10.

24. Anatoly Dobrynin, *In Confidence: Moscow's Ambassador to America's Six Cold War Presidents, 1962–1986* (New York: Times Books, 1995), esp. pp. 207–10, 231–2.

25. Nixon, *Memoirs*, 619.

26. Shevchenko, *Breaking with Moscow*, p. 215.

27. Dobrynin, *In Confidence*, p. 256.

28. On the grain deal see particularly Hersh, *Kissinger*, ch. 37.

29. See the judgment of Keith L. Nelson, *The Making of Détente: Soviet-American Relations in the Shadow of Vietnam* (Baltimore: Johns Hopkins University Press, 1995), p. 146.

30. For troop figures see Marilyn B. Young, *The Vietnam Wars, 1945–1990* (New York: HarperCollins, 1991), pp. 334–5.

31. Quoted in William J. Duiker, *Sacred War: Nationalism and Revolution in a Divided Vietnam* (New York: McGraw-Hill, 1995), p. 234. See also John W. Garver, "Sino-Vietnamese Conflict and the Sino-American Rapprochement," *Political Science Quarterly* 96 (1981): esp. pp. 453–6.

32. Quoted in Arnold R. Isaacs, *Without Honor: Defeat in Vietnam and Cambodia* (Baltimore: Johns Hopkins University Press, 1983), pp. 25–6.

33. George C. Herring, *America's Longest War: The United States and Vietnam, 1950–1975,* 2nd ed. (New York: Knopf, 1986), p. 247.

34. Nixon, *Memoirs,* p. 749.

35. James P. Harrison, "History's Heaviest Bombing," in Jayne S. Werner and Luu Doan Huynh, eds, *The Vietnam War: Vietnamese and American Perspectives* (Armonk, N.Y.: M.E. Sharpe, 1993), pp. 131–3.

36. Nixon, *Public Papers,* 1973, p. 18.

37. Mary Fulbrook, *Anatomy of a Dictatorship: Inside the GDR, 1949–1989* (Oxford: Oxford University Press, 1995), pp. 193–9.

38. Timothy Garton Ash, *In Europe's Name: Germany and the Divided Continent* (London: Jonathan Cape, 1993), pp. 66, 466.

39. Newspaper article of July 15, 1970, quoted in Helga Haftendorn, *Security and Détente: Conflicting Priorities in German Foreign Policy* (New York: Praeger, 1985), p. 190.

40. William E. Griffith, *The Ostpolitik of the Federal Republic of Germany* (Cambridge, Mass.: MIT Press, 1978), p. 191. Chapter 5 of this book offers a good survey of Brandt's *Ostpolitik.*

41. Quotations from Willy Brandt, *People and Politics: The Years 1960–1975,* trans. J. Maxwell Brownjohn (London: Collins, 1978), pp. 399–400.

42. As emphasized by A. James McAdams, *Germany Divided: From the Wall to Reunification* (Princeton, N.J.: Princeton University Press, 1993), pp. 87–95.

43. Quotation is from Willi Stoph, chairman of the GDR Council of Ministers, in Dieter Borkowski, *Erich Honecker: Statthalter Moskaus oder deutscher Patriot?* (München: C. Bertelsmann, 1987), p. 272; see also Fred Oldenburg and Gerhard Wettig, "The Special Status of the GDR in East-West Relations," *East Central Europe* 6/2 (1979): 174–5.

44. See the account in Arnulf Baring, with Manfred Görtemaker, *Machtwechsel: Die Ära Brandt-Scheel* (Stuttgart: Deutsche Verlags-Anstalt, 1982), pp. 420–4.

45. Angela Stent, *From Embargo to Ostpolitik: The Political Economy of West German–Soviet Relations, 1955–1980* (Cambridge: Cambridge University Press, 1981), pp. 192–3.

46. Quoted in McAdams, *Germany Divided,* p. 96.

47. Garton Ash, *In Europe's Name,* pp. 139, 656.

48. Leslie, ed., *The History of Poland since 1863,* 2nd ed. (Cambridge: Cambridge University Press, 1983), pp. 403–21.

49. On which see Garthoff, *Détente and Confrontation*, pp. 127–35, 527–37.

50. Quoted in Keith Middlemas, *Orchestrating Europe: The Informal Politics of European Union, 1973–1995* (London: HarperCollins, 1995), p. 68. See generally Derek W. Urwin, *The Community of Europe: A History of European Integration since 1945* (London: Longman, 1991), pp. 139–79.

51. Speech of September 3, 1971, in Haftendorn, *Security and Détente*, p. 245.

52. Alan Campbell, "Anglo-French Relations a Decade Ago: A New Assessment," *International Affairs* 58 (1982): 432–8.

53. White Paper of July 1971, quoted in David Reynolds, *Britannia Overruled: British Policy and World Power in the Twentieth Century* (London: Longman, 1991), p. 242.

54. See Haig Simonian, *The Privileged Partnership: Franco-German Relations in the European Community* (Oxford: Clarendon, 1985), pp. 367–9.

55. Greece, Portugal, and Spain are usually linked together in accounts of southern Europe's democratic transition. Sometimes Italy has been added, but its shift came much earlier. Turkey is rarely considered, partly because the 1970s marked no sharp rupture with the past, but it seems to me instructive to take these two pairs of countries together.

56. For a general survey see Feroz Ahmad, *The Making of Modern Turkey* (London: Routledge, 1993), esp. chs. 6–9.

57. Mehemet Ali Birand, *The Generals' Coup in Turkey: An Inside Story of 12 September 1980*, trans. by M. A. Diekerdem (London: Brassey's, 1987), pp. 15, 19.

58. A point emphasized by Dankwart A. Rustow, "Political Parties in Turkey: An Overview," in Martin Heper and Jacob M. Landau, eds., *Political Parties and Democracy in Turkey* (London: I. B. Tauris, 1991), pp. 20–21.

59. William Hale, "The Turkish Army in Politics, 1960–1973," in Andrew Finkel and Nükhet Sirman, eds., *Turkish State, Turkish Society* (London: Routledge, 1990), pp. 53–78.

60. Ahmad, *The Making of Modern Turkey*, p. 13.

61. For a good overview, see C. M. Woodhouse, *The Rise and Fall of the Greek Colonels* (London: Granada, 1985).

62. A point emphasized by P. Nikiforos Diamandouros, "Transition to, and Consolidation of, Democratic Politics in Greece: A Tentative Assessment," in Geoffrey Pridham, ed., *The New Mediterranean Democracies: Regime Transition in Spain, Greece and Portugal* (London: Frank Cass, 1984), pp. 53–4.

63. George Stergiou Kaloudis, *The Role of the United Nations in Cyprus from 1964 to 1979* (New York: Peter Lang, 1991), ch. 3.

64. Andrew Wilson, "The Aegean Dispute," in Jonathan Alford, ed., *Greece and Turkey: Adversity in Alliance* (Aldershot: Gower/IISS, 1984), pp. 90–130.

65. Diamandouros, "Democratic Politics in Greece, pp. 59–65.

66. Quoted in Speros Vryonis, Jr., ed., *Greece on the Road to Democracy: From the Junta to PASOK, 1974–1986* (New Rochelle, N.Y.: Orpheus Publishing Inc., 1991), p. 22. See generally chs. 1–2.

67. Tom Gallagher, *Portugal: A Twentieth-Century Interpretation* (Manchester: Manchester University Press, 1983), remains valuable.

68. Quoted in Douglas Porch, *The Portuguese Armed Forces and the Revolution* (London: Croom Helm, 1977), p. 84—still an essential study of the army's role.

69. See Hugo Gill Ferreira and Michael W. Marshall, *Portugal's Revolution: Ten Years On* (Cambridge: Cambridge University Press, 1986), pp. 209-11.

70. A. R. Jones, "Agriculture: Organization, Reform and the EEC," in Allan Williams, ed., *Southern Europe Transformed: Political and Social Change in Greece, Italy, Portugal and Spain* (London: Harper & Row, 1984), pp. 243-4.

71. Robert Harvey, *Portugal: Birth of a Democracy* (London: Macmillan, 1978), p. 2.

72. Themes of Thomas C. Bruneau, "Continuity and Change in Portuguese Politics: Ten Years after the Revolution of 25 April 1974," in Pridham, ed., *The New Mediterranean Democracies*, pp. 72-83.

73. For a lively overview see Paul Preston, *The Triumph of Democracy in Spain* (London: Methuen, 1986).

74. On these themes see Victor M. Pérez-Díaz, *The Return of Civil Society: The Emergence of Democratic Spain* (Cambridge, Mass.: Harvard University Press, 1993), ch. 1.

75. Quoted by Audrey Brassloff, "The Church in Post-Franco Society," in Christopher Abel and Nissa Torrents, eds., *Spain: Conditional Democracy* (London: Croom Helm, 1984), p. 61.

76. Quotations from Woodhouse, *Rise and Fall of the Greek Colonels*, p. 173, and Pérez-Díaz, *Return of Civil Society*, p. 1.

77. Susannah Verney, "Greece and the European Community," in Kevin Featherstone and Dimitrios K. Katsoudas, eds., *Political Change in Greece: Before and After the Colonels* (London: Croom Helm, 1987), pp. 253-70.

78. Stephen E. Ambrose, *Nixon*, vol. 3 (New York: Simon & Schuster, 1991), p. 27.

79. Ambrose, *Nixon*, 2 (1989), pp. 409-12.

80. Transcript in *Watergate: Chronology of a Crisis* (Washington, D.C.: Congressional Quarterly, Inc., 1975), p. 90-A.

81. Gerald Gold, ed., *The White House Transcripts* (New York: Bantam Books, 1974), p. 146.

82. Fred Emery, *Watergate: The Corruption and Fall of Richard Nixon* (London: Jonathan Cape, 1994), p. 334. This is the best recent study of Watergate, drawing on declassified tapes.

83. Nixon, *Memoirs*, p. 1089.

84. Ross Terrill, *Mao: A Biography*, 2nd ed. (New York: Touchstone, 1993), p. 428.

85. Dobrynin, *In Confidence*, pp. 302-3, 310-11, 316-7.

86. Kissinger, *White House Years*, p. 841.

87. Garthoff, *Détente and Confrontation*, p. 349.

88. Quoted anonymously in Isaacs, *Without Honor*, p. 102.

89. Isaacs, *Without Honor*, p. 217.

90. Quoted in Robert S. Litwak, *Détente and the Nixon Doctrine: American Foreign Policy and the Pursuit of Stability, 1969–1976* (Cambridge: Cambridge University Press, 1984), p. 132.

91. Shown to the president himself. See Gerald R. Ford, *A Time to Heal* (London: W. H. Allen, 1979), p. 275.

92. See John Dumbrell, *The Carter Presidency: A Re-evaluation* (Manchester, England: Manchester University Press, 1993), pp. 115–8.

93. Gelman, *The Brezhnev Politburo*, pp. 146–51, 160–2.

94. Kissinger, 1976, quoted in Litwak, *Détente and the Nixon Doctrine*, p. 82.

95. The differences are elucidated in Garthoff, *Détente and Confrontation*, ch. 2.

96. An unnamed Soviet official quoted in Holloway, *The Soviet Union and the Arms Race*, p. 91.

97. Quoted in Roger Morris, *Uncertain Greatness: Henry Kissinger and American Foreign Policy* (London: Quartet Books, 1977), p. 241.

98. Paul E. Sigmund, *The Overthrow of Allende and the Politics of Chile, 1964–1976* (Pittsburgh: University of Pittsburgh Press, 1977), ch. 13.

99. See Edy Kaufman, *Crisis in Allende's Chile: New Perspectives* (New York: Praeger, 1988), pp. 124, 271–2.

100. Points emphasized in Nathaniel Davis, *The Last Two Years of Salvador Allende* (Ithaca, N.Y.: Cornell University Press, 1985), pp. 363–4, 399.

101. U.S. Senate, *Covert Action in Chile, 1963–1973* (Washington, D.C.: Government Printing Office, 1975), pp. 2, 28.

102. Garthoff, *Détente and Confrontation*, pp. 580–1. Ch. 15 of this book provides a judicious overview; see also the narrative in Daniel Spikes, *Angola and the Politics of Intervention: From Local Bush War to Chronic Crisis in Southern Africa* (Jefferson, N.C.: McFarland, 1993).

103. Ford, *A Time to Heal*, p. 373.

104. Quoted in Peter Calvocoressi, *World Politics since 1945*, 5th ed. (London: Longman, 1987), p. 455.

105. Jorge I. Domínguez, *To Make a World Safe for Revolution: Cuba's Foreign Policy* (Cambridge, Mass.: Harvard University Press, 1989), p. 132; and Spikes, *Angola*, pp. 220–1. On the details of Cuban and Soviet policy see documents and analysis in *Cold War International History Project Bulletin* 8–9 (Winter 1996/7): 5–37.

106. Quoted in W. Martin James III, *A Political History of the Civil War in Angola, 1974–1990* (New Brunswick, N.J.: Transaction Publishers, 1992), p. 84. See also James Barber and John Barratt, *South Africa's Foreign Policy: The Search for Status and Security, 1945–1988* (Cambridge: Cambridge Univ. Press, 1990), pp. 190–6.

107. Robert G. Patman, *The Soviet Union in the Horn of Africa: The Diplomacy of Intervention and Disengagement* (Cambridge: Cambridge University Press, 1990), chs. 5–7; and more generally Mulatu Wubneh and Yohannis Abate, *Ethiopia: Transition and Development in the Horn of Africa* (Boulder, Colo.: Westview, 1988).

108. Patman, *The Soviet Union in the Horn of Africa,* p. 254.

109. Quoted in Domínguez, *To Make a World Safe,* p. 2.

110. For an overview see Roderick MacFarquhar's essay in *CHOC,* vol. 15, ch. 4, supplemented on court politics and Mao's health by Zhisui Li, *The Private Life of Chairman Mao: The Memoirs of Mao's Personal Physician* (London: Arrow Books, 1996), chs. 76–92.

111. See the biography by Richard Evans, *Deng Xiaoping and the Making of Modern China,* 2nd ed. (London: Penguin, 1995).

112. Terrill, *Mao,* 425, 430.

113. Li, *Private Life of Chairman Mao,* p. 612.

114. The struggle can be followed in Harry Harding, *China's Second Revolution: Reform after Mao* (Washington, D.C.: Brookings Institution, 1987), ch. 2.

115. Quoted in Nancy Bernkopf Tucker, *Taiwan, Hong Kong, and the United States, 1945–1992* (New York: Twayne, 1994), p. 130.

116. Carter later regretted he had not pushed for his first preference, George Ball, who had served as undersecretary of state to Kennedy and Johnson but was regarded as unacceptable to the Jewish lobby because of his support for a Palestinian homeland. See Douglas Brinkley, "The Rising Stock of Jimmy Carter," *Diplomatic History* 20/4 (Fall 1996): 516.

117. Hamilton Jordan, *Crisis: The Last Year of the Carter Presidency* (London: Michael Joseph, 1982), p. 47.

118. Zbigniew Brzezinski, *Power and Principle: Memoirs of the National Security Adviser, 1977–1981* (London: Weidenfeld & Nicolson, 1983), p. 196.

119. Quoted in Garthoff, *Détente and Confrontation,* p. 771.

120. See David P. Chandler, *The Tragedy of Cambodian History: Politics, War, and Revolution since 1945* (New Haven: Yale University Press, 1991), pp. 300–1.

121. See Ben Kiernan, "China's Ethnic Chinese under Pol Pot: A Case of Systematic Social Discrimination," *Journal of Contemporary Asia* 16/1 (January 1986): 18–29.

122. Quoted in Anne Gilks, *The Breakdown of the Sino-Vietnamese Alliance, 1970–1979* (Berkeley: University of California, 1992), p. 214—a book on which this section draws, together with Min Chen, *The Strategic Triangle and Regional Conflicts: Lessons from the Indochina Wars* (Boulder, Colo.: Lynne Rienner, 1992), ch. 5.

123. William J. Duiker, *Vietnam since the Fall of Saigon,* 2nd ed. (Athens: Ohio University Center of International Studies, 1985), pp. 117–9.

124. Douglas C. Pike, *Vietnam and the Soviet Union: Anatomy of an Alliance* (Boulder, Colo.: Westview Press, 1987), pp. 184–5, 191–2.

125. Quotations from Gaddis Smith, *Morality, Reason, and Power: American Diplomacy in the Carter Years* (New York: Hill and Wang, 1986), p. 97.

126. Gilks, *Breakdown of the Sino-Vietnamese Alliance,* pp. 221–3. Robert S. Ross, *The Indochina Tangle: China's Vietnam Policy, 1975–1979* (New York: Columbia University Press, 1988), pp. 230–2 argues that even this encountered considerable opposition.

127. See King C. Chen, *China's War with Vietnam, 1979: Issues, Decisions, and Implications* (Stanford, Calif.: Hoover Institution Press, 1987), p. 153.

128. Michael Vickery, *Cambodia: 1975–1982* (Sydney: Allen & Unwin, 1984), ch. 3.

129. Kimmo Kiljunen, *Kampuchea: Decade of the Genocide. Report of a Finnish Inquiry Commission* (London: Zed Books, 1984), pp. 30–4. Vickery, *Cambodia*, pp. 184–8, is out of line with most accounts in suggesting only four hundred thousand.

130. Karl D. Jackson, "The Ideology of Total Revolution," in Karl D. Jackson, ed., *Cambodia, 1975–1978: Rendezvous with Death* (Princeton, N.J.: Princeton University Press, 1989), p. 37.

131. Thiounn Mumm, quoted in David P. Chandler, *Brother Number One: A Political Biography of Pol Pot* (Boulder, Colo.: Westview Press, 1992), p. 112; cf. Dmitri Volkogonov, *Lenin: Life and Legacy* (London: HarperCollins, 1994), pp. 408–9.

132. According to Prince Norodom Sihanouk, *War and Hope: The Case for Cambodia* (London: Sidgwick & Jackson, 1980), p. 86.

133. Quoted in Kenneth M. Quinn, "The Pattern and Scope of Violence," in Jackson, ed., *Cambodia*, p. 182.

134. In January 1979. See Garthoff, *Détente and Confrontation*, p. 786.

135. Phrase used by Deputy Foreign Minister Georgy Kornienko, quoted in Strobe Talbott, *Endgame: The Inside Story of SALT II* (New York: Harper & Row, 1979), p. 73.

136. Quoted in Adam Ulam, *Dangerous Relations: The Soviet Union in World Politics, 1970–1982* (New York: Oxford University Press, 1983), p. 236.

137. Quotations from Dobrynin, *In Confidence,* p. 426, and Garthoff, *Détente and Confrontation,* p. 811.

138. Holloway, *Soviet Union and the Arms Race*, pp. 59–60.

139. Quoted in Dumbrell, *The Carter Presidency*, p. 185.

140. For a good overview, see Anthony Hyman, *Afghanistan under Soviet Domination, 1964–1991*, 3rd ed. (London: Macmillan, 1992).

141. Quotations from Diego Cordovez and Selig S. Harrison, *Out of Afghanistan: The Inside Story of the Soviet Withdrawal* (New York: Oxford University Press, 1995), pp. 36–7. Ch. 1 of this book and Garthoff, *Détente and Confrontation*, ch. 26, provide informed accounts using much new Soviet material.

142. Quoted by Odd Arne Westad, "New Russian Evidence on the Soviet Intervention in Afghanistan," *Cold War International History Project Bulletin* 8–9 (Winter 1996/1997): p. 130.

143. Quoted in M. Hassan Kakar, *Afghanistan: The Soviet Invasion and the Afghan Response, 1979–1982* (Berkeley: University of California, 1995), p. 237.

144. Brzezinski, *Power and Principle,* p. 520.

145. Garthoff, *Détente and Confrontation*, pp. 1059–60.

146. *Public Papers of the Presidents of the United States: Jimmy Carter, 1980* (Washington, D.C.: Government Printing Office, 1981), p. 40, cf. pp. 108, 196.

147. Garthoff, *Détente and Confrontation*, p. 1105.

148. Gabriella Grasselli, *British and American Responses to the Soviet Invasion of Afghanistan* (Aldershot, Hampshire: Dartmouth Publishing Company, 1996), pp. 146–7.

149. Christopher R. Hill, *Olympic Politics* (Manchester: Manchester University Press, 1992), p. 31.

150. Richard Espy, *The Politics of the Olympic Games*, 2nd ed. (Berkeley: University of California Press, 1981), p. 175.

151. Quoted in Derick L. Hulme, Jr., *The Political Olympics: Moscow, Afghanistan, and the 1980 U.S. Boycott* (New York: Praeger, 1990), p. 27. This book provides the fullest account of the controversy.

152. Hill, *Olympic Politics*, p. 131; Carter, *Keeping Faith*, p. 489.

153. Rolf Pfeiffer, *Sport und Politik: Die Boycottdiskussionen um die Olympischen Spiele von Mexico City 1968 bis Los Angeles 1984* (Frankfurt am Main: Peter Lang, 1987), p. 387.

154. Allen Guttmann, *The Olympics: A History of the Modern Games* (Urbana: University of Illinois Press, 1992), p. 141.

155. See Odd Arne Westad, "Prelude to Invasion: The Soviet Union and the Afghan Communists, 1978–1979," *International History Review* 16 (1994): esp. 57, 59.

Chapter 11 Israel, Oil, and Islam

1. Michael I. Handel, *The Diplomacy of Surprise: Hitler, Nixon, Sadat* (Cambridge, Mass.: Harvard Center for International Affairs, 1981), pp. 275–9.

2. On these points see Raymond A. Hinnebusch, Jr., *Egyptian Politics under Sadat: The Post-Populist Development of an Authoritarian-Modernizing State* (Cambridge: Cambridge University Press, 1985), pp. 40–53; William B. Quandt, *Peace Process: American Diplomacy and the Arab-Israeli Conflict since 1967* (Washington, D.C.: Brookings Institution, 1993), pp. 135–6.

3. Quotations from David Hirst and Irene Beeson, *Sadat* (London: Faber & Faber, 1981), p. 152.

4. Patrick Seale, with Maureen McConville, *Asad of Syria: The Struggle for the Middle East* (London: I. B. Tauris, 1990), pp. 197–9; Saad el-Shazly, *The Crossing of Suez: The October War, 1973* (London: Third World Centre, 1980), pp. 30–1.

5. Richard Ned Lebow and Janice Gross Stein, *We All Lost the Cold War* (Princeton, N.J.: Princeton University Press, 1994), pp. 164–6; Victor Israelyan, *Inside the Kremlin during the Yom Kippur War* (University Park: Pennsylvania State University Press, 1995), pp. 16–19.

6. See discussion by Michael Russell Rip and Joseph F. Fontanella, "A Window on the Arab-Israeli 'Yom Kippur' War of 1973: Military Photo-Reconnaissance from High Altitude and Space," *Intelligence and National Security* 6 (1991): 65–7.

7. The plans and their execution are described with considerable detail and pride in Shazly, *The Crossing of Suez*, pp. 13–14, 41–52, 149–57.

8. Quoted in Hirst and Beeson, *Sadat*, p. 28.

9. Robert Slater, *Warrior Statesman: The Life of Moshe Dayan* (London: Robson Books, 1991), p. 359.

10. For this and the next paragraph see Lebow and Stein, *We All Lost the Cold War,* chs. 8–10.

11. Quotations in this paragraph from Israelyan, *Inside the Kremlin,* pp. 136–8, 169–70.

12. Lebow and Stein, *We All Lost the Cold War,* pp. 237–8.

13. Walter Isaacson, *Kissinger* (New York: Simon and Schuster, 1992), p. 530.

14. For claims about Nixon's state see Roger Morris, *Haig: The General's Progress* (London: Robson Books, 1982), pp. 257–9; see also Lebow and Stein, *We All Lost the Cold War,* pp. 480–1.

15. Quotations from Anatoly Dobrynin, *In Confidence: Moscow's Ambassador to America's Six Cold War Presidents, 1962–1986* (New York: Times Books, 1995), p. 297; Quandt, *Peace Process,* p. 180.

16. Henry Kissinger, *Years of Upheaval* (London: Weidenfeld & Nicolson and Michael Joseph, 1982), p. 980.

17. Israelyan, *Inside the Kremlin,* pp. 182–3.

18. Howard M. Sachar, *A History of Israel* (New York: Knopf, 1988), p. 787.

19. Michael N. Barnett, *Confronting the Costs of War: Military Power, State, and Society in Egypt and Israel* (Princeton, N.J.: Princeton University Press, 1992), p. 231.

20. Harold Saunders, cited in Seale, *Asad,* p. 244. On Kissinger's diplomacy see Quandt, *Peace Process,* chs. 8–9.

21. On this see, Barnett, *Confronting the Costs of War,* esp. pp. 135–40, 185–96, 218–33.

22. Sasson Sofer, *Begin: Anatomy of Leadership* (Oxford: Basil Blackwell, 1988), p. 93.

23. Ilan Peleg, *Begin's Foreign Policy, 1977–1983: Israel's Move to the Right* (New York: Greenwood, 1987), p. 65. This book and Sofer offer useful accounts of Begin's world-view.

24. Contrast Quandt, *Peace Process,* pp. 267–70, and Saul A. Friedlander, *Sadat and Begin: The Domestic Politics of Peacemaking* (Boulder, Colo.: Westview, 1983), p. 68.

25. Quotations from Hirst and Beeson, *Sadat,* pp. 265, 275.

26. Sofer, *Begin,* pp. 182–3.

27. Peleg, *Begin's Foreign Policy,* pp. 110–1.

28. Jimmy Carter, *Keeping Faith: Memoirs of a President* (New York: Bantam Books, 1982), p. 416.

29. A basic study, on which this section relies, is Helena Cobban, *The Making of Modern Lebanon* (London: Hutchinson, 1985).

30. Quotations from Daniel Pipes, *Greater Syria: The History of an Ambition* (New York: Oxford University Press, 1990), pp. 119, 130, 139.

31. Pipes, *Greater Syria,* p. 175.

32. Quoted in Sofer, *Begin,* p. 206.

33. Peleg, *Begin's Foreign Policy*, pp. 152–5. For a detailed account, see Ze'ev Schiff & Ehud Ya'avi, *Israel's Lebanon War*, trans. by Ina Friedman (New York: Simon and Schuster, 1984).

34. Robert Fisk, *Pity the Nation: Lebanon at War* (London: André Deutsch, 1990), p. 362.

35. Quotations from Colin Shindler, *Israel, Likud and the Zionist Dream: Power, Politics and Ideology from Begin to Netanyahu*, (London: I. B. Tauris, 1995), p. 161, and Sofer, *Begin*, p. 210.

36. Robert Lacey, *The Kingdom* (London: Fontana/Collins, 1982), pp. 5–6, 562.

37. Joan Edelman Spero, *The Politics of International Economic Relations*, 2nd ed. (London: Allen & Unwin, 1982), p. 252.

38. Fiona Venn, *Oil Diplomacy in the Twentieth Century* (London: Macmillan, 1986), p. 11.

39. See N. C. Grill, *Urbanisation in the Arabian Peninsula* (University of Durham: Centre for Middle Eastern Studies, 1984), pp. 12, 40–8; Stephen Gardiner, *Kuwait: The Making of a City* (London: Longman, 1983).

40. Richard F. Nydorp, ed., *Saudi Arabia: A Country Study*, 4th ed. (Washington, D.C.: Government Printing Office, 1984), p. 74.

41. Fouad Al Farsy, *Saudi Arabia: A Case Study in Development*, 2nd ed. (London: Kegan Paul International, 1986), p. 177. In general, see Ragaei El Mallakh, *Saudi Arabia: Rush to Development. Profile of an Energy Economy and Investment* (London: Croom Helm, 1982).

42. Lacey, *The Kingdom*, p. 518.

43. Abdul Rahman Osama, *The Dilemma of Development in the Arabian Peninsula* (London: Croom Helm, 1987), p. 35.

44. Employment data from Khaldoun Hasan al-Naqeeb, *Society and State in the Gulf and Arab Peninsula: A Different Perspective*, trans. L. M. Kenny (London: Routledge, 1990), pp. 86, 112.

45. Al-Naqeeb, *Society and State*, chs. 5–6; also Jill Crystal, *Oil and Politics in the Gulf: Rulers and Merchants in Kuwait and Qatar* (Cambridge: Cambridge University Press, 1990).

46. For this paragraph, see Mordechai Abir, *Saudi Arabia: Government, Society and the Gulf Crisis* (London: Routledge, 1993), esp. chs. 1–6.

47. Homa Katouzian, *The Political Economy of Modern Iran: Despotism and Pseudo-Modernism, 1926–1979* (London: Macmillan, 1981), pp. 257–8, 291–2.

48. William Shawcross, *The Shah's Last Ride: The Story of the Exile, Misadventures and Death of the Emperor* (London: Chatto & Windus, 1989), pp. 46–7.

49. *The Public Papers of the Presidents of the United States: Jimmy Carter, 1977* (Washington, D.C.: Government Printing Office, 1978), p. 2221.

50. Marvin Zonis and Daniel Brumberg, *Khomeini, The Islamic Republic of Iran, and the Arab World* (Cambridge, Mass.: Harvard Center for Middle Eastern Studies, 1987), ch. 1.

51. A point emphasized by Mansour Moaddel, *Class, Politics, and Ideology in the Iranian Revolution* (New York: Columbia University Press, 1993), p. 268.

52. See Shaul Bakhash, *The Reign of the Ayatollahs: Iran and the Islamic Revolution* (London: I. B. Tauris, 1985), p. 49.

53. Richard Cottam, "Inside Revolutionary Iran," *Middle East Journal* 43 (1989): p. 168.

54. Mohammad Reza Pahlavi, *The Shah's Story,* trans. by Teresa Waugh (London: Michael Joseph, 1980), p. 190.

55. Quotations from Dilip Hiro, *Iran under the Ayatollahs* (London: Routledge & Kegan Paul, 1985), p. 100.

56. The phrase in Ambassador William Sullivan's notorious "long telegram" from Teheran on Nov. 9, 1978. For an analysis of U.S. errors see Charles-Philippe David, with Nancy Ann Carrol and Zachary A. Selden, *Foreign Policy Failure in the White House: Reappraising the Fall of the Shah and the Iran-Contra Affair* (New York and London: University Press of America, 1993), Part 2.

57. See Milani, *The Making of Iran's Islamic Revolution,* ch. 8.

58. Gary Sick, *All Fall Down: America's Fateful Encounter with Iran* (London: I. B. Tauris, 1985), p. 220. This book provides a good insider's overview of U.S. policy.

59. Quotations from Dilip Hiro, *The Longest War: The Iran-Iraq Military Conflict* (London: Paladin Books, 1990), pp. 32, 35, on which this section draws in general.

60. Hiro, *Iran under the Ayatollahs,* p. 139.

61. Quoted in Bakhash, *Reign of the Ayatollahs,* p. 97.

62. Professor Ali Dessouki, quoted in Anthony McDermott, *Egypt from Nasser to Mubarak: A Flawed Revolution* (London: Croom Helm, 1988), p. 179.

63. About which the classic tract is Edward Said, *Orientalism* (London: Routledge & Kegan Paul, 1978).

64. Mansour Khalid, *Nimeiri and the Revolution of Dis-May* (London: Kegan Paul International, 1985), p. 255.

65. Quoted in Lillian Craig Harris, *Libya: Qadhafi's Revolution and the Modern State* (Boulder, Colo.: Westview, 1986), p. 57.

66. Brian L. Davis, *Qaddafi, Terrorism, and the Origins of the U.S. Attack on Libya* (New York: Praeger, 1990), p. 3.

67. Lisa Anderson, "Qaddafi's Islam," in John L. Esposito, ed., *Voices of Resurgent Islam* (New York: Oxford University Press, 1983), p. 142.

68. Quoted in Omar Noman, *Pakistan: A Political and Economic History since 1947* (London: Kegan Paul International, 1990), p. 108.

69. Quoted in Shahid Javed Burki, *Pakistan under Bhutto, 1971–1977,* 2nd ed. (London: Macmillan, 1988), p. 212.

70. Quoted in Surendra Nath Kaushik, *Politics of Islamization in Pakistan: A Study of Zia Regime* (New Delhi: South Asian Publishers, 1993), p. 65.

71. Anthony Hyman, *Afghanistan under Soviet Domination, 1964–91,* 3rd ed. (London: Macmillan, 1992), pp. 197–8.

72. Jeff Haynes, *Religion in Third World Politics* (Buckingham: Open University Press, 1993), pp. 134–6.

73. Habiba Zaman, "The Military in Bangladesh Politics," in Chowdury E. Haque, ed., *Bangladesh: Politics, Economy and Society* (Winnipeg, Manitoba: Bangladesh Studies Assemblage, 1987), p. 26.

74. Lawrence Ziring, *Bangladesh from Mujib to Ershad: An Interpretive Study* (Karachi: Oxford University Press, 1992), p. 181. This paragraph draws on Ziring and also Dilara Chowdury, *Constitutional Development in Bangladesh: Stresses and Strains* (Karachi: Oxford University Press, 1994).

75. World Bank, *World Tables, 1994* (Baltimore: Johns Hopkins University Press, 1994), pp. 128–31.

76. See the case study by Santi Rozario, *Purity and Communal Boundaries: Women and Social Change in a Bangladeshi Village* (London: Zed Books, 1992), esp. ch. 11.

77. Quoted in Patrick Bannerman, *Islam in Perspective: A Guide to Islamic Society, Politics and Law* (London and New York: Routledge, 1988), p. 123.

78. Nazih N. Ayubi, *Political Islam: Religion and Politics in the Arab World* (London: Routledge, 1991), p. 177.

79. A point emphasized by Sami Zubaiba, "The Quest for the Islamic State: Islamic Fundamentalism in Egypt and Iran," in Lionel Caplan, ed., *Studies in Religious Fundamentalism* (London: Macmillan, 1987), pp. 48–9.

80. Ayubi, *Political Islam*, p. 226.

81. Quotations from the very good editorial discussion in Elizabeth Warnock Fernea, ed., *Women and the Family in the Middle East: New Voices of Change* (Austin: University of Texas Press, 1985), pp. 220–1.

82. For these contrasting views, see Freda Hussain, ed., *Muslim Women* (London: Croom Helm, 1984), respectively pp. 202, 63.

83. Carla Makhlouf Obermeyer, "Islam, Women, and Politics: The Demography of Arab Countries," *Population and Development Review* 18 (1992): 51.

Chapter 12 Capitalist Revolutions, Asian Style

1. See R. C. O. Matthews, ed., *Slower Growth in the Western World* (London: Heinemann, 1982), pp. 12–13, 129–47.

2. Joan Edelman Spero, *The Politics of International Economic Relations*, 2nd ed. (London: Allen & Unwin, 1982), pp. 103, 105.

3. Andrew Shonfield, ed., *International Economic Relations of the Western World, 1959–1971* Vol. II (London: Oxford University Press, 1976), ch. 6, esp. pp. 176, 182.

4. Alfred Grosser, *The Western Alliance: European-American Relations since 1945*, trans. Michael Shaw (London: Macmillan, 1980), p. 271.

5. Quoted in Susan Strange, "The Dollar Crisis, 1971," *International Affairs* 48 (1972): 205.

6. Walter Galenson, *Trade Union Growth and Decline: An International Study* (Westport, Conn.: Praeger, 1994), p. 2. See generally, Robert J. Flanagan, David W. Soskice, and Lloyd

Ulman, *Unionism, Economic Stabilization, and Incomes Policy: European Experience* (Washington, D.C.: Brookings Institution, 1983), esp. ch. 11.

7. Philip Armstrong, Andrew Glyn and John Harrison, *Capitalism since 1945* (Oxford: Blackwell, 1991), pp. 217–20.

8. Richard P. Mattione, *OPEC's Investments and the International Financial System* (Washington, D.C.: Brookings Institution, 1985), esp. pp. 1, 11, 23, 41, 106–7, 136.

9. For these and subsequent statistics, see Michael Bruno and Jeffrey D. Sachs, *Economics of Worldwide Stagflation* (Oxford: Basil Blackwell, 1985), pp. 155–6.

10. Robert Mundell, "Unemployment, Competitiveness and the Welfare State," in Mario Baldassarri, Luigi Paganetto, and Edmund S. Phelps, eds., *Equity, Efficiency and Growth: The Future of the Welfare State* (London: Macmillan, 1996), p. 146.

11. Spero, *Politics of International Economic Relations*, p. 60.

12. On these distinctions see Bruno and Sachs, *Economics of Worldwide Stagflation*, ch. 11.

13. See Peter Lange, George Ross, Maurizio Vannicelli, *Unions, Change and Crisis: French and Italian Union Strategy and the Political Economy, 1945–1980* (London: Allen & Unwin, 1982), ch. 3. More generally, see Paul Ginsborg, *A History of Contemporary Italy: Society and Politics, 1943–1988* (London: Penguin, 1990), ch. 10.

14. Fiona Venn, *Oil Diplomacy in the Twentieth Century* (London: Macmillan, 1986), table A.2, pp. 176–7.

15. On which see Geoffrey Bolton, *The Oxford History of Australia,* vol. 5, *1952–1988* (Melbourne: Oxford University Press, 1990), chs. 9–10; John Gould, *The Rake's Progress? The New Zealand Economy since 1945* (London: Hodder & Stoughton, 1982), esp. chs. 5, 8.

16. David J. Bell, *The Roots of Disunity: A Study of Canadian Political Culture,* 2nd ed. (Toronto: Oxford University Press, 1992), ch. 5; more generally, Robert Bothwell, Ian Drummond, and John English, *Canada since 1945: Power, Politics and Provincialism,* 2nd ed. (Toronto: University of Toronto Press, 1989), chs. 27–29.

17. Bela Balassa, "The Lessons of East Asian Development: An Overview," *Economic Development and Cultural Change* 36/3, supplement (April 1988): pp. S275–6; cf. Michio Morishima, *Why Has Japan "Succeeded"?: Western Technology and the Japanese Ethos,* 2nd ed. (Cambridge: Cambridge University Press, 1984).

18. Takashi Inoguchi and Daniel I. Okimoto, eds., *The Political Economy of Japan,* vol. 2, *The Changing International Context* (Stanford: Stanford University Press, 1988), pp. 29 (Inoguchi quote) and 230—henceforth *PEJ* 2.

19. Tadashi Fukutake, *The Japanese Social Structure: Its Evolution in the Modern Century,* trans. Ronald P. Dore, 2nd ed. (Tokyo: University of Tokyo Press, 1989), pp. 85 (quote), 86, 99–100.

20. Naohiro Ogawa and Robert D. Retherford, "Prospects for Increased Contraceptive Pill Use in Japan," *Studies in Family Planning* 22 (1991): 378–83.

21. Takatoshi Ito, *The Japanese Economy* (Cambridge, Mass.: MIT Press, 1992), p. 188.

22. On broad contrasts between capitalism in Japan and elsewhere see Charles Hampden-Turner and Alfons Trompenaars, *The Seven Cultures of Capitalism* (New York: Doubleday, 1993), esp. chs. 6–8.

23. G. C. Allen, *A Short Economic History of Modern Japan,* 4th ed. (London: Macmillan, 1981), p. 282; Ito, *Japanese Economy,* p. 227.

24. A contrast emphasized by Rodney Clark, *The Japanese Company* (New Haven: Yale University Press, 1979), pp. 142–3.

25. See Yasusuke Murakami, "The Japanese Model of Political Economy," in Kozo Yamamura and Yasukichi Yasuba, *The Political Economy of Japan,* vol. 1, *The Domestic Transformation,* (Stanford: Stanford University Press, 1987), pp. 62–5—henceforth *PEJ* 1.

26. J. A. A. Stockwin, *Japan: Divided Politics in a Growth Economy,* 2nd ed. (London: Weidenfeld & Nicolson, 1982), pp. 108, 111.

27. Gary D. Allinson, "The Structure and Transformation of Conservative Rule," in Andrew Gordon, ed., *Postwar Japan as History* (Berkeley: University of California Press, 1993), pp. 131–2.

28. Yutaka Kōsai, "The Postwar Japanese Economy, 1945–73," in Peter Duus, ed., *The Cambridge History of Japan,* vol. 6 (Cambridge: Cambridge University Press, 1988), p. 535.

29. Allen, *Short Economic History,* p. 248.

30. Quotations from Murakami, "The Japanese Model of Political Economy," pp. 50, 54.

31. Michael A. Cusumano, *The Japanese Automobile Industry: Technology and Management at Nissan and Toyota* (Cambridge, Mass.: Harvard University Press, 1985), pp. 1, 266. This paragraph draws heavily on Cusumano's book.

32. Harry T. Oshima, "Reinterpreting Japan's Postwar Growth," *Economic Development and Cultural Change* 31 (1982): 24—an article in which this point about mechanization is developed.

33. Statistics from Kōsai, "Postwar Japanese Economy," p. 515.

34. David W. Plath, "MY-CAR-ISMA: Motorizing the Showa Self," in Carol Gluck and Stephen R. Graubard, eds., *Showa: The Japan of Hirohito* (New York: Norton, 1992), pp. 230–1.

35. Fukutake, *Japanese Social Structure,* ch. 15; Balassa and Noland, *Japan in the World Economy,* ch. 4.

36. Fukutake, *Japanese Social Structure,* p. 111.

37. Naohiro Ogawa and Robert D. Retherford, "The Resumption of Fertility Decline in Japan, 1973–92," *Population and Development Review* 19 (1993): 707.

38. Ezra F. Vogel, *Japan's New Middle Class: The Salary Man and His Family in a Tokyo Suburb,* 2nd ed. (Berkeley: University of California Press, 1971), pp. 195–6.

39. Karel van Wolferen, *The Enigma of Japanese Power: People and Politics in a Stateless Nation* (New York: Alfred A. Knopf, 1990), pp. 85, 439–40.

40. *The Military Balance, 1987–1988* (London: Institute for Strategic Studies, 1987), table 5, pp. 216, 220.

41. Shigeto Tsuru, *Japan's Capitalism: Creative Defeat and Beyond* (Cambridge: Cambridge University Press, 1993), pp. 48–52, 78, 129.

42. Håken Hedberg (1969) quoted in Fukutake, *Japanese Social Structure*, p. 187. Statistics from Joan E. Spero, *The Politics of International Economic Relations*, 2nd ed. (London: Allen & Unwin, 1982), p. 252.

43. Ito, *Japanese Economy*, pp. 71, 125–7, 241.

44. Fukutake, *Japanese Social Structure*, p. 191.

45. Tsuru, *Japanese Capitalism*, p. 129.

46. Frank K. Upham, "Unplaced Persons and the Movement for Place," in Gordon, ed., *Postwar Japan*, pp. 338–42.

47. Statistics on crime and social security from Martin Bronfenbrenner and Yasukichi Yasuba, "Economic Welfare," in *PEJ* 1: 119, 131.

48. Spending and deficit figures from Ito, *Japanese Economy*, p. 168.

49. Ito, *Japanese Economy*, p. 241.

50. Figures from Michael Bruno and Jeffrey D. Sachs, *Economics of Worldwide Stagflation* (Oxford: Basil Blackwell, 1985), p. 155.

51. Cusumano, *The Japanese Automobile Industry*, pp. 6, 186.

52. Bela Balassa and Marcus Noland, *Japan in the World Economy* (Washington, D.C.: Institute for International Economics, 1988), pp. 116–8.

53. See discussion in Balassa and Noland, *Japan in the World Economy*, chs. 4–5.

54. See graph in Koichi Hamada and Hugh T. Patrick, "Japan and the International Monetary Regime," in *PEJ* 1, p. 116.

55. Reinhard Drifte, *Japan's Foreign Policy* (London: Routledge, 1990), p. 66.

56. Measured in terms of exchange rates. See Ito, *Japanese Economy*, p. 4.

57. Following the best seller by Ezra F. Vogel, *Japan as Number One: Lessons for America* (Cambridge, Mass.: Harvard University Press, 1979).

58. For statistics in this paragraph on income and exports see Bela Balassa, *Economic Policies in the Pacific Area Developing Countries* (London: Macmillan, 1991), pp. 2, 25.

59. Overviews from different perspectives include: Paul W. Kuznets, "An East Asian Model of Economic Development: Japan, Taiwan, and South Korea," *Economic Development and Cultural Change* 36/3 Supplement (April 1988): S11–43; Robert Wade, *Governing the Market: Economic Theory and the Role of Government in East Asian Industrialization* (Princeton, N.J.: Princeton University Press, 1990); The World Bank, *The East Asian Miracle: Economic Growth and Public Policy* (New York: Oxford University Press, 1993).

60. In the early 1930s, for instance, Taiwan had 2,857 miles of railways compared with 9,400 in the whole of mainland China. Roderick MacFarquhar and John K. Fairbank, eds., *The Cambridge History of China*, vol. 15 (Cambridge: Cambridge University Press, 1991), pp. 815–7.

61. Martin Hart-Landsberg, *The Rush to Development: Economic Change and Political Struggle in South Korea* (New York: Monthly Review Press, 1993), pp. 1–2.

62. World Bank, *The East Asian Miracle*, p. 130.

63. Young Whan Kihl, *Politics and Policies in Divided Korea: Regimes in Contest* (Boulder, Colo.: Westview, 1984), pp. 75–83.

64. On Park see Se-Jim Kim, *The Politics of Military Revolution in Korea* (Chapel Hill: University of North Carolina Press, 1971), pp. 88–92.

65. Hart-Landsberg, *The Rush to Development*, p. 83.

66. Alice M. Amsden, *Asia's Next Giant: South Korea and Late Industrialization* (New York: Oxford University Press, 1989), p. 116.

67. Hart-Landsberg, *Rush to Development*, ch. 7, esp. pp. 145–7, 153–4.

68. Shirley W. Y. Kuo, *The Taiwan Economy in Transition* (Boulder, Colo.: Westview, 1983), pp. 12–13.

69. Kuo, *Taiwan Economy*, p. 135.

70. These Gini coefficients from Kuo, *Taiwan Economy*, pp. 96–7.

71. Balassa, *Economic Policies in the Pacific Area*, p. 101.

72. Wade, *Governing the Market*, pp. 176–7.

73. See generally the stimulating essay by Lawrence B. Krause, "Hong Kong and Singapore: Twins or Kissing Cousins?" in *Economic Development and Cultural Change* 36/3 Supplement (1988): S45–66.

74. A point emphasized by W. G. Huff, *The Economic Growth of Singapore: Trade and Development in the Twentieth Century* (Cambridge: Cambridge University Press, 1994), pp. 367–8.

75. Huff, *The Economic Growth of Singapore*, pp. 319–21.

76. Lawrence B. Krause, Koh Ai Tee, and Lee (Tsao) Yuan, eds., *The Singapore Economy Reconsidered* (Singapore: Institute of Southeast Asian Studies, 1987), pp. 115–7.

77. C. P. Lo, *Hong Kong* (London: Belhaven Press, 1992), p. 174.

78. Lo, *Hong Kong*, p. 63.

79. A. J. Youngson, *Hong Kong: Economic Growth and Policy* (Hong Kong: Oxford University Press, 1992), pp. 21–2.

80. Lo, *Hong Kong*, p. 94.

81. Youngson, *Hong Kong*, p. 136.

82. Henry J. Bruton, *The Political Economy of Poverty, Equity, and Growth: Sri Lanka and Malaysia* (New York: Oxford University Press, 1992), p. 393.

83. Generally see Gordon P. Means, *Malaysian Politics: The Second Generation* (Singapore: Oxford University Press, 1991), and Anne Munro-Kua, *Authoritarian Populism in Malaysia* (London: Macmillan, 1996).

84. Means, *Malaysian Politics*, p. 94.

85. See the portrait in Elliott Kuklick and Dick Wilson, *Thailand's Turn: Profile of a New Dragon* (London: Macmillan, 1992), pp. xv–xxiv.

86. Balassa, *Economic Policies*, p. 196.

87. On which see generally Hal Hill, ed., *Indonesia's New Order: The Dynamics of Socio-Economic Transformation* (Honolulu: University of Hawaii, 1994), ch. 1; and Michael R. J. Vatikiotis, *Indonesian Politics under Suharto: Order, Development and Pressure for Change*, 2nd ed. (London: Routledge, 1994), ch. 1.

88. John G. Taylor, *Indonesia's Forgotten War: The Hidden History of East Timor* (London: Zed Books, 1991), p. ix.

89. Generally see Hill, ed., *Indonesia's New Order*, chs. 2–3; Mari Pangestu, "Economic Policy Reforms in Indonesia," *Indonesian Quarterly* 17 (1989): 218–33; and Graeme J. Hugo, Terence H. Hull, Valerie J. Hull and Gavin W. Jones, *The Demographic Dimension in Indonesian Development* (Singapore: Oxford University Press, 1987), ch. 5.

90. Hal Hill, ed., *Unity and Diversity: Regional Economic Development in Indonesia since 1970* (Singapore: Oxford University Press, 1989), p. 235.

91. Anthony J. Whitten, Herman Haeruman, Hadi S. Alikodra, and Machmud Thohari, *Transmigration and the Environment in Indonesia: The Past, Present and Future* (Gland, Switzerland: IUCN, 1987), p. 3.

92. John Bresnan, *Managing Indonesia: The Modern Political Economy* (New York: Columbia University Press, 1993), pp. 190–1; and Richard Robison, *Indonesia: The Rise of Capital* (London: Unwin Hyman, 1986), pp. 171–2, 376.

93. Bresnan, *Managing Indonesia*, pp. 191–2, 281, 289; see also World Bank, *Adjustment in Africa: Reforms, Results, and the Road Ahead* (New York: Oxford University Press, 1994), pp. 32–3.

94. Hill, ed., *Indonesia's New Order*, p. 104.

95. David I. Steinberg, *Burma: A Socialist Nation of Southeast Asia* (Boulder, Colo.: Westview, 1982), pp. 90–1.

96. Burnham O. Campbell, "Development Trends: A Comparative Analysis of the Asian Experience," in Naohiro Ogawa, Gavin W. Jones, and Jeffrey G. Williamson, eds., *Human Resources in Development along the Asia-Pacific Rim* (Singapore: Oxford University Press, 1993), p. 67.

97. Yong Mun Cheong, "The Political Structures of the Independent States," in Nicholas Tarling, ed., *The Cambridge History of Southeast Asia*, vol. 2 (Cambridge: Cambridge University Press, 1992), p. 449.

98. Balassa, *Economic Policies*, p. 2. In general on the Philippines see John Bresnan, ed., *Crisis in the Philippines: The Marcos Era and Beyond* (Princeton, N.J.: Princeton University Press, 1986).

99. Generally see Carmen Navarro Pedrosa, *Imelda Marcos* (London: Weidenfeld & Nicolson, 1987).

100. Challenged later about his statement by incredulous reporters, Bush insisted, "I'll repeat it and stand by it." See Raymond Bonner, *Waltzing with a Dictator: The Marcoses and the Making of American Policy* (London: Macmillan, 1987), pp. 307–8.

101. Quoted in Bonner, *Waltzing with a Dictator*, p. 355.

102. Quoted in Mark R. Thompson, *The Anti-Marcos Struggle: Personalistic Rule and Democratic Transition in the Philippines* (New Haven: Yale University Press, 1995), pp. 145–6.

103. Pedrosa, *Imelda Marcos*, pp. 219–21.

104. William C. Rempel, *Delusions of a Dictator: The Mind of Marcos as Revealed in His Secret Diaries* (Boston: Little, Brown, 1993), p. xiii; Peter Matthews, ed., *The New Guinness Book of Records, 1995* (London: Guinness Publishing, 1994), p. 190.

105. World Bank, *China 2020* (Washington, D.C.: World Bank, 1997), pp. 2, 4, 13.

106. Nicholas R. Lardy, *Foreign Trade and Economic Reform in China, 1978–1990* (Cambridge: Cambridge University Press, 1992), pp. 1, 13.

107. Barry Naughton, *Growing Out of the Plan: Chinese Economic Reform, 1979–1993* (Cambridge: Cambridge University Press, 1995), p. 245.

108. Yum K. Kwan and Gregory C. Chow, "Estimating Economic Effects of Political Movements in China," *Journal of Comparative Economics* 23 (1996): esp. 204–6 suggest a figure of 2.7.

109. Gregory C. Chow, "Capital Formation and Economic Growth in China," *Quarterly Journal of Economics* 108 (1993): 809–42.

110. Carl Riskin, *China's Political Economy: The Quest for Development since 1949* (Oxford: Oxford University Press, 1991), p. 318.

111. These points are stressed in Andrew G. Walder, ed., *China's Transitional Economy* (Oxford: Clarendon, 1996), pp. 10, 16.

112. Naughton, *Growing Out of the Plan*, pp. 40–2.

113. Dudley L. Poston, Jr., "Fertility Trends in China," in Dudley L. Poston and David Yaukey, eds., *The Population of Modern China* (New York: Plenum Press, 1992), pp. 277–85, quoting from p. 277.

114. See the essays by H. Yan Tien, "Abortion in China: Incidence and Implications," and by Dudley L. Poston, Jr., "Patterns of Contraceptive Use in China," in Poston and Yaukey, eds., *The Population of Modern China*, pp. 287–310 and 311–27.

115. Bill Brugger and Stephen Reglar, *Politics, Economy and Society in Contemporary China* (London: Macmillan, 1994), pp. 292–3.

116. Immanuel C. Y. Hsü, *China without Mao: The Search for a New Order*, 2nd ed. (New York: Oxford University Press, 1990), p. 107.

117. Figures from Naughton, *Growing Out of the Plan*, pp. 89–92.

118. Richard Evans, *Deng Xiaoping and the Making of Modern China* (London: Penguin Books, 1995), p. 200.

119. David S. G. Goodman, *Deng Xiaoping and the Chinese Revolution: A Political Biography* (London: Routledge, 1994), p. 91.

120. On which see Wang Lixin and Joseph Fewsmith, "Bulwark of the Planned Economy: The Structure and Role of the State Planning Commission," in Carol Lee Hamrin and Suisheng Zhao, eds., *Decision-making in Deng's China: Perspectives from Insiders* (Armonk, N.Y.: M.E. Sharpe, 1995), pp. 51–65.

121. Quoted in Naughton, *Growing Out of the Plan*, p. 120.

122. See Naughton, *Growing Out of the Plan*, chs. 5–6.

123. For this background, see Terry Cannon and Alan Jenkins, eds., *The Geography of Contemporary China: The Impact of Deng Xiaoping's Decade* (London: Routledge, 1990), ch. 6.

124. David Wen-Wei Chang, *China under Deng Xiaoping* (London: Macmillan, 1988), pp. 139–40.

125. Riskin, *China's Political Economy*, p. 261.

126. See the argument of Dali L. Yang, *Calamity and Reform in China: State, Rural Society, and Institutional Change since the Great Leap Forward* (Stanford: Stanford University Press, 1996).

127. Naughton, *Growing Out of the Plan*, pp. 111–2 and generally chs. 4–5.

128. John Gittings, *China Changes Face: The Road from Revolution, 1949–1989* (Oxford: Oxford University Press, 1990), pp. 127–8.

129. A point emphasized by Peter Nolan, *China's Rise, Russia's Fall: Politics, Economics and Planning in the Transition from Stalinism* (London: Macmillan, 1995), p. 188.

130. For discussion, see Lardy, *Foreign Trade and Economic Reform*, ch. 3.

131. On the SEZs, see David S. G. Goodman, *China's Regional Development* (London: Routledge, 1989), ch. 7.

132. Joseph Chai, "Consumption and Living Standards in China," in Robert F. Ash and Y. Y. Kueh, eds, *The Chinese Economy under Deng Xiaoping* (Oxford: Clarendon, 1996), pp. 247, 262, 274.

133. James Lull, *China Turned On: Television, Reform and Resistance* (London: Routledge, 1991), pp. 20, 23, 27. The next paragraph follows Lull's book, esp. chs. 5–8.

134. Interviewee quoted in Lull, *China Turned On*, p. 174.

135. Campbell, "Development Trends," p. 67.

136. Vincent Cable, *China and India: Economic Reform and Global Integration* (London: Royal Institute of International Affairs, 1995), p. 37.

137. Statistics from Naohiro Ogawa and Noriko O. Tsuya, "Demographic Change and Human Resource Development in the Asia-Pacific Region: Trends of the 1960s to 1980s and Future Prospects," in Ogawa et al., eds., *Human Resources*, pp. 31 (fertility) and 53 (agricultural work force).

138. Mukesh Eswaran and Ashok Kotwal, *Why Poverty Persists in India: A Framework for Understanding the Indian Economy* (Delhi: Oxford University Press, 1994), p. 122.

139. Ogawa and Tsuya, "Demographic Change," p. 52.

140. Lin Leam Lim, "The Feminization of Labour in the Asia-Pacific Rim Countries," in Ogawa, et al., eds, *Human Resources*, ch. 6, quoting from p. 179.

141. Paul R. Brass, *The Politics of India since Independence*, 2nd ed. (Cambridge: Cambridge University Press, 1994), pp. 151, 177.

142. Raghavendra Rao, *Society, Culture and Population Policy in India* (Delhi: Ajanta Publications, 1989), p. 32.

143. For this and the footnote, see Inder Malhotra, *Indira Gandhi: A Personal and Political Biography* (London: Hodder & Stoughton, 1989), p. 191.

144. Robert W. Stern, *Changing India: Bourgeois Revolution on the Sub-Continent* (Cambridge: Cambridge University Press, 1993), p. 104.

145. Brass, *Politics of India*, p. 104.

146. Sudipta Kaviraj, "Religion, Politics and Modernity," in Upendra Baxi and Bhikhu Parekh, eds., *Crisis and Change in Contemporary India* (New Delhi: Sage, 1995), p. 305.

147. Johari, et al., *Governments and Politics*, pp. 62, 140–7; Susan Bayly, *Caste, Society and Politics in India from the Eighteenth Century to the Modern Age* (Cambridge: Cambridge Univ. Press, 1999), ch. 7.

148. This paragraph draws on Christophe Jaffrelot, *The Hindu Nationalist Movement and Indian Politics, 1925 to the 1990s* (London: Hurst & Co., 1996), chs. 9–12.

149. Cassen, *India: Population, Economy, Society* (London: Macmillan, 1978), p. 323. Ch. 3 of this book, and Rao, *Society, Culture and Population Policy in India*, ch. 4, are basic sources for this paragraph.

150. See generally Geraldine Forbes, *Women in Modern India* (Cambridge: Cambridge University Press, 1996), Ch. 8; and Veena Das, *Critical Events: An Anthropological Perspective on Contemporary India* (Delhi: Oxford University Press, 1995), ch. 4.

151. Sumantra Bose, *States, Nations, Sovereignty: Sri Lanka, India and the Tamil Eelam Movement* (New Delhi: Sage, 1994), pp. 64–5. Generally see Chandra Richard de Silva, *Sri Lanka: A History* (New Delhi: Vikas, 1987), chs. 1, 17–19; and Edgar O'Ballance, *The Cyanide War: Tamil Insurrection in Sri Lanka, 1973–88* (London: Brassey's, 1989).

152. Dennis Austin, *Democracy and Violence in India and Sri Lanka* (London: Pinter, 1994), p. 82, and generally pp. 80–4.

153. Stern, *Changing India*, p. 208.

154. For these points, see Cable, *China and India*, pp. 3–4, 15–16.

155. UN Industrial Development Office, *India: New Dimensions of Industrial Growth* (Oxford: Blackwell, 1990), pp. 70, 86.

156. Figures calculated from J. S. Yadava and Usha V. Reddi, "In the Midst of Diversity: Television in Urban Indian Homes," in James Lull, ed., *World Families Watch Television* (London: Sage, 1988), pp. 122–3.

157. Quoted in Paul Hartmann, B. R. Patil and Anita Dighe, *The Mass Media and Village Life: An Indian Study* (New Delhi: Sage, 1989), p. 204.

158. Neena Behl, "Equalizing Status: Television and Tradition in an Indian Village," in Lull, ed., *World Families*, ch. 6.

159. Ved Mehta, *Rajiv Gandhi and Rama's Kingdom* (New Haven: Yale University Press, 1994), p. 171.

160. Jaffrelot, *Hindu Nationalist Movement*, p. 389.

Chapter 13 Challenges for the West

1. Friedrich A. Hayek, *The Road to Serfdom* (Chicago: University of Chicago, 1976 ed.), p. 17.

2. Jürgen Kohl, "Trends and Problems in Postwar Public Expenditure Development in Western Europe and North America," in Peter Flora and Arnold J. Heidenheimer, eds., *The Development of Welfare States in Europe and America* (New Brunswick, N.J.: Transaction Books, 1981), p. 310.

3. Jens Alber, "Is There a Crisis of the Welfare State? Cross-National Evidence from Europe, North America, and Japan," *European Sociological Review* 4 (1988): 190.

4. Michael Novak, *The Crisis of the Welfare State: Ethics and Economics* (London: Centre for Policy Studies, 1993), pp. 11–12.

5. Milton and Rose Friedman, *Free to Choose: A Personal Statement* (London: Secker & Warburg, 1980).

6. Quoted in Bernard Nossiter, *Britain: A Future That Works* (London: Andre Deutsch, 1978), p. 42.

7. Quoted in Hugo Young, *One of Us: A Biography of Margaret Thatcher* (London: Macmillan, 1989), p. 130.

8. Quoted in Margaret Thatcher, *The Downing Street Years* (London: HarperCollins, 1993), p. 122.

9. Quotations from Robert Dallek, *Ronald Reagan: The Politics of Symbolism* (Cambridge, Mass.: Harvard University Press, 1984), pp. 12, 193.

10. Donald Regan, *From Wall Street to Washington* (New York: Harcourt Brace Jovanovich, 1988), p. 4.

11. Thomas "Tip" O'Neill, with William Novak, *Man of the House: The Life and Political Memoirs of Speaker Tip O'Neill* (New York: Random House, 1987), pp. 360, 363.

12. See Wayne Northcutt, *Mitterrand: A Political Biography* (New York: Holmes and Meier, 1992), from which the de Gaulle story in the footnote is taken (p. 8).

13. Jean-Louis Bianco, quoted in David R. Cameron, "Exchange-Rate Politics in France, 1981–1983," in Anthony Daley, ed., *The Mitterrand Era: Policy Alternatives and Political Mobilization in France* (London: Macmillan, 1996), p. 69.

14. Quoted in Pierre-Alain Muet and Alain Fontenau, *Reflation and Austerity: Economic Policy under Mitterrand,* trans. by Malcolm Slater (London: Berg, 1990), p. xix.

15. Keith Middlemas, *Orchestrating Europe: The Informal Politics of European Integration, 1973–1995* (London: Fontana, 1995), pp. 98–155.

16. Quoted in Franz-Olivier Giesbert, *François Mitterrand, une vie* (Paris: Éditions du Seuil, 1996), p. 430.

17. Olivier Duhamel and Jérôme Jaffré quoted in Daley, ed., *The Mitterrand Era,* p. 2.

18. Peter Holmes, "The Thatcher Government's Overall Economic Performance," in David S. Bell, ed., *The Conservative Government, 1979–84: An Interim Report* (London: Croom Helm, 1985), pp. 15–32.

19. Quotations from David Reynolds, *Britannia Overruled: British Policy and World Power in the Twentieth Century* (London and New York: Longman, 1991), p. 261.

20. David A. Stockman, *The Triumph of Politics: The Crisis in American Government and How It Affects the World* (New York: Avon, 1987), p. 14.

21. Joseph Hogan, "The Federal Budget in the Reagan Era," in Hogan, ed., *The Reagan Years: The Record in Presidential Leadership* (Manchester: Manchester University Press, 1990), pp. 231–2.

22. Robert Higgs, *Crisis and Leviathan: Critical Episodes in the Growth of American Government* (New York: Oxford University Press, 1987), p. 255.

23. Herman van der Wee, *Prosperity and Upheaval: The World Economy, 1945–1980,* trans. by Robin Hogg and Max R. Hall (London: Pelican, 1987), p. 263.

24. Statistics from Robert Devlin, *Debt and Crisis in Latin America: The Supply Side of the Story* (Princeton, N.J.: Princeton University Press, 1989), esp. pp. 24, 41, 44–5, 54.

25. Devlin, *Debt and Crisis in Latin America,* chs. 2–4, esp. pp. 38, 110 (quotation), 146–7.

26. For data in these two paragraphs, see Daniel Yergin, *The Prize: The Epic Quest for Oil, Money, and Power* (New York: Touchstone, 1992), esp. pp. 659–70, 692, 717–8.

27. For a good overview see Howard Handelman, *Mexican Politics: The Dynamics of Change* (New York: St. Martin's, 1997).

28. Quoted in Thomas E. Skidmore and Peter H. Smith, *Modern Latin America,* 3rd ed. (New York: Oxford University Press, 1992), p. 246.

29. Quoted by Vinod K. Aggarwal, "Interpreting the History of Mexico's External Debt Crises," in Barry Eichengreen and Peter H. Lindert, eds., *The International Debt Crisis in Historical Perspective* (Cambridge, Mass.: MIT Press, 1984), p. 148. Generally see Nora Lustig, *Mexico: The Remaking of an Economy* (Washington, D.C.: Brookings Institution, 1992), esp. ch. 1.

30. Quoted in Héctor Aguilar Camín and Lorenzo Meyer, *In the Shadow of the Mexican Revolution: Contemporary Mexican History, 1910–1989,* trans. Luis Alberto Fierro (Austin: University of Texas Press, 1993), p. 216.

31. World Bank, *Latin America and the Caribbean: A Decade after the Debt Crisis* (Washington, D.C.: World Bank, 1993), p. 13.

32. Devlin, *Debt and Crisis,* pp. 45, 183.

33. William R. Cline, *International Debt: Systemic Risk and Policy Response* (Washington, D.C.: Institute for International Economics, 1984), pp. 23–26.

34. Ernest J. Oliveri, *Latin American Debt and the Politics of International Finance* (Westport, Conn.: Praeger, 1992), ch. 4, quoting pp. 90 and 102.

35. "The Crash of 198?," *The Economist,* October 16, 1982, p. 15.

36. World Bank, *Latin America and the Caribbean,* p. 13.

37. Devlin, *Debt and Crisis in Latin America,* p. 23.

38. Data on Mexico in this paragraph and the next from Lustig, *Mexico,* ch. 3.

39. Mercedes González de la Rocha, "Economic Crisis, Domestic Reorganisation and Women's Work in Guadalajara, Mexico," *Bulletin of Latin American Research* 7 (1988): 207–23; see also Sylvia Chant, *Women and Survival in Mexican Cities: Perspectives on Gender, Labour Markets and Low Income Households* (Manchester: Manchester University Press, 1991), ch. 6.

40. Maruja Barrig, "The Difficult Equilibrium between Bread and Roses: Women's Organizations and the Transition from Dictatorship to Democracy in Peru," in Jane S. Jaquette, ed., *The Women's Movement in Latin America: Feminism and the Transition to Democracy* (Boston: Unwin Hyman, 1989), pp. 134, 144.

41. Vivienne Bennett, "The Evolution of Urban Popular Movements in Mexico between 1968 and 1988," in Arturo Escobar and Sonia E. Alvarez, eds., The *Making of Social Movements in Latin America: Identity, Strategy, and Democracy* (Boulder, Colo.: Westview, 1992), pp. 240–59; Carlos B. Gill, ed., *Hope and Frustration: Interviews with Leaders of Mexico's Political Opposition* (Wilmington, Del.: Scholarly Resources, 1992), pp. 48–57.

42. See John D. Wirth, Edson de Oliveria Nunes, and Thomas E. Bogenschild, eds., *State and Society in Brazil: Continuity and Change* (Boulder, Colo.: Westview, 1987), chs. 4–5, esp. pp. 167, 180.

43. Sonia E. Alvarez, *Engendering Democracy in Brazil: Women's Movements in Transition Politics* (Princeton, N.J.: Princeton University Press, 1990).

44. Guillermo O'Donnell and Philippe C. Schmitter, "Tentative Conclusions about Uncertain Democracies," in Guillermo O'Donnell, Philippe C. Schmitter, and Laurence Whitehead, eds., *Transitions from Authoritarian Rule: Prospects for Democracy* (Baltimore: Johns Hopkins University Press, 1986), part IV, p. 22. This volume provides valuable case studies of Latin American transitions, as does Larry Diamond, Juan J. Linz, and Seymour Martin Lipset, eds., *Democracy in Developing Countries*, vol. 4, *Latin America* (Boulder, Colo.: Lynne Rienner, 1989).

45. See Stepan, ed., *Democratizing Brazil*, esp. chs. 1–2.

46. Donald C. Hodges, *Argentina's "Dirty War": An Intellectual Biography* (Austin: University of Texas Press, 1991), pp. 3, 125, 128.

47. See John Simpson and Jana Bennett, *The Disappeared: Voices from a Secret War* (London: Robson Books, 1985).

48. Quoted in Simpson and Bennett, *The Disappeared*, p. 304.

49. Quoted in David Rock, *Argentina, 1516–1987: From Spanish Colonization to the Falklands War and Alfonsín* (London: I. B. Tauris, 1987), p. 378. On wartime policy making, see Lawrence Freedman and Virginia Gamba-Stonehouse, *Signals of War: The Falklands Conflict of 1982* (London: Faber & Faber, 1990).

50. Devlin, *Debt and Crisis in Latin America*, pp. 45, 198.

51. See Robert A. Potash, "The Military under Alfonsín and Menem: The Search for a New Role," in Colin M. Lewis and Nissa Torents, eds., *Argentina in the Crisis Years (1983–1990): From Alfonsín to Menem* (London: Institute of Latin American Studies, 1993), pp. 53–72.

52. See Linz et al., eds, *Democracy in Developing Countries*, vol. 4, ch. 8.

53. Robert Thomson, *Green Gold: Bananas and Dependency in the Eastern Caribbean* (London: Latin American Bureau, 1987), p. vii.

54. Helen Schooley, *Conflict in Central America: Keesing's International Studies* (London: Longman, 1987), p. 268.

55. See generally Jan S. Adams, *A Foreign Policy in Transition: Moscow's Retreat from Central America and the Caribbean, 1985–1992* (Durham, N.C.: Duke University Press, 1992), Ch. 1.

56. Juri Valenta and Esperanza Durán, eds, *Conflict in Nicaragua: A Multidimensional Perspective* (Boston: Allen & Unwin, 1987), pp. 264–6; Yuri Pavlov, *Soviet-Cuban Alliance, 1959–1991* (New Brunswick, N.J.: Transaction Publishers, 1994), pp. 99–101.

57. Quotations from Mark Falcoff, "Afterword," in Howard J. Wiarda and Mark Falcoff, eds., *The Communist Challenge in the Caribbean and Central America* (Washington, D.C.: American Enterprise Institute, 1987), p. 237.

58. Quoted in Cynthia J. Arnson, *Crossroads: Congress, the President, and Central America, 1976–1993,* 2nd ed. (University Park: Pennsylvania State University Press, 1993), p. 128.

59. Quoted in Walter LaFeber, *Inevitable Revolutions: The United States in Central America,* 2nd ed. (New York: Norton, 1993), p. 280.

60. Bob Woodward, *Veil: The Secret Wars of the CIA* (New York: Pocket Books, 1988), pp. 459–60.

61. McFarlane and North quotations from *The Tower Commission Report: The Full Text of the President's Special Review Board* (New York: Bantam Books, 1987), pp. 460, 476.

62. Jorge I. Domínguez, *To Make a World Safe for Revolution: Cuba's Foreign Policy* (Cambridge, Mass.: Harvard University Press, 1989), pp. 162–71.

63. Quoted in Kai P. Schoenhals and Richard A. Melanson, *Revolution and Intervention in Grenada: The New Jewel Movement, the United States, and the Caribbean* (Boulder, Colo.: Westview, 1987), p. 143.

64. For details see Schooley, *Conflict in Central America,* pp. xiii, 208–9.

65. Marvin E. Gettleman, Patrick Lacefield, Louis Menashe, and David Marmelstein, eds., *El Salvador: Central America in the New Cold War,* rev. ed. (New York: Grove Press, 1987), p. 266.

66. Americas Watch, *El Salvador's Decade of Terror Human Rights Since the Assassination of Archbishop Romero* (New Haven: Yale University Press, 1991), p. 138.

67. Schooley, *Conflict in Central America,* pp. xxv, 239.

68. LaFeber, *Inevitable Revolutions,* p. 289.

69. Statistics from Robert A. Pastor, *Integration with Mexico: Options for the United States* (New York: Twentieth Century Fund, 1993), pp. 11–13.

70. Statistics from Scott B. MacDonald, *Dancing on a Volcano: The Latin American Drug Trade* (New York: Praeger, 1988), p. 3, on which these two paragraphs rely.

71. Speech of October 23, 1974, quoted in M. Tamarkin, *The Making of Zimbabwe: Decolonization in Regional and International Politics* (London: Frank Cass, 1990), on which this paragraph relies.

72. Peter Carrington, *Reflect on Things Past: The Memoirs of Lord Carrington* (London: Fontana/Collins, 1989), p. 303. Generally see Henry Wiseman and Alastair M. Taylor, *From Rhodesia to Zimbabwe: The Politics of Transition* (New York: Pergamon, 1981).

73. Anthony Verrier, *The Road to Zimbabwe, 1890–1980* (London: Jonathan Cape, 1986), pp. 149 (quotation), 302–3.

74. Peter Godwin and Ian Hancock, *"Rhodesians Never Die": The Impact of War and Political Change on White Rhodesia, c. 1970–1980* (Oxford: Oxford University Press, 1993), p. 315.

75. Alex Vines, *Renamo: Terrorism in Mozambique* (Bloomington: Indiana University Press, 1991), pp. 111–9; see generally David Birmingham, *Frontline Nationalism in Angola and Mozambique* (London: James Currey, 1992), ch. 5.

76. Keith Somerville, *Southern Africa and the Soviet Union: From Communist International to Commonwealth of Independent States* (London: Macmillan, 1993), esp. pp. 273–92.

77. A comment in 1976 quoted by Alex Thomson, *Incomplete Engagement: U.S. Foreign Policy towards the Republic of South Africa* (Aldershot, Hants: Avebury, 1996), p. 260.

78. Figures from Susannah Smith, *Front Line Africa: The Right to a Future* (Oxford: Oxfam, 1990), pp. 41–50, 334–5.

79. Anthony W. Marx, *Lessons of the Struggle: South African Internal Opposition, 1960–1990* (New York: Oxford University Press, 1992), pp. 62–3.

80. David M. Smith, ed., *Living Under Apartheid: Aspects of Urbanization and Social Change in South Africa* (London: Allen & Unwin, 1982), pp. 27, 91.

81. Quotations from Robert M. Price, *The Apartheid State in Crisis: Political Transformation in South Africa, 1975–1990* (New York: Oxford University Press, 1991), p. 82—a study on which this section draws heavily.

82. Quoted in Patti Waldmeir, *Anatomy of a Miracle: The End of Apartheid and the Birth of the New South Africa* (London: Viking, 1997), p. 56.

83. James Barber and John Barratt, *South Africa's Foreign Policy: The Search for Status and Security, 1945–1988* (Cambridge: Cambridge University Press, 1990), pp. 320–3.

84. Price, *The Apartheid State in Crisis*, p. 228.

85. Quoted in Price, *The Apartheid State in Crisis*, p. 208.

86. Quoted by Shula Marks and Neil Andersson, "The Epidemiology of Violence," in N. Chabani Manganyi and André du Toit, eds, *Political Violence and the Struggle in South Africa* (London: Macmillan, 1990), p. 39.

87. Gill Straker, *Faces in the Revolution: The Psychological Effects of Violence on Township Youth in South Africa* (Cape Town: David Philip, 1992), ch. 5.

88. Omari H. Kokole and Ali A. Mazrui, "Uganda: The Dual Polity and the Plural Society," in Larry Diamond, Juan J. Linz, and Seymour Martin Lipset, eds., *Democracy in Developing Countries*, Vol. 2, *Africa* (Boulder, Colo.: Lynne Rienner, 1988), pp. 259–98.

89. Donald Rothchild and Naomi Chazan, eds., *The Precarious Balance: State and Society in Africa* (Boulder, Colo.: Westview, 1988), p. 26.

90. See obituary in *The Times* (London), November 5, 1996, p. 23.

91. Christopher Clapham, *Africa and the International States System: The Politics of State Survival* (Cambridge: Cambridge University Press, 1996), pp. 88–98; and Michael Clough, *U.S. Policy toward Africa and the End of the Cold War* (New York: Council on Foreign Relations, 1992), pp. 65–6, 78, 81.

92. James D. Tarver, *The Demography of Africa* (Westport, Conn.: Praeger, 1996), esp. pp. 30, 52–4, 69–71, 86, 224.

93. Carl K. Eicher, "Facing Up to Africa's Food Crisis," in John Ravenhill, ed., *Africa in Economic Crisis* (London: Macmillan, 1986), p. 150.

94. John Iliffe, *Africans: The History of a Continent* (Cambridge: Cambridge University Press, 1995), p. 252. Chapter 11 of this study provides a useful guide to the 1980s crisis.

95. Virginia DeLancey, "The Economies of Africa," in April A. Gordon and Donald L. Gordon, eds., *Understanding Contemporary Africa*, 2nd ed. (Boulder, Colo.: Lynne Rienner, 1996), p. 98.

96. Joan E. Spero, *The Politics of International Economic Relations*, 4th ed. (London: Unwin Hyman, 1990), p. 218.

97. William D. Graf, *The Nigerian State: Political Economy, State Class and Political System in the Post-Colonial Era* (London: James Currey, 1988), esp. ch. 11.

98. Robert H. Bates, *Markets and States in Tropical Africa: The Political Basis of Agricultural Policies* (Berkeley: University of California Press, 1981), pp. 6, 122.

99. Iliffe, *Africans*, p. 263.

100. See Moriba Touré and T. O. Fadayomi, eds., *Migrations, Development and Urbanization in Sub-Saharan Africa* (Dakar: CODESRIA, 1992), ch. 2, esp. p. 63.

101. Rothchild and Chazan, eds., *The Precarious Balance*, p. 162; see also David Siddle and Kenneth Swindell, *Rural Change in Tropical Africa: From Colonies to Nation-States* (Oxford: Basil Blackwell, 1990), pp. 102, 145.

102. Sara Berry, "Coping with Confusion: African Farmers' Responses to Economic Instability in the 1970s and 1980s," in Thomas M. Callaghy and John Ravenhill, eds., *Hemmed In: Responses to Africa's Economic Decline* (New York: Columbia University Press, 1993), pp. 248–78.

103. John Lonsdale, "States and Social Processes in Africa: A Historiographical Survey," *African Studies Review* 24 (1981): 139.

104. Jean-François Bayert, *The State in Africa: The Politics of the Belly* (London: Longman, 1993), p. 241.

105. DeLancey, "The Economies of Africa," p. 107.

106. Ravenhill, ed., *Africa in Economic Crisis*, esp. pp. 8–9, 150, 154–5. See more generally the examination by Jean-Philippe Platteau, "The Food Crisis in Africa: A Comparative Structural Analysis," in Jean Drèze and Amartya Sen, eds., *The Political Economy of Hunger*, Vol. 2, *Famine Prevention* (Oxford: Clarendon, 1990), pp. 279–387.

107. John Seaman, "Famine Mortality in Ethiopia and the Sudan," in Etienne van de Walle, Gilles Piston, and Mpembele Sala-Diakanda, eds., *Mortality and Society in Sub-Saharan Africa* (Oxford: Clarendon, 1992), p. 365.

108. Quotations from Peter Gill, *A Year in the Death of Africa* (London: Paladin, 1986), pp. 91, 97. See also *Keesings Contemporary Archives,* March 1986, p. 34214 (on Geldof), and John Iliffe, *The African Poor* (Cambridge: Cambridge University Press, 1987), pp. 250–9.

109. Tony Barnett and Piers Blaikie, *AIDS in Africa: Its Present and Future Impact* (London: Belhaven Press, 1992), esp. pp. 11–14, 20–2.

110. The hypothesis of African genesis is still hotly contested by some African politicians but much evidence points in that direction. See Mirko D. Grmek, *History of AIDS: Emergence and Origin of a Modern Pandemic,* trans. by Russell C. Maulitz and Jacalyn Duffin (Princeton, N.J.: Princeton University Press, 1990), esp. ch. 13.

111. Kenneth P. Kiple, ed., *The Cambridge World History of Human Disease* (Cambridge: Cambridge University Press, 1993), pp. 547–51.

112. Geoffrey Swain and Nigel Swain, *Eastern Europe since 1945* (London: Macmillan, 1993), pp. 181, 183.

113. See Tad Szulc, *Pope John Paul II: The Biography* (New York: Scribner, 1995).

114. Quoted in Trevor Beeson, *Discretion and Valour: Religious Conditions in Russia and Eastern Europe,* 2nd ed. (London: Collins, 1982), p. 187.

115. See generally Timothy Garton Ash, *The Polish Revolution: Solidarity,* 2nd ed. (London: Granta, 1991).

116. Mark Kramer, "Poland 1980–81: Soviet Policy during the 'Polish Crisis,' *Cold War International History Project Bulletin* 5 (1995): quoting from 137. In May 1981, John Paul II was shot and seriously wounded in Rome. The controversy remains unresolved about whether this was the work of a lone fanatic, a member of a Turkish neofascist organization, or an agent of the Bulgarian secret service in league with Andropov's KGB.

117. Claudia Wörmann, *Osthandel als Problem der Atlantischen Allianz: Erfahrungen aus dem Erdgas-Röhren-Geschäft mit der UdSSR* (Bonn: Europa Union Verlag, 1986), p. 109.

118. According to Alexander M. Haig, Jr., *Caveat: Realism, Reagan, and Foreign Policy* (London: Weidenfeld & Nicolson, 1984), p. 252.

119. Quoted in Antony J. Blinken, *Ally versus Ally: America, Europe, and the Siberian Pipeline Crisis* (New York: Praeger, 1987), p. 3—to date the best account of the story.

120. Blinken, *Ally versus Ally,* pp. 50, 59.

121. Margaret Thatcher, *The Downing Street Years* (London: HarperCollins, 1993), p. 256.

122. For background see Jonathan Haslam, *The Soviet Union and the Politics of Nuclear Weapons in Europe, 1969–1987: The Problem of the SS-20* (London: Macmillan, 1989).

123. Zbigniew Brzezinski, *Power and Principle: Memoirs of the National Security Adviser, 1977–1981* (London: Weidenfeld & Nicolson, 1983), p. 306. See generally Milton Leitenberg, "The Neutron Bomb—Enhanced Radiation Warheads," *Journal of Strategic Studies* 5 (1982): 341–69.

124. Helmut Schmidt, *Men and Powers: A Political Retrospective,* trans. by Ruth Hein (London: Jonathan Cape, 1990), p. 181.

125. See Diego Cordovez and Selig S. Harrison, *Out of Afghanistan: The Inside Story of the Soviet Withdrawal* (New York: Oxford University Press, 1995), p. 47.

126. Haslam, *The Soviet Union and the Politics of Nuclear Weapons,* esp. pp. 96–102, 107. See generally Raymond L. Garthoff, *Détente and Confrontation: American-Soviet Relations from Nixon to Reagan,* 2nd ed. (Washington: Brookings Institution, 1994), ch. 25.

127. Gerd Langguth, *Protestbewegung: Entwicklung—Niedergang—Renaissance: Die Neue Linke seit 1968* (Köln: Verlag Wissenschaft und Politik, 1984), p. 257.

128. Strobe Talbott, *Deadly Gambits: The Reagan Administration and the Stalemate in Nuclear Arms Control* (New York: Vintage Books, 1985), p. 4.

129. Quotations from Reagan, *Public Papers of the Presidents of the United States: Ronald Reagan, 1983* (Washington, D.C.: Government Printing Office, 1984), pp. 363–4, 442–3.

130. Martin Anderson, *Revolution: The Reagan Legacy,* 2nd ed. (Stanford: Hoover Institution Press, 1990), pp. 80–3. See generally the account in Donald R. Baucom, *The Origins of SDI, 1944–1983* (Lawrence: University of Kansas Press, 1992), chs. 6–8.

131. McGeorge Bundy, George F. Kennan, Robert S. McNamara, and Gerard Smith, "The President's Choice: Star Wars or Arms Control," *Foreign Affairs* 63/2 (Winter 1984/85): 269.

132. David Z. Robinson, *The Strategic Defense Initiative: Its Effect on the Economy and Arms Control* (New York: New York University Press, 1987), p. 36.

133. TV address, September 5, 1983, in Reagan, *Public Papers, 1983,* p. 1228. See generally Seymour Hersh, *"The Target is Destroyed": What Really Happened to Flight 007 and What America Knew About It* (London: Faber & Faber, 1986).

134. Quotation from Raymond L. Garthoff, *The Great Transition: American-Soviet Relations and the End of the Cold War,* (Washington, D.C.: Brookings Institution, 1994), p. 129.

135. See Christopher Andrew and Oleg Gordievsky, eds., *Instructions from the Centre: Top Secret Files on KGB Operations, 1975–1985* (London: Hodder & Stoughton, 1991), ch. 4.

136. Vladimir E. Shlapentokh, "Moscow's War Propaganda and Soviet Public Opinion," *Problems of Communism* vol. 33/5 (September–October 1984): 88–94.

137. Quoted in David Miller, *Olympic Revolution: The Biography of Juan Antonio Samaranch* (London: Pavilion Books, 1992), p. 88.

138. Earlier comments by German and French spokesmen, quoted by Hans-Erich Au, *Die strategische Verteidigunsinitiative (SDI): Zur politischen Diskussion in der BR Deutschland* (Frankfurt am Main: Peter Lang, 1988), p. 37; and Jonathan Dean, "Europe in the Shadow of Star Wars," in John Tirman, ed., *Empty Promise: The Growing Case Against Star Wars* (Boston: Beacon Press, 1986), p. 163.

139. Quoted in E. P. Thompson, ed., *Star Wars* (Harmondsworth: Penguin, 1985), p. 107.

140. Quoted in Gisèle Charzat, *La militarisation intégrale* (Paris: L'Herne, 1986), p. 145.

141. Edward Reiss, *The Strategic Defense Initiative* (Cambridge: Cambridge University Press, 1992), p. 135.

142. Quotations from A. W. DePorte, *Europe between the Superpowers: The Enduring Balance,* 2nd ed. (New Haven: Yale University Press, 1986), subtitle and p. vii, and John Palmer, *Europe without America: The Crisis in Atlantic Relations* (Oxford: Oxford University Press, 1987), pp. 1–2.

143. Quoted in Geoffrey H. Hartman, ed., *Bitburg in Moral and Political Perspective* (Bloomington: Indiana University Press, 1986), p. 258.

144. Quotations from Richard J. Evans, *In Hitler's Shadow: West German Historians and the Attempt to Escape from the Nazi Past* (London: I. B. Tauris, 1989), pp. 28, 112.

145. Josef Joffe, "The Battle of the Historians," *Encounter* 69/1 (June 1987): 76.

146. Quoted in Shultz, *Turmoil and Triumph*, p. 863.

147. Theodore Draper, *A Very Thin Line: The Iran-Contra Affair* (New York: Hill and Wang, 1991), p. 474.

148. David Mervin, *Ronald Reagan and the American Presidency* (New York: Longman, 1990), p. 159.

149. Quoted in Philip G. Henderson, *Managing the Presidency: The Eisenhower Legacy—from Kennedy to Reagan* (Boulder, Colo.: Westview, 1988), p. 166.

150. *Time*, November 2, 1987, p. 22, also pp. 34–5.

151. *Keesing's Contemporary Archives*, Feb. 1988, pp. 35740–2.

152. *Time*, November 2, 1987, p. 20.

153. *Time*, November 9, 1987, cover, pp. 18, 20, 21.

154. Scarsdale being one of the most affluent of the New York suburbs. Paul Kennedy, *The Rise and Fall of the Great Powers: Economic Change and Military Conflict from 1500 to 2000* (London: Unwin Hyman, 1988), pp. 514, 533.

155. *Newsweek*, February 22, 1988.

Chapter 14 Chips and Genes

1. Alvin M. Weinberg, "Impact of Large-Scale Science on the United States," *Science* 134 (July 21, 1961): 161.

2. Statistics from John Krige and Dominique Pestre, eds., *Science in the Twentieth Century* (Amsterdam: Harwood, 1997), pp. 217, 265, 828.

3. Vannevar Bush, *Science: The Endless Frontier—A Report to the President on a Program for Postwar Scientific Research,* July 1945 (Washington, D.C.: NSF Reprint, 1960), quoting p. 19.

4. Paul Forman, "Behind Quantum Electronics: National Security as Basis for Physical Research in the United States, 1940–1960," *Historical Studies in the Physical and Biological Sciences* 18 (1987): 149–229, esp. 152–3 and 156 (quotation).

5. See Stuart W. Leslie, *The Cold War and American Science: The Military-Industrial Complex at MIT and Stanford* (New York: Columbia University Press, 1993)—a useful, wide-ranging account.

6. Krige and Pestre, eds., *Science in the Twentieth Century,* pp. 767–70.

7. Etel Solingen, ed., *Scientists and the State: Domestic Structures and the International Context* (Ann Arbor: University of Michigan Press, 1994), pp. 78–9.

8. Krige and Pestre, eds., *Science in the Twentieth Century*, pp. 893–5.

9. Solingen, ed., *Scientists and the State*, p. 98.

10. David Holloway, *Stalin and the Bomb: The Soviet Union and Atomic Energy* (New Haven: Yale University Press, 1994), p. 363.

11. For this paragraph see Loren R. Graham, *Science in Russia and the Soviet Union: A Short History* (Cambridge: Cambridge University Press, 1993), esp. chs. 6, 9, and appendix.

12. Mark W. Zacher, with Brent A. Sutton, *Governing Global Networks: International Regimes for Transportation and Communications* (Cambridge: Cambridge University Press, 1996), pp. 179–80, 222.

13. Peter Temin, with Louis Galambos, *The Fall of the Bell System: A Study in Prices and Profits* (Cambridge: Cambridge University Press, 1987), pp. 346–7.

14. These and other figures from Desmond King-Hele et al., eds, *The RAE Table of Earth Satellites 1958–1989*, 4th ed. (Farnborough, Hants: Royal Aircraft Establishment, 1990), pp. iv–vii.

15. Quoted in Paul B. Stares, *The Militarization of Space: U.S. Policy, 1945–1984* (Ithaca, N.Y.: Cornell University Press, 1985), p. 103.

16. In what follows I draw particularly on Günter Paul, *The Satellite Spin-Off: The Achievements of Space Flight*, trans. Alan and Barbara Lacy (New York: Robert B. Luce, 1975).

17. Arthur C. Clarke, "Extra-Terrestrial Relays: Can Rocket Stations Give World-Wide Radio Coverage?" *Wireless World*, vol. 51 (October 1945), pp. 304–8.

18. Interview quoted in William J. Walker, *Space Age* (New York: Random House, 1992), p. 218.

19. Benjamin G. Rader, *In Its Own Image: How Television Has Transformed Sports* (New York: Free Press, 1984), chs. 7–8.

20. John Goldlust, *Playing for Keeps: Sport, the Media and Society* (Melbourne: Longman Cheshire, 1987), pp. 159–64.

21. Robert W. Campbell, "Satellite Communications in the USSR," *Soviet Economy* 1 (1985): 313–39.

22. See Joseph R. Dominick, Barry L. Sherman and Gary A. Copeland, *Broadcasting/Cable and Beyond: An Introduction to Modern Electronic Media*, 2nd ed. (New York: McGraw-Hill, 1993), chs. 3 and 6, esp. pp. 68, 125.

23. Rader, *In Its Own Image*, p. 198.

24. Robert Britt Horowitz, *The Irony of Regulatory Reform: The Deregulation of American Telecommunications* (New York: Oxford University Press, 1989), ch. 8, quoting from p. 245.

25. Statistics from Jonathan Barnard, Narinder Banwait, Phil Cain, and Adam Smith, *Television in Europe to 2006* (London: Zenith Media, 1997), pp. 231, 233.

26. Alex Fynn and Lynton Grant, *Out of Time: Why Football Isn't Working* (London: Simon and Schuster, 1994), ch. 4.

27. Anthony Smith, ed., *Television: An International History* (Oxford: Oxford University Press, 1995), pp. 328–9.

28. Daniel J. Kevles, "Korea, Science, and the State," in Peter Galison and Bruce Hevly, eds., *Big Science: The Growth of Large-Scale Research* (Stanford: Stanford University Press, 1992), p. 314.

29. Temin, with Galambos, *The Fall of the Bell System:* p. 10.

30. Eli Noam, Seisuke Komatsuzaki, and Douglas A. Conn, eds., *Telecommunications in the Pacific Basin: An Evolutionary Approach* (New York: Oxford University Press, 1994), pp. 25–6.

31. Paul, *Satellite Spin-Off,* pp. 53–8.

32. John Bray, *The Communications Miracle: The Telecommunication Pioneers from Morse to the Information Superhighway* (London: Plenum Press, 1995), ch. 17.

33. D. E. N. Davies, C. Hilsum, and A. W. Rudge, eds., *Communications after AD 2000* (London: Chapman and Hall, 1991), pp. 202–3.

34. Noam et al., eds., *Telecommunications in the Pacific Basin,* p. 60.

35. Robert W. Campbell, *Soviet and Post-Soviet Telecommunications: An Industry under Reform* (Boulder, Colo.: Westview, 1995), esp. pp. 15, 22, 95–102.

36. Jürgen Müller and Emilia Nyevrikel, "Closing the Capacity and Technology Gaps in Central and Eastern European Telecommunications," in Bjorn Wellenius and Peter A. Stern, eds., *Implementing Reforms in the Telecommunications Sector: Lessons from Experience* (Aldershot, Hants: Avebury, 1996), p. 354.

37. Wellenius and Stern, eds., *Implementing Reforms in the Telecommunications Sector,* p. 15.

38. Michel Carpentier, Sylvanie Farnoux-Toporkoff, and Christian Garris, *Telecommunications in Transition,* trans. C. P. Skrimshire (New York: John Wiley, 1992), p. 29.

39. Horowitz, *The Irony of Regulatory Reform,* ch. 8, quoting p. 224.

40. The pattern is described in the introduction to Wellenius and Stern, eds., *Implementing Reforms in the Telecommunications Sector.*

41. Colossus's claims are still widely ignored in the United States but see, for instance, Kenneth Flamm, *Creating the Computer: Government, Industry, and High Technology* (Washington, D.C.: Brookings Institution, 1988), pp. 39, 47.

42. Martin Campbell-Kelly and William Aspray, *Computer: A History of the Information Machine* (New York: Basic Books, 1996), is basic for this section.

43. Herman Lukoff, *From Dits to Bits: A Personal History of the Electronic Computer* (Portland, Ore.: Robotics Press, 1979), pp. 127–31.

44. See *Annals of the History of Computing* 5 (1983): 146–7.

45. Emerson W. Pugh, *Building IBM: Shaping an Industry and its Technology* (Cambridge, Mass.: MIT Press, 1995), p. 296.

46. Flamm, *Creating the Computer,* pp. 82–90.

47. Thomas J. Watson, Jr., and Richard Petre, *Father and Son, & Co.: My Life at IBM and Beyond* (London: Bantam Press, 1990), pp. 230–3. On SAGE, see generally the special issue of *Annals of the History of Computing* 5/4 (1983): 319–403.

48. Pugh, *Building IBM*, p. 326, appendix D.

49. Campbell-Kelly and Aspray, *Computer*, p. 140.

50. Lillian Hoddeson, "Research on Crystal Rectifiers during World War II and the Invention of the Transistor," *History and Technology* 11 (1994): 121–30. In general see Ernest Braun and Stuart MacDonald, *Revolution in Miniature: The History and Impact of Semiconductor Electronics*, 2nd ed. (Cambridge: Cambridge University Press, 1982).

51. For the detailed story see Michael Riordan and Lillian Hoddesdon, *Crystal Fire: The Birth of the Information Age* (New York: Norton, 1997).

52. Braun and MacDonald, *Revolution in Miniature*, p. 80; and Thomas J. Misa, "Military Needs, Commercial Realities, and the Development of the Transistor, 1948–1958, in Merritt Roe Smith, ed., *Military Enterprise and Technological Change* (Cambridge, Mass.: MIT Press, 1985), pp. 253–87.

53. Riordan and Hoddesdon, *Crystal Fire*, p. 240.

54. On this, see especially Campbell-Kelly and Aspray, *Computer*, ch. 10.

55. Frank Rose, *West of Eden: The End of Innocence at Apple Computer* (London: Business Books, 1988), p. 11.

56. James Chposky and Ted Leonsis, *Blue Magic: The People, Power and Politics behind the IBM Personal Computer* (London: Grafton Books, 1989), p. 9.

57. Daniel Ichbiah and Susan L. Knepper, *The Making of Microsoft: How Bill Gates and His Team Created the World's Most Successful Software Company* (Rocklin, Calif.: Prima Publishing, 1991), p. 93.

58. *Time*, January 3, 1983, p. 4.

59. Figures from Flamm, *Creating the Computer*, pp. 238, 253.

60. Statistics and quotations from *Time*, January 3, 1983, p. 4.

61. Alan Q. Morton, "Packaging History: The Emergence of the Uniform Product Code (UPC) in the United States, 1970–1975," *History and Technology* 11 (1994): 101–11.

62. See Lawrence G. Roberts, "The Arpanet and Computer Networks," in Adele Goldberg, ed., *A History of Personal Workstations* (New York: ACM Press, 1988), pp. 143–67.

63. Campbell-Kelly and Aspray, *Computer*, ch. 12; and Katie Hafner and Matthew Lyon, *Where Wizards Stay Up Late: The Origins of the Internet* (New York: Simon and Schuster, 1996).

64. Anthony Giddens, *The Nation-State and Violence: Volume Two of a Contemporary Critique of Historical Materialism* (Cambridge: Polity Press, 1985), p. 178.

65. Themes developed by Frank Webster, *Theories of the Information Society* (London: Routledge, 1995), esp. chs. 4–5.

66. Flamm, *Creating the Computer*, esp. pp. 135, 168, 185, 201.

67. Figures from Braun and MacDonald, *Revolution in Miniature*, p. 153.

68. On Japan see P. R. Morris, *A History of the World Semiconductor Industry* (London: Peter Peregrinus, 1990), ch. 7.

69. Peter Dicken, *Global Shift: The Internationalization of Economic Activity*, 2nd ed. (London: Paul Chapman, 1992), p. 360.

70. Barney Warf, "Telecommunications and the Globalization of Financial Services," *The Professional Geographer* 41 (1989): 261–2.

71. Quoted in Adrian Hamilton, *The Financial Revolution: The Big Bang Worldwide* (New York: Viking, 1986), p. 30.

72. Hamilton, *The Financial Revolution*, pp. 42–5, 118.

73. Richard O'Brien, *Global Financial Integration: The End of Geography* (London: Pinter, 1992), p. 7.

74. Loren R. Graham, *Science in Russia and the Soviet Union: A Short History* (Cambridge: Cambridge University Press, 1993), p. 256.

75. Richard W. Judy, "Computing in the USSR: A Comment," *Soviet Economy* 2 (1986): 355–67.

76. Quoted in Karen Dawisha, *Eastern Europe, Gorbachev and Reform: The Great Challenge*, 2nd ed. (Cambridge: Cambridge University Press, 1990), p. 160.

77. Charles S. Maier, *Dissolution: The Crisis of Communism and the End of East Germany* (Princeton, N.J.: Princeton University Press, 1997), p. 73.

78. Judy, "Soviet Computing," 362–3.

79. George P. Shultz, *Turmoil and Triumph: My Years as Secretary of State* (New York: Scribners', 1993), pp. 586–91, 891–3.

80. Quoted in Robert Olby, "The Revolution in Molecular Biology," in R. C. Olby, G. N. Cantor, J. R. R. Christie, and M. J. S. Hodge, eds., *Companion to the History of Modern Science* (London: Routledge, 1990), p. 508.

81. James D. Watson, *The Double Helix*, critical edition, ed. Gunther S. Stent (London: Weidenfeld and Nicolson, 1981), p. 17.

82. Quoted in Horace Freeland Judson, *The Eighth Day of Creation: Makers of the Revolution in Biology* (London: Jonathan Cape, 1979), p. 59.

83. See Lily E. Kay, *The Molecular Vision of Life: Caltech, the Rockefeller Foundation, and the Rise of the New Biology* (New York: Oxford University Press, 1993), pp. 4–6.

84. Francis Crick, *What Mad Pursuit: A Personal View of Scientific Discovery* (London: Weidenfeld and Nicolson, 1988), p. 64.

85. Watson, *Double Helix*, p. 32.

86. Judson, *Eighth Day of Creation*, p. 186.

87. Quoted in Judson, *Eighth Day of Creation*, p. 172.

88. *Nature*, April 25, 1953, pp. 737–41.

89. Quoted in Judson, *Eighth Day of Creation*, p. 347.

90. On this process, see Sahotra Sarkar, "Biological Information: A Skeptical Look at Some Central Dogmas of Molecular Biology," in Sarkar, ed., *The Philosophy and History of Molecular Biology: New Perspectives* (Dordrecht: Kluwer Academic Publishers, 1996), pp. 187–231.

91. Walter Bodmer and Robin McKie, *The Book of Man: The Human Genome Project and the Quest to Discover Our Genetic Heritage* (Oxford: Oxford University Press, 1994), p. 10.

92. Quotations from *Time,* March 9, 1981, pp. 50–1.

93. Robert Teitelman, *Gene Dreams: Wall Street, Academia, and the Rise of Biotechnology* (New York: Basic Books, 1989), p. 4.

94. See Robert Bud, *The Uses of Life: A History of Biotechnology* (Cambridge: Cambridge University Press, 1993), esp. pp. 32–5, 140, 183–4.

95. See Teitelman, *Gene Dreams,* ch. 15.

96. Bud, *The Uses of Life,* p. 192.

97. Here I develop ideas in Teitelman, *Gene Dreams,* pp. 205–7.

98. British Medical Association, *Our Genetic Future: The Science and Ethics of Genetic Technology* (Oxford: Oxford University Press, 1992), p. 210.

99. This paragraph rests on the detailed analysis by Robert M. Cook-Deegan, "The Human Genome Project: The Formation of Federal Policies in the United States, 1986–1990," in Kathi E. Hanna, ed., *Biomedical Politics* (Washington, D.C.: National Academy Press, 1991), pp. 99–168.

100. Quoted in Cook-Deegan, "The Human Genome Project," p. 119.

101. *Time,* March 20, 1989, p. 62.

102. Liz Fletcher and Roy Porter, *A Quest for the Code of Life: Genome Analysis at the Wellcome Trust Genome Campus* (London: Wellcome Trust, 1997), chs. 1 and 4.

103. Walter Bodmer and Robin McKie, *The Book of Man: The Human Genome Project and the Quest to Discover our Genetic Heritage* (Oxford: Oxford University Press, 1997), esp. chs. 4, 10 and 11.

104. Quotations from James D. Watson and John Tooze, eds., *The DNA Story: A Documentary History of Gene Cloning* (San Francisco: W. H. Freeman, 1981), pp. 111–2.

105. Quoted in Krimsky, *Genetic Alchemy,* p. 266.

106. For a good introduction on which this section draws, see John McCormick, *The Global Environmental Movement: Reclaiming Paradise* (London: Belhaven Press, 1989).

107. Figures from Max Nicholson, *The New Environmental Age* (Cambridge: Cambridge University Press, 1987), p. 36.

108. Rachel Carson, *Silent Spring* (London: Penguin, 1982), pp. 256–7.

109. World Commission on Environment and Development, *Our Common Future* (Oxford: Oxford University Press, 1987), p. 43.

110. Sharachchandra M. Lélé, "Sustainable Development: A Critical Review," *World Development* 19 (1991): 607–21.

111. McCormick, *Global Environmental Movement,* pp. 160–1.

112. Murray Feshbach and Alfred Friendly, Jr., *Ecocide in the USSR: Health and Nature under Siege* (London: Aurum Press, 1992), esp. pp. 1–3 and 73–88.

113. McCormick, *Global Environmental Movement*, pp. viii, 125.

114. Quoted in Barton J. Bernstein, "Four Physicists and the Bomb: The Early Years, 1945–1950," *Historical Studies in the Physical and Biological Sciences* 18 (1985): 262.

115. Quotations from Paul Boyer, *By the Bomb's Early Light: American Thought and Culture at the Dawn of the Atomic Age* (New York: Pantheon Books, 1985), pp. 109 (*Herald Tribune*), 121 (Einstein), and 268 (Truman).

116. A theme developed by Margaret Gowing, *Reflections on Atomic Energy History* (Cambridge: Cambridge University Press, 1978), pp. 23–4.

117. See the semiofficial history by Lorna Arnold, *Windscale 1957: Anatomy of a Nuclear Accident* (London: Macmillan, 1992), p. 102.

118. Details were known in the West only in the 1980s. See Feshbach and Friendly, *Ecocide in the USSR*, pp. 174–5.

119. Richard G. Hewlett and Jack M. Holl, *Atoms for Peace and War, 1953–1961: Eisenhower and the Atomic Energy Commission* (Berkeley: University of California Press, 1989), pp. 186–8, 419–22.

120. Alwyn McKay, *The Making of the Atomic Age* (Oxford: OPUS, 1984), pp. 128–30, 133.

121. Quoted in Robert A. Divine, *Eisenhower and the Cold War* (Oxford: Oxford University Press, 1981), p. 111.

122. Speech in September 1954, quoted in Gerard H. Clarfield and William M. Wiecek, *Nuclear America: Military and Civilian Power in the United States* (New York: Harper & Row, 1984), p. 277.

123. Data and quotation from Spencer Weart, *Nuclear Fear: A History of Images* (Cambridge, Mass.: Harvard University Press, 1988), pp. 164–5.

124. Joseph A. Camilleri, *The State and Nuclear Power: Conflict and Control in the Western World* (Brighton, Sussex: Harvester Press, 1984), pp. 62–3.

125. Camilleri, *The State and Nuclear Power*, p. 46.

126. Tony Hall, *Nuclear Politics: The History of Nuclear Power in Britain* (Harmondsworth, Middx: Penguin, 1986), chs. 5–6, quoting p. 91.

127. Statistics in this paragraph from Vaclav Smil and William E. Knowland, eds., *Energy in the Developing World: The Real Energy Crisis* (Oxford: Oxford University Press, 1980), pp. 6–7, 102.

128. Weart, *Nuclear Fears*, p. 159, quoting Waldemar Kaempffert, a veteran science writer at the *New York Times* in January 1947.

129. Camilleri, *The State and Nuclear Power*, chs. 3 and 5.

130. For comparisons see John L. Campbell, *Collapse of an Industry: Nuclear Power and the Contraction of U.S. Policy* (Ithaca, N.Y.: Cornell University Press, 1988), ch. 8.

131. *Report of the President's Commission on the Accident at Three Mile Island* (New York: Pergamon, 1979), pp. 11, 17, 21.

132. Philip L. Cantelon and Robert C. Williams, *Crisis Contained: The Department of Energy at Three Mile Island* (Carbondale: Southern Illinois University Press, 1982), p. xi.

133. See Peter S. Houts, Paul D. Cleary, and Teh-Wei Hu, *The Three Mile Island Crisis: Psychological, Social, and Economic Impacts on the Surrounding Population* (University Park: Pennsylvania State University Press, 1988), pp. 16, 34–5.

134. Feshbach and Friendly, *Ecocide in the USSR*, p. 12.

135. See discussion and statistics in UN Department of Humanitarian Affairs, *DHA News* 16 (September–October 1995): esp. 2, 7.

136. Zhores A. Medvedev, *The Legacy of Chernobyl* (Oxford: Basil Blackwell, 1990), pp. 76 and 289.

137. Martin Walker, *The Waking Giant: The Soviet Union under Gorbachev* (London: Abacus, 1987), pp. 224–6; Feshbach and Friendly, *Ecocide in the USSR*, pp. 143–4.

138. Sir Alan Cottrell, *How Safe is Nuclear Energy?* (London: Heinemann, 1981), p. 113.

139. Quoted in Clarfield and Wiecek, *Nuclear America*, p. 184.

140. Munir Ahmad Khan, "Nuclear Energy and International Cooperation: A Third World Perception of the Erosion of Confidence," in Ian Smart, ed., *World Nuclear Energy: Toward a Bargain of Confidence* (Baltimore: Johns Hopkins University Press, 1982), p. 49.

141. Mitchell Reiss, *Without the Bomb: The Politics of Nuclear Nonproliferation* (New York: Columbia University Press, 1988), p. 28.

142. David Fischer, *Stopping the Spread of Nuclear Weapons: The Past and the Prospects* (London: Routledge, 1992), pp. 5, 251.

143. Reiss, *Without the Bomb*, ch. 5, quoting p. 156.

144. These statistics come from Terence Price, *Political Electricity: What Future for Nuclear Energy?* (Oxford: Oxford University Press, 1990), p. 4.

145. Vaclav Smil, *Energy, Food, Environment: Realities, Myths, Options* (Oxford: Clarendon Press, 1987), p. 82.

146. Quotations from Reiss, *Without the Bomb*, pp. 15–16.

Chapter 15 The Crisis of Communism

1. Quoted in Jonathan Haslam, *The Soviet Union and the Politics of Nuclear Weapons in Europe, 1969–87: The Problem of the SS-20* (London: Macmillan, 1989), p. 151.

2. Leslie Holmes, *Post-Communism: An Introduction* (Cambridge: Polity Press, 1997), p. 4.

3. Quoted in Martin Walker, *The Waking Giant: The Soviet Union under Gorbachev* (London: Abacus, 1987), p. 42.

4. Fiona Venn, *Oil Diplomacy in the Twentieth Century* (London: Macmillan, 1986), table A.2, p. 177.

5. Evgeny M. Andreev, "Life Expectancy and Causes of Death in the USSR," in Wolfgang Lutz, Sergei Scherbov, and Andrei Volkov, eds., *Demographic Trends and Patterns in the Soviet Union before 1991* (London: Routledge, 1994), pp. 288–9.

6. See Archie Brown, "Andropov: Discipline *and* Reform," *Problems of Communism* 32/1 (January–February 1983): pp. 18–31.

7. Quoted in Michael R. Beschloss and Strobe Talbott, *At the Highest Levels: The Inside Story of the End of the Cold War* (Boston: Little, Brown, 1993), p. 6.

8. Walker, *The Waking Giant,* p. 175.

9. Moshe Lewin, *The Gorbachev Phenomenon: A Historical Interpretation* (Berkeley: University of California Press, 1988), p. 31.

10. John Miller, *Mikhail Gorbachev and the End of Soviet Power* (London: Macmillan, 1993), p. 29.

11. Quoted in Archie Brown, *The Gorbachev Factor* (Oxford: Oxford University Press, 1996), p. 18.

12. Jerry F. Hough, *Democratization and Revolution in the USSR, 1985–1991* (Washington, D.C.: Brookings Institution, 1997), p. 15. Cf. Paul Dibb, *The Soviet Union: The Incomplete Superpower,* 2nd ed. (London: Macmillan, 1988), p. 95.

13. Mikhail Gorbachev, *Memoirs* (London: Transworld, 1996), p. 165. For his rise, see Brown, *The Gorbachev Factor,* chs. 2–3.

14. Among the main secondary studies, Miller, *Mikhail Gorbachev,* e.g., pp. 65–70, emphasizes the ways in which Gorbachev learned on the job and responded to pressures, whereas Brown, *The Gorbachev Factor,* e.g., 13, 139, insists on his reformist roots.

15. Quoted in Angus Roxburgh, *The Second Russian Revolution: The Struggle for Power in the Kremlin* (London: BBC Books, 1991).

16. See generally Zhores A. Medvedev, *The Legacy of Chernobyl* (Oxford: Basil Blackwell, 1990).

17. Quoted in Brown, *The Gorbachev Factor,* p. 163.

18. This theme is developed in Andrew Tickle and Ian Welsh, eds., *Environment and Society in Eastern Europe* (London: Longman, 1998), pp. 12–13, 38–41.

19. Stephen White, *Gorbachev in Power* (Cambridge: Cambridge University Press, 1990), pp. 18–19.

20. Eduard Shervardnadze, *The Future Belongs to Freedom,* trans. by Catherine A. Fitzpatrick (London: Sinclair-Stevenson, 1991), p. 39.

21. Donald T. Regan, *For the Record: From Wall Street to Washington* (New York: Harcourt Brace Jovanovich, 1988), pp. 316–7.

22. Raymond L. Garthoff, *The Great Transition: American-Soviet Relations and the End of the Cold War* (Washington, D.C.: Brookings Institution, 1994), p. 774.

23. Margaret Thatcher, *The Downing Street Years* (London: HarperCollins, 1993), pp. 450–1, 768.

24. Donald R. Baucom, *The Origins of SDI, 1944–1983* (Lawrence: University of Kansas Press, 1992), p. 200. Similarly John L. Gaddis, *The United States and the End of the Cold War* (New York: Oxford University Press, 1992), pp. 43–4.

25. A theme developed by Thomas Risse-Kappen, "Did 'Peace Through Strength' End the Cold War?: Lessons from INF," *International Security* 16/1 (Summer 1991): 162–88.

26. Speech to the British Parliament, Dec. 18, 1984, in M. S. Gorbachov, *Speeches and Writings*, vol. 1 (Oxford: Pergamon Press, 1986), quoting pp. 126, 129.

27. Report, June 28, 1988, in Nineteenth CPSU Conference, *Documents and Materials* (Moscow: Novosti, 1988), p. 32.

28. See George E. Hudson, ed., *Soviet National Security Policy under Perestroika* (Boston: Unwin Hyman, 1990), esp. ch. 9.

29. Ronald Reagan, *An American Life* (London: Hutchinson, 1990), p. 588; cf. Garthoff, *The Great Transition*, p. 142.

30. "Everyone roared," wrote Shultz, "including Henry." See George P. Shultz, *Turmoil and Triumph: My Years as Secretary of State* (New York: Scribners', 1993), pp. 991, 1138.

31. Michael Urban, with Vyacheslav Igrunov and Sergei Mitrokhin, *The Rebirth of Politics in Russia* (Cambridge: Cambridge University Press, 1997), ch. 5.

32. See Brian McNair, *Glasnost, Perestroika and the Soviet Media* (London: Routledge, 1991), esp. ch. 4.

33. Quotation from R. W. Davies, *Soviet History in the Gorbachev Revolution* (London: Macmillan, 1989), p. 130.

34. Quotations from Stephen F. Cohen and Katrina vanden Heuvel, eds., *Voices of Glasnost: Interviews with Gorbachev's Reformers* (New York: Norton, 1989), pp. 39, 89.

35. John Morrison, *Boris Yeltsin: From Bolshevik to Democrat* (London: Penguin, 1991), chs. 4–6.

36. See discussion by Stephen Cohen in the introduction to Yegor Ligachev, *Inside Gorbachev's Kremlin* (New York: Pantheon, 1993), esp. pp. viii–ix.

37. Quoted in Roxburgh, *The Second Russian Revolution*, p. 86.

38. 19th CPSU Conference, *Documents and Materials*, pp. 38, 41.

39. For election statistics see Giulietto Chiese, with Douglas Taylor Northrop, *Transition to Democracy: Political Change in the Soviet Union, 1987–1991* (Hanover, N.H.: University Press of New England, 1993), ch. 4.

40. James Eberle, "Understanding the Revolutions in Eastern Europe: A British Perspective and Prospective," in Gwyn Prins, ed., *Spring in Winter: The 1989 Revolutions* (Manchester: Manchester University Press, 1990), p. 197.

41. On debt and growth see Karen Dawisha, *Eastern Europe, Gorbachev and Reform: The Great Challenge*, 2nd ed. (Cambridge: Cambrdige University Press, 1990), pp. 118, 169.

42. Charles Gati, *The Bloc That Failed: Soviet–East European Relations in Transition* (Bloomington: Indiana University Press, 1990), p. 119.

43. A theme developed in Charles S. Maier, *Dissolution: The Crisis of Communism and the End of East Germany* (Princeton, N.J.: Princeton University Press, 1997), ch. 2.

44. See Tomasz Goban-Klas and Pal Kolstø, "East European Mass Media: The Soviet Role," in Odd Arne Westad, Sven Holtsmark, and Iver B. Neumann, *The Soviet Union in Eastern Europe, 1945–89* (New York: St. Martin's, 1994), esp. p. 131.

45. Gorbachev, *Speeches and Writings*, vol. 2 (Oxford: Pergamon Press, 1987), p. 200.

46. Quoted in R. J. Crampton, *Eastern Europe in the Twentieth Century* (London: Routledge, 1994), p. 408.

47. For the background see Diego Cordovez and Selig S. Harrison, *Out of Afghanistan: The Inside Story of the Soviet Withdrawal* (New York: Oxford University Press, 1995).

48. Anatolii Cherniaev, "Gorbachev and the Reunification of Germany: Personal Recollections," in Gabriel Gorodetsky, ed., *Soviet Foreign Policy, 1917–1991: A Retrospective* (London: Frank Cass, 1994), p. 158.

49. This formulation comes from Gati, *Bloc That Failed*, p. 88.

50. Jacques Rupnik, *The Other Europe* (London: Weidenfeld and Nicolson, 1988), p. 260.

51. For an overview see Roger Boyes, *The Naked President: A Political Life of Lech Walesa* (London: Secker & Warburg, 1994), ch. 11.

52. For a detailed account using party archives, see Rudolf L. Tökés, *Hungary's Negotiated Transition: Economic Reform, Social Change, and Political Succession, 1957–1990* (Cambridge: Cambridge University Press, 1996).

53. David Childs, *The GDR: Moscow's German Ally*, 2nd ed. (London: Unwin Hyman, 1988), p. xii.

54. Stasi report cited in Timothy Garton Ash, *In Europe's Name: Germany and the Divided Continent* (London: Jonathan Cape, 1993), p. 202.

55. For figures see Mary Fulbrook, *Anatomy of a Dictatorship: Inside the GDR, 1949–1989* (Oxford: Oxford University Press, 1995), pp. 48–50.

56. Maier, *Dissolution*, pp. 59–60.

57. Quoted in Ash, *In Europe's Name*, p. 371.

58. Figures from Konrad H. Jarausch, *The Rush to German Unity* (New York: Oxford University Press, 1994), pp. 19, 21–2.

59. See Neues Forum Leipzig, *Jetzt oder Nie—Demokratie: Leipziger Herbst '89* (München: C. Bertelsmann, 1990).

60. Quotations from Crampton, *Eastern Europe*, p. 408.

61. *New York Times*, October 25, 1989, quoted in Bernard Gwertzman and Michael T. Kaufman, eds., *The Collapse of Communism* (New York: Times Books, 1990), p. 163.

62. Meeting of November 1, 1989, quoted in Hannes Adomeit, "Gorbachev, German Unification and the Collapse of Empire," *Post-Soviet Affairs* 10 (1994): p. 215.

63. On this still-tangled story, see the documentation in Igor F. Maximytschew and Hans-Hermann Hertle, "Die Maueröffnung: Eine russisch-deutsche Trilogie," *Deutschland Archiv* 27 (1994): esp. 1145–55; also M. E. Sarotte, "Elite Intransigence and the End of the Berlin Wall," *German Politics* 2 (1993): 270–87.

64. See his account in Egon Krenz, with Hartmut König and Gunter Rettner, *Wenn Mauern Fallen. Die Friedliche Revolution: Vorgeschichte—Ablauf—Auswirkungen* (Vienna: Paul Neff, 1990), p. 182.

65. Philip Zelikow and Condoleezza Rice, *Germany Unified and Europe Transformed: A Study in Statecraft*, 2nd ed. (Cambridge, Mass.: Harvard University Press, 1997), p. 101.

66. Robert Darnton, *Berlin Journal, 1989–1990* (New York: Norton, 1990), p. 85.

67. Quoted in Elizabeth Pond, *Beyond the Wall: Germany's Road to Unification* (Washington, D.C.: Brookings Institution, 1993), pp. 90–1.

68. See Richard Crampton, "The Intelligentsia, the Ecology and the Opposition in Bulgaria," *The World Today* 46/2 (February 1990): 23–6; and Charles A. Moser, *Theory and History of the Bulgarian Transition* (Sofia: Free Initiative Press, 1994).

69. Their importance is stressed by Sharon L. Wolchik, *Czechoslovakia in Transition: Politics, Economics and Society* (London: Pinter, 1991), pp. 41–7.

70. Timothy Garton Ash, *We the People: The Revolution of '89 Witnessed in Warsaw, Budapest, Berlin and Prague* (Cambridge: Granta Books, 1990), p. 78.

71. Bernard Wheaton and Zdeněk Kavan, *The Velvet Revolution: Czechoslovakia, 1988–1991* (Boulder, Colo.: Westview, 1992), p. 95.

72. Quoted in Michael Simmons, *The Reluctant President: A Political Life of Václav Havel* (London: Methuen, 1991), p. 151.

73. Statistics from Martyn Rady, *Romania in Turmoil: A Contemporary History* (New York: I. B. Tauris, 1992), pp. 63, 78. This is a good short history of the Ceauşescus' rise and fall.

74. For his architectural megalomania see Mark Almond, *The Rise and Fall of Nicolae and Elena Ceauşescu* (London: Chapmans, 1992), ch. VIII.

75. Trond Gilberg, *Nationalism and Communism in Romania: The Rise and Fall of Ceauşescu's Personal Dictatorship* (Boulder, Colo.: Westview, 1990), p. 177.

76. Matei Calinescu and Vladimir Tismaneanu, "The 1989 Revolution and Romania's Future," in Daniel N. Nelson, ed., *Romania after Tyranny* (Boulder, Colo.: Westview, 1992), p. 15.

77. See Tom Gallagher, *Romania after Ceauşescu: The Politics of Intolerance* (Edinburgh: Edinburgh University Press, 1995), p. 73.

78. Rady, *Romania in Turmoil*, p. 194.

79. Quoted in Pekka Kalevi Hämäläinen, *Uniting Germany: Actions and Reactions* (Aldershot, Hants: Dartmouth, 1994), p. 100.

80. According to his aide, Horst Teltschik, *329 Tage: Innenansichten der Einigung* (Berlin: Siedler, 1991), p. 52. In his own memoirs, Kohl says three to four years: *Ich Wollte Deutschlands Einheit* (Berlin: Propyläen, 1996), p. 167.

81. Jacques Attali, *Verbatim, Tome 3: Chronique des Années 1988–1991* (Paris: Fayard, 1995), p. 369.

82. Jarausch, *The Rush to German Unity* p. 80.

83. Tyll Necker, quoted in Maier, *Dissolution*, p. 226.

84. According to Jarausch, *The Rush to German Unity*, p. 62.

85. Quoted in Pond, *Beyond the Wall*, p. 172.

86. Hans-Dietrich Genscher, *Erinnerungen* (Berlin: Siedler, 1995), p. 729.

87. Maier, *Dissolution*, p. 213.

88. Quoting from Paul J. J. Welfens, ed., *Economic Aspects of German Unification: Expectations, Transition Dynamics and International Perspectives*, 2nd ed. (Berlin: Springer, 1996), p. 40.

89. Quoted in Carl F. Lankowski, ed., *Germany and the European Community: Beyond Hegemony and Containment?* (London: Macmillan, 1994), p. 191.

90. Quoted in Pond, *Beyond the Wall*, p. 172.

91. Quoted in Hämäläinen, *Uniting Germany*, p. 133.

92. Quoted in James A. Baker III, with Thomas M. DeFrank, *The Politics of Diplomacy: Revolution, War and Peace, 1989–1992* (New York: Putnam, 1995), p. 234. See also Beschloss and Talbott, *At the Highest Levels:* esp. pp. 165–8, 187–8, 205.

93. Zelikow and Rice, *Germany Unified and Europe Transformed*, p. 335.

94. For a good discussion see Hannes Adomeit, "Gorbachev, German Unification and the Collapse of Empire," *Post-Soviet Affairs* 10 (1994): esp. 221–5.

95. See Thatcher, *The Downing Street Years* pp. 783, 789, 798.

96. Attali, *Verbatim, tome 3*, pp. 350, 416.

97. Quotations from the final declaration, July 6, 1990, in *New York Times,* July 7, 1990, p. A5.

98. Quoted in Raymond L. Garthoff, *The Great Transition: American-Soviet Relations and the End of the Cold War* (Washington, D.C.: Brookings Institution, 1994), p. 434.

99. Quotation from Paul G. Lewis, *Central Europe since 1945* (London: Longman, 1994), p. 204.

100. George Ross, *Jacques Delors and European Integration* (Cambridge: Polity Press, 1995), p. 39. See generally Richard Corbett, *The Treaty of Maastricht. From Conception to Ratification: A Comprehensive Reference Guide* (London: Longman, 1993).

101. Letter of April 20, 1990, printed in Corbett, *Treaty of Maastricht*, p. 126.

102. Hans-Dietrich Genscher, *Unterwegs zur Einheit: Reden und Dokumente aus bewegter Zeit* (Berlin: Siedler, 1991), p. 261.

103. Quoted in Harald Müller, "German Foreign Policy after Unification," in Paul B. Stares, ed., *The New Germany and the New Europe* (Washington, D.C.: Brookings Institution, 1992), p. 160.

104. For these themes, and a succinct account of the negotiations, see Roy Pryce, "The Treaty Negotiations," in Andrew Duff, John Pinder and Roy Pryce, eds., *Maastricht and Beyond: Building the European Union* (London: Routledge, 1993), pp. 36–52.

105. Quoted in Anthony Seldon, *Major: A Political Life* (London: Phoenix, 1998), p. 167.

106. *The Spectator* (London), July 13, 1990, pp. 8–10.

107. Interview in June 1993, quoted in Charles Grant, *Delors: Inside the House that Jacques Built* (London: Nicholas Brealey, 1993), p. 208.

108. Term used by Lord Mackenzie-Stuart, a former judge of the European Court, quoted by Andrew Duff, "The Main Reforms," in Duff et al., eds., *Maastricht and Beyond*, p. 26.

109. See Marshall I. Goldman, *What Went Wrong with Perestroika*, 2nd ed. (New York: Norton, 1992), pp. 128–39.

110. See generally Anders Åslund, *Gorbachev's Struggle for Economic Reform* (London: Pinter, 1991).

111. See generally Urban, *The Rebirth of Politics in Russia*, chs. 7–8.

112. For a sympathetic explanation of his reasoning, see Brown, *The Gorbachev Factor*, pp. 202–7.

113. Graham Smith, ed., *The Nationalities Question in the Soviet Union* (London: Longman, 1990), pp. v, 363. The essays in this book offer a good overview of the situation just before breakup.

114. See Anatol Lieven, *The Baltic Revolution: Estonia, Latvia, Lithuania and the Path to Independence*, 2nd ed. (New Haven: Yale University Press, 1993), ch. 8.

115. Roman Szporluk, "Dilemmas of Russian Nationalism," *Problems of Communism* 38/4 (July–August 1989): pp. 15–35.

116. *Tass*, March 13, 1989, quoted in Smith, ed., *The Nationalities Question*, p. 16.

117. Quoted in David Pryce-Jones, *The War that Never Was: The Fall of the Soviet Empire, 1985–1991* (London: Weidenfeld and Nicolson, 1995), p. 390.

118. For these opposing views, see Miller, *Mikhail Gorbachev and the End of Soviet Power*, pp. 166–9; and Hough, *Democratization and Revolution*, pp. 393–5.

119. Shevardnadze, *The Future Belongs to Freedom*, p. 203.

120. Compare Brown, *The Gorbachev Factor*, pp. 279–83, with John B. Dunlop, *The Rise of Russia and the Fall of the Soviet Empire* (Princeton, N.J.: Princeton University Press, 1991), pp. 30, 152.

121. Miller, *Mikhail Gorbachev*, p. 192.

122. On the coup, see Martin Sixsmith, *Moscow Coup: The Death of the Soviet System* (London: Simon & Schuster, 1991)—a journalist's "instant history" which is still a useful guide to events; and the documentation in *Putsch: The Diary. Three Days That Collapsed the Empire* (Stevenage, England: Spa Books, 1992). For analysis of the many puzzles, see Dunlop, *Rise of Russia*, ch. 5. and Hough, *Democratization and Revolution*, pp. 322–38.

123. David Remnick, *Lenin's Tomb: The Last Days of the Soviet Empire* (London: Penguin, 1993), p. 357.

124. *Newsweek*, September 2, 1991, p. 56.

125. Quoted in Hough, *Democratization and Revolution*, p. 329. Both he and Dunlop highlight questions about Gorbachev's exact position.

126. Sixsmith, *Moscow Coup*, p. 136.

127. Quoted in Dunlop, *Rise of Russia*, p. 239.

128. Boris Yeltsin, *The View from the Kremlin*, trans. by Catherine A. Fitzpatrick (London: HarperCollins, 1993), p. 57.

129. See the edited transcript printed in Ruslan Khasbulatov, *The Struggle for Russia: Power and Change in the Democratic Revolution,* ed. Richard Sakwa (London and New York: Routledge, 1993), ch. 10.

130. Dunlop, *Rise of Russia,* p. 272.

131. Georgy Shakhnazarov, quoted in Brown, *The Gorbachev Factor,* p. 299.

132. Figures from Barry Naughton, *Growing Out of the Plan: Chinese Economic Reform, 1979–1993* (Cambridge: Cambridge University Press, 1995), pp. 90–1.

133. Ruth Cherrington, *China's Students: The Struggle for Democracy* (London: Routledge, 1991), pp. 55, 71.

134. Baogang He, *The Democratization of China* (London: Routledge, 1996), p. 33.

135. Chen Yizi, "The Decision Process behind the 1986–1989 Political Reforms," in Carol Lee Hamrin and Suisheng Zhao, eds., *Decision-Making in Deng's China: Perspectives from Insiders* (Armonk, N.Y.: M. E. Sharpe, 1995), esp. pp. 136–8.

136. Merle Goldman, *Sowing the Seeds of Democracy in China: Political Reform in the Deng Xiaoping Era* (Cambridge, Mass.: Harvard University Press, 1993), chs. 7–8.

137. For these figures, see Gordon White, *Riding the Tiger: The Politics of Economic Reform in Post-Mao China* (London: Macmillan, 1993), pp. 186–7.

138. Goldman, *Sowing the Seeds,* pp. 232–7.

139. Nan Lin, *The Struggle for Tiananmen: Anatomy of the 1989 Mass Movement* (Westport, Conn.: Praeger, 1992), pp. 38–9.

140. Statistics from Suzanne Pepper, "Educational Reform in the 1980s," in Michael Ying-Mao Kau and Susan H. Marsh, eds., *China in the Era of Deng Xiaoping: A Decade of Reform* (Armonk, N.Y.: M. E. Sharpe, 1993), p. 263.

141. Cherrington, *China's Students,* p. 68.

142. On this I follow Goldman, *Sowing the Seeds,* ch. 10, esp. pp. 266, 277–8.

143. See Michel Oksenberg, Lawrence R. Sullivan, Marc Lambert, eds, *Beijing Spring, 1989: Confrontation and Conflict. Basic Documents* (Armonk, N.Y.: M. E. Sharpe, 1990), docs. 23–5. For accounts of the 1989 crisis, still based on problematic evidence, see Nan Lin, *The Struggle for Tiananmen,* and the Symposium "Tiananmen Square, 1989," in *Problems of Communism* 38/5 (September–October 1989): 1–38.

144. Quoted by Lowell Dittmer, "The Tiananmen Massacre," *Problems of Communism* 38/5 (September–October 1989): 7, from later reports in the Hong Kong press.

145. Quotations from Timothy Brook, *Quelling the People: The Military Suppression of the Beijing Democracy Movement* (New York: Oxford University Press, 1992), p. 31.

146. Quotations from Oksenberg et al., eds., *Beijing Spring,* pp. 290, 310.

147. The importance of this is stressed by Nan Lin, *The Struggle for Tiananmen,* pp. 23–5, 131–2.

148. Cherrington, *China's Students,* p. 171.

149. This paragraph follows Brook, *Quelling the People*, ch. 5, esp. pp. 121–2, 129–30.

150. Quoted in James Lull, *China Turned On: Television, Reform, and Resistance* (London: Routledge, 1991), p. 193. On casualties see also Brook, *Quelling the People*, ch. 6.

151. Government statement by Yuan Mu, June 6, in Oksenberg et al., eds., *Beijing Spring*, p. 363.

152. Lull, *China Turned On*, pp. 215–6. Although not mown down by the tanks—he was pulled away by bystanders—the demonstrator, possibly named Wang Weilin, was sentenced to ten years' imprisonment. See Brook, *Quelling the People*, p. 177.

153. Brook, *Quelling the People*, p. xii.

154. Anders Åslund, *How Russia Became a Market Economy* (Washington, D.C.: Brookings Institution, 1995), p. 16.

155. Hough, *Democratization and Revolution in the USSR*, pp. 15–22; Peter Nolan, *China's Rise, Russia's Fall: Politics, Economics and Planning in the Transition from Stalinism* (London: Macmillan, 1995), ch. 8.

156. Printed in Oksenberg et al., eds., *Beijing Spring*, doc. 53.

157. Quoted in Richard Evans, *Deng Xiaoping and the Making of Modern China* (London: Penguin Books, 1995), p. 307.

158. Naughton, *Growing Out of the Plan*, ch. 10, esp. pp. 303, 331.

159. World Bank, *China 2020: Development Challenges in the New Century* (Washington, D.C.: World Bank, 1997), pp. 3, 6.

160. Nolan, *China's Rise, Russia's Fall*, pp. 17–18.

Chapter 16 States, Wealth, and Order after the Cold War

1. Francis Fukuyama, "The End of History?" *National Interest,* Summer 1989, quoting pp. 3–4.

2. *The Public Papers of the Presidents of the United States: George Bush, 1991* (Washington, D.C.: Government Printing Office, 1992), p. 221.

3. Bill Clinton, *Between Hope and History: Meeting America's Challenges for the 21st Century* (New York: Times Books, 1996), p. 145.

4. See Samuel P. Huntington, *The Third Wave: Democratization in the Late Twentieth Century* (Norman: University of Oklahoma Press, 1991).

5. For the distinction between electoral and liberal democracies see Larry Diamond, "Is the Third Wave Over?" *Journal of Democracy* 7/3 (July 1996): 20–37.

6. Dilip Hiro, *The Longest War: The Iran-Iraq Military Conflict* (London: Paladin, 1990), pp. 1, 250–1.

7. See Efraim Karsh and Inari Rautsi, *Saddam Hussein: A Political Biography* (London: Brassey's, 1991).

8. Bush, *Public Papers, 1990*, p. 1411.

9. I follow here the argument of Musallam Ali Musallam, *The Iraqi Invasion of Kuwait: Saddam Hussein, His State, and International Power Politics* (London: British Academic Press, 1996), modeled on the typology of Kenneth Waltz.

10. Just how real was the threat remains debatable. See Nigel John Ashton, *Eisenhower, Macmillan and the Problem of Nasser: Anglo-American Relations and Arab Nationalism, 1955–1959* (London: Macmillan, 1996), Ch. 15.

11. Hiro, *The Longest War,* pp. 159–60, 250.

12. See Kenneth R. Timmerman, *The Death Lobby: How the West Armed Iraq* (London: Fourth Estate, 1992), p. 397.

13. See Oliver Ramsbotham, "The Conflict in Comparative Perspective," in Alex Danchev and Dan Keohane, eds., *International Perspectives on the Gulf Conflict, 1990–1991* (London: Macmillan, 1994), p. 305.

14. Michael Beschloss and Strobe Talbott, *At the Highest Levels: The Inside Story of the End of the Cold War* (Boston: Little, Brown, 1993), p. 255.

15. Robert J. Lieber, "Oil and Power after the 1991 Gulf War," in Wolfgang F. Danspeckgruber with Charles R. H. Tripp, eds., *The Iraqi Aggression against Kuwait: Strategic Lessons and Implications for Europe* (Boulder, Colo.: Westview, 1996), esp. pp. 159–60.

16. Quoted in Lawrence Freedman and Efraim Karsh, *The Gulf Conflict, 1990–1991* (London: Faber & Faber, 1993), p. 282.

17. H. Norman Schwarzkopf, with Peter Petre, *It Doesn't Take A Hero* (New York: Bantam, 1992), p. 468.

18. Freedman and Karsh, *The Gulf War,* p. 408; Dilip Hiro, *Desert Shield to Desert Storm: The Second Gulf War* (London: HarperCollins, 1992), p. 396, gives the higher death toll.

19. Bush, *Public Papers,* 1991, p. 197.

20. See Edward Luttwak, "The Air War," in Danchev and Keohane, eds., *International Perspectives on the Gulf War,* ch. 10, quoting from p. 227.

21. As even the chairman of his Joint Chiefs of Staff, General Colin Powell, came close to acknowledging. See Colin Powell, with Joseph E. Persico, *My American Journey* (New York: Ballantine Books, 1996), p. 478.

22. See Edgar O'Ballance, *The Kurdish Struggle, 1920–94* (London: Macmillan, 1996), esp. chs. 12–14; and Majid Khadduri and Edmund Ghareeb, *War in the Gulf, 1990–91: The Iraq-Kuwait Conflict and Its Implications* (New York: Oxford Univ. Press, 1997), ch. 12.

23. See F. Robert Hunter, *The Palestinian Uprising: A War by Other Means* (Berkeley: University of California Press, 1991).

24. See Asher Slusser, *In Through The Out Door: Jordan's Disengagement and the Middle Eastern Peace Process* (Washington, D.C.: Washington Institute for Near East Policy, 1990).

25. Andrew Gowers and Tony Walker, *Arafat: The Biography,* 2nd ed. (London: Virgin Books, 1994), ch. 16.

26. Quoted in Omar Massalha, *Towards the Long-Promised Peace* (London: Saqi Books, 1994), p. 42.

27. James A. Baker III, with Thomas M. DeFrank, *The Politics of Diplomacy: Revolution, War and Peace, 1989–1992* (New York: Putnam, 1995), p. 512.

28. Shamir said that, had he won, "I would have conducted the autonomy negotiations for ten years, and in the meantime we would have reached half a million souls in Judea and Samaria." Quoted in M. Graeme Bannerman, "Arabs and Israelis: Slow Walk Toward Peace," *Foreign Affairs* 72/1 (January–February 1993): 150.

29. Quoted in Hemda Ben-Yahuda, "Attitude Change and Policy Transformation: Yitzhak Rabin and the Palestinian Question, 1967–95," in Efraim Karsh, ed., *From Rabin to Netahyahu: Israel's Troubled Agenda* (London: Frank Cass, 1997), p. 208. Generally see David Makovsky, *Making Peace with the PLO: The Rabin Government's Road to the Oslo Accord* (Boulder, Colo.: Westview, 1996), and David Horovitz, ed., *Yitzhak Rabin: Soldier of Peace* (London: Peter Halban, 1996).

30. Quoted in John King, *Handshake in Washington: The Beginning of Middle East Peace?* (London: Ithaca Press, 1994), p. 42.

31. Shimon Peres, with Arye Naor, *The New Middle East* (Shaftesbury, Dorset: Element Books, 1993), pp. 71, 96.

32. See Geoffrey Aronson, *Settlements and the Israel-Palestinian Negotiations: An Overview* (Washington, D.C.: Institute of Palestinian Studies, 1996).

33. For useful overviews see Roger Owen, *State, Power and Politics in the Making of the Modern Middle East* (London: Routledge, 1992), and M. E. Yapp, *The Near East since the First World War*, 2nd ed. (London: Longman, 1995), esp. section IV.

34. Details from Naji Abi-Aad and Michel Grenon, *Instability and Conflict in the Middle East: People, Petroleum and Security Threats* (London: Macmillan, 1997), ch. 9.

35. Abi-Aad and Grenon, *Instability and Conflict,* pp. 50–1.

36. Abi-Aad and Grenon, *Instability and Conflict,* ch. 10.

37. Samuel P. Huntington, "The Clash of Civilizations?" *Foreign Affairs* 72/3 (Summer 1993): quoting 22, 35.

38. Quotations from Augustus Richard Norton, ed., *Civil Society in the Middle East*, vol. 1 (Leiden: E. J. Brill, 1995), p. 20 (Krauthammer); and Martin Kramer, "Fundamentalist Islam at Large: The Drive for Power," *Middle East Quarterly* 3/2 (June 1996): 48.

39. Points emphasized by Saeed Rahnema and Sohrab Behdad, eds., *Iran after the Revolution: Crisis of an Islamic State* (London: I. B. Tauris, 1995), pp. 4–5, and Sami Zubaida, *Islam, The People and the State: Essays on Political Ideas and Movement in the Middle East* (London: Routledge, 1988), p. ix.

40. Robert Mortimer, "Islamists, Soldiers and Democrats: The Second Algerian War," *Middle East Journal* 50/1 (Winter 1996): 19.

41. Martin Stone, *The Agony of Algeria* (London: Hurst & Co., 1997), p. 166—a study on which this section rests.

42. John Waterbury, *Commander of the Faithful: The Moroccan Political Elite* (London: Weidenfeld and Nicolson, 1970), p. 146. See also Andrew J. Pierre and William B. Quandt, *The Algerian Crisis: Policy Options for the West* (Washington, D.C.: Carnegie Endowment for International Peace, 1996), pp. 17–18.

43. See Barry Rubin, *Islamic Fundamentalism in Egyptian Politics* (London: Macmillan, 1990).

44. Graham E. Fuller and Ian O. Lesser, with Paul B. Henze and J. F. Brown, *Turkey's New Geopolitics: From the Balkans to Western China* (Boulder, Colo.: Westview, 1993), p. x. See also Feroz Ahmad, *The Making of Modern Turkey* (London: Routledge, 1993), chs. 9–10.

45. Figures from Anoushiravan Ehteshami, *After Khomeini: The Iranian Second Republic* (London: Routledge, 1995), pp. 93, 100—a book on which this section draws heavily.

46. Asghar Schirazi, *The Constitution of Iran: Politics and the State in the Islamic Republic*, trans. John O'Kane (London: I. B. Tauris, 1997), p. 304.

47. See Fred Halliday, *Islam and the Myth of Confrontation: Religion and Politics in the Middle East* (London: I. B. Tauris, 1995), ch. 7.

48. Quoted in Steven Friedman and Doreen Atkinson, eds., *The Small Miracle: South Africa's Negotiated Settlement* (Johannesburg: Raven Press, 1994), p. 1.

49. Quoted in Willem de Klerk, *F. W. de Klerk: The Man in His Time* (Johannesburg: Jonathan Ball, 1991), p. 34.

50. Dan O'Meara, *Forty Lost Years: The Apartheid State and the Politics of the National Party, 1948–1994* (Athens, Ohio: Ohio University Press, 1996), pp. 354–7.

51. Quoted in de Klerk, *F. W. de Klerk*, p. 27.

52. Figures from Gerhard Mare, "Civil War Regions and Ethnic Mobilisation: Inkatha and Zulu Nationalism in the Transition to South African Democracy," in Paul B. Rich, ed., *Reaction and Renewal in South Africa* (London: Macmillan, 1996), pp. 25, 34.

53. Steven Friedman, ed., *The Long Journey: South Africa's Quest for a Negotiated Settlement* (Johannesburg: Raven Press, 1994), p. 174.

54. Quoted in Patti Waldmeir, *Anatomy of a Miracle: The End of Apartheid and the Birth of the New South Africa* (London: Viking, 1997), p. 213.

55. Quoted in Martin Meredith, *South Africa's New Era: The 1994 Election* (London: Mandarin, 1994), p. 57.

56. Doreen Atkinson, "Brokering a Miracle?: The Multiparty Negotiating Forum," in Friedman and Atkinson, eds., *The Small Miracle*, pp. 35–6.

57. On the conduct of the election, see Steven Friedman and Louise Stack, "The Magic Moment: The 1994 Election," in Friedman and Atkinson, eds., *The Small Miracle*, ch. 12.

58. Quoted in *Keesing's Record of World Events*, May 1994, p. 39990.

59. Martin J. Murray, *The Revolution Deferred: The Painful Birth of Post-Apartheid South Africa* (London: Verso, 1994), ch. 3, esp. pp. 56, 61.

60. R. W. Johnson, "How Free? How Fair?" in R. W. Johnson and Lawrence Schlemmer, eds., *Launching Democracy in South Africa: The First Open Election, April 1994* (New Haven: Yale University Press, 1994), p. 319.

61. Michael Bratton and Nicolas van de Walle, *Democratic Experiments in Africa: Regime Transitions in Comparative Perspective* (Cambridge: Cambridge University Press, 1997), introduction, quoting p. 3.

62. Philippe Hugon, "Les effets des politiques d'adjustement sur les structures politiques africaines," in Gérard Conac, ed., *L'Afrique en transition vers le pluralisme politique* (Paris: Economica, 1993), p. 95.

63. World Bank, *Adjustment in Africa: Reforms, Results, and the Road Ahead* (New York: Oxford University Press, 1994), p. 61.

64. For an overview of these patterns, see Bratton and van de Walle, *Democratic Experiments in Africa*, chs. 3–6, and John A. Wiseman, *The New Struggle for Democracy in Africa* (Aldershot, Hants: Avebury, 1996), chs. 3–5.

65. Wiseman, *The New Struggle for Democracy in Africa*, pp. 126–31; *The Economist*, November 29, 1997, p. 128; and Daniel N. Posner, "Malawi's New Dawn," *Journal of Democracy* 6 (1995): 131–45.

66. Wiseman, *The New Struggle for Democracy in Africa*, pp. 120, 133.

67. World Bank, *Adjustment in Africa*, p. 40.

68. See the discussion in Patrick Nugent, *Big Men, Small Boys and Politics in Ghana: Power, Ideology and the Burden of History* (London: Pinter, 1995), esp. pp. 198–207, 271.

69. David W. Throup and Charles Hornsby, *Multi-Party Politics in Kenya: The Kenyatta and Moi States and the Triumph of the System in the 1992 Election* (Oxford: James Currey, 1998), p. 602.

70. Bratton and van de Walle, *Democratic Experiments in Africa*, p. 233.

71. This section draws heavily on Larry Diamond, Anthony Kirk-Greene, and Oyeleye Oyediran, eds., *Transition without End: Nigerian Politics and Civil Society under Babangida* (Boulder, Colo.: Lynne Rienner, 1997), esp. the introduction and chs. 12, 13, 21.

72. Catherine Besteman and Lee V. Cassanelli, eds., *The Struggle for Land in Southern Somalia: The War Behind the War* (Boulder, Colo.: Westview, 1996), quoting p. 15.

73. Michael Clough, "The United States and Africa: The Policy of Cynical Disengagement," *Current History* 91 (May 1992): 193–8. Generally see Peter J. Schraeder, *United States Foreign Policy toward Africa: Incrementalism, Crisis and Change* (Cambridge: Cambridge University Press, 1994), pp. 175–80.

74. *Guardian Weekly*, January 17, 1993, p. 8.

75. *Keesing's Contemporary Archives*, August 1996, p. 41213.

76. Elias Nyamlell Wakoson, "The Politics of Southern Self-Government, 1972–83," in M. W. Daly and Ahmad Alawad Sikainga, eds., *Civil War in the Sudan* (London: British Academic Press, 1993), pp. 27–50.

77. *Economist*, March 28, 1998, pp. 67–8. See also J. Millard Burr and Robert O. Collins, *Requiem for the Sudan: War, Drought, and Disaster Relief on the Nile* (Boulder, Colo.: Westview, 1995).

78. See Dixon Kamakuma, *Rwanda Conflict: Its Roots and Regional Implications*, 2nd ed. (Kampala: Fountain Publishers, 1997), pp. 32–3.

79. This account follows Gérard Prunier, *The Rwanda Crisis, 1959–1994: History of a Genocide* (London: C. Hurst, 1995), ch. 7.

80. *The Economist,* January 24, 1998, p. 64.

81. Christopher Clapham, *Africa and the International System: The Politics of State Survival* (Cambridge: Cambridge University Press, 1996), pp. 88–98; Peter J. Schraeder, "African International Relations," in April A. Gordon and Donald L. Gordon, eds., *Understanding Contemporary Africa* (Boulder, Colo.: Lynne Rienner, 1996), pp. 146–54.

82. See the argument developed in Basil Davidson, *The Black Man's Burden: Africa and the Curse of the Nation-State* (New York: Times Books, 1992).

83. Daniel C. Bach, "Indigeneity, Ethnicity, and Federalism," in Diamond et al., eds., *Transition without End,* ch. 14, esp. p. 334.

84. Cf. Siegfried Pausewang, "Local Democracy and Central Control," in Abebe Zegeye and Siegfried Pausewang, eds., *Ethiopia in Change: Peasantry, Nationalism and Democracy* (London: British Academic Press, 1994), pp. 209–30.

85. Thomas Callaghy, "Africa: Back to the Future?" in Larry Diamond and Marc F. Plattner, eds., *Economic Reform and Democracy* (Baltimore: Johns Hopkins University Press, 1995), ch. 11, quoting p. 150.

86. John C. Caldwell, I. O. Orubuloye, and Pat Caldwell, "Fertility Transition in Africa: A New Type of Transition?", *Population and Development Review* 18 (1992): 211–42.

87. *International Herald Tribune,* June 24, 1998, pp. 1, 4.

88. See the general discussion in George Philip, "New Economic Liberalism and Democracy in Spanish America," *Government and Opposition,* 29 (1994), 362–77.

89. I follow here the general argument of Stephan Haggard and Robert R. Kaufman, *The Political Economy of Democratic Transitions* (Princeton, N.J.: Princeton University Press, 1995), esp. chs. 5–8.

90. For an overview, see Lois Hecht Oppenheimer, *Politics in Chile: Democracy, Authoritarianism, and the Search for Development* (Boulder, Colo.: Westview, 1993).

91. Quoted in Rob Aitken, Nikki Craske, Gareth A. Jones, and David E. Stansfield, eds., *Dismantling the Mexican State?* (London: Macmillan, 1996), p. xii. See generally Howard Handelman, *Mexican Politics: The Dynamics of Change* (New York: St. Martin's, 1997).

92. See Davide G. Erro, *Resolving the Argentine Paradox: Politics and Development, 1966–1992* (Boulder, Colo.: Lynne Rienner, 1993), chs. 6–7; also Edward E. Epstein, ed., *The New Argentine Democracy: The Search for a Successful Formula* (Westport, Conn.: Praeger, 1992), esp. ch. 10.

93. See Frances Hagopian, *Traditional Politics and Regime Change in Brazil* (Cambridge: Cambridge University Press, 1996), esp. ch. 10.

94. Haggard and Kaufman, *Political Economy of Democratic Transitions,* p. 195.

95. Kurt Weyland, "The Rise and Fall of President Collor and Its Impact on Brazilian Democracy," *Journal of Inter-American Studies and World Affairs* 35 (1993): 25.

96. Celina Souza, *Constitutional Engineering in Brazil: The Politics of Federalism and Decentralization* (London: Macmillan, 1997), p. 80.

97. A theme emphasized by Rachel Sieder, ed., *Central America: Fragile Transition* (London: Macmillan, 1996), esp. pp. 1–6.

98. Dario Moreno, *The Struggle for Peace in Central America* (Gainesville: University Press of Florida, 1994), chs. 4–6.

99. Georges Fauriol and Eva Loser, eds., *Cuba: The International Dimension* (London: Transaction Publishers, 1990), ch. 11.

100. *The Economist,* August 16, 1997, p. 43; see generally Roberto Segre, Mario Coyula, and Joseph L. Scarpaci, *Havana: Two Faces of the Antillean Metropolis* (New York: John Wiley, 1997), ch. 7.

101. *The Economist,* November 22, 1997, pp. 79–80; and *Keesing's Record of World Events,* pp. 40316–7, 41901, 42188–9.

102. For patterns see David E. Hojman, "The Political Economy of Recent Conversions to Market Economics in Latin America," *Journal of Latin American Studies* 26 (1994): 191–219.

103. See Joseph S. Tulchin and Gary Bland, eds., *Peru in Crisis: Dictatorship or Democracy?* (Boulder, Colo.: Lynne Rienner, 1994).

104. Scott Mainwaring and Timothy R. Scully, eds., *Building Democratic Institutions: Party Systems in Latin America* (Stanford: Stanford University Press, 1995), esp. ch. 1.

105. See the comparative discussion in J. Patrick McSherry, *Incomplete Transition: Military Power and Democracy in Argentina* (London: Macmillan, 1997), ch. 1.

106. *The Economist,* December 6, 1997, supplement on "Business in Latin America," p. 9.

107. Andres Oppenheimer, *Bordering on Chaos: Guerrillas, Stockbrokers, Politicians, and Mexico's Road to Prosperity* (Boston: Little, Brown, 1996), pp. 90–3.

108. Oppenheimer, *Bordering on Chaos,* p. xi.

109. Donna Lee Van Cott, ed., *Indigenous Peoples and Democracy in Latin America* (London: Macmillan, 1994), esp. ch. 1.

110. Richard S. Hillman, ed., *Understanding Contemporary Latin America* (Boulder, Colo.: Lynne Rienner, 1997), ch. 11; Arlindo Villaschi, *The Newly Industrialized Countries and the Information Technology Revolution: The Brazilian Experience* (Aldershot, Hants: Avebury, 1994).

111. For this concept, see Claus Offe, "Capitalism by Democratic Design?: Democratic Theory Facing the Triple Transition in East Central Europe," *Social Research* 58 (1991): 865–92.

112. Steven Fish, "Russia's Fourth Transition," in Diamond and Plattner, eds., *The Resurgence of Global Democracy,* pp. 264–75; cf. Leslie Holmes, *Post-Communism: An Introduction* (Cambridge: Polity Press, 1997), pp. 51–2, 270.

113. See Stephen White, Richard Rose, and Ian McAllister, *How Russia Votes* (Chatham, N.J.: Chatham House Publishers, 1997), an excellent study of elections from 1989 to 1996.

114. Boris Yeltsin, *The View from the Kremlin,* trans. Catherine A. Fitzpatrick (London: HarperCollins, 1994), pp. 277–9.

115. Peter Nolan, *China's Rise, Russia's Fall: Politics, Economics and Planning in the Transition from Stalinism* (London: Macmillan, 1995), p. 17.

116. For a vivid portrait, see John Kampfner, *Inside Yeltsin's Russia: Corruption, Conflict, Capitalism* (London: Cassell, 1994).

117. Anders Aslund, *How Russia Became a Market Economy* (Washington, D.C.: Brookings Institution, 1995), p. 5; cf. Grigory Yavlinsky, "Russia's Phoney Capitalism," *Foreign Affairs* 77/3 (May–June 1998): p. 69.

118. Anatol Lieven, *Chechnya: Tombstone of Russian Power* (New Haven: Yale University Press, 1998), p. 169.

119. Raphel Shen, *Restructuring the Baltic Economies: Disengaging Fifty Years of Integration with the USSR* (Westport, Conn.: Praeger, 1994), pp. 214–5.

120. Zanny Minton Beddoes, in *The Economist*, February 7, 1998, Central Asia survey, p. 16.

121. Quoted in Ian Bremmer and Ray Taras, eds., *New States, New Politics: Building the Post-Soviet Nations* (Cambridge: Cambridge University Press, 1997), p. 587.

122. Bremmer and Taras, eds., *New States, New Politics*, pp. 29, 48.

123. Karen Dawisha and Bruce Parrott, *Russia and the New States of Eurasia: The Politics of Upheaval* (Cambridge: Cambridge University Press, 1994), Ch. 8, esp. p. 261.

124. Using the famous phrase of the tsar's interior minister in 1904 about how to avert a revolution. (The Russo-Japanese War led directly to the 1905 revolution!) See Carlotta Gall and Thomas de Waal, *Chechnya: A Small Victorious War* (London: Pan, 1997), pp. xii, 161.

125. Daniel Pipes, "The Event of Our Era: Former Soviet Muslim Republics Change the Middle East," in Michael Mandelbaum, ed., *Central Asia and the World* (New York: Council on Foreign Relations, 1994), p. 85.

126. For a useful guide to the tangled and emotive historiography, see Gale Stokes, John Lampe, and Denison Rusinow, with Julie Mostov, "Instant History: Understanding the Wars of Yugoslav Succession," *Slavic Review* 55 (1996): 136–60.

127. A theme emphasized by Susan L. Woodward, *Balkan Tragedy: Chaos and Dissolution after the Cold War* (Washington, D.C.: Brookings Institution, 1995), ch. 3.

128. Amanda Vickers, *Between Serb and Albanian: A History of Kosovo* (London: Hurst & Co., 1998), chs. 10–14; Aleksa Djilas, "A Profile of Slobodan Milošević," *Foreign Affairs* 72/3 (Summer 1996): 81–96.

129. See generally Noel Malcolm, *Bosnia: A Short History*, 2nd ed. (London: Papermac, 1996).

130. Quoted in Laura Silber and Allan Little, *The Death of Yugoslavia* (London: Penguin Books, 1995), p. 328.

131. For the analogy with Spain, see Sabrina Petra Ramet, "The Yugoslav Crisis and the West," in Ramet and Ljubiša S. Adamovich, eds., *Beyond Yugoslavia: Politics, Economics and Culture in a Shattered Community* (Boulder, Colo.: Westview, 1995), pp. 461–2.

132. Jiří Musil, ed., *The End of Czechoslovakia* (Budapest: Central European University Press, 1995), chs. 12–13, esp. p. 233.

133. Kazimierz Z. Poznanski, *Poland's Protracted Transition: Institutional Change and Economic Growth, 1970–1994* (Cambridge: Cambridge University Press, 1996), p. 289.

134. Marie Lavigne, "Market Economies as Project and Practice," in Jack Hayward and Edward C. Page, eds., *Governing the New Europe* (Cambridge: Polity Press, 1995), p. 116.

135. See Paul Cornish, *Partnership in Crisis: The U.S., Europe and the Fall and Rise of NATO* (London: RIIA/Pinter, 1997).

136. Speech in August 1993, quoted in Michael Mandelbaum, *The Dawn of Peace in Europe* (New York: Twentieth Century Fund Press, 1996), p. 24.

137. Jonathan Haslam, "Russia's Seat at the Table: A Place Denied or A Place Delayed?" *International Affairs* 74 (1998): 124–5.

138. See John Redmond, ed., *The 1995 Enlargement of the European Union* (Aldershot Hants: Ashgate, 1997).

139. Robert A. Jones, *The Politics and Economics of the European Union* (Cheltenham: Edward Elgar, 1996), pp. 147, 285.

140. Heather Grabbe and Kirsty Hughes, *Enlarging the EU Eastwards* (London: RIIA/Pinter, 1998), p. 1.

141. Jones, *The Politics and Economics of the European Union,* ch. 10, esp. p. 193.

142. Roland Czada, "The Treuhandanstalt and the Transition from Socialism to Capitalism," in Arthur Benz and Klaus H. Goetz, eds., *A New German Public Sector?: Reform, Adaptation and Stability* (Aldershot, Hants: Dartmouth, 1996), 93–117.

143. Russell J. Dalton, ed., *Germans Divided: The 1994 Bundestag Elections and the Evolution of the German Party System* (Oxford: Berg, 1996), pp. 12–15.

144. Donald Sassoon, *One Hundred Years of Socialism: The West European Left in the Twentieth Century* (London: Fontana, 1997), pp. 743–4.

145. Tom Mackie, "Parties and Elections," in Hayward and Page, eds., *Governing the New Europe,* p. 175.

146. This paragraph draws heavily on Michael Keating, *The New Regionalism in Western Europe: Territorial Restructuring and Political Change* (Cheltenham: Edward Elgar, 1998).

147. Quoted in *The Economist,* March 9, 1996, p. 33. See also Kishibore Mahbubani, "The West and the Rest," *The National Interest,* Summer 1992: 3–12; and generally Samuel P. Huntington, *The Clash of Civilizations and the Remaking of World Order* (New York: Simon and Schuster, 1996), pp. 103–9.

148. See Yoshikazu Sakamoto, "The Role of Japan in the Future International System," in Armand Clesse, Richard Cooper, and Yoshikazu Sakamoto, eds., *The International System after the Collapse of the East-West Order* (Dordrecht: Martinus Nijhoff, 1994), pp. 555–69.

149. *Economic Survey of Japan, 1992–1993* (Tokyo: Economic Planning Agency, July 1993), pp. 273–4.

150. As calculated by Shigeto Tsuru, *Japan's Capitalism: Creative Defeat and Beyond* (Cambridge: Canto, 1996), p. 160.

151. See *The Times* (London), September 26, 1997, p. 31.

152. See data on financial markets in *The Economist,* January 3, 1998, p. 98; July 4, 1998, p. 138; and, generally, March 7, 1998, supplement on "East Asian Economies."

153. *International Herald Tribune,* June 9, 1998, p. 9.

154. Paul Krugman, "The Myth of Asia's Miracle," *Foreign Affairs* 73/6 (November–December 1994): 62–78, quoting p. 70.

155. See Khoo Boo Teik, *Paradoxes of Mahathirism: An Intellectual Biography of Mahathir Mohamad* (Kuala Lumpur: Oxford University Press, 1995).

156. *Keesing's Record of World Events*, October 1997, pp. 41868–9.

157. This argument is emphasized by essayists in the special section on the Asian Economic Crisis in *World Development* 26/8 (August 1998): 1529–1609.

158. *The Times* (London), May 30, 1998, p. 56. Other figures from *Indonesia in Crisis: A Macroeconomic Update* (World Bank paper, July 16, 1998), on which this paragraph rests.

159. Peter Carey, "Will the Centre Hold?," *The World Today*, 54/7 (July 1998): 176–7.

160. Mark R. Thompson, *The Anti-Marcos Struggle: Personalistic Rule and Democratic Transition in the Philippines* (New Haven: Yale University Press, 1995); and Benedict Anderson, "From Miracle to Crash," *London Review of Books*, April 16, 1998, pp. 3–7.

161. Quoted in the *Sunday Times* (London), February 16, 1997, p. 15. See also Tong Wham Park, "Arms Control between the Two Koreas," *Contemporary Security Policy* 17 (1996): 113–26.

162. Michael C. Williams, *Vietnam at the Crossroads* (London: RIIA/Pinter, 1992), p. 86.

163. World Bank, *China 2020: Development Challenges in the New Century* (Washington: World Bank, 1997), pp. 2–4.

164. World Bank, *World Development Report, 1997* (New York: Oxford University Press, 1997), Table 17.

165. Richard Grant, "Challenges for China," *The World Today* 54/6 (June 1998): pp. 159–60.

166. World Bank, *China 2020*, p. 50.

167. Steven M. Goldstein, "China in Transition: The Political Foundations of Incremental Reform," in Andrew Walder, ed., *China's Transitional Economy* (Oxford: Clarendon, 1996), p. 169.

168. Quoted in Jonathan Dimbleby, *The Last Governor: Chris Patten and the Handover of Hong Kong* (London: Little, Brown, 1997), p. 156.

169. *International Herald Tribune*, June 23, 1998, p. 2. See also David Shambaugh, ed., *Greater China: The Next Superpower?* (Oxford: Oxford University Press, 1995).

170. Jagdish Bhagwati, *India in Transition: Freeing the Economy* (Oxford: Clarendon, 1993), pp. 67–8.

171. Vijay Joshi and I. M. D. Little, *India's Economic Reforms, 1991–2001* (Oxford: Clarendon, 1996), pp. 174–5.

172. On 1998, see the essays on "India defies the Odds" in *Journal of Democracy* 9/3 (July 1998): 3–50; and, more generally, Atul Kothi, ed., *India's Democracy: An Analysis of Changing State-Society Relations* (Princeton, N.J.: Princeton University Press, 1990).

173. See generally Iftikhar H. Malik, *State and Civil Society in Pakistan: Politics of Authority, Ideology and Ethnicity* (London: Macmillan, 1997); and Dilara Choudhury, *Constitutional Development in Bangladesh: Stresses and Strains* (Karachi: Oxford University Press, 1994).

174. World Bank, *World Development Report, 1995* (New York: Oxford University Press, 1995), p. 210.

175. See Barnett R. Rubin, *The Search for Peace in Afghanistan: From Buffer State to Failed State* (New Haven: Yale University Press, 1995).

176. Quoted in *The Times* (London), August 26, 1998, p. 11. For background see William A. Walker, "International Nuclear Relations after the Indian and Pakistani Test Explosions," *International Affairs* 74 (1998): 505–28.

177. Roger C. Thompson, *The Pacific Basin since 1945* (London: Longman, 1994), chs. 5, 8; and Donald Denoon, ed., *The Cambridge History of the Pacific Islanders* (Cambridge: Cambridge University Press, 1997), esp. ch. 10 on "The Nuclear Pacific."

178. See Patrick Massey, *New Zealand: Market Liberalization in a Developed Economy* (London: Macmillan, 1995).

179. *The Economist,* June 13, 1998, p. 101.

180. Geoffrey Sherrington, *Australia's Immigrants, 1788–1988,* 2nd ed. (Sydney: Allen & Unwin, 1990), ch. 5; *The Economist,* September 26, 1998, p. 146.

181. See Geoffrey W. Rice, ed., *The Oxford History of New Zealand,* 2nd ed. (Auckland: Oxford University Press, 1992), ch. 10; and Richard Broome, *Aboriginal Australians: Black Responses to White Dominance, 1788–1994,* 2nd ed. (St. Leonards, N.S.W.: Allen & Unwin, 1994), ch. 12.

182. See Xavier Pons, *A Sheltered Land* (St. Leonards, NSW: Allen & Unwin, 1994), pp. xi–xii.

183. As predicted by Robert A. Heilbronner, "The 'Disappearance' of Capitalism," *World Policy Journal* 15/2 (Summer 1998): 6–7.

Chapter 17 Goods and Values

1. The phrase is from Charles Krauthammer, "The Unipolar Moment," *Foreign Affairs* 70/1 (Winter 1991): 23–33.

2. *Washington Post,* August 13, 1998, p. A28; *The Economist,* June 20, 1998, p. 148.

3. Department of Defense, *Annual Report to the President and Congress, 1994* (Washington, D.C.: Government Printing Office, 1994), p. 16.

4. *The Times* (London), June 26, 1997, p. 31.

5. Ron Watts, "The American Constitution in Comparative Perspective: A Comparison of Federalism in the United States and Canada," *Journal of American History* 74 (1987): p. 777.

6. *Keesing's Record of World Events,* pp. 37519, 39126, 40565–6; see also Robert A. Young, *The Secession of Quebec and the Future of Canada* (Montreal: McGill–Queen's University Press, 1995) on how Canada might react to an independent Quebec.

7. Mortimer B. Zuckerman, "A Second American Century," *Foreign Affairs* 77/3 (May–June 1998): 18–31.

8. Christopher Layne, "Rethinking American Grand Strategy: Hegemony or Balance of Power?" *World Policy Journal* 14/2 (Summer 1998): 8–28.

9. Wyn Q. Bowen and David Dunn, *American Security Policy in the 1990s: Beyond Containment* (Aldershot, Hants: Darmouth, 1996), ch. 5, quoting p. 122.

10. The United States is the only democracy in which voter registration is initiated by the individual, and this makes registration rates unusually low. Although the "motor voter" act of 1993 made registration easier (e.g., when applying for a driver's license), the 1996 election saw nearly ten million *fewer* citizens voting than in 1992. See Alan Grant, *The American Political Process*, 6th ed. (Aldershot, Hants: Aldgate, 1997), pp. 297–9.

11. Ross Perot, *United We Stand: How We Can Take Back Our Country* (New York: Hyperion, 1992), p. 24.

12. See Bob Woodward, *The Choice* (New York: Simon and Schuster, 1996); and Elizabeth Drew, *Showdown: The Struggle between the Gingrich Congress and the Clinton White House* (New York: Simon and Schuster, 1996).

13. Representative James P. Moran, quoted in the *Washington Post* edition of the *Starr Report* (New York: Public Affairs Press, 1998), p. xi.

14. John Brummett, *Highwire: From the Backwoods to the Beltway—The Education of Bill Clinton* (New York: Hyperion, 1994), pp. 268–9.

15. Robert D. Putnam, "Bowling Alone: America's Declining Social Capital," in Larry Diamond and Marc F. Plattner, eds., *The Resurgence of Global Democracy,* 2nd ed. (Baltimore: Johns Hopkins University Press, 1996), pp. 290–303.

16. Quoted by Gavin Esler, *The United States of Anger* (London: Penguin, 1998), p. 173.

17. *The Economist,* April 4, 1998, p. 18.

18. Esler, *United States of Anger,* p. 90.

19. *The Times* (London), April 13, 1998, p. 12.

20. Morris Janowitz, *The Reconstruction of Patriotism: Education for Civic Consciousness* (Chicago: University of Chicago Press, 1983), p. 129.

21. Peter Skerry, *Mexican Americans: The Ambivalent Minority* (New York: Free Press, 1993), pp. 7, 17, 376–7.

22. *International Herald Tribune,* April 24, 1997, p. 3.

23. *Journal of American History* 84 (1997): 566, 578.

24. Statistics from Andrew Hacker, *Two Nations: Black and White, Separate, Hostile, Unequal* (New York: Scribner's, 1992), pp. 67, 99, 103, 162, 181.

25. Quoted in Calvin McLeod Logue and Jean DeHart, eds., *Representative American Speeches, 1996–1997* (New York: H. W. Wilson, 1997), p. 58.

26. Malcolm Waters, *Globalization* (London: Routledge, 1995), p. 1.

27. Roland Robertson, *Globalization: Social Theory and Global Culture* (London: Sage, 1992), p. 8.

28. Data from Network Wizards (http://www.nw.com).

29. *The Economist,* September 19, 1998, survey on "The Millennium Bug," esp. p. 21.

30. A. Jagoda and M. de Villepin, *Mobile Communications* (New York: John Wiley, 1993), chs. 6–7; *The Economist,* March 28, 1998, p. 136.

31. *The Economist*, October 25, 1997, p. 139.

32. Bjorn Wellenius and Peter A. Stern, eds., *Implementing Reforms in the Telecommunications Sector: Lessons from Experience* (Aldershot, Hants: Avebury, 1996), chs. 3, 8.

33. Joan E. Spero and Jeffrey A. Hart, *The Politics of International Economic Relations*, 5th ed. (New York: St. Martin's, 1997), pp. 82–7.

34. Quotations from Kenichi Ohmae, *The End of the Nation State: The Rise of Regional Economics* (London: HarperCollins, 1996), pp. 12 and 17; Robert B. Reich, *The Work of Nations: Preparing Ourselves for 21st-Century Capitalism* (New York: Knopf, 1991), p. 8.

35. Alvin Toffler, *The Third Wave* (New York: William Morrow, 1980), ch. 16; Frances Cairncross, *The Death of Distance: How the Communications Revolution Will Change Our Lives* (Boston: Harvard Business School Press, 1997), p. 279.

36. Quotations from Hans-Peter Martin and Harald Schumann, *The Global Trap: Globalization and the Assault on Democracy and Prosperity* (London: Zed Books, 1997), p. 5; and John Gray, *False Dawn: The Delusions of Global Capitalism* (London: Granta, 1998), p. 207.

37. Spero and Hart, *The Politics of International Economic Relations*, pp. 27, 57; Blanca Heredia, "Prosper or Perish: Development in the Age of Global Capital," *Current History* 96 (November 1997): 384.

38. Quoted in R. J. Johnston, Peter J. Taylor, and Michael J. Watts, ed., *Geographies of Global Change: Remapping the World in the Late Twentieth Century* (Oxford: Blackwell, 1995), p. 50.

39. Paul Hirst and Grahame Thompson, *Globalization in Question: The International Economy and the Possibilities of Governance* (Cambridge: Polity Press, 1996), pp. 68–70.

40. See, e.g., Jeffrey E. Garten, *The Big Ten: The Big Emerging Markets and How They Will Change Our Lives* (New York: Basic Books, 1997).

41. See Robert H. Frank and Philip J. Cook, *The Winner-Take-All Society* (New York: Free Press, 1995).

42. Rebecca M. Blank, *It Takes a Nation: A New Agenda for Fighting Poverty* (Princeton, N.J.: Princeton University Press, 1997), ch. 2; cf. Reich, *Work of Nations*, chs. 16–17.

43. World Bank, *World Development Report, 1995: Workers in an Integrating World* (New York: Oxford University Press, 1995), ch. 18.

44. Hirst and Thompson, *Globalization in Question*, pp. 68–70.

45. Elizabeth Pettit and Bilgin Soylu, with Jonathan Fiske, *The World Telecoms Marketplace, 1998* (Cambridge: Analysis, 1997), pp. 6, 10, 663, 669.

46. George Thomas Kurian, *Fitzroy Dearborn Book of World Rankings* (Chicago: Fitzroy Dearborn, 1998), table 204.

47. Thomas M. Callaghy, "Globalization and Marginalization: Debt and the International Underclass," *Current History* 96 (November 1997): 392–6.

48. Bruno Amoroso, *On Globalization: Capitalism in the 21st Century* (London: Macmillan, 1998), p. 119.

49. Robert W. Cox, "A Perspective on Globalization," in James H. Mittelman, ed., *Globalization: Critical Reflections* (Boulder: Lynne Rienner, 1996), p. 23.

50. Francis Fukuyama, *The End of History and the Last Man* (London: Penguin, 1992), p. 126.

51. David Crystal, *English as a Global Language* (Cambridge: Cambridge University Press, 1997), pp. 4–5, 53–61.

52. James L. Watson, ed., *Golden Arches East: McDonald's in East Asia* (Stanford: Stanford University Press, 1997), p. 3.

53. Benjamin R. Barber, *Jihad vs. McWorld* (New York: Ballantine Books, 1996), p. 4.

54. Toffler, *The Third Wave*, ch. 13.

55. Mike Featherstone, ed., *Global Culture: Nationalism, Globalization and Modernity* (London: Sage, 1990), p. 10.

56. Cf. Peter Golding and Phil Harris, eds., *Beyond Cultural Imperialism: Globalization, Communication and the New International Order* (London: Sage, 1997), p. 5.

57. Geoffrey Nowell-Smith, ed., *The Oxford History of World Cinema* (Oxford: Oxford University Press, 1996), pp. 475–82, 759–63.

58. Crystal, *English as a Global Language*, pp. 105–10.

59. Salman Rushdie, " 'Commonwealth Literature' Does Not Exist," in *Imaginary Homelands: Essays and Criticism, 1981–1991* (London: Granta, 1991), p. 64.

60. Watson, ed., *Golden Arches East*, esp. introduction.

61. Cairncross, *Death of Distance*, p. 186.

62. See the discussion in Gray, *False Dawn*, pp. 121–30.

63. Quotations from Samuel P. Huntington, *The Clash of Civilizations and the Remaking of World Order* (New York: Simon and Schuster, 1996), pp. 306–7.

64. *The Economist*, January 10, 1998, survey on "Travel and Tourism," p. 5.

65. Alma S. Wittlin, *Museums: In Search of a Usable Future* (Cambridge, Mass.: MIT Press, 1970), ch. 5; Flora E. S. Kaplan, ed., *Museums and the Making of "Ourselves": The Role of Objects in National Identity* (London: Leicester University Press, 1994), ch. 4.

66. Donald Horne, *The Great Museum: The Re-presentation of History* (London: Pluto, 1984), p. 29.

67. Robertson, *Globalization*, p. 155.

68. David Cannadine, "The First Hundred Years," in Howard Newby, ed., *The National Trust: The Next Hundred Years* (London: National Trust, 1995), pp. 11, 26.

69. Patrick Wright (1986), quoted in Robert Hewison, *The Heritage Industry: Britain in a Climate of Decline* (London: Methuen, 1987), p. 141.

70. Peter Novick, *That Noble Dream: The "Objectivity Question" and the American Historical Profession* (Cambridge: Cambridge University Press, 1988), quoting pp. 469, 592.

71. See Gyan Prakash, "Writing Post-Orientalist Histories of the Third World: Perspectives from Indian Historiography," *Comparative Studies in Society and History* 32 (April 1990): 383–408.

72. As argued by many analysts, e.g., Ian Clark, *Globalization and Fragmentation: International Relations in the Twentieth Century* (Oxford: Oxford University Press, 1997); and James N. Rosenau, *Along the Domestic-Foreign Boundary: Exploring Governance in a Turbulent World* (Cambridge: Cambridge University Press, 1997).

73. George M. Marsden, *Fundamentalism and American Culture: The Shaping of Twentieth-Century Evangelicalism, 1870–1925* (New York: Oxford University Press, 1980), chs. 15–17, quoting p. 159.

74. See, e.g., Martin A. Marty and R. Scott Appleby, *The Fundamentalism Project,* vol. 5 (Chicago: University of Chicago, 1991–5), pp. 414–5.

75. Jeff Haynes, *Religion in Third World Politics* (Buckingham: Open University Press, 1993), p. 36. On similarities and differences see, e.g., David Martin, "Fundamentalism: An Observational and Definitional *Tour d'Horizon,*" *Political Quarterly* 61 (1990): 129–31; and Harriet A. Harris, *Fundamentalism and Evangelicals* (Oxford: Clarendon Press, 1998), pp. 325–36.

76. Marty and Appleby, *The Fundamentalism Project,* vol. 5, p. 409.

77. See Gilles Kepel, *The Revenge of God: The Resurgence of Islam, Christianity and Judaism in the Modern World,* trans. Alan Braley (Cambridge: Polity Press, 1994).

78. James D. Hunter, "Fundamentalism in Its Global Contours," in Norman J. Cohen, ed., *The Fundamentalist Phenomenon* (Grand Rapids, Mich.: Eerdmans, 1990), p. 57.

79. Steve Bruce, *The Rise and Fall of the New Christian Right: Conservative Protestant Politics in America, 1979–1988* (Oxford: Clarendon, 1990), p. 48.

80. Cf. Marty and Appleby, eds., *Fundamentalism Project,* vol. 5, p. 504.

81. Ralph Reed, *Active Faith: How Christians are Changing the Soul of American Politics* (New York: Free Press, 1996), pp. 6–7; cf. Bruce, *Rise and Fall of the New Christian Right,* pp. vii, 172.

82. See Marty and Appleby, eds., *The Fundamentalism Project,* vol. 4, ch. 6.

83. David Martin, *Tongues of Fire: The Explosion of Protestantism in Latin America* (Oxford: Basil Blackwell, 1990), esp. pp. 50–2, 265–8; and Richard S. Hillman, ed., *Understanding Contemporary Latin America* (Boulder, Colo.: Lynne Rienner, 1997), pp. 308–13.

84. Anthony D. Smith, *National Identity* (London: Penguin, 1991), p. 15.

85. For emphasis of these themes see Lester Kurtz, *Gods in the Global Village: The World Religions in Sociological Perspective* (Thousand Oaks, Calif.: Pine Forks Press, 1995), pp. 191, 234.

86. Quotations from Niels C. Nielsen, Jr., *Fundamentalism, Mythos, and World Religions* (Albany, N.Y.: State University of New York Press, 1993), p. 24; Lionel Caplan, ed., *Studies in Religious Fundamentalism* (London: Macmillan, 1987), introduction, p. 2.

87. Quoted in Kepel, *Revenge of God,* p. 56.

88. On this see Margaret Rose, *The Modern and the Post-Industrial: A Critical Analysis* (Cambridge: Cambridge University Press, 1991), pp. 2, 178.

89. Charles Jencks, *What is Post-Modernism?*, 4th ed. (London: Academy Editions, 1996), p. 30.

90. For New Orleans and Stuttgart, respectively, see David Harvey, *The Condition of Post-Modernity: An Enquiry into the Origins of Cultural Change* (Oxford: Basil Blackwell, 1989), pp. 93–7; and Charles Jencks, *The Language of Post-Modern Architecture*, 6th ed. (London: Academy Editions, 1991), pp. 141–2.

91. Quoted in Didier Eribon, *Michel Foucault*, trans. Betsy Wing (London: Faber & Faber, 1991), p. 210.

92. Quoted in David Lodge, ed., *Modern Criticism and Theory: A Reader* (London: Longman, 1988), p. 107.

93. Umberto Eco, *Reflections on "The Name of the Rose,"* trans. by William Weaver (London: Secker & Warburg, 1985), p. 67.

94. Michel Foucault, *The Order of Things: An Archaeology of the Human Sciences* (London: Tavistock Publications, 1970), quoting pp. xi, 387.

95. Jean-François Lyotard, *The Post-Modern Condition: A Report on Knowledge*, trans. by Geoff Bennington and Brian Massumi (Manchester: Manchester University Press, 1984), pp. 6, 8–9, 17.

96. Linda Hutcheon, *A Poetics of Postmodernism: History, Theory, Fiction* (New York: Routledge, 1988), pp. 239–30.

97. Quoted in Christopher Norris, *Derrida* (London: Fontana, 1987), pp. 236–7.

98. Quoted in Madrun Sarup, *An Introductory Guide to Post-Structuralism and Postmodernism*, 2nd ed. (New York: Harvester Wheatsheaf, 1993), p. 46.

99. Jean Baudrillard, *Selected Writings*, ed. Mark Poster (Cambridge: Polity Press, 1988), p. 170.

100. For an overview, see Ronald N. Giere, *Explaining Science: A Cognitive Approach* (Chicago: Univ. of Chicago Press, 1988), ch. 2.

101. Thomas S. Kuhn, *The Structure of Scientific Revolutions*, 2nd ed. (Chicago: University of Chicago Press, 1970), quoting p. 94.

102. Paul Feyerabend, *Against Method* (London: Verso, 1978), esp. pp. 19, 23, 284–5.

103. Ian Hacking, *Representing and Intervening: Introductory Topics in the Philosophy of Natural Science* (Cambridge: Cambridge University Press, 1983), p. 66.

104. Quotations from W. H. Newton-Smith, *The Rationality of Science* (London: Routledge, 1981), ch. 11. See also Nicholas Jardine, *The Fortunes of Inquiry* (Oxford: Clarendon, 1986).

105. Hacking, *Representing and Intervening*, p. 274.

106. Martin J. Rees, "Origin of the Universe" in A. C. Fabian, ed., *Origins: The Darwin College Lectures* (Cambridge: Cambridge University Press, 1988), p. 12.

107. Steven Weinberg, *The First Three Minutes: A Modern View of the Origin of the Universe*, 2nd ed. (London: HarperCollins, 1993), p. 120.

108. Weinberg, *The First Three Minutes*, chs. 2, 3 and 6; and Joseph Silk, *The Big Bang*, 2nd ed. (New York: W. H. Freeman, 1989), chs. 3–4. For more recent developments, see Alan H.

Guth, *The Inflationary Universe: The Quest for a New Theory of Cosmic Origins* (London: Jonathan Cape, 1997).

109. Comments in 1981, quoted in Stephen Hawking, *A Brief History of Time: From the Big Bang to Black Holes* (New York: Bantam Books, 1988), p. 116.

110. Stephen Hawking, ed., *Stephen Hawking's A Brief History of Time: A Reader's Companion* (New York: Bantam Books, 1992), p. 141.

111. Weinberg, *First Three Minutes*, p. 148.

112. The terms are from Paul Davies, *The Runaway Universe* (London: J. M. Dent & Sons, 1978), p. 165.

113. K. Hufbauer, "Astronomy," in John Krige and Dominique Pestre, eds., *Science in the Twentieth Century* (Amsterdam: Harwood, 1997), p. 637.

114. Stephen Hawking, *The Illustrated A Brief History of Time* (New York: Bantam Press, 1996), foreword.

115. Hawking, *A Brief History of Time*, pp. 116, 140–1, 173–5.

116. See Michael White and John Gribbin, *Stephen Hawking: A Life in Science* (New York: Dutton, 1992).

117. Tony Stark, *Knife to the Heart: The Story of Transplant Surgery* (London: Macmillan, 1996), pp. 21–2, 25–9. This section draws extensively on Stark's book.

118. McFarlane Burnet, *Self and Not-Self: Cellular Immunology*, book 1 (Cambridge: Cambridge University Press, 1969).

119. Joseph M. Silverstein, *A History of Immunology* (San Diego: Academic Press, 1989), pp. 285–91, 344–5.

120. Figures from Stark, *Knife to the Heart*, pp. 89, 104.

121. Renée C. Fox and Judith P. Swazey, with Judith C. Watkins, *Spare Parts: Organ Replacement in American Society* (New York: Oxford University Press, 1992), p. 7.

122. Janis Kuby, *Immunology*, 3rd ed. (New York: W. H. Freeman, 1997), pp. 567–8.

123. On these issue, see David Lamb, *Organ Transplants and Ethics* (New York: Routledge, 1990).

124. Edwards, "The Early Days of In Vitro Fertilization," in A. Th. Alberda, R. A. Gan, and H. M. Vemer, eds., *Pioneers in In Vitro Fertilization* (New York: Parthenon, 1995), pp. 7–23.

125. Jennifer Gunning and Veronica English, *Human In Vitro Fertilization: A Case Study in the Regulation of Medical Innovation* (Aldershot, Hants: Dartmouth, 1993), p. 47.

126. Michael J. Coughlan, *The Vatican, the Law and the Human Embryo* (London: Macmillan, 1987), p. 5; cf. Alberda et al., eds., *Pioneers in In Vitro Fertilization*, pp. 40–2.

127. Ian Kennedy, *Treat Me Right: Essays in Medical Law and Ethics* (Oxford: Clarendon, 1988), p. 119.

128. Gunning and English, *Human In Vitro Fertilization*, ch. 9.

129. See Donald Evans, ed., *Conceiving the Embryo: Ethics, Law and Practice in Human Embryology* (The Hague: Martinus Nijhoff, 1996), pp. 94–5, 124.

130. *Science* 281 (July 24, 1998): 495–6. On the background to Dolly, see Gina Kolata, *Clone: The Road to Dolly and the Path Ahead* (London: Allen Lane, 1997).

131. *Science* 279 (January 30, 1998): 646–8; *Nature* 394 (July 23, 1998): 315–6.

132. Brown, *Gene Cloning*, 3rd ed. (London: Chapman and Hall, 1995), ch. 14.

133. David Rotman, "The Next Biotech Harvest," *Technology Review* 101/5 (September–October 1998): pp. 34–41.

134. *New York Times*, August 18, 1998, C6.

135. Monsanto Company, *1997 Annual Report* (St. Louis, Mo.: Monsanto, 1998), pp. 2–3.

136. *The Times* (London), July 10, 1998, p. 18.

137. Lester R. Brown, ed., *State of the World 1997* (New York: Norton, 1997), chs. 2–3, esp. pp. 24–5, 41 (quotation), 51–2.

138. Donald O. Mitchell, Merlinda D. Ingco, and Ronald C. Duncan, *The World Food Outlook* (Cambridge: Cambridge University Press, 1997), pp. 16, 71, 125.

139. Points emphasized in World Bank, *Food Security for the World* (Washington, D.C.: World Bank, 1996), p. 10.

140. World Bank, *At China's Table: Food Security Options* (Washington, D.C.: World Bank, 1997), esp. pp. 1–5.

141. See Kym Anderson and Chao Yang Peng, "Feeding and Fueling China in the 21st Century," *World Development* 26 (1998): 1429.

142. Brown, ed., *State of the World, 1997*, pp. 28–31.

143. Jan A. Veltrop, "Importance of Dams for Water Supply and Hydropower," in Asit K. Biswas, Mohammed Jellali, and Glenn E. Stout, eds., *Water for Sustainable Development in the Twenty-First Century* (Delhi: Oxford University Press, 1993), pp. 102–15.

144. Tony Whitten, Roehayat Emon Soeriaatmadja, and Suraya A. Afiff, *The Ecology of Java and Bali* (Singapore: Periplus, 1996), p. 53.

145. Asit K. Biswas, "Water Security in the 21st Century: A Global Perspective," in Biswas et al., eds., *Water for Sustainable Development*, p. 15.

146. Mitchell et al., *World Food Outlook*, ch. 12.

147. The following statistics on earth, water, and air come from World Bank, *World Development Report, 1992* (New York: Oxford University Press, 1992), esp. pp. 2–7. See generally Andrew Goudie, *The Human Impact on the Natural Environment*, 4th ed. (Oxford: Blackwell, 1993).

148. *The Economist*, October 4, 1997, pp. 18, 85–6.

149. Goudie, *The Human Impact on the Natural Environment*, p. 367.

150. J. E. Lovelock, *Gaia: A New Look at Life on Earth* (Oxford: Oxford University Press, 1979), p. ix.

151. See the discussion in Mary Douglas, *Risk and Blame: Essays in Cultural Theory* (London: Routledge, 1992), pp. 255–70.

152. J. T. Houghton et al., eds., *Climate Change 1995: The Science of Climate Change* (Cambridge: Cambridge University Press, 1996), pp. 5–6.

153. B. L. Turner II (princ. ed.), *The Earth as Transformed by Human Action: Global and Regional Changes in the Biosphere over the Past 300 Years* (Cambridge: Cambridge University Press, 1990), pp. 6–7.

154. Stephen H. Schneider and Penelope J. Boston, eds., *Scientists on Gaia* (Cambridge, Mass.: MIT Press, 1991), p. xx.

155. See Malcolm Newson, "The Earth as Output: Pollution," in R. J. Johnston, Peter J. Taylor, Michael J. Watts, *Geographies of Global Change: Remapping the World in the Late Twentieth Century* (Oxford: Blackwell, 1995), p. 335.

156. Michael Grubb et al., *The "Earth Summit" Agreements: A Guide and Assessments* (London: RIIA/Earthscan, 1992), pp. 33–4; Cynthia Rosenzweig and Martin L. Parry, "Potential Impact of Climate Change on World Food Supply," *Nature* 367 (January 13, 1994), 133–8.

157. Richard Elliott Benedick, *Ozone Diplomacy: New Directions in Safeguarding the Planet* (Cambridge, Mass.: Harvard University Press, 1991), pp. 8, 211.

158. The contrast on the two issues is examined in Ian Bellany, *The Environment in World Politics: Exploring the Limits* (Cheltenham: Edward Elgar, 1997), pp. 142–57, 168–92. See also Lester B. Lave and Elena Shevakova, "Potential Damage from Climate Changes in the U.S.," *Energy and Environment* 9 (1998): 349–63.

159. See Stanley P. Johnson, ed., *The Earth Summit: The United Nations Conference on Environment and Development* (London: Graham and Trotman, 1993), esp. pp. 1–10.

160. Stephen H. Schneider, "Kyoto Protocol: The Unfinished Agenda," *Climatic Change* 39 (May 1998): 1–21.

161. A dilemma emphasized in Andrew Hurrell, "Brazil and the International Politics of Amazonian Deforestation," in Andrew Hurrell and Benedict Kingsbury, eds., *The International Politics of the Environment: Actors, Interests, and Institutions* (Oxford: Clarendon, 1992), pp. 399–402.

162. Statistics from United Nations Centre for Human Settlements (HABITAT), *An Urbanizing World: Global Report on Human Settlements, 1996* (Oxford: Oxford Univ. Press, 1996), ch. 1.

163. *An Urbanizing World*, ch. 6, esp. pp. 199, 231.

164. A point emphasized in Jorge E. Hardoy, Diana Mitlin, and David Satterthwaite, *Environmental Problems in Third World Cities* (London: Earthscan, 1992), pp. 204–6.

165. On the background, see Peter M. Ward, *Mexico City: The Production and Reproduction of an Urban Environment* (London: Belhaven Press, 1990), esp. chs. 3, 5, and 8.

166. Data from Barry Turner, ed., *The Statesman's Yearbook, 1998–1999* (London: Macmillan, 1998), pp. 1585–7.

167. Roy Porter, *London: A Social History* (London: Hamish Hamilton, 1994), ch. 16.

168. Mission interministérielle de coordination des grandes opérations d'architecture et d'urbanisme, *Architectures Capitales: Paris, 1979–1989* (Paris: Electa, 1987).

169. *The Economist*, December 6, 1997, pp. 27–9.

170. Jonas Rabinovitch and Josef Leitman, "Urban Planning in Curitiba," *Scientific American*, March 1996, pp. 46–53.

171. Richard Rogers, *Cities for a Small Planet*, ed. Philip Gumuchdjian (London: Faber & Faber, 1997), pp. 19, 59–61.

172. Statistics from *An Urbanizing World*, p. 275.

173. *Business Week*, August 5, 1996, pp. 46–7.

174. Alex Mercer, *Disease, Mortality and Population in Transition: Epidemiological-Demographic Change in England since the Eighteenth Century as Part of a Global Phenomenon* (London: Leicester University Press, 1990), ch. 6, esp. pp. 136–7, 148.

175. Robert L. Rabin and Stephen D. Sugarman, eds., *Smoking Policy: Law, Politics, and Culture* (New York: Oxford University Press, 1993), p. 3.

176. James T. Patterson, *The Dread Disease: Cancer and Modern American Culture* (Cambridge, Mass.: Harvard University Press, 1987), pp. 201–2.

177. Stanton A. Glantz, John Slade, Lisa A. Bero, Peter Hanauer, and Deborah E. Barnes, *The Cigarette Papers* (Berkeley: University of California Press, 1996), e.g., pp. 15–23.

178. Jordan Goodman, *Tobacco in History: The Cultures of Dependence* (London: Routledge, 1993), p. 11.

179. Robert A. Kagan and David Vogel, "The Politics of Smoking Regulation: Canada, France, the United States," in Rabin and Sugarman, eds., *Smoking Policy*, ch. 2.

180. Statistics from Goodman, *Tobacco in History*, pp. 10–11.

181. Philippe Fargues, "The Arab World: The Family as Fortress," in André Burguière, Christiane Klapisch-Zuber, Martine Segalen, and Françoise Zonabend, eds., *A History of the Family*, Vol. 2, *The Impact of Modernity*, trans. Sarah Hanbury Tenison (Cambridge: Polity Press, 1996), pp. 356–7.

182. See the essays on "Social Security and Declining Labor Force Participation" in *The American Economic Review* 88/2 (May 1998): 158–78.

183. World Bank, *Averting the Old Age Crisis: Policies to Protect the Old and Promote Growth* (New York: Oxford University Press, 1994), pp. 4, 123.

184. World Bank, *China 2020: Development Challenges in the New Century* (Washington, D.C.: World Bank, 1997), pp. 51–4.

185. Judith Banister, "Implications of the Aging of China's Population," in Dudley L. Poston, Jr., and David Yaukey, eds., *The Population of Modern China* (New York: Plenum Press, 1992), esp. pp. 468, 475.

186. See Imelda Whelehan, *Modern Feminist Thought: From the Second Wave to "Post-Feminism"* (Edinburgh: Edinburgh University Press, 1995), esp. part II.

187. Data on schooling and contraception from Unicef, *The State of the World's Children, 1996* (Oxford: Oxford University Press, 1996), p. 99.

188. Barney Cohen, "The Emerging Fertility Transition in Sub-Saharan Africa," *World Development* 26 (1998): 1431–61.

189. Larry L. Bumpass, "What's Happening to the Family? Interactions between Demography and Institutional Change," *Demography* 27 (1990): quoting 484.

190. Elizabeth Ardayfio-Schandorf, "Household Energy Supply and Rural Women's Work in Ghana," in Janet Henshall Momsen and Vivian Kinnaird, eds., *Different Places, Different Voices: Gender and Development in Africa, Asia and Latin America* (London: Routledge, 1993), pp. 15–29.

191. See Susan P. Joekes, *Women in the World Economy: An INSTRAW Study* (New York: Oxford University Press, 1987), esp. chs. 5–7.

192. *The Economist,* July 18, 1998, supplement on "Women and Work," p. 8.

193. Habitat, *An Urbanizing World,* p. 12.

194. Roderick Phillips, *Putting Asunder: A History of Divorce in Western Society* (Cambridge: Cambridge University Press, 1996), chs. 13–14.

195. Martine Segalen, "The Industrial Revolution: From Proleteriat to Bourgeoisie," in Burguière et al., eds., *A History of the Family,* vol. 2, p. 402.

196. *The Economist,* September 26, 1998, p. 46.

197. See Kath Weston, *Families We Choose: Lesbians, Gays, Kinship* (New York: Columbia University Press, 1991).

198. Colin Spencer, *Homosexuality: A History* (London: Fourth Estate, 1995), pp. 384–9.

199. See generally Burguière et al., eds., *A History of the Family,* vol. 2, chs. 6–8.

200. Ronald Dworkin, *Taking Rights Seriously* (London: Duckworth, 1977), p. xi.

201. Quoted in *Keesings Record of World Events,* p. 39537.

202. R. J. Vincent, *Human Rights and International Relations* (Cambridge: Cambridge University Press, 1986), esp. chs. 3 and 5.

203. Ela Bhatt, quoted in *Time* (European ed.), September 11, 1995, p. 52.

Epilogue

1. Cf. Francis Fukuyama, "The End of History?" *The National Interest,* Summer 1989, pp. 3–18; Eric Hobsbawm, *The Age of Extremes: The Short Twentieth Century, 1914–1991* (London: Michael Joseph, 1994).

2. Giovanni Arrighi, *The Long Twentieth Century: Money, Power, and the Origins of Our Times* (London: Verso, 1995).

3. John Gray, *Enlightenment's Wake: Politics and Culture at the Close of the Modern Age* (London: Routledge, 1995).

4. Robert McC. Adams, "Foreword: The Relativity of Time and Transformation," in B. L. Turner II (princ. ed.), *The Earth as Transformed by Human Action: Global and Regional Changes in the Biosphere Over the Past 300 Years* (Cambridge: Cambridge University Press, 1990), pp. vii–x.

5. Unicef, *The State of the World's Children, 1996* (Oxford: Oxford University Press, 1996), p. 99.

6. Statistics from World Bank, *World Development Report, 1994* (New York: Oxford University Press, 1994), p. 146; George Thomas Kurian, ed., *Fitzroy Dearborn Book of World Rankings* (Chicago: Fitzroy Dearborn, 1998), pp. 256–7.

7. Cf. Paul Hirst and Grahame Thompson, *Globalization in Question: The International Economy and the Possibilities of Governance* (Cambridge: Polity Press, 1996), ch. 2.

8. See John Lewis Gaddis, *The Long Peace: Inquiries into Cold War History* (New York: Oxford University Press, 1987), ch. 8.

9. Estimates by the International Institute for Strategic Studies, quoted in *The Times,* October 15, 1997, p. 15.

10. John C. Caldwell and Pat Caldwell, "Famine in Africa: A Global Perspective," in Etienne van de Walle, Gilles Pison, and Mpembele Sala-Diakanda, eds., *Mortality and Society in Sub-Saharan Africa* (Oxford: Clarendon, 1992), p. 367.

11. A theme of John Iliffe, *Africans: The History of a Continent* (Cambridge: Cambridge University Press, 1995).

12. Nacha Guevara, quoted in John Simpson and Jana Bennett, *The Disappeared: Voices from a Secret War* (London: Robson Books, 1985), p. 13.

Illustration Credits

U.S. National Archives, Washington, D.C.: Plates 1, 3, 4, 6, 9, 10, 11, 15, 17, 18, 19, 20, 22, 33, 35

Courtesy of Presse- und Informationsamt der Bundesregierung, Bonn: Plates 2, 12, 32

Eastfoto: Plate 5

Royal Commonwealth Society Collection. By permission of the Syndics of Cambridge University Library: Plates 7, 16, 26, 41

Courtesy of World Bank: Plates 8, 23, 24, 25, 27, 28, 29, 30, 46, 47

Corbis-Bettmann-UPI: Plates 13, 31, 37

John F. Kennedy Library, Boston, Massachusetts: Plate 14

Li Zhensheng: Plate 21

AP/Wide World Photos: Plates 36, 38, 40

Courtesy of White House Press Office, Washington D.C.: Plate 39

Courtesy of Hayes Davidson/New Millennium Experience Company: Plate 42

Courtesy of the University of Cambridge Computer Laboratory: Plate 43

Courtesy of the Sanger Centre, Hinxton, Cambridgeshire: Plate 44

Courtesy of the University of Cambridge/Findlay Kember: Plate 45

David Burnett/Contact Press Images/PNI: Plate 34

Index